Scott Foresman - Addison Wesley MIDDLE SCHOOL MATH

Course 2

Randall I. Charles John A. Dossey Steven J. Leinwand
Cathy L. Seeley Charles B. Vonder Embse

L. Carey Bolster • Janet H. Caldwell • Dwight A. Cooley • Warren D. Crown
Linda Proudfit • Alma B. Ramírez • Jeanne F. Ramos • Freddie Lee Renfro
David F. Robitaille • Jane Swafford

Teacher's Edition

Volume 2

Chapters 7–12

Needham, Massachusetts
Upper Saddle River, New Jersey
Glenview, Illinois

Math

that Makes Sense...

"I learn best when math is interesting to me."

The Student's Perspective

"If we are to reach all students, we must strive for meaningful, challenging, and relevant learning in the classroom."

The Research Perspective

ISBN 0-13-054207-5
1 2 3 4 5 6 7 8 9 10 04 03 02 01 00

Teacher

The Teacher's Perspective

*"My primary concern in teaching is to help **all** my students succeed."*

from EVERY *Perspective*

What kind of a math program are you looking for? What about your students? And how about mathematics education research? Can one program really satisfy *all* points of view? Through its content, features, and format, *Scott Foresman - Addison Wesley Middle School MATH* recognizes the real-life needs and concerns specific to middle school—supported by research but grounded in real classroom experience.

Welcome to a math program that excels from every perspective—especially yours!

search

Math that Connects to the Student's World

Middle school students have a perspective all their own. We've tapped into their world with experiences and information that grab their attention and don't let go.

"I want to know when I'll use this."

Real, age-appropriate data
Data based on what middle school students buy, eat, study in school, and enjoy permeate every lesson.

Cool themes like *Spiders, Disasters, Food,* and *Whales*
Student-friendly topics blend learning with what kids love.

MathSURF Internet Site
MathSURF's up and so is student interest! Kids can go online to explore text content of every chapter in safe and exciting destinations around the world.

Interactive Math: Lessons and Tools CD-ROM
Interactive lessons for every chapter provide an exciting environment for learning.

Math that Promotes High School Success

Teachers in today's middle schools need a program that prepares their students for high school math. That means rigorous content, including preparation for algebra and geometry, NTCM content and process standards—PLUS practical strategies for taking tests and problem solving.

*"My students need to be prepared for high school math. And let's face it, how they perform is a reflection of how **I** perform!"*

Performance

The building blocks of algebra

Prepare students for success in high school math with instruction in mathematical reasoning.

Course 1—focuses on *numerical reasoning.*

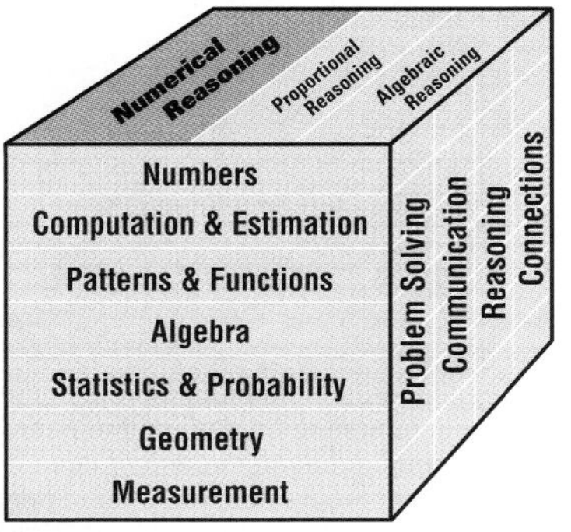

Course 2—focuses on *proportional reasoning.*

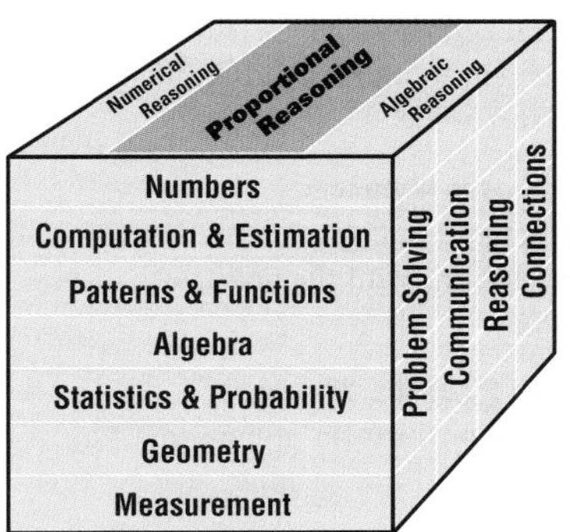

Course 3—focuses on *algebraic reasoning.*

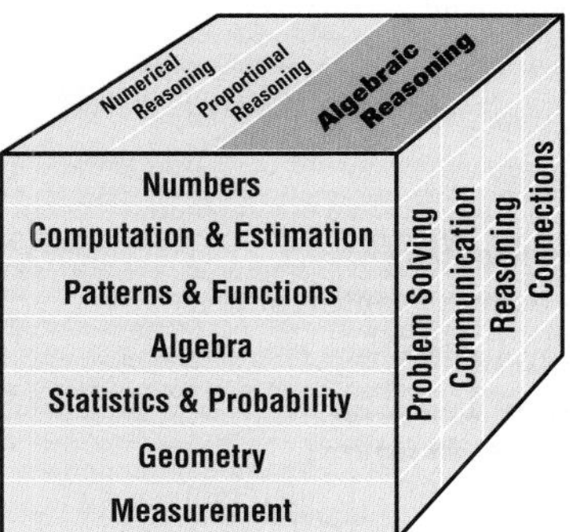

Test prep strategies

The next step in strategies! Helping students be smart about how they take standardized tests builds confidence and leads to success.

Problem solving that's no problem

Sharpen students' problem-solving skills with numerous opportunities to analyze and use the problem-solving process.

A Program that Supports Teaching Success

Teachers in today's middle schools face unique challenges—from improving student performance to adapting to each student's unique learning needs. This program is designed to help you meet those challenges. You'll find help for every teaching need—including *block scheduling* and *interdisciplinary team teaching,* PLUS *outstanding technology,* and more!

Student Edition

Colorful lessons, filled with student-oriented data, have a unique "middle school" look.

Teacher's Edition

Two hardbound volumes provide complete lesson plans plus practical help to meet your every challenge—block scheduling, team teaching, and more.

Teacher's Resource Package

Practice Masters
Exercises reinforce content of every lesson. Also available as a workbook.

Alternative Lessons (Reteaching Masters)
Masters for every lesson offer another look at skills and concepts. Also available as a workbook.

Extend Your Thinking (Enrichment Masters)
Masters enhance thinking skills and creativity in every lesson. Also available as a workbook.

Problem-Solving Masters (for Guided Problem Solving)
Masters guide students step-by-step through one problem from every Student Edition exercise set. Also available as a workbook.

Assessment Sourcebook
Options to help profile students as learners. Includes multiple-choice, short-response, performance, and mixed-format chapter tests, as well as section quizzes and record forms.

Home and Community Connections
Make math a family affair! Booklet with letters in English and Spanish, also provides classroom tips, community projects, and more.

Teacher's Toolkit
Saves time with a variety of Management Resources, plus Teaching Tool Transparencies.

Technology Masters
Computer and calculator activities energize lessons with the power of technology.

Chapter Project Masters
Masters support the on-going project in each Student Edition chapter.

Interdisciplinary Team Teaching
Math across the curriculum! Masters provide an engaging 2-page interdisciplinary lesson for each section.

Review from Last Year Masters
Mini-lessons reteach key prerequisite skills.

Resources to Customize Instruction

Print Resources

Solutions Manual
Manual includes convenient solutions to Student Edition exercises.

Overhead Transparency Package
Daily Transparencies (for Problem of the Day, Review, and Quick Quiz) and Lesson Enhancement Transparencies help enliven class presentations.

Skills Intervention Kit
Innovative resource package for diagnosing students' gaps in basic skills, prescribing an individualized course of study, and monitoring progress. Eight intervention units cover core skills students need to succeed.

Test Taking Tips on Transparencies
Transparencies help you teach test-taking strategies and provide key information on the most widely used standardized tests. Extensive teaching notes provide specific instructional suggestions.

Reading Strategies for Problem Solving Package
Transparencies for instruction and blackline masters for follow-up and practice help connect problem solving to key reading strategies.

SAT 9™ Assessment Package
Practice Quizzes mirroring the SAT 9™ format for each section of the text, Practice Tests simulating the actual SAT 9™ Test, and Teacher's Guides with comprehensive correlations to all the SAT 9™ objectives help you prepare students for testing.

TerraNova™ Assessment Package
Practice Quizzes mirroring the TerraNova™ format for each section of the text, Practice Tests simulating the actual TerraNova™ Test, and Teacher's Guides with comprehensive correlations to all the TerraNova™ objectives help you prepare students for testing.

Block Scheduling Handbook
Practical suggestions let you tailor the program to various block scheduling formats.

Multilingual Handbook
Enhanced math glossary with examples in seven languages provides a valuable resource for teaching. Especially useful with ESL students.

Technology

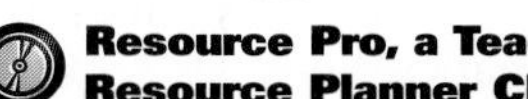

Resource Pro, a Teacher's Resource Planner CD-ROM
The entire Teacher's Resource Package on CD-ROM! Includes an electronic planning guide which allows you to set criteria when planning lessons, customize worksheets, correlate your curriculum to specific objectives, and more!

Interactive Math: Lessons and Tools CD-ROM
Interactive, multimedia lessons with built-in math tools help students explore concepts in enjoyable and involving ways.

MathSURF Web Site
Math on the Web! Provides links to other sites, project ideas, interactive surveys and more.

The Know Zone™ Web Site
Each lesson in the text is supported by an interactive, animated tutorial and each chapter has a practice test. Students are provided incentives for practice and achievement. Teachers are provided class summary and individual student reports. Parents can check on student progress or take a quick math refresher course.

Math Blaster® Pre-Algebra CD-ROM
As students make their way through Dr. Dabbie's eerie mansion, they develop key pre-algebra skills such as logical thinking, estimation, ratios, order of operations, and more.

Wide World of Mathematics™
CD-ROMs and videos demonstrate how math is used in the real world.

TestWorks: Test and Practice CD-ROM
CD-ROM saves hours of test-prep time by generating and customizing tests and worksheets.

Manipulative Kits

Student Manipulative Kit
Quantities of angle rulers, Power Polygons, and other items help students grasp mathematics concepts.

Teacher's Overhead Manipulative Kit
Kit makes demonstrating concepts from an overhead projector easy and convenient.

Authors with Middle School Expertise!

Math that makes sense from every perspective—it's a commitment we've kept in all aspects of this program, including our outstanding team of authors. Their expertise in mathematics education brings to the program extensive knowledge of how middle school students learn math and how best to teach them.

"Students learn and perform better when they are taught in ways that match their own strengths."

Charles B. Vonder Embse

Professor of Mathematics Education and Mathematics

Central Michigan University
Mt. Pleasant, Michigan

Member of NCTM Instructional Issues Advisory Committee

Member of the Advisory Board of Teachers Teaching with Technology (T^3)

Jane Swafford

Professor of Mathematics

Illinois State University
Normal, Illinois

Randall I. Charles

Professor, Department of Mathematics and Computer Science

San Jose State University
San Jose, California

Past Vice-President, National Council of Supervisors of Mathematics

Co-author of two NCTM publications on teaching and evaluating progress in problem solving

Dwight A. Cooley

Assistant Principal

Mary Louise Phillips
Elementary School
Fort Worth, Texas

Member, NCTM Board of Directors

John A. Dossey

Distinguished University Professor of Mathematics

Illinois State University
Normal, Illinois

Past President, NCTM

Guided development of NCTM Standards

Recipient, NCTM Lifetime Achievement Award

Chairman, Conference Board of the Mathematical Sciences

"A program that asks real-life questions provides rich possibilities for students."

Steven J. Leinwand

Mathematics Consultant

Connecticut Department of Education
Hartford, Connecticut

Member, NCTM Board of Directors

Past President, National Council of Supervisors of Mathematics

Cathy L. Seeley

Director of Policy and Professional Development for Texas SSI

University of Texas
Austin, Texas

Texas State Mathematics Supervisor

Writer, Curriculum and Evaluation Standards for School Mathematics

Member, NCTM Board of Directors

Turn the page, for more authors!

More Authors with Middle School Expertise!

Freddie Lee Renfro

Coordinator of Mathematics

Fort Bend Independent School District
Sugarland, Texas

L. Carey Bolster

Director, K–12 Math Projects

Public Broadcasting Service MATHLINE
Alexandria, Virginia

More

"Students construct new learning from a basis of prior knowledge and experience."

Linda Proudfit

University Professor of Mathematics and Computer Education

Governors State University
University Park, Illinois

Janet H. Caldwell

Professor of Mathematics

Rowan University
Glassboro, New Jersey

David F. Robitaille

Professor of Mathematics Education

University of British Columbia
Vancouver, British Columbia,
Canada

Alma Ramírez

Bilingual Mathematics and Science Teacher

Oakland Charter Academy
Oakland, California

"To be successful in high school, students need a solid foundation in mathematical reasoning."

Jeanne F. Ramos

Assistant Principal

Nobel Middle School
Los Angeles, California

Warren D. Crown

Professor of Mathematics Education

Rutgers, The State University of New Jersey
New Brunswick, New Jersey

Expertise

Contributors from Across the Country!

A Nationwide Perspective

Educators from across the country helped shape this program with valuable input about local needs and concerns.

Contributing Writers

Phillip E. Duren
California State University
Hayward, CA

Kathy A. Ross
Loyola University (LaSIP)
New Orleans, LA

Sheryl M. Yamada
Beverly Hills High School
Beverly Hills, CA

Content Reviewers

Ann Boltz
Coldwater, MI

John David Bridges
Greenville, SC

Glenn Bruckhart
Fort Collins, CO

Sharon Bourgeois Butler
Spring, TX

Carol Cameron
Seattle, WA

Steven T. Cottrell
Farmington, UT

Patricia Creel
Lawrenceville, GA

Wendi M. Cyford
New Market, MD

Scott Firkins
Owensboro, KY

Madelaine Gallin
New York, NY

Roy E. Griggs
Boise, ID

Lucy Hahn
Boise, ID

Allison Harris
Seattle, WA

Clay Hutson
Kingsport, TN

Beryl W. Jackson
Alexandria, VA

Janet Jomp
Wilson, NC

Ann P. Lawrence
Marietta, GA

Cheryl McCormack
Indianapolis, IN

Gary McCracken
Tuscaloosa, AL

Allison McNaughton
Marstons Mills, MA

Sandra A. Nagy
Mesa, AZ

Kent Novak
Greene, RI

Jeff C. Nusbaum
Rock Island, IL

Vince O'Connor
Milwaukee, WI

Mary Lynn Raith
Pittsburgh, PA

Kathleen Rieke
Zionsville, IN

Ellen G. Robertson
Norwich, NY

Nancy Rolsen
Worthington, OH

Edith Roos
Helena, MT

Lynn A. Sandro
Cedar Springs, MI

Carol Sims
Arcadia, CA

Paul E. Smith
Newburgh, IN

Donald M. Smyton
Kenmore, NY

Stella M. Turner
Indianapolis, IN

Tommie Walsh
Lubbock, TX

Terri Weaver
Houston, TX

Jacqueline Weilmuenster
Colleyville, TX

Multicultural Reviewers

Mary Margaret Capraro
Hialeah, FL

Robert Capraro
Miami, FL

Bettye Forte
Fort Worth, TX

Hector Hirigoyen
Miami, FL

James E. Hopkins
Auburn, WA

Patricia Locke
Mobridge, SD

Jimmie Rios
Fort Worth, TX

Linda Skinner
Edmond, OK

ESL Reviewers

Anna Uhl Chamot
Washington, DC

Jimmie Rios
Fort Worth, TX

Inclusion Reviewers

Lucy Blood
Amesbury, MA

Janett Borg
Monroe, UT

John David Bridges
Greenville, SC

Edith Roos
Helena, MT

Cross-Curricular Reviewers

Janett Borg
Monroe, UT

Kurt Brorson
Bethesda, MD

Geoffrey Chester
Washington, DC

Trudi Hammel Garland
Orinda, CA

M. Frank Watt Ireton
Washington, DC

Donna Krasnow
Carmel, CA

Chelcie Liu
San Francisco, CA

Edith Roos
Helena, MT

Technology Reviewers

Kurt Brorson
Bethesda, MD

Beverly W. Nichols
Overland Park, KS

Susan Rhodes
Springfield, IL

David L. Stout
Pensacola, FL

TABLE OF CONTENTS

Teacher's Edition

VOLUME 1: CHAPTERS 1–6

VOLUME 2: CHAPTERS 7–12

FROM THE AUTHORS

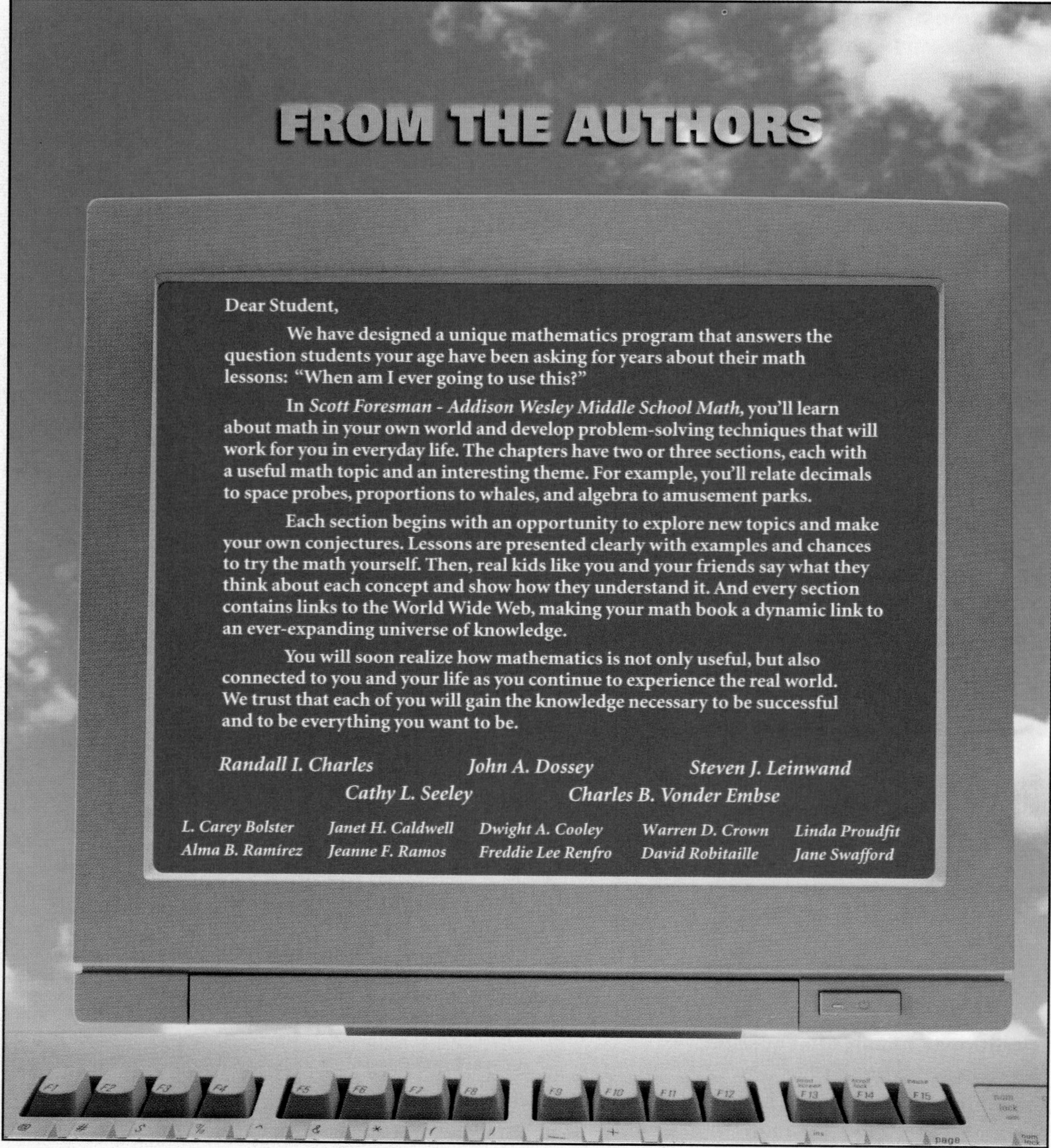

FROM THE AUTHORS

Dear Student,

We have designed a unique mathematics program that answers the question students your age have been asking for years about their math lessons: "When am I ever going to use this?"

In *Scott Foresman - Addison Wesley Middle School Math,* you'll learn about math in your own world and develop problem-solving techniques that will work for you in everyday life. The chapters have two or three sections, each with a useful math topic and an interesting theme. For example, you'll relate decimals to space probes, proportions to whales, and algebra to amusement parks.

Each section begins with an opportunity to explore new topics and make your own conjectures. Lessons are presented clearly with examples and chances to try the math yourself. Then, real kids like you and your friends say what they think about each concept and show how they understand it. And every section contains links to the World Wide Web, making your math book a dynamic link to an ever-expanding universe of knowledge.

You will soon realize how mathematics is not only useful, but also connected to you and your life as you continue to experience the real world. We trust that each of you will gain the knowledge necessary to be successful and to be everything you want to be.

Randall I. Charles *John A. Dossey* *Steven J. Leinwand*
Cathy L. Seeley *Charles B. Vonder Embse*

L. Carey Bolster *Janet H. Caldwell* *Dwight A. Cooley* *Warren D. Crown* *Linda Proudfit*
Alma B. Ramírez *Jeanne F. Ramos* *Freddie Lee Renfro* *David Robitaille* *Jane Swafford*

CHAPTER 1

Making Sense of the World of Data

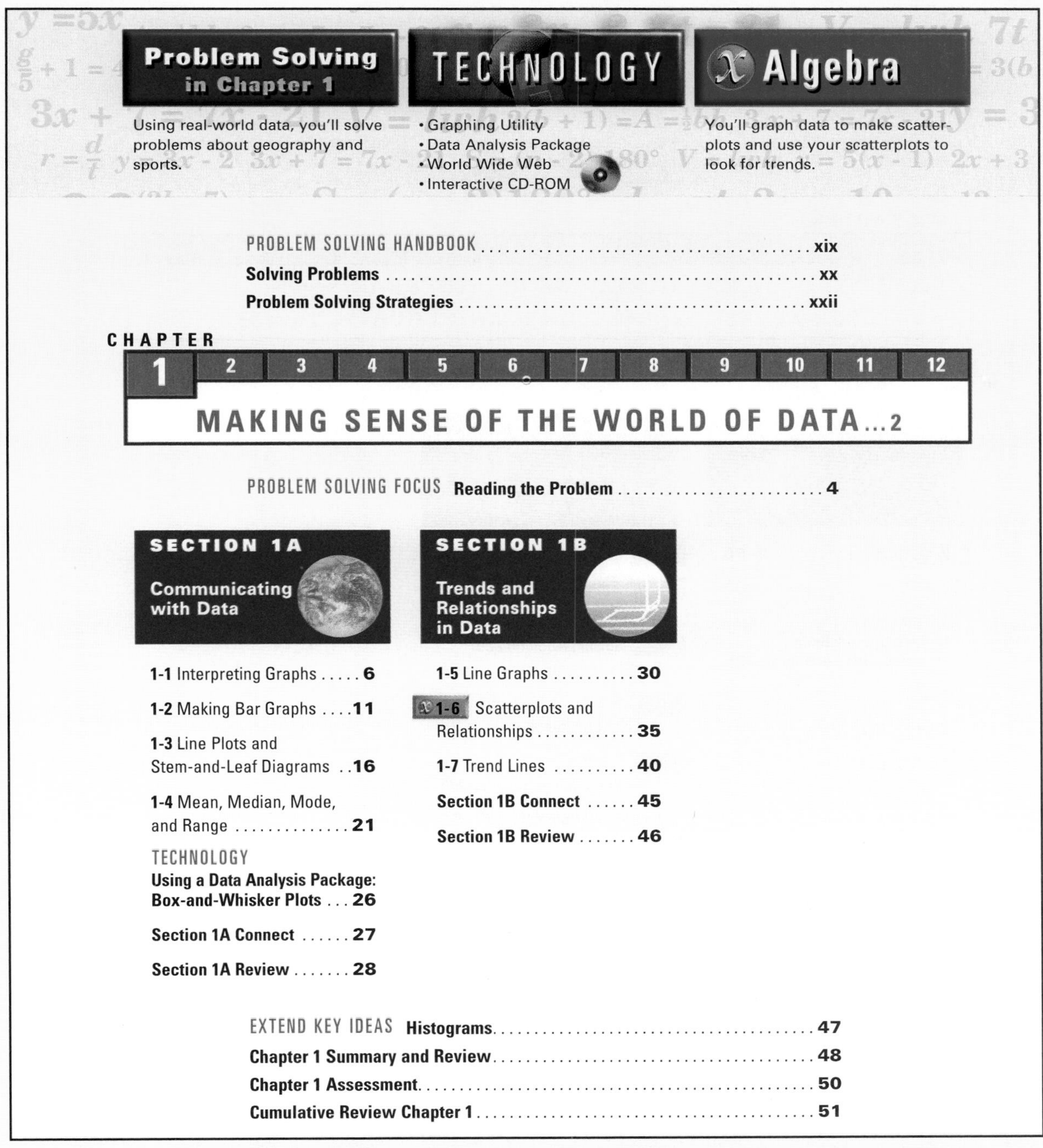

Problem Solving in Chapter 1

Using real-world data, you'll solve problems about geography and sports.

TECHNOLOGY

- Graphing Utility
- Data Analysis Package
- World Wide Web
- Interactive CD-ROM

Algebra

You'll graph data to make scatterplots and use your scatterplots to look for trends.

CHAPTER 2

The Language of Algebra: Formulas, Expressions, and Equations

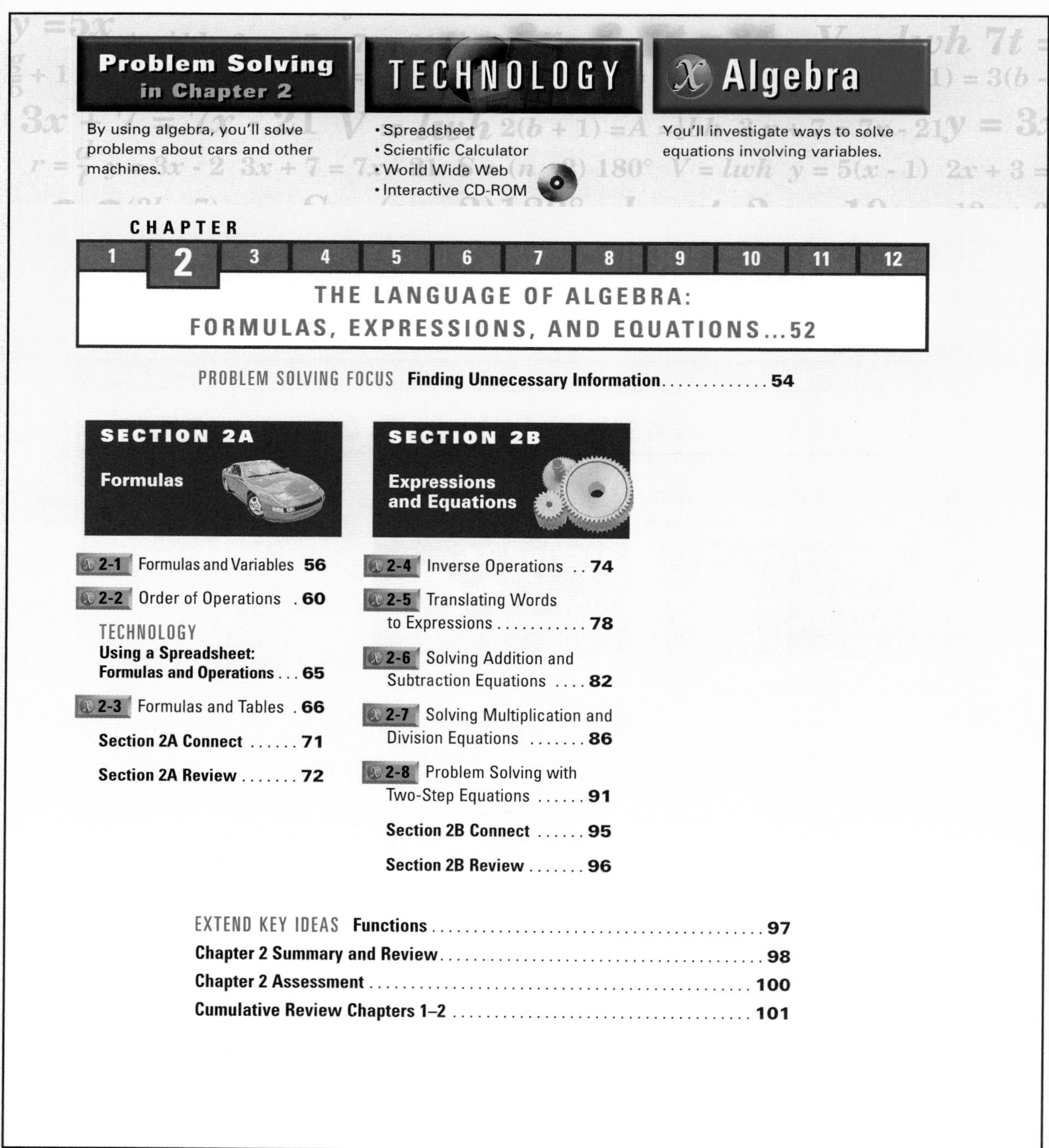

Problem Solving in Chapter 2
By using algebra, you'll solve problems about cars and other machines.

TECHNOLOGY
- Spreadsheet
- Scientific Calculator
- World Wide Web
- Interactive CD-ROM

Algebra
You'll investigate ways to solve equations involving variables.

CHAPTER 1 **2** 3 4 5 6 7 8 9 10 11 12

CHAPTER 3

Number Sense: Decimals and Fractions

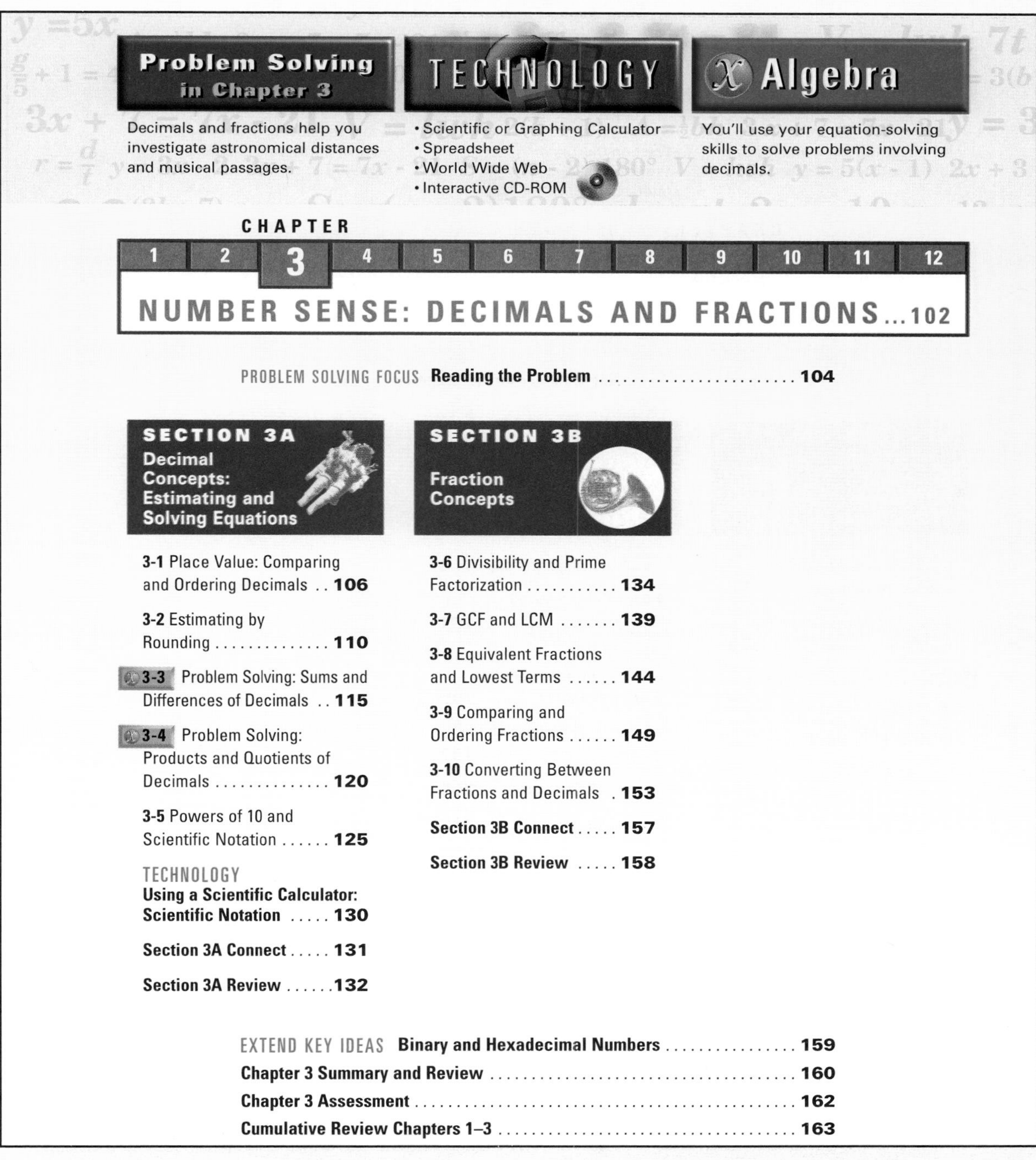

Problem Solving in Chapter 3
Decimals and fractions help you investigate astronomical distances and musical passages.

TECHNOLOGY
- Scientific or Graphing Calculator
- Spreadsheet
- World Wide Web
- Interactive CD-ROM

Algebra
You'll use your equation-solving skills to solve problems involving decimals.

CHAPTER 1 2 **3** 4 5 6 7 8 9 10 11 12

CHAPTER 4

Operations with Fractions

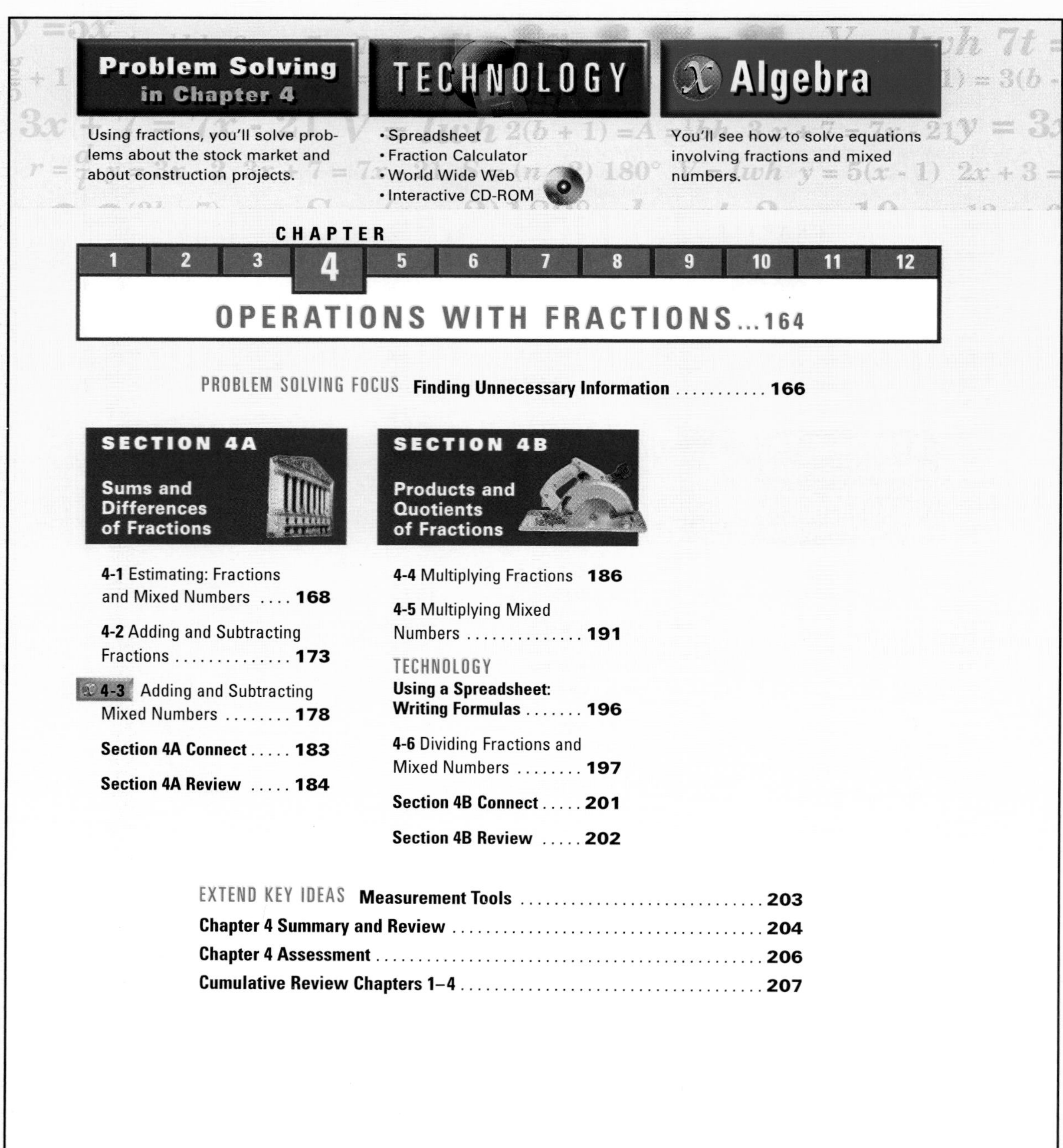

Problem Solving in Chapter 4

Using fractions, you'll solve problems about the stock market and about construction projects.

TECHNOLOGY

- Spreadsheet
- Fraction Calculator
- World Wide Web
- Interactive CD-ROM

Algebra

You'll see how to solve equations involving fractions and mixed numbers.

CHAPTER 1 2 3 **4** 5 6 7 8 9 10 11 12

CHAPTER 5

Geometry and Measurement

You will find that every lesson has four pages of notes. Listed below are additional pages for the teacher.

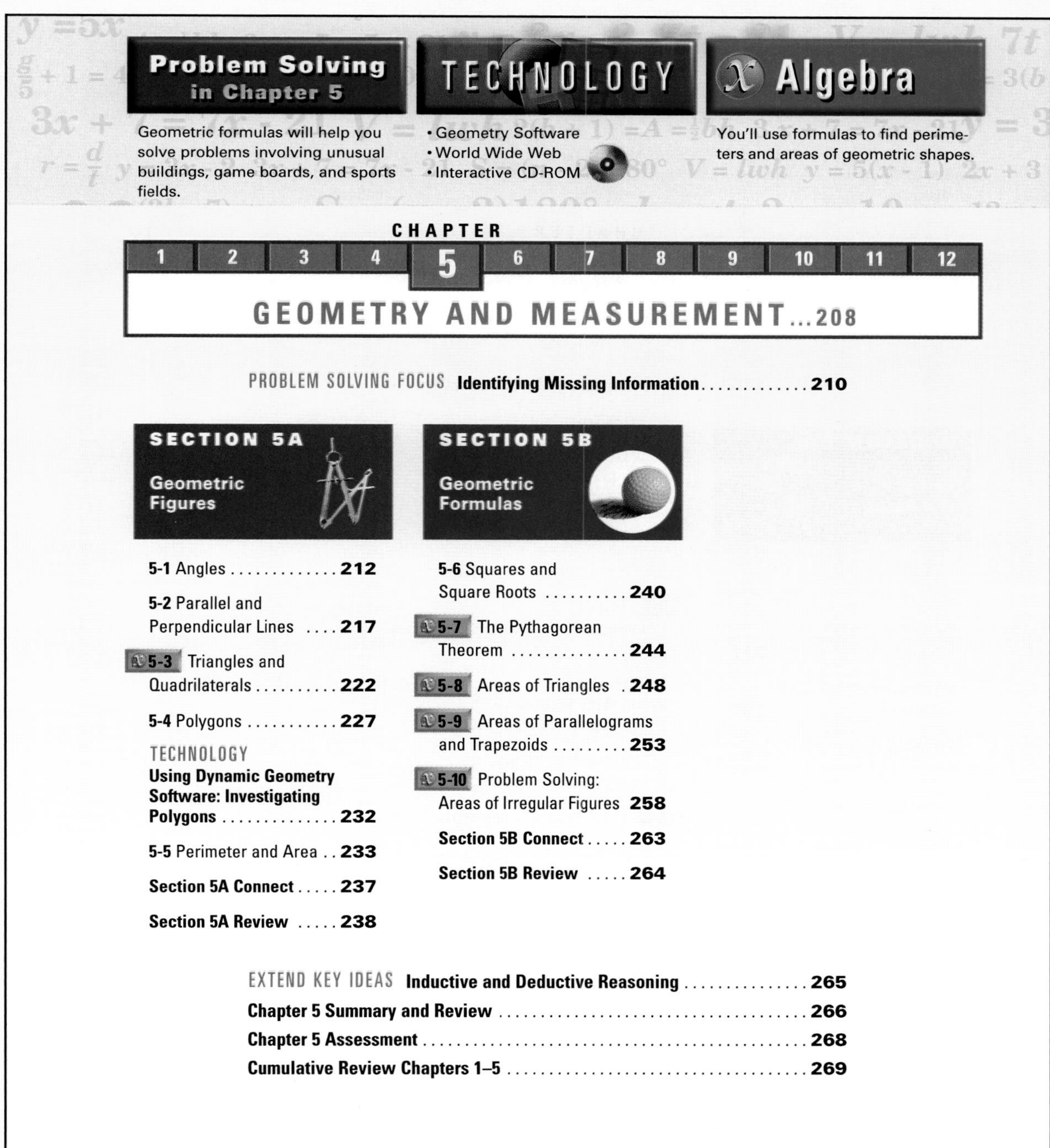

Problem Solving in Chapter 5

Geometric formulas will help you solve problems involving unusual buildings, game boards, and sports fields.

TECHNOLOGY

- Geometry Software
- World Wide Web
- Interactive CD-ROM

Algebra

You'll use formulas to find perimeters and areas of geometric shapes.

CHAPTER 1 2 3 4 5 6 7 8 9 10 11 12

CHAPTER 6

Ratios, Rates, and Proportions

You will find that every lesson has four pages of notes. Listed below are additional pages for the teacher.

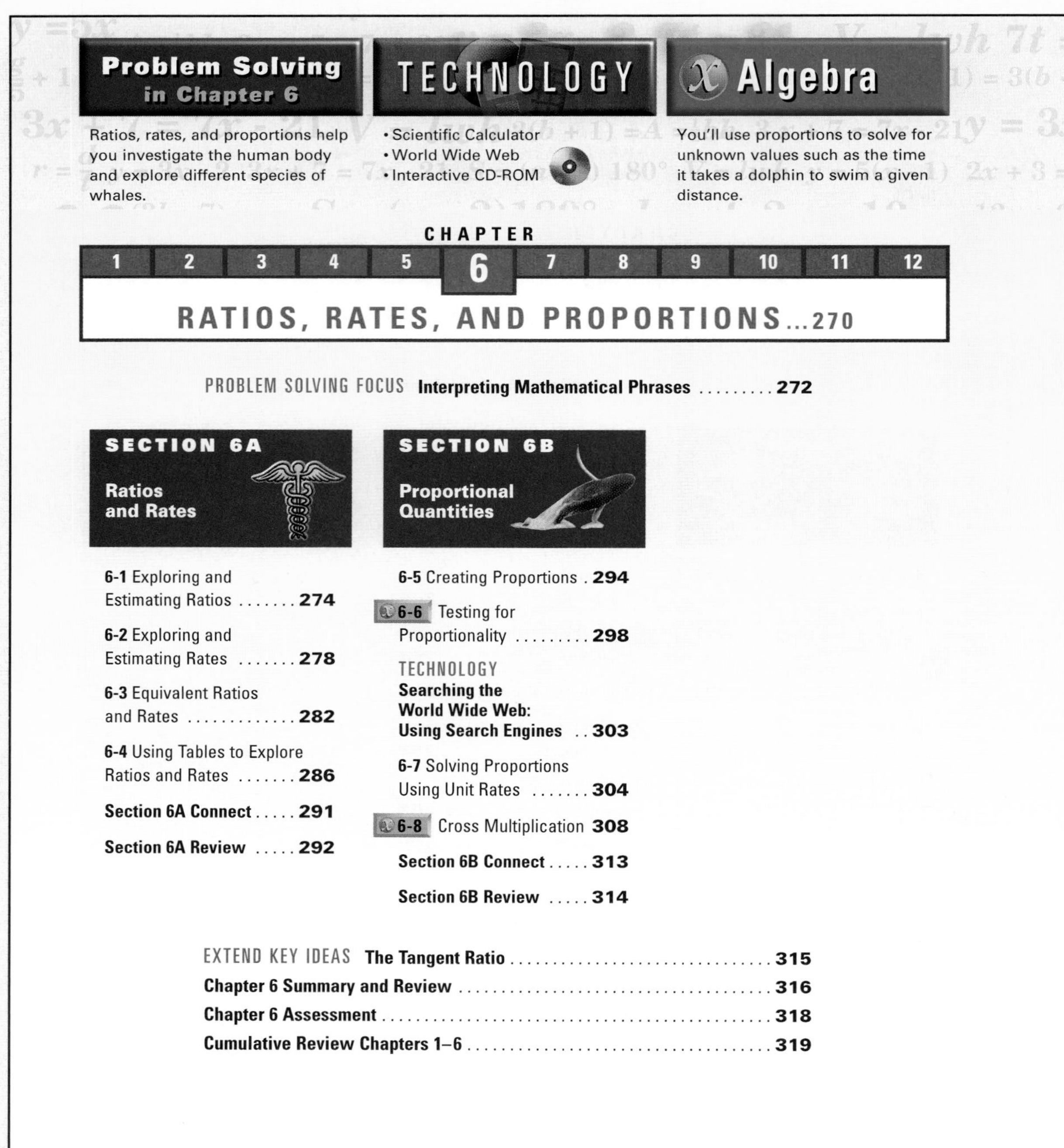

Problem Solving in Chapter 6

Ratios, rates, and proportions help you investigate the human body and explore different species of whales.

TECHNOLOGY

- Scientific Calculator
- World Wide Web
- Interactive CD-ROM

Algebra

You'll use proportions to solve for unknown values such as the time it takes a dolphin to swim a given distance.

CHAPTER 1 2 3 4 5 **6** 7 8 9 10 11 12

CHAPTER 7

Proportion, Scale, and Similarity

Problem Solving in Chapter 7

Maps and models of movie monsters show why scales are useful and important. Rates help you solve problems related to conservation.

TECHNOLOGY

- Geometry Software
- World Wide Web
- Interactive CD-ROM

Algebra

You'll use proportions to solve for unknown lengths in geometric figures, on maps, and on scale models.

CHAPTER 1 2 3 4 5 6 7 8 9 10 11 12

CHAPTER 8

Percents

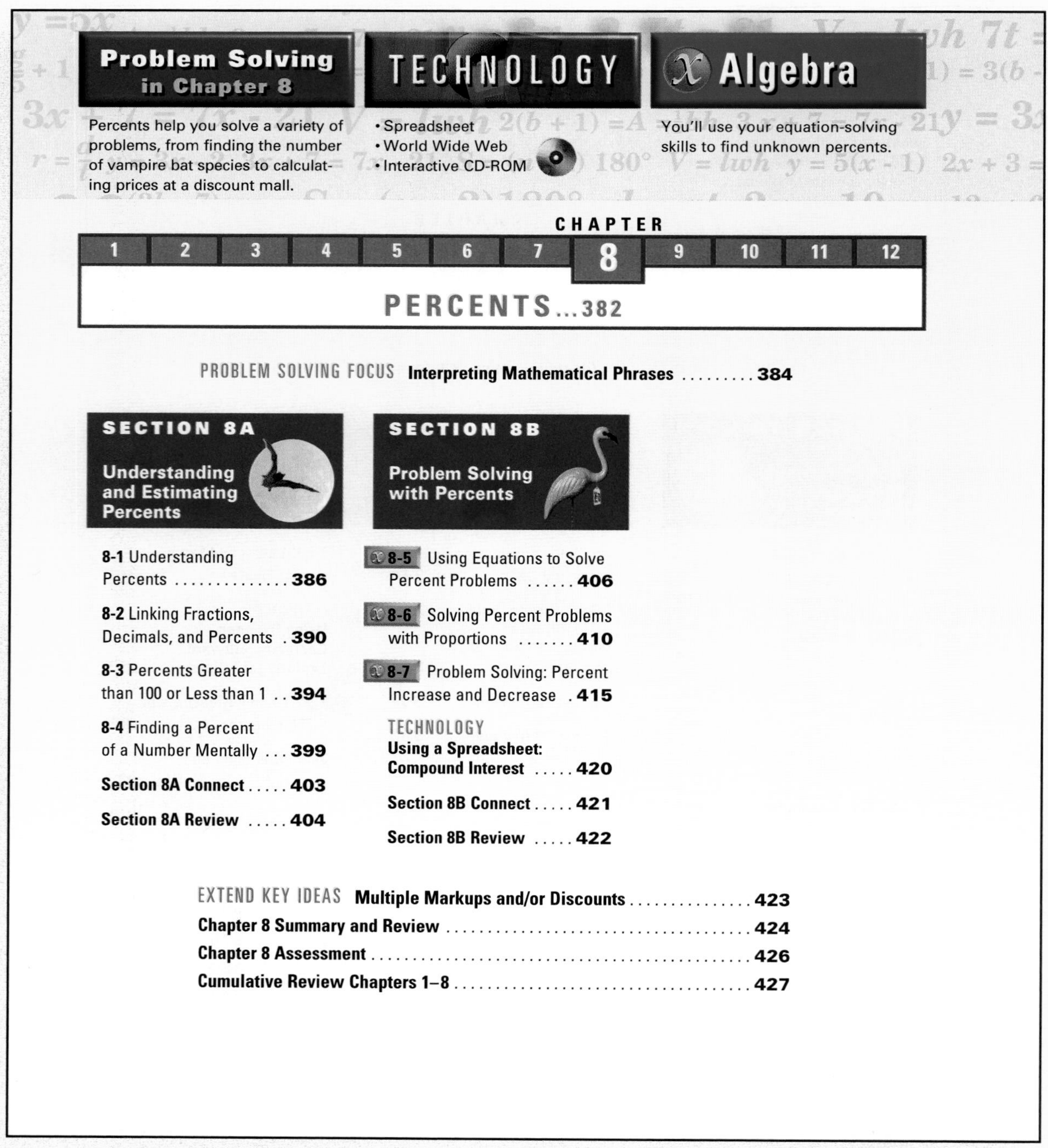

Problem Solving in Chapter 8

Percents help you solve a variety of problems, from finding the number of vampire bat species to calculating prices at a discount mall.

TECHNOLOGY

- Spreadsheet
- World Wide Web
- Interactive CD-ROM

Algebra

You'll use your equation-solving skills to find unknown percents.

CHAPTER 1 2 3 4 5 6 7 8 9 10 11 12

CHAPTER 9

Integers

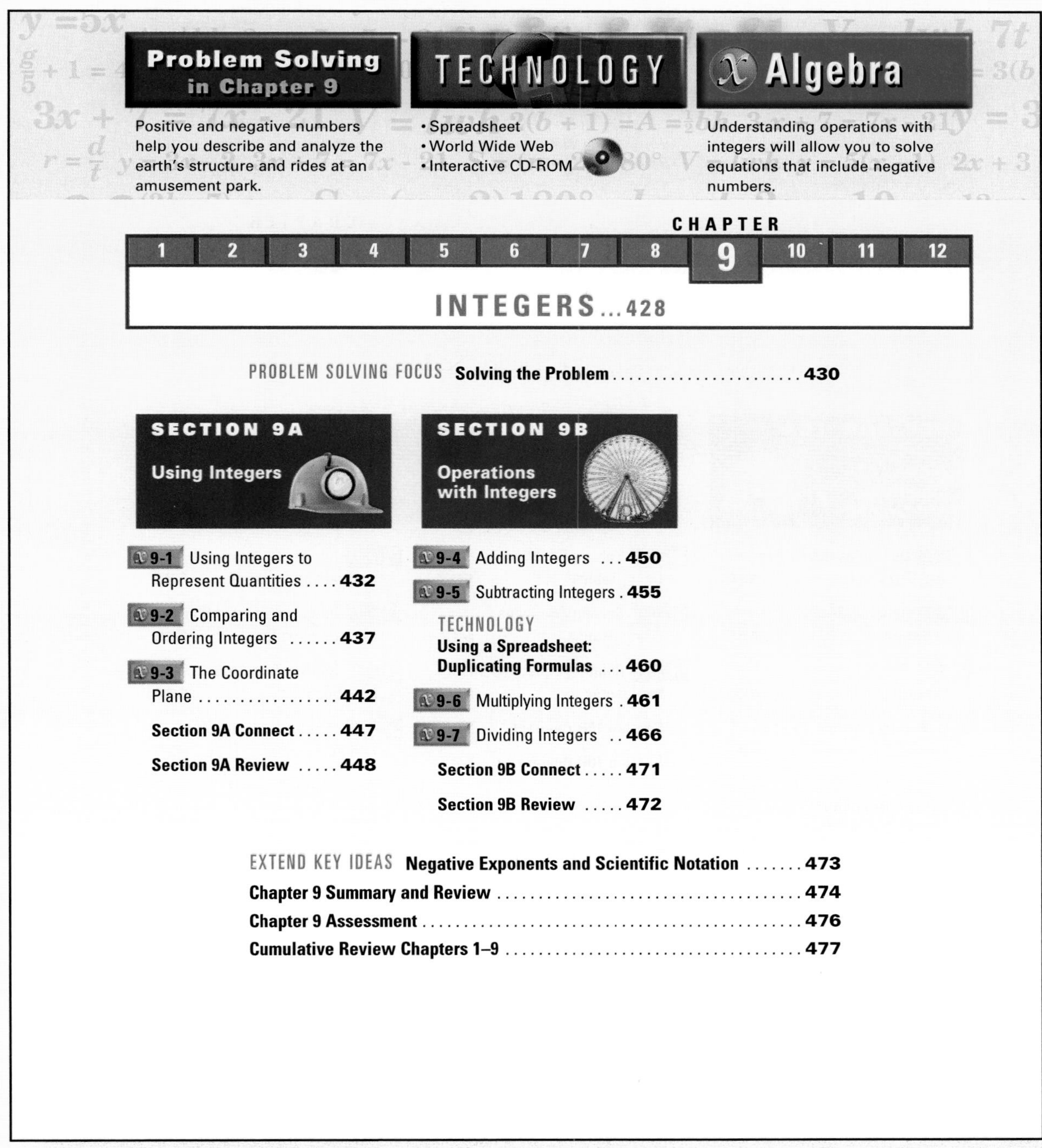

Problem Solving in Chapter 9

Positive and negative numbers help you describe and analyze the earth's structure and rides at an amusement park.

TECHNOLOGY

- Spreadsheet
- World Wide Web
- Interactive CD-ROM

Algebra

Understanding operations with integers will allow you to solve equations that include negative numbers.

CHAPTER 1 2 3 4 5 6 7 8 9 10 11 12

CHAPTER 10

The Patterns of Algebra: Equations and Graphs

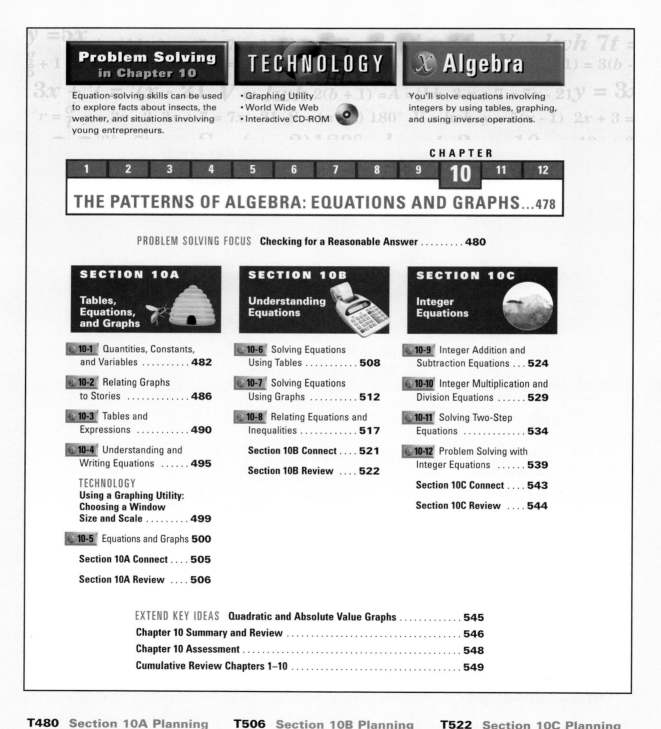

Problem Solving in Chapter 10

Equation-solving skills can be used to explore facts about insects, the weather, and situations involving young entrepreneurs.

TECHNOLOGY

- Graphing Utility
- World Wide Web
- Interactive CD-ROM

Algebra

You'll solve equations involving integers by using tables, graphing, and using inverse operations.

CHAPTER 1 2 3 4 5 6 7 8 9 **10** 11 12

CHAPTER 11

Geometry: Solids, Circles, and Transformations

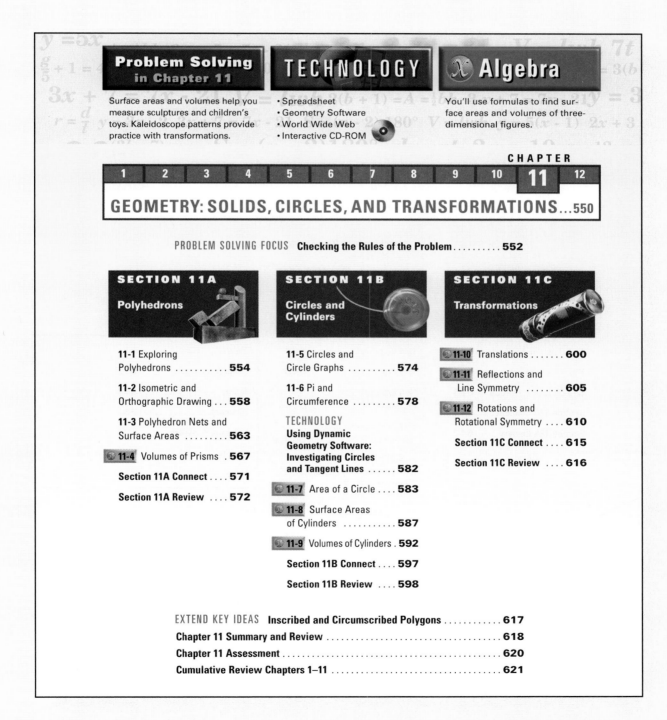

Problem Solving in Chapter 11

Surface areas and volumes help you measure sculptures and children's toys. Kaleidoscope patterns provide practice with transformations.

TECHNOLOGY

- Spreadsheet
- Geometry Software
- World Wide Web
- Interactive CD-ROM

Algebra

You'll use formulas to find surface areas and volumes of three-dimensional figures.

CHAPTER 1 2 3 4 5 6 7 8 9 10 11 12

CHAPTER 12

Counting and Probability

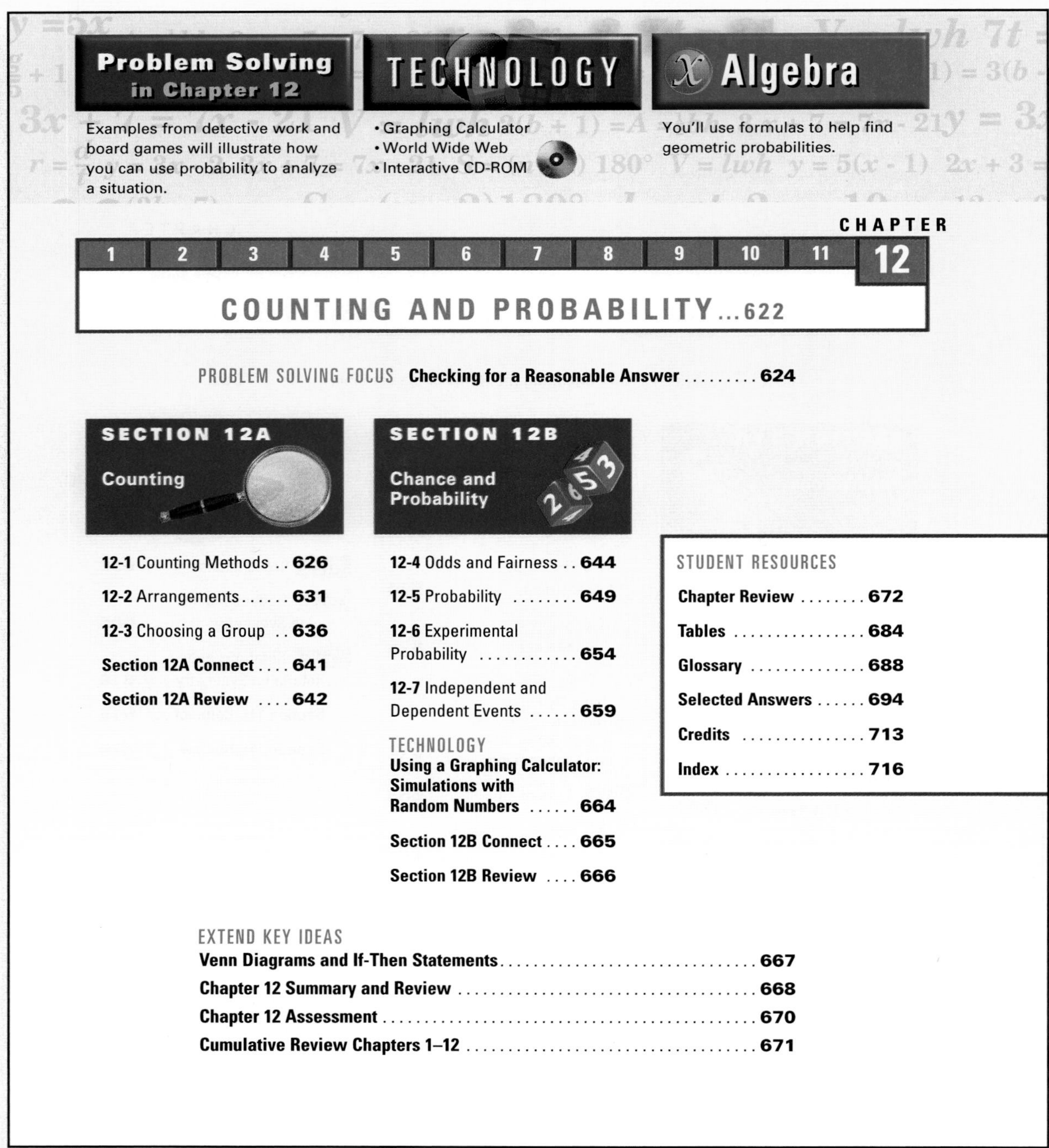

Problem Solving in Chapter 12

Examples from detective work and board games will illustrate how you can use probability to analyze a situation.

TECHNOLOGY

- Graphing Calculator
- World Wide Web
- Interactive CD-ROM

Algebra

You'll use formulas to help find geometric probabilities.

CHAPTER 1 2 3 4 5 6 7 8 9 10 11 12

Pacing Guide

The pacing suggested in the chart at the right assumes one day for most lessons, one day for end-of-section Connect and Review, and two days for end-of-chapter Summary, Review, and Assessment. The same number of days per chapter is used for the block scheduling options. For example, see page 2D.

You may need to adjust pacing to meet the needs of your students and your district curriculum.

	CHAPTER	PAGES	NUMBER OF DAYS
1	Making Sense of the World of Data	2–51	12
2	The Language of Algebra: Formulas, Expressions, and Equations	52–101	13
3	Number Sense: Decimals and Fractions	102–163	16
4	Operations with Fractions	164–207	11
5	Geometry and Measurement	208–269	15
6	Ratios, Rates, and Proportions	270–319	14
7	Proportion, Scale, and Similarity	320–381	16
8	Percents	382–427	12
9	Integers	428–477	13
10	The Patterns of Algebra: Equations and Graphs	478–549	18
11	Geometry: Solids, Circles, and Transformations	550–621	18
12	Counting and Probability	622–671	12
	Total Days		**170**

Materials List

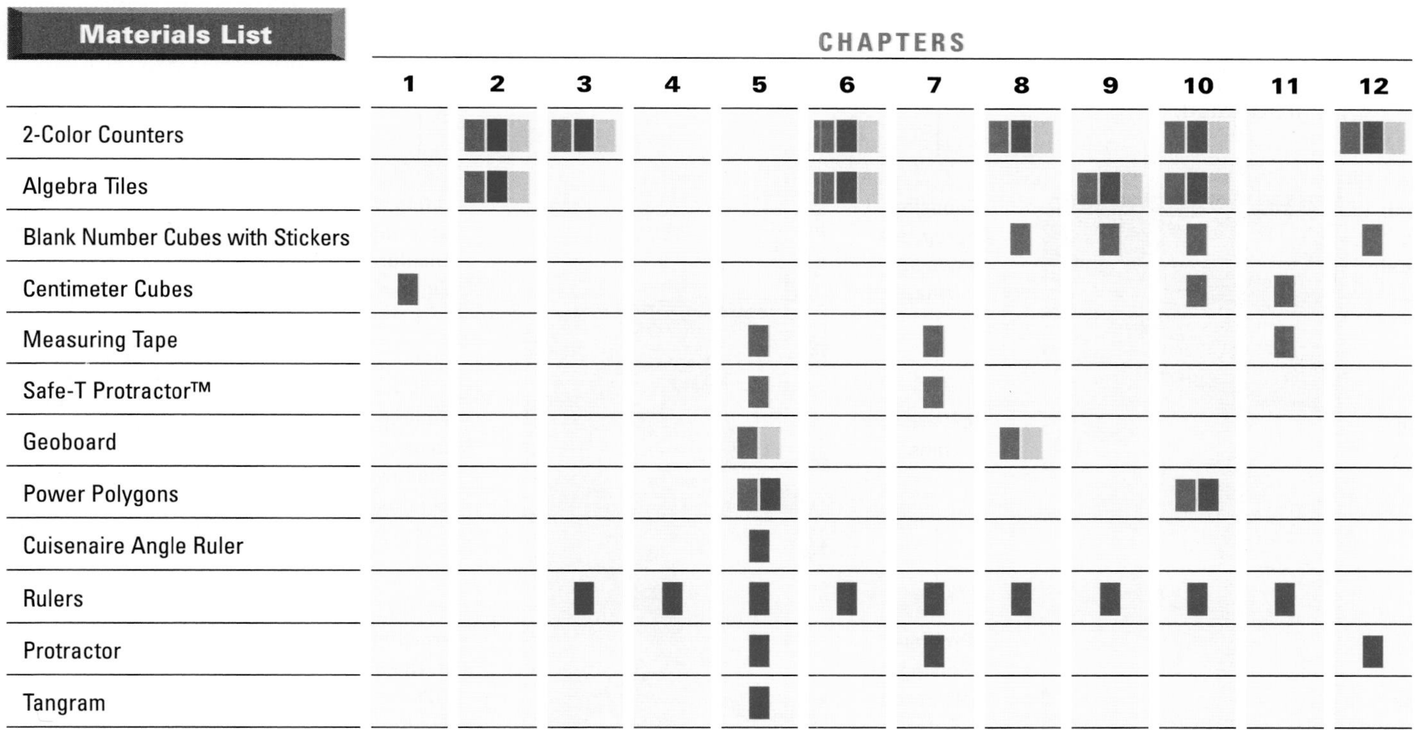

	CHAPTERS 1	2	3	4	5	6	7	8	9	10	11	12
2-Color Counters		S T O	S T O			S T O		S T O		S T O		S T O
Algebra Tiles		S T O				S T O			S T O	S T O		
Blank Number Cubes with Stickers								S	S	S		S
Centimeter Cubes	S									S	S	
Measuring Tape					S		S				S	
Safe-T Protractor™					S		S					
Geoboard					S O			S O				
Power Polygons					S T					S T		
Cuisenaire Angle Ruler					T							
Rulers			T	T	T	T	T	T	T	T	T	
Protractor					T		T					T
Tangram					T							

■ **Student Manipulative Kit** ■ **Teacher's Overhead Manipulative Kit** ■ **Transparencies in Teacher's ToolKit**

PACING AND MATERIALS

Chapter 7 Proportion, Scale, and Similarity

▶ OVERVIEW

Section 7A

Scale Drawings, Maps, and Scales: Students learn to work with scales, compare distances shown on maps, and use maps to solve practical problems. They learn how scale drawings and scale models are created.

7-1 Measurement: Estimating Actual and Scale Distances

7-2 Calculating with Scales

7-3 Problem Solving Using Maps

7-4 Creating Scale Drawings and Scale Models

Section 7B

Dimensional Analysis: Students learn to choose appropriate units when using rate. They learn to use conversion factors to solve problems.

7-5 Choosing Appropriate Rates and Units

7-6 Converting Units

7-7 Problem Solving: Converting Rates

Section 7C

Similarity: Students learn that figures that are scale models of another figure are similar. Students use proportions to find side lengths, perimeters, and area in similar figures.

7-8 Creating and Exploring Similar Figures

7-9 Finding Measures of Similar Figures

7-10 Perimeters and Areas of Similar Figures

Meeting NCTM Standards

Curriculum Standards

S T A N D A R D

Standard			pages
1	**Problem Solving**	Skills and Strategies	322, 335, 336, 348, 350, 367, 369, 370
		Applications	326–327, 331–332, 335–336, 339–340, 341, 347–348, 351–352, 355–356, 357, 363–364, 369–370, 373–374, 375
		Exploration	324, 328, 333, 337, 344, 349, 353, 360, 366, 371
2	**Communication**	Oral	323, 325, 330, 334, 338, 343, 346, 350, 353, 355, 362, *364*, 368, 372, 374
		Written	*322*, 327, 336, 340, 348, 356, 358, 364, 374
		Cooperative Learning	*320, 324, 333, 337, 344, 353, 360, 366, 371*
3	**Reasoning**	Critical Thinking	327, 332, *336,* 340, 352, 356, 364, 370, 374
4	**Connections**	Mathematical	See Standards 5, 7, 12, 13 below.
		Interdisciplinary	Arts & Literature; 320 Science 321, *343*, 345, *346*, 347, 356, 361, *368*; Social Studies 321; History *325*, 335, 338, 342, 345, 351, 374; Fine Arts 339, *359*, 364, *370*; Conservation 352, 355; Literature 325, 342, 351, *362*; Geography *323*, 327, 331, 332, *334*, 339; Language 329; Art 367; Entertainment 320; Industry *343, 359*
		Technology	*323, 343, 359,* 365
		Cultural	320, *330*
5	**Number and Number Relationships**		326, 328–332, *338*, 347, 350–352, 355, 358, 376
7	**Computation and Estimation**		326, *327, 329, 338, 350, 361, 373*
8	**Patterns and Functions**		*374*
10	**Statistics**		347, 356–357
12	**Geometry**		360–377
13	**Measurement**		324–356, 366–376

Italic type indicates Teacher Edition reference.

Teaching Standards

Focus on Questioning

In classroom discourse, questioning is an essential keystone. It is not solely a tool for teachers. Students themselves should

- initiate problems and questions.
- make conjectures and pose solutions.
- question the teacher as well as other students.

Assessment Standards

Focus on Openness

Portfolios The Openness Standard supports the use of regular communication from teacher to student about his or her progress. Portfolios allow students to choose work that exemplifies their understanding and portfolios allow teachers to give feed-back about the quality of this work. Materials from Chapter 7 that students put in their portfolios include

- scale drawings and maps.
- original problems about scale models.
- converting rates.

TECHNOLOGY

For the Teacher

- **Resource Pro, a Teacher's Resource Planner CD-ROM**
  Use the teacher planning CD-ROM to view resources available for Chapter 7. You can prepare custom lesson plans or use the default lesson plans provided.

- **World Wide Web**
  Visit **www.kz.com** to view class summary reports, individual student reports, and more.

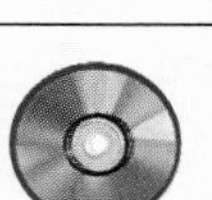

- **TestWorks**
  TestWorks provides ready-made tests and can create custom tests and practice worksheets.

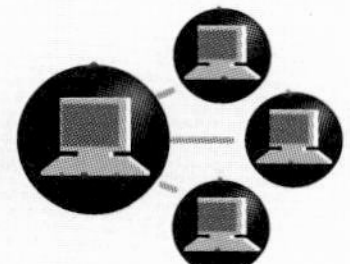

For the Parent

- **World Wide Web**
  Parents can use the Web site at **www.kz.com** to check on student progress or take a quick refresher course.

For the Student

- **Interactive CD-ROM**
  Lesson 7-10 has an *Interactive CD-ROM Lesson*. The *Interactive CD-ROM Journal* and *Interactive CD-ROM Geometry Tool* are also used in Chapter 7.

- **Wide World of Mathematics**
  Lesson 7-2 Algebra: Miniature Books
  Lesson 7-7 Middle School: New York City Marathon
  Lesson 7-10 Geometry: Seeing with Your Hands

- **World Wide Web**
  Use with Chapter and Section Openers; Students can go online to the Scott Foresman-Addison Wesley Web site at **www.mathsurf.com/7/ch7** to collect information about chapter themes. Students can also visit **www.kz.com** for tutorials and practice.

STANDARDIZED - TEST CORRELATION

SECTION 7A

LESSON	OBJECTIVE	ITBS Form M	CTBS 4th Ed.	CAT 5th Ed.	SAT 9th Ed.	MAT 7th Ed.	Your Form
7-1	• Read and understand scales. • Estimate distances from maps using scales.				✘ ✘	✘ ✘	
7-2	• Use scales and scale drawings to calculate actual distances.				✘	✘	
7-3	• Use scales to read maps and make decisions.						
7-4	• Select a reasonable scale for a drawing, map, or model.						

SECTION 7B

LESSON	OBJECTIVE	ITBS Form M	CTBS 4th Ed.	CAT 5th Ed.	SAT 9th Ed.	MAT 7th Ed.	Your Form
7-5	• Select an appropriate scale for a particular situation. • Write reciprocal rates that have the same meaning.						
7-6	• Convert measurements from one unit to another.			✘	✘	✘	
7-7	• Solve problems involving conversion of rates.			✘	✘	✘	

SECTION 7C

LESSON	OBJECTIVE	ITBS Form M	CTBS 4th Ed.	CAT 5th Ed.	SAT 9th Ed.	MAT 7th Ed.	Your Form
7-8	• Identify similar figures. • Write similarity statements.	✘	✘		✘		
7-9	• Find missing side lengths in similar figures. • Use shadows to find the heights of tall objects.				✘		
7-10	• Use the scale factor to find perimeters and areas of similar figures.						

Key: ITBS - Iowa Test of Basic Skills; CTBS - Comprehensive Test of Basic Skills; CAT - California Achievement Test; SAT - Stanford Achievement Test; MAT - Metropolitan Achievement Test

ASSESSMENT PROGRAM

Traditional Assessment

QUICK QUIZZES	SECTION REVIEW	CHAPTER REVIEW	CHAPTER ASSESSMENT FREE RESPONSE	CHAPTER ASSESSMENT MULTIPLE CHOICE	CUMULATIVE REVIEW
TE: pp. 327, 332, 336, 340, 348, 352, 356, 364, 370, 374	SE: pp. 342, 358, 376 *Quiz 7A, 7B, 7C	SE: pp. 378–379	SE: p. 380 *Ch. 7 Tests Forms A, B, E	*Ch. 7 Test Forms C, E	SE: p. 381 *Ch. 7 Test Form F

Alternate Assessment

INTERVIEW	JOURNAL	ONGOING	PERFORMANCE	PORTFOLIO	PROJECT	SELF
p. 364	SE: pp. 332, 342, 348, 352, 356, 358, 370, 376 TE: pp. 327, 352	TE: pp. 324, 328, 333, 337, 344, 349, 353, 360, 366, 371	SE: p. 380 TE: p. 374 *Ch. 7 Tests Forms D, E	TE: pp. 332, 340, 356	SE: pp. 340, 348, 370 TE: pp. 326, 348	TE: pp. 336, 370

*Tests and quizzes are in *Assessment Sourcebook*. Test Form E is a mixed response test. Forms for Alternate Assessment are also available in *Assessment Sourcebook*.

TestWorks: Test and Practice Software

MIDDLE SCHOOL PACING CHART

REGULAR PACING

Day	5 classes per week
1	Chapter 7 Opener; Problem Solving Focus
2	Section **7A** Opener; Lesson **7-1**
3	Lesson **7-2**
4	Lesson **7-3**
5	Lesson **7-4**
6	**7A** Connect; **7A** Review
7	Section **7B** Opener; Lesson **7-5**
8	Lesson **7-6**
9	Lesson **7-7**
10	**7B** Connect; **7B** Review
11	Section **7C** Opener; Lesson **7-8**
12	Technology; Lesson **7-9**
13	Lesson **7-10**
14	**7C** Connect; **7C** Review; Extend Key Ideas
15	Chapter 7 Summary and Review
16	Chapter 7 Assessment Cumulative Review, Chapters 1–7

BLOCK SCHEDULING OPTIONS

Block Scheduling for
Complete Course

Chapter 7 may be presented in

- ten 90-minute blocks
- thirteen 75-minute blocks

Each block consists of a combination of

- Chapter and Section Openers
- Explores
- Lesson Development
- Problem Solving Focus
- Technology
- Extend Key Ideas
- Connect
- Review
- Assessment

For details, see *Block Scheduling Handbook.*

Block Scheduling for
Interdisciplinary Course

Each block integrates math with another subject area.

In Chapter 7, interdisciplinary topics include

- Maps
- Conversation
- Movie Monsters

Themes for Interdisciplinary Team Teaching 7A, 7B, and 7C are

- Maps and Models
- Carbon Dioxide in the Atmosphere
- Measuring Similar Figures

For details, see *Block Scheduling Handbook.*

Block Scheduling for
Lab-Based Course

In each block, 30–40 minutes is devoted to lab activities including

- Explores in the Student Edition
- Connect pages in the Student Edition
- Technology options in the Student Edition
- Reteaching Activities in the Teacher Edition

For details, see *Block Scheduling Handbook.*

Block Scheduling for
Course with *Connected Mathematics*

In each block, investigations from **Connected Mathematics** replace or enhance the lessons in Chapter 7.

Connected Mathematics topics for Chapter 7 can be found in

- *Stretching and Shrinking*
- *Data Around Us*

For details, see *Block Scheduling Handbook.*

INTERDISCIPLINARY BULLETIN BOARD

Set Up

Cut out scale drawings of rooms, houses, and other floor plans from architecture and home decorating magazines. Put them on the bulletin board.

Procedure

Have small groups of students determine the scale used in each drawing. Have them label each drawing with its scale.

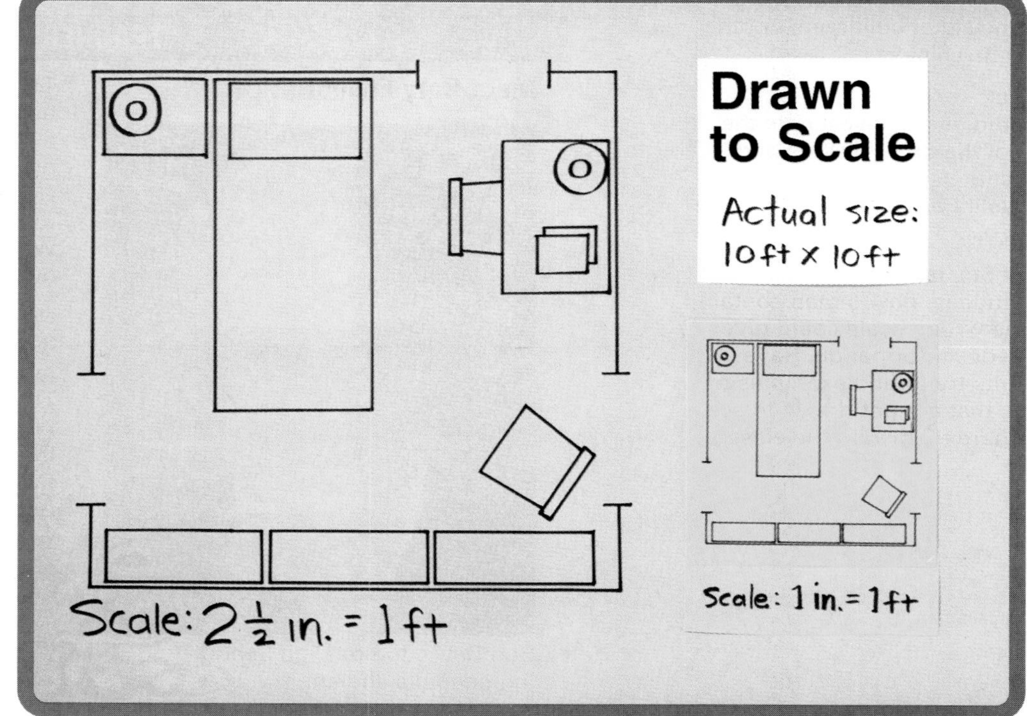

Chapter 7

The information on these pages shows how scale and rates are used in real-life situations.

World Wide Web

If your class has access to the World Wide Web, you might want to use the information found at the Web site addresses given.

Extensions

The following activities do not require access to the World Wide Web.

People of the World
Have students estimate their European shoe size. Then have them determine their actual European shoe size by multiplying the length of their feet in centimeters by $\frac{3}{2}$.

Arts & Literature
Suggest that interested students read *Gulliver's Travels* and report to the class about the size of other objects in the lands of Lilliput and Brobdingnag.

Entertainment
The largest sand castle ever built was 257.5 ft long. Ask students to research sand sculptures and compare the sizes of those built entirely by hand with those built with the aid of bulldozers or other heavy machines.

Science
Ask students to investigate the sizes of the other planets and predict the size of models of the planets if Earth is represented by a golf ball.

Social Studies
Ask students how a map containing the wrong scale could give erroneous information. Have students try to find examples of things that are not drawn to scale and share them with the class.

7 Proportion, Scale, and Similarity

Cultural Link
www.mathsurf.com/7/ch7/people

Entertainment Link
www.mathsurf.com/7/ch7/ent

People of the World

To estimate what your shoe size is in Europe, measure your foot in centimeters and multiply by $\frac{3}{2}$.

Entertainment

A sand castle is a scale model of a "real" castle. The tallest sand castle ever built stood over 23 feet tall! The World Championship Sand Sculpture Competition is held each September in Harrison Hot Springs, British Columbia, Canada.

Arts & Literature

In 1726, Jonathan Swift wrote a book called *Gulliver's Travels*. The hero, Gulliver, travels to two imaginary lands: Lilliput, where people are 6 inches tall, and Brobdingnag, where toddlers are over 40 feet tall.

320

TEACHER TALK

Meet Gary Emmert

Ben Davis Junior High School
Indianapolis, Indiana

To introduce a unit on scale drawing, I use a "treasure map." I begin by drawing a simple map on the overhead without giving a scale or a starting landmark. During a discussion of the map, students realize the importance of these two items. We proceed to find the treasure by introducing a landmark and devising a scale.

Next, I give each group of students a different-colored marble as a treasure to hide inside or outside the classroom. They are directed to draw a map showing a starting landmark, a scale, and the treasure location. Their map must have five right-angle turns, and exactly 150 feet total distance. I provide students with rulers and long measuring tapes. After the maps are completed, groups exchange maps and try to find the treasure. I create a rubric for the activity that evaluates quality and creativity as well as the accuracy of the map.

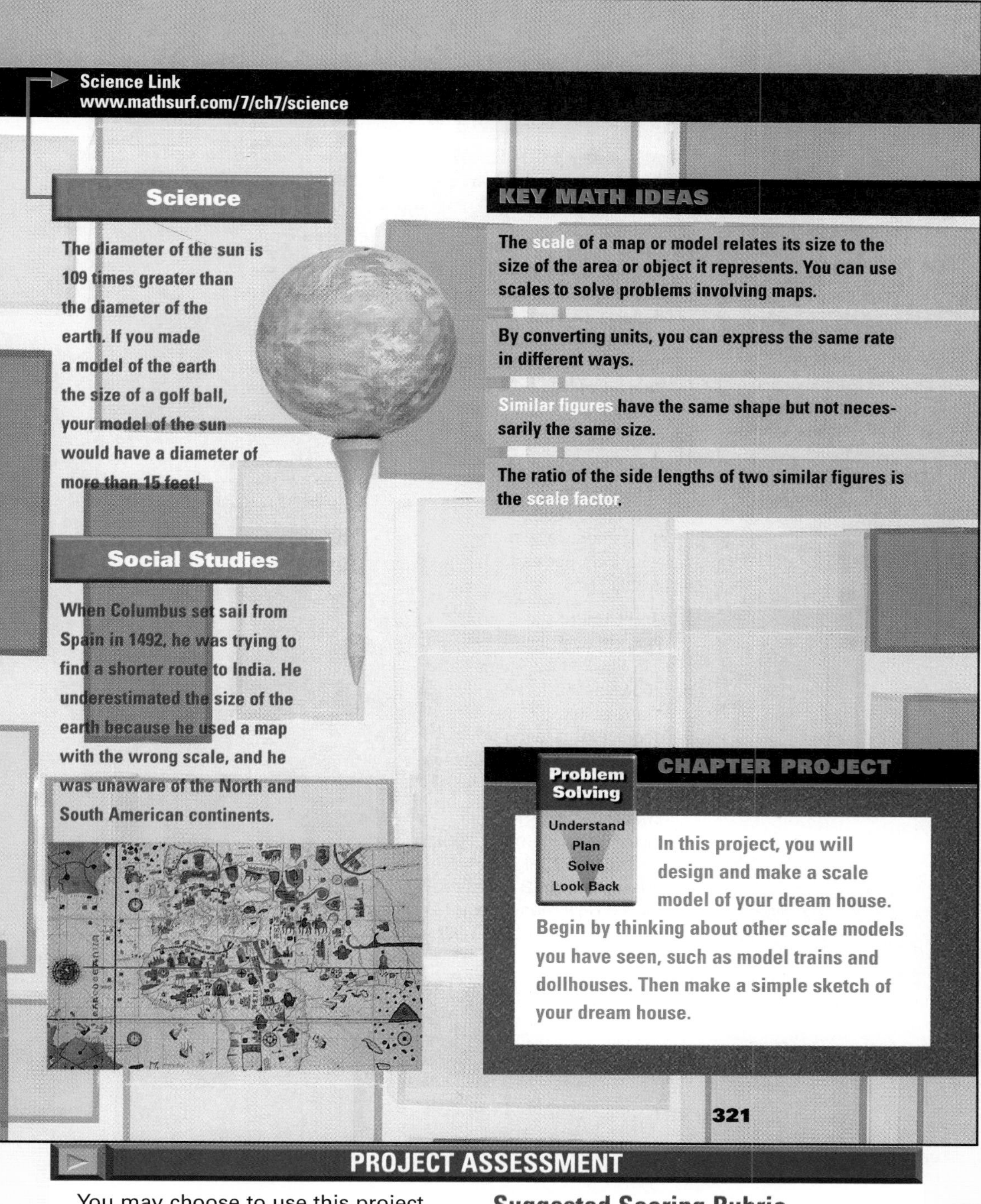

Science Link
www.mathsurf.com/7/ch7/science

Science

The diameter of the sun is 109 times greater than the diameter of the earth. If you made a model of the earth the size of a golf ball, your model of the sun would have a diameter of more than 15 feet!

Social Studies

When Columbus set sail from Spain in 1492, he was trying to find a shorter route to India. He underestimated the size of the earth because he used a map with the wrong scale, and he was unaware of the North and South American continents.

KEY MATH IDEAS

The **scale** of a map or model relates its size to the size of the area or object it represents. You can use scales to solve problems involving maps.

By converting units, you can express the same rate in different ways.

Similar figures have the same shape but not necessarily the same size.

The ratio of the side lengths of two similar figures is the **scale factor**.

CHAPTER PROJECT

Problem Solving
Understand
Plan
Solve
Look Back

In this project, you will design and make a scale model of your dream house. Begin by thinking about other scale models you have seen, such as model trains and dollhouses. Then make a simple sketch of your dream house.

321

PROJECT ASSESSMENT

You may choose to use this project as a performance assessment for the chapter.

Performance Assessment Key

Level 4 Full Accomplishment

Level 3 Substantial Accomplishment

Level 2 Partial Accomplishment

Level 1 Little Accomplishment

Suggested Scoring Rubric

4	•Determines an appropriate scale. •Neatly draws a model and labels all dimensions. •Builds a model or accurately computes the amount of paper needed to do so.
3	•Determines an adequate scale. •Draws an acceptable model with most dimensions labeled. •Attempts to build a model or computes the amount of paper needed.
2	•Attempts, with difficulty, to determine a scale. •Attempts to draw a model but does not show enough dimensions. •Does not make a model or compute the amount of paper needed.
1	•Does not know how to determine an appropriate scale. •Does not attempt to draw a model.

Chapter Project

Students will use their knowledge of scale to design and then make a model of their dream house.

Materials
Ruler, tape measure, construction paper, scissors, tape

Resources
Chapter 7 Project Master

Introduce the Project

- Have students share information about scale models they have seen or built.
- Discuss the kind of information students will need to make a scale model of their dream house, such as the kind of house they want to build and the scale they will use.
- Ask students for suggestions about the kinds of materials they might use in building a model. Talk about sources of information about model building, such as magazines or the Internet.

Project Progress

Section A, page 340 Students measure rooms at home to determine how large they want to make their dream house. Then they decide on an appropriate scale.

Section B, page 348 Students use the scale they picked to make a drawing of their model.

Section C, page 370 Students either build a model of their dream house using construction paper, or they calculate the amount of paper they would need if they were to build the model.

Community Project

A community project for Chapter 7 is available in *Home and Community Connections*.

Cooperative Learning

You may want to use Teaching Tool Transparency 1: Cooperative Learning Checklist with **Explore** and other group activities in this chapter.

Problem Solving Focus

Identifying Missing Information

The Point
Students focus on determining if there is enough information to solve the problem.

Resources
Teaching Tool Transparency 16: Problem-Solving Guidelines

 *Interactive CD-ROM Journal*

About the Page

Using the Problem-Solving Process
In real-life situations, students are often faced with solving problems in which not enough information is given. Students need to be able to determine if they have enough information and what, if any, information is missing. Discuss these suggestions for determining if information is missing:

- Read the problem two or three times before beginning work.
- Decide what information is needed to solve the problem.
- Determine if all the necessary information is given in the problem. If not, where might the information be found?

Ask ...
- What is Problem 1 asking? Do you have enough information to solve the problem? For the ratio of Muresan's height to that of Bogues; No.
- Is there any problem in which enough information is given? Yes; Problem 2

Answers for Problems
1. Needed: The height of Muggsy Bogues.
2. $\approx$ 12.2 rebounds per game.
3. The number of games in which Grant Hill played.
4. The number of 3-point shots Tim Legler made.

Journal
Ask students to write a paragraph describing how they could find the information they need to solve Problem 1.

Problem Solving
Understand
Plan
Solve
Look Back

Identifying Missing Information

As you make a problem-solving plan, you need to be sure you have all the information you need. Sometimes you will encounter a problem that is missing important information.

Problem Solving Focus

Identify any additional information needed to solve each problem. If a problem is not missing any information, give its solution.

1. 7-foot 7-inch, 303-pound Gheorghe Muresan is one of the tallest players in the National Basketball Association. Estimate the ratio of Muresan's height to that of the NBA's shortest player, 132-pound Muggsy Bogues.
2. In the 1995–96 season, David Robinson of the San Antonio Spurs had 1000 rebounds in 82 games. How many rebounds per game is this?
3. Grant Hill of the Detroit Pistons averaged 20.2 points per game in 1995–96. How many points did he score that season?
4. In 1995–96, the NBA's best long-range shooter was Tim Legler of the Washington Bullets. He made 52.2% of his attempts from 3-point range. How many 3-point shots did Legler attempt?

322

Additional Problem

Amy Van Dyken won the women's 100-meter butterfly event in swimming at the 1996 Summer Olympics in Atlanta, Georgia, by only 0.01 second over her nearest competitor, Liu Limin of China. Angel Martino also came in under one minute at 59.23 seconds, securing a third-place finish. What was Amy's time?

1. What does the problem ask you to find? Amy Van Dyken's winning time.
2. Is enough information given to solve the problem? No.
3. What additional information is needed? Where might you find this information? Liu Limin's time; Possible answer: A book or article summarizing 1996 Summer Olympic results.
4. Liu beat Angel by 0.09 second. Knowing this information, how can you find Amy's time? By subtracting 0.09 from Angel's time to find Liu's time (59.14 seconds) and then subtracting 0.01 to find Amy's time (59.13 seconds).

Scale Drawings, Maps, and Scales

LESSON PLANNING GUIDE

Student Edition

Ancillaries*

LESSON		MATERIALS	VOCABULARY	DAILY	OTHER
	Chapter 7 Opener				Ch. 7 Project Master Ch. 7 Community Project Teaching Tool Trans. 1
	Problem Solving Focus				Teaching Tool Trans. 16 *Interactive CD-ROM Journal*
	Section 7A Opener				
7-1	**Measurement: Estimating Actual and Scale Distances**	paper, yardstick or meter stick	scale	7-1	Teaching Tool Trans. 14 Lesson Enhancement Trans. 28
7-2	**Calculating with Scales**	graph paper	scale drawing	7-2	Teaching Tool Trans. 7, 20 Lesson Enhancement Trans. 29 *WW Math*–Algebra
7-3	**Problem Solving Using Maps**	ruler		7-3	Teaching Tool Trans. 14, 21 Lesson Enhancement Trans. 30
7-4	**Creating Scale Drawings and Scale Models**	earth globe, ruler, tape measure		7-4	Teaching Tool Trans. 14, 20 Lesson Enhancement Trans. 31 Ch. 7 Project Master
	Connect	tape measure, ruler			Teaching Tool Trans. 14 Interdisc. Team Teaching 7A
	Review				Practice 7A; Quiz 7A; *TestWorks*

* Daily Ancillaries include Practice, Reteaching, Problem Solving, Enrichment, and Daily Transparency. Teaching Tool Transparencies are in *Teacher's Toolkits*. Lesson Enhancement Transparencies are in *Overhead Transparency Package*.

SKILLS TRACE

LESSON	SKILL	FIRST INTRODUCED GR. 5	GR. 6	GR. 7	DEVELOP	PRACTICE/ APPLY	REVIEW
7-1	**Reading and understanding scales.**			✘ p. 324	pp. 324–325	pp. 326–327	pp. 342, 378, 389, 485
7-2	**Using scales and scale drawings to calculate distance.**			✘ p. 328	pp. 328–330	pp. 331–332	pp. 342, 378, 393, 489
7-3	**Using map scales and making decisions.**			✘ p. 333	pp. 333–334	pp. 335–336	pp. 342, 378, 398, 494

CONNECTED MATHEMATICS

The unit *Stretching and Shrinking (Similarity)*, from the **Connected Mathematics** series, can be used with Section 7A.

INTERDISCIPLINARY TEAM TEACHING

Math and Science/Technology

(Worksheet pages 25–26: Teacher pages T25–T26)

In this lesson, students use scales to interpret and make maps and models.

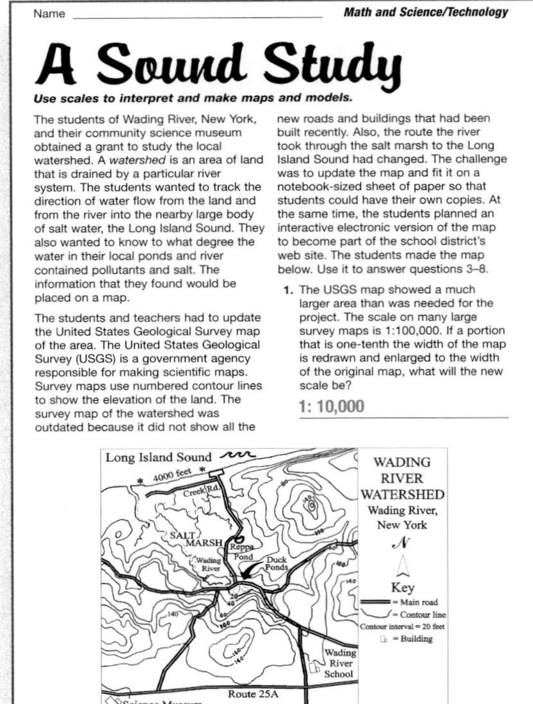

Name ______________________ *Math and Science/Technology*

A Sound Study

Use scales to interpret and make maps and models.

The students of Wading River, New York, and their community science museum obtained a grant to study the local watershed. A *watershed* is an area of land that is drained by a particular river system. The students wanted to track the direction of water flow from the land and from the river into the nearby large body of salt water, the Long Island Sound. They also wanted to know to what degree the water in their local ponds and river contained pollutants and salt. The information that they found would be placed on a map.

The students and teachers had to update the United States Geological Survey map of the area. The United States Geological Survey (USGS) is a government agency responsible for making scientific maps. Survey maps use numbered contour lines to show the elevation of the land. The survey map of the watershed was outdated because it did not show all the new roads and buildings that had been built recently. Also, the route the river took through the salt marsh to the Long Island Sound had changed. The challenge was to update the map and fit it on a notebook-sized sheet of paper so that students could have their own copies. At the same time, the students planned an interactive electronic version of the map to become part of the school district's web site. The students made the map below. Use it to answer questions 3–8.

1. The USGS map showed a much larger area than was needed for the project. The scale on many large survey maps is 1:100,000. If a portion that is one-tenth the width of the map is redrawn and enlarged to the width of the original map, what will the new scale be?

   1: 10,000

Name ______________________ *Math and Science/Technology*

2. The students at Wading River chose to enlarge one square portion of the survey map. They decided to use standard paper, $8\frac{1}{2}$ inches by 11 inches, and display it horizontally. The square map would be on the left and the title and key along the right side in a panel.

   a. In order to leave a $\frac{1}{2}$ inch margin on all the edges, what are the largest dimensions the square map can have?

   $7\frac{1}{2}$ in. $\times$ $7\frac{1}{2}$ in.; $8\frac{1}{2} - (\frac{1}{2} + \frac{1}{2}) =$ $7\frac{1}{2}$ in.

   b. What is the width of the side panel in which to write the key?

   $2\frac{1}{2}$ in.; $11 - 7\frac{1}{2} - (\frac{1}{2} + \frac{1}{2}) =$ $2\frac{1}{2}$ in.

3. Use the scale that you have made to find the distance in thousands of feet from the Science Museum to Wading River School. Write this distance. If there are 5,280 feet in a mile, what is the distance rounded to the nearest mile?

   12,000 feet; 2 miles

4. Students measured the salinity (saltiness) of the water in different locations and were surprised by their findings. Both the Duck Ponds and Reppa Pond had a salinity of 0.0. They also found them to be low in pollutants. Both are clean, freshwater ponds. The salt marsh and the Sound had a salinity of 1.0. Which freshwater pond is closest to the Sound? How far is it from the Sound?

   Reppa Pond; about 4,570 ft away from the Sound.

5. When it rained, students actually watched the flow of water down hillsides and toward the Sound. Find the highest point on the map. Using your scale, about how far is that point from the Long Island Sound?

   about 3,720 feet

6. Some students built clay models to show the runoff along the hillsides. If they made a scale model of that hill, they would make layers to show each contour line.

   a. What is the highest contour line on that hill?

   180 feet

   b. If a clay model of the hill was going to be six inches high, how many feet of elevation would each inch represent?

   30 feet

7. Get together with some friends or classmates to make a contour map of the area in which you live. Determine in which direction water flows. If you wish, make a three-dimensional model of the area. Make sure all measurements are to scale. Indicate the elevations of places such as where you live, your school, and nearby hills. For valuable information, visit the United States Geological Survey online at www.usgs.gov/.

BIBLIOGRAPHY

FOR TEACHERS

American Recycling Market. *The Official Recycled Products Guide*. Ogdensburg, NY: 1991.

Mango, Karin. *Mapmaking*. New York, NY: Messner, 1984.

The Earth Works Group. *50 Simple Things Kids Can Do to Recycle*. Berkeley, CA: Earthworks Press, 1994.

The Earth Works Group. *50 Simple Things You Can Do to Save the Earth*. Kansas City, MO: Andrew & McMeel, 1990.

FOR STUDENTS

Peters, Arno. *Peters Atlas of the World*. New York, NY: Harper & Row, 1990.

Swift, Jonathan. *Gulliver's Travels*. New York, NY: Knopf, 1991.

SECTION 7A

Scale Drawings, Maps, and Scales

▶ Geography Link ▶ www.mathsurf.com/7/ch7/maps

Never Mind— I'll Draw It Myself!

Imagine finding your way to an unfamiliar place across town without a map. Now imagine that you're going across a continent instead of across town; you can't take a plane, car, or bus; and you're not sure you'll make it back alive. Sound like fun?

In 1804, Meriwether Lewis and William Clark set out from St. Louis on exactly this kind of trip. With the help of native people, they traveled from St. Louis to the Pacific Ocean and back—without a map! As they traveled, guided by a Shoshone woman, Sacajawea, Lewis and Clark recorded information so *they* could make a map of the region. They talked to Native Americans, observed the sun and stars, noted important landmarks, and estimated distances. The map they produced was extremely accurate.

Accurate mapmaking requires careful mathematics. You will learn about many of the skills mapmakers use. Then, like Lewis and Clark, you'll make a map of previously unmapped territory!

Captains Lewis & Clark holding a Council with the Indians

1 The Lewis and Clark expedition traveled about 8000 miles in 2 years, 4 months. How many miles per month is this?

2 Two towns separated by 20 mi are 1 in. apart on a map. How far apart should the mapmaker draw two towns that are separated by 60 mi? Explain your reasoning.

323

Where are we now?

In Chapter 6, students used ratios and rates to compare quantities.

They learned how to

- find missing terms in pairs of equivalent ratios.
- deal with rates as special ratios.
- use ratios to create proportions.
- use equal ratios to solve proportions.
- solve proportions by using cross-products.

Where are we going?

In Section 7A, students will

- use ratios to compare distances shown on maps.
- use scales to calculate distances on various models.
- use scales to read maps.
- select a reasonable scale for a drawing, map, or model.

Section 7A

Theme: Maps

World Wide Web

If your class has access to the World Wide Web, you might want to use the information found at the Web site address given. The interdisciplinary link relates to the topics discussed in this section.

About the Page

This page introduces the theme of the section, maps, and discusses the maps made by Lewis and Clark when they explored the west.

Ask ...

- Have you ever tried to read a road map?
- How does a road map differ from other maps you have seen?
- What is a scale of a map? The relationship between the distances on a map and the corresponding actual distances.

Extension

The following activity does not require access to the World Wide Web.

Geography

A variety of maps including globes, road maps, wall maps, relief maps, Mercator maps, and so on, are in use today. Have students research the various types of maps, describe how they are used, and show examples of these maps.

Answers for Questions

1. About 286 miles per month.
2. Three inches; 60 miles is 3 • 20 miles, so map distance is 3 • 1 inch.

Connect

On page 341, students create a map of their classroom.

7-1 Lesson Organizer

Objectives

- Read and understand scales.
- Estimate distances from maps using scales.

Vocabulary

- Scale

Materials

- Explore: Paper, yardstick or meter stick

NCTM Standards

- 1–5, 7, 13

Review

Solve for *x*.

1. $\frac{5}{12} = \frac{x}{36}$ $x = 15$
2. $\frac{6}{x} = \frac{8}{4}$ $x = 3$
3. $\frac{24}{30} = \frac{16}{x}$ $x = 20$

Available on Daily Transparency 7-1

Lesson Link

Ask students to describe some of the ways in which they have used ratios. Identify those that involve comparing quantities. Explain that ratios can also be used to compare actual distances with distances shown on maps.

1 Introduce

Explore

You may wish to use Teaching Tool Transparency 14: Rulers with **Explore**.

The Point

Students explore issues involved in choosing a scale by making a map of an area around their school.

Ongoing Assessment

Check that students choose appropriate distances to measure or estimate, make realistic estimates, and measure distances correctly.

7-1 Measurement: Estimating Actual and Scale Distances

You'll Learn ...

- to read and understand scales
- to estimate distances from maps using scales

... How It's Used

Travel planners need to be able to read distances from maps to organize trips.

Vocabulary

scale

Lesson Link You've used ratios to compare quantities. Now you'll see how ratios are used to compare actual distances with distances shown on maps.

Explore Maps

A Map Is a Snap!

Materials: Paper, Yardstick or meter stick

1. Choose an area around your school you would like to map.
2. Before beginning a detailed map, make a rough sketch of the area you chose. Estimate or measure important distances and record the locations of significant landmarks.
3. Draw your map. Make it as accurate as you can.
4. How did you decide how large to make objects on your map and how far apart to draw them?
5. Most people cannot draw a perfect map. Does any part of your map look distorted? If so, how can you tell?
6. Did you use ratios or proportions to draw your map? Explain.

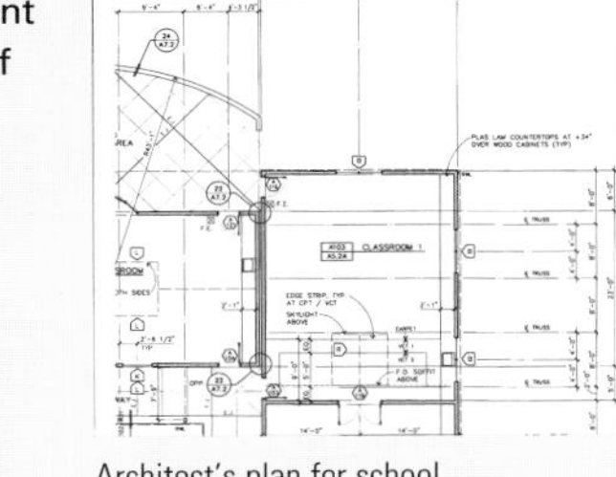

Architect's plan for school

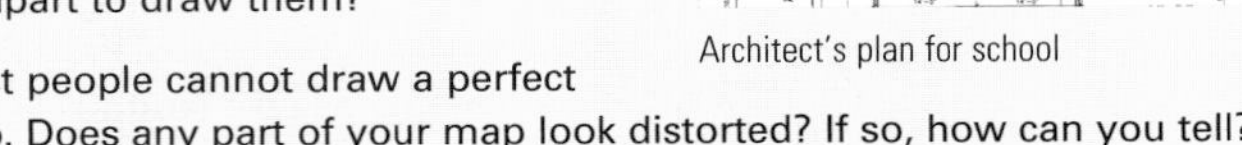

Learn Estimating Actual and Scale Distances

The ratio used to reduce real roads, cities, and countries so they fit on a map is the **scale**. The scale is the ratio of the distance between two points on the map to the actual distance between the points.

Suppose a 10 mi long road has a length of 1 in. on a map. Here are three ways to write the map's scale:

$\frac{1 \text{ in.}}{10 \text{ mi}}$ 1 in.:10 mi   1 in. = 10 mi

MEETING INDIVIDUAL NEEDS

Resources

- 7-1 Practice
- 7-1 Reteaching
- 7-1 Problem Solving
- 7-1 Enrichment
- 7-1 Daily Transparency
  - Problem of the Day
  - Review
  - Quick Quiz
- Teaching Tool Transparency 14
- Lesson Enhancement Transparency 28

Learning Modalities

Verbal Have students write a short story based on one of the maps they created in this lesson.

Visual Have students use a computer drafting program to make their maps

Inclusion

Students with visual/perceptual problems may have difficulty isolating relevant information on maps. It may be helpful for them to use a marker to highlight the points involved in a problem, cover the map with tracing paper and copy the points, connect the points with a straight line, and use the traced image to help them solve the problem. In severe cases, you may wish to use simplified maps.

Bring in sample maps and demonstrate how a scale is represented.

Add new vocabulary to reference book.

Examples

1 Lewis and Clark traveled from St. Louis to the Pacific coast. These points are actually about 1800 miles apart. Estimate the scale of the map.

On the map, St. Louis is about 2 in. from the Pacific coast. The scale is about

$\frac{2 \text{ in.}}{1800 \text{ mi}}$, or $\frac{1 \text{ in.}}{900 \text{ mi}}$.

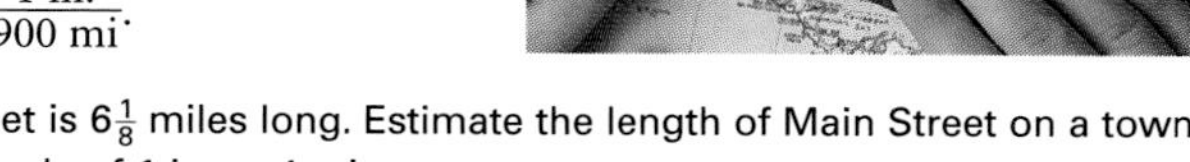

2 Main Street is $6\frac{1}{8}$ miles long. Estimate the length of Main Street on a town map with a scale of 1 in. = 4 mi.

A 4-mile road is 1 in. long on the map. So 2 mi is $\frac{1}{2}$ in. long and 6 mi (3 times as far) is $1\frac{1}{2}$ in. long on the map. Main Street's length of $6\frac{1}{8}$ mi is about $1\frac{1}{2}$ in. on the map.

Try It

Estimate the map length of a 15 mi road on a map with a scale of $\frac{1 \text{ in.}}{8 \text{ mi}}$. A little less than 2 inches: ≈ 1.9 inches

Example 3

A map uses a scale of 2 cm:5 km. Estimate the actual length of a road whose map length is 5.5 cm.

Every 2 cm represents 5 km, so 6 cm would represent 15 km. A length of 5.5 cm represents a little less than 15 km.

A good estimate for the length of the road is about 14 km.

Try It

A map uses the scale 2 cm = 75 km. If the Suez Canal is 3.9 cm long on the map, estimate the actual length of the Suez Canal. ≈ 150 km

▶ Literature Link

Almost every town in the United States has a Main Street. Sinclair Lewis (1885–1951) wrote a novel called *Main Street* that presented a grim picture of small-town life.

The metric system of measurement was developed in France after the French Revolution. One meter was defined as one ten-millionth of the distance from the North Pole to the Equator.

Check Your Understanding

1. Why is it important to know the scale of a map?
2. You begin a map with a scale of 1 in.:500 ft, then find that it will be too large to fit your paper. How would you change the scale? Explain.
3. Would two maps of Utah have the same shape even if the scales were different? Explain.

For Groups That Finish Early
Map another area, using the same proportions as in this map.
Answers may vary.

Answers for Explore
1–3. Answers may vary.
4. By comparing the size of the objects to the size of the paper and seeing how far apart they were in relation to each other.
5. Answers may vary.
6. Yes; Used proportions to keep relative sizes the same.

2 Teach

Learn

You might want to use Lesson Enhancement Transparency 28 with **Learn.**

Alternate Examples

1. On a map of South Africa, the distance from Johannesburg to Victoria Falls is about 3 cm. The actual distance is about 900 km. Estimate the scale of the map.

   The scale is about $\frac{3 \text{ cm}}{900 \text{ km}}$, or $\frac{1 \text{ cm}}{300 \text{ km}}$.

2. Market Street is $7\frac{1}{2}$ miles long. Estimate the length of Market Street on a town map with a scale of 1 in. = 2 mi.

   Since a 2-mi road is 1 in. long, a road almost 8 mi long will have a map length of about 4 in.

3. A map uses a scale of 3 cm:500 km. Estimate the actual length for which the map length is 10 cm.

   Every 3 cm represents 500 km, so 9 cm would represent 1500 km and 1 more cm would represent a little less than 200 km, for a total of 1700 km.

3 Practice and Assess

Check

Answers for Check Your Understanding
1. To see about how far apart places on the map really are.
2. Possible answer: Change the scale so that 1 in. represents more than 500 ft. Then the drawing will be smaller.
3. Yes; Both maps show the same territory.

MATH EVERY DAY

▶ Problem of the Day

Jacque is taller than Sandy. Meg is shorter than Evan. Kayla is taller than Jacque, but shorter than Evan. Sandy is not the shortest of the five people. List the five people, from tallest to shortest. Possible answer: Evan, Kayla, Jacque, Sandy, Meg

Available on Daily Transparency 7-1

An Extension is provided in the transparency package.

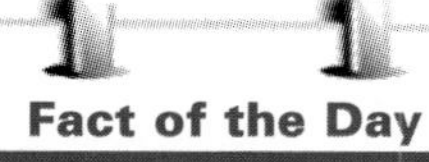

Fact of the Day

Sacajawea, Shoshone guide for the Lewis and Clark expedition, was about 17 years old at the time. She also was their interpreter and helped obtain supplies.

Mental Math

Do these mentally.

1. $\frac{3}{4} + 1\frac{1}{2}$ $2\frac{1}{4}$
2. $5 - 2\frac{2}{3}$ $2\frac{1}{3}$
3. 6.4 + 7.3 13.7
4. 7.1 − 1.4 5.7

7-1 Exercises and Applications

Assignment Guide

- **Basic**
  1–8, 11,14,15, 18, 19–33 odds
- **Average**
  1, 2–20 evens, 21, 22–34 evens
- **Enriched**
  1–9 odds, 12–21, 23–33 odds

Exercise Notes

Exercise 13

Estimation Students may have a wide range of answers to this problem, depending upon the estimation strategy used. For example, a student might think that 1 cm is about 300 km and South America is about 30 cm long, so its actual length is about 300 • 30, or 9000 km.

Exercise Answers

2. $\frac{2 \text{ in.}}{75 \text{ mi}}$, 2 in. = 75 mi
3. 1 in.:225 mi, $\frac{1 \text{ in.}}{225 \text{ mi}}$
4. 1 cm:30 km, 1 cm = 30 km
5. 6 cm = 100 km, $\frac{6 \text{ cm}}{100 \text{ km}}$
6. 5 in.:5 mi, 5 in. = 5 mi

Reteaching

Activity

Materials: Maps showing your town

- Find at least three different maps that show your town. Find the scale on each of the maps. Are they the same or different? Why?
- Find all the towns within a map distance of 3 in. of your town. How far away is the farthest town on each map?
- Find a town 100 mi from your own. Use the scale to find the map distance between the towns and then measure the distance on the map to check your work.

7-1 Exercises and Applications

PRACTICE 7-1

Practice and Apply

1. **Getting Started** Follow these steps to estimate the distance between two cities shown $5\frac{1}{8}$ inches apart on a map with a scale of 1 in. = 15 mi.
   a. Determine the number of miles represented by 5 inches. **75 miles**
   b. Estimate the number of miles represented by $\frac{1}{8}$ inch. ≈ **1.9 miles**
   c. Add the numbers you found to estimate the total actual distance. ≈ **76.9 miles**

Number Sense Write each scale in two other ways.

2. 2 in.:75 mi
3. 1 in. = 225 mi
4. $\frac{1 \text{ cm}}{30 \text{ km}}$
5. 6 cm:100 km
6. $\frac{5 \text{ in.}}{5 \text{ mi}}$

Use the following measurements to estimate the scale of each map.

7. A 60 mi road is 5 in. long. **1 in.:10–12 mi**
8. A 110 km wide park is 22 cm wide. **1 cm:5 km**
9. A 75 mi trail is $10\frac{1}{2}$ in. long. **1 in.:7–8 mi**
10. A 4866 km wide continent is 3 cm wide. **1 cm:1600–2000 km**

Estimation Estimate each map distance.

11. A bullet train travels 192 kilometers between the Japanese cities of Hiroshima and Kokuru. About how long will the train line appear on a map with the scale $\frac{1 \text{ cm}}{100 \text{ km}}$? ≈ **2 cm**
12. New York City is 205 miles from Washington, DC. About how far apart will these cities appear on a map with the scale of 1 in.:50 mi? ≈ **4 in.**
13. A map uses the scale 1 cm = 319 km. If South America is 27.7 cm long on the map, estimate the actual length of South America. ≈ **9000 km**

Use the map and a ruler to estimate each straight-line distance in miles.

14. Boise City to Forgan ≈ **105 mi**
15. Hardesty to Kenton ≈ **100 mi**
16. Tyrone to Guymon ≈ **25 mi**

PRACTICE

Name ______________________

Practice 7-1

Measurement: Estimating Actual and Scale Distances

Write each scale in two other ways.

1. 1 in. : 25 mi — **$\frac{1 \text{ in.}}{25 \text{ mi}}$, 1 in. = 25 mi**
2. 3 cm = 100 km — **$\frac{3 \text{ cm}}{100 \text{ km}}$, 3 cm : 100 km**
3. $\frac{2 \text{ in.}}{17 \text{ mi}}$ — **2 in. : 17 mi, 2 in. = 17 mi**
4. 5 cm : 8 km — **$\frac{5 \text{ cm}}{8 \text{ km}}$, 5 cm = 8 km**
5. 4 in. = 21 mi — **$\frac{4 \text{ in.}}{21 \text{ mi}}$, 4 in. : 21 mi**
6. $\frac{1 \text{ cm}}{85 \text{ km}}$ — **1 cm : 85 km, 1 cm = 85 km**

Use the following measurements to find the scale of each map.

7. A 540-mile river is 10 inches long. **$\frac{1 \text{ in.}}{54 \text{ mi}}$**
8. A 15-km street is 3 cm long. **1 cm : 5 km**
9. A 2-mile-wide park is 5 inches wide. **5 in. = 2 mi**
10. A 390-km freeway is 13 cm long. **$\frac{1 \text{ cm}}{30 \text{ km}}$**
11. A 375-km railroad route is 15 cm long. **1 cm = 25 km**

Geography Estimate each map distance.

12. Dallas, Texas, is 803 miles from Chicago, Illinois. About how far apart will these cities appear on a map with scale 1 in. = 40 mi? **About 20 in.**
13. Shanghai, China, is 1229 km from Hong Kong. About how far apart will these cities appear on a map with scale 1 cm : 500 km? **About 2.5 cm**
14. **Science** The largest scale model of our solar system features a "Sun" at the Lakeview Museum in Peoria, Illinois. "Jupiter" is located about 20,600 feet away from the museum. The actual distance between the Sun and Jupiter is about 480,000,000 miles. Estimate the scale of the model solar system. **About 1 ft : 23,000 mi**

RETEACHING

Name ______________________

Alternative Lesson 7-1

Measurement: Estimating Actual and Scale Distances

The ratio used to reduce real roads, cities, and countries so they fit on a map is the **scale.** The scale is the ratio of the distance between two points on the map to the actual distance between the points.

Example 1

Use these measurements to estimate the scale of Carly's map.

The actual distance between Claremont and Rampart is about 16 miles. On the map, the distance is about 2 inches. Write as a ratio.

Distance on map → / Actual distance → $\frac{2 \text{ in.}}{16 \text{ mi}} = \frac{1 \text{ in.}}{8 \text{ mi}}$

So, the scale of Carly's map can be written as $\frac{1 \text{ in.}}{8 \text{ mi}}$ or 1 in.:8 mi or 1 in. = 8 mi.

Try It Use the following measurements to find the scale of each map. Write each scale in three ways.

a. A 60-mile road is 15 inches long.
   Distance on map → / Actual distance → $\frac{15 \text{ in.}}{60 \text{ mi}} = \frac{1 \text{ in.}}{4 \text{ mi}}$
   $\frac{1 \text{ in.}}{4 \text{ mi}}$, 1 in.:4 mi, 1 in. = 4 mi.
b. A 25-kilometer trail is 2 inches long.
   $\frac{2 \text{ in.}}{25 \text{ km}}$, 2 in.:25 km, 2 in. = 25 km.

Example 2

On a map, the distance between Claremont and Westview is $1\frac{1}{2}$ inches. The scale of the map is 1 in.:8 mi. What is the actual length of the road?

Since the distance between Claremont and Westview on the map is $1\frac{1}{2}$ inches, multiply $1\frac{1}{2}$ and the number of miles per inch: $1\frac{1}{2} \times 8 = 12$.

So, the actual distance between Claremont and Westview is 12 miles.

Try It

c. Find the actual length of a road that measures $3\frac{1}{4}$ inches on a map with a scale of 1 in. = 8 mi. **26 mi**
d. Find th϶ actual length of a woodland path that measures $2\frac{1}{2}$ centimeters on a map with a scale of 1 cm:5 km. **12.5 km**

17. Geography The students at Clissold Elementary School in Chicago, Illinois, painted a map of the world on their playground. The United States, which is about 3000 miles wide, measures 25 feet across on the playground map. Estimate the scale of their map.

18. **Test Prep** Two towns are 146 miles apart. About how far apart will they appear on a map with the scale 1 in. = 45 mi? **B**

Ⓐ 2 in. Ⓑ 3 in. Ⓒ 45 in. Ⓓ 135 in.

Problem Solving and Reasoning

19. Critical Thinking Yellowstone Lake, in Wyoming, is the largest high-altitude lake in North America, measuring 20 mi long and 14 mi wide. About how long and wide would Yellowstone Lake appear on a map with the scale 1 in. = 3 mi? **≈ 7 in. long, ≈ 5 in. wide**

20. Communicate Fantasy novels such as J. R. R. Tolkien's *The Hobbit* often contain maps of imaginary lands. Draw your own map of an imaginary world. Include as much detail as you like. When you are finished, write a scale next to your map. Explain how you calculated your scale.

21. Critical Thinking GPS A group of artists produced a miniature model of New York City in which every detail of the city is modeled at a much smaller scale. A 1200 ft tall building measures just 1 ft tall in the model. Express the scale used in the model in in. per ft. **1 in.:100 ft**

PROBLEM SOLVING 7-1

Mixed Review

Estimate each sum or difference. *[Lesson 4-1]*

22. $\frac{1}{5} + \frac{3}{8} \approx \frac{1}{2}$ **23.** $\frac{2}{3} - \frac{1}{7} \approx \frac{1}{2}$ **24.** $\frac{1}{6} - \frac{1}{9} \approx 0$ **25.** $\frac{5}{12} + \frac{3}{7} \approx 1$ **26.** $\frac{1}{7} + \frac{4}{5} \approx 1$

27. $\frac{2}{9} - \frac{1}{13} \approx 0$ **28.** $\frac{4}{5} - \frac{1}{6} \approx 1$ **29.** $\frac{5}{11} + \frac{1}{8} \approx \frac{1}{2}$ **30.** $\frac{7}{15} + \frac{2}{3} \approx 1$ **31.** $\frac{11}{12} + \frac{1}{20} \approx 1$

Find the area of each trapezoid or parallelogram. *[Lesson 5-9]*

32.

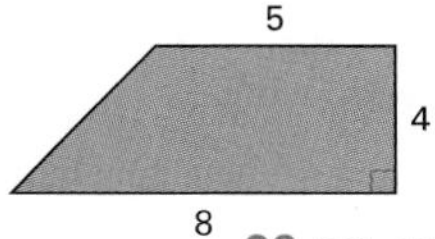

26 sq. units

33.

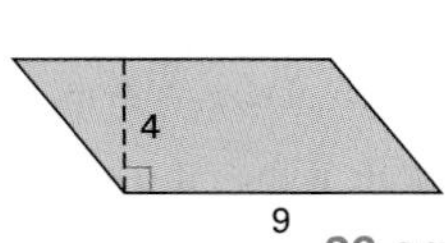

36 sq. units

34.

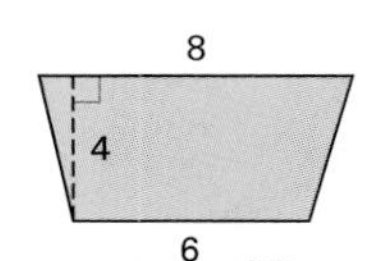

28 sq. units

Exercise Notes

■ Exercises 22–31

Estimation Encourage students to think about whether the answer is close to 0, close to $\frac{1}{2}$, close to 1, or close to $1\frac{1}{2}$. Students may have reasonable estimates that are different from those given in the answer key.

Exercise Answers

17. ≈ 1 ft:100 mi.

20. Answers may vary.

Alternate Assessment

You may want to use the *Interactive CD-ROM Journal* with this assessment.

Journal Have students write about what they learned about scale in this lesson. Ask them to include hints for beginners that might help them select an appropriate scale for a map, find the scale given a map, or find a distance when given a scale.

Quick Quiz

1. Two towns are $3\frac{1}{2}$ inches apart on a map. The scale of the map is 1 inch = 30 miles. What is the actual distance between the towns? 105 miles
2. Two trees are 175 yards apart. On Sandy's map, they are 7 cm apart. What is the scale of Sandy's map? 1 cm = 25 yards
3. A map has a scale of 2 cm = 90 km. The distance between two lakes is actually 225 km. How far apart are they on the map? 5 cm

Available on Daily Transparency 7-1

PROBLEM SOLVING

Name ______________________

Guided Problem Solving 7-1

GPS **PROBLEM 21, STUDENT PAGE 327**

A group of artists produced a miniature model of New York City in which every detail of the city is modeled at a much smaller scale. A 1200 ft tall building measures just 1 ft tall in the model. Express the scale used in the model in in. per ft.

— Understand —

1. How tall is the model? **1 foot tall.**
2. How tall is the actual building? **1200 feet tall.**
3. What will your ratio of the scale compare? **Height of model to actual height of building.**
4. What units of measure are used in the scale? **in. and ft**

— Plan —

5. Which ratio best represents the scale of the model? **b**

   a. $\frac{12 \text{ ft}}{1200 \text{ ft}}$ **b.** $\frac{12 \text{ in.}}{1200 \text{ ft}}$ **c.** $\frac{12 \text{ in.}}{12 \text{ ft}}$

6. How can you rewrite the ratio so that the first number in the ratio is 1 inch? **Divide both parts of the ratio by 12.**

— Solve —

7. Write a sentence to express the scale in inches per foot. **The scale used in the model can be expressed as $\frac{1 \text{ in.}}{100 \text{ ft}}$.**

— Look Back —

8. Use the ratio you expressed in Item 7. Find the number of inches that would represent 1200 ft. Is it equivalent to 1 ft? **12 in.; Yes.**

SOLVE ANOTHER PROBLEM

A 100-yard football field is displayed in a model that is 6 inches long. Express the scale used in the model in inches per foot.

$\frac{1 \text{ in.}}{50 \text{ ft}}$

ENRICHMENT

Name ______________________

Extend Your Thinking 7-1

Critical Thinking

The legendary Paul Bunyan's giant blue ox, Babe, stood 42 ax handles tall at the shoulder and measured 40 ax handles between his horns. The length from head to tail measured 61 ax handles. Six ax handles measure about 21 feet in length.

1. About how many feet tall is Babe from the shoulder to the ground? **≈ 147** ft
2. About how many feet is the distance between Babe's horns? **≈ 140** ft
3. About how many feet long is Babe from head to tail? **≈ 213.5** ft
4. About $\frac{1}{3}$ of Babe's total height is made up of his head and horns.
   - **a.** About how many ax handles will he measure from the tip of his horns to the bottom of his feet? **≈ 63 ax handles.**
   - **b.** About how many feet will he measure from the tip of his horns to the bottom of his feet? **≈ 220.5 feet**
5. Paul is planning to build a new barn. What size stall will he need to build for Babe? Estimate the dimensions in both feet and ax handles. **Possible answer: Greater than 63 ax handles tall, 40 ax handles wide, and 61 ax handles long; greater than 220.5 ft tall, 140 ft wide, and 213.5 ft long.**
6. If the barn door measures 75 ft wide and 150 ft tall, will Babe be able to get through? Explain. **No, Babe measures 140 feet between the horns, so the door is not wide enough. Babe's height is 220.5 ft, so the door must be at least that high.**
7. What is the ratio of your height to Babe's height, including the horns? Draw a sketch in proportion of you and Babe. **Answers will vary. Check students' work.**
8. Paul's ax has a cutting edge that is about half as long as the ax handle. About how many inches is the cutting edge? **≈ 21 inches**

7-2 Lesson Organizer

Objective

- Use scales and scale drawings to calculate actual distances.

Vocabulary

- Scale drawing

Materials

- Graph paper

NCTM Standards

- 1–5, 7, 13

Review

Write each fraction as a decimal.

1. $\frac{5}{8}$ 0.625
2. $\frac{14}{5}$ 2.8

Write each decimal as a fraction.

3. 0.75 $\frac{3}{4}$
4. 2.2 $\frac{11}{5}$

Available on Daily Transparency 7-2

Lesson Link

Ask students to think of places other than maps where knowing the scale is important. Discuss why scale is useful in these situations.

1 Introduce

Explore

You may wish to use Lesson Enhancement Transparency 29 and Teaching Tool Transparency 7: $\frac{1}{4}$-Inch Graph Paper with **Explore**.

The Point
Students see how scales are used to make a scale drawing.

Ongoing Assessment
Check that students trace the compass rose carefully, position it appropriately, and enlarge it in all directions.

7-2 Calculating with Scales

You'll Learn ...

- to use scales and scale drawings to calculate actual distances

... How It's Used

Mapmakers use scales as they determine the size a map will be.

Vocabulary

scale drawing

Lesson Link You've learned how scales are used to relate map distances to actual distances. The concept of scale can also be applied to various kinds of drawings, diagrams, and even three-dimensional models. ◄

Explore Scale Drawings

Materials: Graph paper

Growing Roses

A *compass rose* is the design on a map that shows which direction is north.

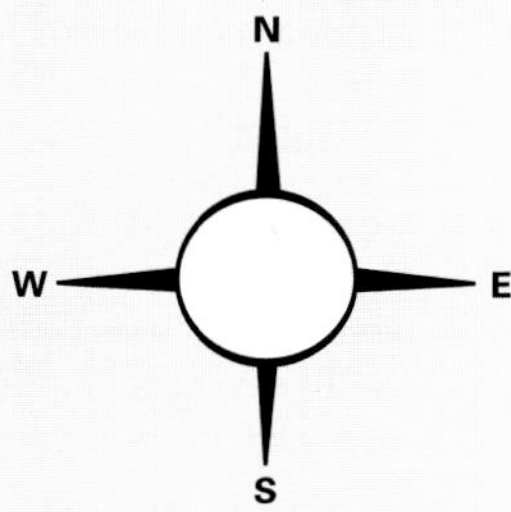

1. Trace the drawing of the compass rose onto your graph paper near the top of the page.
2. Using the grid marks on your paper as a guide, draw another compass rose whose length is twice that of the original. What is the scale of this drawing?
3. Draw a third compass rose whose length is twice that of the one you drew in Step 2. What is the scale of this drawing compared to the original compass rose? How can you tell?
4. Use the original compass rose to draw a fourth one, with a scale of 3 to 1. How did you decide how long and how wide to make your drawing?
5. Suppose that a drawing of the original compass rose has a length of 9 in. What scale do you think was used?

Learn Calculating with Scales

A  **scale drawing** is often used to illustrate something that is too large or too small to show actual size. A map is one kind of scale drawing.

A drawing's scale is the ratio of a length in the drawing to the actual length it represents. When the units are the same, they can be omitted from the scale. For example, a scale of 1 in.:5 in. can be stated as 1:5 or $\frac{1}{5}$.

MEETING INDIVIDUAL NEEDS

Resources

7-2 Practice
7-2 Reteaching
7-2 Problem Solving
7-2 Enrichment
7-2 Daily Transparency
Problem of the Day
Review
Quick Quiz
Teaching Tool Transparencies 7, 20
Lesson Enhancement Transparency 29

Wide World of Mathematics
Algebra: Miniature Books

Learning Modalities

Kinesthetic Have students determine the scale of an image on an overhead projector and then predict the measures of other objects. Students can check their work by actually measuring the projected images.

Social Have students sit back-to-back. One student makes a drawing on graph paper. That student then gives verbal directions to the partner for drawing the same figure enlarged (or reduced) by a scale of 1:5. The students compare the figures to see if they match.

Challenge

Have students determine how large the props would need to be for a film such as *Honey, I Shrunk the Kids*. For example, have students imagine that a child is "shrunk" small enough to fit into a spoon in a cereal bowl. How big would the cereal bowl prop have to be? How long would the spoon be? How large would cereal flake props be?

Example 1

Jaime drew a picture of his car using a scale of 1 in.:4 ft. Measure his drawing and find the actual length of the car.

The length of the drawing is 3 in.

Since the scale means every inch on the drawing represents 4 ft, the length of the car is 3 times 4 ft, or 12 ft.

The actual length of the car is 12 ft.

Try It

Find the actual height of Jaime's car. 5 feet

DID YOU KNOW?

The Transporter, used to carry Saturn V rockets at the Kennedy Space Center in Florida, measures 131 ft 4 in. by 114 ft.

When you make a drawing or model that is smaller than the real thing, it is a *reduction*. A scale represents a reduction when the first number is *less* than the second number. When the first number in the scale is greater, the scale represents an *enlargement*.

Reduction Scale: 1:2

Original

Enlargement Scale: 2:1

Example 2

A bolt is 1.2 cm long. Find the length of an enlarged technical drawing of this bolt at a scale of 15:2.

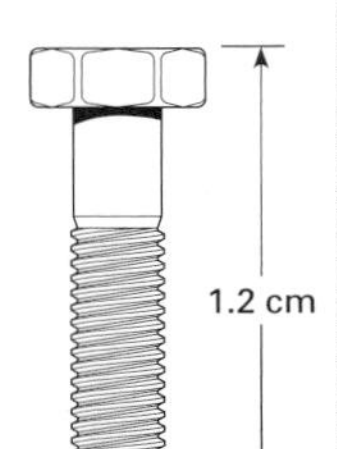

The actual length is 1.2 cm. Let x be the length of the drawing.

$$\frac{\text{scale length}}{\text{actual length}} = \frac{x \text{ cm}}{1.2 \text{ cm}} = \frac{15}{2}$$

$2x = 1.2 \cdot 15$ Write the cross products.

$2x = 18$ Multiply.

$\frac{2x}{2} = \frac{18}{2}$ To undo multiplying by 2, divide by 2.

$x = 9$ Divide.

The new drawing has a length of 9 cm.

Language Link

Our word *scale* comes from the Latin word *scalae,* which means "staircase." A scale works in steps to change sizes up or down.

MATH EVERY DAY

Problem of the Day

Each day, Whitney does one more sit-up than she did the day before. At the end of one week she had done 77 sit-ups. How many sit-ups did she do the first day? 8 sit-ups

Available on Daily Transparency 7-2

An Extension is provided in the transparency package.

Fact of the Day

In about 2300 B.C., the Babylonians made maps that still exist today. These maps were cut on clay tiles.

Estimation

Estimate.

1. 3.45 + 2.04 + 41.00 About 46.5
2. 89.3 − 47.83 About 40
3. 3.1 × 19.97 About 60
4. 56.734 ÷ .788 About 70

For Groups That Finish Early

Give the scale of the compass rose in Step 4 compared to the one in Step 2 and in Step 3. Answers may vary.

Follow Up

Discuss various student responses to Steps 3 and 4. Ask students to explain how they figured out the answer in Step 5.

Answers for Explore

2. Drawing should be twice the length and width of original; Scale = 2:1.
3. Drawing should be 4 times the length and width of original; Scale = 4:1; If you multiply by 2 and then by 2 again, result is multiplying by 4.
4. Drawing should be 3 times the length and width of original; Since scale is 3:1, multiplied original length and width by 3.
5. About 6 to 1.

2 Teach

Learn

Use students' drawings of the compass rose to explain scale notation. Explain that units are not always needed. Give examples of reductions and enlargements.

Alternate Examples

1. Sally drew a picture of her birdhouse using a scale of 1 in.:6 in. The drawing was 4 in. high. How tall was the birdhouse?

   Since every inch on the drawing represents 6 in., the height of the birdhouse is 6 times 4 in., or 24 in.

2. A picture hook is 2.6 cm long. Find the length of an enlarged technical drawing of this picture hook at a scale of 15:2.

   $$\frac{\text{scale length}}{\text{actual length}} = \frac{x \text{ cm}}{2.6 \text{ cm}} = \frac{15}{2}$$

   $2x = 2.6 \cdot 15$

   $2x = 39$

   $x = 19.5$ cm

   The enlarged drawing has a length of 19.5 cm.

Students use two methods to solve a problem. One student uses cross products to solve a proportion, while the other uses multiplication. Students can choose the method that they prefer.

Answers for What Do You Think?

1. The scale is given as 1 in.:80 mi, so the answer must be in miles.
2. Yes; $\frac{\text{actual length}}{\text{scale length}} = \frac{x \text{ mi}}{0.75 \text{ in.}} = \frac{80 \text{ mi}}{1 \text{ in.}}$

3 Practice and Assess

Check

Some students may have trouble with placing the actual length in the correct location in a proportion. It may be helpful to note that, in the scale, the actual length is always on the bottom.

Answers for Check Your Understanding

1. Possible answer: Set the scale measurement over the unknown measurement equal to the scale and solve the proportion.
2. Possible answer: The scale drawing will become smaller. Each scale inch now represents a much larger part of the actual object.
3. Possible answer: The scale drawing will become larger. Each scale cm now represents a much smaller part of the actual object. The drawing is 4 times as big.

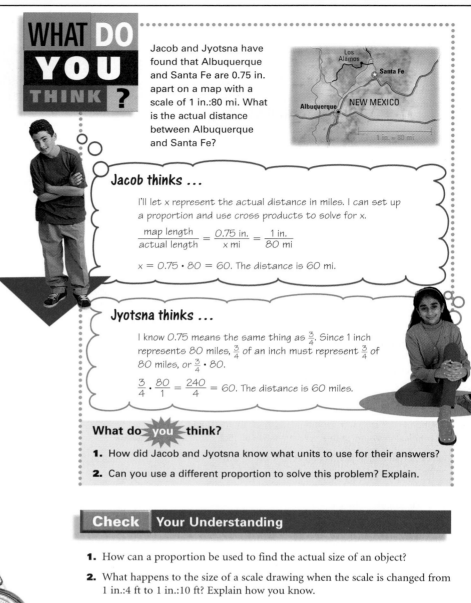

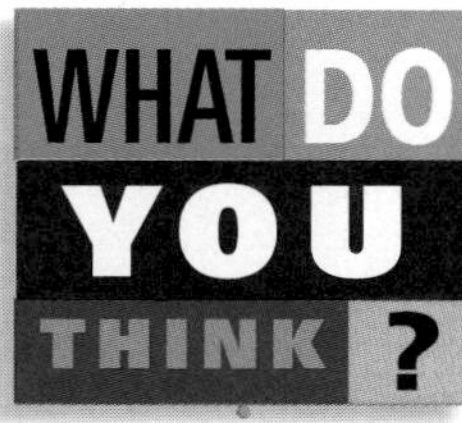

Jacob and Jyotsna have found that Albuquerque and Santa Fe are 0.75 in. apart on a map with a scale of 1 in.:80 mi. What is the actual distance between Albuquerque and Santa Fe?

Jacob thinks . . .

I'll let x represent the actual distance in miles. I can set up a proportion and use cross products to solve for x.

$\frac{\text{map length}}{\text{actual length}} = \frac{0.75 \text{ in.}}{x \text{ mi}} = \frac{1 \text{ in.}}{80 \text{ mi}}$

$x = 0.75 \cdot 80 = 60$. The distance is 60 mi.

Jyotsna thinks . . .

I know 0.75 means the same thing as $\frac{3}{4}$. Since 1 inch represents 80 miles, $\frac{3}{4}$ of an inch must represent $\frac{3}{4}$ of 80 miles, or $\frac{3}{4} \cdot 80$.

$\frac{3}{4} \cdot \frac{80}{1} = \frac{240}{4} = 60$. The distance is 60 miles.

What do you think?

1. How did Jacob and Jyotsna know what units to use for their answers?
2. Can you use a different proportion to solve this problem? Explain.

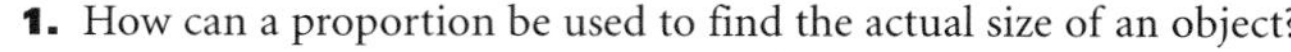

Check Your Understanding

1. How can a proportion be used to find the actual size of an object?
2. What happens to the size of a scale drawing when the scale is changed from 1 in.:4 ft to 1 in.:10 ft? Explain how you know.
3. What is the impact on a scale drawing when the scale is changed from $\frac{1 \text{ cm}}{20 \text{ m}}$ to $\frac{1 \text{ cm}}{5 \text{ m}}$? Explain.

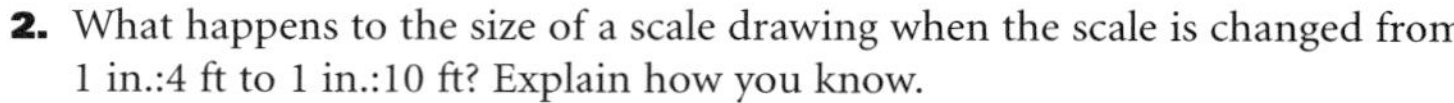

MEETING MIDDLE SCHOOL CLASSROOM NEEDS

Tips from Middle School Teachers

My students like to bring in examples of scale models or scale drawings that they use in their hobbies. I put as many as I can on the bulletin board and use their examples as sources of problems.

Team Teaching

Work with an industrial-arts teacher to have students build models of items by measuring and scaling down by proportions. Display the completed models and their labels giving the proportional sizing.

Cultural Connection

Scale models of buildings and other structures are popular as souvenirs around the world, from the Eiffel Tower in Paris (984 ft tall) to the first pyramid in ancient Egypt, the Step Pyramid, built in 2650 B.C. to a height of about 200 ft. Ask students to decide what an appropriate scale might be for a souvenir scale model of these structures. Using centimeter cubes might help students decide on a scale.

7-2 Exercises and Applications

Practice and Apply

1. **Getting Started** Follow these steps to calculate the actual length of a house if the model uses the scale 1 cm = 3 m.
   a. Measure the length of the scale model.
   b. Let x be the actual length in meters. Use your measurement and the scale of the model to set up the following proportion:
   $$\frac{\text{scale length (cm)}}{x\text{ m}} = \frac{1\text{ cm}}{3\text{ m}}$$
   c. Cross multiply. Write the actual length of the house.

Number Sense Measure the scale drawing and find the width of the bedroom for each scale.

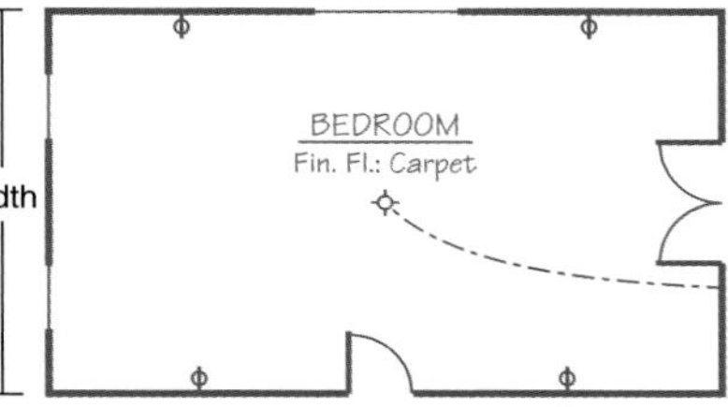

2. 1 in. = 7 ft **10.5 ft**
3. 1 in. = $8\frac{1}{2}$ ft **12.75 ft**
4. 1 in. = $9\frac{3}{4}$ ft **$14\frac{5}{8}$ ft**
5. 1 in. = 12.25 ft **18.375 ft**

A model airplane is 6 cm long. Use each scale to find the length of the actual airplane.

6. Scale: 1 cm = 2 m **12 m**
7. Scale: 1 cm = $3\frac{1}{3}$ m **20 m**
8. Scale: 2 cm = 9 m **27 m**
9. **Geography** Dallas is $7\frac{1}{2}$ in. from Houston on a map of Texas with a scale of $\frac{3\text{ in.}}{100\text{ mi}}$. What is the actual distance from Dallas to Houston? **250 mi**
10. When the leaders of Fort Wayne, Indiana, decided to build a huge playground called Kids Crossing, they asked students for ideas. Many students made scale drawings showing the equipment and rides they wanted. If a student made a drawing of a slide with a scale of 1 in. = 8 ft, how long would the slide actually be if it was drawn $2\frac{1}{2}$ in. long? **20 ft**

Solve for x in each proportion.

11. $\frac{5\text{ in.}}{x} = \frac{3\text{ in.}}{12\text{ ft}}$ **x = 20 ft**
12. $\frac{7\text{ cm}}{x} = \frac{10\text{ cm}}{84\text{ km}}$ **x = 58.8 km**
13. $\frac{1.4\text{ in.}}{25\text{ mi}} = \frac{7\text{ in.}}{x}$ **x = 125 mi**
14. $\frac{8\text{ cm}}{300\text{ km}} = \frac{3.2\text{ cm}}{x}$ **x = 120 km**

PRACTICE 7-2

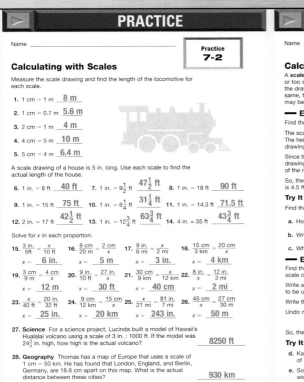

PRACTICE

Name ____________________

Practice 7-2

Calculating with Scales

Measure the scale drawing and find the length of the locomotive for each scale.

1. 1 cm = 1 m **8 m**
2. 1 cm = 0.7 m **5.6 m**
3. 2 cm = 1 m **4 m**
4. 4 cm = 5 m **10 m**
5. 5 cm = 4 m **6.4 m**

A scale drawing of a house is 5 in. long. Use each scale to find the actual length of the house.

6. 1 in. = 8 ft **40 ft**
7. 1 in. = $9\frac{1}{2}$ ft **$47\frac{1}{2}$ ft**
8. 1 in. = 18 ft **90 ft**
9. 1 in. = 15 ft **75 ft**
10. 1 in. = $6\frac{1}{4}$ ft **$31\frac{1}{4}$ ft**
11. 1 in. = 14.3 ft **71.5 ft**
12. 2 in. = 17 ft **$42\frac{1}{2}$ ft**
13. 1 in. = $12\frac{3}{4}$ ft **$63\frac{3}{4}$ ft**
14. 4 in. = 35 ft **$43\frac{3}{4}$ ft**

Solve for x in each proportion.

15. $\frac{3\text{ in.}}{5\text{ft}} = \frac{x}{10\text{ ft}}$ x = **6 in.**
16. $\frac{8\text{ cm}}{20\text{ m}} = \frac{2\text{ cm}}{x}$ x = **5 m**
17. $\frac{9\text{ in.}}{6\text{ mi}} = \frac{x}{2\text{ mi}}$ x = **3 in.**
18. $\frac{15\text{ cm}}{3\text{ km}} = \frac{20\text{ cm}}{x}$ x = **4 km**
19. $\frac{3\text{ cm}}{9\text{ m}} = \frac{4\text{ cm}}{x}$ x = **12 m**
20. $\frac{9\text{ in.}}{10\text{ ft}} = \frac{27\text{ in.}}{x}$ x = **30 ft**
21. $\frac{30\text{ cm}}{9\text{ km}} = \frac{x}{12\text{ km}}$ x = **40 cm**
22. $\frac{8\text{ in.}}{x} = \frac{12\text{ in.}}{3\text{ mi}}$ x = **2 mi**
23. $\frac{x}{40\text{ ft}} = \frac{20\text{ in.}}{32\text{ ft}}$ x = **25 in.**
24. $\frac{9\text{ cm}}{12\text{ km}} = \frac{15\text{ cm}}{x}$ x = **20 km**
25. $\frac{x}{21\text{ mi}} = \frac{81\text{ in.}}{7\text{ mi}}$ x = **243 in.**
26. $\frac{45\text{ cm}}{x} = \frac{27\text{ cm}}{30\text{ m}}$ x = **50 m**

27. **Science** For a science project, Lucinda built a model of Hawaii's Hualalai volcano using a scale of 3 in. : 1000 ft. If the model was $24\frac{3}{4}$ in. high, how high is the actual volcano? **8250 ft**

28. **Geography** Thomas has a map of Europe that uses a scale of 1 cm = 50 km. He has found that London, England, and Berlin, Germany, are 18.6 cm apart on this map. What is the actual distance between these cities? **930 km**

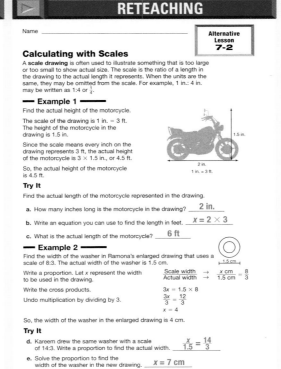

RETEACHING

Name ____________________

Alternative Lesson 7-2

Calculating with Scales

A **scale drawing** is often used to illustrate something that is too large or too small to show actual size. The scale is the ratio of a length in the drawing to the actual length it represents. When the units are the same, they may be omitted from the scale. For example, 1 in.: 4 in. may be written as 1:4 or $\frac{1}{4}$.

— Example 1 —

Find the actual height of the motorcycle.

The scale of the drawing is 1 in. = 3 ft. The height of the motorcycle in the drawing is 1.5 in.

Since the scale means every inch on the drawing represents 3 ft, the actual height of the motorcycle is 3 × 1.5 in., or 4.5 ft.

So, the actual height of the motorcycle is 4.5 ft.

1.5 in.
2 in.
1 in. = 3 ft.

Try It

Find the actual length of the motorcycle represented in the drawing.

a. How many inches long is the motorcycle in the drawing? **2 in.**
b. Write an equation you can use to find the length in feet. **$x = 2 \times 3$**
c. What is the actual length of the motorcycle? **6 ft**

— Example 2 —

Find the width of the washer in Ramona's enlarged drawing that uses a scale of 8:3. The actual width of the washer is 1.5 cm.

1.5 cm

Write a proportion. Let x represent the width to be used in the drawing. $\frac{\text{Scale width}}{\text{Actual width}} \begin{matrix}\rightarrow\\ \rightarrow\end{matrix} \frac{x\text{ cm}}{1.5\text{ cm}} = \frac{8}{3}$

Write the cross products. $3x = 1.5 \times 8$

Undo multiplication by dividing by 3. $\frac{3x}{3} = \frac{12}{3}$

$x = 4$

So, the width of the washer in the enlarged drawing is 4 cm.

Try It

d. Kareem drew the same washer with a scale of 14:3. Write a proportion to find the actual width. **$\frac{x}{1.5} = \frac{14}{3}$**
e. Solve the proportion to find the width of the washer in the new drawing. **$x = 7$ cm**

7-2 Exercises and Applications

Assignment Guide

- **Basic**
  1, 2–16 evens, 17, 20–26 evens
- **Average**
  1–15 odds, 16–18, 21–27 odds
- **Enriched**
  3–15 odds, 16–19, 21–27 odds

Exercise Notes

Exercises 6, 8 and 10

Extension Have students discuss different ways of solving these problems. Some students may have multiplied in each exercise. Others first may have found that 1 cm = 4.5 m in exercise 8, and then multiplied. Still others may have set up proportions for all of the problems. Discuss the advantages and disadvantages of each procedure.

Exercise Answers

1. a. 2.9 cm
   b. $\frac{2.9\text{ cm}}{x\text{ m}} = \frac{1\text{ cm}}{3\text{ m}}$
   c. The house is 8.7 m long.

Reteaching

Activity

Materials: Map

Work together in groups of 4

- Each of two people should pick a location on the map.
- Another person should estimate the actual distance between the locations.
- A fourth person should measure the map distance and use the map scale to determine the actual distance.
- Take turns so that each person in the group has a chance to determine the actual distance.

Exercise Notes

■ Exercise 15

Geography You may wish to use Teaching Tool Transparency 20: Map of the World with this exercise.

■ Exercise 18

Extension Ask students to think of situations in which they might want to use different scales for the same scale drawing (e.g., matching fabrics, wallpaper and border, three sizes of bears).

Exercise Answers

15. 2860 km: 12 cm = 4 × 3 cm so the actual distance = 4 × 715 km.

18. Answers may vary.

19. Possible answer: 1 in.:5 ft; The model would be 8 in. long—small enough for a 5-year-old to play with but not so small that the child could swallow it.

Alternate Assessment

Portfolio Have students choose a scale drawing or map that they have created for their portfolio. Ask students to write about what they learned by making the scale drawing or map.

▶ Quick Quiz

1. A model of a house uses the scale 1 in. = 10 ft. The model is 4.5 in. long. How long is the house? 45 feet
2. An airplane has a wingspan of 120 ft. How large would the wingspan be on a scale drawing that uses a scale of 1 in. = 15 ft? 8 in.
3. Helen's little brother has a scale model of a *Tyrannosaurus rex.* The tag says that it uses a scale of 2 cm = 3 m. If the model is 9.5 cm long from head to tail, how big was the real dinosaur? 14.25 m

Available on Daily Transparency 7-2

PROBLEM SOLVING 7-2

15. Geography Enrique has found that Lagos, Nigeria, is 12 cm from Casablanca, Morocco, on an African map with a scale of 3 cm:715 km. Find the actual distance from Lagos to Casablanca. Explain how you found your answer.

16. Test Prep A scale model of a truck uses the scale 1 in. = 8 ft. The model is 2.75 in. long. How long is the actual truck? C

Ⓐ 18 ft Ⓑ 20 ft Ⓒ 22 ft Ⓓ 24 ft

Problem Solving and Reasoning

17. Critical Thinking Stan Herd is an artist who plants flowers and grains on large fields to create "crop art." This photo shows a work called *Saginaw Grant.*

GPS

Herd often makes a scale drawing before planting seeds and flowers. If a sketch measures 6.4 in. × 10.2 in. at a scale of 1 in. = 25 ft, what will be the dimensions of his "crop art"? 160 ft × 255 ft

18. Critical Thinking Make a scale drawing of an object and write three different scales next to the drawing. Calculate the actual size of the object you drew based on each of the three scales.

19. Journal A *Tyrannosaurus rex* was about 40 ft long from head to tail. Suppose you wanted to make a toy *Tyrannosaurus* for a five-year-old. What scale would you use? Explain how you chose your scale. Tell why the toy shouldn't be too large or too small.

Mixed Review

Find the sum or difference. Write your answers in lowest terms. *[Lesson 4-2]*

20. $\frac{2}{21} + \frac{3}{7}$ $\frac{11}{21}$ **21.** $\frac{5}{6} - \frac{4}{5}$ $\frac{1}{30}$ **22.** $\frac{2}{3} - \frac{1}{9}$ $\frac{5}{9}$ **23.** $\frac{11}{12} + \frac{1}{15}$ $\frac{59}{60}$ **24.** $\frac{1}{3} + \frac{2}{3}$ 1

Find the area of each figure. *[Lesson 5-10]*

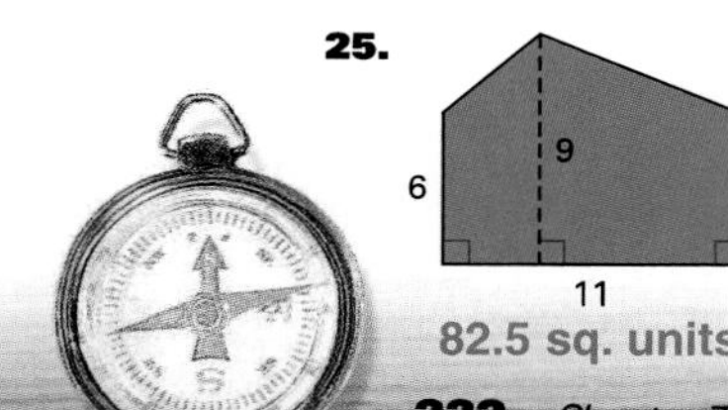

25. 9, 6, 6, 11 — 82.5 sq. units

26. 7, 5, 7, 7, 3, 3 — 50.5 sq. units

27. 14, 6, 4, 5, 7, 7, 3 — 71 sq. units

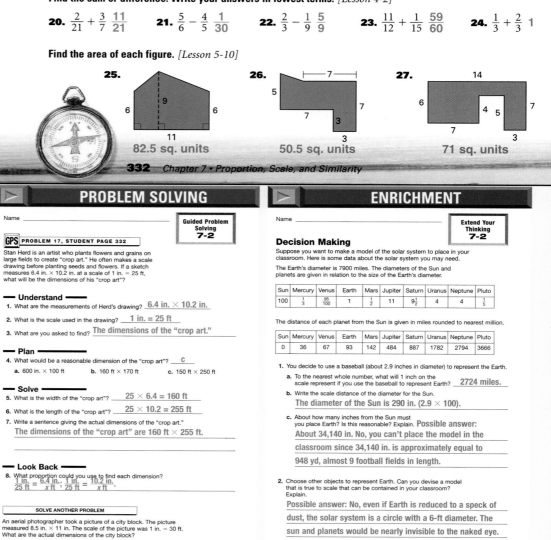

PROBLEM SOLVING

Name ____________________

Guided Problem Solving 7-2

GPS PROBLEM 17, STUDENT PAGE 332

Stan Herd is an artist who plants flowers and grains on large fields to create "crop art." He often makes a scale drawing before planting seeds and flowers. If a sketch measures 6.4 in. × 10.2 in. at a scale of 1 in. = 25 ft, what will be the dimensions of his "crop art"?

— Understand —

1. What are the measurements of Herd's drawing? 6.4 in. × 10.2 in.
2. What is the scale used in the drawing? 1 in. = 25 ft
3. What are you asked to find? The dimensions of the "crop art."

— Plan —

4. What would be a reasonable dimension of the "crop art"? C

   a. 600 in. × 100 ft b. 160 ft × 170 ft c. 150 ft × 250 ft

— Solve —

5. What is the width of the "crop art"? 25 × 6.4 = 160 ft
6. What is the length of the "crop art"? 25 × 10.2 = 255 ft
7. Write a sentence giving the actual dimensions of the "crop art." The dimensions of the "crop art" are 160 ft × 255 ft.

— Look Back —

8. What proportion could you use to find each dimension? $\frac{1 \text{ in.}}{25 \text{ ft}} = \frac{6.4 \text{ in.}}{x \text{ ft}}$; $\frac{1 \text{ in.}}{25 \text{ ft}} = \frac{10.2 \text{ in.}}{x \text{ ft}}$.

SOLVE ANOTHER PROBLEM

An aerial photographer took a picture of a city block. The picture measured 8.5 in. × 11 in. The scale of the picture was 1 in. = 30 ft. What are the actual dimensions of the city block?

255 ft × 330 ft

ENRICHMENT

Name ____________________

Extend Your Thinking 7-2

Decision Making

Suppose you want to make a model of the solar system to place in your classroom. Here is some data about the solar system you may need.

The Earth's diameter is 7900 miles. The diameters of the Sun and planets are given in relation to the size of the Earth's diameter.

Sun	Mercury	Venus	Earth	Mars	Jupiter	Saturn	Uranus	Neptune	Pluto
100	$\frac{1}{3}$	$\frac{95}{100}$	1	$\frac{1}{2}$	11	$9\frac{1}{2}$	4	4	$\frac{1}{5}$

The distance of each planet from the Sun is given in miles rounded to nearest million.

Sun	Mercury	Venus	Earth	Mars	Jupiter	Saturn	Uranus	Neptune	Pluto
0	36	67	93	142	484	887	1782	2794	3666

1. You decide to use a baseball (about 2.9 inches in diameter) to represent the Earth.

   a. To the nearest whole number, what will 1 inch on the scale represent if you use the baseball to represent Earth? 2724 miles.

   b. Write the scale distance of the diameter for the Sun.
   The diameter of the Sun is 290 in. (2.9 × 100).

   c. About how many inches from the Sun must you place Earth? Is this reasonable? Explain. Possible answer: About 34,140 in. No, you can't place the model in the classroom since 34,140 in. is approximately equal to 948 yd, almost 9 football fields in length.

2. Choose other objects to represent Earth. Can you devise a model that is true to scale that can be contained in your classroom? Explain.
   Possible answer: No, even if Earth is reduced to a speck of dust, the solar system is a circle with a 6-ft diameter. The sun and planets would be nearly invisible to the naked eye.

Problem Solving Using Maps

7-3

▶ Lesson Link You have learned how scales relate map distances to actual distances. Maps can be used to solve many practical problems, including choosing the best route and determining arrival times. ◀

You'll Learn ...

■ to use scales to read maps and make decisions

... How It's Used

Schedulers for railroads and airlines need to be able to solve problems using maps to design efficient schedules.

Explore Problem Solving Using Maps

Drive and Deliver!

Materials: Ruler

You are the delivery person for Furniture Paradise, location F on the map. You must make the following deliveries today, and you need to plan your route so you can deliver the furniture efficiently.

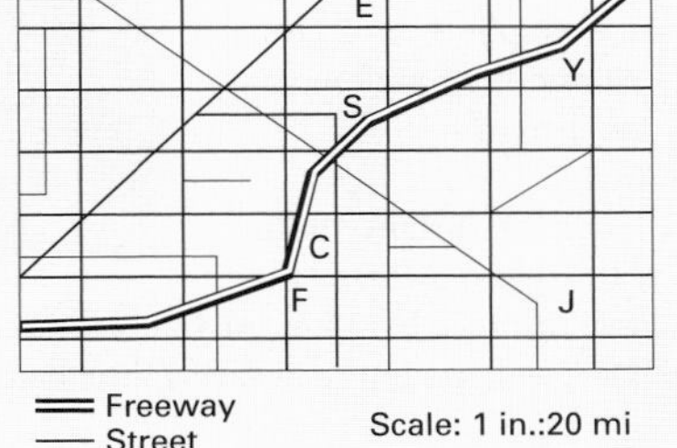

═ Freeway
— Street

Scale: 1 in.:20 mi

Name	Location	To Be Delivered
Mr. Chavez	C	Dining table and chairs
Mrs. Smith	S	Couch
Mr. Yamamoto	Y	Entertainment center
Ms. Jones	J	Bookcases
Mr. Edwards	E	Desk, filing cabinet

1. What information can you get from the map that will help you plan your route?
2. What other information would you want before planning your route?
3. Using the map to help you, plan an efficient delivery route. Give a short written explanation of how you decided on this route.
4. Mr. Edwards calls and asks what time you expect to get to his office. If you plan to start your route at 9:00 A.M., what should you tell him? Explain your answer.
5. How can you estimate the time it will take to get somewhere? How can a map help you make such an estimate?

7-3 Lesson Organizer

Objective

- Use scales to read maps and make decisions.

Materials

- Explore: Ruler

NCTM Standards

- 1–4, 13

▶ Review

Solve for x.

1. $3x + 5 = 17$ $x = 4$
2. $2 = 5x - 3$ $x = 1$
3. $\frac{1}{3}x = 4$ $x = 12$

Available on Daily Transparency 7-3

▶ Lesson Link

Review with students what they have learned about scales on maps. Also review the $d = rt$ formula and related formulas.

1 Introduce

Explore

You may wish to use Lesson Enhancement Transparency 30 and Teaching Tool Transparency 14: Rulers with **Explore**.

The Point
Students see how a map can be used to determine an efficient route and estimate travel time.

Ongoing Assessment
Check that students know average speeds on freeways and streets; ask them how far they could go in a specified time.

For Groups That Finish Early
The freeway has exits only at F and S. How will you modify your route? How much longer will it take?
Answers will vary.

Answers for Explore on next page.

MEETING INDIVIDUAL NEEDS

Resources

7-3 Practice
7-3 Reteaching
7-3 Problem Solving
7-3 Enrichment
7-3 Daily Transparency
  Problem of the Day
  Review
  Quick Quiz

Teaching Tool Transparencies 14, 21

Lesson Enhancement Transparency 30

Learning Modalities

Kinesthetic Have students refer to clock faces to determine the number of minutes in common fractional parts of an hour ($\frac{1}{2}, \frac{1}{3}, \frac{2}{3}, \frac{1}{4}, \frac{3}{4}, \frac{1}{5}, \frac{1}{6}$), and then have them look for patterns that would help them use a calculator for more difficult fractions.

Individual Ask students to reflect on what they understand well at this point about problem solving with maps and what they need to work on.

English Language Development

Be aware that, because of language differences, students may have learned the formula relating distance, rate, and time with different variable names.

The *Multilingual Handbook* with its glossary of math terms, illustrations, and worked-out examples, can help you with students who have limited English language skills. The glossary is provided in several languages.

Answers for Explore

1. Location and distances of delivery destinations.
2. When someone can receive the goods, amount of traffic.
3. C, S, Y, E, J; Travel on the freeway as much as possible.
4. Around 11:30 A.M. (assuming 60 mi/hr on the freeway, 30 mi/hr on streets, and 30 minutes per delivery).
5. By using distance and an estimate of average speed. A map can help you estimate the distance.

2 Teach

Learn

Alternate Examples

1. Use the map and information in Example 1. If Dave's rate was 12 km/hr when would he arrive?

   At 12 km/hr, the ride takes about 65 minutes. He will arrive about 4:20 P.M.

2. Mary's mother needs to be at work by 9 A.M. She can drive about 40 mi/hr on the 10-mi freeway route and about 30 mi/hr on the 12-mi street route. Which route is faster, and when should she leave?

   The freeway route is 10 mi, so the time needed is $\frac{\text{distance}}{\text{rate}} = \frac{10}{40} = \frac{1}{4}$ hour. The street route is 12 mi, so the time needed is $\frac{\text{distance}}{\text{rate}} = \frac{12}{30} = \frac{2}{5}$ hour. The freeway route is faster. She must leave $\frac{1}{4}$ hour before 9 A.M., at 8:45 A.M.

3 Practice and Assess

Check

Answers for Check Your Understanding

1. Possible answer: By showing distances and routes. You can estimate travel time if you know the distance and the type of road you will be using.
2. Possible answer: If you recognize places, you can use your knowledge about their distance apart to estimate the scale.

Learn Problem Solving Using Maps

Remember

distance = rate × time

time = $\frac{\text{distance}}{\text{rate}}$

[Page 58]

A map can be an important problem-solving tool. You can use the formula time = $\frac{\text{distance}}{\text{rate}}$ and your knowledge of scale to solve problems.

Example 1

Dave leaves school at 3:15 P.M. and rides his bicycle to the library at 15 km/hr. The scale of the map is 1 cm:2 km. At about what time will he arrive?

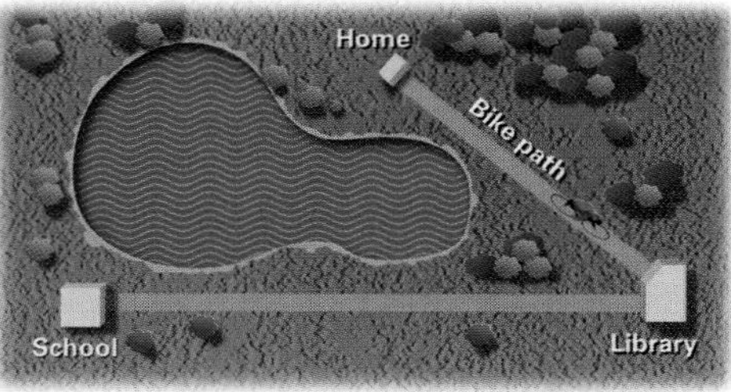

The map distance to the library is 6.5 cm, so the real distance is 13 km. At 15 km/hr, the ride takes a little less than an hour. Dave will get to the library a little before 4:15 P.M.

Try It

Dave leaves the library at 4:55 P.M. and rides home at a rate of about 12 km/hr. At about what time do you expect him to get home? About 5:35 P.M.

DID YOU KNOW?

There are many different kinds of maps. Some simply show street plans and names. Others, called *relief maps,* show the actual contours of the land—how high it is and how steep the roads are.

Example 2

Antoinette is on a hike with her nature club. The hikers need to arrive at their campsite before 6:00 P.M. They can take a steep 11 km trail or a flatter 17 km trail. The hikers average 3 km/hr on the steep trail and 4 km/hr on the flatter one. Which trail is faster, and when should they leave?

The time needed to hike the flat trail is $\frac{\text{distance}}{\text{rate}} = \frac{17}{4} = 4\frac{1}{4}$ hr. (The time is in hours because the rate is in kilometers per *hour.*)

The steep trail is 11 km long, so the time to hike it is $\frac{\text{distance}}{\text{rate}} = \frac{11}{3} = 3\frac{2}{3}$ hr.

The steeper trail is faster. The hikers must leave $3\frac{2}{3}$ hr before 6:00. Since $\frac{2}{3}$ hr is 40 minutes, they must leave at 2:20 P.M.

Check Your Understanding

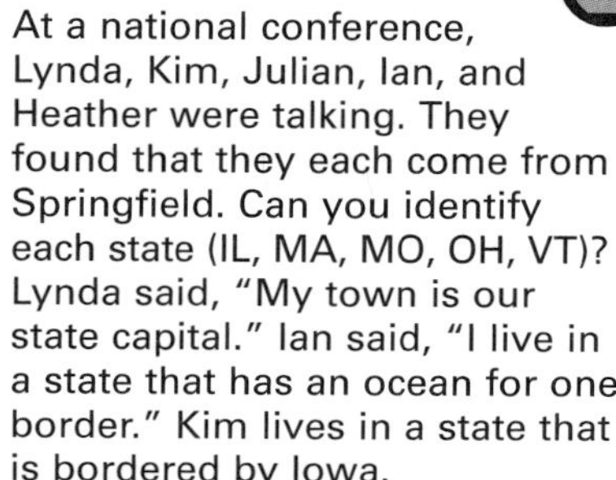

1. How do maps make planning easier?
2. How can you estimate the scale for a map if it is not given?

MATH EVERY DAY

Problem of the Day

At a national conference, Lynda, Kim, Julian, Ian, and Heather were talking. They found that they each come from Springfield. Can you identify each state (IL, MA, MO, OH, VT)? Lynda said, "My town is our state capital." Ian said, "I live in a state that has an ocean for one border." Kim lives in a state that is bordered by Iowa. "Our state capital is Montpelier," commented Heather. (Hint: Use a map!) Lynda, IL; Ian, MA; Kim, MO; Heather, VT; Julian, OH

Available on Daily Transparency 7-3

An Extension is provided in the transparency package.

Fact of the Day

Ptolemy, an Egyptian scholar, produced a geography book that included maps of the world in the year 150. His maps were the first to be mathematically accurate.

Mental Math

Do these mentally.

1. $\frac{2}{3} \cdot 9$ 6
2. $\frac{1}{2} \div \frac{1}{6}$ 3
3. $5\frac{1}{2} \cdot 4$ 22
4. $6\frac{3}{4} \div \frac{1}{4}$ 27

7-3 Exercises and Applications

Practice and Apply

1. **Getting Started** Follow these steps to find what time Shuichi will arrive home if he leaves the library at 3:30 P.M. and walks at 4 km/hr.

   a. On a map with a scale of 1 cm = 2 km, the library is 3 cm from Shuichi's home. Calculate the actual distance from the library to Shuichi's home. **6 km**

   b. Use $\frac{\text{distance}}{\text{rate}} = \text{time}$ to calculate how long Shuichi's walk takes. **$1\frac{1}{2}$ hours**

   c. Use the answer to **b** and the departure time of 3:30 P.M. to determine when Shuichi arrives home. **5:00 P.M.**

Ferdinand left home at 3:00 P.M. and traveled 150 mi. Find his arrival time for each of the following speeds.

2. 25 mi/hr **9:00 P.M.**
3. 30 mi/hr **8:00 P.M.**
4. 40 mi/hr **6:45 P.M.**
5. 55 mi/hr **≈ 5:45 P.M.**
6. 15 mi/hr **≈ 1:00 A.M.**

7. Lisa's family plans to go to a movie theater downtown at 8:00 P.M. They can drive 40 mi/hr on King Expressway.

   a. What is the expressway distance from their home to the theater? **≈ 30 mi**

   b. How long will it take them to get from home to the theater? **≈ 45 min**

   c. When do they need to leave to get to the movie by 8:00 P.M.? **≈ 7:15 P.M.**

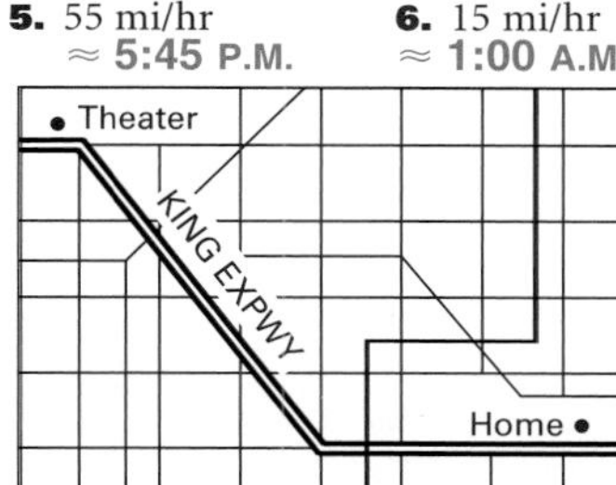

Scale: 1 in. = 12 mi

8. **Problem Solving** Carly is planning a trip from Appleton to Shore City. She can drive at an average speed of 50 mi/hr or take a train that averages 40 mi/hr. The driving distance between the cities is 180 mi. The train takes a more direct route, so the rail distance is 140 mi.

   a. Which method of travel is faster? Explain how you decided.

   b. If Carly chooses the faster method and leaves Appleton at 2:00 P.M., when will she arrive in Shore City?

9. **History** Pony Express riders delivered mail between St. Joseph, Missouri, and Sacramento, California, a distance of 1966 miles. A day's ride could cover 75 miles or more.

   a. If a rider began at 7:30 A.M. and rode at an average speed of 15 mi/hr for 75 mi, when would his ride end? **12:30 P.M.**

   b. If a rider began at 2:30 P.M. and rode 80 mi at 15 mi/hr, when would his ride end? **7:50 P.M.**

PONY EXPRESS!
CHANGE OF TIME! REDUCED RATES!
10 Days to San Francisco!
LETTERS
OFFICE, 84 BROADWAY,
NEW YORK,
Up to 4 P. M. every TUESDAY.
Up to 2½ P. M. every SATURDAY.
TELEGRAMS
EXPRESS CHARGES.
WELLS, FARGO & CO., Ag'ts.

PRACTICE 7-3

7-3 Exercises and Applications

Assignment Guide

- Basic
  1–4, 8–12 evens, 19–24
- Average
  1, 2–6 evens, 7–12, 15–23 odds
- Enriched
  4–13, 14–24 evens

Exercise Notes

Exercises 2-6

Error Prevention Some students may reverse the distance and rate when they are computing the time. Encourage students to estimate and to consider whether their answers are reasonable.

Exercise Answers

8. a. The train is faster. It would take 3.6 hr by car, but only 3.5 hr by train.

   b. 5:30 P.M.

Reteaching

Activity

- As a salesperson for Modern American Toys and Habitats (MATH), you are based in Philadelphia (Ph). You must visit Boston, Washington, D.C., New York City, and Pittsburgh.
- You can drive to each city (average speed 50 mi/hr), take a train (average speed 75 mi/hr), or combine train travel with driving by renting a car. You would like to spend about 10–12 hours a day traveling and working.
- Plan a route that begins and ends in Philadelphia. How many days would you need for your trip? Answers will vary.

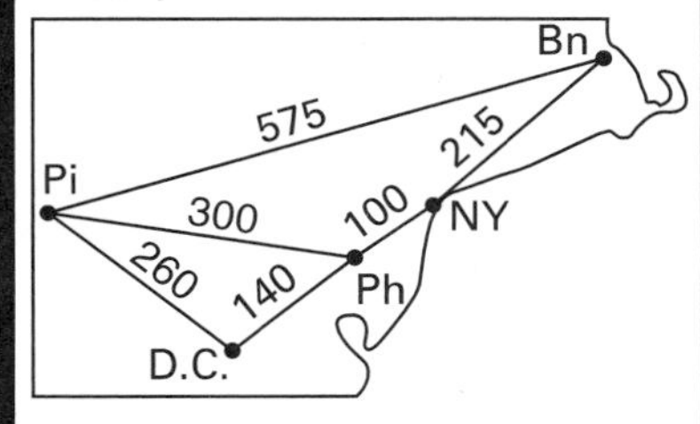

PRACTICE

Name ______________________ **Practice 7-3**

Problem Solving Using Maps

Margaret left home at 8:00 A.M. and traveled 120 miles. Find her arrival time for each of the following speeds.

1. 30 mi/hr **12:00 noon**
2. 45 mi/hr **10:40 A.M.**
3. 72 mi/hr **9:40 A.M.**
4. 40 mi/hr **11:00 A.M.**
5. 60 mi/hr **10:00 A.M.**
6. 50 mi/hr **10:24 A.M.**

7. After a camping trip, Anh drove 75 miles home at a rate of 60 mi/hr. If he arrived home at 8:30 P.M., what time did he begin his drive? **7:15 P.M.**

8. Scott drove 115 miles from Cleveland, Ohio to Pittsburgh, Pennsylvania, at a rate of 69 mi/hr. If he arrived in Pittsburgh at 11:30 A.M., what time did he leave Cleveland? **9:50 A.M.**

9. Carol and Mike have decided to go see a movie which is playing tonight at 9:00 P.M. at both Cinema Six and Acme Theater. Cinema Six is 20 miles away on the freeway, where the speed limit is 60 mi/hr. Acme Theater is only 10 miles away, but the speed limit on the road to Acme Theater is 25 mi/hr.

   a. Which theater should they choose if they want to get there in the shortest time? Explain how you decided.
   Cinema Six; Possible answer: It takes 20 min to drive to Cinema Six and 24 min to drive to Acme Theater.

   b. What time do they need to leave to get to the theater you chose in part a? **By 8:40 P.M.**

10. The Yamada family plans to go to a ball game at 7:30 P.M. They drive 45 mi/hr on Atlantic Parkway.

    Stadium
    Atlantic Pkwy
    Yamada home
    Scale: 1 in. = 16 mi

    a. What is the distance from home to the stadium? **24 mi**

    b. How long will it take them to get from home to the stadium? **32 min**

    c. When do they need to leave to get to the stadium at 7:30 P.M.? **6:58 P.M.**

11. Howard plans to drive from Seattle Washington, to Portland, Oregon, a road distance of 172 miles. He needs to be in Portland by 11:45 A.M. If he drives at a rate of 60 mi/hr, what is the latest time he can leave Seattle? **8:53 A.M.**

RETEACHING

Name ______________________ **Alternative Lesson 7-3**

Problem Solving Using Maps

You can use this formula to find the time for a given trip:

$$\text{time} = \frac{\text{distance}}{\text{rate}}$$

If you know the distance a trip is and how fast you will travel, you can divide to find the time it will take.

Example

Leanne rode her mountain bike a distance of 20 miles at a rate of 8 mi/hr. How many hours did she ride? If she left at 3:00 P.M., what time did she finish?

Use the formula to find the number of hours Leanne rode.

$$\text{time} = \frac{\text{distance}}{\text{rate}} = \frac{20}{8} = 2.5$$

The ride took 2.5 hours. Since she left at 3:00 P.M., and rode for 2.5 hours, it was 5:30 P.M. when she finished.

Try It Fumiko is driving 175 mi to Hanover on a business trip. She averages 50 mi/hr when traveling. If she needs to be in Hanover by 2:00 P.M., at what time should she leave?

a. How long is the trip? **175 mi**

b. At what rate does she travel? **50 mi/hr**

c. Use the formula to find how long the trip will take. **3.5 hr**

d. Did Fumiko leave before or after 2:00 P.M.? **Before**

e. At what time should Fumiko leave? **10:30 A.M.**

Find the time it would take to travel each distance at the given rate.

f. 75 mi at 25 mi/hr **3 hr**
g. 120 km at 80 km/hr **1.5 hr**
h. 240 mi at 60 mi/hr **4 hr**
i. 217 km at 35 km/hr **6.2 hr**
j. 70 mi at 50 mi/hr **1.4 hr**
k. 390 km at 65 km/hr **6 hr**
l. 35 mi at 20 mi/hr **1.75 hr**
m. 385 km at 55 km/hr **7 hr**
n. 540 mi at 60 mi/hr **9 hr**
o. 520 km at 80 km/hr **6.5 hr**

Exercise Notes

■ Exercises 11 and 13

Geography You may wish to use Teaching Tool Transparency 21: Map of the United States with these exercises.

Extension Have students estimate the answers to these problems.

■ Exercises 14–22

Extension Have students estimate the answers to these problems before (or instead of) computing the exact answer.

Exercise Answers

23. 3 pounds:1 dollar; $\frac{\text{3 pounds}}{\text{1 dollar}}$; 3 pounds to 1 dollar.

24. 11 people:2 tables; $\frac{\text{11 people}}{\text{2 tables}}$; 11 people to 2 tables.

Alternate Assessment

Self Assessment Ask students to critique their work in developing their delivery routes in **Explore.** Have them also address other things they might have considered or other approaches they might have taken.

► Quick Quiz

1. Maria left home at 10 A.M. and traveled 130 mi to her mother's home at 50 mi/hr. What time did she arrive? 12:36 P.M.
2. Marty's flight from New York to Chicago took 2.5 hr. If it is about 700 miles from New York to Chicago, then what was the average speed of the plane? 280 mi/hr

Available on Daily Transparency 7-3

PROBLEM SOLVING 7-3

10. **Test Prep** Maria-Teresa left the library at 5:30 P.M. and began biking at the rate of 20 km/hr. By what time had she biked 35 kilometers? **D**

Ⓐ 6:04 P.M. Ⓑ 6:05 P.M. Ⓒ 6:25 P.M. Ⓓ 7:15 P.M.

Problem Solving and Reasoning

11. **Critical Thinking** Sela is a truck driver traveling from Dallas, Texas, to Buffalo, New York. The road distance on her map is $5\frac{1}{2}$ in. and the map's scale is 1 in.:250 mi. Her truck gets 11 mi/gal.

a. What is the actual distance Sela will drive? **1,375 mi**

b. How much gasoline will Sela use on her trip? **125 gallons**

c. What will fuel cost for the trip if the price is $1.30 per gallon? **$162.50**

12. **Choose a Strategy** GPS Students at Northampton East High School in North Carolina designed an electric car. At top speed, the car can travel for 6 hr. Then its batteries must be recharged for 6 hr. If this car travels 1440 miles, when would the car arrive if it left on Tuesday at noon? (Assume the driver travels at a speed of 65 mi/hr.) **≈ 4:00 A.M. Thursday**

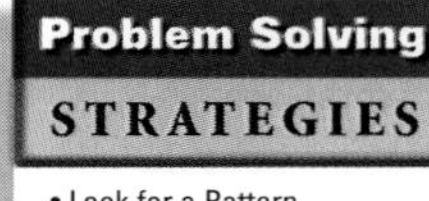

Problem Solving STRATEGIES

- Look for a Pattern
- Make an Organized List
- Make a Table
- Guess and Check
- Work Backward
- Use Logical Reasoning
- Draw a Diagram
- Solve a Simpler Problem

13. **Communicate** Using an atlas, plan a "fantasy trip" from your home to a place in the United States you would like to visit. Calculate how long the trip would take at an average speed of 30 mi/hr. Finally, write a trip *itinerary* (plan), telling what time you would leave and when you would reach your destination. **Answers may vary**

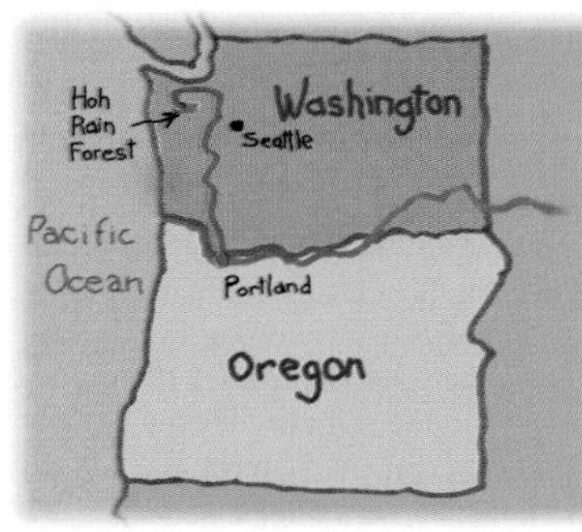

Mixed Review

Find each sum or difference. *[Lesson 4-3]*

14. $6\frac{2}{3} + 2\frac{1}{2}$ **$9\frac{1}{6}$** **15.** $8\frac{3}{5} - 5\frac{4}{5}$ **$2\frac{4}{5}$** **16.** $1\frac{1}{4} + 2\frac{4}{7}$ **$3\frac{23}{28}$** **17.** $3\frac{5}{8} - 2\frac{3}{7}$ **$1\frac{11}{56}$** **18.** $12\frac{4}{11} + \frac{1}{3}$ **$12\frac{23}{33}$**

19. $5\frac{4}{9} + 10\frac{6}{7}$ **$16\frac{19}{63}$** **20.** $3\frac{1}{9} - 1\frac{7}{8}$ **$1\frac{17}{72}$** **21.** $13\frac{3}{7} + 4\frac{2}{3}$ **$18\frac{2}{21}$** **22.** $10\frac{11}{12} - 3\frac{1}{3}$ **$7\frac{7}{12}$**

Write each ratio in three ways. *[Lesson 6-1]*

23. 3 pounds for 1 dollar **24.** 11 people for 2 tables

► PROBLEM SOLVING

Name ______

Guided Problem Solving 7-3

GPS **PROBLEM 12, STUDENT PAGE 336**

Students at Northampton East High School in North Carolina designed an electric car. At top speed, the car can travel for 6 hr. Then its batteries must be recharged for 6 hr. If this car travels 1440 miles, when would the car arrive if it left on Tuesday at noon? (Assume the driver travels at a speed of 65 mi/hr.)

— Understand —

1. Underline what you are asked to find.

— Plan —

2. Complete the table that shows how many miles were traveled at the end of each 6-hour period.

Hours	6	12	18	24	30	36	42
Miles	390	390	780	780	1170	1170	1560

3. The electric car travels 1440 miles in all. How many more miles would it have traveled in 42 hours? **120 miles.**
4. About how many hours does it take to travel the distance in Item 3? **About 2 hours.**
5. About how many hours did the trip take? **About 40 hours.**

— Solve —

6. At what time did the car arrive? **About 4 A.M. Thursday.**

— Look Back —

7. How can you solve this problem using different steps in order to see if your answer is reasonable? **Subtract 1170 miles from 1440 miles, traveling about 270 miles in 4 hours. Add 4 hours to 36 hours traveled. Total trip time is about 40 hours; Arrive about 4 A.M.**

SOLVE ANOTHER PROBLEM

Suppose the driver of the car left at 10 A.M. on Monday and traveled 1050 miles. About what time would they arrive at the destination? **About 2 P.M. Tuesday.**

► ENRICHMENT

Name ______

Extend Your Thinking 7-3

Critical Thinking

The map below shows a section of Rudy's new home town placed on a grid. Each square on the grid measures 1 mile on each side.

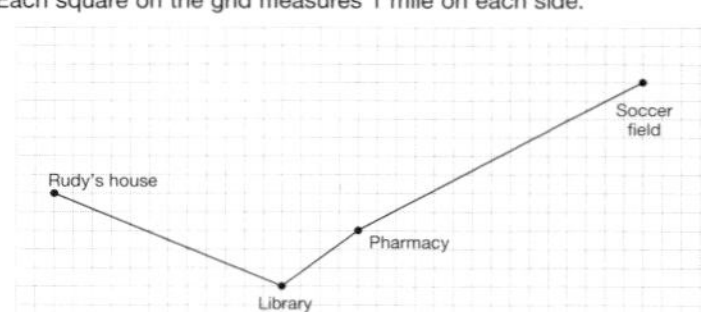

Rudy plans to go to the library, then to the pharmacy, and then to the soccer field. How many miles will the trip be? He does not have a ruler to measure map distance.

Use what you know about right triangles to help Rudy find the distance to each destination. First draw a line on the grid map that goes south 5 miles. Then draw another line that goes east 12 miles to the library. You now have a right triangle.

1. Write the Pythagorean Theorem. Use it to find the distance from Rudy's house to the library. **$a^2 + b^2 = c^2$; $5^2 + 12^2 = c^2$; $13 = c$; 13 mi**
2. Create another right triangle on the grid map that will allow you to find the distance from the library to the pharmacy.
   a. What are the measurements of the legs of the triangle? **3 mi; 4 mi**
   b. How far is it from the library to the pharmacy? **5 mi**
3. Create another right triangle on the grid map to find the distance from the pharmacy to the soccer field.
   a. What are the measurements of the legs of the triangle? **8 mi; 15 mi**
   b. How far is it from the pharmacy to the soccer field? **17 mi**
4. How far did Rudy travel from his home to the soccer field? **35 mi**
5. Rudy returns home by retracing his route. He needs to be home by 6 P.M. What time must he leave the soccer field if he averages 50 mi/hr on the drive home? **No later than 5:18 P.M.**

Creating Scale Drawings and Scale Models

7-4

▶ Lesson Link You've used scales to interpret maps and other scale drawings. Now you'll choose appropriate scales for scale drawings and scale models. ◀

You'll Learn ...

■ to select a reasonable scale for a drawing, map, or model

... How It's Used

Craftspeople who construct models of ships, automobiles, or other objects need to determine a scale to create an authentic reproduction of the desired size.

Explore Creating Scale Drawings

In Search of a Flat Earth

Materials: Earth globe, Ruler, Tape measure

Mapmakers have used many different methods to project the globe of the earth onto a flat surface. One of these methods is the Mercator projection, used to make the map shown at right.

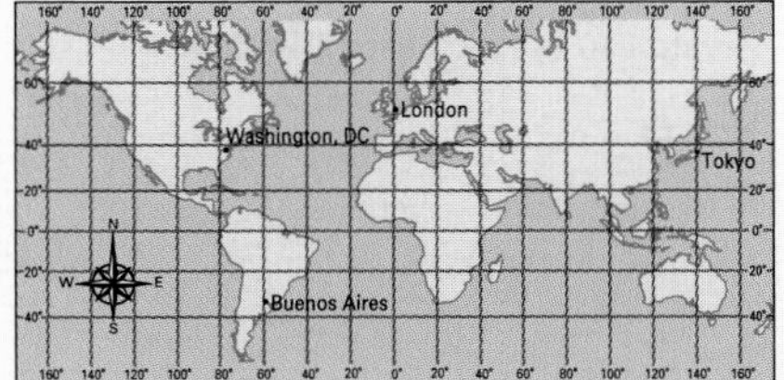

1. Do you think the Mercator map is distorted? How can you tell?
2. Washington, DC, is 5218 mi away from Buenos Aires, Argentina. Use this fact to calculate the scales of the map and the globe.
3. The distance from London, England, to Tokyo, Japan, is 5940 mi. Calculate the scales again, using London and Tokyo.
4. How are your results related to your answer to Step 1? Did any of your results surprise you? Explain.

Learn Creating Scale Drawings and Scale Models

Fitting the round Earth onto a flat map has challenged people for centuries. In fact, it is impossible to do this without some distortion.

Fortunately, when mapping small regions or making scale drawings or models, distortion is not a significant problem, and the fit problem is solved simply by choosing a good scale. The scale must be small enough to fit the available space. It should be large enough to show important details.

MEETING INDIVIDUAL NEEDS

Resources

- 7-4 Practice
- 7-4 Reteaching
- 7-4 Problem Solving
- 7-4 Enrichment
- 7-4 Daily Transparency
  - Problem of the Day
  - Review
  - Quick Quiz
- Teaching Tool Transparencies 14, 20
- Lesson Enhancement Transparency 31
- Chapter 7 Project Master

Learning Modalities

Verbal Have students make a poster showing the steps involved in making a scale drawing or scale model. The students should illustrate each step along the way.

Visual Have students use oranges to experiment with different ways of making maps of the earth. Note that distances can be relatively correct within a small area.

English Language Development

Have students add terms relating to scale, scale models, and scale drawings to their file of vocabulary words and definitions on index cards.

7-4 Lesson Organizer

Objective

- Select a reasonable scale for a drawing, map, or model.

Materials

- Explore: Earth globe, ruler, tape measure

NCTM Standards

- 1–4, 7, 13

▶ Review

Perform each operation.

1. $\frac{3}{4} \cdot \frac{8}{9}$ $\frac{2}{3}$
2. $4\frac{1}{2} \cdot 3\frac{1}{5}$ $14\frac{2}{5}$
3. $\frac{4}{5} \div \frac{1}{3}$ $2\frac{2}{5}$
4. $3\frac{2}{3} \div 1\frac{2}{3}$ $2\frac{1}{5}$

Available on Daily Transparency 7-4

1 Introduce

Explore

You may wish to use Teaching Tool Transparencies 14: Rulers, and 20: Map of the World, or Lesson Enhancement Transparency 31 with **Explore.**

The Point

Students see that a Mercator map does not use a consistent scale, and therefore distorts distances.

Ongoing Assessment

Check that students are not discouraged if they get different scales in Steps 2 and 3. You might suggest that students convert the scales to the form 1 in.:_____ to make comparisons easier. Encourage students to have faith in their results.

For Groups That Finish Early

Estimate the distance between London, England, and Buenos Aires, Argentina.

Answers may vary.

Answers for Explore on next page.

Answers for Explore

1. Yes: Greenland appears bigger than the U.S.
2. The globe scale depends on the globe used. Map scale is about $\frac{5}{8}$ in.:5218 mi = 1 in.:8348.8 mi.
3. Globe scale same as in Step 2. Map scale about $1\frac{1}{8}$ in.:5940 mi = 1 in.:5280 mi.
4. Since the scale of the map is not consistent, the map is distorted. The results may be surprising because the measurements taken do not appear to include especially distorted regions.

2 Teach

Learn

Alternate Examples

1. Mandy is making a scale drawing of an airplane on an $8\frac{1}{2}$ in. × 11 in. sheet of paper. The actual plane is 12 ft high and 66 ft long. What scale should she use?

   If Mandy uses $\frac{11\text{ in.}}{66\text{ ft}} = \frac{1\text{ in.}}{6\text{ ft}}$, the height of 12 ft would result in a drawing 2 in. high.

2. Al is enlarging a 12 cm × 18 cm map to fit on a poster 51 cm × 81 cm. What is the largest scale he can use?

   Largest scale for width $= \frac{\text{poster width}}{\text{actual width}} = \frac{51\text{ cm}}{12\text{ cm}} = 4.25:1$

   Largest scale for height $= \frac{\text{poster height}}{\text{actual height}} = \frac{81\text{ cm}}{18\text{ cm}} = 4.5:1$

   The largest possible scale is 4.25:1.

3 Practice and Assess

Check

Answers for Check Your Understanding

1. Possible answer: Size of the actual object, size of the paper, and amount of detail needed.
2. Possible answer: They help to represent objects in proportion so they can be compared and understood.
3. If the 16.5 cm length is multiplied by 8, the corresponding poster length is 132 cm, too long to fit on the 100 cm length of the poster.

Example 1

Gerald is making a scale drawing of a locomotive on an $8\frac{1}{2}$ in. × 11 in. sheet of paper turned sideways. The actual locomotive is 12 ft tall and 22 ft long. What scale should he use if he wants the drawing to be as large as possible?

The length of the drawing must be 11 in. or less. If Gerald makes the drawing 11 in. long, the scale is

$$\frac{\text{scale length}}{\text{actual length}} = \frac{11\text{ in.}}{22\text{ ft}} = \frac{1\text{ in.}}{2\text{ ft}}$$

Check that the other dimension also fits the paper. At 1 in.:2 ft, the drawing's height will be 6 in., which easily fits the paper's $8\frac{1}{2}$ in. height.

Gerald can use a scale of 1 in.:2 ft.

Try It

Marbella wants to sketch a dog that is 33 in. tall and 44 in. long on a 3 in. by 5 in. index card. What scale should she use if she wants to make the largest possible sketch? ≈ **1:11**

History Link

The first practical locomotive was designed and built by George Stephenson in 1829. It was called the *Rocket* and ran from Stockton to Darlington, in the north of England.

Example 2

Heidi is designing a 60 cm × 100 cm poster showing a rectangular 7.5 cm × 16.5 cm calculator. What is the largest scale she can use?

Both dimensions of the calculator must fit. Find the largest scale possible for each dimension and choose the *lesser of the two.*

$$\text{Largest scale for width to fit} = \frac{\text{poster width}}{\text{actual width}} = \frac{60\text{ cm}}{7.5\text{ cm}} = 8:1$$

$$\text{Largest scale for height to fit} = \frac{\text{poster height}}{\text{actual height}} = \frac{100\text{ cm}}{16.5\text{ cm}} \approx 6:1$$

The largest possible scale is 6:1.

MENTAL MATH

When deciding on a scale, it's helpful to make an estimate of the object's actual size and the paper's dimensions. Then divide to see how many times one fits into the other.

Check Your Understanding

1. When you make a scale drawing, what factors help you decide on a good scale to use?
2. Why are scale drawings useful?
3. In Example 2, why was 6:1 chosen for the largest possible scale instead of 8:1?

MATH EVERY DAY

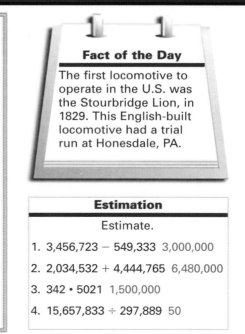

Problem of the Day

The Earth has an average distance of about 93,000,0000 miles from the Sun. Make a diagram showing the Sun and the Earth with distances drawn to scale on an $8\frac{1}{2}$-by-11-inch piece of paper. What scale would you use? Why? Possible answer: Scale: 1 in. = 11,000,000 mi because the paper is $8\frac{1}{2}$ inches wide and $8\frac{1}{2}$ times 11 million = 93.5 million miles.

Available on Daily Transparency 7-4

An Extension is provided in the transparency package.

Fact of the Day

The first locomotive to operate in the U.S. was the Stourbridge Lion, in 1829. This English-built locomotive had a trial run at Honesdale, PA.

Estimation

Estimate.

1. 3,456,723 − 549,333 3,000,000
2. 2,034,532 + 4,444,765 6,480,000
3. 342 • 5021 1,500,000
4. 15,657,833 ÷ 297,889 50

7-4 Exercises and Applications

Practice and Apply

1. **Getting Started** Follow these steps to find the largest scale that can be used to enlarge the picture at right to make a 21 in. × 36 in. poster.

   a. Measure the height of the picture in inches.

   b. Use the formula scale $= \frac{\text{scale length}}{\text{actual length}}$ to find the scale that gives you a height of 36 in.

   c. Measure the width of the picture. Find the scale that gives you a width of 21 in.

   d. Choose the smaller of your scale calculations in **b** and **c**.

A giraffe can be as much as 18 ft tall. Find the maximum scale you can use for a model giraffe if it must fit in a:

2. Room with a 9 ft ceiling **6 in.:1 ft**
3. 6 ft tall crate **1 ft:3 ft**
4. 2 ft tall toy box **1 ft:9 ft**
5. 5 in. tall zoo diorama **1 in.:3.6 ft**
6. Determine an appropriate scale to make a scale drawing of this figure that fills an $8\frac{1}{2}$ in. × 11 in. sheet of paper. Then make the scale drawing. **≈ 13:1** 
7. **Fine Arts** When developed, most film used by photographers makes negatives that measure about 24 mm high and 35 mm wide. These negatives are used to make prints that measure about 102 mm × 153 mm. What is the approximate scale of the prints? **≈ 4.25:1**
8. **Geography** Oregon is approximately 400 miles from east to west and 300 miles from north to south. What is the largest scale that can be used to fit a map of Oregon on a sheet of $8\frac{1}{2}$ in. × 11 in. paper, if:

   a. The 11 in. side runs north-south **≈ 1 in.:48 mi**

   b. The $8\frac{1}{2}$ in. side runs north-south **≈ 1 in.:36 mi**

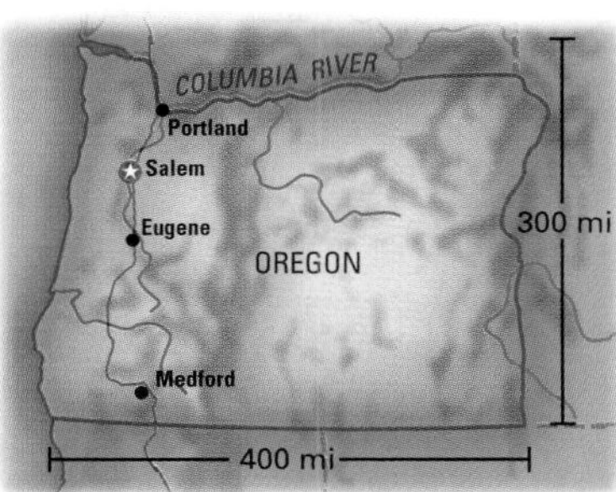

9. **Estimation** Estimate the scale of the Oregon map. **1 in.:200 mi**
10. **Test Prep** Which of these scales is the largest that could be used to make a scale drawing of a 26 in. × 35 in. photo on a 3 in. × 5 in. card? **C**

    Ⓐ 1:6　　Ⓑ 1:8

    Ⓒ 1:9　　Ⓓ 1:12

PRACTICE 7-4

7-4 Exercises and Applications

Assignment Guide

- **Basic** 1–5, 8–11, 14–28 evens
- **Average** 1–11, 15–29 odds
- **Enriched** 2–13, 15–29 odds

Exercise Notes

Exercise 7

Fine Arts One method for making prints larger than their negatives is by projection printing. The negative is placed in an enlarger, which projects the image onto printing paper, much like an overhead projector throwing an image onto a screen. To increase the size of the print, you increase the distance between negative and paper.

Exercise 8

Error Prevention Warn students to be careful to check that both north-south and east-west will fit on the page.

Exercise Answers

1. a. 2.5 in.
   b. 1 in.:14.4 in.
   c. 2.0 in.; 1 in.:10.5 in.
   d. Scale is 1:10.5.

PRACTICE

Name ______________________

Practice 7-4

Creating Scale Drawings and Scale Models

The Statue of Liberty is 152 ft tall. Find the maximum scale you can use for a model of the Statue of Liberty if the model must fit in a:

1. room with an 8-foot ceiling <u>1 : 19</u>
2. 4-inch tall toy box <u>1 in. : 38 ft</u>
3. 12-foot-tall crate <u>3 : 38</u>
4. hotel lobby with a 38-ft ceiling <u>1 : 4</u>
5. Determine an appropriate scale to make a scale drawing of this figure on an $8\frac{1}{2}$-in. × 11-in. sheet of paper. Then make the scale drawing on a separate sheet of paper.

   <u>Possible answer: 1 in. : 6 in.</u>
6. **Geography** Utah is approximately 275 miles from east to west and 350 miles from north to south. What is the largest scale that can be used to fit a map of Utah on an $8\frac{1}{2}$-in. × 11-in. sheet of paper, if:

   a. the 11-in. side runs north-south

   <u>17 in. : 550 mi or about 1 in. : 32.4 mi</u>

   b. the $8\frac{1}{2}$-in. side runs north-south

   <u>17 in. : 700 mi or about 1 in. : 41.2 mi</u>
7. A $3\frac{1}{2}$-in. × 5-in. photograph is enlarged to a 28-in. × 40 in. poster. What is the scale of the poster? <u>8 : 1</u>
8. A painting measures 45 cm × 55 cm. What is the largest scale that can be used to create a print of this painting if the print must fit in a 20-cm × 25-cm frame? <u>4 : 9</u>
9. Estimate the scale of the map whose scale of miles is shown. Scale: 0 10 20 30 miles <u>3 in. : 80 mi</u>
10. A postage stamp measures $\frac{7}{8}$ in. × 1 in. Find the largest scale that can be used to make an enlargement of the stamp on a 3-in. × 5-in. note card. <u>24 : 7</u>
11. Determine an appropriate scale to make a scale drawing of this figure on a 4-in. × 6-in. note card. Then make the scale drawing on a separate sheet of paper.

    <u>Possible answer: 1 in. : 4 in.</u>

RETEACHING

Name ______________________

Alternative Lesson 7-4

Creating Scale Drawings and Scale Models

Before selecting a scale for a scale drawing, you must often consider the space you have available for making the drawing.

Example

Lars wants to enlarge a drawing of a race car. The drawing measures 3 in. × 5 in. Find the maximum scale he can use for the enlargement if it must fit on a 24 in. × 30 in. poster.

Find the largest possible scale for width to fit. $\frac{24 \text{ in.}}{3 \text{ in.}} = \frac{8}{1}$ ← Poster width ← Actual width

Using a scale of 8:1, the new dimensions would be: Width: 3 in. × 8 = 24 in. Length: 5 in. × 8 = 40 in.

This scale will not work since the new length is too long to fit the length of the poster.

Find the largest possible scale for length to fit. $\frac{30 \text{ in.} \div 5}{5 \text{ in.} \div 5} = \frac{6}{1}$ ← Poster length ← Actual length

Using a scale of 6:1, the new dimensions of 18 in. by 30 in. will fit on the poster.

So, the maximum scale Lars can use is 6:1.

Try It Suppose you have a poster that measures 36 in. high and 24 in. wide. You want to have it reduced to fit on a greeting card that measures 6 in. high and 3 in. wide. What scale will you use?

a. Find the largest possible scale to accommodate the width. $\frac{\text{Card width}}{\text{Poster width}} = \frac{3}{24} = \frac{1}{8}$

b. Find the largest possible scale to accommodate the height. $\frac{\text{Card height}}{\text{Poster height}} = \frac{6}{36} = \frac{1}{6}$

c. How wide will the card be if you use the largest possible height scale? <u>4 in.</u>

d. Will the drawing fit on a 3 in. × 6 in. card? Explain.

<u>No, the reduced 4 in. by 6 in. drawing will not fit on a 3 in. × 6 in. card.</u>

e. What scale will you need to use? Explain.

<u>The scale of 1:8, since the reduced 3 in. × $4\frac{1}{2}$ in. drawing will fit on a 3 in. × 6 in. card.</u>

Reteaching

Activity

Materials: Ruler

- Draw a small picture of something you like.
- Find an appropriate scale to enlarge your picture to fit on an 8.5 in. by 11 in. piece of paper.
- Enlarge your picture.

Exercise Notes

Exercise 12

Error Prevention Remind students that, if no units are given, then the same units are assumed for both parts of the scale.

Project Progress

You may want to have students use Chapter 7 Project Master.

Exercise Answers

12. Divide 982,000 by 5,280.

13. a. ≈ 1:7,326,300,000

b. ≈ 20.4 m

c. ≈ 812.1 m

d. ≈ 0.06m = 6 cm

24. 20 pages per day

25. 3 sections per day

26. 33 desks per classroom

27. 33.4 miles per gallon

28. 5 meters per second

29. 24 cans per case

Alternate Assessment

Portfolio Have students make up their own problems (with answers) about creating scale drawings and scale models.

➤ Quick Quiz

1. An elephant is about 12 ft tall. Find the maximum scale you can use for a model elephant if it must fit into a 10-in. high zoo diorama. 1 in. = 1.2 ft
2. A 3 in. × 5 in. photo is to be enlarged to fit on paper that is 8.5 in. × 11 in. What is the largest scale that can be used?
1 in. = 2.2 in.

Available on Daily Transparency 7-4

PROBLEM SOLVING 7-4

Problem Solving and Reasoning

11. Critical Thinking The Oscar Mayer Wienermobile has been a traveling advertisement for the past 60 years. The 27 ft long Wienermobile looks like a large hot dog sitting on a bun. A hot dog measures about 5 in. in length. What is the scale of the Wienermobile compared to a real hot dog?

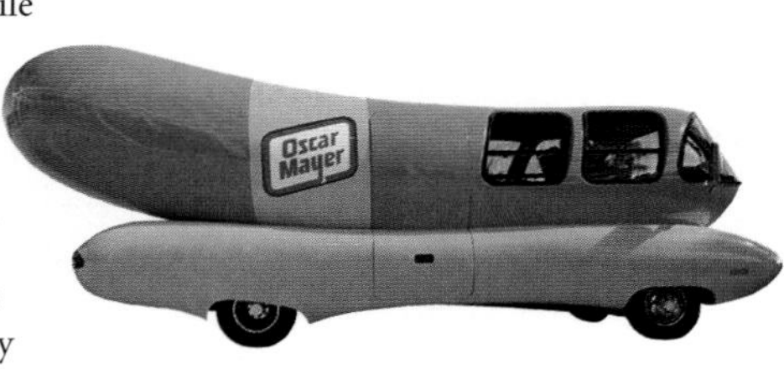

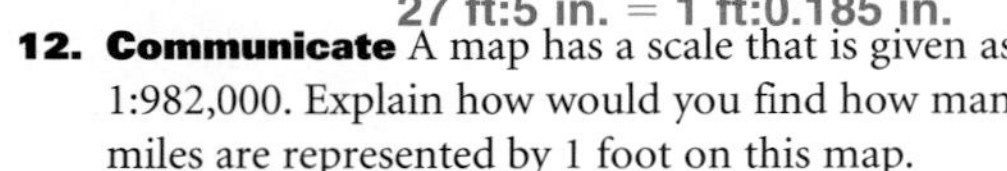

27 ft:5 in. = 1 ft:0.185 in.

12. Communicate A map has a scale that is given as 1:982,000. Explain how would you find how many miles are represented by 1 foot on this map.

13. Critical Thinking In a scale model of the solar system, a penny (0.019 m in diameter) is used to represent the sun, which is 139,200 km in diameter.

a. Determine the scale being used for this model.

b. On average, Earth is 149,600,000 km from the sun. How far from the penny should Earth be in the model?

c. On average, Pluto is 5,950,000,000 km from the sun. How far from the penny should Pluto be in the model?

d. The moon is about 400,000 km from Earth. How far away from Earth should it be in the model?

Mixed Review

Solve each equation. Check your answer. *[Lesson 2-7]*

14. $m \cdot 6 = 72$ $m = 12$ **15.** $\frac{q}{5} = 12$ $q = 60$ **16.** $6s = 42$ $s = 7$ **17.** $15 = 3 \cdot n$ $n = 5$ **18.** $11p = 121$ $p = 11$

19. $t \cdot 2 = 42$ $t = 21$ **20.** $5x = 5$ $x = 1$ **21.** $47r = 94$ $r = 2$ **22.** $3 = \frac{u}{7}$ $u = 21$ **23.** $8 = \frac{w}{5}$ $w = 40$

Express each rate as a unit rate. *[Lesson 6-2]*

24. 40 pages read in 2 days **25.** 15 sections in 5 days **26.** 132 desks in 4 classrooms

27. 334 miles for 10 gallons **28.** 20 meters in 4 seconds **29.** 48 cans in 2 cases

Project Progress

Decide which rooms you want in your dream house. Then decide how big you want each room to be. (Measuring rooms in your own home can help you do this.) Determine an appropriate scale for your project.

Problem Solving
Understand
Plan
Solve
Look Back

PROBLEM SOLVING

Name ____________

Guided Problem Solving 7-4

GPS PROBLEM 11, STUDENT PAGE 340

The Oscar Mayer Wienermobile has been a traveling advertisement for the past 60 years. The 27 ft long Wienermobile looks like a large hot dog sitting on a bun. A hot dog measures about 5 in. in length. What is the scale of the Wienermobile compared to a real hot dog?

— Understand —

1. What is the length of the Wienermobile? 27 ft
2. What is the length of a real hot dog? About 5 in.
3. What are you asked to find? The scale of the Wienermobile compared to a real hot dog.

— Plan —

4. Which ratio represents the Wienermobile compared to a real hot dog? c

a. $\frac{5 \text{ in.}}{60 \text{ ft}}$ b. $\frac{27 \text{ ft}}{60 \text{ yr}}$ c. $\frac{27 \text{ ft}}{5 \text{ in.}}$ d. $\frac{60 \text{ yr}}{5 \text{ in.}}$

5. What will you divide by so that the scale length of the hot dog is 1 in.? Divide by 5.

— Solve —

6. What is the scale of the Wienermobile compared to the length of a real hot dog?
$\frac{27 \text{ ft}}{5 \text{ in.}} = \frac{5.4 \text{ ft}}{1 \text{ in.}}$

— Look Back —

7. What is the scale of the real hot dog compared to the Wienermobile?
$\frac{5 \text{ in.}}{27 \text{ ft}} = \frac{0.185 \text{ in.}}{1 \text{ ft}}$

SOLVE ANOTHER PROBLEM

The Space Shuttle is 56 m tall. A model of the Space Shuttle is 84 cm tall. What is the scale of the model compared to the Space Shuttle? $\frac{84 \text{ cm}}{56 \text{ m}} = \frac{1.5 \text{ cm}}{1 \text{ m}}$

ENRICHMENT

Name ____________

Extend Your Thinking 7-4

Decision Making

Suppose you are asked to plan a poster that will be enlarged for a mural in the chemistry lab and reduced for flyers that advertise the school science fair. The wall mural will be 15 ft long and 10 ft high. The flyers will be on $8\frac{1}{2}$ by 11 inch paper. Plan the size of the poster so that the enlargement and reduction will be as easy as possible to make.

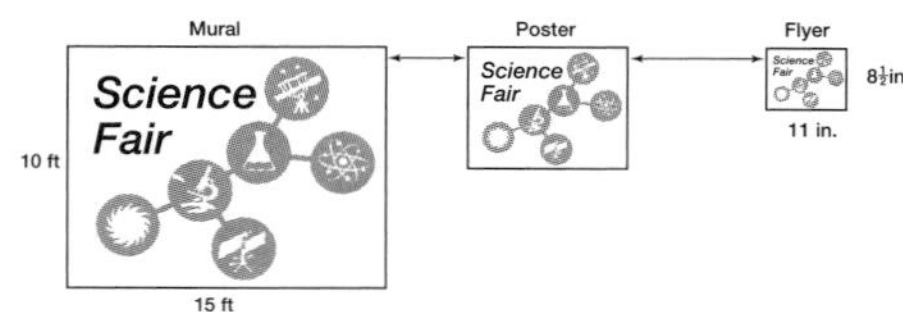

1. What is the length:width ratio for the wall mural? 15 ft:10 ft or 3:2
2. What is the length:width ratio for the flyer? 11 in.:$8\frac{1}{2}$ in.
3. Are the ratios for the mural and flyer the same? No.
4. Suppose you decide to use $\frac{3}{2}$ as the ratio for the poster. What are some possible dimensions for your poster using this ratio? Possible answer: 30 in. long, 20 in. high.
5. Will your poster completely fill the wall space when it is enlarged for the mural? Explain. Yes, because each can be expressed in a length:width ratio as 3:2.
6. Will your poster completely fill the paper when it is reduced for the flyer? Explain. Possible answer: No, its length:width ratio cannot be expressed as 3:2. So, the reduced poster will be slightly wider than 11 in. and slightly shorter than $8\frac{1}{2}$ in.
7. Will you be able to write the name of the school on the flyer? If so, where will it go? Possible answer: Yes, at the bottom or top of the flyer.

At the beginning of Section 7A, you saw that Lewis and Clark were able to create a map of an unfamiliar territory. Now you will create a map of a very familiar territory—your classroom. You can use what you've learned about maps and scales to make a very accurate map.

Never Mind—I'll Draw It Myself!

Materials: Tape measure, Ruler

Your younger sister wants to know what your math classroom is like. When she becomes confused by your explanations, you decide to make a scale drawing so you can *show* her how it's arranged.

1. Without taking any measurements, make a rough sketch of your classroom. Show details such as doors, windows, chalkboards, and your teacher's desk.

2. What other information will you need to make an accurate scale drawing?

3. How can you be sure the drawing will fit on a single sheet of paper? Make some measurements and decide what scale to use.

4. Make any other measurements you need, then make a final drawing. Be as accurate as you can.

5. Are you pleased with your drawing? If not, tell what you would do differently the next time.

6. If you needed to make a scale drawing of your school, how would you obtain the measurements you needed? How would you decide on a scale?

7A Connect

Never Mind—I'll Draw It Myself!

The Point

In *Never Mind—I'll Draw It Myself!* on page 323 students discussed map making. Now they will create a map of their classroom.

Materials

Tape measure, ruler

Resources

Teaching Tool Transparency 14: Rulers

About the Page

Have students work in pairs to complete the measurements and draw the map.

- Tell students to write the measurements on their sketch as they measure each section of the classroom.
- Discuss with students how the size of the paper they use will help determine the scale.
- Discuss why the scale would change if students make a scale drawing of the school on the same size paper they use for the scale drawing of the classroom.

Ongoing Assessment

Check that students have drawn a reasonable sketch, measured accurately, and selected a reasonable scale for their drawing.

Extension

All classrooms have desks or tables and other furniture in the room. Ask students to measure the furniture in their classroom, apply the scale they used in the drawing, and add the furnishings to their scale drawing.

Answers for Connect

1. Student-generated sketch.
2. Measurements
3. By choosing an appropriate scale.
4. Student-generated drawing.
5. Answers will vary.
6. Use a large tape measure to find the dimensions of the school, or obtain a blueprint of the floor plan. Compare size of paper to actual dimensions.

7A Review

Review Correlation

Item(s)	Lesson(s)
1–3	7-1
4	7-2
5, 6	7-1
7	7-2
8	7-1
9	7-4
10	7-3

Test Prep

Test-Taking Tip

Tell students to read labels on answers carefully. Here, they can eliminate Answer D immediately because distances on a map would not be in kilometers.

Answers for Review

1. $\frac{4 \text{ in.}}{200 \text{ mi}}$, 4 in. = 200 mi
2. $\frac{17 \text{ in.}}{510 \text{ mi}}$, 17 in.:510 mi
3. 10 cm:4 km, 10 cm = 4 km
4. a. 17 in. by 17 in.
   b. 28.5 in. by 28.5 in.
   c. 7 ft by 7 ft
9. ≈ 1:2.2; divide 24 by 11 ≈ 2.2, then check that this scale will work for other dimensions.

Section 7A Review

REVIEW 7A

Number Sense Give two other ways to write each scale.

1. 4 in.:200 mi **2.** 17 in. = 510 mi **3.** $\frac{10 \text{ cm}}{4 \text{ km}}$

4. Measure the miniature reproduction of a painting. Find its actual dimensions given the following scales.

a. 1 in. = 8.5 in. **b.** 1 in. = 14.25 in. **c.** 1 in. = $3\frac{1}{2}$ ft

Piet Mondrian, *Large composition*, 1919

Use the following measurements to find the scale of each map.

5. A 400 km state border is 2 cm long. **1 cm:200 km**

6. A 260 mi bike trail is 3 in. long. **1 in.:86.67 mi**

7. History The Pyramid of the Sun, in Mexico, is about 200 ft tall. If a model of the pyramid uses a scale of 1.5 in.:5 ft, how tall is the model? **60 in.**

8. Literature In Jonathan Swift's *Gulliver's Travels,* Gulliver travels to Brobdingnag, the land of the giants. Gulliver says that a Brobdingnagian "took about ten yards at every stride." Assume that Gulliver's stride is about 2 ft long. Estimate the scale if:

a. Gulliver is viewed as a reduced scale model of the giant **2 ft:10 yd**

b. The giant is viewed as an enlarged scale model of Gulliver **10 yd:2 ft**

9. Journal In an atlas, a map of Korea is $13\frac{1}{2}$ in. × 24 in. Sheila needs to fit a copy of this map onto a 9 in. × 11 in. report cover. What is the largest scale she can use? Explain how you found your answer.

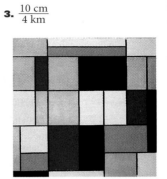

Test Prep

On a multiple choice test, check that your answers make sense. Even if you cannot solve a problem, you may be able to use common sense to eliminate answers.

10. Berlin, Germany, is 811 km from Stockholm, Sweden. About how far apart will these cities appear on a map with the scale 3 cm = 200 km? **A**

Ⓐ 12 cm Ⓑ 27 cm Ⓒ 270 cm Ⓓ 12 km

Resources

Practice Masters
Section 7A Review

Assessment Sourcebook
Quiz 7A

TestWorks
Test and Practice Software

PRACTICE

Name ______________ Practice

Section 7A Review

Give two other ways to write each scale. **Possible answers:**

1. 2 cm : 5 km $\frac{2 \text{ cm}}{5 \text{ km}}$, 2 cm = 5 km
2. 3 in. = 40 mi $\frac{3 \text{ in.}}{40 \text{ mi}}$, 3 in. : 40 mi
3. $\frac{1 \text{ cm}}{250 \text{ km}}$ 1 cm : 250 km, 1 cm = 250 km
4. 4 in. : 50 mi $\frac{4 \text{ in.}}{50 \text{ mi}}$, 4 in. = 50 mi

Use the following measurements to find the scale of each map.

5. A 15-mi road is 4 in. long. 4 in. = 15 mi
6. A 120-km river is 6 cm long. $\frac{1 \text{ cm}}{20 \text{ km}}$
7. Measure the height of the gingerbread man shown. Find the height of the actual cookie for each of the following scales.

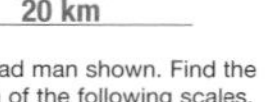

a. 1 in. = 2 in. 3 in. b. 1 in. = 5 in. $7\frac{1}{2}$ in.

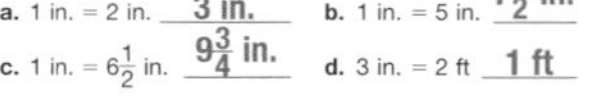

c. 1 in. = $6\frac{1}{2}$ in. $9\frac{3}{4}$ in. d. 3 in. = 2 ft 1 ft

8. The Transamerica Pyramid in San Francisco, California, is 260 m tall. If a model of this building uses a scale of 5 cm = 13 m, how tall is the model? 100 cm or 1 m
9. Peter has both an LP and a CD copy of his favorite album. The LP cover art measures $12\frac{3}{8}$ in. on each side. The CD insert measures $4\frac{3}{4}$ in. on each side.
   a. Estimate the scale if the LP cover is viewed as an enlarged copy of the CD insert. 99 : 38 or about 2.6 : 1
   b. Estimate the scale if the CD insert is viewed as a reduced copy of the LP cover 38 : 99 or about 1 : 2.6
10. A tree trunk makes an angle of 72° with the ground. A pole making an angle of 55° with the ground is used to support the tree. What angle does the pole make with the tree? *[Lesson 5-3]*

53°

11. **Health** The average secretary burns 88 calories every 60 minutes while working. How many calories are burned in 21 minutes? *[Lesson 6-3]* 30.8 calories

Section 7B

Dimensional Analysis

LESSON PLANNING GUIDE

Student Edition | **Ancillaries***

LESSON		MATERIALS	VOCABULARY	DAILY	OTHER
	Section 7B Opener				
7-5	**Choosing Appropriate Rates and Units**	tape measure, stopwatch		7-5	Teaching Tool Trans. 2, 3 Ch. 7 Project Master
7-6	**Converting Units**		conversion factor	7-6	
7-7	**Problem Solving: Converting Rates**			7-7	*WW Math*–Middle School
	Connect				Interdisc. Team Teaching 7B
	Review				Practice 7B; Quiz 7B; *TestWorks*

* Daily Ancillaries include Practice, Reteaching, Problem Solving, Enrichment, and Daily Transparency. Teaching Tool Transparencies are in *Teacher's Toolkits*. Lesson Enhancement Transparencies are in *Overhead Transparency Package*.

SKILLS TRACE

LESSON	SKILL	FIRST INTRODUCED GR. 5	GR. 6	GR. 7	DEVELOP	PRACTICE/ APPLY	REVIEW
7-4	**Selecting reasonable scales.**			✗ p. 337	pp. 337–338	pp. 339–340	pp. 358, 378, 402, 498
7-5	**Selecting scales and writing reciprocal rates.**	✗			pp. 344–346	pp. 347–348	pp. 358, 379, 409, 581
7-6	**Converting measurements between units.**	✗			pp. 349–350	pp. 351–352	pp. 358, 379, 414, 586
7-7	**Solving problems involving conversion of rates.**		✗		pp. 353–354	pp. 355–356	pp. 358, 379, 419, 591

CONNECTED MATHEMATICS

The unit *Data Around Us (Number Sense)*, from the **Connected Mathematics** series, can be used with Section 7B.

INTERDISCIPLINARY TEAM TEACHING

Math and Science/Technology

(Worksheet pages 27–28: Teacher pages T27–T28)

In this lesson, students use and convert rates and units to solve problems involving carbon dioxide in the atmosphere.

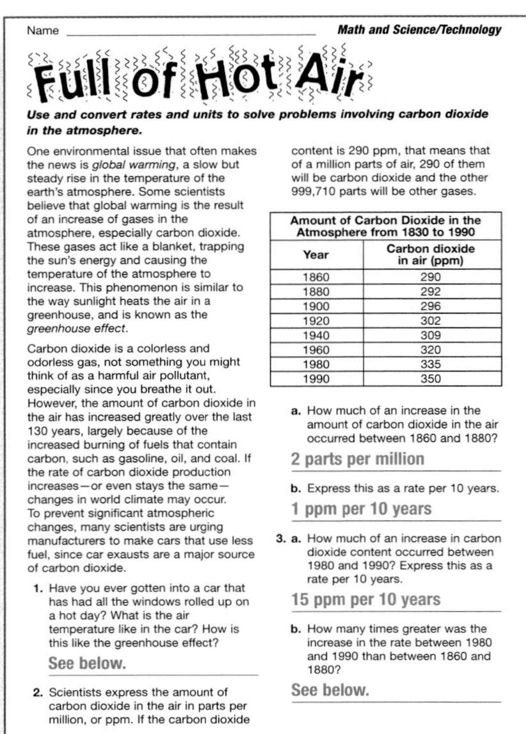

Name ______________________ *Math and Science/Technology*

Full of Hot Air

Use and convert rates and units to solve problems involving carbon dioxide in the atmosphere.

One environmental issue that often makes the news is *global warming*, a slow but steady rise in the temperature of the earth's atmosphere. Some scientists believe that global warming is the result of an increase of gases in the atmosphere, especially carbon dioxide. These gases act like a blanket, trapping the sun's energy and causing the temperature of the atmosphere to increase. This phenomenon is similar to the way sunlight heats the air in a greenhouse, and is known as the *greenhouse effect*.

Carbon dioxide is a colorless and odorless gas, not something you might think of as a harmful air pollutant, especially since you breathe it out. However, the amount of carbon dioxide in the air has increased greatly over the last 130 years, largely because of the increased burning of fuels that contain carbon, such as gasoline, oil, and coal. If the rate of carbon dioxide production increases—or even stays the same—changes in world climate may occur. To prevent significant atmospheric changes, many scientists are urging manufacturers to make cars that use less fuel, since car exausts are a major source of carbon dioxide.

1. Have you ever gotten into a car that has had all the windows rolled up on a hot day? What is the air temperature like in the car? How is this like the greenhouse effect?

See below.

2. Scientists express the amount of carbon dioxide in the air in parts per million, or ppm. If the carbon dioxide content is 290 ppm, that means that of a million parts of air, 290 of them will be carbon dioxide and the other 999,710 parts will be other gases.

Amount of Carbon Dioxide in the Atmosphere from 1830 to 1990

Year	Carbon dioxide in air (ppm)
1860	290
1880	292
1900	296
1920	302
1940	309
1960	320
1980	335
1990	350

a. How much of an increase in the amount of carbon dioxide in the air occurred between 1860 and 1880?

2 parts per million

b. Express this as a rate per 10 years.

1 ppm per 10 years

3. a. How much of an increase in carbon dioxide content occurred between 1980 and 1990? Express this as a rate per 10 years.

15 ppm per 10 years

b. How many times greater was the increase in the rate between 1980 and 1990 than between 1860 and 1880?

See below.

Name ______________________ *Math and Science/Technology*

4. In a typical car, burning 1 gallon of gasoline produces about 20 pounds of carbon dioxide.

a. At this rate, how many pounds of carbon dioxide would a car release in a year, if it burned 800 gallons of gasoline?

16,000 lb; $\frac{1 \text{ gal}}{20 \text{ lb}} = \frac{800 \text{ gal}}{x}$;

$x = 16{,}000$

b. If 1 ton = 2,000 pounds, express your answer in tons per year.

See below.

c. If a household has two cars, each using 800 gallons of gasoline a year, about how many tons of carbon dioxide would the vehicles release in one year? In three years?

See below.

5. More fuel-efficient cars release less carbon dioxide than less fuel-efficient cars. On average, the amount of carbon dioxide emitted over a car's lifetime is about 26 tons for a car that gets 45 miles to the gallon, and about 38 tons for a car that gets 28 miles to the gallon. In tons, about how many times more carbon dioxide is emitted from the car that gets 28 miles to the gallon than the car that gets 45 miles to the gallon?

See below.

6. Some people advocate planting trees to reduce the amount of the carbon dioxide in the atmosphere. In the process of photosynthesis, green plants such as trees absorb carbon dioxide from the air. As a tree gets older, it gets bigger and absorbs more carbon dioxide. To approximate the amount of carbon dioxide absorbed by a tree, some scientists use the following equation:

A tree's carbon dioxide intake in pounds per year = (4.3 × tree's age in years) − 70. Each tree species has an average yearly rate of increase in diameter, which can help a scientist to estimate the age of an individual tree.

a. Many schoolyards contain trees that were planted 40 years ago. Estimate how many pounds of carbon dioxide one of these trees uses in a year.

102 pounds; (4.3 × 40) − 70

b. If there are 100 trees that are 40 years old on the school grounds, how many pounds of carbon dioxide do they use per year? Express your answer to the nearest ton.

10,200 pounds; 5 tons

7. a. Do some research and make a list of some of the things other than cars that produce carbon dioxide.

See below.

b. Draw a diagram of your block or immediate neighborhood showing sources of carbon dioxide. Include the number of houses, apartments, and cars found there. Calculate how much carbon dioxide is produced per year using the following data: a residential house, or apartment of equal size, that is heated by burning fuel oil may release up to 6.5 tons of carbon dioxide per year; a car will release up to 8 tons per year. If other kinds of fuel are used where you live, do some research to find out how much carbon dioxide is produced per year by the burning of other kinds of fuel.

Answers

1. The car windows have allowed sunlight into the car, which heats the air inside. The warm air is trapped inside the car, similar to the way the sun's energy is trapped by gases in Earth's atmosphere.

3. b. The rate between 1980 and 1990 is 15 times greater than the rate between 1860 and 1880.

4. b. 8 tons of carbon dioxide per year

   c. 16 tons per year; 48 tons over three years

5. About $1\frac{1}{2}$ times more carbon dioxide: $38 \div 26 \approx 1.46 \approx 1.5$

7. a. Possible answers: factories, forest fires, power plants, buses, trucks, airplanes, people, animals, home furnaces.

   b. Among the fuels students may consider are natural gas, coal, and wood.

BIBLIOGRAPHY

FOR TEACHERS

American Recycling Market. *The Official Recycled Products Guide*. Ogdensburg, NY: 1991.

Mango, Karin. *Mapmaking*. New York, NY: Messner, 1984.

The Earth Works Group. *50 Simple Things Kids Can Do to Recycle*. Berkeley, CA: Earthworks Press, 1994.

The Earth Works Group. *50 Simple Things You Can Do to Save the Earth*. Kansas City, MO: Andrew & McMeel, 1990.

FOR STUDENTS

All "Trashed" Out. Springfield, IL: Illinois Dept. of Energy and Natural Resources, 1992.

Verne, Jules. *Twenty Thousand Leagues Under the Sea*. Pleasantville, NY: Reader's Digest Assoc. 1990.

Schouweiler, Tom. *The Exxon-Valdez Oil Spill*. San Diego, CA: Lucent Books, 1991.

SECTION 7B

Dimensional Analysis

Science Link | Industry Link | www.mathsurf.com/7/ch7/conservation

Oceans cover most of the earth's surface. So why should you conserve water? First of all, ocean water is too salty to drink; we can only drink water from lakes, wells, or reservoirs. And even in a rainy climate, wasting water hurts the environment. It takes energy and chemicals to treat waste water, pump clean water to your home, and heat water for your showers.

The book 50 Simple Things You Can Do to Save the Earth, *by The EarthWorks Group, contains many water conservation tips. According to this book (which is printed on recycled paper), your family can save up to 20,000 gallons of water per year by doing simple things such as not running the faucet while you brush your teeth or wash the dishes.*

When you work with a number of gallons per year or pounds of paper per tree, you are using rates. You'll explore many different rates that have to do with conservation and the environment.

1 How much water do you use in an 8-minute shower if the water runs at a rate of 5 gallons per minute?

2 If your family saves 20,000 gallons of water per year, will they save more or less than 20,000 gallons per day? Explain how you know.

343

Where are we now?

In Section 7A, students learned how to use ratios to solve problems.

They learned how to

- use ratios to compare distances shown on maps.
- use scales to calculate distances on various models.
- use scales to read maps.
- select a reasonable scale for a drawing, map, or model.

Where are we going?

In Section 7B, students will

- choose appropriate rates for different situations.
- convert measurements from one unit to another.
- use conversion factors to convert from one rate to another.

Section 7B

Theme: Conservation

World Wide Web

If your class has access to the World Wide Web, you might want to use the information found at the Web site addresses given. The interdisciplinary links relate to the topics discussed in this section.

About the Page

This page introduces the theme of the section, conservation, and discusses water conservation and treatment.

Ask ...

- Are you doing anything in your home to conserve water? What things could you be doing?
- Does your community have any water conservation programs such as limiting the days or times you can water the lawn?
- Why does wasting water hurt the environment?
- Do you recycle paper? How does recycling help the environment?

Extensions

The following activities do not require access to the World Wide Web.

Science
Have students investigate and report on the water supply in your community. Ask them to determine the source of the water, how it is stored, how it is purified, and its cost.

Industry
The nuclear power industry uses a tremendous amount of water to cool the reactors. Students might research this industry and learn how it conserves water.

Answers for Questions

1. 40 gallons
2. Less; A day is a shorter period of time.

Connect

On page 357, students analyze the water saved when a family uses conservation measures.

7-5 Lesson Organizer

Objectives

- Select an appropriate rate for a particular situation.
- Write reciprocal rates that have the same meaning.

Materials

- Explore: Tape measure, stopwatch

NCTM Standards

- 1–2, 4–5, 13

▶ Review

Express each as a unit rate.

1. 12 pencils for $3.00
   4 pencils per dollar
2. 114 miles in 3 hours
   38 miles per hour
3. 42 computers for 105 students 0.4 computers per student

Available on Daily Transparency 7-5

1 Introduce

Explore

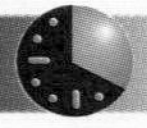

The Point
Students use collected data to estimate a rate. They then use that rate in calculations.

Ongoing Assessment
Check for students who have difficulty because they use the reciprocals of rates; suggest to the student that if a rate does not seem to fit the situation, they should check to see if its reciprocal rate is more appropriate. Some students might be helped by drawing diagrams and labeling distances and times.

7-5 Choosing Appropriate Rates and Units

You'll Learn ...

- to select an appropriate rate for a particular situation
- to write reciprocal rates that have the same meaning

... How It's Used

Chefs may need to convert recipes given in small units (such as cups and ounces) to larger ones (such as quarts and pounds) when they cook for a large number of people.

▶ Lesson Link You know what rates are and how to use rates to solve problems. Now you will choose appropriate rates for different situations. ◀

Explore Using Rates

Shake Across America!

Materials: Tape measure, Stopwatch

An environmental group is organizing a "Handshake Across America." They plan to have people line up from New York to Los Angeles and pass a handshake from east to west.

1. Have several members of your class form a line. Count how many students are in the line and measure its length.
2. Start a handshake at one end of the line. Use a stopwatch to find out how long the handshake takes to reach the end of the line.
3. Use your results from Step 1 to estimate the number of students per foot. Explain why this number is a rate.
4. The road distance from Los Angeles to New York is 2825 miles, or almost 15,000,000 ft. About how many people need to be in the line?
5. Use your results from Step 2 to estimate the speed of the handshake. How did you choose your units for this rate?
6. Estimate when the handshake would have to start so it ends on midnight in Los Angeles. Explain how you found your answer. What rates did you use to help solve this problem?

Learn Choosing Appropriate Rates and Units

It's important to choose appropriate units when you use a rate. If the speedometer in your family's car read 40,000 inches per minute, it would be hard to tell whether you're speeding or blocking traffic. But if it reads 30 miles per hour, you have a better idea of how fast you're traveling.

MEETING INDIVIDUAL NEEDS

Resources

7-5 Practice
7-5 Reteaching
7-5 Problem Solving
7-5 Enrichment
7-5 Daily Transparency
Problem of the Day
Review
Quick Quiz
Teaching Tool Transparencies 2, 3
Chapter 7 Project Master

Learning Modalities

Musical Have students create jingles or raps supporting recycling. Each jingle should include information involving rates.

Visual Have students use objects or draw diagrams that show rates.

English Language Development

Some students will confuse *ratio* and *rate* since the words are very similar. Point out that a ratio is a comparison of two quantities. When these quantities involve different units, the ratio is called a rate. Therefore, every rate is a ratio, but not every ratio is a rate.

Example 1

What are appropriate units for measuring a snail's speed?

Rates that describe speeds, such as miles per hour, have a distance unit per time unit. Snails are slow, so it is best to use a shorter unit of distance.

Appropriate units for a snail's speed might be feet per hour or inches per minute.

Try It

What are appropriate units for measuring:

a. The speed of a jet airplane? **miles per hour**

b. The rate at which you do homework? **problems per hour**

▶ Science Link

Snails are mollusks. The "horns" on a snail's head are actually its eyes. They can be extended to look around and can be retracted when the snail retreats into its shell.

Rates can be expressed in different ways that have the same meaning. The most useful way to express a rate depends on the problem you are solving.

Example 2

At a recycling center, you are paid 2.5 cents per can. Does this rate mean the same thing as 40 cans per dollar? Give a situation where each rate is useful.

If you recycle 40 cans at 2.5 cents each, you are paid $40 \times 2.5 = 100$ cents, or one dollar. The rates have the same meaning.

If you want to know *how much money* you will get for 120 cans, it's easier to use the 2.5 cents per can rate:

$120 \times 2.5 = 300$ cents ($3.00)

If you want to know *how many cans* you need to earn $10, you'd use 40 cans per dollar:

$10 \times 40 = 400$ cans

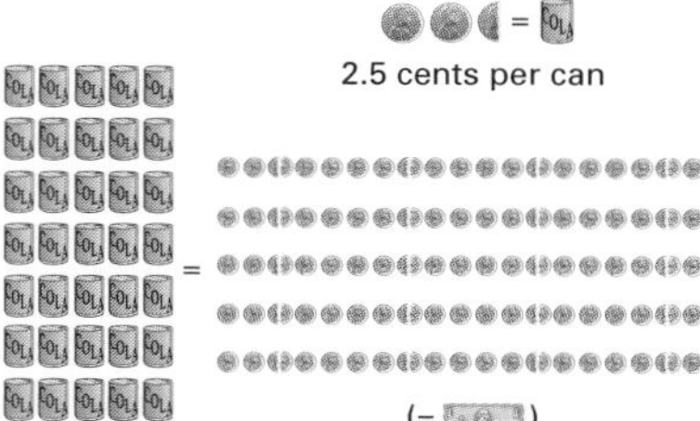

▶ History Link

Aluminum was once one of the most expensive metals on earth. In the 1820s, a pound of aluminum sold for more than $500!

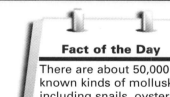

Try It

Ollie the collie eats 3 cups of dog food per day. Does this rate have the same meaning as Ollie eating at a rate of $\frac{1}{3}$ of a day per cup? **Yes**

MATH EVERY DAY

▶ Problem of the Day

Light travels about 186,000 miles per second. If a beam of light started on the day you were born, how far has it traveled now? Check students' answers. For a 12-year-old, about 70,400,000,000,000 miles.

Available on Daily Transparency 7-5

An Extension is provided in the transparency package.

Fact of the Day

There are about 50,000 known kinds of mollusks, including snails, oysters, clams, and octopuses. There may be more than 80,000 kinds of snails.

Mental Math

Do these mentally.

1. $1.2 + 0.34$ 1.54
2. $6 - 3.4$ 2.6
3. $3 \cdot 4.5$ 13.5
4. $5.5 \div 0.5$ 11

For Groups That Finish Early

Discuss whether or not your answer for step 6 reflects the situation accurately.

Answers may vary.

Answers for Explore

1. Answers may vary.
2. Answers may vary.
3. Answer is the number in line divided by its length; A rate because the units are different.
4. Answer is the rate from Step 3 multiplied by 15,000,000.
5. Answer is the length of the line divided by the time; Units may be feet per second because those are the units the tape measure and stop-watch provided.
6. Time it takes is 15,000,000 divided by the speed from Step 5, and starting time is this time (in hours) subtracted from 12:00.

2 Teach

Learn

Ask students to describe some situations in which they use rates. For each situation, ask them what an appropriate or inappropriate rate would be and why.

Alternate Examples

1. What is an appropriate unit for measuring a sprinter's speed?

   Sprinters run short distances, so appropriate units might be feet per second or meters per second.

2. You are paid 5 cents for each plastic bottle at the recycling center. Does this rate have the same meaning as 20 bottles per dollar? Give a situation in which each rate is useful.

   If you want to know *how much money* you will get for 35 bottles, it's easier to use the 5 cents per bottle rate: $35 \times 5 = 175$ cents ($1.75)

   If you want to know *how many bottles* you need to earn $10, it's easier to use 20 bottles per dollar: $10 \times 20 = 200$ bottles

Alternate Example

3. The average American produces 3.5 pounds of garbage daily. Give a reciprocal rate that has the same meaning. Then give a reciprocal *unit* rate.

   Find a reciprocal rate by exchanging the numerator and the denominator. $\frac{3.5 \text{ pounds}}{1 \text{ day}}$ means the same thing as $\frac{1 \text{ day}}{3.5 \text{ pounds}}$.

   To convert $\frac{1 \text{ day}}{3.5 \text{ pounds}}$ to a unit rate, divide the numerator and denominator by 3.5.
   $\frac{1 \text{ day}}{3.5 \text{ lb}} = \frac{1 \text{ day} \div 3.5}{3.5 \text{ lb} \div 3.5} = \frac{0.29 \text{ day}}{1 \text{ lb.}}$
   The reciprocal unit rate is about 0.29 day per pound.

3 Practice and Assess

Check

You may wish to ask students to give examples of problems involving the rates in question 1 and then identify what they are looking for and which rate would be easier to use.

Answers for Check Your Understanding

1. 6 pounds per day means that 6 pounds are used in 1 day, and 6 days per pound means that $\frac{1}{6}$ pound is used in 1 day. The first is useful when you need to find weight for a given time period, and the second when you need to find number of days for a given weight.
2. Possible answer: When something is moving slowly, for instance, lava flow from a certain kind of volcano.
3. Possible answer: Refund per can, bottles per day, pounds of paper per week.

Remember
Customary Units
8 fluid ounces (fl oz) = 1 cup
4 cups = 1 quart (qt)
128 fl oz = 4 qt = 1 gallon (gal)
16 ounces (oz) = 1 pound (lb)
2000 lb = 1 ton
[Previous Course]

The rates in Example 2, $\frac{2.5 \text{ cents}}{1 \text{ can}}$ and $\frac{40 \text{ cans}}{1 \text{ dollar}}$, have the same meaning, but they are not equal. Although they may not look like it, they are *reciprocals*!

$\frac{2.5 \text{ cents}}{1 \text{ can}} \xrightarrow{\text{reciprocal}} \frac{1 \text{ can}}{2.5 \text{ cents}}$ Exchange numerator and denominator.

$= \frac{1 \text{ can} \times 40}{2.5 \text{ cents} \times 40} = \frac{40 \text{ cans}}{100 \text{ cents}} = \frac{40 \text{ cans}}{1 \text{ dollar}}$ Write an equivalent unit rate.

Example 3

A low-flow faucet aerator can save 2 gallons of water per minute. Give a reciprocal rate that has the same meaning. Then give a reciprocal *unit* rate.

Find a reciprocal rate by exchanging the numerator and the denominator. $\frac{2 \text{ gal}}{1 \text{ min}}$ means the same thing as $\frac{1 \text{ min}}{2 \text{ gal}}$.

To convert $\frac{1 \text{ min}}{2 \text{ gal}}$ to a unit rate, divide the numerator and denominator by 2.

$$\frac{1 \text{ min}}{2 \text{ gal}} = \frac{1 \text{ min} \div 2}{2 \text{ gal} \div 2} = \frac{\frac{1}{2} \text{ min}}{1 \text{ gal}} = \frac{0.5 \text{ min}}{\text{gal}}$$

The reciprocal unit rate is $\frac{1}{2}$ minute per gallon or 0.5 minutes per gallon.

Remember
Metric Units
1000 meters (m) = 1 kilometer (km)
100 centimeters (cm) = 1 m
1000 grams (g) = 1 kilogram (kg)
[Previous Course]

Try It

Jorge recycles 25 pounds of newspapers, cans, and bottles per week. Give a reciprocal rate that has the same meaning. Then give the reciprocal *unit* rate.
$\frac{1 \text{ wk}}{25 \text{ lb}}$; $\frac{0.04 \text{ wk}}{1 \text{ lb}}$

Check Your Understanding

1. How are the rates 6 pounds per day and 6 days per pound different? When would each be useful?
2. Describe a situation where you would want to know the number of hours per mile instead of miles per hour.
3. Name some rates that would help you plan improvements to a recycling program.

MEETING MIDDLE SCHOOL CLASSROOM NEEDS

Tips from Middle School Teachers

I find that my students understand better why we use certain rates for certain kinds of problems by looking at one or two situations in depth. I usually have them consider two equivalent rates, such as 40 miles per hour and 1.5 minutes per mile. Working in groups, they create and solve problems involving these rates and then share these with each other.

Team Teaching

Ask the other teachers on your team to call attention to rates, reciprocal rates, and unit rates. Here are some suggestions:

Social studies: inflation rates, unemployment rates

Language: reading rates

Science: speeds of objects (falling, rolling), pulse rates, speed of sound or light, speed of vehicles.

Science Connection

Land snails lay down a track of slime to make movement easier. Snails have only one means of locomotion whether on land or in the water—a muscle on the bottom of the snail's foot. Snails search for food with a ribbonlike tongue that may have many thousand denticles (little teeth). The tongue is projected from the mouth and is drawn along rocks or leaves to find algae or decaying matter. Carnivorous snails can bore through the shells of other snails.

7-5 Exercises and Applications

Practice and Apply

1. **Getting Started** Find the reciprocal unit rate for 20 miles per gallon.
   a. Write 20 miles per gallon as a fraction.
   b. Find a reciprocal rate by exchanging the numerator and the denominator.
   c. The rate you found in **b** is a reciprocal, but it is not a unit rate. To convert it to a unit rate, divide its numerator and denominator by the number in the denominator.

Number Sense Suggest appropriate units for each rate. You may use the same units more than once.

2. The speed of a bicycle rider **miles per hour**
3. The rate at which a car uses gasoline **gallons per mile**
4. The rate at which your heart beats **beats per minute**
5. The rate of pay for a baby-sitter **dollars per hour**
6. The rate at which a family recycles aluminum cans **cans per week**

Give a unit rate that describes each situation.

7. 75 quarts of soup for 150 students
8. 4 pounds of bananas for $1.00
9. 100 meters in 10 seconds
10. 400 raisins in 20 cookies

Do the rates in each pair have the same meaning? Write *Yes* or *No*.

11. $\frac{2\text{ ft}}{\text{sec}}, \frac{0.5\text{ sec}}{\text{ft}}$ **Yes**
12. $\frac{25\text{ mi}}{\text{gal}}, \frac{25\text{ gal}}{\text{mi}}$ **No**
13. $\frac{25¢}{\text{lb}}, \frac{4\text{ lb}}{\text{dollar}}$ **Yes**
14. $\frac{7\text{ days}}{\text{week}}, \frac{\frac{1}{7}\text{ week}}{\text{day}}$ **Yes**

For each rate, give a reciprocal unit rate that has the same meaning.

15. $\frac{5\text{ lb}}{\$1}$ **$\frac{\$0.20}{1\text{ lb}}$**
16. $\frac{15\text{ mi}}{\text{hr}}$ **$\frac{4\text{ min}}{1\text{ mile}}$**
17. $\frac{2\text{ weeks}}{\text{ton}}$ **$\frac{0.5\text{ ton}}{\text{week}}$**
18. $\frac{25\text{ gal}}{\text{day}}$ **$\frac{0.04\text{ day}}{\text{gal}}$**

19. **Science** According to *50 Simple Things Kids Can Do to Save the Earth,* about 20 *species* (types) of plants and animals become extinct every week. (Not all scientists agree with this estimate.) Does this rate have the same meaning as $\frac{0.2\text{ days}}{\text{species}}$? **No**

African Elephant Population 1979–1992

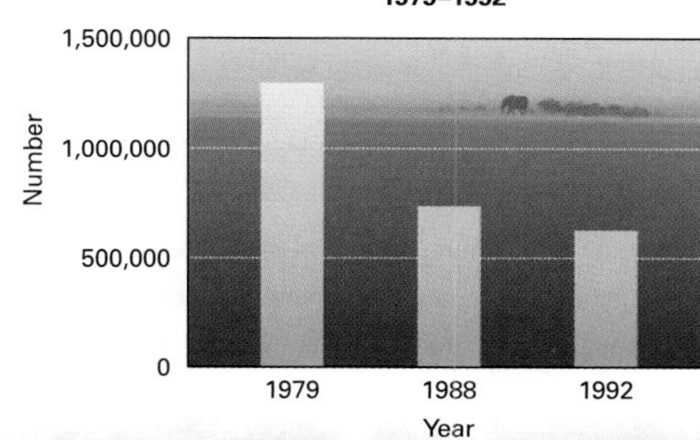

The African elephant is a threatened species

PRACTICE 7-5

7-5 Exercises and Applications

Assignment Guide

- **Basic** 1–6, 8–18 evens, 20, 23, 24–34 evens
- **Average** 1–19 odds, 20–23, 25–33 odds
- **Enriched** 2–18 evens, 19–23, 24–34 evens

Exercise Notes

Exercise 7

Error Prevention Suggest that students convert units, if possible, rather than use fractions or decimals; remind them that 2 pints = 1 quart.

Exercise Answers

1. a. $\frac{20\text{ miles}}{1\text{ gallon}}$
   b. $\frac{1\text{ gallon}}{20\text{ miles}}$
   c. $\frac{0.05\text{ gallons}}{1\text{ mile}}$
7. 1 pint of soup per student.
8. $0.25 for 1 pound of bananas.
9. 10 meters per second.
10. 20 raisins per cookie.

Reteaching

Activity

Materials: A daily newspaper, scale

- Estimate the number of pounds of newspaper a family gets in a week by weighing a daily paper. Then multiply that weight by 3 to get the weight of a Sunday paper.
- Add daily and Sunday weights to find weight of papers for one week. Write your answer as a unit rate. Unit rate is pounds per week.
- Use the unit rate to estimate the number of pounds of newspaper a family gets in one year. Unit rate is pounds per year.
- If you are paid 12 cents a pound for newspapers, how much would you earn in a year from recycling the family's newspapers? Write your answer as a unit rate. Multiply above answer by 0.12. Unit rate is dollars per year.

PRACTICE

Name ______________________ **Practice 7-5**

Choosing Appropriate Rates and Units

Suggest appropriate units for each rate. You may use the same units more than once. **Possible answers:**

1. The speed of a roller coaster **miles per hour**
2. The rate at which water comes out of a hose **gallons per hour**
3. The rate at which a child grows **inches per year**
4. The amount of music a radio station plays **songs per hour**

Give a unit rate that describes each situation.

5. 200 miles in 4 hours **$\frac{50\text{ mi}}{\text{hr}}$**
6. 80 students for 16 computers **$\frac{5\text{ students}}{\text{computer}}$**
7. $96.00 for 12 hours of work **$\frac{\$8.00}{\text{hr}}$**
8. 42 books shared by 14 people **$\frac{3\text{ books}}{\text{person}}$**

Do the rates in each pair have the same meaning? Write *yes* or *no*.

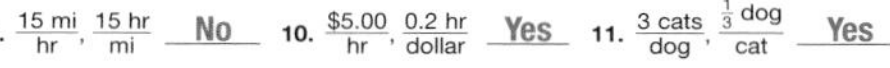

9. $\frac{15\text{ mi}}{\text{hr}}, \frac{15\text{ hr}}{\text{mi}}$ **No**
10. $\frac{\$5.00}{\text{hr}}, \frac{0.2\text{ hr}}{\text{dollar}}$ **Yes**
11. $\frac{3\text{ cats}}{\text{dog}}, \frac{\frac{1}{3}\text{ dog}}{\text{cat}}$ **Yes**
12. $\frac{12\text{ in.}}{\text{ft}}, \frac{\frac{1}{12}\text{ ft}}{\text{in.}}$ **Yes**
13. $\frac{2\text{ oz}}{\text{cookie}}, \frac{\frac{1}{2}\text{ oz}}{\text{cookie}}$ **No**
14. $\frac{1\text{ ft}}{\text{sec}}, \frac{1\text{ sec}}{\text{ft}}$ **Yes**

For each rate, give a reciprocal unit rate that has the same meaning.

15. $\frac{4\text{ tomatoes}}{\text{lb}}$ **$\frac{0.25\text{ lb}}{\text{tomato}}$**
16. $\frac{100\text{ beats}}{\text{min}}$ **$\frac{0.01\text{ min}}{\text{beat}}$**
17. $\frac{20\text{ mi}}{\text{hr}}$ **$\frac{0.05\text{ hr}}{\text{mi}}$**
18. $\frac{0.08\text{ hr}}{\text{dollar}}$ **$\frac{\$12.50}{\text{hr}}$**
19. $\frac{\frac{1}{8}\text{ teacher}}{\text{student}}$ **$\frac{8\text{ students}}{\text{teacher}}$**
20. $\frac{40\text{ gal}}{\text{min}}$ **$\frac{0.025\text{ min}}{\text{gal}}$**

21. The average American worker needs to work about $\frac{1}{2}$ hour to earn enough money to buy a Barbie doll. Is this rate equivalent to 2 Barbie dolls per hour? **Yes**
22. In 1990, there were, on the average, about 2.5 persons per American household. Find the number of households per person. **$\frac{0.4\text{ households}}{\text{person}}$**

RETEACHING

Name ______________________ **Alternative Lesson 7-5**

Choosing Appropriate Rates and Units

You can express a rate in different ways by using various unit combinations. Sometimes a unit rate can help you solve problems.

Example 1

What are appropriate units for measuring how far someone walks?

The following are equivalent rates using different units.

$$\frac{5\text{ miles}}{2\text{ hours}} = \frac{8800\text{ yards}}{120\text{ minutes}} = \frac{26{,}400\text{ feet}}{7200\text{ seconds}}$$

Of the three equivalent rates, $\frac{5\text{ miles}}{2\text{ hours}}$ is the most appropriate way to express the rate at which someone walks.

Try It Match each rate with the most appropriate units.

a. Food eaten by a parakeet each day **iii**
b. The speed of a turtle **iv**
c. The speed of a cougar **i**
d. Meat used by the school cafeteria each day **ii**

i. miles per hour
ii. pounds per day
iii. ounces per day
iv. inches per minute

Example 2

Give a reciprocal unit rate for $\frac{40\text{ mi}}{60\text{ min}}$.

Step 1: Write the rate as a reciprocal. $\frac{40\text{ mi}}{60\text{ min}} \rightarrow \frac{60\text{ min}}{40\text{ mi}}$

Step 2: Divide numerator and denominator by the denominator. $\frac{60\text{ min} \div 40}{40\text{ mi} \div 40} = \frac{1.5\text{ min}}{1\text{ mi}}$

The reciprocal unit rate is 1.5 minutes per mile.

Try It For each rate, give a reciprocal unit rate.

	Rate	Reciprocal	Reciprocal Unit Rate
e.	$\frac{\$16}{120\text{ oz}}$	$\frac{120\text{ oz}}{\$16}$	$\frac{7.5\text{ oz}}{\$1}$
f.	$\frac{4\text{ cars}}{16\text{ persons}}$	$\frac{16\text{ people}}{4\text{ cars}}$	$\frac{4\text{ people}}{1\text{ car}}$
g.	$\frac{24\text{ m}}{60\text{ sec}}$	$\frac{60\text{ sec}}{24\text{ m}}$	$\frac{2.5\text{ sec}}{1\text{ m}}$
h.	$\frac{60\text{ mi}}{3\text{ gal}}$	$\frac{3\text{ gal}}{60\text{ mi}}$	$\frac{0.05\text{ gal}}{1\text{ mi}}$
i.	$\frac{3\text{ hr}}{66\text{ mi}}$	$\frac{66\text{ mi}}{3\text{ hr}}$	$\frac{22\text{ mi}}{1\text{ hr}}$

Exercise Notes

■ Exercise 21

Extension Have students monitor one of the rates they suggest for one time period (day, hour, week). Then have them create and solve problems based on their data.

■ Exercise 22

Problem-Solving Tip You may want to use Teaching Tool Transparencies 2 and 3: Guided Problem Solving, pages 1–2.

Project Progress

You may want to have students use Chapter 7 Project Master.

Exercise Answers

21. Possible answer: Minutes per shower, flushes per day, watts per lamp.

22. $\frac{2}{15}$ hour per mile $= \frac{8 \text{ min}}{\text{mile}}$

23. Yes; $\frac{20 \text{ min}}{\text{hour}} = \frac{1}{3}$, $\frac{15 \text{ miles}}{45 \text{ miles}} = \frac{1}{3}$

29. 3 millimeters per second.

30. 20 pages per day.

31. 33 desks per classroom.

32. $9.33 per T-shirt.

33. 1000 mL per L.

34. 10 decades per century.

Alternate Assessment

Project Have groups of students collect data from the school, such as paper used per day, milk cartons used per day or food thrown out each day. Then have them analyze the data and prepare a report suggesting ways to reduce these rates.

➤ Quick Quiz

1. What are appropriate units for measuring the growth rate of a seedling?
   Inches or centimeters per week or day.
2. Give a unit rate that describes 420 raisins in 20 scoops.
   21 raisins per scoop.
3. Give a reciprocal unit rate that has the same meaning as 25 feet per second.
   $\frac{1}{25}$ second per foot or 0.04 seconds per foot.

Available on Daily Transparency 7-5

PROBLEM SOLVING 7-5

20. **Test Prep** Which of the following units are most appropriate for the rate of newspaper recycling in Illinois? B

Ⓐ Miles per hour　　Ⓑ Tons per week

Ⓒ Ounces per month　　Ⓓ Years per pound

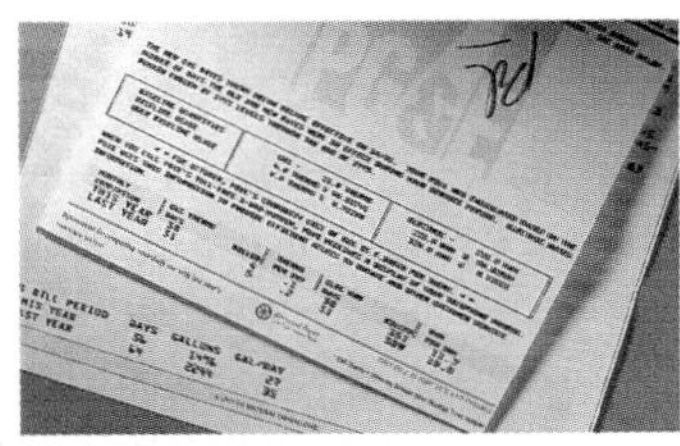

Problem Solving and Reasoning

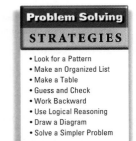

21. Journal Suppose you want to examine your family's energy and water use. You plan to find out how efficiently your family uses these resources, and what changes you might make to increase efficiency. Name rates that will be helpful in carrying out your plan.

22. **Choose a Strategy** One of the earliest auto races was the *Chicago Times-Herald* race of 1895, covering 55 miles from Chicago, Illinois, to Evanston, Illinois. The winner, J. Frank Duryea, averaged $7\frac{1}{2}$ miles per hour. Write a reciprocal unit rate for that average speed that has the same meaning.

Problem Solving STRATEGIES
- Look for a Pattern
- Make an Organized List
- Make a Table
- Guess and Check
- Work Backward
- Use Logical Reasoning
- Draw a Diagram
- Solve a Simpler Problem

23. **Communicate** GPS Two buses leave your school to take students on field trips. One bus travels for 20 minutes, covering 15 miles. The other travels 45 miles in one hour. Did both buses travel at the same rate? Explain your answer.

Mixed Review

Solve each equation. Check your answer. *[Lesson 2-7]*

24. $m \cdot 8 = 56$ $m = 7$ **25.** $\frac{q}{3} = 25$ $q = 75$ **26.** $9s = 144$ $s = 16$ **27.** $18 = 6 \cdot n$ $n = 3$ **28.** $7p = 84$ $p = 12$

Express each rate as a unit rate. *[Lesson 6-2]*

29. 15 millimeters in 5 seconds　　**30.** 160 pages read in 8 days

31. 231 desks in 7 classrooms　　**32.** $27.99 for 3 T-shirts

33. 2,000 mL in 2 L　　**34.** 60 decades in 6 centuries

Project Progress

Using the measurements and decisions you made earlier, set up and solve proportions to determine the scaled-down sizes of the rooms and features to be included in a scale model of your dream house. Make a drawing of your model.

Problem Solving
Understand
Plan
Solve
Look Back

PROBLEM SOLVING

Name ______________

Guided Problem Solving 7-5

GPS **PROBLEM 23, STUDENT PAGE 348**

Two buses leave your school to take students on field trips. One bus travels for 20 minutes, covering 15 miles. The other travels 45 miles in one hour. Did both buses travel at the same rate? Explain your answer.

— Understand —

1. Underline the time and distance traveled by each bus.
2. How can you tell if the rates are the same? They both have the same unit rate.

— Plan —

3. Which rate is usually used to describe vehicle travel? c
   a. $\frac{\text{hours}}{\text{miles}}$　b. $\frac{\text{minutes}}{\text{miles}}$　c. $\frac{\text{miles}}{\text{hours}}$
4. Use $\frac{1}{3}$ hr to represent 20 min. Which rate represents the first bus? a
   a. 15 mi:$\frac{1}{3}$ hr　b. 20 min:$\frac{1}{3}$ hr
5. Write the rate in Item 4 as a unit rate. $\frac{45 \text{ mi}}{1 \text{ hr}}$
6. Write the unit rate for the second bus. $\frac{45 \text{ mi}}{1 \text{ hr}}$

— Solve —

7. Write both unit rates to see if they are equal. $\frac{45 \text{ mi}}{1 \text{ hr}} = \frac{45 \text{ mi}}{1 \text{ hr}}$.
8. Did both buses travel at the same rate? Explain. Yes. Both unit rates are equal, so the buses are traveling at the same rate.

— Look Back —

9. Write the rate using miles:minutes. Are they equal?
   $\frac{15 \text{ mi}}{20 \text{ min}} = \frac{45 \text{ mi}}{60 \text{ min}}$. They are equal.

SOLVE ANOTHER PROBLEM

Jared's dog eats 12 cans of food in 4 days. Keisha's dog eats 56 cans of food in 2 weeks. Are the dogs eating their food at the same rate? Explain.
No. The unit rates, $\frac{3 \text{ cans}}{1 \text{ day}}$ and $\frac{4 \text{ cans}}{1 \text{ day}}$, are not equal.

ENRICHMENT

Name ______________

Alternative Lesson 7-6

Converting Units

The table at the right shows measurements that represent the same amount. You can use them to create **conversion factors** to convert measurements from one unit to another.

Remember: If the numerator and denominator of a fraction are equivalent, the fraction is equal to 1. Multiplying by a conversion factor equal to 1 can change units but will not change values.

100 centimeters = 1 meter
1000 meters = 1 kilometer
12 inches = 1 foot
3 feet = 1 yard
16 ounces = 1 pound
4 quarts = 1 gallon
60 seconds = 1 minute
60 minutes = 1 hour
24 hours = 1 day
7 days = 1 week
365 days = 1 year

— Example —

Convert 4 feet to inches.

Use the table to find the equal measures: 12 inches = 1 foot.

When choosing a conversion factor, the unit you want to convert is in the *denominator* of the conversion factor.

$\frac{4 \text{ feet}}{1} = \frac{4 \text{ feet}}{1} \times \frac{12 \text{ inches}}{1 \text{ foot}} = \frac{48 \text{ inches}}{1}$

So, 4 feet is equal to 48 inches.

Try It Convert 45 minutes to hours.

a. Write the equivalent measures you will use. 60 minutes = 1 hour
b. Write the conversion factor. $\frac{1 \text{ hour}}{60 \text{ minutes}}$
c. Multiply by your conversion factor. Then change the fraction to a decimal.
   $\frac{45 \text{ minutes}}{1} \times \frac{1 \text{ hour}}{60 \text{ min}} = \frac{45}{60}$　45 min = 0.75 hr

Convert 3 pounds to ounces.

d. Write the equivalent measures you will use. 16 ounces = 1 pound
e. Write the conversion factor. $\frac{16 \text{ ounces}}{1 \text{ pound}}$
f. Multiply by your conversion factor.
   $\frac{3 \text{ pounds}}{1} \times \frac{16 \text{ oz}}{1 \text{ lb}} = \frac{48}{1}$　3 lb = 48 oz

Converting Units

7-6

▶ Lesson Link You've chosen appropriate units for rates. Now you'll convert measurements from one unit to another. ◀

Explore Converting Units

How Old Are You?

Are you closer to one million seconds old or one billion seconds old?

1. What is your age in years? In days? In hours?
2. Find your age in seconds.
3. How many years equal one million seconds? One billion seconds?
4. Is your age closer to a million seconds or a billion seconds? Explain.

You'll Learn ...

■ to convert measurements from one unit to another

... How It's Used

Travelers going from one country to another need to convert their money into the local currency. Knowing the conversion rate helps them manage their money.

Vocabulary

conversion factor

Learn Converting Units

You know that 2 days = 48 hours because there are 24 hours in a day.

$$2 \text{ days} \times \frac{24 \text{ hr}}{1 \text{ day}} = 48 \text{ hours} \qquad 48 \text{ hr} \times \frac{1 \text{ day}}{24 \text{ hr}} = 2 \text{ days}$$

The fractions shown above, $\frac{24 \text{ hr}}{1 \text{ day}}$ and $\frac{1 \text{ day}}{24 \text{ hr}}$, are called **conversion factors** because they can be used to convert measurements from one unit to another.

A conversion factor equals 1 because its numerator equals its denominator (1 day is the same thing as 24 hours). So multiplying a quantity by a conversion factor changes only its units, not its value.

When choosing a conversion factor, be sure the unit you want to convert is in the *denominator* of the conversion factor.

To convert days to hours:

$$2 \text{ days} \times \frac{24 \text{ hr}}{1 \text{ day}} = 48 \text{ hours}$$

To convert hours to days:

$$48 \text{ hr} \times \frac{1 \text{ day}}{24 \text{ hr}} = 2 \text{ days}$$

MEETING INDIVIDUAL NEEDS

Resources

- **7-6** Practice
- **7-6** Reteaching
- **7-6** Problem Solving
- **7-6** Enrichment
- **7-6** Daily Transparency
  - Problem of the Day
  - Review
  - Quick Quiz

Learning Modalities

Kinesthetic Have students actually measure objects using two different units and then use their measures to find the conversion factor.

Individual Have students rate themselves on their ability to convert measurements from one unit to another before and after the lesson. Ask them to describe what they still need to improve.

Challenge

Many students enjoy working with very large (or very small) numbers. Do more "million" problems: How high would a stack of a million sheets of paper be? How much would a million grains of rice weigh? Students will find it easier to do these problems if, instead of weighing one grain of rice, for example, they weigh 100 grains.

7-6 Lesson Organizer

Objective

■ Convert measurements from one unit to another.

Vocabulary

■ Conversion factor

NCTM Standards

■ 1–5, 13

▶ Review

Give each missing number.

1. 1 mi = ______ ft 5280
2. 1 lb = ______ oz 16
3. 1 m = ______ cm 100
4. 1 kg = ______ g 1000

Available on Daily Transparency 7-6

1 Introduce

Explore

The Point

Students explore unit conversion by deciding whether they are closer in age to a million seconds or a billion seconds.

Ongoing Assessment

Have students make a prediction before actually doing the computations. Some students may use estimation, while others compute answers exactly with a calculator.

For Groups That Finish Early

Describe what rates you used for finding your answers. Explain how you converted from one rate to another.

Answers may vary.

Answers for Explore

1. Possible answer: 12 years; ≈ 4380 days; ≈ 105,120 hours.
2. ≈ 378,432,000 seconds.
3. ≈ 0.0317 years; ≈ 31.7 years.
4. A million seconds; 12 is closer to 0.03 than to 31.7.

2 Teach

Learn

Alternate Examples

1. Sandy walked 4 km. How many meters did she walk?

   There are 1000 m in 1 km, so there are two possible conversion factors: $\frac{1000 \text{ m}}{1 \text{ km}}$ or $\frac{1 \text{ km}}{1000 \text{ m}}$.

   Choose the factor that has the unit you want to convert in the denominator. You want to convert km, so choose the first factor.

   $4 \textbf{ km} \times \frac{1000\text{m}}{1 \textbf{ km}} = \frac{4000}{1} \text{ m}$

   $= 4000 \text{ m}$

   Sandy walked 4000 meters.

2. Each year, the average American sends about 76,000 pounds of garbage to landfills. How many tons is this? You want to convert *pounds,* so use the conversion factor $\frac{\text{a1 ton}}{2{,}000 \text{ pounds}}$.

   $76{,}000 \textbf{ lb} \times \frac{1 \text{ ton}}{2{,}000 \textbf{ lb}} =$

   $\frac{76{,}000}{2{,}000} \text{ tons} = 38 \text{ tons}$

3 Practice and Assess

Check

Answers for Check Your Understanding

1. If lb is in the numerator of what you are converting, use $\frac{16 \text{ oz}}{1 \text{ lb}}$ to convert to oz; If oz is in the numerator, use $\frac{1 \text{ lb}}{16 \text{ oz}}$.
2. If the unit is in the denominator, then it factors out when you multiply.

Examples

1 The reticulated python is the world's longest snake. Many of these pythons are more than 20 feet long. Convert 20 feet to inches.

There are 12 inches in 1 foot, so there are two possible conversion factors:

$\frac{12 \text{ in.}}{1 \text{ ft}} \quad \frac{1 \text{ ft}}{12 \text{ in.}}$

Choose the factor that has the unit you want to convert in the denominator. You want to convert *feet,* so choose the first factor.

$\frac{20 \textbf{ ft} \times 12 \text{ in.}}{1 \textbf{ ft}} = (20 \times 12) \text{ inches} = 240 \text{ inches}$

20 feet is equal to 240 inches.

Problem Solving TIP

Check to make sure your answer makes sense.

2 In 1989, the tanker *Exxon Valdez* spilled 70 million pounds of crude oil into Prince William Sound, Alaska. Convert 70 million pounds to tons.

There are 2000 pounds in 1 ton. You want to convert *pounds,* so use the conversion factor $\frac{1 \text{ ton}}{2000 \text{ lb}}$.

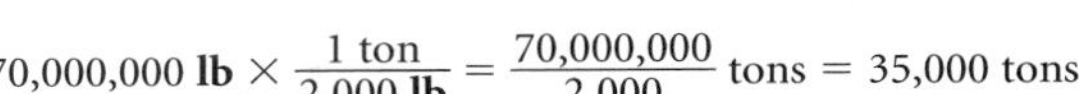

$70{,}000{,}000 \textbf{ lb} \times \frac{1 \text{ ton}}{2{,}000 \textbf{ lb}} = \frac{70{,}000{,}000}{2{,}000} \text{ tons} = 35{,}000 \text{ tons}$

The tanker spilled 35,000 tons of oil.

Remember

Converting to different units may give you a rate with a very large number. You may want to use scientific notation when you write this number. [Page 126]

Try It

a. The Student Senate met for 180 minutes. Convert this time to hours. **3 hours**

b. In baseball, the distance between bases is 90 feet. Convert this distance to yards. **30 yd**

Check Your Understanding

1. How do you decide whether to use the conversion factor $\frac{16 \text{ oz}}{1 \text{ lb}}$ or $\frac{1 \text{ lb}}{16 \text{ oz}}$?

2. When you choose a conversion factor, why should the unit you want to convert from be in the denominator of the conversion factor?

MATH EVERY DAY

Problem of the Day

Suppose you travel *Around the World in 80 Days.* The circumference of the world is about 25,000 miles. At what average speed (in miles per hour) would you be traveling? Round your answer to the nearest whole number. About 13 miles per hour

Available on Daily Transparency 7-6

An Extension is provided in the transparency package.

Fact of the Day

Jeanne Calment of Arles, France, set a record for the longest life span. She was 125 years old in 1995. Until she was injured at age 100, she traveled by bicycle.

Estimation

Estimate.

1. 23,569 + 305,444 329,000
2. 501,003 − 2999.87 498,000
3. 4,500 • 3.52 16,000
4. 203 ÷ 19.88 10

7-6 Exercises and Applications

Practice and Apply

1. **Getting Started** Convert 3,000 meters to kilometers.
   - **a.** There are 1,000 meters in a kilometer. Write two fractions involving meters and kilometers that can be used as conversion factors.
   - **b.** Choose the conversion factor that has the unit you want to convert from in the denominator.
   - **c.** To convert 3,000 meters to kilometers, multiply 3,000 meters by the conversion factor you chose in **b**.

Number Sense Write two conversion factors involving each pair of units. (Use the information on page 346 if you do not remember how some of these units compare.)

2. Inches, feet **3.** Days, years **4.** Centimeters, meters

5. Pounds, ounces **6.** Gallons, quarts **7.** Grams, kilograms

Operation Sense Convert each quantity to the given units. (Use the information on page 346 if you do not remember how some of these units compare.)

8. 2 weeks to days 14 days **9.** 20 feet to inches 240 in.

10. 275 centimeters to meters 2.75 m **11.** 672 ounces to pounds 42 lb

12. 12 minutes to hours 0.2 hr **13.** 8 quarts to gallons 2 gal

14. 500 meters to kilometers 0.5 km **15.** 150 inches to feet 12.5 ft

16. 7 pounds to ounces 112 oz **17.** 10 gallons to quarts 40 qt

18. History The *cubit* was the basic unit of length used to build the pyramids of ancient Egypt. One cubit was the distance from the tip of the middle finger to the elbow. Use your arm and hand to measure the length of one cubit in inches. Write two conversion factors for your measurements.

19. Literature *Twenty Thousand Leagues Under the Sea* is a famous novel by Jules Verne. A league is about 3.45 miles. Convert 20,000 leagues to feet.

GPS

PRACTICE 7-6

7-6 Exercises and Applications

Assignment Guide

- **Basic**
  1–21 odds, 24, 25–33 odds
- **Average**
  2–18 evens, 19–22, 26–34 evens
- **Enriched**
  3–33 odds

Exercise Notes

Error Prevention Some students may make errors if they try to take shortcuts in solving these problems. Encourage students to consider whether their answers are reasonable. Suggest that they write out the conversion factors if they are making errors.

Exercise Answers

1. a. $\frac{1000 \text{ m}}{1 \text{ km}}$ and $\frac{1 \text{ km}}{1000 \text{ m}}$
   b. $\frac{1 \text{ km}}{1000 \text{ m}}$
   c. 3 km
2. $\frac{12 \text{ inches}}{1 \text{ foot}}, \frac{1 \text{ foot}}{12 \text{ inches}}$
3. $\frac{365 \text{ days}}{1 \text{ year}}, \frac{1 \text{ year}}{365 \text{ days}}$
4. $\frac{100 \text{ centimeters}}{1 \text{ meter}}, \frac{1 \text{ meter}}{100 \text{ centimeters}}$
5. $\frac{1 \text{ pound}}{16 \text{ ounces}}, \frac{16 \text{ ounces}}{1 \text{ pound}}$
6. $\frac{1 \text{ gallon}}{4 \text{ quarts}}, \frac{4 \text{ quarts}}{1 \text{ gallon}}$
7. $\frac{1000 \text{ grams}}{1 \text{ kilogram}}, \frac{1 \text{ kilogram}}{1000 \text{ grams}}$

18. Possible answer: $\frac{17.5 \text{ inches}}{1 \text{ cubit}}, \frac{1 \text{ cubit}}{17.5 \text{ inches}}$

19. 364,320,000 feet

PRACTICE

Name ____________________ **Practice 7-6**

Converting Units

Write two conversion factors involving each pair of units. (Use the chart on page 346 of your textbook if you do not remember how some of these units compare.)

1. feet, yards $\frac{3 \text{ ft}}{1 \text{ yd}}, \frac{1 \text{ yd}}{3 \text{ ft}}$ **2.** minutes, seconds $\frac{1 \text{ min}}{60 \text{ sec}}, \frac{60 \text{ sec}}{1 \text{ min}}$

3. meters, kilometers $\frac{1000 \text{ m}}{1 \text{ km}}, \frac{1 \text{ km}}{1000 \text{ m}}$ **4.** fluid ounces, cups $\frac{8 \text{ fl oz}}{1 \text{ cup}}, \frac{1 \text{ cup}}{8 \text{ fl oz}}$

5. weeks, days $\frac{1 \text{ week}}{7 \text{ days}}, \frac{7 \text{ days}}{1 \text{ week}}$ **6.** tons, pounds $\frac{1 \text{ ton}}{2000 \text{ lb}}, \frac{2000 \text{ lb}}{1 \text{ ton}}$

7. ounces, pounds $\frac{16 \text{ oz}}{1 \text{ lb}}, \frac{1 \text{ lb}}{16 \text{ oz}}$ **8.** minutes, hours $\frac{60 \text{ min}}{1 \text{ hr}}, \frac{1 \text{ hr}}{60 \text{ min}}$

9. gallons, quarts $\frac{1 \text{ gal}}{4 \text{ qt}}, \frac{4 \text{ qt}}{1 \text{ gal}}$ **10.** miles, feet $\frac{1 \text{ mi}}{5280 \text{ ft}}, \frac{5280 \text{ ft}}{1 \text{ mi}}$

Convert each quantity to the given units. (Use the chart on page 346 of your textbook if you do not remember how some of these units compare.)

11. 5.8 meters to centimeters 580 cm **12.** 21 days to hours 504 hr

13. 63 feet to inches 756 in. **14.** 45 kilometers to meters 45,000 m

15. 150 hours to minutes 9000 min **16.** 487 grams to kilograms 0.487 kg

17. 93 yards to feet 279 ft **18.** 360 hours to days 15 days

19. 24 fluid ounces to cups 3 cups **20.** 21 gallons to quarts 84 qt

21. 1500 pounds to tons 0.75 ton **22.** 78 inches to feet 6.5 ft

23. 2.5 kilograms to grams 2500 g **24.** 165 centimeters to meters 1.65 m

25. 49 days to weeks 7 weeks **26.** 64 gallons to fluid ounces 8192 fl oz

27. United States farms produced 2,460,000,000 bushels of soybeans in 1994. How many quarts is this? (A bushel is 32 quarts.) 78,720,000,000 quarts

28. In 1994, Brian Berg set a record by building an 81-story "house" using standard playing cards. The house was $15\frac{2}{3}$ ft tall. How many inches is this? 188 in.

RETEACHING

Name ____________________ **Alternative Lesson 7-6**

Converting Units

The table at the right shows measurements that represent the same amount. You can use them to create **conversion factors** to convert measurements from one unit to another.

Remember: If the numerator and denominator of a fraction are equivalent, the fraction is equal to 1. Multiplying by a conversion factor equal to 1 can change units but will not change values.

100 centimeters =	1 meter
1000 meters =	1 kilometer
12 inches =	1 foot
3 feet =	1 yard
16 ounces =	1 pound
4 quarts =	1 gallon
60 seconds =	1 minute
60 minutes =	1 hour
24 hours =	1 day
7 days =	1 week
365 days =	1 year

Example

Convert 4 feet to inches.

Use the table to find the equal measures: 12 inches = 1 foot.

When choosing a conversion factor, the unit you want to convert is in the *denominator* of the conversion factor.

$$\frac{4 \text{ feet}}{1} = \frac{4 \text{ feet}}{1} \times \frac{12 \text{ inches}}{1 \text{ foot}} = \frac{48 \text{ inches}}{1}$$

So, 4 feet is equal to 48 inches.

Try It Convert 45 minutes to hours.

a. Write the equivalent measures you will use. 60 minutes = 1 hour

b. Write the conversion factor. $\frac{1 \text{ hour}}{60 \text{ minutes}}$

c. Multiply by your conversion factor. Then change the fraction to a decimal.

$\frac{45 \text{ minutes}}{1} \times \frac{1 \text{ hour}}{60 \text{ min}} = \frac{45}{60}$ 45 min = 0.75 hr

Convert 3 pounds to ounces.

d. Write the equivalent measures you will use. 16 ounces = 1 pound

e. Write the conversion factor. $\frac{16 \text{ ounces}}{1 \text{ pound}}$

f. Multiply by your conversion factor.

$\frac{3 \text{ pounds}}{1} \times \frac{16 \text{ oz}}{1 \text{ lb}} = \frac{48}{1}$ 3 lb = 48 oz

Reteaching

Activity

Materials: Penny, ruler, scale

- Measure the height of a penny in mm. How high would a stack of one million pennies be in mm? cm? m? km?
  One penny is about 1.5 mm high. One million pennies ≈ 1,500,000 mm ≈ 150,000 cm ≈ 1500 m ≈ 1.5 km.
- Weigh the penny in grams. How much would one million pennies weigh in g? kg?
  One penny weighs about 28 grams. One million pennies ≈ 28,000,000 g ≈ 28,000 kg

Exercise Notes

Exercise 22

Extension Have students convert the answer to miles; the Kentucky Derby is 1.25 miles long.

Exercise Answers

20. 2880 ounces

21. C

22. a. $\frac{1 \text{ yard}}{36 \text{ inches}}$

b. $1\frac{2}{3}$ yards; 540 inches

c. $\frac{660 \text{ feet}}{1 \text{ furlong}}$

d. 6600 feet

23. No, Since the week is the longer time period, there are fewer weeks until vacation than there are days.

24. 8

25. 4.00452×10^4

26. 5.38334892×10^8

27. 4.3567×10

28. 3.87657633×10^6

29. 5.77×10^2

30. 8.0×10^2

31. 4.03770×10^2

32. 3.008903×10^2

33.

4	8	12	16	20	24
5	10	15	20	25	30

34.

60	30	12	6	4	2
90	45	18	9	6	3

Alternate Assessment

Journal Have students write about what was helpful to them when converting units. Ask each student to make up and solve two problems involving different types of units.

➤ Quick Quiz

Convert each quantity to the given units.

1. 28 days to weeks 4 weeks
2. 54 in. to ft 4.5 ft
3. 3 lb to oz 48 oz
4. 150 min to hr 2.5 hours
5. 8 kg to g 8000 g

Available on Daily Transparency 7-6

The information in Exercises 20 and 21 comes from *50 Simple Things You Can Do to Save the Earth.*

20. Conservation The average office worker in the United States throws away 180 pounds of recyclable paper every year. How many ounces is this?

21. Test Prep The energy saved from recycling one glass bottle would light a 100-watt bulb for 4 hours. How many minutes is this?

Ⓐ $\frac{1}{15}$ minute Ⓑ $1\frac{2}{3}$ minutes Ⓒ 240 minutes Ⓓ 6,000 minutes

PROBLEM SOLVING 7-6

Problem Solving and Reasoning

22. Number Sense There are 12 inches in a foot and 3 feet in a yard.

a. What relationship involving inches and yards could you use to convert inches to yards in one step?

b. Use a conversion factor to make each conversion in one step: 60 inches to yards; 15 yards to inches.

c. There are 220 yards in a furlong. What conversion factor could you use to convert furlongs to feet?

d. In the Kentucky Derby, horses race a distance of 10 furlongs. Convert this distance to feet.

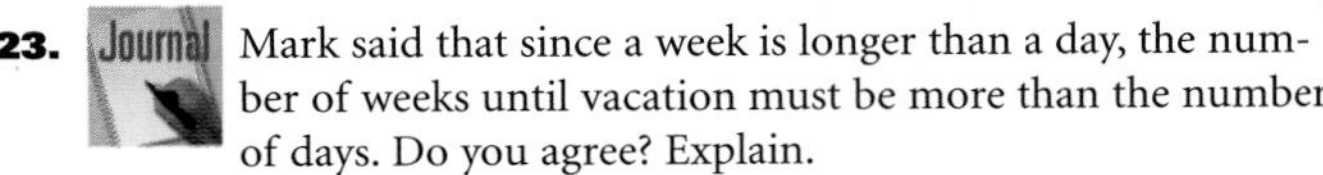

23. Journal Mark said that since a week is longer than a day, the number of weeks until vacation must be more than the number of days. Do you agree? Explain.

24. Critical Thinking There are 2 pints in a quart. How many pints are there in a gallon?

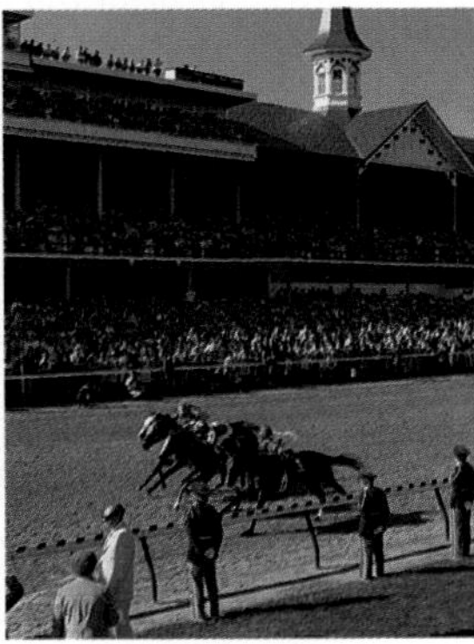

The Kentucky Derby

Mixed Review

Write each number in scientific notation. *[Lesson 3-5]*

25. 40,045.2 **26.** 538,334,892 **27.** 43.567 **28.** 3,876,576.33

29. 577 **30.** 800 **31.** 403.770 **32.** 300.8903

Complete the tables. *[Lesson 6-4]*

33. Using multiplication, complete the table to find 5 ratios equivalent to $\frac{4}{5}$.

4	8	12	16	20	24
5					

34. Using division, complete the table to find 5 ratios equivalent to $\frac{60}{90}$.

60	30	12	6	4	2
90					

PROBLEM SOLVING

Name ______________ **Guided Problem Solving 7-6**

GPS **PROBLEM 19, STUDENT PAGE 351**

Twenty Thousand Leagues Under the Sea is a famous novel by Jules Verne. A league is about 3.45 miles. Convert 20,000 leagues to feet.

— Understand —

1. How many miles is equal to a league? 3.45 miles.
2. What are you asked to do? Convert 20,000 leagues to feet.

— Plan —

3. How many miles are there in 20,000 leagues? 69,000 miles.
4. How many feet are there in a mile? 5280 feet.
5. What will you need to do to find how many feet in a league? Multiply 69,000 by 5280.

— Solve —

6. How many feet are in 20,000 leagues? 364,320,000 feet.
7. Write the title of Verne's novel using feet in place of leagues. Three Hundred Sixty-Four Million, Three Hundred Twenty Thousand Feet Under the Sea.

— Look Back —

8. Estimate to see if your answer is reasonable. Possible answer: $20,000 \times 4 = 80,000$; $80,000 \times 5000 = 400,000,000$; 364,320,000 is close to 400,000,000, so the answer is reasonable.

SOLVE ANOTHER PROBLEM

Convert 15,000 leagues to feet. 15,000 leagues = 273,240,000 feet.

ENRICHMENT

Name ______________ **Extend Your Thinking 7-6**

Visual Thinking

On another sheet of paper, trace and cut out these shapes.

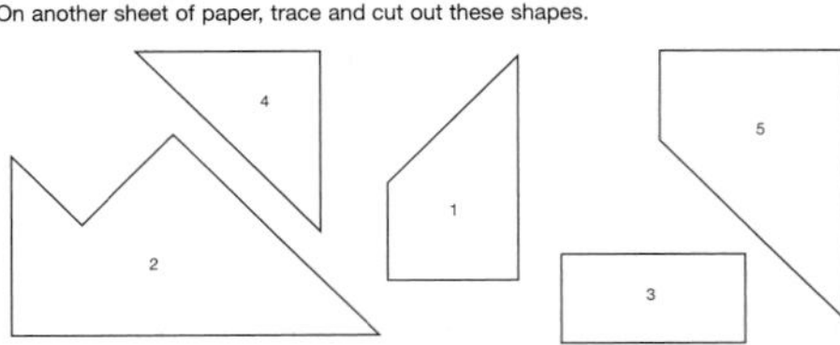

1. Use the shapes to make a square. Use each piece only once. Show your solution at the right.

2. Use the shapes to make a triangle. Use each piece only once. (Hint: Pieces may be flipped over.) Show your solution at the right.

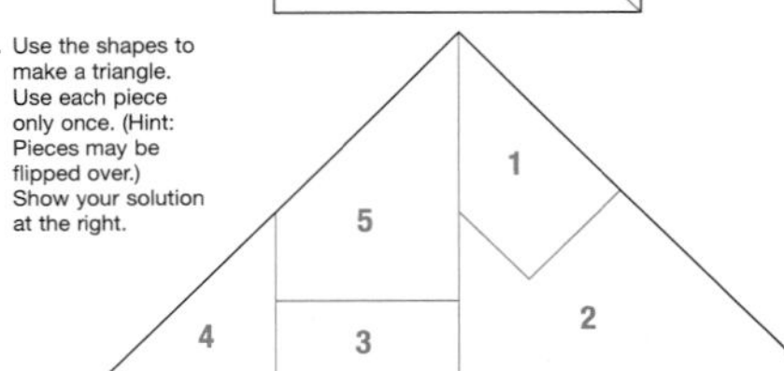

Pieces 4 & 5 are flipped over.

Problem Solving: Converting Rates

7-7

▶ Lesson Link You've seen how to use a conversion factor to convert from one unit to another. Now you will use conversion factors to convert from one rate to another. ◀

You'll Learn ...

- to solve problems involving conversion of rates

... How It's Used

Physicists use rate conversions to express speeds, forces, and masses in different units.

Explore Converting Rates

Drastic Plastic

According to *50 Simple Things You Can Do to Save the Earth,* an average person in the United States uses about 190 pounds of plastic every year.

U.S. Plastic Recycling, 1993 (Millions of tons)

Recovered–0.7

Unrecovered–18.6

1. Give two reciprocal conversion factors that involve pounds and ounces.
2. Use the appropriate conversion factor to find the number of ounces of plastic used by each person in a year.
3. In the last lesson, you saw how to convert feet to inches and pounds to tons. How are those conversions different from the conversion in Step 2? Why are conversions such as the one in Step 2 useful?
4. How could you convert your answer in Step 2 to give the number of ounces of plastic the average person in the United States uses each day? What is this number?
5. Based on the information in the circle graph, about how much of this plastic is recycled? (Hint: Use the graph and your answer to Step 4 to set up a proportion.)

Learn Problem Solving: Converting Rates

Every rate contains two units. 50 miles per hour 18 **holidays** per **year**

You can use conversion factors to convert from one rate to another. If you need to change a unit in the *numerator* of the rate, choose a conversion factor with that unit in the *denominator,* and vice-versa.

$$\frac{\text{miles}}{\text{hour}} \cdot \frac{\text{feet}}{\text{mile}} = \frac{\text{feet}}{\text{hour}}$$

$$\frac{\text{miles}}{\text{hour}} \cdot \frac{\text{hours}}{\text{day}} = \frac{\text{miles}}{\text{day}}$$

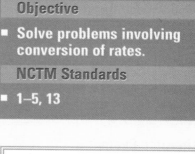

7-7 Lesson Organizer

Objective

- Solve problems involving conversion of rates.

NCTM Standards

- 1–5, 13

▶ Review

1. $\frac{2}{3} + \frac{4}{5}$ $\frac{22}{15} = 1\frac{7}{15}$
2. $2\frac{5}{6} - 1\frac{3}{4}$ $1\frac{1}{12}$
3. $3\frac{1}{4} \cdot 2\frac{1}{2}$ $\frac{65}{8} = 8\frac{1}{8}$
4. $7\frac{1}{3} \div 2\frac{2}{3}$ $\frac{11}{4} = 2\frac{3}{4}$

Available on Daily Tansparency 7-7

1 Introduce

Explore

The Point

Students solve a problem involving conversion of rates to determine how much plastic each person uses per day.

Ongoing Assessment

You may wish to have students estimate the answer to Step 4 before beginning their computations. It also may be helpful to have students write the two reciprocal conversion factors for years and days in Step 4 before choosing which to use.

For Groups That Finish Early

Describe when *pounds of plastic recycled per year* would be a useful rate to use. When would *ounces per day* be useful?

Answers may vary.

Answers for Explore

1. $\frac{1\text{ lb}}{16\text{ oz}}$; $\frac{16\text{ oz}}{1\text{ lb}}$
2. $\frac{3040\text{ ounces}}{\text{year}}$
3. The conversion in Step 2 is a rate conversion; These conversions are used to express rates in appropriate units.
4. Multiply by $\frac{1\text{ year}}{365\text{ days}}$; About 8.33 ounces per day.
5. About 0.3 ounces.

MEETING INDIVIDUAL NEEDS

Resources

- **7-7** Practice
- **7-7** Reteaching
- **7-7** Problem Solving
- **7-7** Enrichment
- **7-7** Daily Transparency
  - Problem of the Day
  - Review
  - Quick Quiz

Wide World of Mathematics Middle School: New York City Marathon

Learning Modalities

Logical Have students list as many possible equivalent rates as they can for a given rate.

Social Have students work in groups to prepare explanations of specific problems for the class.

Inclusion

Some students may have difficulty when more than one unit must be changed in a problem. Have them write down the intermediate units so they can focus on each piece of the problem separately.

Begin with simple conversions, such as "If you attend school 30 hours a week, how many hours do you attend per day?" Demonstrate the steps; then allow students to ask for your help as they work on problems.

2 Teach

Learn

Note: To help keep track of units, some students might want to "cancel" common units in rates and conversion factors. In Example 1, the unit "week" could be crossed off because it appears in a denominator and in a numerator. Point out that we can't truly "cancel" units and that this technique must be done carefully to avoid errors.

Alternate Examples

1. Harry's family receives about 65 pieces of junk mail each week. How many pieces per day is this?

   There are 7 days in a week. To convert $\frac{\text{pieces}}{\text{week}}$ to $\frac{\text{pieces}}{\text{day}}$, use the conversion factor that has weeks in the numerator.
   $\frac{65 \text{ pieces}}{1 \text{ week}} \cdot \frac{1 \text{ week}}{7 \text{ days}} = \frac{65 \text{ pieces}}{7 \text{ days}} \approx$ 9.29 pieces per day.

2. A typical American family throws away about 540 pounds of metal each year. How many ounces per day is this?

   First, convert from pounds per year to pounds per day.
   $\frac{540 \text{ lb}}{1 \text{ yr}} \cdot \frac{1 \text{ yr}}{365 \text{ days}} = \frac{540 \text{ lb}}{365 \text{ days}} \approx$ 1.48 pounds per day.

   Then, convert from pounds per day to ounces per day.
   $\frac{1.48 \text{ lb}}{1 \text{ day}} \cdot \frac{16 \text{ oz}}{1 \text{ lb}} = \frac{1.48 \cdot 16 \text{ oz}}{\text{day}} =$ 23.68 ounces per day.

3 Practice and Assess

Check

Answers for Check Your Understanding

1. The conversion factor is equal to 1.
2. Multiply by $\frac{5280 \text{ feet}}{\text{mile}}$ and $\frac{1 \text{ hour}}{3600 \text{ seconds}}$; Larger number.

Every week, half a million trees are used for Sunday newspapers. That's an entire forest!

Example 1

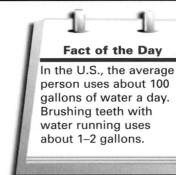

It takes more than 5,000,000 trees to print one week's worth of newspapers for the United States. How many trees per day is this?

There are 7 days in a week. To convert

$$\frac{\text{trees}}{\textbf{week}} \text{ to } \frac{\text{trees}}{\textbf{day}}$$

use the conversion factor that has weeks in the numerator.

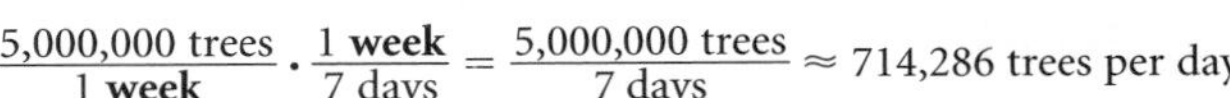

$$\frac{5{,}000{,}000 \text{ trees}}{1 \textbf{ week}} \cdot \frac{1 \textbf{ week}}{7 \text{ days}} = \frac{5{,}000{,}000 \text{ trees}}{7 \text{ days}} \approx 714{,}286 \text{ trees per day}$$

Printing the newspapers uses about 714,286 trees per day.

Try It

a. Convert 714,286 trees per day to trees per hour. ≈29,762 trees per hour

b. Convert 12 meters per second to millimeters per second. 12,000 millimeters per second

c. Convert 12,000 millimeters per second to millimeters per minute. 720,000 millimeters per minute

If you need to change *both* units in a rate, you can make the change one step at a time.

MENTAL MATH

When making conversions, decide whether the units you are converting to are larger or smaller than the original ones. This will help you see if your answer is reasonable.

Example 2

A standard showerhead uses about 6 gallons of water per minute. How many ounces per second is this? (A gallon contains 128 fluid ounces.)

First, convert from gallons per minute to gallons per second.

$$\frac{6 \text{ gal}}{1 \textbf{ min}} \cdot \frac{1 \textbf{ min}}{60 \text{ sec}} = \frac{6 \text{ gal}}{60 \text{ sec}}$$

Then convert from gallons per second to ounces per second.

$$\frac{6 \textbf{ gal}}{60 \text{ sec}} \cdot \frac{128 \text{ oz}}{1 \textbf{ gal}} = \frac{768 \text{ oz}}{60 \text{ sec}} = 12.8 \text{ ounces per second}$$

A standard showerhead uses 12.8 fluid ounces of water per second.

Try It

a. Convert 65 kilometers per hour to meters per minute. ≈1083.3 meters per minute

b. Convert $2.40 per pound to cents per ounce. 15 cents per ounce

MATH EVERY DAY

Problem of the Day

In the early 1900s in Buganda (Uganda), Africa, cowrie shells were used as money. Here is a transaction that might have happened in the early 1900s. Five thousand cowrie shells were exchanged for two cows. The cows were then traded for ten goats. Five of the goats were then traded for four spears made by the local blacksmith. At that time, how many cowrie shells was a spear worth? 625 shells

Available on Daily Transparency 7-7

An Extension is provided in the transparency package.

Fact of the Day

In the U.S., the average person uses about 100 gallons of water a day. Brushing teeth with water running uses about 1–2 gallons.

Mental Math

Do these mentally.

1. $\frac{2}{3} \cdot 6$ 4
2. $\frac{3}{4} \div \frac{1}{8}$ 6
3. $4 - 1\frac{2}{3}$ $2\frac{1}{3}$

Check Your Understanding

1. Why do you get an equivalent rate when you multiply a rate by a conversion factor?
2. Explain how you would convert miles per hour to feet per second. Would the new number be larger or smaller?

7-7 Exercises and Applications

PRACTICE 7-7

Practice and Apply

1. **Getting Started** Follow the steps below to convert 16 gallons per day to quarts per day.
   a. Use 1 gal = 4 quarts to give two conversion factors of the form $\frac{?\text{ gal}}{?\text{ qt}}$ and $\frac{?\text{ qt}}{?\text{ gal}}$.
   b. Since $\frac{16\text{ gal}}{1\text{ day}}$ has gallons in the numerator, choose the conversion factor from **a** that has gallons in the denominator.
   c. Multiply $\frac{16\text{ gal}}{1\text{ day}}$ by the correct conversion factor. The result is the rate in quarts per day.

Operation Sense Convert each rate to an equivalent rate.

2. 40 kilometers per hour to kilometers per minute
3. 128 inches per second to feet per second
4. 0.45 kilograms per pound to grams per pound
5. 36 fluid ounces per day to cups per day
6. 28 feet per second to miles per hour

The information in Exercises 7–10 comes from *50 Simple Things You Can Do to Save the Earth.*

7. Every year 50 million flea collars are thrown away. How many flea collars are thrown away per day?
8. The average person in the United States uses about 640 pounds of paper each year. How much is this in ounces per year?
9. Homeowners in the United States use more than 25 million pounds of pesticides on their lawns every year. Convert this rate to ounces per hour.
10. People in the United States throw away 2.5 million plastic bottles per hour. How many bottles per year do we throw away?

PRACTICE

Name ____________

Practice 7-7

Problem Solving: Converting Rates

Convert each rate to an equivalent rate.

1. 35 pounds per minute to pounds per hour — 2100 pounds per hour
2. $72.00 per hour to dollars per minute — $1.20 per minute
3. 75 feet per second to feet per minute — 4500 feet per minute
4. 2.54 centimeters per inch to meters per inch — 0.0254 meters per inch
5. 90 quarts per hour to quarts per minute — 1.5 quarts per minute
6. 28.35 grams per ounce to grams per pound — 453.6 grams per pound
7. 7.2 inches per second to feet per second — 0.6 feet per second
8. $1.44 per gallon to cents per quart — 36¢ per quart
9. $8.00 per pound to dollars per ounce — $0.50 per ounce

Science Use conversion factors to complete the table.

	Name of Animal	Maximum Speed (mi/hr)	Maximum Speed (ft/sec)
10.	Elk	45	66
11.	Grizzly bear	30	44
12.	Spider	1.17	1.716
13.	Three-toed sloth	0.15	0.22
14.	Squirrel	12	17.6

15. The average North American consumes about 26 barrels of petroleum per year, and the average African consumes about one barrel of petroleum per year. Convert these rates to gallons per day. (One barrel is 42 gallons.)

    North America: About 2.99 gal per day

    Africa: About 0.115 gal per day

16. In 1994, American farmers produced 133.8 bushels of corn per acre of corn crops. Convert this rate to pecks per square foot. (A bushel is equal to 4 pecks, and an acre is equal to 43,560 square feet.)

    About 0.0123 pecks per square foot

RETEACHING

Name ____________

Alternative Lesson 7-7

Problem Solving: Converting Rates

You can use conversion factors to convert from one rate to another. It is important to note whether the unit you wish to change is in the *numerator* or in the *denominator*.

To change a unit in the numerator of a rate, choose a conversion factor with that unit in the denominator. To change a unit in the denominator of a rate, choose a conversion factor with that unit in the numerator.

Example 1

Convert 7 feet per hour to inches per hour.

Use 12 inches = 1 foot to convert from feet to inches.

$$\frac{7\text{ feet}}{1\text{ hour}} \times \frac{12\text{ inches}}{1\text{ foot}} = \frac{7\text{ feet} \times 12\text{ inches}}{1\text{ hour} \times 1\text{ foot}} = \frac{84\text{ inches}}{1\text{ hour}}$$

So, 7 feet per hour is equal to 84 inches per hour.

Try It Convert 12 quarts per day to gallons per day.

a. Write the conversion factor. $\frac{1\text{ gallon}}{4\text{ quarts}}$

b. Multiply by the conversion factor. Then write the new rate.

$$\frac{12\text{ quarts}}{1\text{ day}} \times \frac{1\text{ gallon}}{4\text{ quarts}} = \frac{3\text{ gallons}}{1\text{ day}}$$ 3 gal per day.

Example 2

Convert 56 packages per week to packages per day.

Use 1 week = 7 days to convert from week to days.

$$\frac{56\text{ packages}}{1\text{ week}} \times \frac{1\text{ week}}{7\text{ days}} = \frac{56\text{ packages} \times 1\text{ week}}{1\text{ week} \times 7\text{ days}} = \frac{56\text{ packages}}{7\text{ days}}$$

Divide both numerator and denominator by 7 to find the packages per day.

So, 56 packages per week is equal to 8 packages per day.

Try It Convert 50 feet per minute to feet per second.

c. Write the fraction for your conversion factor. $\frac{1\text{ minute}}{60\text{ seconds}}$

d. Multiply by your conversion factor. Then write the new rate.

$$\frac{50\text{ feet}}{1\text{ minute}} \times \frac{1\text{ minute}}{60\text{ seconds}} = \frac{5\text{ feet}}{6\text{ seconds}}$$

50 feet per minute = $\frac{5}{6}$ feet per second

7-7 Exercises and Applications

Assignment Guide

- **Basic** 1–11 odds, 12–14, 16, 17–25 odds
- **Average** 2–10 evens, 11–16, 18–24 evens
- **Enriched** 4–16, 17–25 odds

Exercise Notes

Exercise 6

Error Prevention Students may wish to change this rate first to feet per minute, then feet per hour, then miles per hour.

Exercise Answers

1. a. $\frac{1\text{ gal}}{4\text{ qt}}$; $\frac{4\text{ qt}}{1\text{ gal}}$
   b. $\frac{4\text{ qt}}{1\text{ gal}}$
   c. $\frac{64\text{ qt}}{1\text{ day}}$
2. $\approx \frac{2}{3}$ km per min.
3. $\approx 10\frac{2}{3}$ ft per sec.
4. 450 grams per pound.
5. $4\frac{1}{2}$ cups per day.
6. $\approx$ 19.09 miles per hour.
7. $\approx$ 137,000 flea collars per day.
8. $\approx$ 10,240 ounces per year.
9. $\approx$ 46,000 ounces per hour.
10. $\approx$ 21.9 billion bottles per year.

Reteaching

Activity

Suppose you use 20 sheets of notebook paper each school day.

- How many sheets do you use each school year? (Assume 180 school days = 1 school year.) 3600 sheets per year.
- A 200-sheet package of paper is $\frac{3}{4}$ inch high. How high a stack of paper do you use each month? (Assume 20 school days = 1 month.) $1\frac{1}{2}$ inches per month.
- The weight of 200 sheets of paper is 15 ounces. How many pounds of paper per school year do you use? 16.875 pounds per school year.

Exercise Notes

■ Exercises 12–14

Error Prevention Have students look at their answers for all three problems to see if they are reasonable.

Exercise Answers

12. ≈ 102.7 feet per second.

13. ≈ 216.8 miles per hour.

14. ≈ 58.67 feet per second.

21.

5	10	15	20
3	6	9	12

$\frac{5}{3} = \frac{10}{6}; \frac{10}{6} = \frac{15}{9}; \frac{15}{9} = \frac{20}{12}$

22.

1	2	3	4
2	4	6	8

$\frac{1}{2} = \frac{2}{4}; \frac{2}{4} = \frac{3}{6}; \frac{3}{6} = \frac{4}{8}$

23.

11	22	33	44
44	88	132	176

$\frac{11}{44} = \frac{22}{88}; \frac{22}{88} = \frac{33}{132}; \frac{33}{132} = \frac{44}{176}$

24.

4	8	12	16
7	14	21	28

$\frac{4}{7} = \frac{8}{14}; \frac{8}{14} = \frac{12}{21}; \frac{12}{21} = \frac{16}{28}$

25.

27	9	3	54
36	12	4	72

$\frac{27}{36} = \frac{9}{12}; \frac{9}{12} = \frac{3}{4}; \frac{3}{4} = \frac{54}{72}$

Alternate Assessment

Portfolio Have students select examples of tasks they have completed in this section that illustrate what they have learned about rates and converting rates.

► Quick Quiz

Convert each rate to an equivalent rate.

1. 50 inches per minute to inches per hour
   3000 inches per hour.
2. 50 inches per minute to feet per minute
   4.17 feet per minute.
3. 30 kilometers per hour to meters per minute
   500 meters per minute.

Available on Daily Transparency 7-7

PROBLEM SOLVING 7-7

11. **Test Prep** The United States is the leading garbage-producing nation on earth, with an average of 864 kg of waste produced by each person per year. On average, how much waste is produced by each person in the United States in a month? **A**

Ⓐ 72 kg Ⓑ 8,640 kg Ⓒ 10,380 kg Ⓓ 315,360 kg

Science **Some of the world's fastest animals are endangered species. Use conversion factors to complete the table.**

	Name of Animal	Maximum Speed (mi/hr)	Maximum Speed (ft/sec)
12.	Cheetah	70	
13.	Peregrine falcon		318
14.	Mountain zebra	40	

Problem Solving and Reasoning

15. Journal An ad for Spudz Potato Chips claims, "In 1995, Spudz lovers bought 329,000,000 pounds of Spudz Potato Chips. That's over 901,000 pounds a day, 625 pounds a minute, and 10 pounds a second!" Assuming the number 329,000,000 is correct, check the truth of this claim. Are the numbers exact or estimates? **True; Estimates**

16. **Critical Thinking** Do you use more water for a shower or for a bath? GPS Suppose you always use 250 L of water for a bath and your shower uses 15 L of water per minute.

a. How many minutes would a 150 L shower take? **10 minutes**

b. What is the greatest whole number of minutes you can shower and still use less water than you would use taking a bath? **16 minutes**

Mixed Review

Use >, <, or = to compare each pair of numbers. *[Lesson 3-9]*

17. $\frac{13}{52}$ [<] $\frac{5}{16}$ **18.** $\frac{8}{9}$ [>] $\frac{43}{50}$ **19.** $\frac{23}{92}$ [=] $\frac{1}{4}$ **20.** $\frac{32}{512}$ [<] $\frac{2}{17}$

For each ratio, make a table and create three equal ratios. Then use your ratios to write three proportions. *[Lesson 6-5]*

21. $\frac{5}{3}$ **22.** $\frac{1}{2}$ **23.** $\frac{11}{44}$ **24.** $\frac{4}{7}$ **25.** $\frac{27}{36}$

PROBLEM SOLVING

Name ______________________

Guided Problem Solving 7-7

GPS **PROBLEM 16, STUDENT PAGE 356**

Do you use more water for a shower or for a bath? Suppose you always use 250 L of water for a bath and your shower uses 15 L of water per minute.

a. How many minutes would a 150 L shower take?

b. What is the greatest whole number of minutes you can shower and still use less water than you would use taking a bath?

— Understand —

1. How much water is used for a bath? **250 liters.**
2. What determines the amount of water used for a shower?
   How long the shower runs.

— Plan —

3. Which expression shows time spent showering if x represents liters of water. **b**

   a. $15x$ **b.** $\frac{x}{15}$ **c.** $\frac{150}{x}$ **d.** $150x$

4. Use your expression to complete the table showing number of liters of water used for showers lasting 10 minutes to 20 minutes.

Minutes	10	11	12	13	14	15	16	17	18	19	20
Liters of water	150	165	180	195	210	225	240	255	270	285	300

— Solve —

5. How many minutes would a 150-L shower take? **10 minutes.**
6. What is the greatest number of minutes you can shower and still use less water than you would use taking a bath? **16 minutes.**

— Look Back —

7. In the table above, which amount of water used for showering was closest to 250 L? Explain why this was *not* the correct solution.
   255 L; 255 L is more than, not less than, water used for bath.

SOLVE ANOTHER PROBLEM

Rosetta installed a low-flow shower head that uses 12 L of water per minute. How long can she shower and still use less water than taking a 250-L bath? **20 minutes.**

ENRICHMENT

Name ______________________

Extend Your Thinking 7-7

Patterns in Measurement

On the planet of Zoran, the following four units are used for measuring length: lipp, mutt, pial, and wird. Their relationships are shown in the table at the right.

I lipp = 6 mutts
1 mutt = 9 pials
1 pial = 3 wirds

1. Use a conversion factor to convert 324 wirds to pials.
   $\frac{324 \text{ wirds}}{1} \times \frac{1 \text{ pial}}{3 \text{ wirds}} = 108$ **pials.**
2. Use a conversion factor to convert 108 pials to mutts.
   $\frac{108 \text{ pials}}{1} \times \frac{1 \text{ mutt}}{9 \text{ pials}} = 12$ **mutts.**
3. Use a conversion factor to convert 12 mutts to lipps.
   $\frac{12 \text{ mutts}}{1} \times \frac{1 \text{ lipp}}{6 \text{ mutts}} = 2$ **lipps.**
4. Which of the units is the smallest? **Wird.**
5. Which of the units is the largest? **Lipp.**
6. What pattern do you notice about the quantity of units as you convert from the smallest unit to the largest unit?
   There are fewer units of a larger measure.
7. Use a conversion factor to convert 8 lipps to mutts.
   $\frac{8 \text{ lipps}}{1} \times \frac{6 \text{ mutts}}{1 \text{ lipp}} = 48$ **mutts.**
8. Use a conversion factor to convert 48 mutts to pials.
   $\frac{48 \text{ mutts}}{1} \times \frac{9 \text{ pials}}{1 \text{ mutt}} = 432$ **pials.**
9. Use a conversion factor to convert 432 pials to wirds.
   $\frac{432 \text{ pials}}{1} \times \frac{3 \text{ wirds}}{1 \text{ pial}} = 1296$ **wirds.**
10. What pattern do you notice about the quantity of units as you convert from the largest unit to the smallest unit?
    The quantity of units is more.
11. What general statement can you make about the quantity of units relative to their size?
    The larger the unit, the smaller the quantity and vice versa.

Section 7B Connect

You've investigated different rates and units. Now you will use what you have learned about rates to see if a claim about the amount of water a family can save is true.

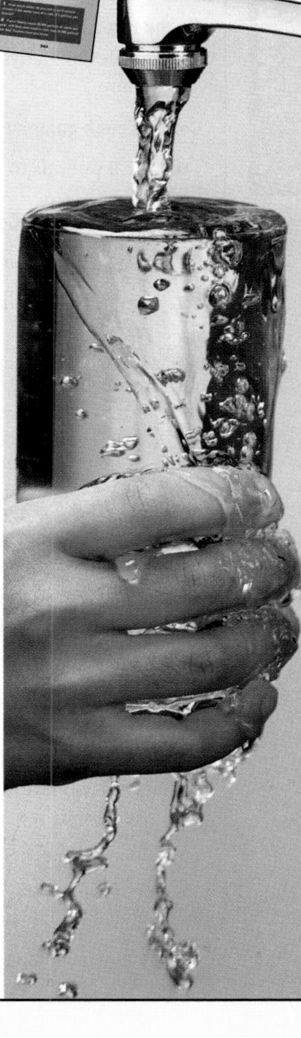

Water, Water Everywhere

According to *50 Simple Things You Can Do to Save the Earth,* a family can save 20,000 gallons of water per year by taking a few simple conservation measures. Here are four suggestions the book makes:

- Just wet and rinse your toothbrush when you brush.
- When you wash dishes, fill the basin instead of running the tap.
- Use a bucket and a hose with a shut-off nozzle when you wash the car.
- When shaving, fill the sink with water instead of keeping the water running.

The table shows savings for a family of four (with one adult who shaves).

Activity	Savings Rate (gal/min)	Time (min)	How Often
Brushing teeth	4	1	8 times a day (4 people)
Washing dishes	4	6	Once a day
Washing car	3	30	Once a week
Shaving	4	2	Once a day (one person)

1. How much car washing water can be saved per week? Per day?

2. How much tooth brushing water can be saved each day? How much dish washing water? How much shaving water?

3. Use the above answers to find the total daily water savings. Then decide whether a family could actually save 20,000 gallons of water a year. Explain how you found your answer.

Water, Water, Everywhere

The Point

In *Water, Water Everywhere* on page 343, students explored ways for saving water. Now they will use their understanding of rate to determine the validity of claims made about the conservation measures discussed.

About the Page

- Review the table with the class to ensure that students understand it. Point out that the car is washed once a week, while brushing teeth, washing dishes, and shaving are daily activities.
- Discuss the idea that the savings rate multiplied by the time spent equals the amount saved.

Ongoing Assessment

Check that students have determined the correct daily or weekly savings before they attempt to find annual savings.

Extension

Have students determine the amount of water their family could save using the information given on the chart. Remind them to count the number of people in their families and how often each person brushes his or her teeth, the number of cars and how often they are washed, the number of people who shave, and so on. Ask students if their families could save more or less water than the family described in the example.

Answers for Connect

1. Possible answers: 90 gallons per week; About 12.9 gallons per day.
2. Possible answers: Tooth brushing: 32 gallons per day; Dish washing: 24 gallons per day; Shaving: 8 gallons per day.
3. Possible answers: Total savings: 76.9 gallons per day or ≈ 28,000 gallons per year; Added the individual per-day savings and multiplied by 365.

7B Review

Review Correlation

Item(s)	Lesson(s)
1–7	7-5
8–10	7-6
11–17	7-7

Test Prep

Test-Taking Tip

Tell students to make lists of measurements into which each given measurement could be changed. Here, pounds could be changed to ounces or tons, and hours could be changed to minutes, seconds, or days.

Answers for Review

1. Possible answer: Pages per hour.
2. Possible answer: Miles per hour.
3. $\frac{2.5 \text{ students}}{1 \text{ pizza}}$, $\frac{0.4 \text{ pizza}}{1 \text{ student}}$; Possible answer: The first is more useful as it tells you how many students 1 pizza will feed.

11. 600 miles per day.
12. 760 cents per hour.
13. 2880 gallons per day.
14. 2.1 meters per minute.
15. ≈ 208 ounces per year.
16. Possible answer: 1 person eats ≈ 6 square feet per year which sounds reasonable. Find square feet eaten by 1 person in 1 day and multiply by 365 to find 1 year.

Section 7B Review

REVIEW 7B

Number Sense Suggest appropriate units for each rate.

1. The rate at which a book is read
2. The speed of a train
3. **Logic** Suppose there are 32 pizzas for 80 students. Write two unit rates that describe this situation. Which one of your rates is more useful?

Do the rates in each pair have the same meaning? Write *Yes* or *No*.

4. $\frac{2 \text{ miles}}{\text{day}}, \frac{0.5 \text{ days}}{\text{mile}}$ Yes
5. $\frac{\$0.40}{\text{lb}}, \frac{3 \text{ lb}}{\$1}$ No
6. $\frac{10 \text{ mi}}{\text{hr}}, \frac{0.25 \text{ hr}}{\text{mi}}$ No
7. $\frac{4 \text{ ft}}{\text{sec}}, \frac{0.25 \text{ sec}}{\text{ft}}$ Yes

Convert each quantity to the given units.

8. 4,000 pounds to tons 2 tons
9. 84 hours to days 3.5 days
10. 43 meters to centimeters 4300 cm

Operation Sense Convert each rate to an equivalent rate.

11. 25 miles per hour to miles per day
12. $7.60 per hour to cents per hour
13. 2 gallons per minute to gallons per day
14. 3.5 centimeters per second to meters per minute
15. According to *50 Simple Things You Can Do to Save the Earth,* a mature tree consumes up to 13 pounds of carbon dioxide per year. Convert this rate to ounces per year.

16.  Journal Suppose you hear a claim that people in the United States eat 100 acres of pizza per day. Convert this rate into reasonable units so you can evaluate this claim. Explain how you chose your units. One acre contains 43,560 square feet, and the population of the United States is about 260 million.

Test Prep

When finding an equivalent rate on a multiple choice test, you can eliminate choices that do not involve similar units. For example, when converting miles per hour, the answer must involve distance per time.

17. Which rate is equivalent to 3 pounds per hour? B

Ⓐ 1200 oz/km Ⓑ 0.8 oz/min Ⓒ 4.4 ft/sec Ⓓ 11.25 oz/mile

Resources

Practice Masters
Section 7B Review

Assessment Sourcebook
Quiz 7B

TestWorks
Test and Practice Software

PRACTICE

Name ______________________

Practice

Section 7B Review

Suggest appropriate units for each rate. Possible answers:

1. The rate at which someone mows a lawn square feet per minute
2. The rate of pay for a secretary dollars per hour
3. A craftsman made 18 flower pots in 6 days. Write two unit rates that describe this situation. Is one of your rates more useful?
$\frac{3 \text{ pots}}{\text{day}}, \frac{\frac{1}{3} \text{ day}}{\text{pot}}$; Possible answer: Both rates can be useful

Do the rates in each pair have the same meaning? Write *yes* or *no*.

4. $\frac{25 \text{ gal}}{\text{min}}, \frac{25 \text{ min}}{\text{gal}}$ No
5. $\frac{\$1.60}{\text{hr}}, \frac{0.625 \text{ hr}}{\text{dollar}}$ Yes
6. $\frac{100 \text{ L}}{\text{day}}, \frac{0.01 \text{ day}}{\text{L}}$ Yes
7. $\frac{40 \text{ mi}}{\text{hr}}, \frac{0.025 \text{ hr}}{\text{mi}}$ Yes
8. $\frac{5 \text{ tons}}{\text{week}}, \frac{\frac{1}{5} \text{ ton}}{\text{week}}$ No
9. $\frac{\$4.00}{\text{ft}}, \frac{\frac{1}{4} \text{ ft}}{\text{dollar}}$ Yes

Convert each quantity to the given units.

10. 6.42 kilograms to grams 6420 g
11. 12 centimeters to meters 0.12 m
12. 64 fluid ounces to quarts 2 qt
13. 45 hours to seconds 162,000 sec

Convert each rate to an equivalent rate.

14. 24 ounces per minute to pounds per minute 1.5 pounds per minute
15. $2.50 per minute to dollars per hour $150.00 per hour
16. 21 pounds per foot to pounds per inch 1.75 pounds per inch
17. The average American eats 150 pounds of canned food per year. Convert this rate to ounces per day. ≈ 6.58 ounces per day
18. A steel shelving unit uses a diagonal brace to prevent wobbling. Find the length of the brace. *[Lesson 5-7]* 53 in.

45 in.
28 in.

19. **Fine Arts** Pablo Picasso produced about 13,500 paintings during his 78-year career. Assuming that he painted at a consistent rate for his entire career, estimate the number of paintings he produced during the last 12 years. *[Lesson 6-7]* About 2400 paintings

Similarity

LESSON PLANNING GUIDE

Student Edition / Ancillaries*

LESSON		MATERIALS	VOCABULARY	DAILY	OTHER
	Section 7C Opener				
7-8	**Creating and Exploring Similar Figures**	protractor, metric ruler, graph paper	similar figures, corresponding sides, corresponding angles, scale factor	7-8	Teaching Tool Trans. 6, 7, 14, 15 Lesson Enhancement Trans. 32 Technology Master 30
	Technology	Dynamic geometry software			*Interactive CD-ROM Geometry Tool*
7-9	**Finding Measures of Similar Figures**	protractor, ruler		7-9	Teaching Tool Trans. 14, 15 Lesson Enhancement Trans. 33 Technology Master 31 Ch. 7 Project Master
7-10	**Perimeters and Areas of Similar Figures**	graph paper		7-10	Teaching Tool Trans. 7 Technology Master 32 *Interactive CD-ROM Lesson 7* *WW Math*–Geometry
	Connect	graph paper with large squares			Lesson Enhancement Trans. 34 Teaching Tool Trans. 7 Interdisc. Team Teaching 7C
	Review				Practice 7C; Quiz 7C; *TestWorks*
	Extend Key Ideas				
	Chapter 7 Summary and Review				
	Chapter 7 Assessment				Ch. 7 Tests Forms A–F *TestWorks*; Ch. 7 Letter Home
	Cumulative Review, Chapters 1–7				Cumulative Test Ch. 1–7

* Daily Ancillaries include Practice, Reteaching, Problem Solving, Enrichment, and Daily Transparency. Teaching Tool Transparencies are in *Teacher's Toolkits*. Lesson Enhancement Transparencies are in *Overhead Transparency Package*.

SKILLS TRACE

LESSON	SKILL	FIRST INTRODUCED GR. 5	GR. 6	GR. 7	DEVELOP	PRACTICE/ APPLY	REVIEW
7-8	**Identifying similar figures.**		✘		pp. 360–362	pp. 363–364	pp. 376, 379, 596
7-9	**Finding missing lengths in similar figures.**		✘		pp. 366–368	pp. 369–370	pp. 376, 379, 436, 604
7-10	**Using scale factors with perimeter and area.**			✘ p. 371	pp. 371–372	pp. 373–374	pp. 376, 379, 441, 609

CONNECTED MATHEMATICS

The unit *Stretching and Shrinking (Similarity)*, from the **Connected Mathematics** series, can be used with Section 7C.

INTERDISCIPLINARY TEAM TEACHING

Math and Science/Technology

(Worksheet pages 29–30: Teacher pages T29–T30)

In this lesson, students measure similar figures using dinosaur model data.

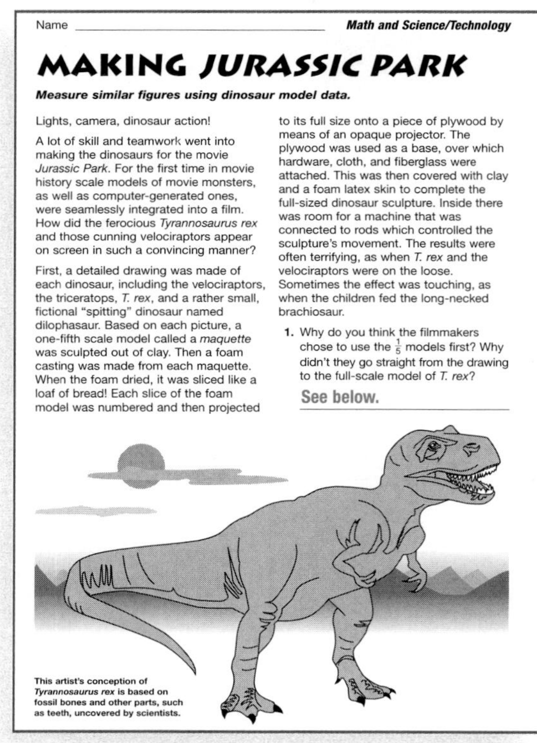

Name ______________________ *Math and Science/Technology*

MAKING *JURASSIC* PARK

Measure similar figures using dinosaur model data.

Lights, camera, dinosaur action!

A lot of skill and teamwork went into making the dinosaurs for the movie *Jurassic Park*. For the first time in movie history scale models of movie monsters, as well as computer-generated ones, were seamlessly integrated into a film. How did the ferocious *Tyrannosaurus rex* and those cunning velociraptors appear on screen in such a convincing manner?

First, a detailed drawing was made of each dinosaur, including the velociraptors, the triceratops, *T. rex*, and a rather small, fictional "spitting" dinosaur named dilophasaur. Based on each picture, a one-fifth scale model called a *maquette* was sculpted out of clay. Then a foam casting was made from each maquette. When the foam dried, it was sliced like a loaf of bread! Each slice of the foam model was numbered and then projected to its full size onto a piece of plywood by means of an opaque projector. The plywood was used as a base, over which hardware, cloth, and fiberglass were attached. This was then covered with clay and a foam latex skin to complete the full-sized dinosaur sculpture. Inside there was room for a machine that was connected to rods which controlled the sculpture's movement. The results were often terrifying, as when *T. rex* and the velociraptors were on the loose. Sometimes the effect was touching, as when the children fed the long-necked brachiosaur.

1. Why do you think the filmmakers chose to use the $\frac{1}{5}$ models first? Why didn't they go straight from the drawing to the full-scale model of *T. rex*?
   See below.

This artist's conception of *Tyrannosaurus rex* is based on fossil bones and other parts, such as teeth, uncovered by scientists.

Name ______________________ *Math and Science/Technology*

2. The $\frac{1}{5}$ scale model *T. rex* was 4 feet tall and 8.5 feet long. What were the height and length of the final 13,000-pound, full-sized mechanical version of *T. rex*?
   20 feet high by 42.5 feet long

3. *Jurassic Park* was shot on the island of Kauai, Hawaii. However, the sequence in which the *T. rex* breaks through the perimeter fence and chases the jeep was actually shot on a sound stage. The stage area was a rectangle that measured 135 × 240 feet.
   a. What is the longest continuous straight length of road or fence that could be set up and shot on this sound stage?
   240 feet
   b. Jungle appeared in the background along the perimeter of the set. How long was the entire perimeter of the sound stage?
   750 feet

4. When an entire brachiosaur was on screen, it was computer generated. But a mechanical neck and head puppet was used in the close-up shots where the children are up in the tree feeding the brachiosaur. The head puppet was 8 feet tall. This represented approximately $\frac{2}{13}$ of the animal's total height. How tall was the whole animal?
   $\frac{2}{13} = \frac{8}{x}$; $x = 52$ feet

5. The set of the "control room" was dominated by an extraordinarily large 6 × 8 foot computer monitor which was controlled by a computer in the next room.
   a. What is the image area of the computer screen?
   48 square feet
   b. Some desktop computer monitors are about 12 × 16 inches. How many times larger is the image area of the control room monitor compared to such a desktop computer monitor?
   The area of the smaller screen is 192 in.^{2}, while that of the larger screen is 6,912 in.^{2} or 36 times greater; or in feet: $1 \times 1\frac{1}{3} = 1\frac{1}{3}$ ft^2; $48 \div 1\frac{1}{3} = 36$

6. Do some research to find a good picture of a velociraptor. Use an opaque projector or other means to enlarge the picture and paint a wall mural of this smart little dinosaur. If you were to make your velociraptor life-sized, how tall would it be, and how big would you make its sharp front claws? Use this scale model information. A $\frac{1}{10}$ scale model velociraptor sold as official *Jurassic Park* merchandise is 5 inches high and 7 inches long (including a $4\frac{1}{2}$ inch tail section), with a half-inch front claw.
   50 inches high, 70 inches long (with 45 inches of tail) and a 5-inch claw

Answers

1. Possible answers: Making a large, three-dimensional dinosaur sculpture is expensive. Errors can be costly to correct. By making a small, low-cost model first, technicians can test the model under different conditions, find problems, and then correct them inexpensively.

BIBLIOGRAPHY

FOR TEACHERS

American Recycling Market. *The Official Recycled Products Guide*. Ogdensburg, NY: 1991.

Mango, Karin. *Mapmaking*. New York, NY: Messner, 1984.

The Earth Works Group. *50 Simple Things Kids Can Do to Recycle*. Berkeley, CA: Earthworks Press, 1994.

The Earth Works Group. *50 Simple Things You Can Do to Save the Earth*. Kansas City, MO: Andrew & McMeel, 1990.

FOR STUDENTS

Dodge, Venus. *The New Dolls' House Do-It-Yourself Book*. New York, NY: Newton Abbott, 1993.

Van Hise, James. *Hot Blooded Dinosaur Movies*. Las Vegas, NV: Pioneer Books, 1993.

Section 7C

SECTION 7C

Similarity

▶ Industry Link ▶ Fine Arts Link ▶ www.mathsurf.com/7/ch7/movie_monsters

LARGER THAN LIFE

Have you ever wondered how monster and science fiction movies such as *King Kong* and *Star Wars* were created? The creatures in these movies appear to be taller than a house, and it's hard to find a 24 foot tall actor who is willing to wear an ape suit!

In these movies, directors used scale models of the "monsters." The original version of *King Kong* was filmed using a model only 18 inches tall! Today, computers are replacing scale models. When you see a spaceship in an old *Star Trek* episode, you can be sure you're looking at a model. But recent films like *Jurassic Park* have been made using computers.

The scale models used in moviemaking are mathematically similar to the "real" objects they replace. By learning about the properties of similar figures, you can understand how these models compare to the things they represent.

1 In the movie *Honey, I Shrunk the Kids*, humans become smaller than insects. How do you think the models of insects used in this movie were different from the models of Godzilla and King Kong?

2 King Kong was supposed to be 24 feet tall. What scale was used to make the 18 in. scale model?

359

Where are we now?

In Section 7B, students learned to choose appropriate units when using a rate.

They learned how to

- choose appropriate rates for different situations.
- convert measurements from one unit to another.
- use conversion factors to convert from one rate to another.

Where are we going?

In Section 7C, students will

- identify similar figures and write similarity statements.
- find side lengths in similar figures.
- use shadows to find the heights of tall objects.
- use the scale factor to find the perimeters and areas of similar figures.

Theme: Movie Monsters

World Wide Web

If your class has access to the World Wide Web, you might want to use the information found at the Web site address given. The interdisciplinary links relate to the topics discussed in this section.

About the Page

This page introduces the theme of the section, movie monsters, and discusses the scale models used to create the illusions shown in these films.

Ask ...

- Have you seen any of the movies mentioned?
- Have you ever wondered how the creatures in *Jurassic Park* were created?
- Why would moviemakers need to know about scale?

Extensions

The following activities do not require access to the World Wide Web.

Industry
Making movies is big business. Pixar is a company that has computerized the characters and animation seen in movies such as *Toy Story*. Have students research the techniques used to create their favorite movie monster or science fiction character.

Fine Arts
Artists, computer specialists, graphic designers, producers, and directors are just a few of the many professionals involved in creating and producing movies. Ask students to investigate and report on one aspect of moviemaking.

Answers for Questions

1. Possible answer: They were larger than the original insects.
2. Possible answer: 1 in.:16 in.

Connect

On page 375, students use both the grid and projection methods to enlarge a picture.

7-8 Lesson Organizer

Objectives

- Identify similar figures.
- Write similarity statements.

Vocabulary

- Similar figures, corresponding sides, corresponding angles, scale factor

Materials

- Explore: Protractor, metric ruler, graph paper

NCTM Standards

- 1–4, 7, 12

Review

Solve each equation.

1. $x - 3 = 13$ $x = 16$
2. $2x = 24$ $x = 12$
3. $\frac{x}{5} = 3$ $x = 15$
4. $2x - 1 = 3$ $x = 2$

Available on Daily Transparency 7-8

1 Introduce

Explore

You may want to use Teaching Tool Transparencies 7: cm Graph Paper, 14: Rulers, and 15: Protractor, or 6: Cuisenaire Angle Ruler with **Explore**.

The Point

Students see that *adding* the same length to each side of a polygon changes its shape, but *multiplying* each side length by the same number produces a figure with the same shape.

Ongoing Assessment

Check that students add 3 cm to each segment in Step 2, and that they use the protractor properly.

7-8 Creating and Exploring Similar Figures

You'll Learn ...

- to identify similar figures
- to write similarity statements

... How It's Used

Photographers produce similar figures when they enlarge or reduce their pictures.

Vocabulary

similar figures

corresponding sides

corresponding angles

scale factor

▶ Lesson Link You've seen that a scale drawing has the same shape as the original but a different size. Now you'll look at geometric figures that also have the same shape but not necessarily the same size. ◀

Explore Similar Shapes

Oh, Give Me a Home ...

Materials: Protractor, Metric ruler, cm graph paper

1. On your paper, draw a small "house" with five sides. Measure the length of each segment.
2. Add 3 cm to each length, then draw another house with the new dimensions. (Make sure both diagonal sides are the right length.)
3. Draw a third house, adding another 4 cm to each segment in the second house. Do your houses have the same shape?

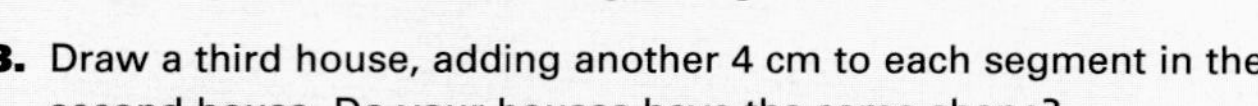

4. Measure the angles in your houses. What do you notice?
5. Now draw a fourth house by doubling each length in the original house. Does this house have the same shape as the original house?
6. Measure the angles in your fourth house. What do you notice now?

Learn Creating and Exploring Similar Figures

The scale model used to make *King Kong* looked like the "real" Kong but was a different size.

If one geometric figure is a scale model of another, the figures are **similar figures**. Similar figures have the same shape, but not necessarily the same size.

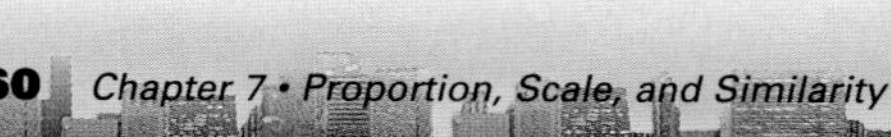

MEETING INDIVIDUAL NEEDS

Resources

- 7-8 Practice
- 7-8 Reteaching
- 7-8 Problem Solving
- 7-8 Enrichment
- 7-8 Daily Transparency
  - Problem of the Day
  - Review
  - Quick Quiz
- Teaching Tool Transparencies 7, 14, and 15 or 6
- Lesson Enhancement Transparency 32
- Technology Master 30

Learning Modalities

Visual You may want to trace similar figures onto two overhead transparencies and lay the transparencies on top of each other to show that the corresponding angles are congruent.

Kinesthetic Have students trace the figures in the text, label them, and cut them out. Then students can flip, slide, and turn the figures to gain a better understanding of similarity. They may also find it useful to use a copy machine to enlarge and reduce figures.

English Language Development

Students for whom English is a second language might not completely understand "same shape." Have students draw or model their understanding of similarity to check their comprehension.

The *Multilingual Handbook* with its glossary of math terms, illustrations, and worked-out examples, can help you with students who have limited English language skills. The glossary is provided in multiple languages.

Matching sides and angles of similar figures are called **corresponding sides** and **corresponding angles**. The measures of these sides and angles are related in a special way.

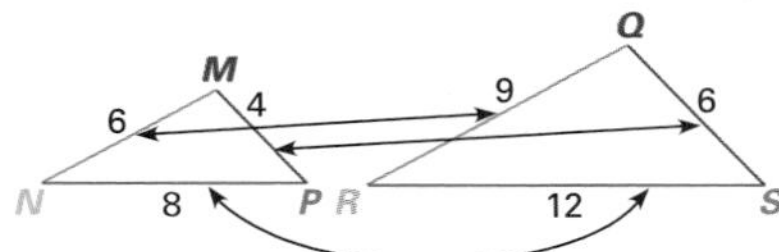

> **Remember**
> Congruent angles have equal measures.
> [Page 214]

DEFINITION OF SIMILARITY

Figures are similar if their corresponding angles are congruent and the lengths of their corresponding sides have equal ratios.

The ratio of corresponding side lengths is the **scale factor** of the figures. It has the same meaning as the map and model scales you worked with earlier. The scale factor from $\triangle MNP$ to $\triangle QRS$ is $\frac{3}{2}$, since $\frac{9}{6} = \frac{6}{4} = \frac{12}{8} = \frac{3}{2}$.

Example 1

A movie uses a model skyscraper that is similar to a real one. Find the scale factor from the actual skyscraper to the model.

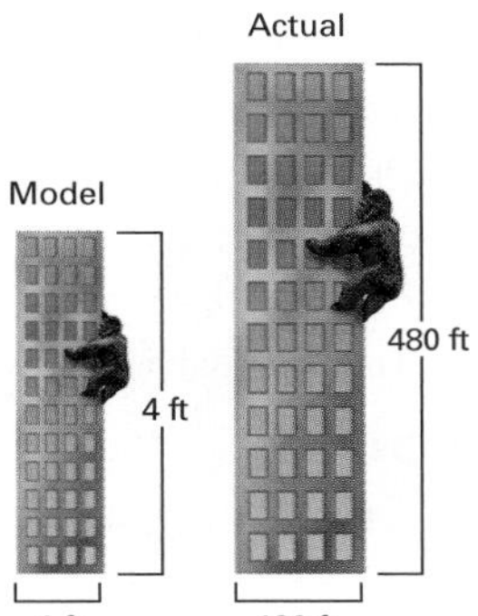

In similar figures, the ratio of any pair of corresponding side lengths can be used to find the scale factor. You can use the buildings' heights *or* widths to find the scale factor.

Using heights:

$$\frac{\text{model height}}{\text{actual height}} = \frac{4}{480} = \frac{1}{120}$$

Using widths:

$$\frac{\text{model width}}{\text{actual width}} = \frac{1}{120}$$

The scale factor from the actual skyscraper to the model is $\frac{1}{120}$.

> **Science Link**
> The largest ape in the world is the gorilla. An adult male usually weighs between 300 and 400 pounds.

The statement $\triangle ABC \sim \triangle EFD$ says that $\triangle ABC$ is similar to $\triangle EFD$. The order of the letters shows the corresponding parts. When you write a similarity statement, be sure to list the parts in the right order.

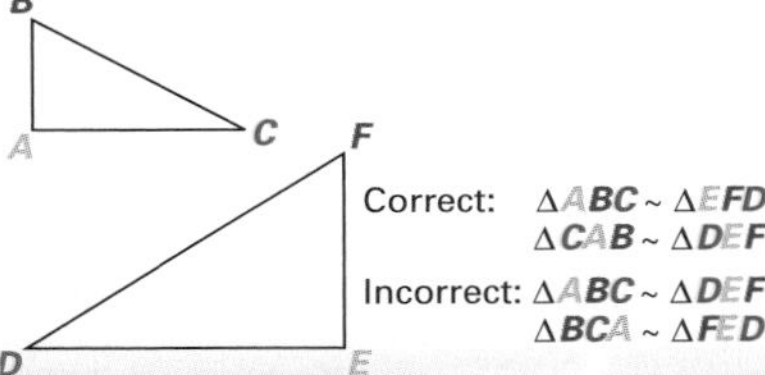

MATH EVERY DAY

Problem of the Day

How many similar triangles are in the figure below?

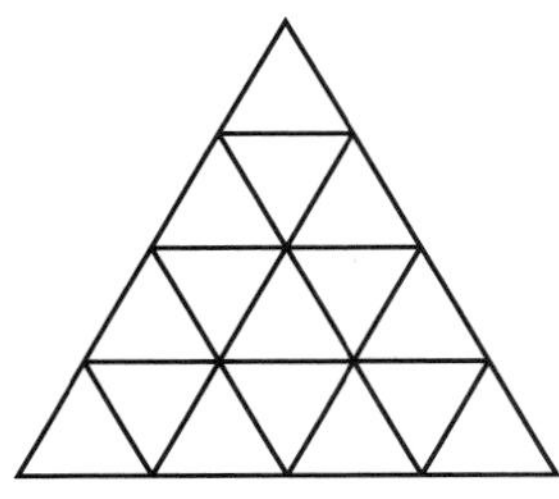

26 triangles

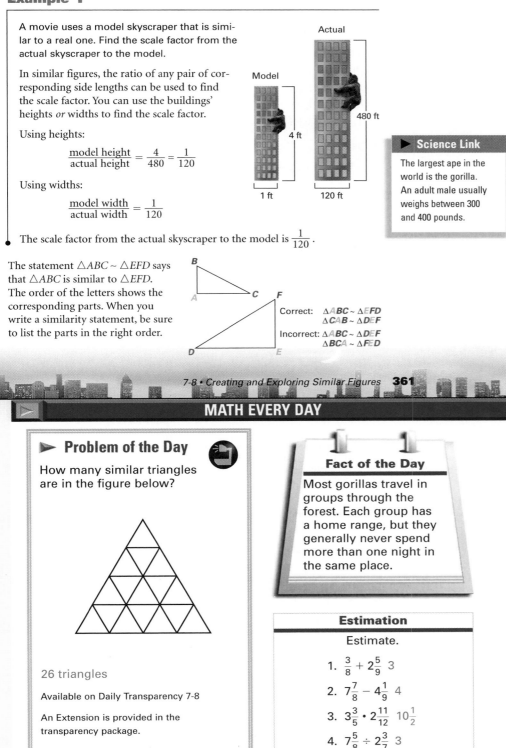

Available on Daily Transparency 7-8

An Extension is provided in the transparency package.

Fact of the Day

Most gorillas travel in groups through the forest. Each group has a home range, but they generally never spend more than one night in the same place.

Estimation

Estimate.

1. $\frac{3}{8} + 2\frac{5}{9}$ 3
2. $7\frac{7}{8} - 4\frac{1}{9}$ 4
3. $3\frac{3}{5} \cdot 2\frac{11}{12}$ $10\frac{1}{2}$
4. $7\frac{5}{8} \div 2\frac{3}{7}$ 3

For Groups That Finish Early

Suppose you enlarged a picture of a house by multiplying each length of the original picture by 20. Would this house have the same shape as the original? Yes What can you say about the measures of the angles? They are equal.

Answers for Explore

1.

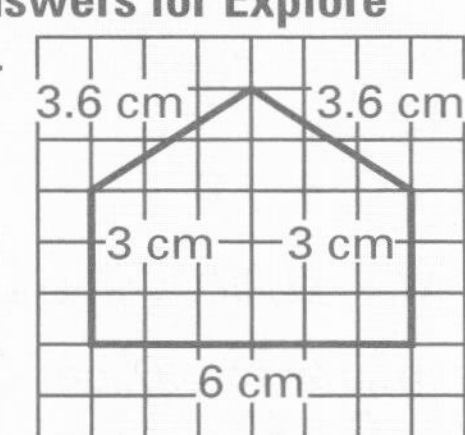

2.

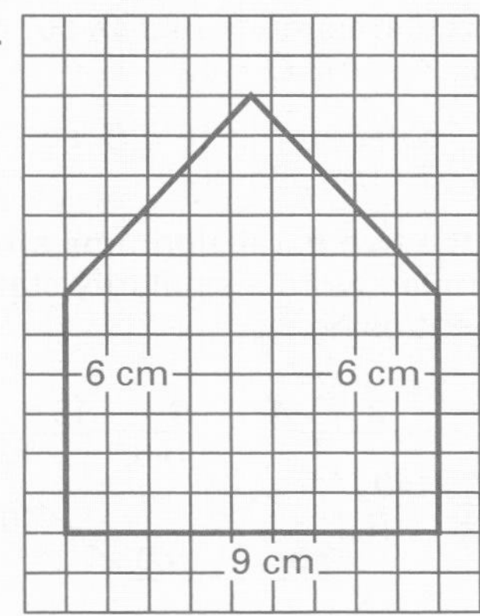

Answers for Steps 3–6 on page C1.

2 Teach

Learn

You might want to use Lesson Enhancement Transparency 32 with **Learn**.

Alternate Example

1. A disaster movie uses a model of a school. The real school is 50 ft high and 220 ft long; the model is 5 ft high and 22 ft long. Find the scale factor from the model school to the real school. Use the heights or lengths to find the scale factor.

   Using heights:
   $$\frac{\text{actual height}}{\text{model height}} = \frac{50}{5} = 10$$
   Using lengths:
   $$\frac{\text{actual length}}{\text{model length}} = \frac{220}{22} = 10$$
   The scale factor from the model to the real school is 10.

Alternate Examples

2. $\Delta CAT \sim \Delta DOG$. Find the measures of $\angle D$, $\angle O$, and $\angle G$.

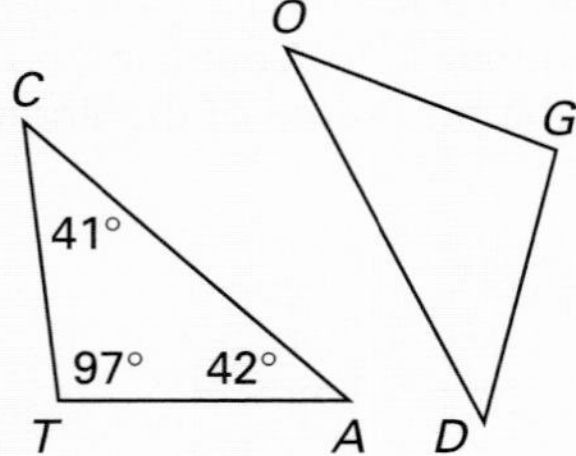

Since $\Delta CAT \sim \Delta DOG$, you know:

$\angle C$ corresponds to $\angle D$, so $m\angle C = m\angle D = 41°$.

$\angle A$ corresponds to $\angle O$, so $m\angle A = m\angle O = 42°$.

$\angle T$ corresponds to $\angle G$, so $m\angle T = m\angle G = 97°$.

3. If the two parallelograms are similar, write a similarity statement using ~.

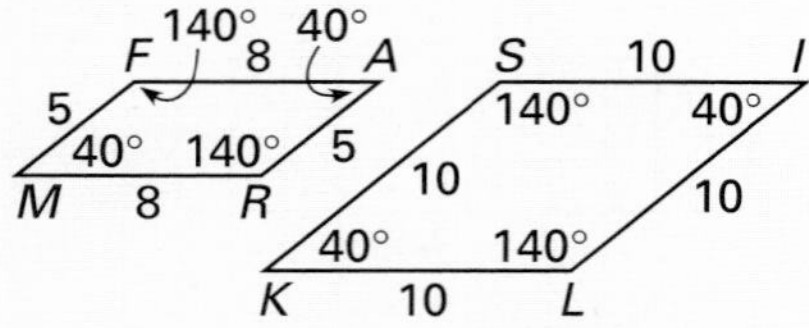

Check that corresponding angles are congruent.

$\angle F \cong \angle S$; $\angle A \cong \angle I$; $\angle R \cong \angle L$; $\angle M \cong \angle K$.

Check that corresponding side lengths have equal ratios.

$\frac{10}{5} = 2$, $\frac{10}{8} = \frac{5}{4}$,

$\frac{10}{5} = 2$,

$\frac{10}{8} = \frac{5}{4}$.

They are not similar.

3 Practice and Assess

Check

Answers for Check Your Understanding

1. Similar figures have the same shape.
2. Yes; No.
3. Possible answer: In everyday use, *similar* means "almost alike." Differences may be slight. Mathematically, *similar* always means having corresponding angles congruent and corresponding side lengths proportional.

Study TIP

To check whether you understand the definition of a geometric term, see if you can draw a picture that illustrates the definition.

Example 2

$\triangle PQR \sim \triangle TUS$. Find the measures of $\angle S$, $\angle T$, and $\angle U$.

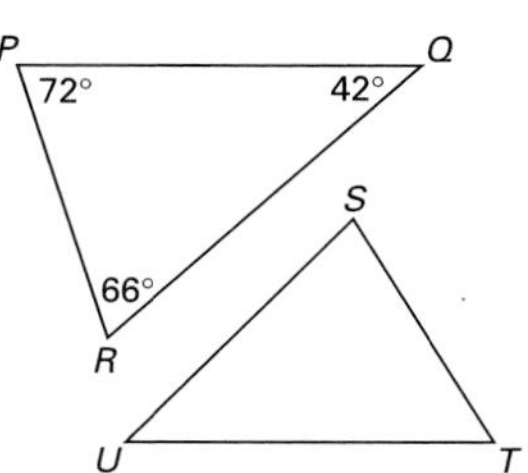

Since $\triangle PQR \sim \triangle TUS$, you know:

$\angle T$ corresponds to $\angle P$, so $m\angle T = m\angle P = 72°$.

$\angle U$ corresponds to $\angle Q$, so $m\angle U = m\angle Q = 42°$.

$\angle S$ corresponds to $\angle R$, so $m\angle S = m\angle R = 66°$.

To see if two figures are similar, check that their corresponding angles are congruent *and* their corresponding side lengths have equal ratios.

Example 3

Tell whether the trapezoids are similar. If they are, write a similarity statement using ~.

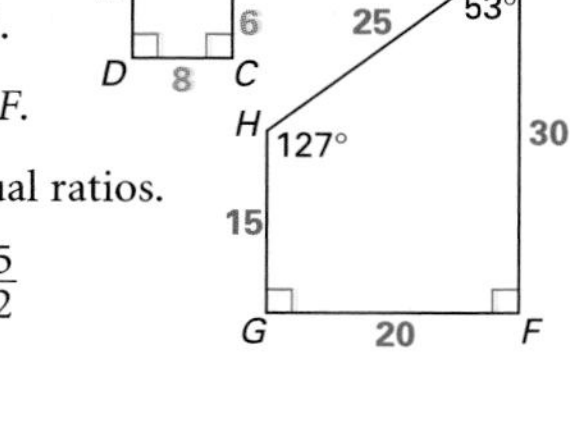

Check that corresponding angles are congruent.

$\angle A \cong \angle E$; $\angle B \cong \angle H$; $\angle C \cong \angle G$; and $\angle D \cong \angle F$.

Check that corresponding side lengths have equal ratios.

$\frac{25}{10} = \frac{5}{2}$ $\quad \frac{30}{12} = \frac{5}{2}$ $\quad \frac{20}{8} = \frac{5}{2}$ $\quad \frac{15}{6} = \frac{5}{2}$

The trapezoids are similar: $ABCD \sim EHGF$.

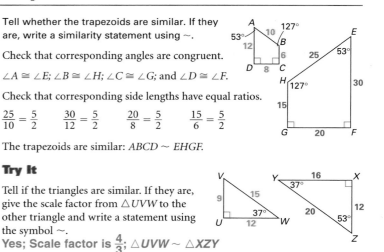

Try It

Tell if the triangles are similar. If they are, give the scale factor from $\triangle UVW$ to the other triangle and write a statement using the symbol ~.

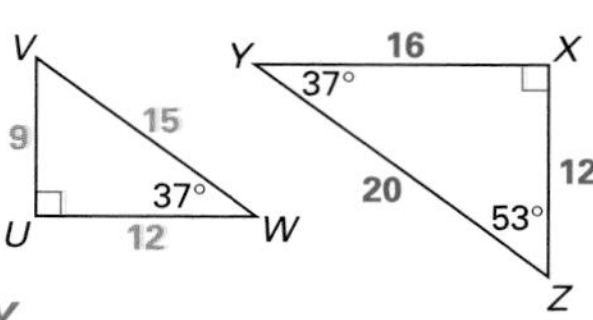

Yes; Scale factor is $\frac{4}{3}$; $\triangle UVW \sim \triangle XZY$

Check Your Understanding

1. Why must similar figures have congruent corresponding angles?
2. Are all squares similar? Are all rectangles similar?
3. How does the everyday use of the word *similar* differ from the mathematical use of the word?

MEETING MIDDLE SCHOOL CLASSROOM NEEDS

Tips from Middle School Teachers

I like to have each student draw a picture using coordinates and then enlarge his or her pictures for a bulletin-board display.

Team Teaching

Work with an art teacher and have the students create designs using similar figures.

Literature Connection

H. G. Wells often is considered the father of modern science fiction. He began writing science stories in 1894, and wrote about traveling in submarines and airplanes long before they were invented. Among his well-known publications are *The Time Machine* in 1895, *The Island of Dr. Moreau* in 1896, *The Invisible Man* in 1897, *The War of the Worlds* in 1898, and *The First Men in the Moon* in 1901.

7-8 Exercises and Applications

Practice and Apply

1. **Getting Started** Follow the steps to check that the two triangles are similar and to find the scale factor from $\triangle ABC$ to the other triangle.

a. Decide how the figures correspond. Which angle corresponds to $\angle A$? To $\angle B$? To $\angle C$?

b. Check that each angle has the same measure as its corresponding angle.

c. Which side corresponds to $\overline{AB}$? Find the ratio of that side's length to the length of $\overline{AB}$. Repeat for $\overline{BC}$ and $\overline{AC}$.

d. Check that all three ratios are equal. What is the scale factor from $\triangle ABC$ to the other triangle?

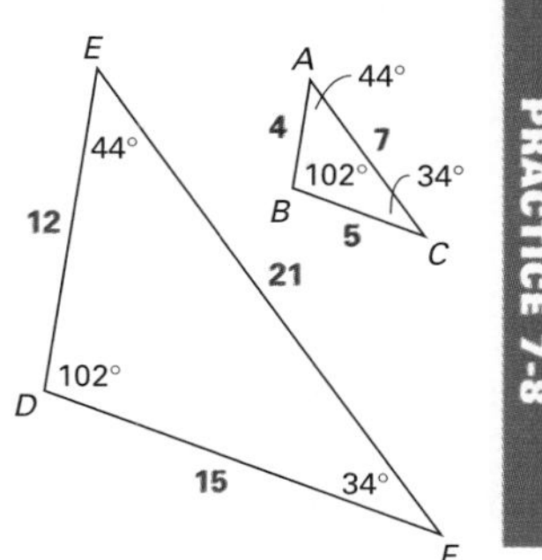

Geometry Tell if the figures are similar. If they are, write a similarity statement using ~ and give the scale factor. If they're not, explain why not.

2.

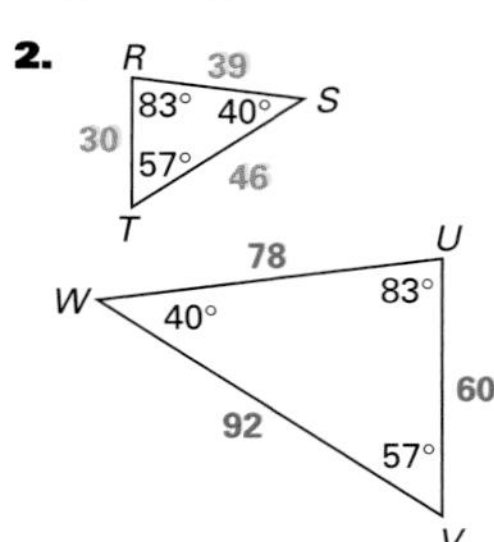

3.

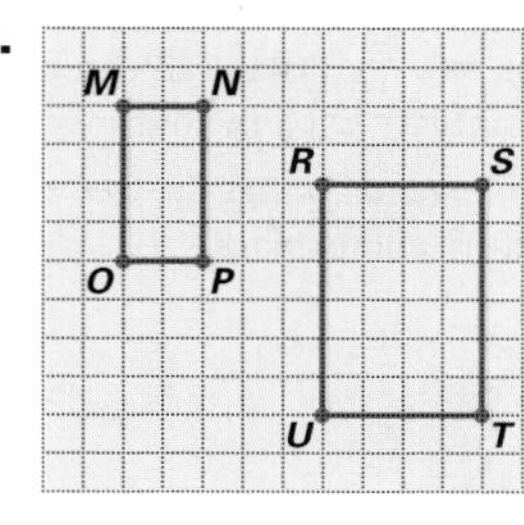

4.

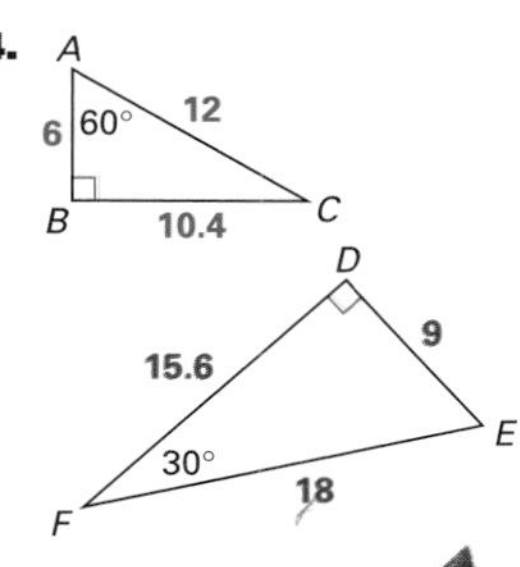

5. Draw two rectangles that are similar and two that are not similar. **Answers may vary**

6. Tammy drew the two monsters shown. Are they mathematically similar? Explain why or why not.
No; Because they are not exactly the same shape.

7. Suppose $\triangle UVW \sim \triangle ZYX$. If $m\angle X = 96°$, $m\angle Y = 46°$, and $m\angle Z = 38°$, find the measures of $\angle U$, $\angle V$, and $\angle W$.
$m\angle U = 38°$; $m\angle V = 46°$; $m\angle W = 96°$

8. GPS Suppose $\triangle ABC \sim \triangle DEF$. The length of $\overline{AB}$ is 8, the length of $\overline{BC}$ is 10, the length of $\overline{CA}$ is 12, and the length of $\overline{DE}$ is 12. Find the lengths of $\overline{EF}$ and $\overline{FD}$.

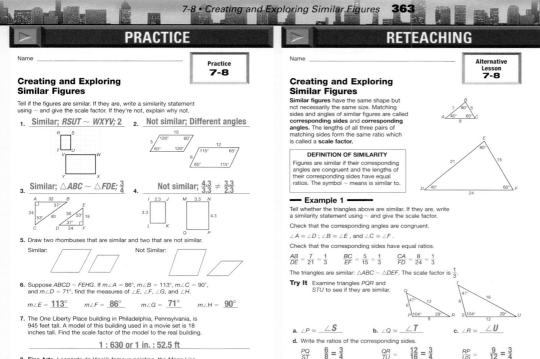

PRACTICE 7-8

PRACTICE

Name ______________________

Practice 7-8

Creating and Exploring Similar Figures

Tell if the figures are similar. If they are, write a similarity statement using ~ and give the scale factor. If they're not, explain why not.

1. **Similar; $RSUT \sim WXYV$; 2**
2. **Not similar; Different angles**

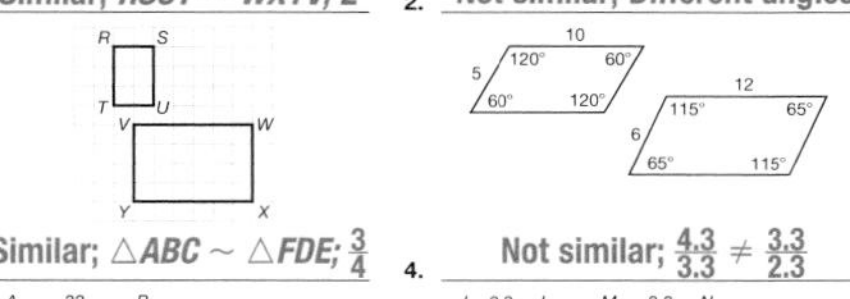

3. **Similar; $\triangle ABC \sim \triangle FDE$; $\frac{3}{4}$**
4. **Not similar; $\frac{4.3}{3.3} \neq \frac{3.3}{2.3}$**

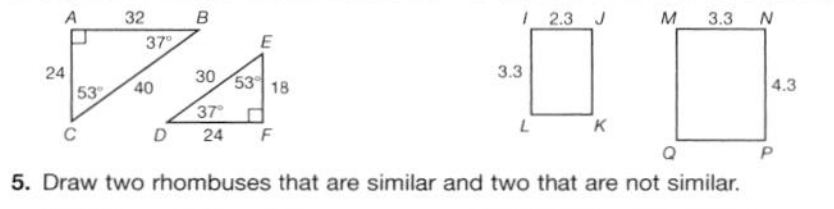

5. Draw two rhombuses that are similar and two that are not similar.

Similar: Not Similar:

6. Suppose $ABCD \sim FEHG$. If $m\angle A = 86°$, $m\angle B = 113°$, $m\angle C = 90°$, and $m\angle D = 71°$, find the measures of $\angle E$, $\angle F$, $\angle G$, and $\angle H$.

$m\angle E =$ **113°** $m\angle F =$ **86°** $m\angle G =$ **71°** $m\angle H =$ **90°**

7. The One Liberty Place building in Philadelphia, Pennsylvania, is 945 feet tall. A model of this building used in a movie set is 18 inches tall. Find the scale factor of the model to the real building.

1 : 630 or 1 in. : 52.5 ft

8. **Fine Arts** Leonardo da Vinci's famous painting, the *Mona Lisa*, measures 53 cm × 77.5 cm. Suppose a postcard reproduction of the painting measures 12 cm × 17 cm. Is the postcard similar to the original? Explain.

No. Possible explanation: $\frac{12}{53} \neq \frac{17}{77.5}$

RETEACHING

Name ______________________

Alternative Lesson 7-8

Creating and Exploring Similar Figures

Similar figures have the same shape but not necessarily the same size. Matching sides and angles of similar figures are called **corresponding sides** and **corresponding angles.** The lengths of all three pairs of matching sides form the same ratio which is called a **scale factor.**

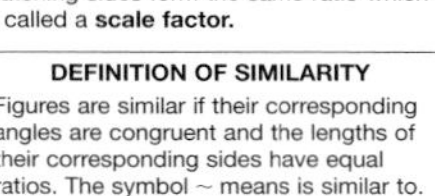

DEFINITION OF SIMILARITY

Figures are similar if their corresponding angles are congruent and the lengths of their corresponding sides have equal ratios. The symbol ~ means is similar to.

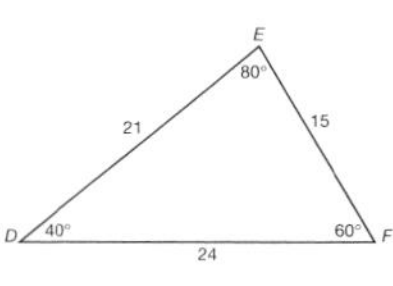

Example 1

Tell whether the triangles above are similar. If they are, write a similarity statement using ~ and give the scale factor.

Check that the corresponding angles are congruent.

$\angle A \cong \angle D$; $\angle B \cong \angle E$, and $\angle C \cong \angle F$.

Check that the corresponding sides have equal ratios.

$\frac{AB}{DE} = \frac{7}{21} = \frac{1}{3}$ $\frac{BC}{EF} = \frac{5}{15} = \frac{1}{3}$ $\frac{CA}{FD} = \frac{8}{24} = \frac{1}{3}$

The triangles are similar: $\triangle ABC \sim \triangle DEF$. The scale factor is $\frac{1}{3}$.

Try It Examine triangles *PQR* and *STU* to see if they are similar.

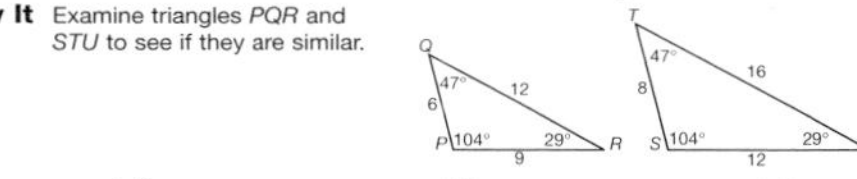

a. $\angle P \cong$ **$\angle S$** b. $\angle Q \cong$ **$\angle T$** c. $\angle R \cong$ **$\angle U$**

d. Write the ratios of the corresponding sides.

$\frac{PQ}{ST}$ **$\frac{6}{8} = \frac{3}{4}$** $\frac{QR}{TU} =$ **$\frac{12}{16} = \frac{3}{4}$** $\frac{RP}{US} =$ **$\frac{9}{12} = \frac{3}{4}$**

e. Are the ratios equal? **Yes.**

f. Are the triangles similar? Explain. **Yes, The ratios of the corresponding sides are equal and the corresponding angles are congruent.**

7-8 Exercises and Applications

Assignment Guide

- Basic
  1–9, 11, 14–22 evens
- Average
  1–13, 15–23 odds
- Enriched
  2–14, 15–23 odds

Exercise Notes

Exercises 2 and 4

Error Prevention Some students may not recognize figures as similar when one of the figures has been turned. Suggest that they trace and cut out the figures. The cut-outs can be turned to any orientation.

Exercise Answers

1. a. $\angle E$, $\angle D$, $\angle F$.
   b. Corresponding angles are congruent.
   c. $\overline{ED}$, $\frac{3}{1}$; $\overline{DF}$, $\frac{3}{1}$; $\overline{EF}$, $\frac{3}{1}$.
   d. The ratios are the same; Scale factor is $\frac{3}{1}$ or $\frac{1}{3}$.
2. $\Delta RST \sim \Delta UWV$, $\frac{2}{1}$ or $\frac{1}{2}$.
3. *MNPO* is not similar to *RSTU*. $RS = 2(MN)$, $RU = \frac{3}{2}(MO)$.
4. $\Delta ABC \sim \Delta EDF$; $\frac{3}{2}$ or $\frac{2}{3}$.
8. The length of $\overline{EF}$ is 15; The length of $\overline{FD}$ is 18.

Reteaching

Activity

Materials: Protractor, graph paper, metric ruler

- Work with a partner. Draw a diagram on graph paper. Then shrink or enlarge your picture and record the scale factor. Do not show your work to your partner.
- Give your partner directions for drawing your picture. Do not look at your partner's drawing.
- Compare all three drawings. Label the points. Are all three figures similar? If they are similar, write three similarity statements and give the scale factors. If they are not similar, explain why not.

Exercise Notes

Exercise 13

Error Prevention Students who have difficulty with this problem may find it helpful to act out the problem with actual objects.

Exercise Answers

12. Yes; To be similar, corresponding sides must be in the same proportion. It is possible to draw figures with corresponding angles congruent but with corresponding sides not proportional.

13.

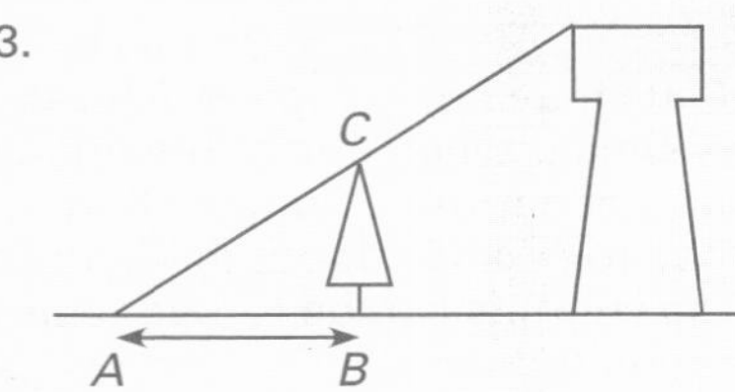

Anywhere on line segment $\overline{AB}$.

14. 1; Each side has been multiplied by 1 to maintain the congruence.

Alternate Assessment

Interview Ask students to record their response to the following question on an audiotape: How can you tell whether two figures are similar or not?

▶ Quick Quiz

1. $\Delta ARK \sim \Delta DIP$. If $m\angle A = 44°$, $m\angle R = 72°$, and $m\angle K = 64°$, find the measures of $\angle D$, $\angle I$, and $\angle P$.
   $m\angle D = 44°$
   $m\angle I = 72°$
   $m\angle P = 64°$.
2. Draw and label two triangles that are similar. Answers may vary.
3. Sharon is enlarging a 3″ × 5″ map to poster size. Would a 20″ × 32″ poster be similar to the original map?
   No, $\frac{20}{3} \approx 6.67$ and $\frac{32}{5} = 6.4$.

Available on Daily Transparency 7-8

PROBLEM SOLVING 7-8

9. In the movie *Ghostbusters,* the massive Stay-Puft Marshmallow Man terrorized New York City. A child's toy version of the Marshmallow Man is 10 inches tall. Assume that the Marshmallow Man was supposed to be 800 feet tall. Find the scale factor from the toy to the "real" monster. $\frac{1 \text{ in.}}{80 \text{ ft.}}$

10. Fine Arts Motion pictures can be projected onto a screen, played on a videotape machine, broadcast over television, and even shown in clips on a computer. Which of these rectangular screens is similar to a computer screen that measures 10 in. by 14 in.? b and c

a. A miniature TV screen 2 in. by 3 in.

b. A TV monitor 17.5 in. by 24.5 in.

c. A movie screen 20 ft by 28 ft

11. Test Prep Which similarity statement is *not* correct? B

Ⓐ $\Delta EFG \sim \Delta RTS$ Ⓑ $\Delta GEF \sim \Delta STR$

Ⓒ $\Delta GFE \sim \Delta STR$ Ⓓ $\Delta FGE \sim \Delta TSR$

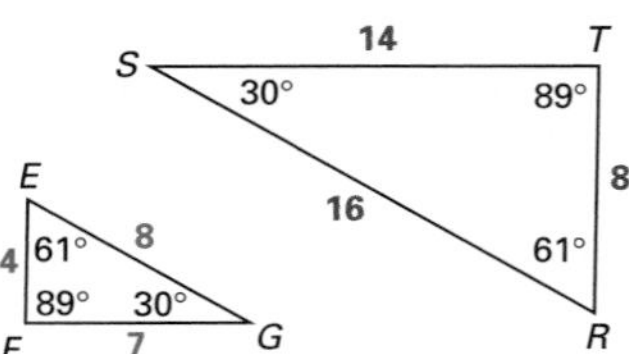

Problem Solving and Reasoning

12. Critical Thinking Do you think two quadrilaterals can have four pairs of congruent angles but not be similar? Explain your answer.

13. Communicate Where would you stand so that the tree appears taller than the lighthouse? Draw a picture and explain. Answers may vary.

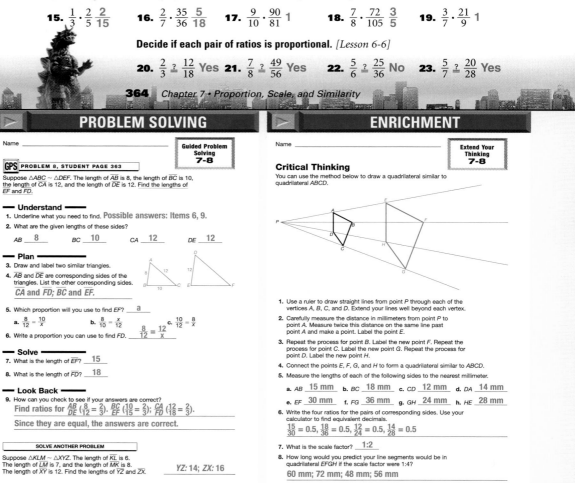

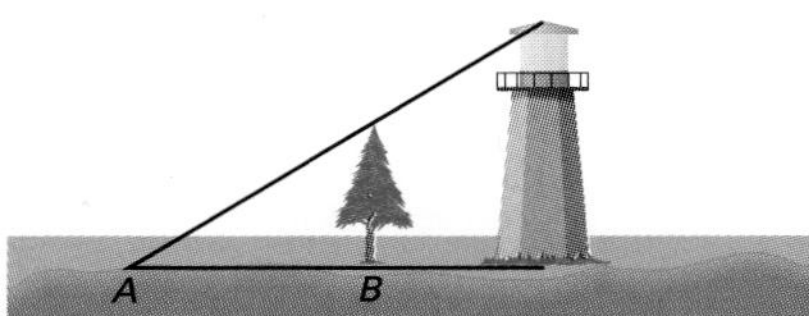

14. Critical Thinking Similar figures that have the same size are *congruent figures.* What is the scale factor for two congruent figures? Explain.

Mixed Review

Find each product. Write your answers in lowest terms. *[Lesson 4-4]*

15. $\frac{1}{3} \cdot \frac{2}{5}$ $\frac{2}{15}$ **16.** $\frac{2}{7} \cdot \frac{35}{36}$ $\frac{5}{18}$ **17.** $\frac{9}{10} \cdot \frac{90}{81}$ 1 **18.** $\frac{7}{8} \cdot \frac{72}{105}$ $\frac{3}{5}$ **19.** $\frac{3}{7} \cdot \frac{21}{9}$ 1

Decide if each pair of ratios is proportional. *[Lesson 6-6]*

20. $\frac{2}{3} \stackrel{?}{=} \frac{12}{18}$ Yes **21.** $\frac{7}{8} \stackrel{?}{=} \frac{49}{56}$ Yes **22.** $\frac{5}{6} \stackrel{?}{=} \frac{25}{36}$ No **23.** $\frac{5}{7} \stackrel{?}{=} \frac{20}{28}$ Yes

---

PROBLEM SOLVING

Name ______

Guided Problem Solving 7-8

GPS PROBLEM 8, STUDENT PAGE 363

Suppose $\triangle ABC \sim \triangle DEF$. The length of $\overline{AB}$ is 8, the length of $\overline{BC}$ is 10, the length of $\overline{CA}$ is 12, and the length of $\overline{DE}$ is 12. Find the lengths of $\overline{EF}$ and $\overline{FD}$.

— Understand —

1. Underline what you need to find. Possible answers: Items 6, 9.
2. What are the given lengths of these sides?

AB 8 BC 10 CA 12 DE 12

— Plan —

3. Draw and label two similar triangles.
4. $\overline{AB}$ and $\overline{DE}$ are corresponding sides of the triangles. List the other corresponding sides. $\overline{CA}$ and $\overline{FD}$; $\overline{BC}$ and $\overline{EF}$.

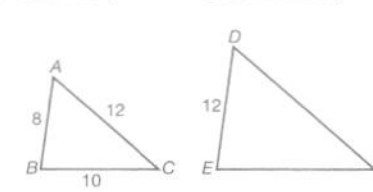

5. Which proportion will you use to find EF? a

a. $\frac{8}{12} = \frac{10}{x}$ b. $\frac{8}{10} = \frac{x}{12}$ c. $\frac{10}{12} = \frac{8}{x}$

6. Write a proportion you can use to find FD. $\frac{8}{12} = \frac{12}{x}$

— Solve —

7. What is the length of $\overline{EF}$? 15
8. What is the length of $\overline{FD}$? 18

— Look Back —

9. How can you check to see if your answers are correct?
Find ratios for $\frac{AB}{DE}$ $(\frac{8}{12} = \frac{2}{3})$. $\frac{BC}{EF}$ $(\frac{10}{15} = \frac{2}{3})$; $\frac{CA}{FD}$ $(\frac{12}{18} = \frac{2}{3})$.
Since they are equal, the answers are correct.

SOLVE ANOTHER PROBLEM

Suppose $\triangle KLM \sim \triangle XYZ$. The length of $\overline{KL}$ is 6. The length of $\overline{LM}$ is 7, and the length of $\overline{MK}$ is 8. The length of $\overline{XY}$ is 12. Find the lengths of $\overline{YZ}$ and $\overline{ZX}$. YZ: 14; ZX: 16

ENRICHMENT

Name ______

Extend Your Thinking 7-8

Critical Thinking

You can use the method below to draw a quadrilateral similar to quadrilateral *ABCD*.

1. Use a ruler to draw straight lines from point *P* through each of the vertices *A*, *B*, *C*, and *D*. Extend your lines well beyond each vertex.
2. Carefully measure the distance in millimeters from point *P* to point *A*. Measure twice this distance on the same line past point *A* and make a point. Label the point *E*.
3. Repeat the process for point *B*. Label the new point *F*. Repeat the process for point *C*. Label the new point *G*. Repeat the process for point *D*. Label the new point *H*.
4. Connect the points *E*, *F*, *G*, and *H* to form a quadrilateral similar to *ABCD*.
5. Measure the lengths of each of the following sides to the nearest millimeter.

a. AB 15 mm b. BC 18 mm c. CD 12 mm d. DA 14 mm
e. EF 30 mm f. FG 36 mm g. GH 24 mm h. HE 28 mm

6. Write the four ratios for the pairs of corresponding sides. Use your calculator to find equivalent decimals.
$\frac{15}{30} = 0.5$, $\frac{18}{36} = 0.5$, $\frac{12}{24} = 0.5$, $\frac{14}{28} = 0.5$
7. What is the scale factor? 1:2
8. How long would you predict your line segments would be in quadrilateral *EFGH* if the scale factor were 1:4?
60 mm; 72 mm; 48 mm; 56 mm

TECHNOLOGY

Using Dynamic Geometry Software • Exploring Dilations

Problem: How can you construct a polygon similar to a given polygon using a scale factor of 2.5?

You can use dynamic geometry software to construct the polygon. A *dilation* is an enlargement or reduction of a geometric figure. A dilation results in a figure similar to the original figure.

1. **Use your software to make a triangle. Then choose "numerical edit" from the label menu and type 2.5 somewhere outside the triangle.**

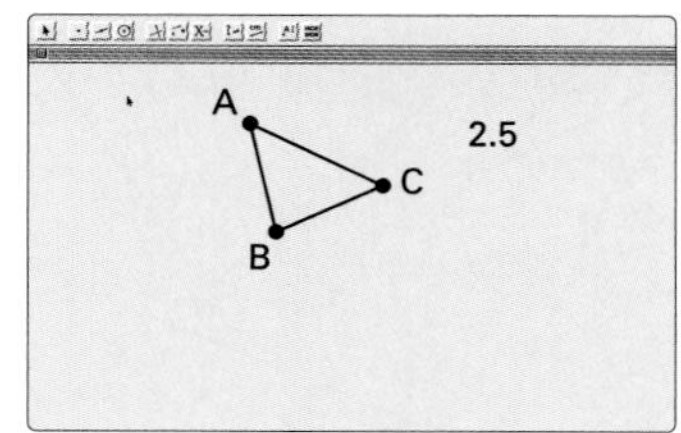

2. **Create a dilation of the triangle. Make point *A* the center of the dilation and use a scale factor of 2.5.**

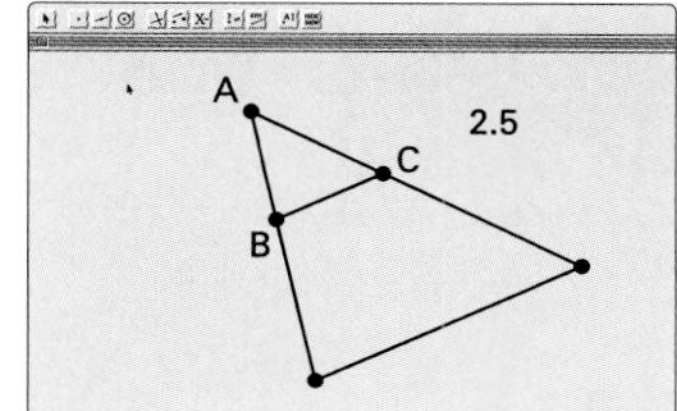

Solution: The result of the dilation is a triangle that is similar to $\triangle ABC$ using a scale factor of 2.5.

TRY IT

a. Use geometry software to draw a triangle. Then use a dilation to construct a similar triangle using a scale factor of 3. Sketch the result.

b. Use geometry software to draw a rectangle. Then use a dilation to construct a similar rectangle using a scale factor of $\frac{1}{2}$. Sketch the result.

ON YOUR OWN

- What do you think would happen if you dilated a figure using a scale factor of 7, then reduced the dilation using a scale factor of $\frac{1}{7}$? Use geometry software to test your idea.
- Why do you think you need to type a number before the computer can do the dilation?

Technology

Using Dynamic Geometry Software • Exploring Dilations

The Point
Students use dynamic geometry software to create larger or smaller similar figures.

Materials
Dynamic geometry software

Resources

Interactive CD-ROM Geometry Tool

About the Page

- You might want to work through this lesson before using it with your class so you can modify the steps to match the software you are planning to use.
- If students are not familiar with the dynamic software, you might want to demonstrate some of the basic features.
- In Step 2, have students also try clicking on points *B* and *C,* and observe the resulting figures.

Ask ...
How could you make a similar figure that is smaller than the original? Enter a number less than 1 for the scale factor.

Answers for Try It
a. See student sketches.
b. See student sketches.

On Your Own

- For the first question, ask why 7 and $\frac{1}{7}$ were chosen. Then ask what other pairs of numbers could have been chosen to illustrate the point. Because they are reciprocals of each other; Possible answers: 2 and $\frac{1}{2}$, 3 and $\frac{1}{3}$, or any pair of reciprocals.
- Ask students what would have been the result in the first question if 8 and $\frac{1}{4}$ had been chosen. The resulting figure would be twice the size of the original.

Answers for On Your Own

- The result of the second dilation is identical to the original figure.
- The number designates the size of the enlargement or reduction relative to the original figure.

7-9 Lesson Organizer

Objectives

- Find missing side lengths in similar figures.
- Use shadows to find the heights of tall objects.

Materials

- Explore: Protractor, ruler

NCTM Standards

- 1–4, 12, 13

➤ Review

1. Draw a triangle with sides of 5 cm and 5 cm, and a base of 6 cm.
2. Use the Pythagorean Theorem to find the height of your triangle. 4 cm
3. Find the area of the triangle. 12 cm^2
4. Find the perimeter of the triangle. 16 cm

Available on Daily Transparency 7-9

1 Introduce

Explore

You might want to use Lesson Enhancement Transparency 33 and Teaching Tool Transparencies 14: Rulers and 15: Protractor with **Explore**.

The Point
Students measure sides and angles in order to decide which triangles are similar.

Ongoing Assessment
Some students may need assistance in organizing their data; you may wish to provide a chart that structures their work.

7-9 Finding Measures of Similar Figures

You'll Learn ...

- to find missing side lengths in similar figures
- to use shadows to find the heights of tall objects

... How It's Used

The methods geographers use to find the height of a mountain are based on similar triangles

▶ Lesson Link You've seen that similar figures have the same shape, but not necessarily the same size. Now you'll use proportions to find side lengths in similar figures. ◀

Explore Measures of Similar Figures

Maybe It Just LOOKS Similar!

Materials: Protractor, Ruler

1. Find all pairs of similar triangles in the set of six triangles. For each pair, write a similarity statement, using ~, and find a scale factor.

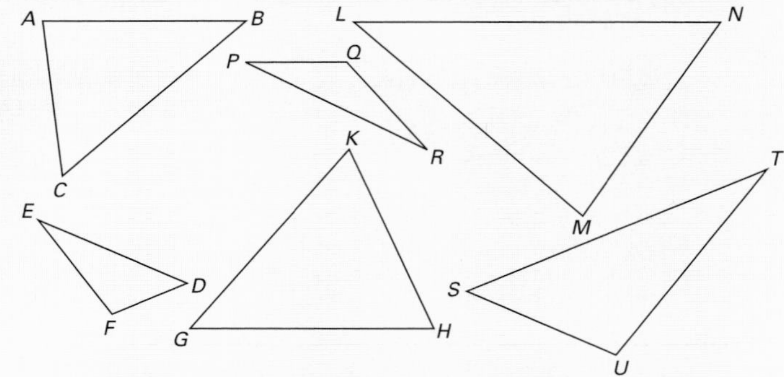

2. For each pair of similar triangles, write a paragraph explaining why you're sure they are similar.
3. Suppose $\triangle XYZ \sim \triangle ABC$ and the scale factor from $\triangle XYZ$ to $\triangle ABC$ is 3. Find the angle measures and side lengths in $\triangle XYZ$.

Learn Finding Measures of Similar Figures

You can use proportions to solve problems about side lengths of similar figures.

By applying this idea, you may be able to find a real-world length or distance that you would not be able to measure with a ruler or tape measure. This technique is called *indirect measurement.*

MEETING INDIVIDUAL NEEDS

Resources

- **7-9** Practice
- **7-9** Reteaching
- **7-9** Problem Solving
- **7-9** Enrichment
- **7-9** Daily Transparency
  - Problem of the Day
  - Review
  - Quick Quiz
- Teaching Tool Transparencies 14, 15
- Technology Master 31
- Lesson Enhancement Transparency 33
- Chapter 7 Project Master

Learning Modalities

Visual Use colored chalk to highlight corresponding sides of similar figures.

Kinesthetic Have students use pattern blocks or tangram pieces to make designs and then enlarge or reduce the design so it fits on a particular size of paper.

Social Ask a student to do a presentation for the class on a hobby that involves using similar figures—photography, quilting, dollhouses, etc.

Inclusion

Some students may be able to recognize similar figures when they are side by side but not when the figures are turned or flipped. Make a set of cardboard triangles in different shapes, each of which can be "matched" with at least one other similar triangle. Mix the cards randomly and have students pick up and match them to form similar pairs. Or, let students use tracing paper to copy a second figure so they might rotate it to see the relationship to the first figure.

Examples

1 If $\triangle ABC \sim \triangle DEF$, find x, the length of $\overline{EF}$.

The triangles are similar, so corresponding side lengths are proportional.

$\frac{12}{15} = \frac{x}{10}$ Write a proportion.

$120 = 15x$ Find the cross products.

$\frac{120}{15} = \frac{15x}{15}$ To undo multiplication by 15, divide both sides by 15.

$8 = x$ Divide.

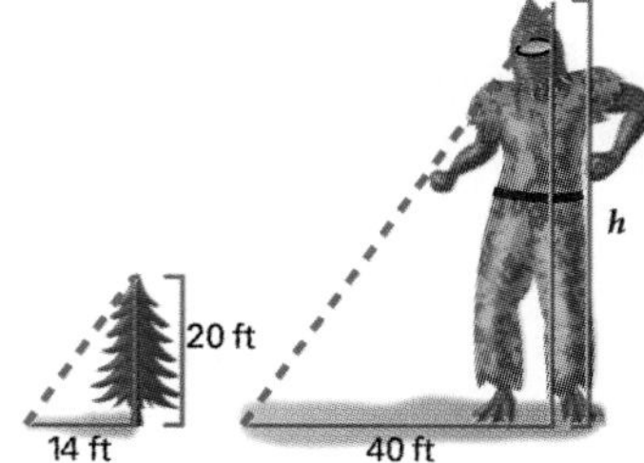

The length of $\overline{EF}$ is 8 units.

2 Director I. M. Skerry is making a new movie, *Shadows of Terror.* In one scene, the shadow of a 20-foot-tall tree is 14 feet long. At the same time, the monster's shadow is 40 feet long. How tall is the monster?

Because the sun's rays come in at the same angle, the triangles formed by the objects and their shadows are similar.

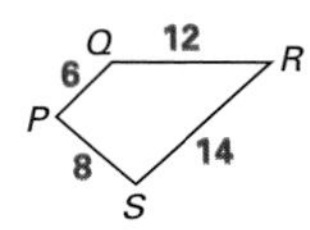
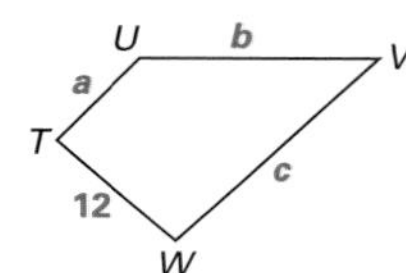

$\frac{h}{20} = \frac{40}{14}$ Write a proportion.

$14h = 800$ Find the cross products.

$\frac{14h}{14} = \frac{800}{14}$ To undo multiplication by 14, divide both sides by 14.

$h \approx 57.14$ Divide.

The monster is about 57.14 feet (nearly 57 feet 2 inches) tall.

Try It

$PQRS \sim TUVW$. Find a, b, and c.

$a = 9, b = 18, c = 21$

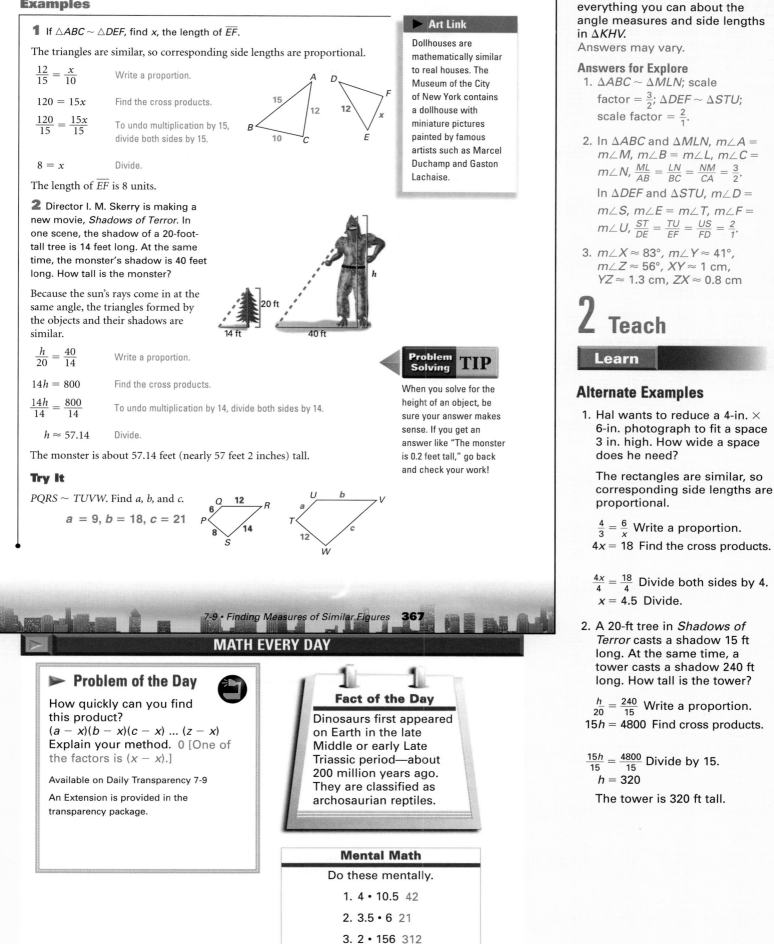

▶ Art Link

Dollhouses are mathematically similar to real houses. The Museum of the City of New York contains a dollhouse with miniature pictures painted by famous artists such as Marcel Duchamp and Gaston Lachaise.

Problem Solving TIP

When you solve for the height of an object, be sure your answer makes sense. If you get an answer like "The monster is 0.2 feet tall," go back and check your work!

For Groups That Finish Early

Suppose $\Delta KHV \sim \Delta KGH$. Tell everything you can about the angle measures and side lengths in ΔKHV.

Answers may vary.

Answers for Explore

1. $\Delta ABC \sim \Delta MLN$; scale factor $= \frac{3}{2}$; $\Delta DEF \sim \Delta STU$; scale factor $= \frac{2}{1}$.
2. In ΔABC and ΔMLN, $m\angle A = m\angle M$, $m\angle B = m\angle L$, $m\angle C = m\angle N$, $\frac{ML}{AB} = \frac{LN}{BC} = \frac{NM}{CA} = \frac{3}{2}$. In ΔDEF and ΔSTU, $m\angle D = m\angle S$, $m\angle E = m\angle T$, $m\angle F = m\angle U$, $\frac{ST}{DE} = \frac{TU}{EF} = \frac{US}{FD} = \frac{2}{1}$.
3. $m\angle X \approx 83°$, $m\angle Y \approx 41°$, $m\angle Z \approx 56°$, $XY \approx 1$ cm, $YZ \approx 1.3$ cm, $ZX \approx 0.8$ cm

2 Teach

Learn

Alternate Examples

1. Hal wants to reduce a 4-in. × 6-in. photograph to fit a space 3 in. high. How wide a space does he need?

   The rectangles are similar, so corresponding side lengths are proportional.

   $\frac{4}{3} = \frac{6}{x}$ Write a proportion.
   $4x = 18$ Find the cross products.

   $\frac{4x}{4} = \frac{18}{4}$ Divide both sides by 4.
   $x = 4.5$ Divide.

2. A 20-ft tree in *Shadows of Terror* casts a shadow 15 ft long. At the same time, a tower casts a shadow 240 ft long. How tall is the tower?

   $\frac{h}{20} = \frac{240}{15}$ Write a proportion.
   $15h = 4800$ Find cross products.

   $\frac{15h}{15} = \frac{4800}{15}$ Divide by 15.
   $h = 320$

   The tower is 320 ft tall.

MATH EVERY DAY

▶ Problem of the Day

How quickly can you find this product?
$(a - x)(b - x)(c - x) \ldots (z - x)$
Explain your method. 0 [One of the factors is $(x - x)$.]

Available on Daily Transparency 7-9

An Extension is provided in the transparency package.

Fact of the Day

Dinosaurs first appeared on Earth in the late Middle or early Late Triassic period—about 200 million years ago. They are classified as archosaurian reptiles.

Mental Math

Do these mentally.

1. 4 • 10.5 42
2. 3.5 • 6 21
3. 2 • 156 312

Students see two methods for finding the missing side lengths in similar figures. They can decide which of the two methods they prefer.

Answers for What Do You Think?

1. Because each uses the correct scale factor, Wendy's method is actually the same as Luis's without naming a variable.
2. $\frac{18}{25}$ foot

3 Practice and Assess

Check

Be sure that students understand that maps involve similar figures, the one on the map and the one in the real world. Also, you may find that students need to draw a diagram for the second question.

Answers for Check Your Understanding

1. The land and the map are similar figures with a scale factor equal to the scale of the map.
2. Measure your shadow and the shadow of the tower. Set up a proportion and solve it.

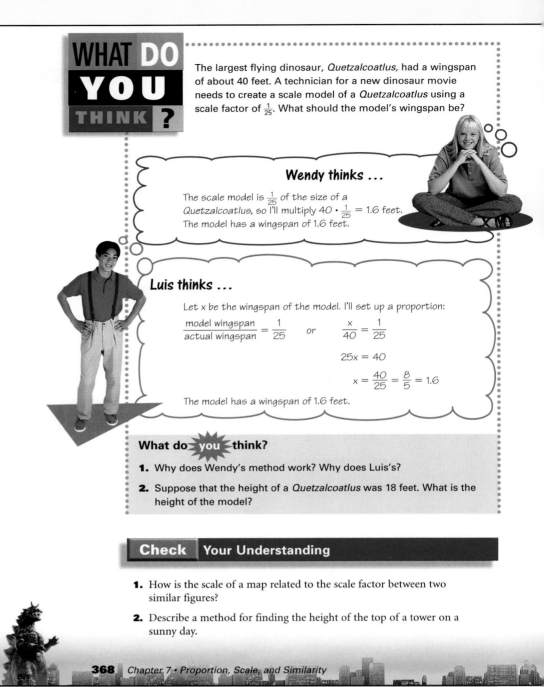

The largest flying dinosaur, *Quetzalcoatlus,* had a wingspan of about 40 feet. A technician for a new dinosaur movie needs to create a scale model of a *Quetzalcoatlus* using a scale factor of $\frac{1}{25}$. What should the model's wingspan be?

Wendy thinks ...

The scale model is $\frac{1}{25}$ of the size of a *Quetzalcoatlus*, so I'll multiply $40 \cdot \frac{1}{25} = 1.6$ feet. The model has a wingspan of 1.6 feet.

Luis thinks ...

Let x be the wingspan of the model. I'll set up a proportion:

$$\frac{\text{model wingspan}}{\text{actual wingspan}} = \frac{1}{25} \quad \text{or} \quad \frac{x}{40} = \frac{1}{25}$$

$$25x = 40$$

$$x = \frac{40}{25} = \frac{8}{5} = 1.6$$

The model has a wingspan of 1.6 feet.

What do you think?

1. Why does Wendy's method work? Why does Luis's?
2. Suppose that the height of a *Quetzalcoatlus* was 18 feet. What is the height of the model?

Check Your Understanding

1. How is the scale of a map related to the scale factor between two similar figures?
2. Describe a method for finding the height of the top of a tower on a sunny day.

MEETING MIDDLE SCHOOL CLASSROOM NEEDS

Tips from Middle School Teachers

I ask my students to think about how they use similar figures in their lives. Sometimes they bring in pictures for the bulletin board, and sometimes I just ask them to write about this in their journals.

Team Teaching

Work with related arts teachers to identify situations in which the measures of similar figures need to be determined.

Science Connection

For a long time, dinosaurs, even flying ones like *Quetzalcoatlus*, were thought to be reptiles. Several paleontologists now think that dinosaurs actually are more closely related to birds. Here are some reasons: Dinosaurs could stand upright, like birds, while the legs of reptiles, such as lizards and crocodiles, usually go out to the sides. Dinosaur bones are more like bird bones than reptile bones. Some paleontologists even found fossilized feathers near dinosaur bones.

7-9 Exercises and Applications

Practice and Apply

1. **Getting Started** If $ABCD \sim EFGH$, follow the steps to find x, the length of $\overline{EF}$.
   a. Which side in $ABCD$ corresponds to $\overline{EF}$? $\overline{AB}$
   b. Give the ratio of x to the length of the corresponding side in $ABCD$. $\frac{x}{18}$
   c. Which side of $EFGH$ has a known length? $\overline{HE}$
   d. Which side of $ABCD$ corresponds to the side you named in **c**? Give the ratio of these corresponding sides. $\overline{DA}$; $\frac{1}{3}$
   e. The ratios in **b** and **d** are equal. Write and solve a proportion to find x. $\frac{x}{18} = \frac{1}{3}$; $x = 6$

Find x in each pair of similar figures.

2. $\triangle ABC \sim \triangle DEF$ $x = 2.5$

3. $GHIJ \sim KLMN$ $x = 45$

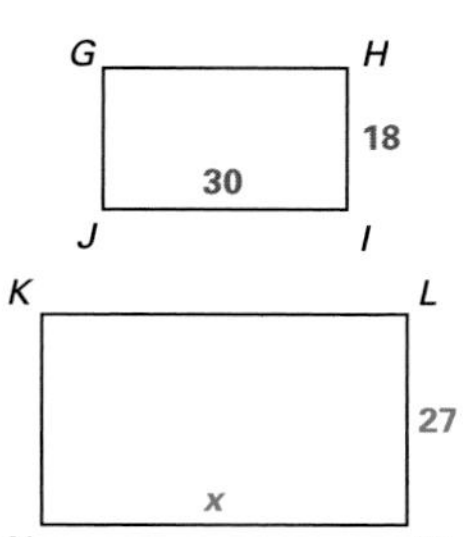

4. $x = 3.75$ cm

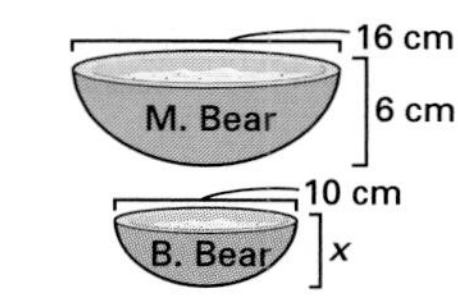

5. **Problem Solving** In *Terror of the Bird Thing,* the Bird Thing casts a shadow that is 60 m long. Diane is 150 cm tall. If Diane's shadow is 180 cm long, how tall is the Bird Thing? 50 m

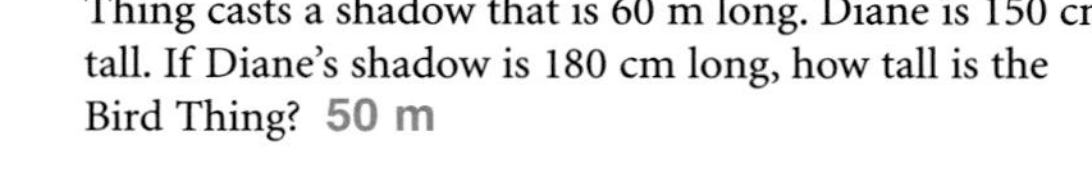

Find the missing side lengths in each pair of similar figures.

6. $\triangle RST \sim \triangle UVW$

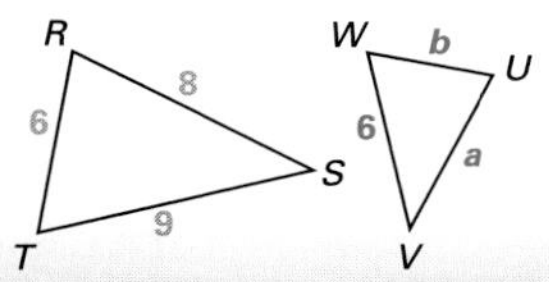

7. $EFGH \sim JKLM$

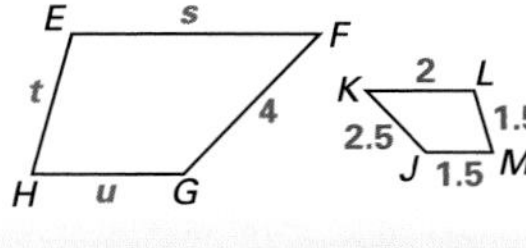

8. $\triangle NPQ \sim \triangle RST$

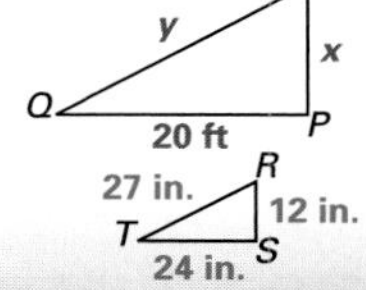

PRACTICE

Name ____________________

Practice 7-9

Finding Measures of Similar Figures

Find x in each pair of similar figures.

1. $\triangle UVW \sim \triangle XYZ$ $x =$ 22.5
2. $JKLM \sim QRST$ $x =$ 14
3. $\triangle DEF \sim \triangle GHI$ $x =$ 20

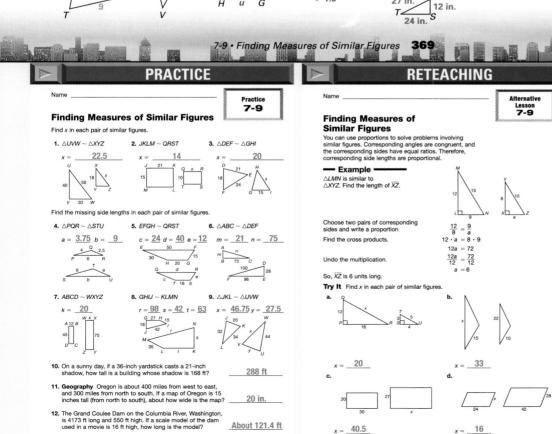

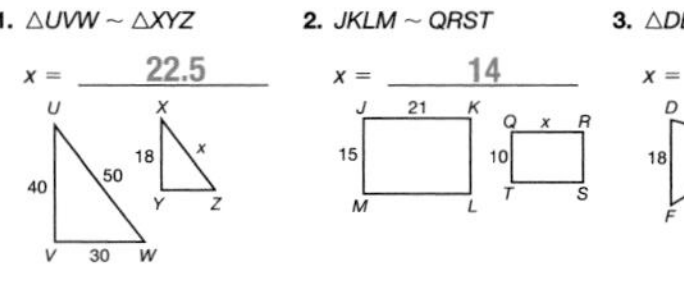

Find the missing side lengths in each pair of similar figures.

4. $\triangle PQR \sim \triangle STU$ $a =$ 3.75 $b =$ 9
5. $EFGH \sim QRST$ $c =$ 24 $d =$ 40 $e =$ 12
6. $\triangle ABC \sim \triangle DEF$ $m =$ 21 $n =$ 75

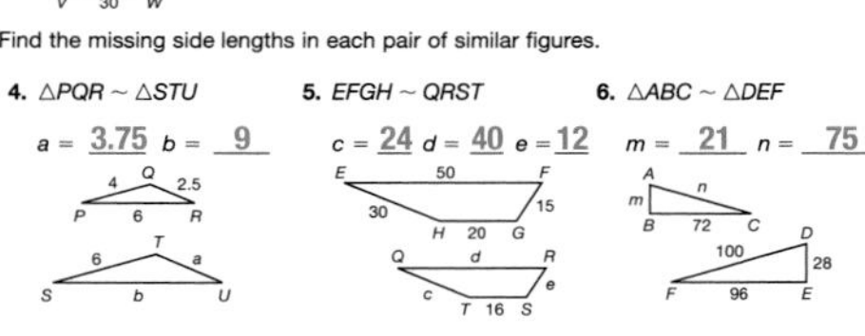

7. $ABCD \sim WXYZ$ $k =$ 20
8. $GHIJ \sim KLMN$ $r =$ 98 $s =$ 42 $t =$ 63
9. $\triangle JKL \sim \triangle UVW$ $x =$ 46.75 $y =$ 27.5

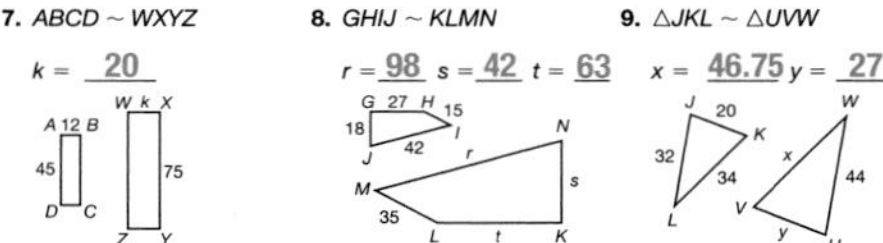

10. On a sunny day, if a 36-inch yardstick casts a 21-inch shadow, how tall is a building whose shadow is 168 ft? 288 ft

11. **Geography** Oregon is about 400 miles from west to east, and 300 miles from north to south. If a map of Oregon is 15 inches tall (from north to south), about how wide is the map? 20 in.

12. The Grand Coulee Dam on the Columbia River, Washington, is 4173 ft long and 550 ft high. If a scale model of the dam used in a movie is 16 ft high, how long is the model? About 121.4 ft

RETEACHING

Name ____________________

Alternative Lesson 7-9

Finding Measures of Similar Figures

You can use proportions to solve problems involving similar figures. Corresponding angles are congruent, and the corresponding sides have equal ratios. Therefore, corresponding side lengths are proportional.

Example

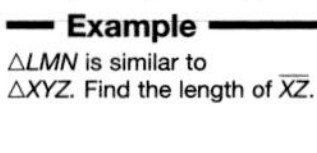

$\triangle LMN$ is similar to $\triangle XYZ$. Find the length of $\overline{XZ}$.

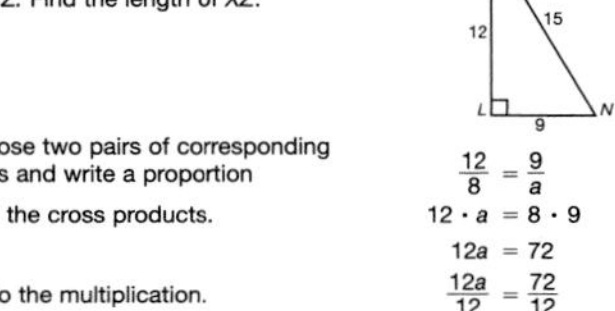

Choose two pairs of corresponding sides and write a proportion $\frac{12}{8} = \frac{9}{a}$

Find the cross products. $12 \cdot a = 8 \cdot 9$

$12a = 72$

Undo the multiplication. $\frac{12a}{12} = \frac{72}{12}$

$a = 6$

So, $\overline{XZ}$ is 6 units long.

Try It Find x in each pair of similar figures.

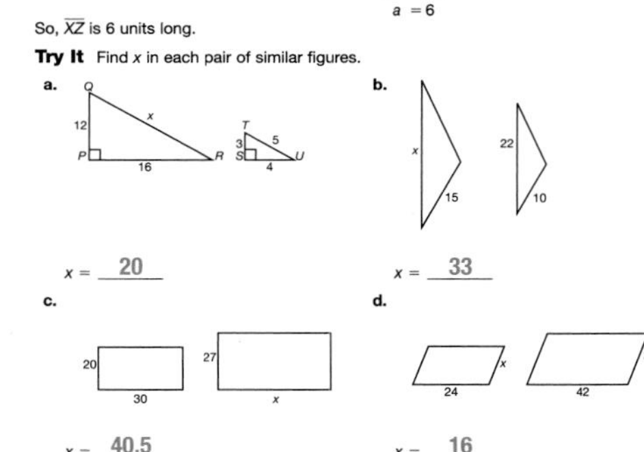

a. $x =$ 20
b. $x =$ 33
c. $x =$ 40.5
d. $x =$ 16

7-9 Exercises and Applications

Assignment Guide

- Basic
  1–9, 12, 14–20 evens
- Average
  2–10, 12, 13–21 odds
- Enriched
  2–13, 15–21 odds

Exercise Answers

6. $a = 5\frac{1}{3}$; $b = 4$.
7. $t = 2.4$; $u = 2.4$; $s = 3.2$.
8. $x = 10$ ft, $y = 22.5$ ft

Reteaching

Activity

Materials: Ruler, protractor

- The design below is going to be enlarged. The side of the square will be 10.5 cm. What is the scale factor? How long will the hypotenuse of each right triangle be?

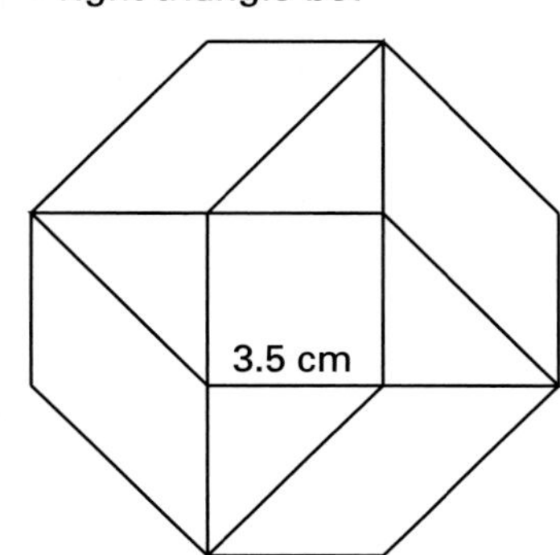

Scale factor is 3:1, hypotenuse about 15 cm

- The design also needs to be reduced, so that the side of the square is 1 cm. What is the scale factor? How long will the hyptenuse be? Scale factor is 1:3.5, hypotenuse will be about 1.4 cm.

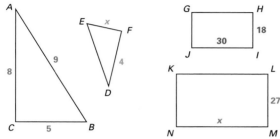

Exercise Notes

■ Exercise 11

Fine Arts Explain that sometimes part of a photo is cropped out, (cut off) when it is enlarged or reduced in order to make a nicer photo.

■ Exercise 13

Error Prevention It may be helpful for students to draw two equilateral triangles with the same orientation, so that it is easy to match corresponding sides and vertices.

Project Progress

You may want to have students use Chapter 7 Project Master.

Exercise Answers

11. No; By making the enlargement 5 in. × 7.14 in. and then cropping to size.

12. 48 m. Set up a proportion $\frac{ED}{8} = \frac{90}{15}$ and solve.

13. Yes. All corresponding angles are congruent and the scale factor will be the same for all three sides.

Alternate Assessment

Self Assessment Ask students to write about what they think is most difficult about this lesson. Have them make up examples of "easy" and "hard" problems and solve them.

► Quick Quiz

1. Two rectangles are similar. The width of the smaller rectangle is 2 cm and its length is 5 cm. The width of the larger rectangle is 9 cm. What is the length of the larger rectangle? 22.5 cm
2. $BEAR \sim POST$; $BE = 4$ in. and $PO = 5$ in. If $EA = 7$ in., how long is OS? 8.75 in.

Available on Daily Transparency 7-9

PROBLEM SOLVING 7-9

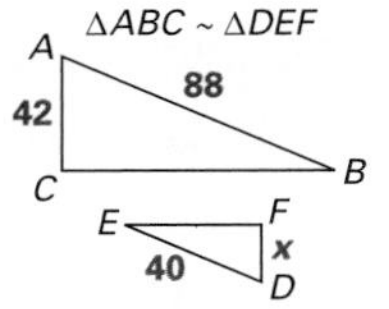

9. **Test Prep** What proportion could you use to solve for x? **A**

Ⓐ $\frac{42}{x} = \frac{88}{40}$ Ⓑ $\frac{x}{42} = \frac{88}{40}$ Ⓒ $\frac{40}{42} = \frac{x}{88}$ Ⓓ $\frac{40}{x} = \frac{42}{88}$

$\triangle ABC \sim \triangle DEF$; A, B, C; 42, 88; E, F, D; 40, x

10. Ashok has enlarged an 8 in. × 10 in. photograph to make a poster. If his poster's length is 25 in., what is its width? **20 in.**

Problem Solving and Reasoning

11. 

A photo processing lab offers to enlarge 3.5 in. × 5 in. photos to 5 in. × 7 in. Are these rectangles similar? If not, how can the photo lab make the enlargements? Explain.

12. **Choose a Strategy** You need to find the distance across the Ralimis River. If $\triangle ABC \sim \triangle DEC$, what is the distance across the river from E to D? Explain how you solved this problem.

Problem Solving STRATEGIES
- Look for a Pattern
- Make an Organized List
- Make a Table
- Guess and Check
- Work Backward
- Use Logical Reasoning
- Draw a Diagram
- Solve a Simpler Problem

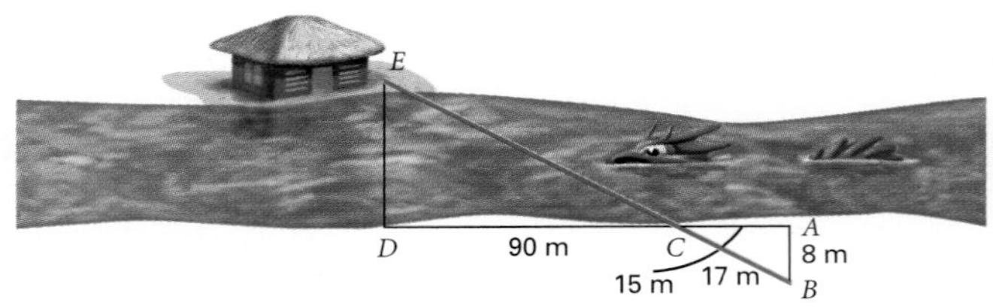

13. **Critical Thinking** Maribel says that any two equilateral triangles are similar. Is she right? If she is, explain why. If she is not, sketch two equilateral triangles that are not similar.

Mixed Review

Find each product. *[Lesson 4-5]*

14. $2\frac{3}{4} \cdot 1\frac{2}{3}$ $4\frac{7}{12}$ 15. $5\frac{7}{8} \cdot 3\frac{4}{3}$ $25\frac{11}{24}$ 16. $2\frac{5}{9} \cdot 7\frac{1}{10}$ $18\frac{13}{90}$ 17. $3\frac{4}{5} \cdot 6\frac{1}{2}$ $24\frac{7}{10}$ 18. $10\frac{5}{8} \cdot 3\frac{5}{12}$ $36\frac{29}{96}$

Find each unit rate. *[Lesson 6-7]*

19. 200 words in 5 minutes **40 words per minute**
20. 14 days in 7 months **2 days per month**
21. $16.99 for 10 gallons **$1.699 per gallon**

Project Progress

If possible, build the scale model of your dream house using construction paper, scissors, and tape. If this is not possible, find how much paper you would need to build your house by calculating the areas of the walls, ceiling, and roof.

Problem Solving: Understand, Plan, Solve, Look Back

PROBLEM SOLVING

Name ______________________ **Guided Problem Solving 7-9**

GPS **PROBLEM 12, STUDENT PAGE 370**

You need to find the distance across the Ralimis River. If $\triangle ABC \sim \triangle DEC$, what is the distance across the river from E to D? Explain how you solved this problem.

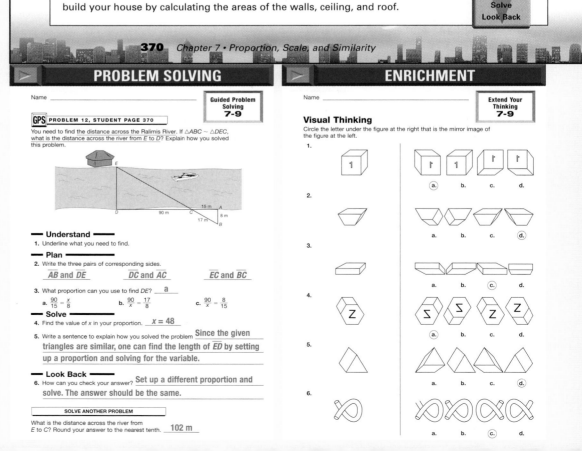

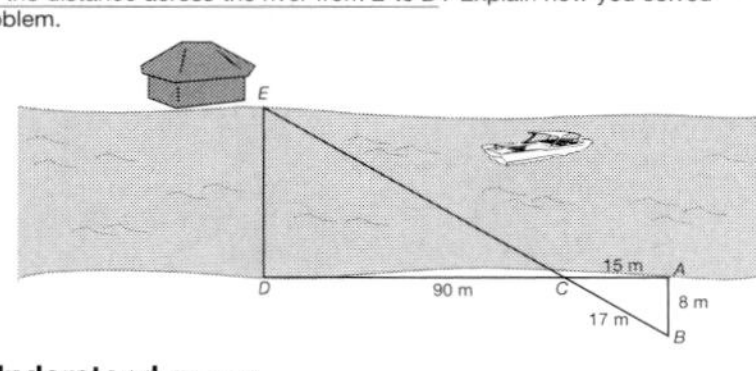

— Understand —

1. Underline what you need to find.

— Plan —

2. Write the three pairs of corresponding sides.
$\overline{AB}$ and $\overline{DE}$ $\overline{DC}$ and $\overline{AC}$ $\overline{EC}$ and $\overline{BC}$

3. What proportion can you use to find DE? **a**
a. $\frac{90}{15} = \frac{x}{8}$ b. $\frac{90}{x} = \frac{17}{8}$ c. $\frac{90}{x} = \frac{8}{15}$

— Solve —

4. Find the value of x in your proportion. **$x = 48$**

5. Write a sentence to explain how you solved the problem **Since the given triangles are similar, one can find the length of $\overline{ED}$ by setting up a proportion and solving for the variable.**

— Look Back —

6. How can you check your answer? **Set up a different proportion and solve. The answer should be the same.**

SOLVE ANOTHER PROBLEM

What is the distance across the river from E to C? Round your answer to the nearest tenth. **102 m**

ENRICHMENT

Name ______________________ **Extend Your Thinking 7-9**

Visual Thinking

Circle the letter under the figure at the right that is the mirror image of the figure at the left.

1. (a.) b. c. d.

2. 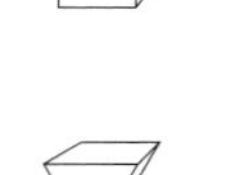
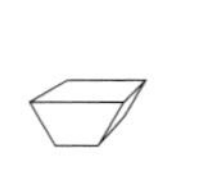
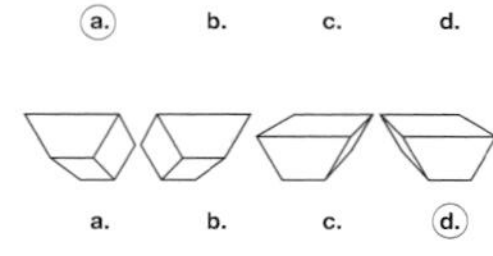
a. b. c. (d.)

3. 
a. b. (c.) d.

4. 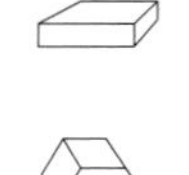

(a.) b. c. d.

5. 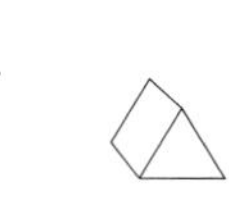
a. b. c. (d.)

6. 

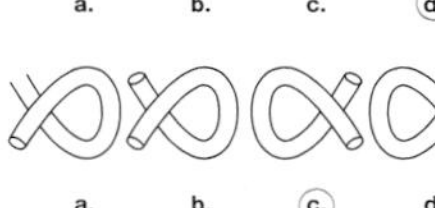
a. b. (c.) d.

Perimeters and Areas of Similar Figures

7-10

▶ Lesson Link You've learned how to find side lengths of similar figures. Now you'll explore perimeters and areas of similar figures. ◀

You'll Learn ...

■ to use the scale factor to find perimeters and areas of similar figures

... How It's Used

People who frame artwork need to know how the size of a painting affects its area and perimeter.

Explore Perimeters and Areas

If It's a Lot, It Can't Be Little

Materials: Graph paper

Celluloid Creatures Studios has asked you to investigate the costs of buying and fencing different-sized lots. Lot space costs $100 per square foot. Fencing costs $12 per foot.

1. Let one grid square represent 10 ft by 10 ft. Sketch a 50 ft × 200 ft lot. Find the lot space cost, the fencing cost, and the total cost of the lot.
2. Sketch a 100 ft × 200 ft lot and a 100 ft × 400 ft foot lot. For each, find the lot space cost, the fencing cost, and the total cost.
3. Compare the lot space, fencing, and total costs of the three lots. What do you notice? Which of the larger lots would you say is "twice as big" as the original?
4. What geometric measurement is associated with the fencing of the lot? What measurement is associated with the size of the lot?

Learn Perimeters and Areas of Similar Figures

The ratio of the perimeters of two similar figures is equal to the ratio of the side lengths—the scale factor. The ratio of their areas is equal to the *square* of the scale factor.

MEETING INDIVIDUAL NEEDS

Resources

7-10 Practice
7-10 Reteaching
7-10 Problem Solving
7-10 Enrichment
7-10 Daily Transparency
- Problem of the Day
- Review
- Quick Quiz

Teaching Tool Transparency 7
Technology Master 32

 *Interactive CD-ROM Lesson 7*

 *Wide World of Mathematics Geometry:* Seeing with Your Hands

Learning Modalities

Verbal Point out that the perimeter ratio is the same as the scale factor, just as the units for perimeter are the same as the units for the length of a line segment. The area ratio is the square of the scale factor, and area units are square units.

Visual Have students show how many copies of a figure fit in an enlargement to reinforce the area ratio as the square of the scale factor.

Kinesthetic Have students use pattern blocks or color tiles to generate similar figures. They then can compute the perimeter and area of each figure by counting.

Challenge

Have students predict how volume ratios would change in relationship to scale factors and then investigate using cubes.

INTERACTIVE LESSON

7-10 Lesson Organizer

Objective

- Use the scale factor to find perimeters and areas of similar figures.

Materials

- Graph paper

NCTM Standards

- 1–4, 7, 12, 13

▶ Review

Simplify.

1. 4^3 64
2. 3^4 81
3. $\sqrt{25}$ 5
4. $\sqrt{121}$ 11

Available on Daily Transparency 7-10

1 Introduce

Explore

You may wish to use Teaching Tool Transparency 7: $\frac{1}{4}$-Inch Graph Paper with **Explore.**

The Point

Students draw three different rectangles, and find the perimeter and area of each. They discover that doubling both dimensions creates a similar figure whose perimeter is twice that of the original and whose area is four times as great.

Ongoing Assessment

Listen to students' use of mathematical language; some will use the terms "area" and "perimeter," while others will talk about "space inside" or "distance around."

For Groups That Finish Early

Choose a 2-digit number and sketch, on graph paper, as many rectangles as you can that have that number of units as perimeter. Determine which has the least area and which has the greatest. Answers may vary.

Answers for Explore on page C1

2 Teach

Learn

Alternate Examples

1. A movie ad is 2 in. × 3 in. You want to enlarge it to make a poster. If the scale factor from the poster to the ad is 12, predict the ratio of their areas. Check your prediction by calculating the areas.

   Prediction: The ratio of the areas should be $12^2 = 144$.
   Calculation:
   Ad area $= 2 \times 3 = 6$ in^2
   Poster area $= 24 \times 36 = 864$ in^2
   The ratio of the areas is $\frac{864}{6} = \frac{144}{1}$.

2. The perimeter of the larger of two similar figures is 48 cm and its area is 60 cm^2. The scale factor from the larger to the smaller is $\frac{2}{3}$. Find the perimeter and area of the smaller figure.

   Perimeter $= 48 \times \frac{2}{3} = 32$ cm

   Area $= 60 \times (\frac{2}{3})^2$

   $= 60 \times \frac{4}{9}$

   ≈ 26.67 cm^2

3 Practice and Assess

Check

Answers for Check Your Understanding

1. Original side $= s$ and area $= s \cdot s = s^2$; New side $= 2s$, and area $= 2s \cdot 2s = 4s^2$.
2. No. If it did, it would have 4 times the area.

An original movie poster from *Godzilla 1985* is now worth about $125.

Examples

1 A designer is making two similar versions of a movie poster. If the scale factor from the smaller poster to the larger is 3, predict the ratio of their areas. Check your prediction by calculating the areas.

Prediction: Since the scale factor is 3, the ratio of the areas should be $3^2 = 9$.

Calculation: The area of the smaller poster is $4 \cdot 3 = 12$ square units. The area of the larger is $12 \cdot 9 = 108$ square units. The ratio of the areas is $\frac{108}{12} = 9$.

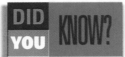

2 The perimeter of the larger of these similar figures is 38 cm and its area is 50 cm^2. The scale factor from the larger to the smaller is $\frac{3}{5}$. Find the perimeter and area of the smaller figure.

Multiply by the scale factor to find the perimeter of the smaller figure.

Perimeter $= 38 \cdot \frac{3}{5} = 22.8$ cm.

Multiply by the *square* of the scale factor to find the area of the smaller figure.
Area $= 50 \cdot \left(\frac{3}{5}\right)^2 = 50 \cdot \frac{9}{25} = 18$ cm^2.

Try It

The perimeter of the smaller of these similar figures is 64 units and its area is 44 square units. The scale factor from the smaller figure to the larger is $\frac{3}{2}$. Find the perimeter and area of the larger figure.
Perimeter = 96 units; Area = 99 square units

Check Your Understanding

1. Explain why doubling the side length of a square quadruples its area.
2. If one similar rectangle has twice the area of another, does it have twice the length and width? Explain.

MATH EVERY DAY

Problem of the Day

Start with a large cube and paint all of the sides. Cut the cube into 27 smaller cubes.

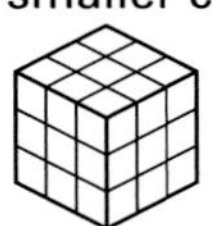

You mix up the smaller cubes and draw one without looking. What are the chances that you draw a cube that has been painted on exactly 1 side? 2 sides? 3 sides? 4 sides? 0 sides?
1 side—6 out of 27; 2 sides—12 out of 27; 3 sides—8 out of 27; 4 sides—0 out of 27; 0 sides—1 out of 27

Available on Daily Transparency 7-10

An Extension is provided in the transparency package.

Fact of the Day

Between 1915 and 1920, the film industry gradually moved from the east coast to Hollywood. This began the era of the large film studios.

Estimation

Estimate.

1. $\frac{3}{5} + \frac{5}{11} - \frac{1}{4}$ $\frac{3}{4}$
2. $4\frac{19}{20} - 2\frac{1}{8}$ 3
3. $4.576 \cdot 3.998$ 18

7-10 Exercises and Applications

Practice and Apply

1. **Getting Started** Two rectangles are similar. The scale factor from the smaller to the larger is 3. The smaller rectangle has perimeter 14 and area 28. Follow the steps to find the perimeter and area of the larger rectangle.
   a. The ratio of the perimeters is equal to the scale factor. Multiply the small rectangle's perimeter by the scale factor to find the large rectangle's perimeter. 42
   b. Square the scale factor. This is the ratio of the areas. 9
   c. Multiply the small rectangle's area by the ratio in **b** to find the large rectangle's area. 252 square units

Geometry Predict the ratio of the areas of each pair of similar figures. Check your predictions by calculating the areas.

2. Scale factor 2
   4

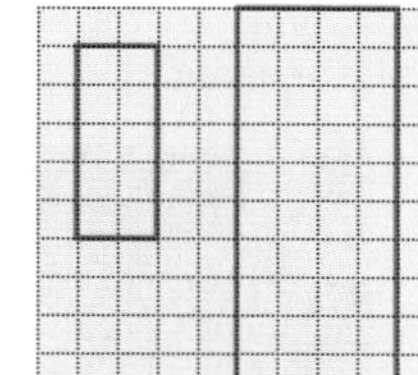

3. Scale factor 4
   16

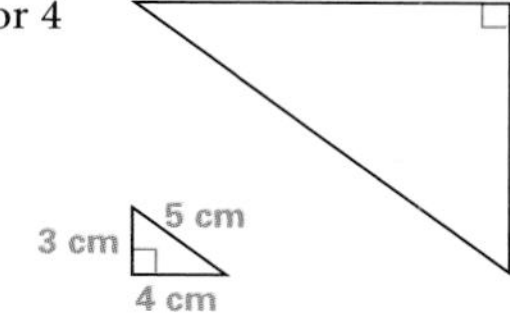

4. An artist is drawing a larger version of the monster in this poster. The scale factor from this figure to the enlargement is $\frac{7}{3}$. If this figure has an area of 108 cm^2, what will the area of the larger one be? Explain.

INCREDIBLE, UNSTOPPABLE TITAN OF TERROR!
GODZILLA
It's Alive!
KING
MONSTERS!

Suppose two figures are similar. For each scale factor from the smaller to the larger, find the unknown perimeter and area.

5. Scale factor = 3, perimeter of smaller = 10 cm, area of smaller = 6 cm^2. Find the perimeter and area of the larger figure.
6. Scale factor = 5, perimeter of larger = 120 in., area of larger = 172 in^2. Find the perimeter and area of the smaller figure.
7. Scale factor = $\frac{3}{2}$, perimeter of smaller = 14 ft, area of smaller = 26 ft^2. Find the perimeter and area of the larger figure.

7-10 Exercises and Applications

Assignment Guide

- **Basic** 1–11, 13, 14, 16, 19–26
- **Average** 1—18, 19–25 odds
- **Enriched** 2–18, 20–26 evens

Exercise Notes

Exercises 2 and 3

Estimation Have students estimate the ratio of the areas before computing each area.

Exercise Answers

4. 588 cm^2; The ratio of the areas is $\frac{49}{9}$.
5. Perimeter = 30 cm; Area = 54 cm^2
6. Perimeter = 24 in.; Area = 6.88 in^2
7. Perimeter = 21 ft; Area = 58.5 ft^2

PRACTICE

Name ______________________

Practice 7-10

Perimeters and Areas of Similar Figures

Predict the ratio of the areas of each pair of similar figures. Check your predictions by calculating the areas.

1. scale factor 3
   area ratio = 9
2. scale factor $\frac{1}{2}$
   area ratio = $\frac{1}{4}$
3. scale factor $\frac{4}{3}$
   area ratio = $\frac{16}{9}$

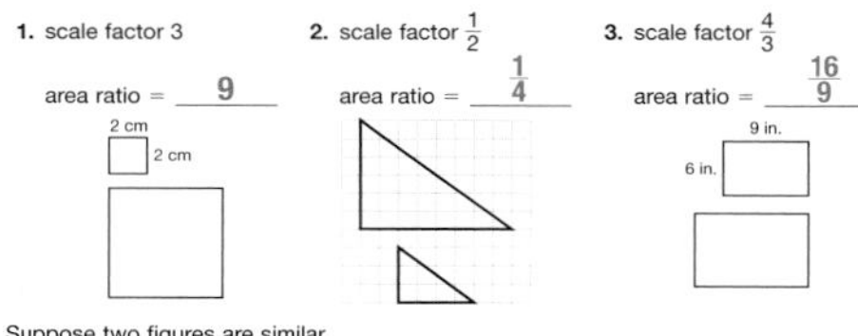

Suppose two figures are similar.

4. scale factor = 4, perimeter of smaller = 30 in.; area of smaller = 22 in^2
   Find the perimeter and area of the larger figure.
   perimeter = 120 in. area = 352 in^2
5. scale factor = $\frac{5}{3}$, perimeter of larger = 24 m; area of larger = 20 m^2
   Find the perimeter and area of the smaller figure.
   perimeter = 14.4 m area = 7.2 m^2

Perimeter and area ratios of similar figures are given. Find each scale factor.

6. perimeter ratio = 81
   scale factor = 81
7. area ratio = 16
   scale factor = 4
8. perimeter ratio = 100
   scale factor = 100
9. A common postage stamp has perimeter $3\frac{3}{4}$ in. and area $\frac{7}{8}$ in. Find the perimeter and area of a scale drawing of this stamp if the scale factor is 8.
   perimeter = 30 in. area = 56 in^2
10. All circles are similar. The diameter of a long-playing record is about $\frac{5}{2}$ times the diameter of a compact disc. If the area of a compact disc is about 115 cm^2, estimate the area of a record.
    About 690 cm^2

RETEACHING

Name ______________________

Alternative Lesson 7-10

Perimeters and Areas of Similar Figures

The ratio of the perimeters of two similar figures is equal to the ratio of the side lengths, which is the scale factor. The ratio of their areas is equal to the *square* of the scale factor.

Example

Find the perimeter and area of the figures at the right. The scale factor is 3.

Add the lengths of the sides to find the perimeter of the small rectangle.	$4 + 5 + 4 + 5 = 18$
Multiply by the scale factor to find the perimeter of the large rectangle.	$18 \times 3 = 54$
Check your work by adding the lengths of the sides.	$12 + 15 + 12 + 15 = 54$
Add the lengths of the sides to find the area of the small rectangle.	20 square units
Multiply by the square of the scale factor to find the area of the large rectangle. Check your work by counting square units.	$3^2 \times 20 = 9 \times 20 = 180$ square units

So, the perimeter of the small rectangle is 18 units and its area is 20 square units. The perimeter of the large rectangle is 54 units and its area is 180 square units.

Try It Find the perimeter and area of the figures at the right. The scale factor is $\frac{1}{2}$.

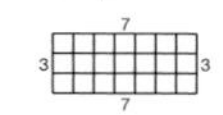

a. Find the perimeter of the large figure. 40 units.
b. Multiply the perimeter of the large figure by the scale factor to find the perimeter of the small figure. The perimeter is:
   20 units; $\frac{1}{2} \times 40 = 20$
c. Find the area of the large figure.
   84 square units.
d. Multiply the area of the large figure by the *square* of the scale factor to find the area of the small figure. The area is:
   21 square units; $(\frac{1}{2})^2 \times 84 = 21$

Reteaching

Activity

Materials: Graph paper

- Make a small drawing on grid paper, using only straight lines. Find the perimeter and area. Answers will vary.
- Make a second drawing by tripling the length of each line segment. Predict the perimeter and area. Check your prediction by finding the perimeter and area by counting. Answers will vary; Perimeter should be 3 times perimeter in Step 1; Area should be 9 times area in Step 1.

Exercise Answers

14. It is not clear whether Jacob is referring to the individual dimensions of length and width, the perimeter, or the area; Possible answer: "twice as big" usually means twice as long and twice as wide, which actually means four times as big in area.

16. It would take 0.64 gallons; The scale factor is 2, so the area ratio is 4.

Alternate Assessment

Performance Have students demonstrate their understanding of how perimeter and area are affected by scale factors by drawing a diagram of similar figures and explaining the relationships.

▶ Quick Quiz

1. Two figures are similar. The scale factor from the smaller to the larger is 4. The perimeter of the smaller is 36. What is the perimeter of the larger? 144
2. Two figures are similar, with a scale factor from the larger to the smaller of $\frac{5}{8}$. The area of the larger is 128 square inches. What is the area of the smaller? 50 in^2.
3. The area ratio of two figures is 49. What is the scale factor? 7

Available on Daily Transparency 7-10

PROBLEM SOLVING 7-10

Perimeter and area ratios of similar figures are given. Find each scale factor.

8. Perimeter ratio = 100 **100**

9. Area ratio = 25 **5**

10. Area ratio = 81 **9**

11. Perimeter ratio = 0.62 **0.62**

12. History The ancient temple Angkor Wat was built by the Khmer people of Cambodia. The temple's enclosure is a rectangle 1000 meters long and 850 meters wide. If a museum model of the temple is built using a scale factor of $\frac{1}{8}$, what will the area of the model be? **13,281.25 m^2**

13. Test Prep The ratio of the areas of two similar rectangles is $\frac{36}{25}$. What is the ratio of their perimeters? **B**

Ⓐ $\frac{5}{6}$ Ⓑ $\frac{6}{5}$ Ⓒ $\frac{25}{36}$ Ⓓ $\frac{36}{25}$

Problem Solving and Reasoning

14. Communicate Jacob tells Renata that one of his school photographs is twice as big as another one. Renata asks Jacob what he means by "twice as big." Explain why Renata might be confused. What do you think people usually mean when they say one thing is "twice as big" as another?

15. Critical Thinking On a movie set, a 2-meter tall Godzilla casts a shadow whose area is 3 m^2. If the "real" Godzilla is 50 meters tall, what is the area of his shadow? **1875 m^2**

16. Critical Thinking GPS You find that it takes 0.16 gallons of paint to paint a rectangular wall whose length is 6 ft and whose height is 8 ft. How much paint will you need to paint a wall whose length is 12 ft and whose height is 16 ft? Explain how you found your answer.

Mixed Review

Find each quotient. Write your answers in lowest terms. *[Lesson 4-6]*

17. $\frac{3}{4} \div 1\frac{2}{3}$ **$\frac{9}{20}$** **18.** $5\frac{1}{2} \div 2\frac{3}{4}$ **2** **19.** $1\frac{1}{9} \div \frac{1}{3}$ **$3\frac{1}{3}$** **20.** $\frac{1}{2} \div \frac{5}{12}$ **$1\frac{1}{5}$** **21.** $32 \div \frac{1}{2}$ **64**

Solve each proportion. *[Lesson 6-8]*

22. $\frac{x}{14} = \frac{4}{7}$ **$x = 8$** **23.** $\frac{p}{12} = \frac{3}{4}$ **$p = 9$** **24.** $\frac{5}{11} = \frac{m}{22}$ **$m = 10$** **25.** $\frac{12}{n} = \frac{6}{5}$ **$n = 10$** **26.** $\frac{b}{3} = \frac{2}{4}$ **$b = \frac{3}{2}$**

PROBLEM SOLVING

Name ____________________

Guided Problem Solving 7-10

GPS PROBLEM 16, STUDENT PAGE 374

You find that it takes 0.16 gallons of paint to paint a rectangular wall whose length is 6 ft and whose height is 8 ft. How much paint will you need to paint a wall whose length is 12 ft and whose height is 16 ft?

— Understand —

1. What are the dimensions of the wall you painted? **6 ft × 8 ft**
2. What are the dimensions of the wall you are planning to paint? **12 ft × 16 ft**
3. Underline what you are asked to find.

— Plan —

4. What is the ratio of the
   a. length of the smaller wall to the length of the larger wall? **$\frac{6}{12}$**
   b. height of the smaller wall to the height of the larger wall? **$\frac{8}{16}$**
5. Are the ratios you found in Items 3 and 4 equal? **Yes, both equal $\frac{1}{2}$.**
6. How is the ratio of the areas of two similar figures related to the scale factor? **The ratio is the square of the scale factor.**

— Solve —

7. How many times greater is the area of the wall you are planning to paint than the area of the wall you have painted? **4**
8. How much paint will you use for the larger wall? **0.64 gal**

— Look Back —

9. What other strategy can you use to help you solve the problem? **Possible answer: Draw a Diagram, Solve a Simpler Problem.**

SOLVE ANOTHER PROBLEM

You have wallpapered a section of wall that measures 4 ft high and 7 ft wide. You now need to wallpaper a wall that measures 20 ft high and 35 ft wide. The amount of wallpaper that you will need for the larger wall is how many times the amount of wallpaper that you have already used? **25 times.**

ENRICHMENT

Name ____________________

Extend Your Thinking 7-10

Patterns in Geometry

You have explored the relationships between perimeter and area in similar figures. Now you will explore volume of similar figures.

To find the volume of a rectangular prism (box), multiply length × width × height. The formula is $V = lwh$. Volume is given in cubic units. For example, the volume is labeled in^3 if the dimensions are given in inches.

1. Find the volume of each rectangular prism.

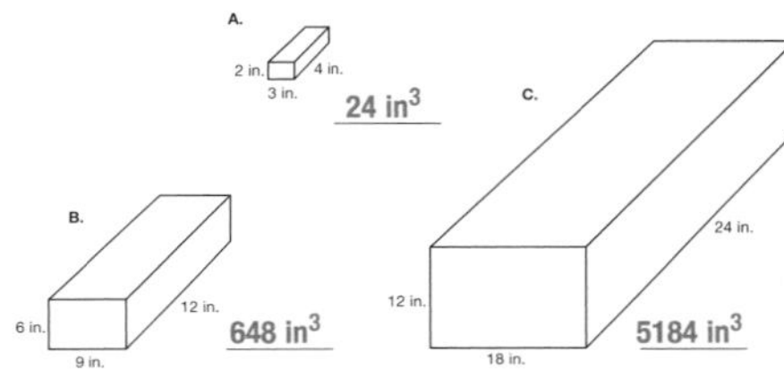

2. What is the scale factor of Prism C to Prism B? **2:1**
3. What is the ratio of the volume in simplest form of Prism C to Prism B? **8:1**
4. Write the ratio in Item 3 using exponents. **2^3:1**
5. How is the ratio of the volume and the scale factor related? **Volume ratio is the scale factor cubed ($8 = 2^3$).**
6. What is the scale factor of Prism A to Prism B? **1:3**
7. What is the ratio of the volume in simplest form of Prism A to Prism B? **$\frac{1}{27}$**
8. Write the ratio in Item 7 as using exponents. **1:3^3**
9. How is the ratio of the volume and the scale factor related? **Volume ratio is the scale factor cubed ($\frac{1}{27} = \frac{1}{3^3}$).**
10. What pattern do you notice? **The volume ratio is equal to the scale factor cubed.**

You have seen that an enlargement or reduction of a figure is similar to the original. Now you will use two different methods to enlarge a drawing.

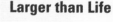

Larger than Life

Materials: Graph paper (with larger squares than those in drawing)

The drawing shows a simplified drawing of Rodan, who co-starred with Godzilla in several 1960s movies. You will use two methods—the *grid* method and the *projection* method—to enlarge this drawing.

1. In the grid method, you enlarge one piece of the picture at a time. Use an 8 × 8 area on your graph paper to make a larger copy of Rodan. Each square in your drawing should look like the corresponding square in the original.
2. To use the projection method:

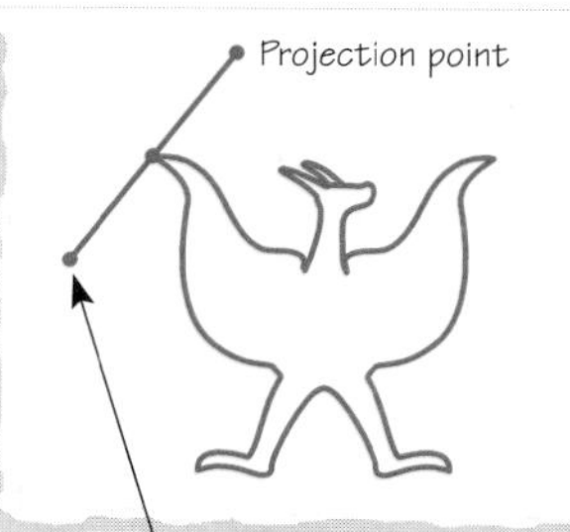

   a. Trace the original drawing onto an $8\frac{1}{2}$ in. × 11 in. sheet of paper. The top of your tracing should be about $2\frac{1}{2}$ in. from the top of the paper.

   b. Mark dots on your tracing. These dots will be your guide for the enlargement. Mark key points, like the tips of the wings.

   c. Draw a dot near the top of your paper. This is the *projection point.* Draw a line from this point through each dot on your drawing. Mark a new dot twice as far from the projection point as the original dot.

   d. Using the new dots as a guide, sketch a larger drawing. What is the scale factor from the enlargement to the original?
3. How can each of these methods be used to make a drawing triple the size of the original? One-fourth the size of the original?

Larger than Life

The Point

In *Larger than Life* on page 359, students discussed scale models. Now they will use both the grid and projection methods to enlarge a picture.

Materials

Graph paper (with larger squares than those in the drawing)

Resources

Lesson Enhancement Transparency 34

Teaching Tool Transparency 7: $\frac{1}{4}$-Inch Graph Paper

About the Page

- Discuss the two methods for enlarging the drawing to be sure students understand what they are to do.
- Demonstrate and discuss the projection method so that students have a clear understanding of how to determine the key points and where to make the necessary dots.
- Ask students what they would do if they wanted to make the picture twice as large or half as large as the original. This should help them in understanding Question 3.

Ongoing Assessment

For both methods, check that students have enlarged the drawing correctly.

Extension

Have students make drawings triple the size of the original and $\frac{1}{4}$ the size of the original using both methods. Have them measure the resulting pictures to determine if they are correctly enlarged or reduced. Ask students which method they prefer and why.

Answers for Connect

1. Student drawings should be rough enlargements of the original, with each square in the enlargement resembling the corresponding square in the original drawing.
2. d. The scale factor is 2.

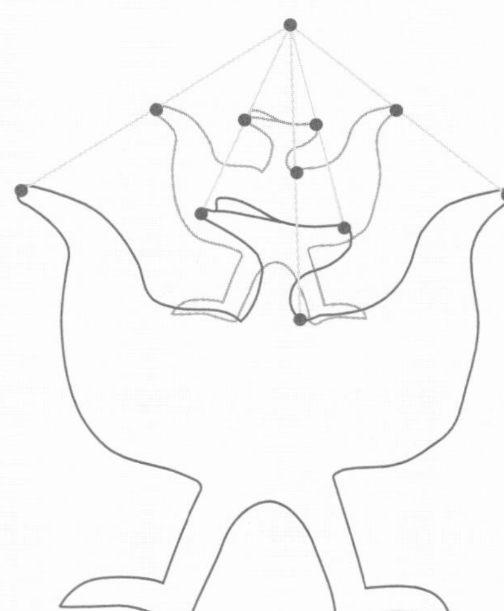

3. First method: Make the side of each square about 3 times the original square; make the side of each square $\frac{1}{4}$ of the side of the original square. Second method: Make new dots three times the distance from the projection point; make new dots $\frac{1}{4}$ times the distance from the projection point.

7C Review

Review Correlation

Item(s)	Lesson(s)
1–3	7-8
4	7-9
5	7-10
6	7-9
7	7-6
8	7-9

Test Prep

Test-Taking Tip

Tell students that drawing and labeling a sketch of given information can help them select a correct answer. Here, they can draw and label two rectangles with the widths and heights labeled.

Answers for Review

1. Yes. $\Delta XYZ \sim \Delta RQP$; 2
2. No. Sides are not proportional.
3. No. Everything is unchanged except the parallel sides.
4. 1.2 m
6. $13\frac{1}{3}$ ft.; Possible answer: Set up and solve the proportion $\frac{10 \text{ in.}}{18 \text{ in.}} = \frac{\text{shadow length}}{24 \text{ feet}}$.
7. $12\frac{1}{3}$ miles per minute.

Section 7C Review

REVIEW 7C

Geometry Tell if the figures are similar. If they are, write a similarity statement using ~ and give the scale factor. If they're not, explain why not.

1.

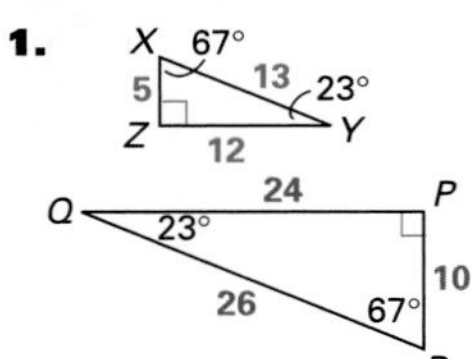

2.

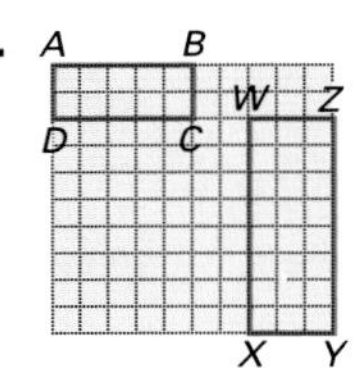

3.

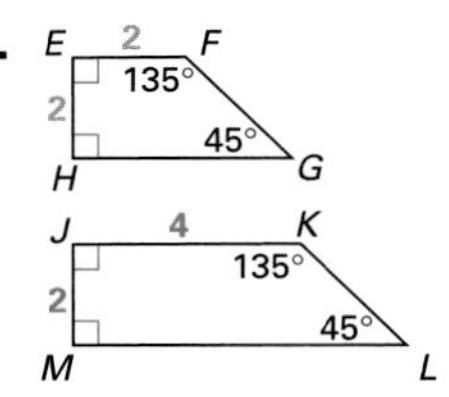

4. The mother and baby elephant shown are approximately similar. Assume the mother is 2.8 m tall and 4.2 m long. If the baby is 1.8 m long, how tall is it?

5. Two rectangles are similar, and the scale factor from the smaller to the larger is 2. The perimeter of the smaller rectangle is 20 ft and its area is 24 ft^2. Find the perimeter and area of the larger rectangle.
perimeter = 40 ft, area = 96 ft^2

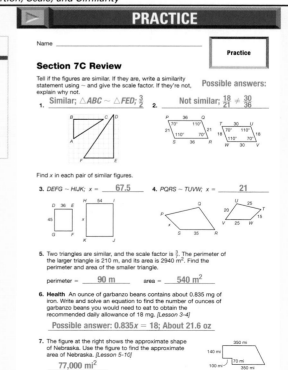

6. Journal In the original *King Kong*, Kong was supposed to be 24 feet tall. If the 18-inch-tall model of Kong cast a 10-inch-long shadow during one scene, how long would the shadow of the "real" Kong have been? Explain how you solved this problem.

7. **Operation Sense** Convert 740 miles per hour to miles per minute.

Test Prep

When you're asked to find a side length in a pair of similar figures on a multiple choice test, setting up a proportion can help you work more quickly.

8. Pat uses a photocopy machine to enlarge a drawing that is 6 cm wide and 8 cm long. If the enlargement has a width of 10.5 cm, what is its length? Choose the proportion that will help you find the correct answer. B

Ⓐ $\frac{6}{x} = \frac{10.5}{8}$ Ⓑ $\frac{6}{10.5} = \frac{8}{x}$ Ⓒ $\frac{6}{x} = \frac{8}{10.5}$ Ⓓ $\frac{x}{6} = \frac{8}{10.5}$

Resources

Practice Masters
Section 7C Review

Assessment Sourcebook
Quiz 7C

TestWorks
Test and Practice Software

PRACTICE

Name ______________________ Practice

Section 7C Review

Tell if the figures are similar. If they are, write a similarity statement using ~ and give the scale factor. If they're not, explain why not. Possible answers:

1. Similar; $\triangle ABC \sim \triangle FED$; $\frac{3}{2}$
2. Not similar; $\frac{18}{21} \neq \frac{30}{36}$

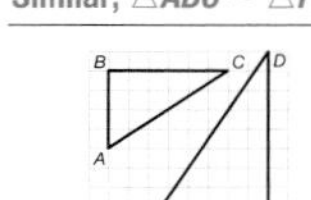

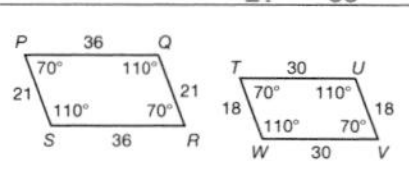

Find x in each pair of similar figures.

3. $DEFG \sim HIJK$; x = 67.5
4. $PQRS \sim TUVW$; x = 21

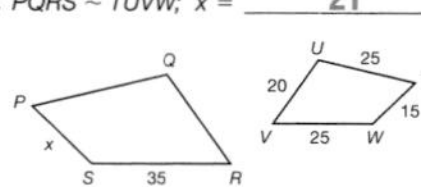

5. Two triangles are similar, and the scale factor is $\frac{3}{7}$. The perimeter of the larger triangle is 210 m, and its area is 2940 m^2. Find the perimeter and area of the smaller triangle.

perimeter = 90 m area = 540 m^2

6. **Health** An ounce of garbanzo beans contains about 0.835 mg of iron. Write and solve an equation to find the number of ounces of garbanzo beans you would need to eat to obtain the recommended daily allowance of 18 mg. *[Lesson 3-4]*

Possible answer: $0.835x = 18$; About 21.6 oz

7. The figure at the right shows the approximate shape of Nebraska. Use the figure to find the approximate area of Nebraska. *[Lesson 5-10]*

77,000 mi^2

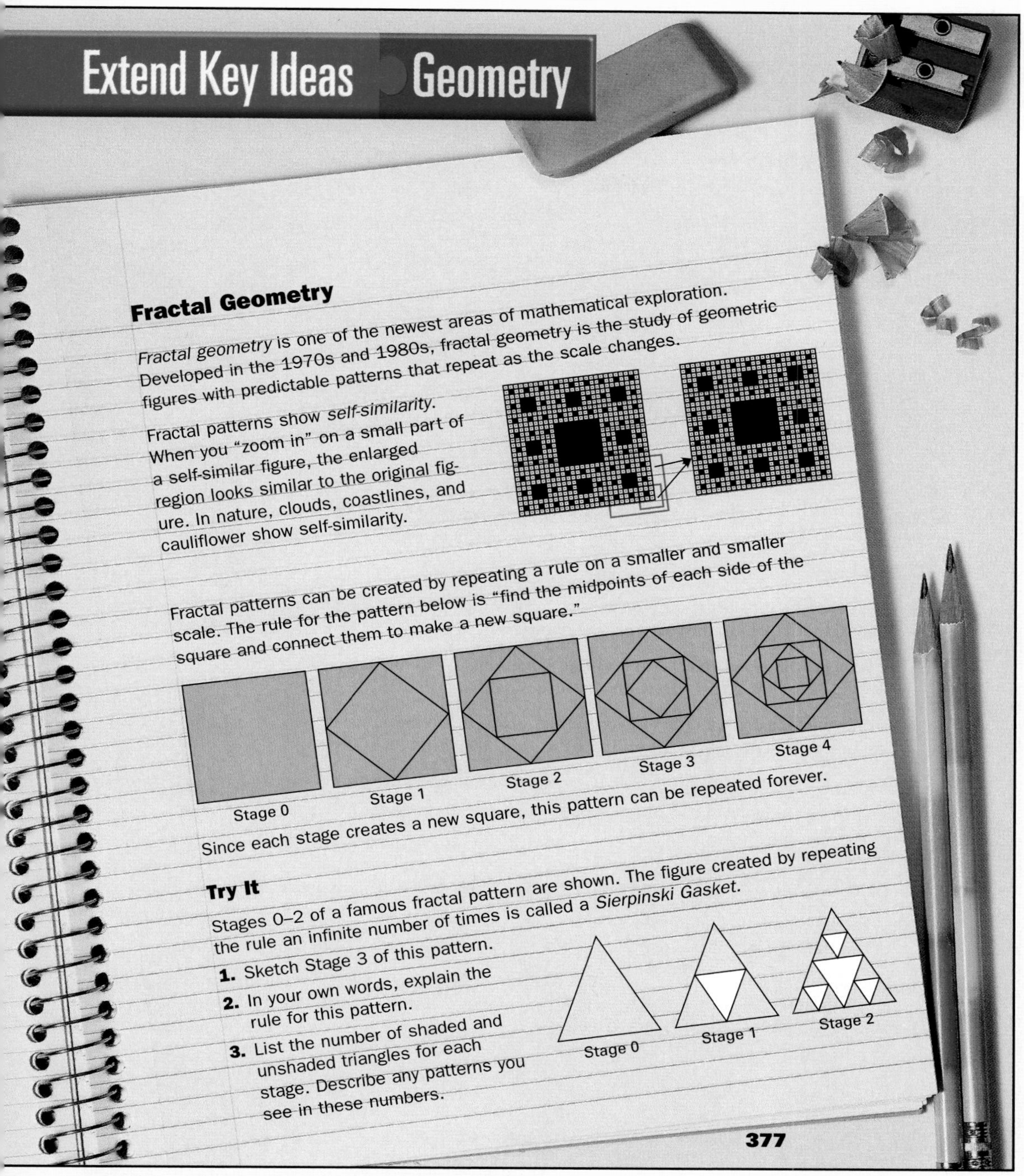

Fractal Geometry

Fractal geometry is one of the newest areas of mathematical exploration. Developed in the 1970s and 1980s, fractal geometry is the study of geometric figures with predictable patterns that repeat as the scale changes.

Fractal patterns show *self-similarity.* When you "zoom in" on a small part of a self-similar figure, the enlarged region looks similar to the original figure. In nature, clouds, coastlines, and cauliflower show self-similarity.

Fractal patterns can be created by repeating a rule on a smaller and smaller scale. The rule for the pattern below is "find the midpoints of each side of the square and connect them to make a new square."

Stage 0 Stage 1 Stage 2 Stage 3 Stage 4

Since each stage creates a new square, this pattern can be repeated forever.

Try It

Stages 0–2 of a famous fractal pattern are shown. The figure created by repeating the rule an infinite number of times is called a *Sierpinski Gasket.*

1. Sketch Stage 3 of this pattern.
2. In your own words, explain the rule for this pattern.
3. List the number of shaded and unshaded triangles for each stage. Describe any patterns you see in these numbers.

Stage 0 Stage 1 Stage 2

377

Extend Key Ideas

Fractal Geometry

The Point

Students are introduced to the concept of self-similarity as it pertains to fractal geometry.

About the Page

- Bring in some pictures created by using fractals. Give students the opportunity to figure out the rule for themselves.
- Have students create their own fractal and find whether classmates can figure out the rule.

Ask ...

- Describe fractals in your own words.
- How would you create Stage 5 of the squares pattern? Connect the midpoints of the sides of the smallest square from Stage 4 to create a new square.

Extension

Programs have been written for the Sierpinski Gasket, or Sierpinski Triangle, as it is sometimes called, for graphing calculators. Try to locate one and program your graphing calculator to create the pattern.

Answers for Try It

1. 

2. For each shaded triangle, use the midpoints of its sides as the vertices of a new, unshaded triangle.

3.

Stage	0	1	2	3
Shaded triangles	1	3	9	27
Unshaded triangles	0	1	4	13

The number of shaded triangles at any stage is always equal to the previous number multiplied by 3 (= 3 to the power of the stage number). The number of unshaded triangles at any stage is always equal to the total number of triangles at the previous stage.

Chapter 7 Summary and Review

Review Correlation

Item(s)	Lesson(s)
1	7-1
2, 3	7-2
4	7-1
5	7-3
6	7-4
7, 8	7-5
9	7-6
10	7-7
11	7-8
12, 13	7-10

For additional review, see page 678.

Answers for Review

1. 1 in.:25 mi; 1 in. = 25 mi
2. $x = 8$ yd
3. 450 ft
4. 14 cm = 63 km or 1 cm = 4.5 km
5. 4:27 P.M.
6. 9:26 or 1:2.89
7. Answers may vary.
8. 0.2 seconds per foot
9. 6 miles per minute
10. ≈ 1.5 cents per second
11. Similar; $ABCD \sim HEFG$; Scale factor 2:1
12. Perimeter = 28 in.; Area = 80 in.^{2}
13. Perimeter ratio = 9; Scale factor = 9

Chapter 7 Summary and Review

Graphic Organizer

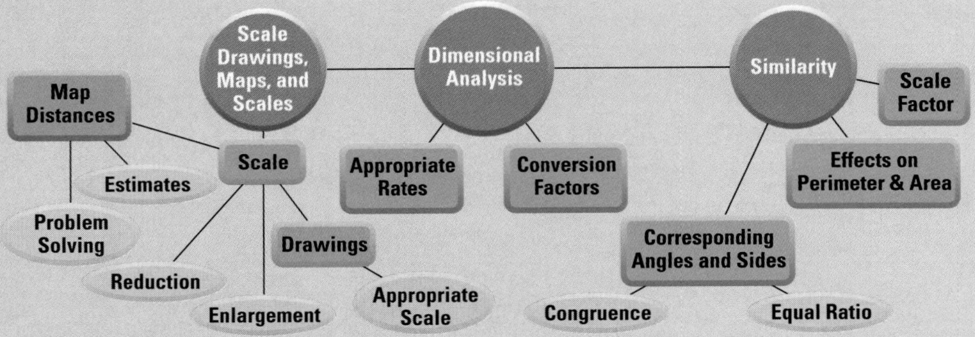

Section 7A Scale Drawings, Maps, and Scales

Summary

- The **scale** of a map is the ratio of the distance between two points on the map to the actual distance between the points.
- A **scale drawing** is often used to illustrate something that is too large or too small to show actual size. A map is one kind of scale drawing.
- A drawing's scale is the ratio of a length in the drawing to the actual length it represents. When the units are the same, they can be omitted.
- A map can be an important problem-solving tool. You can solve problems by using the formula time $= \frac{\text{distance}}{\text{rate}}$ and your knowledge of scale.

Review

1. Write the scale $\frac{1 \text{ in.}}{25 \text{ mi}}$ in two other ways.
2. Solve the proportion $\frac{14 \text{ in.}}{x} = \frac{21 \text{ in.}}{12 \text{ yd}}$ for x.
3. A model train is 35 in. long. Find the length of the actual train if the scale is 7 in.:90 ft.
4. Find the scale of a map if a 63 km wide canyon is 14 cm wide on the map.
5. Devesh left school at 3:45 P.M. and rode his bike home at a rate of 10 mi/hr. If his home is 7 mi away from school, when did he arrive?
6. A model of a 26 ft tall dinosaur has to fit into a museum with 9 ft ceilings. Suggest an appropriate scale for the model.

Resources

Practice Masters
Cumulative Review Chapters 1–7

PRACTICE

Name ____________________ Practice

Cumulative Review Chapters 1–7

Find the GCF and LCM. *[Lesson 3-7]*

1. 57, 76 GCF: 19 LCM: 228
2. 60, 100 GCF: 20 LCM: 300
3. 84,144 GCF: 12 LCM: 1008
4. 25, 35 GCF: 5 LCM: 175
5. 64, 112 GCF: 16 LCM: 448
6. 126, 56 GCF: 14 LCM: 504

Solve each equation. *[Lesson 4-3]*

7. $t - 4\frac{6}{7} = 3\frac{2}{7}$ $t =$ $8\frac{1}{7}$
8. $c - 2\frac{1}{2} = 5\frac{3}{7}$ $c =$ $7\frac{13}{14}$
9. $p - 3\frac{2}{9} = 21\frac{4}{9}$ $p =$ $24\frac{2}{3}$
10. $u + 12\frac{1}{6} = 21\frac{19}{24}$ $u =$ $9\frac{5}{8}$

Classify each figure in as many ways as you can. *[Lesson 5-3]*

11. Quadrilateral, trapezoid
12. Obtuse isosceles triangle
13. Right scalene triangle

A model train is 30 in. long. Use each scale to find the length of the actual train. *[Lesson 7-2]*

14. scale: 1 in. = 8 ft actual length: 240 ft
15. scale: 1 in. = 12 ft actual length: 360 ft
16. scale: 2 in. = 15 ft actual length: 225 ft

Find the missing side lengths in each pair of similar figures. *[Lesson 7-9]*

17. $ABCD \sim EFGH$ $x =$ 64
18. $\triangle IJK \sim \triangle LMN$ $p =$ 36 $q =$ 45
19. $PQRS \sim TUVW$ $a =$ 20 $b =$ 50 $c =$ 30

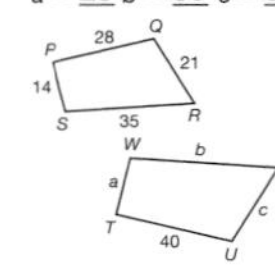

Chapter 7 Summary and Review

Section 7B Dimensional Analysis

Summary

- For any rate, you can find the reciprocal unit rate by exchanging the numerator and denominator, then converting to a unit rate.
- **Conversion factors** are fractions that can be used to convert units. If you need to convert a unit in the *numerator* of a rate, multiply by a conversion factor that has that unit in the *denominator,* and vice versa.

Review

7. Suggest appropriate units for a rate that describes the growth rate of a plant.

8. Give a reciprocal unit rate that has the same meaning as 5 feet per second.

9. Convert 360 miles per hour to miles per minute.

10. Dr. Acevedo earns $55 per hour. Convert this rate to cents per second.

Section 7C Similarity

Summary

- **Similar** figures have the same shape but not necessarily the same size.
- Matching sides and angles of similar figures are **corresponding sides** and **corresponding angles.** Figures are similar if the corresponding angles are congruent and corresponding side lengths have equal ratios.
- The statement $\triangle ABC \sim \triangle DEF$ means that $\triangle ABC$ is similar to $\triangle DEF$. The order of the letters shows the corresponding parts.
- You can use proportions to find side lengths in similar figures.
- The ratio of the perimeters of two similar figures is equal to the scale factor. The ratio of their areas is equal to the *square* of the scale factor.

Review

11. Tell whether the figures on the grid are similar. If they are, write a similarity statement using ~ and give the scale factor. If they're not, explain why not.

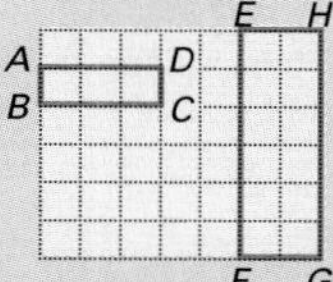

12. Two triangles are similar, with scale factor 4. The smaller triangle has perimeter 7 in. and area 5 in^2. Find the perimeter and area of the larger triangle.

13. Two similar octagons have an area ratio of 81. Find the perimeter ratio and the scale factor from the smaller to the larger.

Chapter 7 Assessment

Assessment Correlation

Item(s)	Lesson(s)
1, 3	7-1
2	7-2
4	7-5
5	7-4
6	7-3
7	7-6
8	7-7
9	7-8
10, 12	7-10
11, 14, 15	7-9
13	7-7

Answers for Assessment

4. Possible answer: miles per hour

7. $\frac{60 \text{ seconds}}{\text{minute}}$ and $\frac{1 \text{ minute}}{60 \text{ seconds}}$.

9. Not similar; There are no congruent corresponding angles.

10. Area ratio = 169; Scale factor = 13

12. Perimeter = 6; Area = 2.

13. 1,080,000,000 kilometers per hour

14. $m\angle D = 34°$; $m\angle E = 82°$; $m\angle F = 64°$

Answers for Performance Task

Possible answers:

$\frac{1 \text{ bushel}}{4 \text{ pecks}}$, $\frac{1 \text{ bushel}}{32 \text{ quarts}}$, $\frac{1 \text{ bushel}}{64 \text{ pints}}$,

$\frac{4 \text{ pecks}}{1 \text{ bushel}}$, $\frac{32 \text{ quarts}}{1 \text{ bushel}}$, $\frac{64 \text{ pints}}{1 \text{ bushel}}$,

$\frac{1 \text{ peck}}{8 \text{ quarts}}$, $\frac{1 \text{ peck}}{16 \text{ pints}}$, $\frac{8 \text{ quarts}}{1 \text{ peck}}$,

$\frac{16 \text{ pints}}{1 \text{ peck}}$, $\frac{1 \text{ quart}}{2 \text{ pints}}$, $\frac{2 \text{ pints}}{1 \text{ quart}}$

Chapter 7 Assessment

1. St. Louis is 240 miles from Memphis. About how far apart will these cities appear on a map with the scale 1 in.:40 mi? **6 in.**

2. A model of a building is 64 cm tall, with the scale 8 cm:11 m. Find the height of the actual building. **88 m**

3. Find the scale of a map if a 10 mile road is shown as 25 inches long. **25 in. = 10 mi or 5 in. = 2 mi**

4. Suggest appropriate units for a rate that tells how fast a dog can run.

5. A bicycle measures 42 in. by 54 in. What is the largest scale that can be used to make a scale drawing of the bicycle to fit in a 3 in. by 5 in. note card? **1:14**

6. Carolyn plans to bicycle to her cousin's home, 26 miles away. She needs to arrive at 3:45 P.M. If she rides at an average rate of 14 miles per hour, when should she leave? **About 1:53 P.M.**

7. Write two conversion factors involving seconds and minutes.

8. Convert $45 per hour to dollars per minute. **$0.75 per minute**

9. Tell whether the figures *ABCD* and *EFGH* are similar. If they are, write a similarity statement using ~ and give the scale factor. If they're not, explain why not.

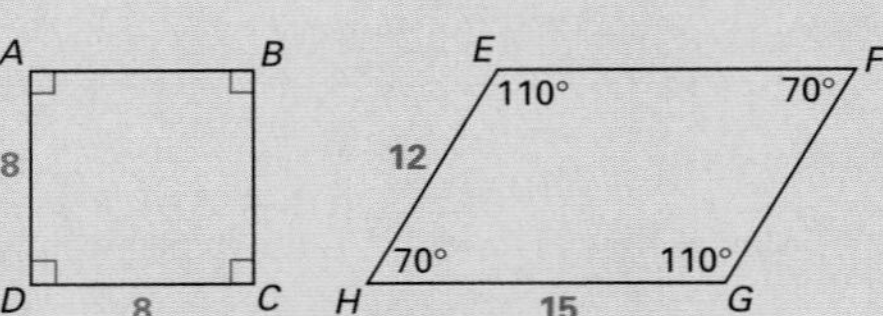

10. Two similar figures have a perimeter ratio of 13. Find the scale factor and the area ratio.

11. $\triangle HIJ \sim \triangle MLK$. Find the missing side lengths. **$a = 21.6$; $b = 19.2$**

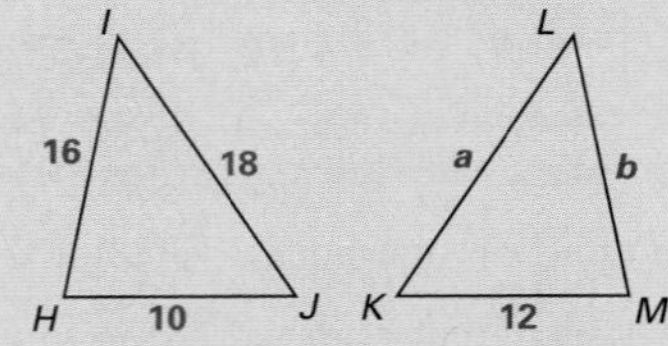

12. Two rectangles are similar, with scale factor 5. The larger rectangle has perimeter 30 and area 50. Find the perimeter and area of the smaller one.

13. Light travels at the rate of 300,000,000 meters per second. Convert this to kilometers per hour.

14. $\triangle JKL \sim \triangle FED$. If $m\angle J = 64°$, $m\angle K = 82°$, and $m\angle L = 34°$, find $m\angle D$, $m\angle E$, and $m\angle F$.

15. When Julianne's shadow is 4 feet long, Greuso's shadow is 22 feet long. If Julianne is 5 feet tall, how tall is Greuso? **27.5 feet**

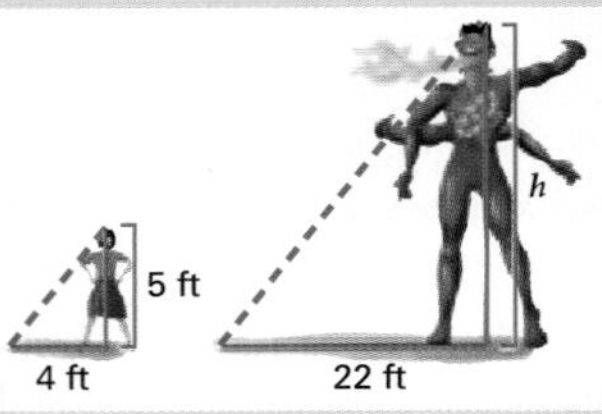

Performance Task

Use the following information to write as many conversion factors as you can: A bushel is 4 pecks. A peck is 8 quarts. A quart is 2 pints.

380 *Chapter 7 • Proportion, Scale, and Similarity*

Resources
Assessment Sourcebook
Chapter 7 Tests
Forms A and B (free response)
Form C (multiple choice)
Form D (performance assessment)
Form E (mixed response)
Form F (cumulative chapter test)
 *TestWorks Test and Practice Software*
Home and Community Connections
Letter Home for Chapter 7 in English and Spanish

Cumulative Review Test Prep

Cumulative Review Chapters 1–7 — Test Prep

Performance Assessment

Choose one problem.

SPACE SCHOOL

Space station Vega 9 has been in orbit for 15 years. Its first generation of children are entering their teens. You are an architect designing a math classroom for Vega 9. Make a scale drawing of your classroom of the future. Show the scale, and label the drawing to explain the items in your classroom and how they work.

You Be the Guide!

Your school has a summer exchange program with a Japanese school. You are excited because one of the students is coming to stay with you. Use maps to plan a 10 day vacation in which you will show your guest around your city and state. Allow time for travel and sightseeing. Write a letter to the student describing your travel plans. Include a map to show her where you will be going.

I'VE BEEN WORKING ON THE RAILROAD

The Transcontinental Railroad was completed in 1869. Many Chinese and Irish laborers died during its construction. Union Pacific crews, working west from Nebraska, laid about 349 miles of track during the three years from 1866 to 1869. Central Pacific crews laid about 18 miles per month during this time. Write a newspaper article about the construction of the railroad. Include a double bar graph comparing each year's total distance for the two crews. Be sure to tell how much track each crew had laid by the time the railroad was finished.

Shadow of Castle Doom

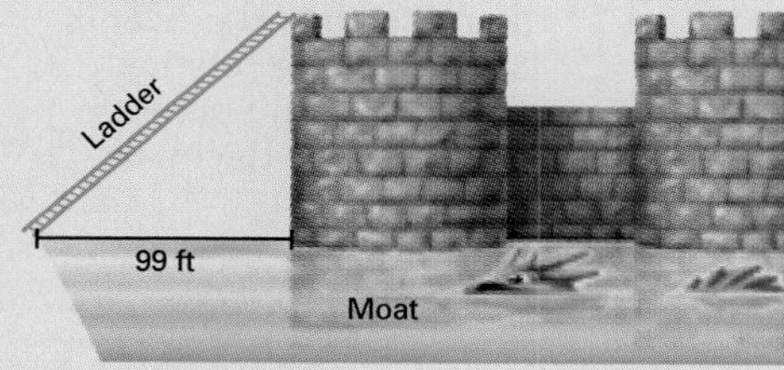

Lady Fenestra, who is 5 ft 6 in. ($5\frac{1}{2}$ ft) tall, must rescue the handsome Don Wannabe from Castle Doom. She plans to place a ladder over the moat to the top of the tower. The moat is 99 feet wide. Lady Fenestra finds that her shadow is 8 ft long when the shadow of the castle tower just covers the moat. How tall is the tower? How long a ladder will Lady Fenestra need? Explain how you found each answer.

About Performance Assessment

The Performance Assessment options:

- provide teachers with an alternate means of assessing students.
- address different learning modalities.
- allow students to choose one problem. Teachers may encourage students to choose the most challenging problem.

Learning Modalities
Space School **Individual** Students undertake the problem of designing a classroom for a space station.
You Be the Guide **Social** Students plan a sightseeing trip for a foreign-exchange student.
I've Been Working on the Railroad **Verbal** Students write a newspaper article comparing two rates in a contest.
Shadow of Castle Doom **Logical** Students reason through relationships in a drawing to explain and solve a problem.

Answer for Assessment
• Shadow of Castle Doom

The tower is about 68.1 feet high. She will need about a 120.2-foot ladder. Possible explanation: Use proportions for actual height and shadow length to find the height of the tower. Use the Pythagorean Theorem (with the tower height and shadow length as legs) to find the length of the ladder.

I've Been Working on the Railroad

Score	Criteria
4	•Writes an interesting newspaper article about the construction of the railroad. •Includes an accurate, well-drawn, clearly labeled double bar graph.
3	•Writes newspaper article about the construction of the railroad. •Includes an adequately labeled double bar graph.
2	•Writes newspaper article including some of the relevant data. •Attempts to draw double bar graph.
1	•Makes little or no attempt to write newspaper article, or fails to include required data. •Makes a poor or no attempt to draw a double bar graph.

Suggested Scoring Rubric

See key on page 321.

Space School

Score	Criteria
4	•Drawing is clearly labeled. •Well-chosen scale is stated and accurately applied. •Shows some imagination as to what a future classroom might look like.
3	•Drawing is clearly labeled. •Scale is clearly stated and accurately applied.
2	•Some labeling has been done. •Scale is stated and an attempt is made to use the scale accurately.
1	•Drawing is poorly or not labeled. •Scale is not stated or is incorrectly used.

Rubric for **You Be the Guide!** on page C1.

Chapter 8

▶ OVERVIEW

Percents

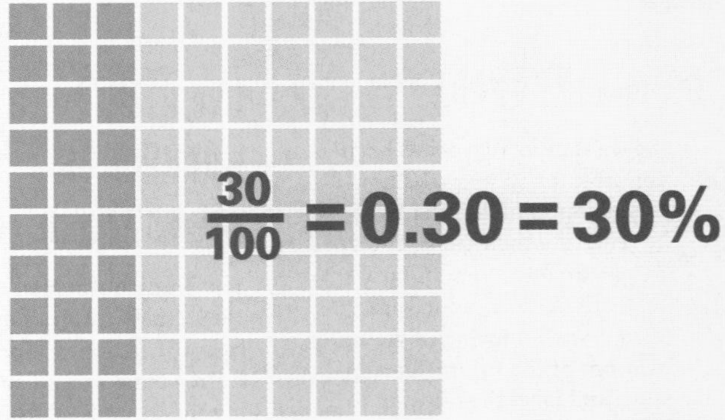

Section 8A

Understanding and Estimating Percents: Students learn to compare quantities using percents. They learn the relationships between percents, fractions, and decimals.

8-1 Understanding Percents

8-2 Linking Fractions, Decimals, and Percents

8-3 Percents Greater than 100 or Less than 1

8-4 Finding a Percent of a Number Mentally

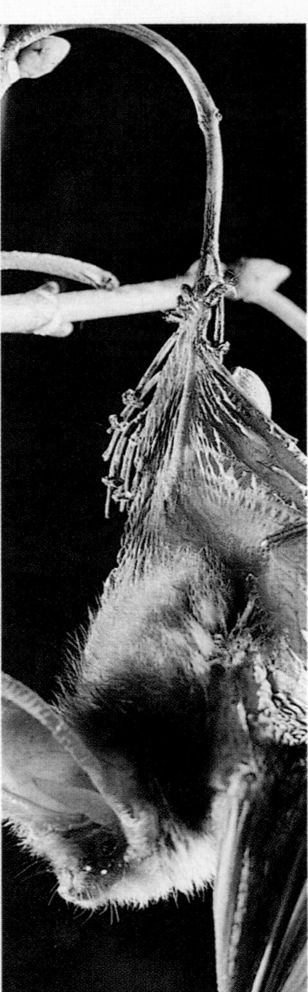

Section 8B

Problem Solving with Percents: Students use equations and proportions to solve problems involving percents. They use percents to describe amounts of increase or decrease.

8-5 Using Equations to Solve Percent Problems

8-6 Solving Percent Problems with Proportions

8-7 Problem Solving: Percent Increase and Decrease

Meeting NCTM Standards

Curriculum Standards

STANDARD			pages
1	**Problem Solving**	Skills and Strategies	384, 397, 398, 400, 402, *408,* 409, 413, 414, 416, 419
		Applications	388–389, 392–393, 397–398, 401–402, 403, 408–409, 413–414, 418–419, 421
		Exploration	386, 390, 394, 399, 406, 410, 415
2	**Communication**	Oral	385, 387, 391, 393, 396, 400, 402, 405, 407, 412, 417
		Written	389, 393, 398, 402, 404, 409, 414, 419, 422
		Cooperative Learning	*386, 390, 394, 399, 402, 406, 410, 412, 415*
3	**Reasoning**	Critical Thinking	389, 393, 398, 401, 402, 409, 412, 414
4	**Connections**	Mathematical	See Standards 5–10, 12, 13 below.
		Interdisciplinary	Social Studies 382, *396, 398,* 408; Science 382, *385,* 387, 392, 397, 401, 404, 413, *417,* 418; Entertainment 383; History 387, *392,* 413, 416, 422; Consumer 389, *405,* 408, 409, 418, 422; Health *393*; Geography 398; Music 407; Fine Arts 382, 388
		Technology	*384, 389,* 405, 411, 420
		Cultural	383, *412*
5	**Number and Number Relationships**		386–404, 409, 410–419
6	**Number Systems and Number Theory**		388, 397
7	**Computation and Estimation**		*391*, 392, 399–404, *407*, 410–419
8	**Patterns and Functions**		413, 423
9	**Algebra**		406–409
10	**Statistics**		392, 414, 420
12	**Geometry**		419
13	**Measurement**		388

Italic type indicates Teacher Edition reference.

Teaching Standards

Focus on Classroom Environment

Teachers should create a learning environment that fosters the development of each student's mathematical power. This includes

- providing and structuring the time necessary to grapple with significant ideas.
- providing a context that encourages the development of mathematical skill.

Assessment Standards

Focus on Equity

Ongoing Assessment The Equity Standard couples high expectations for all students with the opportunity and support necessary for them to reach those levels. Ongoing Assessment provides a means of support as teachers focus on each student's progress as he or she is processing new mathematical information. Ongoing assessment in Chapter 8 probes students'

- understanding of **Explore** activities.
- ability to use estimation with percent.

TECHNOLOGY

For the Teacher

- **Resource Pro, a Teacher's Resource Planner CD-ROM**
  Use the teacher planning CD-ROM to view resources available for Chapter 8. You can prepare custom lesson plans or use the default lesson plans provided.

- **World Wide Web**
  Visit **www.kz.com** to view class summary reports, individual student reports, and more.

- **Test Works**
  TestWorks provides ready-made tests and can create custom tests and practice worksheets.

For the Parent

- **World Wide Web**
  Parents can use the web site at **www.kz.com** to check on student progress or take a quick refresher course.

For the Student

- **Interactive CD-ROM**
  Lesson 8-2 has an *Interactive CD-ROM Lesson.* The *Interactive CD-ROM Journal* and *Spreadsheet/Grapher Tool* are also used in Chapter 8.

- **World Wide Web**
  Use with Chapter and Section Openers; Students can go online to the Scott Foresman-Addison Wesley Web site at **www.mathsurf.com/7/ch8** to collect information about chapter themes. Students can also visit **www.kz.com** for tutorials and practice.

STANDARDIZED - TEST CORRELATION

SECTION 8A

LESSON	OBJECTIVE	ITBS Form M	CTBS 4th Ed.	CAT 5th Ed.	SAT 9th Ed.	MAT 7th Ed.	Your Form
8-1	• Compare quantities by using percents.	✘	✘		✘	✘	
8-2	• Understand the relationships between percents, fractions, and decimals.	✘	✘	✘	✘	✘ ✘	
8-3a	• Use percents that are less than 1%.	✘		✘	✘	✘	
3b	• Use percents that are greater than 100%.						
8-4	• Use mental math to find a percent of a number.						

SECTION 8B

LESSON	OBJECTIVE	ITBS Form M	CTBS 4th Ed.	CAT 5th Ed.	SAT 9th Ed.	MAT 7th Ed.	Your Form
8-5	• Use equations to solve problems involving percents.	✘	✘	✘	✘	✘	
8-6	• Use proportions to solve percent problems.					✘	
8-7	• Solve problems involving percent increase and percent decrease.			✘		✘	

Key: ITBS - Iowa Test of Basic Skills; CTBS - Comprehensive Test of Basic Skills; CAT - California Achievement Test; SAT - Stanford Achievement Test; MAT - Metropolitan Achievement Test

ASSESSMENT PROGRAM

Traditional Assessment

QUICK QUIZZES	SECTION REVIEW	CHAPTER REVIEW	CHAPTER ASSESSMENT FREE RESPONSE	CHAPTER ASSESSMENT MULTIPLE CHOICE	CUMULATIVE REVIEW
TE: pp. 389, 393, 398, 402, 409, 414, 419	SE: pp. 404, 422 *Quiz 8A, 8B	SE: pp. 424–425	SE: p. 426 *Ch. 8 Tests Forms A, B, E	*Ch. 8 Tests Forms C, E	SE: p. 427 *Ch. 8 Test Form F

Alternate Assessment

INTERVIEW	JOURNAL	ONGOING	PERFORMANCE	PORTFOLIO	PROJECT	SELF
TE: p. 402	SE: pp. 389, 398, 404, 409, 414, 419, 422 TE: pp. 384, 389, 393	TE: pp. 386, 390, 394, 399, 406, 410, 415	SE: p. 426 TE: p. 398 *Assessment Resources*, *Ch. 8 Tests Forms D, E	TE: p. 419	SE: pp. 402, 414 TE: p. 383	TE: p. 409

*Tests and quizzes are in *Assessment Sourcebook*. Test Form E is a mixed response test. Forms for Alternate Assessment are also available in *Assessment Sourcebook*.

TestWorks: Test and Practice Software

MIDDLE SCHOOL PACING CHART

REGULAR PACING

Day	5 classes per week
1	Chapter 8 Opener; Problem Solving Focus
2	Section **8A** Opener; Lesson **8–1**
3	Lesson **8–2**
4	Lesson **8–3**
5	Lesson **8–4**
6	**8A** Connect, **8A** Review
7	Section **8B** Opener; Lesson **8–5**
8	Lesson **8–6**
9	Lesson **8–7**; Technology
10	**8B** Connect; **8B** Review; Extend Key Ideas
11	Chapter 8 Summary and Review
12	Chapter 8 Assessment; Cumulative Review, Chapters 1–8

BLOCK SCHEDULING OPTIONS

Block Scheduling for
Complete Course

Chapter 8 may be presented in

- seven 90-minute blocks
- ten 75-minute blocks

Each block consists of a combination of

- Chapter and Section Openers
- Explores
- Lesson Development
- Problem Solving Focus
- Technology
- Extend Key Ideas
- Connect
- Review
- Assessment

For details, see *Block Scheduling Handbook.*

Block Scheduling for
Interdisciplinary Course

Each block integrates math with another subject area.

In Chapter 8, interdisciplinary topics include

- Bats
- Discount Malls

Themes for Interdisciplinary Team Teaching 8A and 8B are

- Interpreting Hard Drive Scans
- Heart Disease

For details, see *Block Scheduling Handbook.*

Block Scheduling for
Lab-Based Course

In each block, 30–40 minutes is devoted to lab activities including

- Explores in the Student Edition
- Connect pages in the Student Edition
- Technology options in the Student Edition
- Reteaching Activities in the Teacher Edition

For details, see *Block Scheduling Handbook.*

Block Scheduling for
Course with *Connected Mathematics*

In each block, investigations from **Connected Mathematics** replace or enhance the lessons in Chapter 8.

Connected Mathematics topics for Chapter 8 can be found in

- *Comparing and Scaling*

For details, see *Block Scheduling Handbook.*

INTERDISCIPLINARY BULLETIN BOARD

Set Up

Display a large outline of your state on a bulletin board. Write your state's name and total population. Provide an atlas or other resource material for researching population figures about your state.

Procedure

- Have small groups of students determine the percentage of the state's population living in the major cities throughout the state.
- Groups should write the name of a city in the correct location on the map and show the percentage of the state's population living there.

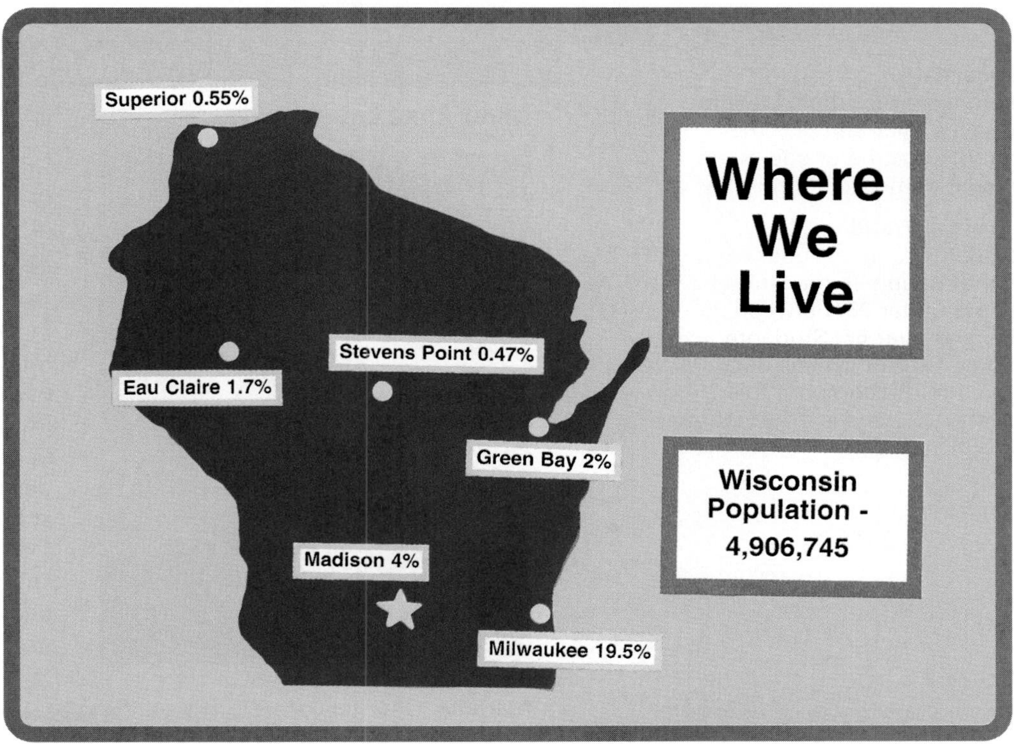

Chapter 8

The information on these pages shows how percents are used in real-life situations.

World Wide Web

If your class has access to the World Wide Web, you might want to use the information found at the Web site addresses given.

Extensions

The following activities do not require access to the World Wide Web.

Science
Have students find how the humidity in the air affects the weather. Suggest they compare a hot, muggy day in summer to a cool day in winter.

Social Studies
Have students find China on a map. Ask them to use library resources to find other products China produces.

Arts & Literature
Ask students to research the Guggenheim Museum. For whom is it named? Who designed it? What type of art is exhibited?
Established in 1937 by Solomon R. Guggenheim; Current building designed by Frank Lloyd Wright in 1959; Contains one of the world's largest collections of abstract art.

Entertainment
Have students pick their favorite basketball player and find the percent of shots he or she made in a recent game.

People of the World
Ask students to investigate what percent of people in the United States are under 25, between 25 and 65, and over 65. Students might use current census data. They also might compare this data with U.S. census information from 1890.

8 Percents

Science Link
www.mathsurf.com/7/ch8/science

Arts & Literature Link
www.mathsurf.com/7/ch8/arts

Science

The relative humidity is a measure of the amount of water the air can hold at a particular temperature. The warmer it is, the more water the air can hold. A relative humidity of 85% at 90°F is wetter than a relative humidity of 85% at 40°F.

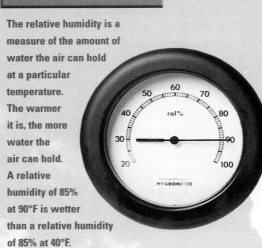

Arts & Literature

The Guggenheim Museum in New York City has a spiraling gallery that increases in height at a 3% grade.

Social Studies

China produced 2,915,000 of the 10,333,000 metric tons of pears grown in one year. This is about 28% of the world's pear production.

382

TEACHER TALK

Meet Anne Lawrence

East Cobb Middle School
Marietta, Georgia

To illustrate percent in a fun way, I purchase packages of M & M's® or Smarties®. I buy a package for each group of students, or, if the packages are small, one package for each student.

Initially each group (or each student) determines the total number of candies in the package. Then, working with the ratio $\frac{\text{part}}{\text{whole}}$, they determine what fraction of the total each color represents. Students compute $\frac{\text{part}}{\text{whole}}$ to obtain a decimal, and then they change the decimal to a percent. Finally I have students add to show that their percents total 100%. This activity transfers knowledge from ratio to fraction to decimals to percent. Later it can also be used with probability.

Entertainment Link
www.mathsurf.com/7/ch8/ent

Entertainment

Lisa Leslie, a center on the United States 1996 Olympic women's basketball team, shot 86% from the field in the gold medal game against Brazil. She made 12 of the 14 shots she took.

People of the World

50% of the people in the world are under the age of 25.

KEY MATH IDEAS

A percent is a ratio that describes a part of 100.

You can use the fact that *percent* means "out of 100" to help you rewrite a percent as a fraction or decimal.

Problems about money often involve percents. You can set up proportions or use other kinds of equations to solve a problem with percents.

You can use percents to describe an increase or decrease in a number.

CHAPTER PROJECT

Problem Solving
Understand
Plan
Solve
Look Back

In this project, you will plan a picnic for young children in a hospital. You must make sure that your meal is nutritious and appealing. To begin the project, make a list of some of the foods you might want to serve.

PROJECT ASSESSMENT

You may choose to use this project as a performance assessment for the chapter.

Performance Assessment Key

Level 4 Full Accomplishment

Level 3 Substantial Accomplishment

Level 2 Partial Accomplishment

Level 1 Little Accomplishment

Suggested Scoring Rubric

Level	Criteria
4	• Meal and costs are appropriate. • Bar graph shows correct percents. • Calories and grams of fat are accurate and, if necessary, meal is adjusted to fit given guidelines.
3	• Meal and costs are adequate. • Bar graph shows percents. • Calories and grams of fat are given and, if necessary, meal is adjusted.
2	• An attempt is made to suggest a meal and find costs. • Bar graph is not entirely accurate. • Some calories and grams of fat are given. Meal is not adjusted.
1	• Meal suggestions do not fit guidelines and costs are not accurate. • Bar graph is not accurate. • Calories and grams of fat, if given, are not accurate.

Chapter Project

Students plan a nutritious and appealing picnic for children in a hospital.

Resources
Chapter 8 Project Master

Introduce the Project

- Talk about the kinds of foods that might be appealing, easy to serve, and nutritious.
- Ask students what other things they might consider in planning foods for a picnic, such as calorie count, ease of preparation, and ease of transportation.
- Talk about where students might get more information about food preparation and nutrition, such as cookbooks, magazines, and the Internet.

Project Progress

Section A, page 402 Students list picnic items and the total cost of each item. They make a bar graph showing what percent of the total cost each item represents.

Section B, page 414 Students determine the calories and grams of fat in a typical teenager's diet and in their picnic meal. They ascertain whether the picnic meal fits within given guidelines.

Community Project

A community project for Chapter 8 is available in *Home and Community Connections.*

Cooperative Learning

You may want to use Teaching Tool Transparency 1: Cooperative Learning Checklist with **Explore** and other group activities in this chapter.

Problem Solving Focus

Interpreting Mathematical Phrases

The Point
Students focus on translating words into symbols to help solve a given math problem.

Resources
Teaching Tool Transparency 16: Problem-Solving Guidelines

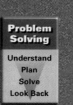

 *Interactive CD-ROM Journal*

About the Page

Using the Problem-Solving Process
In order to solve a problem, students often need to interpret words such as "half as much as," replacing them with appropriate mathematical symbols. Discuss the following suggestions for interpreting phrases:

- Read the problem two or three times before beginning work.
- Identify the key phrases that can be translated into math symbols.
- Translate the phrases and do any appropriate computation.

Ask ...
- What is the key mathematical phrase in Problem 1? How do you interpret it? Three times as many; Multiply by 3.
- In Problem 2, why is the answer 6 chilies, not 8 chilies? The phrase "how many more chilies" suggests subtracting the 2 chilies Doreen already has from the total number she needs.
- In Problem 3, do you need to determine the number of pieces of papadum Reggie plans to make? No

Answers for Problems
1. $3 \times 2 = 6$ cups.
2. $4 \times 2 - 2 = 6$ more chilies.
3. $5 \times \frac{1}{2} = 2\frac{1}{2}$ teaspoons.
4. $24 \times \frac{2}{3} = 16$ people.

Journal
Ask students to write and solve a problem that uses several word phrases that must be translated into mathematical phrases to solve the problem.

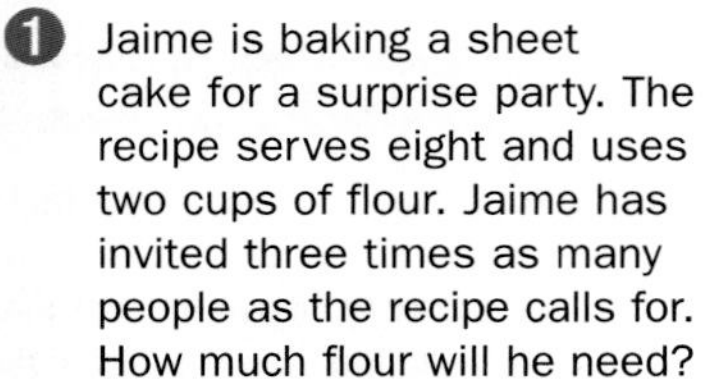

Interpreting Mathematical Phrases

When making a problem-solving plan, you need to translate words into mathematical symbols. For example, the phrase "half as much as" can mean "$\times \frac{1}{2}$," and "four times as many" can mean "$\times 4$."

Problem Solving Focus

For each problem below, write the answer and the arithmetic you used to find the answer. (For example, if you added 5 to 7 to get 12, write "5 + 7 = 12.")

1. Jaime is baking a sheet cake for a surprise party. The recipe serves eight and uses two cups of flour. Jaime has invited three times as many people as the recipe calls for. How much flour will he need?
2. Doreen is bringing Salsa Verde Cruda to the party. Her recipe for this uncooked green sauce makes one and one-half cups of salsa. Doreen decides to make four times this amount. If the recipe calls for two serrano chilies, how many more chilies than this should she buy?
3. Reggie decides to make papadum, a spicy crispbread popular in India. He usually uses $\frac{1}{2}$ teaspoon of cumin seed to make 10 pieces of papadum. If he wants to make 5 times this many pieces, how much cumin should he use?
4. Huynh, who doesn't like to cook, volunteered to bring drinks. She estimates that $\frac{2}{3}$ of the 24 people who are coming to the party will want milk with their cake. How many people should she buy milk for?

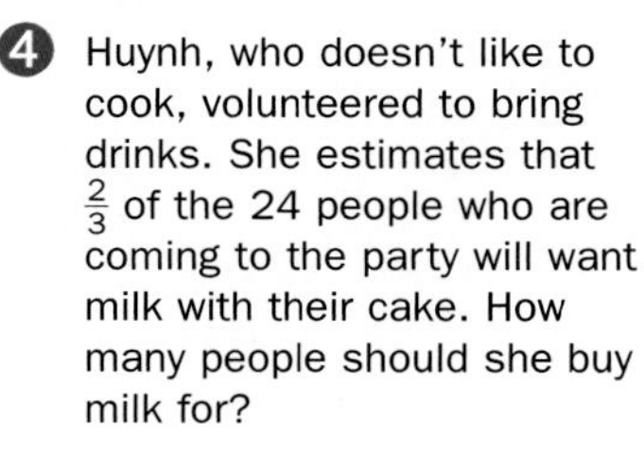

384

Additional Problem

In 1993 there were about 14.9 million inline skaters in the U.S. By 1996 this number doubled. About how many inline skaters were there in 1996?

1. What does the problem ask you to find? An estimate of the number of inline skaters in 1996.
2. What word phrase must be translated into a mathematical phrase? What does this phrase tell you to do? "This number doubled" suggests multiplying by 2.
3. Can you use an estimate to solve the problem? Explain. Yes, because the question says "about how many?"
4. How would you solve the problem? Possible answers: $2 \times 14.9 = 29.8$ million skaters, or estimate, $2 \times 15 = 30$ million skaters.

Understanding and Estimating Percents

LESSON PLANNING GUIDE

Student Edition

Ancillaries*

LESSON		MATERIALS	VOCABULARY	DAILY	OTHER
	Chapter 8 Opener				Ch. 8 Project Master Ch. 8 Community Project Teaching Tool Trans. 1
	Problem Solving Focus				Teaching Tool Trans. 16 *Interactive CD-ROM Journal*
	Section 8A Opener				
8-1	**Understanding Percents**	graph paper	percent	8–1	Teaching Tool Trans. 7, 11 Technology Master 33
8-2	**Linking Fractions, Decimals, and Percents**			8–2	Technology Master 34 *Interactive CD-ROM Lesson 8*
8-3	**Percents Greater than 100 or Less than 1**	graph paper		8–3	Teaching Tool Trans. 7 Lesson Enhancement Trans. 35 Technology Master 35
8-4	**Finding a Percent of a Number Mentally**			8-4	Teaching Tool Trans. 20 Ch. 8 Project Master
	Connect				Teaching Tool Trans. 14 Lesson Enhancement Trans. 36 Interdisc. Team Teaching 8A
	Review				Practice 8A; Quiz 8A; *Testworks*

* Daily Ancillaries include Practice, Reteaching, Problem Solving, Enrichment, and Daily Transparency. Teaching Tool Transparencies are in *Teacher's Toolkits.* Lesson Enhancement Transparencies are in *Overhead Transparency Package.*

SKILLS TRACE

LESSON	SKILL	FIRST INTRODUCED GR. 5	GR. 6	GR. 7	DEVELOP	PRACTICE/APPLY	REVIEW
8-1	**Comparing by using percents.**			✘ p. 386	pp. 386–387	pp. 388–389	pp. 404, 424, 446, 504
8-2	**Relating percents, fractions, and decimals.**		✘		pp. 390–391	pp. 392–393	pp. 404, 424, 454, 511
8-3	**Using percents less than 1% and greater than 100%.**			✘ p. 394	pp. 394–396	pp. 397–398	pp. 404, 424, 459, 516
8-4	**Using mental math to find a percent of a number.**			✘ p. 399	pp. 399–400	pp. 401–402	pp. 404, 425, 465, 520

CONNECTED MATHEMATICS

The unit *Comparing and Scaling, (Ratio, Proportion and Percent),* from the **Connected Mathematics** series can be used with Section 8A.

INTERDISCIPLINARY TEAM TEACHING

Math and Science/Technology

(Worksheet pages 31–32: Teacher pages T31–T32)

In this lesson, students use percentages to interpret a hard-drive scan on a computer.

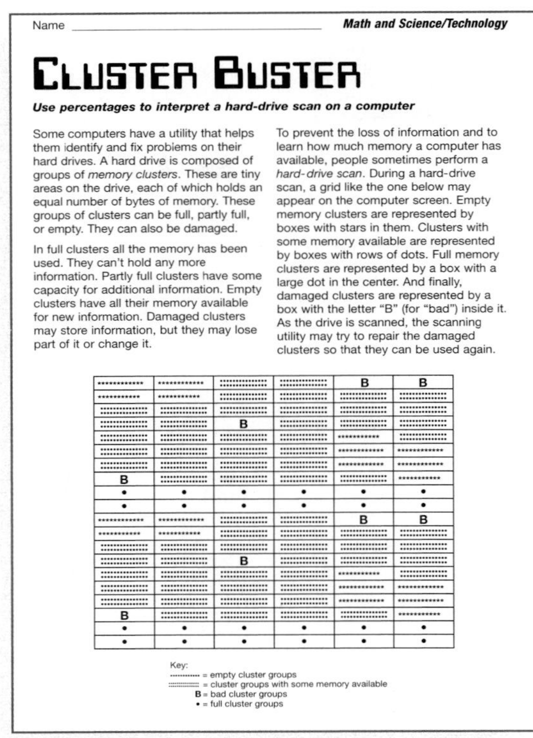

Name ____________________ ***Math and Science/Technology***

CLUSTER BUSTER

Use percentages to interpret a hard-drive scan on a computer

Some computers have a utility that helps them identify and fix problems on their hard drives. A hard drive is composed of groups of *memory clusters*. These are tiny areas on the drive, each of which holds an equal number of bytes of memory. These groups of clusters can be full, partly full, or empty. They can also be damaged.

In full clusters all the memory has been used. They can't hold any more information. Partly full clusters have some capacity for additional information. Empty clusters have all their memory available for new information. Damaged clusters may store information, but they may lose part of it or change it.

To prevent the loss of information and to learn how much memory a computer has available, people sometimes perform a *hard-drive scan*. During a hard-drive scan, a grid like the one below may appear on the computer screen. Empty memory clusters are represented by boxes with stars in them. Clusters with some memory available are represented by boxes with rows of dots. Full memory clusters are represented by a box with a large dot in the center. And finally, damaged clusters are represented by a box with the letter "B" (for "bad") inside it. As the drive is scanned, the scanning utility may try to repair the damaged clusters so that they can be used again.

************	************	::::::::::::::	::::::::::::::	B	B
***********	***********	::::::::::::::	::::::::::::::	::::::::::::::	::::::::::::::
::::::::::::::	::::::::::::::	::::::::::::::	::::::::::::::	::::::::::::::	::::::::::::::
::::::::::::::	::::::::::::::	B	::::::::::::::	::::::::::::::	::::::::::::::
::::::::::::::	::::::::::::::	::::::::::::::	::::::::::::::	***********	::::::::::::::
::::::::::::::	::::::::::::::	::::::::::::::	::::::::::::::	************	************
::::::::::::::	::::::::::::::	::::::::::::::	::::::::::::::	************	************
B	::::::::::::::	::::::::::::::	::::::::::::::	::::::::::::::	***********
•	•	•	•	•	•
•	•	•	•	•	•
************	************	::::::::::::::	::::::::::::::	B	B
***********	***********	::::::::::::::	::::::::::::::	::::::::::::::	::::::::::::::
::::::::::::::	::::::::::::::	::::::::::::::	::::::::::::::	::::::::::::::	::::::::::::::
::::::::::::::	::::::::::::::	B	::::::::::::::	::::::::::::::	::::::::::::::
::::::::::::::	::::::::::::::	::::::::::::::	::::::::::::::	***********	::::::::::::::
::::::::::::::	::::::::::::::	::::::::::::::	::::::::::::::	************	************
::::::::::::::	::::::::::::::	::::::::::::::	::::::::::::::	************	************
B	::::::::::::::	::::::::::::::	::::::::::::::	::::::::::::::	***********
•	•	•	•	•	•
•	•	•	•	•	•

Key:
············ = empty cluster groups
:::::::::::: = cluster groups with some memory available
B = bad cluster groups
• = full cluster groups

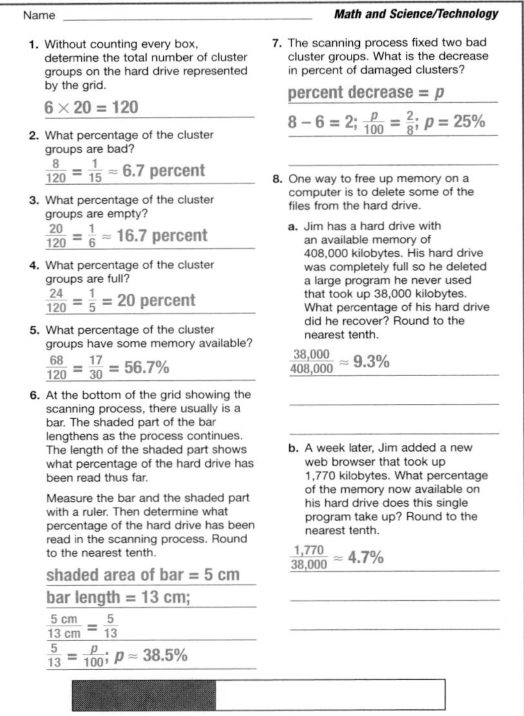

Name ____________________ ***Math and Science/Technology***

1. Without counting every box, determine the total number of cluster groups on the hard drive represented by the grid.

$6 \times 20 = 120$

2. What percentage of the cluster groups are bad?

$\frac{8}{120} = \frac{1}{15} \approx 6.7$ percent

3. What percentage of the cluster groups are empty?

$\frac{20}{120} = \frac{1}{6} \approx 16.7$ percent

4. What percentage of the cluster groups are full?

$\frac{24}{120} = \frac{1}{5} = 20$ percent

5. What percentage of the cluster groups have some memory available?

$\frac{68}{120} = \frac{17}{30} = 56.7\%$

6. At the bottom of the grid showing the scanning process, there usually is a bar. The shaded part of the bar lengthens as the process continues. The length of the shaded part shows what percentage of the hard drive has been read thus far.

Measure the bar and the shaded part with a ruler. Then determine what percentage of the hard drive has been read in the scanning process. Round to the nearest tenth.

shaded area of bar = 5 cm

bar length = 13 cm;

$\frac{5 \text{ cm}}{13 \text{ cm}} = \frac{5}{13}$

$\frac{5}{13} = \frac{p}{100}$; $p \approx 38.5\%$

7. The scanning process fixed two bad cluster groups. What is the decrease in percent of damaged clusters?

percent decrease = p

$8 - 6 = 2$; $\frac{p}{100} = \frac{2}{8}$; $p = 25\%$

8. One way to free up memory on a computer is to delete some of the files from the hard drive.

a. Jim has a hard drive with an available memory of 408,000 kilobytes. His hard drive was completely full so he deleted a large program he never used that took up 38,000 kilobytes. What percentage of his hard drive did he recover? Round to the nearest tenth.

$\frac{38{,}000}{408{,}000} \approx 9.3\%$

b. A week later, Jim added a new web browser that took up 1,770 kilobytes. What percentage of the memory now available on his hard drive does this single program take up? Round to the nearest tenth.

$\frac{1{,}770}{38{,}000} \approx 4.7\%$

BIBLIOGRAPHY

FOR TEACHERS

Eyewitness Visual Dictionaries. *The Visual Dictionary of Buildings*. London, England: Dorling Kindersley, 1992.

Kenney, Margaret J. and Hirsch, Christian R. *Discrete Mathematics Across the Curriculum*. Palo Alto, CA: Dale Seymour Publications, 1996.

Pappas, Theoni. *The Joy of Mathematics*. San Carlos, CA: Wide World Publishing/Tetra House, 1989.

Spangler, David. *Math for Real Kids*. Glenview, IL: Good Year Books, 1997.

FOR STUDENTS

Graham, Gary L. *Bats of the World*. Racine, WI: Western Publishing, 1994.

Kalec, Donald G. *The Home and Studio of Frank Lloyd Wright*. Oak Park, IL: F. L. Wright Foundation, 1982.

McDonald, Mary Ann. *Flying Squirrels*. Mankato, MN: Child's World, 1993.

Milton, Joyce. *Bats: Creatures of the Night*. New York, NY: Gosset & Dunlap, 1993.

SECTION 8A Understanding and Estimating Percents

▶ Science Link ▶ www.mathsurf.com/7/ch8/bats

To the Batcave!

It's just before dusk. You're standing near the Congress Avenue Bridge in Austin, Texas. Suddenly you hear a whirring sound. What looks like a cloud of smoke pours out from underneath the bridge.

But it's not smoke, it's *bats*—1.5 *million* bats, the largest urban bat colony in North America. Austin's bats make up a small part of the 100 million free-tailed bats that migrate north from Mexico each spring to raise their young.

Many countries have legends about bats that attack people. Actually, most bats are harmless and many are extremely beneficial to humans. One little brown bat may eat 600 mosquitoes in one hour—an average of one insect every six seconds!

Mathematical information can help people separate fact from fiction. As you learn more about bats you'll begin your study of *percents,* which are an important way to communicate mathematical information.

1 Write 1.5 million in scientific notation.

2 Give an example showing how mathematics can help people tell fact from fiction.

3 How could you use mathematics to compare Austin's free-tailed bat population to Austin's human population?

385

Where are we now?

In Grade 6 students studied percent as part of the Ratio, Proportion, Percent chapter.

They learned to

- estimate with percents.
- connect percents, fractions, and decimals.
- find a percent of a whole number.

Where are we going?

In Grade 7, Section 8A, students will

- compare quantities using percents.
- relate fractions, decimals, and percents.
- use percents less than 1% and greater than 100%.
- find the percent of a number mentally.

Theme: Bats

World Wide Web

If your class has access to the World Wide Web, you might want to use the information found at the Web site address given. The interdisciplinary link relates to the topics discussed in this section.

About the Page

This page introduces the theme of the section, bats, and discusses bat migration, eating habits, and legends.

Ask ...

- Have you ever seen a bat?
- When are bats usually seen? At night; they are nocturnal.

Extension

The following activity does not require access to the World Wide Web.

Science

Bats are mammals that resemble birds. Have students list ways that bats differ from birds and list characteristics bats have in common with birds. Possible answers: Differ: Bats have fur, not feathers; bat babies are born live, not hatched; bats have a nose and mouth, not a beak. In common: both can fly, some migrate, some eat insects.

Answers for Questions

1. 1.5×10^6
2. Possible answers: Statistics gathered about bat species show that most eat insects or fruit. Very few live on animals' blood, and none live on human blood.
3. Possible answer: Use division to decide how many times more there are of one than the other.

Connect

On page 403, students apply what they have learned about percents to data about the Mexican free-tailed bat.

8-1 Lesson Organizer

Objective

- Compare quantities by using percents.

Vocabulary

- Percent

Materials

- Explore: Graph paper

NCTM Standards

- 1–6, 13

Review 

Write each fraction in lowest terms.

1. $\frac{6}{12}$ $\frac{1}{2}$
2. $\frac{3}{15}$ $\frac{1}{5}$
3. $\frac{15}{18}$ $\frac{5}{6}$

Write each fraction as an equivalent fraction with a denominator of 100:

4. $\frac{4}{25}$ $\frac{16}{100}$
5. $\frac{3}{20}$ $\frac{15}{100}$

Available on Daily Transparency 8-1

1 Introduce

Explore  

You may want to use Teaching Tool Transparency 7: $\frac{1}{4}$-Inch Graph Paper and Teaching Tool Transparency 11: 10 × 10 Grids with **Explore**.

The Point
Students recognize the relationship between the 10 by 10 grid and the decimal or fractional representation and see advantages to using 100 as a consistent benchmark for comparing numbers.

Ongoing Assessment
Check for students who have trouble in Step 2. Remind them that 0.8 means eight-tenths or eight-out-of-ten; check to see that they are shading eight out of each ten squares in the grid.

8-1 Understanding Percents

You'll Learn ...

- to compare quantities by using percents

... How It's Used

Marketing specialists use percents to measure the opinions of potential customers.

Vocabulary

percent

Lesson Link You've studied several methods for comparing quantities, including rates, ratios, and scales. Now you'll compare quantities by measuring them in relation to 100. ◄

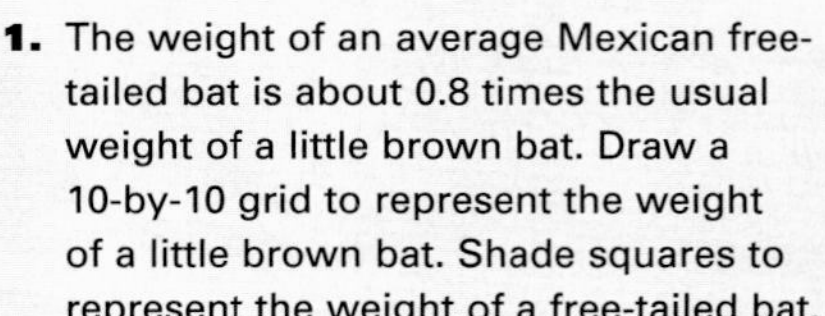

Explore — Comparing Numbers Using Grids

Free Tails and Long Ears

Materials: Graph paper

Red bat

1. The weight of an average Mexican free-tailed bat is about 0.8 times the usual weight of a little brown bat. Draw a 10-by-10 grid to represent the weight of a little brown bat. Shade squares to represent the weight of a free-tailed bat.
2. Repeat Step 1 using a 10-by-4 grid to represent the little brown bat. Then repeat Step 1 using a 6-by-5 grid. Which of the three grids was easiest to use? Why?
3. The length of an average long-eared bat is about $\frac{3}{10}$ the length of a typical red bat. Draw a 10-by-10 grid to represent the length of a red bat. Shade squares to represent the length of a long-eared bat.
4. Repeat Step 3 using a grid size of your choice.
5. Compare your Step 3 and Step 4 grids with those of other students. What is the advantage of using a 10-by-10 grid?

Learn — Understanding Percents

There are 60 shaded squares on this 10-by-10 grid. So $\frac{60}{100}$ of the squares are shaded. You can say that 60 **percent** (written 60%) of the grid squares are shaded. A percent is a ratio that describes a part of 100. 60% means "60 *per hundred*." So 100% represents a whole.

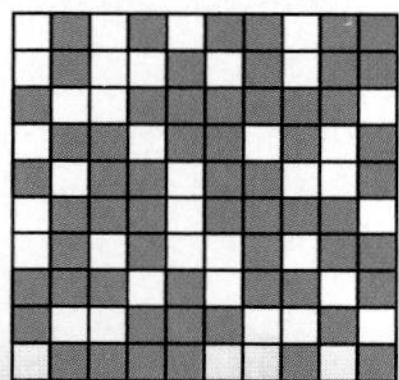

MEETING INDIVIDUAL NEEDS

Resources

- 8-1 Practice
- 8-1 Reteaching
- 8-1 Problem Solving
- 8-1 Enrichment
- 8-1 Daily Transparency
  - Problem of the Day
  - Review
  - Quick Quiz
- Teaching Tool Transparencies 7, 11
- Technology Master 33

Learning Modalities

Kinesthetic Students can use geoboards and rubber bands in place of the grid paper in the lesson. For some students, the geoboard will provide a more "concrete" and meaningful representation.

Social Have groups of 4 students try to throw a crumpled sheet of paper into a trash can from 10 feet away 5, 10, 20, and 25 times, respectively. Then have the students represent their accuracy first with fractions ($\frac{3}{5}$ or $\frac{13}{25}$, for example) and then with percents (60% or 52%).

English Language Development

Be sure students understand the meaning of the word *percent*. The word literally means "for every hundred," so 60 *percent* means *60 for every hundred*. Understanding the meaning of the word will actually help the students use the concept.

Ask Spanish-speaking students for the Spanish equivalent (*por ciento*) and its literal translation *for a hundred*.

Example 1

Use percents to compare the sizes of the tennis court and the picnic area.

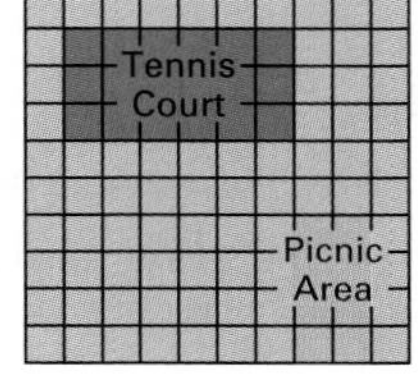

The tennis court occupies 18 out of 100 squares. That's 18% of the park. The picnic area occupies 8 out of 100 squares. That's 8% of the park.

To compare ratios with different denominators, you can write each ratio with a denominator of 100. Then compare the percents.

History Link

Percents used to be written as fractions, with the numerators over 100. Gradually, the bar of the fraction and the 100 blended together to become the percent sign we use today.

Example 2

Little brown bats spend about $\frac{11}{20}$ of their hibernation period in light sleep and about $\frac{2}{5}$ in a state of complete inactivity called "deep torpor." Use percents to compare the amount of time spent in each type of hibernation.

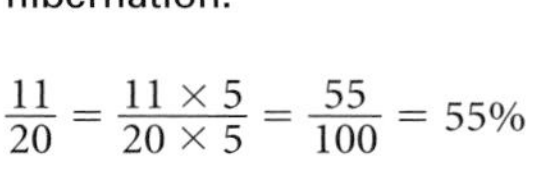

$$\frac{11}{20} = \frac{11 \times 5}{20 \times 5} = \frac{55}{100} = 55\%$$

Rewrite both fractions with denominators of 100.

$$\frac{2}{5} = \frac{2 \times 20}{5 \times 20} = \frac{40}{100} = 40\%$$

During hibernation, little brown bats are in light sleep about 55% of the time and in deep torpor about 40% of the time. They spend more of their time in light sleep.

Science Link

Bats are the only mammals that can truly fly. The "flying" squirrel really only glides from tree to tree, using membranes attached to its legs.

Try It

Use percents to compare.

a. $\frac{1}{2}$ and $\frac{3}{5}$ $\frac{1}{2} = 50\%; \frac{3}{5} = 60\%; \frac{1}{2} < \frac{3}{5}$

b. $\frac{7}{10}$ and $\frac{3}{4}$ $\frac{7}{10} = 70\%; \frac{3}{4} = 75\%; \frac{7}{10} < \frac{3}{4}$

c. $\frac{13}{20}$ and $\frac{16}{25}$ $\frac{13}{20} = 65\%; \frac{16}{25} = 64\%; \frac{13}{20} > \frac{16}{25}$

Check Your Understanding

1. If all the squares on a grid are shaded, what percent of them are shaded?

2. What percent of the votes in an election would guarantee a win? Explain.

MATH EVERY DAY

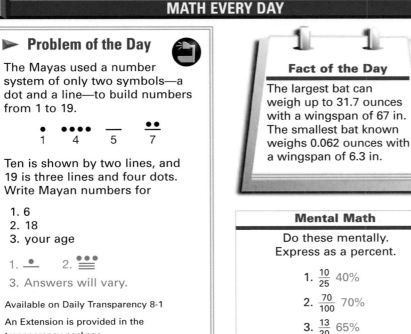

Problem of the Day

The Mayas used a number system of only two symbols—a dot and a line—to build numbers from 1 to 19.

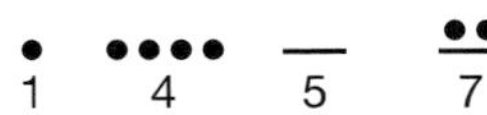

Ten is shown by two lines, and 19 is three lines and four dots. Write Mayan numbers for

1. 6
2. 18
3. your age

1. (one dot over one line) 2. (three dots over three lines)
3. Answers will vary.

Available on Daily Transparency 8-1

An Extension is provided in the transparency package.

Fact of the Day

The largest bat can weigh up to 31.7 ounces with a wingspan of 67 in. The smallest bat known weighs 0.062 ounces with a wingspan of 6.3 in.

Mental Math

Do these mentally. Express as a percent.

1. $\frac{10}{25}$ 40%
2. $\frac{70}{100}$ 70%
3. $\frac{13}{20}$ 65%

Answers for Explore

1–2. See page C2.

3.

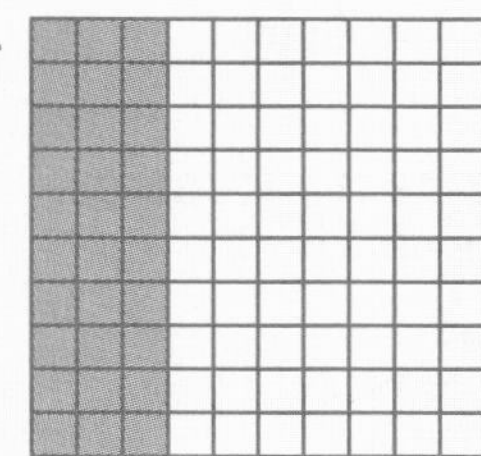

4. Possible answer:

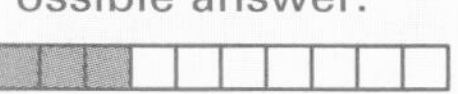

5. It is easier to see that each student has shaded the same fractions of the grid.

2 Teach

Learn

Alternate Examples

1.

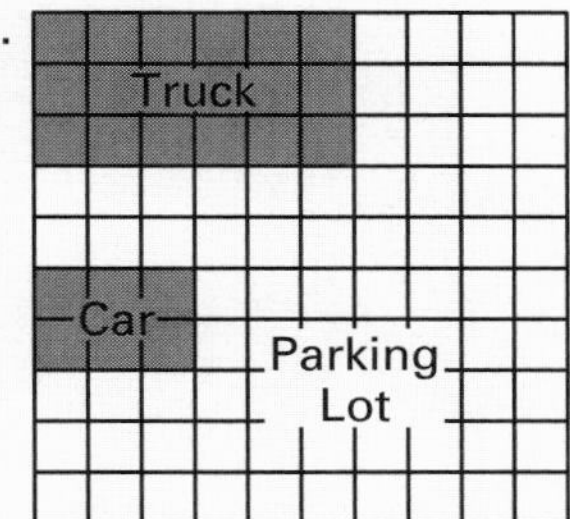

Use percents to compare the sizes of the two vehicles in the parking lot.

The car occupies 6 out of 100 squares. That's 6% of the lot. The truck occupies 18 of the 100 squares, or 18%.

2. Seventh graders typically spend about $\frac{1}{4}$ of their day in school and $\frac{1}{5}$ of their day watching TV. Use percents to compare the amount of time spent in each activity.

$\frac{1}{4} = \frac{25}{100} = 25\%$

$\frac{1}{5} = \frac{20}{100} = 20\%$

3 Practice and Assess

Check

Answers for Check Your Understanding

1. 100%
2. More than 50%; If there are two candidates, one must receive more than $\frac{1}{2}$ of the votes.

8-1 Exercises and Applications

Assignment Guide

- **Basic**
  1–8, 12–13, 17–23, 30–32, 34–48 evens
- **Average**
  2–26 evens, 27–31, 32–48 evens
- **Enriched**
  3–19 odds, 20–34, 35–49 odds

Exercise Notes

Exercise 20

Fine Arts Originally, Escher studied to be an architect, but after a short time, he switched to the decorative and graphic arts.

Exercise Answers

12. $\frac{6}{20} = 30\%, \frac{3}{10} = 30\%; \frac{6}{20} = \frac{3}{10}$
13. $\frac{11}{25} = 44\%, \frac{1}{2} = 50\%; \frac{11}{25} < \frac{1}{2}$
14. $\frac{1}{4} = 25\%, \frac{6}{25} = 24\%; \frac{1}{4} > \frac{6}{25}$
15. $\frac{3}{4} = 75\%, \frac{4}{5} = 80\%; \frac{3}{4} < \frac{4}{5}$
16. $\frac{7}{10} = 70\%, \frac{18}{25} = 72\%; \frac{7}{10} < \frac{18}{25}$

8-1 Exercises and Applications

PRACTICE 8-1

Practice and Apply

1. **Getting Started** Follow these steps to write $\frac{7}{25}$ as a percent.

a. *Percent* means "out of 100," so you need to write a fraction equal to $\frac{7}{25}$ with a denominator of 100. What number do you need to multiply 25 by to get 100? 4

b. Use your answer to **a** to rewrite $\frac{7}{25}$ with a denominator of 100. $\frac{28}{100}$

c. Write the numerator of your fraction in **b** with a percent sign. 28%

Express each fraction as a percent.

2. $\frac{47}{100}$ 47% **3.** $\frac{75}{100}$ 75% **4.** $\frac{25.5}{100}$ 25.5% **5.** $\frac{48.3}{100}$ 48.3% **6.** $\frac{8}{10}$ 80%

7. $\frac{15}{20}$ 75% **8.** $\frac{4}{25}$ 16% **9.** $\frac{13.5}{100}$ 13.5% **10.** $\frac{2}{5}$ 40% **11.** $\frac{3.2}{4}$ 80%

Number Sense Use percents to compare.

12. $\frac{6}{20}$ and $\frac{3}{10}$ **13.** $\frac{11}{25}$ and $\frac{1}{2}$ **14.** $\frac{1}{4}$ and $\frac{6}{25}$ **15.** $\frac{3}{4}$ and $\frac{4}{5}$ **16.** $\frac{7}{10}$ and $\frac{18}{25}$

Use percents to compare the shaded areas on each grid.

17.
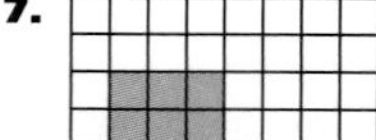
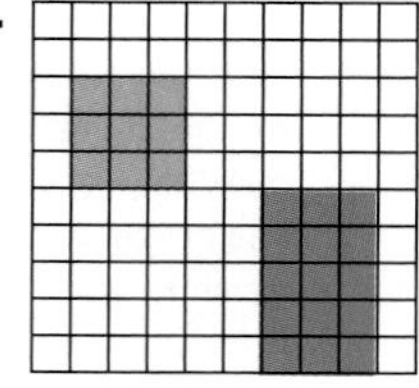
9% < 15%

18.
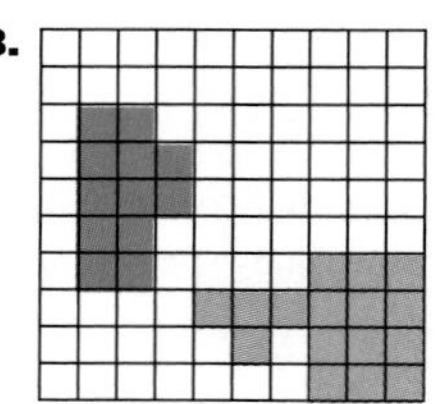
12% < 16%

19.
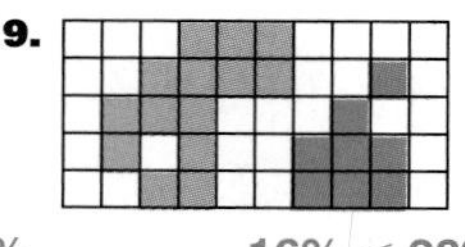
16% < 28%

20. **Fine Arts** M. C. Escher was a Dutch artist who made many prints using interlocking figures called *tessellations.* About what percent of the Escher print shown is made up of black bats? ≈ 20%

M. C. Escher, *Symmetry Drawing*

Measurement There are 100 cm in a meter. Express each length as a percent of a meter.

21. 1 cm 1% **22.** 50 cm 50% **23.** 63 cm 63%

24. 37.5 cm 37.5% **25.** 100 cm 100% **26.** 20.1 cm 20.1%

PRACTICE

Name ______________________ **Practice 8-1**

Understanding Percents

Express each fraction as a percent.

1. $\frac{21}{100}$ 21% 2. $\frac{38}{100}$ 38% 3. $\frac{7}{10}$ 70% 4. $\frac{11}{20}$ 55%
5. $\frac{9}{25}$ 36% 6. $\frac{21}{50}$ 42% 7. $\frac{3.7}{25}$ 14.8% 8. $\frac{18.2}{25}$ 72.8%

Use percents to compare.

9. $\frac{1}{4}$ and $\frac{1}{5}$ 25 % > 20 %
10. $\frac{17}{20}$ and $\frac{22}{25}$ 85 % < 88 %
11. $\frac{3}{10}$ and $\frac{17}{50}$ 30 % < 34 %
12. $\frac{7}{25}$ and $\frac{13}{50}$ 28 % > 26 %
13. $\frac{3}{4}$ and $\frac{19}{25}$ 75 % < 76 %
14. $\frac{13}{20}$ and $\frac{6}{10}$ 65 % > 60 %

Use percents to compare the shaded areas on each grid.

15. 28 % < 30 % 16. 16 % > 12 % 17. 32 % < 36 %

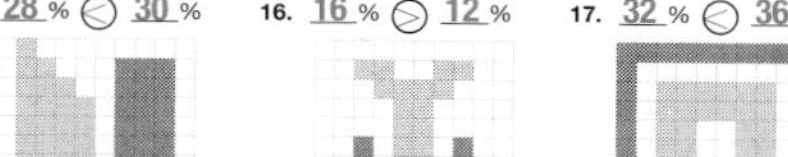

Measurement There are 100 cm in a meter. Express each length as a percent of a meter.

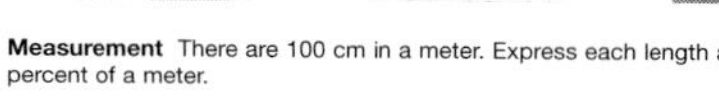

18. 5 cm 5% 19. 70 cm 70% 20. 48.5 cm 48.5% 21. 2.8 cm 2.8%

Consumer Express each amount of money as a percent of a dollar.

22. 8 pennies 8% 23. 4 dimes and a nickel 45%
24. 3 quarters and 4 pennies 79% 25. 2 quarters and 3 nickels 65%
26. **Science** In the wild, only 1 out of 5 cottontail rabbits lives to be six months old. What percent is this? 20%

RETEACHING

Name ______________________ **Alternative Lesson 8-1**

Understanding Percents

A **percent** is a ratio that describes a part of 100. So, 50 percent, written 50%, means "50 *per hundred.*" To compare ratios, write each ratio with a denominator of 100. Then compare the percents.

Example 1

Express $\frac{9}{50}$ as a percent.

Write an equivalent fraction with 100 as the denominator. Since 50 × 2 = 100, multiply the numerator and denominator by 2. $\frac{9}{50} = \frac{9 \times 2}{50 \times 2} = \frac{18}{100}$

Write the numerator of the fraction as a percent. $\frac{18}{100} = 18\%$

So, $\frac{9}{50} = 18\%$.

Try It Express each ratio as a percent.

a. $\frac{17}{20} = \frac{17 \times 5}{20 \times 5} = \frac{85}{100}$

Write the numerator of your fraction with a percent sign. 85%

b. $\frac{16}{25}$ 64% c. $\frac{2}{5}$ 40% d. $\frac{6}{20}$ 30% e. $\frac{1}{4}$ 25%

Example 2

Use percents to compare $\frac{11}{20}$ and $\frac{1}{2}$.

Write each as an equivalent fraction with 100 as the denominator.

Since 20 × 5 = 100, multiply the numerator and the denominator of $\frac{11}{20}$ by 5. $\frac{11}{20} = \frac{11 \times 5}{20 \times 5} = \frac{55}{100} = 55\%$

Since 2 × 50 = 100, multiply the numerator and the denominator of $\frac{1}{2}$ by 2. $\frac{1}{2} = \frac{1 \times 50}{2 \times 50} = \frac{50}{100} = 50\%$

Write the numerator of each fraction as a percent and compare the percents. 55% > 50%

So, $\frac{11}{20} > \frac{1}{2}$.

Try It Use percents to compare $\frac{7}{10}$ and $\frac{3}{4}$. Write your answer using >, <, or =.

f. $\frac{7}{10} = \frac{7 \times 10}{10 \times 10} = \frac{70}{100} = 70\%$

g. $\frac{3}{4} = \frac{3 \times 25}{4 \times 25} = \frac{75}{100} = 75\%$

h. $\frac{7}{10}$ < $\frac{3}{4}$

Reteaching

Activity

Materials: 2-color counters

- Use twenty-five 2-color counters. Toss them gently into the air and let them drop onto a table.
- Tell what fraction of the counters landed on each of the two colors. Then write those two fractions as percents. Do the two percents add up to 100%?
- Do the experiment again. This time use only ten counters.

Consumer **Express each amount of money as a percent of a dollar.**

27. A penny **28.** Two nickels **29.** Four quarters **30.** Three dimes and a nickel

31. **Test Prep** Which percent is equal to $\frac{15}{25}$? D

Ⓐ 4% Ⓑ 15% Ⓒ 25% Ⓓ 60%

Problem Solving and Reasoning

32. **Critical Thinking** About 70% of all species of bats eat insects. About what percent of bat species do *not* eat insects? Explain how you found your answer.

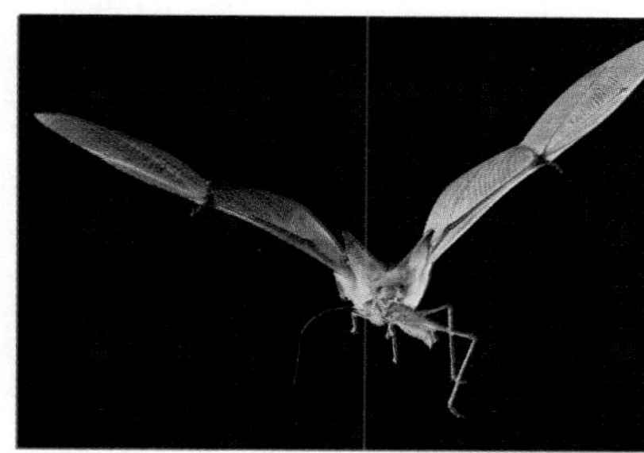

Pallid bat

33. Journal In 1972, the 26th Amendment to the Constitution lowered the voting age from 21 to 18. In 1968, 3 out of 5 eligible voters voted. This ratio is called the *voter turnout.* In 1972, voter turnout changed to 11 out of 20 eligible voters.

a. Use percents to compare the voter turnouts for these elections.

b. Explain why allowing 18- to 20-year-olds to vote might have affected the voter turnout in this way. Then give another possible explanation for the change in voter turnout.

34. **Critical Thinking** Although some bats living in the United States migrate during the cold months of the year, other bats spend the winter hibernating in caves. Most bats in the United States hibernate from early October until the end of April. What percent of the year is this?

GPS

$58\frac{1}{3}$% of a year

Mixed Review

Write each decimal as a fraction in lowest terms. *[Lesson 3-10]*

35. 0.352 $\frac{44}{125}$ **36.** 0.15 $\frac{3}{20}$ **37.** 0.5505 $\frac{1101}{2000}$ **38.** 0.125 $\frac{1}{8}$ **39.** 0.6125 $\frac{49}{80}$

Write each fraction as a decimal. *[Lesson 3-10]*

40. $\frac{3}{7}$ $0.\overline{428571}$ **41.** $\frac{3}{8}$ 0.375 **42.** $\frac{7}{10}$ 0.7 **43.** $\frac{23}{50}$ 0.46 **44.** $\frac{6}{17}$ ≈ 0.352941176 **45.** $\frac{32}{96}$ $0.\overline{3}$

Use the measurements to find the scale of each map. *[Lesson 7-1]*

46. A 40 mi road is 8 cm long. 1 cm:5 mi **47.** A 50 m pool is 2.5 cm long. 1 cm:20 m

48. A 2.7 mi lake is 1.5 in. long. 1 in.:1.8 mi **49.** A 100 ft building is 5 in. wide. 1 in.:20 ft

PROBLEM SOLVING 8-1

Exercise Notes

Exercise 33

History The 26th Amendment was passed during the Vietnam War. Many people felt that young people who could be drafted into the armed forces should have the right to vote.

Exercise Answers

27. 1% of a dollar.

28. 10% of a dollar.

29. 100% of a dollar.

30. 35% of a dollar.

32. 30%; Non-insect-eating bats = All bats (100%) − insect-eating bats (70%) = 30%.

33. a. 3 out of 5 = 60%; 11 out of 20 = 55%. The voter turnout decreased by 5%.

b. 18-to 20-year-olds might have had a lower turnout than other age groups, lowering the overall turnout; Voters in general might have been less interested in the 1972 election.

Alternate Assessment

You may want to use the *Interactive CD-ROM Journal* with this assessment.

Journal Have students make a list of five places where they have seen percents used and then write down the actual numbers that were used as percents.

Quick Quiz

1. Convert $\frac{3}{5}$ to a percent.
   60%
2. Use percents to compare $\frac{4}{25}$ and $\frac{1}{5}$. 16% < 20%
3. What percent of a dollar is 3 quarters and a nickel?
   80%

Available on Daily Transparency 8-1

PROBLEM SOLVING

Name ____________

Guided Problem Solving 8-1

GPS PROBLEM 34, STUDENT PAGE 389

Although some bats living in the United States migrate during the cold months of the year, other bats spend the winter hibernating in caves. Most bats in the United States hibernate from early October until the end of April. What percent of the year is this?

— Understand —

1. What are you asked to find? Percent of the year bats hibernate.
2. What months do most bats hibernate? October through April.

— Plan —

3. How many months do most bats hibernate? 7 months.
4. How many months are in a year? 12 months.
5. Write a fraction to show the part of a year most bats hibernate. $\frac{7}{12}$

— Solve —

6. Divide 100 by the denominator of your fraction in Item 5 to prepare to write an equivalent fraction. $8\frac{1}{3}$
7. Complete the equation to write an equivalent fraction to the one you wrote in Item 5. $\frac{7}{12} \times \frac{8\frac{1}{3}}{8\frac{1}{3}} = \frac{58\frac{1}{3}}{100}$
8. Write the percent of the year that most bats hibernate. $58\frac{1}{3}$%

— Look Back —

9. Why do you need to know that the dates are *early* October and the *end* of April and not just October and April? Possible answer: To better estimate the time spent hibernating. Late October to early April would be 2 months shorter.

SOLVE ANOTHER PROBLEM

Some students attend school from early September until the end of May. What percent of the year is this? 75%

ENRICHMENT

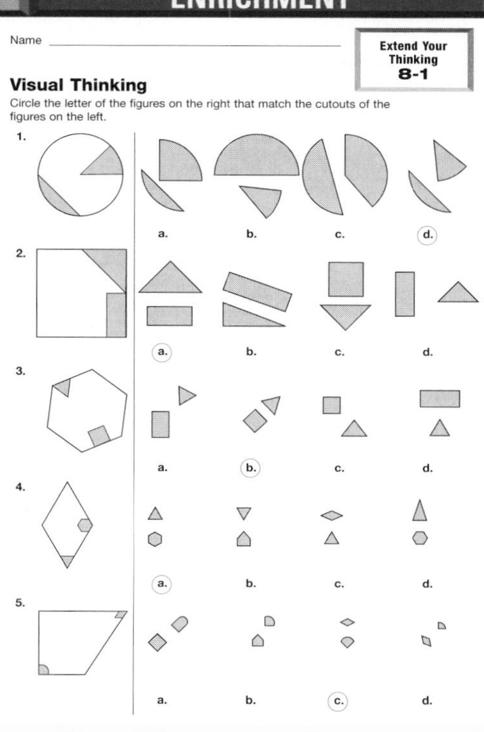

Name ____________

Extend Your Thinking 8-1

Visual Thinking

Circle the letter of the figures on the right that match the cutouts of the figures on the left.

1. a. b. c. (d.)
2. (a.) b. c. d.
3. a. (b.) c. d.
4. (a.) b. c. d.
5. a. b. (c.) d.

INTERACTIVE LESSON

8-2 Lesson Organizer

Objective

- Understand the relationships between percents, fractions, and decimals.

NCTM Standards

- 1–5, 7

Review

Write each decimal as a fraction in lowest terms:

1. 0.3 $\frac{3}{10}$
2. 0.56 $\frac{14}{25}$

Write each fraction as a decimal:

3. $\frac{47}{100}$ 0.47
4. $\frac{7}{50}$ 0.14

Available on Daily Transparency 8-2

1 Introduce

Explore

The Point
Students discover ways to convert fractions into decimals and then into percents.

Ongoing Assessment
Some students may have trouble when they get to the sixth column which contains the fraction $\frac{11}{50}$. Check students' work to be sure that, from habit established in the first five columns, they do not simply write 0.11 and 11%.

For Groups That Finish Early
Write several different equivalent fractions that could be answers in the top row for the last two columns. Possible answers: $\frac{12}{100}$, $\frac{6}{50}$, $\frac{3}{25}$ and $\frac{80}{100}$, $\frac{8}{10}$, $\frac{4}{5}$. Which are in lowest terms? $\frac{3}{25}$ and $\frac{4}{5}$. Which are easiest to visualize? Those in lowest terms.

8-2 Linking Fractions, Decimals, and Percents

You'll Learn ...

- to understand the relationships between percents, fractions, and decimals

... How It's Used

Machinists use relationships between decimals and fractions when selecting drill bits.

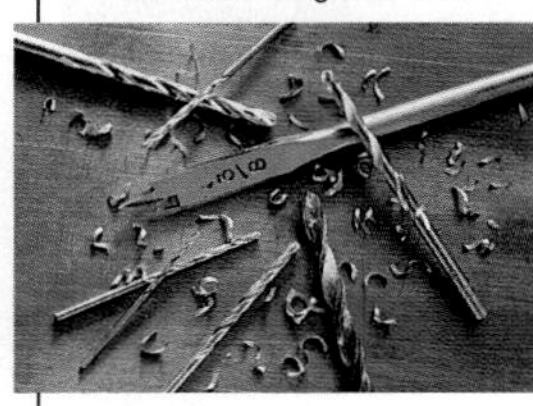

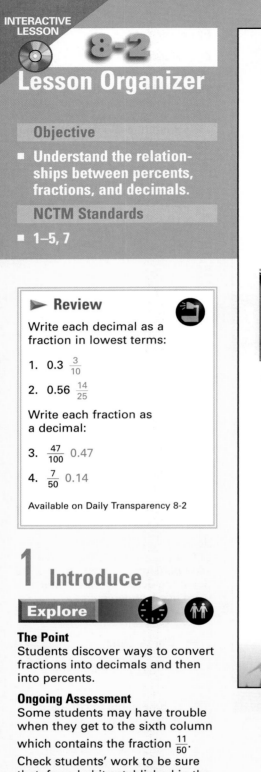

Lesson Link You've seen that percents are ratios. Now you'll look at relationships among percents, fractions, and decimals.

Explore Fractions, Decimals, and Percents

Making Sense of Percents

1. Copy the table. Use the patterns in the first two columns to complete the table.

Fraction	$\frac{91}{100}$	$\frac{23}{100}$	$\frac{67}{100}$			$\frac{11}{50}$		
Decimal	0.91	0.23		0.39			0.12	
Percent	91%	23%			87%			80%

2. Explain how you can write a two-digit decimal such as 0.91 as a percent.
3. Explain how you can write a percent as a fraction.

Learn Linking Fractions, Decimals, and Percents

You can use the fact that *percent* means "out of 100" to rewrite a percent as a fraction.

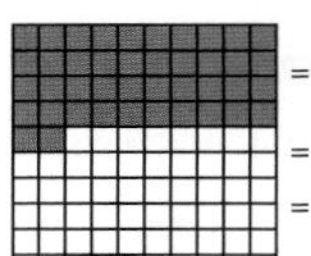

Example 1

About 30% of the tree species in the world's tropical regions are pollinated by bats. Rewrite 30% as a fraction.

$30\% = \frac{30}{100}$ Write the percent as a fraction using 100 as the denominator.

$= \frac{3}{10}$ Rewrite the fraction in lowest terms.

MEETING INDIVIDUAL NEEDS

Resources

- 8-2 Practice
- 8-2 Reteaching
- 8-2 Problem Solving
- 8-2 Enrichment
- 8-2 Daily Transparency
  - Problem of the Day
  - Review
  - Quick Quiz
- Technology Master 34

Interactive CD-ROM Lesson 8

Learning Modalities

Visual Have students use 10 × 10 grids and draw vertical lines to divide the grid into fifths. Then have them shade $\frac{3}{5}$ of the whole grid and write the percent that they shaded by counting the number of shaded small squares. 60%

Kinesthetic Use the same activity as shown above for Visual learners, but use geoboards for more tactile learners. The whole geoboard can represent the unit grid, and students can place a rubber band on the board to enclose $\frac{3}{5}$.

Challenge

Have students use given percents to describe the class as a whole. For instance, Use a non-debatable fact to finish this sentence: "60% of this class is ..." or, "Less than 10% of this class is ..."

Notice that 0.42 and 42% both mean "42 hundredths." Since the *second* place to the right of the decimal point is the hundredths place, you can rewrite decimals and percents by moving the decimal point *two* places.

42.% = 0.42.

42% = 0.42

0.42 = .42.%

0.42 = 42%

Remember

If you know percent names for key fractions, you can use mental math to find the percent names for many others.

$\frac{1}{100} = 1\%$ $\frac{1}{10} = 10\%$

$\frac{1}{5} = 20\%$ $\frac{1}{4} = 25\%$

$\frac{1}{3} = 33\frac{1}{3}\%$ $\frac{1}{2} = 50\%$

[Previous Course]

Examples

2 Write 0.63 as a percent.

To write a decimal as a percent, move the decimal point two places to the *right*.

0.63 = 63%

3 In 1996, about 7.2% of the people living in the United States were between the ages of 10 and 14. Write 7.2% as a decimal.

To write a percent as a decimal, move the decimal point two places to the *left*. Annex zeros as needed.

7.2% = 0.07.2

7.2% = 0.072

You've used division to rewrite fractions in decimal form. By taking one more step, you can also rewrite a fraction as a percent.

Example 4

Little brown bats flap their wings about $\frac{3}{4}$ as fast as pipistrelle bats do. Write the fraction as a decimal and as a percent.

$\frac{3}{4} = 3 \div 4 = 0.75$ Use division to rewrite the fraction as a decimal.

$= 75\%$ Write the decimal as a percent.

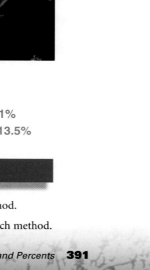

Little brown bat

Try It

a. Write 54% as a fraction. $\frac{27}{50}$

b. Write 0.91 as a percent. 91%

c. Write $\frac{3}{5}$ as a percent. 60%

d. Write 0.135 as a percent. 13.5%

Check Your Understanding

1. What are two ways to write 0.47 as a percent? Explain each method.

2. Describe two ways you could rewrite $\frac{23}{50}$ as a percent. Explain each method.

Follow Up

Ask volunteers to share their written answers to Steps 2 and 3. The answers should come from generalizations about the chart.

Answers for Explore

1. See page C2.
2. To change 0.91 to a percent, move the decimal place two places to the right to get 91%.
3. To change a percent to a fraction, write the percent over 100 and reduce to lowest terms.

2 Teach

Learn

Alternate Examples

1. About 70% of the students in one class have brown hair. Rewrite 70% as a fraction with 100 as the denominator. Then rewrite the fraction in lowest terms.

   $70\% = \frac{70}{100} = \frac{7}{10}$

2. Write 0.39 as a percent.

   Move the decimal point two places to the right.

   0.39 = 39%

3. About 3.4% of the people in one town live in mobile homes. Write 3.4% as a decimal.

   Move the decimal point two places to the left.

   3.4% = 0.034

4. About $\frac{3}{10}$ of the households in America have at least one cat. Write the fraction as a decimal and a percent.

   $\frac{3}{10} = 3 \div 10 = 0.3 = 30\%$

3 Practice and Assess

Check

Answers for Check Your Understanding

1. Move the decimal point two places to the right or multiply by 100.
2. Multiply numerator and denominator by 2: $\frac{23}{50} \times \frac{2}{2} = \frac{46}{100} = 46\%$; or divide 23 by 50 and move the point two places to the right: $23 \div 50 = 0.46 = 46\%$.

MATH EVERY DAY

Problem of the Day

Jon caught a fish that weighed twice as much as Felicia's fish. Andre's fish weighed two kg more than Beth's. Jon's fish weighed half as much as Andre's. Felicia's fish weighed 2.1 kg. How much did Beth's fish weigh? 6.4 kg

Available on Daily Transparency 8-2

An Extension is provided in the transparency package.

Fact of the Day

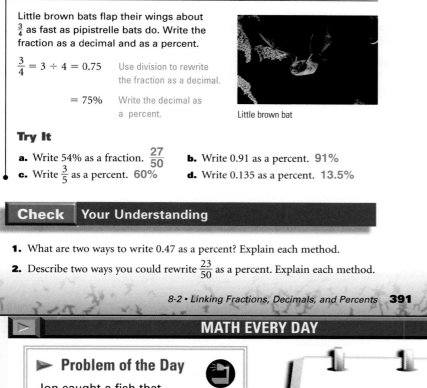

Bats that live in a temperate climate have been known to live as long as 30 years.

Estimation

Estimate the percents for these fractions:

Possible Answers:

1. $\frac{3}{7}$ About 40%
2. $\frac{9}{13}$ About 75%
3. $\frac{4}{9}$ About 45%

8-2 Exercises and Applications

Assignment Guide

- **Basic**
  1–39 odds, 40, 43–55 odds
- **Average**
  1–35 odds, 37–41, 43–61 odds
- **Enriched**
  2–38 evens, 39–42, 44–60 evens

Exercise Notes

Exercise 37

History The first population census in the United States began in 1790. Fewer than 4 million people lived in the United States at that time.

Exercise Answers

38.

Kind of Trash	Plastic	Glass
Percent	59%	12%
Fraction	$\frac{59}{100}$	$\frac{3}{25}$
Decimal	0.59	0.12

Kind of Trash	Metal	Paper	Other
Percent	11%	11%	7%
Fraction	$\frac{11}{100}$	$\frac{11}{100}$	$\frac{7}{100}$
Decimal	0.11	0.11	0.07

Reteaching

Activity

Materials: 10 × 10 grids, number cubes

- Use two number cubes of different colors. Let one color represent tens and the other color represent ones.
- Toss the cubes. Read the number you rolled.
- Shade that number of squares on a 10 × 10 grid.
- Write the fraction, decimal, and percent shown by the shaded squares.

8-2 Exercises and Applications

PRACTICE 8-2

Practice and Apply

1. **Getting Started** Follow these steps to write $\frac{3}{16}$ as a percent.
   a. Write $\frac{3}{16}$ as a decimal by dividing 3 by 16. 0.1875
   b. Rewrite your answer to **a** as a percent by moving the decimal point two places to the right. 18.75%

Write each percent as a decimal.

2. 60% 0.6 **3.** 75% 0.75 **4.** 30% 0.3 **5.** 5% 0.05 **6.** 1% 0.01

7. 100% 1.0 **8.** 8.9% 0.089 **9.** 14.3% 0.143 **10.** 25.5% 0.255 **11.** $47\frac{1}{2}$% 0.475

Write each percent as a fraction in lowest terms.

12. 50% $\frac{1}{2}$ **13.** 20% $\frac{1}{5}$ **14.** 30% $\frac{3}{10}$ **15.** 85% $\frac{17}{20}$ **16.** 98% $\frac{49}{50}$

17. 55% $\frac{11}{20}$ **18.** 65% $\frac{13}{20}$ **19.** 28% $\frac{7}{25}$ **20.** 12.5 % $\frac{1}{8}$ **21.** 37.5% $\frac{3}{8}$

Write each decimal as a percent.

22. 0.86 86% **23.** 0.08 8% **24.** 0.1 10% **25.** 0.875 87.5% **26.** 1.0 100%

Write each fraction as a percent. Where necessary, use a repeating decimal to help express your percent.

27. $\frac{1}{2}$ 50% **28.** $\frac{3}{4}$ 75% **29.** $\frac{4}{9}$ $44.\overline{4}$% **30.** $\frac{1}{4}$ 25% **31.** $\frac{4}{5}$ 80%

32. $\frac{3}{8}$ 37.5% **33.** $\frac{9}{20}$ 45% **34.** $\frac{8.5}{25}$ 34% **35.** $\frac{6.2}{40}$ 15.5% **36.** $\frac{7}{9}$ $77.\overline{7}$%

37. Estimation The 1920 U.S. Census found the United States population to be about 106.02 million. Indiana had a population of about 2.93 million. Estimate the percent of the United States population that lived in Indiana. ≈ 3%

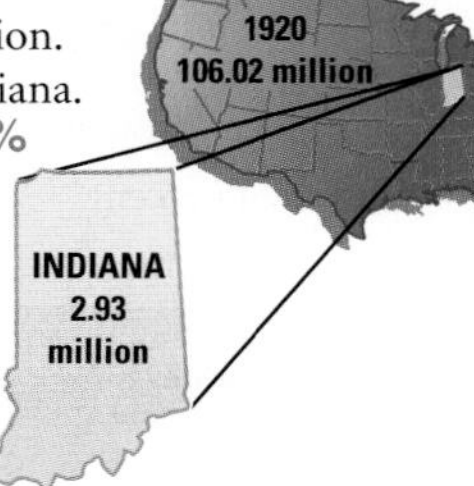

38. Science Each fall, volunteers pick up trash from beaches around the United States. The table shows each kind of trash they find and the percent of total trash it represents. Express each percent as a fraction and as a decimal.

Kind of Trash	Plastic	Glass	Metal	Paper	Other
Percent of Total	59%	12%	11%	11%	7%

PRACTICE

Name ________________

Practice 8-2

Linking Fractions, Decimals, and Percents

Write each percent as a decimal.

1. 83% 0.83 2. 65% 0.65 3. 24% 0.24 4. 7% 0.07
5. 12.7% 0.127 6. 8.75% 0.0875 7. $62\frac{1}{2}$% 0.625 8. $33\frac{1}{3}$% $0.\overline{3}$
9. 2.9% 0.029 10. 18.3% 0.183 11. 99% 0.99 12. $23\frac{1}{4}$% 0.2325

Write each percent as a fraction in lowest terms.

13. 93% $\frac{93}{100}$ 14. 45% $\frac{9}{20}$ 15. 62% $\frac{31}{50}$ 16. 44% $\frac{11}{25}$
17. 10% $\frac{1}{10}$ 18. 62.5% $\frac{5}{8}$ 19. 94% $\frac{47}{50}$ 20. 40% $\frac{2}{5}$
21. 32% $\frac{8}{25}$ 22. 25% $\frac{1}{4}$ 23. 70% $\frac{7}{10}$ 24. 87.5% $\frac{7}{8}$

Write each decimal as a percent.

25. 0.47 47% 26. 0.41 41% 27. 0.34 34% 28. 0.215 21.5%
29. 0.3 30% 30. 0.07 7% 31. 0.999 99.9% 32. 0.085 8.5%

Write each fraction as a percent. Where necessary, use a repeating decimal to help express your percent.

33. $\frac{2}{5}$ 40% 34. $\frac{14}{25}$ 56% 35. $\frac{11}{20}$ 55% 36. $\frac{19}{50}$ 38%
37. $\frac{17}{100}$ 17% 38. $\frac{2}{3}$ $66.\overline{6}$% 39. $\frac{7}{10}$ 70% 40. $\frac{3}{5}$ 60%

41. In 1994, there were 10,057 commercial radio stations in the United States. Of these, 926 stations were devoted to talk (including news, business, or sports). What percent of commercial radio stations were devoted to talk? About 9.2%

42. **Geography** The table lists the percent of the world's land in each continent. Express each percent as a fraction and a decimal.

Continent	Africa	Antarctica	Asia	Australia	Europe	N. America	S. America
Percent of total	20	9	30	5	7	16	9
Fraction	$\frac{1}{5}$	$\frac{9}{100}$	$\frac{3}{10}$	$\frac{1}{20}$	$\frac{7}{100}$	$\frac{4}{25}$	$\frac{9}{100}$
Decimal	0.2	0.09	0.3	0.05	0.07	0.16	0.09

RETEACHING

Name ________________

Alternative Lesson 8-2

Linking Fractions, Decimals, and Percents

A ratio can be written as a fraction, a decimal, or a percent. Since percent means per 100, you can write the percent as a fraction with a denominator of 100. Then rewrite the fraction in lowest terms.

Rewrite decimals and percents by moving the decimal point two places. Move the decimal point to the left to write a percent as a decimal. Move the decimal point to the right to write a decimal as a percent.

Example 1

Write 40% as a fraction in lowest terms.

Since per cent means per 100, you can write the percent as a fraction with a denominator of 100. $40\% = \frac{40}{100}$

Then rewrite the fraction in lowest terms. $\frac{40}{100} = \frac{40 \div 20}{100 \div 20} = \frac{2}{5}$

So, 40% = $\frac{2}{5}$.

Try It Write each percent as a fraction in lowest terms.

a. 65% = $\frac{65}{100} = \frac{13}{20}$ b. 24% = $\frac{6}{25}$ c. 17% = $\frac{17}{100}$

Example 2

Write 21% as a decimal.

Move the decimal point two places to the left to write a percent as a decimal. 21.% = 0.21

So, 21% = 0.21.

Try It Write each percent as a decimal.

d. 73% 0.73 e. 25% 0.25 f. 68% 0.68 g. 5% 0.05

Example 3

Write 0.91 as a percent.

Move the decimal point two places to the right to write a decimal as a percent. 0.91 = 91.%

So, 0.91 = 91%.

Try It Write each decimal as a percent.

h. 0.13 13% i. 0.59 59% j. 0.03 3% k. 0.8 80%

39. **Test Prep** What percent is exactly equal to $\frac{1}{3}$? C

Ⓐ 30% Ⓑ 33% Ⓒ $33\frac{1}{3}$% Ⓓ 34%

Problem Solving and Reasoning

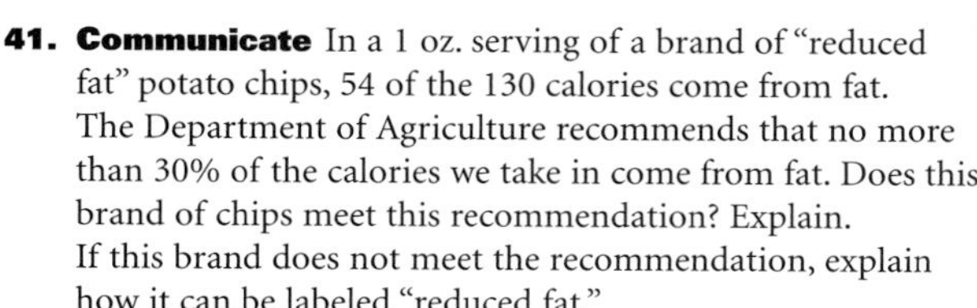

40. Critical Thinking Many bats hibernate during the winter. A wide-awake bat may breathe 200 times per minute; a hibernating bat may breathe 23 times per minute. The bat's normal heart rate of 400 beats per minute often slows to about 25 beats per minute during hibernation. Express the breathing rate and heart rate of a hibernating bat as fractions, decimals, and percents of the corresponding rates for an active bat.

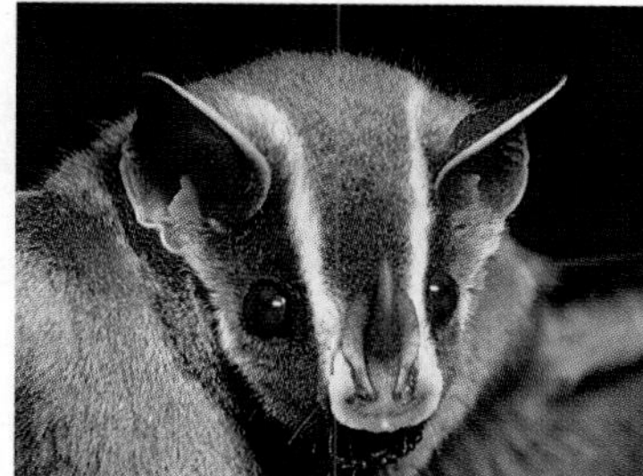

Tent bat

41. Communicate In a 1 oz. serving of a brand of "reduced fat" potato chips, 54 of the 130 calories come from fat. The Department of Agriculture recommends that no more than 30% of the calories we take in come from fat. Does this brand of chips meet this recommendation? Explain. If this brand does not meet the recommendation, explain how it can be labeled "reduced fat."

42. Critical Thinking Seventeen of the 42 species of bats found in the United States are on the endangered species list. What percent of the species of bats found in the United States are endangered? Round your answer to the nearest percent. 40%

Mixed Review

Estimate each sum or difference. *[Lesson 4-1]*

43. $\frac{4}{9} + \frac{3}{7} \approx 1$ **44.** $\frac{4}{5} - \frac{1}{3} \approx \frac{1}{2}$ **45.** $\frac{7}{8} - \frac{1}{9} \approx 1$ **46.** $\frac{1}{14} + \frac{1}{5} \approx 0$ **47.** $\frac{3}{7} + \frac{1}{8} \approx \frac{1}{2}$

48. $\frac{3}{20} - \frac{9}{100} \approx 0$ **49.** $\frac{5}{8} - \frac{1}{6} \approx \frac{1}{2}$ **50.** $\frac{2}{3} + \frac{3}{11} \approx 1$ **51.** $\frac{4}{15} + \frac{1}{9} \approx \frac{1}{2}$ **52.** $\frac{7}{9} + \frac{6}{17} \approx 1\frac{1}{2}$

Solve for *x* in each proportion. *[Lesson 7-2]*

53. $\frac{3 \text{ in.}}{12 \text{ mi}} = \frac{x}{100 \text{ mi}}$ $x = 25$ in. **54.** $\frac{4.2 \text{ cm}}{17 \text{ km}} = \frac{8 \text{ cm}}{x}$ $x \approx 32.38$ km **55.** $\frac{x}{40 \text{ mi}} = \frac{5 \text{ in.}}{250 \text{ mi}}$ $x = 0.8$ in.

56. $\frac{x}{7 \text{ ft}} = \frac{8 \text{ in.}}{14 \text{ ft}}$ $x = 4$ in. **57.** $\frac{22 \text{ mm}}{x} = \frac{11 \text{ mm}}{125 \text{ m}}$ $x = 250$ m **58.** $\frac{42 \text{ cm}}{1 \text{ km}} = \frac{28 \text{ cm}}{x}$ $x = \frac{2}{3}$ km ≈ 0.67 km

59. $\frac{x}{14 \text{ cm}} = \frac{7.5 \text{ mm}}{2 \text{ cm}}$ $x = 52.5$ mm **60.** $\frac{1 \text{ ft}}{25 \text{ mi}} = \frac{12 \text{ ft}}{x}$ $x = 300$ mi **61.** $\frac{0.1 \text{ mm}}{5 \text{ km}} = \frac{2.2 \text{ mm}}{x}$ $x = 110$ km

PROBLEM SOLVING 8-2

PROBLEM SOLVING

Name ______________________

Guided Problem Solving 8-2

GPS **PROBLEM 40, STUDENT PAGE 393**

Many bats hibernate during the winter. A wide-awake bat may breathe 200 times per minute; a hibernating bat may breathe 23 times per minute. The bat's normal heart rate of 400 beats per minute often slows to about 25 beats per minute during hibernation. Express the breathing rate and heart rate of a hibernating bat as fractions, decimals, and percents of the corresponding rates for active bats.

— Understand —

1. What is the breathing rate of a hibernating bat? 23 times per min.
2. What is the breathing rate of an active bat? 200 times per min.
3. What is the heart rate of a hibernating bat? 25 beats per min.
4. What is the heart rate of an active bat? 400 beats per min.
5. Which ratio are you asked to find for each rate? a

   a. $\frac{\text{hibernating rate}}{\text{active (wide-awake) rate}}$ b. $\frac{\text{active (wide-awake) rate}}{\text{hibernating rate}}$

— Plan —

6. Write the ratio for the breathing rate. 23:200 For the heart rate. 25:400

— Solve —

7. Write the answer for **5a** as a

   a. fraction. $\frac{23}{200}$ b. decimal. 0.115 c. percent. 11.5%

8. Write the answer for **5b** as a

   a. fraction. $\frac{25}{400} = \frac{1}{16}$ b. decimal. 0.0625 c. percent. 6.25%

— Look Back —

9. Write each of your answers in fraction form. Are they all equal?
   $\frac{23}{200}, \frac{23}{200}, \frac{23}{200}; \frac{1}{16}, \frac{1}{16}, \frac{1}{16}$; Yes.

SOLVE ANOTHER PROBLEM

There are 50 travel books in the library. Of these, 17 are about international travel. Express the ratio of international books to travel books as a fraction, a decimal, and a percent. $\frac{17}{50}$, 0.34, 34%

ENRICHMENT

Name ______________________

Extend Your Thinking 8-2

Critical Thinking

Use the clues below to complete the Venn Diagram. Write the number that would appear in each section. The total is 100.

1. 0.5 of the total is in the entire area of Circle A. 50
2. 45% of the total is in the entire area of Circle B. 45
3. $\frac{13}{20}$ of the total is in the entire area of Circle C. 65
4. 0.15 of the total is in Circles A and B. 15
5. 27% of the total is in Circles A and C. 27
6. $\frac{6}{25}$ of the total is in Circles B and C. 24
7. 0.09 of the total is in Circles A and B, but *not* in Circle C. 9
8. 21% of the total is in Circles A and C, but *not* in Circle B. 21
9. 0.18 of the total is in Circles B and C, but *not* in Circle A. 18
10. $\frac{3}{50}$ of the total is in Circles A, B, and C. 6
11. Write the numbers in each section of the Venn Diagram.

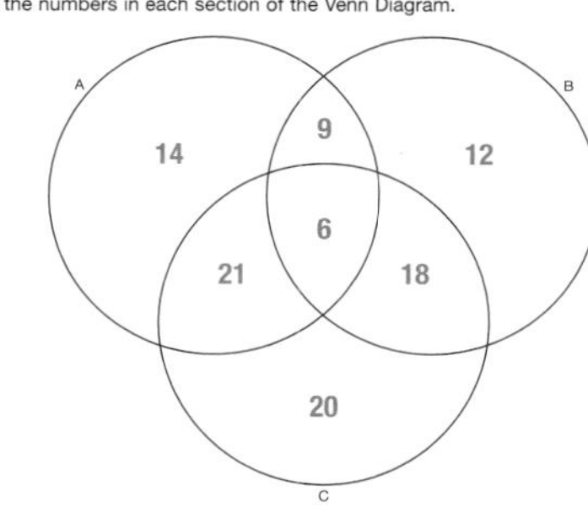

Exercise Notes

■ Exercise 41

Health Explain that the limit of 30% of calories that come from fat refers to an overall diet. A single food may have more or less than this amount.

Extension You might have students check the Nutrition Facts labels on foods and chart the percents of various nutrients in different types of foods.

Exercise Answers

40. $\frac{\text{hibernating breathing rate}}{\text{active breathing rate}} = \frac{23}{200} =$ 0.115 = 11.5%

$\frac{\text{hibernating heart rate}}{\text{active heart rate}} = \frac{1}{16} =$ 0.0625 = 6.25%

41. No; 54 of 130 calories = 41.5%. There must have been a brand of chips for which more than 41.5% of the calories came from fat. The manufacturer changed the recipe to have fewer fat calories, but not enough to meet the recommended levels.

Alternate Assessment

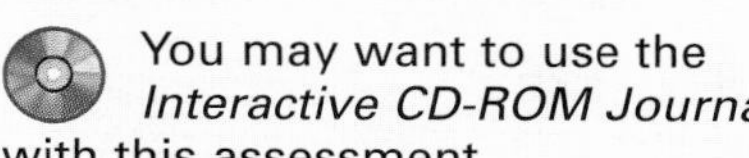

You may want to use the *Interactive CD-ROM Journal* with this assessment.

Journal Have students respond to the following question in their math journals.

Look at the five places you named in your last journal entry where you have seen percents used. In which of those places could fractions or decimals have been used as well? Write each of the the percents you named as a fraction and as a decimal.

➤ Quick Quiz

1. Write 4.7% as a decimal. 0.047
2. Write $\frac{3}{15}$ as both a decimal and a percent. 0.2, 20%
3. Write the portion of time that you sleep every day as a fraction, decimal, and percent of a 24-hour day. Answers will vary but should be approximately $\frac{1}{3}$, 0.33, and 33%.

Available on Daily Transparency 8-2

Lesson Organizer

Objectives

- Use percents that are less than 1%.
- Use percents that are greater than 100%.

Materials

- Explore: Graph paper

NCTM Standards

- 1–6

Review

Write each fraction as a decimal:

1. $\frac{23}{1000}$ 0.023
2. $\frac{478}{100}$ 4.78
3. $\frac{612}{1000}$ 0.612
4. $\frac{5}{4}$ 1.25
5. $\frac{7}{25}$ 0.28

Available on Daily Transparency 8-3

1 Introduce

Explore

You may want to use Teaching Tool Transparency 7: $\frac{1}{4}$-Inch Graph Paper with **Explore**.

The Point
Students use an area model to explore percents that are greater than 100% or less than 1%.

Ongoing Assessment
For Question 2, check that students use as the denominator the total number of *half* squares: 200. Then, in Question 3, they should try to find an equivalent fraction that has a denominator of 100.

For Groups That Finish Early
Describe some comparisons that might result in percents that are less than 1% or greater than 100%. Answers might include comparing all of the people in the country to the number who live in our town.

8-3 Percents Greater than 100 or Less than 1

You'll Learn ...

- to use percents that are less than 1%
- to use percents that are greater than 100%

... How It's Used

Home buyers pay close attention to changes of fractions of a percent in interest rates. The higher the interest rate is, the more money they'll pay on their mortgage each month.

► Lesson Link The percents you've used so far range from 1% to 100%. Now you'll use percents that are less than 1% and greater than 100%. ◄

Explore Large and Small Percents

Made in the Shade

Materials: Graph paper

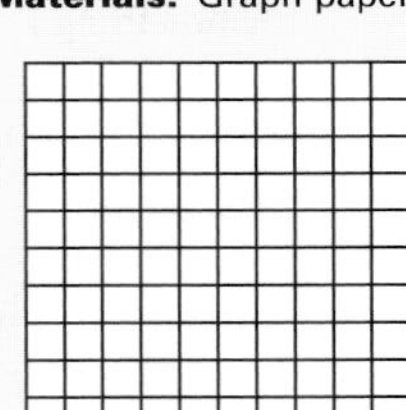

1. Draw a 10-by-10 grid. What percent of the grid does one square represent?
2. Shade half a square. How many half-squares can fit on a grid? What fraction compares one half-square with the total number of half-squares?
3. What percent of a 10-by-10 grid does a half-square represent?
4. Using two grids, shade 120 squares. What percent of one 10-by-10 grid do the squares represent?
5. If you shade *less than one square* on a 10-by-10 grid, what can you say about the percent you have shaded? If you shade *more than one complete grid*, what can you say about the percent?

Learn Percents Greater than 100 or Less than 1

Suppose that, during the first hour of feeding, a little brown bat ate 400 insects.

During the second hour, it ate 600 insects, 150% of the number eaten during the first.

During the third hour, it ate 1 insect, $\frac{1}{4}$% of the number eaten during the first.

100%

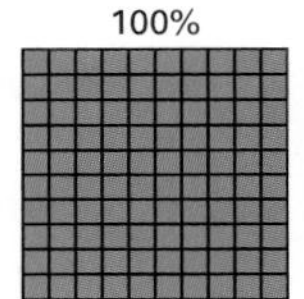

1 square = 4 insects

150%

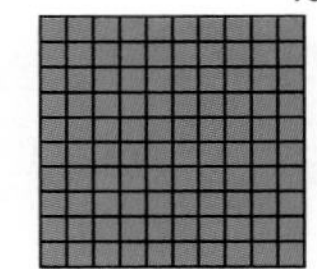

$\frac{1}{4}$%

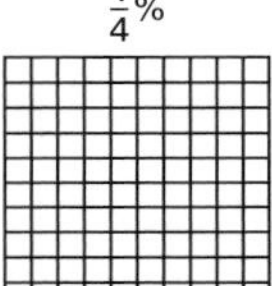

MEETING INDIVIDUAL NEEDS

Resources

- 8-3 Practice
- 8-3 Reteaching
- 8-3 Problem Solving
- 8-3 Enrichment
- 8-3 Daily Transparency
  - Problem of the Day
  - Review
  - Quick Quiz
- Lesson Enhancement Transparency 35
- Teaching Tool Transparencies 7, 20
- Technology Master 35

Learning Modalities

Logical Ask students to formulate a response to the question, "When you find what percent one number is of another, how can you tell whether the answer will be less than 100% or greater than 100%?" Use questions like this to encourage logical thinkers to find and analyze patterns.

Social Have students play a game similar to bingo. Make bingo boards showing percents. Then make "exercise cards" that can be answered with percents on the boards. Let a student read a randomly selected exercise card while other students search for and cover the correct percent on their bingo cards.

Challenge

Have students compute the percent of each day that they spend in the following activities: sleeping, in school, eating, brushing teeth, homework, exercising, watching TV, tying shoes, and passing between classes.

You can express a percent that is less than 1% or greater than 100% as a decimal and as a fraction.

Examples

1 Write 0.3% as a decimal and as a fraction.

To rewrite a percent as a decimal, move the decimal point two places to the left. Annex zeros as needed.

0.3% = 0.00.3

0.3% = 0.003

To rewrite as a fraction:

$0.3\% = \frac{0.3}{100}$ Rewrite with a denominator of 100.

$= \frac{0.3 \times 10}{100 \times 10}$ Rewrite the numerator as a whole number.

$= \frac{3}{1000}$ Simplify.

2 Write 140% as a decimal and as a fraction.

To rewrite a percent as a decimal, move the decimal point two places to the left.

140% = 1.40 = 1.4

To rewrite as a fraction:

$140\% = \frac{140}{100}$ Rewrite with a denominator of 100.

$= \frac{140 \div 20}{100 \div 20}$ To rewrite in lowest terms, divide by the GCF of 140 and 100.

$= \frac{7}{5}$, or $1\frac{2}{5}$ Simplify.

Test Prep

When you rewrite decimals as percents and vice versa, remember that the number will look greater in percent form. This will help you remember which way to move the decimal point.

You may be able to use mental math to rewrite decimals or fractions as percents.

Remember

You can find the greatest common factor of two numbers by listing all the factors of each and finding the greatest factor that is in both lists. **[Page 139]**

Example 3

A large flying fox bat eats about 2.5 times its weight in fruit each night. Write 2.5 as a percent.

Think: 100% = the flying fox's weight.

So 2.5 = 2.5 × 100% = 250%.

Flying fox bat

Try It

Write as a fraction and as a decimal. **a.** 0.4% $\frac{1}{250}$, 0.004 **b.** 125% $1\frac{1}{4}$, 1.25

MATH EVERY DAY

Problem of the Day

I am thinking of a four-digit number. The number is divisible by 8 and 9. The digits increase by one as you read from left to right. What number am I thinking of? Possible answer: 3456

Available on Daily Transparency 8-3

An Extension is provided in the transparency package.

Fact of the Day

Some bats that live in temperate regions migrate to warmer climates in winter. Bats can fly up to 1000 miles to their destination.

Mental Math

Do these mentally.
Write each as a percent:

1. $\frac{3}{200}$ 1.5%
2. 1.52 152%
3. $\frac{6}{1000}$ 0.6%

Answers for Explore

1. 1%
2. 200; $\frac{1}{200}$
3. $\frac{1}{2}\%$
4.

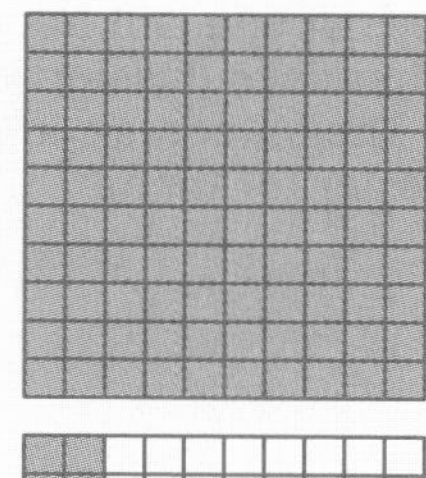

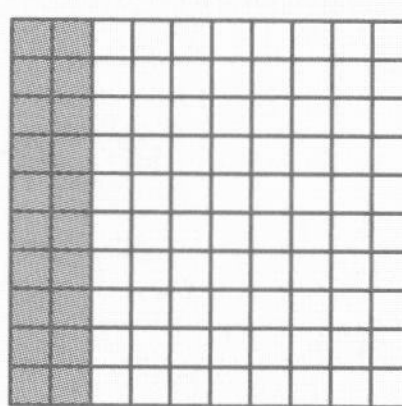

120%

5. The percent is less than 1%; The percent is greater than 100%.

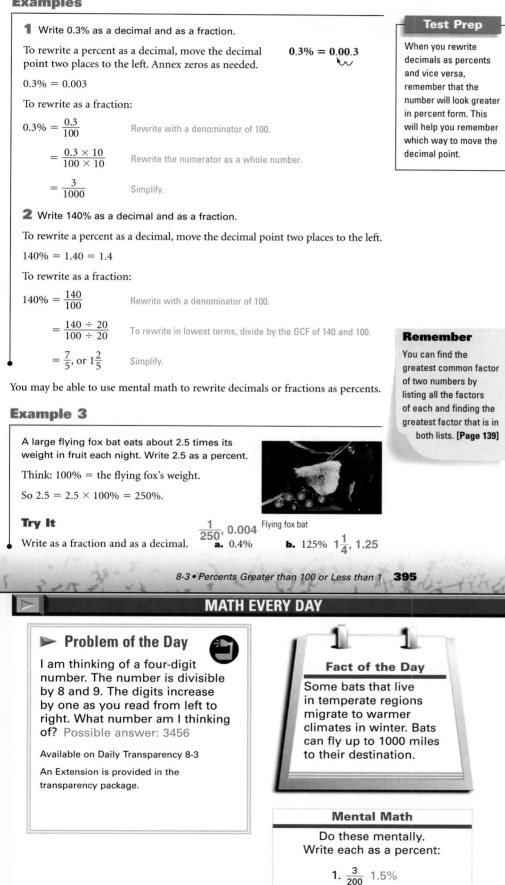

2 Teach

Learn

Alternate Examples

You may want to use Lesson Enhancement Transparency 35 with **Learn**.

1. Write 0.6% as a decimal and as a fraction.

   0.6% = 0.006

   To rewrite as a fraction:

   $0.6\% = \frac{0.6}{100} = \frac{0.6 \times 10}{100 \times 10}$

   $= \frac{6}{1000}$

2. Write 125% as a decimal and as a fraction.

   125% = 1.25

   To rewrite as a fraction:

   $125\% = \frac{125}{100} = \frac{5}{4}$ or $1\frac{1}{4}$

3. About 1.6 times as many people go to see men's college basketball games as go to professional games. Write 1.6 as a percent.

   Think 100% = attendance at pro games.

   So, 1.6 = 1.6 × 100% = 160%.

Students see two methods for converting a fraction less than one hundredth into a percent. One method uses equivalent fractions and the other uses division with a calculator. The students can decide which is easier for them.

Answers for What Do You Think?

1. To make the denominator = 100.
2. $1 \div 1000 = \frac{1}{1000} = 0.001$
3. Possible answer: Reason that $\frac{1}{100} = 1\%$, so $\frac{1}{1000}$ is $\frac{1}{10}$ of 1%, or 0.1%.

3 Practice and Assess

Check

Be sure that students understand that percents can be less than 1% and greater than 100%. These questions focus on the conditions that produce such percents.

Answers for Check Your Understanding

1. The players will have to give more than their usual best effort.
2. The numerator is greater than the denominator.
3. Less than 1%: If there are 2 or more zeros after the decimal point; 0.003 = 0.3%. Greater than 100%: If the number in front of the decimal point is greater than 0; 2.5 = 250%.

Not many species of bats live on islands. There are about 1000 species of bats, but only one of them is native to Hawaii. Lorena and Brett need to know what percent of the species of bats are native to Hawaii.

Lorena thinks ...

I'll write the ratio as a fraction. One out of 1000 = $\frac{1}{1000}$. If I divide the numerator and denominator by 10, the fraction will be out of 100:

$\frac{1 \div 10}{1000 \div 10} = \frac{0.1}{100}$

So 0.1% of the species of bats are native to Hawaii.

Brett thinks ...

I'll use my calculator to put the ratio into decimal form: 1 ÷ 1000 = 0.001. To rewrite this number as a percent, I move the decimal point two places to the right.

So 0.1% of the species of bats are native to Hawaii.

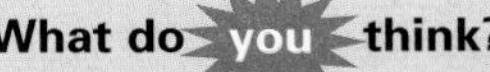

What do you think?

1. Why did Lorena divide the numerator and denominator of her fraction by 10?
2. How else could Brett have known that 1 ÷ 1000 equals 0.001?
3. How else could you solve this problem?

Check Your Understanding

1. A soccer coach said, "To win this game, you've got to give 110%." What did the coach mean?
2. Compare the numerator and denominator of a fraction that is greater than 100%.
3. How can you decide whether a decimal is less than 1%? More than 100%? Give an example for each case.

MEETING MIDDLE SCHOOL CLASSROOM NEEDS

Tips from Middle School Teachers

I like to relate fractions and percents to other areas, such as art. I give students graph paper and have them design their own mosaics. I then have them share their mosaics with the class and describe patterns they have incorporated into their designs. Of course, I always require that they talk about what percent of the total is composed of various components.

Team Teaching

Have the other teachers on your team point out to students where percents are used in their subject areas.

Social Studies Connection

Social scientists use percents all the time in survey activities. Their ability to describe a population in terms of what percent of people will vote for a certain candidate or what percent is below the poverty line help us understand our country better. Ask the students to pay attention to newscasts to find examples of percents and to report them in class.

8-3 Exercises and Applications

Practice and Apply

1. **Getting Started** Follow these steps to write 0.8% as a fraction.
   a. Rewrite 0.8% as a fraction with a denominator of 100. $\frac{0.8}{100}$
   b. Rewrite the fraction as an equivalent fraction with a whole number numerator. $\frac{8}{1000}$
   c. If necessary, simplify the fraction. $\frac{1}{125}$

Number Sense Classify each fraction or decimal as: (A) less than 1%, (B) greater than 100%, or (C) between 1% and 100%.

2. $\frac{240}{100}$ B **3.** $\frac{1}{200}$ A **4.** $\frac{1}{4}$ C **5.** $\frac{3}{2}$ B **6.** $\frac{4}{1000}$ A

7. 0.75 C **8.** 1.05 B **9.** 0.0001 A **10.** 0.015 C **11.** 3.0001 B

Number Sense Use >, <, or = to compare the numbers in each pair.

12. 3 [=] 300% **13.** 9% [>] 0.009 **14.** $\frac{1}{5}$ [=] 20% **15.** 0.5% [<] 0.05 **16.** 1.5 [>] 95%

Write each fraction as a percent.

17. $\frac{0.3}{1000}$ 0.03% **18.** $\frac{105}{100}$ 105% **19.** $\frac{350}{100}$ 350% **20.** $\frac{\frac{1}{3}}{100}$ $0.\overline{3}\%$ **21.** $\frac{13}{10}$ 130%

22. $\frac{90}{10}$ 900% **23.** $\frac{70}{25}$ 280% **24.** $\frac{13}{20}$ 65% **25.** $\frac{1}{125}$ 0.8% **26.** $\frac{5}{4}$ 125%

Write each decimal as a percent.

27. 0.007 0.7% **28.** 5.0 500% **29.** 0.00125 0.125% **30.** 3.015 301.5% **31.** 0.0604 6.04%

Write each percent as a decimal.

32. 0.1% 0.001 **33.** 125% 1.25 **34.** 1000% 10.0 **35.** $\frac{1}{5}$% 0.002 **36.** $\frac{3}{4}$% 0.0075

37. $6\frac{1}{2}$% 0.065 **38.** 205% 2.05 **39.** $\frac{3}{8}$% 0.00375 **40.** 0.43% 0.0043 **41.** 0.0067% 0.000067

42. Science Of the approximately 1000 species of bats, only 3 are vampire bats—bats that feed on the blood of living animals. About what percent of bat species are vampire bats? 0.3%

Common vampire bat

43. Problem Solving In 1993, there were 1,316,291 dogs registered with the American Kennel Club in the top 50 breeds. Of those, 3,519 were Schipperkes. What percent of the dogs were Schipperkes? ≈ 0.27%

8-3 Exercises and Applications

Assignment Guide

- **Basic** 1–43 odds, 45–46, 49–61 odds
- **Average** 1–45 odds, 46–47, 49 –61 odds
- **Enriched** 2–42 evens, 44–48, 50–60 evens

Exercise Notes

Exercise 42

Science In the Western Hemisphere, vampire bats live mostly in Central and South America, although a few live as far north as Mexico. They feed on the blood of animals, mainly cattle. After wounding their prey with their razor-sharp teeth, they lap up the blood as a cat laps milk.

Exercise 43

The Schipperke is a Belgian breed of dog. The name means "little captain" because these dogs once guarded canal barges and hurried the horses that pulled them.

PRACTICE 8-3

PRACTICE

Name ______________________ **Practice 8-3**

Percents Greater Than 100 or Less Than 1

Classify each of the following as: (A) less than 1%, (B) greater than 100%, or (C) between 1% and 100%.

1. $\frac{1}{2}$ (C) 2. $\frac{4}{3}$ (B) 3. $\frac{2}{300}$ (A) 4. $\frac{3}{10}$ (C)
5. 10.8 (B) 6. 0.7 (C) 7. 1.4 (B) 8. 0.06 (C)
9. 1.03 (B) 10. 0.009 (A) 11. 0.635 (C) 12. 0.0053 (A)

Use >, <, or = to compare the numbers in each pair.

13. $\frac{1}{4}$ (>) 20% 14. $\frac{1}{2}$% (<) 50 15. 0.008 (<) 8% 16. 35% (<) $\frac{3}{8}$
17. 150% (>) $\frac{5}{4}$ 18. 3 (=) 300% 19. $\frac{7}{250}$ (>) 0.3% 20. 650% (<) 7

Write each fraction as a percent.

21. $\frac{7}{5}$ 140% 22. $\frac{137}{100}$ 137% 23. $\frac{0.8}{100}$ 0.8%
24. $\frac{21}{4}$ 525% 25. $\frac{17}{10}$ 170% 26. $\frac{65}{40}$ 162.5%
27. $\frac{37}{20}$ 185% 28. $\frac{7}{500}$ 1.4% 29. $\frac{9}{8}$ 112.5%

Write each decimal as a percent.

30. 0.003 0.3% 31. 1.8 180% 32. 0.0025 0.25%
33. 5.3 530% 34. 0.0041 0.41% 35. 0.083 8.3%
36. 0.0009 0.09% 37. 0.83 83% 38. 20 2000%

Write each percent as a decimal.

39. 175% 1.75 40. 120% 1.2 41. $\frac{2}{5}$% 0.004
42. $\frac{5}{8}$% 0.00625 43. 750% 7.5 44. $8\frac{1}{4}$% 0.0825

45. **Social Science** In 1990, the population of Kansas was 2,477,574, which included 21,965 Native Americans. What percent of the people living in Kansas were Native Americans? About 0.89%

46. **Science** The mass of Earth is $\frac{1}{318}$ of the mass of Jupiter. What percent is this? About 0.31%

RETEACHING

Name ______________________ **Alternative Lesson 8-3**

Percents Greater Than 100 or Less Than 1

You can express a percent that is less than 1% or greater than 100% as a decimal and as a fraction. A percent that is less than 1% is a quantity that is less than $\frac{1}{100}$. A percent that is greater than 100% is a quantity that is greater than 1.

Example 1

Write 0.5% as a decimal and as a fraction.

Move the decimal point two places to the left to write a percent as a decimal. Annex zeros as needed. 0.5% = 0.005

Since per cent means per 100, you can write the percent as a fraction with a denominator of 100. $0.5\% = \frac{0.5}{100}$

Then rewrite the numerator as a whole number. Since 10 × 0.5 = 5, multiply the numerator and the denominator by 10. Then simplify. $\frac{0.5}{100} = \frac{0.5 \times 10}{100 \times 10} = \frac{5}{1000} = \frac{1}{200}$

So, $0.5\% = 0.005 = \frac{1}{200}$.

Try It Write each as a fraction and a decimal.

a. 0.01% $\frac{1}{10,000}$; 0.0001 b. 0.45% $\frac{9}{2000}$; 0.0045
c. 0.2% $\frac{1}{500}$; 0.002 d. 0.67% $\frac{67}{10,000}$; 0.0067

Example 2

Write 125% as a decimal and as a fraction.

Move the decimal point two places to the left to write a percent as a decimal. Annex zeros as needed. 125% = 1.25

Since per cent means per 100, you can write the percent as a fraction with a denominator of 100. $125\% = \frac{125}{100}$

Then simplify. $\frac{125}{100} = \frac{125 \div 25}{100 \div 25} = \frac{5}{4} = 1\frac{1}{4}$

So, $125\% = 1.25 = 1\frac{1}{4}$.

Try It Write each as a fraction and a decimal.

e. 150% $\frac{3}{2} = 1\frac{1}{2}$; 1.5 f. 225% $\frac{9}{4} = 2\frac{1}{4}$; 2.25
g. 186% $\frac{93}{50} = 1\frac{43}{50}$; 1.86 h. 201% $\frac{201}{100} = 2\frac{1}{100}$; 2.01

Reteaching

Activity

Materials: Geoboard, rubberbands

- Make a 10 × 10 square on a geoboard. Then make the smallest square you can make inside the first square. What percent of the large square does the small square represent? 1%
- Make a triangle that is one-half of that smallest square. What percent of the large square does that triangle represent? $\frac{1}{2}$%
- What percent of the triangle does the small square represent? 200%

Exercise Notes

■ Exercise 44

Social Studies You may wish to use Teaching Tool Transparency 20: Map of the World with this exercise. Have a volunteer locate Luxembourg and compare its size to the total land area of the world.

Exercise Answers

46. 200; Solve the proportion $\frac{\frac{1}{2}}{100} = \frac{1}{x}$.

47. To write a percent as a decimal, move the point two places to the left. To write a percent as a fraction, write the percent over 100 and reduce to lowest terms.

Alternate Assessment

Performance Assessment Have students work in small groups to write paragraph answers to this question:

What would be your reaction to an advertisement from a local electronics superstore announcing a big storewide sale with all merchandise 50% off?

Quick Quiz

Write these decimals as percents:

1. 0.007 0.7%
2. 3.5 350%

Write these fractions as percents:

3. $\frac{20}{5}$ 400%
4. $\frac{4}{1000}$ 0.4%
5. The population of the United States is about 260 million people. The population of Wyoming is about 470,000. What percent of the country's population is that of Wyoming? 0.18%

Available on Daily Transparency 8-3

PROBLEM SOLVING 8-3

44. Geography The world's total land area is about 57.9 million square miles. Luxembourg has an area of 999 square miles. What percent of the world's total land area does Luxembourg occupy? ≈ 0.0017%

45. **Test Prep** The decimal 0.0125 is equal to what fraction and what percent? B

Ⓐ $\frac{1}{8}$; 1.25% Ⓑ $\frac{1}{80}$; 1.25%

Ⓒ $\frac{1}{125}$; 125% Ⓓ $\frac{1}{12.5}$; 12.5%

Problem Solving and Reasoning

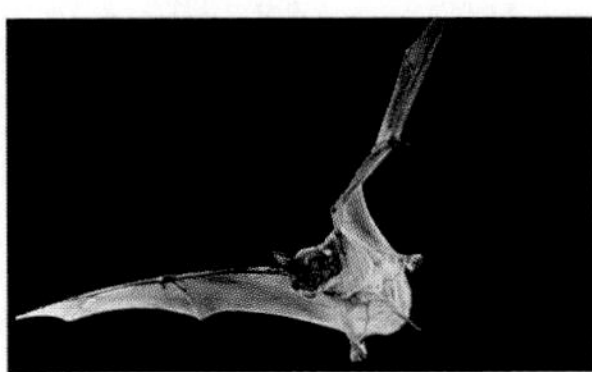

Problem Solving
STRATEGIES
• Look for a Pattern
• Make an Organized List
• Make a Table
• Guess and Check
• Work Backward
• Use Logical Reasoning
• Draw a Diagram
• Solve a Simpler Problem

46. Choose a Strategy GPS A small percent of bats carries rabies—generally about $\frac{1}{2}$%. In how large a group of bats would you expect to find exactly one bat carrying rabies? Explain how you found your answer.

47.  Write a step-by-step explanation of how you can write a percent as a decimal and as a fraction. Explain why each method works.

48. Critical Thinking Eagle Creek Cave in Arizona once housed what was probably the largest bat colony ever to exist in the United States. About 30 million Mexican free-tailed bats lived in this cave in 1963. Because of vandalism and other disturbances, only 30,000 bats remain. What percent of the 1963 population lives in Eagle Creek Cave today? 0.1%

Mexican free-tailed bat

Mixed Review

Find each sum or difference. Rewrite in lowest terms. *[Lesson 4-2]*

49. $\frac{2}{3}+\frac{1}{4}$ $\frac{11}{12}$ **50.** $\frac{3}{5}-\frac{1}{7}$ $\frac{16}{35}$ **51.** $\frac{1}{4}+\frac{4}{9}$ $\frac{25}{36}$ **52.** $\frac{5}{8}-\frac{3}{11}$ $\frac{31}{88}$ **53.** $\frac{4}{7}+\frac{1}{3}$ $\frac{19}{21}$

54. $\frac{3}{5}+\frac{1}{7}$ $\frac{26}{35}$ **55.** $\frac{2}{13}-\frac{1}{39}$ $\frac{5}{39}$ **56.** $\frac{12}{13}+\frac{1}{5}$ $1\frac{8}{65}$ **57.** $\frac{2}{5}-\frac{1}{30}$ $\frac{11}{30}$ **58.** $\frac{23}{24}+\frac{1}{2}$ $1\frac{11}{24}$

Elena leaves her house at 2:30 P.M. to visit Mio. Mio lives 2.5 miles away. Find the time Elena will arrive using each method of transportation. *[Lesson 7-3]*

59. Walking at 3 mi/hr 3:20 P.M. **60.** Jogging at 6.5 mi/hr ≈ 2:53 P.M. **61.** Bicycling at 10 mi/hr 2:45 P.M.

398 *Chapter 8 • Percents*

PROBLEM SOLVING

Name ______ Guided Problem Solving 8-3

GPS PROBLEM 46, STUDENT PAGE 398

A small percent of bats carries rabies—generally about $\frac{1}{2}$%. In how large a group of bats would you expect to find exactly one bat carrying rabies? Explain how you found your answer.

— Understand —

1. Underline what you are asked to find.
2. What percent of bats carries rabies? About $\frac{1}{2}$%.

— Plan —

3. Write $\frac{1}{2}$% as a fraction. $\frac{0.5}{100}$
4. Write your fraction from Item 3 with a whole number in the numerator. $\frac{5}{1000}$
5. Explain what your fraction means by giving the number of bats that may have rabies and the group size. Possible answer: About 5 bats in a group of 1000 bats have rabies.

— Solve —

6. Write an equivalent fraction to the fraction you wrote in Item 4 with a numerator of 1. $\frac{1}{200}$
7. About how large would you expect a group of bats to be if one bat carries rabies? 200 bats.
8. Explain how you found your answer. Possible answer: Write $\frac{1}{2}$% as a fraction. Then find an equivalent fraction with a numerator of 1.

— Look Back —

9. Does your answer mean that every group of bats this size will have exactly one bat with rabies? Explain. Possible answer: No, it is only an average. Some groups will have more than one rabid bat and others will have none.

SOLVE ANOTHER PROBLEM

Of all people surveyed, $\frac{1}{4}$% did not favor a proposed land development project. How large would the survey group have to be so that this percent would represent exactly one person? 400 people.

ENRICHMENT

Name ______ Extend Your Thinking 8-3

Visual Thinking

Estimate the percentage of the figure that is shaded. Then circle the approximate percent on the right.

Accept any reasonable choice.

1. 25% (a.) 33% b. 75% c. 90% d.
2. 60% a. 25% b. 50% c. 37.5% (d.)
3. 43% a. 50% b. $33\frac{1}{3}$% (c.) 25% d.
4. 25% a. 40% b. 55% (c.) 70% d.
5. 50% a. $66\frac{2}{3}$% (b.) 30% c. 80% d.
6. 40% a. $33\frac{1}{3}$% b. 25% c. 14% (d.)
7. 90% a. 80% (b.) 70% c. 60% d.

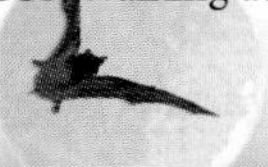

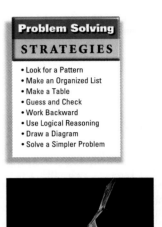

Finding a Percent of a Number Mentally

8-4

▶ Lesson Link You've learned the meaning of percent. Now you'll use mental math to find an exact percent of a number and to estimate a percent. ◀

You'll Learn ...

- to use estimation and mental math to find a percent of a number

... How It's Used

Salespeople need to find percents quickly to determine discounts.

Explore | Finding Percents

Waiter, There's a Bat in My Soup!

When you eat at a restaurant, you usually *tip* the waiter. Tips are figured as a percent of the total bill. The better the service, the bigger the tip.

Tipping Guide

Service	Tip
Excellent	20%
Average	15%
Below Average	10%
Poor	5%

1. What fraction in lowest terms is equal to 10%?
2. Use this fraction and mental math to calculate the tip you would leave for below-average service if your bill were \$40. Explain how you calculated the tip.
3. How can you mentally calculate a tip for excellent service? For poor service? What tip would you leave on a bill of \$60 for these types of service?
4. What tip would you leave for average service on a bill of \$30? Explain.
5. Diners often round their bill to a convenient number before calculating the tip. For a bill of \$46.97, estimate the tip you would leave for each type of service.

Learn | Finding a Percent of a Number Mentally

You can use percents such as 50%, 10%, and 1% to find other percents mentally.

50% of a number is $\frac{1}{2}$ of the number, which means $\frac{1}{2}$ *times* the number.

10% of a number is $\frac{1}{10}$ of the number.

10% of 270 = 27.0. or 27

Decimal point moves one to the left.

1% of a number is $\frac{1}{100}$ of the number.

1% of 270 = 2.70. or 2.7

Decimal point moves two to the left.

MEETING INDIVIDUAL NEEDS

Resources

8-4 Practice
8-4 Reteaching
8-4 Problem Solving
8-4 Enrichment
8-4 Daily Transparency
Problem of the Day
Review
Quick Quiz
Teaching Tool Transparency 20
Chapter 8 Project Master

Learning Modalities

Visual When attempting to mentally compute a percent of a number, it might help students to draw a rectangle showing the whole number and then shade a section that corresponds to the percent.

Verbal Have students repeat aloud the various ways that they can use 10% to compute other percents. For instance 20% is twice 10%, 5% is half of 10%, and so on.

Social Have students describe to a partner their method for mentally finding 15% of a number.

Inclusion

Students who have fine-motor control difficulties may be able to use a geoboard to demonstrate percent concepts instead of the graph paper that is suggested in several activities for this lesson.

8-4 Lesson Organizer

Objective

- Use mental math to find a percent of a number.

NCTM Standards

- 1–5, 7

▶ Review

Use mental math to find these answers:

1. $\frac{1}{2}$ of 72 36
2. $\frac{1}{10}$ of 472 47.2
3. 7 × 40 280
4. 420 − 85 335

Available on Daily Transparency 8-4

▶ Lesson Link

Discuss some of the uses of percent that the students have named in the past few days. Ask students to compute some easy percents mentally. For instance, in a 50%-off sale, what would a \$20 sweater be sold for? \$10

1 Introduce

Explore

The Point
Students use mental computation of simple percents, using 10% as a bridge to the computation of 5%, 15%, and 20%.

Ongoing Assessment
In Steps 3, 4, and 5, check that students first figure out 10% of the bill, and then use that figure to compute the other percents.

For Groups That Finish Early
Suppose that your state has a 6% sales tax on restaurant bills. Use mental math strategies to compute the tax on a bill for \$50.00. \$3

Follow Up
Ask volunteers to share their general strategies for these problems. Emphasize that by knowing how much 10% of a number is, you can also easily determine twice that (20%) or half of that (5%).

Answers for Explore on next page.

Answers for Explore

1. $\frac{1}{10}$
2. \$4; $\frac{1}{10}$ of \$40 is \$4.
3. Excellent service: Find 10% and double it; Poor service: Find 10% and halve it; Excellent: \$12; Poor: \$3.
4. \$4.50; 10% of \$30 = \$3; 5% of \$30 = \$1.50; \$3 + \$1.50 = \$4.50.
5. Excellent: \$10; Normal: \$7.50; Below average: \$5; Poor: \$2.50.

2 Teach

Learn

Alternate Examples

1. Use mental math to find 40% of 360.

   Think: 40% = 50% − 10%. 50% of 360 is 180. 10% of 360 is 36. So, 40% of 360 is 180 − 36 = 144.

2. New Jersey's population density is 1000 people per square mile. Iowa's is about 5% of that figure. What is Iowa's population density?

   Think: 10% of 1000 is 100. So 5% of 1000 must be half of 100, or 50. Iowa's population density is 50 people per sq mi.

3. Use mental math to find 30% of 700.

   Think: 30% equals 3 times 10%. 10% of 700 is 70. So, 30% of 700 is 3 times 70 = 210.

4. A restaurant bill was \$56. If the service was average, how much tip would you leave?

   Think: 15% is 10% plus 5%. 10% of 56 is \$5.60. 5% is half of that, or \$2.80. So, 15% is \$5.60 + \$2.80 = \$8.40.

3 Practice and Assess

Check

Answers for Check Your Understanding

1. First find 10%; Then halve it to find 5%; Add the two for 15%.
2. Yes. $\frac{35}{100} \times 55 = 35 \times \frac{1}{100} \times 55$
   $= 35 \times \frac{55}{100}$
   $= \frac{55}{100} \times 35$
   Multiplication is commutative.

Examples

1 Use mental math to find 60% of 480.

Think: 60% equals 50% + 10%.

50% (half) of 480 is 240. 10% (one-tenth) of 480 is 48.

So 60% of 480 is 240 + 48 = 288.

2 The normal heart rate of a little brown bat is 400 beats per minute. During hibernation, the heart rate falls to about 5% of normal. Use mental math to find the hibernation heart rate.

Little brown bats

Think: 10% of 400 is 40. So 5% of 400 must be half of 40, or 20.

The hibernation heart rate is about 20 beats per minute.

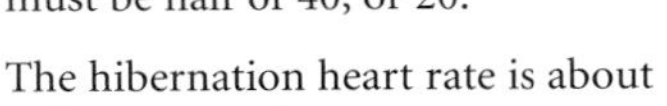

3 Using mental math, estimate 68% of 612.

Think: 68% is close to 70%. 612 is close to 600.

Think: 70% of a number is 7 times 10% of the number.

10% of 600 is 60.

So 68% of 612 is about 7 times 60 or 420.

4 A restaurant bill was \$42. Find the tip for average service.

The usual tip for average service is 15%.

Think: 15% is 10% plus 5%. 5% is half of 10%.

10% of \$42.00 is \$4.20. 5% is half of that, or \$2.10.

So 15% of \$42.00 is \$4.20 + \$2.10 = \$6.30.

DID YOU KNOW?

Many bats use a form of sonar, called *echolocation*, to navigate at night. The time interval before they hear an echo from their cry tells them how close they are to an object. Dolphins, killer whales, and mobile robots also use echolocation.

Problem Solving TIP

When you find a percent mentally, think about how you can break it down into pieces involving 100%, 50%, 10%, and 1%.

Try It

Use mental math to find each percent.

a. 50% of 6 3 **b.** 20% of 80 16 **c.** 5% of 300 15 **d.** 90% of 500 450

Check Your Understanding

1. Explain how you can calculate 15% of a number mentally.
2. Is 35% of 55 the same as 55% of 35? Explain.

MATH EVERY DAY

Problem of the Day

To deliver papers, Jeffrey follows this route. Start at home, go six blocks north, then five blocks east. Next go two blocks north, one block west, and then seven blocks south. Finally, he goes one block west. How many blocks and in which direction must Jeffrey walk to get back home? Possible answer: One block south and three blocks west

Available on Daily Transparency 8-4

An Extension is provided in the transparency package.

Fact of the Day

In 1901 a large cloud of bats seen flying from a cave in the Guadalupe Mountains led to the discovery of the Carlsbad Caverns in southeastern New Mexico.

Estimation

Estimate a 15% tip for the following restaurant bills:

1. \$43.90 \$6.60
2. \$51.52 \$7.50
3. \$65.87 \$10.00

8-4 Exercises and Applications

Practice and Apply

1. **Getting Started** Follow these steps to find 15% of 34,000 mentally.
   - a. Find 10% of 34,000 by moving the decimal point one place to the left. 3,400
   - b. Take half of your answer to **a.** 1,700
   - c. Add your answers from **a** and **b.** 5,100

Find 50%, 10%, and 1% of each number.

2. 27,000 13,500; 2,700; 270 **3.** 5800 2,900; 580; 58 **4.** 120 60; 12; 1.2 **5.** 244 122; 24.4; 2.44 **6.** 73 36.5; 7.3; 0.73

Number Sense Use mental math to find each percent of 8,200.

7. 15% 1,230 **8.** 5% 410 **9.** 70% 5,740 **10.** 25% 2,050 **11.** 40% 3,280 **12.** 90% 7,380

Use mental math to find each percent.

13. 25% of 500 125 **14.** 10% of $40 $4 **15.** 80% of $70 $56 **16.** 30% of 600 180 **17.** 5% of 2100 105

18. 15% of $8.00 $1.20 **19.** 60% of 400 240 **20.** 90% of 240 216 **21.** 5% of 700 35 **22.** 15% of $22.00 $3.30

Estimation Estimate each percent.

23. 10% of 39 ≈ 4 **24.** 48% of 58 ≈ 29 **25.** 15% of 79.7 ≈ 12 **26.** 91% of 198 ≈ 180 **27.** 22% of 9896 ≈ 2000

28. Science Only 3% of what were originally 8,000,000 Mexican free-tailed bats are now living in Carlsbad Caverns in New Mexico. How many Mexican free-tailed bats are now living in Carlsbad Caverns? (*Hint:* First find 1% of the original number of bats.) 240,000

Mexican free-tailed bats, Carlsbad Caverns

29. **Test Prep** Choose the expression that would best help you estimate 47% of 237. C

Ⓐ 40% of 237 Ⓑ 40% of 240
Ⓒ 50% of 240 Ⓓ 50% of 250

Problem Solving and Reasoning

30. Critical Thinking In 1993, the world's population was approximately 5.5 billion people. About 15% spoke Mandarin Chinese as their primary language, about 6% spoke Hindi, and about 2% spoke German. Use mental math to find the number of native speakers of each language.

PRACTICE 8-4

8-4 Exercises and Applications

Assignment Guide

- **Basic**
  1–4, 7–9, 13–17, 23–25, 28–30, 32–40
- **Average**
  1–5, 8–10, 15–20, 24–26, 28–30, 35–40
- **Enriched**
  2–6, 9–12, 18–22, 25–29, 31–32, 36–43

Exercise Notes

Exercise 29

Test Prep If some students choose B or D, point out that these expressions could be used, but that 50% of 240 (120) is a closer estimate.

Exercise Answers

30. 825,000,000 speak Mandarin; 330,000,000 speak Hindi; 110,000,000 speak German.

PRACTICE

Name ____________

Practice 8-4

Finding a Percent of a Number

Find 50%, 10%, and 1% of each number.

1. 2,400 1,200; 240; 24 2. 36 18; 3.6; 0.36 3. 580 290; 58; 5.8 4. 60 30; 6; 0.6

5. 14,000 7,000; 1,400; 140 6. 620 310; 62; 6.2 7. 21 10.5; 2.1; 0.21 8. 122 61; 12.2; 1.22

Use mental math to find each percent of 4800.

9. 10% 480 10. 40% 1920 11. 25% 1200 12. 20% 960

13. 5% 240 14. 75% 3600 15. 15% 720 16. 90% 4320

Use mental math to find each percent.

17. 5% of 300 15 18. 75% of 6000 4500 19. 20% of 800 160 20. 60% of 700 420

21. 40% of $90 $36 22. 10% of 450 45 23. 50% of 28 14 24. 30% of 200 60

Estimate each answer.

25. 30% of 808 About 240 26. 11% of 128 About 14 27. 44% of 764 About 340 28. 10% of 382 About 38

29. 49% of 1737 About 850 30. 62% of 923 About 570 31. 71% of 416 About 300 32. 15% of 620 About 90

33. **Social Science** In 1993, 904,292 people immigrated to the United States. 7.3% of the immigrants came from mainland China. How many people immigrated to the U.S. from mainland China in 1993? About 66,000

34. **Science** It is estimated that there are about 20,000 native plant species in the United States. About 21% of these species are threatened with extinction. How many native plant species are threatened with extinction? About 4,200

RETEACHING

Name ____________

Alternative Lesson 8-4

Finding a Percent of a Number Mentally

You can use percents such as 50%, 10%, and 1% to find other percents mentally.

Example 1

Use mental math to find each percent.

a. 50% of 80 b. 10% of 63 c. 1% of 78

a. Since 50% is $\frac{1}{2}$, you can either find $\frac{1}{2}$ of 80 or you can divide 80 by 2. $50\% \text{ of } 80 = \frac{1}{2} \times 80 = 80 \div 2 = 40$

b. Since 10% is 0.1 you can multiply 63 by 0.1. Move the decimal point one place to the left. $10\% \text{ of } 63 = 0.1 \times 63 = 6.3$

c. Since 1% is 0.01 you can multiply 78 by 0.01. Move the decimal point two places to the left. $1\% \text{ of } 78 = 0.01 \times 78 = 0.78$

So, 50% of 80 is 40, 10% of 63 is 6.3, and 1% of 78 is 0.78.

Try It Use mental math to find each percent.

a. 50% of 62 31 b. 50% of 120 60 c. 10% of 59 5.9

d. 10% of 30 3 e. 1% of 147 1.47 f. 1% of 18 0.18

Example 2

Use mental math to find each percent.

a. 40% of 90
Think: 40% equals 4 times 10%.
10% of 90 is 9.
So, 40% of 90 is 4 times 9, or 36.

b. 5% of 60
Think: 5% equals $\frac{1}{2} \times 10\%$
10% of 60 is 6.
So 5% of 60 would be half of 6, or 3.

Try It Use mental math to find each percent.

g. 70% of 40 28 h. 20% of 350 70 i. 90% of 400 360

j. 5% of 20 1 k. 5% of 160 8 l. 30% of 280 84

m. 5% of 130 6.5 n. 5% of 66 3.3 o. 60% of 90 54

Reteaching

Activity

Materials: Graph paper

- To find 10% of 70, draw a rectangle that has 70 squares in it. Then shade 1 out of every 10 squares.
- How many squares are shaded? 7 This number is 10% of 70. Use this answer to find 20% of 70. 14

Use the same method to find 20% of 60, 20% of 80, and 5% of 60. 12, 16, 3

Exercise Notes

■ Exercise 43

Social Studies You may want to use Teaching Tool Transparency 20: Map of the World with this exercise. Have a volunteer locate Puerto Rico and compare its size to the size of other islands.

Exercise Answers

31. a. 2,000,000 died; 2,000,000 survived.
    b. 500,000 died; 1,500,000 returned to Texas.
    c. 37.5%; Divide 1,500,000 by 4,000,000 and move the point two places to the right.

32. a. Vanilla: 480,000,000 gallons; Chocolate: 160,000,000 gallons; Chocolate chip: 80,000,000 gallons.
    b. 1.8 gallons.

Project Progress

You may want to have students use Chapter 8 Project Master.

Alternate Assessment

Interview Have students pair up to interview each other regarding their approaches to tipping in restaurants. They can start with this question:

> If you went out to eat and were given a bill for $55, how would you decide how much of a tip to leave?

► Quick Quiz

1. Find 50% of 74. 37
2. Find 15% of 80. 12
3. Find 90% of 780. 702
4. About how much tip would you leave in a restaurant for a meal that cost $36? Why? About $5.40; Estimated 15%

Available on Daily Transparency 8-4

PROBLEM SOLVING 8-4

31. Communicate A female Mexican free-tailed bat living in Texas usually produces one baby, called a *pup,* per year. A large colony of these bats can have 4,000,000 pups.

Bat pups in leaf

a. One year, 50% of the pups were eaten by predators or died during the migration to Mexico. How many pups died? How many survived?

b. 25% of the remaining pups died during the winter or on the return migration in the spring. How many of these pups died? How many returned to Texas?

c. What percent of the original 4,000,000 pups returned to Texas? Explain how you solved this problem.

32. Critical Thinking GPS People in the United States eat about 1.6 billion (1,600,000,000) gallons of ice cream each year. About 30% of this ice cream is vanilla, about 10% is chocolate, and about 5% is chocolate chip.

a. Use mental math to find the number of gallons sold for each flavor.

b. There are about 260 million people in the United States. On the average, how many gallons of vanilla ice cream does each one eat in a year?

Mixed Review

Evaluate each expression. *[Lesson 5-6]*

33. 16^2 256 **34.** 12^2 144 **35.** 23^2 529 **36.** 100^2 10,000 **37.** 1^2 1

38. $\sqrt{49}$ 7 **39.** $\sqrt{484}$ 22 **40.** $\sqrt{\frac{1}{4}}$ $\frac{1}{2}$ **41.** $\sqrt{361}$ 19 **42.** $\sqrt{324}$ 18

43. The island of Puerto Rico measures about 100 miles from east to west and 32 miles from north to south. What is the largest scale that can be used to fit a map of Puerto Rico on an $8\frac{1}{2}$ in. by 14 in. sheet of paper if the 14 in. side runs east-west? *[Lesson 7-4]*
14 in.:100 mi ≈ 1 in.:7.1 mi

ATLANTIC OCEAN
San Juan
Bayamón
Carolina
Caguas
Mayagüez
PUERTO RICO
Ponce
0
?
N
W
E
S

Project Progress

Make a table of the items on your picnic list. Have a column that lists the total cost for each item, and add up the costs. Make a bar graph that shows the percent of the total cost that each item represents.

Problem Solving
Understand
Plan
Solve
Look Back

PROBLEM SOLVING

Name ____________

Guided Problem Solving 8-4

GPS **PROBLEM 32, STUDENT PAGE 402**

People in the United States eat about 1.6 billion (1,600,000,000) gallons of ice cream each year. About 30% of this ice cream is vanilla, about 10% is chocolate, and about 5% is chocolate chip.

a. Use mental math to find the number of gallons sold for each flavor.

b. There are about 260 million people in the United States. On the average, how many gallons of vanilla ice cream does each one eat in a year?

— Understand —

1. Circle the information you need.

— Plan —

2. Which of the ice cream sales is the easiest one to find? Why? Chocolate; Move decimal point in number one place to the left.

3. How can you use your answer to Item 2 to find the other quantities? Multiply the answer by 3 to find 30%, by half to find 5%.

4. Will you multiply or divide to find the average amount eaten? Divide.

— Solve —

5. About how many gallons of vanilla is sold? 480,000,000 gal.
   Chocolate? 160,000,000 gal. Chocolate chip? 80,000,000 gal.

6. On the average, about how many gallons of vanilla ice cream does each person in the United States eat each year? ≈ 1.85 gal.

— Look Back —

7. Add the sales of chocolate and chocolate chip ice cream. Why should the sum equal one half of the sales of vanilla ice cream? 240,000,000 gal.; Sum is 15% of total sales, which is half of the 30% of vanilla sales.

SOLVE ANOTHER PROBLEM

About 55% of the 1.6 billion gallons of ice cream sold is flavors other than vanilla, chocolate, and chocolate chip.

a. Find the number of gallons sold for these flavors. ≈ 880,000,000 gal.

b. On the average, how many gallons of these flavors does each of 260 million people eat in a year? ≈ 3.38 gal.

ENRICHMENT

Name ____________

Extend Your Thinking 8-4

Decision Making

A library conducted a survey of the community about the kind of novels they read most often. A total of 40,000 people were surveyed. The results are shown in the circle graph at the right.

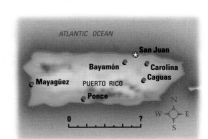

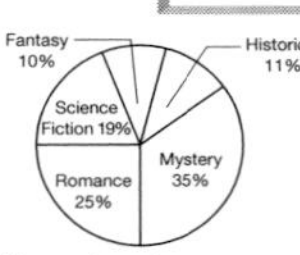

1. Use the information in the circle graph to find the number of people preferring each kind of book. Use mental math.

Kind of Novel	Percent of Community	Number of People in Community	Budget
Fantasy	10%	4,000	25,000
Historical	11%	4,400	27,500
Science Fiction	19%	7,600	47,500
Romance	25%	10,000	62,500
Mystery	35%	14,000	87,500

Possible answers: Items 2, 3, and 4

2. Why is a circle graph a good way to show percent information? Since the circle represents 100% of the whole, it gives a visual idea of how the data relates to the whole.

3. You can spend $250,000 on new library books. Write the amount you would spend for each kind of book in the table. Explain. Spend the same percentage as the kind of books preferred.

4. A patron gave the library $50,000 to expand the children's fiction section. How would you decide which kinds of books to buy? Would you use the survey results above? Use children's books recommended by various national groups. Survey results probably aren't valid for children, since adults are more likely to be surveyed.

Section 8A Connect

In this section, you've learned how to find a percent of a number mentally. You've also linked percents, fractions, and decimals. Now you'll use these skills to learn more about the Mexican free-tailed bat.

To the Batcave!

Materials: Inch ruler

1. The photo shows a swarm of Mexican free-tailed bats leaving Bracken Cave to feed near Comfort, Texas. Estimate the percent of the photo covered by bats.
2. If this photo were completely filled with bats, it might show about 1000 bats. Estimate the number of bats in the photo.
3. Bracken Cave has the largest concentration of bats in the world. Twenty million adult female bats live in the cave. About what percent of the bats in the cave are shown in the photo?
4. Bats arrive at the cave in early spring after migrating 1500 miles from Mexico. On their nightly feeding flights, they fly up to 3% of this migration distance from the cave. Using the map, find the town farthest from the cave that a bat could reach in one night.

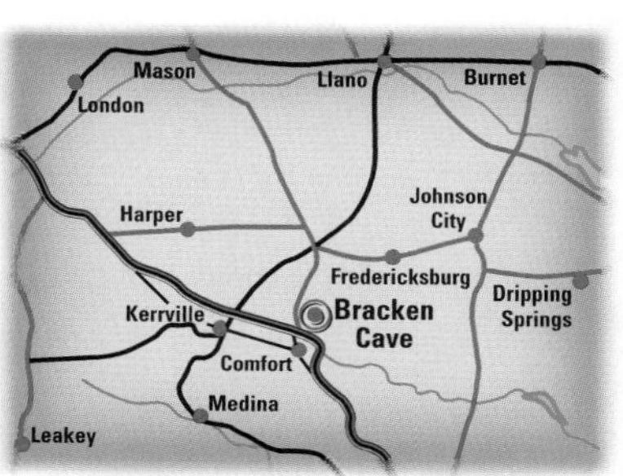

Scale: 1 in. = 40 mi

Answers for Connect

1. Possible answer: 50%
2. Possible answers: 500; Found 50% of 1000
3. Possible answer: 0.0025%
4. Dripping Springs

To the Batcave!

The Point

In *To the Batcave!* on page 385, students learned interesting facts about bats. Now they will use percents in problems relating to the bat population in Bracken Cave in Texas.

Materials

Inch ruler

Resources

Lesson Enhancement Transparency 36
Teaching Tool Transparency 14: Rulers.

About the Page

- Ask students if they think more or less than half of the photo is covered by bats. What percent represents half of something? 50%
- If 50% of the photo were covered with bats, how many bats would be in the photo? 500
- How would you find what percent 500 is of 20 million? Divide 500 by 20,000,000.
- Discuss the map with the students. Ask them how to determine the distance that the bats can travel in one day. Ask how they can find this distance on the map. First find 3% of 1500 mi: 45 mi. On the map, 1 in. = 40 mi, so $1\frac{1}{8}$ in. = 45 mi. Measure $1\frac{1}{8}$ inch in all directions from Bracken Cave.

Ongoing Assessment

Check that students have made reasonable estimates of the number and percent of bats in the photo. Check that students have determined that bats can fly up to 45 miles from the cave.

Extension

If bats travel as many miles per day when they are migrating as they fly on their nightly feeding flights, about how long does it take them to migrate from Mexico to Bracken Cave? $33\frac{1}{3}$ days

8A Review

Review Correlation

Item(s)	Lesson(s)
1–9, 11–13	8-1, 8-2
10, 14, 15	8-3
16	8-1
17–20, 22–25	8-2
21, 26	8-3
27–31	8-4
32	8-1
33, 34	8-4

Test Prep

Test-Taking Tip

Tell students to use mental math whenever they can to save time on a test. In this problem, they need only to move a decimal point in order to find the answer.

Answers for Review

16. 84% identify their pups; 16% do not.

33. Possible answer: Move the decimal point two places to the left to find 1%, then multiply by the required percent.

Section 8A Review

REVIEW 8A

Number Sense Write each fraction or decimal as a percent.

1. 0.17 17% **2.** $\frac{14}{50}$ 28% **3.** $\frac{6}{20}$ 30% **4.** $\frac{23}{25}$ 92% **5.** $\frac{17.9}{25}$ 71.6%

6. $\frac{7}{100}$ 7% **7.** $\frac{3}{5}$ 60% **8.** $\frac{35}{25}$ 140% **9.** $\frac{456}{1000}$ 45.6% **10.** $\frac{5}{1000}$ 0.5%

11. 0.89 89% **12.** 0.04 4% **13.** 0.498 49.8% **14.** 0.0001 0.01% **15.** 3.07 307%

16. **Science** "Maternity" caves may contain thousands of baby bats. Scientists know about 21 out of every 25 mother bats can identify their baby bats, or pups, from among thousands of similar bats. About what percent of mother bats identify their pups? About what percent do not?

Number Sense Write each percent as a decimal.

17. 30% 0.3 **18.** 6% 0.06 **19.** 423% 4.23 **20.** 1050% 10.5 **21.** 0.1% 0.001

Write each percent as a fraction in lowest terms.

22. 25% $\frac{1}{4}$ **23.** 70% $\frac{7}{10}$ **24.** 92% $\frac{23}{25}$ **25.** 306% $3\frac{3}{50}$ **26.** 0.5% $\frac{1}{200}$

Use mental math to find each percent.

27. 10% of 850 85 **28.** 50% of 2468 1234 **29.** 15% of $36 $5.40 **30.** 80% of 140 112 **31.** 5% of 6100 305

32. **Estimation** Many species of bats have "nose leaves." These may aid in locating prey by sensing sound waves reflected from the prey to the bats' noses. Other species have plain noses. If there are 355 species of plain-nosed bats and a total of 986 species, estimate the percent of plain-nosed bat species. ≈ 35%

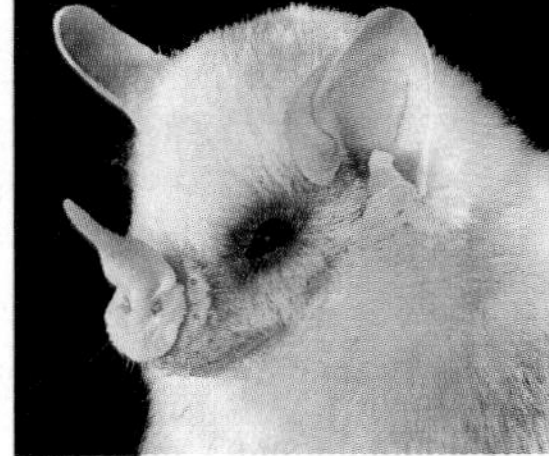
Honduran white bat

33. 

In your own words, explain how you can use mental math to find a percent of a number.

Test Prep

When you're asked to find a percent on a multiple choice test, using mental math can help you work more quickly.

34. What is 1% of $700? A

Ⓐ $7.00 Ⓑ $70,000 Ⓒ $0.07 Ⓓ $0.70

Resources

Practice Masters
Section 8A Review

Assessment Sourcebook
Quiz 8A

TestWorks
Test and Practice Software

PRACTICE

Name ______________________ Practice

Section 8A Review

Write each fraction or decimal as a percent.

1. 0.38 38% 2. $\frac{2}{5}$ 40% 3. $\frac{36}{40}$ 90% 4. $\frac{3}{20}$ 15%

5. $\frac{13}{250}$ 5.2% 6. $\frac{63}{50}$ 126% 7. 0.423 42.3% 8. 5.5 550%

9. Carolyn correctly answered 43 out of 50 problems on a multiple choice test.

What percent of the problems did she answer correctly? 86%

What percent did she answer incorrectly? 14%

Write each percent as a decimal.

10. 42% 0.42 11. 25% 0.25 12. 160% 1.6 13. 0.05% 0.0005

14. 0.12% 0.0012 15. 9.5% 0.095 16. 850% 8.5 17. 0.4% 0.004

Write each percent as a fraction in lowest terms.

18. 67% $\frac{67}{100}$ 19. 125% $\frac{5}{4}$ 20. 0.2% $\frac{1}{500}$ 21. 28% $\frac{7}{25}$

22. 65% $\frac{13}{20}$ 23. 70% $\frac{7}{10}$ 24. 0.68% $\frac{17}{2500}$ 25. 230% $\frac{23}{10}$

Use mental math to find each percent.

26. 20% of 65 13 27. 40% of 120 48 28. 65% of 700 455 29. 90% of 400 360

30. A drug manufacturer claims that 512 out of 633 doctors who were surveyed recommend using the manufacturer's product. Estimate the percent of surveyed doctors who recommend using this product. About 80%

31. The average American ate 12.3 pounds of cookies and crackers in 1993. How many ounces is this? *[Lesson 7-6]* About 197 oz

32. Hans drove from Buffalo, New York, to Pittsburgh, Pennsylvania, a road distance of 219 miles. His average speed was 50 mi/hr, and he arrived in Pittsburgh at 6:30 P.M. What time did he leave Buffalo? *[Lesson 7-3]* At about 2:07 P.M.

Section 8B

Problem Solving with Percents

LESSON PLANNING GUIDE

Student Edition | **Ancillaries***

LESSON		MATERIALS	VOCABULARY	DAILY	OTHER
	Section 8B Opener				
8-5	**Using Equations to Solve Percent Problems**	graph paper		8-5	Teaching Tool Trans. 2, 3, 7 Lesson Enhancement Trans 37 Technology Master 36
8-6	**Solving Percent Problems with Proportions**	inch ruler		8-6	Teaching Tool Trans. 14, 22 Ch. 8 Project Master
8-7	**Problem Solving: Percent Increase and Decrease**		percent increase, percent decrease, percent change	8-7	Teaching Tool Trans. 2, 3 Technology Master 37
	Technology	spreadsheet software			*Interactive CD-ROM Spreadsheet/Grapher Tool*
	Connect				Lesson Enhancement Trans. 38 Interdisc. Team Teaching 8B
	Review				Practice 8B; Quiz 8B; *TestWorks*
	Extend Key Ideas				
	Chapter 8 Summary and Review				
	Chapter 8 Assessment				Ch. 8 Tests Forms A–F *TestWorks*; Ch. 8 Letter Home
	Cumulative Review Chapters 1–8				Cumulative Review Ch. 1–8

* Daily Ancillaries include Practice, Reteaching, Problem Solving, Enrichment, and Daily Transparency. Teaching Tool Transparencies are in *Teacher's Toolkits*. Lesson Enhancement Transparencies are in *Overhead Transparency Package*.

SKILLS TRACE

LESSON	SKILL	FIRST INTRODUCED GR. 5	GR. 6	GR. 7	DEVELOP	PRACTICE/ APPLY	REVIEW
8-5	**Using equations to solve percent problems.**			✘ p. 406	pp. 406–407	pp. 408–409	pp. 422, 425, 470
8-6	**Using proportions to solve percent problems.**			✘ p. 410	pp. 410–412	pp. 413–414	pp. 422, 425, 528, 614
8-7	**Solving percent increase and percent decrease problems.**			✘ p. 415	pp. 415–417	pp. 418–419	pp. 422, 425, 533

CONNECTED MATHEMATICS

The unit *Comparing and Scaling, (Ratio, Proportion and Percent)*, from the **Connected Mathematics** series can be used with Section 8B.

INTERDISCIPLINARY TEAM TEACHING

Math and Science/Technology

(Worksheet pages 33–34: Teacher pages T33–T34)

In this lesson, students use percentages to examine the risk of heart disease.

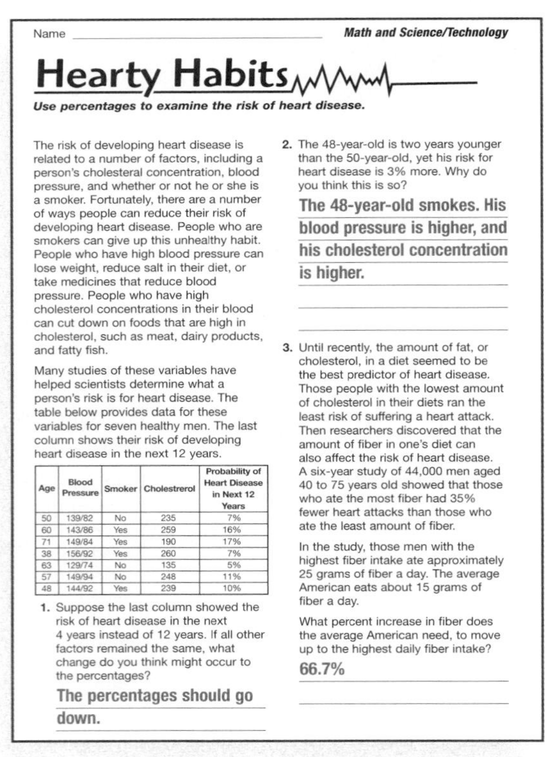

Name ______________________ *Math and Science/Technology*

Hearty Habits

Use percentages to examine the risk of heart disease.

The risk of developing heart disease is related to a number of factors, including a person's cholesteral concentration, blood pressure, and whether or not he or she is a smoker. Fortunately, there are a number of ways people can reduce their risk of developing heart disease. People who are smokers can give up this unhealthy habit. People who have high blood pressure can lose weight, reduce salt in their diet, or take medicines that reduce blood pressure. People who have high cholesterol concentrations in their blood can cut down on foods that are high in cholesterol, such as meat, dairy products, and fatty fish.

Many studies of these variables have helped scientists determine what a person's risk is for heart disease. The table below provides data for these variables for seven healthy men. The last column shows their risk of developing heart disease in the next 12 years.

Age	Blood Pressure	Smoker	Cholestrerol	Probability of Heart Disease in Next 12 Years
50	139/82	No	235	7%
60	143/86	Yes	259	16%
71	149/84	Yes	190	17%
38	156/92	Yes	260	7%
63	129/74	No	135	5%
57	149/94	No	248	11%
48	144/92	Yes	239	10%

1. Suppose the last column showed the risk of heart disease in the next 4 years instead of 12 years. If all other factors remained the same, what change do you think might occur to the percentages?

   The percentages should go down.

2. The 48-year-old is two years younger than the 50-year-old, yet his risk for heart disease is 3% more. Why do you think this is so?

   The 48-year-old smokes. His blood pressure is higher, and his cholesterol concentration is higher.

3. Until recently, the amount of fat, or cholesterol, in a diet seemed to be the best predictor of heart disease. Those people with the lowest amount of cholesterol in their diets ran the least risk of suffering a heart attack. Then researchers discovered that the amount of fiber in one's diet can also affect the risk of heart disease. A six-year study of 44,000 men aged 40 to 75 years old showed that those who ate the most fiber had 35% fewer heart attacks than those who ate the least amount of fiber.

   In the study, those men with the highest fiber intake ate approximately 25 grams of fiber a day. The average American eats about 15 grams of fiber a day.

   What percent increase in fiber does the average American need, to move up to the highest daily fiber intake?

   66.7%

Name ______________________ *Math and Science/Technology*

4. Fiber is found in many cereals, fruits, and vegetables. The researchers estimated that for every 10-gram increase in daily fiber intake, a person could reduce the risk of heart disease by about 20%.

   a. Suppose that the 50-year-old man shown in the table increases his daily fiber intake by 10 grams. What will his new risk for heart disease be?

   20% of 7% = $0.2 \times .07$ = 0.014; 0.014×100 = 1.4 %; 7% − 1.4 % = 5.6%

   b. The 48-year-old man wants to add 15 grams of fiber to his daily diet. What will his new risk for heart disease be?

   If a 10 g increase reduces the risk by 20%, then a 15 g increase reduces the risk by 30%. $1.5 \times 20\%$ = 30%; 30% of 10% = 0.3×0.1 = .03; 0.03×100 = 3%; 10 % − 3% = 7%

   c. The 60-year-old man has decreased his daily fiber intake by 10 grams. What is his new risk for heart disease?

   20% of 16% = 0.2×0.16 = .032; $.032 \times 100$ = 3.2%; 16% + 3.2% = 19.2%

5. a. The 71-year-old man stopped smoking for more than one year. All other variables shown in the table remained the same. By stopping smoking he lowered his risk for a heart attack to 12%. What percent decrease in his risk for a heart attack has occurred?

   17% − 12% = 5%; $\frac{5}{17} \times 100 \approx 29.4\%$

   b. The 57-year-old man started smoking a year ago and has not stopped. All other variables shown in the table remained the same. Smoking increased his risk for heart disease to 15%. What percent increase in his risk for heart disease has occurred?

   15% − 11% = 4%; $\frac{4}{11} \times 100 \approx 36.4\%$

   c. Suppose that all variables in the table for the 38-year-old remained the same, except that his cholesterol had gone down to 140. This lowered his chances for heart disease to 3% in the next 12 years. What percent decrease in his risk for a heart attack has occurred?

   7% − 3% = 4%; $\frac{4}{7} \times 100 \approx 57.1\%$

6. What other factors can influence the risk for heart disease? Are the risks the same for males and females? Do some research in the library. Then report on the subject.

   See below.

Answers

6. Answers will vary. Amount of exercise and weight have a lot to do with the risk for heart disease. So does whether a person has diabetes or not. Women are currently at a lower risk for heart disease than men. Recent studies have correlated stressful environments, race, and other factors with the disease.

BIBLIOGRAPHY

FOR TEACHERS

Eyewitness Visual Dictionaries. *The Visual Dictionary of Buildings*. London, England: Dorling Kindersley, 1992.

Kenney, Margaret J. and Hirsch, Christian R. *Discrete Mathematics Across the Curriculum*. Palo Alto, CA: Dale Seymour Publications, 1996.

Pappas, Theoni. *The Joy of Mathematics*. San Carlos, CA: Wide World Publishing/Tetra House, 1989.

Spangler, David. *Math for Real Kids*. Glenview, IL: Good Year Books, 1997.

FOR STUDENTS

Mackay, James A. *The Guinness Book of Stamps*. New York, NY: Canopy Books, 1992.

Miller, Marilyn F. *Behind the Scenes at the Shopping Mall*. Austin, TX: Raintree Steck-Vaughn, 1996.

SECTION 8B

Problem Solving with Percents

▶ Consumer Link ▶ www.mathsurf.com/7/ch8/malls

THEY'RE ALL AT THE MALL!

Question: What's shaped like an alligator and sells plastic flamingos at a fraction of the original price?

Answer: Sawgrass Mills, the world's biggest outlet and discount mall. Located near Fort Lauderdale, Florida, at the edge of the Everglades, Sawgrass Mills is built in the shape of an alligator. When you enter the parking lot, you see signs decorated with yellow toucans, pink flamingos, and other tropical birds. Shoppers stroll down paths lined with palmetto trees. Tropical scents and sounds fill the air. But although they're having fun, the shoppers are serious about saving money.

Outlet and discount stores have become very popular in recent years. Despite the low prices, store owners make money because they have so many customers. And smart shoppers can find terrific bargains, especially if they're good at calculating discounts. That's one of the skills you'll learn in this section.

1 Why might a large business be able to sell items more cheaply than a small one?

2 A cash register can calculate the correct discount on an item. Why is it important for a shopper to be able to calculate a discount?

3 A sign in a store says, "All Merchandise 50% Off!" What does the sign mean?

405

Where are we now?

In Section 8A, students linked percents, fractions, and decimals and made models of fractions and decimals to solve percent problems.

They learned how to

- compare quantities using percents.
- relate fractions, decimals, and percents.
- use percents less than 1% and greater than 100%.
- find the percent of a number mentally.

Where are we going?

In Section 8B, students will

- use equations to solve percent problems.
- use proportions to solve percent problems.
- use percents to describe amounts of increase or decrease.

Section 8B

Theme: Discount Malls

World Wide Web

If your class has access to the World Wide Web, you might want to use the information found at the Web site address given. The interdisciplinary link relates to the topics discussed in this section.

About the Page

This page introduces the theme of the section, discount malls, and discusses shopping at outlet and discount stores.

Ask ...

- Why do you think people shop at discount stores?
- What is a discount? A reduction made from the regular price.
- Why do you think manufacturers sell some of their merchandise in outlet and discount stores? Possible answer: To sell merchandise that retail stores did not buy or have returned.

Extension

The following activity does not require access to the World Wide Web.

Consumer

Have students research the growth and development of discount stores or outlet malls. If there is a mall nearby, have them determine such things as its size, the number of stores it contains, and its unique features, such as restaurants or theaters. Have students report their findings to the class.

Answers for Questions

1. Possible answer: They sell to large numbers of customers.
2. Possible answer: To be sure that the correct discount is given. Sometimes cash registers are not programmed correctly.
3. Every item is on sale for half of its old price.

Connect

On page 421, students use the floor area of stores in a shopping center to find rental costs.

8-5 Lesson Organizer

Objective

- Use equations to solve problems involving percents.

Materials

- Explore: Graph paper

NCTM Standards

- 1–5, 7, 9

Review

Solve these equations for x.

1. $4x = 20$ $x = 5$
2. $7.3x = 35.04$ $x = 4.8$
3. $x + 23 = 87$ $x = 64$
4. $57 = 19x$ $x = 3$

Available on Daily Transparency 8-5

1 Introduce

Explore

You might use Lesson Enhancement Transparency 37 and Teaching Tool Transparency 7: Graph Paper with **Explore**.

The Point

Students visualize percent of a number by seeing a 10 by 10 grid as the whole and a partially shaded grid as a percent of the whole.

Ongoing Assessment

Students may not see how 100 squares could represent anything other than 100 things. As they look at the shaded squares in the $40 grid ask, "If you paid $40 for all the shaded squares, how much would each square cost?" $0.50

Answers for Explore

1. The first grid shows 100% shaded. This represents the total regular price of a Mogulrider. The second grid has only 80 of 100 squares shaded, or 80%. This represents the sale price.
2. Each square is worth $0.50; The regular price is $50.00; 80 squares represent $40. $40 \div 80 = 0.5$ and $100 \bullet 0.5 = 50$.

8-5 Using Equations to Solve Percent Problems

You'll Learn ...

- to use equations to solve problems involving percents

... How It's Used

People working at oil refineries make gasolines by mixing percents of different chemical compounds.

▶ Lesson Link You've used models, fractions, and decimals to solve percent problems. Now you'll use equations to solve problems involving percents. ◀

Explore Percent Equations

Materials: Graph paper

Think Snow!

It hasn't snowed for weeks, and the S'No Joke Mall is having a sale!

1. Mogulrider snowboards now sell for $40, which is 80% of the regular price. Explain how the grids show the regular price and the sale price of a Mogulrider.

Regular price

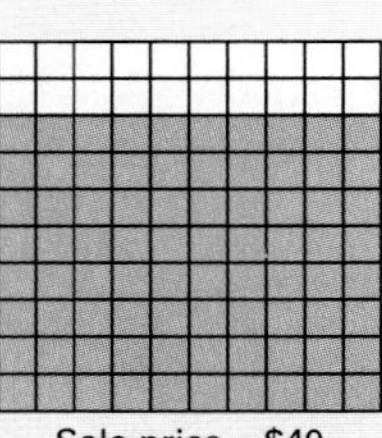

Sale price = $40

2. What is the value of each square? What is the regular price of Mogulriders? How do you know?
3. Crisis! Two more weeks of warm weather! The prices of Slippenslider snowboards are *slashed!* The new price of $48 is 60% of the original price. Use grids to show the regular price and the sale price of a Slippenslider. Then find the regular price of the board.
4. Explain how you can use grids to find the original price of an item if you know the sale price and the percent off.

Learn Using Equations to Solve Percent Problems

Sometimes it's easiest to solve percent problems by writing and solving an equation. Here are two helpful hints for translating percent problems into equations.

- Remember that *of* usually means *times*.
- Rewrite percents as decimals.

What number	is	25%	of	200?
x	=	0.25	$\cdot$	200
x	=	50		

MEETING INDIVIDUAL NEEDS

Resources

- 8-5 Practice
- 8-5 Reteaching
- 8-5 Problem Solving
- 8-5 Enrichment
- 8-5 Daily Transparency
  - Problem of the Day
  - Review
  - Quick Quiz
- Lesson Enhancement Transparency 37
- Teaching Tool Transparencies 2, 3, 7
- Technology Master 36

Learning Modalities

Visual Use the two-grid method of visualizing a number that is a certain percent of another number.

Verbal Help students translate from word problems to mathematical equations by highlighting and discussing the mathematical meanings of the words *is* (equals) and *of* (multiply).

Social Have pairs of students play a game with number cubes. One student rolls two cubes and the other has to make up a percent sentence about the two numbers. For example, if a 3 and a 6 are rolled, the student could say, "3 is 50% of 6."

English Language Development

Students with limited English proficiency may have trouble reading the word problems in this lesson. Pair them with other students who can read and discuss the problems with them.

Have students write new words found in word problems in a notebook or on vocabulary cards.

Example 1

What percent of 48 is 15?

Let p = the percent.	Choose a variable.
p percent of 48 is 15.	Reword the statement.
$p \cdot 48 = 15$	Translate to an equation.
$\frac{p \cdot 48}{48} = \frac{15}{48}$	Use inverse operations.
$p = 0.3125 = 31.25\%$	Divide. Write the decimal as a percent.

15 is 31.25% of 48.

> **Remember**
> When you convert a decimal to a percent, move the decimal point two places to the right.
> **[Page 391]**

A percent *discount* describes how much you save off the original price. The percent of the original price you pay is 100% minus the percent discount.

Example 2

A Fats Domino CD is on sale at Disk Cellar at a 35% discount. The sale price is \$8.06. Find the regular price.

The new price is 100% − 35% = 65% of the original price.

Let r = the regular price.

\$8.06 is 65% of the regular price.

$8.06 = 0.65 \cdot r$

$\frac{8.06}{0.65} = \frac{0.65r}{0.65}$

$12.40 = r$

The regular price is \$12.40.

Try It

a. What percent of 120 is 36? 30% **b.** 12% of what number is 9? 75

> **▶ Music Link**
> Fats Domino was one of the most important rock-and-roll musicians of the 1950s. His records, which included "Blueberry Hill" and "Ain't That a Shame," sold over 65 million copies. Domino was named to the Rock and Roll Hall of Fame in 1986.

Check Your Understanding

1. Do the questions "What is 20% of 40?", "20 is what percent of 40?", and "20 is 40% of what number?" mean the same thing? Explain.
2. Write a percent problem you would solve using mental math. Write another you would use an equation to solve. Explain your thinking.

MATH EVERY DAY

▶ Problem of the Day

Shelia has some baseball cards she wants to put in plastic sheets. She has some sheets that hold nine cards and some that hold eight cards. If she fills the eight-card sheets, she will have two cards left over. If she fills the nine-card sheets, she will use one less sheet, but have three cards left over. She has fewer than 100 cards. How many cards does Shelia have? 66 cards

Available on Daily Transparency 8-5

An Extension is provided in the transparency package.

Fact of the Day

The Rock and Roll Hall of Fame and Museum was not built until 1995. The impressive Cleveland building was designed by I. M. Pei and cost \$92 million.

Estimation

Estimate the following numbers.

1. 163% of 55 90
2. 43 is what percent of 60? 70%
3. 52 is about 40% of what number? 130

Answers for Explore

3.

Regular price

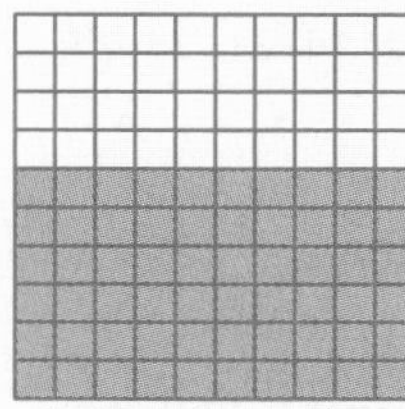

Sale price = \$48

Regular price is \$80.00.

4. Use the sale price grid to find the value of 1 square, then multiply by 100.

2 Teach

Learn

Alternate Examples

1. What percent of 64 is 18?

   $p \bullet 64 = 18$

   $\frac{p \bullet 64}{64} = \frac{18}{64}$

   $p = 0.28125 = 28.125\%$

   18 is 28.125% of 64.

2. The discount on a certain CD is 20%. If the sale price is \$11.60, what was the original price?

   The new price is 100% − 20% = 80% of the original price.

   $11.60 = 0.8 \bullet r$

   $\frac{11.60}{0.8} = \frac{0.8 \bullet r}{0.8}$

   $14.50 = r$

   The regular price is \$14.50.

3 Practice and Assess

Check

Answers for Check Your Understanding

1. No. The first asks for 20% of 40; The second asks for 20 expressed as a percent of 40; The last asks for the number that 20 is 40% of.
2. Possible answer: Mental math: What is 50% of 236? Just divide by 2. Equation: 35 is 62% of what number? This answer is not obvious.

8-5 Exercises and Applications

Assignment Guide

- Basic
  1–15 odds, 18, 20, 22–27
- Average
  1–15 odds, 16–20, 21–27 odds
- Enriched
  2–12 evens, 14–21, 24–27

Exercise Notes

Exercise 20

Problem-Solving Tip You may wish to use Teaching Tool Transparencies 2 and 3: Guided Problem Solving pages 1–2.

Exercise Answers

1. a. Let regular price be r.
   b. $25.20 is 60% of the regular price.
   c. $25.20 = 0.6 \cdot r$
   d. $\frac{25.20}{0.6} = \frac{0.6}{0.6} \cdot r$
   e. $r = 42$. The regular price is $42.00.

14. Answers will vary. Any pair of numbers where the second is greater than the first.

Reteaching

Activity

Materials: 10 × 10 grids, calculator

- Solve Exercises 6, 11, and 13 using the method in **Explore**.
- Check your answers using a calculator.

Exercise 6: The value of each square is 1.5, and $1.5 \times 100 = 150$, so 30% of 150 is 45.

Exercise 11: The value of each square is 2, and $2 \times 100 = 200$, so 89% of 200 is 178.

Exercise 13: The value of each square is 120, and $120 \times 100 = 12{,}000$, so 0.1% of 12,000 is 12.

8-5 Exercises and Applications

Practice and Apply

1. **Getting Started** Follow these steps to find the regular price of an item that sells for $25.20, which is 60% of the regular price.

a. Choose a variable for the regular price.

b. Reword the problem using the following format: ____ is ____ percent of the regular price.

c. Translate the problem to an equation.

d. Use the inverse operation.

e. Solve for the variable. State the regular price of the item.

Solve each problem. If necessary, round answers to the nearest tenth.

2. What percent of 78 is 39? **50%**

3. What percent of 70 is 22? **31.4%**

4. 55% of 985 is what number? **541.8**

5. 9% of 600 is what number? **54**

6. 30% of what number is 45? **150**

7. 11% of what number is 36? **327.3**

8. What percent of 72 is 67? **93.1%**

9. 95% of 40 is what number? **38**

10. 240% of 58 is what number? **139.2**

11. 89% of what number is 178? **200**

12. What percent of 780 is 3.9? **0.5%**

13. 0.1% of what number is 12? **12,000**

14. **Logic** In the following sentence, fill in the blanks with numbers so that the answer is greater than 100 percent.

What percent of ____ is ____?

15. **Consumer** Superplex Cinemas give students a 25% discount off the regular ticket price of $7.00. GPS

a. What percent of the regular price is the student price? **75%**

b. What is the student ticket price? **$5.25**

16. **Social Studies** A student at West Milford High School, in New Jersey, was concerned because food in the school cafeteria was served on plastic foam trays rather than recyclable paper trays. She polled students to see if they would pay 5¢ extra for paper trays. Of those students, 85% responded that they would be willing to pay the extra nickel. If 480 students were polled, how many were willing to pay extra for paper trays? **408 students**

PRACTICE 8-5

PRACTICE

Name ____________

Practice 8-5

Using Equations to Solve Percent Problems

Solve each problem. If necessary, round answers to the nearest tenth.

1. What percent of 64 is 48? 75%
2. 16% of 130 is what number? 20.8
3. 25% of what number is 24? 96
4. What percent of 18 is 12? 66.7%
5. 48% of 83 is what number? 39.8
6. 40% of what number is 136? 340
7. What percent of 530 is 107? 20.2%
8. 74% of 643 is what number? 475.8
9. 62% of what number is 84? 135.5
10. What percent of 84 is 50? 59.5%
11. 37% of 245 is what number? 90.7
12. 12% of what number is 105? 875
13. What percent of 42 is 7.5? 17.9%
14. 98% of 880 is what number? 862.4
15. 7% of what number is 63? 900
16. What percent of 95 is 74? 77.9%
17. Cafe Mediocre offers senior citizens a 15% discount off its regular price of $8.95 for the dinner buffet.
    a. What percent of the regular price is the price for senior citizens? 85%
    b. What is the price for senior citizens? $7.61
18. In 1990, 12.5% of the people in Oregon did not have health insurance. If the population of Oregon was 2,880,000, how many people were uninsured? 360,000

RETEACHING

Name ____________

Alternative Lesson 8-5

Using Equations to Solve Percent Problems

You can write equations to solve percent problems by substituting amounts into the statement: "____% of ____ is ____?"

Example 1

64% of 50 is what number?

Choose a variable for the unknown amount.	Let n = unknown number
Reword the statement, ____% of ____ is ____.	64% of 50 is n
Write an equation.	$64\% \cdot 50 = n$
Write the percent as a decimal.	$0.64 \cdot 50 = n$
Multiply to solve for n.	$32 = n$

So, 64% of 50 is 32.

Try It

a. Write an equation for: 9% of 150 is what number. 0.09 · 150 = n

b. Solve the equation to find 9% of 150 is what number? 13.5

c. 48% of 250 is what number? 120

d. 82% of 75 is what number? 61.5

e. 16% of 50 is what number? 8

f. 32% of 800 is what number? 256

Example 2

What percent of 36 is 18?

Choose a variable for the unknown amount.	Let p = unknown percent.
Reword the statement, ____% of ____ is ____.	p % of 36 is 18.
Write an equation.	$36 \cdot p = 18$
Divide each side by 36.	$36 \cdot \frac{p}{36} = \frac{18}{36}$
Simplify and write the decimal as a percent.	$p = 0.5 = 50\%$

So, 18 is 50% of 36.

Try It

g. Reword the statement: What percent of 75 is 12? p % of 75 is 12

h. Use the statement to find what percent of 75 is 12. 16%

i. What percent of 60 is 18? 30%

j. What percent of 50 is 35? 70%

17. **Consumer** Two candle stores are having a sale. Advertisements for Cut-Rate Candles say, "At Least 10% Off All Candles!" Flyers for Wick World say, "Up to 75% Off All Candles!" Which store is having the better sale? Explain.

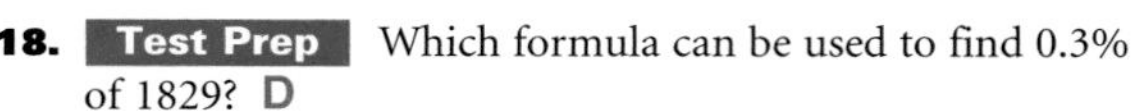

18. **Test Prep** Which formula can be used to find 0.3% of 1829? D

Ⓐ 3×1829 Ⓑ 0.3×1829

Ⓒ 0.03×1829 Ⓓ 0.003×1829

Problem Solving and Reasoning

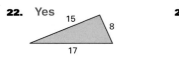

19. **Journal** The table gives data about U.S. physicians in 1994.

Physicians in the United States, 1994		
Sex	**Total**	**Under 35 Years Old**
Male	551,151	90,528
Female	133,263	43,204

a. What percent of U.S. physicians in 1994 were women?

b. What percent of U.S. physicians under 35 years old were women?

c. Compare your answers to **a** and **b.** Make a prediction about the percent of female physicians in the future. Explain your reasoning.

20. **Choose a Strategy** Find all the whole-number percents of 182 that would equal a number less than 18. Explain how you found your answer.

21. **Critical Thinking** If 25% of a number is 45, is the number greater than or less than 45? If 150% of a number is 45, is the number greater than or less than 45? Explain how you can tell.

Problem Solving STRATEGIES

- Look for a Pattern
- Make an Organized List
- Make a Table
- Guess and Check
- Work Backward
- Use Logical Reasoning
- Draw a Diagram
- Solve a Simpler Problem

Mixed Review

Determine if each triangle is a right triangle. *[Lesson 5-7]*

22. Yes (sides 15, 8, 17)

23. Yes (sides 26, 10, 24)

24. No

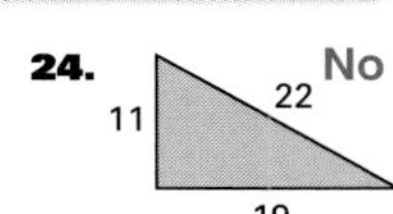

Number Sense **Suggest appropriate units for each rate.** *[Lesson 7-5]*

25. Your breathing rate **26.** The price of potatoes **27.** The speed of ketchup coming out of a bottle

PROBLEM SOLVING 8-5

Exercise Answers

17. It is not possible to tell from the advertisements. Cut-Rate Candles' discount is 10% or more; Wick World's discount is 75% or less. These overlap and no decision can be made.

19. a. ≈ 19.47% were women.

b. ≈ 32.31%

c. The percent will be higher; The percent of young female physicians is higher than the overall percent, so, if the trend continues, the overall percent will increase.

20. 1%, 2%, 3%, 4%, 5%, 6%, 7%, 8%, 9%. All percents must be less than 10%, since 10% of 182 = 18.2.

21. Greater than 45. Less than 45. In the first case, 45 = 25% of some number. 25% is less than 1, so 45 is only a part of the number. In the second case, 45 = 150% of some number. 150% is more than 1, so 45 is more than the number.

25. Possible answer: Breaths per minute.

26. Possible answer: Cents per pound.

27. Possible answer: Cubic centimeters per minute.

Alternate Assessment

Self Assessment Have students write about what they understand about percent problems. Ask them to look over the exercises on these pages and write as many different types of percent problems as they can think of.

PROBLEM SOLVING

Name ____________ **Guided Problem Solving 8-5**

GPS PROBLEM 15, STUDENT PAGE 408

Superplex Cinemas gives students a 25% discount off the regular ticket price of $7.00.

a. What percent of the regular price is the student price?

b. What is the student ticket price?

Understand

1. What is the regular price? $7.00

2. What percent is the student discount? 25%

Plan

3. What percent of the regular price is $7.00? 100%

4. Complete the equation to find what percent of the regular price is the student price?

100 % − 25 % = 75 %

5. Write an equation to find the student price. $0.75 \cdot 7.00 = n$

6. What is a reasonable student ticket price? c

a. $12.75 b. $7.00 c. $5.25 d. $2.75

Solve

7. Solve the equation from Item 5. $n = 5.25$

8. Write the student ticket price and what percent it is of the regular price. $5.25; 75%

Look Back

9. How can you find the student ticket price without first finding what percent it is of the regular price? Possible answer: Find 25% of $7 ($1.75). Subtract from $7.00 ($5.25).

SOLVE ANOTHER PROBLEM

A sweater is selling at a 35% discount off the regular price of $55.

a. What percent of the regular price is the sale price? 65%

b. What is the sale price of the sweater? $35.75

ENRICHMENT

Name ____________ **Extend Your Thinking 8-5**

Critical Thinking

Use what you know about finding percents and writing equations to find multiple percents of a number.

1. What is 25% of 40% of 45?

a. What is 40% of 45? 18

b. What is 25% of your answer to Question 1a? 4.5

2. a. What is 25% of 45? 11.25

b. What is 40% of your answer to Question 2a? 4.5

3. a. What is 25% of 40%? 10%

Possible answers: Items 4–7

b. What is 45 multiplied by your answer to Question 3a? 4.5

4. Compare how you found the answers to Questions 1, 2, and 3. What are the similarities? What are the differences?

They have same factors and same products. The order in which the factors are multiplied differs.

5. How can you use this observation to solve percent problems, such as 50% of 140% of 200 mentally?

Use factors that are easy to compute mentally, such as 50% of 200 (100). Then find 140% of 100 (140).

6. If 50% of 120% of 30% of a number is 108, what is the number? Show how you found your answer.

50% of 120% is 60%. 30% of 60% is 18%.

$0.18 \cdot x = 108$. $x = 600$.

7. If 40% of 60% of 25% of a number is 54, what is the number? Show how you found your answer.

25% of 60% is 15%. 40% of 15% is 6%.

$0.06 \cdot x = 54$. $x = 900$.

Quick Quiz

1. 140% of 55 is what number? 77

2. 15% of what number is 67? 446.6

3. What percent of 22 is 8? 36.4%

4. Winter parkas are on sale at a 40% discount. They now sell for $58.80. What was their original price? $98

Available on Daily Transparency 8-5

8-6 Lesson Organizer

Objective

- Use proportions to solve percent problems.

Materials

- Explore: Inch ruler

NCTM Standards

- 1–5, 7, 8, 10

Review

Solve each proportion. Round to the nearest tenth if necessary.

1. $\frac{r}{35} = \frac{21}{235}$ $r = 3.1$
2. $\frac{65}{n} = \frac{476}{37}$ $n = 5.1$
3. $\frac{6}{35} = \frac{m}{47}$ $m = 8.1$
4. $\frac{42}{89} = \frac{420}{x}$ $x = 890$

Available on Daily Transparency 8-6

Lesson Link

Remind the students that a proportion is an equation stating that two ratios are equal.

1 Introduce

Explore

You may want to use Teaching Tool Transparency 14: Rulers with **Explore**.

The Point

Students see that a ratio comparing the number of one type of store to the total number of stores is equal to the percent of stores of that type. This proportion is the basis for the problem-solving method used in this lesson.

Ongoing Assessment

Check that students accurately compute the percents in Step 2. Be sure they understand that the total number of stores (125) must be used in each computation.

8-6 Solving Percent Problems with Proportions

You'll Learn ...

- to use proportions to solve percent problems

... How It's Used

Printers combined different percents of four basic colors to produce all the colors you see in this book.

Lesson Link You've solved percent problems by solving equations. Now you'll use proportions to solve problems involving percents.

Explore Solving Percent Problems

Materials: Inch ruler, Graph paper

Attention, Shoppers!

The brochure lists the types of stores at Lakeside Mall.

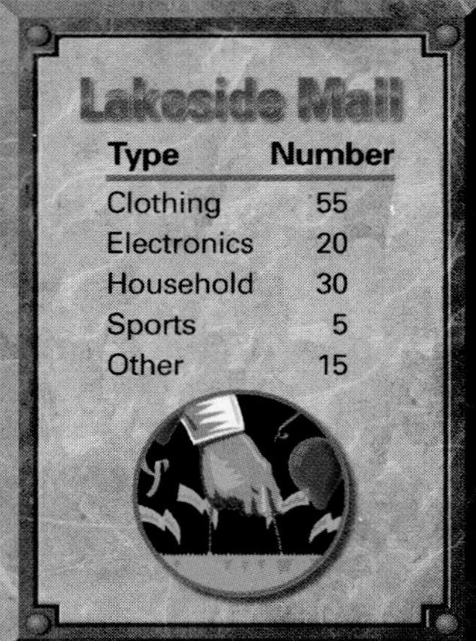

Lakeside Mall

Type	Number
Clothing	55
Electronics	20
Household	30
Sports	5
Other	15

1. What is the total number of stores at the mall?
2. Use an equation to find the percent of each type of store.
3. Draw a 10 unit by 10 unit square on graph paper. Your drawing will contain 100 squares.
4. Divide the large square into 5 regions that represent the percent of different types of stores. Label each region. Explain how you divided the square.
5. Write a fraction comparing the *number* of clothing stores to the total number of stores. Then rewrite the *percent* of stores that are clothing stores as a fraction. Are these fractions equal?

Learn Solving Percent Problems with Proportions

You know how to solve percent problems by using equations. However, it's sometimes easier to set up and solve these equations as proportions.

You can rewrite a percent as a fraction whose denominator is 100. This is one fraction in the proportion. The other comes from information in the problem.

MEETING INDIVIDUAL NEEDS

Resources

- 8-6 Practice
- 8-6 Reteaching
- 8-6 Problem Solving
- 8-6 Enrichment
- 8-6 Daily Transparency
  - Problem of the Day
  - Review
  - Quick Quiz
- Teaching Tool Transparencies 14, 22
- Chapter 8 Project Master

Learning Modalities

Logical Emphasize the importance of placing numbers in their correct positions in a proportion. In a percent proportion, one ratio will generally have the percent (known or unknown) as its first term and 100 as its second term. The terms of the other ratio must be in the same relative order, with the term representing the "whole" in the same position as 100.

Social Have pairs of students describe to each other their understandings of the two methods already studied for solving percent problems: using equations and using proportions. Have them decide which they think is easier.

Inclusion

Students who are not motivated may need to be shown the usefulness of mathematics in their lives. Percent is a topic that they confront all the time in stores, in newspaper advertisements, and on the radio. Help the students write their own problems about things they would like to buy.

Examples

1 What number is 47% of 280? Solve using a proportion.

Estimate: 47% is close to 50%, which is $\frac{1}{2}$. Half of 280 is 140. 47% of 280 should be a little less than 140.

Let n = the number. Choose a variable.

$\frac{47}{100} = \frac{n}{280}$ Write a proportion.

$13{,}160 = 100n$ Find the cross products.

$\frac{13{,}160}{100} = \frac{100n}{100}$ Use inverse operations.

$131.6 = n$ Divide.

131.6 is 47% of 280.

2 Sam chose a jacket from a "45% Off" rack. The original price was $35.00. When the clerk rang up the sale, the price, before tax, was $23.80. What percent discount did Sam get? Is this the correct discount?

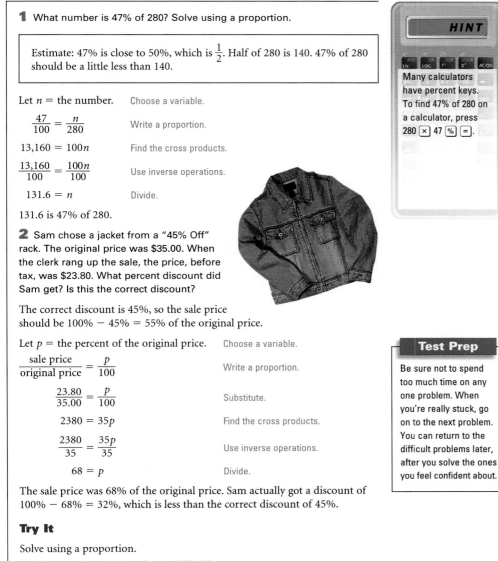

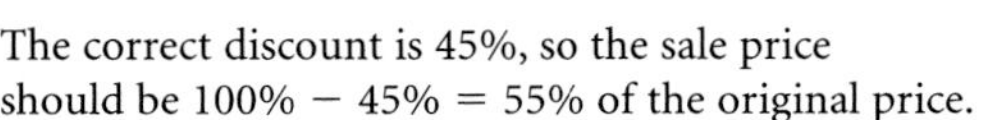

The correct discount is 45%, so the sale price should be 100% − 45% = 55% of the original price.

Let p = the percent of the original price. Choose a variable.

$\frac{\text{sale price}}{\text{original price}} = \frac{p}{100}$ Write a proportion.

$\frac{23.80}{35.00} = \frac{p}{100}$ Substitute.

$2380 = 35p$ Find the cross products.

$\frac{2380}{35} = \frac{35p}{35}$ Use inverse operations.

$68 = p$ Divide.

The sale price was 68% of the original price. Sam actually got a discount of 100% − 68% = 32%, which is less than the correct discount of 45%.

HINT

Many calculators have percent keys. To find 47% of 280 on a calculator, press 280 [×] 47 [%] [=].

Test Prep

Be sure not to spend too much time on any one problem. When you're really stuck, go on to the next problem. You can return to the difficult problems later, after you solve the ones you feel confident about.

Try It

Solve using a proportion.

a. What number is 78% of 221? 172.38

b. If there are 16 girls in a class of 30, what percent of the students are girls? $53.\overline{3}\%$

MATH EVERY DAY

Problem of the Day

Fill in the squares below with the digits 1 through 9 so that each number sentence (horizontal and vertical) is true. Note that each digit will be used exactly once.

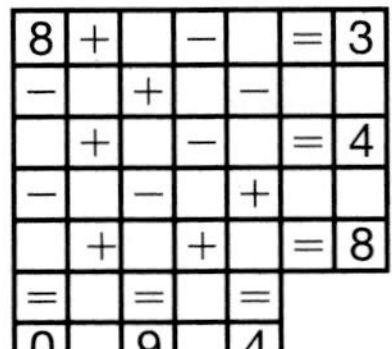

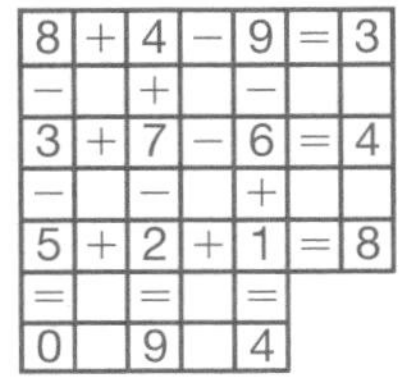

Available on Daily Transparency 8-6

An Extension is provided in the transparency package.

Fact of the Day

Edmonton, the capital city of the Canadian province of Alberta, is the fifth largest city in Canada with a population of over 600,000.

Mental Math

Do these mentally.

1. What is 50% of 124? 62
2. What percent of 244 is 61? 25%
3. 23 is 20% of what number? 115

For Groups That Finish Early

Can your drawing of the square with the allocated spaces be an actual map of the mall? Why or why not? It could not be a map of a mall; stores of each type usually are scattered, and there is no allowance for common spaces.

Answers for Explore

1. 125 stores
2. Clothing: 44%; Electronics: 16%; Household: 24%; Sports: 4%; Other: 12%.

3–4. Possible drawing:

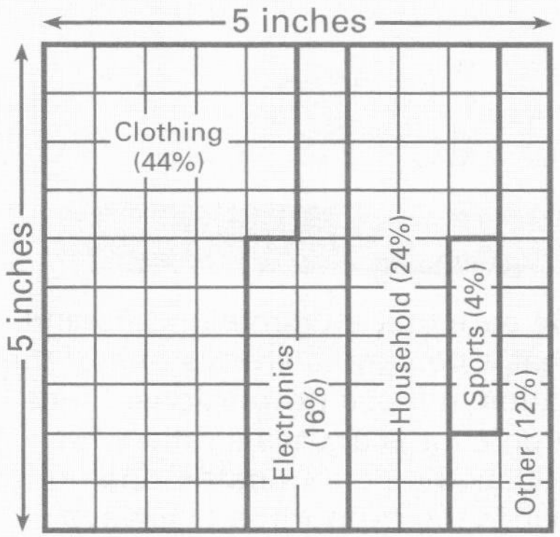

Each small square = 1%.

5. $\frac{55}{125}$; $\frac{44}{100}$; Yes, both equal $\frac{11}{25}$.

2 Teach

Learn

You may want to use Teaching Tool Transparency 22: Scientific Calculator with Example 1.

Alternate Examples

1. What number is 23% of 240?

   Estimate: 23% is close to 25% which is $\frac{1}{4}$. One-fourth of 240 is 60. 23% of 240 should be a little less than 60.

   $\frac{23}{100} = \frac{n}{240}$

   $5520 = 100n$

   $\frac{5520}{100} = \frac{100n}{100}$

   $55.2 = n$; 55.2 is 23% of 240.

2. A sweater originally priced at $45.00 was sold for $24.75. Find the percent discount.

   $\frac{\text{sale price}}{\text{original price}} = \frac{p}{100}$

   $\frac{24.75}{45.00} = \frac{p}{100}$

   $2475 = 45p$

   $\frac{2475}{45} = \frac{45p}{45}$

   $55 = p$; The sale price was 55% of the original price. The discount was 100% − 55% = 45%.

Alternate Examples

3. John collected 35% of all of the contributions in his class for a local charity. He collected $213.50 by himself. How much was raised by the whole class?

$$\frac{\text{John's amount}}{\text{Class amount}} = \frac{35}{100}$$

$$\frac{213.50}{c} = \frac{35}{100}$$

$35c = 21350$

$c = 610$

The class collected $610.00.

3 Practice and Assess

Check

Be sure that students understand that a percent is always one of the ratios in these proportions. Since a percent is always a ratio with 100 as the denominator, one number in the proportion is always compared to 100.

Answers for Check Your Understanding

1. 100; Because 100% always represents the whole amount in any situation.
2. The percent that Juanita is finding is more than 100%.

DID YOU KNOW?

West Edmonton Mall opened on September 15, 1981. In addition to its stores, it contains 19 movie theaters, 5 amusement areas, a chapel, and a hotel. It cost more than $1.1 billion to build!

Example 3

The largest shopping center in the United States is the Mall of America in Bloomington, Minnesota. The largest shopping center in the world is the West Edmonton Mall in Alberta, Canada.

West Edmonton Mall

The Mall of America has 350 stores. This is 43.75% of the number in the West Edmonton Mall. How many stores are there in the West Edmonton Mall?

Let e = number of stores in the West Edmonton Mall. — Choose a variable.

$\frac{\text{Mall of America stores}}{e} = \frac{43.75}{100}$ — Write a proportion.

$\frac{350}{e} = \frac{43.75}{100}$ — Substitute.

$35{,}000 = 43.75e$ — Find the cross products.

$\frac{35{,}000}{43.75} = \frac{43.75e}{43.75}$ — Use inverse operations.

$800 = e$ — Divide.

There are 800 stores in the West Edmonton Mall.

Try It

Solve using a proportion.

a. 41 is 25% of what number? 164

b. In 1988, there were about 735,000 African elephants. This was about 56% of the number of African elephants in 1979. How many African elephants were there in 1979? 1,312,500 African elephants

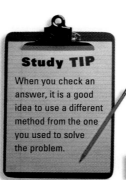

Study TIP

When you check an answer, it is a good idea to use a different method from the one you used to solve the problem.

Check Your Understanding

1. When you use a proportion to solve a percent problem, one of the four numbers is always the same. Which is it, and why is it always the same?
2. Juanita was using a proportion to find a percent of a number. She noticed that her proportion involved an improper fraction. If Juanita set up the proportion correctly, what does this tell you?

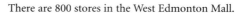

MEETING MIDDLE SCHOOL CLASSROOM NEEDS

Tips from Middle School Teachers

To integrate the study of percents with statistics, I ask students to vote on their favorite brands of jeans, athletic shoes, or other popular items. We then show the results, as percents, in bar and circle graphs.

I also have the students bring in ads for their favorite brands, especially ads that show a percent-off sale. We calculate the sale price (to check the store's computation) and then add sales tax to find the final cost.

Cooperative Learning

Students can work in pairs to improve their estimation skills. Prepare cards with problems involving percents. Print the answers on the backs of the cards. One student holds up a card; the other estimates the answer. The first student then says "higher" or "lower" and the second student revises the original estimate. The game continues until the second student has come within some prearranged small range of the answer (say, within 0.5 of the actual answer). Students try to minimize the number of guesses to arrive at the answer.

Cultural Connection

Korea is a very popular place to shop in Asia. The unit of currency in Korea is the won and, although exchange rates vary, about 800 won equal one U.S. dollar. Ask students to determine about how many U.S. dollars they would have to pay in Seoul, Korea, for a piece of pottery that has a price of 160,000 won. $200

8-6 Exercises and Applications

Practice and Apply

1. **Getting Started** 52 is 38% of what number? Follow these steps to solve using a proportion.
   a. Choose a variable. x
   b. Write a proportion involving 38% rewritten as a fraction. $\frac{38}{100} = \frac{52}{x}$
   c. Multiply to find the cross products. $38x = 5200$
   d. Use the inverse operation. $\frac{38x}{38} = \frac{5200}{38}$
   e. Solve for the variable. Round your answer to the nearest tenth. **136.8**

Operation Sense Write a proportion and solve each problem. If necessary, round answers to the nearest tenth.

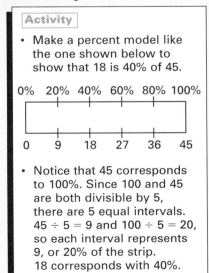

2. What number is 70% of 45? **31.5**
3. What number is 23% of 75? **17.3**
4. 45 is what percent of 90? **50%**
5. 7 is what percent of 77? **9.1%**
6. 15 is 25% of what number? **60**
7. 43 is 18% of what number? **238.9**
8. What number is 75% of 125? **93.8**
9. 60 is what percent of 25? **240%**
10. 39 is 150% of what number? **26**
11. 25 is what percent of 752? **3.3%**
12. 19 is 95% of what number? **20**
13. What number is 0.5% of 490? **2.5**
14. In part because of the popularity of outlet malls, about 300 of the 1800 traditional retail malls across the United States may close in the next few years. Find the percent of retail malls that may close. $16\frac{2}{3}\%$
15. **Science** The bee hummingbird is the smallest bird. It can weigh as little as 2 grams. The largest bird, the ostrich, can weigh as much as 150 kilograms. What percent of the weight of a bee hummingbird is the weight of an ostrich? **7,500,000%**
    GPS
16. **Problem Solving** The U.S. Postal Service handles 170,000,000,000 pieces of mail each year. This is 40% of the world's total. How many pieces of mail are sent each year? **425,000,000,000**
17. **Patterns** The fraction $\frac{1}{3}$ is equal to $33\frac{1}{3}\%$. Name three other fractions that equal $33\frac{1}{3}\%$. **Possible answer:** $\frac{4}{12}, \frac{8}{24}, \frac{16}{48}$

PRACTICE 8-6

8-6 Exercises and Applications

Assignment Guide

- Basic
  1–9, 14–16, 20–30 evens
- Average
  1–19 odds, 20–22, 23–29 odds
- Enriched
  2–12 evens, 14–22, 24–30 evens

Exercise Notes

Exercises 2–13

Estimation Have students estimate answers before doing computations.

Exercise 15

Science More than 300 species of hummingbirds are known. They live only in the Western Hemisphere, but only about 19 kinds live in the U.S. Their wings can move as fast as 60 to 70 times per second.

Exercise 16

History Many ancient civilizations, including the Chinese, Egyptians, Assyrians, and Persians, had well-organized mail systems. Generally, however, these postal systems could be used only by government officials.

PRACTICE

Name ______________________

Practice 8-6

Solving Percent Problems with Proportions

Write a proportion and solve each problem. If necessary, round answers to the nearest tenth.

1. What number is 18% of 95? $\frac{x}{95} = \frac{18}{100}$; 17.1
2. 37 is what percent of 50? $\frac{37}{50} = \frac{x}{100}$; 74%
3. 12 is 20% of what number? $\frac{12}{x} = \frac{20}{100}$; 60
4. What number is 54% of 82? $\frac{x}{82} = \frac{54}{100}$; 44.3
5. 89 is what percent of 395? $\frac{89}{395} = \frac{x}{100}$; 22.5%
6. 33 is 16% of what number? $\frac{33}{x} = \frac{16}{100}$; 206.3
7. What number is 90% of 84? $\frac{x}{84} = \frac{90}{100}$; 75.6
8. 108 is what percent of 647? $\frac{108}{647} = \frac{x}{100}$; 16.7%
9. 64 is 178% of what number? $\frac{64}{x} = \frac{178}{100}$; 36.0
10. What number is 46% of 835? $\frac{x}{835} = \frac{46}{100}$; 384.1
11. 861 is what percent of 513? $\frac{861}{513} = \frac{x}{100}$; 167.8%
12. 19 is 0.7% of what number? $\frac{19}{x} = \frac{0.7}{100}$; 2714.3
13. A store that normally sells a compact stereo system for $128 is having a sale. Everything is discounted 35%. How much can you save by buying the stereo during the sale? $44.80
14. In 1990, 17,339,000 Americans spoke Spanish at home. If 54.4% of non-English speakers spoke Spanish, find the number of non-English speakers. About 31,873,000
15. **Measurement** An acre is 4,840 square yards. A hectare is 11,960 square yards. What percent of a hectare is an acre? About 40.5%

RETEACHING

Name ______________________

Alternative Lesson 8-6

Solving Percent Problems with Proportions

You can rewrite a percent as a fraction whose denominator is 100. That fraction can be written as part of a proportion to solve percent problems.

— Example 1 —

What number is 35% of 42?

Choose a variable. Write the percent as a fraction.	Let n = unknown number; $35\% = \frac{35}{100}$
Write a proportion.	$\frac{35}{100} = \frac{n}{42}$
Find the cross products.	$1470 = 100n$
Use inverse operations.	$\frac{1470}{100} = \frac{100n}{100}$
Divide.	$14.7 = n$

So, 35% of 42 is 14.7.

Try It

a. Write 125% as a fraction. $\frac{125}{100}$

b. Write a proportion for: 125% of 96 is what number? $\frac{125}{100} = \frac{n}{96}$

c. What number is 125% of 96? 120

d. What number is 75% of 80? 60

— Example 2 —

What percent of 15 is 60?

Choose a variable for the unknown amount.	Let $\frac{p}{100}$ = unknown percent
Write a proportion.	$\frac{p}{100} = \frac{60}{15}$
Find the cross products.	$15p = 6000$
Use inverse operations.	$\frac{15p}{15} = \frac{6000}{15}$
Divide.	$p = 400$

So, 60 is $\frac{400}{100}$ or 400% of 15.

Try It Solve each problem.

e. Write a proportion for: What percent of 125 is 5? $\frac{p}{100} = \frac{5}{125}$

f. Solve the proportion to find what percent of 125 is 5. 4%

g. What percent of 40 is 26? 65%

h. What percent of 30 is 18? 60%

Reteaching

Activity

- Make a percent model like the one shown below to show that 18 is 40% of 45.

0% 20% 40% 60% 80% 100%

0 9 18 27 36 45

- Notice that 45 corresponds to 100%. Since 100 and 45 are both divisible by 5, there are 5 equal intervals. $45 \div 5 = 9$ and $100 \div 5 = 20$, so each interval represents 9, or 20% of the strip. 18 corresponds with 40%.
- Make similar models to show that 40% of 120 = 48 and 25% of 96 = 24.

Project Progress

You may want to have students use Chapter 8 Project Master.

Exercise Answers

21. Korean travelers spend about 189% of U.S. travelers' spending, and 120% of South Africans' spending. South Africans spend $83\frac{1}{3}$% of Koreans' spending, and 158% of U.S. travelers' spending. U.S. travelers spend about 53% of Korean travelers' spending, and $63\frac{1}{3}$% of South African travelers' spending.

22. First way: $10\% = \frac{1}{10}$, $520 \div 10 = 52$; Second way: $\frac{x}{520} = \frac{10}{100}$; The first way seems more efficient since it involves just one division.

Alternate Assessment

Ongoing Write a letter to the parents and guardians of your students informing them that you've been working on percent and on estimating percents of a number. Ask them to reinforce your work at home by having their children make estimates of percents when they occur in the everyday life of the family: when leaving a tip in a restaurant, when deciding how much a $50 pair of sneakers costs in a 30%-off sale, and so on.

► Quick Quiz

Write a proportion to solve each problem.

1. What number is 34% of 127? 43.18
2. 45 is 80% of what number? 56.25
3. 51 is what percent of 85? 60%
4. CD World is having a "20 percent off" sale. How much would a CD cost that normally costs $16.95? $13.56

Available on Daily Transparency 8-6

PROBLEM SOLVING 8-6

18. Problem Solving A factory-outlet shoe store sells items at discounts ranging from 20% to 70%. If a pair of shoes that usually costs $45 is sold at a 25% discount, how much can you save by purchasing the shoes from this store? **$11.25**

19. Statistics The weight of a nickel is 80% of the weight of a quarter.

a. If a nickel weighs 5 grams, how much does a quarter weigh? **6.25 grams**

b. A dime weighs 50% as much as a nickel does. What is the weight of a dime? **2.5 grams**

20. Test Prep 25 is approximately what percent of 23? **D**

Ⓐ 0.92% Ⓑ 1.1% Ⓒ 92% Ⓓ 109%

Problem Solving and Reasoning

21. Critical Thinking Tourists from Korea spend an average of $360 shopping when they travel abroad. Travelers from South Africa spend less—an average of $300 per person. Travelers from the United States average only about $190. Using percents, compare tourist spending for pairs of these countries. Report on all possible combinations.

22. Journal Describe two different ways to solve: "What number is 10% of 520?" Then explain which method seems to be the more efficient way to solve the problem.

Mixed Review

Find the missing measurements for the following triangles. *[Lesson 5-8]*

23. $b = ?$, $h = 14$ cm, $A = 70$ cm^2 **$b = 10$ cm**

24. $b = 4$ in., $h = 15$ in., $A = ?$ **$A = 30$ in^2**

25. $b = 11$ m, $h = ?$, $A = 66$ m^2 **$h = 12$ m**

26. $b = ?$, $h = 1$ ft, $A = 0.5$ ft^2 **$b = 1$ ft**

Convert each rate to an equivalent rate. *[Lesson 7-6]*

27. 2 feet per second to feet per minute **120 feet per minute**

28. 30 kilometers per hour to meters per hour **30,000 meters per hour**

29. 2.54 centimeters per inch to centimeters per foot **30.48 centimeters per foot**

30. 60 dollars per hour to dollars per minute **$1.00 per minute**

Project Progress

Consult a nutrition book to find out how many calories and grams of fat a typical teenager should consume each day. Then find the calories and grams of fat your picnic meal would contain. If your meal has less than 20% or more than 35% of either amount, change your meal to bring it within those limits.

Problem Solving
Understand
Plan
Solve
Look Back

PROBLEM SOLVING

Name ____________

Guided Problem Solving 8-6

GPS PROBLEM 15, STUDENT PAGE 413

The bee hummingbird is the smallest bird. It can weigh as little as 2 grams. The largest bird, the ostrich, can weigh as much as 150 kilograms. What percent of the weight of a bee hummingbird is the weight of an ostrich?

— Understand —

1. What is the weight of a bee hummingbird? 2 grams.
2. What is the weight of an ostrich? 150 kilograms.
3. Are the weights given in the same units? No.
4. Which bird weighs more? Ostrich.

— Plan —

5. Is an ostrich's weight more or less than 100% of a hummingbird's weight? Explain. Possible answer: More than 100% because 150 kg > 2 g.
6. How many grams are in a kilogram? 1000 grams.
7. What is the weight of an ostrich in grams? 150,000 grams.
8. Write a ratio of an ostrich's weight to a hummingbird's weight. $\frac{150{,}000}{2}$

— Solve —

9. Write a proportion to find the missing percent. $\frac{150{,}000}{2} = \frac{p}{100}$
10. Solve the proportion to find the percent. $p = 7{,}500{,}000$; 7,500,000%

— Look Back —

11. Write and solve an equation to find the percent. Verify that your answer is the same. $2p = 150{,}000$; $p = 75{,}000$; So the percent is 7,500,000.

SOLVE ANOTHER PROBLEM

An average adult's stride is 2.5 feet. A mile is 1760 yards. What percent of an average adult's stride is one mile? 211,200%

ENRICHMENT

Name ____________

Extend Your Thinking 8-6

Patterns in Data

You can graph some percents and use the graph to estimate other values. Use these interest rates and principal amounts to find the annual amount of interest due on each loan. Then graph your results.

Possible answers: Items 2–5

1. You borrow money and pay 15% interest. Solve to find the interest due for each loan amount.

a. 15% of 100 15
b. 15% of 80 12
c. 15% of 40 6
d. 15% of 60 9

2. Graph each of your solutions from Question 1. Connect the points. Label the line 15%.

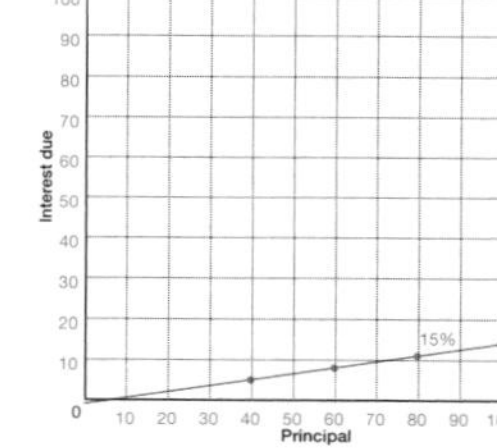

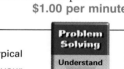

3. Describe the graph. It is a line that has a positive slope. It does not have a steep slope.
4. How can you use the graph to estimate 15% of 65.2? Find the point on the graph that is above 65.2. Interest is the corresponding value on the vertical axis. The interest is about $10.00.
5. Why might it be helpful to graph this information? To help you decide if you can afford the interest on a specific loan.
6. Choose another interest rate and find the interest for these principal amounts. Then graph your solutions. Check students' answers.

a. ______ of 100 ______ b. ______ of 80 ______
c. ______ of 40 ______ d. ______ of 60 ______

7. Use the graph for the interest rate you chose to predict the annual interest due for a loan of $25. Check students' answers.

Problem Solving: Percent Increase and Decrease

8-7

▶ Lesson Link You've used several different strategies to solve percent problems. Now you'll use percents to describe amounts of increase or decrease. ◀

Explore Percent Increase and Decrease

Pencil Ups and Downs

You're the manager of Just Pencils. You've decided to raise the price of Dazzlers and lower the price of Yellow Classics. Both sell for 20¢.

1. Decide on a new price for Dazzlers. Then copy the table and complete the first row. Express the values in the last three columns as percents.

Old Price	New Price	Price Change	$\frac{\text{New Price}}{\text{Old Price}}$	$\frac{\text{Price Change}}{\text{Old Price}}$	$\frac{\text{Price Change}}{\text{New Price}}$
20¢					
20¢					

2. Complete the second row of the table for Yellow Classics, *lowering* the price exactly as much as you raised the price of Dazzlers.

3. Repeat Steps 1 and 2, using a different price change.

4. Describe any patterns you see in your tables. Which percent stays the same whether you raise or lower the price?

You'll Learn ...

■ to solve problems involving percent increase and percent decrease

... How It's Used

Retailers need to know how much they can discount the price of an item on sale without losing money.

Vocabulary

percent increase

percent decrease

percent change

Learn Problem Solving: Percent Increase and Decrease

When a number changes, you can use a **percent increase** or **percent decrease** to describe the size of the change. A percent increase or decrease is always based on the original amount.

Solving the proportion $\frac{\text{percent change}}{100} = \frac{\text{amount of change}}{\text{original amount}}$ is one way to find the **percent change**.

25% decrease 25% increase

\$30 ←— − \$10 ←— \$40 backpack —→ + \$10 —→ \$50

(original price)

MEETING INDIVIDUAL NEEDS

Resources

8-7 Practice
8-7 Reteaching
8-7 Problem Solving
8-7 Enrichment
8-7 Daily Transparency
Problem of the Day
Review
Quick Quiz
Teaching Tool Transparencies 2 and 3
Technology Master 37

Learning Modalities

Social Have students bring in advertising circulars that list both the regular prices and the sales prices of things they would like to buy. They can then work in groups to put together a poster of these objects and label each with the percent decrease in price.

Individual You may want to help students develop self-pacing and goal-setting skills by asking them to choose their own assignment from this lesson. Let them determine how many of each type of exercise they need to do to master the skills involved. They can then write down their rationale for the numbers they've chosen.

English Language Development

Encourage students to write as much as possible. Writing about math helps clarify thinking, increases language skills, and reinforces math skills. Have them write about their approaches to solving percent problems. Focus on the content rather than grammar when reading students' writing. Comment in writing on the ideas students express.

8-7 Lesson Organizer

Objective

■ Solve problems involving percent increase and percent decrease

Vocabulary

■ Percent increase, percent decrease, percent change

NCTM Standards

■ 1–2, 4–5, 7, 12

▶ Review

Solve each proportion.

1. $\frac{z}{354} = \frac{34}{177}$ $z = 68$
2. $\frac{45}{734} = \frac{54}{d}$ $d = 880.8$

Find the area of each rectangle.

3. $l = 7$ cm; $w = 7$ cm
 49 cm^2
4. $l = 4$ in.; $w = 12$ in.
 48 in^2

Available on Daily Transparency 8-7

1 Introduce

Explore

The Point

Students see that only the percent change computed by dividing by the original amount represents percent increases and decreases consistently.

Ongoing Assessment

Be sure that students write the amounts in the last three columns as percents. Help them find the patterns in the numbers.

Answers for Explore on next page.

For Groups That Finish Early
Write an ad for the Just Pencils store, telling about price increases and decreases. Use the most effective percents from the tables.

Follow Up
Ask volunteers to share the patterns they identified in response to Step 4. Ask why they think the $\frac{\text{Price Change}}{\text{Old Price}}$ percent stays the same.

Answers for Explore

1–3. See page C2.

4. The sum of $\frac{\text{Price Change}}{\text{Old Price}}$ and $\frac{\text{New Price}}{\text{Old Price}}$ is 100% for a price reduction. The difference of $\frac{\text{Price Change}}{\text{Old Price}}$ and $\frac{\text{New Price}}{\text{Old Price}}$ is 100% for a price increase. $\frac{\text{Price Change}}{\text{Old Price}}$ is the same value for a price increase or reduction.

2 Teach

Learn

Alternate Examples

1. After Cathy joined the basketball team, the team's average points per game increased from 57 to 72. Find the percent increase.

   Amount of change: $72 - 57 = 15$

   $\frac{p}{100} = \frac{15}{57}$

   $57p = 1500$

   $\frac{57p}{57} = \frac{1500}{57}$

   $p \approx 26.3\%$

   There was a 26.3% increase.

2. The team had committed an average of 29 fouls per game. After Cathy joined, they committed 17% fewer fouls. What was the team's average number of fouls per game after Cathy joined them?

   The amount of change is 17% of the original average.

   $c = 0.17 \cdot 29$

   $c = 4.93$

   To find the new average, subtract the amount of change from the previous average: $29 - 4.93 = 24.07$

   The team averaged about 24 fouls per game after Cathy joined them.

Answers for Try It

a. 60%

b. 29¢

Example 1

After the holiday season, the average number of customers per day at the Game Galaxy store decreased from 612 to 450. Find the percent decrease.

Solve for p to find the percent decrease.

amount of change $= 612 - 450 = 162$

$\frac{p}{100} = \frac{162}{612}$ ← amount of change / ← original amount

$612p = 16{,}200$

$\frac{612p}{612} = \frac{16{,}200}{612}$

$p \approx 26.5$

There was a 26.5% decrease in the number of customers after the holidays.

When you know the *percent* change, you can use an equation to solve for the *amount* of change.

Example 2

Los Angeles air violated federal carbon monoxide standards on 47 days in 1990. By 1993, this number was 57% lower, largely due to pollution control devices on cars. What was the number of "bad air" days in 1993?

First find the amount of change (c).

The amount of change is 57% of the 1990 total. — Reword the question.

$c = 0.57 \cdot 47$ — Translate to an equation.

$c = 26.79 \approx 27$ — Multiply. Round to a whole number of days.

This is the amount of change, not the 1993 total. To find the new amount, subtract the amount of change from the original number.

$47 - 27 = 20$

There were 20 "bad air" days in Los Angeles in 1993.

Problem Solving TIP

Another way to find the number of "bad air" days is to subtract 57% from 100%, then find 43% of 47.

History Link

The first U.S. postage stamps were issued on July 1, 1847. The 5¢ stamp showed Benjamin Franklin; the 10¢, George Washington.

Try It

a. During the holiday season, daily sales at Game Galaxy grew from \$125,000 to \$200,000. Find the percent increase.

b. The price of a first-class postage stamp was 10¢ in 1974. By 1991, the price had risen 190%. Find the 1991 price of a first-class stamp.

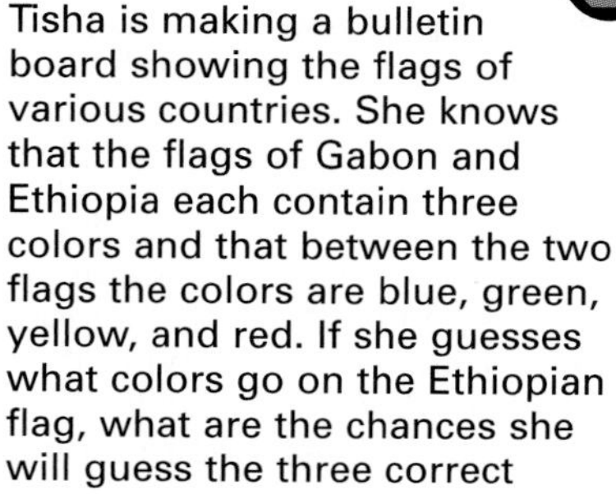

MATH EVERY DAY

Problem of the Day

Tisha is making a bulletin board showing the flags of various countries. She knows that the flags of Gabon and Ethiopia each contain three colors and that between the two flags the colors are blue, green, yellow, and red. If she guesses what colors go on the Ethiopian flag, what are the chances she will guess the three correct colors on her first try? 1 out of 4

Available on Daily Transparency 8-7

An Extension is provided in the transparency package.

Fact of the Day

Los Angeles, home to over 3,485,000 people, has an inadequate public transportation system. As a result, exhaust from many automobiles helps cause the smog.

Mental Math

Mentally find the percent increase or decrease for each change.

1. 25 increased to 50 100%
2. 32 increased to 48 50%
3. 100 decreased to 67 33%
4. 72 decreased to 0 100%

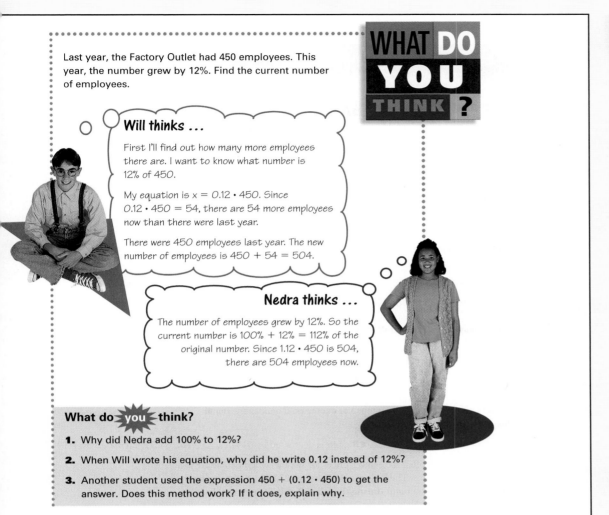

Last year, the Factory Outlet had 450 employees. This year, the number grew by 12%. Find the current number of employees.

First I'll find out how many more employees there are. I want to know what number is 12% of 450.

My equation is $x = 0.12 \cdot 450$. Since $0.12 \cdot 450 = 54$, there are 54 more employees now than there were last year.

There were 450 employees last year. The new number of employees is $450 + 54 = 504$.

The number of employees grew by 12%. So the current number is 100% + 12% = 112% of the original number. Since $1.12 \cdot 450$ is 504, there are 504 employees now.

1. Why did Nedra add 100% to 12%?
2. When Will wrote his equation, why did he write 0.12 instead of 12%?
3. Another student used the expression $450 + (0.12 \cdot 450)$ to get the answer. Does this method work? If it does, explain why.

Check Your Understanding

1. Suppose the number of shoppers at a mall decreased by 100% from one year to the next. What would this mean? What might have happened?
2. Is it possible for an amount of increase to be greater than the original amount? If so, what do you know about the percent increase?

Students see two methods for calculating the number that corresponds to a percent increase. One method computes the number that represents the change and adds it to the original number. The other method uses just one step by multiplying the original number by a percent greater than 100%. The students can talk about the advantages of each technique and decide which is easier for them.

Answers for What Do You Think?

1. So that her answer included the original employees.
2. If he had not, he would have found the increase to be 12 times the original number of employees.
3. Yes; This adds the original number to 12% of the original number.

3 Practice and Assess

Check

Be sure that students understand that 100% means all of an amount, so a 100% decrease means everything is gone, while a 100% increase means that the amount has doubled.

Answers for Check Your Understanding

1. There are now no shoppers at the mall. The mall may have closed down.
2. Yes. The percent increase must be greater than 100%.

MEETING MIDDLE SCHOOL CLASSROOM NEEDS

Tips from Middle School Teachers

There is an obvious connection between this chapter and consumerism. I encourage students to keep a log of the sales and other uses of percent that they see outside of school. I use advertising circulars and brochures that the students bring in to create the problems solved in class. I also let the students write problems for each other using local store advertisements as data.

Science Connection

Work with a science teacher when discussing percents. The students could find the percents, by weight, of the thirteen elements that make up the human body: oxygen 64.5%, carbon 18%, hydrogen 10%, nitrogen 3%, calcium 2%, phosphorus 0.9%, potassium 0.35%, sulfur 0.25%, sodium 0.15%, chlorine 0.15%, magnesium 0.05%, iodine trace, iron trace.

Team Teaching

Work with a language arts teacher to have students write descriptive paragraphs about ads and how they can be misinterpreted.

Assignment Guide

- Basic
  1–25 odds, 26–28, 29–35 odds
- Average
  1–25 odds, 26–29, 32, 34
- Enriched
  2–26 evens, 27–35

Exercise Notes

Exercise 22

Science The tiger is an endangered species. Wild tigers are found only in Asia, but tigers are easy to breed and raise in zoos. Today enough tigers are born in captivity so that no more wild tigers need to be captured for zoos.

Reteaching

Activity

Materials: 2-color counters, calculator

- Work with a partner. Put some red counters on your desk. Have your partner put some yellow counters on your desk.
- Write the ratio of the number of yellow counters to the total number of counters.
- Using a calculator, divide the numerator by the denominator and multiply by 100. The answer is the percent increase.
- Have your partner start over with a group of red and yellow counters. Take away the yellow counters.
- Write the ratio of yellow counters to the original number of counters. Using a calculator, divide the numerator by the denominator. Multiply by 100. The result is the percent decrease.

PRACTICE 8-7

8-7 Exercises and Applications

Practice and Apply

1. **Getting Started** The number of cars in a mall parking lot grew from 140 at 10:00 to 259 at 11:00. Find the percent increase.
   a. Find the amount of change by subtracting the smaller value from the larger value. 119
   b. Write a proportion using $\frac{\text{percent change}}{100} = \frac{\text{amount of change}}{\text{original amount}}$. $\frac{c}{100} = \frac{119}{140}$
   c. Find the cross products. $140c = 11{,}900$
   d. Use the inverse operation to solve for the percent change. 85%

Find each percent increase or decrease. If necessary, round answers to the nearest tenth.

2. 15 is increased to 20. 33.3%
3. 96 is decreased to 72. 25%
4. 13.5 is increased to 27. 100%
5. 125 is decreased to 2. 98.4%
6. 360 is increased to 361. 0.3%
7. 84 is decreased to 28. 66.7%

Find each amount of increase or decrease. If necessary, round answers to the nearest tenth.

8. 55 is increased by 20%. 11
9. 75 is decreased by 40%. 30
10. 58 is increased by 72%. 41.8
11. 28 is increased by 150%. 42
12. 506 is decreased by 57%. 288.4
13. 37.6 is decreased by 25%. 9.4

Find the new amount after each increase or decrease. If necessary, round answers to the nearest tenth.

14. $48 is increased by 35%. $64.80
15. 446 is decreased by 91%. 40.1
16. 84.5 is increased by 110%. 177.5
17. **Consumer** Hotels often have lower prices for seasons when people are less likely to take vacations. The Welcome Inn charges $52.00 a night during the summer, but $40.00 a night during the fall. What is the percent decrease? $\approx$ 23.1%

Consumer Sales tax is an amount of increase. Find the amount of sales tax and the total price (including sales tax) for each of the following. If necessary, round answers to the nearest cent.

18. $8.99, 6% sales tax Tax: $0.54; Price: $9.53
19. $53.49, 8.25% sales tax Tax: $4.41; Price: $57.90
20. $108.05, 5% sales tax Tax: $5.40; Price: $113.45
21. $79.98, 6.5% sales tax Tax: $5.20; Price: $85.18
22. **Science** The world's tiger population was probably about 125,000 in 1900. The number of tigers has declined about 95% since then. About how many tigers are there now? 6,250

PRACTICE

Name ____________

Practice 8-7

Problem Solving: Percent Increase and Decrease

Find each percent of increase or decrease. If necessary, round answers to the nearest tenth.

1. 12 is increased to 18. 50%
2. 36 is decreased to 24. 33.3%
3. 175 is increased to 208. 18.9%
4. 642 is decreased to 499. 22.3%

Find each amount of increase or decrease. If necessary, round answers to the nearest tenth.

5. 63 is increased by 40% 25.2
6. 93 is decreased by 17%. 15.8
7. 817 is increased by 62%. 506.5
8. 539 is decreased by 38%. 204.8

Find the new amount after each increase or decrease. If necessary, round answers to the nearest tenth.

9. 103 is increased by 28%. 131.8
10. $21 is decreased by 40%. $12.6
11. $65 is increased by 182%. $183.3
12. 417 is decreased by 8%. 383.6

Consumer Sales tax is an amount of increase. Find the amount of sales tax and the total price (including sales tax) for each of the following. If necessary, round answers to the nearest cent.

13. $17.50; 7% sales tax
    tax: $1.23 total: $18.73
14. $21.95; 4.25% sales tax
    tax: $0.93 total: $22.88

Geometry For each pair of similar figures, find the percent increase or decrease in area from figure A to figure B.

15. 44% increase A. 35, 25 B. 42, 30
16. 51% decrease A. 50 cm, 50 cm B. 35 cm, 35 cm
17. **Social Science** In 1990, there were 31,224,000 Americans of age 65-and-over. This population is expected to increase 71% by 2020. What is the expected 65-and-over population in 2020? About 53,393,000

RETEACHING

Name ____________

Alternative Lesson 8-7

Problem Solving: Percent Increase and Decrease

When a number changes, the **percent change** describes the size of the change. If the new amount is larger, it is a **percent increase.** If the new amount is smaller, it is a **percent decrease.** A percent change is always based on the original amount.

— Example 1 —

Find the percent of increase when 240 is increased to 264.

Find the amount of the increase. $264 - 240 = 24$

Write a proportion to solve the problem. Let p = percent increase $\frac{p}{100} = \frac{24}{240}$ ← amount of change / ← original amount

Find the cross products. $240p = 2400$

Use inverse operations. $\frac{240p}{240} = \frac{2400}{240}$

Divide. $p = 10$

The percent of increase is 10%.

Try It Find the percent of decrease when 200 is decreased to 150.

a. Find the amount of change. $200 - 150 = 50$
b. Write a proportion using $\frac{\text{percent change}}{100} = \frac{\text{amount of change}}{\text{original amount}}$. $\frac{p}{100} = \frac{50}{200}$
c. Find cross products. $200p = 5{,}000$
d. Find the percent change. 25%

Find each percent increase or decrease.

e. 20 is increased to 30. 50%
f. 75 is decreased to 18. 76%

— Example 2 —

Find the amount of increase when 20 is increased by 15%.

Find the amount of change (c). $c = 0.15 \cdot 20$

Multiply. $c = 3$

The amount of increase is 3.

Try It Find each amount of increase or decrease.

g. 24 is increased by 25%. 6
h. 55 is decreased by 60%. 33

Geometry **For each pair of similar figures, find the percent increase or decrease in area from Figure A to Figure B.**

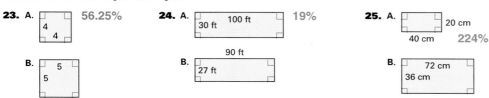

23. A. 4 by 4 square — 56.25%
B. 5 by 5 square

24. A. 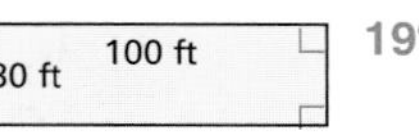

19%

B. 

25. A. 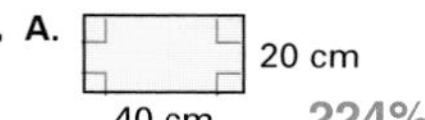

224%

B. 72 cm by 36 cm

26. **Problem Solving** A softball diamond is a 60 ft by 60 ft square. The sides of a baseball diamond are 50% longer than this. What is the percent increase in the area from the softball diamond to the baseball diamond? 125%

27. **Test Prep** The price of a computer game is \$39.99. If the sales tax is 6%, its total cost is: C

Ⓐ \$39.99 × 0.06 Ⓑ \$39.99 + 0.06 Ⓒ \$39.99 × 1.06 Ⓓ \$39.99 + 1.06

Problem Solving and Reasoning

28. **Choose a Strategy** In 1916, 18,353,022 people voted in the U.S. presidential election. In 1919, the Nineteenth Amendment gave women the right to vote. The 1920 election had 26,768,613 voters. What was the percent increase in the number of voters? Round to the nearest percent. 46%

29. **Problem Solving** Many people collect coins. The highest price ever paid for a coin is \$1,500,000, for a 1907 U.S. Double Eagle \$20 gold coin. What is the percent increase in the value of this coin since 1907? 7,499,900%

30. Journal An item originally cost \$10. It was discounted 50%, then discounted 25% off the *reduced* price. What is the sale price of the item? How much would the sale price be if the *original* price had been reduced 75%? Why isn't a 50% discount followed by a 25% discount the same thing as a 75% discount?

Problem Solving STRATEGIES
- Look for a Pattern
- Make an Organized List
- Make a Table
- Guess and Check
- Work Backward
- Use Logical Reasoning
- Draw a Diagram
- Solve a Simpler Problem

PROBLEM SOLVING 8-7

Mixed Review

Find the area of each figure. *[Lesson 5-9]*

31. 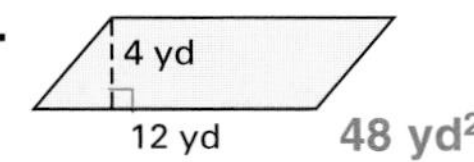

48 yd²

32. 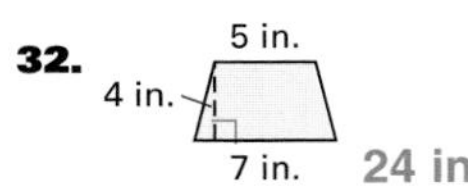

24 in²

33. 8 in., 3 in., 6 in. — 21 in²

Convert each rate into the equivalent rate. *[Lesson 7-7]*

34. 2.5 milliliters per minute to milliliters per day — 3600 milliliters per day

35. 42 feet per second to miles per hour — 28.$\overline{63}$ miles per hour

Exercise Notes

Exercise 28

Problem-Solving Tip You may want to use Teaching Tool Transparencies 2 and 3: Guided Problem Solving, pages 1 and 2.

Exercise Answers

30. \$3.75; \$2.50; Because the base quantity (or the 100%) is not the same in each case.

Alternate Assessment

Portfolio Have students look back over this chapter and all of the work they have completed to pick the work that they think best reflects their understanding of the concepts involved with percent. They may want to choose as their journal entry Exercise 30 from this lesson as a nice summary discussion.

Quick Quiz

Find the new number after each change.

1. 43 increased by 60% 68.8
2. 72 decreased by 55% 32.4

Find each percent increase or decrease.

3. 44 increased to 55 25%
4. 30 is decreased to 12? 60%

Available on Daily Transparency 8-7

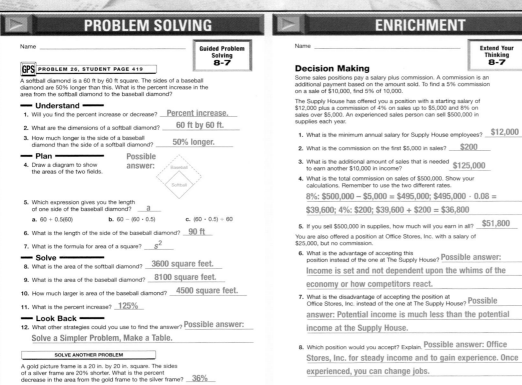

PROBLEM SOLVING

Name ________ **Guided Problem Solving 8-7**

GPS PROBLEM 26, STUDENT PAGE 419

A softball diamond is a 60 ft by 60 ft square. The sides of a baseball diamond are 50% longer than this. What is the percent increase in the area from the softball diamond to the baseball diamond?

Understand

1. Will you find the percent increase or decrease? Percent increase.
2. What are the dimensions of a softball diamond? 60 ft by 60 ft.
3. How much longer is the side of a baseball diamond than the side of a softball diamond? 50% longer.

Plan

4. Draw a diagram to show the areas of the two fields. Possible answer: (Baseball, Softball)
5. Which expression gives you the length of one side of the baseball diamond? a
 a. 60 + 0.5(60) b. 60 − (60 · 0.5) c. (60 · 0.5) ÷ 60
6. What is the length of the side of the baseball diamond? 90 ft
7. What is the formula for area of a square? s^2

Solve

8. What is the area of the softball diamond? 3600 square feet.
9. What is the area of the baseball diamond? 8100 square feet.
10. How much larger is area of the baseball diamond? 4500 square feet.
11. What is the percent increase? 125%

Look Back

12. What other strategies could you use to find the answer? Possible answer: Solve a Simpler Problem, Make a Table.

SOLVE ANOTHER PROBLEM

A gold picture frame is a 20 in. by 20 in. square. The sides of a silver frame are 20% shorter. What is the percent decrease in the area from the gold frame to the silver frame? 36%

ENRICHMENT

Name ________ **Extend Your Thinking 8-7**

Decision Making

Some sales positions pay a salary plus commission. A commission is an additional payment based on the amount sold. To find a 5% commission on a sale of \$10,000, find 5% of 10,000.

The Supply House has offered you a position with a starting salary of \$12,000 plus a commission of 4% on sales up to \$5,000 and 8% on sales over \$5,000. An experienced sales person can sell \$500,000 in supplies each year.

1. What is the minimum annual salary for Supply House employees? \$12,000
2. What is the commission on the first \$5,000 in sales? \$200
3. What is the additional amount of sales that is needed to earn another \$10,000 in income? \$125,000
4. What is the total commission on sales of \$500,000. Show your calculations. Remember to use the two different rates. 8%: \$500,000 − \$5,000 = \$495,000; \$495,000 · 0.08 = \$39,600; 4%: \$200; \$39,600 + \$200 = \$36,800
5. If you sell \$500,000 in supplies, how much will you earn in all? \$51,800

You are also offered a position at Office Stores, Inc. with a salary of \$25,000, but no commission.

6. What is the advantage of accepting this position instead of the one at The Supply House? Possible answer: Income is set and not dependent upon the whims of the economy or how competitors react.
7. What is the disadvantage of accepting the position at Office Stores, Inc. instead of the one at The Supply House? Possible answer: Potential income is much less than the potential income at the Supply House.
8. Which position would you accept? Explain. Possible answer: Office Stores, Inc. for steady income and to gain experience. Once experienced, you can change jobs.

Technology

Using a Spreadsheet • Compound Interest

The Point
Students use a spreadsheet to calculate interest compounded annually for a certain number of years.

Materials
Spreadsheet software

Resources

Interactive CD-ROM Spreadsheet/Grapher Tool

About the Page
Explain the difference between compound interest and simple interest: If $100 is invested at 10%, after 1 year there is $110 in the account. At the end of the second year, with simple interest, another $10 (10% of $100) is earned so there is $120 in the account. With compound interest, $11 (10% of $110) is earned so there is $121 in the account. With compound interest, the investor earns interest on the original amount plus interest already earned.

Ask ...
- In Step 3, why copy the formula into the other cells? Because the formula calculates the interest earned for the year and adds it to the current principal.
- How would you determine what the investment would be worth earning 6% interest? Change .04 to .06.
- How would you determine what the investment would be worth after 8 years? Copy the formula into five more rows.

Answers for Try It
a. $148.02
b. $793.44

On Your Own
For the second question, to calculate simple interest, the formula in B4 would have to be changed to = B2*.04 + B3, and the formula in B5 would have to be changed to = B2*.04 + B4. Why? The interest is calculated on the original amount each year.

Answers for On Your Own
- The percent must be entered in decimal form. Entering 4 gives you 400% interest.
- 112; 49 cents less than the result with compound interest.

TECHNOLOGY

Using a Spreadsheet • Compound Interest

Problem: How much would an investment of $100 earning 4% interest each year be worth after 3 years?

You can use a spreadsheet to help answer this question.

1 Enter the amount of the original investment and the year numbers into the spreadsheet as shown.

	A	B
1	Year	Amount
2	0	100
3	1	
4	2	
5	3	

2 If your investment earns 4% interest per year, it increases by 4% of the beginning amount each year. In cell B3, enter the formula = B2*.04+B2. **This calculates the interest for Year 1 and adds it to the original amount.**

	A	B
1	Year	Amount
2	0	100
3	1	104
4	2	
5	3	

3 Copy your formula from cell B3 and paste it into cells B4 and B5.

	A	B
1	Year	Amount
2	0	100
3	1	104
4	2	108.16
5	3	112.49

Solution: The investment will be worth $112.49 after 3 years.

This investment earns *compound* interest because each year you also earn interest on the previous interest, not just on the original amount.

TRY IT

a. How much would an investment of $100 earning 4% interest each year be worth in 10 years?

b. How much would an investment of $500 earning 8% interest each year be worth after 6 years?

ON YOUR OWN

- In 2, why was B2 multiplied by .04 and not by 4?
- If you earn *simple* interest, interest is paid only on the original amount. How much would the $100 investment in the problem be worth if it earned 4% simple interest for three years? Compare your answer to the result of 3.

In this section, you've applied percents to many different shopping situations. Now you'll apply what you've learned to a problem that faces every store owner in a mall: What's a fair rent to pay?

They're All at the Mall!

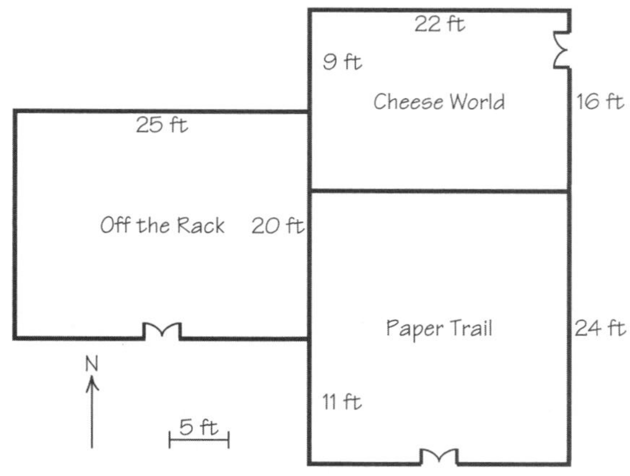

1. At the Northeast Ridgemont Megamall, store owners are charged $1.60 per square foot each month in rent. Calculate the area of each store and its rent charge.
2. Off the Rack has expanded its business and needs more floor space. The store owner was able to negotiate an agreement with Cheese World and Paper Trail to move its wall 5 feet to the east. Draw a dashed line to represent the placement of the new wall.
3. Find the percent increase or decrease in the area of each store.
4. By what amount should Off the Rack's rent increase? How much should the rents of Cheese World and Paper Trail decrease? Explain your reasoning.

They're All at the Mall!

The Point

In *They're All at the Mall!* on page 405, students discussed shopping malls. Now they will investigate the cost of renting space in a mall.

Resources

Lesson Enhancement Transparency 38

About the Page

- Review the formula for finding area of a rectangle.
- Discuss the original floor plan and the dimensions of each store with students.
- If students have difficulty determining how to expand the Off the Rack store, demonstrate the placement of the dashed line representing the new wall.
- Have students determine the dimensions of the new stores before they find the increase or decrease in the size and the corresponding rentals.
- Remind students to compare the amount of change to the original amount to determine percent of increase or decrease.

Ongoing Assessment

Check that students have determined the rent for both the original and new stores, and calculated the percent of increase or decrease correctly.

Extension

Assume that the store owner increases the rent per square foot by $0.20 per month. What rent would Off the Rack have to pay for its expanded floor space? Rent for 600 square feet would cost $1080 per month.

Answers for Connect

1. Off the Rack: area = 500 square feet; rent = $800.

   Cheese World: area = 352 square feet; rent = $563.20.

   Paper Trail: area = 528 square feet; rent = $844.80.

2. 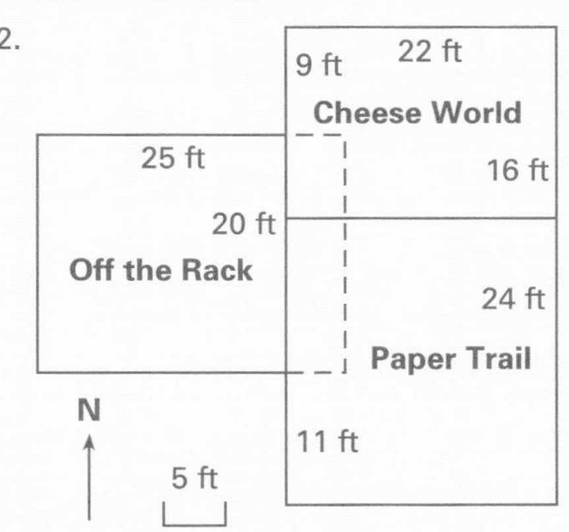

3. Off the Rack: increase 20%; Cheese World: decrease 9.9%; Paper Trail: decrease 12.3%.
4. Off the Rack: up $160; Cheese World: down $56; Paper Trail: down $104. Each square foot gained raises the rent by $1.60. Each square foot lost lowers the rent by $1.60.

8B Review

Review Correlation

Item(s)	Lesson(s)
1–10	8-5, 8-6
11	8-7
12–16	8-4
17	8-4, 8-5, 8-6
18	8-7

Test-Taking Tip
Tell students that sometimes they must pose and answer an intermediary step before they can answer a question.

Answers for Review

10. Book Warehouse. Booksellers' price is 70% of $25, or $17.50. The Book Warehouse price is 85% of $20, or $17.00.
17. Possible answer:
First way: Since 80% = 0.8, multiply 50 by 0.8.
Second way: Since 80% = 8 • 10%, find 10% of 50, then multiply by 8.
Third way: Find 1% of 50, then multiply by 80.
Each method gives the correct answer: 40.

Section 8B Review

REVIEW 8B

Solve each problem. If necessary, round answers to the nearest tenth.

1. What percent of 108 is 24? 22.2%
2. 45% of 820 is what number? 369
3. 17% of 620 is what number? 105.4
4. 30% of what number is 33? 110
5. What percent of 44 is 55? 125%
6. 0.2% of 1100 is what number? 2.2
7. 125% of what number is 84? 67.2
8. What percent of 408 is 3? 0.7%
9. **Consumer** Backstage Pass ticket agency sells concert tickets for their face value plus an 8% service fee. If the face value of a ticket is $22.00, what is the total charge, including the service fee? $23.76
10. A best-selling book that usually sells for $25.00 at Booksellers, Ltd., is on sale at a 30% discount. The same book usually sells for $20.00 at Book Warehouse, which is having a 15% off sale. Where would you buy the book? Explain how you decided.
11. **History** According to *The Good Old Days—They Were Terrible!*, by Otto Bettmann, an 1893 survey of 18 public schools in Brooklyn, New York, found that many teachers had 90 or more students. In 1993, the average number of students per teacher in New York was 15.2. What is the percent decrease from 90 to 15.2? $83\frac{1}{9}\%$

Use mental math to find each percent. *[Lesson 8-4]*

12. 25% of 240 60
13. 10% of $50 $5
14. 60% of 120 72
15. 15% of $32 $4.80
16. 5% of 7200 360
17.  Use three different methods to find 80% of 50. Give a short written explanation telling why each method works.

Test Prep

When solving a percent change problem on a multiple choice test, remember to compare the change to the original number.

18. There are 820 math books in a school bookstore. After the first hour of school, 697 books are left. What is the percent decrease in the number of books? C

Ⓐ 1.5% Ⓑ 1.76% Ⓒ 15% Ⓓ 17.6%

Resources

Practice Masters
Section 8B Review
Assessment Sourcebook
Quiz 8B
 *TestWorks*
Test and Practice Software

PRACTICE

Name ____________ Practice

Section 8B Review

Solve each problem. If necessary, round answers to the nearest tenth.

1. What percent of 95 is 18? 18.9%
2. 68% of 68 is what number? 46.2
3. 43% of what number is 26? 60.5
4. What percent of 72 is 65? 90.3%
5. 27% of 582 is what number? 157.1
6. 59% of what number is 222? 376.3
7. What percent of 803 is 719? 89.5%
8. 215% of 78 is what number? 167.7
9. 77% of what number is 213? 276.6
10. What percent of 643 is 4.5? 0.7%
11. 85% of 468 is what number? 397.8
12. 93% of what number is 745? 801.1
13. What percent of 37 is 5? 13.5%
14. 4% of 890 is what number? 35.6
15. **Consumer** The Better Sweater Store sells a wool sweater for $37.95, plus 6.5% state sales tax. If you buy this sweater, how much will you pay? $40.42
16. A new top-selling compact disc is marked 25% off at Raspy Music, where the disc normally sells for $16.97. The same disc sells for $14.47 at Broken Records, where you have a coupon for 10% off anything in the store. Where would you buy the CD? Explain how you decided.
Possible answer: Buy at Raspy Music, because $12.73 at Raspy Music is less than $13.02 at Broken Records.
17. The number of Americans who speak Yiddish at home decreased from 320,380 in 1980 to 213,064 in 1990. Find the percent decrease. About 33.5%
18. The slowest-moving crab in the world may be the *Neptune pelagines*. One of these crabs took 29 years to travel the 101.5 miles from the Red Sea to the Mediterranean Sea along the Suez Canal. If this crab maintained a constant rate, how long did it take to travel the first 40 miles? *[Lesson 6-3]* About 11.4 years
19. In 1935, Amelia Earhart made history by being the first woman to fly alone from Honolulu, Hawaii, to the U.S. mainland. Her average speed was about 133 miles per hour. Convert this rate to feet per second. *[Lesson 7-7]* About 195 ft/sec

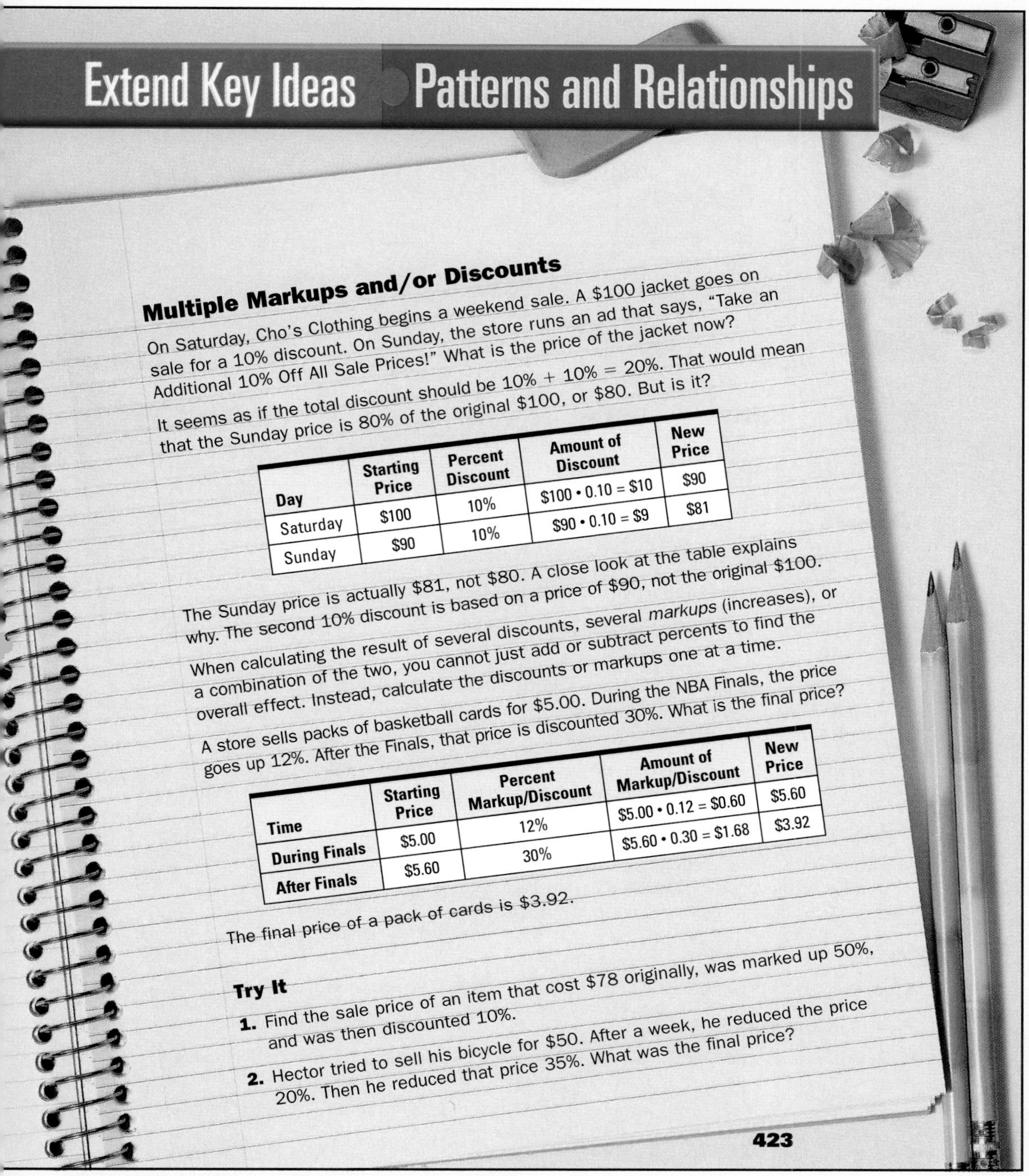

Extend Key Ideas • Patterns and Relationships

Multiple Markups and/or Discounts

On Saturday, Cho's Clothing begins a weekend sale. A $100 jacket goes on sale for a 10% discount. On Sunday, the store runs an ad that says, "Take an Additional 10% Off All Sale Prices!" What is the price of the jacket now?

It seems as if the total discount should be 10% + 10% = 20%. That would mean that the Sunday price is 80% of the original $100, or $80. But is it?

Day	Starting Price	Percent Discount	Amount of Discount	New Price
Saturday	$100	10%	$100 • 0.10 = $10	$90
Sunday	$90	10%	$90 • 0.10 = $9	$81

The Sunday price is actually $81, not $80. A close look at the table explains why. The second 10% discount is based on a price of $90, not the original $100.

When calculating the result of several discounts, several *markups* (increases), or a combination of the two, you cannot just add or subtract percents to find the overall effect. Instead, calculate the discounts or markups one at a time.

A store sells packs of basketball cards for $5.00. During the NBA Finals, the price goes up 12%. After the Finals, that price is discounted 30%. What is the final price?

Time	Starting Price	Percent Markup/Discount	Amount of Markup/Discount	New Price
During Finals	$5.00	12%	$5.00 • 0.12 = $0.60	$5.60
After Finals	$5.60	30%	$5.60 • 0.30 = $1.68	$3.92

The final price of a pack of cards is $3.92.

Try It

1. Find the sale price of an item that cost $78 originally, was marked up 50%, and was then discounted 10%.
2. Hector tried to sell his bicycle for $50. After a week, he reduced the price 20%. Then he reduced that price 35%. What was the final price?

423

Multiple Markups and/or Discounts

The Point

Students learn that multiple markups and discounts must be calculated individually, rather than by adding the percents.

About the Page

Consumers can be misled by advertisements in which multiple discounts are offered. This lesson will help students become better informed consumers.

Ask ...

- Why isn't a 10% discount and an additional 10% discount equivalent to a 20% discount? Because the second 10% is calculated on the already reduced price, not on the original price, as is the first 10% discount.
- With a 20% discount and an additional 10% discount, are you actually getting more or less than a 30% discount? Less, since the 10% is discounted from a lesser amount than the 20% discount.
- With a 20% markup and an additional 10% markup, are you actually paying more or less than a 30% markup? More, since the 10% is marked up from a greater amount than the 20% markup.

Extension

Find a promotion in which a store advertises taking an additional percent off of an already reduced price. Estimate the original costs of two items, and calculate the new sale prices.

Answers for Try It

1. $105.30
2. $26.00

Chapter 8 Summary and Review

Review Correlation

Item(s)	Lesson(s)
1, 2	8-1
3–6	8-2
7, 8	8-3
9–12	8-4
13–21	8-5, 8-6
22–24	8-7

For additional review, see page 679.

Chapter 8 Summary and Review

Graphic Organizer

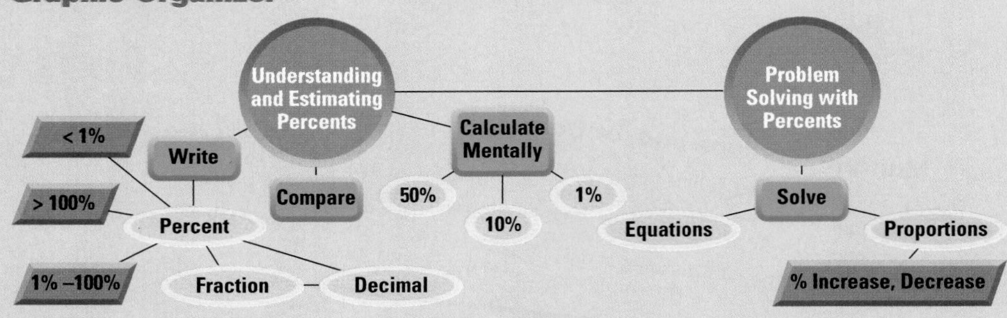

Section 8A Understanding and Estimating Percents

Summary

- A **percent** is a ratio that compares a number with 100.
- Percents can be written as fractions or as decimals.
- To rewrite a percent as a fraction, write the percent over 100 and rewrite in lowest terms.
- To rewrite a percent as a decimal, move the decimal point two places to the left. To rewrite a decimal as a percent, move the decimal point two places to the right.
- To rewrite a fraction as a percent, first use division to rewrite it as a decimal, then move the decimal point two places to the right.
- A percent can be greater than 100% or less than 1%.
- You can find 50% of a number mentally by taking half of it; 10% of the number by moving the decimal point one place to the left; and 1% by moving the decimal point two places to the left.

Review

1. Write $\frac{27}{100}$ as a percent. **27%**

2. Use percents to compare $\frac{1}{4}$ and $\frac{1}{5}$. **$\frac{1}{4} = 25\%; \frac{1}{5} = 20\%; \frac{1}{4} > \frac{1}{5}$**

3. Rewrite 22% as a fraction. **$\frac{11}{50}$**

4. Rewrite 86% as a decimal. **0.86**

5. Rewrite 0.73 as a percent and a fraction. **73%, $\frac{73}{100}$**

6. Rewrite 45% as a fraction and as a decimal. **$\frac{9}{20}$, 0.45**

Resources

Practice Masters
Cumulative Review Chapters 1–8

PRACTICE

Name ____________________ **Practice**

Cumulative Review Chapters 1–8

Express each fraction in lowest terms. *[Lesson 3-8]*

1. $\frac{8}{12}$ $\frac{2}{3}$ **2.** $\frac{24}{28}$ $\frac{6}{7}$ **3.** $\frac{55}{75}$ $\frac{11}{15}$ **4.** $\frac{21}{96}$ $\frac{7}{32}$

5. $\frac{30}{84}$ $\frac{5}{14}$ **6.** $\frac{32}{144}$ $\frac{2}{9}$ **7.** $\frac{15}{75}$ $\frac{1}{5}$ **8.** $\frac{42}{108}$ $\frac{7}{18}$

Find each product or quotient. Reduce to lowest terms. *[Lessons 4-5 and 4-6]*

9. $3\frac{1}{3} \cdot 1\frac{1}{2}$ 5 **10.** $13 \div 4\frac{2}{7}$ $3\frac{1}{30}$ **11.** $6\frac{3}{10} \cdot \frac{1}{3}$ $2\frac{1}{10}$ **12.** $2\frac{1}{3} \div 1\frac{8}{9}$ $1\frac{4}{17}$

13. $1\frac{5}{9} \div 3\frac{3}{5}$ $\frac{35}{81}$ **14.** $2\frac{3}{4} \cdot 3\frac{1}{2}$ $9\frac{5}{8}$ **15.** $19\frac{1}{6} \div 3\frac{5}{6}$ 5 **16.** $4 \cdot 6\frac{3}{8}$ $25\frac{1}{2}$

Find the sum of the measures of the angles in each polygon. *[Lesson 5-4]*

17. trapezoid 360° **18.** hexagon 720°

19. 9-sided polygon 1260° **20.** 17-sided polygon 2700°

Convert each rate to an equivalent rate. *[Lesson 7-7]*

21. 27 pounds per day to ounces per day 432 ounces per day

22. 45 kilograms per hour to grams per hour 45,000 grams per hour

23. 63 quarts per week to quarts per day 9 quarts per day

24. 154 feet per second to miles per hour 105 miles per hour

Write each percent as a fraction in lowest terms. *[Lesson 8-2]*

25. 12% $\frac{3}{25}$ **26.** 50% $\frac{1}{2}$ **27.** 38% $\frac{19}{50}$ **28.** 45% $\frac{9}{20}$

29. $66\frac{2}{3}\%$ $\frac{2}{3}$ **30.** 27% $\frac{27}{100}$ **31.** $12\frac{1}{2}\%$ $\frac{1}{8}$ **32.** 4% $\frac{1}{25}$

Solve each problem. If necessary, round answers to the nearest tenth. *[Lesson 8-6]*

33. What number is 26% of 83? 21.6 **34.** 4.3 is what percent of 738? 0.6%

35. 69 is 17% of what number? 405.9 **36.** What number is 135% of 216? 291.6

37. 57 is what percent of 188? 30.3% **38.** 817 is 93% of what number? 878.5

Chapter 8 Summary and Review

Section 8A Understanding and Estimating Percents *continued*

7. Rewrite 0.8% as a fraction and as a decimal. $\frac{1}{125}$, 0.008

8. Rewrite 125% as a fraction and as a decimal. $\frac{5}{4}$, 1.25

9. Find 10% and 1% of 2400 mentally. 240, 24

10. Find 60% of 460 mentally. 276

11. Find 5% of 280 mentally. 14

12. Find 15% of $44 mentally. $6.60

Section 8B Problem Solving with Percents

Summary

- You can solve a percent problem by writing and solving an equation or by using a proportion.
- To solve a percent problem using proportions, write the percent as a ratio with a denominator of 100 and use it to form one side of the proportion. Use the data in the problem to write the other ratio. Then use cross products to help solve the problem.
- Increases and decreases in value can be measured as percents. To calculate a percent increase or decrease, use this proportion:
  $\frac{\text{percent change}}{100} = \frac{\text{amount of change}}{\text{original amount}}$.

Review

13. 40% of 50 is what number? 20

14. What percent of 65 is 30? ≈ 46.2%

15. 18% of what number is 12? $66\frac{2}{3}$

16. 160% of 115 is what number? 184

17. A bike is on sale for $170. This is 80% of the regular price. Find the regular price. $212.50

18. A $20 T-shirt is on sale at a 25% discount. What is the sale price of the shirt? $15.00

19. At a shopping mall, 45% of 220 stores sell clothing. How many clothing stores are there? 99

20. During a flu epidemic, 146 students out of the 680 who attend Lincoln Middle School were absent. What percent were absent? ≈ 21.5%

21. DeJuan bought a $15.00 CD on sale for $12.60. What percent is this of the regular price? What percent discount did he get? 84%; 16%

22. During the first week of school, Ms. Yamada's math class increased from 26 to 32 students. What was the percent increase? ≈ 23.1%

23. A fashion buyer for Great Gear, Inc. bought 250 dresses for $45 each. Great Gear sold the dresses for $59 each. What was the percent increase? $31\frac{1}{9}$%

24. There were 124 students at a baseball game. By the time the score was 15 to 1, only 32 students were left. Find the percent decrease in the number of students. ≈ 74.2%

Chapter 8 Assessment

Assessment Correlation

Item(s)	Lesson(s)
1, 3, 4	8-2
2	8-1
5–8	8-3
9, 11, 12	8-4
10, 13–15	8-5, 8-6
16–18	8-7

Answer for Performance Task

Note: Fractions are given in lowest terms; students may give other equivalent fractions.

Vitamin A: 0.25, $\frac{1}{4}$

Calcium: 0.04, $\frac{1}{25}$

Iron: 0.8, $\frac{4}{5}$

Vitamin D: 0.1, $\frac{1}{10}$

Copper: 0.02; $\frac{1}{50}$

Niacin: 0.35, $\frac{7}{20}$

Phosphorus: 0.12, $\frac{3}{25}$

Vitamin B_{12}: 0.15, $\frac{3}{20}$

Chapter 8 Assessment

1. Of the 42 species of bats in the United States, 33 live in Texas. What percent of U.S. bat species live in Texas? $\approx$ **78.6%**
2. Use percents to compare $\frac{17}{20}$ and $\frac{4}{5}$. $\frac{17}{20} = 85\%; \frac{4}{5} = 80\%; \frac{17}{20} > \frac{4}{5}$
3. Write 0.95 as a percent and as a fraction. **95%, $\frac{19}{20}$**
4. List from smallest to greatest: $\frac{3}{8}$, 32%, and 0.36. **32%, 0.36, $\frac{3}{8}$**
5. Suppose 0.5% of the bats in a cave have rabies. What fraction of the bats is this? $\frac{1}{200}$
6. The sales tax in Green County is 6%. Your total bill for an item would be what percent of its original price? **106%**
7. Only 5 of 850 concert tickets were not sold. Was the percent of unsold tickets greater or less than 1%? **Less than 1%**
8. At birth, a Mexican free-tailed bat weighs $\frac{1}{3}$ as much as its mother. At that time, the mother's weight is what percent of the baby's weight? **300%**
9. If a dinner bill were $43.80, how much would a 15% tip be? **$6.57**
10. Jorge has exactly $20. If the sales tax is 7%, can he buy a shirt that is priced at $19.95? Explain. **No; Price with tax would be $21.35.**
11. Use mental math to find 20% of 530. **106**
12. Is 48% of 65 the same as 65% of 48? Explain. **Yes:** $\frac{48}{100} \times 65 = \frac{48 \times 65}{100} = \frac{65}{100} \times 48$
13. Rick scored 76% on a history quiz. His score was 25% higher on the next quiz. What did he score on the second quiz? **95%**
14. What percent of 640 is 280? **43.75%**
15. Which is greater: 6% of 24 or 85% of 1.5? **6% of 24**
16. A skateboard that normally sells for $84.99 is on sale for $70.00. By what percent has it been marked down? $\approx$ **17.6%**
17. After Toni received a salary increase of 4%, her salary was $35,360. What was her salary before the raise? **$34,000**
18. By what percent does the area of an 8 ft by 6 ft rectangle change if its length and width are both increased by 50%? **It increases by 125%.**

Performance Task

The label on a cereal box lists the nutritional content of the product. Give each of the figures in two other ways.

CRUNCHY BITS

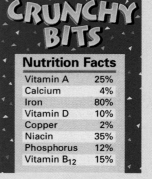

Nutrition Facts	
Vitamin A	25%
Calcium	4%
Iron	80%
Vitamin D	10%
Copper	2%
Niacin	35%
Phosphorus	12%
Vitamin B_{12}	15%

426 *Chapter 8 • Percents*

Resources

Assessment Sourcebook

Chapter 8 Tests
- Forms A and B (free response)
- Form C (multiple choice)
- Form D (performance assessment)
- Form E (mixed response)
- Form F (cumulative chapter test)

TestWorks
Test and Practice Software

Home and Community Connections
- Letter Home for Chapter 8 in English and Spanish

Cumulative Review Chapters 1–8

Test Prep

Multiple Choice

Choose the best answer.

1. Find the mode for the set of data: 38, 33, 37, 36, 36, 12, 16, 32. *[Lesson 1-4]* C

Ⓐ 25 Ⓑ 26 Ⓒ 36 Ⓓ 38

2. Solve: $5.2x = 18.2$ *[Lesson 3-4]* B

Ⓐ $x = 3$ Ⓑ $x = 3.5$

Ⓒ $x = 23.4$ Ⓓ $x = 94.64$

3. Find the prime factorization for 1680. *[Lesson 3-6]* C

Ⓐ $4^2 \cdot 3 \cdot 5 \cdot 7$ Ⓑ $2^4 \cdot 7 \cdot 15$

Ⓒ $2^4 \cdot 3 \cdot 5 \cdot 7$ Ⓓ $5 \cdot 6 \cdot 7 \cdot 8$

4. Find the product of $1\frac{1}{2} \times 1\frac{2}{3} \times 2\frac{1}{5}$. *[Lesson 4-5]* D

Ⓐ $2\frac{4}{7}$ Ⓑ $3\frac{2}{7}$ Ⓒ $4\frac{2}{12}$ Ⓓ $5\frac{1}{2}$

5. Fill in the blank: The *complement* of an acute angle is always a(n) _____ angle. *[Lesson 5-1]* A

Ⓐ Acute Ⓑ Obtuse

Ⓒ Right Ⓓ Straight

6. Which of these sets of lengths could form the sides of a right triangle? *[Lesson 5-7]* B

Ⓐ 8 m, 13 m, 18 m

Ⓑ 15 m, 20 m, 25 m

Ⓒ 7 m, 12 m, 17 m

Ⓓ 9 m, 16 m, 21 m

7. Which of these ratios is *not* equivalent to 24:45? *[Lesson 5-7]* B

Ⓐ 8:15 Ⓑ 12:23 Ⓒ 16:30 Ⓓ 48:90

8. Solve: $\frac{p}{18} = \frac{25}{48}$ *[Lesson 6-8]* C

Ⓐ $p = 5$ Ⓑ $p = 23$

Ⓒ $p = 9.375$ Ⓓ $p = 34.56$

9. Which of these rates is faster than 35 miles per hour? *[Lesson 7-6]* C

Ⓐ 1 mile in 3 minutes

Ⓑ 1250 feet in 30 seconds

Ⓒ 10 miles in 15 minutes

Ⓓ 48 feet per second

10. Which set of conversion factors changes meters per hour into centimeters per minute? *[Lesson 7-7]* B

Ⓐ $\frac{\text{meters}}{\text{hour}} \cdot \frac{\text{centimeters}}{\text{meter}} \cdot \frac{\text{minutes}}{\text{hour}}$

Ⓑ $\frac{\text{meters}}{\text{hour}} \cdot \frac{\text{centimeters}}{\text{meter}} \cdot \frac{\text{hours}}{\text{minute}}$

Ⓒ $\frac{\text{meters}}{\text{hour}} \cdot \frac{\text{hours}}{\text{centimeter}} \cdot \frac{\text{meters}}{\text{minute}}$

Ⓓ $\frac{\text{meters}}{\text{hour}} \cdot \frac{\text{hours}}{\text{minute}} \cdot \frac{\text{meters}}{\text{centimeter}}$

11. Which fraction is equivalent to 36%? *[Lesson 8-2]* C

Ⓐ $\frac{1}{36}$ Ⓑ $\frac{3}{6}$ Ⓒ $\frac{9}{25}$ Ⓓ $\frac{100}{36}$

12. Maria's stamp collection has increased in value by 125% since 1992, when it was worth $440. What is it worth now? *[Lesson 8-3]* B

Ⓐ $2432 Ⓑ $990

Ⓒ $665 Ⓓ $115

13. The sales tax is 7%. How much tax did Ranjit pay for a sweatshirt that cost $25? *[Lesson 8-5]* C

Ⓐ $1750 Ⓑ $17.50

Ⓒ $1.75 Ⓓ $0.175

Cumulative Review Test Prep

About Multiple-Choice Tests

The Cumulative Review found at the end of Chapters 2, 4, 6, 8, 10, and 12 can be used to prepare students for standardized tests.

Students sometimes do not perform as well on standardized tests as they do on other tests. There may be several reasons for this related to the format and content of the test.

- **Format**
  Students may have limited experience with multiple-choice tests. For some questions, such tests are harder because having options may confuse the student.
- **Content**
  A standardized test may cover a broader range of content than normally covered on a test, and the relative emphasis given to various strands may be different than given in class. Also, some questions may assess general aptitude or thinking skills and not include specific pieces of mathematical content.

It is important not to let the differences between standardized tests and other tests shake your students' confidence.

▶ OVERVIEW

Integers

-2 + 5 = 3

-10 -9 -8 -7 -6 -5 -4 -3 -2 -1 0 1 2 3 4 5 6 7 8 9 10

Section 9A

Using Integers: Students learn the basic properties of integers and use integers to represent real-life quantities. They learn to plot numbers that are less than zero.

9-1 Using Integers to Represent Quantities

9-2 Comparing and Ordering Integers

9-3 The Coordinate Plane

Section 9B

Operations with Integers: Students learn to add, subtract, multiply, and divide integers.

9-4 Adding Integers

9-5 Subtracting Integers

9-6 Multiplying Integers

9-7 Dividing Integers

Meeting NCTM Standards

Curriculum Standards

STANDARDS

	Standard		pages
1	**Problem Solving**	Skills and Strategies	429, 430, 433, 441, 446, 459, 467
		Applications	435–436, 440–441, 445–446, 447, 453–454, 458–459, 464–465, 469–470, 471
		Exploration	432, 437, 442, 450, 455, 461, 466
2	**Communication**	Oral	431, 434, 439, 441, 444, 449, 453, *454*, 457, 464, 468, *470*
		Written	*430*, 436, 446, 448, 454, 459, 465, 470, 472
		Cooperative Learning	*428*, *432*, *437*, *442*, *450*, *455*, *461*, *466*
3	**Reasoning**	Critical Thinking	436, *441*, 446, 454, 459, 465, 470
4	**Connections**	Mathematical	See Standards 5–10, 12 below.
		Interdisciplinary	Science; 428, *431*, 435, *436*, *439*, 440, 448, 454, *463*, 464, 469, 472; Entertainment 428; Social Studies 428–429; Arts & Literature 428–429; Industry 434, 445, *449*; Geography *431*, 434, 436, 448, *457*, 458, *464*, *468*, *470;* History 444, *449*, *454*, 456, 472; Sports 465; Consumer *454*, *470*
		Technology	430, 433, 436, 449, *452*, 459, 460
		Cultural	428, *434*
5	**Number and Number Relationships**		432–473
6	**Number Systems and Number Theory**		432–473
7	**Computation and Estimation**		433, 458, *459*, 465
8	**Patterns and Functions**		430, 445, 454, 458, *461*, 464, *465*, *470*, 473
9	**Algebra**		458
10	**Statistics**		442–448, 458, 460, 469, 470
12	**Geometry**		445
13	**Measurement**		432–447

Italic type indicates Teacher Edition reference.

Teaching Standards

Focus on Analysis of Teaching

Assessment of students and analysis of instruction are interconnected. Teachers should

- monitor students' learning on an ongoing basis in order to assess and adjust their teaching.
- be willing to revise and adapt their short-term and long-range plans.

Assessment Standards

Focus on Mathematics

Interviews The Mathematics Standard encourages teachers to present students with opportunities to solve realistic problems and to gather information about the skills and concepts they have learned from observing the process of solving the problem. A realistic problem with rich mathematics embedded in can be the basis of a teacher-student interview. In Chapter 9 students verbalize rules for finding sums, differences, products and quotients of integers.

TECHNOLOGY

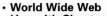

For the Teacher

- **Resource Pro, a Teacher's Resource Planner CD-ROM**
  Use the teacher planning CD-ROM to view resources available for Chapter 9. You can prepare custom lesson plans or use the default lesson plans provided.

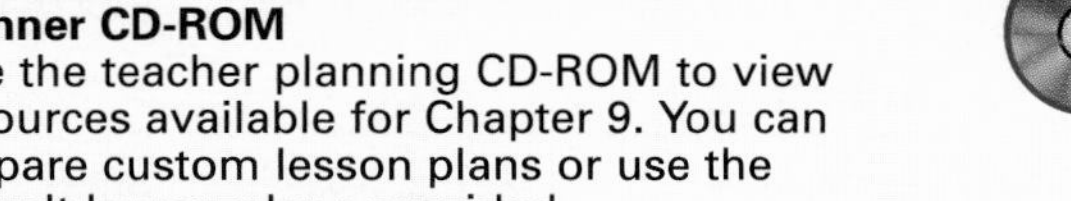

- **World Wide Web**
  Visit **www.kz.com** to view class summary reports, individual student reports, and more.

- **TestWorks**
  TestWorks provides ready-made tests and can create custom tests and practice worksheets.

For the Parent

- **World Wide Web**
  Parents can use the Web site at **www.kz.com** to check on student progress or take a quick refresher course.

For the Student

- **Interactive CD-ROM**
  Lesson 9-4 has an *Interactive CD-ROM Lesson*. The *Interactive CD-ROM Journal* and *Interactive CD-ROM Spreadsheet/Grapher Tool* are also used in Chapter 9.

- **Wide World of Mathematics**
  Lesson 9-3 Algebra: Living in 64 Squares
  Lesson 9-4 Middle School: Integer Football

- **World Wide Web**
  Use with Chapter and Section Openers;
  Students can go online to the Scott Foresman-Addison Wesley Web site at **www.mathsurf.com/7/ch9** to collect information about chapter themes. Students can also visit **www.kz.com** for tutorials and practice.

STANDARDIZED - TEST CORRELATION

SECTION 9A

LESSON	OBJECTIVE	ITBS Form M	CTBS 4th Ed.	CAT 5th Ed.	SAT 9th Ed.	MAT 7th Ed.	Your Form
9-1	• Use integers to represent real-life quantities.	✘		✘			
	• Find the opposite of an integer.					✘	
	• Find the absolute value of an integer.					✘	
9-2	• Compare and order integers.	✘	✘	✘	✘	✘	
9-3	• Graph points on a coordinate plane.						

SECTION 9B

LESSON	OBJECTIVE	ITBS Form M	CTBS 4th Ed.	CAT 5th Ed.	SAT 9th Ed.	MAT 7th Ed.	Your Form
9-4	• Add integers.	✘	✘	✘			
9-5	• Subtract integers.		✘	✘			
9-6	• Multiply integers.		✘	✘			
9-7	• Divide integers.		✘	✘			

Key: ITBS - Iowa Test of Basic Skills; CTBS - Comprehensive Test of Basic Skills; CAT - California Achievement Test; SAT - Stanford Achievement Test; MAT - Metropolitan Achievement Test

ASSESSMENT PROGRAM

Traditional Assessment

QUICK QUIZZES	SECTION REVIEW	CHAPTER REVIEW	CHAPTER ASSESSMENT FREE RESPONSE	CHAPTER ASSESSMENT MULTIPLE CHOICE	CUMULATIVE REVIEW
TE: pp. 436, 441, 446, 454, 459, 465, 470	SE: pp. 448, 472 *Quiz 9A, 9B	SE: pp. 474–475	SE: p. 476 *Ch. 9 Tests Forms A, B, E	*Ch. 9 Tests Forms C, E	SE: p. 477 *Ch. 9 Test Form F; Quarterly Test Ch. 1–9

Alternate Assessment

INTERVIEW	JOURNAL	ONGOING	PERFORMANCE	PORTFOLIO	PROJECT	SELF
TE: pp. 454, 470	SE: pp. 436, 446, 448, 454, 472 TE: pp. 430, 436, 459, 465	TE: pp. 432, 437, 442, 450, 455, 461, 466	SE: p. 476 *Ch. 9 Tests Forms D, E	p. 446	SE: pp. 446, 470 TE: p. 429	TE: p. 441

*Tests and quizzes are in *Assessment Sourcebook*. Test Form E is a mixed response test. Forms for Alternate Assessment are also available in *Assessment Sourcebook*.

TestWorks: Test and Practice Software

MIDDLE SCHOOL PACING CHART

REGULAR PACING

Day	5 classes per week
1	Chapter 9 Opener; Problem Solving Focus
2	Section **9A** Opener; Lesson **9-1**
3	Lesson **9-2**
4	Lesson **9-3**
5	**9A** Connect; **9A** Review
6	Section **9B** Opener; Lesson **9-4**
7	Lesson **9-5** Technology
8	Lesson **9-6**
9	Lesson **9-7**
10	**9B** Connect; **9B** Review; Extend Key Ideas
11	Chapter 9 Summary and Review
12	Chapter 9 Assessment
13	Cumulative Review, Chapters 1–9

BLOCK SCHEDULING OPTIONS

Block Scheduling for Complete Course

Chapter 9 may be presented in

- eight 90-minute blocks
- ten 75-minute blocks

Each block consists of a combination of

- Chapter and Section Openers
- Explores
- Lesson Development
- Problem Solving Focus
- Technology
- Extend Key Ideas
- Connect
- Review
- Assessment

For details, see *Block Scheduling Handbook*.

Block Scheduling for Interdisciplinary Course

Each block integrates math with another subject area.

In Chapter 9, interdisciplinary topics include

- Geology
- Amusement Parks

Themes for Interdisciplinary Team Teaching 9A and 9B are

- Properties of Water
- Calorie Intake

For details, see *Block Scheduling Handbook*.

Block Scheduling for Lab-Based Course

In each block, 30–40 minutes is devoted to lab activities including

- Explores in the Student Edition
- Connect pages in the Student Edition
- Technology options in the Student Edition
- Reteaching Activities in the Teacher Edition

For details, see *Block Scheduling Handbook*.

Block Scheduling for Course with *Connected Mathematics*

In each block, investigations from **Connected Mathematics** replace or enhance the lessons in Chapter 9.

Connected Mathematics topics for Chapter 9 can be found in

- *Accentuate the Negative*

For details, see *Block Scheduling Handbook*.

INTERDISCIPLINARY BULLETIN BOARD

Set Up

Post a large outline map of the world with a vertical number line next to it. The number line should have 0 ft, sea level, at its midpoint. It should show positive increments of 5,000 ft up to 30,000 ft and negative increments of 500 ft down to 1500 ft.

Procedure

For each of the seven continents, have groups of students:

- Find out the highest and lowest elevation points.
- Indicate the elevations in feet on the number line.
- On the map, show the countries or areas in which the points are located. Use a + symbol to indicate the highest point above sea level and a – symbol to indicate the lowest point below sea level.

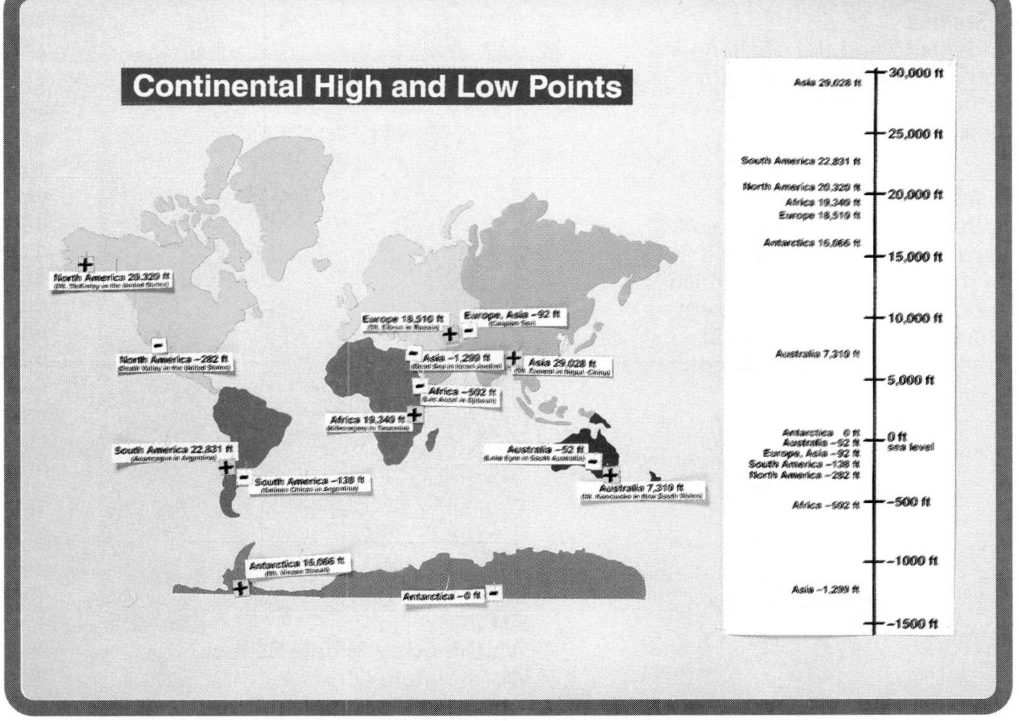

Chapter 9

The information on these pages shows how integers and coordinate grids are applied in real-life situations.

World Wide Web

If your class has access to the World Wide Web, you might want to use the information found at the Web site addresses given.

Extensions

The following activities do not require access to the World Wide Web.

People of the World
Talk about how a negative economic growth rate would affect a country.

Science
Have students find the temperatures at which water freezes and boils, both in Celsius and Fahrenheit. Have them find out the coldest temperature recorded in their city and in the United States. 0°C, 32°F; 100°C, 212°F; Answers may vary.

Entertainment
Ask students to describe their favorite games and TV game shows and tell whether negative numbers are used in scoring the games.

Social Studies
Ask students to find the Challenger Deep on a map and then to determine other ocean depths in the same vicinity.

Arts & Literature
Suggest that students work in groups of four to make a grid map of the neighborhood in which their school is located. Have them show three or four nearby buildings in relationship to the school.

9 Integers

Cultural Link
www.mathsurf.com/7/ch9/people

Science Link
www.mathsurf.com/7/ch9/science

People of the World

In 1993, the annual growth rate in the Russian economy was −12%. The growth rate in the economy of Chile was +6%.

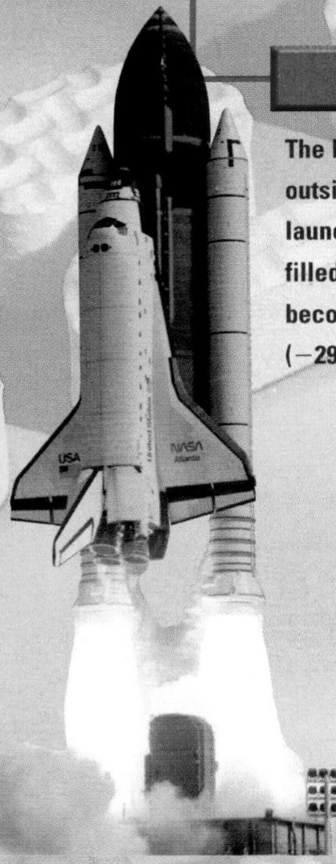

Science

The largest fuel tank on the outside of the rocket that launches the space shuttle is filled with liquid oxygen. Oxygen becomes a liquid at −183°C (−297°F).

Entertainment

In golf, *par* is the score a good player would normally get on a particular hole. Scores above par are shown with positive numbers, those below par are shown with negative numbers. The more negative a golf score is, the better it is.

428

TEACHER TALK

Meet Nancy Rolsen

Worthingway Middle School
Worthington, Ohio

Students seem to gain a better understanding of positive and negative numbers through active participation. When comparing and ordering integers, I give each student a large index card with an integer written on it and have them form a human number line by standing in the order of their integers. I put masking tape on the floor to make a number line and we mark off the integers in equal intervals. At the beginning of the unit I use the number line for comparing and ordering integers. Later I have students show addition of integers on this number line.

To introduce graphing ordered pairs of integers, I separate the room into four quadrants with masking tape and use students' desks as coordinate points. Then I call on students by giving the coordinates of their desks. I also give directions such as, "Will all students with y-coordinate of 2 stand." I note that a horizontal row of students is standing.

Social Studies Link
www.mathsurf.com/7/ch9/social

Social Studies

The Challenger Deep, in the Pacific Ocean, is the deepest point in the world's oceans. The elevation of the Challenger Deep is −35,839 ft.

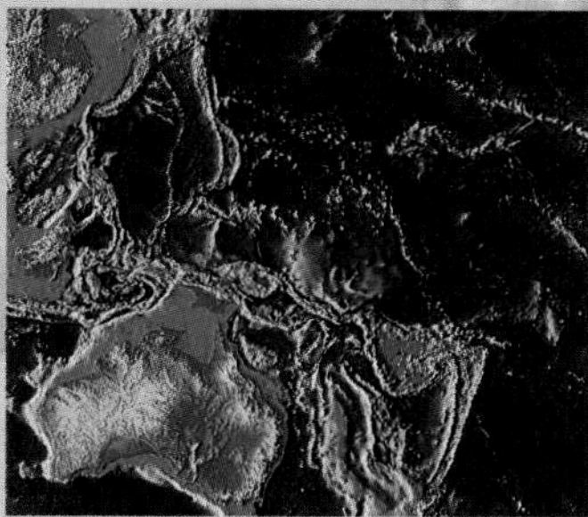

Arts & Literature

Architects use grids to lay out floor plans for new buildings.

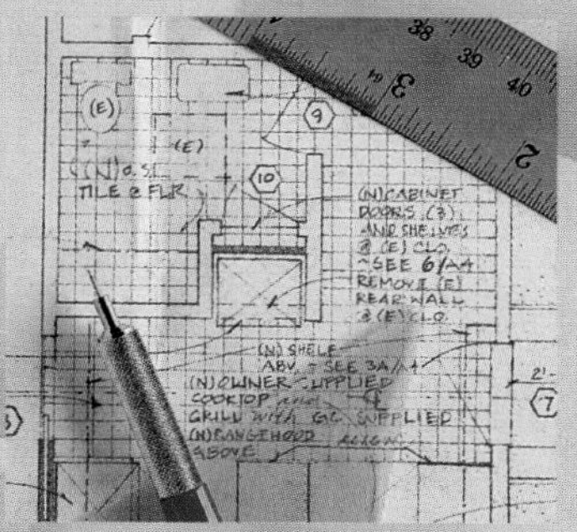

KEY MATH IDEAS

An integer is a whole number, positive or negative. Negative integers are written with a − sign.

The absolute value of an integer tells its distance from 0.

Ordered pairs can be represented by points on a coordinate plane.

When you add or subtract integers, you must take their signs into account. You can use number lines or algebra tiles to model integer addition and subtraction.

The product or quotient of two integers with the same sign is positive. The product or quotient of two integers with different signs is negative.

CHAPTER PROJECT

Problem Solving

Understand
Plan
Solve
Look Back

In this project, you'll create a personal time line showing dates that are important to you. Begin the project by drawing a number line. Put the date you were born above the center of the line and write a zero below it.

429

PROJECT ASSESSMENT

You may choose to use this project as a performance assessment for the chapter.

Performance Assessment Key

Level 4 Full Accomplishment

Level 3 Substantial Accomplishment

Level 2 Partial Accomplishment

Level 1 Little Accomplishment

Suggested Scoring Rubric

4	•Drawing shows an excellent grasp of a time line showing dates before and after a zero point. •At least 10 carefully researched dates are correctly placed on the line.
3	•Drawing shows an understanding of the structure of a time line. •Eight to ten dates are correctly placed on the line.
2	•Drawing shows partial understanding of the structure of a time line. •Fewer than 8 dates are shown, some of which are incorrectly placed.
1	•Little attempt is made to draw an adequate time line. •Fewer than 5 dates are shown, some or all of which are incorrectly placed.

Chapter Project

Students create a time line that shows important dates in their lives.

Resources
Chapter 9 Project Master.

Introduce the Project

- Ask students to describe a time line and explain what it shows. Illustrate how to make a time line for your classroom day, using noon as zero.
- Discuss dates that might be important to students. Point out that they can be dates of things that occurred before they were born.
- Talk about sources of information for dates that students do not know, such as their parents or relatives, encyclopedias, or the Internet.

Project Progress

Section A, page 446 Students begin their time line by making tick marks to represent years before and after their birth. Then they decide what dates to include on the time line.

Section B, page 470 Students complete their time line using the events they identified earlier. They also illustrate the time line with art or pictures.

Community Project

A community project for Chapter 9 is available in *Home and Community Connections.*

Cooperative Learning

You may want to use Teaching Tool Transparency 1: Cooperative Learning Checklist with **Explore** and other group activities in this Chapter.

Problem Solving Focus

Solving the Problem

The Point
Students focus on different ways to solve the same problem. They choose a method that works best.

Resources
Teaching Tool Transparency 16: Problem-Solving Guidelines

 *Interactive CD-ROM Journal*

About the Page

Using the Problem-Solving Process
Once students have read a problem and identified what they are to find, they must decide how to solve it. More than one approach might be possible, and sometimes one way seems more logical or easier. Discuss these suggestions for deciding how to solve a problem:

- Identify what the problem is asking.
- Ask if a diagram, pattern, table, or other method would help organize the information given.
- Choose the method that seems best. Not all people will select the same method.

Ask …
- When is drawing a picture a good way to solve a problem? Possible answer: When the problem involves patterns.
- When does making a table help you solve a problem? Possible answer: When there appears to be a relationship or pattern in the numbers given.
- How can you combine these two methods to solve the staircase problem? Possible answer: Draw a few diagrams to see what is happening; then make a table to show the pattern.
- How would you use logic to explain the number of triangles? Each answer is the square of the number of rows; $5^2 = 25$

Answer for Problems
1. 25

Journal

Ask students to write a paragraph explaining the method they used for solving the triangle problem and why they chose this method.

Problem Solving
Understand
Plan
Solve
Look Back

Solving the Problem

There is often more than one way to solve a problem. When you solve a problem, you may find that one plan works more easily than another. An important part of good problem solving is choosing a strategy that is easy to work with.

Problem Solving Focus

The following problem has already been solved using three different methods.

Squares can be used to make staircase patterns, as shown. Find the number of squares in a six-step staircase pattern.

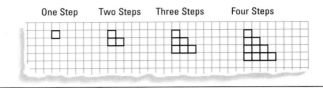

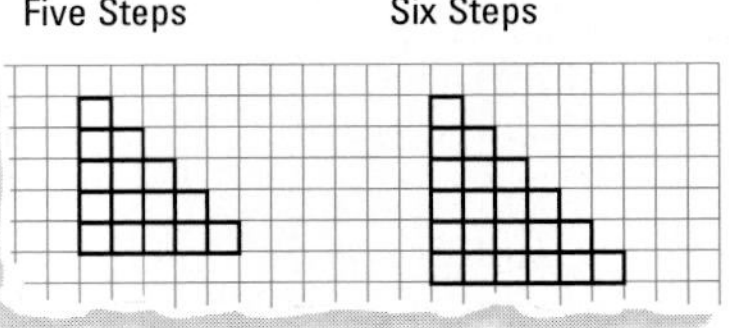

Draw a diagram

By counting squares, you see that there are 21 steps in a six-step staircase.

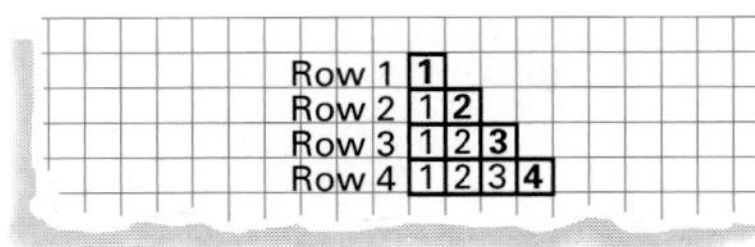

Look for a pattern

Making a table can show a pattern in the results.

Number of Steps	1	2	3	4
Number of Squares	1	3	6	10
Increase	–	2	3	4

When you add a step, the number of squares always increases by the number of steps in the new staircase. So there are 10 + **5** = 15 steps in a **five**-step staircase, and there are 15 + **6** = 21 steps in a **six**-step staircase.

Use logical reasoning

Each row of the staircase has the same number of squares as its row number.

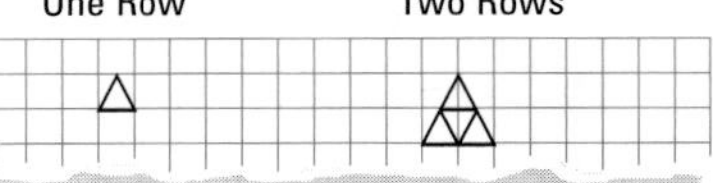

So a six-step staircase has 1 + 2 + 3 + 4 + 5 + 6 = 21 steps.

Solve the following problem. You may use one of the above methods or a method of your own.

 How many small triangles does it take to build a triangle five rows high?

One Row
Two Rows

Additional Problem

Kara is on a baseball team with 9 players. After they win a game, each person on the team does a high five with each other person on the team. How many high fives do they do?

1. Describe how you could solve the problem by drawing a diagram. Possible answer: Let a dot represent each player and draw lines to represent the high fives.
2. How could you use a pattern to solve the problem? Possible answer: Find the number of high fives for 2, 3, and 4 players and look for a pattern.
3. How could you use logic? Possible answer: Notice the pattern. Multiply the number of players by the number that is one less. Then divide by 2. For 9 players, $9 \times 8 \div 2 = 36$.
4. Which method do you like best? Did you think of another possible way to solve the problem? Answers may vary.

Section 9A

Using Integers

LESSON PLANNING GUIDE

Student Edition / **Ancillaries***

LESSON		MATERIALS	VOCABULARY	DAILY	OTHER
	Chapter 9 Opener				Ch. 9 Project Master Ch. 9 Community Project Teaching Tool Trans. 1
	Problem Solving Focus				Teaching Tool Trans. 16 *Interactive CD-ROM Journal*
	Section 9A Opener				
9-1	**Using Integers to Represent Quantities**		negative numbers, origin, opposite numbers, integers, absolute value	9-1	Teaching Tool Trans. 5 Lesson Enhancement Trans. 39
9-2	**Comparing and Ordering Integers**			9-2	Teaching Tool Trans. 2, 3, 5
9-3	**The Coordinate Plane**	tracing paper, ruler	coordinate system, *x*-*y* coordinate plane, *x*-axis, *y*-axis, origin, quadrants, ordered pair, *x*-coordinate, *y*-coordinate	9-3	Teaching Tool Trans. 8 Lesson Enhancement Transparencies 40–42 Chapter 9 Project Master *WW Math*–Algebra
	Connect	graph paper			Teaching Tool Trans. 8 Interdisc. Team Teaching 9A
	Review				Practice 9A; Quiz 9A; TestWorks

* Daily Ancillaries include Practice, Reteaching, Problem Solving, Enrichment, and Daily Transparency. Teaching Tool Transparencies are in *Teacher's Toolkits*. Lesson Enhancement Transparencies are in *Overhead Transparency Package*.

SKILLS TRACE

LESSON	SKILL	FIRST INTRODUCED GR. 5	GR. 6	GR. 7	DEVELOP	PRACTICE/ APPLY	REVIEW
9-1	**Applying integers and absolute value.**		✗		pp. 432–434	pp. 435–436	pp. 448, 474, 516, 542
9-2	**Comparing and ordering integers.**		✗		pp. 437–439	pp. 440–441	pp. 448, 474, 485, 520
9-3	**Graphing points on a coordinate plane.**		✗		pp. 442–444	pp. 445–446	pp. 448, 474, 489, 557

CONNECTED MATHEMATICS

Investigation 1 in the unit *Accentuate the Negative (Integers)*, from the **Connected Mathematics** series, can be used with Section 9A.

INTERDISCIPLINARY TEAM TEACHING

Math and Science/Technology

(Worksheet pages 35–36: Teacher pages T35–T36)

In this lesson, students use integers and coordinates to understand the properties of water.

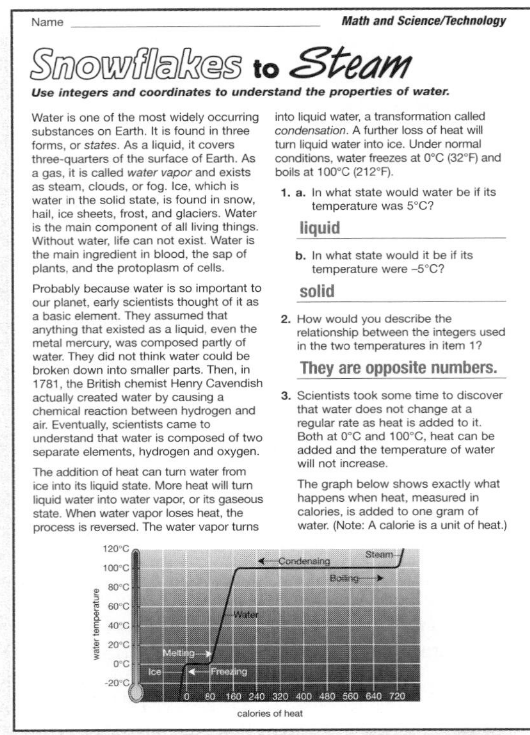

Name ______________________ *Math and Science/Technology*

Snowflakes to Steam

Use integers and coordinates to understand the properties of water.

Water is one of the most widely occurring substances on Earth. It is found in three forms, or *states*. As a liquid, it covers three-quarters of the surface of Earth. As a gas, it is called *water vapor* and exists as steam, clouds, or fog. Ice, which is water in the solid state, is found in snow, hail, ice sheets, frost, and glaciers. Water is the main component of all living things. Without water, life can not exist. Water is the main ingredient in blood, the sap of plants, and the protoplasm of cells.

Probably because water is so important to our planet, early scientists thought of it as a basic element. They assumed that anything that existed as a liquid, even the metal mercury, was composed partly of water. They did not think water could be broken down into smaller parts. Then, in 1781, the British chemist Henry Cavendish actually created water by causing a chemical reaction between hydrogen and air. Eventually, scientists came to understand that water is composed of two separate elements, hydrogen and oxygen.

The addition of heat can turn water from ice into its liquid state. More heat will turn liquid water into water vapor, or its gaseous state. When water vapor loses heat, the process is reversed. The water vapor turns into liquid water, a transformation called *condensation*. A further loss of heat will turn liquid water into ice. Under normal conditions, water freezes at 0°C (32°F) and boils at 100°C (212°F).

1. a. In what state would water be if its temperature was 5°C?

   liquid

   b. In what state would it be if its temperature were –5°C?

   solid

2. How would you describe the relationship between the integers used in the two temperatures in item 1?

   They are opposite numbers.

3. Scientists took some time to discover that water does not change at a regular rate as heat is added to it. Both at 0°C and 100°C, heat can be added and the temperature of water will not increase.

The graph below shows exactly what happens when heat, measured in calories, is added to one gram of water. (Note: A calorie is a unit of heat.)

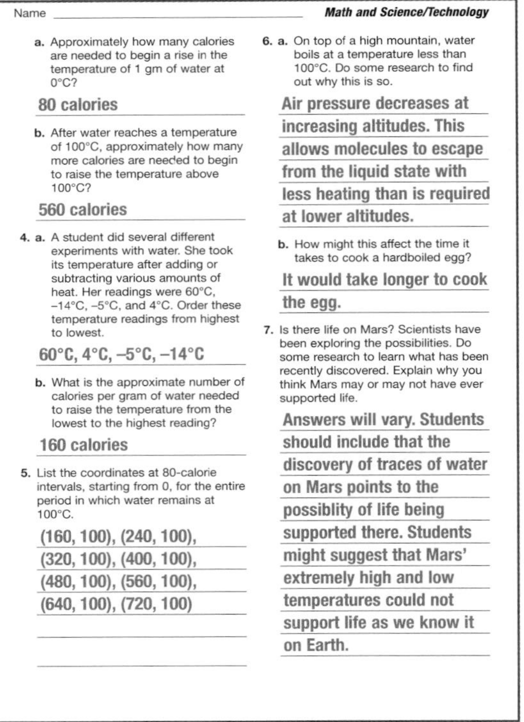

Name ______________________ *Math and Science/Technology*

a. Approximately how many calories are needed to begin a rise in the temperature of 1 gm of water at 0°C?

80 calories

b. After water reaches a temperature of 100°C, approximately how many more calories are needed to begin to raise the temperature above 100°C?

560 calories

4. a. A student did several different experiments with water. She took its temperature after adding or subtracting various amounts of heat. Her readings were 60°C, –14°C, –5°C, and 4°C. Order these temperature readings from highest to lowest.

   60°C, 4°C, –5°C, –14°C

   b. What is the approximate number of calories per gram of water needed to raise the temperature from the lowest to the highest reading?

   160 calories

5. List the coordinates at 80-calorie intervals, starting from 0, for the entire period in which water remains at 100°C.

   (160, 100), (240, 100), (320, 100), (400, 100), (480, 100), (560, 100), (640, 100), (720, 100)

6. a. On top of a high mountain, water boils at a temperature less than 100°C. Do some research to find out why this is so.

   Air pressure decreases at increasing altitudes. This allows molecules to escape from the liquid state with less heating than is required at lower altitudes.

   b. How might this affect the time it takes to cook a hardboiled egg?

   It would take longer to cook the egg.

7. Is there life on Mars? Scientists have been exploring the possibilities. Do some research to learn what has been recently discovered. Explain why you think Mars may or may not have ever supported life.

   Answers will vary. Students should include that the discovery of traces of water on Mars points to the possiblity of life being supported there. Students might suggest that Mars' extremely high and low temperatures could not support life as we know it on Earth.

BIBLIOGRAPHY

FOR TEACHERS

Edgerton, Lynne T. *The Rising Tide: Global Warming and World Sea Levels.* Washington, DC: Island Press, 1991.

Fibonacci, Leonardo. *The Book of Squares.* Boston, MA: Academic Press, 1987.

Flint, David. *Weather and Climate: Experiments with Geography.* New York, NY: Watts, 1991.

Ritchie, David. *The Encyclopedia of Earthquakes and Volcanoes.* New York, NY: Facts on File, 1994.

Willoughby, Stephen. *Mathematics Education for a Changing World.* Alexandria, VA: ASCD, 1990.

FOR STUDENTS

Descartes, Rene. *The Geometry of Rene Descartes.* New York, NY: Dover Publications, 1954.

Florence, Ronald. *The Perfect Machine: Building the Palomar Telescope.* New York, NY: HarperCollins, 1994.

Robinson, Fay. *Space Probes to the Planets.* Morton Grove, IL: A. Whitman & Co., 1993.

Verne, Jules. *Journey to the Center of the Earth.* New York, NY: Bantam Books, 1991.

SECTION 9A

Using Integers

Science Link | Geography Link | www.mathsurf.com/7/ch9/geology

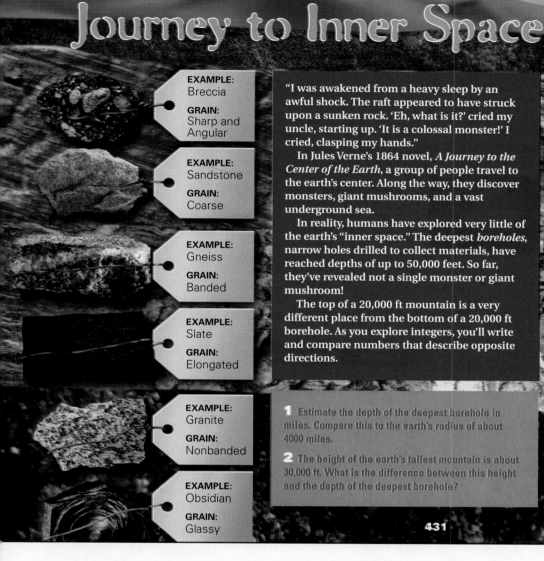

Journey to Inner Space

EXAMPLE: Breccia
GRAIN: Sharp and Angular

EXAMPLE: Sandstone
GRAIN: Coarse

EXAMPLE: Gneiss
GRAIN: Banded

EXAMPLE: Slate
GRAIN: Elongated

EXAMPLE: Granite
GRAIN: Nonbanded

EXAMPLE: Obsidian
GRAIN: Glassy

"I was awakened from a heavy sleep by an awful shock. The raft appeared to have struck upon a sunken rock. 'Eh, what is it?' cried my uncle, starting up. 'It is a colossal monster!' I cried, clasping my hands."

In Jules Verne's 1864 novel, *A Journey to the Center of the Earth*, a group of people travel to the earth's center. Along the way, they discover monsters, giant mushrooms, and a vast underground sea.

In reality, humans have explored very little of the earth's "inner space." The deepest *boreholes*, narrow holes drilled to collect materials, have reached depths of up to 50,000 feet. So far, they've revealed not a single monster or giant mushroom!

The top of a 20,000 ft mountain is a very different place from the bottom of a 20,000 ft borehole. As you explore integers, you'll write and compare numbers that describe opposite directions.

1 Estimate the depth of the deepest borehole in miles. Compare this to the earth's radius of about 4000 miles.

2 The height of the earth's tallest mountain is about 30,000 ft. What is the difference between this height and the depth of the deepest borehole?

431

Where are we now?

In Grade 6, students used integers to describe and compare real-world relationships. They explored the idea of integers as opposites.

They learned how to

- express profit and loss by positive and negative integers.
- operate with integers.
- graph integers on the coordinate plane.

Where are we going?

In Grade 7 Section 9A, students will

- find the opposite of an integer.
- find the absolute value of an integer.
- compare and order integers.
- graph points with positive and negative coordinates on a coordinate plane.

Theme: Geology

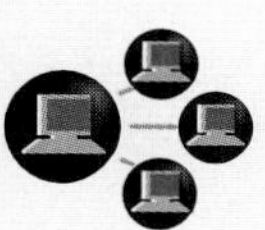

World Wide Web

If your class has access to the World Wide Web, you might want to use the information found at the Web site address given. The interdisciplinary links relate to topics discussed in this section.

About the Page

This page introduces the theme of the section, geology, and discusses exploring the earth's "inner space."

Ask ...

- How many feet are in a mile? Have scientists drilled more than a mile into the earth's crust? 5,280 ft; Yes, 50,000 ft is more than 9 miles.
- How would you show that the top of a mountain is above sea level and the bottom of a borehole is below sea level? Possible answer: Use "+" for above sea level and "−" for below it.

Extensions

Science
Geology deals with the history of the earth and its life forms. Some areas of geology are geophysics, geochemistry, mineralogy, and paleontology. Have students research an area of geology that interests them.

Geography
Have interested students find the highest and lowest points in the United States and write the altitudes using integers. Highest: Mt. McKinley, AK, +20,320 ft; Lowest: Death Valley, CA, −282 ft.

Answers for Questions

1. Possible answer: About 10 mi; Very small compared to the earth's radius.
2. About 80,000 ft

Connect

On page 447, students examine the relationship between temperature and depth in the earth's interior.

Lesson Organizer

Objectives

- Use integers to represent real-world quantities.
- Find the opposite of an integer.
- Find the absolute value of an integer.

Vocabulary

- Negative numbers, origin, opposite numbers, integers, absolute value

NCTM Standards

- 1–7

Review

Find each difference.

1. 3022 − 2960 62
2. 12,009 − 3588 8421
3. 4802 − 67 4735
4. 5551 − 3692 1859
5. 18,440 − 5678 12,762

Available on Daily Transparency 9-1

1 Introduce

Explore

You may wish to use Lesson Enhancement Transparency 39 with **Explore.**

The Point
Students explore numbers above and below a zero point. Showing these points on a vertical number line helps show the relative values of these numbers.

Ongoing Assessment
Check that students understand the relationship between the distances above sea level and the distances below sea level.

9-1 Using Integers to Represent Quantities

You'll Learn ...

- to use integers to represent real-world quantities
- to find the opposite of an integer
- to find the absolute value of an integer

... How It's Used

Sailors need to know ocean and harbor depths to prevent their ships from running aground.

Vocabulary

negative numbers
origin
opposite numbers
integers
absolute value

Lesson Link Most of the numbers you've studied so far have been greater than zero. Now you'll explore numbers that are less than zero. ◄

Explore Numbers Less than Zero

Hills and Valleys

In Plaquemines Parish, Louisiana, a borehole was drilled to 22,570 ft below sea level. Sea level is the average height of the earth's oceans.

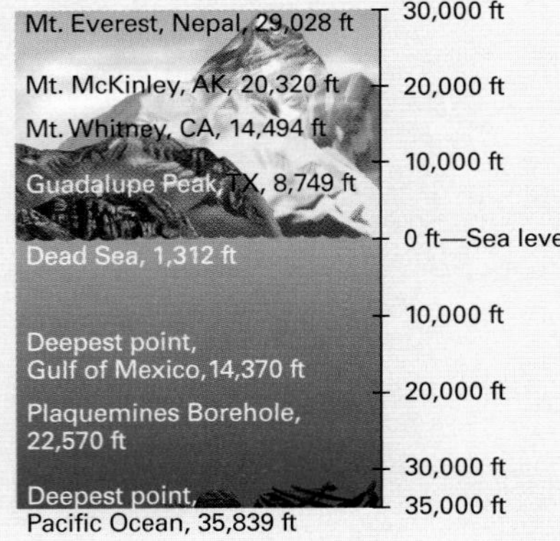

1. Which landmarks are below sea level? Above sea level?
2. Which is closer to sea level, the deepest point in the Gulf of Mexico or Mt. Whitney? How much closer?
3. Which is farther from sea level, Mt. McKinley or the Plaquemines borehole? How much farther?
4. Describe a way to show the difference between numbers of feet above sea level and below sea level.

Learn Using Integers to Represent Quantities

A vertical number line can be used to compare heights and depths.

+3000 ft
+2000 ft
+1000 ft
0 ft—Sea level
−1000 ft
−2000 ft
−3000 ft

Positive numbers

Zero is neither positive nor negative

Negative numbers

MEETING INDIVIDUAL NEEDS

Resources

- 9-1 Practice
- 9-1 Reteaching
- 9-1 Problem Solving
- 9-1 Enrichment
- 9-1 Daily Transparency
  - Problem of the Day
  - Review
  - Quick Quiz
- Teaching Tool Transparency 5
- Lesson Enhancement Transparency 39

Learning Modalities

Logical So that students will realize that negative numbers arise naturally in many situations, be sure to present as many examples as possible in this first lesson on integers. In addition to those examples in the column notes and student pages, you might discuss rocket-launch countdowns, changes in stock prices, business profits and losses, and so on.

Visual Number lines provide a semi-concrete model of integers that will help students grasp and retain the important ideas in this lesson. Allow students to use them as long as they wish.

English Language Development

Review the meanings of the terms below by encouraging students to give examples of each in relation to positive and negative integers. Correct any misconceptions and clarify the meanings with additional examples if necessary.

above, below	loss, gain	forward, backward
decrease, increase	up, down	withdrawal, deposit

Positive numbers, such as +1000, are greater than zero. They are usually written without a positive (+) sign. **Negative numbers**, such as −2000, are less than zero. The zero point on a number line is the **origin**.

Example 1

The greatest recorded altitude for a bird in flight, a Ruppell's vulture, is 37,000 feet above sea level. A leatherback turtle once dove 3,973 feet below sea level. Use signs to write each number.

Ruppell's vulture

You can use positive numbers to represent heights and negative numbers to represent depths.

Height of vulture: +37,000 Depth of turtle: −3,973

Problem Solving TIP

When you're deciding how to represent a number as an integer, remember that numbers *below* or *less than* the zero point are negative.

A number line can be drawn horizontally. The farther to the right a number is, the greater it is; the farther to the left it is, the less it is.

Opposite numbers are the same distance from zero. −2 and 2 are opposites because they are both 2 units from zero.

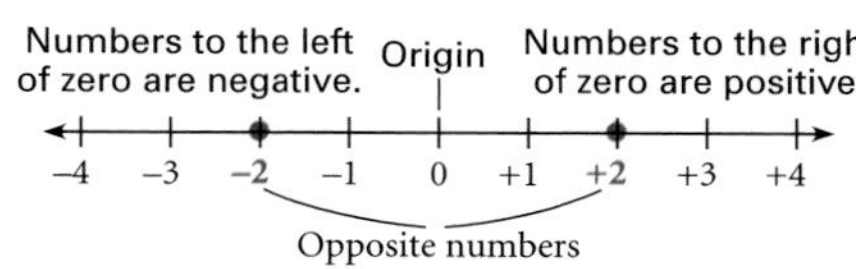

Whole numbers and their opposites are **integers**. Zero is a whole number, so it is an integer.

HINT

A calculator can show negative numbers. To show −3, enter 3, then press the +/− key. On a graphing calculator, use the (−) key.

Example 2

On seven runs, a football running back gained 6, 2, −4, 0, −2, −1, and 4 yards. Which numbers are positive? Negative? Which pairs of numbers are opposites?

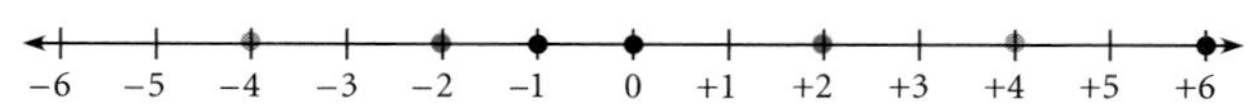

2, 4, and 6 are to the right of zero, so they are positive.

−4, −2, and −1 are to the left of zero, so they are negative.

−4 and 4 are opposites. −2 and 2 are opposites.

Try It

Which of the numbers −3, 5, 0, −1, 4, −5, and 3 are positive? Negative? Which pairs of numbers are opposites? 3, 4, 5; −1, −3, −5; −3 and 3, −5 and 5

MATH EVERY DAY

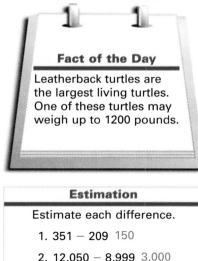

Problem of the Day

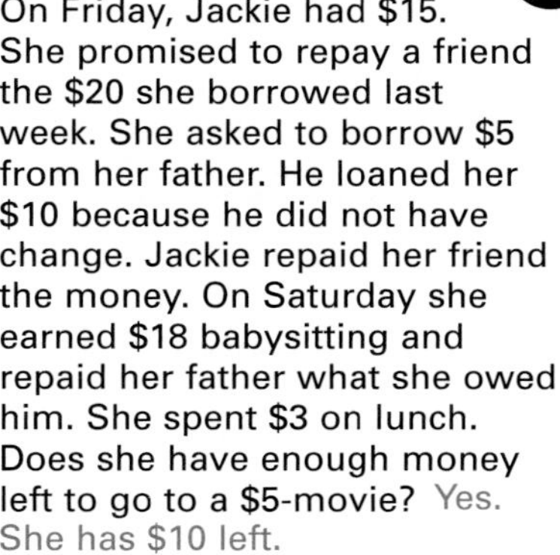

On Friday, Jackie had $15. She promised to repay a friend the $20 she borrowed last week. She asked to borrow $5 from her father. He loaned her $10 because he did not have change. Jackie repaid her friend the money. On Saturday she earned $18 babysitting and repaid her father what she owed him. She spent $3 on lunch. Does she have enough money left to go to a $5-movie? Yes. She has $10 left.

Available on Daily Transparency 9-1

An Extension is provided in the transparency package.

Fact of the Day

Leatherback turtles are the largest living turtles. One of these turtles may weigh up to 1200 pounds.

Estimation

Estimate each difference.

1. 351 − 209 150
2. 12,050 − 8,999 3,000
3. 4002 − 3809 200
4. 762 − 49 710
5. 950 − 905 40

For Groups That Finish Early

Which is closer to sea level, Mt. McKinley or Mt. Whitney? Mt. Whitney How much closer? 5826 ft Which point is farther below sea level, the Plaquemines borehole or the deepest point in the Pacific Ocean, and how much farther? The deepest point in the Pacific Ocean, 13,269 ft.

Answers for Explore

1. Below sea level: Dead Sea, Deepest point in Gulf of Mexico, Plaquemines borehole, Deepest point in Pacific Ocean; Above sea level: Mt. Everest, Mt. McKinley, Mt. Whitney, Guadalupe Peak
2. Deepest point in Gulf of Mexico; 124 ft closer
3. Plaquemines borehole; 2250 ft farther
4. Possible answers: Label each number; Use negative numbers; Make the deepest point in the Pacific Ocean 0 ft.

2 Teach

Learn

You may wish to use Teaching Tool Transparency 5: Number Lines with Examples 1 and 2.

Alternate Examples

1. The highest temperature ever recorded in California was 134°F in 1913. The lowest temperature ever recorded in California was 45°F below zero in 1937. Use signs to write each number.

   Highest temperature: +134°F

   Lowest temperature: −45°F

2. In eight carries, Ken gained 5, 3, −4, −3, 2, 4, −2, and 6 yards. Which numbers are positive? Negative? Which pairs of numbers are opposites?

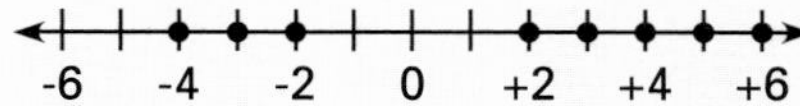

   5, 3, 2, 4, and 6 are to the right of zero, so they are positive.

   −4, −3, and −2 are to the left of zero, so they are negative.

   −4 and 4 are opposites.

   3 and −3 are opposites.

   2 and −2 are opposites.

Alternate Examples

3. Lake Assal, in Africa, is at about −570 feet. How far is this from sea level?

   $|-570| = 570$

   The lake bottom is about 570 feet from sea level.

3 Practice and Assess

Check

Give students a variety of integers and ask for the absolute values to ensure that they understand the concept.

Answers for Check Your Understanding

1. Possible answers: Measuring distance under water; Subtracting too much from a bank account; Walking backward from a starting point.
2. 0; A negative number; A positive number.

Geography Link

The top of Mt. Everest is at an elevation of 29,028 feet, and the Challenger Deep, the deepest point in the world's oceans, is at −35,839 feet. The Challenger Deep is 6,811 feet—almost 1.3 miles—deeper than Mt. Everest is tall.

If you fly from Chicago to Cleveland, you travel 340 miles. If you fly from Chicago to Des Moines, you go the same distance, but in the opposite direction. Do you travel −340 miles?

No! Des Moines and Cleveland are *both* 340 miles from Chicago. No matter what direction you travel, distance is a positive number.

Like distances on a map, distances on a number line are always positive.

The **absolute value** of a number is its distance from zero. Bars are used to show absolute value.

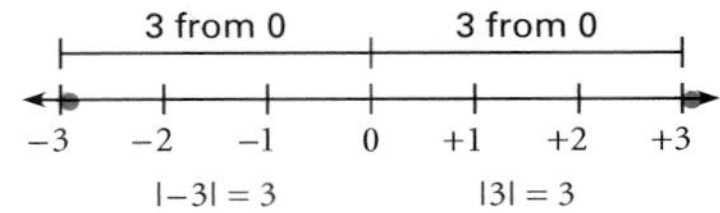

$|2| = 2$ $\qquad |-17| = 17$

The absolute value of a negative number is its (positive) opposite. The absolute value of a positive number or 0 is the number itself.

Industry Link

The only operating diamond mine in the United States is in Arkansas, near the Tennessee border. It operates as a tourist attraction.

Example 3

The world's deepest mine is in South Africa. The bottom of this mine shaft is at −12,600 feet. How far is this from sea level?

The absolute value of a number is its distance from zero.

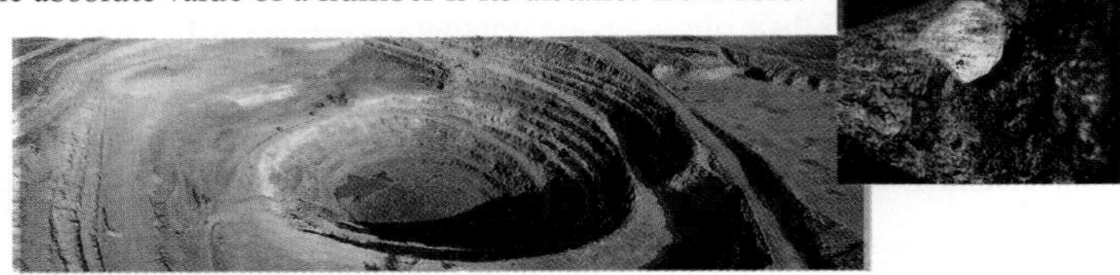

$|-12{,}600| = 12{,}600$

The bottom of the mine is 12,600 feet from sea level.

Try It

Find each absolute value. **a.** $|-17|$ 17 **b.** $|5.25|$ 5.25 **c.** $|-3298|$ 3298 **d.** $|0|$ 0

Check Your Understanding

1. Describe some real-life situations where you might use negative numbers.
2. What is the opposite of zero? Of a positive number? Of a negative number?

MEETING MIDDLE SCHOOL CLASSROOM NEEDS

Tips from Middle School Teachers

I like to have students, working in small groups, look in newspapers and magazines to find examples of the use of positive and negative integers. Then I have them prepare a report of their findings to share with the class.

Cultural Connection

The climate in many parts of Russia is very harsh. At Verkhoyansk in the northeast, the mean January temperature is −58°F, while the lowest recorded temperature there is −90°F. At Eureka, in Canada's high Arctic, winter temperatures average −35°F, and summer temperatures average 43°F. Invite students to discuss how living in very cold climates influences daily life. You might also ask students how much colder it is in January in Verkhoyansk than in their local area.

Team Teaching

Invite a science teacher to discuss various types of mines, for example, coal mines, copper mines, or diamond mines. Discuss the common depths for the mines and have students use integers to express the depths.

9-1 Exercises and Applications

Practice and Apply

1. **Getting Started** **a.** Graph each of the numbers $-1, 3, 0, 1, -5, 4,$ and -3 on a horizontal number line.
   b. Which numbers are positive? 1, 3, 4
   c. Which numbers are negative? $-1, -3, -5$
   d. Which pairs of numbers are opposites? -1 and 1, -3 and 3

Tell whether each number is an integer. Write *Yes* or *No*.

2. -3 Yes 3. 4.1 No 4. $-\frac{1}{2}$ No 5. 0 Yes 6. -3.14 No

Number Sense **Use signs to write each number.**

7. A borehole 31,441 feet deep $-31,441$
8. Earned $10 $+10$
9. Lost 6 yards -6
10. 5280 feet above sea level $+5280$
11. 2 units to the left of the origin on a horizontal number line -2
12. 9 units above the origin on a vertical number line $+9$

Write the opposite of each integer.

13. 3 -3 14. -23 23 15. -222 222 16. 250 -250 17. 5640 -5640

Find each absolute value.

18. $|23|$ 23 19. $|-23|$ 23 20. $|-66|$ 66 21. $|66|$ 66 22. $|-1089|$ 1089

23. $|-4771|$ 4771 24. $|650|$ 650 25. $|2435|$ 2435 26. $|-1000|$ 1000 27. $|-90{,}121|$ 90,121

28. **Science** North American geologists and geophysicists have drilled boreholes to see if temperatures at different depths are related to global warming. The table shows the depths of some of the boreholes they have drilled. Write an integer to represent each depth. $-1000, -160, -710, -220$

Location	Western Canada	Western Utah	Northeast United States	Alberta, Canada
Borehole Depth (m)	1000	160	710	220

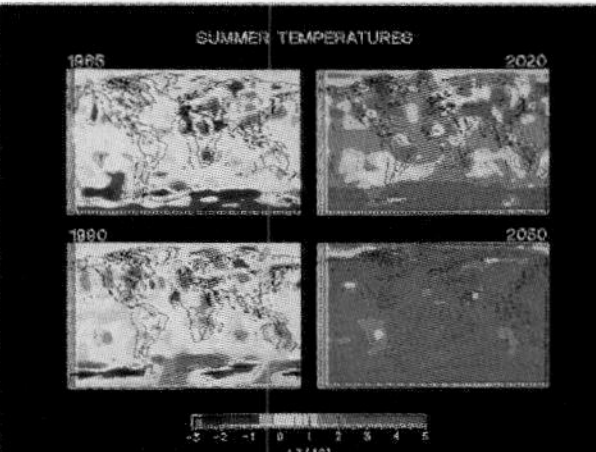

PRACTICE 9-1

PRACTICE

Name ______________________

Practice 9-1

Using Integers to Represent Quantities

Tell whether each number is an integer. Write *Yes* or *No*.

1. 64 Yes 2. -9.31 No 3. $-2\frac{1}{2}$ No 4. 16.7 No
5. -37 Yes 6. $\frac{27}{3}$ Yes 7. 10.01 No 8. $\frac{3}{8}$ No

Use signs to write each number.

9. Spent $23 $-\$23$
10. Gained 12 yards +12 yd
11. 14 degrees below zero $-14°$
12. Profit of $640 +$640
13. The distance from 0 to -4 on a number line $+4$
14. 7 units below the origin on a vertical number line -7

Write the opposite of each integer.

15. 42 -42 16. -163 163 17. -24 24 18. 69 -69
19. -39 39 20. 7 -7 21. -572 572 22. 18 -18

Find each absolute value.

23. $|-12|$ 12 24. $|23|$ 23 25. $|-42|$ 42 26. $|-58|$ 58
27. $|937|$ 937 28. $|-37|$ 37 29. $|2640|$ 2640 30. $|1329|$ 1329

31. **Science** The table gives the deepest recorded underwater dives of animals, as reported in the 1997 *Guinness Book of World Records*. Use an integer to represent the height of each animal during its dive. (The height at sea level is 0 ft.)

Animal	Depth (ft)	Height (ft)
Elephant Seal	5017	-5017
Leatherback Turtle	3973	-3973
Emperor Penguin	1584	-1584
Human (without equipment)	428	-428

32. **Science** The average surface temperature on Mercury is 332°F. On Pluto, it is -355°F.
   a. Find the absolute value of each temperature. 332°F; 355°F
   b. Which temperature is closer to 0°F? 332°F

RETEACHING

Name ______________________

Alternative Lesson 9-1

Using Integers to Represent Quantities

The number line at the right shows the **whole numbers** (zero and the **positive numbers**). The arrow indicates that the numbers go on without end.

0 1 2 3 4 5

When you extend the number line to the left, you can also represent **negative numbers**, those numbers less than zero. They are always written with a negative sign. **Opposite numbers**, such as 3 and –3, are the same distance from zero on the number line. The absolute value of a number is its distance from zero.

–5 –4 –3 –2 –1 0 1 2 3 4 5

Whole numbers and their opposites are **integers.**

Example 1

Write the opposite of –8.

Find the absolute value $|-8|$.

–8 is eight units to the left of zero.
8 is eight units to the right of zero.

–8 –7 –6 –5 –4 –3 –2 –1 0 1 2 3 4 5 6 7 8

Opposites

So, the opposite of –8 is 8, and $|-8| = 8$.

Try It Write the opposite of each integer.

a. –5 5 b. 10 –10 c. 12 –12

Find the absolute value of each number.

d. –7 7 e. 15 15 f. –35 35

Example 2

Use signs to write each number: 9 degrees above zero and 9 degrees below zero.

Positive 9 represents a temperature of 9 degrees *above* 0.
Negative 9 represents a temperature of 9 degrees *below* 0.

So, the increase is represented as 9 and the decrease is represented by –9.

Try It Use signs to write each number.

g. Loss of 5 pounds –5
   Gain of 5 pounds 5
h. 7 steps forward 7
   7 steps backward –7
i. 3 flights up 3
   2 flights down –2
j. Gain of 21 yards 21
   Loss of 14 yards –14

9-1 Exercises and Applications

Assignment Guide

- **Basic**
  1–27 odds, 30, 32, 35–39 odds
- **Average**
  2–28 evens, 30, 32, 33, 34–38 evens
- **Enriched**
  9–27 odds, 28–33, 35–39 odds

Exercise Notes

Exercises 13–27

Error Prevention Remind students that numbers without signs are positive.

Exercise 28

Science Environmental scientists are concerned that changes in the atmosphere, especially those caused by human activity, could cause the temperature of the earth's surface to rise to a dangerous degree. It is feared that icecaps could melt and cause sea levels to rise, thus flooding coastal cities.

Exercise Answers

1. a.

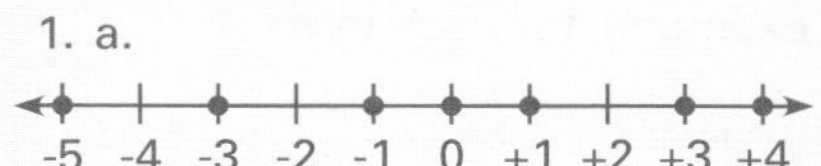

Reteaching

Activity

Materials: Ruler

- In golf, a score that is used as a standard is called *par*. Scores can be above par, below par, or even with par. Use your ruler to draw a line on your paper, and mark off equal intervals. Label the middle mark as "par," the marks to the left "below par," and the marks to the right "above par."
- What number represents even with par? 0 Mark that number on your line.
- What number represents 4 above par? +4 Mark that number on your line.
- What number represents 4 below par? –4 Mark that number on your line. Now fill in all the missing numbers on your number line.

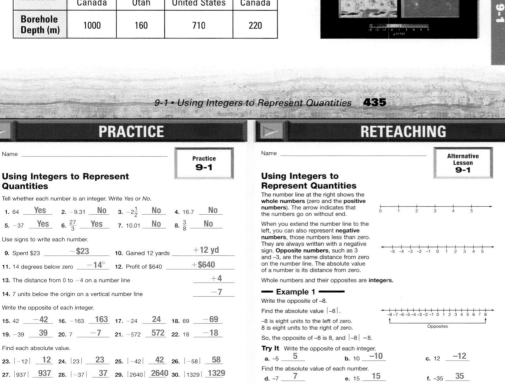

Exercise Notes

■ Exercise 31

Science Two active volcanoes in the United States outside Alaska and Hawaii are Lassen Peak in California and Mt. St. Helens in Washington.

Exercise Answers

32. Crust: 0–25 mi; Mantle: −25 to −1825 mi; Outer core: −1825 to −3225 mi; Inner core: −3225 mi

33. Possible answers:
  a. Time lost tying a shoe instead of running.
  b. Store discount.
  c. Temperature in Minnesota in January.
  d. Distance walked backwards for every step forward.

Alternate Assessment

You may want to use the *Interactive CD-ROM Journal* with this assessment.

Journal Have students give definitions in their own words for *integers*, *opposites*, and *absolute value*. Have them give examples for each term.

► Quick Quiz

1. Give the opposite of each integer.
  a. −5 5
  b. 3 −3
  c. 0 0
  d. −18 18
2. Give each absolute value.
  a. |−52| 52
  b. |13| 13
  c. |14.6| 14.6
  d. |0| 0

Available on Daily Transparency 9-1

29. Geography The hottest recorded temperature on Earth was 136°F, at Al' Aziziyah, Libya. The coldest was −129°F, at Vostok, Antarctica. Find the absolute value of each temperature and tell which is closer to zero. 136°; 129°; −129°

30. Test Prep Find the set of numbers that contains the opposites of 37, −7, and −54. B

Ⓐ −37, −7, −54   Ⓑ −37, 7, 54   Ⓒ 37, −7, 54   Ⓓ 37, 7, −54

Problem Solving and Reasoning

31. Critical Thinking The volcano Mauna Kea, on the island of Hawaii, is the world's tallest mountain from base to peak. Mauna Kea's base is 19,680 feet below the ocean's surface. Its peak is 13,796 feet above sea level. Write integers representing the height of Mauna Kea above sea level and its depth below sea level. 13,796; −19,680

Mauna Kea

32. Critical Thinking GPS The earth is covered with a rocky *crust,* which can be 25 miles thick. Underneath this is an 1800-mile-thick *mantle* of heavier rock. Below the mantle is a liquid *outer core,* about 1400 miles thick. The center of the earth is a solid *inner core.*

Use integers to describe the minimum and maximum depths of each region. (You will be able to give only the minimum depth of the inner core.)

33.  Write about a situation each measurement might represent.

a. −30 seconds   **b.** −$20   **c.** −39°F   **d.** −12 yards

Mixed Review

Write each ratio in three ways. If possible, write in lowest terms. *[Lesson 6-1]*

34. 4 days out of 7 days $\frac{4}{7}$, 4:7, 4 to 7

35. 2 socks for every uniform $\frac{2}{1}$, 2:1, 2 to 1

36. 1 teacher for every 30 students $\frac{1}{30}$, 1:30, 1 to 30

37. 12 servings for 10 people $\frac{6}{5}$, 6:5, 6 to 5

Find *x* in each pair of similar figures. *[Lesson 7-9]*

38. $x = 7$

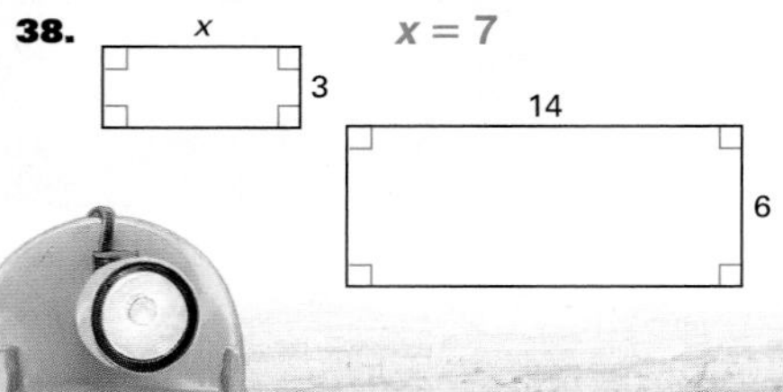

39. $x = 15$

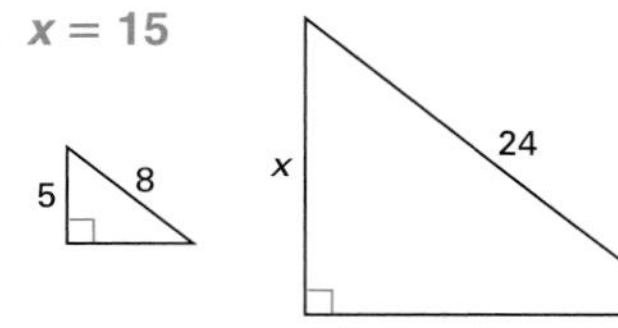

PROBLEM SOLVING 9-1

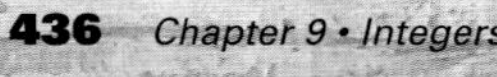

PROBLEM SOLVING

Name ______

Guided Problem Solving 9-1

GPS PROBLEM 32, STUDENT PAGE 436

The earth is covered with a rocky *crust*, which can be 25 miles thick. Underneath this is an 1800-mile-thick *mantle* of heavier rock. Below the mantle is a liquid *outer core*, about 1400 miles thick. The center of the earth is a solid *inner core*.

Use integers to describe the minimum and maximum depths of each region. (You will be able to give only the minimum depth of the inner core.)

— Understand —

1. How many layers will you need to describe? 4 layers.
2. Underline which layer will not have a maximum depth.

— Plan —

3. How can you find the minimum depth for each layer? The maximum depth? Minimum: add thicknesses above the given layer. Maximum: add minimum and thickness of given layer.

— Solve —

4. Use integers to describe the minimum and maximum depth of each region.
  a. Crust 0 miles, min.; −25 miles, max.
  b. Mantle −25 miles, min.; −1825 miles, max.
  c. Outer core −1825 miles, min.; −3225 miles, max.
  d. Inner core −3225 miles, min.; no max.

— Look Back —

5. What strategy might help you solve this problem? Draw a Diagram.

SOLVE ANOTHER PROBLEM

Jo made a deep dive in four stages. She dived 52 feet, then 37 feet lower, then 43 feet lower, and finally 24 feet lower. Use an integer to express her position after each dive.

−52 ft, −89 ft, −132 ft, −156 ft

ENRICHMENT

Name ______

Extend Your Thinking 9-1

Visual Thinking

An analogy is a statement that compares properties of two pairs of objects as in the following example.

Example: is to as is to

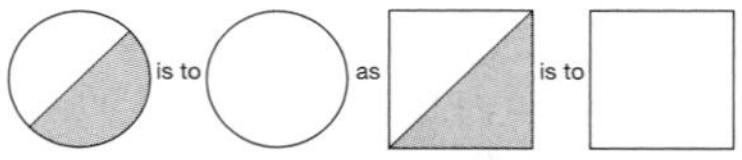

Circle the letter of the figure on the right that correctly completes the analogy on the left.

1. is to as is to   a. b. ⓒ d.
2. is to as is to   ⓐ b. c. d.
3. is to as is to   a. b. c. ⓓ
4. is to as is to   a. ⓑ c. d.
5. is to as is to   ⓐ b. c. d.

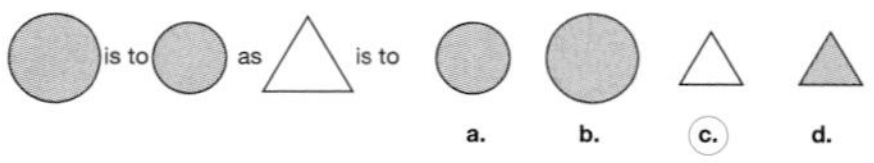

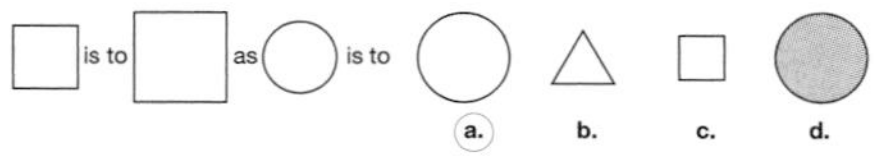

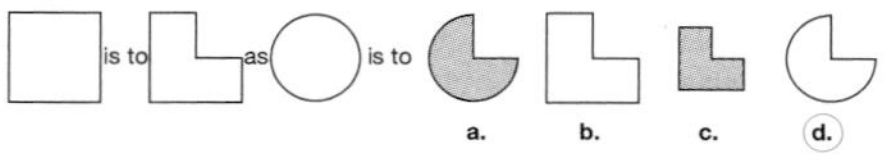

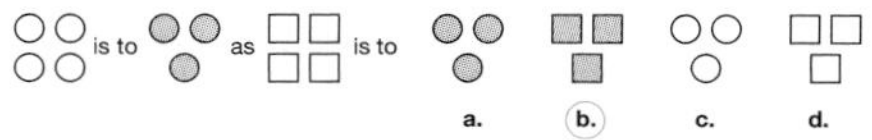

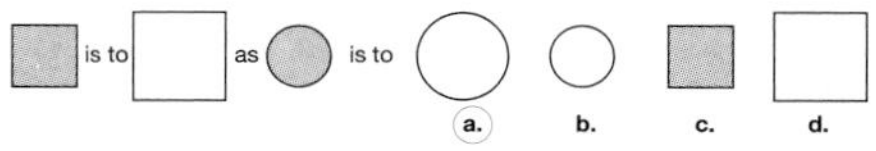

Comparing and Ordering Integers

9-2

▶ Lesson Link In the last lesson, you used integers to represent real-world quantities. Now you'll compare and order integers. ◀

You'll Learn ...

■ to compare and order integers

... How It's Used

Quality control workers compare positive and negative numbers to tell whether a product is within desired limits.

Explore Comparing and Ordering Integers

Forecast: Windy and Colder

Have you ever noticed that a cold day feels *colder* when the wind blows? For example, a 50 mi/hr wind makes a 35°F temperature feel like 0°F.

The *wind chill temperature* tells us how cold it feels. The chart shows actual and wind chill temperatures on a day in February, 1996.

City	Cody, WY	St. Paul, MN	Helena, MT	Idaho Falls, ID	Key West, FL
Temperature	–12°F	5°F	–16°F	0°F	73°F
Wind Chill Temperature	–25°F	–10°F	–30°F	–12°F	73°F

1. Which city had the higher actual temperature, Cody or St. Paul? How do you know?
2. Sketch a vertical thermometer and mark the ten temperatures on it.
3. Which temperature was the coldest? The warmest?
4. Which city had a *higher* wind chill temperature that day, Helena or Idaho Falls? Which temperature was farther from 0°? Explain.

Learn Comparing and Ordering Integers

The average January temperature in Chicago is -3°C. The average July temperature is 24°C. As any Chicagoan can tell you, a positive number is always greater than a negative number.

If two integers have different signs, it's easy to decide which is greater. However, it's more difficult to compare two negative integers.

MEETING INDIVIDUAL NEEDS

Resources

9-2 Practice
9-2 Reteaching
9-2 Problem Solving
9-2 Enrichment
9-2 Daily Transparency
Problem of the Day
Review
Quick Quiz
Teaching Tool Transparencies 2, 3, 5

Learning Modalities

Logical Ask students what is always true when comparing a positive number and a negative number. They should realize that they can write an inequality without considering the numerical part of the number because the positive number is naturally greater than the negative number.

Visual Students often have difficulty writing inequalities. Remind them that the symbols $<$ and $>$ each open to the greater number. As with all integer work, number lines are invaluable in helping students with comparisons.

Social Have students work in pairs to complete Steps 1–4 in **Explore**.

Challenge

Have students research typical temperatures in your area and prepare a report to present to the class.

Lesson Organizer

Objective

■ Compare and order integers.

NCTM Standards

■ 1–2, 4–6

▶ Review

Use $<$, $>$, or $=$ to compare each pair of numbers.

1. 505 ☐ 550 $<$
2. 10.9 ☐ 9.01 $>$
3. 0.053 ☐ 0.503 $<$
4. 403 ☐ 94 $>$
5. 3.5 ☐ 3.50 $=$

Available on Daily Transparency 9-2

1 Introduce

Explore

You may wish to use Teaching Tool Transparency 5: Number Lines with this lesson.

The Point
By comparing temperatures, students see that a number that is more negative than a second number is *less than* the second number. They also compare distances of positive and negative numbers from zero, reinforcing the concept of absolute value.

Ongoing Assessment
Have students note that for each city, the wind chill temperature is less than or equal to the actual temperature.

For Groups That Finish Early
Use your thermometer drawings to give the differences between the wind chill and actual temperatures for each city. Cody, 13°F; St. Paul, 15°F; Helena, 14°F; Idaho Falls, 12°F; Key West, 0°F

Answers for Explore on next page.

Follow Up
Have a volunteer draw and label a thermometer on the chalkboard to list the five cities' temperatures. Use this thermometer for discussion.

Answers for Explore

1. St. Paul; 5°F is above 0, while −12°F is below 0.
2. See page C2.
3. Coldest: −30°F; Warmest: 73°F
4. The wind chill temperature in Idaho Falls was closer to 0°F, so it was warmer; Helena's was farther from 0°F.

2 Teach

Learn

Alternate Examples

1. Write an inequality to tell which is less, −6 or −1.

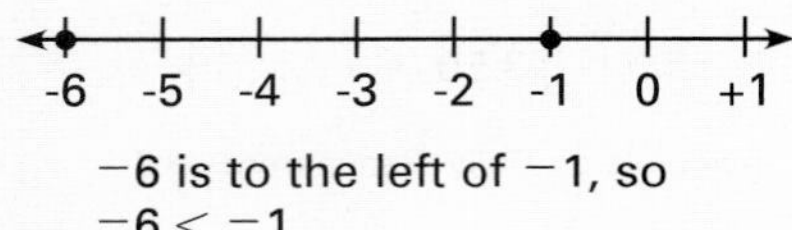

−6 is to the left of −1, so −6 < −1.

2. Order these lowest U.S. monthly temperatures from coldest to warmest:

February, −66°F
April, −36°F
June, 2°F
August, 10°F
October, −33°F
December, −59°F

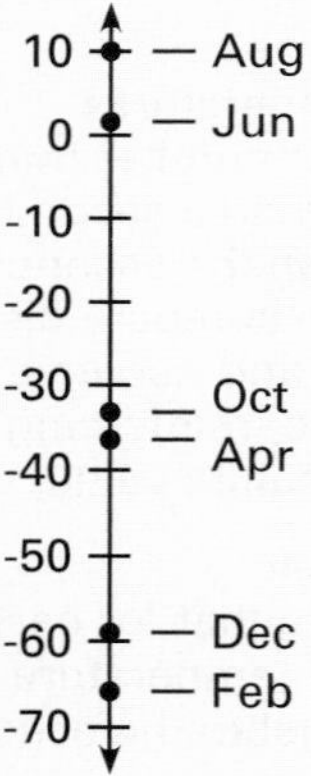

From coldest to warmest they are −66°F, −59°F, −36°F, −33°F, 2°F, and 10°F.

Remember
The symbol < means less than; > means greater than. [Previous course]

You can use a number line to compare integers.

On a horizontal number line, the farther *to the right* a number is, the greater it is.

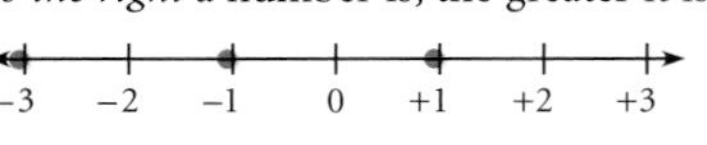

−1 is to the right of −3, so −1 > −3.

−1 is to the left of +1, so −1 < +1.

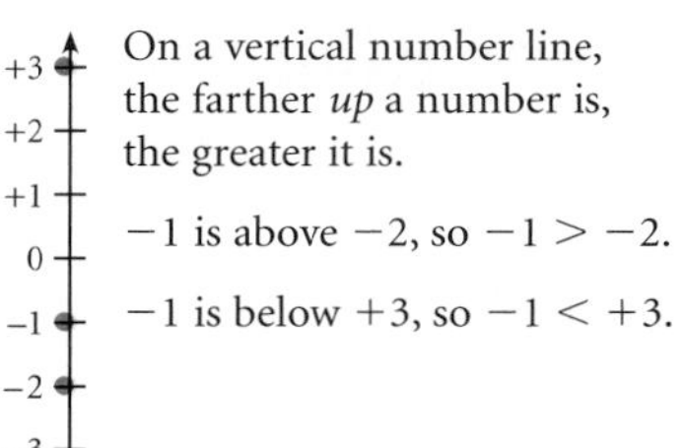

On a vertical number line, the farther *up* a number is, the greater it is.

−1 is above −2, so −1 > −2.

−1 is below +3, so −1 < +3.

On a number line, the farther to the left or farther down a number is, the *less* it is. So a negative number close to zero such as −2 is *greater* than −25,000.

Examples

1 Write an inequality to tell which is greater, −7 or −2.

−2 is to the right of −7, so −2 > −7.

2 Order the depths of these mines from deepest to least deep: Kolar, India, −8,604 ft; Western Deep, South Africa, −12,600 ft; Nova Lima, Brazil, −8,052; Boksburg, South Africa, −11,248 ft.

The number line shows these depths.

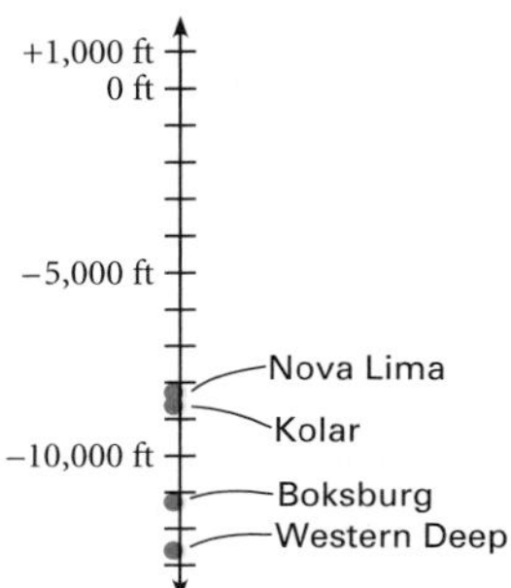

From deepest to least deep, the depths are −12,600 ft, −11,248 ft, −8,604 ft, and −8,052 ft.

Try It

a. Which is warmer, −67°F or 45°F? 45°F

b. Write an inequality to tell which number is greater, −22 or −1. −1 > −22

c. Order the depths of these Rocky Mountain caves from deepest to least deep: Papoose, −252 m; Sunray, −245 m; Silvertip, −313 m; Big Brush, −262 m. −313, −262, −252, −245

DID YOU KNOW?
Marble Bar, Australia, had 160 consecutive days where the temperature exceeded 100°F. Langdon, North Dakota, had 92 days in a row where the temperature dropped below freezing (0°C).

MATH EVERY DAY

Problem of the Day

In Holland an ice-skating race known as the *Elfstedentocht* is held each year. In 1954, a Dutch schoolteacher finished the 124-mile course in 7 hours, 35 minutes. What was his average speed in miles per hour? Round your answer to the nearest tenth. 16.4 mi/hr

Available on Daily Transparency 9-2

An Extension is provided in the transparency package.

Fact of the Day

The greatest change in temperature in one day is a drop of about 100 degrees, from 44°F to −56°F. It occurred in Browning, MT, on January 23–24, 1916.

Mental Math

Tell which is greater.

1. 562 or −563 562
2. −43 or 41 41
3. 3 or −399 3
4. −79 or −81 −79

Jacob and Winona were asked to compare January temperatures for four cities by ordering them from lowest to highest.

City	Albany, NY	Bismarck, ND	Duluth, MN	Fairbanks, AK
Average January Low Temperature	16°F	−2°F	0°F	−20°F

Jacob thinks ...

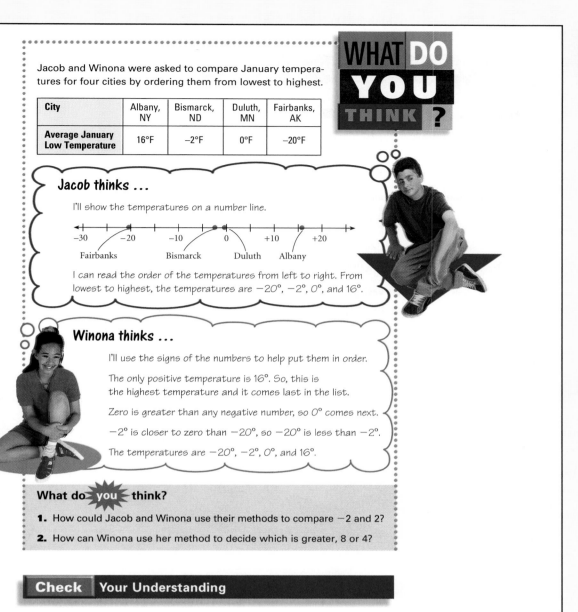

I'll show the temperatures on a number line.

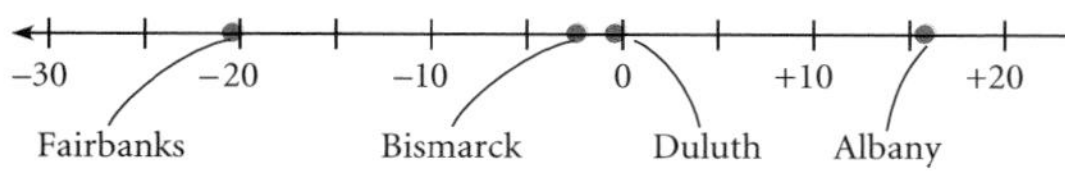

I can read the order of the temperatures from left to right. From lowest to highest, the temperatures are −20°, −2°, 0°, and 16°.

Winona thinks ...

I'll use the signs of the numbers to help put them in order.

The only positive temperature is 16°. So, this is the highest temperature and it comes last in the list.

Zero is greater than any negative number, so 0° comes next.

−2° is closer to zero than −20°, so −20° is less than −2°.

The temperatures are −20°, −2°, 0°, and 16°.

What do you think?

1. How could Jacob and Winona use their methods to compare −2 and 2?
2. How can Winona use her method to decide which is greater, 8 or 4?

Check Your Understanding

1. Explain why −5,000 is greater than −1,000,000.
2. What is the greatest negative integer?

Students see two methods for ordering a set of integers. The first involves plotting the integers on a number line for comparison, while the second employs using the signs of the integers and their positions in relation to zero.

Answers for What Do You Think?

1. The number line would show that 2 is farther to the right than −2, so 2° is higher; 2 is positive and −2 is negative, so 2° must be higher.
2. 8 is farther to the right than 4, so it is greater.

3 Practice and Assess

Check

On the chalkboard write ten or twelve pairs of integers and ask students to compare them using both *greater than* and *less than.*

Answers for Check Your Understanding

1. Possible answer: −5,000 is to the right of −1,000,000, so −5,000 is greater.
2. −1

MEETING MIDDLE SCHOOL CLASSROOM NEEDS

Tips from Middle School Teachers

I bring in newspaper stock-market reports and discuss with students the meanings of the negative and positive numbers. Then I have them use only the integer values to discuss inequalities. This helps them to realize that integers can be used in daily life.

Science Connection

Wind makes us feel colder because it carries away the air around us that our body heat has warmed, and it evaporates the moisture on our skin.

You might want to reproduce part or all of the following table of wind chill temperatures.

Wind Chill Temperatures

Wind speed (mph)	Thermometer reading (°F) 30	20	10	0	-10	-20	-30
5	27	19	7	-5	-15	-26	-36
10	16	3	-9	-22	-34	-46	-58
15	9	-5	-18	-31	-45	-58	-72
20	4	-10	-24	-39	-53	-67	-81
25	1	-15	-29	-44	-59	-74	-88
30	-2	-18	-33	-49	-64	-79	-93
35	-4	-20	-35	-52	-67	-82	-97
40	-5	-21	-37	-53	-69	-84	-100
45	-6	-22	-38	-54	-70	-85	-102

9-2 Exercises and Applications

Assignment Guide

- **Basic**
  1–23 odds, 24, 26–28, 31–35 odds
- **Average**
  2–24 evens, 25, 27, 28, 30–34 evens
- **Enriched**
  6–24 evens, 25–29, 30–34 evens

Exercise Notes

Exercises 17–18

Error Prevention Remind students to find the absolute values *before* comparing.

Exercise Answers

1. a.

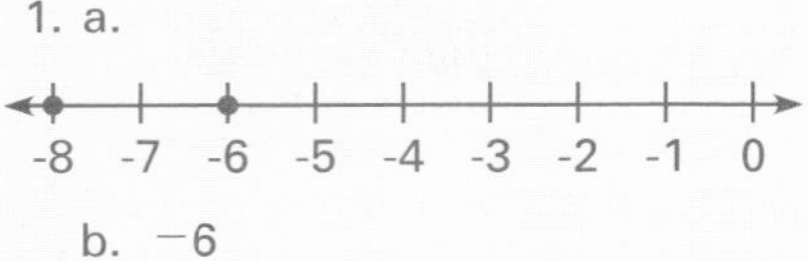

b. −6

Reteaching

Activity

Materials: Number line labeled −6 to 6, small container holding 2 yellow number cubes for positive integers and 2 red number cubes for negative integers

- Shake two number cubes out of the container, and write two sentences, if possible, comparing the two numbers shown.
- If you have trouble writing the sentences, place the number cubes in the correct positions on your number line to help you. Remember, yellow cubes represent positive integers and red cubes represent negative integers.
- Replace the cubes and repeat the comparisons. How many sentences will you write if the numbers shown are the same? 1

9-2 Exercises and Applications

Practice and Apply

1. **Getting Started** Follow these steps to determine which number is greater, −6 or −8.
   a. Draw a number line. Locate −6 and −8.
   b. Determine which number is farther to the right. This is the greater number.

Number Sense Using the number line, write an inequality to tell which number is greater.

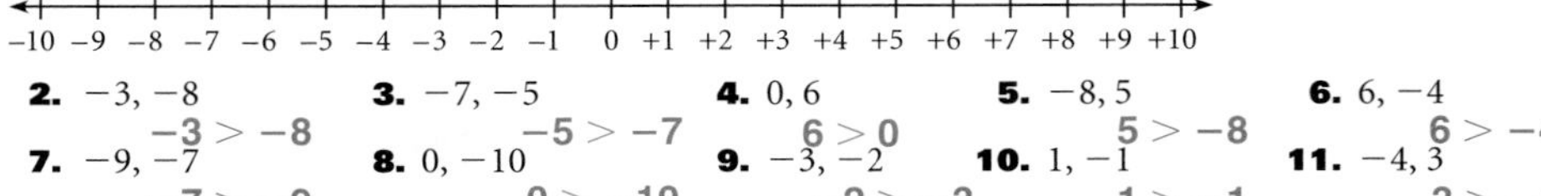

2. −3, −8   −3 > −8
3. −7, −5   −5 > −7
4. 0, 6   6 > 0
5. −8, 5   5 > −8
6. 6, −4   6 > −4
7. −9, −7   −7 > −9
8. 0, −10   0 > −10
9. −3, −2   −2 > −3
10. 1, −1   1 > −1
11. −4, 3   3 > −4

Use >, <, or = to compare each pair of numbers.

12. −4 [<] 5
13. −4 [<] 0
14. −34 [<] −25
15. −679 [>] −769
16. −901 [>] −910
17. |5| [=] |−5|
18. |−56| [<] |−61|
19. −100 [>] −104

Order each set of numbers from greatest to least.

20. −2°, 12°, 54°, 0°, −18°, −5°   54°, 12°, 0°, −2°, −5°, −18°
21. $12, −$7, $11, $0, −$2, −$5, $8 $12, $11, $8, $0, −$2, −$5, −$7
22. 32°, −24°, −10°, 0°, 212°   212°, 32°, 0°, −10°, −24°
23. −3551, −3155, −3515, −3151, −3555   −3151, −3155, −3515, −3551, −3555
24. **Science** The map shows the depth below sea level of several boreholes. −11,357, −31,911, −25,600, −2,000
    a. Represent each depth as an integer.
    b. Order the integers in **a** from least to greatest. −31,911, −25,600, −11,357, −2,000

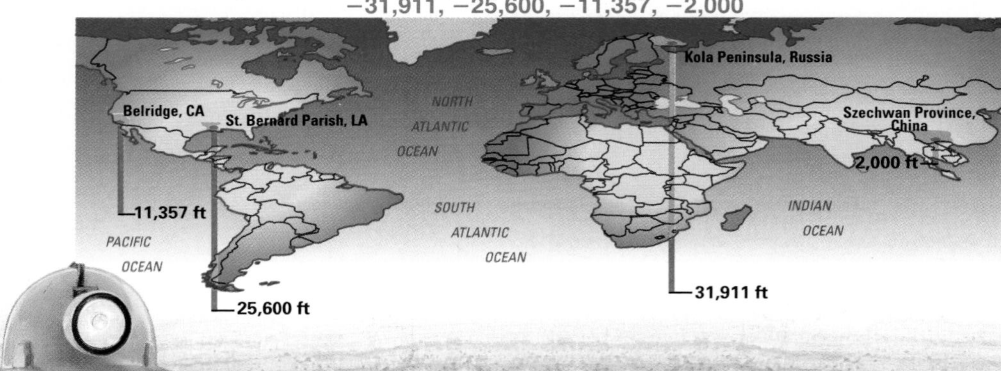

PRACTICE 9-2

PRACTICE

Name ____________

Practice 9-2

Comparing and Ordering Integers

Using the number line, write an inequality to tell which number is greater.

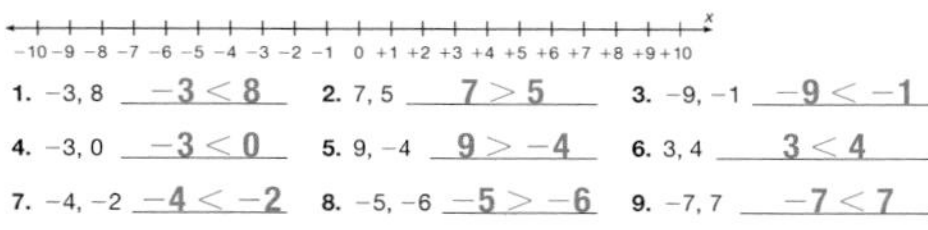

1. −3, 8   −3 < 8
2. 7, 5   7 > 5
3. −9, −1   −9 < −1
4. −3, 0   −3 < 0
5. 9, −4   9 > −4
6. 3, 4   3 < 4
7. −4, −2   −4 < −2
8. −5, −6   −5 > −6
9. −7, 7   −7 < 7

Use >, <, or = to compare each pair of numbers.

10. −12 (<) 17
11. −64 (<) −46
12. 367 (>) −376
13. −23 (>) −32
14. −123 (>) −321
15. 14 (>) −15
16. 37 (<) 73
17. 265 (>) −265
18. 412 (<) 421
19. −98 (<) −89
20. −21 (<) 21
21. −482 (<) −284
22. |−65| (>) |64|
23. |15| (>) |−14|
24. |18| (=) |−18|
25. |−84| (<) |−86|

Order each set of numbers from greatest to least.

26. −42, 24, 58, −16, 44, −46   58, 44, 24, −16, −42, −46
27. −$8, $11, −$12, $7, −$10, $9 $11, $9, $7, −$8, −$10, −$12
28. 0°, 6°, −16°, −26°, −36°, 46°   46°, 6°, 0°, −16°, −26°, −36°
29. The chart shows the daily average minimum temperatures for fall and winter in McGrath, Alaska.
    a. Complete the table by representing each temperatura as an integer.

Month	Ave. Min. Temp. (°F)	Integer Temp. (°F)
October	18 above zero	18
November	4 below zero	−4
December	15 below zero	−15
January	18 below zero	−18
February	14 below zero	−14
March	3 below zero	−3

b. Order the integers in **a** from least to greatest.

−18, −15, −14, −4, −3, 18

RETEACHING

Name ____________

Alternative Lesson 9-2

Comparing and Ordering Integers

You can use a number line to compare integers. For any two integers on the number line, the one farther to the right is greater and the one farther to the left is less.

Example 1

Use >, <, or = to compare each pair of numbers.

a. −3 □ 2   b. −4 □ −7

Find both numbers on the number line.   Find both numbers on the number line.

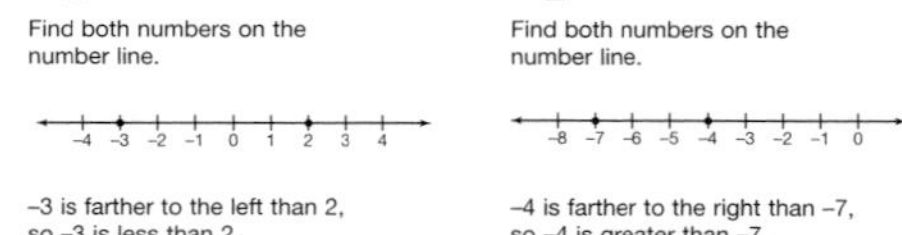

−3 is farther to the left than 2, so −3 is less than 2.

−3 < 2.

−4 is farther to the right than −7, so −4 is greater than −7.

−4 > −7

Try It Use >, <, or = to compare each pair of numbers. You can use a number line to help you.

a. −7 [<] 7   b. 3 [<] 5   c. −8 [<] −5   d. 4 [>] −9

Example 2

Order 8, −4, 0, −7, 6, −5 in order from least to greatest.

Place a point on the number line for each number.
Then list the numbers in order beginning with the number on the left.

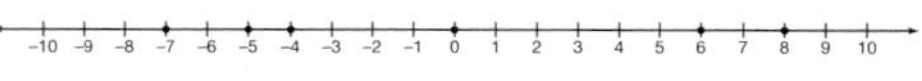

The integers in order from least to greatest are: −7, −5, −4, 0, 6, 8.

Try It Order each set of numbers from least to greatest. You can use a number line to help you.

e. −1, 4, 2, −8, 7, 0   −8, −1, 0, 2, 4, 7
f. 5, −9, 3, 1, −3, −5   −9, −5, −3, 1, 3, 5
g. −6, −8, 2, 5, −7, −1   −8, −7, −6, −1, 2, 5
h. −6, 4, −9, 3, 0, −1   −9, −6, −1, 0, 3, 4

25. **Logic** Fill in the blanks with *sometimes, always,* or *never.*

a. A positive integer is _____ greater than a negative integer. Always

b. The absolute value of a positive integer is _____ greater than the absolute value of a negative integer. Sometimes

c. If two integers are positive, the one closer to zero is _____ greater. Never

d. Zero is _____ greater than any negative integer. Always

26. **Problem Solving** The table shows minimum estimated surface temperatures for several planets. Order the temperatures from greatest to least.
890°F, −130°F, −190°F, −240°F, −300°F, −390°F

Planet	Mercury	Venus	Earth	Mars	Jupiter	Pluto
Temperature	−300°F	890°F	−130°F	−190°F	−240°F	−390°F

27. **Test Prep** Determine which statement is true. B

Ⓐ −13 > −4 Ⓑ −18 < −12 Ⓒ −2 > 0 Ⓓ −14 < −16

Problem Solving and Reasoning

28. **Choose a Strategy** The table shows elevations of the *lowest* points in five states. Write each as an integer, then order from least to greatest.
0, −282, 3350, −8, 3099; −282, −8, 0, 3099, 3350

State	Alabama	California	Colorado	Louisiana	Wyoming
Lowest Point	Sea level	282 ft below sea level	3350 ft	8 ft below sea level	3099 ft

Problem Solving STRATEGIES
- Look for a Pattern
- Make an Organized List
- Make a Table
- Guess and Check
- Work Backward
- Use Logical Reasoning
- Draw a Diagram
- Solve a Simpler Problem

29. **Communicate** Changes in stock prices are listed using positive and negative numbers. For instance, "$-1\frac{1}{2}$" means that a share lost \$1.50 in value. Explain what each price change means.

a. $-2\frac{3}{4}$ Lost \$2.75 **b.** $-3\frac{1}{4}$ Lost \$3.25 **c.** $+1\frac{1}{4}$ Gained \$1.25 **d.** -4 Lost \$4.00

Mixed Review

Express each rate as a unit rate. *[Lesson 6-2]*

30. 360 miles on 12 gallons 30 miles per gallon

31. 30 pages in 60 minutes A half a page per minute

32. 24 sets of markers for 3 classrooms 8 sets per classroom

33. 10 hours of homework in 5 days 2 hours per day

Find the perimeter and area of each figure. *[Lesson 7-10]*

34. Scale factor 1.5

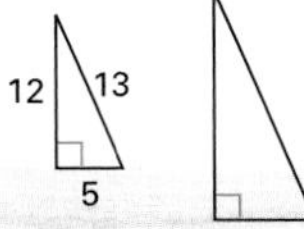

35. Scale factor 3

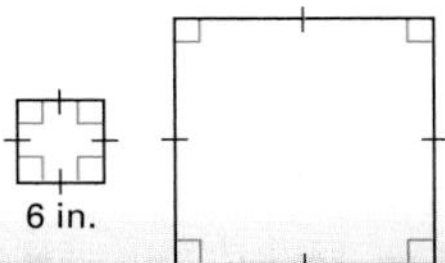

PROBLEM SOLVING 9-2

Exercise Notes

Exercise 27

Test Prep In all but the correct choice, B, the comparisons are correct for the *absolute values* of the integers.

Exercise 28

Problem Solving Tip You may wish to use Teaching Tool Transparencies 2 and 3: Guided Problem Solving, pages 1–2.

Exercises 34–35

Error Prevention You may have to remind students of the definition of *scale factor.*

Exercise Answers

34. Perimeter of first: 30; Area of first: 30; Perimeter of second: 45; Area of second: 67.5.

35. Perimeter of first: 24; Area of first: 36; Perimeter of second: 72; Area of second: 324.

Alternate Assessment

Self Assessment Ask each student to evaluate his or her ability to compare and order integers. They might include answers to questions like the following: How is comparing and ordering integers similar to comparing and ordering whole numbers? How is it different?

Quick Quiz

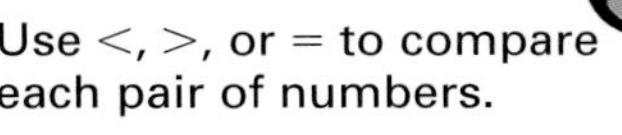

Use <, >, or = to compare each pair of numbers.

1. −18 ☐ −81 >
2. −342 ☐ 0 <
3. −55 ☐ 44 <
4. −29 ☐ −30 >
5. Order −5, 12, −13, 6, and −10 from least to greatest. −13, −10, −5, 6, 12

Available on Daily Transparency 9-2

PROBLEM SOLVING

Name ______________________ **Guided Problem Solving 9-2**

GPS PROBLEM 24, STUDENT PAGE 440

The chart shows the depth below sea level of several boreholes.

a. Represent each depth as an integer.

b. Order the integers in part a from least to greatest.

Location	Depth
Belridge, California	11,357 ft
Kola Peninsula, Russia	31,911 ft
St. Bernard Parish, Louisiana	25,600 ft
Szechwan Province, China	2,000 ft

— Understand —

1. Underline what you are asked to do. Possible answers: Items 3, 7.

— Plan —

2. Which depths can be represented by a negative integer?
All, because all depths are *below* sea level.

3. How can you tell which of two negative integers is less?
Use a number line to compare.

— Solve —

4. Write the integers to represent each depth. California, −11,357; Russia, −31,911; Louisiana, −25,600; China, −2,000

5. Mark each integer on the number line.

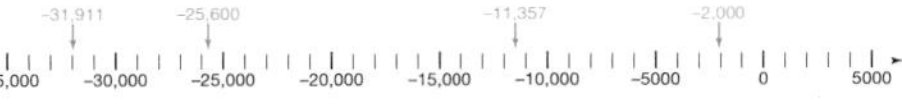

6. Write the integers in order from least to greatest.
−31,911, −25,600, −11,357, −2,000

— Look Back —

7. How could you order the negative integers without using a number line?
Order absolute values from greatest to least.

SOLVE ANOTHER PROBLEM

The chart shows the depth below sea level of several locations. Order the integers from least to greatest.
−1312, −512, −282, −131

Location	Depth
Dead Sea	1312 ft
Valdes Peninsula	131 ft
Death Valley	282 ft
Lake Assal	512 ft

ENRICHMENT

Name ______________________ **Extend Your Thinking 9-2**

Critical Thinking

You can use the same rules to compare and order positive and negative fractions and decimals that you learned when comparing and ordering integers on the number line. Remember:

> On a number line, the farther to the right an integer is, the greater it is. The farther to the left an integer is, the less it is.

Beth and Leroy used a number line to order $\frac{1}{2}$, $-\frac{1}{8}$, and −0.75 from least to greatest.

Beth's way	Leroy's way
She changed −0.75 to a fraction ($-0.75 = -\frac{75}{100} = -\frac{3}{4}$). Then she located fractions on a number line.	He changed $\frac{1}{2}$ and $-\frac{1}{8}$ to decimals ($\frac{1}{2} = 0.5$ and $-\frac{1}{8} = -0.125$). Then he the located the decimals on a number line.
Number line: $-\frac{7}{8}$ … $\frac{7}{8}$, marked at $-\frac{3}{4}$, $-\frac{1}{8}$, $\frac{1}{2}$	Number line: −0.75 … 0.75, marked at −0.75, −0.125, 0.5
She listed the fractions from left to right to order them from least to greatest and changed $-\frac{3}{4}$ back to −0.75.	He listed the decimals from left to right to order them from least to greatest and changed −0.125 and 0.5 back to fractions.
$-\frac{3}{4}, -\frac{1}{8}, \frac{1}{2}$ ↓ ↓ ↓ $-0.75, -\frac{1}{8}, \frac{1}{2}$	−0.75, −0.125, 0.5 ↓ ↓ ↓ $-0.75, -\frac{1}{8}, \frac{1}{2}$

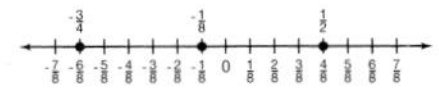

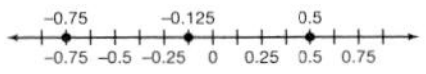

1. Choose either Beth's or Leroy's way to order each set of numbers from least to greatest. Draw a number line if necessary.

a. $0.25, -\frac{1}{2}, -\frac{5}{8}$ $-\frac{5}{8}, -\frac{1}{2}, 0.25$

b. $\frac{1}{3}, 0.7, -\frac{5}{6}$ $-\frac{5}{6}, \frac{1}{3}, 0.7$

c. $\frac{1}{4}, -0.625, -\frac{5}{12}$ $-0.625, -\frac{5}{12}, \frac{1}{4}$

d. $0.12, -0.12, -0.35, \frac{17}{31}$ $-0.35, -0.12, 0.12, \frac{17}{31}$

e. $-\frac{25}{41}, \frac{13}{50}, -\frac{14}{22}, -0.516$ $-\frac{14}{22}, -\frac{25}{41}, -0.516, \frac{13}{50}$

2. In which exercises did you use Beth's way? Leroy's way? Explain.
Possible answer: Beth's–first three, the fractions can easily be shown on a number line. Leroy's–others, the fractions are not as easily shown on a number line.

9-3 Lesson Organizer

Objective

- Graph points on a coordinate plane.

Vocabulary

- Coordinate system, *x*-*y* coordinate plane, *x*-axis, *y*-axis, origin, quadrants, ordered pair, *x*-coordinate, *y*-coordinate

Materials

- Explore: Tracing paper, ruler

NCTM Standards

- 1–6, 8, 10, 12

Review

Make a scatterplot of the data.

Age (years)	5	10	15	20	25
Shoe size	5	4	7	8	8

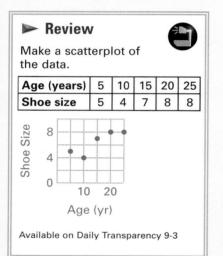

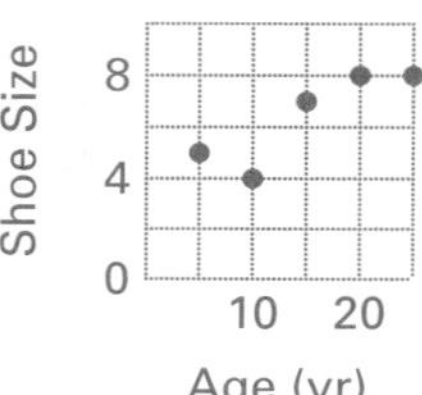

Available on Daily Transparency 9-3

1 Introduce

Explore

You may wish to use Lesson Enhancement Transparency 40 with **Explore**. Teaching Tool Transparency 8: Coordinate Grids may also be used with this lesson.

The Point
Students use negative coordinates to locate a point and also see that the coordinates of a point on a grid depend on the location of the origin.

Ongoing Assessment
Check that students can identify the negative values for the positions of the borehole on their grids.

9-3 The Coordinate Plane

You'll Learn ...

- to graph points on a coordinate plane

... How It's Used

Archaeologists use grids to record the locations of the artifacts they find at a dig site.

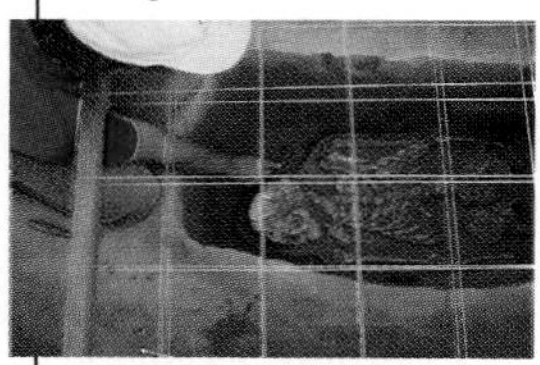

Vocabulary

coordinate system
x-*y* coordinate plane
x-axis
y-axis
origin
quadrants
ordered pair
x-coordinate
y-coordinate

▶ Lesson Link You've made scatterplots by plotting points with positive coordinates. Now you'll plot points with negative coordinates. ◀

Explore The Coordinate Plane

X Marks the Spot

Materials: Tracing paper, Ruler

An oil company plans to drill a borehole near Odessa, Texas. It needs to give a precise description of its location.

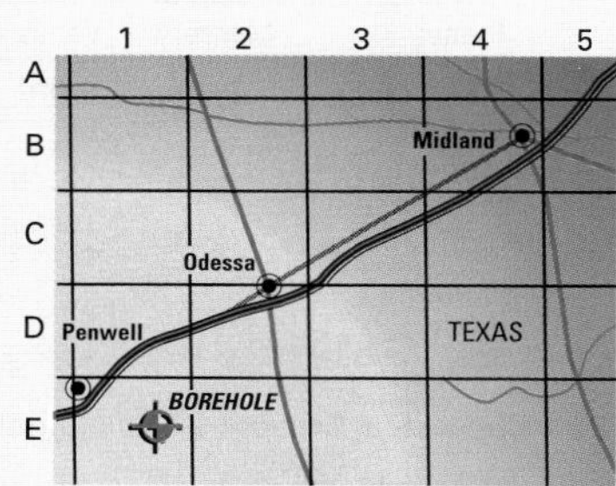

1. Use the letters and numbers on the map to describe Midland's location.
2. Now describe the location of the borehole.
   a. Draw intersecting vertical and horizontal number lines on your tracing paper. Let the intersection point be the origin of both lines.
   b. Place the tracing paper so the origin is over Midland. Be sure your vertical number line points north.
   c. Use the integers on your lines to describe the location of the borehole. Explain how you found your answer.
3. Move your tracing paper so the origin is over Odessa. What is the location of the borehole now?

Learn The Coordinate Plane

Maps often use a grid of numbers and letters to help locate landmarks. The Parliament Building in Victoria, British Columbia, is located at R38 on the map.

MEETING INDIVIDUAL NEEDS

Resources

- 9-3 Practice
- 9-3 Reteaching
- 9-3 Problem Solving
- 9-3 Enrichment
- 9-3 Daily Transparency
  - Problem of the Day
  - Review
  - Quick Quiz
- Teaching Tool Transparency 8
- Lesson Enhancement Transparencies 40–42
- Chapter 9 Project Master

Wide World of Mathematics
Algebra: Living in 64 Squares

Learning Modalities

Kinesthetic If the desks in your classroom are arranged in rows and columns, choose a central location as the origin of a coordinate grid. Designate a row and a column as the two axes. Then have students identify their positions with coordinates or ask which student's seat is identified by a set of coordinates.

Visual Bring in to class a variety of street, county, and state maps. Have students identify locations of specific landmarks or cities. Then give locations and have students supply landmarks and cities for them.

Challenge

Have students draw a figure or a picture on a coordinate grid and then list the coordinates of the vertices so that their classmates can connect them to form the same figure.

You can locate points with a similar **coordinate system** of intersecting horizontal and vertical number lines.

The ***x-y* coordinate plane** is based on two number lines. The horizontal line is the ***x*-axis** and the vertical line is the ***y*-axis**. They intersect at the **origin** of the coordinate plane.

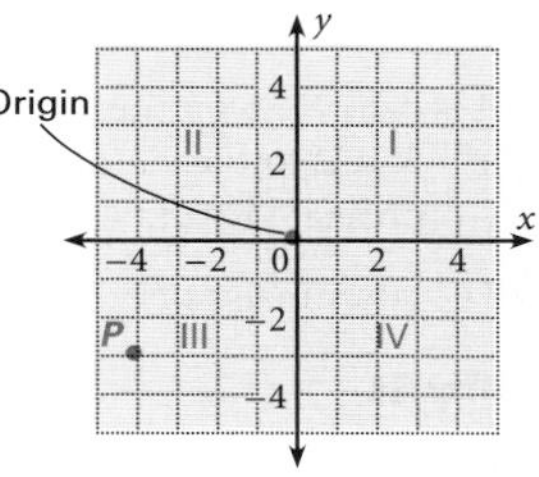

The axes divide the plane into four **quadrants**, numbered I, II, III, and IV. Point *P* is in quadrant III.

The axes are not in any quadrant.

Any point can be described by an **ordered pair**, such as $(-3, 5)$. The first number is the ***x*-coordinate**. It tells how far to the left or right of the origin the point is, as measured along the *x*-axis. The ***y*-coordinate** tells how far up or down the point is, as measured along the *y*-axis. The origin itself is at $(0, 0)$.

Study TIP

You can use alphabetical order to remember the directions of the axes. *Horizontal* (*x*) comes before *vertical* (*y*).

Examples

Plot each point on a coordinate plane.

1 $(4, -3)$

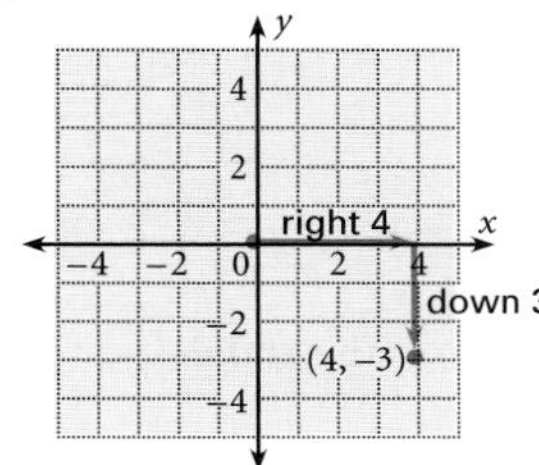

Start at the origin. Move 4 units to the right on the *x*-axis. Then move 3 units down (parallel to the *y*-axis). Plot the point.

2 $(-400, 0)$

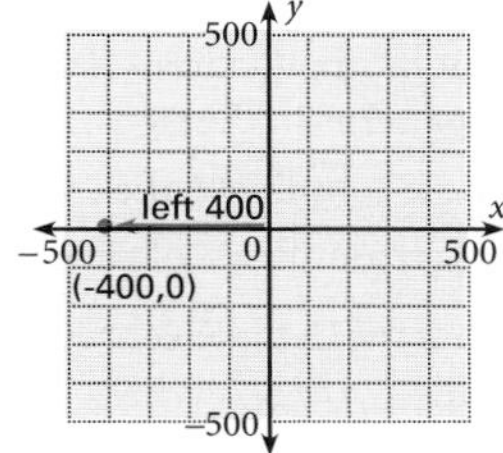

Start at the origin. Move 400 units to the left on the *x*-axis. Plot the point. (Since the *y*-coordinate is 0, do not move up or down.)

Test Prep

When you graph points on a coordinate plane, remember that *x* comes before *y*, so the *x*-coordinate is the first of the two numbers in the ordered pair.

Try It

Plot each point on the same coordinate plane.

a. $(-3, 4)$ **b.** $(4, -3)$ **c.** $(2, 0)$ **d.** $(0, -5)$

e–h. Name the quadrant or axis that contains each point in **a–d**.

e. II f. IV g. *x*-axis h. *y*-axis

MATH EVERY DAY

Problem of the Day

Sofia is older than Pablo, who is older than Quincy. Milton is younger than Ralph, but older than Sofia. Each of these people wrote his or her name on a card and dropped it into a hat. What are the chances of picking the oldest of the five people if a name is drawn without looking? One out of five. It is not necessary to find out who is oldest.

Available on Daily Transparency 9-3

An Extension is provided in the transparency package.

Fact of the Day

Oil wells were first dug in Germany between 1857 and 1859, but the oil industry started in 1859 when Edwin L. Drake drilled a well near Titusville, PA.

Mental Math

Tell in which quadrant or on which axis each point is located.

1. $(-5, 0)$ *x*-axis
2. $(-4, 3)$ quadrant II
3. $(2, -6)$ quadrant IV
4. $(0, -7)$ *y*-axis

For Groups That Finish Early

Place the origin of your number lines over Penwell and describe the location of the borehole. The horizontal component should be positive and the vertical component negative.

Answers for Explore

1. B4

2–3. Answers may vary; Both horizontal and vertical components should be negative.

2 Teach

Learn

You may wish to use Lesson Enhancement Transparencies 41 and 42 with **Learn.**

Alternate Examples

Plot each point.

1. $(-4, 2)$

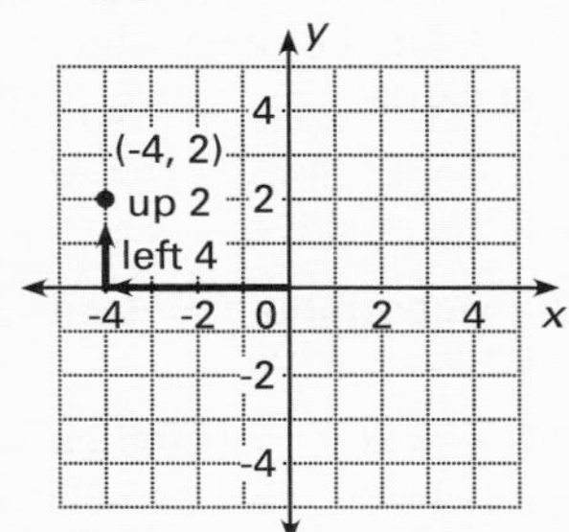

Start at the origin. Move 4 units to the left and 2 units up. Plot the point.

2. $(0, -30)$

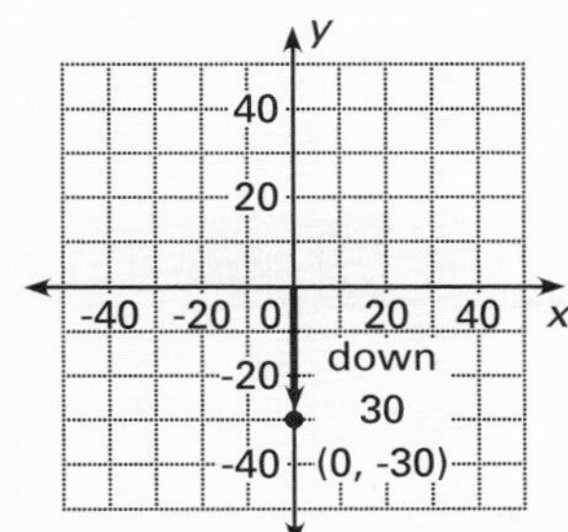

Start at the origin. Do not move right or left. Move 30 units down. Plot the point.

Answers for Try It

a–d.

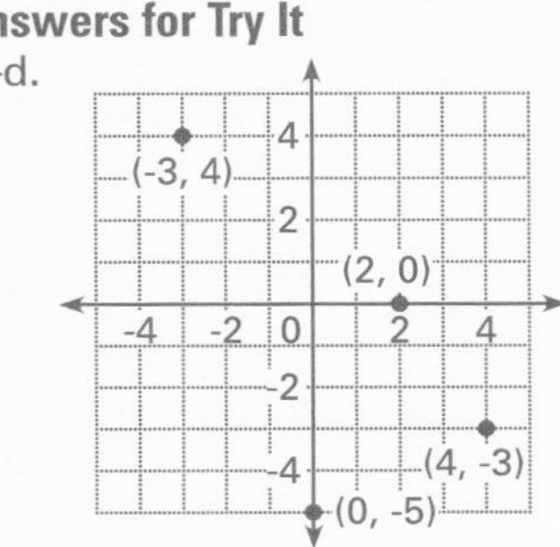

Alternate Examples

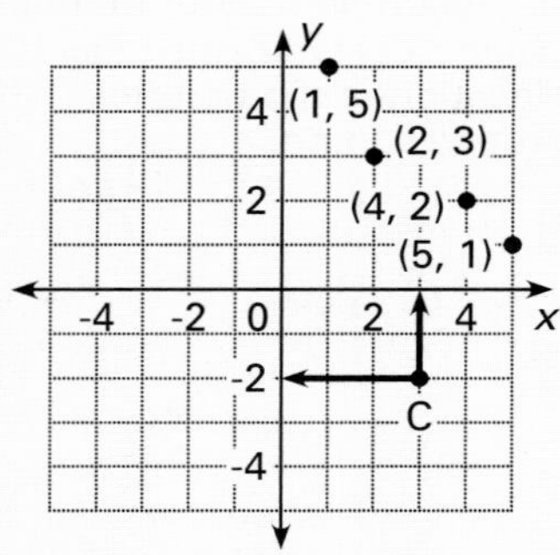

3. Find the coordinates of point C on the grid above.

   C is below 3 on the x-axis, so its x-coordinate is 3. C is to the right of −2 on the y-axis, so its y-coordinate is −2.

   The coordinates of point *C* are (3, −2)

4. Look at the above grid. What are the signs of the *x*- and *y*-coordinates of points in quadrant I?

   Four points in quadrant I are plotted. Notice these patterns in the signs:

   - The *x*-coordinate of each point is positive.
   - The *y*-coordinate of each point is positive.
   - The *x*- and *y*-coordinates of any point in quadrant I are positive.

Answers for Try It, Example 3
B(−4, 1), *C*(1, 3), *D*(0, −3), *E*(2, −2)

3 Practice and Assess

Check

Answers for Check Your Understanding

1. 0; 0
2. There has to be both an *x*-coordinate and a *y*-coordinate.
3. No; (−4, 5) is in quadrant II, and (5, −4) is in quadrant IV.

History Link

The *x*-*y* coordinate plane is known as the *Cartesian* coordinate system. This name honors its originator, the French philosopher and mathematician René Descartes.

Example 3

Find the coordinates of point *A*.

A is below −5 on the *x*-axis, so its *x*-coordinate is −5. *A* is to the left of −4 on the *y*-axis, so its *y*-coordinate is −4.

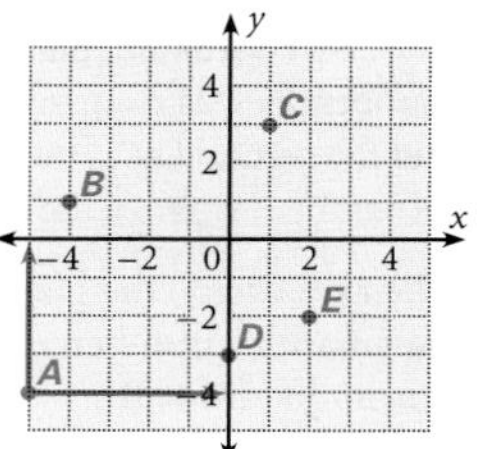

The coordinates of point *A* are (−5, −4).

Try It

Using the grid for Example 3, find the coordinates of points *B*, *C*, *D*, and *E*.

You can tell which quadrant a point is in from the signs of its *x*- and *y*-coordinates. For example, quadrant I contains all points that are to the right of and above the origin. So any point whose coordinates are both positive must be in quadrant I.

Study TIP

Remember that quadrants with positive *x*-values are to the right of the origin, and those with positive *y*-values are above the origin.

Example 4

What are the signs of the *x*- and *y*-coordinates of points in quadrant II?

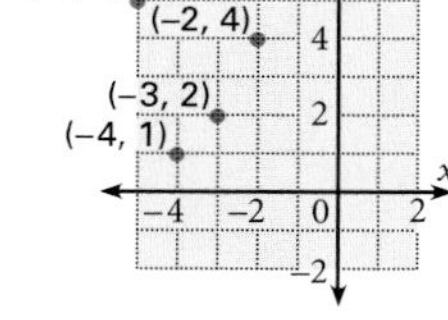

Four points in quadrant II are plotted. Notice these patterns in the signs:

- The *x*-coordinate of each point is negative.
- The *y*-coordinate of each point is positive.

In quadrant II, the *x*-coordinate of any point is negative and the *y*-coordinate is positive.

Try It

What are the signs of the *x*- and *y*-coordinates of points in quadrant III?
***x*-coordinates negative; *y*-coordinates negative**

Check Your Understanding

1. What is the *x*-coordinate of a point on the *y*-axis? What is the *y*-coordinate of a point on the *x*-axis?
2. On a number line, the coordinate of the origin is 0. Why does the origin on a coordinate plane have coordinates (0, 0)?
3. Is the point (−4, 5) the same as the point (5, −4)? Explain.

MEETING MIDDLE SCHOOL CLASSROOM NEEDS

Tips from Middle School Teachers

I have students look in textbooks from other courses or in newspapers and magazines for examples of 4-quadrant graphs. I then display the graphs in class.

I point out to students that quadrants I, II, III, and IV are labeled in a counterclockwise direction starting with I in the upper right quadrant of the coordinate plane.

Team Teaching

Ask the social studies teachers to discuss with students the times in which Descartes lived, with references to Sir Isaac Newton and Galileo.

History Connection

René Descartes, who originated the Cartesian coordinate system, lived from 1596 to 1650. He is often called the founder of modern philosophy.

9-3 Exercises and Applications

Practice and Apply

1. **Getting Started** Follow these steps to plot the point $(-3, -5)$.
   a. Draw and label a horizontal x-axis and a vertical y-axis.
   b. Since the x-coordinate is negative, move 3 units *to the left* on the x-axis.
   c. Since the y-coordinate is negative, move 5 spaces *down,* parallel to the y-axis.
   d. Plot the point.

Find the coordinates of each point.

2. A **(4, 3)** 3. B **(0, 0)** 4. C **(−3, −5)** 5. D **(−2, 0)** 6. E **(−4, 2)** 7. F **(3, −1)**

8. **Patterns** What are the signs of the x- and y-coordinates of points in quadrant IV?
   x-coordinate is positive and y-coordinate is negative

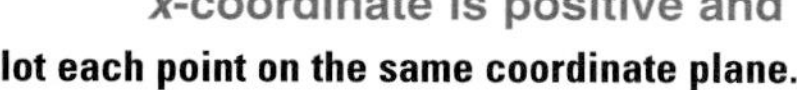

Plot each point on the same coordinate plane.

9. $(4, 4)$ 10. $(-2, 0)$ 11. $(3, -1)$ 12. $(-1, -5)$ 13. $(0, -3)$

Plot each point on the same coordinate plane.

14. $(16, -6)$ 15. $(20, 14)$ 16. $(-5, 10)$ 17. $(-11, 9)$ 18. $(-14, -12)$

19. **Industry** The depth of a geologic formation is not always the same. Two hundred feet from point A, the formation shown is 100 feet deep. It is 200 feet deep at a distance of 500 feet from A.
   GPS
   a. Use two ordered pairs to describe this data. Let the x-coordinate of each point be the distance from A and the y-coordinate be the depth of the formation. **(200, −100) (500, −200)**
   b. Plot these ordered pairs on a coordinate plane. Choose a scale that fits the data.

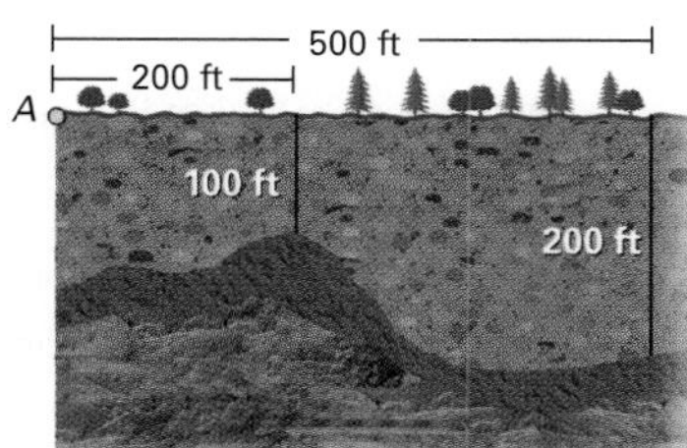

20. **Geometry** Draw a trapezoid on a coordinate plane so that each of its vertices is in a different quadrant. Label the coordinates of each point.

Logic Name the quadrant that contains each point.

21. $(7, -3)$ **IV** 22. $(-4, -9)$ **III** 23. $(6, 3)$ **I** 24. $(-5, 8)$ **II** 25. $(-2, -2)$ **III**
26. $(17, 26)$ **I** 27. $(40, -60)$ **IV** 28. $(-324, 119)$ **II** 29. $(404, 15)$ **I** 30. $(-628, -705)$ **III**

PRACTICE 9-3

PRACTICE

Name ______________

Practice 9-3

The Coordinate Plane

Find the coordinates of each point.

1. S **(1, −5)** 2. T **(4, 0)**
3. U **(2, 3)** 4. V **(−3, 2)**
5. W **(0, −3)** 6. X **(5, −4)**
7. Y **(−4, −1)** 8. Z **(−4, 4)**

Plot each point on the same coordinate plane.

9. (2, −4) 10. (0, 4)
11. (−3, 2) 12. (0, 0)
13. (−2, 0) 14. (−1, −3)
15. (5, 3) 16. (4, −1)

Plot each point on the same coordinate plane.

17. (8, 10) 18. (−14, 6)
19. (0, −12) 20. (2, −16)
21. (−5, 16) 22. (−12, −14)
23. (−18, −4) 24. (10, −13)

Name the quadrant or axis that contains each point.

25. (7, −12) **IV** 26. (16, 21) **I** 27. (−83, 12) **II** 28. (−61, −35) **III**
29. (−31, 24) **II** 30. (0, 3) **y-axis** 31. (−18, −25) **III** 32. (47, −38) **IV**
33. (16, −18) **IV** 34. (−7, 23) **II** 35. (−7, 0) **x-axis** 36. (17, 35) **I**

37. Plot the points (2, −2), (3, 4), (−1, 2), and (−2, −4) on the coordinate plane. Connect the points, in order, to form a polygon. What kind of polygon is formed? Be as specific as possible.
   Parallelogram

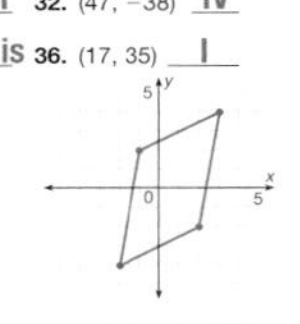

RETEACHING

Name ______________

Alternative Lesson 9-3

The Coordinate Plane

The ***x-y* coordinate plane** is based on two number lines. The horizontal line is the ***x*-axis**, and the vertical line is the ***y*-axis.** They intersect at the zero point on each number line. This point is called the **origin**. The axes divide the plane into four **quadrants.**

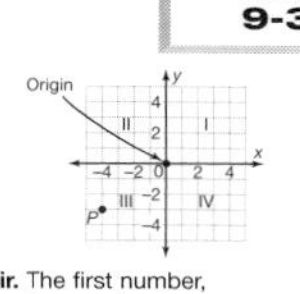

Any point, P, can be described by an **ordered pair.** The first number, the ***x*-coordinate**, tells how far to the left (for a negative number) or right (for a positive number) of the origin the point is. The ***y*-coordinate** tells how far up (for a positive number) or down (for a negative number) the point is. The origin is always labeled (0, 0).

Example 1

Plot point A (–3, 4).

Move left 3 units. Move up 4 units.
(–3, 4)

Example 2

Find the coordinates of point B.

Point B is located 5 units to the left of the origin (–5 on the x-axis) and 3 units down (–3 on the y-axis).

So, the coordinates of point B are (–5, –3).

Try It Plot each point on the coordinate plane.

a. K (1, 4) b. L (–2, 3)
c. M (0, –4) d. N (–4, –5)

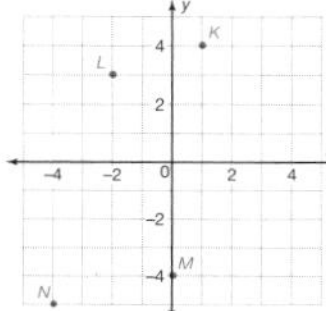

Describe in words each point's position. Then give its coordinates.

e. C **3 units right; 5 units up; (3, 5)**
f. D **4 units left; 2 units down; (–4, –2)**

9-3 Exercises and Applications

Assignment Guide

- **Basic**
  1–31 odds, 32, 35–43 odds
- **Average**
  2–18 evens, 19, 20–30 evens, 31–33, 36–44 evens
- **Enriched**
  2–18 evens, 19–25, 31–34, 36–44 evens

Exercise Notes

Exercise 20

Error Prevention You may need to review properties of trapezoids.

Exercise Answers

Answers for Exercises 1, 9–18, 19b, and 20 on pages C2 and C3.

Reteaching

Activity

Materials: Graph paper, 4 number cubes (2 yellow for positive integers and 2 red for negative integers), bag

- In the center of your graph paper, draw and label vertical and horizontal number lines from −6 to 6, intersecting at the origin.
- Put the four number cubes in a bag and, without looking, pick one. Toss it and place it on the corresponding point on the x-number line. Pick another cube, toss it, and place it on the corresponding point on the y-number line.
- Draw a vertical line through the point on the x-number line and a horizontal line through the point on the y-number line. The two lines intersect at the point indicated by the two number cubes. Mark this point with the numbers on the cubes.
- Repeat the procedure until you have plotted eight or ten points in all.

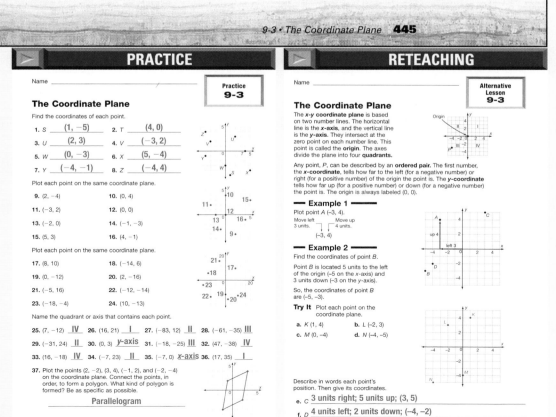

Project Progress

You may want to have students use Chapter 9 Project Master.

Exercise Answers

32.

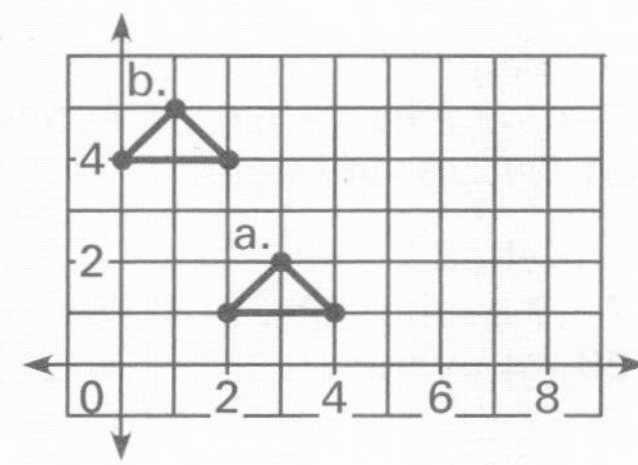

c. The new figure is the same size and shape but it is moved 2 units to the left and 3 units up.

33. Cairo: 30° north, 31° east; Zanzibar: 6° south, 39° east

34.

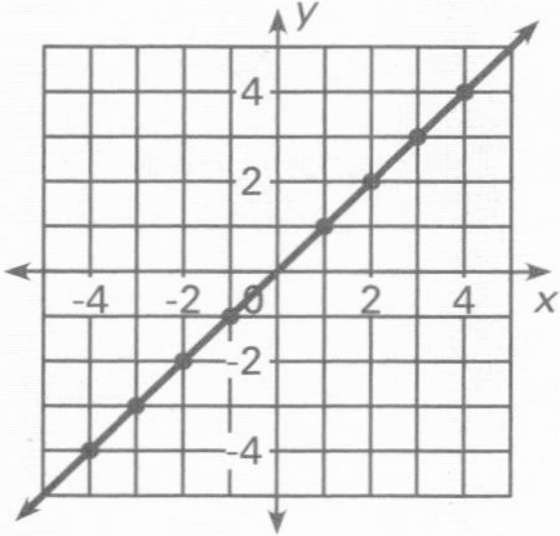

The line is diagonal and cuts quadrants I and III in half. It passes through the origin.

Alternate Assessment

Portfolio Have students plot a point in each quadrant on a coordinate grid and give the coordinates of the point. Then have them describe the coordinates of points in each quadrant as positive or negative. Suggest that they put the graph in their portfolios for reference.

Quick Quiz

Plot and label each point on the same coordinate plane.

A. $(-5, 0)$ B. $(3, -1)$

C. $(0, -4)$ D. $(-1, 2)$

E. $(3, 3)$

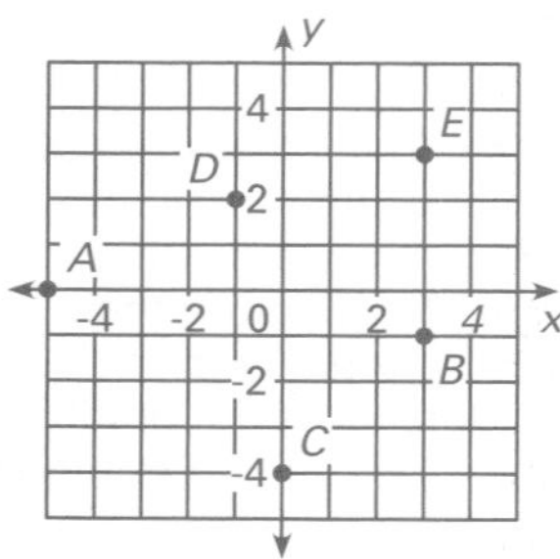

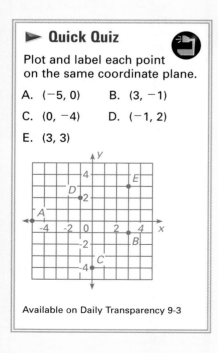

Available on Daily Transparency 9-3

31. **Test Prep** In which quadrant would you find $(-6, -3)$? **C**

Ⓐ I Ⓑ II Ⓒ III Ⓓ IV

Problem Solving and Reasoning

32. Critical Thinking Follow these steps to *translate* a geometric figure. A translation moves a figure but does not change its size or shape.

a. Plot the ordered pairs (4, 1), (3, 2), and (2, 1). Connect the points.

b. Make three new ordered pairs by subtracting 2 from the *x*-coordinates and adding 3 to the *y*-coordinates of the original points. Plot these points and connect them.

c. Describe the new figure. How does it compare to the original?

33. Critical Thinking The *latitude-longitude* system describes locations on the earth's surface. Latitude measures degrees north or south of the equator. Longitude measures degrees east or west of a line called the *prime meridian.* For instance, Dakar is at 15° north, 17° west.

Use the map to give the approximate latitude and longitude of Cairo and Zanzibar.

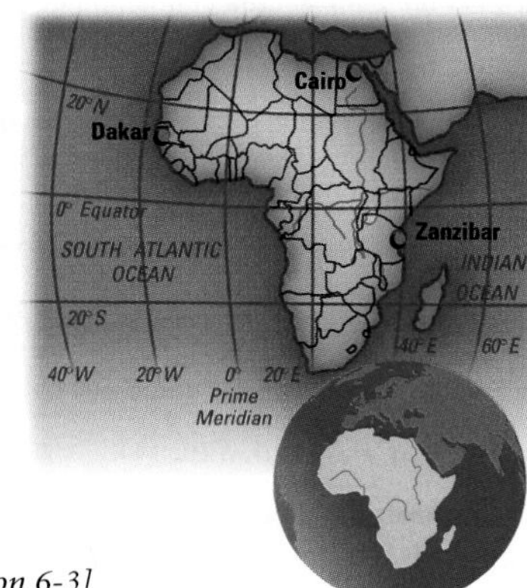

34. Journal On a coordinate plane, plot all the points whose *x*-coordinates and *y*-coordinates are equal. Connect the points. Describe the result.

Mixed Review

Multiply and divide to find two ratios equivalent to each ratio. *[Lesson 6-3]*

35. $\frac{8}{22}$ **$\frac{4}{11}$, $\frac{16}{44}$** **36.** $\frac{6}{14}$ **$\frac{3}{7}$, $\frac{12}{28}$** **37.** $\frac{20}{42}$ **$\frac{10}{21}$, $\frac{40}{84}$** **38.** $\frac{18}{20}$ **$\frac{9}{10}$, $\frac{36}{40}$** **39.** $\frac{42}{100}$ **$\frac{21}{50}$, $\frac{84}{200}$**

Express each fraction as a percent. *[Lesson 8-1]*

40. $\frac{9}{12}$ **75%** **41.** $\frac{67}{100}$ **67%** **42.** $\frac{4}{25}$ **16%** **43.** $\frac{17}{50}$ **34%** **44.** $\frac{4}{5}$ **80%**

Project Progress

Put tick marks on your time line to the left and right of the origin. Use these marks to represent years before and after your birth. List events and dates you'd like to include on your time line. Ask your parents or look in books to find out about events that happened before you were born.

Problem Solving
Understand
Plan
Solve
Look Back

PROBLEM SOLVING 9-3

PROBLEM SOLVING

Name ______________________

Guided Problem Solving 9-2

GPS PROBLEM 24, STUDENT PAGE 440

The chart shows the depth below sea level of several boreholes.

a. Represent each depth as an integer.

b. Order the integers in part **a** from least to greatest.

Location	Depth
Belridge, California	11,357 ft
Kola Peninsula, Russia	31,911 ft
St. Bernard Parish, Louisiana	25,600 ft
Szechwan Province, China	2,000 ft

— Understand —

1. Underline what you are asked to do. **Possible answers: Items 3, 7.**

— Plan —

2. Which depths can be represented by a negative integer?
All, because all depths are *below* sea level.

3. How can you tell which of two negative integers is less?
Use a number line to compare.

— Solve —

4. Write the integers to represent each depth. **California, –11,357; Russia, –31,911; Louisiana, –25,600; China, –2,000**

5. Mark each integer on the number line.

6. Write the integers in order from least to greatest.
–31,911, –25,600, –11,357, –2,000

— Look Back —

7. How could you order the negative integers without using a number line?
Order absolute values from greatest to least.

SOLVE ANOTHER PROBLEM

The chart shows the depth below sea level of several locations. Order the integers from least to greatest.
–1312, –512, –282, –131

Location	Depth
Dead Sea	1312 ft
Valdes Peninsula	131 ft
Death Valley	282 ft
Lake Assal	512 ft

ENRICHMENT

Name ______________________

Extend Your Thinking 9-3

Critical Thinking

Figure A below is a mirror image of Figure B. Mathematicians refer to a mirror image as a reflection image. In this case, it reflects over the *y*-axis.

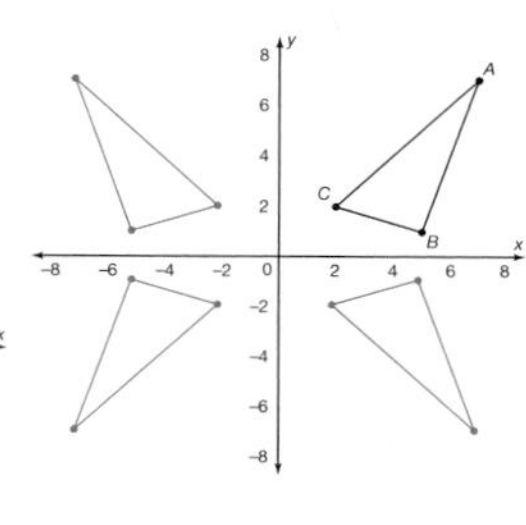

Use the coordinate grid at the right when answering questions 1–4.

1. Give the coordinates of each point.

a. *A* **(7, 7)** b. *B* **(5, 1)** c. *C* **(2, 2)**

2. Change the sign of each *x*-coordinate—if positive, change to negative; and if negative, change to positive. Plot the new points and connect them. Describe the new figure.
(–7, 7), (–5, 1), (–2, 2); Possible answer: It is a mirror image of original figure and reflects over the *y*-axis.

3. Predict what will happen to the original figure if you change the signs of the *y*-coordinates. Plot the points to test your prediction.
Possible answer: It will be a mirror image and reflect over the *x*-axis. (7, –7), (5, –1), (2, –2)

4. Plot a mirror image of the original figure in Quadrant III. Give the coordinates of each point and describe what you did to find them.
(–7, –7), (–5, –1), (–2, –2); Possible answer: Changed signs of the *x*-coordinates in Quadrant IV or changed signs of the *y*-coordinates in Quadrant II.

Section 9A Connect

You've used integers to describe and compare real-world quantities. Now you'll learn about a relationship between depth and temperature as you examine measurements that were taken when a giant drill bored deep into the earth.

Journey to Inner Space

Materials: Graph paper

As they descended to the center of the earth, Jules Verne's fictional characters found the temperature unexpectedly comfortable. Ten thousand feet below sea level, the temperature was about 63°F. Now you'll see what temperatures are *really* like in the earth's interior. The following data comes from measurements taken during the drilling of a borehole in South Africa.

Depth (ft)	Temp. (°F)	Depth (ft)	Temp. (°F)	Depth (ft)	Temp. (°F)
−2094	75.4	−597	68.6	−3644	82.9
−4747	88.2	−8937	110.3	−6860	100.1
−9904	114.0	−5806	92.6	−7912	105.6

1. Write each pair of data values as an ordered pair, with depth as the x-coordinate and temperature as the y-coordinate.

2. Order the points according to temperature, from coldest to hottest.

3. Order the points according to depth, from deepest to least deep.

4. Are the sets of points you made in Steps 2 and 3 in the same order?

5. Plot the points on a coordinate graph. What patterns do you notice?

6. Use your graph to predict the temperature at each depth. Explain how you made your predictions.

a. −5000 ft **b.** −20,000 ft **c.** Sea level

EXAMPLE: Breccia
GRAIN: Sharp and Angular

EXAMPLE: Sandstone
GRAIN: Coarse

EXAMPLE: Gneiss
GRAIN: Banded

EXAMPLE: Slate
GRAIN: Elongated

EXAMPLE: Granite
GRAIN: Nonbanded

EXAMPLE: Obsidian
GRAIN: Glassy

Answers for Connect

1. (−2094, 75.4), (−4747, 88.2), (−9904, 114.0), (−597, 68.6), (−8937, 110.3), (−5806, 92.6), (−3644, 82.9), (−6860, 100.1), (−7912, 105.6)
2. (−597, 68.6), (−2094, 75.4), (−3644, 82.9), (−4747, 88.2), (−5806, 92.6), (−6860, 100.1), (−7912, 105.6), (−8937, 110.3), (−9904, 114.0)
3. (−9904, 114.0), (−8937, 110.3), (−7912, 105.6), (−6860, 100.1), (−5806, 92.6), (−4747, 88.2), (−3644, 82.9), (−2094, 75.4), (−597, 68.6)
4. No, the order is reversed.
5. 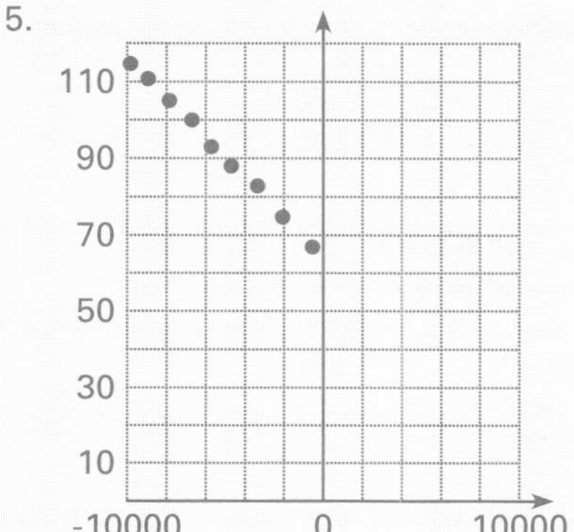

As the altitude decreases, the temperature increases.
6. a. 90°F; Between the temperatures for −5806 ft and −4747 ft.
   b. 165°F; Extended a best-fit line.
   c. 65°F; Extended a best-fit line.

9A Connect

Journey to Inner Space

The Point

Students talked about boreholes in *Journey to Inner Space* on page 431. Now they examine the relationship between depth and temperature measurements recorded during the drilling of a borehole.

Materials

Graph paper

Resources

Teaching Tool Transparency 8: Coordinate Grids

About the Page

- Discuss the table with students to be sure they understand the information given.
- Review ordering negative numbers.
- Review the quadrants on the coordinate graph. Remind students that negative values are to the left of the origin on the x-axis and down from the origin on the y-axis.
- Ask students to examine the numbers they are going to graph. Help them determine how they are going to label the axes.

Ongoing Assessment

Check that students have ordered the pairs and plotted the points correctly.

Extension

Have students research the relationship between distance above sea level and temperature. How much does the temperature increase or decrease as you travel into the atmosphere?

9A Review

Review Correlation

Item(s)	Lesson(s)
1–10	9-1
11–14	9-2
15	9-1
16–20	9-3
21	9-1
22	9-2
23	9-3

Test Prep

Test-Taking Tip

Tell students to examine graphs and drawings carefully before answering questions. Here, the axes have different scales, and neither is in units of 1.

Answers for Review

16–20.

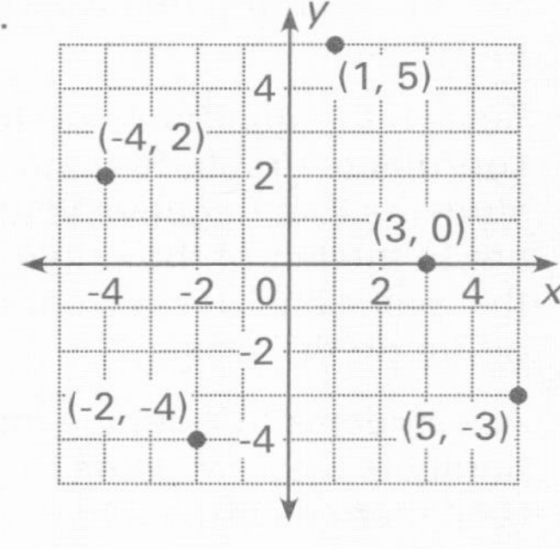

21. Possible answer: The absolute value of a number tells how far the number is from zero on a number line. The opposite of a number is the same distance from zero as the number itself but is always on the other side of zero.

Section 9A Review

Number Sense Write the opposite of each integer.

1. -4 4 **2.** 50 -50 **3.** 0 0 **4.** -726 726 **5.** 201 -201

Find each absolute value.

6. $|-6|$ 6 **7.** $|6|$ 6 **8.** $|-1800|$ 1800 **9.** $|613|$ 613 **10.** $|-24{,}789|$ 24,789

Use $>$, $<$, or $=$ to compare each pair of numbers.

11. -3 [$>$] -8 **12.** -12 [$<$] 12 **13.** -702 [$>$] -720 **14.** 0 [$<$] $|-10|$

15. Science The depth of the bottom of the earth's crust varies from 5 to 25 miles below sea level. Write integers to represent these two numbers. $-5, -25$

Crust

Plot each point on the same coordinate plane.

16. (1, 5) **17.** $(-2, -4)$ **18.** $(5, -3)$ **19.** (3, 0) **20.** $(-4, 2)$

21. Journal In your own words, explain the difference between the *absolute value* of a number and the *opposite* of a number.

22. Geography The table shows the lowest point of every continent except Antarctica. Order the elevations from lowest to highest. $-1312, -509, -282, -131, -92, -52$

Continent	Africa	North America	South America	Asia	Australia	Europe
Location	Lake Assal	Death Valley	Vakles Peninsula	Dead Sea	Lake Eyre	Caspian Sea
Lowest Elevation (ft)	–509 ft	–282 ft	–131 ft	–1312 ft	–52 ft	–92 ft

REVIEW 9A

Test Prep

When you're asked to find the coordinates of a point on a multiple choice test, be sure to pay attention to the scales on the axes.

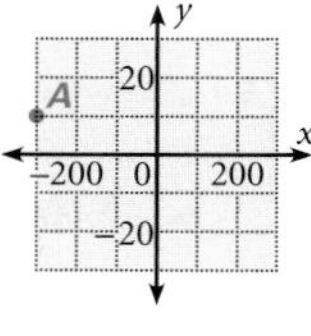

23. What are the coordinates of point *A*? C

Ⓐ $(-3, 1)$ Ⓑ $(3, -1)$ Ⓒ $(-300, 10)$ Ⓓ $(-300, -100)$

Resources

Practice Masters
Section 9A Review

Assessment Sourcebook
Quiz 9A

TestWorks
Test and Practice Software

PRACTICE

Name ______________________ Practice

Section 9A Review

Write the opposite of each integer.

1. 15 -15 2. -8 8 3. 27 -27 4. -58 58
5. -367 367 6. 222 -222 7. 638 -638 8. -412 412

Find each absolute value.

9. $|37|$ 37 10. $|-41|$ 41 11. $|86|$ 86 12. $|-101|$ 101
13. $|-648|$ 648 14. $|-3841|$ 3841 15. $|2163|$ 2163 16. $|-484|$ 484

Use $>$, $<$, or $=$ to compare each pair of numbers.

17. 38 ($>$) -83 18. -47 ($>$) -52 19. -85 ($>$) -95 20. 637 ($<$) 763
21. -321 ($<$) -312 22. 418 ($>$) -481 23. $|18|$ ($<$) $|-21|$ 24. $|-17|$ ($>$) $|-15|$

Plot each point on the same coordinate plane.

25. $(-4, -2)$ 26. $(3, -3)$
27. (3, 1) 28. $(-1, 4)$
29. $(0, -2)$ 30. (2, 3)

31. In 1968, John Gruener and R. Neal Watson used scuba equipment to dive to a depth of 437 ft below sea level. Use an integer to represent their height during the dive. -437 ft

32. During its first half-year, Anita's business earned monthly profits of $-\$3285$, $-\$680$, \$329, \$567, $-\$240$, and \$980. (A negative number represents a loss.) Order the dollar amounts from lowest to highest.
$-\$3285, -\$680, -\$240, \$329, \$567, \$980$

33. **Geography** The area of Peru is about $3\frac{4}{25}$ times the area of Paraguay. If Paraguay has an area of 157,000 mi^2, what is the area of Peru? *[Lesson 4-5]* About 496,000 mi^2

34. In 1964, Steve's Cheese of Denmark, Wisconsin, made a cheddar cheese weighing $17\frac{1}{2}$ tons. The milk used to make the cheese equalled the daily production of 16,000 cows. How many tons of cheddar cheese could be made using the daily production of milk from 3,200 cows? *[Lesson 6-8]* $3\frac{1}{2}$ tons

Section 9B

Operations with Integers

LESSON PLANNING GUIDE

Student Edition

Ancillaries*

LESSON		MATERIALS	VOCABULARY	DAILY	OTHER
	Section 9B Opener				
9-4	**Adding Integers**	algebra tiles	additive inverse, zero pair	9-4	Teaching Tool Trans. 12, 13 *Interactive CD-ROM Lesson 9* *WW Math*–Middle School
9-5	**Subtracting Integers**	algebra tiles		9-5	Teaching Tool Transparencies 2, 3, 5, 12, 13
	Technology	spreadsheet software			*Interactive CD-ROM Spreadsheet/ Grapher Tool*
9-6	**Multiplying Integers**			9-6	Lesson Enhancement Trans. 43
9-7	**Dividing Integers**			9-7	Ch. 9 Project Master
	Connect				Interdisc. Team Teaching 9B
	Review				Practice 9B; Quiz 9B; *TestWorks*
	Chapter 9 Summary and Review				
	Chapter 9 Assessment				Ch. 9 Tests Forms A–F; *TestWorks*; Ch. 9 Letter Home
	Cumulative Review Chapters 1–9				Cumulative Review Ch. 1–9 Quarterly Test Ch. 1–9

* Daily Ancillaries include Practice, Reteaching, Problem Solving, Enrichment, and Daily Transparency. Teaching Tool Transparencies are in *Teacher's Toolkits*. Lesson Enhancement Transparencies are in *Overhead Transparency Package*.

SKILLS TRACE

LESSON	SKILL	FIRST INTRODUCED GR. 5	GR. 6	GR. 7	DEVELOP	PRACTICE/ APPLY	REVIEW
9-4	**Adding integers.**		✗		pp. 450–452	pp. 453–454	pp. 472, 475, 494
9-5	**Subtracting integers.**		✗		pp. 455–457	pp. 458–459	pp. 472, 475, 498
9-6	**Multiplying integers.**		✗		pp. 461–463	pp. 464–465	pp. 472, 475, 504
9-7	**Dividing integers.**		✗		pp. 466–468	pp. 469–470	pp. 472, 475, 511

CONNECTED MATHEMATICS

Investigations 2–4 in the unit *Accentuate the Negative (Integers)*, from the **Connected Mathematics** series, can be used with Section 9B.

INTERDISCIPLINARY TEAM TEACHING

Math and Science/Technology

(Worksheet pages 37–38: Teacher pages T37–T38)

In this lesson, students add, subtract, and multiply integers to determine calorie intake.

Name ______________ *Math and Science/Technology*

Weighty Issues

Add, subtract, and multiply integers to determine calorie intake.

You probably know that overeating, or eating an unbalanced diet rich in fats and carbohydrates, tends to make you gain weight and that exercise can help you lose it. Why? Part of the answer can be summed up in a single word—calories. Whether you gain or lose weight depends partly on the calories you take in with the foods you eat and the calories you use up as you exercise.

An adult weighing 128 pounds who leads a life of normal activity needs about 1,700 calories to stay at that weight. If that person reduces his or her calorie intake to about 1,200 a day, without changing other factors, he or she is likely to lose about a pound per week. People your age, who tend to be very active and are growing, need 2,200–2,500 calories a day to stay healthy.

What would happen if the adult began exercising instead of dieting? He or she would also tend to lose weight.

Many people combine dieting and increased exercise in a weight-loss program. One way to keep track of progress in such a program is to add and subtract calories on a number line. The chart at right is like a vertical number line. It shows the calories gained or lost by eating certain kinds and amounts of food or doing certain kinds of exercise for one hour. WARNING: If you are considering a weight-reduction program, you must consult a doctor or nutritionist before you begin. Young growing people in particular require a balanced diet that contains enough calories to support normal growth and development.

Food/Exercise	Calories
1 cup milk	+149
1 medium garlic roll	+104
1 cup veal stew	+101
1 cup vegetable soup	+85
1 cup spaghetti with sauce	+78
1 medium tangerine	+44
playing pool	–144
bowling	–275
badminton	–330
aerobic dance, moderate	–350
aerobic dance, intense	–460
basketball	–474

1. Why are all the exercises shown as negative integers?
   All lead to calories lost, rather than gained.

2. a. What is the total number of calories gained or lost by playing an hour of basketball and an hour of pool?
   618 calories lost

   b. What is the total number of calories gained or lost by eating two garlic rolls with a cup of milk and going bowling for an hour?
   82 calories gained

Name ______________ *Math and Science/Technology*

c. What is the total number of calories gained or lost by playing badminton for 2 hours and eating a tangerine?
   616 calories lost

3. The table below shows 60-minute exercises, the amount of calories each uses up, and the approximate number of times each must be performed for the person to lose 1 pound.

Exercise (60 min)	Calories Used Up	Number of Hours to Lose a Pound
basketball	474	7
intense aerobics	460	7
moderate aerobics	350	9
badminton	330	10
bowling	275	11
playing pool	144	22

a. Suppose the person reduced calorie intake by 500 calories per week for a month. During the month, the person also played 20 hours of badminton. How much weight is the person likely to have lost?
   6 pounds

b. Suppose the person did not decrease calorie intake, but increased activity by playing basketball 14 hours in one month. How much weight would the person be likely to have lost?
   2 pounds

4. An adult who weighed 142 pounds wanted to go on an intensive diet and exercise program. His goal was to lose 20 pounds. He now takes in about 1,900 calories a day, which keeps his weight stable.

The table below shows three calorie-reduction programs. Each program results in the loss of a varying number of pounds.

Amount Daily Calories Reduced	Weight Loss per Month (in pounds)
700	6
500	4
400	3

a. In the first month, the dieter kept to the 700-calorie reduction for the first two weeks but went back to his 1,900 calories a day for all of the last two weeks. How much weight was he likely to have lost that first month?
   3 pounds

b. Suppose the person added 700 calories to his daily diet on the first month? Estimate what he would have weighed at the end of the month.
   148 pounds

5. As stated before, this person wants to lose 20 pounds. Design a diet and exercise plan for the person. List daily calorie reduction, the amount and kind of exercise, and the number of months it will take the person to lose the 20 pounds.
   See below.

6. Do some research on bulemia and anorexia, two eating disorders that are more common among young people than adults. Make an oral report to the class describing each disorder, its causes, symptoms, effects, and treatment. If you wish, you can do this in groups of 4, each student in the group addressing one of the topics.

Answers

5. Answers will vary. One possibility would be a 700-calorie reduction diet for 3 months plus medium aerobics six times a month during each of the 3 months.

BIBLIOGRAPHY

FOR TEACHERS

Edgerton, Lynne T. *The Rising Tide: Global Warming and World Sea Levels.* Washington, DC: Island Press, 1991.

Fibonacci, Leonardo. *The Book of Squares.* Boston, MA: Academic Press, 1987.

Flint, David. *Weather and Climate: Experiments with Geography.* New York, NY: Watts, 1991.

Ritchie, David. *The Encyclopedia of Earthquakes and Volcanoes.* New York, NY: Facts on File, 1994.

Willoughby, Stephen. *Mathematics Education for a Changing World.* Alexandria, VA: ASCD, 1990.

FOR STUDENTS

Lafferty, Peter. *Heat and Cold.* Tarrytown, NY: Benchmark Books, 1996.

Silverstein, Herma. *Scream Machines: Roller Coasters Past, Present and Future.* New York, NY: Walker, 1986.

Time-Life for Children. *Pterodactyl Tunnel, Amusement Park Math.* Alexandria, VA: Time-Life for Children, 1993.

The Visual Encyclopedia. London, England: Dorling Kindersley, 1995.

SECTION 9B

Operations with Integers

▷ Industry Link ▷ History Link ▷ www.mathsurf.com/7/ch9/amusement_parks

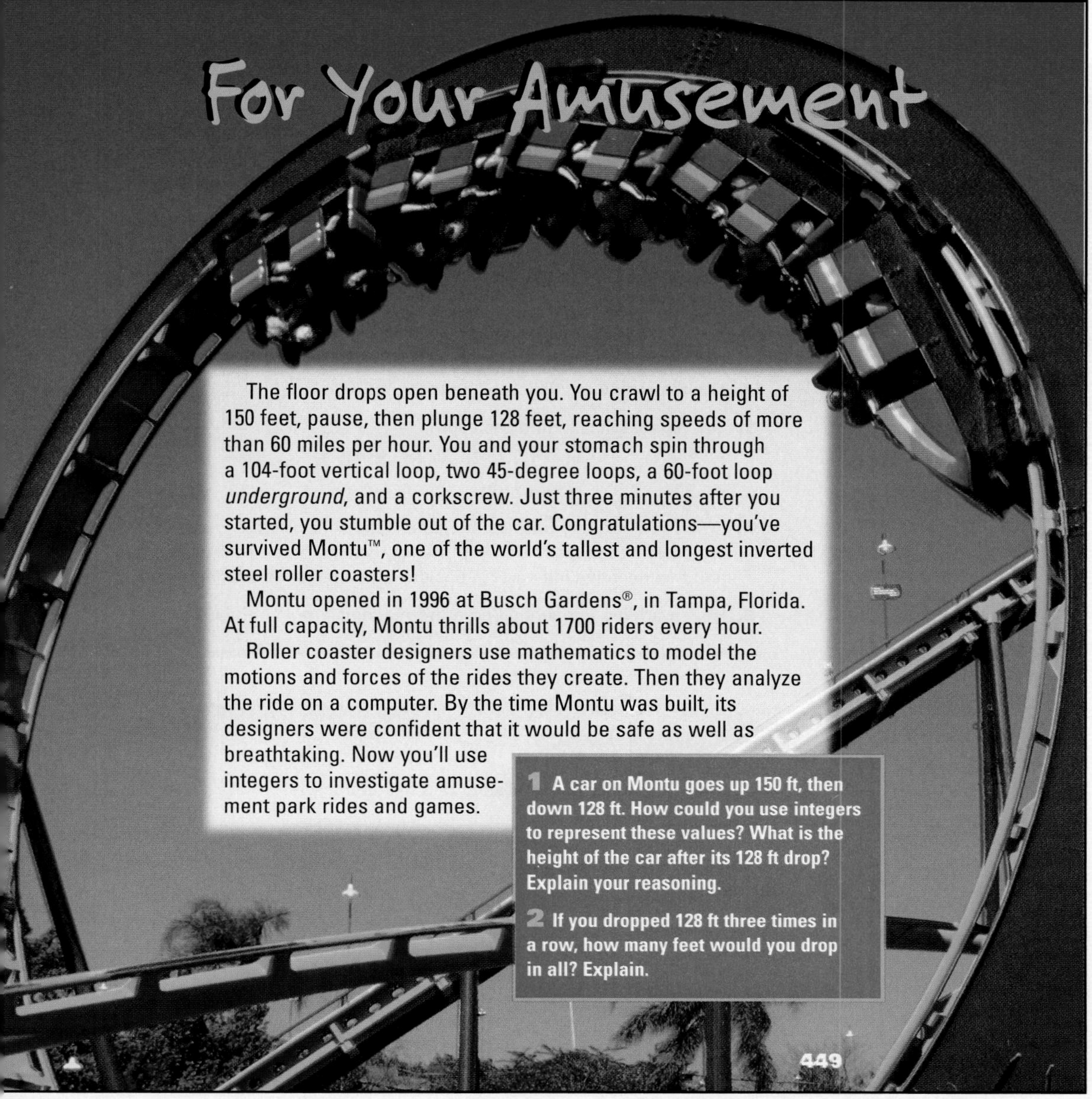

For Your Amusement

The floor drops open beneath you. You crawl to a height of 150 feet, pause, then plunge 128 feet, reaching speeds of more than 60 miles per hour. You and your stomach spin through a 104-foot vertical loop, two 45-degree loops, a 60-foot loop *underground*, and a corkscrew. Just three minutes after you started, you stumble out of the car. Congratulations—you've survived Montu™, one of the world's tallest and longest inverted steel roller coasters!

Montu opened in 1996 at Busch Gardens®, in Tampa, Florida. At full capacity, Montu thrills about 1700 riders every hour.

Roller coaster designers use mathematics to model the motions and forces of the rides they create. Then they analyze the ride on a computer. By the time Montu was built, its designers were confident that it would be safe as well as breathtaking. Now you'll use integers to investigate amusement park rides and games.

1 A car on Montu goes up 150 ft, then down 128 ft. How could you use integers to represent these values? What is the height of the car after its 128 ft drop? Explain your reasoning.

2 If you dropped 128 ft three times in a row, how many feet would you drop in all? Explain.

449

Where are we now?

In Section 9A, students explored ways in which integers are used.

They learned how to

- find the opposite of an integer.
- find the absolute value of an integer.
- compare and order integers.
- graph points on a coordinate plane.

Where are we going?

In Section 9B, students will

- add integers.
- subtract integers.
- multiply integers.
- divide integers.

Theme: Amusement Parks

World Wide Web

If your class has access to the World Wide Web, you might want to use the information found at the Web site address given. The interdisciplinary links relate to the topics discussed in this section.

About the Page

This page introduces the theme of the section, amusement parks, and discusses the motion and forces of amusement park rides.

Ask ...

- Have you ever been scared on a ride in an amusement park? If so, describe your experience.
- Why do roller coaster designers use mathematics to plan rides? To be sure the rides are safe.

Extensions

The following activities do not require access to the World Wide Web.

Industry
Before opening a park or building a ride, the owners do market research to find out what people enjoy and how much they will pay. Survey 10 friends. Ask them to tell you their 3 favorite amusement park rides. Graph the results.

History
Tell students that the first roller coasters were ice-covered wooden slides built in Russia in the 15th century. Ask them to research when the first roller coaster appeared in the United States. It was built at Coney Island in New York City in 1884.

Answers for Questions

1. 150 and -128; 22 ft; $150 + (-128) = 22$ ft above starting elevation.
2. Possible answer: 384 feet; $3 \times 128 = 384$

Connect

On page 471, students write problems to show how integer operations relate to amusement park rides.

INTERACTIVE LESSON

9-4 Lesson Organizer

Objective

- Add integers.

Vocabulary

- Additive inverse, zero pair

Materials

- Explore: Algebra tiles

NCTM Standards

- 1–6, 8

Review

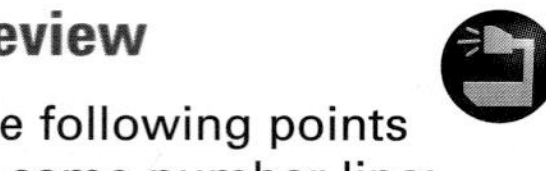

Plot the following points on the same number line: −5, 0, 3, −1, 2, 6

Available on Daily Transparency 9-4

Lesson Link

Ask students to tell when they might move forward or backward a given number of units. They might suggest playing board games or "Mother, May I?" and gaining or losing yardage in football. Explain that adding integers is a similar process.

1 Introduce

Explore

You may wish to use Teaching Tool Transparencies 12 and 13: Algebra Tiles (red) and Algebra Tiles (yellow) with this lesson.

The Point

Students use algebra tiles to explore the addition of integers.

Ongoing Assessment

Check that students understand that $1 + (-1) = 0$. Ask: "If you take 1 step forward and 1 step back, where do you end up? How far have you moved?"

9-4 Adding Integers

You'll Learn ...

- to add integers

... How It's Used

Weather forecasters use integers to describe changes in temperatures and barometric pressures.

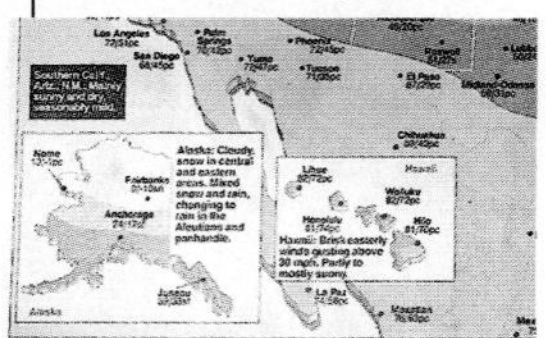

Vocabulary

additive inverse

zero pair

Lesson Link In the last section, you learned basic properties of integers. Now you'll see how to add integers. ◄

Explore Adding Integers

It All Adds Up!

Materials: Algebra tiles

Adding Integers

- To model $2 + (-3)$, model positive integers with yellow tiles and negative integers with red tiles.
- $+1 + (-1) = 0$, so you can remove any yellow-red pair without changing the value of the pile.
- Use the remaining tile(s) to find the sum.

+2 + (−3)

= 0

= 0

+2 + (−3) = −1

1. Use algebra tiles to find each sum.
   - **a.** $2 + 1$
   - **b.** $-1 + (-2)$
   - **c.** $3 + (-1)$
   - **d.** $-1 + 2$
   - **e.** $1 + (-2)$
   - **f.** $-4 + 2$
2. When you add two positive integers, is the sum positive, negative, or impossible to predict? Can you predict the sign of the sum when you add two negative integers? A positive and a negative integer? Explain.
3. How is adding integers different from adding whole numbers?

Learn Adding Integers

You can use a number line or algebra tiles to add integers.

Number Line

To add a *positive* number, move to the right.

To add a *negative* number, move to the left.

−1 + 3

−3 −2 −1 0 +1 +2 +3

+3 + (−5)

Algebra Tiles

Use yellow tiles to represent positive integers and red tiles to represent negative integers.

Remove yellow-red pairs. The number of tiles left is the sum.

MEETING INDIVIDUAL NEEDS

Resources

- 9-4 Practice
- 9-4 Reteaching
- 9-4 Problem Solving
- 9-4 Enrichment
- 9-4 Daily Transparency
  - Problem of the Day
  - Review
  - Quick Quiz

Teaching Tool Transparencies 12, 13

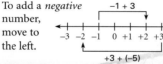

Interactive CD-ROM Lesson 9

Wide World of Mathematics Middle School: Integer Football

Learning Modalities

Visual Use number lines extensively in this lesson to reinforce the concept of adding integers. Especially lead students to see that 1 and –1 form a zero pair as does any other pair of opposites.

Kinesthetic The use of algebra tiles is especially important in presenting a very concrete experience in the removal of zero pairs.

Inclusion

Materials: plastic number lines, crayons

Give students plastic number lines with numbers permanently marked from –25 to 25 and a wax crayon that produces marks that can be easily wiped off later. Have students model the addition of integers on this number line. Remind them to start at the first integer and move to the right if the second addend is positive and to the left if the second addend is negative.

Example 1

Use a number line and algebra tiles to add: $-2 + (-4)$

Number Line

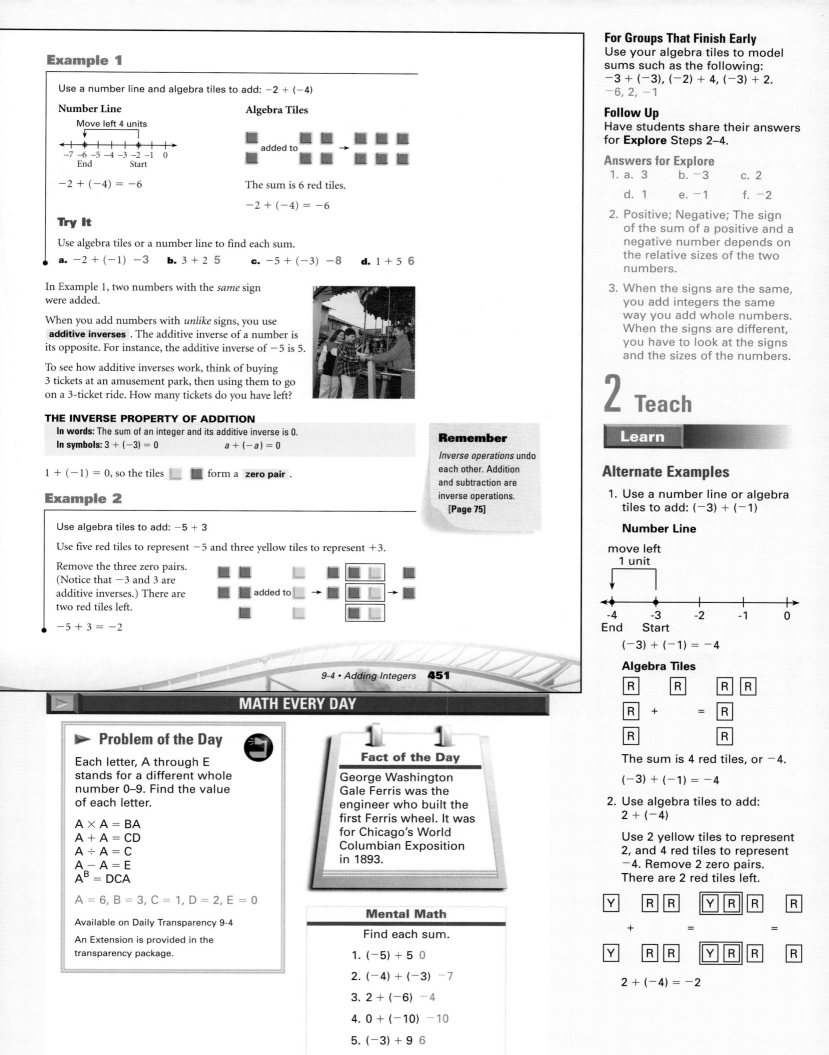

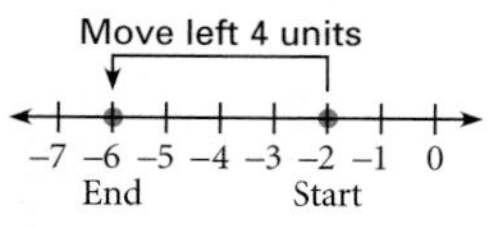

$-2 + (-4) = -6$

Algebra Tiles

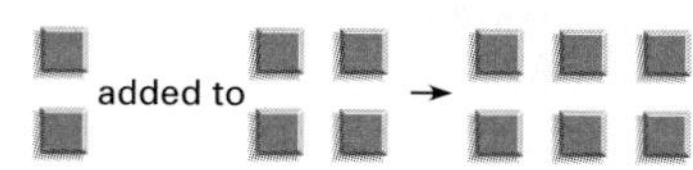

The sum is 6 red tiles.

$-2 + (-4) = -6$

Try It

Use algebra tiles or a number line to find each sum.

a. $-2 + (-1)$ −3 **b.** $3 + 2$ 5 **c.** $-5 + (-3)$ −8 **d.** $1 + 5$ 6

In Example 1, two numbers with the *same* sign were added.

When you add numbers with *unlike* signs, you use **additive inverses**. The additive inverse of a number is its opposite. For instance, the additive inverse of −5 is 5.

To see how additive inverses work, think of buying 3 tickets at an amusement park, then using them to go on a 3-ticket ride. How many tickets do you have left?

THE INVERSE PROPERTY OF ADDITION

In words: The sum of an integer and its additive inverse is 0.
In symbols: $3 + (-3) = 0$ $a + (-a) = 0$

$1 + (-1) = 0$, so the tiles 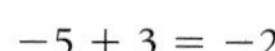 form a **zero pair**.

Remember

Inverse operations undo each other. Addition and subtraction are inverse operations.
[Page 75]

Example 2

Use algebra tiles to add: $-5 + 3$

Use five red tiles to represent −5 and three yellow tiles to represent +3.

Remove the three zero pairs. (Notice that −3 and 3 are additive inverses.) There are two red tiles left.

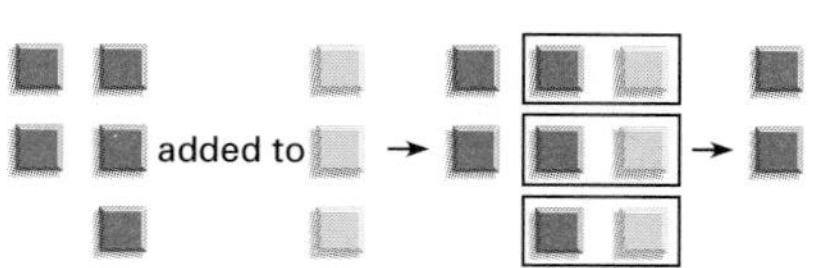

$-5 + 3 = -2$

MATH EVERY DAY

Problem of the Day

Each letter, A through E stands for a different whole number 0–9. Find the value of each letter.

A × A = BA
A + A = CD
A ÷ A = C
A − A = E
A^B = DCA

A = 6, B = 3, C = 1, D = 2, E = 0

Available on Daily Transparency 9-4

An Extension is provided in the transparency package.

Fact of the Day

George Washington Gale Ferris was the engineer who built the first Ferris wheel. It was for Chicago's World Columbian Exposition in 1893.

Mental Math

Find each sum.

1. $(-5) + 5$ 0
2. $(-4) + (-3)$ −7
3. $2 + (-6)$ −4
4. $0 + (-10)$ −10
5. $(-3) + 9$ 6

For Groups That Finish Early

Use your algebra tiles to model sums such as the following: $-3 + (-3)$, $(-2) + 4$, $(-3) + 2$.
−6, 2, −1

Follow Up

Have students share their answers for **Explore** Steps 2–4.

Answers for Explore

1. a. 3 b. −3 c. 2 d. 1 e. −1 f. −2
2. Positive; Negative; The sign of the sum of a positive and a negative number depends on the relative sizes of the two numbers.
3. When the signs are the same, you add integers the same way you add whole numbers. When the signs are different, you have to look at the signs and the sizes of the numbers.

2 Teach

Learn

Alternate Examples

1. Use a number line or algebra tiles to add: $(-3) + (-1)$

Number Line

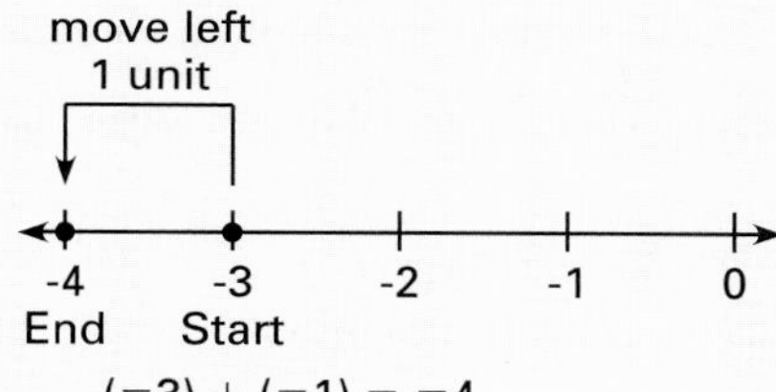

$(-3) + (-1) = -4$

Algebra Tiles

R R R R
R + = R
R R

The sum is 4 red tiles, or −4.

$(-3) + (-1) = -4$

2. Use algebra tiles to add: $2 + (-4)$

Use 2 yellow tiles to represent 2, and 4 red tiles to represent −4. Remove 2 zero pairs. There are 2 red tiles left.

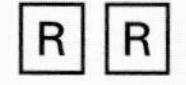
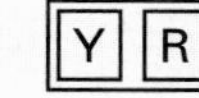

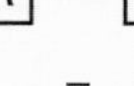

$2 + (-4) = -2$

Alternate Examples

3. Cathy won a token for each basket she made. She spent 5 tokens and made 7 shots. Use a number line to find how many more tokens she had when she finished than when she began.

   Use negative numbers for tokens spent and positive numbers for tokens won.

   $-5 + 7 = 2$

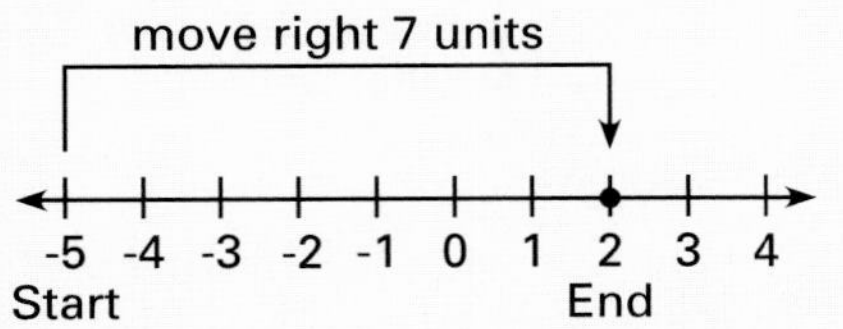

   Cathy had 2 tokens more than when she began.

4. Find the sum.

   $-9 + (-15)$

   Add the absolute values.
   $9 + (15) = 24$

   Use the sign of the numbers.
   $-9 + (-15) = -24$

5. Find the sum.

   $(-18) + 14$

   Subtract the absolute values.
   $18 - 14 = 4$

   Use the sign of the number with the greater absolute value.
   $(-18) + 14 = -4$

3 Practice and Assess

Check

Have students perform a variety of integer additions to be sure they can apply the rules on this page.

Answers for Check Your Understanding

1. Subtract the absolute values of the two numbers and use the sign of the number with the greater absolute value.
2. The sum of the numbers in a zero pair is 0.

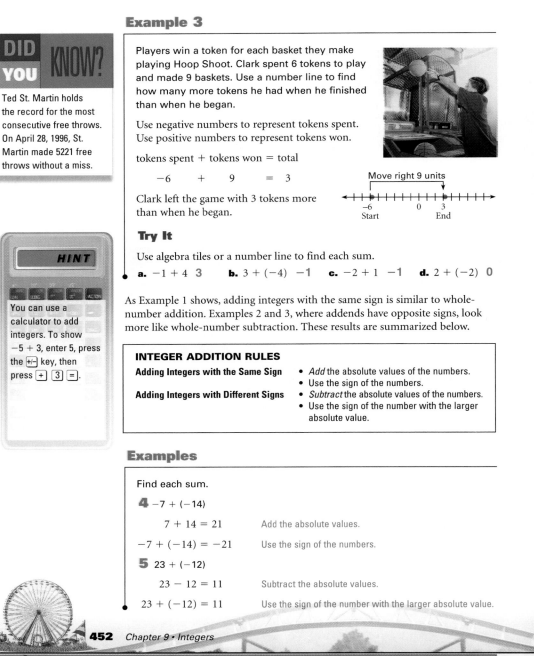

Ted St. Martin holds the record for the most consecutive free throws. On April 28, 1996, St. Martin made 5221 free throws without a miss.

Example 3

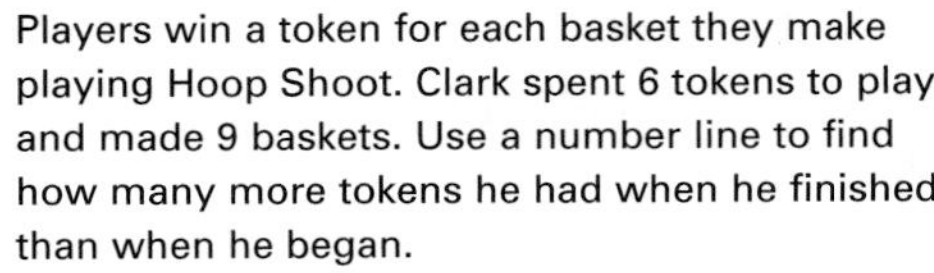

Players win a token for each basket they make playing Hoop Shoot. Clark spent 6 tokens to play and made 9 baskets. Use a number line to find how many more tokens he had when he finished than when he began.

Use negative numbers to represent tokens spent. Use positive numbers to represent tokens won.

tokens spent + tokens won = total

$-6 \quad + \quad 9 \quad = \quad 3$

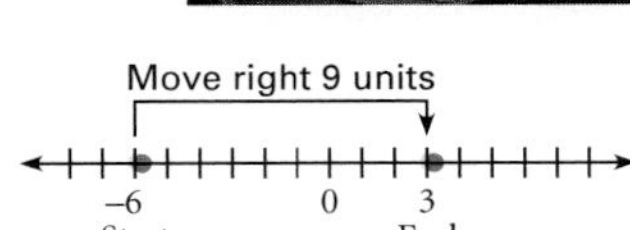

Clark left the game with 3 tokens more than when he began.

Try It

Use algebra tiles or a number line to find each sum.

a. $-1 + 4$ **3** **b.** $3 + (-4)$ **−1** **c.** $-2 + 1$ **−1** **d.** $2 + (-2)$ **0**

You can use a calculator to add integers. To show $-5 + 3$, enter 5, press the +/− key, then press + 3 =.

As Example 1 shows, adding integers with the same sign is similar to whole-number addition. Examples 2 and 3, where addends have opposite signs, look more like whole-number subtraction. These results are summarized below.

INTEGER ADDITION RULES

Adding Integers with the Same Sign	• *Add* the absolute values of the numbers. • Use the sign of the numbers.
Adding Integers with Different Signs	• *Subtract* the absolute values of the numbers. • Use the sign of the number with the larger absolute value.

Examples

Find each sum.

4 $-7 + (-14)$

$7 + 14 = 21$ — Add the absolute values.

$-7 + (-14) = -21$ — Use the sign of the numbers.

5 $23 + (-12)$

$23 - 12 = 11$ — Subtract the absolute values.

$23 + (-12) = 11$ — Use the sign of the number with the larger absolute value.

MEETING MIDDLE SCHOOL CLASSROOM NEEDS

Tips from Middle School Teachers

When I teach integer addition, I always use number lines, explaining that each integer has two parts, the sign which tells which direction to move and the numerical part whose absolute value tells the number of units or distance to move.

Technology Connection

If you decide to have students use calculators to find sums of integers in this lesson, be sure that they all know the correct procedure for entering a negative sign on their own particular machine.

Team Teaching

Ask physical education teachers to discuss with students the concept of *par* and the method of keeping score in golf by listing shots above and below par.

Check Your Understanding

1. How do you find the sum of two integers with different signs?
2. How is the Zero Property of Addition related to the idea of zero pairs?

9-4 Exercises and Applications

Practice and Apply

1. **Getting Started** Follow these steps to find $2 + (-5)$ using algebra tiles.
   a. Sketch two positive tiles. Color them yellow (or leave them empty).
   b. Sketch five negative tiles. Color them red (or shade them in).
   c. Remove zero pairs.
   d. Count the remaining tiles. Write the sum. -3

Write the addition problem and the sum for each model.

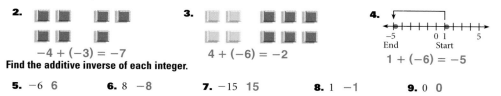

2. 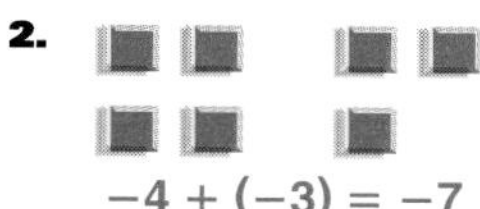
$-4 + (-3) = -7$

3. 
$4 + (-6) = -2$

4. Number line from -5 to 5: -5 End, 0, 1 Start, 5
$1 + (-6) = -5$

Find the additive inverse of each integer.

5. -6 6 6. 8 -8 7. -15 15 8. 1 -1 9. 0 0

Use algebra tiles or a number line to find each sum.

10. $2 + 4$ 6 11. $-7 + (-3)$ -10 12. $6 + (-2)$ 4 13. $-4 + 9$ 5 14. $6 + (-6)$ 0

15. $9 + (-5)$ 4 16. $-5 + 8$ 3 17. $-4 + (-6)$ -10 18. $7 + (-8)$ -1 19. $-4 + 4$ 0

Operation Sense Find each sum.

20. $-16 + 37$ 21 21. $23 + (-12)$ 11 22. $-25 + (-15)$ -40

23. $-81 + 35$ -46 24. $64 + (-23)$ 41 25. $97 + (-75)$ 22

26. $42 + 14$ 56 27. $-55 + (-55)$ -110 28. $123 + (-60)$ 63

29. Binh spent 15 game tokens in an amusement park arcade. She won 11 tokens while she was playing the games. If she has no tokens left when she leaves the arcade, how many did she buy while she was playing the games? Explain your answer.

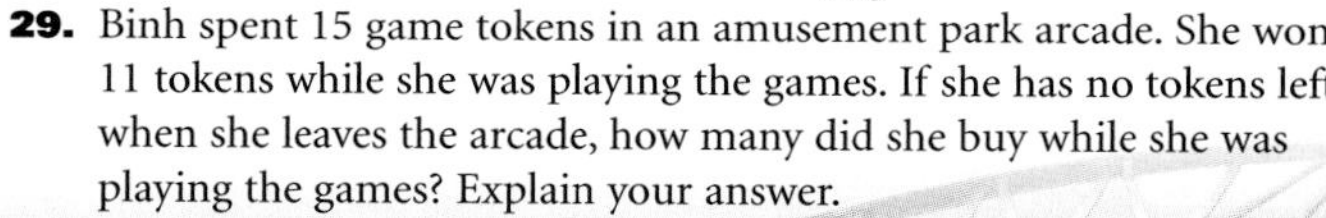

PRACTICE 9-4

9-4 Exercises and Applications

Assignment Guide

- Basic
  1–4, 5–27 odds, 33–47 odds
- Average
  3–4, 5–47 odds
- Enriched
  3–4, 6–32 evens, 33–36, 38–48 evens

Exercise Notes

Exercises 10–19

Extension Have students use algebra tiles if they used number lines and vice versa.

Exercise Answers

1. a.–b. 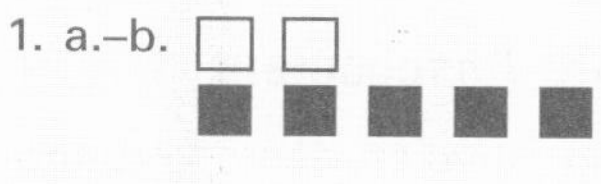

c. 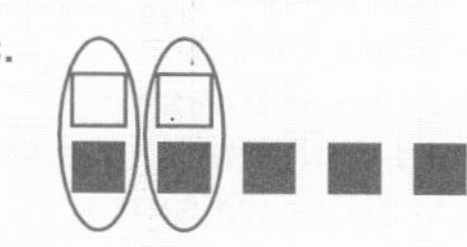

29. $-15 + 11 = -4$, so she must have bought 4 in order to leave with 0.

Reteaching

Activity

Materials: Container holding 4 number cubes: 2 yellow for positive integers and 2 red for negative integers, small object

- Draw and label a number line from -12 to 12.
- Shake a cube out of the container, and place an object on the corresponding point on the number line. Remember, yellow cubes represent positive integers and red cubes represent negative integers.
- Shake out another cube, and move the object the number of units indicated by the number showing on the cube. Move right if the cube is yellow and left if the cube is red.
- The point at which you stop is the sum of the two numbers on the cubes. Repeat the steps to find the sums of different integers, and write an addition equation for each sum.

PRACTICE

Name ____________

Practice 9-4

Adding Integers

Write the addition problem and the sum for each model. The lighter tiles represent positive numbers.

1. $-3 + 4 = 1$ 2. $2 + (-5) = -3$ 3. $5 + (-7) = -2$

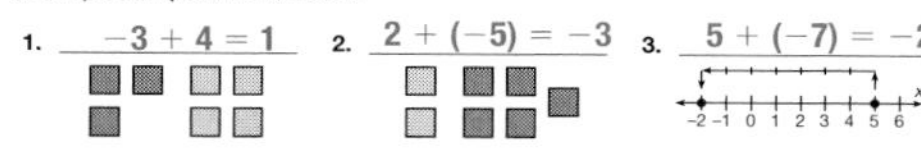

Find the additive inverse of each integer.

4. 7 -7 5. -9 9 6. 37 -37 7. 14 -14
8. -16 16 9. -23 23 10. 41 -41 11. -28 28

Use algebra tiles or a number line to find each sum.

12. $7 + (-4)$ 3 13. $-1 + (-3)$ -4 14. $3 + 2$ 5 15. $-7 + 8$ 1
16. $-6 + (-1)$ -7 17. $-1 + (-2)$ -3 18. $-4 + 9$ 5 19. $-8 + 6$ -2

Find each sum.

20. $58 + 57$ 115 21. $-110 + 19$ -91 22. $-49 + (-106)$ -155
23. $16 + (-47)$ -31 24. $-40 + 16$ -24 25. $35 + (-40)$ -5
26. $-36 + (-58)$ -94 27. $-17 + 13$ -4 28. $-146 + 16$ -130
29. $10 + (-30)$ -20 30. $-25 + (-21)$ -46 31. $-66 + (-13)$ -79

Write the next integer in each pattern.

32. $-12, -9, -6,$ -3 33. $6, -2, -10,$ -18 34. $-20, -16, -12,$ -8
35. $10, 5, 0,$ -5 36. $-11, -16, -21,$ -26 37. $-11, -7, -3,$ 1

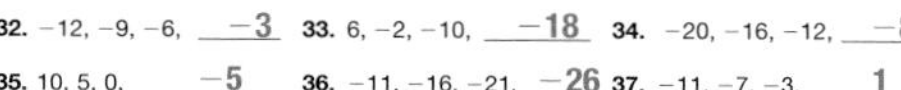

38. A diver is at a depth of 14 ft below sea level. If she is lifted to 10 ft above her present position, will she be above or below sea level? Write an addition problem and the sum to explain your answer. Below; $-14 + 10 = -4$

39. The average daily minimum temperature in International Falls, Minnesota, is 38°F warmer in March than in January. If the temperature in January is -10°F, what is the temperature in March? 28°F

RETEACHING

Name ____________

Alternative Lesson 9-4

Adding Integers

You can think of adding integers as making moves on a number line. Adding a positive number indicates a movement to the right. Adding a negative integer indicates a movement to the left. Numbers that are opposites are **additive inverses.**

Examples

a. Use the number line to find $7 + 5$.

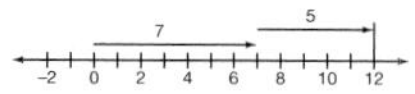

Start at 0. Move 7 units to the right. Then move 5 more units to the right.

So, $7 + 5 = 12$.

b. Use the number line to find $-3 + (-4)$.

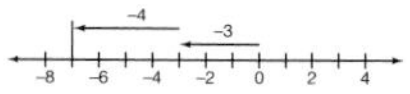

Start at 0. Move 3 units to the left. Then move 4 more units to the left.

So, $-3 + (-4) = -7$.

c. Use the number line to find $-3 + 6$.

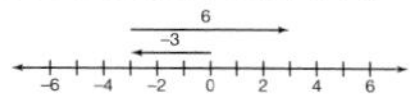

Start at 0. Move 3 units to the left. Then move 6 units to the right.

So, $-3 + 6 = 3$.

d. Use the number line to find $5 + (-7)$.

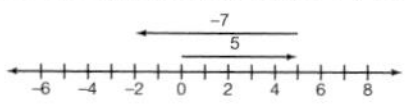

Start at 0. Move 5 units to the right. Then move 7 units to the left.

So, $5 + (-7) = 2$.

Try It Use the number find each sum.

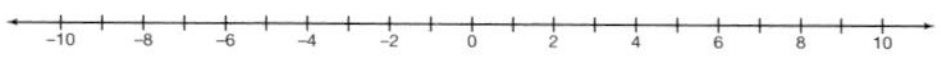

a. $-2 + 7 =$ 5 b. $3 + (-5) =$ -2 c. $5 + 3 =$ 8
d. $7 + (-8) =$ -1 e. $8 + (-8) =$ 0 f. $-3 + (-2) =$ -5
g. $-4 + 9 =$ 5 h. $2 + (-9) =$ -7 i. $3 + (-1) =$ 2
j. $-6 + (-2)$ -8 k. $4 + 5 =$ 9 l. $-8 + 5 =$ -3
m. $7 + 3 =$ 10 n. $-3 + (-2) =$ -5 o. $5 + (-4) =$ 1
p. $-7 + 4 =$ -3 q. $-5 + (-5) =$ -10 r. $9 + 2 =$ 11

Exercise Notes

■ Exercise 34

Science Mercury is a very heavy element, weighing more than 13 times an equal volume of water. Stone, iron, and lead can float on it.

Consumer During the 15th to 20th centuries, mercury was used for medicinal purposes. People did not realize then that those uses were harmful, because mercury is toxic. Mercury should never be handled, since it can be absorbed through the skin. Today, mercury is used in electrical switches and thermometers.

■ Exercise 35

History The original Ferris wheel could accommodate more than 2000 people at one time.

Alternate Assessment

Interview Have students verbalize the rules for adding integers. Have them give examples of adding integers with the same signs and with different signs.

► Quick Quiz

Find each sum.

1. $-23 + (-23)$ -46
2. $(-14) + 14$ 0
3. $0 + (-9)$ -9
4. $-33 + 28$ -5
5. $20 + (-7)$ 13

Available on Daily Transparency 9-4

Patterns Write the next integer in each pattern.

30. $-18, -14, -10,$ ____ -6 **31.** $8, 2, -4,$ ____ -10 **32.** $-8, -1, 6,$ ____ 13

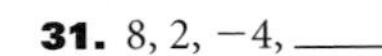

33. **Test Prep** A football team gains 7 yards on one play, then loses 15 yards on the next. What is the team's total gain? B

Ⓐ 8 yards Ⓑ -8 yards Ⓒ 22 yards Ⓓ -22 yards

34. Science Although mercury is a metal, it is a liquid at room temperature. Mercury melts at about -39°C. If the temperature of a block of mercury starts at -54°C and increases by 22°C, does the mercury melt? Explain your answer. Yes; -54°C is colder than -39°C, and -32°C is warmer.

Problem Solving and Reasoning

35. Critical Thinking GPS The first Ferris wheel operated at Chicago's World's Columbian Exposition in 1893. The top of the Ferris wheel was 264 feet above the ground.

a. Bertram's car was at the top of the Ferris wheel. Then it descended 127 feet. Write a sum you could use to find the height of Bertram's car after this descent. $264 + (-127)$

b. How far off the ground was Bertram? 137 ft

36.  Write an addition equation using one positive integer and one negative integer so that:

a. The sum is positive $5 + (-4) = 1$

b. The sum is negative $5 + (-6) = -1$

c. The sum is zero $5 + (-5) = 0$

d. The sum is -14 $5 + (-19) = -14$

Mixed Review

Use multiplication or division to complete each table. *[Lesson 6-4]*

37. Find five ratios equivalent to $\frac{3}{7}$.

3	6	9	12	15	18
7	14	21	28	35	42

38. Find five ratios equivalent to $\frac{60}{96}$.

60	30	20	15	10	5
96	48	32	24	16	8

Write each percent as a fraction in lowest terms. *[Lesson 8-2]*

39. 50% $\frac{1}{2}$ **40.** 80% $\frac{4}{5}$ **41.** 5% $\frac{1}{20}$ **42.** 36% $\frac{9}{25}$ **43.** 45% $\frac{9}{20}$

44. 98% $\frac{49}{50}$ **45.** 11.2% $\frac{14}{125}$ **46.** 47% $\frac{47}{100}$ **47.** 52% $\frac{13}{25}$ **48.** 0.5% $\frac{1}{200}$

PROBLEM SOLVING 9-4

PROBLEM SOLVING

Name ____

Guided Problem Solving 9-4

GPS PROBLEM 35, STUDENT PAGE 454

The first Ferris wheel operated at Chicago's World's Columbian Exposition in 1893. The top of the Ferris wheel was 264 feet above the ground.

a. Bertram's car was at the top of the Ferris wheel. Then it descended 127 feet. Write a sum you could use to find the height of Bertram's car after this descent.

b. How far off the ground was Bertram?

— Understand —

1. How far is the top of the Ferris wheel from the ground? 264 ft
2. How far did Bertram's car descend from the top of the Ferris wheel? 127 ft
3. What are you asked to do and to find? Write a sum that can be used to find height after descent. Find the height.

— Plan —

4. Write each distance as a positive or negative number.
   a. Top of Ferris wheel from the ground 264 ft
   b. How far the Ferris wheel descended -127 ft

— Solve —

5. Write a sum to find the height of Bertram's car after its descent. $264 + (-127) = 137$
6. How far off the ground was Bertram after the Ferris wheel descended from the top? 137 ft

— Look Back —

7. Describe another way to find a solution to part b. Subtract 127 from 246.

SOLVE ANOTHER PROBLEM

The Sears Tower located in Chicago is 110 stories tall. Keisha was on the top floor and used the elevator to descend 98 stories. Write a sum to find the floor Keisha was on after she got off the elevator. What floor was she on?
$110 + (-98) = 12$; 12th floor.

ENRICHMENT

Name ____

Extend Your Thinking 9-4

Decision Making

Carlos decided to join a hockey league. The annual fee is $500 and can be paid in 4 installments. He chooses to take beginner hockey lessons which cost $10 per week.

He has these choices of equipment that he can buy from each of the following stores. The more expensive equipment is usually chosen by the more experienced skaters.

Sam's Pro Shop: Skates, $395; Stick, $65; Helmet, $105; Pads, $214; Gloves, $135
Don's Sports: Skates, $120; Stick, $60; Helmet, $85; Pads, $85; Gloves, $80
Economy Sports: Skates, $65; Stick, $10; Helmet, $70; Pads, $60; Gloves, $20
Hockey Shop: Skates, $100; Stick, $65; Helmet, $90; Pads, $80; Gloves, $45

He has saved $500 and can save an additional $20 each week.

1. From which shops can Carlos buy a complete package of equipment with the money he now has?
   Don's Sports, Economy Sports, and Hockey Shop.
2. From which shops can Carlos buy a complete package of equipment and have enough money left to pay the first installment for the league fee and the first week of hockey lessons? Explain.
   League installment fee and a lesson cost $135. $500 – $135 leaves $365 for equipment. Economy Sports equipment costs $225. Others cost more than $365.
3. Hockey season begins in 7 months. If Carlos chooses to buy all his equipment at Sam's Pro Shop, will he be able to afford the first installment for the league fee and the first installment for lessons? Explain.
   Yes; he will have $1060 ($914 for equipment, $125 for fee installment, and $10 for first lesson).
4. From which shop would you advise Carlos to purchase his equipment? Explain.
   Possible answer: Economy Sports so he has money for the league fee and can begin playing immediately. He can buy better equipment when he is sure he enjoys the sport.

Subtracting Integers

9-5

▶ Lesson Link In the last lesson, you added integers. Now you'll explore integer subtraction. ◀

You'll Learn ...

■ to subtract integers

... How It's Used

Business owners need to add and subtract integers to see whether their business is making or losing money.

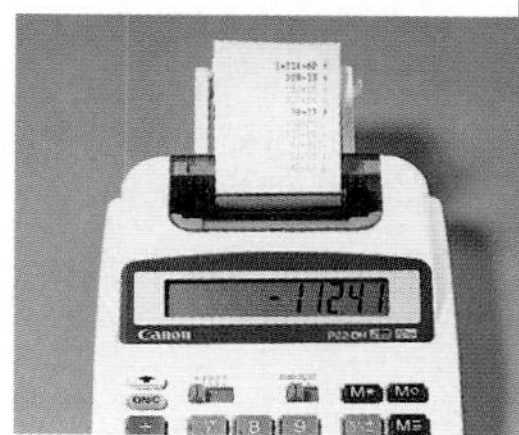

Explore Subtracting Integers

What Difference Does It Make?

Materials: Algebra tiles

Subtracting Integers

- To model 2 − 3, use algebra tiles to model the first number in the difference.
- The second number in the difference tells you how many tiles to "take away." If you do not have enough to take away, add yellow-red pairs until you have the right number.
- Take away the number of tiles equal to the second number in the difference. Use the remaining tile(s) to write the difference.

2 − 3
Now there are 3 positive tiles to take away.
Take away 3 tiles.
2 − 3 = −1

1. Use algebra tiles to find each difference.

a. 5 − 3 **b.** −7 − (−2) **c.** −6 − (−4)

d. 2 − 3 **e.** 2 − (−3) **f.** −3 − (−5)

2. Why can you add yellow-red pairs to the original number of tiles?

3. When you subtract a negative integer from a number, how does the result compare to the original number? Explain why this happens.

Learn Subtracting Integers

You can model subtraction with algebra tiles. To subtract a number, take away that number of tiles. To subtract 5 − 3:

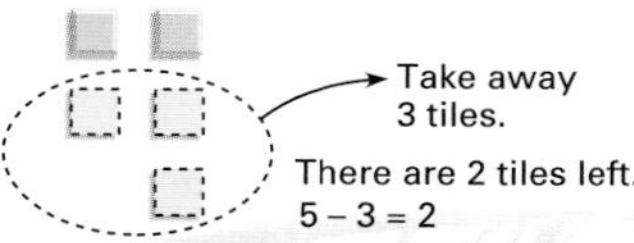

Start with 5 positive tiles.
Take away 3 tiles.
There are 2 tiles left.
5 − 3 = 2

9-5 Lesson Organizer

Objective

- Subtract integers.

Materials

- Explore: Algebra tiles

NCTM Standards

▶ Review

Find each sum.

1. 8 + (−7) 1
2. (−15) + 9 −6
3. 13 + (−22) −9
4. (−16) + 23 7
5. (−19) + (−8) −27

Available on Daily Transparency 9-5

1 Introduce

Explore

You might want to use Teaching Tool Transparency 5: Number Lines, and Teaching Tool Transparencies 12 and 13: Algebra Tiles (red) and Algebra Tiles (yellow) with this lesson.

The Point

Students use algebra tiles to model subtracting integers.

Ongoing Assessment

Check that students understand the inverse relationship between addition and subtraction and how they might represent the operations on a number line or with tiles.

For Groups That Finish Early

Write a sum for each difference and a difference for each sum:

5 + (−1) 5 − 1
(−3) − 2 −3 + (−2)
4 − (−4) 4 + 4
6 + (−3) 6 − 3

Answers for Explore on next page.

MEETING INDIVIDUAL NEEDS

Resources

9-5 Practice
9-5 Reteaching
9-5 Problem Solving
9-5 Enrichment
9-5 Daily Transparency
Problem of the Day
Review
Quick Quiz

Teaching Tool Transparencies 2, 3, 5, 12, 13

Learning Modalities

Verbal Encouraging students to verbalize the rules for adding and subtracting integers will help them remember the algorithms.

Kinesthetic The use of large number lines on the classroom floor is very conceptual and enjoyable for students. Be sure to give many examples of both addition and subtraction of integers to ensure their understanding, stressing that subtraction and addition are inverse operations.

English Language Development

The use of patterns such as that below may help students with limited English proficiency to understand the concept of integer subtraction. Encourage them to extend the pattern and to write a corresponding addition for each subtraction sentence.

10 − 3 = 7	10 − (−1) = 11
10 − 2 = 8	10 − (−2) = 12
10 − 1 = 9	10 − (−3) = 13
10 − 0 = 10	

Answers for Explore

1. a. 2 b. −5
   c. −2 d. −1
   e. 5 f. 2
2. Yellow-red pairs are equal to zero, so adding them does not change the value of the pile.
3. The result is greater than the original number; Possible explanation: If you take away a debt from someone, they are better off than before.

2 Teach

Learn

Have students use algebra tiles to model several more subtractions involving various combinations of signs.

Alternate Examples

1. Use algebra tiles to subtract: $-4 - (-7)$

   Start with 4 negative tiles. You do not have 7 negative tiles to take away. To get 7 negative tiles, add 3 zero pairs. Since you are adding zero, the value is not changed.

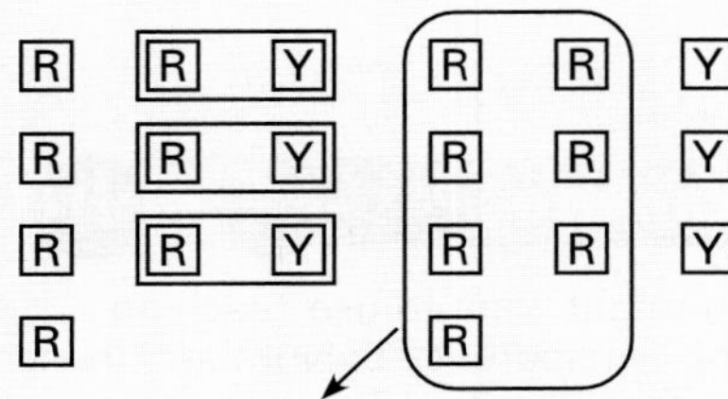

   Now subtract by taking away 7 negative tiles. There are 3 positive tiles left. $-4 - (-7) = 3$.

2. Use a number line to subtract: $2 - (-3)$

   To subtract a negative number, move to the right.

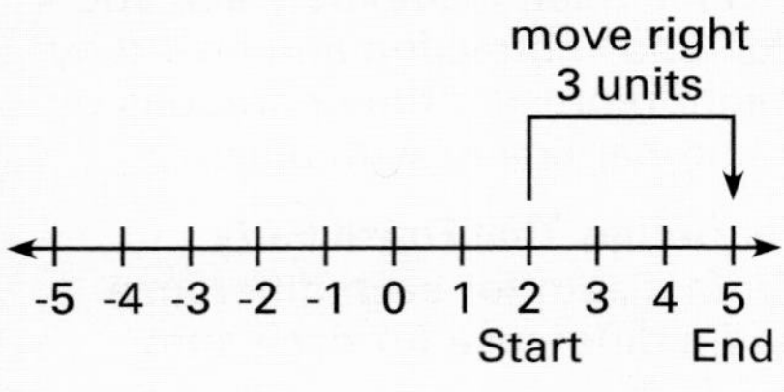

   $2 - (-3) = 5$

When you use algebra tiles to subtract integers, you may not have enough tiles to take away. You can add zero pairs to provide the tiles you need.

History Link

The Italian mathematician Leonardo Fibonacci published *Liber Abaci* (The Book of Numbers) in A.D. 1202. In it, he explained that "5 diminished by 8" would result in "a debt of 3." This is one of the earliest known references to a negative number.

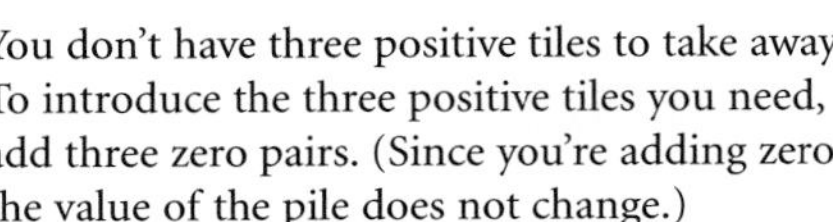

Example 1

Use algebra tiles to subtract: $-2 - 3$

Start with two negative tiles.

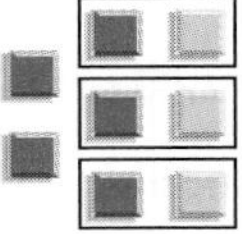

You don't have three positive tiles to take away. To introduce the three positive tiles you need, add three zero pairs. (Since you're adding zero, the value of the pile does not change.)

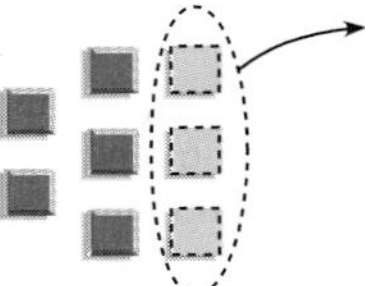

Now subtract by taking away three positive tiles. There are five negative tiles left.

$-2 - 3 = -5$

Try It

Use algebra tiles to find each difference.

a. $4 - 3$ 1 **b.** $2 - 5$ −3 **c.** $-3 - 3$ −6 **d.** $-2 - (-6)$ 4

You can use a number line to subtract integers. When you subtract a positive number, the difference is *less* than the original number, so you move to the *left*. To subtract a negative number, move to the *right*.

Example 2

Use a number line to subtract: $-6 - (-4)$

Start at −6. To subtract *negative* 4, move four units to the *right*.

$-6 - (-4) = -2$

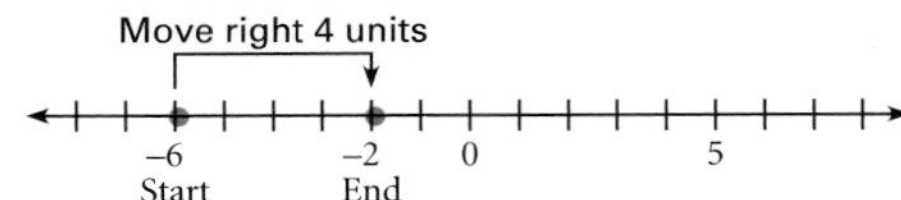

Try It

Use a number line to find each difference.

a. $5 - 3$ 2 **b.** $-2 - 3$ −5 **c.** $-1 - (-4)$ 3 **d.** $0 - (-2)$ 2

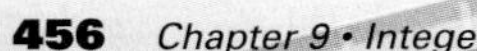

MATH EVERY DAY

Problem of the Day

The fastest 100-yard sack race winner completed the race in 14.4 seconds. How fast was that in miles per hour? Round your answer to the nearest tenth.
14.2 mi/hr

Available on Daily Transparency 9-5

An Extension is provided in the transparency package.

Fact of the Day

Coney Island became an amusement center in the 1880s. It is located in Brooklyn, NY.

Mental Math

Give each subtraction as an addition.

1. $-4 - 4$ $-4 + (-4)$
2. $-4 - (-3)$ $-4 + 3$
3. $2 - 6$ $2 + (-6)$
4. $0 - (-10)$ $0 + 10$

You can use a number line to show a very important relationship between integer addition and subtraction.

Compare the subtraction problem $-4 - (-3)$ to the addition problem $-4 + 3$.

To subtract negative 3, move *right*. To add positive 3, move *right*.

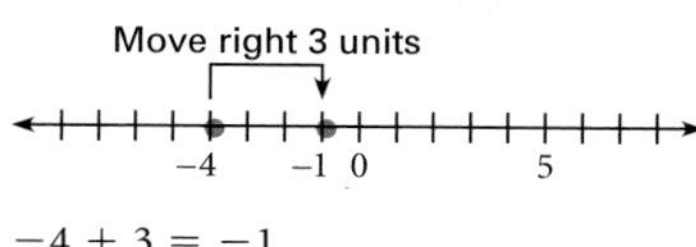

$-4 - (-3) = -1$ $-4 + 3 = -1$

In both cases, you start at the same point, move in the same direction, and get the same answer. This idea is summarized in the following property:

Subtracting a number is the same as adding its opposite.

Example 3

During the biggest drop of the Mean Streak roller coaster at Cedar Point®, in Sandusky, Ohio, your altitude changes by −155 feet. The longest drop of the Texas Giant™, at Six Flags® Over Texas, has a −137 ft change. How much farther do you drop on the Mean Streak?

$-155 - (-137) = -155 + 137$ Rewrite as addition.

$= |-155| - |137|$ The integers have different signs. Subtract their absolute values.

$= 155 - 137$

$= 18$, but write -18 Take the sign of the number with the larger absolute value.

You drop 18 feet farther on the Mean Streak.

Try It

The Drop Zone™ Stunt Tower at Paramount's Great America® has a free-fall altitude change of −129 ft. It replaces the Edge™, which had a −60 ft change. How much farther do you free-fall in the Drop Zone? **69 feet**

DID YOU KNOW?

The Mean Streak can reach speeds of 65 miles per hour.

Check Your Understanding

1. How is subtraction related to addition?

2. Michelle subtracted a negative integer from another integer. Was her answer greater than or less than the original integer? Explain your answer.

MEETING MIDDLE SCHOOL CLASSROOM NEEDS

Tips from Middle School Teachers

To ensure thorough understanding, I have students use concrete materials such as algebra tiles and number lines to model integer operations for as long as they wish.

Team Teaching

Ask science teachers to discuss the effects of air pressure and water pressure on the human body at great elevations and at deep distances under water, respectively.

Geography Connection

The cities of Huron, South Dakota, and Bismarck, North Dakota, both have a range of more than 150°F for lowest and highest temperatures, while Portland, Oregon, and Helena, Montana, both have a range of more than 140°F.

Alternate Examples

3. The coldest temperature ever recorded in Alaska was −80°F and in Florida was −2°F. How much colder was the Alaska temperature than the Florida temperature?

$-80 - (-2)$

Rewrite as addition.
$-80 - (-2) = -80 + 2$

Subtract absolute values.
$80 - 2 = 78$

Use the sign of the number with the greater absolute value.
$-80 + 2 = -78$

The Alaska temperature was 78°F colder than the Florida temperature.

3 Practice and Assess

Check

Have students perform a variety of integer subtractions to be sure they can apply the property on this page. Also check that they are performing the resulting additions correctly. You may need to review the rules for adding integers.

Answers for Check Your Understanding

1. Subtracting is the same as adding the opposite.
2. Greater than; Subtracting a negative integer is the same as adding the absolute value of the negative integer.

9-5 Exercises and Applications

Assignment Guide

- **Basic**
  1–25 odds, 29–31, 33–51 odds
- **Average**
  2–26 evens, 29–31, 34–52 evens
- **Enriched**
  6-26 evens, 27–32, 34–52 evens

Exercise Notes

Exercises 25–28

Estimation Students may use a guess-and-check strategy to find the unknowns.

Exercise Answers

1. a–b.

c. □ □ □ □ □

29. Alaska: 180, California: 179, Hawaii: 86, North Dakota: 181, West Virginia: 149; Widest: North Dakota; Narrowest: Hawaii

Reteaching

Activity

Materials: 4 number cubes: 2 yellow for positive integers and 2 red for negative integers

- Draw and label a number line from -12 to 12. Put the 4 number cubes in a bag. Without looking, pick one. Toss it and place it on the corresponding point on the number line.
- Pick another cube, toss it, and move the first cube the number of units indicated by the number on the second cube. Since subtraction is the inverse of addition, move in the direction opposite that indicated on the cube. That is, move *left* if the 2nd cube is *yellow* and *right* if it is *red*. The point at which you stop is the difference of the two numbers on the cubes.

9-5 Exercises and Applications

Practice and Apply

1. **Getting Started** Follow these steps to find the difference $1 - (-4)$ by using algebra tiles.

a. Draw a positive algebra tile to represent 1.

b. You don't have 4 negative tiles to take away, so sketch 4 zero pairs.

c. Subtract by taking away 4 negative tiles.

d. Count the remaining tiles. Write the difference. 5

Use algebra tiles to find each difference.

2. $3 - (-3)$ 6 **3.** $-5 - 4$ −9 **4.** $-2 - 7$ −9

Use a number line to find each difference.

5. $5 - (-5)$ 10 **6.** $-3 - (-4)$ 1 **7.** $8 - (-4)$ 12

Operation Sense **Find each difference.**

8. $-12 - 33$ −45 **9.** $42 - (-14)$ 56 **10.** $-39 - (-45)$ 6 **11.** $-60 - (-120)$ 60 **12.** $85 - (-30)$ 115

13. $-18 - 3$ −21 **14.** $22 - (-17)$ 39 **15.** $52 - 82$ −30 **16.** $-75 - (-75)$ 0 **17.** $-147 - (-56)$ −91

18. $-67 - 136$ −203 **19.** $271 - (-312)$ 583 **20.** $-430 - (-650)$ 220 **21.** $43 + (-15) - (-102)$ 130

Patterns **Write the next integer in each pattern.**

22. 5, 0, −5, ____ −10 **23.** 13, 4, −5, ____ −14 **24.** 16, 2, −12, ____ −26

Find the unknown number in each difference.

25. $-23 - x = -35$ 12 **26.** $7 - y = -5$ 12

27. $-7 - w = 0$ −7 **28.** $11 - z = 26$ −15

29. **Geography** The table shows the highest and lowest temperatures ever recorded in several states. Find the temperature range for each state. Which state has the widest range? The narrowest range?

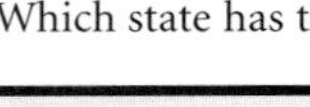

Extreme Temperatures

State	Alaska	California	Hawaii	North Dakota	West Virginia
High Temperature	100°F	134°F	100°F	121°F	112°F
Low Temperature	−80°F	−45°F	14°F	−60°F	−37°F

Death Valley, California

PRACTICE 9-5

PRACTICE

Name ______________________

Practice 9-5

Subtracting Integers

Use algebra tiles to find each difference.

1. $-7 - 2$ −9 2. $7 - (-3)$ 10 3. $-4 - (-3)$ −1 4. $3 - (-4)$ 7
5. $-4 - (-1)$ −3 6. $-4 - 5$ −9 7. $3 - 7$ −4 8. $-3 - (-7)$ 4

Use a number line to find each difference.

9. $1 - (-6)$ 7 10. $2 - 4$ −2 11. $8 - 3$ 5 12. $-6 - 1$ −7
13. $-1 - (-1)$ 0 14. $4 - 7$ −3 15. $8 - (-1)$ 9 16. $0 - 2$ −2

Find each difference.

17. $-38 - 50$ −88 18. $-110 - 118$ −228 19. $-16 - (-34)$ 18
20. $10 - 73$ −63 21. $10 - (-78)$ 88 22. $-12 - 15$ −27
23. $-24 - (-56)$ 32 24. $-56 - 42$ −98 25. $13 - 100$ −87

Write the next integer in each pattern.

26. 15, 3 −9, −21 27. −8, −11, −14, −17 28. 17, 12, 7, 2
29. 12, 5, −2, −9 30. 4, −6, −16, −26 31. 18, 10, 2, −6

Find the unknown number in each difference.

32. $9 - y = 12$ −3 33. $-34 + x = -23$ 11 34. $32 + z = -13$ −45

35. **Geography** The table shows the highest and lowest elevations of each continent. Find the range of elevations for each continent by subtracting the low elevation from the high elevation.

Continent	Africa	Antarctica	Asia	Europe	N. America	S. America	Australia
High el. (m)	5895	4897	8848	5642	6194	6960	2228
Low el. (m)	−156	−2538	−400	−28	−86	−40	−16
Range (m)	6051	7435	9248	5670	6280	7000	2244

Which continent has the widest range? Asia

Which continent has the narrowest range? Australia

RETEACHING

Name ______________________

Alternative Lesson 9-5

Subtracting Integers

You have learned how to add integers using the number line. Study the number lines below to see how addition of integers relates to subtraction of integers.

$7 - 4 = 3$ $7 + (-4) = 3$

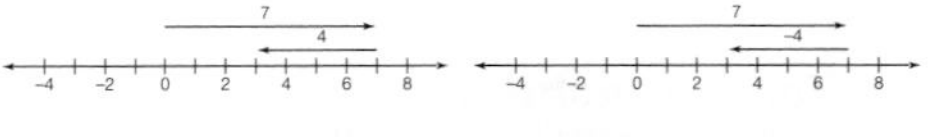

These results can be summarized in the following property.

Subtracting a number is the same as adding its opposite.

Example

Find −3 − 5.

Rewrite as addition. Then add.

So −3 − 5 = −8.

−3 − 5 (− Change to addition. 5 — Change to the opposite.)
−3 + (−5) = −8

Try It Find 7 − (−8).

a. What is the opposite of −8? 8

b. Rewrite as addition. Then add. 7 + 8 = 15

Find −6 − 5.

c. What is the opposite of 5? −5

d. Rewrite as addition. Then add. −6 + −5 = −11

Find −4 − (−3).

e. What is the opposite of −3? 3

f. Rewrite as addition. Then add. −4 + 3 = −1

Find each difference.

g. 9 − (−5) = 14 h. −4 − 6 = −10 i. −3 − (−8) = 5
j. 3 − 8 = −5 k. −6 − (−10) = 4 l. 5 − (−2) = 7
m. −4 − (−12) = 8 n. 10 − (−4) = 14 o. −9 − 7 = −16

30. **Test Prep** A professional golfer scores 5 under par (-5), 3 under par, 6 under par, and 4 under par for the four days of a tournament. What is her total score? C

Ⓐ $+18$ Ⓑ $+8$ Ⓒ -18 Ⓓ -8

Problem Solving and Reasoning

31. Choose a Strategy Evaluate the following expressions if $x = -10$ and $y = 20$. Write an equation for each expression.

a. $x - y$ $-10 - 20 = -30$ **b.** $y - x$ $20 - (-10) = 30$ **c.** $x - x$ $-10 - (-10) = 0$ **d.** $y - y$ $20 - 20 = 0$

Problem Solving STRATEGIES

- Look for a Pattern
- Make an Organized List
- Make a Table
- Guess and Check
- Work Backward
- Use Logical Reasoning
- Draw a Diagram
- Solve a Simpler Problem

32. Critical Thinking The climb from the start to the top of the first hill on the I Scream, You Scream roller coaster is 115 ft.

a. What is the change in altitude for drop A, where the coaster plunges into an underground tunnel (from 115 ft to -17 ft)? -132 ft

b. Find the changes for each of the other climbs and drops (B–E).

c. How did you find the change for climb E? B: 80 ft, C: -69 ft, D: 33 ft, E: -32 ft

It is the descent between 27 and -5, which is a drop of 32 ft.

Mixed Review

Use factor trees to find the prime factorization of the following numbers. If possible, express multiple factors as exponents. *[Lesson 3-6]*

33. 1024 2^{10} **34.** 132 $2^2 \times 3 \times 11$ **35.** 66 $2 \times 3 \times 11$ **36.** 375 3×5^3 **37.** 144 $2^4 \times 3^2$

38. 210 $2 \times 3 \times 5 \times 7$ **39.** 2730 $2 \times 3 \times 5 \times 7 \times 13$ **40.** 192 $2^6 \times 3$ **41.** 96 $2^5 \times 3$ **42.** 2310 $2 \times 3 \times 5 \times 7 \times 11$

Write each decimal as a percent. *[Lesson 8-3]*

43. 0.52 52% **44.** 0.17 17% **45.** 0.9 90% **46.** 0.07 7% **47.** 2.43 243%

48. 1 100% **49.** 9.87654 987.654% **50.** 0.00003 0.003% **51.** 10.2 1020% **52.** 0.1053 10.53%

PROBLEM SOLVING 9-5

Exercise Notes

Exercise 30

Test Prep If students choose A, they have used positive numbers instead of negative. If they choose B, they have used -5 for 5 under par but positive integers for the other scores.

Exercise 31

Problem-Solving Tip You may wish to use Teaching Tool Transparencies 2 and 3: Guided Problem Solving, pages 1–2.

Estimation Students may use guess and check to write the desired equations.

Exercises 33–42

Error Prevention You may need to review with students the process of finding prime factorizations and the use of exponents.

Alternate Assessment

You may want to use the *Interactive CD-ROM Journal* with this assessment.

Journal Have students write the rules for adding integers from Lesson 9-4 and the property of subtraction presented in this lesson, giving examples to illustrate each rule or property.

Quick Quiz

Find each difference.

1. $-29 - (-29)$ 0
2. $-11 - 11$ -22
3. $0 - (-9)$ 9
4. $-3 - (-28)$ 25
5. $20 - 32$ -12

Available on Daily Transparency 9-5

PROBLEM SOLVING

Name ____________________

Guided Problem Solving 9-5

GPS PROBLEM 29, STUDENT PAGE 458

The table shows the highest and lowest temperatures ever recorded in several states. Find the temperature range for each state. Which state has the widest range? The narrowest range?

Extreme Temperatures					
State	Alaska	California	Hawaii	North Dakota	West Virginia
High Temperature	100°F	134°F	100°F	121°F	112°F
Low Temperature	−80°F	−45°F	14°F	−60°F	−37°F

Understand

1. What is meant by the widest range? The narrowest range?
The greatest difference and the least difference between the high and low temperatures.

Plan

2. How can you find each temperature range? b
 a. Add high and low temperatures. b. Subtract low from high temperature.

Solve

3. Find the temperature range for each state.
 a. Alaska 180°F b. California 179°F c. Hawaii 86°F
 d. North Dakota 181°F e. West Virginia 149°F
4. Which state has the widest range? The narrowest? N. Dakota; Hawaii

Look Back

5. Use a calculator to check your calculations.

SOLVE ANOTHER PROBLEM

The table shows the highest and lowest temperatures ever recorded in Illinois, Nevada, and Florida. Which state has the widest range? Nevada; Florida

Extreme Temperatures (in °F)			
State	Illinois	Florida	Nevada
High Temperature	117°F	109°F	122°F
Low Temperature	−35°F	−2°F	−50°F

ENRICHMENT

Name ____________________

Extend Your Thinking 9-5

Visual Thinking

There are many polygons in this figure.

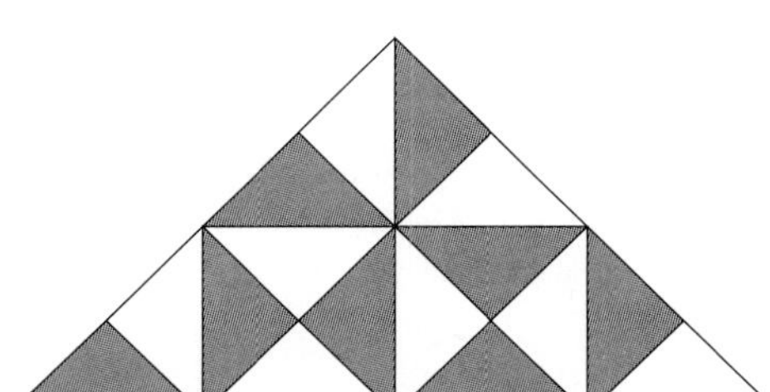

Complete the chart below to find the number of each type of polygon.

Polygon	Number in Figure
Triangle	40
Square	9
Rectangle (includes square)	18
Parallelogram (includes rectangle)	26
Trapezoid	41
All Quadrilaterals	67

Technology

Using a Spreadsheet • Duplicating Formulas

The Point

Students discover the usefulness of the copy feature of a spreadsheet software program.

Materials

Spreadsheet software

Resources

Interactive CD-ROM Spreadsheet/Grapher Tool

About the Page

Emphasize that what really makes the copy feature of a spreadsheet program useful is that it automatically changes a formula to reflect the appropriate rows or columns. For example, if the formula = B2 + B3 was entered into B4 and then copied into C4, the formula would be adjusted to = C2 + C3.

Ask ...

- If the data for June was entered into column G, what would you do in cell G4? Copy the formula from cell F4.
- What would be the new formula in cell G4? = G2/G3

Answers for Try It

Wk 1: ≈ 2.9 drinks per day

Wk 2: = 3/day

Wk 3: ≈ 3.4/day

Wk 4: ≈ 2.7/day

Wk 5: ≈ 2.6/day

Wk 6: ≈ 3.3/day

Wk 7: ≈ 3.1/day

Wk 8: ≈ 3.7/day

Wk 9: = 4/day

Wk 10 ≈ 3.4/day

Wk 11: ≈ 4.3/day

Wk 12: ≈ 4.9/day

Wk 13: ≈ 6.9/day

On Your Own

The second question points out the capability of a spreadsheet to act similarly to a word processor—text may be copied and pasted into new locations.

TECHNOLOGY

Using a Spreadsheet • Duplicating Formulas

Problem: Magdalena's family owns a cafe. The sales totals for the first five months of the year are shown. What are the average sales per day each month?

You can use your spreadsheet's ability to duplicate formulas to answer this question.

Jan.	$7050
Feb.	$5784
Mar.	$8992
Apr.	$7231
May	$9067

1 Enter the data and the number of days in each month into the spreadsheet.

Then, to find January sales per day, divide the value in cell B2 by the number of days in cell B3. This formula is =B2/B3. Enter it into cell B4, and press return.

	A	B	C	D	E	F
1	Month	January	February	March	April	May
2	Sales	7050	5784	8992	7231	9067
3	Days in month	31	28	31	30	31
4	Sales per day	227.42				

2 To find sales per day for the other months, you could enter =C2/C3 into cell C4, =D2/D3 into cell D4, and so on. But, except for the letters, these formulas are the same as the one used in cell B4. In this case, you can COPY the formula and PASTE it into cells C4 through F4. The spreadsheet automatically updates the cell references—if you look in cell E4, it shows the formula =E2/E3.

	B
1	January
2	7050
3	31
4	227.42

	A	B	C	D	E	F
1	Month	January	February	March	April	May
2	Sales	7050	5784	8992	7231	9067
3	Days in month	31	28	31	30	31
4	Sales per day	227.42	206.57	290.06	241.03	292.48

Solution: The sales per day are shown in the last row of the table.

TRY IT

Misha's Market is open every day. In the first 13 weeks of the year, customers bought 20, 21, 24, 19, 18, 23, 22, 26, 28, 24, 30, 34, and 48 Super Sleety drinks. Use a spreadsheet to find the average sold per day for each week.

ON YOUR OWN

▶ Why is it helpful to be able to copy and paste formulas in a spreadsheet?

▶ You can also copy and paste numbers in a spreadsheet. Suppose Magdalena's family owned a second restaurant and wanted to find out its sales per day for the first four months. What numbers from the spreadsheet shown in 1 would it be useful to copy and paste?

460

Answers for On Your Own

1. When you have many similar calculations, you do not have to retype the formula several times.
2. Since the number of days per month does not change, you could copy and paste row 3 (Days per month) into the table for the second restaurant instead of retyping the information.

Multiplying Integers

9-6

▶ Lesson Link You know how to add and subtract integers. Now you'll investigate multiplication of integers. ◀

You'll Learn ...

- to multiply integers

... How It's Used

Civil engineers use integer multiplication when they calculate the forces on a bridge.

Explore Multiplying Integers

One Good Turn Deserves Another

Latasha videotaped her sister Tonya riding a Ferris wheel. During the first half of the ride, the wheel turned forward (clockwise). During the second half of the ride, the wheel turned backward. Later, the girls played the video on their VCR.

1. On the video, did the wheel appear to turn forward or backward during the first half of the ride?

2. Did the wheel appear to turn forward or backward during the second half of the ride?
3. For fun, the girls decided to run the video backward. Did the wheel appear to turn forward or backward during the first half of the ride? How did the wheel appear to turn during the second half of the ride? Explain.
4. Using your answers to Questions 1–3, copy and complete the table. Describe any patterns you notice.

Ferris Wheel Motion	Forward	Backward	Forward	Backward
VCR Motion	Forward	Forward	Backward	Backward
Apparent Motion of Wheel				

MEETING INDIVIDUAL NEEDS

Resources

9-6 Practice
9-6 Reteaching
9-6 Problem Solving
9-6 Enrichment
9-6 Daily Transparency
Problem of the Day
Review
Quick Quiz

Lesson Enhancement Transparency 43

Learning Modalities

Logical Use patterns to illustrate integer multiplication. Multiplying a given number by a negative integer is the opposite of multiplying the given number by a positive integer, so the products are opposites of each other.

Visual Using the concept of multiplication as repeated addition with number lines is a good approach to the teaching of integer multiplication.

English Language Development

The use of patterns such as those below may help students with limited English proficiency to understand the concept of integer multiplication. Encourage them to extend the patterns and then give rules in their own words.

$4 \cdot 2 = 8$	$-4 \cdot 2 = -8$
$4 \cdot 1 = 4$	$-4 \cdot 1 = -4$
$4 \cdot 0 = 0$	$-4 \cdot 0 = 0$
$4 \cdot (-1) = -4$	$-4 \cdot (-1) = 4$
$4 \cdot (-2) = -8$	$-4 \cdot (-2) = 8$
$4 \cdot (-3) = -12$	$-4 \cdot (-3) = 12$

9-6 Lesson Organizer

Objective

- Multiply integers.

NCTM Standards

- 1–8

▶ Review

Find each sum.

1. $-8 + (-8) + (-8)$ −24
2. $-1 + (-1) + (-1) + (-1) + (-1)$ −5
3. $3 + 3 + 3 + 3 + 3 + 3$ 18
4. $-16 + (-16) + (-16)$ −48
5. $-5 + (-5) + (-5) + (-5) + (-5)$ −25

Available on Daily Transparency 9-6

1 Introduce

Explore

The Point

Students use their imaginations to visualize what happens when a video is run backward. They then describe the patterns they find. These patterns mirror the sign rules for integer multiplication and division.

Ongoing Assessment

Have students give an integer to describe 3 bank deposits of $10 each. 30 Then have them give an integer for 3 withdrawals of $10 each. −30 Repeat with questions about equal gains and equal losses of yardage in a football game, equal gains and equal losses of weight, and so on. Have them describe the patterns they see.

For Groups That Finish Early

Imagine situations in a football video in which the quarterback is running forward with the ball and when he is dropping back to pass. Describe the apparent motions if the video is run backward. They will be the reverse of the actual motions.

Answers for Explore on next page.

Answers for Explore

1. Forward
2. Backward
3. Backward; Forward; The direction of the wheel was opposite to how it actually went.
4. Forward; Backward; Backward; Forward; When the video is run forward, the direction of the wheel appears the same as it actually turned. When the video is run backward, the direction of the wheel appears to be the opposite of the actual direction.

2 Teach

Learn

You may wish to use Lesson Enhancement Transparency 43 with **Learn.**

Relate the rules for integer multiplication to the patterns found in the **Explore** table. Ask students to describe which motions represent positive integers. Forward wheel, forward video Then have them describe the motions that represent negative integers. Backward wheel, backward video.

Alternate Examples

Find each product.

1. $4 \bullet 13$

   Both numbers are positive, so the product is positive.
   $4 \bullet 13 = 52$

2. $-5 \bullet 15$

   -5 is negative and 15 is positive, so the product is negative.
   $-5 \bullet 15 = -75$

3. $6 \bullet (-12)$

   6 is positive and -12 is negative, so the product is negative.
   $6 \bullet (-12) = -72$

Learn Multiplying Integers

When you multiply two integers, you need to know whether the product is positive or negative. There are four cases to think about:

First Number	Second Number	Example
+	+	$2 \cdot 3$
+	−	$2 \cdot (-3)$
−	+	$-2 \cdot 3$
−	−	$-2 \cdot (-3)$

The first case is easy. From arithmetic, you know *the product of two positive numbers is positive.*

You can use algebra tiles to investigate the second case.

Think: $2 \cdot (-3)$ means "two groups of negative three."

There are six red tiles, so $2 \cdot (-3) = -6$.

From the Commutative Property of Multiplication, you know that the order of multiplication does not affect the product. For the third case, $-3 \cdot 2$ must also equal -6. Therefore, *the product of two integers with different signs is negative,* and $-2 \cdot 3$ also equals -6.

Test Prep

When you're preparing for a test on integer operations, review your basic addition, subtraction, multiplication, and division facts for whole numbers.

Examples

Find each product.

1 $12 \cdot 5$

Both numbers are positive, so the product is positive.

$12 \cdot 5 = 60$

2 $-6 \cdot 8$

-6 is negative and 8 is positive, so the product is negative.

$-6 \cdot 8 = -48$

3 $7 \cdot (-2)$

7 is positive and -2 is negative, so the product is negative.

$7 \cdot (-2) = -14$

Try It

Find each product.

a. $-4 \cdot 4$ -16 **b.** $10 \cdot 2$ 20 **c.** $9 \cdot (-6)$ -54

d. $-11 \cdot 3$ -33 **e.** $28 \cdot (-5)$ -140 **f.** $-19 \cdot 0$ 0

MATH EVERY DAY

Problem of the Day

You throw three darts at the target below. Assume you hit the target with all three darts.

1. What is the minimum score you can get? The maximum?
2. If you get one dart in each area, what will your total score be?

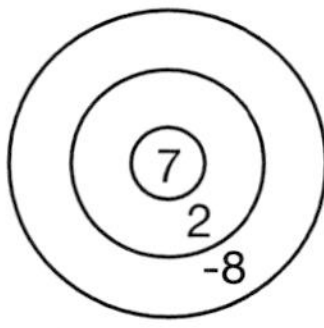

1. −24; 21, 2. 1

Available on Daily Transparency 9-6

An Extension is provided in the transparency package.

Fact of the Day

Camcorders are combination video cameras and tape recorders. Lightweight video recorders use 8-mm tapes or VHS videotapes.

Mental Math

Tell the sign of each product

1. $-44 \bullet (-14)$ positive
2. $-50 \bullet 3$ negative
3. $24 \bullet (-63)$ negative
4. $20 \bullet 10$ positive
5. $-33 \bullet (-9)$ positive

Example 4

When the 32 passengers on a roller coaster went through a loop, an average of 65¢ in change fell out of each of their pockets. How much money did the passengers lose in all?

Use −65 to represent a loss of 65¢.

$32 \cdot (-65) = -2080$ The factors have opposite signs, so the product is negative.

The passengers lost 2080¢, or $20.80.

To decide what happens when both numbers are negative, study the pattern in the table. What predictions can you make about $-3 \cdot (-1)$ and $-3 \cdot (-2)$?

-3×4	=	−12
-3×3	=	−9
-3×2	=	−6
-3×1	=	−3
-3×0	=	0
$-3 \times (-1)$	=	?
$-3 \times (-2)$	=	?

Each product is 3 more than the preceding one. Continuing the pattern, $-3 \cdot (-1) = 3$ and $-3 \cdot (-2) = 6$. This shows that *the product of two negative integers is positive.*

Here is a summary of rules for multiplying integers.

Study TIP

You can remember that the product of two negative numbers is positive by imagining their two minus signs forming a plus sign.

INTEGER MULTIPLICATION RULES
- The product of two numbers with the same sign is positive.
- The product of two numbers with different signs is negative.

Examples

5 Multiply: $-34 \cdot (-9)$

Both numbers have the same sign, so the product is positive.

$-34 \cdot (-9) = 306$

6 Multiply: $-2 \cdot (-3) \cdot (-4)$

$-2 \cdot (-3) \cdot (-4) = 6 \cdot (-4)$ The signs are the same, so the product is positive.

$6 \cdot (-4) = -24$ The signs are different, so the product is negative.

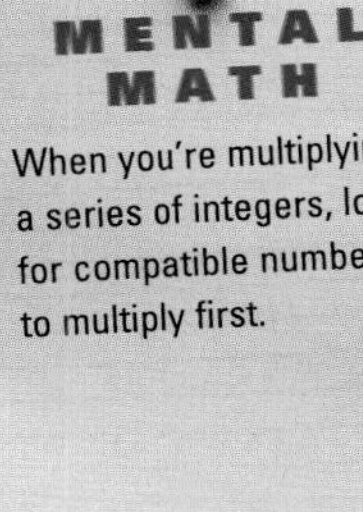

MENTAL MATH

When you're multiplying a series of integers, look for compatible numbers to multiply first.

Try It

Find each product.

a. $-4 \cdot (-8) \cdot 2$ 64 **b.** $5 \cdot 3 \cdot (-2)$ −30 **c.** $6 \cdot (-2) \cdot (-2)$ 24

MEETING MIDDLE SCHOOL CLASSROOM NEEDS

Tips from Middle School Teachers

Some of my students have no trouble with addition and subtraction of integers but become confused with multiplication. I provide concrete examples and use the idea of repeated addition.

Science Connection

When two gears are connected so that one turns clockwise, the second moves counterclockwise. If a third gear is added, it moves clockwise. This can be compared to multiplying a series of negative numbers: the product of two negative numbers is positive; the product of three is negative, the product of four is positive, and so on.

Team Teaching

Invite a communications or fine-arts teacher to show students how to make a videotape. Students might prepare a show that they can record.

Alternate Examples

4. Before a storm, the temperature dropped 2 degrees per hour for 5 hours. What was the total change in temperature?

   Let −2 represent the change per hour.

   $5 \cdot (-2) = -10$

   The factors have opposite signs, so the product is negative.

   The change in temperature was −10 degrees.

5. Multiply: $-28 \cdot (-6)$.

   Both numbers have the same sign, so the product is positive.

   $-28 \cdot (-6) = 168$.

6. Multiply: $-4 \cdot (-5) \cdot (-3)$

   The signs of the first two factors are the same, so their product is positive.

   $-4 \cdot (-5) \cdot (-3) = 20 \cdot (-3)$

   The signs of the two remaining factors are different, so their product is negative.

   $20 \cdot (-3) = -60$

3 Practice and Assess

Check

- Write a positive integer on the chalkboard. Ask students to name integers whose product with the original is negative. Then have them name integers whose product with the original is positive.
- Now write a negative integer on the chalkboard. Ask students to name integers whose product with the original is negative. Then have them name integers whose product with the original is positive.
- In each case, have students supply the product.

9-6 Exercises and Applications

Assignment Guide

- **Basic** 1–10, 11–23 odds, 28–32, 35–49 odds
- **Average** 1–7, 12–28 evens, 29–33, 36–50 evens
- **Enriched** 1–7, 13–29 odds, 30–34, 35–49 odds

Answers for Check Your Understanding

1. The product of two positive numbers is positive and the product of two negative numbers is also positive. The products are the same.
2. They are either both positive or both negative; One is positive and the other is negative.

Exercise Notes

Exercises 23–27

Extension Ask students to determine the sign of each product before computing.

Exercise 28

Geography Horseshoe Falls is the part of Niagara Falls located in Canada. The American part of Niagara Falls is called the American Falls.

Reteaching

Activity

Materials: 4 number cubes: 2 yellow for positive integers and 2 red for negative integers, bag

- Draw and label a number line from −36 to 36. Put the four number cubes in the bag. Without looking, pick two cubes. Toss them and find the product of the two numbers that show.
- What will the sign of the product be if you toss two red cubes? + Two yellow cubes? + One red cube and one yellow cube? −
- If you have trouble deciding on the sign, use the number line. For instance, if you toss 3 and 5, make 3 moves of 5 units to the right. 15 If you toss −3 and 5, make 5 moves of 3 units to the left. −15

Check Your Understanding

1. Explain why $3 \cdot 4 = -3 \cdot (-4)$.
2. What can you say about the signs of two numbers if their product is positive? Negative?

9-6 Exercises and Applications

Practice and Apply

Getting Started Copy and complete each pattern.

1.	2.	3.
$4 \times 4 = 16$	$-5 \times 3 = -15$	$-9 \times 3 = ?$ **−27**
$4 \times 3 = 12$	$-5 \times 2 = -10$	$-9 \times 2 = -18$
$4 \times 2 = ?$ **8**	$-5 \times 1 = ?$ **−5**	$-9 \times 1 = -9$
$4 \times 1 = ?$ **4**	$-5 \times 0 = 0$	$-9 \times 0 = ?$ **0**
$4 \times 0 = 0$	$-5 \times (-1) = ?$ **5**	$-9 \times (-1) = ?$ **9**
$4 \times (-1) = ?$ **−4**	$-5 \times (-2) = ?$ **10**	$-9 \times (-2) = ?$ **18**
$4 \times (-2) = ?$ **−8**	$-5 \times (-3) = ?$ **15**	$-9 \times (-3) = 27$

Operation Sense Give the sign of each product.

4. $+ \times +$ **+**
5. $+ \times -$ **−**
6. $- \times +$ **−**
7. $- \times -$ **+**

Operation Sense Find each product.

8. $8 \cdot 9$ **72**
9. $-8 \cdot (-9)$ **72**
10. $-8 \cdot 9$ **−72**
11. $8 \cdot (-9)$ **−72**
12. $-8 \cdot 0$ **0**
13. $-5 \cdot (-9)$ **45**
14. $12 \cdot (-3)$ **−36**
15. $-20 \cdot 5$ **−100**
16. $-14 \cdot (-10)$ **140**
17. $27 \cdot (-5)$ **−135**
18. $-81 \cdot 1$ **−81**
19. $-25 \cdot (-5)$ **125**
20. $100 \cdot (-10)$ **−1000**
21. $-16 \cdot 7$ **−112**
22. $-50 \cdot (-50)$ **2500**
23. $-2 \cdot (-2) \cdot (-2)$ **−8**
24. $-5 \cdot 2 \cdot (-3)$ **30**
25. $-7 \cdot 3 \cdot 4$ **−84**
26. $10 \cdot (-6) \cdot (-5)$ **300**
27. $8 \cdot (-8) \cdot 8$ **−512**
28. **Science** The underlying rock ledge of Canada's Horseshoe Falls is cut back about 2 ft each year by erosion.
    a. Write the erosion rate as a negative integer. **−2**
    b. Calculate how much the rock ledge will erode over a seven-year period. **−14 feet**

PRACTICE 9-6

PRACTICE

Name ______________ **Practice 9-6**

Multiplying Integers

Find each product.

1. −2 · (−16) **32**	2. −29 · 3 **−87**	3. −11 · 21 **−231**
4. 3 · 19 **57**	5. −2 · 16 **−32**	6. −10 · 12 **−120**
7. −2 · (−6) **12**	8. −8 · (−18) **144**	9. 13 · (−26) **−338**
10. −2 · 6 **−12**	11. −3 · 28 **−84**	12. −2 · (−2) **4**
13. −27 · 28 **−756**	14. 2 · (−3) **−6**	15. −2 · (−5) **10**
16. 2 · (−6) **−12**	17. 12 · (−14) **−168**	18. −14 · (−10) **140**
19. 46 · (−6) **−276**	20. −4 · 4 **−16**	21. −13 · 2 **−26**
22. −17 · (−4) **68**	23. 19 · 5 **95**	24. 16 · (−14) **−224**
25. −11 · (−34) **374**	26. 2 · (−34) **−68**	27. −17 · (−5) **85**
28. 9 · (−10) **−90**	29. 2 · (−13) **−26**	30. −16 · 3 **−48**
31. −17 · 19 **−323**	32. −17 · (−36) **612**	33. −22 · 4 **−88**
34. −9 · (−19) **171**	35. 4 · (−8) **−32**	36. −14 · (−2) **28**
37. −6 · (−23) **138**	38. −9 · 3 **−27**	39. −18 · 9 **−162**
40. −16 · 7 **−112**	41. −38 · 18 **−684**	42. −32 · (−6) **192**
43. −25 · (−10) **250**	44. −13 · 20 **−260**	45. 2 · (−9) **−18**
46. −9 · 11 **−99**	47. −4 · (−2) **8**	48. −11 · (−24) **264**

49. In 1995, Nigeria was losing its forest cover at the rate of 4000 km^2 per year.
    a. Write the deforestation rate as a negative integer. **−4000 km^2 per yr**
    b. Calculate the change in the amount of forest in a 5-year period. **−20,000 km^2**
50. Tabitha withdrew $85 a month from her savings account for seven months. What was the change in her balance? **−$595**

RETEACHING

Name ______________ **Alternative Lesson 9-6**

Multiplying Integers

When you multiply two integers, you need to know whether the product is positive or negative. The sign of the product depends on the signs of the factors.

	Signs of Integers	Answer is:
Multiply	Same sign →	+
	Different sign →	−

Example

Find −8 · 3.

a. What is the sign of the product? **−**
b. Multiply the absolute values. **24** c. Write the product. **−24**

So, −8 · 3 = −24.

Try It Find −5 · (−7).

d. What is the sign of the product? **+**
e. Multiply the absolute values. **35** f. Write the product. **35**

Find 8 · 4.

g. What is the sign of the product? **+**
h. Multiply the absolute values. **32** i. Write the product. **32**

Find 7 · (−8).

j. What is the sign of the product? **−**
k. Multiply the absolute values. **56** l. Write the product. **−56**

Find each product.

m. 4 · −3 = **−12** n. 6 · (−2) = **−12** o. −9 · (−5) = **45**
p. 12 · 4 = **48** q. −7 · (−6) = **42** r. −3 · 12 = **−36**

Tell whether each product will be positive or negative.

s. Positive × positive **Positive.** t. Positive × negative **Negative.**
u. Negative × negative **Positive.** v. Negative × positive **Negative.**

29. Sports A hockey player's plus-minus rating compares the number of goals scored by his or her team (plus) to the number scored by the opponents (minus) while he or she is playing. In 1996, eight players on the San Jose Sharks had an average plus-minus rating of -17. What was the total of their ratings? **−136**

30. Estimation Estimate the product $-5 \cdot 19 \cdot (-11)$. GPS Explain how you made your estimate.

1000; $-5 \times 20 = -100$ and $-100 \times -10 = 1000$

31. Test Prep Miguel withdrew \$20 per week from his bank account for 4 weeks. Which expression shows the change in his account balance? **C**

Ⓐ $-20 + 4$ Ⓑ $-20 - 4$ Ⓒ -20×4 Ⓓ $-20 \div 4$

Problem Solving and Reasoning

32. Communicate In this exercise, you will look for patterns in powers of negative numbers.

a. Evaluate $(-2)^2, (-2)^3, (-2)^4, (-2)^5$, and $(-2)^6$. **4, −8, 16, −32, 64**

b. Evaluate $(-3)^2, (-3)^3, (-3)^4, (-3)^5$, and $(-3)^6$. **9, −27, 81, −243, 729**

c. What patterns do you notice in your results? Explain why the patterns make sense.

33. Communicate How is multiplying integers like multiplying whole numbers? How is it different?

34. Critical Thinking Suppose an amusement park bought a merry-go-round for \$92,000, and 42,512 people paid \$2 each to ride the merry-go-round in its first year of operation. Ignoring the cost of operation, how much money did the park earn or lose on this ride in its first year? **Lost \$6976**

Mixed Review

Find the GCF for each pair of numbers. *[Lesson 3-7]*

35. 45, 75 **15** **36.** 132, 55 **11** **37.** 68, 187 **17** **38.** 76, 361 **19**

39. 147, 168 **21** **40.** 51, 129 **3** **41.** 273, 54 **3** **42.** 36, 72 **36**

Use mental math to find each percent. *[Lesson 8-4]*

43. 15% of 400 **60** **44.** 10% of 42 **4.2** **45.** 75% of 120 **90** **46.** 20% of 40 **8**

47. 5% of 30 **1.5** **48.** 80% of 50 **40** **49.** 15% of \$36 **\$5.40** **50.** 60% of 200 **120**

PROBLEM SOLVING 9-6

Exercise Notes

Exercise 32

Error Prevention Students may need to write all the factors to determine each power in parts a and b.

Exercise Answers

32. c. When a negative number is raised to an even exponent, the result is positive; when it is raised to an odd exponent, the result is negative.

33. You can multiply integers as you would whole numbers, but you have to look at the signs to figure out what sign the product is.

Alternate Assessment

Journal Have students write the rules for multiplying integers, giving examples of each case.

Quick Quiz

Find each product.

1. $-6 \cdot (-9)$ 54
2. $-5 \cdot 14$ −70
3. $22 \cdot (-4)$ −88
4. $-13 \cdot 0$ 0
5. $2 \cdot (-4) \cdot 7$ −56

Available on Daily Transparency 9-6

PROBLEM SOLVING

Name ______________

Guided Problem Solving 9-6

GPS **PROBLEM 34, STUDENT PAGE 465**

Suppose an amusement park bought a merry-go-round for \$92,000, and 42,512 people paid \$2 each to ride the merry-go-round in its first year of operation. Ignoring the cost of operation, how much money did the park earn or lose on this ride in its first year?

— Understand —

1. Underline what you are asked to find.
2. How much money did the park pay for the merry-go-round? **\$92,000**
3. How many rode the merry-go-round the first year? **42,512 people.**

— Plan —

3. Which expression represents the money paid for rides the first year? **a**
   a. $2 \times 42{,}512$ **b.** $2 \times 92{,}000$
4. How can you determine if the park earned or lost money in its first year? **Subtract the cost of the merry-go-round from the money paid for the rides the first year.**
5. Which estimate best represents the money earned or lost by the park? **a**
   a. Loss: \$90,000 – \$85,000 = \$5,000 **b.** Earned \$90,000 + \$5,000 = \$95,000
6. How much money was paid for rides the first year? **\$85,024**
7. What did the park earn or lose on this ride in its first year? **Lose \$6976.**

— Look Back —

8. How can you tell if your answer is reasonable? **Possible answer: 6976 is close to the estimate of 5000 in Item 5.**

SOLVE ANOTHER PROBLEM

It costs Ervin \$15 to have his lawn mowed every two weeks for the 16 weeks of summer. He plans to buy a lawn mower for \$175 and cut his own lawn this summer. How much money will he save or lose the first year? **Lose \$55.**

ENRICHMENT

Name ______________

Extend Your Thinking 9-6

Patterns in Numbers

The multiplication table below is separated into four sections with × in the center.

		Column −3							Column 3			
−25	−20	15	−10	−5	5	0	5	10	15	20	25	
−20	−16	−12	−8	−4	4	0	4	8	12	16	20	
−15	−12	−9	−6	−3	3	0	3	6	9	12	15	Row 3
−10	−8	−6	−4	−2	2	0	2	4	6	8	10	
−5	−4	−3	−2	−1	1	0	1	2	3	4	5	
0	0	0	0	0	0	0	0	0	0	0	0	
−5	−4	−3	−2	−1	×	0	1	2	3	4	5	
5	4	3	2	1	−1	0	−1	−2	−3	−4	−5	
10	8	6	4	2	−2	0	−2	−4	−6	−8	−10	
15	12	9	6	3	−3	0	−3	−6	−9	−12	−15	Row −3
20	16	12	8	4	−4	0	−4	−8	−12	−16	−20	
25	20	15	10	5	−5	0	−5	−10	−15	−20	−25	

1. What pattern do you see as you read the numbers from top to bottom in Column 3? As you read from right to left in Column 3? **The numbers decrease by 3 when going from top to bottom and from right to left.**
2. Complete Row 3 and Column 3 by applying the pattern in the table to the upper left section and to the bottom right section. Complete Row −3 and Column −3. Then complete the table.
3. How does the table show the rules for multiplying positive and negative numbers? **Possible answer: Quadrant I shows positive × positive; Quadrants II and IV show positive × negative; Quadrant III shows negative × negative.**

9-7 Lesson Organizer

Objective

- Divide integers.

NCTM Standards

- 1–6, 10

Review

Find each product.

1. −8 • 3 −24
2. 5 • −7 −35
3. −3 • (−6) 18
4. −16 • 3 −48
5. −9 • (−7) 63

Available on Daily Transparency 9-7

Lesson Link

Discuss with students the operations of multiplication and division. Ask them to explain how the two operations are related. They are inverse operations.

1 Introduce

Explore

The Point

Students find the mean for a set of negative integers as an intuitive approach to dividing with integers.

Ongoing Assessment

Have students give an integer to describe the mean for bank deposits of $10, $20, $30, and $20. 20 Then have them give an integer to describe the mean for bank withdrawals of $10, $20, $30, and $20. −20

For Groups That Finish Early

Use your calculators to find the mean of the numbers in the **Explore** table. −163.6 ft

Follow Up

Have students discuss their reasoning as they answered **Explore** Steps 2–5.

9-7 Dividing Integers

You'll Learn ...

- to divide integers

... How It's Used

Bank officers calculate average income and expenses when they evaluate a credit card or loan application.

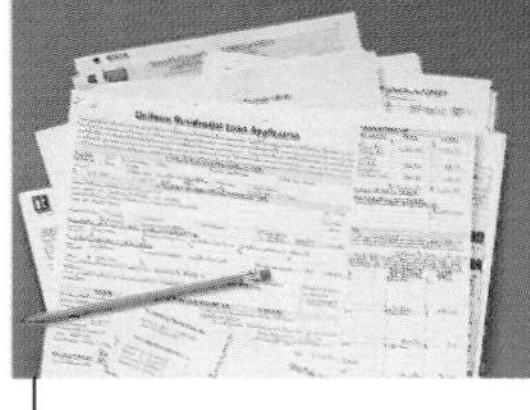

Lesson Link You know how to add, subtract, and multiply integers. Now you'll use your knowledge of multiplication to develop division rules for integers.

Explore Dividing Integers

A Pretty Mean Drop

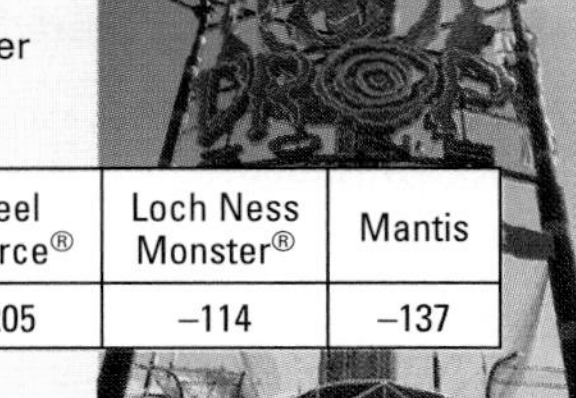

The table gives altitude changes for free-fall drops in five amusement park rides.

1. Plot these altitude changes on a number line.

Name of Ride	Desperado	Drop Zone™	Steel Force®	Loch Ness Monster®	Mantis
Change (ft)	−225	−137	−205	−114	−137

2. Estimate a point on the line that represents the mean of these changes. How did you choose the point? Is the mean positive or negative? (Recall that the mean of a data set is the sum of the values divided by the number of values.)
3. Without adding, tell whether the sum of the changes is positive or negative. Explain how you decided.
4. Without dividing, tell whether the sum of the changes divided by 5 is positive or negative. Explain how you know.
5. Two rides not listed above have altitude changes of −100 ft and −200 ft. Find the mean change for these rides. How did you find the mean?

Learn Dividing Integers

Multiplication and division are inverse operations. If you know the product of two numbers, you can find two quotients.

3 • 4 = 12

12 ÷ 4 = 3 12 ÷ 3 = 4

MEETING INDIVIDUAL NEEDS

Resources

- 9-7 Practice
- 9-7 Reteaching
- 9-7 Problem Solving
- 9-7 Enrichment
- 9-7 Daily Transparency
  - Problem of the Day
  - Review
  - Quick Quiz
- Chapter 9 Project Master

Learning Modalities

Logical Some students respond well to the use of patterns to illustrate integer division. Dividing a given number by a negative integer is the opposite of dividing the given number by a positive integer, so the quotients are opposites of each other.

Individual Have volunteers tell about their experiences playing golf or miniature golf or about visiting a large amusement park.

English Language Development

Pair each student of limited English ability with a student who is more proficient in English. Have them review the rules for multiplying integers and then write and complete groups of exercises like the following.

4 • 4 = 16, so 16 ÷ 4 = ______. 4

4 • (−4) = −16, so −16 ÷ 4 = ______. −4

−4 • 4 = −16, so −16 ÷ −4 = ______. 4

−4 • (−4) = 16, so 16 ÷ (−4) = ______. −4

Examples

Use the given product to find each quotient.

1 $8 \cdot 6 = 48$	**2** $-2 \cdot 4 = -8$	**3** $-3 \cdot (-2) = 6$	**4** $9 \cdot (-6) = -54$
$48 \div 8 = ?$	$-8 \div 4 = ?$	$6 \div (-3) = ?$	$-54 \div (-6) = ?$
$48 \div 8 = 6$	$-8 \div 4 = -2$	$6 \div (-3) = -2$	$-54 \div (-6) = 9$

Try It

Use the given product to find each quotient.

a. $7 \cdot 4 = 28$ $28 \div 7 = ?$ 4 **b.** $5 \cdot (-3) = -15$ $-15 \div (-3) = ?$ 5 **c.** $-2 \cdot 9 = -18$ $-18 \div 9 = ?$ −2 **d.** $-3 \cdot (-3) = 9$ $9 \div (-3) = ?$ −3

Because of the relationship between multiplication and division, the rules for dividing integers are the same as those for multiplying integers.

INTEGER DIVISION RULES
- The quotient of two numbers with the same sign is positive.
- The quotient of two numbers with different signs is negative.

Example 5

Shelley played miniature golf at an amusement park. *Par* is a typical number of strokes (shots) for a hole. Scores above par are positive, scores below par are negative.

On the first five holes, Shelley's scores were −2, −1, +1, −2, and −1. What was her mean score for these holes?

To find the mean, divide the total score by the number of holes.

$$\frac{-2 + (-1) + 1 + (-2) + (-1)}{5} = \frac{-5}{5} = -1$$

Shelley's mean score for the first five holes was −1 (1 under par).

Problem Solving TIP

You can use additive inverses to simplify sums of integers. In Example 5, you can first add −1 and +1 to make 0, then add the remaining numbers.

Try It

Here are the results of six plays for the Elbmuf Junior High football team. Find the mean gain per play.

−3, −5, 19, −7, −24, −4 −4

MATH EVERY DAY

Problem of the Day

When you mix concrete for a driveway or patio, you must use the correct mixture of cement (measured in sacks), sand, and gravel. Sand and gravel are measured in cubic feet. The ratio of cement to sand to gravel is written as cement:sand:gravel. For example, a ratio of 1:2:3 would mean 1 sack of cement to 2 ft^3 of sand to 3 ft^3 of gravel.

How much sand and gravel should be mixed with 5.5 sacks of cement for a 1:3:4 mix?
16.5 ft^3, 22 ft^3

Available on Daily Transparency 9-7

An Extension is provided in the transparency package.

Fact of the Day

Carlsbad Caverns in New Mexico form the largest underground cave system. The levels range from 750 ft to more than 1300 ft below the surface.

Mental Math

Tell the sign of each quotient.

1. $-44 \div (-4)$ positive
2. $-50 \div 25$ negative
3. $24 \div (-6)$ negative
4. $20 \div 20$ positive
5. $-33 \div (-11)$ positive

Answers for Explore

1.

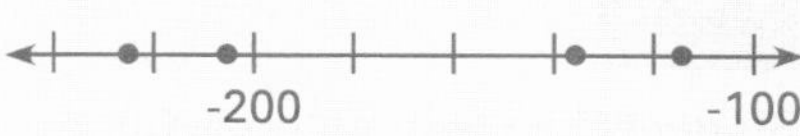

2. Possible answers: −170; It is about halfway between −114 and −225; Negative
3. The integers are all negative, so the sum must be negative.
4. Negative; Restate the problem as "5 multiplied by a negative number must be negative," so the number must be negative.
5. −150; Add the numbers and restate the problem as "2 multiplied by a number is −300," so the number must be −150.

2 Teach

Learn

Review the rules for integer multiplication. Write a number of multiplication equations on the chalkboard. Have students give two related division equations for each multiplication equation.

Alternate Examples

Use the given product to find each quotient.

1. $4 \cdot 9 = 36$
   $36 \div 9 = ?$
   $36 \div 9 = 4$
2. $-8 \cdot 3 = -24$
   $-24 \div 3 = ?$
   $-24 \div 3 = -8$
3. $-5 \cdot (-9) = 45$
   $45 \div (-5) = ?$
   $45 \div (-5) = -9$
4. $8 \cdot -7 = -56$
   $-56 \div (-7) = ?$
   $-56 \div (-7) = 8$
5. During the last week, stock for The Daisy Chain reflected these changes: −2, 2, −1, 3, and 3. What was the mean change for the 5 days?
   $$\frac{-2 + 2 + (-1) + 3 + 3}{5} = \frac{5}{5} = 1$$
   The mean change for The Daisy Chain stock was 1 point per day.

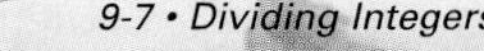

Students see two methods for finding a missing factor. One involves dividing and using a sign rule for integers, and the other finds a factor which will yield the given product.

Answers for What Do You Think?

1. No; He ignored them only at first; then he looked at them to decide what sign the quotient should have.
2. Andy: 56 divided by 28 is 2. 56 and 28 are both positive, so the speed is 2 feet per minute; Jyotsna: 2 times 28 is 56. 28 is positive and a positive product comes from two positive numbers, so the speed is 2 feet per minute.

3 Practice and Assess

Check

Students often assign a negative value to the quotient of two negative integers. Have them check their quotients by writing the corresponding multiplication equations.

Answers for Check Your Understanding

1. They're the same.
2. They're different.

With their spelunking club, Andy and Jyotsna want to explore a cave passage whose elevation is −56 ft. They plan to descend at a rate of −8 ft/min. They need to know how long it will take to reach the cave.

Andy thinks ...

I'll ignore the positive and negative signs.

56 divided by 8 is 7.

The two integers −56 and −8 have the same sign, so the quotient is positive 7.

It will take us 7 minutes to reach the passage.

Jyotsna thinks ...

I'll turn this into a multiplication problem.

We'll go −56 feet at −8 feet per minute.

Since rate × time = distance, I need to know what number times −8 is −56. I know 56 is 8 times 7. A negative product must come from two numbers with different signs, so the number I'm looking for is positive 7.

It will take us 7 minutes to reach the passage.

What do you think?

1. Did Andy really ignore the positive and negative signs? Explain.
2. After exploring the cave, Andy and Jyotsna took 28 minutes to return to the surface. How would each calculate the speed of their ascent?

Check Your Understanding

1. The quotient of two integers is positive. What do you know about the signs of the integers?
2. The quotient of two integers is negative. What do you know about the signs of the integers?

MEETING MIDDLE SCHOOL CLASSROOM NEEDS

Tips from Middle School Teachers

To help students recognize the inverse relationship between multiplication and division, I ask them to tell how they check the answer to a division problem. They quickly see the relationship and are then able to formulate rules for dividing integers by considering the related multiplications.

Geography Connection

The number of people visiting Disneyland in 1995 was nearly the 1995 population of New York City, while the number of people visiting the EPCOT Center in 1995 was greater than the 1995 population of Los Angeles.

Team Teaching

Ask science teachers to discuss how caves might have been formed. Students might research features such as stalactites and stalagmites.

9-7 Exercises and Applications

Practice and Apply

1. **Getting Started** Altitude changes for the longest drops of some of the world's largest roller coasters are shown. Follow these steps to find the average change.

a. Add the four altitude changes. −724 ft **b.** Divide the sum by 4 to find the average change. −181 ft

c. Write your answer as an integer. −181 **d.** Does this represent a drop or a rise? A drop

Operation Sense Give the sign of each quotient.

2. $+ \div +$ + **3.** $+ \div -$ − **4.** $- \div +$ − **5.** $- \div -$ +

Use the given product to find each quotient.

6. $7 \cdot 4 = 28$; $28 \div 4 = ?$ 7

7. $-3 \cdot 17 = -51$; $-51 \div 17 = ?$ −3

8. $-7 \cdot (-9) = 63$; $63 \div (-7) = ?$ −9

9. $8 \cdot (-4) = -32$; $-32 \div (-4) = ?$ 8

Find each quotient.

10. $-18 \div (-9)$ 2 **11.** $-18 \div 9$ −2 **12.** $0 \div (-8)$ 0 **13.** $16 \div (-2)$ −8 **14.** $-63 \div (-7)$ 9

15. $-81 \div (-1)$ 81 **16.** $-40 \div 10$ −4 **17.** $80 \div (-5)$ −16 **18.** $-105 \div 5$ −21 **19.** $-300 \div (-20)$ 15

20. $400 \div 0$ Undefined **21.** $-1000 \div 125$ −8 **22.** $-256 \div (-16)$ 16 **23.** $-56 \div 7 \div (-2)$ 4

24. **Science** A cold wave gripped much of the United States during the first week of February 1996. The lowest temperatures in four Ohio cities that week were: Cleveland, −10°F; Cincinnati, −11°F; Columbus, −3°F; Toledo, −8°F. What was the average lowest temperature for these cities? −8°

25. **Statistics** Antonio had scores of −1, −2, −1, −2, 0, 2, −1, −2, and −2 for nine holes on a miniature golf course. What was his mean score? −1

GPS

PRACTICE 9-7

PRACTICE

Name ______________________

Practice 9-7

Dividing Integers

Use the given product to find each quotient.

1. $11 \cdot (-7) = -77$; $-77 \div (-7) =$ 11
2. $7 \cdot 14 = 98$; $98 \div 7 =$ 14
3. $-5 \cdot 10 = -50$; $-50 \div 10 =$ −5
4. $3 \cdot (-6) = -18$; $-18 \div (-6) =$ 3

Find each quotient.

5. $56 \div (-8)$ −7	6. $-196 \div (-14)$ 14	7. $-10 \div (-10)$ 1
8. $-117 \div (-9)$ 13	9. $-49 \div (-7)$ 7	10. $-63 \div 7$ −9
11. $-40 \div 4$ −10	12. $-18 \div (-3)$ 6	13. $7 \div (-7)$ −1
14. $-120 \div (-8)$ 15	15. $-4 \div (-1)$ 4	16. $-50 \div (-10)$ 5
17. $-40 \div (-8)$ 5	18. $-99 \div 9$ −11	19. $-117 \div 9$ −13
20. $44 \div (-4)$ −11	21. $-24 \div 8$ −3	22. $-40 \div 10$ −4
23. $18 \div (-6)$ −3	24. $180 \div 15$ 12	25. $-48 \div (-8)$ 6
26. $-84 \div (-14)$ 6	27. $-84 \div 7$ −12	28. $-91 \div (-7)$ 13
29. $9 \div (-3)$ −3	30. $-144 \div 12$ −12	31. $10 \div (-10)$ −1
32. $-70 \div 10$ −7	33. $117 \div (-13)$ −9	34. $-36 \div 9$ −4
35. $-3 \div (-1)$ 3	36. $120 \div (-10)$ −12	37. $-24 \div (-4)$ 6
38. $8 \div (-8)$ −1	39. $-28 \div (-4)$ 7	40. $-112 \div (-8)$ 14
41. $-36 \div 6$ −6	42. $-126 \div (-14)$ 9	43. $-77 \div (-11)$ 7
44. $-143 \div 11$ −13	45. $-22 \div (-11)$ 2	46. $-48 \div 8$ −6
47. $-44 \div 4$ −11	48. $-117 \div (-13)$ 9	49. $-112 \div 8$ −14

50. Some typical daily low temperatures for Alaska cities in February are: Anchorage, 12°F; Fairbanks, −14°F; Kotzebue, −12°F; Gulkana, −7°F; and Nome, −4°F. What is the average of these temperatures? −5°F

51. Over a 6-year period, a business reported annual profits of \$8 million, −\$5 million, −\$9 million, \$3 million, and −\$7 million, and −\$2 million. What was the mean annual profit? −\$2 million

RETEACHING

Name ______________________

Alternative Lesson 9-7

Dividing Integers

You know how to find the sign when you multiply two integers. The same rules apply when you divide integers.

Multiply or Divide	Signs of Integers	Answer is:
	Same sign →	+
	Different sign →	−

Example

Find 9 ÷ (–3).

a. What is the sign of the quotient? −

b. Divide the absolute values 3 c. Write the quotient. −3

So, 9 ÷ (–3) = –3.

Try It Find –12 ÷ 3.

d. What is the sign of the quotient? −

e. Divide the absolute values. 4 f. Write the quotient. −4

Find 21 ÷ 7.

g. What is the sign of the quotient? +

h. Divide the absolute values. 3 i. Write the quotient. 3

Find –32 ÷ (–8).

j. What is the sign of the quotient? +

k. Divide the absolute values. 4 l. Write the quotient. 4

Find each quotient.

m. 18 ÷ (–6) = −3 n. –24 ÷ (–3) = 8 o. –35 ÷ (–7) = 5

p. –40 ÷ 8 = −5 q. 28 ÷ (–7) = −4 r. 81 ÷ 9 = 9

Tell whether each quotient will be positive or negative.

s. Positive ÷ positive = Positive. t. Positive ÷ negative = Negative.

u. Negative ÷ positive = Negative. v. Negative ÷ negative = Positive.

Assignment Guide

- Basic 1–9, 10–24 evens, 25–27, 30–40 evens
- Average 2–9, 11–25 odds, 26, 27–41 odds
- Enriched 3–25 odds, 26–28, 29–41 odds

Exercise Notes

Exercises 6–9

Enrichment Have students give another division equation for each exercise. For 6: $28 \div 7 = 4$
For 7: $-51 \div (-3) = 17$;
For 8: $63 \div (-9) = -7$;
For 9: $-32 \div 8 = -4$

Reteaching

Activity

Materials: Algebra tiles

- To model $12 \div 3$, take 12 yellow tiles and make 3 equal groups. How many are in each group? 4 yellow tiles You could also make groups of 3. How many groups are there? 4 groups The quotient is the same for both cases.
- For $-12 \div 3$, take 12 red tiles and make 3 equal groups. How many are in each group? 4 red tiles
- For $-12 \div (-3)$, take 12 red tiles and make groups of −3. How many groups are there? 4 groups
- $12 \div (-3)$ is the *opposite* of $-12 \div (-3)$, so its quotient is the opposite of 4. What is that quotient? −4

Exercise Notes

■ Exercise 26

Test Prep Students should use the rules for dividing integers to determine that the quotient must be positive and then realize that any positive number is greater than any negative number.

■ Exercise 28

Consumer Disneyland opened in 1955 in Anaheim, CA, while Walt Disney World opened in 1971 in Orlando, FL. Tokyo Disneyland opened in 1983, and Euro Disneyland opened in Paris in 1992.

Project Progress

You may want to have students use Chapter 9 Project Master.

Exercise Answers

28. 1993–1994 change: Magic Kingdom −800,000; Disneyland −1,100,000; EPCOT −300,000; Disney-MGM no change; Average change: −550,000

1994–1995 change: Magic Kingdom 1,700,000; Disneyland 3,800,000; EPCOT 1,000,000; Disney-MGM 1,500,000; Average change: 2,000,000

The average change was greater in 1994–1995. The 1993–1994 change is negative because fewer people came to the parks in 1994 than in 1993. The 1994–1995 change is positive because more people came to the parks in 1995 than in 1994.

Alternate Assessment

Interview Have students work in pairs and interview each other about computing with integers. If possible, have them use a tape recorder for the interviews.

Also have students insert the rules for dividing integers in their journals, giving examples, as they did for the other operations.

Quick Quiz

Find each quotient.

1. −56 ÷ (−7) 8
2. −35 ÷ 5 −7
3. 24 ÷ (−4) −6
4. −48 ÷ (−12) 4
5. 42 ÷ (−3) −14

Available on Daily Transparency 9-7

---

26. **Test Prep** If you divide one negative number by another, the quotient is: A

Ⓐ Greater than either number Ⓑ Less than either number

Ⓒ Equal to one of the numbers Ⓓ Not enough information to tell

Problem Solving and Reasoning

27. Communicate What is the mean of five negative integers and their opposites? Explain how you know.
0; The sum of any number and its opposite is 0, and 0 divided by 10 is 0.

28. Critical Thinking The table gives *Amusement Business* magazine's estimated 1993–1995 attendance figures for the four best attended amusement and theme parks in the United States.

Find the average change in attendance for these parks from 1993 to 1994. Compare this to the average change from 1994 to 1995. Express your answers as integers, and explain what their signs mean.

Park Attendance, 1993–1995

	1993	1994	1995
The Magic Kingdom®	12,000,000	11,200,000	12,900,000
Disneyland®	11,400,000	10,300,000	14,100,000
EPCOT®	10,000,000	9,700,000	10,700,000
Disney–MGM Studios	8,000,000	8,000,000	9,500,000

Mixed Review

Express each fraction in lowest terms. *[Lesson 3-8]*

29. $\frac{33}{75}$ $\frac{11}{25}$ **30.** $\frac{10}{20}$ $\frac{1}{2}$ **31.** $\frac{9}{45}$ $\frac{1}{5}$ **32.** $\frac{12}{48}$ $\frac{1}{4}$ **33.** $\frac{52}{65}$ $\frac{4}{5}$ **34.** $\frac{4}{4}$ 1 **35.** $\frac{5}{25}$ $\frac{1}{5}$ **36.** $\frac{240}{375}$ $\frac{16}{25}$

Solve each problem. If necessary, round answers to the nearest tenth. *[Lesson 8-5]*

37. What percent of 56 is 28? 50% **38.** 20% of what number is 5? 25 **39.** 11% of 200 is what number? 22

40. 16% of 50 is what number? 8 **41.** What percent of 144 is 36? 25% **42.** 45% of 40 is what number? 18

PROBLEM SOLVING 9-7

Project Progress

Use your list of events to complete your time line. Illustrate your time line by cutting out or drawing pictures to show different events. Make a list showing the time that passed between several pairs of events on your time line. Include events before and after your birth, and in your future.

Problem Solving
Understand
Plan
Solve
Look Back

PROBLEM SOLVING

Name ______________

Guided Problem Solving 9-7

GPS PROBLEM 25, STUDENT PAGE 469

Antonio had scores of –1, –2, –1, –2, 0, 2, –1, –2, and –2 for nine holes on a miniature golf course. What was his mean score?

— Understand —

1. What are you asked to find? Antonio's mean score.
2. What is the definition of mean? Average.

— Plan —

3. Which method would you use to find the mean? c
   - a. Choose the score that appears most often.
   - b. List all scores in order. Then find the middle number.
   - c. Add the scores. Then divide by the number of scores.

— Solve —

4. Add Antonio's scores. –9
5. How many holes did Antonio play? 9
6. Find the mean. –1
7. Write a sentence that answers the question.
   Possible answer: Antonio's mean score was –1.

— Look Back —

8. Why do you think your answer is reasonable? Possible answer: –1 falls in the range of scores from –2 to 2.

SOLVE ANOTHER PROBLEM

Heidi had scores of –1, 1, –2, 0, 2, 1, –2, –1, and 2 for nine holes on a miniature golf course. What was her mean score?

Heidi's mean score was 0.

ENRICHMENT

Name ______________

Extend Your Thinking 9-7

Patterns in Data

Temperatures can be measured as degrees Celsius (°C) or degrees Fahrenheit (°F). Sometimes you need to convert from one scale to the other.

You can use this formula to convert Celsius to Fahrenheit. Substitute any Celsius temperature into the formula for C and solve to find the comparable Fahrenheit temperature, F.

$$F = \frac{9C}{5} + 32$$

You can use this formula to convert Fahrenheit to Celsius. Substitute any Fahrenheit temperature into the formula for F and solve to find the comparable Celsius temperature, C.

$$C = \frac{5(F - 32)}{9}$$

Boiling point of water
Normal body temperature
Warm day
Freezing point of water
Cold day

Convert each temperature to degrees Fahrenheit.

1. 0°C = 32 °F 2. –1°C = 30.2 °F

3. –2°C = 28.4 °F 4. –5°C = 23 °F
5. –10°C = 14 °F 6. –15°C = 5 °F
7. –20°C = –4 °F 8. –25°C = –13 °F
9. Look at the negative Celsius temperatures. What pattern do you notice in the signs of their corresponding Fahrenheit temperatures. < 32°

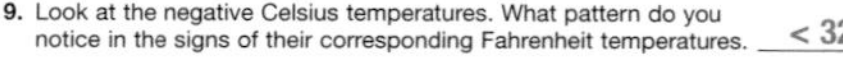

Convert each temperature to degrees Celsius. Round to nearest tenth.

10. 40°F = 4.4 °C 11. 34°F = 1.1 °C 12. 33°F = 0.6 °C
13. 32°F = 0 °C 14. 31°F = –0.6 °C 15. 30°F = –1.1 °C
16. 0°F = –17.8 °C 17. –5°F = –20.6 °C 18. –10°F = –23.3 °C
19. Look at the Fahrenheit temperatures less than 32°F. What pattern do you notice in the signs of their corresponding Celsius temperatures?
   The signs are all negative.
20. Why do you think these patterns occur?
   Possible answer: Since 0°C and 32°F are freezing temperatures for water, any temperature below is shown by a negative number.

Section 9B Connect

You've added, subtracted, multiplied, and divided integers. Now you'll show how these integer operations relate to the "real" world of roller coasters, water slides, and merry-go-rounds.

For Your Amusement

Your class has just been put in charge of an amusement park, and you're part of the public relations (PR) team. Your job is to explain the relationship between mathematics and amusement parks to other students.

1. Write four problems involving mathematics in your amusement park.
   - Each problem should involve a different operation (+, −, ×, ÷).
   - One problem should involve a ride, one should involve a game, and one should involve money.
   - The fourth problem can be about a topic of your choice.
   - At least two of the problems should involve negative integers.
2. Solve each of your problems in writing. Be sure to show your solutions clearly so other students can learn from them. Explain how you know your solutions are correct.
3. Prepare a presentation of your problems and solutions that you could give to your class.

471

9B Connect

For Your Amusement

The Point

In *For Your Amusement* on page 449, students were introduced to the motions and forces of amusement park rides. Now, they relate integers to the world of amusement parks.

About the Page

- Ask students if they think writing specific types of problems clearly is an easy assignment.
- Review the types of problems that are to be written so that students clearly understand what they are to do.
- Tell students to pretend they are writing a letter to possible investors in the park. They will have to write problems involving possible gains and losses of money. Remind students to write the problems so that they can be understood and solved by someone else.
- Suggest that students show solutions on a separate piece of paper.

Ongoing Assessment

Check that students have written problems and solutions clearly and correctly.

Extension

Have students exchange their set of problems with another student. Ask each student to determine if the problem writer followed the directions when writing the problems. Have students solve the problems they were given. The writer of the problems should then check the answers.

Answers for Connect

1–3. Answers may vary.

9B Review

Section 9B Review

Review Correlation

Item(s)	Lesson(s)
1, 5, 9	9-4
2, 8, 11, 16	9-5
3, 7, 10, 12, 15, 17	9-6
4, 6, 13, 14, 18, 19	9-7
20–24	9-3
25, 27	9-5
26, 28	9-7

Test Prep

Test-Taking Tip

Tell students to use rounding and estimation to help them save time on a test. Here, rounding and estimation can help them choose the sign of the answer and an estimate of the magnitude.

Answers for Review

20–24.

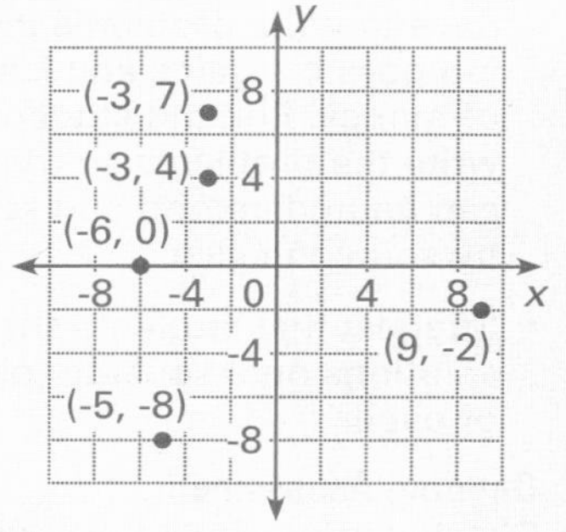

25. Answers may vary.

REVIEW 9B

Find each sum, difference, product, or quotient.

1. $7 + (-7)$ 0 **2.** $-9 - (-3)$ −6 **3.** $5 \cdot (-10)$ −50 **4.** $-24 \div 6$ −4 **5.** $-11 + 20$ 9

6. $-24 \div (-3)$ 8 **7.** $-15 \cdot (-10)$ 150 **8.** $-37 - 47$ −84 **9.** $-59 + (-181)$ −240 **10.** $-17 \cdot 101$ −1717

11. $108 - (-274)$ 382 **12.** $-17 \cdot (-1001)$ 17,017 **13.** $288 \div (-18)$ −16 **14.** $0 \div (-52)$ 0 **15.** $17 \cdot (-10{,}001)$ −170,017

Evaluate each expression.

16. $3 + (-4) - 8$ −9 **17.** $(-2)(-8)(-10)$ −160 **18.** $16 \div (-2) \div (-4)$ 2 **19.** $-5 + 6 \div (-2) + (-4) \cdot (-2)$ 0

Plot each point on the same coordinate plane. *[Lesson 9-3]*

20. $(-3, 7)$ **21.** $(-5, -8)$ **22.** $(9, -2)$ **23.** $(-6, 0)$ **24.** $(-3, 4)$

25. 

Explain why subtracting an integer gives the same result as adding its opposite. You may wish to draw algebra tiles or number lines to illustrate your explanation.

26. History After Chicago's World's Columbian Exposition in 1893, the number of amusement parks in the United States grew rapidly. By 1919, there were about 1520 parks. Because of the Great Depression, which began in 1929, only 400 were left by 1935. Find the rate of change in the number of parks from 1919 to 1935. Give your answer in parks per year. −70 parks per year

27. Science The highest temperature ever recorded was 136°F (58°C), in Libya. The lowest ever recorded was −129°F (−89°C), in Antarctica. Find the difference between these extreme temperatures in °F and in °C. 265°F; 147°C

Test Prep

When you're asked to find the mean (average) of several integers on a multiple choice test, you can use mental math to estimate the sign and size of the answer. By doing this, you may be able to eliminate some answer choices.

28. What is the mean of −29, −12, 39, −48, and 20? B

Ⓐ −60 Ⓑ −6 Ⓒ −0.6 Ⓓ 6

Resources

Practice Masters
Section 9B Review

Assessment Sourcebook
Quiz 9B

TestWorks
Test and Practice Software

PRACTICE

Name ____________________ **Practice**

Section 9B Review

Find each sum, difference, product, or quotient.

1. $-135 \div 15$ −9 2. $-57 + 29$ −28 3. $3 \cdot (-5)$ −15
4. $21 - (-137)$ 158 5. $64 \div (-8)$ −8 6. $-76 + (-84)$ −160
7. $-20 \cdot (-16)$ 320 8. $-40 - 28$ −68 9. $-30 \div 3$ −10
10. $-26 + (-31)$ −57 11. $-5 \cdot 2$ −10 12. $38 - 59$ −21
13. $96 \div 8$ 12 14. $30 + (-60)$ −30 15. $8 \cdot (-2)$ −16

Evaluate each expression.

16. $6 + (-4) - (-8)$ 10 17. $3 \cdot (-5) \cdot 7$ −105 18. $-6 \cdot 10 \div (-15)$ 4
19. $-3 + (-7) \cdot (-4)$ 25 20. $64 \div (-4) + 12$ −4 21. $-28 \div (-7) \cdot (-4)$ −16
22. $4 \cdot (-9) - (-25)$ −11 23. $-2 + (-9) - (-15)$ 4 24. $36 \div (-12) + (-6)$ −9

25. **Science** Temperatures on the moon can be as high as 273°F (134°C) and as low as −274°F (−170°C). Find the difference between these extreme temperatures in °F and °C. 547°F; 304°C

26. Stephan is playing a card game. He started out with 100 points, and then he scored +20, −15, +30, −5, and −40 points. Then his score was tripled because he held all the aces. What was his final score? 270

27. The population of Buffalo, New York, was about 580,000 in 1950 and 328,000 in 1990. Find the average rate of change of the population (in people per year) from 1950 to 1990. −6300 people per year

28. Rebecca is buying new carpet for the section of her home that is shown. How many square feet of carpet will she need? *[Lesson 5-10]* 348 ft²

14 ft, 10 ft, 5 ft, 12 ft, 4 ft, 25 ft

29. In 1980, independent presidential candidate John Anderson won 6.6% of the popular vote. He received about 5,720,000 votes. How many people voted in this election? *[Lesson 8-6]* About 86,700,000 people

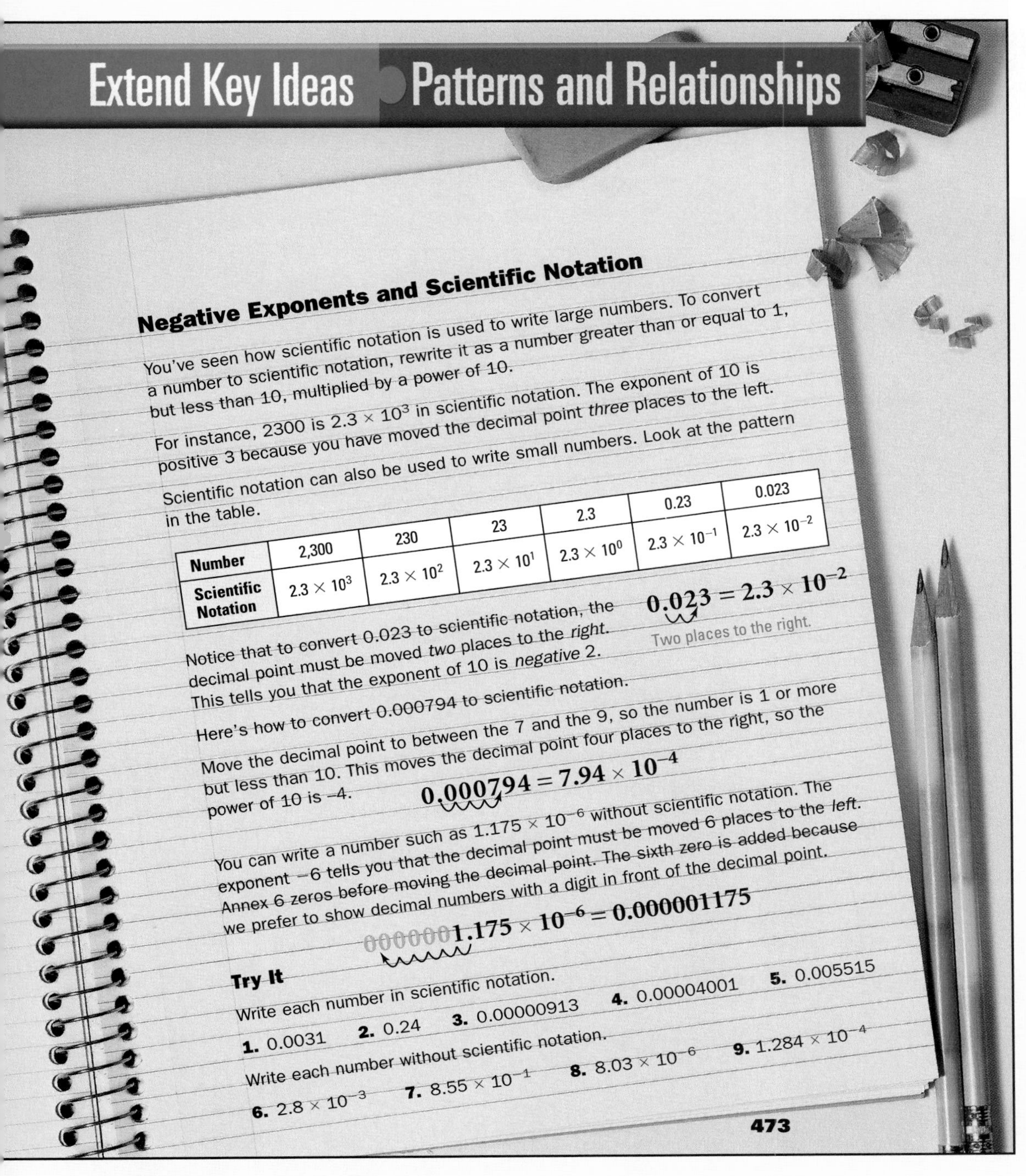

Extend Key Ideas • Patterns and Relationships

Negative Exponents and Scientific Notation

You've seen how scientific notation is used to write large numbers. To convert a number to scientific notation, rewrite it as a number greater than or equal to 1, but less than 10, multiplied by a power of 10.

For instance, 2300 is 2.3×10^3 in scientific notation. The exponent of 10 is positive 3 because you have moved the decimal point *three* places to the left.

Scientific notation can also be used to write small numbers. Look at the pattern in the table.

Number	2,300	230	23	2.3	0.23	0.023
Scientific Notation	2.3×10^3	2.3×10^2	2.3×10^1	2.3×10^0	2.3×10^{-1}	2.3×10^{-2}

Notice that to convert 0.023 to scientific notation, the decimal point must be moved *two* places to the *right*. This tells you that the exponent of 10 is *negative* 2.

$$0.023 = 2.3 \times 10^{-2}$$

Two places to the right.

Here's how to convert 0.000794 to scientific notation.

Move the decimal point to between the 7 and the 9, so the number is 1 or more but less than 10. This moves the decimal point four places to the right, so the power of 10 is –4.

$$0.000794 = 7.94 \times 10^{-4}$$

You can write a number such as 1.175×10^{-6} without scientific notation. The exponent –6 tells you that the decimal point must be moved 6 places to the *left*. Annex 6 zeros before moving the decimal point. The sixth zero is added because we prefer to show decimal numbers with a digit in front of the decimal point.

$$0000001.175 \times 10^{-6} = 0.000001175$$

Try It

Write each number in scientific notation.

1. 0.0031 **2.** 0.24 **3.** 0.00000913 **4.** 0.00004001 **5.** 0.005515

Write each number without scientific notation.

6. 2.8×10^{-3} **7.** 8.55×10^{-1} **8.** 8.03×10^{-6} **9.** 1.284×10^{-4}

473

Answers for Try It

1. 3.1×10^{-3}
2. 2.4×10^{-1}
3. 9.13×10^{-6}
4. 4.001×10^{-5}
5. 5.5515×10^{-3}
6. 0.0028
7. 0.855
8. 0.00000803
9. 0.0001284

Extend Key Ideas

Negative Exponents and Scientific Notation

The Point

Students use negative exponents to write numbers in scientific notation.

About the Page

If students are having trouble knowing the correct exponent when converting a number to scientific notation, you might ask them the following question. Once the decimal has been moved to make the number between 1 and 10, how does the decimal point have to move to recreate the original number? If it has to be moved to the left, the exponent will be negative; if to the right, the exponent will be positive.

Ask ...

- For a very small number in scientific notation, would you expect the exponent to be positive or negative? Why? Negative; this moves the decimal point to the left, which makes the number smaller.
- Describe how to write the number 0.000034 in scientific notation. To make a number ≥ 1 but < 10, move the decimal point 5 places to the right, so the exponent is -5: 3.4×10^{-5}. Or, to make a number ≥ 1 but < 10, place the decimal point between the 3 and 4. To make the original number, the decimal point has to move 5 places to the left, so the exponent is -5: 3.4×10^{-5}.

Extension

Search through your science text for occurrences of very small numbers. If the number is not in scientific notation, convert it to scientific notation. If it is in scientific notation, convert it to a decimal. Try to find five examples.

Chapter 9 Summary and Review

Review Correlation

Item(s)	Lesson(s)
1–4	9-1
5, 6	9-2
7–8	9-3
9–12	9-4
13	9-5
14	9-6
15, 16	9-7
17	9-6

For additional review, see page 680.

Answers for Review

6. −8, −4, 0, 10, 18

7. Possible answer:

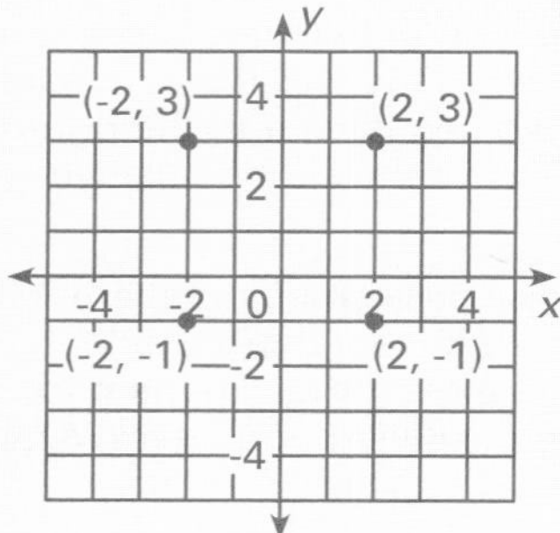

8.

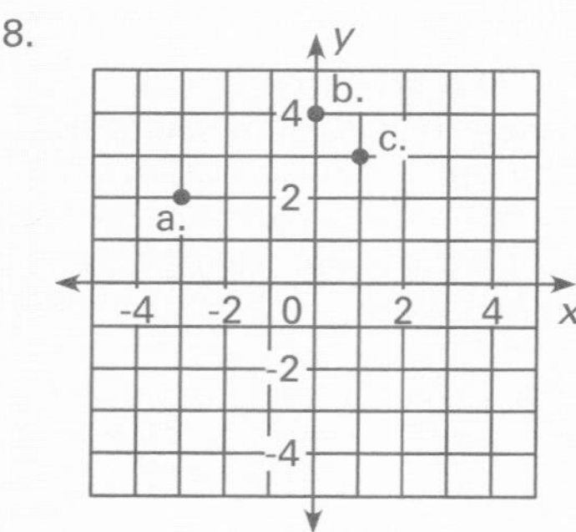

Chapter 9 Summary and Review

Graphic Organizer

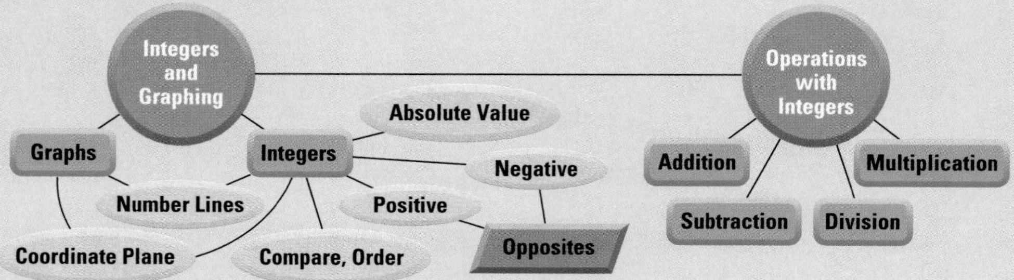

Section 9A Using Integers

Summary

- A **number line** can be horizontal or vertical. Its zero point is the **origin**.
- **Positive numbers** are greater than zero. **Negative numbers** are less than zero and are written with a − sign.
- Distances on a number line are always positive. The **absolute value** of a number is its distance from zero.
- Whole numbers (including zero) and their opposites are **integers.**
- The ***x-y* coordinate plane** is based on a horizontal number line (x-axis) and a vertical number line (y-axis). The axes intersect at the **origin.**
- Any point can be described by an **ordered pair,** like $(-3, 5)$. The first number (the ***x*-coordinate**) tells how far to the left or right of the origin the point is. The ***y*-coordinate** tells how far up or down the point is.

Review

1. Tell whether −1.75 is an integer. No
2. Use a sign to write the number: lost $25 −$25
3. Write the opposite of 42. −42
4. Find the absolute value: $|-87|$ 87
5. Use >, <, or = to compare the numbers: −18 [>] −91
6. Order the set of numbers from least to greatest: 18, −4, 0, 10, −8
7. Draw a square so that each of its vertices is in a different quadrant. Label the coordinates of each vertex.
8. Plot each point on the same coordinate plane.
   a. $(-3, 2)$ **b.** $(0, 4)$ **c.** $(1, 3)$

Resources

Practice Masters
Cumulative Review Chapters 1–9

Assessment Sourcebook
Quarterly Test Chapters 1-9

PRACTICE

Name ____________________

Practice

Cumulative Review Chapters 1–9

Convert to a fraction in lowest terms. *[Lesson 3-10]*

1. 0.63 $\frac{63}{100}$ 2. 0.75 $\frac{3}{4}$ 3. 0.56 $\frac{14}{25}$ 4. 0.45 $\frac{9}{20}$
5. 0.6 $\frac{3}{5}$ 6. 0.375 $\frac{3}{8}$ 7. 0.124 $\frac{31}{250}$ 8. 0.36 $\frac{9}{25}$
9. 0.888 $\frac{111}{125}$ 10. 0.98 $\frac{49}{50}$ 11. 0.413 $\frac{413}{1000}$ 12. 0.175 $\frac{7}{40}$

Find the missing length in each right triangle. *[Lesson 5-7]*

13. t = 45 m 14. x = 24 in. 15. m = 4.5 cm 16. q = 73 ft

Consumer Use unit prices to find the better buy. Underline the correct choice. *[Lesson 6-2]*

17. Oranges: $1.44 for 3 lb or $2.50 for 5 lb
18. Granola cereal: $1.68 for 12 oz or $2.47 for 19 oz
19. Magazines: $21 for 12 issues or $44 for 24 issues
20. Blueberries: $2.98 for 2 baskets or $3.98 for 3 baskets

Perimeter and area ratios of similar figures are given. Find each scale factor. *[Lesson 7-10]*

21. Perimeter ratio = $\frac{49}{25}$ Scale factor = $\frac{49}{25}$
22. Area ratio = 16 Scale factor = 4
23. Perimeter ratio = 0.36 Scale factor = 0.36
24. Perimeter ratio = 81 Scale factor = 81
25. Area ratio = $\frac{9}{100}$ Scale factor = $\frac{3}{10}$
26. Area ratio = 2.25 Scale factor = 1.5

Find each sum, difference, product, or quotient. *[Lessons 9-4 to 9-7]*

27. $-21 + (-168)$ −189 28. $-41 - (-51)$ 10 29. $126 + (-146)$ −20
30. $30 \div (-6)$ −5 31. $53 + (-12)$ 41 32. $37 - (-44)$ 81

Section 9B Operations with Integers

Summary

- You can use a number line to add integers. To add a positive number, move right. To add a negative number, move left.
- Algebra tiles can be used to represent integers. The tiles ▢ ■ form a **zero pair**. You can use algebra tiles to add or subtract integers. After all zero pairs are removed, the tiles left represent the sum or difference.
- The **additive inverse** of an integer is its opposite. The **Inverse Property of Addition** says that the sum of an integer and its additive inverse is 0.
- To add two integers with the same sign, add their absolute values and use the sign of the numbers. To add two integers with different signs, subtract their absolute values and use the sign of the number with the larger absolute value. To subtract an integer, add its opposite.
- To multiply two integers, multiply their absolute values and then decide the correct sign. The product is positive if the numbers have the same sign; it is negative if they have different signs.
- To divide two integers, divide their absolute values and then decide the correct sign. The quotient is positive if the numbers have the same sign; it is negative if they have different signs.

Review

9. Write the addition problem and the sum modeled in the picture.

10. Use algebra tiles or a number line to find the sum $3 + (-7)$.

11. Write the next integer in the pattern: $-16, -10, -4,$ ____ 2

12. Find each sum.

a. $-2 + 8$ 6 b. $-7 + (-4)$ -11

c. $-41 + (-24)$ -65 d. $-25 + (-62) + 25$ -62

13. Find each difference.

a. $4 - 7$ -3 b. $-2 - (-6)$ 4

c. $-73 - 28$ -101 d. $-85 - (-97) - 12$ 0

14. Find each product.

a. $-7 \cdot 12$ -84 b. $-10 \cdot (-4)$ 40

c. $21 \cdot 6 \cdot (-2)$ -252 d. $32 \cdot (-3) \cdot (-5)$ 480

15. Find each quotient.

a. $110 \div (-5)$ -22 b. $-32 \div (-8)$ 4

c. $-54 \div 9$ -6 d. $168 \div 4 \div 2$ 21

16. Wanda's business lost \$42,000 over a period of eight years. What was the average annual loss? $-\$5250$

17. The lowest point in the United States is Death Valley, California, 282 ft below sea level. The highest point is Mt. McKinley, Alaska, 20,320 ft above sea level. Subtract to find the range of elevations. 20,602 ft

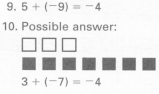

Answers for Review

9. $5 + (-9) = -4$

10. Possible answer:

$3 + (-7) = -4$

Chapter 9 Assessment

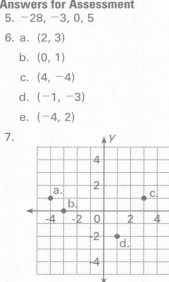

Assessment Correlation

Item(s)	Lesson(s)
1–3	9-1
4, 5	9-2
6–8	9-3
9	9-5
10, 11	9-4
12	9-4, 9-5, 9-6, 9-7
13	9-4, 9-5
14	9-6

Answers for Assessment

5. −28, −3, 0, 5
6. a. (2, 3)
   b. (0, 1)
   c. (4, −4)
   d. (−1, −3)
   e. (−4, 2)

7.

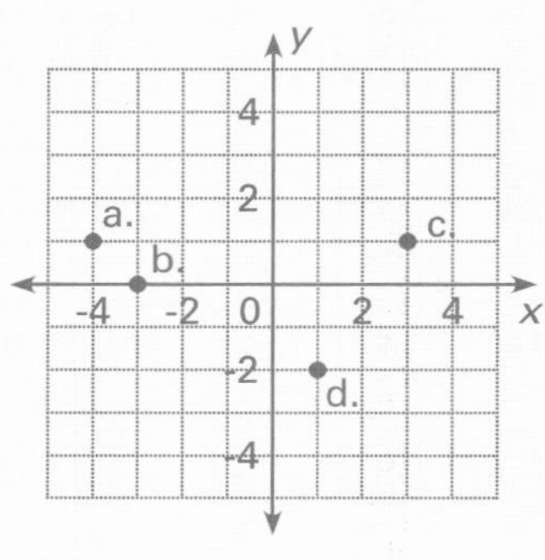

8. Quadrant III
10. −4 + (−7) = −11
11. Possible answer:

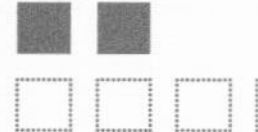

−2 + 6 = 4

Answers for Performance Task

Possible answer:

-2	3	-4
-3	-1	1
2	-5	0

Students' magic squares may vary.

Chapter 9 Assessment

1. Use a sign to write the number: 23 degrees below zero −23°
2. Write the opposite of −54. 54
3. Find the absolute value: |−327| 327
4. Use >, <, or = to compare the pair of numbers: 5 [>] −21
5. Order the set of numbers from least to greatest: 5, −28, −3, 0
6. Find the coordinates of each point.
   a. *A* b. *B* c. *C* d. *D* e. *E*
7. Plot each point on the same coordinate plane.
   a. (−4, 1) b. (−3, 0) c. (3, 1) d. (1, −2)
8. Name the quadrant or axis that contains (−18, −12).
9. Write the next integer in the pattern: 17, 8, −1, ____ −10
10. Write the addition problem and the sum modeled in the picture.

11. Use algebra tiles or a number line to find the sum −2 + 6.
12. Find each sum, difference, product, or quotient.
    a. −2 + 5 3 b. 17 + (−11) 6 c. −26 + (−31) −57 d. 5 − (−4) 9
    e. −23 − 8 −31 f. −75 − 53 −128 g. −13 · (−7) 91 h. 8 · (−11) −88
    i. −5 · (−6) · (−7) −210 j. −50 ÷ 25 −2 k. 78 ÷ (−6) −13 l. −93 ÷ (−3) 31
13. Gerry's bank account has a balance of $146. What will his balance be after he deposits $100 and then withdraws $33? $213
14. Fill in the blank with *sometimes, always,* or *never:* The product of two negative integers is ____ greater than the product of a negative integer and a positive integer. Always

Performance Task

The figure on the left is called a *magic square* because the whole numbers in each row, column, and diagonal add up to the same number. Use integers to complete a copy of the magic square on the right. Then make up a magic square of your own that contains positive and negative integers.

6	7	2
1	5	9
8	3	4

	3	−4
	−1	
2		

Performance Assessment Key

See key on page 429.

Resources

Assessment Sourcebook
Chapter 9 Tests
- Forms A and B (free response)
- Form C (multiple choice)
- Form D (performance assessment)
- Form E (mixed response)
- Form F (cumulative chapter test)

TestWorks
Test and Practice Software

Home and Community Connections
Letter Home for Chapter 9 in English and Spanish

Answers for Performance Assessment (page 477)

• **The Big Chill**

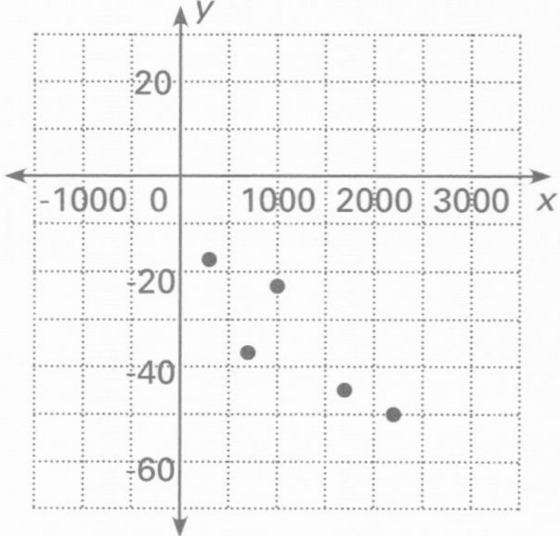

Possible answer: As the elevation increases, the temperature decreases; Between 500 and 1000 feet

Cumulative Review Chapters 1–9 Test Prep

Performance Assessment

Choose one problem.

Good Game!

Check students' games.

Design your own board or card game that uses integer addition, subtraction, multiplication, and division to determine the number of points a player has. The game can involve skill, chance, or a combination of the two.

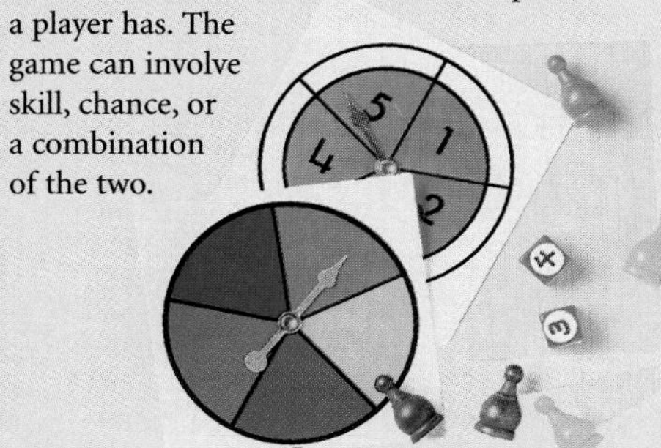

THE BIG CHILL

The table shows the lowest known temperatures for five states and the elevations of the places where they occurred, to the nearest hundred meters. Graph this data on a coordinate plane, then describe any patterns you see. Predict the elevation for a record low temperature of −33°F.

State	Elev. (m)	Temp. (°F)
California	1,700	−45°
Georgia	300	−17°
New Mexico	2,200	−50°
Texas	1,000	−23°
West Virginia	700	−37°

What Goes Up May Come Down

You can show negative values on a bar graph by drawing bars that go below the horizontal axis. Draw a bar graph that shows last week's performance of the stocks in Mr. Takagi's portfolio.

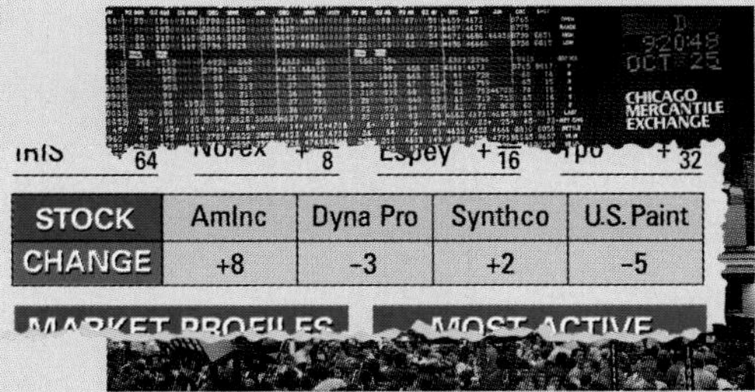

STOCK	AmInc	Dyna Pro	Synthco	U.S. Paint
CHANGE	+8	−3	+2	−5

HOME, SWEET HOME

Draw a simple pentagonal house on a coordinate plane. Place the tip of the "roof" on the y-axis, the corners of the roof in quadrants I and II, and the bottom of the house in quadrants III and IV. Draw a second house by doubling the coordinates of each vertex of your original house. Compare the shapes, perimeters, and areas of the two houses.

Cumulative Review Test Prep

About Performance Assessment

The Performance Assessment options ...

- provide teachers with an alternate means of assessing students.
- address different learning modalities.

Teachers may encourage students to choose the most challenging problem.

Learning Modalities
Good Game **Individual** Students design their own game.
The Big Chill **Logical** Students make predictions based on graphs.
What Goes Up May Come Down **Visual** Students draw bar graphs that represent positive and negative numbers.
Home, Sweet Home **Verbal** Students write a comparison of two drawings and solve a problem.

Suggested Scoring Rubric

Good Game!

Score	Criteria
4	•Game is designed neatly, with an organizational pattern. •Scoring uses integers and the four operations. •Game involves skill and/or chance.
3	•Game is designed neatly, with an organizational pattern. •Scoring uses integers and the four operations. •Game involves some skill and/or chance.
2	•Game lacks organization. •Scoring uses integers and three operations. •Game involves some skill and/or chance.
1	•Game lacks organization. •Scoring rules fail to provide adequate details. •No skill and/or chance is involved.

Answers for Assessment

Answer for The Big Chill on page 476.

- **What Goes Up May Come Down**

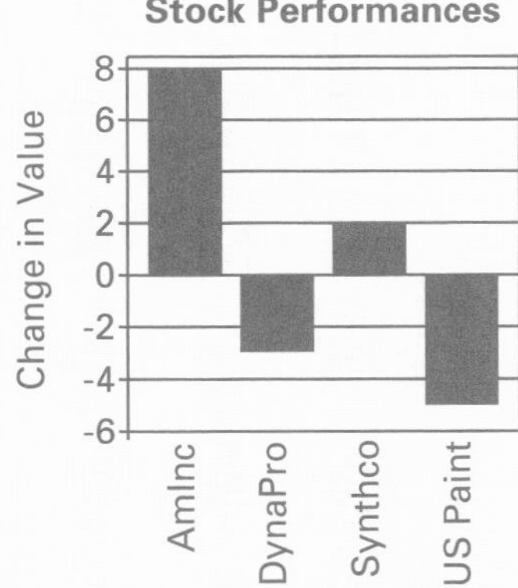

- **Home Sweet Home**

Possible answer:

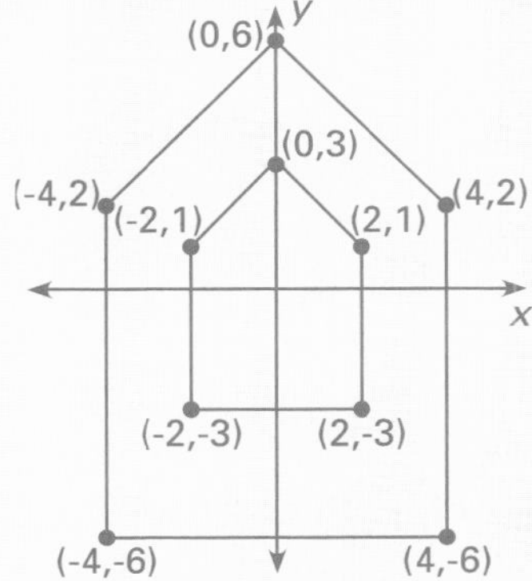

The shapes are similar. The second house has twice the perimeter and four times the area of the first house.

The Patterns of Algebra:

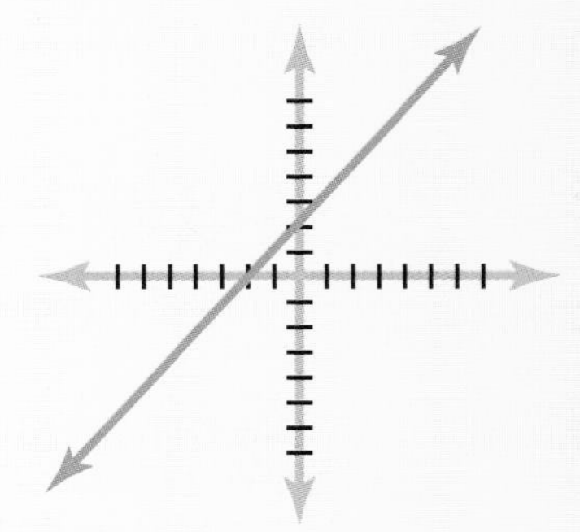

Equations and Graphs

▶ OVERVIEW

Section 10A

Tables, Equations, and Graphs: Students use variables, graphs, and tables to show relationships. They write equations and draw graphs to describe the relationship between two quantities.

10-1 Quantities, Constants, and Variables

10-2 Relating Graphs to Stories

10-3 Tables and Expressions

10-4 Understanding and Writing Equations

10-5 Equations and Graphs

Section 10B

Understanding Equations: Students use tables and graphs to solve one- and two-step equations. They graph inequalities on a number line.

10-6 Solving Equations Using Tables

10-7 Solving Equations Using Graphs

10-8 Relating Equations and Inequalities

Section 10C

Integer Equations: Students use algebra to solve equations involving integers.

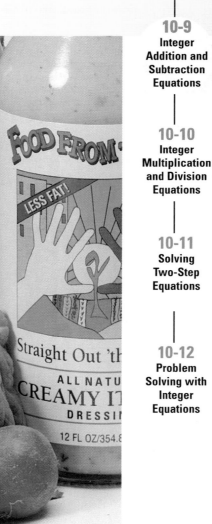

10-9 Integer Addition and Subtraction Equations

10-10 Integer Multiplication and Division Equations

10-11 Solving Two-Step Equations

10-12 Problem Solving with Integer Equations

Meeting NCTM Standards

Curriculum Standards

STANDARD			pages
1	**Problem Solving**	Skills and Strategies	479, 480, 484, 489, 494, 504, *510,* 511, 513, 515, 520, 528, *532,* 533, 538, 540
		Applications	484–485, 488–489, 493–494, 497–498, 503–504, 505, 510–511, 515–516, 519–520, 521, 527–528, 532–533, 537–538, 541–542, 543
		Exploration	482, 486, 490, 495, 500, 508, 512, 517, 524, 529, 534, 539
2	**Communication**	Oral	481, 487, 492, 497, 502, 507, 514, 523, 536
		Written	485, 489, 498, 504, 511, 516, 522, 533, 542
		Cooperative Learning	*478, 482, 486, 490, 495, 500, 508, 512, 517, 524, 529, 534, 539*
3	**Reasoning**	Critical Thinking	485, 489, 494, 498, 504, 516, 520, 528, 533, 538, 542
4	**Connections**	Mathematical	See Standards 5, 7, 8, 9, 12, 13.
		Interdisciplinary	Social Studies 479, 485, 527; Science 478, *481,* 483, *485,* 487, *492,* 493, *502,* 503, 520, 523, 527, 532, 536, 537, 541, 544; Arts & Literature *478,* 479, 511, *514*; Entertainment 478; History 506, 513, 531; Language 509; Industry *481, 507,* 510, 516, 519, 522, *526,* 541; Consumer 533; Geography *523, 531,* 536
		Technology	480, 499, 525
		Cultural	478
5	**Number and Number Relationships**		484, 488, 498, 504, 520, 533
7	**Computation and Estimation**		*483, 491, 501,* 510, *513,* 515, 522, *525, 535*
8	**Patterns and Functions**		490–522, 533
9	**Algebra**		482–545
10	**Statistics**		493, 500, 505, 511
12	**Geometry**		485, *494,* 510, 533, 538
13	**Measurement**		484

Italic type indicates Teacher Edition reference.

Teaching Standards

Focus on Student Discourse

The teacher of mathematics should promote classroom discourse in which students

•listen to, respond to, and question the teacher and one another.

•use a variety of tools to reason, make connections, solve problems, and communicate.

Assessment Standards

Focus on Inferences

Portfolios The Inferences Standard invites teachers to use cumulative knowledge about students when commenting on tasks recently completed. A portfolio of student work provides concrete evidence of student's growth in mathematical reasoning, communication, and problem solving. Examples of work students are asked to put in their portfolios from Chapter 10 include

- stories about graphs.
- graphs used to solve equations.

TECHNOLOGY

For the Teacher

- **Resource Pro, a Teacher's Resource Planner CD-ROM**
  Use the teacher planning CD-ROM to view resources available for Chapter 10. You can prepare custom lesson plans or use the default lesson plans provided.

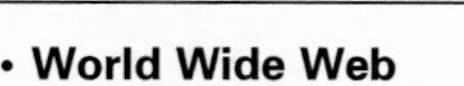

- **World Wide Web**
  Visit **www.kz.com** to view class summary reports, individual student reports, and more.

- **Test Works**
  TestWorks provides ready-made tests and can create custom tests and practice worksheets.

For the Parent

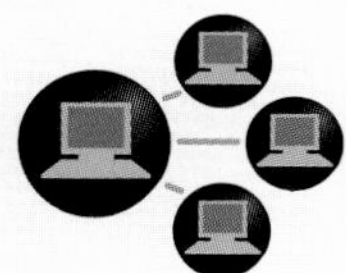

- **World Wide Web**
  Parents can use the web site at **www.kz.com** to check on student progress or to take a quick refresher course.

For the Student

- **Interactive CD-ROM**
  Lesson 10-7 has an *Interactive CD-ROM Lesson.* The *Interactive CD-ROM Journal* and *Interactive CD-ROM Equation Grapher Tool* are also used in Chapter 10.

- **Wide World of Mathematics**
  Lesson 10-1 Algebra: Rube Goldberg Machines
  Lesson 10-3 Algebra: La Quebrada Divers
  Lesson 10-4 Algebra: Endangered Species
  Lesson 10-5 Algebra: Investing for College

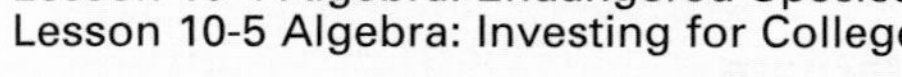

- **World Wide Web**
  Use with Chapter and Section Openers; Students can go online to the Scott Foresman-Addison Wesley Web site at **www.mathsurf.com/7/ch10** to collect information about chapter themes. Students can also visit **www.kz.com** for tutorials and practice.

STANDARDIZED - TEST CORRELATION

SECTION 10A

LESSON	OBJECTIVE	ITBS Form M	CTBS 4th Ed.	CAT 5th Ed.	SAT 9th Ed.	MAT 7th Ed.	Your Form
10-1	• Identify variables and constants.	✘	✘	✘	✘	✘	
10-2	• Match a graph to a story. • Write a story for a graph.	✘ ✘	✘ ✘	✘ ✘	✘ ✘	✘ ✘	
10-3	• Write rules for sequences. • Identify arithmetic and geometric sequences.			✘ ✘	 ✘	✘ ✘	
10-4	• Write an equation from a table of values.			✘			
10-5	• Draw the graph of an equation.						

SECTION 10B

LESSON	OBJECTIVE	ITBS Form M	CTBS 4th Ed.	CAT 5th Ed.	SAT 9th Ed.	MAT 7th Ed.	Your Form
10-6	• Use tables to solve equations.			✘		✘	
10-7	• Use graphs to solve equations.						
10-8	• Graph inequalities on a number line. • Write the inequality represented by a graph.						

SECTION 10C

LESSON	OBJECTIVE	ITBS Form M	CTBS 4th Ed.	CAT 5th Ed.	SAT 9th Ed.	MAT 7th Ed.	Your Form
10-9	• Solve addition and subtraction equations involving positive and negative integers.	✘	✘	✘			
10-10	• Solve multiplication and division problems involving positive and negative integers.	✘	✘	✘			
10-11	• Solve two-step equations involving positive and negative integers.						
10-12	• Solve real-world problems by using integer equations.						

Key: ITBS - Iowa Test of Basic Skills; CTBS - Comprehensive Test of Basic Skills; CAT - California Achievement Test; SAT - Stanford Achievement Test; MAT - Metropolitan Achievement Test

ASSESSMENT PROGRAM

Traditional Assessment

QUICK QUIZZES	SECTION REVIEW	CHAPTER REVIEW	CHAPTER ASSESSMENT FREE RESPONSE	CHAPTER ASSESSMENT MULTIPLE CHOICE	CUMULATIVE REVIEW
TE: pp. 485, 489, 494, 498, 504, 511, 516, 520, 528, 533, 538, 542	SE: pp. 506, 522, 544 *Quiz 10A, 10B, 10C	SE: pp. 546–547	SE: p. 548 *Ch. 10 Tests Forms A, B, E	*Ch. 10 Tests Forms C, E	SE: p. 549 *Ch. 10 Test Form F

Alternate Assessment

INTERVIEW	JOURNAL	ONGOING	PERFORMANCE	PORTFOLIO	PROJECT	SELF
TE: pp. 511, 528	SE: pp. 485, 489, 506, 511, 522, 533 TE: pp. 480, 485, 494, 504, 533	TE: pp. 482, 486, 490, 495, 500, 508, 512, 517, 524, 529, 534, 539	SE: p. 548 *Ch. 10 Tests Forms D, E	TE: pp. 489, 498, 516, 542	SE: pp. 504, 520, 538 TE: p. 479	TE: pp. 494, 520, 538

*Tests and quizzes are in *Assessment Sourcebook*. Test Form E is a mixed response test. Forms for Alternate Assessment are also available in *Assessment Sourcebook*.

TestWorks: Test and Practice Software

MIDDLE SCHOOL PACING CHART

REGULAR PACING

Day	5 classes per week
1	Chapter 10 Opener; Problem Solving Focus
2	Section **10A** Opener; Lesson **10-1**
3	Lesson **10-2**
4	Lesson **10-3**
5	Lesson **10-4**; Technology
6	Lesson **10-5**
7	**10A** Connect; **10A** Review
8	Section **10B** Opener; Lesson **10-6**
9	Lesson **10-7**
10	Lesson **10-8**
11	**10B** Connect; **10B** Review
12	Section **10C** Opener; Lesson **10-9**
13	Lesson **10-10**
14	Lesson **10-11**
15	Lesson **10-12**
16	**10C** Connect; **10C** Review; Extend Key Ideas
17	Chapter 10 Summary and Review
18	Chapter 10 Assessment; Cumulative Review, Chapters 1–10

BLOCK SCHEDULING OPTIONS

Block Scheduling for
Complete Course

Chapter 10 may be presented in

- eleven 90-minute blocks
- fourteen 75-minute blocks

Each block consists of a combination of

- Chapter and Section Openers
- Explores
- Lesson Development
- Problem Solving Focus
- Technology
- Extend Key Ideas
- Connect
- Review
- Assessment

For details, see *Block Scheduling Handbook.*

Block Scheduling for
Interdisciplinary Course

Each block integrates math with another subject area.

In Chapter 10, interdisciplinary topics include

- Insects
- Young Entrepreneurs
- Weather

Themes for Interdisciplinary Team Teaching 10A, 10B, and 10C are

- Monarch Butterflies
- The Computer Business
- Weather Data

For details, see *Block Scheduling Handbook.*

Block Scheduling for
Lab-Based Course

In each block, 30–40 minutes is devoted to lab activities including

- Explores in the Student Edition
- Connect pages in the Student Edition
- Technology options in the Student Edition
- Reteaching Activities in the Teacher Edition

For details, see *Block Scheduling Handbook.*

Block Scheduling for
Course with *Connected Mathematics*

In each block, investigations from **Connected Mathematics** replace or enhance the lessons in Chapter 10.

Connected Mathematics topics for Chapter 10 can be found in

- *Variables and Patterns*
- *Moving Straight Ahead*
- *Accentuate the Negative*

For details, see *Block Scheduling Handbook.*

INTERDISCIPLINARY BULLETIN BOARD

Set Up

Set up a bulletin board with three columns labeled "Animal," "5 years," and "Graph." Provide resource materials for research on animal populations.

Procedure

- Have small groups of students research the number of offspring well-known wild animals have per year. Animals might include raccoon, squirrel, wolf, bear, deer, coyote, groundhog, fox, rabbit.
- Tell students to imagine that 5 years have passed by. Groups should write an equation to show the relationship between the number of years that pass (y) and the number of offspring produced by a particular pair of wild animals (o).
- Groups should draw a picture of the animal. Next to the picture, they should write the equation and then draw a graph of the equation.

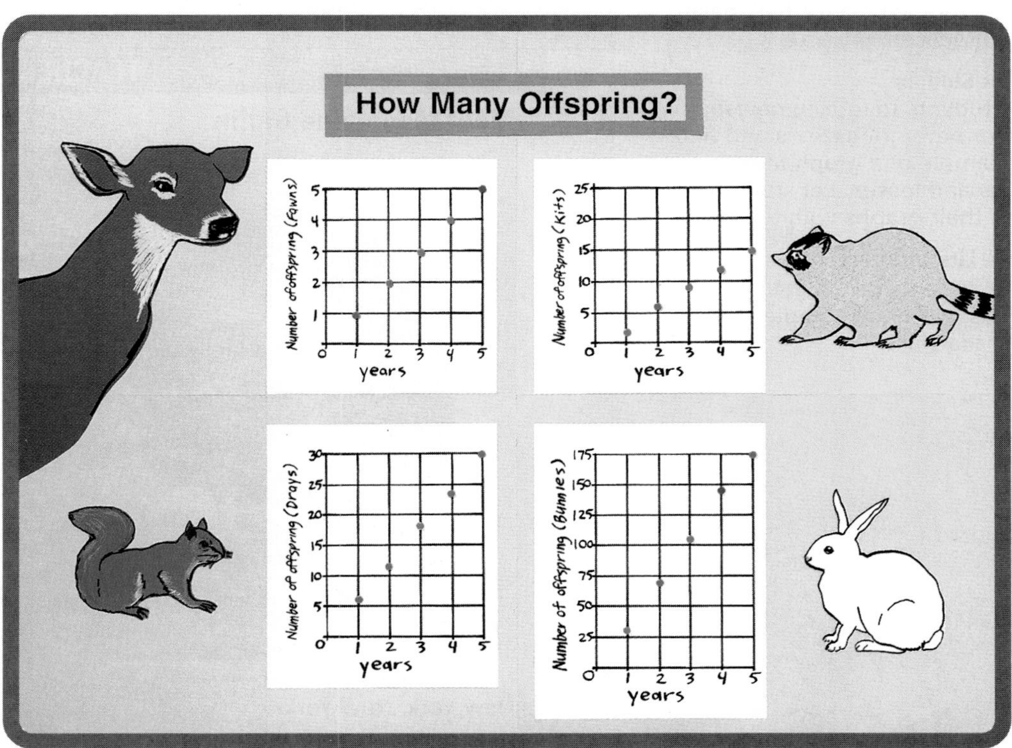

Chapter 10

The information on these pages shows how patterns and rules are used in real-life situations.

World Wide Web

If your class has access to the World Wide Web, you might want to use the information found at the Web site addresses given.

Extensions

The following activities do not require access to the World Wide Web.

People of the World
Ask students to describe things that are sold in much the same way as described here, that is, by the unit weight. Possible answer: Meat and vegetables are often sold by the pound.

Science
Ask students to give Fahrenheit and Celsius temperatures with which they are familiar, such as the freezing point of water or the boiling point of water. 0°C, 32°F; 100°C, 212°F

Entertainment
Ask students to work with partners to make up their own "dream team" for one of these sports: football, basketball, baseball, or soccer.

Social Studies
Ask students to look in newspapers or news magazines and find an example of a graph that shows profits and losses. Let students share their graphs with the class.

Arts & Literature
Have students investigate fractals and find examples to show the class.

10 The Patterns of Algebra: Equations

Science Link
www.mathsurf.com/7/ch10/science

People of the World

In fifteenth-century Italy, the merchant's key was a rule used to determine how much a quantity of an item would cost. The merchant would find the unit cost and multiply it by the quantity that the customer wanted.

Science

To convert Fahrenheit temperatures to Celsius, subtract 32 and multiply the result by $\frac{5}{9}$. The only temperature that is the same in both scales is $-40°$.

Entertainment

In fantasy sports leagues, people "pick teams" of professional athletes. Formulas are used to analyze the athletes' performances and to see whose team did the best.

478

TEACHER TALK

Meet Madelaine Gallin

Manhattan District #5
New York, New York

I introduce linear functions by playing the game, "Guess My Rule." I begin by placing numbers in a 2-column chart headed by a star and a circle. The students suggest numbers to put in the star column and I place a number in the circle column based on a rule I have devised. The numbers students give need not be consecutive; it is often better to select numbers at random. As students begin to "discover" the rule, I have those who think they know it respond by identifying the circle value when given a star value. When students state the rule, I insist that they express it in a full sentence, such as "The circle is four more than the star." After using examples with several different rules, I exchange the shapes for variables and do several more examples. We then transfer each rule into a linear equation, such as $y = x + 4$.

and Graphs

Arts & Literature Link
www.mathsurf.com/7/ch10/arts

Social Studies

Businesspeople use graphs to show trends in their company's profits.

Arts & Literature

Fractal patterns like the one shown below are generated by mathematical rules. Some fractals are made by substituting coordinates for many different points into an equation, then tracing the results for each point.

KEY MATH IDEAS

Quantities whose values can change are **variables**. Those whose values do not change are **constants**. The relationship between two variables can be shown in a table or graph.

A **sequence** is a pattern of numbers. By writing an algebraic rule for a sequence, you can find any of its terms.

You can solve an equation by using a graph or a table. If you find the value of the known variable on the graph or in the table, you can read the value of the unknown variable.

You can also solve an equation involving integers by using algebra tiles or algebraic symbols. When solving by these methods, you must always do the same thing to both sides of the equation.

CHAPTER PROJECT

Problem Solving
Understand
Plan
Solve
Look Back

In this project, you'll investigate the population of your city, town, or state. Begin by choosing the population you're interested in. Then do some research to find this population for several different years.

Chapter Project

Students investigate trends in the population of their city, town, or state over a period of time.

Resources
Chapter 10 Project Master

Introduce the Project

- Discuss where students might find information about the past and present populations of the area they selected.
- Tell students that they are going to use their population data to show trends, so they may want to find data for equal intervals, such as each census year during the 20th century.

Project Progress

Section A, page 504 Students put their population data in a table and try to find an equation that fits, or almost fits, the data.

Section B, page 520 Students make a scatterplot showing their data and the graph of the equation they wrote earlier.

Section C, page 538 Using data for their place of residence, students predict a population for the future and then estimate when this number will be reached.

Community Project

A community project for Chapter 10 is available in *Home and Community Connection.*

Cooperative Learning

You may want to use Teaching Tool Transparency 1: Cooperative Learning Checklist with **Explore** and other group activities in this chapter.

PROJECT ASSESSMENT

You may choose to use this project as a performance assessment for the chapter.

Performance Assessment Key

Level 4 Full Accomplishment

Level 3 Substantial Accomplishment

Level 2 Partial Accomplishment

Level 1 Little Accomplishment

Suggested Scoring Rubric

4
- Appropriate data is recorded.
- Equation fits data well.
- Scatterplot is accurate.
- Future population fits data.

3
- Appropriate data is recorded.
- Equation is acceptable.
- Scatterplot is acceptable.
- Future population and projected date are acceptable.

2
- Appropriate data is recorded.
- Has difficulty writing equation.
- Scatterplot is acceptable.
- Future population does not adequately fit data.

1
- Records some data.
- Does not write an equation.
- Scatterplot is inadequate.
- No future population or date given.

Problem Solving Focus

Checking for a Reasonable Answer

The Point
Students focus on using estimation to evaluate the reasonableness of an answer.

Resources
Teaching Tool Transparency 16: Problem-Solving Guidelines

 *Interactive CD-ROM Journal*

About the Page

Using the Problem-Solving Process
Once students have determined an answer to a problem, they need to see if the answer makes sense and is reasonable. To determine if the answer is reasonable, they can use estimation. Discuss the following suggestions for the Look Back step:

- Determine what the problem asked you to find.
- Review the steps you used to solve the problem and check your arithmetic.
- Estimate the answer and decide if your calculated answer is reasonable based on the estimate.

Ask ...
- In Problem 2, is Mount Kanchenjunga higher or lower than Pike's Peak? Explain. Higher, because Mount Kanchenjunga is almost twice as tall as Pike's Peak.
- What equation could you write to solve Problem 4? Could you solve the problem in another way? $2x - 6 = 1000$; Yes, for example, by working backward.

Answers for Problems
1. Too low; Should be 23,034 ft.
2. Close enough; Should be 28,208 ft.
3. Too high; Should be 24,674 ft.
4. Close enough; Should be 503 m.
5. Too low; Should be 609.3 m.
6. Too high; Should be 94 m.

Journal

Ask students to write a paragraph discussing the purpose of the Look Back step in problem solving.

Problem Solving
Understand
Plan
Solve
Look Back

Checking for a Reasonable Answer

It is important to look back at your answer to a problem to make sure it's reasonable. You can use an estimate to evaluate the reasonableness of your exact answer.

Problem Solving Focus

Each of the problems below has an answer, but the answer is not exactly right. Tell if each answer is "close enough," "too low," or "too high," and explain why.

1. The tallest mountain in the world, Mount Everest, is 29,028 ft tall. It is located on the border of China and Nepal. The tallest mountain in the Americas is Aconcagua, which is 5,994 ft shorter than Mount Everest. How tall is Aconcagua?
Answer: 21,100 ft

2. Mount Kanchenjunga, on the border between Nepal and Sikkim, is 12 ft less than twice as tall as Pike's Peak in Colorado. If Pike's Peak is 14,110 ft tall, how tall is Mount Kanchenjunga?
Answer: 28,200 ft

3. What is the mean of the heights of Mount Everest and Alaska's 20,320 ft Mount McKinley, the tallest mountain in the United States?
Answer: 26,300 ft

4. The highest waterfall in the world is 1000-meter-tall Angel Falls in Venezuela. It is 6 meters less than twice as tall as Takkakaw Falls in British Columbia, Canada. What is the height of Takkakaw Falls?
Answer: 500 meters

5. The second- and third-highest waterfalls in the world are 914-meter-tall Tugela Falls in South Africa and Cuquenán Falls in Venezuela. The height of Cuquenán Falls is $\frac{2}{3}$ of the height of Tugela Falls. How tall is Cuquenán Falls?
Answer: 400 meters

6. Sutherland Falls, in New Zealand, is 580 meters tall. It is 486 meters taller than Lower Yellowstone Falls, in Wyoming. How tall is Lower Yellowstone Falls?
Answer: 200 meters

480

Additional Problem

The longest railroad tunnel in the world is in Japan. It is called the Seikan Tunnel and is 33 miles long. It is one mile longer than four times the length of the longest railroad tunnel in the United States, the New Cascade Tunnel in Washington. How long is the New Cascade Tunnel?

1. Is an estimate of 34 miles too low, too high, or close enough? Explain. Too high; the New Cascade Tunnel is shorter than the Seikan Tunnel.
2. Is an estimate of 20 miles too low, too high, or close enough? Too high; the New Cascade Tunnel is only about a fourth as long as the Seikan Tunnel.
3. Estimate the length of the New Cascade Tunnel. Possible answer: $32 \div 4 = 8$; 8 miles

Tables, Equations, and Graphs

LESSON PLANNING GUIDE

Student Edition / **Ancillaries**

LESSON		MATERIALS	VOCABULARY	DAILY	OTHER
	Chapter 10 Opener				Ch. 10 Project Master Ch. 10 Community Project Teaching Tool Trans. 1
	Problem Solving Focus				Teaching Tool Trans. 16 *Interactive CD-ROM Journal*
	Section 10A Opener				
10-1	**Quantities, Constants, and Variables**		constant	10-1	Teaching Tool Trans. 21 *WW Math*–Algebra
10-2	**Relating Graphs to Stories**		increasing graph, decreasing graph, constant graph	10-2	Lesson Enhancement Trans. 44
10-3	**Tables and Expressions**	centimeter cubes or graph paper	sequence, term, arithmetic sequence, geometric sequence	10-3	Teaching Tool Trans. 7 Technology Master 44
10-4	**Understanding and Writing Equations**			10-4	Technology Master 45
	Technology	graphing calculator			Teaching Tool Trans. 23 *Interactive CD-ROM Equation Grapher Tool*
10-5	**Equations and Graphs**			10-5	Teaching Tool Trans. 8 Lesson Enhance. Trans. 45, 46 Technology Master 46 Ch. 10 Project Master *WW Math*–Middle School
	Connect	graph paper			Lesson Enhancement Trans. 47
	Review				Practice/Quiz 10A; *TestWorks*

SKILLS TRACE

LESSON	SKILL	FIRST INTRODUCED GR. 5	GR. 6	GR. 7	DEVELOP	PRACTICE/APPLY	REVIEW
10-1	**Identifying variable and constants.**		✘		pp. 482–483	pp. 484–485	pp. 506, 546, 562
10-2	**Relating graphs and stories.**			✘ p. 486	pp. 486–487	pp. 488–489	pp. 506, 546, 566
10-3	**Writing rules for sequences.**		✘		pp. 490–492	pp. 493–494	pp. 506, 546, 570
10-4	**Writing equations for tables.**			✘ p. 495	pp. 495–496	pp. 497–498	pp. 506, 546, 577
10-5	**Graphing equations.**			✘ p. 500	pp. 500–502	pp. 503–504	pp. 506, 546, 581

CONNECTED MATHEMATICS

Investigations 1–4 in the unit *Variables and Patterns (Introducing Algebra)*, from the **Connected Mathematics** series, can be used with Section 10A.

INTERDISCIPLINARY TEAM TEACHING

Math and Science/Technology

(Worksheet pages 39–40: Teacher pages T39–T40)

In this lesson, students write expressions and make graphs using constants and variables from monarch butterfly migration data.

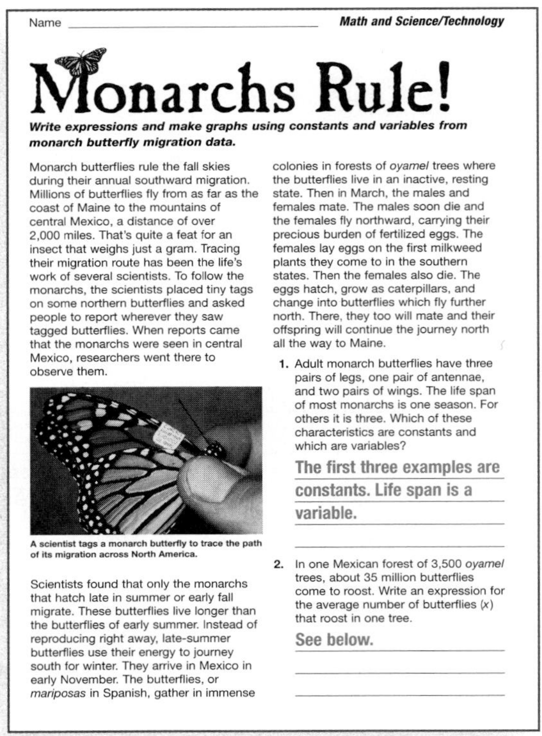

Name ______________________ *Math and Science/Technology*

Monarchs Rule!

Write expressions and make graphs using constants and variables from monarch butterfly migration data.

Monarch butterflies rule the fall skies during their annual southward migration. Millions of butterflies fly from as far as the coast of Maine to the mountains of central Mexico, a distance of over 2,000 miles. That's quite a feat for an insect that weighs just a gram. Tracing their migration route has been the life's work of several scientists. To follow the monarchs, the scientists placed tiny tags on some northern butterflies and asked people to report wherever they saw tagged butterflies. When reports came that the monarchs were seen in central Mexico, researchers went there to observe them.

A scientist tags a monarch butterfly to trace the path of its migration across North America.

Scientists found that only the monarchs that hatch late in summer or early fall migrate. These butterflies live longer than the butterflies of early summer. Instead of reproducing right away, late-summer butterflies use their energy to journey south for winter. They arrive in Mexico in early November. The butterflies, or *mariposas* in Spanish, gather in immense colonies in forests of *oyamel* trees where the butterflies live in an inactive, resting state. Then in March, the males and females mate. The males soon die and the females fly northward, carrying their precious burden of fertilized eggs. The females lay eggs on the first milkweed plants they come to in the southern states. Then the females also die. The eggs hatch, grow as caterpillars, and change into butterflies which fly further north. There, they too will mate and their offspring will continue the journey north all the way to Maine.

1. Adult monarch butterflies have three pairs of legs, one pair of antennae, and two pairs of wings. The life span of most monarchs is one season. For others it is three. Which of these characteristics are constants and which are variables?

The first three examples are constants. Life span is a variable.

2. In one Mexican forest of 3,500 *oyamel* trees, about 35 million butterflies come to roost. Write an expression for the average number of butterflies (x) that roost in one tree.

See below.

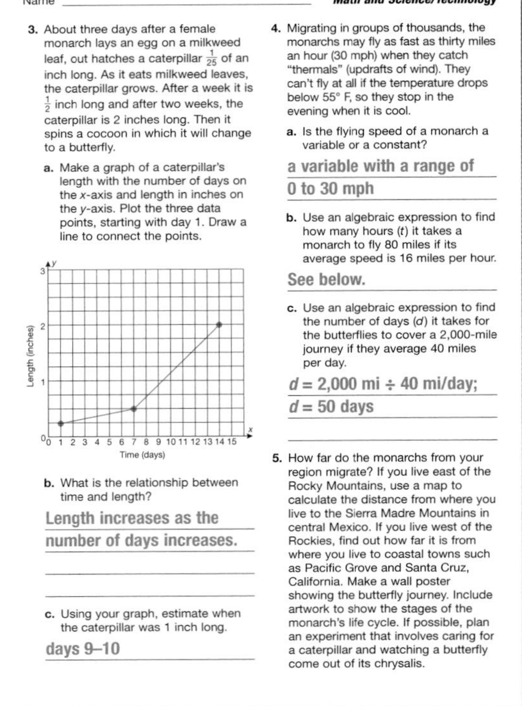

Name ______________________ *Math and Science/Technology*

3. About three days after a female monarch lays an egg on a milkweed leaf, out hatches a caterpillar $\frac{1}{25}$ of an inch long. As it eats milkweed leaves, the caterpillar grows. After a week it is $\frac{1}{2}$ inch long and after two weeks, the caterpillar is 2 inches long. Then it spins a cocoon in which it will change to a butterfly.

a. Make a graph of a caterpillar's length with the number of days on the x-axis and length in inches on the y-axis. Plot the three data points, starting with day 1. Draw a line to connect the points.

b. What is the relationship between time and length?

Length increases as the number of days increases.

c. Using your graph, estimate when the caterpillar was 1 inch long.

days 9–10

4. Migrating in groups of thousands, the monarchs may fly as fast as thirty miles an hour (30 mph) when they catch "thermals" (updrafts of wind). They can't fly at all if the temperature drops below 55° F, so they stop in the evening when it is cool.

a. Is the flying speed of a monarch a variable or a constant?

a variable with a range of 0 to 30 mph

b. Use an algebraic expression to find how many hours (t) it takes a monarch to fly 80 miles if its average speed is 16 miles per hour.

See below.

c. Use an algebraic expression to find the number of days (d) it takes for the butterflies to cover a 2,000-mile journey if they average 40 miles per day.

d = 2,000 mi ÷ 40 mi/day;
d = 50 days

5. How far do the monarchs from your region migrate? If you live east of the Rocky Mountains, use a map to calculate the distance from where you live to the Sierra Madre Mountains in central Mexico. If you live west of the Rockies, find out how far it is from where you live to coastal towns such as Pacific Grove and Santa Cruz, California. Make a wall poster showing the butterfly journey. Include artwork to show the stages of the monarch's life cycle. If possible, plan an experiment that involves caring for a caterpillar and watching a butterfly come out of its chrysalis.

Answers

2. 3,500 x = 35,000,000; x = 35,000,000/3,500 = 10,000 per tree

4. b. 5 hours; time = distance ÷ speed;
t = 80 mi ÷ 16 mi/hr = 5 hr.

BIBLIOGRAPHY

FOR TEACHERS

Huxley, Anthony, ed. *Standard Encyclopedia of the World's Mountains.* New York, NY: Putnam, 1962.

O'Toole, Christopher, ed. *The Encyclopedia of Insects.* New York, NY: Facts on File, 1986.

Robinson, Andrew. *Earth Shock: Hurricanes, Volcanoes, Earthquakes, Tornadoes and Other Forces of Nature.* New York, NY: Thames and Hudson, 1993.

Ryden, Hope. *Wild Animals of Africa ABC.* New York, NY: Lodestar Books, 1989.

Thomas, Lowell. *Lowell Thomas' Book of High Mountains.* New York, NY: J. Messner, 1964.

FOR STUDENTS

Bramwell, Martyn. *Mountains.* New York, NY: Franklin Watts, 1994.

Penner, Lucille Recht. *Monster Bugs.* New York, NY: Random House, 1996.

Roop, Peter. *Going Buggy!: Jokes About Insects.* Minneapolis, MN: Lerner Publications, 1986.

Wood, Jenny. *Waterfalls: Nature's Thundering Splendor.* Milwaukee, WI: G. Stevens Children's Books, 1991.

Section 10A

SECTION 10A Tables, Equations, and Graphs

▶ Science Link ▶ Industry Link ▶ www.mathsurf.com/7/ch10/insects

Howdy, Ant Bee!

A summer picnic in a city park—what could be nicer? Unfortunately, these outings can turn into a battle for the survival of the fittest. While you're brushing the ants off your fruit salad with one hand and slapping mosquitoes with the other, you're trying to dodge a swarm of bees who think your insect repellent smells like a flower!

When most people think of insects, only the annoying ones come to mind. Yet of the more than one million species of insects, probably less than 2% are pests. In fact, many of these six-legged creatures are essential to our survival. About one-third of our food is a direct result of insect pollination of plants.

Entomologists use mathematics to model insect behavior and the growth of insect populations. Now you will investigate many of the mathematical tools these scientists use.

1 There are about 4600 species of mammals. How many times more species of insects are there?

2 Suppose an adult human consumes 2100 food calories in a day. On average, how many of these calories are a direct result of insect pollination?

481

Where are we now?

In Grade 6, students worked with variables and variable expressions.

They learned how to

- write expressions using variables.
- translate words into mathematical expressions.
- write and solve equations.

Where are we going?

In Grade 7 Section 10A students will

- identify variables and constants.
- analyze graphs.
- identify arithmetic and geometric sequences.
- write an equation from a table of values.
- graph equations.

Theme: Insects

World Wide Web

If your class has access to the World Wide Web, you might want to use the information found at the Web site address given. The interdisciplinary links relate to topics discussed in this section.

About the Page

This page introduces the theme of the section, insects, and discusses insect behavior and the impact of insects on our survival.

Ask ...

- Why are insects important?
  Possible answers: Pollination, provide food for other animals.
- What are some insect pests? What makes them pests?
  Possible answers: Mosquitoes, bees, wasps, locusts, termites; They sting, destroy property, carry disease, destroy crops.

Extensions

The following activities do not require access to the World Wide Web.

Science

Many insects are invaluable for the part they play in the pollination of flowers. Other insects, such as bees and silk worms, are a source of food and other products. Ask students to list examples of helpful insects and explain why the insects are helpful.

Industry

The damage done to the farming industry by insect pests can be devastating and has led to a variety of methods of controlling these insects. Ask students to research such methods and report their findings to the class.

Answers for Questions

1. About 200
2. 700

Connect

On page 505, students use graphs and tables to analyze the nutritional content of edible insects and other animals.

10-1 Lesson Organizer

Objective

- Identify variables and constants.

Vocabulary

- Constant

NCTM Standards

- 1–4, 9, 12, 13

Review

Do the following amounts remain the same at all times?

1. Number of ounces in a pound Yes
2. Weight of a baby No
3. Height of a tree No
4. Length of a week Yes

Available on Daily Transparency 10-1

1 Introduce

Explore

The Point
Students decide if certain numbers describing houseflies can change or if the numbers always stay the same. This leads to the distinction between a variable and a constant.

Ongoing Assessment
Watch for students who think they actually have to find the numbers described before Step 7.

For Groups That Finish Early
Give one more example of an insect-related number that can change and one that stays the same. Possible answers: The length of a praying mantis can change, but the number of eyes of a praying mantis stays the same.

10-1 Quantities, Constants, and Variables

You'll Learn ...

- to identify variables and constants

... How It's Used

The quantities measured by medical tests are variables that can be used to diagnose illnesses.

Vocabulary

constant

▶ Lesson Link You've used variables to help you solve many different types of problems. Now you'll take a closer look at variables and other numbers. ◀

Explore Types of Numbers

Flying Lesson

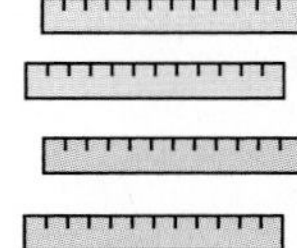

Think about each of the numbers described below. Make a table showing the numbers that can change and those that always stay the same.

1. Number of legs on a normal housefly
2. Amount of food eaten by a housefly in one day
3. Distance a housefly flies in an hour
4. Weight of a male housefly
5. Number of wings on a normal housefly
6. Add other fly-related numbers to your table. Include at least one number that stays the same and another that can change.
7. Give the actual value of any number in Step 6 that you know about. What do you notice about all of these numbers?

Learn Quantities, Constants, and Variables

A *quantity* is anything that can be measured by a number. The number of inches in a foot and the number of ladybugs on a leaf are quantities. The *value* for the first of these quantities is 12 inches; the second value might be 1 ladybug.

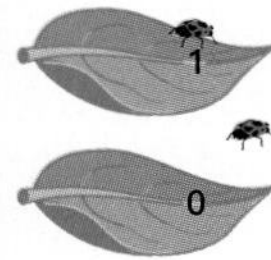

As you've seen, quantities whose values may change are called *variables*. Quantities whose values cannot change are called **constants**.

MEETING INDIVIDUAL NEEDS

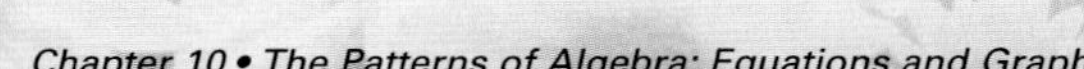

Resources

- 10-1 Practice
- 10-1 Reteaching
- 10-1 Problem Solving
- 10-1 Enrichment
- 10-1 Daily Transparency
  - Problem of the Day
  - Review
  - Quick Quiz
- Teaching Tool Transparency 21

Wide World of Mathematics Algebra: Ticker-Tape Parade

Learning Modalities

Verbal Have students write a paragraph for one of the following titles: *Constants That I Use* or *Variables in My Life.*

Social Have a group of students collect data about how they use numbers over a 24-hour period and then make a presentation to the class about the results. They should explain which numbers are variables and which are constants.

Inclusion

Some students are confused by the fact that letters used to name variables are different from one problem to the next. Point out that when students define a variable, they can use any convenient letter. Often the first letter of the word naming the quantity is chosen as the variable, but any letter can be used.

Examples

Tell whether each quantity is a variable or a constant.

1 The number of times a butterfly's wings beat in one minute

The number of beats in a minute can change, so this quantity is a variable.

2 The number of antennae on a butterfly

Butterflies always have two antennae, so this quantity is a constant.

Try It

Tell whether each quantity is a variable or a constant.

a. Your height Variable

b. The number of centimeters in a meter Constant

c. The number of locusts in a swarm Variable

d. The number of quarters in a dollar Constant

Science Link

A swarm of locusts may contain 28 billion insects, weighing a total of 70 tons.

Although variables can take on different values, you can make an educated guess at a reasonable *range* of values for many real-world quantities.

Examples

For each quantity, define a variable and give a range of reasonable values.

3 The length of a cricket

Let c = the length of a cricket. By looking at a ruler, you can estimate that c is between 1 cm and 4 cm.

4 The number of songs on a CD

Let s = the number of songs. For most CDs, s is between 8 and 15.

Try It

For each quantity, define a variable and give a range of reasonable values.

a. The time it takes to get to school

b. The wingspan of a butterfly

Check Your Understanding

1. Explain the difference between variable and constant quantities.

2. Why do you think we use letters instead of numbers to represent the values of variable quantities?

MATH EVERY DAY

Problem of the Day

What comes next in this series? [Hint: Think of words.]

8, 5, 4, 9, 1, 7, 6, ___, ___

3, 2 [arranged alphabetically]

Available on Daily Transparency 10-1

An Extension is provided in the transparency package.

Fact of the Day

The eyes of the housefly are compound and may have as many as 4000 facets. They pick up light changes and movement more than images.

Estimation

Estimate.

1. 4,592 + 2,344 − 1,002 6,000
2. 4222 • 39 160,000
3. 648,668 ÷ 772 800

Answers for Explore

1. Same
2. Change
3. Change
4. Change
5. Same
6. Answers may vary.
7. Answers may vary; Possible answer: You can give values only if the number does not change.

2 Teach

Learn

Alternate Examples

Tell whether each quantity is a variable or a constant.

1. The number of insects caught in a spider's web

   The number can change, so this quantity is a variable.

2. The number of legs on a spider

   Spiders have eight legs, so this quantity is a constant.

For each quantity, define a variable and give a range of reasonable values.

3. The length of a caterpillar

   Let c = the length of a caterpillar. The length of most caterpillars is between 2 cm and 6 cm.

4. The number of pages in a novel

   Let p = the number of pages in a novel. For most novels, p is between 100 and 500.

Answers for Try It

Possible answers:

a. Let T = the time it takes to get to school; Between 5 and 60 minutes.

b. Let W = wingspan of a butterfly; Between 1 cm and 10 cm.

3 Practice and Assess

Check

Answers for Check Your Understanding

1. The value of a variable can change. The value of a constant can't. Variables have a range of values. Constants only have one value.
2. The value of a variable is usually a number, and having one number represent another number could be confusing.

10-2 Lesson Organizer

Objectives

- Match a graph to a story.
- Write a story for a graph.

Vocabulary

- Increasing graph, decreasing graph, constant graph

NCTM Standards

- 1–4, 9

Review

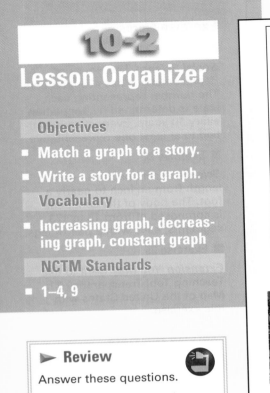

Answer these questions.

What is probably true about a car if the amount of gasoline in its tank

1. stays the same over a long period of time? The car is standing still.
2. decreases steadily? The car is moving.
3. increases rapidly? The tank is being filled.

Available on Daily Transparency 10-2

1 Introduce

Explore

You may want to use Lesson Enhancement Transparency 44 with **Explore.**

The Point
Students use a graph to answer questions about how the number of bees in a hive changes over a period of time. By doing this, students develop their sense of what increasing, decreasing, and constant portions of a graph represent.

Ongoing Assessment
Be sure students understand that each point on the graph represents an ordered pair, where the first number represents time and the second number represents the number of bees at that time.

For Groups That Finish Early
Make a new graph that would require a different story about the bees in the hive.
Answers may vary.

10-2 Relating Graphs to Stories

You'll Learn ...

- to match a graph to a story
- to write a story for a graph

... How It's Used

Quality control experts analyze graphs to decide when product quality is declining and a manufacturing process needs to be corrected.

Vocabulary
increasing graph
decreasing graph
constant graph

► Lesson Link You've investigated quantities that can change. Now you'll explore a way to show relationships between variables visually. ◄

Explore Relating Graphs to Stories

Breaking Out of Hives

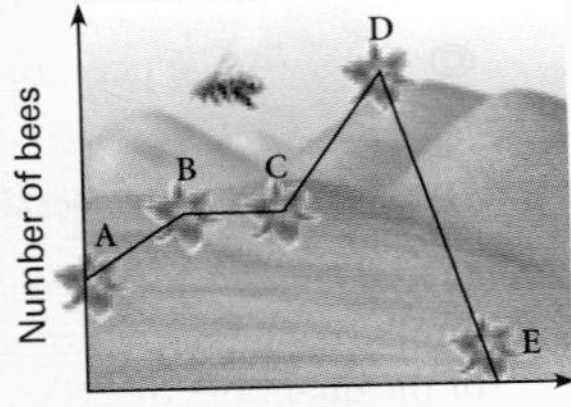

1. The graph shows the population of bees in a hive over time. Look at the change in the graph between points A and B. Explain what might have happened during this time period.
2. In what way did the population change between points B and C? Explain what might have happened between these times.
3. How is the increase in the number of bees between points C and D different from that between points A and B?
4. What might have happened between point D and point E?

Learn Relating Graphs to Stories

The direction of a graph can show a relationship between the quantities on its axes.

When the graph is **increasing** from left to right, the quantities on the axes go up together.

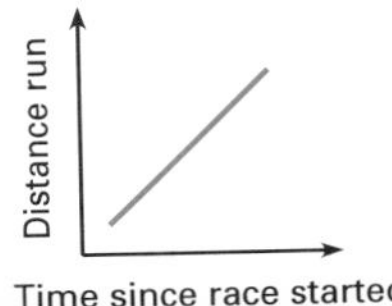

When the graph is **decreasing**, one quantity goes down when the other goes up.

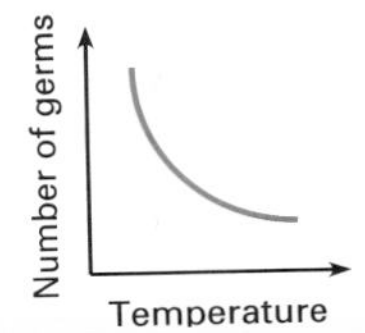

When the graph is **constant**, one quantity stays the same when the other changes.

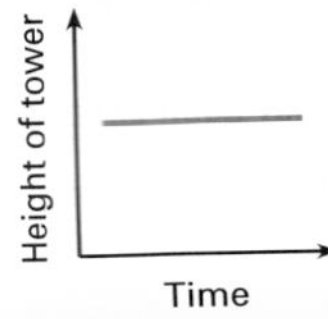

MEETING INDIVIDUAL NEEDS

Resources

10-2 Practice
10-2 Reteaching
10-2 Problem Solving
10-2 Enrichment
10-2 Daily Transparency
Problem of the Day
Review
Quick Quiz
Lesson Enhancement Transparency 44

Learning Modalities

Verbal Have students develop a "model story" that matches a graph that is increasing, one for a graph that is decreasing, and one for a graph that stays constant.

Kinesthetic Have students act out the stories they develop for specific graphs.

Social Have students swap stories and critique each other's work.

Inclusion

Avoid presenting too much information in one graph. Students with vision problems may have difficulty distinguishing relevant characteristics.

Example 1

A bee flies from the hive to the flower garden, stays a while to get some pollen, and then flies back to the hive. Which graph could show its flight?

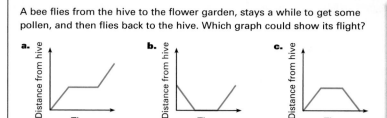

a. Distance from hive / Time

b.

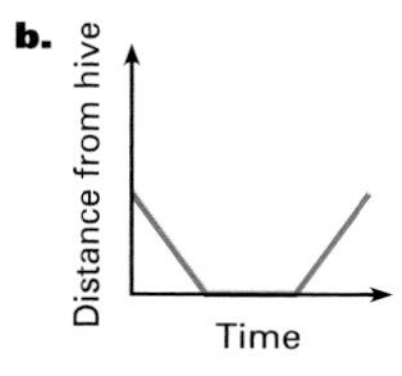

c.

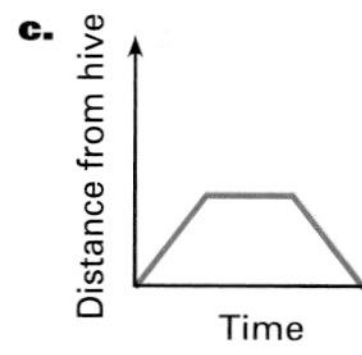

When the bee leaves, its distance from the hive *increases.* Then it stops at the garden, so the graph is *constant.* As the bee returns to the hive, the distance *decreases.* The answer is **c.**

Try It

Another bee was at the flower garden. It flew to the hive, stayed a while, and then flew back to the garden. Which of the graphs above could show its flight? b

Example 2

The graph shows the number of homework exercises Leilani did one night. Tell a story that fits the graph.

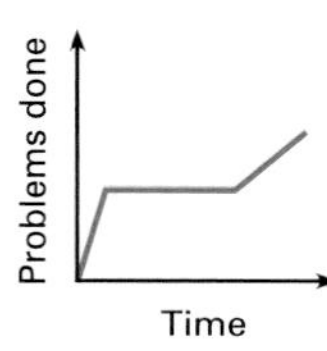

Leilani did about half of the exercises. Then she stopped doing homework while she talked to her friend. Next, she did the rest of the problems, but worked more slowly than she had at first.

Try It

The graph shows the number of students in a classroom over time. Tell a story that fits the graph.

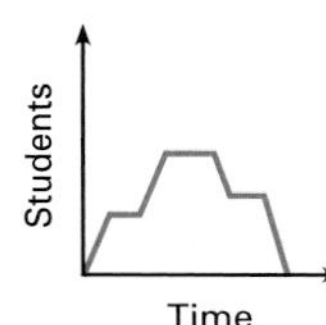

Check Your Understanding

1. How can you tell from a graph whether two quantities have an increasing relationship? A decreasing relationship? A constant relationship?
2. None of the graphs in this lesson had numbers on their axes. How is it possible to get useful information from these graphs?

Science Link

Domesticated bees make honey in manufactured hives. There are three types of bee in each hive: one queen, who lays all of the eggs; hundreds of males, called *drones;* and 50,000 or more female workers.

Answers for Explore

1. The population increased.
2. The population stayed the same; The number of bees born was the same as the number leaving the hive or dying.
3. The population increased more over less time.
4. Bees left the hive to start a new colony.

2 Teach

Learn

Alternate Examples

1. A bee flies from the hive to the flower garden, stays awhile to get some pollen, then flies still farther to the vegetable garden. Which graph in Example 1 could show its flight?

   When the bee leaves, its distance from the hive *increases*. Then it stops at the garden, so the graph is *constant*. Then the distance *increases* as the bee flies to the vegetable garden. The answer is a.

2. Tell a story that fits the second graph (b) in Example 1.

   A bee flies from the flower garden back to the hive, stays awhile to rest, then flies back to the flower garden.

Answers for Try It

The classroom's occupancy over time: Increased from empty, didn't change, increased, didn't change, decreased, didn't change, decreased to empty.

MATH EVERY DAY

Problem of the Day

A boxed set of silverware comes with 8 place settings and several serving pieces. A place setting consists of a knife, a dinner fork, a salad fork, a teaspoon, and a soup spoon. Also included is an extra teaspoon for each place setting. There are $\frac{1}{2}$ as many serving pieces as there are knives. How many pieces of silverware are in the box?

52 pieces [$8 \times 6 + 4 = 52$]

Available on Daily Transparency 10-2

An Extension is provided in the transparency package.

Fact of the Day

Most species of bees are solitary, but about 1000 or more species are communal. They live in small colonies that have a queen and a few daughter workers.

Mental Math

Do these mentally.

1. $750 + 288 + 250$ 1288
2. $18{,}003 - 998$ 17,005
3. $7 \cdot 49$ 343
4. $4536 \div 9$ 504

3 Practice and Assess

Check

Answers for Check Your Understanding

1. As you move from left to right on the graph, the points get higher if the relationship is increasing, get lower if decreasing, and stay the same height if constant.
2. You can still tell whether the quantities increase, decrease, or stay the same and you can compare a change on one part of the graph to a change on another part.

10-2 Exercises and Applications

Assignment Guide

- **Basic** 1–8, 10–13, 15–22
- **Average** 1–7, 9, 11–22
- **Enriched** 1–7, 9, 11–14, 16–22

Exercise Notes

Exercises 6–7

Extension Have students tell other stories to match each graph.

Exercise Answers

Possible answers are given for Exercises 2–11.

2. The width of the mound or the number of termites inside.
3. The length of a side.
4. The amount it spends.
5. The age of the teenager.
8. After some time, you drink some juice. Then you wait awhile and drink more later.
9. You start at home with a full gas tank and drive awhile. You stop, then drive until the tank is empty. You fill the tank.
10. For some time there is no pollen. Then it starts to increase. The amount levels off, then it starts to decrease. Eventually, there is none again.
11.

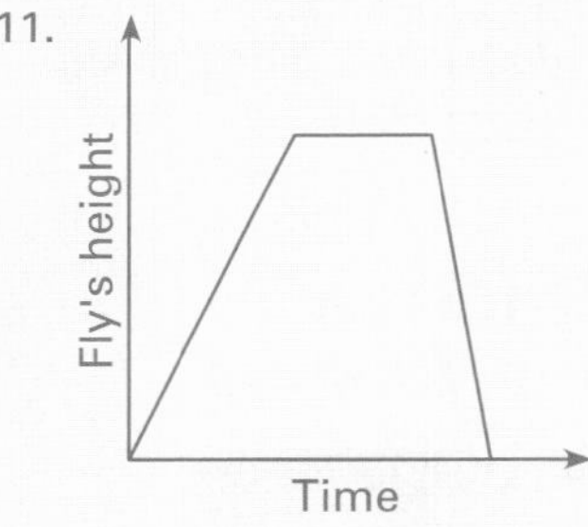

Reteaching

Activity

Work with a partner. Each person should draw a graph similar to one of those in Examples 1–2 or Exercises 6–7 and then exchange graphs. Pretend each of you is a TV announcer. Tell a story that matches the graph you are given by your partner.

PRACTICE 10-2

10-2 Exercises and Applications

Practice and Apply

1. **Getting Started** You're flying from Tulsa to Oklahoma City. As the time increases, tell whether each of the following quantities increases, decreases, or stays constant.
   a. The miles remaining to Oklahoma City Decreases
   b. The amount of fuel in the airplane Decreases
   c. The number of pilots on the airplane Stays constant
   d. The miles from Tulsa Increases

Number Sense Name another quantity that each given quantity might depend on.

2. The height of a termite mound
3. The area of a square
4. The amount of money a business makes
5. The height of a teenager

Termite mound

For Exercises 6 and 7, choose the graph that best shows the story.

6. You notice a few fleas on your dog. You decide they'll probably go away on their own. Instead, the problem gets much worse! b

a. 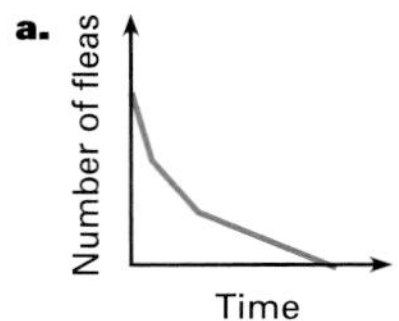

b. 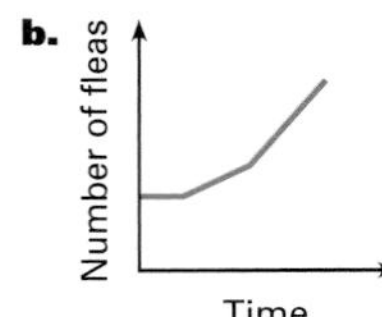

c. 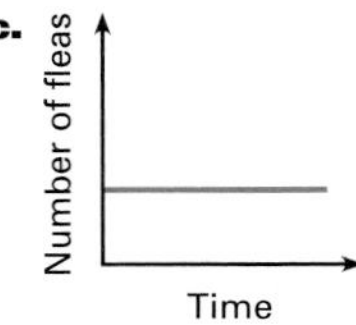

7. You bicycle to your friend's apartment and stay there for lunch. Then the two of you ride to an arcade and play some games. After you finish, you ride straight home. a

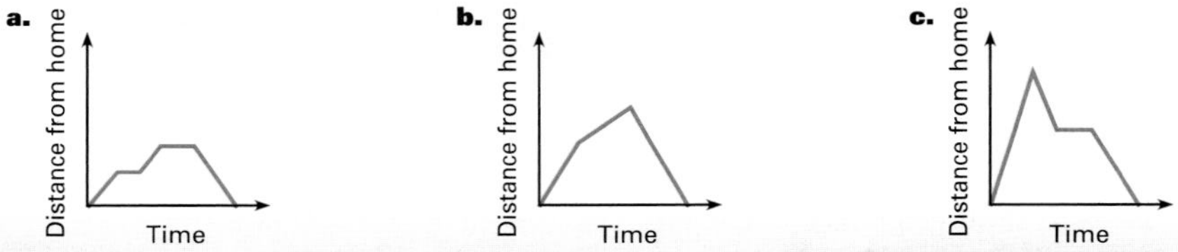

a. 

b. 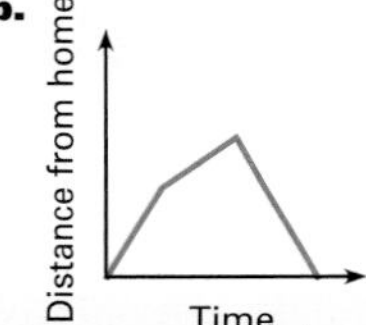

c. 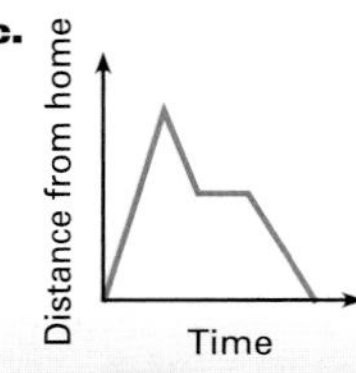

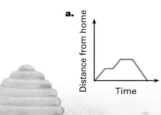

PRACTICE

Name ______________

Practice 10-2

Relating Graphs to Stories

Name another quantity that each given quantity might depend on.

Possible answers:

1. The number of houses on a city block Length of the block
2. The volume of a cube Length of a side
3. The amount of a paycheck Number of hours worked
4. A student's score on a test Number of hours studied

In Exercises 5 and 6, choose the graph that best shows the story.

5. You catch the flu, so your temperature increases. As you regain your health, your temperature returns to normal.

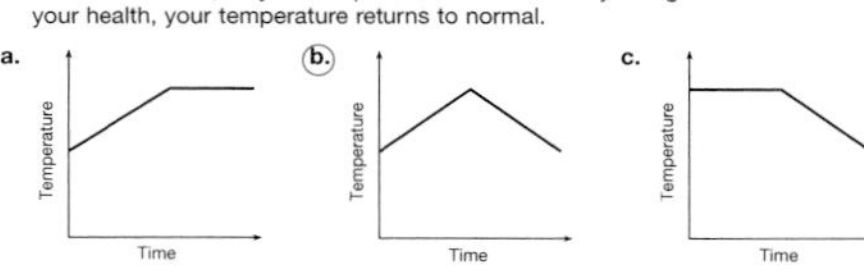

6. You leave for school in the morning. When you get halfway to school, you suddenly realize that you've left an important paper at home. You return home, and then go to school.

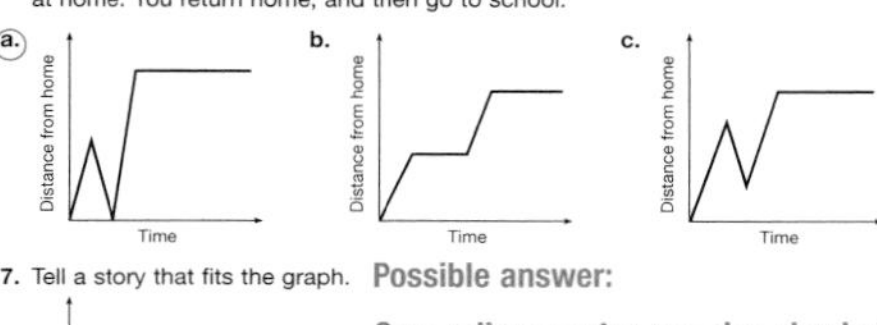

7. Tell a story that fits the graph. Possible answer:

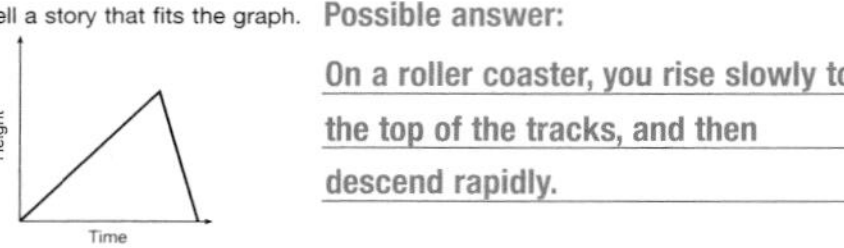

On a roller coaster, you rise slowly to the top of the tracks, and then descend rapidly.

RETEACHING

Name ______________

Alternative Lesson 10-2

Relating Graphs to Stories

The direction of a graph can show a relationship between the quantities on its axes. The relationship can be described as **increasing**, **decreasing**, or **constant**. For example, the first graph below shows quantities that increase, the second graph shows quantities that decrease, and the third graph shows quantities that are constant.

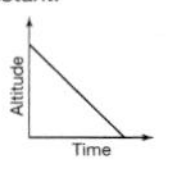

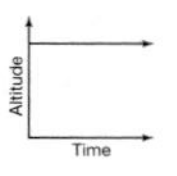

Example

Choose the graph that best shows this story.

A family drove all morning, stopped for lunch, drove all afternoon, and stopped overnight in a motel.

A. 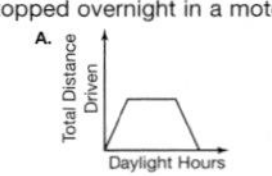

B. 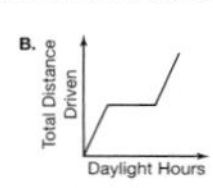

C. 

While driving, the graph increases. When the car stops, the graph is constant. It increases again while driving in the afternoon, and is constant when the family stops at the motel. Graph B shows this relationship.

Try It

a. Circle the graph that best shows this story.

Jeremy rides his bike to the mall. After shopping at the mall, he rides to Karen's house and plays a game of chess. Then he rides home.

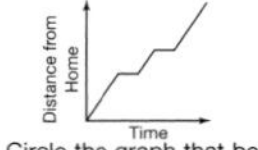

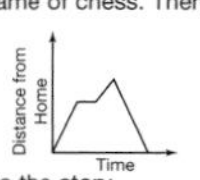

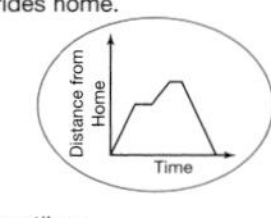

b. Circle the graph that best shows the story.

The number of bacteria in a culture dish steadily grows until an antibiotic is added to the dish. The number of bacteria shows a dramatic decrease, then begins to grow again.

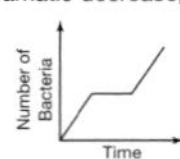

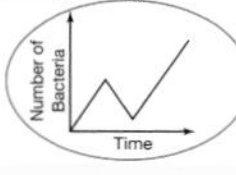

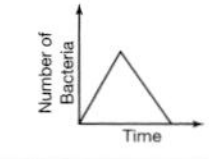

For Exercises 8–10, tell a story that fits each graph.

8. 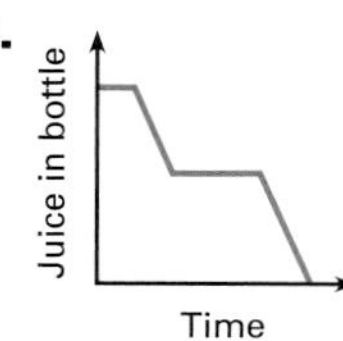

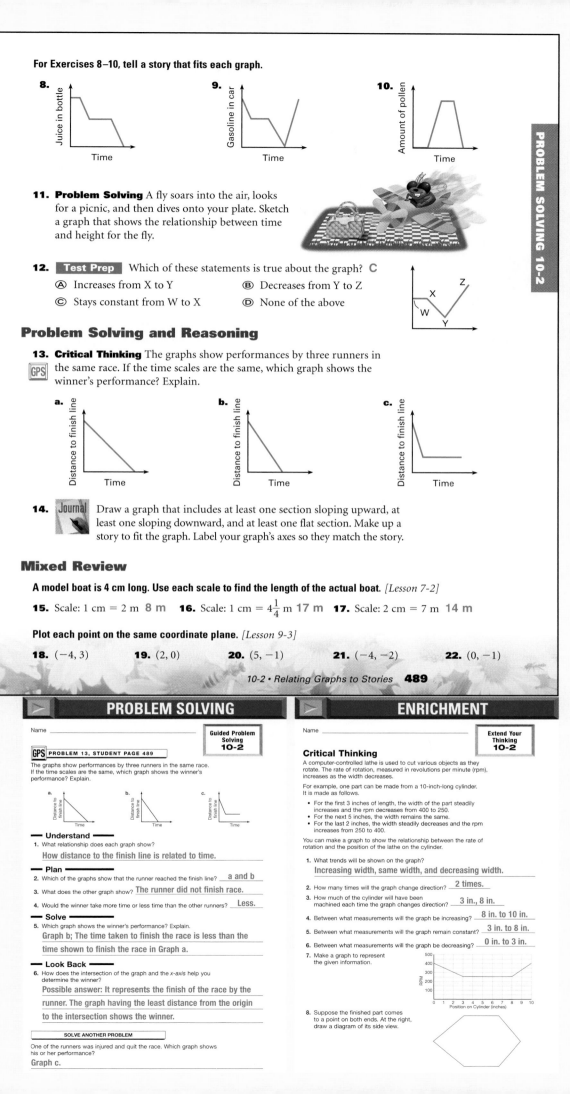

9. 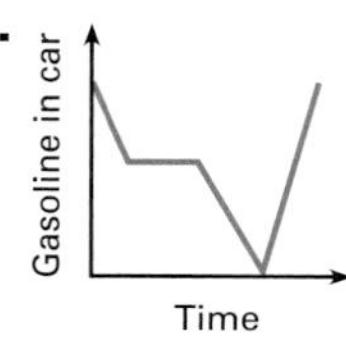

10. 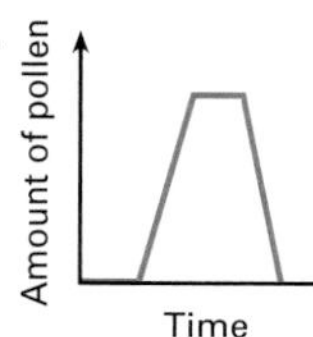

11. Problem Solving A fly soars into the air, looks for a picnic, and then dives onto your plate. Sketch a graph that shows the relationship between time and height for the fly.

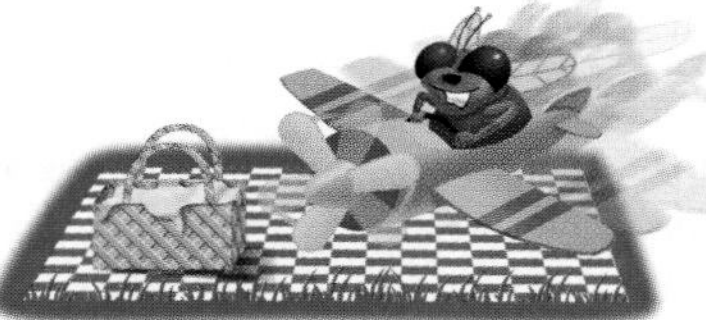

12. **Test Prep** Which of these statements is true about the graph? C

Ⓐ Increases from X to Y Ⓑ Decreases from Y to Z

Ⓒ Stays constant from W to X Ⓓ None of the above

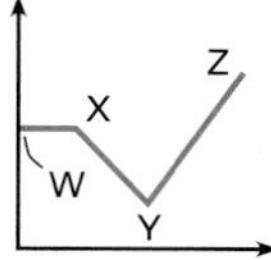

Problem Solving and Reasoning

13. Critical Thinking GPS The graphs show performances by three runners in the same race. If the time scales are the same, which graph shows the winner's performance? Explain.

a. 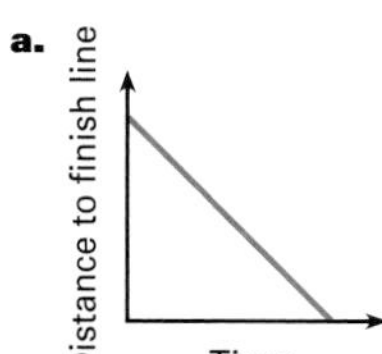

b. 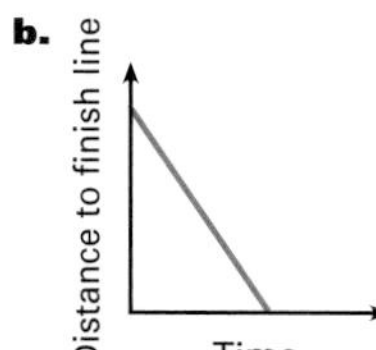

c. 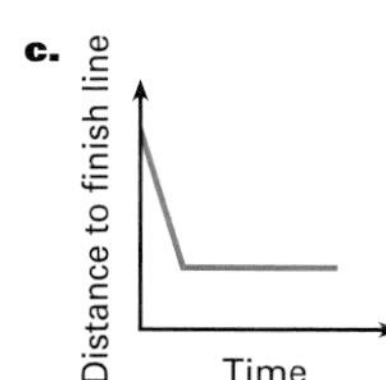

14. Journal Draw a graph that includes at least one section sloping upward, at least one sloping downward, and at least one flat section. Make up a story to fit the graph. Label your graph's axes so they match the story.

Mixed Review

A model boat is 4 cm long. Use each scale to find the length of the actual boat. *[Lesson 7-2]*

15. Scale: 1 cm = 2 m 8 m **16.** Scale: 1 cm = $4\frac{1}{4}$ m 17 m **17.** Scale: 2 cm = 7 m 14 m

Plot each point on the same coordinate plane. *[Lesson 9-3]*

18. (−4, 3) **19.** (2, 0) **20.** (5, −1) **21.** (−4, −2) **22.** (0, −1)

PROBLEM SOLVING 10-2

PROBLEM SOLVING

Name ______

Guided Problem Solving 10-2

GPS PROBLEM 13, STUDENT PAGE 489

The graphs show performances by three runners in the same race. If the time scales are the same, which graph shows the winner's performance? Explain.

a. b. 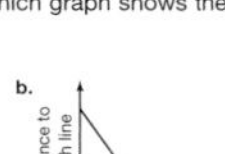 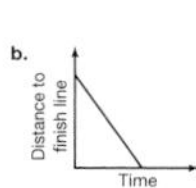 c. 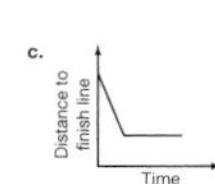

Understand

1. What relationship does each graph show?
How distance to the finish line is related to time.

Plan

2. Which of the graphs show that the runner reached the finish line? a and b
3. What does the other graph show? The runner did not finish race.
4. Would the winner take more time or less time than the other runners? Less.

Solve

5. Which graph shows the winner's performance? Explain.
Graph b; The time taken to finish the race is less than the time shown to finish the race in Graph a.

Look Back

6. How does the intersection of the graph and the *x*-axis help you determine the winner?
Possible answer: It represents the finish of the race by the runner. The graph having the least distance from the origin to the intersection shows the winner.

SOLVE ANOTHER PROBLEM

One of the runners was injured and quit the race. Which graph shows his or her performance?
Graph c.

ENRICHMENT

Name ______

Extend Your Thinking 10-2

Critical Thinking

A computer-controlled lathe is used to cut various objects as they rotate. The rate of rotation, measured in revolutions per minute (rpm), increases as the width decreases.

For example, one part can be made from a 10-inch-long cylinder. It is made as follows.

- For the first 3 inches of length, the width of the part steadily increases and the rpm decreases from 400 to 250.
- For the next 5 inches, the width remains the same.
- For the last 2 inches, the width steadily decreases and the rpm increases from 250 to 400.

You can make a graph to show the relationship between the rate of rotation and the position of the lathe on the cylinder.

1. What trends will be shown on the graph?
Increasing width, same width, and decreasing width.
2. How many times will the graph change direction? 2 times.
3. How much of the cylinder will have been machined each time the graph changes direction? 3 in., 8 in.
4. Between what measurements will the graph be increasing? 8 in. to 10 in.
5. Between what measurements will the graph remain constant? 3 in. to 8 in.
6. Between what measurements will the graph be decreasing? 0 in. to 3 in.
7. Make a graph to represent the given information.

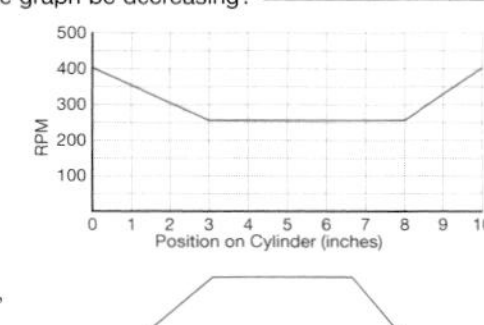

8. Suppose the finished part comes to a point on both ends. At the right, draw a diagram of its side view.

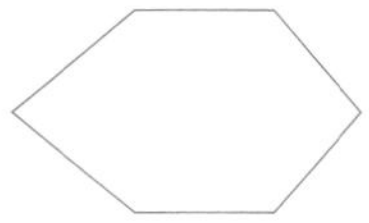

Exercise Answers

13. Graph b; When the distance to the finish line was 0, the time spent was shortest.

14. Answers may vary.

18–22.

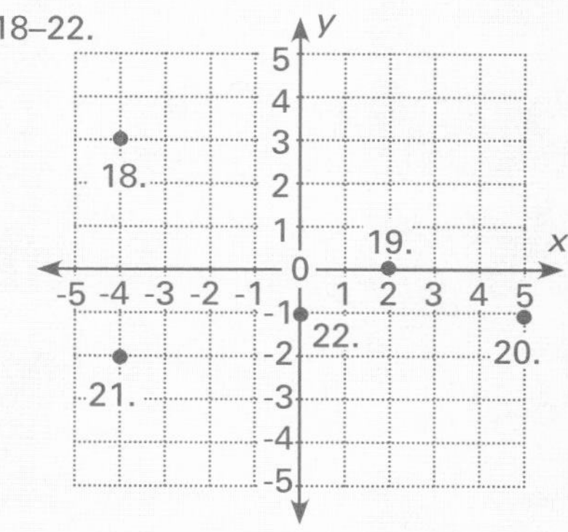

Alternate Assessment

Portfolio Have students select their favorite story about a graph and add it to their portfolios. Ask them to write about why it is their favorite and what they learned from doing it.

Quick Quiz

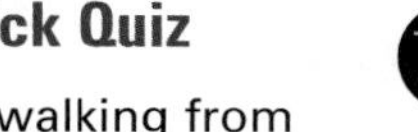

You are walking from home to school. As the time increases, tell whether each quantity increases, decreases, or stays constant.

1. The number of blocks from school Decreases
2. The number of houses you have passed Increases
3. The number of books you are carrying Stays constant

Tell a story that fits this graph.

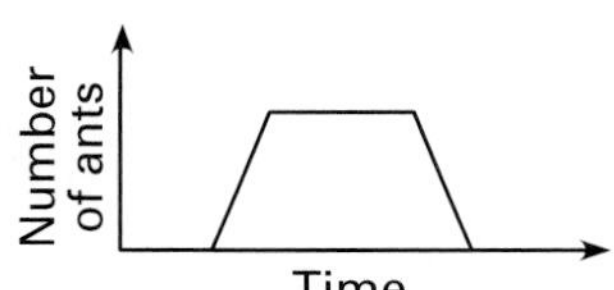

Possible answer: At first, there were no ants. Then someone dropped part of a cookie and lots of ants came and ate the cookie. The ants started to leave. Finally, all of the ants were gone.

Available on Daily Transparency 10-2

10-3 Lesson Organizer

Objectives

- Write rules for sequences.
- Identify arithmetic and geometric sequences.

Vocabulary

- Sequence, term, arithmetic sequence, geometric sequence

Materials

- Explore: Centimeter cubes or graph paper

NCTM Standards

- 1–4, 7, 8, 9

Review

Look for a pattern. How would you find the next number in each set?

1. 4, 7, 10, 13, ... Add 3.
2. 4, 8, 16, 32, ... Multiply by 2.
3. 20, 16, 12, 8, ... Subtract 4.
4. 1000, 500, 250, 125, ... Divide by 2.

Available on Daily Transparency 10-3

1 Introduce

Explore

You may want to use Teaching Tool Transparency 7: $\frac{1}{4}$-Inch Graph Paper with **Explore**.

The Point
Students use cubes or graph paper to make a sequence of figures. They find the pattern, predict the number of cubes in the 100th figure, and develop a general rule.

Ongoing Assessment
Watch for students who have difficulty relating the number of cubes to the figure number.

For Groups That Finish Early
If the first figure had 3 cubes, the second 6, and the third 9, what is the pattern? The number of cubes is three times the figure number.

10-3 Tables and Expressions

You'll Learn ...

- to write rules for sequences
- to identify arithmetic and geometric sequences

... How It's Used

Biologists use sequences to analyze population growth.

Vocabulary

sequence
term
arithmetic sequence
geometric sequence

Lesson Link You've seen how graphs can show relationships between quantities. Now you'll see how those relationships can be shown in a table.

Explore Tables

Patterns, Patterns Everywhere

Materials: Centimeter cubes or graph paper

1. Use cubes to build the figures shown, or sketch them on graph paper.

1st 2nd 3rd

2. Continue the pattern. How many cubes would it take to make the fourth figure? The fifth? Organize your findings in a table.

Figure Number (n)	1	2	3	4	5	6
Number of Cubes	2	4	6			

3. Describe any patterns you see in your table.
4. Predict the number of cubes in the 100th figure. Explain how you made your prediction.
5. If we use the variable n to represent the number of a figure, how could we use n to describe the number of cubes? Explain.

Learn Tables and Expressions

As you've seen, you can use tables to write equivalent fractions. The fractions in this table can be used to create several proportions.

The numerators and denominators in the table both show consistent patterns. Lists of numbers like these are called **sequences**. The numbers 4, 8, 12, 16, ... form a sequence. Each number in the sequence is a **term**.

		1•2	1•3	1•4
Numerator	1	2	3	4
Denominator	4	8	12	16
		4•2	4•3	4•4

Sequences often follow patterns that can be described by an expression. Looking at the numerical position (number) of a term can help you find the pattern.

MEETING INDIVIDUAL NEEDS

Resources

- **10-3** Practice
- **10-3** Reteaching
- **10-3** Problem Solving
- **10-3** Enrichment
- **10-3** Daily Transparency
  - Problem of the Day
  - Review
  - Quick Quiz

Teaching Tool Transparency 7

Technology Master 44

Learning Modalities

Visual Have students develop posters that show examples of arithmetic, geometric, and other sequences.

Kinesthetic Have students use manipulatives such as pattern blocks and centimeter cubes to represent sequences like those in Exercises 11–18 and 20–24.

Individual Ask students to think about any tips or techniques that might help them to understand this lesson better.

Challenge

Have students make up tables for two-step rules such as $2k + 3$ and challenge each other to find the rule.

Examples

1 Write an expression describing the rule for the numbers in the sequence 6, 7, 8, 9, 10, 11, ... Then give the 100th number in the sequence.

Make a table pairing a term number to each number in the sequence.

Term Number (n)	1	2	3	4	5	6	...	n
	↓ + 5	↓ + 5	↓ + 5	↓ + 5	↓ + 5	↓ + 5		↓ + 5
Number in Sequence	6	7	8	9	10	11	...	?

In words, the rule is "*add five to the term number.*" This translates to $n + 5$.

The 100th number in the sequence is $100 + 5 = 105$.

2 Silk is a fabric made from silkworm cocoons. Write a rule showing the relationship between the number of silk kimonos and the number of cocoons. Then tell how many cocoons it would take to make 12 kimonos.

Number of Kimonos (k)	1	2	3	4	5	...	k
Number of Cocoons	1700	3400	5100	6800	8500	...	?

In words, the rule is "*multiply the number of kimonos by 1700.*" This translates to the expression $1700k$.

So, to make 12 kimonos, it would take $1700 \cdot 12 = 20{,}400$ silkworm cocoons!

DID YOU KNOW?

A silkworm is not a worm. It is the larval stage of an Asiatic moth.

3 Write a rule showing the relationship between the figure number and the number of squares.

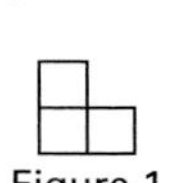
Figure 1

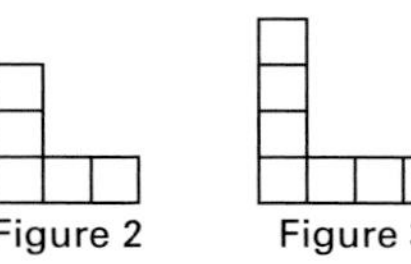
Figure 2 Figure 3

Make a table to show the relationship.

Figure Number (n)	1	2	3	...	n
Number of Squares	3	5	7	...	?

In words, the rule is "*add one to twice the figure number.*" (This is because two more squares are added to the corner square each time.) This translates to the expression $2n + 1$.

Try It

Write an expression describing the rule for the numbers in the sequence 3, 6, 9, 12, ... $3n$

MATH EVERY DAY

Problem of the Day

What is the area of the shaded part of the square? Round to the nearest tenth.

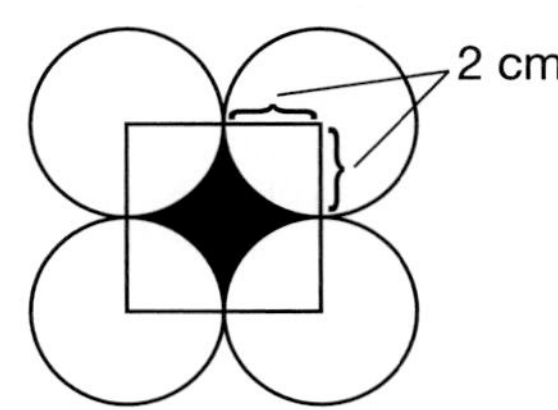

3.4 cm² (The area of each quarter circle is $\frac{1}{4} \times (\pi \times 4)$. The area of the square is 4×4. So, the area of the shaded portion is $16 - 4 \times \pi$, or about 3.4 cm².

Available on Daily Transparency 10-3

An Extension is provided in the transparency package.

Fact of the Day

The finest quality silk is produced by silkworm caterpillars that feed on mulberry leaves. When mature, these caterpillars measure about 3 inches long.

Estimation

Estimate.

1. $5\frac{5}{8} + 4\frac{1}{2} - 3\frac{2}{11}$ 8
2. $6\frac{7}{8} \cdot 9\frac{9}{10}$ 70
3. $6\frac{7}{8} \div 9\frac{9}{10}$ $\frac{7}{10}$

Answers for Explore

2.

Figure No.	1	2	3	4	5
No. of Cubes	2	4	6	8	10

3. The numbers of cubes are multiples of 2.
4. 200; $100 \cdot 2 = 200$
5. $2n$; The number of cubes is twice the number of the figure.

2 Teach

Learn

Alternate Examples

1. Write an expression describing the rule for the sequence 9, 10, 11, 12, ... Then give the 100th number in the sequence.

Make a table.

Term Number	1	2	3	...	n
	↓+8	↓+8	↓+8		↓+8
Number in Sequence	9	10	11	...	?

The rule is, *"add 8 to the term number."* This translates to $n + 8$. The 100th number in the sequence is $100 + 8 = 108$.

2. Write a rule showing the relationship between a number of spiders and the number of legs the spiders have. Then tell how many legs 125 spiders have.

Number of Spiders	1	2	3	4	...	s
Number of Legs	8	16	24	32	...	?

The rule is, *"Multiply the number of spiders by 8."* This translates to the expression $8s$. So, 125 spiders have 1000 legs.

3. Write a rule showing the relationship between the figure number and the number of triangles.

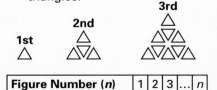

1st 2nd 3rd

Figure Number (n)	1	2	3	...	n
Number of Triangles	1	4	9		?

In words, the rule is *"square the figure number."* This translates to the expression n^2.

Alternate Examples

4. The rule for a sequence is 4^n. Make a table showing the first four terms.

   Make a table and fill in the term numbers. Use the rule to complete the table.

n	1	2	3	4
4^n	4	16	64	256

5. Tell whether the sequence is arithmetic, geometric, or neither. Then give the next two terms.

   2, 6, 18, 54, ...

   Each term is three times the previous term, so the sequence is geometric. The next two terms are 54 • 3 = 162 and 162 • 3 = 486.

Answer for Try It, Example 4

x	1	2	3	4	5	6
$10x$	10	20	30	40	50	60

3 Practice and Assess

Check

Students need to understand that expressions represent verbal rules in a kind of shorthand.

Answers for Check Your Understanding

1. The rule often depends on the term number. It's sometimes easier to see the pattern.
2. If the rule is complicated and is confusing to write out in words.

If you are given an expression describing the rule for a sequence, you can make a table of numbers in the sequence.

Example 4

The rule for a sequence is 2^n. Make a table showing the first 4 terms.

Make a table and fill in the term numbers. Use the rule to complete the table.

Term Number (n)	1	2	3	4
Number in Sequence, 2^n	$2^1 = 2$	$2^2 = 4$	$2^3 = 8$	$2^4 = 16$

Try It

The rule for a sequence is $10x$. Make a table showing the first 6 terms.

Study TIP

Be sure to check several of the known terms in a sequence when looking for a rule. Different sequences can start the same way.

In Example 1, the terms in the second row of the table form the sequence 6, 7, 8, 9, 10, 11, ... In this sequence, each term is 1 more than the previous term. Sequences where the difference between consecutive terms is always the same are **arithmetic sequences**.

In Example 4, each term in the sequence 2, 4, 8, 16, ... was 2 times as large as the previous one. Sequences like these are **geometric sequences**.

Arithmetic Sequence

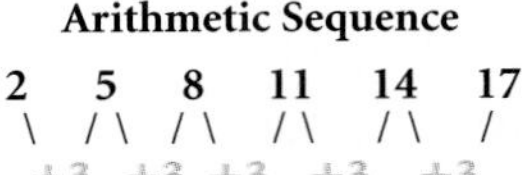

Each term is 3 **more than** the previous term.

Geometric Sequence

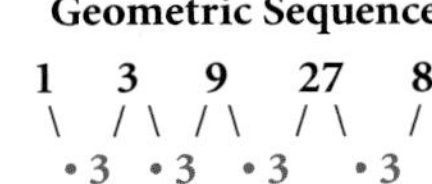

Each term is 3 **times as much as** the previous term.

Example 5

Tell whether the sequence is arithmetic, geometric, or neither. Then give the next two terms.

18, 23, 28, 33, 38, ...

Each term is 5 more than the previous one, so the sequence is arithmetic. The next two terms are 38 + 5 = 43 and 43 + 5 = 48.

Check Your Understanding

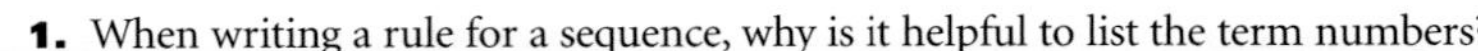

1. When writing a rule for a sequence, why is it helpful to list the term numbers?
2. Why might it be useful to describe a rule for a sequence with an expression?

MEETING MIDDLE SCHOOL CLASSROOM NEEDS

Tips from Middle School Teachers

It seems to help my students find the rules for sequences if they think of a function machine. I tell them that I'm going to put in the "address" (term number) and the machine (rule) will tell me what number "lives there."

Team Teaching

Work with an art teacher to develop patterns similar to those used in Exercises 8–10.

Science Connection

Termites are sometimes called white ants. They feed on wood and can destroy buildings and furniture.

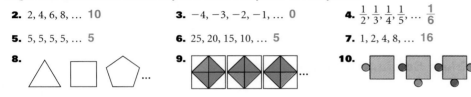

10-3 Exercises and Applications

Practice and Apply

1. **Getting Started** Follow the steps to describe the rule for the numbers in the sequence 7, 14, 21, 28, 35, ….

   a. Make a table with two rows. In the first row, list term numbers 1, 2, 3, 4, 5, and n.

   b. Fill in the first five numbers in the second row with the numbers in the sequence. Leave the cell under n blank.

   c. Compare each number in the sequence to its term number. When you recognize a pattern, write an expression using n to describe the rule. Test your rule to be sure it works.

Logic Give the next term in each sequence or the next picture in each pattern.

2. 2, 4, 6, 8, … 10
3. −4, −3, −2, −1, … 0
4. $\frac{1}{2}, \frac{1}{3}, \frac{1}{4}, \frac{1}{5}, \ldots$ $\frac{1}{6}$
5. 5, 5, 5, 5, … 5
6. 25, 20, 15, 10, … 5
7. 1, 2, 4, 8, … 16
8. 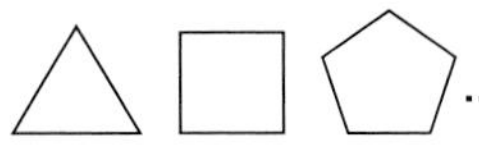
9. 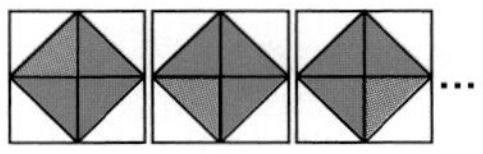
10. 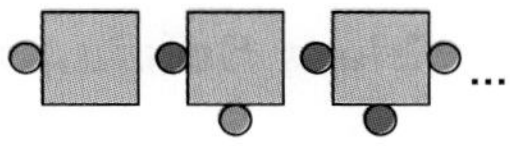

Write an expression describing the rule for each sequence. Then give the 100th term for the sequence.

11. 11, 12, 13, 14, … $n + 10$; 110
12. 4, 8, 12, 16, … $4n$; 400
13. $\frac{1}{2}, 1, \frac{3}{2}, 2, \ldots$ $\frac{n}{2}$; 50
14. 9, 18, 27, 36, … $9n$; 900
15. 0.1, 0.2, 0.3, 0.4, … $\frac{n}{10}$; 10
16. −5, −4, −3, −2, … $n - 6$; 94
17. 1, 4, 9, 16, … n^2; 10,000
18. 3, 5, 7, 9, … $2n + 1$; 201

19. **Science** A queen termite can lay 8000 eggs a day for years, making it the insect with the greatest reproduction rate.

Days	1	2	3	4	5	6	7
Total Eggs	8,000	16,000	24,000	32,000	40,000	48,000	56,000

   a. Write a rule showing the relationship between the number of days and the number of eggs.

   b. How many eggs can the queen termite lay in one year? Explain how you found your answer.

Make a table showing the first four terms of the sequence for each rule.

20. $6n$
21. $n + 8$
22. $-7x$
23. $2c + 5$
24. 3^n

PRACTICE 10-3

10-3 Exercises and Applications

Assignment Guide

- **Basic**
  1–10, 11–23 odds, 26–29, 34, 37–49 odds
- **Average**
  1, 2–10 evens, 11–30, 34, 36–50 evens
- **Enriched**
  2–24 evens, 26–35, 36–50 evens

Exercise Notes

Exercises 11–18

Error Prevention Some students may give incorrect expressions. Remind them that each number in the sequence has a corresponding term number, beginning with 1 for the first number. It might be helpful to make tables.

Exercise Answers

1. a–c

Term Number, n	1	2	3	4	5	n
Number in Sequence	7	14	21	28	35	$7n$

8. 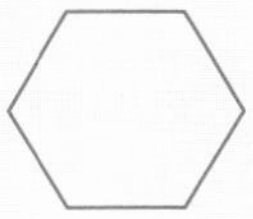
9. 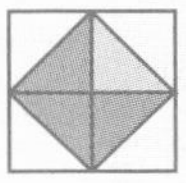
10. 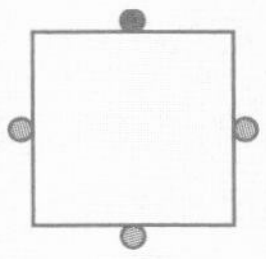

19–24. See page C3.

PRACTICE

Name ______________________

Practice 10-3

Tables and Expressions

Give the next term in each sequence or the next picture in each pattern.

1. 4, 8, 12, 16, 20, …
2. −20, −18, −16, −14, −12, …
3. 8, −8, 8, −8, 8, …
4. 3, 6, 12, 24, 48, …
5. 
6. 

Write an expression describing the rule for each sequence. Then give the 100th term for the sequence.

7. 35, 36, 37, 38, … Expression: $n + 34$ 100th term: 134
8. 8, 10, 12, 14, … Expression: $2n + 6$ 100th term: 206
9. 1.5, 3, 4.5, 6, … Expression: $1.5n$ 100th term: 150

Make a table showing the first 4 terms of the sequence for each rule.

10. $n + 20$

n	1	2	3	4
$n + 20$	21	22	23	24

11. $3n - 5$

n	1	2	3	4
$3n - 5$	−2	1	4	7

Tell whether each sequence is arithmetic, geometric, or neither. Then give the next term.

12. −5, 25, −125, 625, −3,125, … Geometric
13. $\frac{1}{3}, \frac{1}{6}, \frac{1}{9}, \frac{1}{12}$, $\frac{1}{15}$, … Neither

14. A pattern of squares is shown. 

   a. Sketch the 4th and 5th figure in this pattern. 

   b. Make a table comparing the figure number to the number of squares. Write an expression for the number of squares in the nth figure. $3n + 2$

Figure number	1	2	3	4	5
Number of Squares	5	8	11	14	17

   c. How many squares would there be in the 80th figure? 242

RETEACHING

Name ______________________

Alternative Lesson 10-3

Tables and Expressions

Lists of numbers that show consistent patterns are called **sequences**. Each number in the sequence is a **term**.

Example 1

Give the next two terms in this sequence: 6, 12, 18, 24, 30 …

Term number	1	2	3	4	5
Term	6	12	18	24	30

The rule is "*multiply the term number by 6.*"

So, the next two terms will be 36 and 42.

Try It Give the next two terms in this sequence: 4, 8, 12, 16, 20, …

a. What will you multiply the term number by to find the corresponding term? 4

b. Let n = term number. Write an expression that shows this relationship. $4n$

c. How will you find the sixth term in the sequence? The seventh term? Multiply each term number by 4.

d. What are the sixth and seventh terms? 24, 28

Give the next two terms in this sequence: 5, 7, 9, 11, 13, …

e. Let n = term number. Circle the expression that gives the rule for this sequence.

$2n + 1$ $n - 3$ ($2n + 3$) $n + 3$

f. How will you find the sixth term in the sequence? The seventh term? Multiply each term number by 2, then add 3.

g. What are the sixth and seventh terms? 15, 17

Let n = term number. Circle the expression that gives the rule for each sequence.

h. 2, 5, 8, 11, 14 … $2n - 1$ ($3n - 1$) $3n + 1$

i. 1, 4, 9, 25, 36, … $n + 5$ (n^2) $n^2 - 1$

j. 5, 10, 15, 20, 25 … ($5n$) n^5 $n + 5$

Reteaching

Activity

Materials: Graph paper

Use graph paper to draw the next two figures in the pattern. Then complete the table.

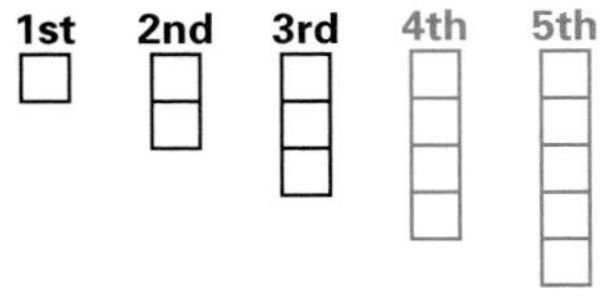

Figure Number	1	2	3	4	5
Total Number of Segments	4	7	10	13	16

Which of the following expressions describes the rule for the sequence, where n is the figure number? C

A. $3n - 1$ B. $4n$ C. $3n + 1$

Exercise Notes

Exercises 27–33

Extension Have students describe the rule for each pattern in words and, where possible, using an expression.

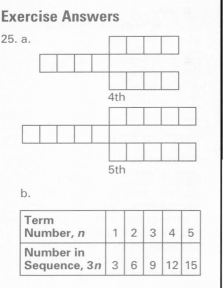

Exercise Answers

25. a.

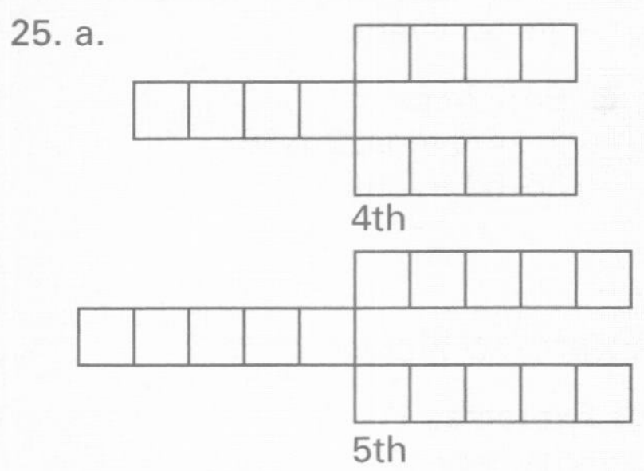

b.

Term Number, n	1	2	3	4	5
Number in Sequence, $3n$	3	6	9	12	15

c. 300

27. Arithmetic; 9, 11.
28. Geometric; 32, 64.
29. Arithmetic; 55, 66.
30. Neither; 111,111, 1,111,111.
31. Geometric; 100,000; 1,000,000.
32. Geometric; −243, 729.
33. Neither; $\frac{5}{6}, \frac{6}{7}$.
34. 80, 84, 88, 92
35. 625,000,000; If n is the nth generation, the number of flies after the nth generation has hatched is 2×50^n.

Alternate Assessment

You may want to use the *Interactive CD-ROM Journal* with this assessment.

Journal Ask students to write about what they found difficult in this lesson. They should include an example of a problem that was hard for them.

Quick Quiz

1. Give the next term: 13, 17, 21, 25,... 29
2. Write an expression that gives the rule for the sequence: 6, 12, 18, 24,... $6n$
3. Show the first four terms of the sequence $2k - 3$. −1, 1, 3, 5

Available on Daily Transparency 10-3

PROBLEM SOLVING 10-3

25. A pattern of squares is shown.

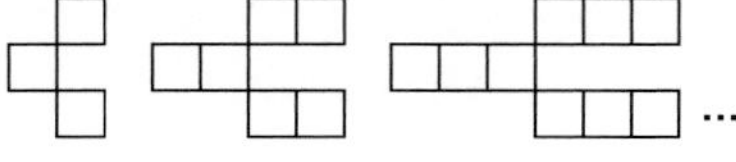

a. Sketch the fourth and fifth figure in this pattern.

b. Make a table comparing the figure number to the number of squares. Write an expression for the number of squares in the nth figure.

c. How many squares would there be in the 100th figure?

26. **Test Prep** The cicada was once a terrible pest in the United States. It would appear in large numbers, devour trees, then disappear for 17 years. If a swarm was seen in 1980, in which of these sequences of years is the cicada likely to appear? B

Ⓐ 1917, 2017, 2117 Ⓑ 1997, 2014, 2031

Ⓒ 1980, 1981, 1982 Ⓓ 2000, 2017, 2034

Tell whether each sequence is arithmetic, geometric, or neither. Then give the next two terms.

27. 1, 3, 5, 7, … **28.** 2, 4, 8, 16, … **29.** 11, 22, 33, 44, …

30. 11, 111, 1,111, 11,111, … **31.** 10, 100, 1,000, 10,000, …

32. −3, 9, −27, 81, … **33.** $\frac{1}{2}, \frac{2}{3}, \frac{3}{4}, \frac{4}{5}, \ldots$

Problem Solving and Reasoning

34. **Choose a Strategy** The fifth term of an arithmetic sequence is 96. The difference between consecutive terms is 4. Find the first four terms.

35. **Critical Thinking** Suppose a female fruit fly (generation 1) lays 100 eggs in her lifetime. If half of those eggs contain female flies, each of which survives to lay 100 eggs, how many flies will there be in the fifth generation? Explain your answer.

Problem Solving STRATEGIES

- Look for a Pattern
- Make an Organized List
- Make a Table
- Guess and Check
- Work Backward
- Use Logical Reasoning
- Draw a Diagram
- Solve a Simpler Problem

Mixed Review

Wilson left home at 3:00 P.M. and traveled 60 miles. Find his arrival time for each of the following speeds. *[Lesson 7-3]*

36. 15 mi/hr 7:00 P.M. **37.** 10 mi/hr 9:00 P.M. **38.** 20 mi/hr 6:00 P.M. **39.** 25 mi/hr 5:24 P.M. **40.** 48 mi/hr 4:15 P.M.

Operation Sense **Find each sum.** *[Lesson 9-4]*

41. 22 + (−14) 8 **42.** −27 + (−12) −39 **43.** −49 + 22 −27 **44.** −51 + 45 −6

45. −71 + 23 −48 **46.** 88 + (−53) 35 **47.** −102 + (−77) −179

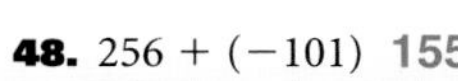

48. 256 + (−101) 155 **49.** (−127) + (−341) −468 **50.** −917 + (−497) −1414

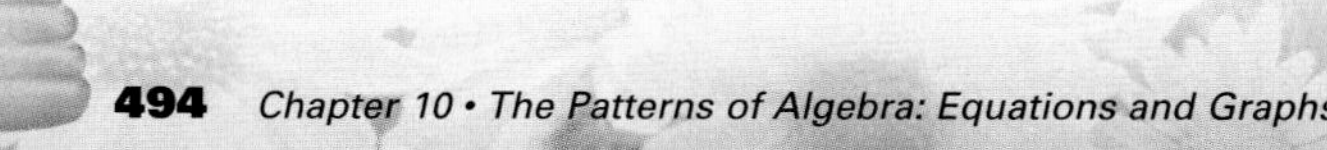

PROBLEM SOLVING

Name ______________

Guided Problem Solving 10-3

GPS PROBLEM 34, STUDENT PAGE 494

The fifth term of an arithmetic sequence is 96. The difference between consecutive terms is 4. Find the first four terms.

— Understand —

1. What is an arithmetic sequence? A sequence of numbers that has the same difference between consecutive terms.
2. How can you find consecutive terms in an arithmetic sequence? b
   a. Multiply each previous term by the difference.
   b. Add the difference to each previous term.
3. What is the fifth term of the arithmetic sequence? 96

— Plan —

4. Which strategies can help you find the first four terms? c
   a. Work Backward b. Draw a Diagram c. Either a or b
5. How much more is 96 than the amount of the fourth term? 4 more.
6. How can you find the fourth term? Subtract 4 from 96.
7. How can you find the third term, the second term, and the first term? Third: subtract 4 from fourth term; Second: subtract 4 from third term; First: subtract 4 from second term.

— Solve —

8. Find the first four terms of the sequence. 80, 84, 88, 92

— Look Back —

9. How can you decide if your answers are reasonable? Possible answer: Check to see that difference between consecutive terms is 4.

SOLVE ANOTHER PROBLEM

The fifth term of a geometric sequence is 567. Each term is three times the previous term. Find the first four terms in the sequence.

7, 21, 63, 189

ENRICHMENT

Name ______________

Extend Your Thinking 10-3

Patterns in Geometry

In 1202, Leonardo Fibonacci, an Italian mathematician, described a mathematical sequence that is named after him, the Fibonacci Sequence.

The first ten numbers in the sequence are given below.

1 1 2 3 5 8 13 21 34 55

1. How are the first two terms related to the third term? The third term is equal to the sum of the first two terms.
2. How are the second and third terms related to the fourth term? The fourth term is equal to the sum of the second and third terms.
3. How are the third and fourth terms related to the fifth term? The fifth term is equal to the sum of the third and fourth terms.
4. What general rule can you make for finding each successive term? Add the last two known terms to find the next term.

Additional patterns can be found in the Fibonacci Sequence.

5. Complete the table for the given three consecutive terms of the sequence. Then choose two additional sets of three consecutive terms of the sequence and complete the table for them.

Consecutive terms	Product of first and third terms	Square of second term
1, 2, 3	3	4
2, 3, 5	10	9
Possible 3, 5, 8	24	25
answers: 5, 8, 13	65	64

6. What pattern do you notice in the numbers in the second and third columns for each set of consecutive terms? They have a difference of one.
7. Is the smaller number always in the same column? No.

Understanding and Writing Equations

10-4

▶ Lesson Link You've written expressions to describe sequences. Now you'll see how to write equations to describe the relationship between two quantities. ◀

You'll Learn ...

■ to write an equation from a table of values

... How It's Used

Equations allow spreadsheets to calculate values automatically.

Explore Showing Relationships with Tables

Faster than a Speeding Beetle?

Some of the fastest-moving insects are beetles. The table shows how fast one type of beetle can crawl.

Time (sec)	1	2	3	4	5	...	t
Distance (in.)	4	8	12	16	20	...	?

1. Describe any patterns you see in the table. Write an expression using t for the final box in the distance row.
2. Use words to describe the relationship between the distance traveled and the time.
3. If this beetle crawled for 60 seconds, how far would it go?
4. How long would it take this beetle to crawl 36 inches?
5. Explain how you found your answers to Steps 3 and 4. What is different about the questions asked in these steps?

Learn Understanding and Writing Equations

When two expressions name the same quantity, we can link them with an equation. Writing an equation is an important way to show a relationship between variables.

The geometric formulas you've worked with are equations. For instance, since the perimeter of a square is four times the length of a side, we write $p = 4s$. The equal sign shows that p and $4s$ always have the same value.

MEETING INDIVIDUAL NEEDS

Resources

10-4 Practice
10-4 Reteaching
10-4 Problem Solving
10-4 Enrichment
10-4 Daily Transparency
- Problem of the Day
- Review
- Quick Quiz

Technology Master 45

Learning Modalities

Verbal Have students write a letter to a younger student in which they explain what they have learned in this lesson.

Social Have students work in groups to find a verbal rule arising from a real-life situation. Have them develop an equation and use the equation to find at least six pairs of values.

Challenge

Augustus De Morgan, an English mathematician who lived in the 1800s once said, "I was x years old in the year x^2." In what year was he born? 1806

If a person born in the 1900s will be x years old in the year x^2, in what year was the person born? The person will be 45 in the year 45^2, which is 2025. Therefore the person was born in 2025 − 45, or 1980.

10-4 Lesson Organizer

Objective

■ Write an equation from a table of values.

NCTM Standards

■ 1–4, 8, 9

▶ Review

Evaluate each expression for the given value of the variable.

1. $4x - 5$, $x = 6$ 19
2. $3 + 2a$, $a = 1.25$ 5.5
3. $100k - 47$, $k = 250$ 24,953

Available on Daily Transparency 10-4

1 Introduce

Explore

The Point

Students use a table of values to write an expression for a distance in terms of time. They use that expression to help find times for given distances. These are important steps in developing skills in writing and solving equations.

Ongoing Assessment

Watch for students who multiply 36 by 4 to find the answer in Step 4 instead of dividing 36 by 4.

For Groups That Finish Early

How long would it take the beetle to crawl 3 yards? 27 seconds

Answers for Explore

1. The numbers in the distance row are the multiples of 4. Each distance is 4 times the number above it. $4t$
2. Four inches traveled in one second.
3. 240 in.
4. 9 sec
5. Use the fact that $4t$ equals the distance traveled, where t equals how long it traveled. In Step 3, you use multiplication. In step 4, you use division.

2 Teach

Learn

Alternate Examples

1. Write an equation to show the relationship between x and y. Use the equation to find y when $x = 5$.

x	1	2	3	4
y	−4	−3	−2	−1

Notice that each y-value is equal to five less than the corresponding x-value. The equation is $y = x - 5$.

To find y when $x = 5$, substitute 5 into the equation for x.

$y = x - 5 = 5 - 5 = 0$

When $x = 5$, $y = 0$.

2. Write an equation to describe the relationship between the number of leaves a caterpillar eats and the number of hours required. Use the equation to find the number of hours it takes to eat 1000 leaves.

Number of Leaves Eaten	1	2	3	4
Number of Hours	8	16	24	32

Let e = the number of leaves eaten and h = the number of hours required. The table shows that the caterpillar needs 8 hours to eat each leaf. The equation is $h = 8e$.

To find the number of hours it takes to eat 1000 leaves, substitute 1000 for e.

$h = 8 \cdot 1000 = 8000$ hours.

It takes 8000 hours for a caterpillar to eat 1000 leaves.

3. Make a table of six pairs of values for the equation $y = 4x - 2$.

Choose six x-values, then substitute each into $y = 4x - 2$ to find the y-values.

x	1	2	3	4	5	6
y	2	6	10	14	18	22

Answers for Try It

Possible answer:

y	1	2	3	4	5	6
p	20	40	60	80	100	120

Test Prep

When you're writing an equation to model a real-world situation, be sure the equation gives results that make sense.

Examples

1 Write an equation to show the relationship between x and y. Use the equation to find y when $x = 9$.

x	1	2	3	4
y	1	4	9	16

Notice that each y-value is equal to the *square* of its x-value. The equation $y = x^2$ shows this relationship.

To find y when $x = 9$, substitute 9 into the equation for x.

$y = 9^2 = 81$. When $x = 9$, $y = 81$.

2 Write an equation to describe the relationship between the number of trips a bee makes and the amount of pollen it carries to its hive. Use the equation to find the amount of pollen the bee can carry in 12 trips.

Trips	Pollen (mg)
1	25
2	50
3	75
4	100

Let t = the number of trips, and p = the amount of pollen. The table shows that the bee carries 25 mg of pollen in each trip. The equation is $p = 25t$.

To find the amount of pollen carried in 12 trips, substitute 12 for t.

$p = 25(12) = 300$ mg

The bee can carry 300 mg of pollen in 12 trips.

Try It

Write an equation to show the relationship between x and y. Then use the equation to find the value of y when $x = 17$. 

x	1	2	3	4	5
y	0.25	0.5	0.75	1	1.25

You can use equations to make tables of values.

Example 3

Make a table of six pairs of values for the equation $y = 3x + 2$.

Choose six x-values, then substitute each into $y = 3x + 2$ to find the y-values.

x	1	2	3	4	5	6
y	5	8	11	14	17	20

Try It

A bee colony needs about 20 kg of pollen each year. In y years, it will need $20y$, so $p = 20y$. Make a table of six pairs of values for this equation.

MATH EVERY DAY

Problem of the Day

Each number on the face of a number cube is even and divisible by 9. What is the probability that a number on the number cube is divisible by 6? 1; If the numbers are even and divisible by 9, then they have both 2 and 3 as factors. Therefore, they are all divisible by 6.

Available on Daily Transparency 10-4

An Extension is provided in the transparency package.

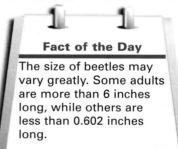

Fact of the Day

The size of beetles may vary greatly. Some adults are more than 6 inches long, while others are less than 0.602 inches long.

Mental Math

Do these mentally.

1. 25 • 45 • 4 4500
2. 9909 ÷ 9 1101
3. 728 + 445 + 272 1445

Check Your Understanding

1. How does an equation show a relationship between quantities?
2. What does an equation tell you that a table of values does not? What information is in a table of values that isn't shown in an equation?

10-4 Exercises and Applications

PRACTICE 10-4

Practice and Apply

1. **Getting Started** Follow the steps to make a table of five values for the equation $y = 3x - 4$.
   a. Make a table with two rows (or columns). Begin the first with the letter x, then fill in five x-values of your choice.
   b. Begin the second row (or column) with the letter y. Substitute the first x-value into the equation. Simplify to find the y-value for this x-value.
   c. Repeat until you complete the table.

For each table, write an equation to show the relationship between x and y. Use the equation to find y when $x = 7$.

2.

x	1	2	3	4
y	3	4	5	6

$y = x + 2$; $y = 9$

3.

x	1	2	3	4
y	−5	−10	−15	−20

$y = -5x$; $y = -35$

Complete each table. Then write an equation to show the relationship between the variables.

4.

r	D
40	80
50	100
55	110
60	
65	

5.

n	C
0	0
2	7.00
4	14.00
6	
8	

6.

s	A
1	1
2	4
3	9
4	
6	

7.

t	d
1	35
2	70
3	
4	
5	

Make a table of six pairs of values for each equation.

8. $y = 2x$
9. $y = x + 8$
10. $c = -7b$
11. $k = g - 3$
12. $y = \frac{1}{3}x$
13. $y = 3x + 1$
14. $d = -14t - 22$
15. $y = 0.22x$
16. $y = -x$
17. $h = \frac{k}{4} + 1$

PRACTICE

Name ______________________

Practice 10-4

Understanding and Writing Equations

For each table, write an equation to show the relationship between x and y. Use the equation to find y when $x = 7$.

1. $y = 8x$

x	1	2	3	4	7
y	8	16	24	32	56

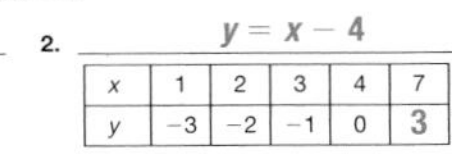

2. $y = x - 4$

x	1	2	3	4	7
y	−3	−2	−1	0	3

Complete each table, and write an equation to show the relationship between the variables.

3. $t = s + 15$

s	3	5	7	15	50
t	18	20	22	30	65

4. $b = 7a$

a	10	20	30	80	100
b	70	140	210	560	700

5. $c = 3.14d$

d	1	2	3	7	12
c	3.14	6.28	9.42	21.98	37.68

6. $q = 12p$

p	0	2	4	9	20
q	0	24	48	108	240

Make a table of five pairs of values for each equation. Possible answers:

7. $y = x - 12$

x	1	2	3	4	5
y	−11	−10	−9	−8	−7

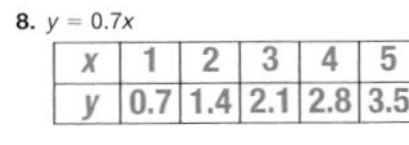

8. $y = 0.7x$

x	1	2	3	4	5
y	0.7	1.4	2.1	2.8	3.5

9. $p = 5m - 3$

m	1	2	3	4	5
p	2	7	12	17	22

10. $v = \frac{u}{5} + 7$

u	0	5	10	15	20
v	7	8	9	10	11

11. **Science** The relationship between the amount of time a zebra runs at maximum speed and the distance it covers is shown.

Time (min)	3	6	9	12	15
Distance (mi)	2	4	6	8	10

a. Write an equation to describe this relationship. Possible answer: $d = \frac{2}{3}t$

b. Use the equation to find the distance the zebra would travel in 48 minutes. 32 mi

RETEACHING

Name ______________________

Alternative Lesson 10-4

Understanding and Writing Equations

An equation is used to show that two expressions name the same quantity. You can use equations to show a relationship between variables.

Example 1

Write an equation to show the relationship between x and y. Use the equation to find y when $x = 8$.

x	1	2	3	4	5	6
y	4	8	12	16	20	24

Find the rule. The value of y is 4 times the value of x.

This equation shows the relationship between x and y. $y = 4x$

To find y when $x = 8$, substitute 8 into the equation for x. $y = 4 \cdot 8 = 32$

When $x = 8$, $y = 32$.

Try It Write an equation to show the relationship between x and y.

x	3	4	5	6	7	8
y	−2	−1	0	1	2	3

a. What number will you add to x or multiply x by to find the value of y? Write the rule. Add −5.

b. Write an equation showing this relationship. $y = x - 5$

Example 2

Make a table of six pairs of values for the equation $y = x - 4$.

Choose six values for x and substitute each into $y = x - 4$.

x	3	4	5	6	7	8
	↓ 3 − 4 = −1	↓ 4 − 4 = 0	↓ 5 − 4 = 1	↓ 6 − 4 = 2	↓ 7 − 4 = 3	↓ 8 − 4 = 4
y	−1	0	1	2	3	4

Try It

c. Make a table of six pairs for the equation $y = 2x + 1$. Possible answer:

x	0	1	2	3	4	5
y	1	3	5	7	9	11

10-4 Exercises and Applications

Assignment Guide

- **Basic** 1–12, 19–20, 22–30 evens
- **Average** 2–12, 18–20, 22–30 evens
- **Enriched** 3–7 odds, 13–21, 23–31 odds

3 Practice and Assess

Check

Answers for Check Your Understanding

Possible Answers

1. An equation shows that the quantity on the left of the equals sign is always equal to the quantity on the right.
2. An equation represents a rule by which one can find a missing value; A table can show specific values that make the equation true.

Exercise Answers

Answers for Exercises 1 and 4–17 on page C3.

Reteaching

Activity

Materials: Number cube

Play this game with a partner. For each round, take turns doing the following:

- Toss a number cube twice and write the numbers in the following equation.

  $y =$ ______ $x +$ ______

- Then toss the number cube five times to generate five x-values. Use your equation to find the y-value for each x-value and record your results in a table.
- Add all the y-values to find your score for this round.
- The person with the highest total score after three rounds wins the game.

Exercise Notes

■ Exercise 19

Test Prep If students select A, they have looked at the first number pair only. If they select B, they are reversing the order of the variables in the equation.

Exercise Answers

20. a. 1, 3, 6, 10, 15

b. 1, 3, 6, 10, 15; The results are the same. The rule gives the sum of the first n whole numbers.

Alternate Assessment

Portfolio Have students pick one or two exercises that best exemplify the concepts of this lesson.

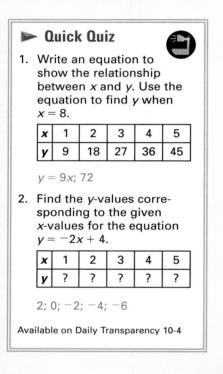

► Quick Quiz

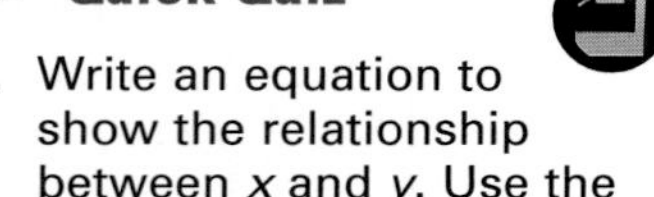

1. Write an equation to show the relationship between x and y. Use the equation to find y when $x = 8$.

x	1	2	3	4	5
y	9	18	27	36	45

$y = 9x$; 72

2. Find the y-values corresponding to the given x-values for the equation $y = -2x + 4$.

x	1	2	3	4	5
y	?	?	?	?	?

2; 0; −2; −4; −6

Available on Daily Transparency 10-4

PROBLEM SOLVING 10-4

18. The relationship between the number of jumps a locust makes and the distance it covers is shown. Write an equation to describe this relationship. Then use the equation to find the distance the locust would cover in 25 jumps. $d = 20j$; 500 in.

Jumps	1	2	3	4	5	6
Distance (in.)	20	40	60	80	100	120

19. **Test Prep** GPS As shown in the table, the cost of boarding a cat in a kennel depends on the number of days it stays.

Days	2	4	5	7
Cost ($)	6	12	15	21

Which equation represents the relationship between cost and number of days? C

Ⓐ $C = d + 4$ Ⓑ $C = \frac{d}{3}$ Ⓒ $C = 3d$ Ⓓ $C = 6d$

Problem Solving and Reasoning

20. **Critical Thinking** An important rule for a mathematical sequence is $\frac{n(n+1)}{2}$.

a. Find the first five terms of this sequence.

b. Find the sums $1 + 2$, $1 + 2 + 3$, $1 + 2 + 3 + 4$, and $1 + 2 + 3 + 4 + 5$. Compare your results to the sequence in **a.** Why is this rule important?

21. **Communicate** Draw a square pattern of your own invention, like the ones shown on page 490 and 491. Label each figure with a number. Answers may vary

a. If you can, write an equation that describes the pattern. If you can't, explain why not.

b. Find the number of squares in the 100th figure in your pattern.

Mixed Review

A bottlenose dolphin can be 12 feet long. Find the maximum scale you can use for a model dolphin if it must fit in each of the following. *[Lesson 7-4]*

22. A 6 ft long crate 1:2

23. A 3 in. long toy box 1 in.:4 ft

24. A 50 ft long exhibit hall 1:0.24

25. A 5 in. long carton 1 in.:2.4 ft

Operation Sense Find each difference. *[Lesson 9-5]*

26. $37 - 58$ −21

27. $-10 - (-15)$ 5

28. $-79 - 32$ −111

29. $51 - (-51)$ 102

30. $171 - 239$ −68

31. $481 - (-308)$ 789

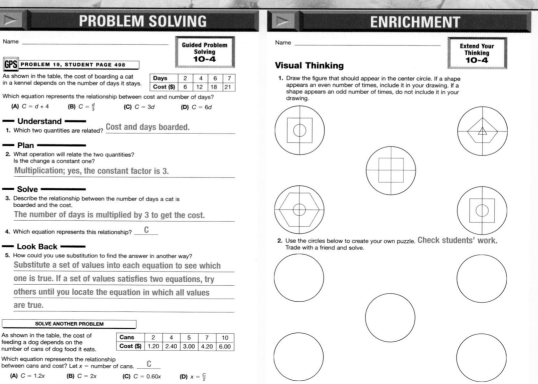

PROBLEM SOLVING

Name ______________________

Guided Problem Solving 10-4

GPS PROBLEM 19, STUDENT PAGE 498

As shown in the table, the cost of boarding a cat in a kennel depends on the number of days it stays.

Days	2	4	6	7
Cost ($)	6	12	18	21

Which equation represents the relationship between cost and number of days?

(A) $C = d + 4$ **(B)** $C = \frac{d}{3}$ **(C)** $C = 3d$ **(D)** $C = 6d$

— Understand —

1. Which two quantities are related? Cost and days boarded.

— Plan —

2. What operation will relate the two quantities? Is the change a constant one? Multiplication; yes, the constant factor is 3.

— Solve —

3. Describe the relationship between the number of days a cat is boarded and the cost. The number of days is multiplied by 3 to get the cost.

4. Which equation represents this relationship? C

— Look Back —

5. How could you use substitution to find the answer in another way? Substitute a set of values into each equation to see which one is true. If a set of values satisfies two equations, try others until you locate the equation in which all values are true.

SOLVE ANOTHER PROBLEM

As shown in the table, the cost of feeding a dog depends on the number of cans of dog food it eats.

Cans	2	4	5	7	10
Cost ($)	1.20	2.40	3.00	4.20	6.00

Which equation represents the relationship between cans and cost? Let x = number of cans. C

(A) $C = 1.2x$ **(B)** $C = 2x$ **(C)** $C = 0.60x$ **(D)** $x = \frac{C}{2}$

ENRICHMENT

Name ______________________

Extend Your Thinking 10-4

Visual Thinking

1. Draw the figure that should appear in the center circle. If a shape appears an even number of times, include it in your drawing. If a shape appears an odd number of times, do not include it in your drawing.

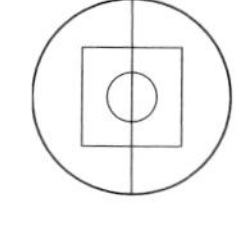

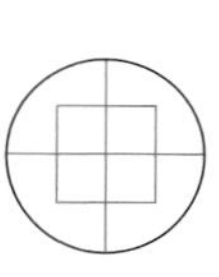

2. Use the circles below to create your own puzzle. Trade with a friend and solve. Check students' work.

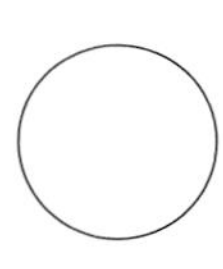

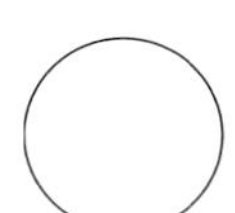

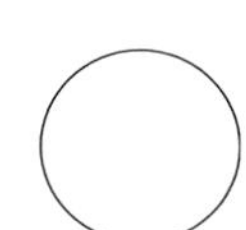

TECHNOLOGY

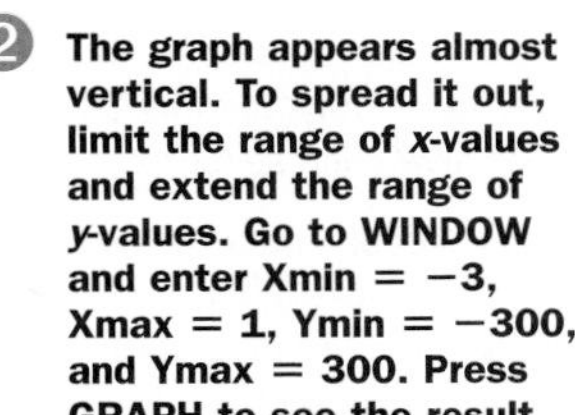

Using a Graphing Utility • Choosing a Window Size and Scale

Problem: How can you select an appropriate viewing "window" for the graph of $y = 100x + 250$?

You can use a graphing utility to investigate this question.

1 **Enter the function $y = 100x + 250$ as Y1. Go to ZOOM and select the standard window, then press GRAPH to graph the function.**

2 **The graph appears almost vertical. To spread it out, limit the range of x-values and extend the range of y-values. Go to WINDOW and enter Xmin = −3, Xmax = 1, Ymin = −300, and Ymax = 300. Press GRAPH to see the result.**

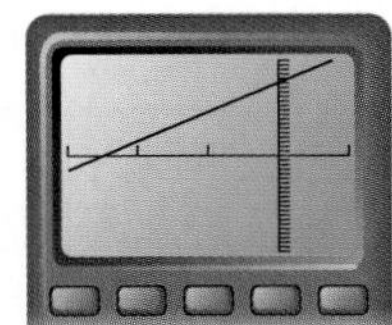

3 **Notice that the "tick marks" are very spread out on the x-axis and very close together on the y-axis. To change this, go to WINDOW. Change Xscl to 0.5 and Yscl to 50. Press GRAPH to see the result.**

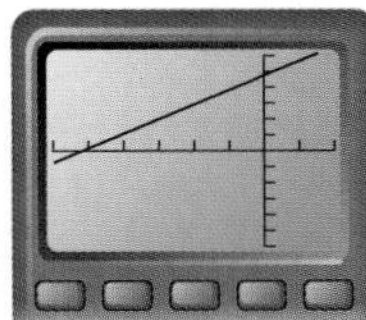

Solution: Values that give an appropriate viewing window are Xmin = −3, Xmax = 1, Ymin = −300, Ymax = 300, Xscl = 0.5, and Yscl = 50.

TRY IT

Determine an appropriate viewing window for each graph.

a. $y = 200x - 100$
b. $y = 0.25x + 10$
c. $y = x^2 + 2$

ON YOUR OWN

▶ What do Xmin, Xmax, Ymin, Ymax, Xscl, and Yscl mean?

▶ If you and a friend graphed $y = 25x - 100$ using different values for the viewing window, would the graphs look the same? Explain.

499

Answers for On Your Own

1. Xmin and Ymin are the least x-value and y-value. Xmax and Ymax are the greatest x-value and y-value. Xscl and Yscl are the scales for each axis, they tell how far apart the tick marks are on the axes.
2. The graphs would not look the same. The graphs would have the same general shape, but one would be steeper or flatter than the other.

Technology

Using a Graphing Utility • Choosing a Window Size and Scale

The Point

Students discover that an appropriate viewing window is important for understanding a graph.

Materials

Graphing utility

Resources

Interactive CD-ROM Equation Grapher Tool

Teaching Tool Transparency 23: Graphing Calculator

About the Page

- You may want to work through this lesson before using it with your class so you can modify the steps to match the software you are planning to use.
- The viewing window is an important consideration when analyzing a graph. The graph may be distorted or not even shown if the viewing window is not appropriate.
- Students sometimes assume that calculators can do everything, but figuring out the viewing window is definitely the responsibility of the user.

Ask ...

- If a diagonal line looks vertical, how should the viewing window be changed? Narrow the range of the x-axis.
- If a diagonal line looks horizontal, how should the viewing window be changed? Narrow the range of the y-axis.

Answers for Try It

a. Xmin = −5, Xmax = 5, Xscl = 1, Ymin = −100, Ymax = 1000, Ysci = 100.

b. Xmin = −10, Xmax = 10, Xscl = 1, Ymin = 0, Ymax = 20, Yscl = 1.

c. Xmin = −5, Xmax = 5, Xsci = 1, Ymin = 0, Ymax = 30, Ysci = 2.

On Your Own

For Question 2, the graphs may appear the same if the viewing windows are proportional.

10-5 Lesson Organizer

Objective

- Draw the graph of an equation.

NCTM Standards

- 1–4, 7, 8, 9

Review

Plot each point on a coordinate grid.

1. (3, −4)
2. (−2, −5)
3. (−1, 0)

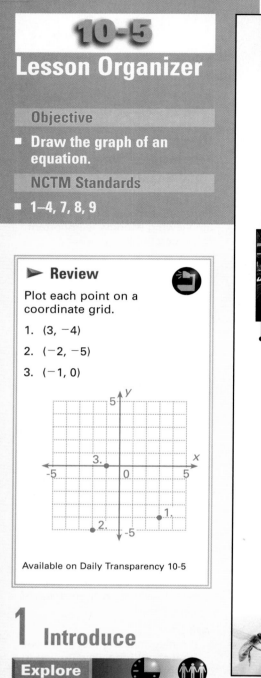

Available on Daily Transparency 10-5

1 Introduce

Explore

You may want to use Lesson Enhancement Transparency 45 with **Explore.**

The Point
Students read information from two scatterplots concerning hives and honey production, use it to complete two tables, and then use the relationships to answer questions about honey production of two kinds of bees. This experience helps students see the connection between data in tables and points on graphs.

Ongoing Assessment
Some students may read values directly from the graph and thus have approximate answers (25, 50, 75, 100, 125 for Step 1). Others will use the rule rather than the graph to find the answers in Steps 1 and 2 ; these students will have exact answers.

10-5 Equations and Graphs

You'll Learn ...

- to draw the graph of an equation

... How It's Used

Sound recording engineers use three-dimensional sound graphs when recording albums.

▶ Lesson Link You've seen how equations and graphs show how quantities are related. Now you'll see how you can draw a graph of an equation. ◀

Explore Showing Relationships in Graphs

These Bees Are "Killer"!

Honey is produced in the United States mostly by European-type bees, often called honeybees. They average 24 kg of honey per hive each season.

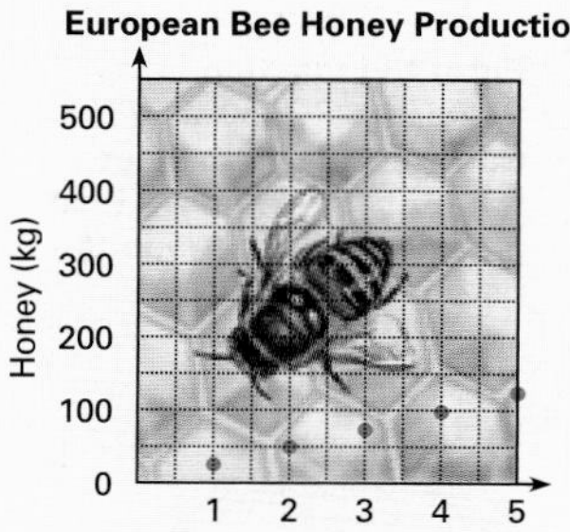

1. The scatterplot shows the amount of honey produced by 1 hive, 2 hives, 3 hives, 4 hives, and 5 hives of European bees in one season. Copy the table below, then use the scatterplot to complete it.

European Bee Honey Production					
Hives	1	2	3	4	5
Honey (kg)					

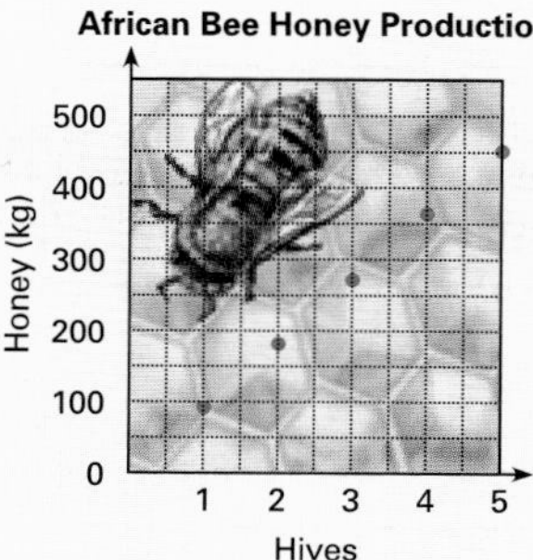

2. African ("killer") bees produce up to 90 kg of honey per hive, as shown in the scatterplot. Make and complete a table like the one above for African bee honey production.
3. If a beekeeper has 10 European honeybee hives, approximately how many kg of honey would they produce in one season? How much honey could she get from 10 African bee hives? Explain.
4. Assuming that African bees are safe, should the beekeeper change bees? Why or why not? Explain how the tables and scatterplots support your choice.

MEETING INDIVIDUAL NEEDS

Resources

10-5 Practice
10-5 Reteaching
10-5 Problem Solving
10-5 Enrichment
10-5 Daily Transparency
Prob. of the Day
Review
Quick Quiz
Teaching Tool Trans. 8
Lesson Enhancement Transparencies 45, 46
Technology Master 46
Chapter 10 Project Master

Wide World of Mathematics
Middle School: Balancing the Budget

Learning Modalities

Kinesthetic Lay out a coordinate grid on your classroom floor, in the gym, or outside. Assign different x-values to students (both positive and negative) and have them stand on the x-axis at their values. When you say an equation out loud (such as $y = 2x$), each student evaluates the expression ($2x$) for their x-value and moves to the appropriate point on the grid.

Visual Have pairs of students prepare posters with the graphs for different equations. Use the posters to compare the graphs of equations that are linear or not and those that go through the origin or not.

Inclusion

Students with visual or perceptual problems may have difficulty with reading values from graphs or with plotting points. Allow these students to work with someone else who can help them draw the graphs or let them use a graphing calculator or a graphing program on the computer.

Learn Equations and Graphs

To make a scatterplot from data in a table, you can write the data as ordered pairs and plot the points on a coordinate plane.

Graphing an equation is similar to creating a scatterplot. You can begin by making a table of values, then plotting the ordered pairs these values represent.

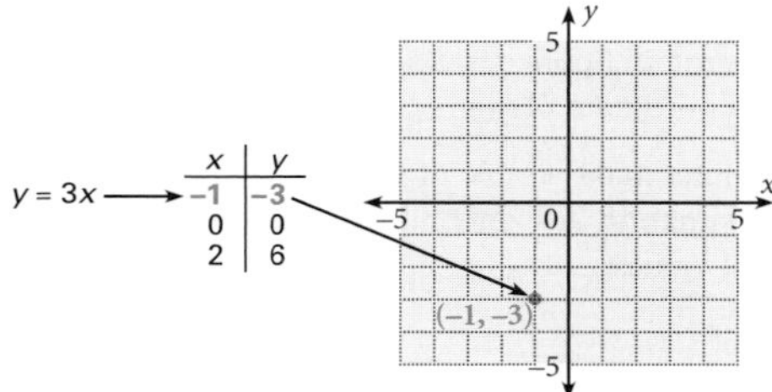

Example 1

Graph the equation $y = 3x$ on a coordinate plane.

First make a table of values. Choose several values for x. It's a good idea to include 0 and a negative value.

x	y
−1	−3
0	0
1	3
2	6
3	9

Next, plot the ordered pairs $(-1, -3)$, $(0, 0)$, $(1, 3)$, $(2, 6)$, and $(3, 9)$ represented by the table.

All of these points fall in a line.

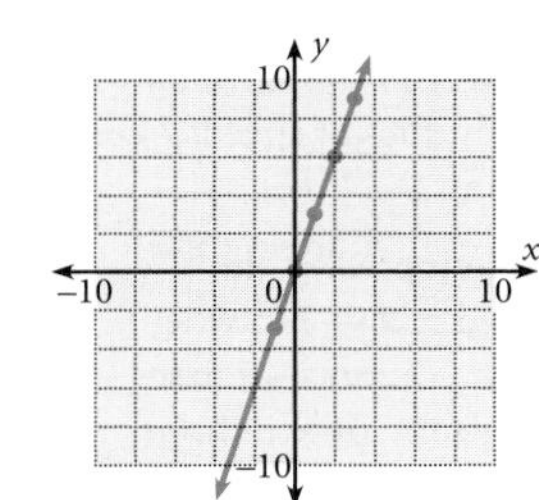

Although these points are on the graph of the equation, they are not the *only* points on the graph. Although the math would not have been as easy, we could have used x-values like $2\frac{1}{2}$ and 1.0001.

To show that points between and beyond the ones in the table are also on the graph, we connect the points.

Remember

Remember that the product of two numbers with the same sign is positive, and the product of two numbers with different signs is negative. **[Page 463]**

Try It

Graph each equation on a coordinate plane.

a. $y = 5x$ **b.** $y = x + 4$ **c.** $y = -2x$

You can use graphs to model relationships in the real world. However, when you do this, be sure the values you choose for your table make sense in the real-world situation.

MATH EVERY DAY

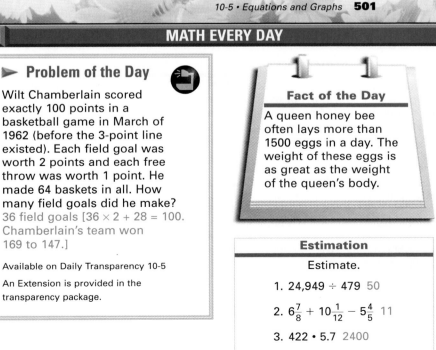

Problem of the Day

Wilt Chamberlain scored exactly 100 points in a basketball game in March of 1962 (before the 3-point line existed). Each field goal was worth 2 points and each free throw was worth 1 point. He made 64 baskets in all. How many field goals did he make? 36 field goals [$36 \times 2 + 28 = 100$. Chamberlain's team won 169 to 147.]

Available on Daily Transparency 10-5

An Extension is provided in the transparency package.

Fact of the Day

A queen honey bee often lays more than 1500 eggs in a day. The weight of these eggs is as great as the weight of the queen's body.

Estimation

Estimate.

1. $24{,}949 \div 479$ 50
2. $6\frac{7}{8} + 10\frac{1}{12} - 5\frac{4}{5}$ 11
3. $422 \cdot 5.7$ 2400

For Groups That Finish Early

What type of figure is formed if you connect the points that are plotted in each scatterplot? A line. Extend the figures to go through the points found in Step 3; are they still straight lines? Yes.

Answers for Explore

1.

Hives	1	2	3	4	5
Honey (kg)	24	48	72	96	120

2.

Hives	1	2	3	4	5
Honey (kg)	90	180	270	360	450

3. European: 240 kg; African: 900 kg; For each bee, multiply the average number of kilograms produced per season by 10.
4. Yes; African bees produce more honey. Corresponding points on the scatterplot for the African bees are higher and corresponding amounts of honey in the table are greater.

2 Teach

Learn

You may want to use Learning Enhancement Transparency 46 and Teaching Tool Transparency 8: Coordinate Grids with **Learn.**

Alternate Examples

1. Graph the equation $y = -2x$ on a coordinate plane.

   First, make a table of values. Choose several values for x, including 0 and a negative value.

x	−1	0	1	2	3
y	2	0	−2	−4	−6

   Next, plot the ordered pairs $(-1, 2)$, $(0, 0)$, $(1, -2)$, $(2, -4)$, and $(3, -6)$. Finally, connect the points to form a line.

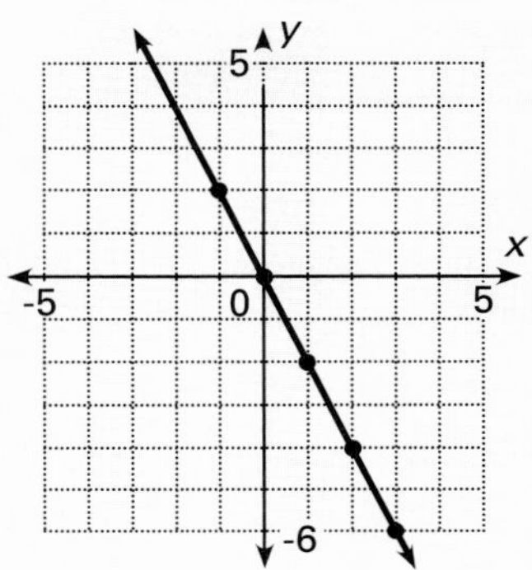

Answers for Try It on page C3.

Alternate Examples

2. Suppose a female aphid lays 50 eggs each week. An equation to represent this relationship is $e = 50a$, where e represents the number of eggs and a represents the number of weeks. Graph this equation on a coordinate plane.

   First, make a table of values. Since this is a real-world situation, use only positive values for a.

a	0	1	2	3	4
e	0	50	100	150	200

   Then, graph the points in the table on a coordinate plane and connect the points.

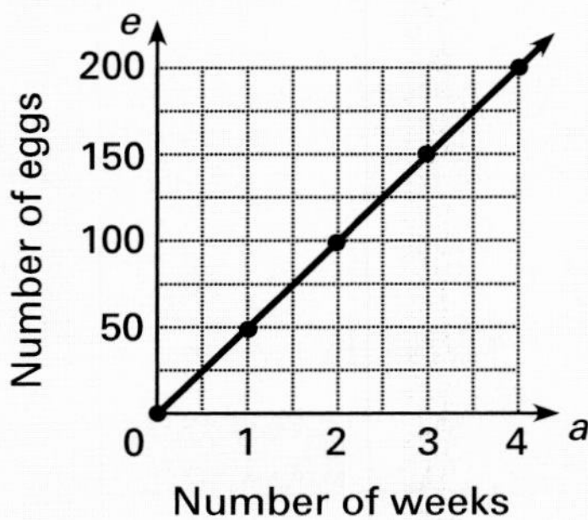

Answers for Try It

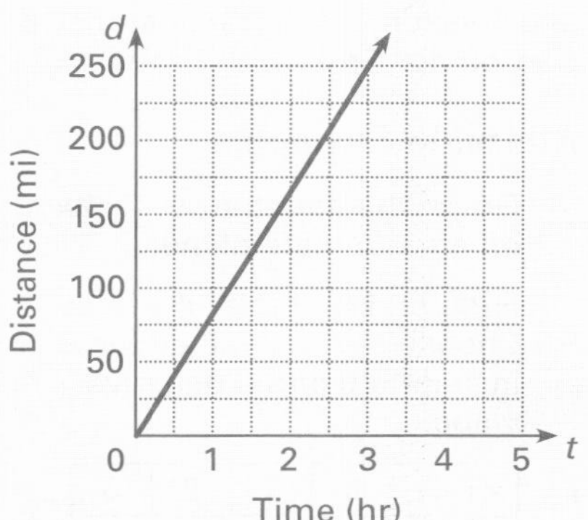

3 Practice and Assess

Check

Possible Answers

1. Answers may vary.
2. Possible answer: Temperature versus time.

Dragonfly wings move at a rate of 30–50 beats per second. The wings of a housefly, which have a different structure, move at 200 wingbeats per second.

Example 2

A dragonfly can reach speeds of 50 km/hr. An equation to represent the dragonfly's speed is $d = 50t$, where d represents the distance in kilometers and t represents the time in hours. Graph this equation on a coordinate plane.

First make a table of values. For this situation, use only non-negative t-values.

Time (hr)	Distance (km)
0	0
1	50
2	100
3	150
4	200
5	250

Then graph the points in the table on a coordinate plane and connect the points.

Notice that this graph is shown only in the first quadrant, since negative numbers do not make sense in this situation.

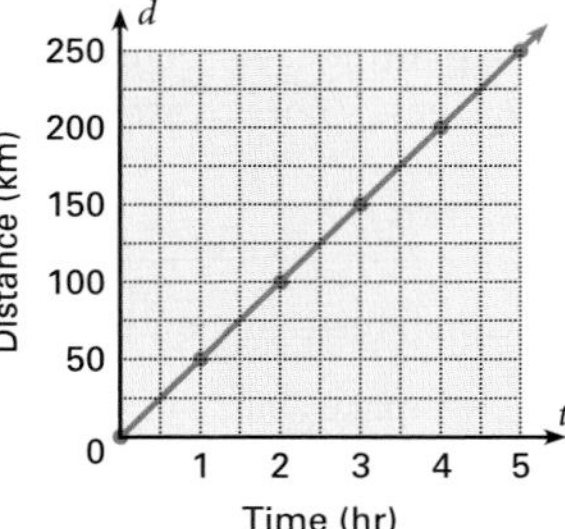

Try It

The fastest insect in the world, a type of horsefly, flies at speeds of up to 87 mi/hr.

An equation to represent the horsefly's speed is $d = 87t$, where d represents the distance in miles and t represents the time in hours. Graph this equation on a coordinate plane.

Check Your Understanding

1. In your own words, describe a method for graphing an equation.
2. Give an example of a graph of a real-world situation that would *not* be in the first quadrant only.

MEETING MIDDLE SCHOOL CLASSROOM NEEDS

Tips from Middle School Teachers

My students enjoy graphing equations that arise from classroom situations, no matter how silly they are. For example, sometimes we'll graph the relationship between the number of people in the room and the number of feet in the room. Another time, I may give every student ten centimeter cubes and ask them to graph the relationship between the number of people and the number of cubes.

Team Teaching

Work with the science teacher to identify equations that students can graph. Students might graph the equations used to convert temperatures from Celsius to Fahrenheit or vice versa. Alternatively, they might conduct experiments with mealworms, ladybugs, or crickets (how far do they fly/jump/crawl in a given period of time) and try to describe the relationships they find using equations.

Science Connection

Honey bees are social insects that cannot survive outside a communal setting. The number of worker bees in a typical colony varies from spring to summer and may exceed 80,000 by early summer.

10-5 Exercises and Applications

Practice and Apply

1. **Getting Started** Follow the steps to graph the equation $y = 2x + 3$.

a. Make a table with two rows (or columns). Begin the first with the letter x, then fill in several x-values of your choice. Include at least one negative value and zero.

b. Begin the second row (or column) with the letter y. Then substitute the first x-value into the equation. Simplify to find the y-value for this x-value. Write this y-value next to its corresponding x-value.

c. Repeat until you complete the table.

d. Each x-y pair of values in the table represents a point. Plot these points on a coordinate plane. Then connect the points to show the graph.

In Exercises 2–5, a table of points is given for each equation. Graph each equation on a coordinate plane.

2. $y = x + 2$

x	y
−1	1
0	2
1	3
2	4
3	5

3. $y = 4x$

x	y
−2	−8
0	0
1	4
2	8
4	16

4. $y = x - 1$

x	y
−1	−2
0	−1
3	2
4	3
5	4

5. $y = -2x + 5$

x	y
−2	9
0	5
2	1
4	−3
6	−7

Graph each equation on a coordinate plane.

6. $y = 2x$ **7.** $y = x + 1$ **8.** $y = -3x$ **9.** $y = 4x - 5$ **10.** $y = x$

11. Look at the graphs for the equations in Exercises 2–10. Compare the equations whose graphs go through the origin to the equations whose graphs do not. What do you notice?

12. Science The Goliath beetle is the world's heaviest insect. One Goliath beetle can weigh 3.5 ounces. An equation to represent the weight of several Goliath beetles is $w = 3.5b$, where w represents the weight in ounces and b represents the number of beetles. Graph this equation.

PRACTICE 10-5

10-5 Exercises and Applications

Assignment Guide

- **Basic**
  1, 2–12 evens, 18–20, 22–36 evens
- **Average**
  2–6, 11–14, 17–20, 23–35 odds
- **Enriched**
  3–11 odds, 12–21, 22–36 evens

Exercise Notes

Exercises 6–10

Error Prevention Some students may still need help substituting values for variables in expressions. Point out that only the variable is replaced by a number; the signs between variables are operation signs that must remain.

Exercise Answers

Answers for Exercises 1–12 on page C4.

1a-c: Check students' work. Tables may vary. See page C4 for graph.

Reteaching

Activity

Materials: Pattern blocks

The equation $p = 2n + 2$ shows the relationship between p, the perimeter, and n, the number of square pieces used for the pattern below.

1st 2nd 3rd

Continue the pattern to find the missing numbers in each table. Then graph the points on a coordinate plane and connect them.

No. of Squares	1	2	3	4	5
Perimeter	4	6	8	10	12

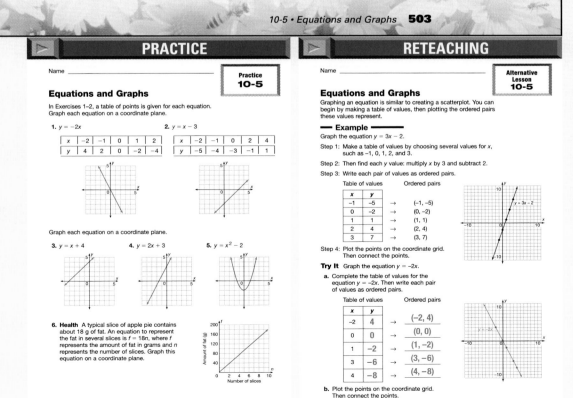

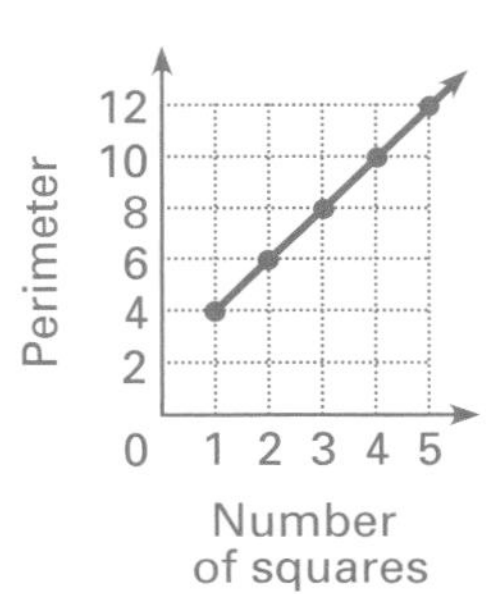

PRACTICE

Name ____________

Practice 10-5

Equations and Graphs

In Exercises 1–2, a table of points is given for each equation. Graph each equation on a coordinate plane.

1. $y = -2x$

x	−2	−1	0	1	2
y	4	2	0	−2	−4

2. $y = x - 3$

x	−2	−1	0	2	4
y	−5	−4	−3	−1	1

Graph each equation on a coordinate plane.

3. $y = x + 4$ **4.** $y = 2x + 3$ **5.** $y = x^2 - 2$

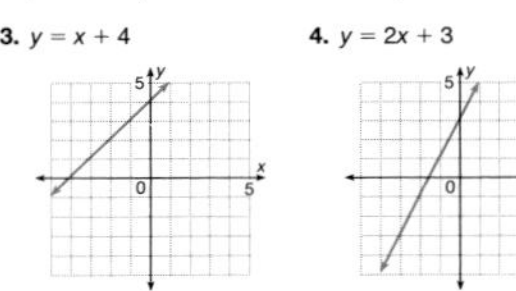

6. Health A typical slice of apple pie contains about 18 g of fat. An equation to represent the fat in several slices is $f = 18n$, where f represents the amount of fat in grams and n represents the number of slices. Graph this equation on a coordinate plane.

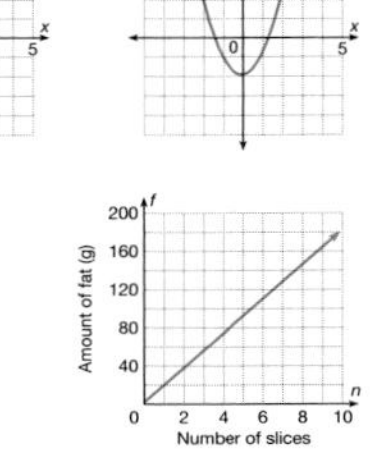

RETEACHING

Name ____________

Alternative Lesson 10-5

Equations and Graphs

Graphing an equation is similar to creating a scatterplot. You can begin by making a table of values, then plotting the ordered pairs these values represent.

Example

Graph the equation $y = 3x - 2$.

Step 1: Make a table of values by choosing several values for x, such as −1, 0, 1, 2, and 3.

Step 2: Then find each y value: multiply x by 3 and subtract 2.

Step 3: Write each pair of values as ordered pairs.

x	y		Ordered pairs
−1	−5	→	(−1, −5)
0	−2	→	(0, −2)
1	1	→	(1, 1)
2	4	→	(2, 4)
3	7	→	(3, 7)

Step 4: Plot the points on the coordinate grid. Then connect the points.

Try It Graph the equation $y = -2x$.

a. Complete the table of values for the equation $y = -2x$. Then write each pair of values as ordered pairs.

x	y		Ordered pairs
−2	4	→	(−2, 4)
0	0	→	(0, 0)
1	−2	→	(1, −2)
3	−6	→	(3, −6)
4	−8	→	(4, −8)

b. Plot the points on the coordinate grid. Then connect the points.

Exercise Notes

■ Exercises 13–16

Error Prevention Students may not plot enough points to see the pattern for these graphs. Encourage them to plot at least six points, including some negative values for *x*.

Project Progress

You may want to have students use Chapter 10 Project Master.

Exercise Answers

Answers for Exercises 13–17 on page C4 and for Exercises 19–21 on page C5.

Alternate Assessment

You may want to use the *Interactive CD-ROM Journal* with this assessment.

Journal Have students explain how to graph an equation.

▶ Quick Quiz

Graph each equation on a coordinate plane.

1. $y = 5x$
2. $y = 2x - 1$

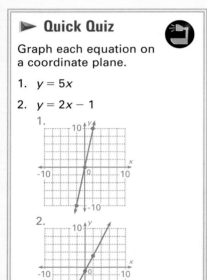

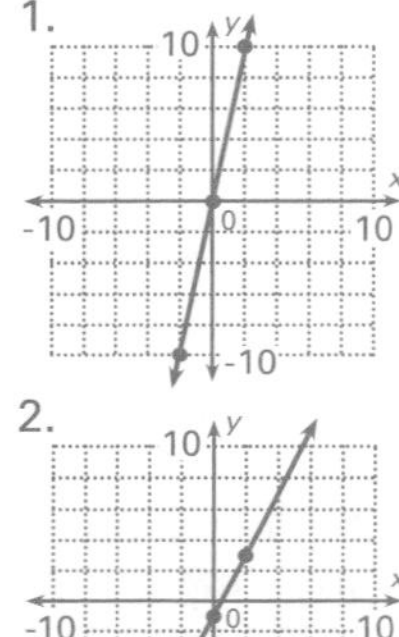

Available on Daily Transparency 10-5

Graph each equation on the same coordinate plane.

13. $y = \frac{1}{2}x$ **14.** $y = \frac{1}{2}x - 1$ **15.** $y = \frac{1}{2}x + 1$ **16.** $y = \frac{1}{2}x - 3$

17. What do you notice about the graphs in Exercises 13–16?

18. **Test Prep** Which of these equations has a graph that contains the origin? B

Ⓐ $y = x + 2$ Ⓑ $y = 2x$ Ⓒ $y = 2x + 1$ Ⓓ $y = x - 2$

PROBLEM SOLVING 10-5

Problem Solving and Reasoning

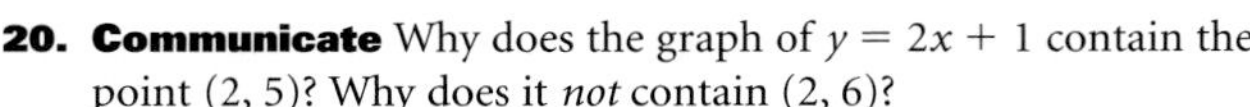

19. **Critical Thinking** When an insect is active, its heart can beat at a rate of 140 beats per minute. When it is inactive and cold, its heart rate can slow to 1 beat per hour. GPS

a. Write an equation to represent each of these rates.

b. Graph both equations on the same coordinate plane. Describe similarities and differences between these graphs. How can you tell by looking which graph represents the lesser rate?

20. **Communicate** Why does the graph of $y = 2x + 1$ contain the point (2, 5)? Why does it *not* contain (2, 6)?

21. **Critical Thinking** Graph each pair of equations on the same coordinate plane.

a. $y = 2x$ and $y = -2x$ **b.** $y = 3x$ and $y = -3x$ **c.** $y = 10x$ and $y = -10x$

d. Describe the differences between the graphs in each pair.

Mixed Review

Number Sense Use percents to compare. *[Lesson 8-1]*

22. $\frac{61}{100}$ and $\frac{3}{5}$ **23.** $\frac{9}{20}$ and $\frac{1}{2}$ **24.** $\frac{1}{4}$ and $\frac{4}{25}$ **25.** $\frac{1}{4}$ and $\frac{1}{5}$ **26.** $\frac{3}{10}$ and $\frac{7}{25}$

22. $\frac{61}{100} = 61\%; \frac{3}{5} = 60\%; \frac{61}{100} > \frac{3}{5}$
23. $\frac{9}{20} = 45\%; \frac{1}{2} = 50\%; \frac{9}{20} < \frac{1}{2}$
24. $\frac{1}{4} = 25\%; \frac{4}{25} = 16\%; \frac{1}{4} > \frac{4}{25}$
25. $\frac{1}{4} = 25\%; \frac{1}{5} = 20\%; \frac{1}{4} > \frac{1}{5}$
26. $\frac{3}{10} = 30\%; \frac{7}{25} = 28\%; \frac{3}{10} > \frac{7}{25}$

Operation Sense Find each product. *[Lesson 9-6]*

27. $7 \cdot 9$ 63 **28.** $-3 \cdot (-5)$ 15 **29.** $-4 \cdot 11$ −44 **30.** $6 \cdot (-10)$ −60 **31.** $-16 \cdot 0$ 0

32. $42 \cdot (-10)$ −420 **33.** $-12 \cdot (-9)$ 108 **34.** $-5 \cdot 23$ −115 **35.** $18 \cdot (-15)$ −270 **36.** $-1 \cdot -1 \cdot -1$ −1

Project Progress

Create a table of the population data you found for your city, town, or state. Then see if you can find an equation that fits the data. If there is no exact equation, see if you can find an equation that comes close. (*Hint:* It may help to number the years from 0 instead of using the actual dates.)

Problem Solving
Understand
Plan
Solve
Look Back

PROBLEM SOLVING

Name ____________

Guided Problem Solving 10-5

GPS **PROBLEM 19, STUDENT PAGE 504**

When an insect is active, its heart can beat at a rate of 140 beats per minute. When it is inactive and cold, its heart rate can slow to 1 beat per hour.

a. Write an equation to represent each of these rates.

b. Graph both equations on the same coordinate plane. Describe similarities and differences between these graphs. How can you tell by looking which graph represents the lesser rate?

— Understand —

1. How many heart beats are there when an insect is

a. active? $\frac{140 \text{ beats}}{1 \text{ min}}$ b. inactive? $\frac{1 \text{ beat}}{1 \text{ hr}}$

— Plan —

2. How many heart beats are there per minute when an insect is inactive? C

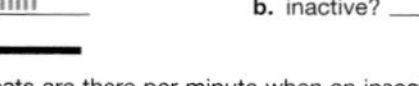

a. $\frac{60 \text{ beats}}{1 \text{ min}}$ b. $\frac{30 \text{ beats}}{60 \text{ min}}$ c. $\frac{\frac{1}{60} \text{ beat}}{1 \text{ min}}$

— Solve —

3. Use *b* for beats and *m* for minutes. Write the equation that represents the

a. active heartbeat. $b = 140m$ b. inactive heartbeat. $b = \frac{m}{60}$

4. Graph the equations.

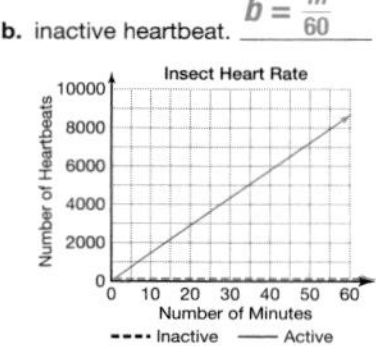

5. Describe the similarities and differences. One is steep; other is flat.

6. How can you tell by looking which graph represents the lesser rate? Graph with the flatter slope.

— Look Back —

7. Do you have to graph the equations to tell which rate is the lesser one? Explain. No, the equations show which is a lesser rate.

SOLVE ANOTHER PROBLEM

An adult's heart can beat at a rate of 4800 times per hour. A new baby's heart can beat at a rate of 140 times per minute. Write an equation to represent each of these as $\frac{\text{beats}}{\text{hour}}$. Which represents the greater rate?

$r = \frac{4800 \text{ beats}}{1 \text{ hour}}$; $r = \frac{8400 \text{ beats}}{1 \text{ hour}}$; new baby's heart rate.

ENRICHMENT

Name ____________

Extend Your Thinking 10-5

Critical Thinking

The letter in each circle represents a digit from 1 to 9. Where two circles intersect and a number is given, the number is the sum of the values of the letters in those two circles. Find the value of each letter. Hint: There are two circles labeled A and two labeled E. The value of a letter is the same each time it occurs in the puzzle.

— Example —

Possible values of *x* and *y*:
$x = 1, y = 4; x = 4, y = 1;$
$x = 2, y = 3; x = 3, y = 2$

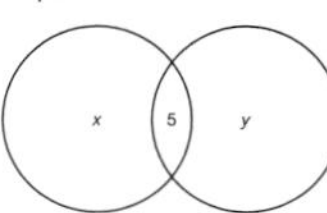

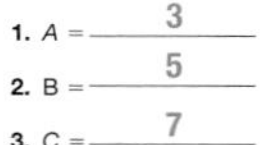

1. *A* = 3
2. B = 5
3. C = 7
4. *D* = 9
5. *E* = 2
6. *F* = 4
7. G = 6
8. *H* = 8
9. *I* = 1

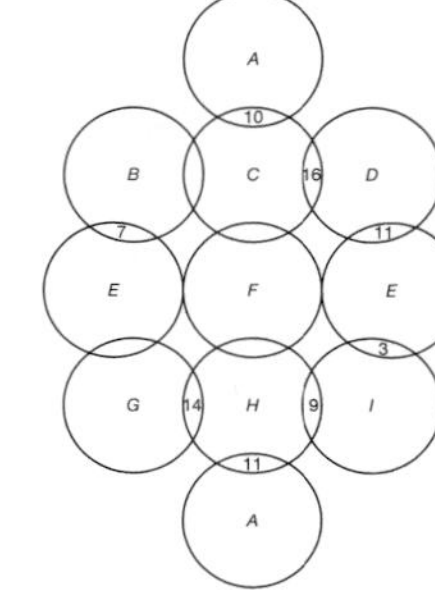

10. Write at least six expressions using the variables above that show values equal to 12. For example, $D - A + G = 12$.

Possible answers: $A + D, F + H, B + C, I + E + D, E + A + C, A + F + B, F + C + I, D - I + F, G \div E + D, A \times E + G, F \times B - H, H \div I + F, D - F + F + A$

Section 10A Connect

You've analyzed relationships between quantities by using graphs, tables, and equations. Now you'll apply those skills to add some spice to your diet.

Howdy, Ant Bee!

Materials: Graph paper

Have you ever swallowed an insect accidentally? You may have felt a little uneasy at the time, but you got the better of the deal. In fact, many insects are good for you!

The following table gives nutritional information for 1-ounce servings of different types of animals.

Nutritional Content of Edible Insects and Other Animals

	Energy (cal)	Protein (g)	Calcium (mg)	Iron (mg)
Daily Requirements (adult)	2850	37	1000	18
Termites	172	4.0	11.3	2.1
Weevils	159	1.9	52.7	3.7
Beef (lean ground)	62	7.8	3.4	1.0
Chicken (roasted white meat)	47	9.0	3.1	0.4
Fish (broiled cod)	48	8.1	8.8	0.3

1. Make a table and a graph of the amount of iron in 1, 2, 3, 4, and 5 ounces of termites.

2. Use your graph or your table to find the approximate amount of iron in $4\frac{1}{2}$ ounces of termites. Explain how you found your answer.

3. Approximately how many ounces of termites would an adult have to eat to get the minimum daily requirement of iron?

4. How many ounces of fish would you have to eat to get as much calcium as there is in 1 ounce of weevils?

5. Approximately how many ounces of weevils would an adult have to eat to get the minimum daily requirement of calcium?

6. Compare the amounts of each type of food that you would need to eat to get an adult's minimum requirement of calories. What do you notice?

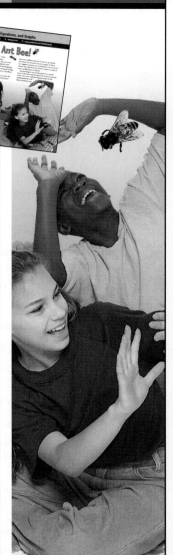

505

Answers for Connect

1.

Termites (oz)	Iron (mg)
1	2.1
2	4.2
3	6.3
4	8.4
5	10.5

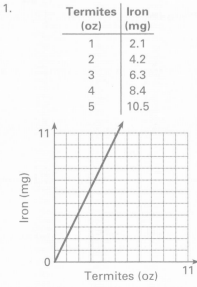

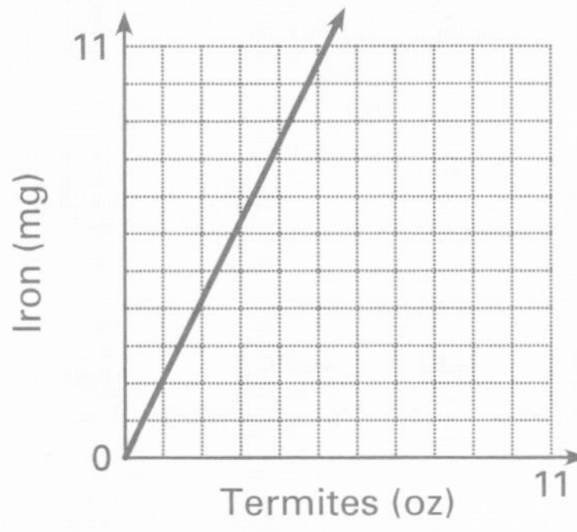

2. 9.45 mg; Use the graph to find the point (4.5, y) or use the table to find the middle point between 8.4 and 10.5.

3. About 9 oz

4. About 6 oz

5. About 20 oz

6. Termites: 16.6 ounces; Weevils: 17.9 ounces; Beef: 46.0 ounces; Chicken: 60.6 ounces; Fish: 59.4 ounces. You need less of the termites and weevils than you do of the beef, chicken, or fish.

Howdy, Ant Bee!

The Point

In *Howdy, Ant Bee!* on page 481, students discussed insects as food and as instruments for pollination. Now they will analyze the nutritional content of edible insects and other animals.

Resources

Lesson Enhancement Transparency 47

About the Page

- Review the information given on the table. Confirm that information given compares one-ounce servings of all items listed.
- Ask students which foods on the table they would prefer to eat.
- Discuss the nutritional value of foods and the daily requirements needed to maintain a healthy body.

Ongoing Assessment

Check that students have correctly determined the amount of each food needed to provide the minimum daily requirement of protein.

Extension

Have students research the minimum daily requirements for persons in their age group of protein, fat, and carbohydrates and the most common vitamins and minerals. Ask students how they could determine if they are eating a diet that provides the daily requirements.

10A Review

Review Correlation

Item(s)	Lesson(s)
1	10-2
2–5	10-3
6, 7	10-4
8–12	10-5
13	10-4, 10-5
14	10-3

Test Prep

Test-Taking Tip

Tell students that on some test questions, numbers can be related to each other in ways not related to the four basic operations. Examples are relationships between odd numbers, even numbers, squares of numbers, and prime numbers. In this problem, all of the numbers are prime.

Answers for Review

8.

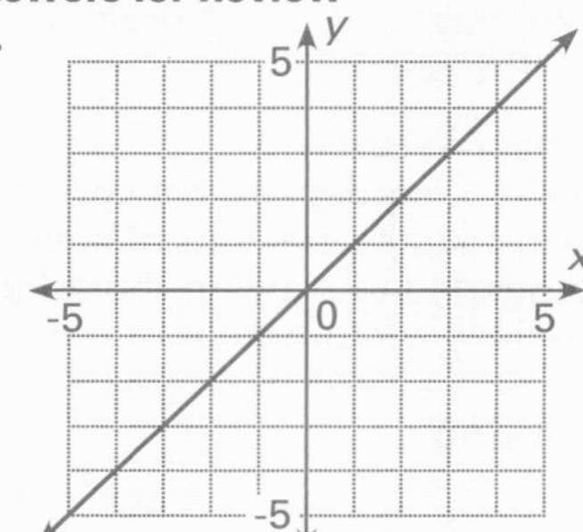

9.

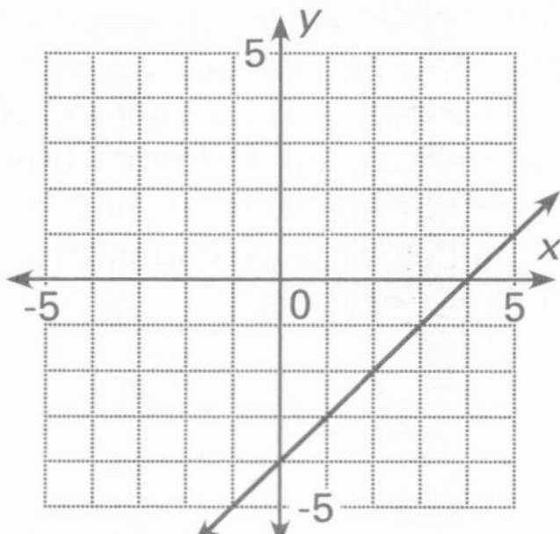

10.

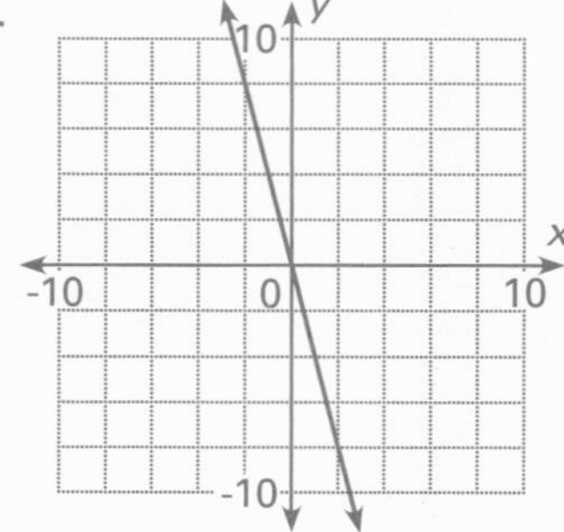

Answers for Exercises 11–13 on page C5.

Section 10A Review

REVIEW 10A

1. **History** In 1519, Ferdinand Magellan left Spain on a voyage around the world. After Magellan died in the Philippines, Juan del Cano assumed command. He waited until the ships were repaired, then returned to Spain in 1522. Which graph could show this voyage? b

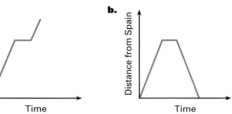

a.

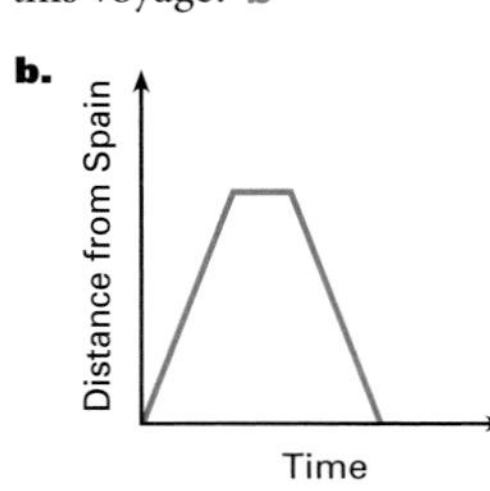

b.

Distance from Spain

Time

Write an expression describing the rule for each sequence. Then give the 100th term for the sequence.

2. 4, 5, 6, 7, … $n + 3$; 103
3. 2, 4, 6, 8, … $2n$; 200
4. 0.3, 0.6, 0.9, 1.2, … $\frac{3n}{10}$; 30
5. −5, −10, −15, −20, … $-5n$; −500

For each table, write an equation to show the relationship between *x* and *y*. Use the equation to find *y* when *x* = 9.

6.

x	1	2	3	4
y	3	6	9	12

$y = 3x$; 27

7.

x	1	2	3	4
y	−5	−4	−3	−2

$y = x - 6$; 3

Graph each equation on a coordinate plane.

8. $y = x$
9. $y = x - 4$
10. $y = -4x$
11. $y = 2x + 2$
12. $y = -x$

13.  Explain the relationship between an equation, a table of values for the equation, and the graph of the equation.

Test Prep

When asked to find the next number in a sequence on a multiple choice test, remember that the sequence may follow a rule that can't be written as an expression.

14. What is the next number in the sequence 2, 3, 5, 7, 11, …? B

Ⓐ 12 Ⓑ 13 Ⓒ 14 Ⓓ 15

Resources

Practice Masters
Section 10A Review

Assessment Sourcebook
Quiz 10A

 *TestWorks*
Test and Practice Software

PRACTICE

Name ______________________ **Practice**

Section 10A Review

1. Tell whether the depth of water in a bathtub is a variable or a constant. Variable

2. A person making deliveries rode an elevator from the lobby to the 17th floor to deliver a package. She then rode to the 9th floor to make another delivery, and then she returned to the lobby. Which graph could represent this story?

a. b. (c.)

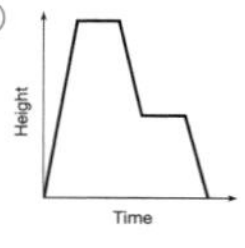

Height

Time

Write an expression describing the rule for each sequence. Then give the 100th term for the sequence.

3. −6, −12, −18, −24, ⋯

Expression: $-6n$ 100th term: −600

4. −8, −7, −6, −5, ⋯

Expression: $n - 9$ 100th term: 91

5. Write an equation to show the relationship between x and y. Use the equation to find y when $x = 9$.

x	1	2	3	4	9
y	7	8	9	10	15

$y = x + 6$

Graph each equation on a coordinate plane.

6. $y = -4x$
7. $y = x - 3$
8. $y = -2x + 4$

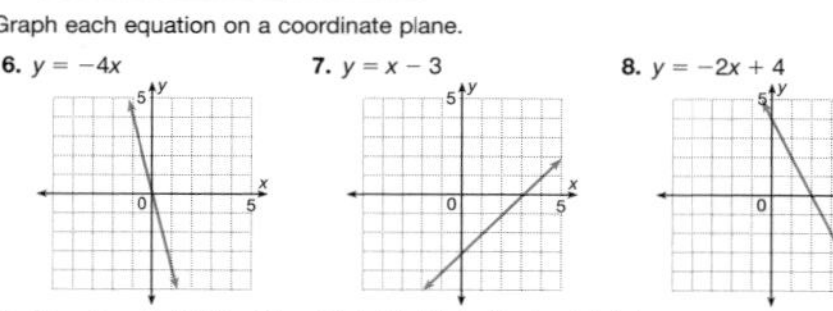

9. Dave traveled 271 mi from Philadelphia to Boston. He left at 10:00 A.M. and drove at 60 mi/hr. What time did he arrive? *[Lesson 7-3]* 2:31 P.M.

10. **Science** Ice melts at 32°F. If the temperature of a block of ice increases 35°F from −10°F, does the ice melt? Explain your answer. *[Lesson 9-4]*

No. Possible answer: $-10 + 35 = 25$, and $25 < 32$.

Understanding Equations

LESSON PLANNING GUIDE

Student Edition

Ancillaries*

LESSON		MATERIALS	VOCABULARY	DAILY	OTHER
	Section 10B Opener				
10-6	**Solving Equations Using Tables**			10-6	Teaching Tool Trans. 2, 3 Technology Master 47 *WW Math*–Middle School
10-7	**Solving Equations Using Graphs**	graphing utility		10-7	Teaching Tool Trans. 8, 28 Technology Master 48 *Interactive CD-ROM Lesson 10*
10-8	**Relating Equations and Inequalities**		inequality, solutions of an inequality	10-8	Teaching Tool Trans. 5 Ch. 10 Project Master
	Connect	graph paper			Teaching Tool Trans. 7
	Review				

* Daily Ancillaries include Practice, Reteaching, Problem Solving, Enrichment, and Daily Transparency. Teaching Tool Transparencies are in *Teacher's Toolkits*. Lesson Enhancement Transparencies are in *Overhead Transparency Package*.

SKILLS TRACE

LESSON	SKILL	FIRST INTRODUCED GR. 5	GR. 6	GR. 7	DEVELOP	PRACTICE/ APPLY	REVIEW
10-6	**Using tables to solve equations.**			✘ p. 508	pp. 508–509	pp. 510–511	pp. 522, 547, 591
10-7	**Using graphs to solve equations.**			✘ p. 512	pp. 512–514	pp. 515–516	pp. 522, 547, 586
10-8	**Graphing inequalities on a number line.**			✘ p. 517	pp. 517–518	pp. 519–520	pp. 522, 547, 596

CONNECTED MATHEMATICS

Investigations 1–5 in the unit *Moving Straight Ahead (Linear Relationships)*, from the **Connected Mathematics** series, can be used with Section 10B.

INTERDISCIPLINARY TEAM TEACHING

Math and Social Studies

(Worksheet pages 41–42: Teacher pages T41–T42)

In this lesson, students solve equations and relate inequalities using data from the computer industry.

Name ____________________ ***Math and Social Studies***

Computer Business Has Growing Pains

Solve equations and relate inequalities using data from the computer industry.

The computer industry is sometimes compared to a teenager! Like many teenagers, the computer business is growing quickly, its ideas are ever-changing, and its direction is sometimes unpredictable. This has led to the "growing pains" of some large computer companies. Added to the youthful image is the fact that many of the industry's most inventive minds began their careers when they were barely out of their teens. Bill Gates, chairman of Microsoft, started his software business when he was only twenty. He is now the world's richest man. Steve Jobs and Steve Wozniak started Apple Computer out of a family garage. Mike Dell, of Dell Computer Corporation, started out by selling computers from his college dormitory room. Pamela Lopker started her own software company in her early twenties and is now the richest self-made woman in America.

The computer business is very different from other businesses because its technology changes so rapidly. More powerful computer chips to run programs faster are being developed all the time. Newer chips mean that new hardware (computers) and software (programs) can also be developed and brought out to the market in record time. The astonishing variety of computer applications affect how we work and play and has changed our society forever.

1. a. Make a list of some of the ways in which computers affect your everyday life.

Possible answers: helps with homework; entertains; speeds communication.

b. Make a list of the characteristics that people might have who would be interested in starting a computer business.

Possible answers: interest in computers, intelligence, ambition, motivation, ability to work hard and see a project through.

2. Mike Dell was the first person to get the idea of selling computers over the phone. Today he is a billionaire. When he first started in the 1980s, he made $80,000 in sales a month! If the average sale was $2,000, write an equation and solve for the number of computers, c, he sold each month.

$c = \frac{\$80,000}{\$2,000} = 40$ or

$2,000c = 80,000$

Name ____________________ ***Math and Social Studies***

3. Steve Jobs and Steve Wozniak started Apple Computer in 1976 with just $1,350. In 1977, they had orders for $1 million worth of computers. In 1978, they took orders for $10 million when the price of their computer was $1,200. Write and solve an equation to represent the total number of computers Apple sold, *c*, between 1976 and 1978. Round your answer.

$c = \frac{\$11,000,000}{\$1,200} = 9,167$ or

$1,200c = 11,000,000$

4. In 1981, IBM came out with the first personal computer, or PC. The IBM PC was soon imitated with "clones" made by Compaq and Hewlett-Packard. By the mid-1980s, Gateway 2000 and Dell Computer were selling personal computers over the phone and by mail.

The table shows the approximate total value of the stock of each computer company in 1997.

Company	Stock Value in Billions of Dollars
IBM	75
Compaq	21
Gateway 2000	4
Dell	8
Apple	3
Hewlett-Packard	50

a. IBM and Hewlett-Packard are the computer industry's giants. Write an algebraic equation to express the value of Hewlett-Packard, *h*, compared to that of IBM, *i*.

$h = \frac{50}{75} \times i$; $h = \frac{2}{3} \times i$

b. Gateway 2000 and Dell compete in the mail-order computer market. Write an algebraic equation to express the value of Dell, *d*, compared to that of Gateway 2000, *g*.

$d = 2g$

5. In January 1997, leading personal computer companies began to advertise their prices for computers that use the new powerful MMX chip.

Company	Starting Prices of Computers using the MMX chip
Compaq	$1,299
Hewlett-Packard	$1,399
IBM	$2,399
Gateway 2000	$ 2,149
Dell	

Dell will use the chip in its home-office computer. This computer is better equipped and more expensive than the comparable Compaq or HP. However, Dell will sell it more cheaply than IBM or Gateway 2000. Write an inequality to show the price range of the Dell computer, *d*, with the MMX chip.

$\$1,399 < d < \$2,149$

6. Do some research to find a large computer catalogue, such as *Computer Shopper*. Find a line of computer hardware or software in which you have an interest. Make a list of prices that different manufacturers offer for the same or comparable products. Visit a computer store and see how store prices compare to the prices in the mail-order catalogue. Put the information you have gathered into a table.

BIBLIOGRAPHY

FOR TEACHERS

Huxley, Anthony, ed. *Standard Encyclopedia of the World's Mountains*. New York, NY: Putnam, 1962.

O'Toole, Christopher, ed. *The Encyclopedia of Insects*. New York, NY: Facts on File, 1986.

Robinson, Andrew. *Earth Shock: Hurricanes, Volcanoes, Earthquakes, Tornadoes and Other Forces of Nature*. New York, NY: Thames and Hudson, 1993.

Ryden, Hope. *Wild Animals of Africa ABC*. New York, NY: Lodestar Books, 1989.

Thomas, Lowell. *Lowell Thomas' Book of High Mountains*. New York, NY: J. Messner, 1964.

FOR STUDENTS

Brattina, Anita F. *Diary of a Small Business Owner: A Personal Account of How I Built a Profitable Business*. New York, NY: AMACOM, 1996.

Ichbiah, Daniel. *The Making of Microsoft: How Bill Gates and His Team Created the World's Most Successful Software Company*. Rocklin, CA: Prima Publications, 1991.

Selden, George. *The Cricket in Times Square*. Santa Barbara, CA: Cornerstone Books, 1990.

SECTION 10B

Understanding Equations

▶ Industry Link ▶ www.mathsurf.com/7/ch10/entrepreneurs

IT IS MY BUSINESS!

It started as a garden in South Central Los Angeles. In 1992, after riots devastated their community, 38 Crenshaw High School students cleared a patch of weeds and began to raise vegetables. They sold some for scholarship money and donated some to homeless shelters. Then they had an idea: We know vegetables, so let's make salad dressing!

Biology teacher Tammy Bird helped the students. The group experimented until they found the right recipe. They got advice from Norris Bernstein, founder of Bernstein's salad dressings. Finally they set up their own company, Food From the 'Hood. In 1994, more than 2000 grocery stores began selling their product, Straight Out 'the Garden salad dressing.

When they graduate, the students receive their profits as scholarship money. Food From the 'Hood is on target to earn $50,000 for its student owners! Now you'll see how young entrepreneurs like the owners of Food From the 'Hood use mathematics in their businesses.

1. Explain how you calculate the profit for a business if you know its income and its costs.
2. How do you think the student owners of Food From the 'Hood use mathematics in their business?

507

Where are we now?

In Section 10A, students identified arithmetic and geometric sequences. They wrote and graphed equations.

They learned how to

- identify variables and constants.
- analyze graphs.
- identify arithmetic and geometric sequences.
- write an equation from a table of values.
- graph equations.

Where are we going?

In Section 10B, students will

- use tables to solve equations.
- use graphs to solve equations.
- graph inequalities on a number line.
- write inequalities represented on a graph.

Theme: Young Entrepreneurs

World Wide Web

If your class has access to the World Wide Web, you might want to use the information found at the Web site address given. The interdisciplinary link relates to topics discussed in this section.

About the Page

This page introduces the theme of the section, young entrepreneurs, and discusses a group of students who started a business.

Ask ...

- What is an entrepreneur? One who organizes, manages, and assumes the risk of a business.
- What is "the market" for any product? The people who would potentially buy the product.

Extension

The following activity does not require access to the World Wide Web.

Industry
Have students investigate companies that were founded by young entrepreneurs, such as Microsoft, founded by Bill Gates.

Answers for Questions

1. Possible answer: Subtract the costs from the income.
2. To calculate income, profit, and expenses, gather and display sales data, and so on.

Connect

On page 521, students study the problems that might be faced by students who own businesses.

10-6 Lesson Organizer

Objective

- Use tables to solve equations.

NCTM Standards

- 1–2, 4, 7, 8, 9, 12

Review

Find the number that is halfway between each pair of numbers.

1. 6 and 8 7
2. 30 and 50 40
3. 80 and 160 120
4. 9 and 12 10.5

Available on Daily Transparency 10-6

1 Introduce

Explore

The Point
Students write an equation and use it to make a table of values relating the number of necklaces sold to the total cost. Then they use the table or the equation to find the cost for different numbers of necklaces.

Ongoing Assessment
Watch for students who are not able to find the cost for 24 necklaces because the quantity *24 necklaces* is not in the table.

For Groups That Finish Early
How many necklaces would Solangel need to sell in order to make $3000? 600.

Answers for Explore
Possible Answers

1. $c = 5n$
2. See page C5 for table. 7 necklaces would cost $35; 24 necklaces would cost $120.
3. $n = 10$; Looked in the table for $c = \$50$ and found the number of necklaces for this amount.

10-6 Solving Equations Using Tables

You'll Learn ...

- to use tables to solve equations

... How It's Used

Taxpayers look up the amount of tax they owe in large tables. These tables show the solutions to "income tax equations."

▶ Lesson Link You've made tables of values and drawn graphs of equations. Now you'll use tables and graphs to solve equations. ◀

Explore Tables and Equations

Up to Her Necklace in Sales!

As a seventh-grader, Solangel Brujan of New York City borrowed $50 and began a jewelry business. In just 3 years, she made $3000. One item she stocked was a faux-pearl necklace that sold for $5.

1. Let n be the number of "pearl" necklaces purchased by one customer. Let c be the customer's total cost. Write an equation showing the relationship between these variables.
2. Make a table showing how much 1 to 12 necklaces would cost. How much would 7 necklaces cost? 24 necklaces? Explain.
3. How many necklaces would Solangel have to sell to pay back the amount she borrowed? Explain how you found the answer.

Learn Solving Equations Using Tables

By using a table of x and y values for an equation, you can read the x-value that goes with a specific y-value.

Example 1

Make a table of values for $y = x + 2$. Use x-values of -1, 0, 1, 2, 3, and 4. Then find the value of x when y is 1, 3, and 6.

x	−1	0	1	2	3	4
y	1	2	3	4	5	6

To make the table, substitute each x-value into the equation.

When $y = 1$, $x = -1$; when $y = 3$, $x = 1$; and when $y = 6$, $x = 4$.

MEETING INDIVIDUAL NEEDS

Resources

10-6 Practice
10-6 Reteaching
10-6 Problem Solving
10-6 Enrichment
10-6 Daily Transparency
- Problem of the Day
- Review
- Quick Quiz

Teaching Tool Transparencies 2, 3
Technology Master 47

Wide World of Mathematics Middle School: The Census

Learning Modalities

Logical Have students use spreadsheets to solve problems like those in this lesson. With the computer, they can change the x-values more easily.

Individual Ask each student to reflect upon his/her progress so far, for example, what do they understand well? where are they having difficulty? what can they do to improve?

Challenge

Students who need additional challenges may enjoy working with quadratic equations, like $y = x^2 + 5$. Using tables to estimate solutions can be quite difficult in some cases.

You can use a table of values to solve an equation. To solve $8 = x + 5$, first make a table for the *related* equation $y = x + 5$. Then find the x-value for $y = 8$.

Example 2

Use a table to solve $14 = 3x - 4$.

x	−2	0	2	4	6	8
y	−10	−4	2	8	14	20

The related equation is $y = 3x - 4$. A table for this equation is shown.

From the table, $x = 6$ when $y = 14$.

Try It

Make and use a table to solve each equation.

a. $7 = x - 3$ $x = 10$ **b.** $42 = -7x$ $x = -6$ **c.** $15 = 3k + 2$ $k = 4\frac{1}{3}$ **d.** $-6 = 2x + 8$ $x = -7$

▶ Language Link

The word *entrepreneur* comes from the French *entreprendre*, which means "to undertake."

You may be able to use a table to estimate the solution to an equation.

Example 3

The MelMaps Company was started by 11-year-old Melissa Gollick of Denver. Melissa uses a computer to draw maps for real estate firms. Each map sells for $40. How many maps does she need to sell to earn $280?

Let m = the number of maps. We need to solve $280 = 40m$.

Let y = the amount earned. The table gives values for $y = 40m$.

Maps, m	2	4	6	8	10
Income, y ($)	80	160	240	320	400

$y = 280$ does not appear in the table. However, you can *estimate* that 280 is halfway between 240 and 320.

In the m-row, the value halfway between 6 and 8 is 7. Melissa must sell 7 maps.

DID YOU KNOW?

Bill Gates co-founded Microsoft in 1975, when he was 20. By 1996, he was the richest person in the United States. His fortune was worth 18 *billion* dollars, which is enough to give everyone in Elko, Nevada, a million dollars and have more than $3 billion left over!

Check Your Understanding

1. What is the related equation for $14 = 7x$? How are these equations "related"?

2. In Example 3, how could we check whether 7 maps is the correct answer?

MATH EVERY DAY

▶ Problem of the Day

The African oil palm grows up to 80 feet tall and produces 200 pounds of fruit in a year. A Brazilian palm has the largest fronds (leaves) in the plant kingdom. These fronds are 6 feet longer than $\frac{4}{5}$ the height of the African oil palm. The Brazilian palm fronds are 1 foot narrower than $\frac{1}{4}$ of the height of the African oil palm. Find the length and width of the Brazilian palm fronds. 70 feet by 19 feet

Available on Daily Transparency 10-6

An Extension is provided in the transparency package.

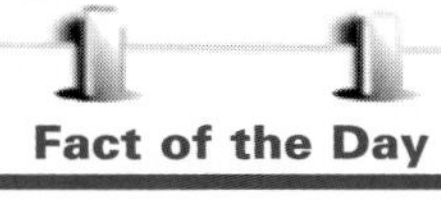

Fact of the Day

To produce a cultured pearl, a mother-of-pearl bead is placed into a pearl oyster. The bead is at least 75% of the diameter of the cultured pearl desired.

Mental Math

Do these mentally.

1. $6.7 + 7.3 + 4.3$ 18.3
2. $10 - 5.6$ 4.4
3. $2.6 \cdot 8$ 20.8
4. $0.0848 \div 0.4$ 0.212

2 Teach

Learn

Alternate Examples

1. Make a table of values for $y = -3x$. Use x-values of −1, 0, 1, 2, 3, and 4. Then find the value of x when y is −6, −3, and 3.

   To make the table, substitute each x-value into the equation.

x	−1	0	1	2	3	4
y	3	0	−3	−6	−9	−12

   When $y = -6$, $x = 2$.
   When $y = -3$, $x = 1$.
   When $y = 3$, $x = -1$.

2. Use a table to solve $9 = 2x + 3$.

   The related equation is $y = 2x + 3$. A table is shown.

   From the table, $x = 3$ when $y = 9$.

x	−1	0	1	2	3	4
y	1	3	5	7	9	11

3. How many $25 tickets must be sold to earn $225?

   Let x = the number of tickets. Solve $25x = 225$.

   The table gives values for $y = 25x$.

x	2	4	6	8	10
y	50	100	150	200	250

   y = $225 does not appear in the table. Estimate that 225 is halfway between 200 and 250. In the x-row, the value halfway between 8 and 10 is 9.

   Nine tickets must be sold.

3 Practice and Assess

Check

Answers for Check Your Understanding

1. $y = 7x$; They have the same right side (involving x), but the specific value 14 is replaced by a variable.
2. Substitute $m = 7$ into $y = 40m$ and see whether $y = 280$.

10-6 Exercises and Applications

Assignment Guide

- **Basic**
  1–11, 13, 15–18, 21–27, 31–40
- **Average**
  1–11, 13, 15–18, 20, 23–29, 31–40
- **Enriched**
  2–10, 12, 14–20, 24–40

Exercise Notes

Exercise 19

Problem-Solving Tip You may want to use Teaching Tool Transparencies 2 and 3: Guided Problem Solving, pages 1–2.

Exercise Answers

1. b.

x	1	2	3	4	5
y	4	5	6	7	8

6. $x = -1\frac{1}{2}$; $y = 3$ is halfway between $y = 4$ and $y = 2$, so the x-value is halfway between $x = -2$ and $x = -1$.

15. a. (C-values rounded to the nearest tenth)

d	1	2	3	4	5
C	3.1	6.3	9.4	12.6	15.7

b. $d \approx 3\frac{1}{2}$

Reteaching

Activity

Materials: Centimeter ruler

- Let c be the number of centimeters and m be the corresponding number of millimeters. Write an equation showing the relationship between these variables. (Hint: Look at your ruler. How many millimeters are in one centimeter?) $m = 10c$
- Make a table showing how many millimeters there are in 1 to 5 centimeters.

c	1	2	3	4	5
m	10	20	30	40	50

- How many millimeters are in 4 cm? 3.5 cm? 1.5 cm? 40, 35, 15

10-6 Exercises and Applications

PRACTICE 10-6

Practice and Apply

1. **Getting Started** Follow the steps to solve $8 = x + 3$ by using a table.
   a. Write the related equation for $8 = x + 3$ by replacing 8 with y. $y = x + 3$
   b. Make a table of values for the related equation.
   c. Look for a y-value of 8 in your table. The x-value for this y-value is the solution to the equation. $x = 5$

The table below represents the equation $y = -2x$. Use it to solve the related equations below the table.

x	−2	−1	0	1	2	3	4	6	8
y	4	2	0	−2	−4	−6	−8	−12	−16

2. $-6 = -2x$ $x = 3$
3. $-2x = 4$ $x = -2$
4. $0 = -2x$ $x = 0$
5. $-2x = -8$ $x = 4$
6. **Estimation** Use the table above to estimate the solution to $3 = -2x$. Explain how you found your answer.

Make and use a table to solve each equation.

7. $4 = x - 2$ $x = 6$
8. $3x = 9$ $x = 3$
9. $-16 = 5r + 4$ $r = -4$
10. $200 = 10n - 50$ $n = 25$

Estimation Make and use a table to estimate the solution to each equation.

11. $7 = 2x$ $x = 3\frac{1}{2}$
12. $-5b = 18$ $b \approx -3\frac{1}{2}$
13. $-17 = 3z - 2$ $z = -5$
14. $3\frac{1}{2} = 2k - 7$ $k = 5\frac{1}{4}$
15. **Geometry** Recall that the circumference of a circle is equal to π times its diameter, so $C = \pi d$.
    a. Make a table of values for $C = \pi d$.
    b. Use your table to estimate the diameter of a circle whose circumference is 11 cm.

16. **Industry** Champ Cookies and Things is a business that began in a Washington, DC, school in 1987. Students bought the supplies, baked the cookies, and packaged and sold the cookies. Suppose the ingredients for one dozen cookies cost 35¢. Use a table to decide how many dozen cookies could be made for \$7.70. GPS
    22 dozen

PRACTICE

Name ____________

Practice 10-6

Solving Equations Using Tables

The table below represents the equation $y = 3x + 4$. Use it to solve the related equations below the table.

x	−4	−3	−2	−1	0	1	2	3	4
y	−8	−5	−2	1	4	7	10	13	16

1. $10 = 3x + 4$ $x =$ 2
2. $-5 = 3x + 4$ $x =$ −3
3. $3x + 4 = 16$ $x =$ 4
4. $-8 = 3x + 4$ $x =$ −4
5. Use the table above to estimate the solution to $8 = 3x + 4$. Explain how you found your answer.
   $\approx 1\frac{1}{2}$; Possible answer: If y is between 7 and 10, then x is between 1 and 2.

Make and use a table to solve each equation.

6. $20 = 5x$ $x =$ 4
7. $19 = x + 12$ $x =$ 7
8. $-6 = -3x$ $x =$ 2
9. $-5 = -2x + 5$ $x =$ 5
10. $-54 = 7x - 12$ $x =$ −6
11. $8 = -8x$ $x =$ −1
12. $3 = x - 5$ $x =$ 8
13. $2x - 3 = 9$ $x =$ 6

Make and use a table to estimate the solution to each equation.

14. $30 = 7x$ $x \approx 4\frac{1}{2}$
15. $35 = 5x + 7$ $x \approx 5\frac{1}{2}$
16. $-4x = 10\frac{1}{2}$ $x \approx -2\frac{1}{2}$
17. $-18 = 3x - 4$ $x \approx -4\frac{1}{2}$
18. Suppose a trapezoid has height 10, and one of its bases has length 7. Then the area is given by $A = \frac{1}{2} \cdot 10(7 + x)$, or $A = 35 + 5x$, where x is the length of the other base.
    a. Make a table of values for $A = 35 + 5x$. Possible answer:

x	2	4	6	8	10	12
A	45	55	65	75	85	95

    b. Use your table to estimate the value of x for one of these trapezoids with area 78. About $8\frac{1}{2}$

RETEACHING

Name ____________

Alternative Lesson 10-6

Solving Equations Using Tables

By using a table of x and y values for an equation, you can read the x-value that goes with a specific y-value. You can also use a table of values to solve an equation.

Example 1

Make and use a table to solve the equation $15 = 4x - 1$.

Step 1: Write the *related* equation by replacing 15 with y. → $y = 4x - 1$

Step 2: Make a table of values for x and y.

x	−1	0	1	2	3	4	5	6
y	−5	−1	3	7	11	15	19	23

If y is 15, then x is 4.

Try It Make and use a table to solve $7 = 2x + 1$.

a. Write the related equation. $y = 2x + 1$

b. Complete the table of values for x and y.

x	−1	0	1	2	3	4	5	6
y	−1	1	3	5	7	9	11	13

c. Solve the equation for x. $x = 3$

Make and use a table to solve $7 = 3x - 2$.

d. Write the related equation. $y = 3x - 2$

e. Complete the table of values for x and y.

x	−1	0	1	2	3	4	5	6
y	−5	−2	1	4	7	10	13	16

f. Solve the equation for x. $x = 3$

Make and use a table to solve $8 = 5x + 3$.

g. Write the related equation. $y = 5x + 3$

h. Complete the table of values for x and y.

x	−1	0	1	2	3	4	5	6
y	−2	3	8	13	18	23	28	33

i. Solve the equation for x. $x = 1$

17. Literature In *The Cricket in Times Square,* by George Selden, Mario talks to his mother and father about crickets while he sells newspapers at their newsstand. (Excerpt below from *The Cricket in Times Square* (New York: Farrar, Straus and Giroux, 1960). Copyright ©1960 by George Selden Thompson.)

"So you spend less time playing with cricketers, you'll sell more papers," said Mama.

"Oh now, now," Papa soothed her. "Mario couldn't help it if nobody buys."

"You can tell the temperature with crickets too," said Mario. "You count the number of chirps in a minute, divide by four, and add forty. They're very intelligent."

Make a table to find the number of times a cricket would chirp in a minute if the temperature were 90°F. 200 times

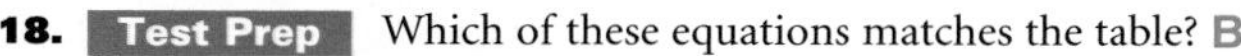

18. Test Prep Which of these equations matches the table? B

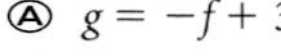

Ⓐ $g = -f + 3$ Ⓑ $g = 1 - 2f$

Ⓒ $g = 2f - 1$ Ⓓ $g = 2 - 3f$

f	−1	0	1	2
g	3	1	−1	−3

PROBLEM SOLVING 10-6

Problem Solving and Reasoning

19. Choose a Strategy Some tables don't come from equations, but they can still be used to make predictions. Use the table to predict the percent of women in the United States who will be working by the year 2000. Explain how you made your prediction.

Women 16 and Over in the Civilian Labor Force

Year	1930	1940	1950	1960	1970	1980	1990
Percent	22.0	25.4	33.9	37.7	43.3	51.5	57.5

Problem Solving STRATEGIES

- Look for a Pattern
- Make an Organized List
- Make a Table
- Guess and Check
- Work Backward
- Use Logical Reasoning
- Draw a Diagram
- Solve a Simpler Problem

20.  When you use a table to solve an equation, how do you decide which *x*-values to use? (*Hint:* Would you choose different values to solve $12 = 3x$ than to solve $27{,}954 = 3x$?)

Mixed Review

Write each percent as a decimal. *[Lesson 8-2]*

21. 50% 0.5 **22.** 20% 0.2 **23.** 90% 0.9 **24.** 2% 0.02 **25.** 7% 0.07

26. 120% 1.2 **27.** 5.6% 0.056 **28.** 22.2% 0.222 **29.** 84.62% 0.8462 **30.** $12\frac{1}{2}$% 0.125

Find each quotient. *[Lesson 9-7]*

31. $-12 \div (-4)$ 3 **32.** $-12 \div 4$ −3 **33.** $0 \div (-17)$ 0 **34.** $22 \div (-2)$ −11 **35.** $-56 \div (-8)$ 7

36. $-44 \div (-1)$ 44 **37.** $-60 \div 15$ −4 **38.** $80 \div (-12)$ $-6\frac{2}{3}$ **39.** $-170 \div 5$ −34 **40.** $-300 \div 0$ Undefined

Exercise Notes

Exercise 19

Error Prevention Students may try to find a pattern in the differences between the *y*-values. Encourage them to look for a more general way to approach this problem, by considering the average increase.

Exercise Answers

19. Possible answer: about 63.4%; Average change in a decade ≈ 5.9%, 57.5 + 5.9 = 63.4.

20. Test numbers to find ones that give values close to the desired number; choose a range of these numbers.

Alternate Assessment

Interview Have students observe each other as they solve problems like those in Exercises 7–14. Ask the person doing the problem to think aloud, while the other person observes. At the end of each problem, ask the observer to comment on what the "doer" did well and what he/she needs to work on.

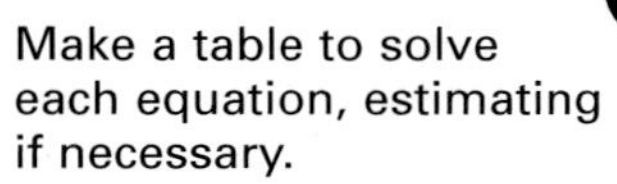

Quick Quiz

Make a table to solve each equation, estimating if necessary.

1. $8 = 4x - 12$ $x = 5$
2. $-4 = 4x - 12$ $x = 2$
3. $-2 = 4x - 12$ $x = 2.5$

Available on Daily Transparency 10-6

PROBLEM SOLVING

Name ____________

Guided Problem Solving 10-6

GPS PROBLEM 16, STUDENT PAGE 510

Champ Cookies and Things is a business that began in a Washington, DC, school in 1987. Students bought the supplies, baked the cookies, and packaged and sold the cookies. Suppose the ingredients for one dozen cookies cost 35¢. Use a table to decide how many dozen cookies could be made for $7.70.

— Understand —

1. How much do the ingredients cost to make one dozen cookies? 35¢
2. Underline what you are asked to find.

— Plan —

3. Will you use negative numbers in your table? Explain. No, you can't make a negative number of cookies.
4. Complete the tables below to help you decide the answer to the question.

Number of dozen	1	2	3	4	5	10	12	14
Cost ($)	0.35	0.70	1.05	1.40	1.75	3.50	4.20	4.90

Number of dozen	16	18	20	22	24	26	28	30
Cost ($)	5.60	6.30	7.00	7.70	8.40	9.10	9.80	10.50

— Solve —

5. How many dozen cookies could be made for $7.70? 22 dozen.

— Look Back —

6. How can you use division to check your answer? Divide: $7.70 ÷ 22 = $0.35, the cost for 1 dozen.

SOLVE ANOTHER PROBLEM

Suppose a package of three disks costs $1.95. Complete the table to find how many packages can be bought for $9.75. 5 packages.

Package of disks	1	2	3	4	5	6	7
Cost ($)	1.95	3.90	5.85	7.80	9.75	11.70	13.65

ENRICHMENT

Name ____________

Extend Your Thinking 10-6

Visual Thinking

Many of the shapes are exactly alike.

1. Circle the shape that has no match.
2. How many different shapes can you find? 26 different shapes.

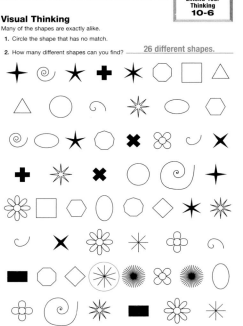

INTERACTIVE LESSON

10-7 Lesson Organizer

Objective

- Use graphs to solve equations.

Materials

- Explore: Graphing utility

NCTM Standards

- 1–4, 7, 8, 9

Review

For each equation, find the values of y when $x = -2$, 0, 2, and 4.

1. $y = -4x$ 8, 0, −8, −16
2. $y = 4x - 10$ −18, −10, −2, 6

Available on Daily Transparency 10-7

1 Introduce

Explore  

You may want to use Teaching Tool Transparencies 8: Coordinate Grids, and 23: Graphing Calculator with this lesson.

The Point
Students learn to solve an equation by graphing it on a graphing calculator. They use TRACE to find x-values corresponding to specific y-values.

Ongoing Assessment
Students with limited experience in using the graphing utility may need to have its use demonstrated before beginning **Explore**. Students may also need guidance in selecting an appropriate viewing window, such as [0, 1500] by [−1000,5000]. On many graphing utilities, it may not be possible to find y-values of 0 and 4500 without zooming or changing the viewing window to look at a smaller part of the graph.

For Groups That Finish Early
Suppose the store manager finds that the store earns only $3 for each rack sold. Write the new equation relating x and y and use the graphing utility to find the break-even point. $y = 3x - 1000$, about 333 cookie racks

10-7 Solving Equations Using Graphs

You'll Learn ...

- to use graphs to solve equations

... How It's Used

Materials scientists "design" the metals and plastics that products are made from. They consult graphs to decide whether a material will be a solid, liquid, or gas at a particular temperature and pressure.

▶ Lesson Link You've used tables and graphs to solve one-step equations. Now you'll use these methods to solve two-step equations. ◀

Explore Equations and Graphs

Racking Up the Profits

Materials: Graphing utility

In 1992, Lizzie Denis and Louise Kramer of St. Paul, Minnesota, decided that cookies take too long to bake in a single-layer pan. So the two 11-year-olds invented the Double Decker Baking Rack. Their company, L&L Products, markets the rack through stores and catalogs. It sells for about $20.

Suppose a store buys $1000 worth of racks and earns $4 for each rack sold. The store's manager wants to know how many racks the store needs to sell:

- To break even ($0 profit)
- To make $4500

1. Let x represent the number of racks sold, and let y represent the amount of money made. Write an equation in the form $y =$ ______ relating x and y. Remember to subtract the original $1000 investment.
2. Graph the equation on a graphing utility. Describe the graph.

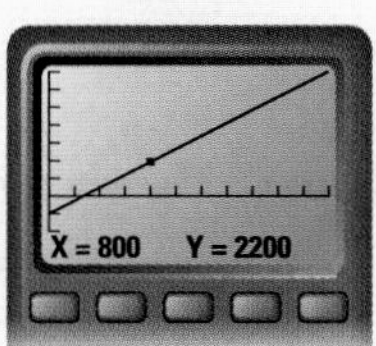

3. To find out how many racks need to be sold to reach the break-even point ($0 profit), use TRACE to move along your graph until the y-value equals 0. What is the x-value? What does this tell you?
4. Use TRACE to find out how many racks need to be sold for the store to earn $4500.

MEETING INDIVIDUAL NEEDS

Resources

10-7 Practice
10-7 Reteaching
10-7 Problem Solving
10-7 Enrichment
10-7 Daily Transparency
Problem of the Day
Review
Quick Quiz
Teaching Tool Transparencies 8, 23
Technology Master 48
Interactive CD-ROM Lesson 10

Learning Modalities

Kinesthetic Use "human graphs" to solve equations. Mark off a coordinate plane on the floor of the classroom and assign x-values to a few students. When an equation is written on the board, these students evaluate the expression for their x-value and move to that location. Connect the students with a ribbon or rope. Have another student find the x-value corresponding to a particular y-value by starting at the y-value on the y-axis, walking to the ribbon or cord, turning, and walking to the x-axis to read the corresponding x-value.

Visual Have students use a graphing utility to solve more realistic problems involving equations. Point out that a graphing utility is especially useful when numbers are not easy to work with.

Challenge

Have students use a graphing utility to solve more complex equations, such as $7 = 3x^2 + 2x - 5$. This will demonstrate the power of the graphing utility more clearly.

Learn Solving Equations Using Graphs

Just as you can with a table, you can use a graph to find the value of x that goes with a particular value of y.

Example 1

Graph $y = -2x$. Then find the values of x when y is -2 and 4.

x	-1	0	1	2
y	2	0	-2	-4

Make a table of a few values for the equation.

Plot the points on a coordinate plane and connect them.

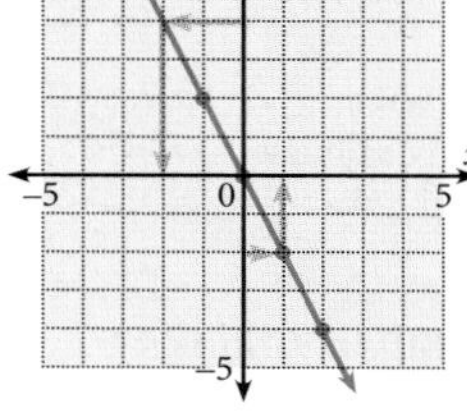
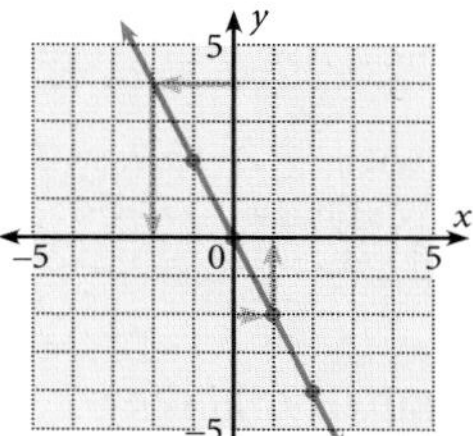

To find the value of x when $y = -2$, go to -2 on the y-axis. Then move across to the line. When you reach the line, move up to the x-axis.

When $y = -2$, $x = 1$.

You can use the same method to find the value of x when $y = 4$. In this case, you need to move *down* from the line to reach the x-axis.

When $y = 4$, $x = -2$.

You can use a graph to solve an equation.

Example 2

Use a graph to solve $16 = 3x - 8$.

Graph the *related* equation $y = 3x - 8$.

x	-2	0	2	4
y	-14	-8	-2	4

Go to 16 on the y-axis. Move across to the line, then down to the x-axis. You reach the x-axis at 8.

The solution is $x = 8$.

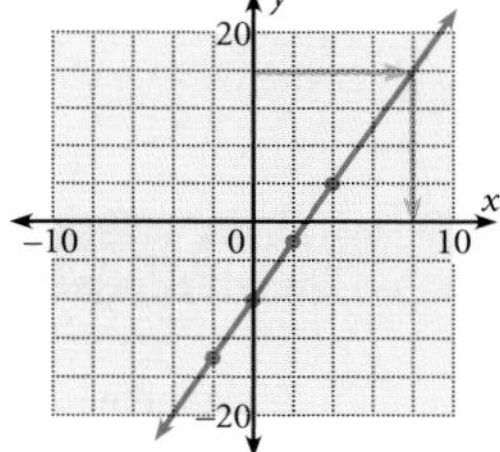

Try It

Use a graph to solve each equation.

a. $4 = x - 2$ $x = 6$

b. $12 = -3x$ $x = -4$

c. $-10 = 4x + 2$ $x = -3$

▶ History Link

In 1903, an African American, Maggie Lena Walker, became the first female bank president in the United States. She founded Saint Luke's Penny-Saving bank in Richmond, Virginia. During the Great Depression, Walker's bank merged with others to become the Richmond Consolidated Bank and Trust.

Problem Solving TIP

Be sure you make the scale on the y-axis large enough to include the value you're looking for—here, the y-axis needed to include 16.

MATH EVERY DAY

▶ Problem of the Day

Draw the next figure.

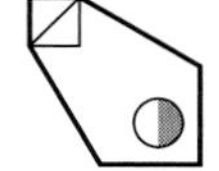 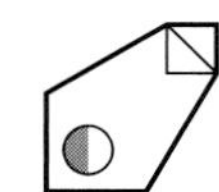 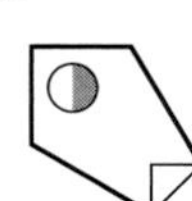

Possible answer:

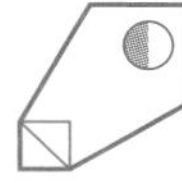

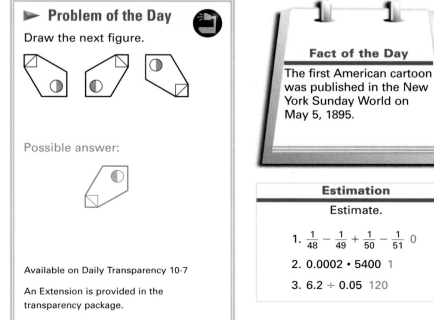

Available on Daily Transparency 10-7

An Extension is provided in the transparency package.

Fact of the Day

The first American cartoon was published in the New York Sunday World on May 5, 1895.

Estimation

Estimate.

1. $\frac{1}{48} - \frac{1}{49} + \frac{1}{50} - \frac{1}{51}$ 0
2. $0.0002 \cdot 5400$ 1
3. $6.2 \div 0.05$ 120

Answers for Explore

Possible Answers

1. $y = 4x - 1000$
2. Graph is a straight line that slants up to the right.
3. $x = 250$; Need to sell 250 racks to recover $1000 investment.
4. $y = 1375$

2 Teach

Learn

Alternate Examples

1. Graph $y = x - 5$. Then find the value of x when y is -2 and 0.

   Make a table. Plot the points and connect them.

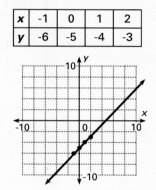

x	-1	0	1	2
y	-6	-5	-4	-3

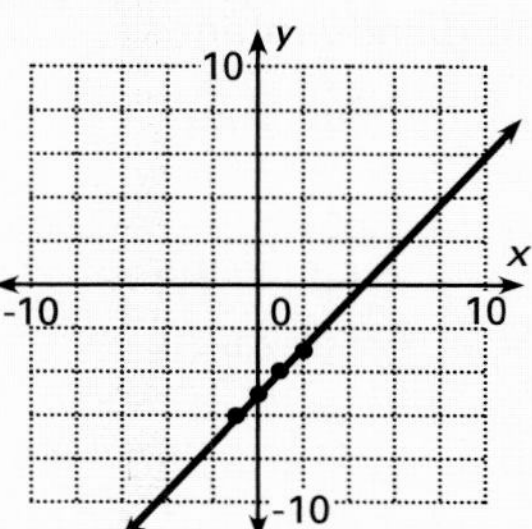

   To find the value of x when $y = -2$, go to -2 on the y-axis. Move across to the line and then move up to the x-axis. When $y = -2$, $x = 3$. Similarly, when $y = 0$, $x = 5$.

2. Use a graph to solve $5 = -3x - 10$.

   Make a table of values for the related equation $y = -3x - 10$. Plot and connect the points.

x	-1	0	1	2
y	-7	-10	-13	-16

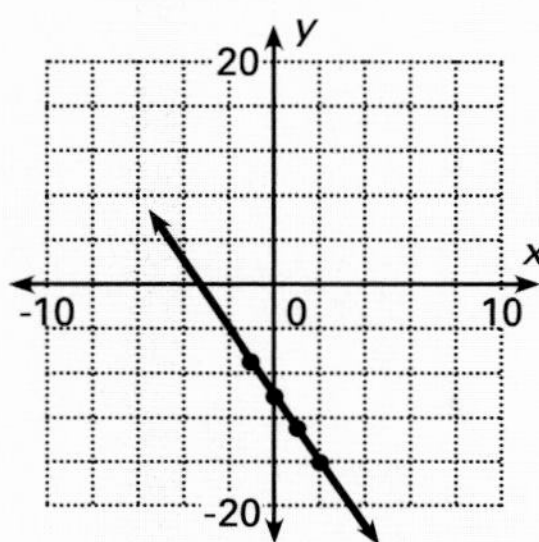

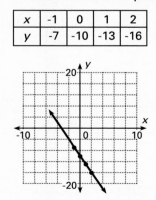

   Go to 5 on the y-axis. Move across to the line, then down to the x-axis. You hit the x-axis at -5. The solution is $x = -5$.

Students see two methods of solving an equation. One method uses a table of values, and the other uses a graph. Students can decide which of the two methods is easier for them.

Answers for What Do You Think?

1. This was the one-day profit.
2. Profit was $10 for each comic book sold less the $65 paid.

3 Practice and Assess

Check

Students should understand that both tables and graphs are useful strategies for solving equations, but that each strategy has advantages and disadvantages.

Answers for Check Your Understanding

1. Answers may vary. Tables may be more effective for a limited range of values, graphs for a wider range.
2. If you move horizontally, the y-value does not change, so you find a point with the y-value you're looking for.

Ben Narasin is the founder of Boston Prepatory Co. sportswear. He got his first taste of big business at age 12 when he paid $65 to buy and sell comics at a comic book convention. His one-day profit: $2500!

Suppose you pay $65 to sell n comic books at an average profit of $10. Your profit, p, is given by $p = 10n - 65$. How many comic books would you need to sell to earn $2500?

Will thinks ...

I'll use the equation $p = 10n - 65$ to make a table.

Number of Comics Sold, n	50	100	150	200	250	300
Profit, p ($)	435	935	1435	1935	2435	2935

At $p = 2435$, $n = 250$. 2500 is a little more than 2435, so I'll estimate $n = 260$. I'd need to sell about 260 comic books.

Kimberly thinks ...

I'll graph the equation $p = 10n - 65$ first.

Starting at $p = 2500$ on the "Profit" axis, I'll move over to the line, then down. I end at about 260 on the "Comic Books" axis.

I'd need to sell about 260 comic books.

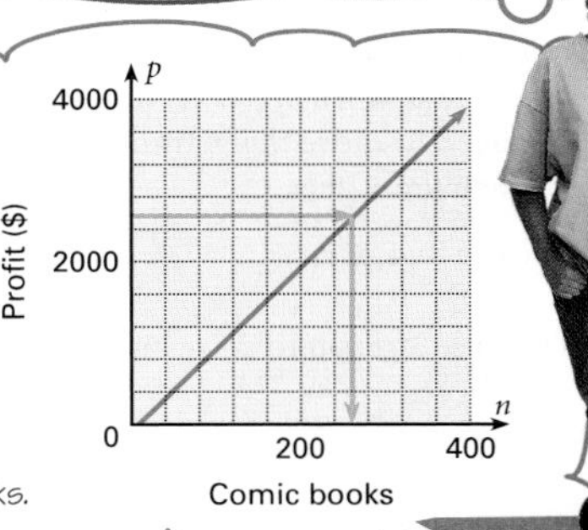

What do you think?

1. Why did Will and Kimberly both look for $p = 2500$?
2. Why does $p = 10n - 65$ give the amount of profit?

Check Your Understanding

1. Is it easier to use a table or a graph to estimate solutions? Explain.
2. When you solve an equation by graphing, why do you need to move across to the graph from a point on the y-axis instead of moving up or down?

MEETING MIDDLE SCHOOL CLASSROOM NEEDS

Tips from Middle School Teachers

This lesson provides an excellent opportunity to do some real-world problems that will help students be better consumers. I use information about different cable TV plans, different phone companies, and different banks to set up situations in which graphs can be used to solve equations. Frequently, the students find that different plans are better for different people, depending on how much of a particular service they are going to be using regularly.

Team Teaching

Work with the social studies teachers to identify consumer education situations in which graphs can be used to solve equations. Show them how a graphing utility can be useful in solving these problems.

Literature Connection

The first real comic book was published in 1929. Thirteen issues of *The Funnies* were published, and the colored pages were of newspaper size. In 1934, *Famous Funnies* was the first comic book to be sold on newstands.

10-7 Exercises and Applications

Practice and Apply

Getting Started A graph of $y = x + 3$ is shown at the right. Use it to solve the related equations.

1. $2 = x + 3$ $x = -1$ **2.** $x + 3 = -1$ $x = -4$ **3.** $4 = x + 3$ $x = 1$ **4.** $x + 3 = 0$ $x = -3$

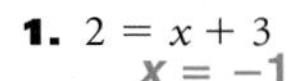

5. Estimation Use the graph to estimate the solution to $\frac{1}{2} = x + 3$. Explain how you found your answer.

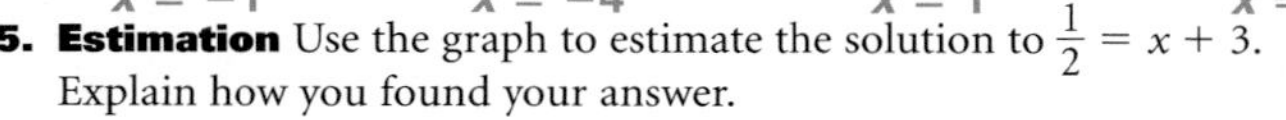

6. Follow the steps to solve $10 = 3x - 2$ by graphing.

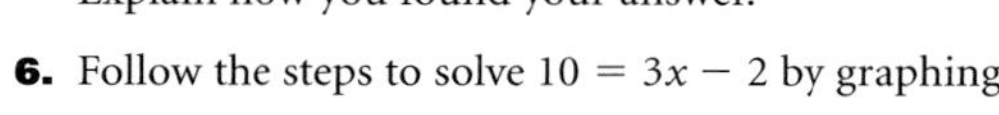

a. Write the related equation for $10 = 3x - 2$ by replacing 10 with y. $y = 3x - 2$

b. Make a table of values for the related equation.

c. Plot the points in your table on a coordinate plane. Connect the points.

d. Start at 10 on the y-axis of your coordinate plane. Go across until you reach the graph. Then drop vertically to the x-axis and read the solution. $x = 4$

Use a graph to solve each equation.

7. $5 = x + 3$ $x = 2$ **8.** $2x = 8$ $x = 4$ **9.** $-5 = 3p - 2$ $p = -1$ **10.** $500 = 8n - 100$ $n = 75$

Estimation Use a graph to estimate the solution to each equation.

11. $6 = 2x - 3$ $x = 4\frac{1}{2}$ **12.** $-7 = 4x + 2$ $x = -2\frac{1}{4}$ **13.** $35 = -3t - 11$ $t = -15\frac{1}{3}$ **14.** $22.75 = 5n - 8$ $n \approx 6.2$

15. Problem Solving When you *lease* an automobile, you return it to the dealer after you have driven it for a certain amount of time. Suppose a car lease requires an initial payment of \$1500 and payments of \$300 at the end of each month. After how many months will the total cost of the lease be \$4500? Use a graph to answer this question. 10 months

16. Test Prep Darryl is going on a business trip. His company allows him \$140 per day in expenses, up to a total of \$1000. Which equation can Darryl use to find the greatest number of days his expenses can last? A

Ⓐ $1000 = 140d$ Ⓑ $1000 = \frac{d}{140}$

Ⓒ $d = 140 \cdot 1000$ Ⓓ $1000 = \frac{140}{d}$

PRACTICE

Name ____________________

Practice 10-7

Solving Equations Using Graphs

1. Follow the steps to solve $1 = -2x + 3$ by graphing. Possible answer:

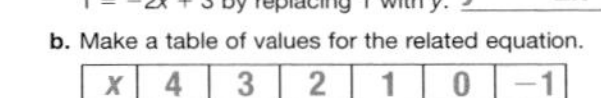

a. Write the related equation for $1 = -2x + 3$ by replacing 1 with y. $y = -2x + 3$

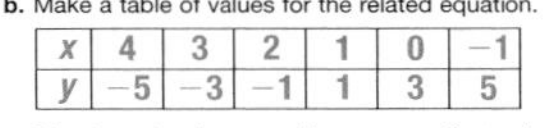

b. Make a table of values for the related equation.

x	4	3	2	1	0	−1
y	−5	−3	−1	1	3	5

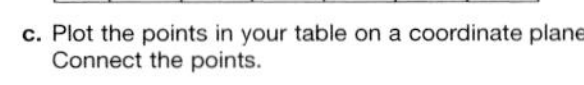

c. Plot the points in your table on a coordinate plane. Connect the points.

d. Start at 1 on the y-axis of your coordinate plane. Go across until you reach the graph. Then, drop vertically to the x-axis, and read the solution. $x =$ 1

2. Use your graph above to estimate the solution to $-3\frac{1}{2} = -2x + 3$.

$x \approx 3\frac{1}{4}$; Possible answer: When $y = -3\frac{1}{2}$, $x \approx 3\frac{1}{4}$.

Use a graph to solve each equation. Possible answers:

3. $-4x = 12$ $x =$ −3 4. $17 = -2x + 9$ $x =$ −4 5. $-15 = 3x - 6$ $x =$ −3 6. $11 = -5x - 4$ $x =$ −3

7. $10 = 2k - 4$ $k =$ 7 8. $p + 6 = 11$ $p =$ 5 9. $-13 = 5h - 3$ $h =$ −2 10. $-5 = -4m + 7$ $m =$ 3

Use a graph to estimate the solution to each equation.

11. $6 = 4x + 17$ $x \approx$ −3 12. $15 = -3u + 8$ $u \approx$ −2 13. $-10 = 7p - 5$ $p \approx$ −1 14. $15 = -5b + 8$ $b \approx$ −1

15. The MaxiTaxi Company charges \$1.00 per mile, plus a base charge of \$2.50 per trip. The cost, c, to travel d miles is given by $c = d + 2.5$.

a. Graph this equation.

b. Melinda paid \$8.00 for her taxi ride. How far did she go? 5.5 mi

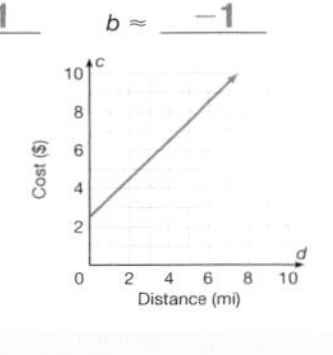

RETEACHING

Name ____________________

Alternative Lesson 10-7

Solving Equations Using Graphs

You can use a graph to find the value of x that goes with a particular value of y. You can also use a graph to solve an equation.

Example

Use a graph to solve $9 = 2x - 1$.

Step 1: Write the *related* equation by replacing 9 with y. → $y = 2x - 1$

Step 2: Make a table of values for x and y.

x	−1	0	1	2	3
y	−3	−1	1	3	5

Step 3: Plot and connect the points.

Step 4: Locate 9 on the y-axis. Move across to the line you drew.

Step 5: Move straight down to the x-axis. The number on the x-axis is 5.

The solution is $x = 5$.

Try It Use a graph to solve $-3 = x + 2$.

a. Write the related equation. $y = x + 2$

b. Complete the table of values for x and y.

x	−1	0	1	2	3
y	1	2	3	4	5

c. Plot and connect the points. Use the related equation to label the graph.

d. Locate −3 on the y-axis. Move across to the line you drew. What number is on the x-axis? −5

e. What is the solution? $x = -5$

Use a graph to solve $4 = x - 3$.

f. Write the related equation. $y = x - 3$

g. Complete the table of values for x and y. Then plot and connect the points on the above grid. Use the related equation to label the graph.

x	0	1	2	3	4	5
y	−3	−2	−1	0	1	2

h. What is the solution? $x = 7$

10-7 Exercises and Applications

Assignment Guide

- **Basic** 1–9, 11, 12, 15, 16, 19–33 odds
- **Average** 1–11, 13, 15–17, 19, 20–34 evens
- **Enriched** 1–5, 7–10, 12, 14–19, 20–34 evens

Exercise Answers

5. $x = -2\frac{1}{2}$; Go to $\frac{1}{2}$ on the y-axis, then move left to the line, then down to the x-axis.

6. b.

x	−1	0	1	2	3
y	−5	−2	1	4	7

c.

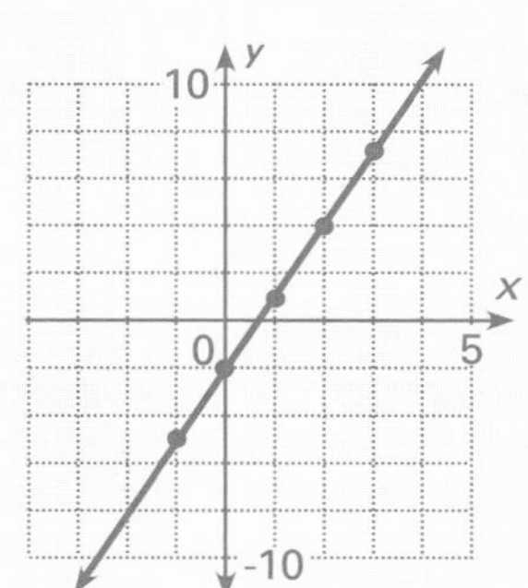

Reteaching

Activity

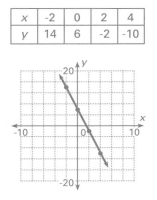

Materials: Graph paper, ruler, uncooked spaghetti

- Make a table of values for the equation $y = -4x + 6$. Then plot the points on a coordinate plane and use your ruler to connect them.

x	-2	0	2	4
y	14	6	-2	-10

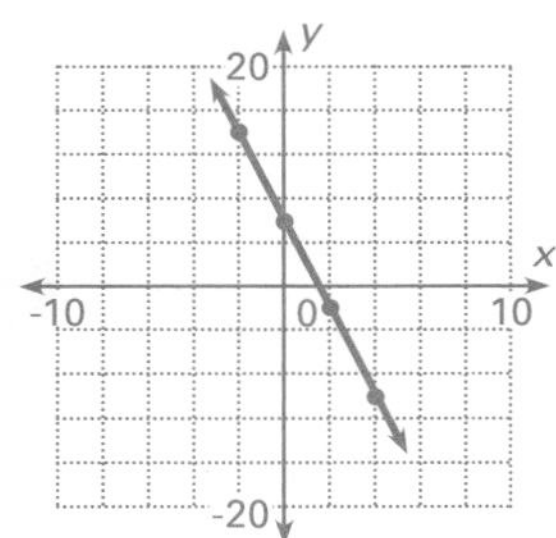

- Lay a piece of spaghetti horizontally across the grid at $y = -6$. Where it crosses your graph, lay another piece of spaghetti vertically. To solve $-6 = -4x + 6$, read the x-value for the second piece of spaghetti. $x = 3$

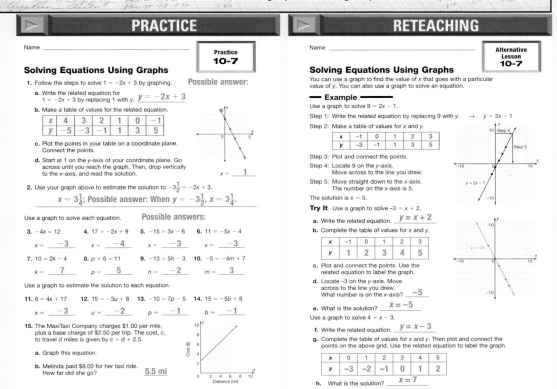

Exercise Notes

Exercise 19

Consumer Have students find out about bank charges in your community. Compare which banks charge less in which circumstances by making graphs for each.

Exercise Answers

17. a. $2n$ dollars

b. $1,200

c. $y = 2n - 1200$

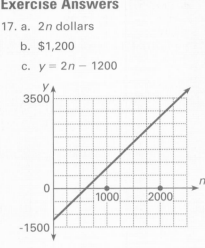

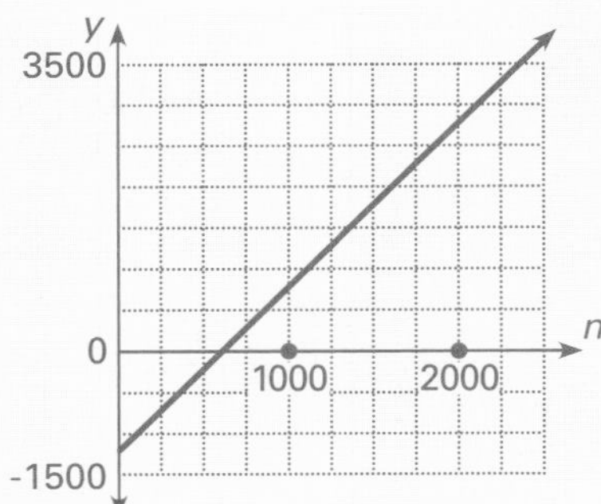

d. 2100 items; Go to 3000 on the y-axis, then move right to the line, then down to the n-axis.

18. a. $50,000: at least 3334 toys; $125,000: at least 8334 toys; $250,000: at least 16,667 toys.

b. Might use the table to show specific numbers and the graph to show general trends; The graph is more visual, the table can show more precise numbers.

19. a. $A = 5 + 0.25c$

b. $7.50

c. 15 checks; Make a table or graph to help solve $8.75 = 5 + 0.25x$.

Alternate Assessment

Portfolio Have students choose one or two exercises that best exemplify the concepts of this lesson.

Quick Quiz

Solve each equation by graphing.

1. $-1 = 2x + 9$ $x = -5$
2. $0 = -5x - 10$ $x = -2$
3. $4 = -3x + 6$ $x = \frac{2}{3}$

Available on Daily Transparency 10-7

PROBLEM SOLVING 10-7

17. **Industry** When she was in fifth grade, Alexia Abernathy of Cedar Rapids, Iowa, invented the Oops! Proof™ spill-proof bowl. She gets part of the money from the sales of her bowl.

Suppose a family spends $1200 developing an invention, and that they earn $2.00 for each one sold.

a. How much money does the family earn if n items are sold?

b. What were the family's expenses?

c. *Profit* is the difference between money earned *(income)* and expenses. Write an equation for the profit. Graph the equation.

d. How many items must be sold to have a profit of $3000? Explain how you found your answer.

Problem Solving and Reasoning

18. **Critical Thinking** You are a vice president at a toy company. You are going to make a presentation about a new toy that sells for $15.

a. You think people will want to know how many toys the company would need to sell to make $50,000, $125,000, and $250,000. Prepare a graph and a table to answer these questions. What are the answers?

b. In the actual presentation, when might you use the table? When might you use the graph? Explain the advantages and disadvantages of each.

19. **Communicate** Suppose a bank charges its customers $5.00 each month plus a $0.25 fee for each check they write during that month.

a. Write an equation for the total amount the bank would charge a customer in one month.

b. How much would a customer be charged if she wrote 10 checks in a month?

c. If a customer were charged $8.75, how many checks did he write? Explain.

Mixed Review

Write each fraction as a percent. *[Lesson 8-3]*

20. $\frac{1}{1000}$ 0.1% **21.** $\frac{135}{100}$ 135% **22.** $\frac{920}{100}$ 920% **23.** $\frac{\frac{1}{2}}{100}$ 0.5% **24.** $\frac{57}{10}$ 570%

Write the opposite of each integer. *[Lesson 9-1]*

25. 7 −7 **26.** −5 5 **27.** −417 417 **28.** 550 −550 **29.** −114 114

30. 5,040 −5,040 **31.** −22,714 22,714 **32.** 101 −101 **33.** 4×10^4 -4×10^4 **34.** 0 0

PROBLEM SOLVING

Name ____________

Guided Problem Solving 10-7

GPS PROBLEM 15, STUDENT PAGE 515

When you *lease* an automobile, you return it to the dealer after you have driven it for a certain amount of time. Suppose a car lease requires an initial payment of $1500 and payments of $300 at the end of each month. After how many months will the total cost of the lease be $4500? Use a graph to answer this question.

Possible answers: Items 5 and 8

— Understand —

1. Write the amount of each payment.

   a. Initial payment $1500 b. Monthly payment $300

2. Underline what you are asked to find.

— Plan —

3. Which equation shows the cost (y) of the lease after x months? C

   a. $y = 1500x + 300$ b. $1500 = x + 300$ c. $y = 1500 + 300x$

4. Complete the table of values.

x	1	2	3	4
y	1800	2100	2400	2700

5. What scale will you use for your graph?

   x-axis: 1 unit = 1 month

   y-axis: 1 unit = $300

— Solve —

6. Plot and connect the points from the table in Item 4.

7. After how many months will the total cost of the lease be $4500? 10

— Look Back —

8. How can you check your answer? Substitute the answer into the equation for x and make sure y is equal to 4500.

SOLVE ANOTHER PROBLEM

The initial payment on a car lease is $1200. Each monthly payment is $250. Graph the data on the grid above to find how many months it will be until the cost of the lease is $2700. 6 months.

ENRICHMENT

Name ____________

Extend Your Thinking 10-7

Decision Making

Many banks have different types of checking accounts available. The type of account you open depends upon how many checks you write each month and how much money you plan to keep in your account.

Here are the charges from one bank:

Basic Account	$5 per month, plus $0.10 per check
Student Account	$0.20 per check for the first 10 checks each month, $1 per check for each check over 10
$1000 Minimum Balance Account	$0.10 per check

1. Make a graph that shows the monthly fees related to the number of checks written for each type of account.

2. Suppose you are a student who writes about 5 checks per month.

   a. Which account will you open? Student account.

   b. About how much will your monthly fees be? About $1.

3. Suppose you are a student who writes 20 checks per month.

   a. Which account will open? Possible answer: Basic account.

   b. How much will your monthly fees be? Possible answer: $7.00

   c. Suppose you have $1000 earning 4.8% interest each year. Should you open the $1000 minimum balance checking account instead of the basic account? Explain. If so, how much money will you save?

   Possible answer: Yes. Savings in fees by switching from basic to minimum balance are $5.00. You lose the $4.00/month interest you were earning bringing the actual savings per month to $1.00.

Relating Equations and Inequalities

10-8

▶ Lesson Link You've used tables and graphs to solve equations. Now you'll use your knowledge of equations to solve inequalities. ◀

Explore Inequalities

Net Profits

As high school juniors, Rachel Rief and Margaret Kowalski founded FUNdamentals Summer Soccer Camp Just-For-Girls in Yakima, Washington. They charged \$22 per player for a week of soccer training.

1. Make a table showing the income for training 1 to 10 players. Let n represent the number of players.
2. In your table, find the value(s) of n that will produce an income that is:
   a. Equal to \$110 b. Less than \$110 c. Greater than \$110
3. Explain how you found these values from your table.

You'll Learn ...

- to graph inequalities on a number line
- to write the inequality represented by a graph

... How It's Used

Inequalities are used to describe how long you can talk on a telephone before the rates change.

Vocabulary

inequality

solutions of an inequality

Learn Relating Equations and Inequalities

An equation consists of two expressions separated by an equal sign. Two expressions separated by an inequality sign form an **inequality**. Examples of inequalities include $4 + 3 < 12$, $5 - 2 \leq 3$, and $x + 12 \geq 15$.

The **solutions of an inequality** are the values that make the inequality true. They can be graphed on a number line. A filled-in circle shows that the number below it satisfies the inequality.

$x > -2$ ("greater than")

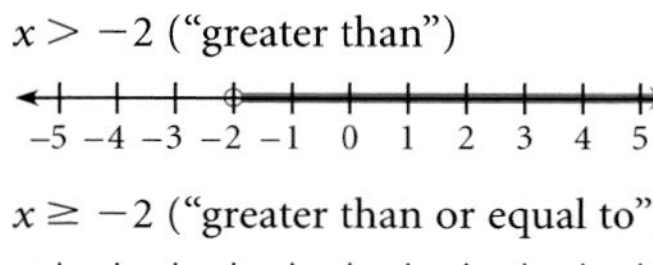

$x < -2$ ("less than")

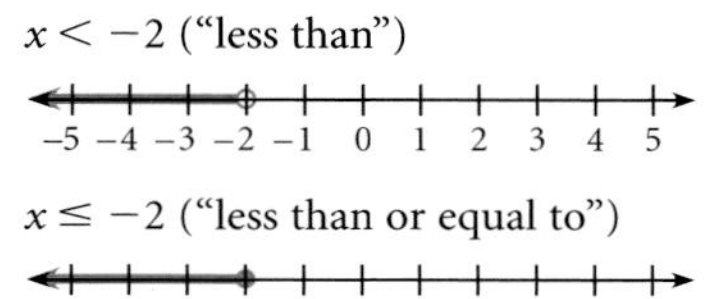

$x \geq -2$ ("greater than or equal to")

$x \leq -2$ ("less than or equal to")

MEETING INDIVIDUAL NEEDS

Resources

10-8 Practice
10-8 Reteaching
10-8 Problem Solving
10-8 Enrichment
10-8 Daily Transparency
- Problem of the Day
- Review
- Quick Quiz

Teaching Tool Transparency 5
Chapter 10 Project Master

Learning Modalities

Verbal Have students make a checklist to help them graph inequalities. Their checklists should include questions to ask themselves as they draw the graphs.

Visual Before drawing the arrow when graphing an inequality, some students may find it helpful to first locate points on the number line that satisfy the inequality.

Social Have students take turns drawing the graphs of an inequality on a number line and then telling what inequality is graphed.

Inclusion

Some students may have difficulty in drawing accurate number lines. It may be helpful to give them a handout that has number lines already drawn, with intervals marked but not yet labeled.

10-8 Lesson Organizer

Objectives

- Graph inequalities on a number line.
- Write the inequality represented by a graph.

Vocabulary

- Inequality, solutions of an inequality

NCTM Standards

- 1–4, 8, 9

▶ Review

True or false?

1. $5 < 8$ True
2. $7 > -7$ True
3. $-10 > 0$ False
4. $10 < -10$ False

Available on Daily Transparency 10-8

1 Introduce

Explore

You may want to use Teaching Tool Transparency 5: Number Lines with this lesson.

The Point

Students make a table and use it to solve an equation and two related inequalities.

Ongoing Assessment

Watch for students who forget they are looking for the number of players (n) rather than the income.

Answers for Explore

1. See page C5.
2. a. 5 players
   b. Less than 5 players
   c. More than 5 players
3. Look in the table for income of \$110, less than \$110, and greater than \$110. For each find the corresponding number(s) of players.

2 Teach

Learn

Alternate Examples

1. Graph the inequality $x \leq 4$ on a number line.

   The x values less than 4 are to the left of 4. Since the inequality has a less than *or equal to* sign, the circle is filled in.

2. Write an inequality for the graph.

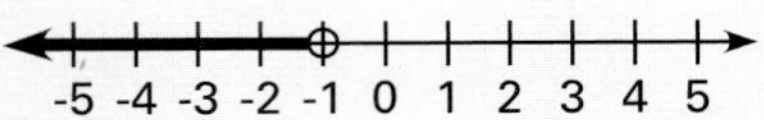

   The inequality includes points less than -1, but does not include -1. The inequality $x < -1$ fits the graph.

3. Write a real-world statement for the inequality $k > 225$.

   The statement shows a quantity greater than 225. So, the statement "We sold more than 225 notebooks last week" fits.

4. Write an inequality for the statement "We made less than $500 in ticket sales last week." Graph the inequality.

   Let p = profits. So $p < \$500$.

   The arrow points to the left because the inequality is "less than." The circle is open.

Answers for Try It

Example 2

a.

Example 4

3 Practice and Assess

Check

Answers for Check Your Understanding

1. Check that values covered by the arrow make the inequality true. If the circle is filled in, check that value also.
2. Yes; If an x-value is greater than 4, then 4 must be less than that value.

Remember

The numbers on a horizontal number line increase from left to right. [Page 437]

Examples

1 Graph the inequality $x \geq 3$ on a number line.

The x values *greater* than 3 are to the right of 3. Since the inequality has a greater than *or equal to* sign, the circle is filled in.

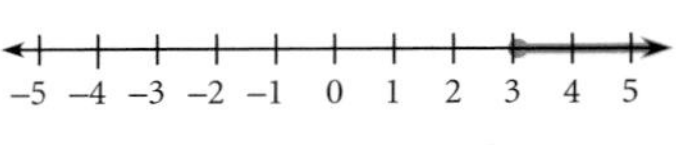

2 Write an inequality for the graph.

The inequality includes points less than 1, but does not include 1.

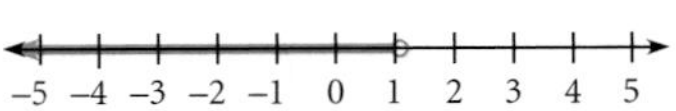

The inequality $x < 1$ fits the graph.

Try It

a. Graph the inequality $x \leq -1$.

b. Write an inequality for the graph. $x > -3$

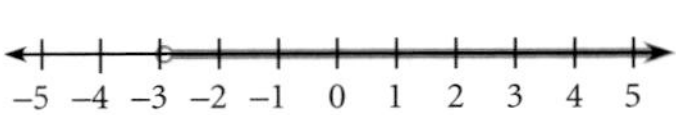

Study TIP

The larger end of the inequality sign opens toward the larger number.

Examples

3 Write a real-world statement for the inequality $n < 150$.

The statement shows a quantity that is less than 150. So a statement like "The number of skateboards sold last week was less than 150" fits the inequality.

4 Write an inequality for the statement "Last week's profits were greater than $800." Graph the inequality.

Let p = profits. — Define a variable.

$p > 800$ — Use an inequality symbol to write an inequality.

The arrow points to the right because the inequality is "greater than." The circle is open.

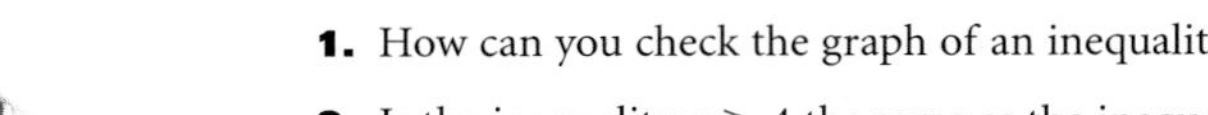

Try It

Write an inequality for the statement "The cost of advertising soccer camp was less than $450." Graph the inequality. $A < 450$

Check Your Understanding

1. How can you check the graph of an inequality?
2. Is the inequality $x > 4$ the same as the inequality $4 < x$? Explain.

MATH EVERY DAY

Problem of the Day

Larry left Kent at noon traveling toward Pearl City at 40 miles per hour. Betsy left Pearl City at 2 P.M. traveling toward Kent on the same road that Larry was on. Betsy drove at 50 miles per hour. Betsy and Larry passed each other at 4 P.M. How far apart are Kent and Pearl City on the road that Larry and Betsy took? 260 miles

Available on Daily Transparency 10-8

An Extension is provided in the transparency package.

Fact of the Day

The game of soccer was first played in England in the 19th century. The first World Cup Soccer competition to be played in the United States was in 1994.

Mental Math

Do these mentally.

1. 25% of 200 50
2. 15% of 80 12
3. 50% of 84 42

10-8 Exercises and Applications

Practice and Apply

1. **Getting Started** Follow the steps to graph the inequality $x \leq -3$.
   a. Draw a number line that includes -3.
   b. Make a circle at -3. Since the inequality includes the "equal to" possibility, fill in the circle.
   c. Since x-values *less than* -3 make the inequality true, draw an arrow that starts at the filled-in circle and goes to the left.

Graph each inequality on a number line.

2. $x > 1$ **3.** $x \geq 0$ **4.** $k \leq 4$ **5.** $t > -3$ **6.** $x \geq 7$
7. $p \leq 40$ **8.** $r > 25$ **9.** $d \geq 100$ **10.** $n < -32$ **11.** $v \geq 2{,}000$

For each inequality, tell whether the number in bold is a solution.

12. $x > 4$; **8** Yes **13.** $z > -12$; **−13** No **14.** $x + 4 \geq 7$; **3** Yes **15.** $2m \leq -5$; **−3** Yes **16.** $2x + 1 < 0$; **−1** Yes

Write an inequality for each graph.

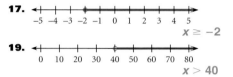

17. $x \geq -2$

18. $x < -1$

19. $x > 40$

20. $x \leq -9$

Write a real-world statement for each inequality.

21. $n > 150$ **22.** $t \leq 12$ **23.** $g \geq 90$ **24.** $t \leq 0.06$ **25.** $s \leq 65$

26. Industry Stephen Lovett started his own car-washing business at age 13. Within 5 years, it grew into a custom cleaning and car detailing business. Lovett charged up to \$80 to work on a car.
   a. Write an inequality to represent the amount Lovett charged to work on a car.
   b. Draw a graph of the inequality you wrote in **a.**

Write and graph an inequality for each statement.

27. Every item in the store costs a dollar or less! $C \leq 1$

28. The population of China is at least 1,000,000,000 people.

10-8 Exercises and Applications

Assignment Guide

- **Basic**
  1–11 odds, 12–20, 21–27 odds, 28–31, 33–46
- **Average**
  2–10 evens, 12–20, 22–28 evens, 30–46
- **Enriched**
  2–10 evens, 12–20, 22–26 evens, 28–46

PRACTICE 10-8

Exercise Notes

Exercises 2–11

Error Prevention The choice of an open or closed circle on inequality graphs is difficult for some students. Have students check their work by rereading the inequality and comparing it to the graph.

Project Progress

You may want to have students use Chapter 10 Project Master.

Exercise Answers

Answers for Exercises 1–11 and 21–28 on page C5.

PRACTICE

Name ______________________

Practice 10-8

Relating Equations and Inequalities

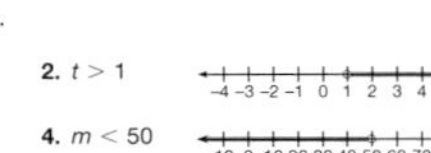

Graph each inequality on a number line.

1. $x \leq 3$ 2. $t > 1$
3. $q \geq -10$ 4. $m < 50$

For each inequality, tell whether the number in bold is a solution.

5. $x < 7$; **7** No 6. $p > -3$; **3** Yes 7. $k \geq 5$; **0** No
8. $3z \leq 12$; **4** Yes 9. $n - 5 > 3$; **6** No 10. $2g + 8 \geq 3$; **−1** Yes

Write an inequality for each graph.

11. $x > -2$ 12. $z \leq 30$

Write a real-world statement for each inequality. Possible answers:

13. $d \geq 60$ It is at least 60 mi away.
14. $p < 200$ The price is under \$200.

Write and graph an inequality for each statement.

15. You can walk there in 20 minutes or less. $t \leq 20$

16. Each prize is worth over \$150. $v > 150$

17. **Science** A species of catfish, *malapterurus electricus,* can generate up to 350 volts of electricity.
   a. Write an inequality to represent the amount of electricity generated by the catfish. $e \leq 350$
   b. Draw a graph of the inequality you wrote in **a**.

RETEACHING

Name ______________________

Alternative Lesson 10-8

Relating Equations and Inequalities

Two expressions separated by an inequality sign form an **inequality**. An inequality shows that the two expressions *are not* equal. Unlike the equations you have worked with, an inequality has many solutions.

The **solutions of an inequality** are the values that make the inequality true. They can be graphed on a number line. A filled-in circle shows that the number below it satisfies the inequality. For example:

$x > -2$ ("greater than") $x < -2$ ("less than")
$x \geq -2$ ("greater than or equal to") $x \leq -2$ ("less than or equal to")

Example

Graph the inequality $x > 4$.

The inequality is read as "x is greater than 4." Since all numbers to the right of 4 are greater than 4, you can draw an arrow from 4 to the right. Since 4 is not greater than itself, use an open circle on 4.

Try It Graph the inequality $x \leq -3$.

a. Write the inequality in words. x is less than or equal to −3.
b. Will the circle at −3 be filled in? Yes; −3 satisfies inequality.
c. Graph the solution.

Graph the inequality $x \geq -1$.

d. Write the inequality in words. x is greater than or equal to −1.
e. Will the circle at −1 be filled in? Yes; −1 satisfies inequality.
f. Graph the solution.

Graph the inequality $x < 3$.

g. Write the inequality in words. x is less than 3.
h. Will the circle at 3 be filled in? No.
i. Graph the solution.

Reteaching

Activity

Materials: 16 index cards, markers, rulers

Play this matching game with a partner.

- Write each of the following inequalities on a different index card. Then graph each one on a different card.
  $x < 1$, $x > 1$, $x < -1$, $x > -1$, $x \leq 1$, $x \geq 1$, $x \leq -1$, $x \geq -1$
- Shuffle the cards and place them face down on your desk in four rows of four.
- One player turns over two cards to try to find a match of an inequality with its graph. If successful, that player removes the two cards and plays again. If the player is not successful, the other player gets a turn. The person with the most pairs at the end wins.

Exercise Notes

Exercise 32

Error Prevention It may be helpful for students to think of absolute value as the distance from zero on the number line.

Exercise Answers

29. No; Numbers less than 60 solve the first inequality, numbers greater than 60 solve the second.

30. a. $T < -39$

b. $T > 2210$

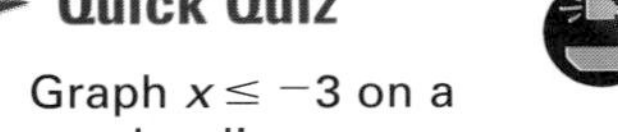

32. False; This means the same thing as $5 < 3$, which is false.

33. Tables may vary; Any values of x greater than 4 solve the inequality.

34. a. If $n = 0$ or 1

b. If $n > 1$ or $n < 0$

c. Never

Alternate Assessment

Self Assessment Have students make up four different inequalities involving $>$, $<$, $\geq$, and $\leq$. Then have them graph each inequality on a number line.

Quick Quiz

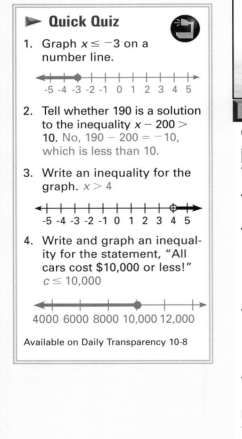

1. Graph $x \leq -3$ on a number line.

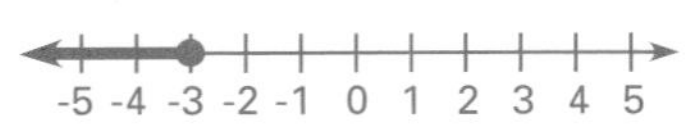

2. Tell whether 190 is a solution to the inequality $x - 200 > 10$. No, $190 - 200 = -10$, which is less than 10.

3. Write an inequality for the graph. $x > 4$

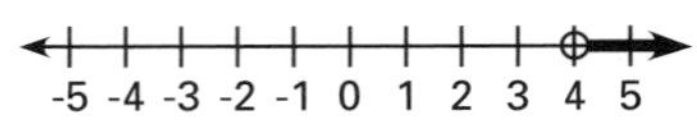

4. Write and graph an inequality for the statement, "All cars cost $10,000 or less!" $c \leq 10{,}000$

Available on Daily Transparency 10-8

PROBLEM SOLVING 10-8

29. Number Sense If $20 + 40 > m$, is $m > 20 + 40$? Explain your answer.

30. Science Most elements have a freezing point and a boiling point. Below the freezing point, the element is a solid. Above the boiling point, the element is a gas. Write and graph an inequality to show each temperature range.

a. The freezing point of mercury is −39°C. For what temperatures is mercury a solid?

b. The boiling point of silver is 2210°C. For what temperatures is silver a gas?

Mercury is the only metal that is a liquid at room temperature.

31. **Test Prep** Which of these values for c makes $c + 0.25 < 19.75$ true? A

Ⓐ 19 Ⓑ 19.75 Ⓒ 20 Ⓓ 20.25

Problem Solving and Reasoning

32. Communicate Is the statement $|-5| < |3|$ true or false? Explain.

33. Critical Thinking Make a table of the *equation* $x + 3 = y$. Then use your table to investigate the *inequality* $x + 3 > 7$. Find at least three values of x that make this inequality true. (You may need to add a few entries to your original table.)

34. Critical Thinking Answer each question for the integers −5 to 5. It may help to make a table.

GPS

a. When is $n = n^2$? **b.** When is $n < n^2$? **c.** When is $n > n^2$?

Mixed Review

Estimate each answer. *[Lesson 8-4]*

35. 10% of 41 4 **36.** 52% of 74 37 **37.** 15% of \$13.92 \$2.10 **38.** 26% of 392 100

Use >, <, or = to compare each pair of numbers. *[Lesson 9-2]*

39. -3 [<] 3 **40.** -7 [<] 0 **41.** -27 [<] -26 **42.** -1 [>] -905

43. -707 [>] -770 **44.** $|17|$ [=] $|-17|$ **45.** $|-27|$ [>] $|-26|$ **46.** 1 [>] $-1{,}000{,}000$

Project Progress

Make a table and a scatterplot of the population data you've gathered. If you've written an equation to fit your data, show the graph of that equation on your scatterplot.

Problem Solving
Understand
Plan
Solve
Look Back

PROBLEM SOLVING

Name ____________

Guided Problem Solving 10-8

GPS PROBLEM 34, STUDENT PAGE 520

Answer each question for the integers −5 to 5. It may help to make a table.

a. When is $n = n^2$? b. When is $n < n^2$? c. When is $n > n^2$?

— Understand —

1. For each of the three questions, what two values will you need to compare? n and n^2

— Plan —

2. Suppose n is a negative integer. Will n^2 be positive or negative? Explain. Positive; product of two negative integers is positive.

3. Make a table of values for n from −5 to 5 and for each n^2.

n	−5	−4	−3	−2	−1	0	1	2	3	4	5
n^2	25	16	9	4	1	0	1	4	9	16	25

— Solve —

4. Compare the n and n^2 values.

a. When is $n = n^2$? When $n = 0$ or 1.

b. When is $n < n^2$? When $n = -5, -4, -3, -2, -1, 2, 3, 4, 5$.

c. When is $n > n^2$? Never.

— Look Back —

5. What other strategy could you use to find the answer? Possible answer: Guess and Check, Draw a Diagram.

SOLVE ANOTHER PROBLEM

Answer each question for the integers −3 to 3.

a. When is $n = n^3$? When $n = -1, 0, 1$.

b. When is $n < n^3$? When $n = 2$ or 3.

c. When is $n > n^3$? When $n = -2$ or -3.

ENRICHMENT

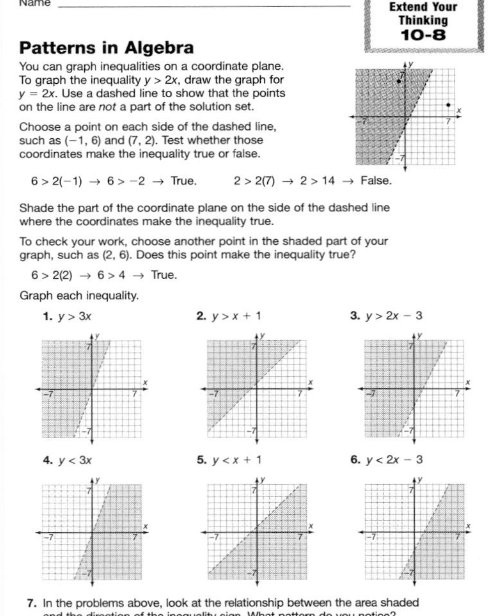

Name ____________

Extend Your Thinking 10-8

Patterns in Algebra

You can graph inequalities on a coordinate plane. To graph the inequality $y > 2x$, draw the graph for $y = 2x$. Use a dashed line to show that the points on the line are *not* a part of the solution set.

Choose a point on each side of the dashed line, such as (−1, 6) and (7, 2). Test whether those coordinates make the inequality true or false.

$6 > 2(-1) \rightarrow 6 > -2 \rightarrow$ True. $2 > 2(7) \rightarrow 2 > 14 \rightarrow$ False.

Shade the part of the coordinate plane on the side of the dashed line where the coordinates make the inequality true.

To check your work, choose another point in the shaded part of your graph, such as (2, 6). Does this point make the inequality true?

$6 > 2(2) \rightarrow 6 > 4 \rightarrow$ True.

Graph each inequality.

1. $y > 3x$ 2. $y > x + 1$ 3. $y > 2x - 3$

4. $y < 3x$ 5. $y < x + 1$ 6. $y < 2x - 3$

7. In the problems above, look at the relationship between the area shaded and the direction of the inequality sign. What pattern do you notice? When $y > x$, shade above the line; when $y < x$, shade below the line.

You've seen some of the ways businesses can use tables, graphs, and equations. Now you'll apply what you've learned to questions that could face the student owners of Food From the 'Hood.

It IS My Business!

Materials: Graph paper

Food From the 'Hood earns $1.25 on each bottle of Creamy Italian or Honey Mustard salad dressing it sells at the full retail price.

1. Write an equation relating the income to the number of bottles sold.
2. Make a table showing the income from sales of 20, 40, 60, 80, and 100 bottles. Use the table to draw a graph.
3. Estimate the number of bottles that must be sold to make $105. Explain how you made your estimate.

Food From the 'Hood has a goal of earning $50,000 in 1996–1997, which will be distributed as scholarship money to the student owners when they graduate.

4. Suppose that Food From the 'Hood has expenses of $35,000 and earns $1.25 for every bottle of salad dressing it sells. Write a two-step equation to show that its income minus its expenses gives a profit of $50,000.
5. Solve the equation you wrote in Step 4. What is your solution, and what does it mean? Explain how you solved the equation.

It IS My Business!

The Point
Students read about a student-owned business in *It IS My Business* on page 507. Now they analyze the earnings, expenses, and profit of the business.

Materials
Graph paper

Resources
Teaching Tool Transparency 7: $\frac{1}{4}$-Inch Graph Paper

About the Page

- Ask students how much they would earn if they sold 2 bottles of salad dressing, 3 bottles, and so on. Then ask how they would determine the earnings on n bottles.
- Discuss with students how a company determines its profit. Remind them that a business has expenses and that expenses must be paid out of earnings before the business can claim a profit.
- Suggest to students who are having trouble writing an equation that they write their equation in words first and then substitute numbers and variables in the word equation.

Ongoing Assessment
Check that students have written correct equations for Steps 1 and 4 and solved the equation in Step 5 correctly.

Extension

Suppose that Food From the 'Hood earns $0.60 on each bottle of dressing it sells. How many bottles of salad dressing would they have to sell if their expenses were $35,000 and they wanted to earn a profit of $50,000? 141,667

Answers for Connect

1. $i = 1.25b$
2.

bottles (b)	20	40	60	80	100
income (i)	25	50	75	100	125

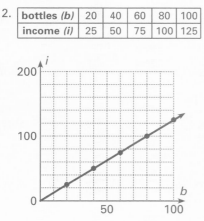

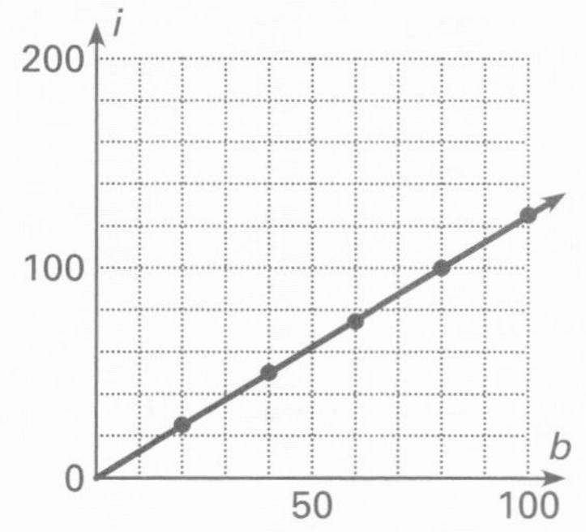

3. About 85 bottles; Students may use the table or their graph to make this estimate.
4. $50{,}000 = 1.25b - 35{,}000$
5. $b = 68{,}000$; The students would need to sell 68,000 bottles of salad dressing to make a profit of $50,000; Possible explanation: Used inverse operations. Added 35,000 to each side to undo subtraction, then divided both sides by 1.25 to undo multiplication.

10B Review

Section 10B Review

REVIEW 10B

The table represents the equation $y = -2x + 6$. Use it to solve the related equations beneath the table.

x	−2	−1	0	1	2	3	4	5	6
y	10	8	6	4	2	0	−2	−4	−6

1. $6 = -2x + 6$ $x = 0$ **2.** $-2x + 6 = -2$ $x = 4$ **3.** $10 = -2x + 6$ $x = -2$ **4.** $-2x + 6 = 0$ $x = 3$

The graph of $y = 5x + 30$ is shown at the right. Use it to solve the related equations.

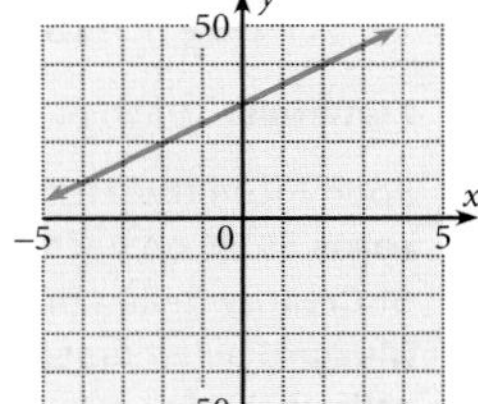

5. $30 = 5x + 30$ $x = 0$ **6.** $40 = 5x + 30$ $x = 2$ **7.** $5x + 30 = 10$ $x = -4$

8. Estimation Use the graph to estimate the solution to $25 = 5x + 30$. $x = -1$

9. 

Explain the difference between an equation and an inequality.

10. The cost of a plane ticket from Anchorage, Alaska, to Biloxi, Mississippi, is greater than \$500. Write and graph an inequality for this statement.

11. Industry When she was 13, Amy Kumpel and her friends began making pillows and having them autographed by famous people. The pillows were sold at an auction, and the proceeds went to benefit homeless children.

a. The pillows sold for an average of about \$72. Write an equation for the amount of money, m, made from selling p pillows.

b. Make a table of values for your equation in **a.** Use the table to estimate the number of pillows sold to make \$4000.

Write an expression describing the rule for each sequence. Then give the 100th term for the sequence. *[Lesson 10-3]*

12. −2, −1, 0, 1, … $n - 3$; 97 **13.** 6, 12, 18, 24, … $6n$; 600 **14.** 0.2, 0.4, 0.6, 0.8, … $0.2n$; 20 **15.** 1, 8, 27, 64, … n^3; 1,000,000

Test Prep

When you're asked a question about an inequality on a multiple choice test, remember to consider negative numbers, fractions, and zero.

16. Which of these inequalities is *always* true for any number n? C

Ⓐ $n^2 > n$ Ⓑ $2n > n$ Ⓒ $n + 4 > n$ Ⓓ $-n < n$

Review Correlation

Item(s)	Lesson(s)
1–4	10-6
5–8	10-7
9, 10	10-8
11	10-6
12–15	10-3
16	10-8

Test Prep

Test-Taking Tip

Tell students that they can always pick test numbers to see if a relationship holds true for each of the test numbers. Here, students can test 0, a positive integer, a negative integer, and a fraction.

Answers for Review

9. An equation shows that the expressions on opposite sides of the = sign have the same value. An inequality shows that one of the expressions is less than (or less than or equal to) the other.

10. $t > 500$

11. a. $m = 72p$

b.

Pillows (p)	Money (m)
10	\$720
20	\$1440
30	\$2160
40	\$2880
50	\$3600
60	\$4320

Need to sell about 55 pillows to make \$4,000.

Resources

Practice Masters
Section 10B Review

Assessment Sourcebook
Quiz 10B

TestWorks
Test and Practice Software

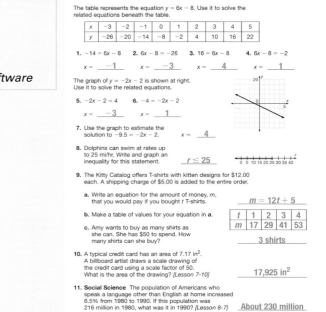

PRACTICE

Name ______________ Practice

Section 10B Review

The table represents the equation $y = 6x - 8$. Use it to solve the related equations beneath the table.

x	−3	−2	−1	0	1	2	3	4	5
y	−26	−20	−14	−8	−2	4	10	16	22

1. $-14 = 6x - 8$ $x =$ −1 **2.** $6x - 8 = -26$ $x =$ −3 **3.** $16 = 6x - 8$ $x =$ 4 **4.** $6x - 8 = -2$ $x =$ 1

The graph of $y = -2x - 2$ is shown at right. Use it to solve the related equations.

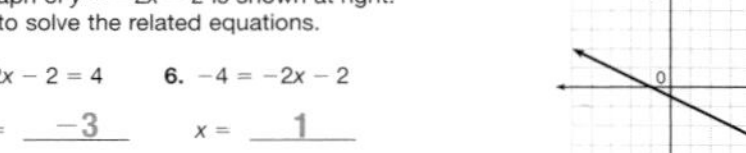

5. $-2x - 2 = 4$ $x =$ −3 **6.** $-4 = -2x - 2$ $x =$ 1

7. Use the graph to estimate the solution to $-9.5 = -2x - 2$. $x \approx$ 4

8. Dolphins can swim at rates up to 25 mi/hr. Write and graph an inequality for this statement. $r \leq 25$

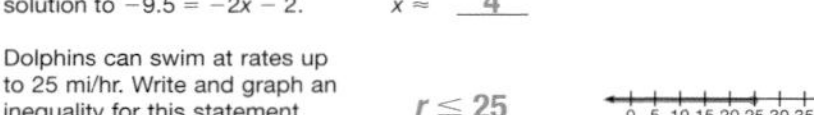

9. The Kitty Catalog offers T-shirts with kitten designs for \$12.00 each. A shipping charge of \$5.00 is added to the entire order.

a. Write an equation for the amount of money, m, that you would pay if you bought t T-shirts. $m = 12t + 5$

b. Make a table of values for your equation in **a**.

t	1	2	3	4
m	17	29	41	53

c. Amy wants to buy as many shirts as she can. She has \$50 to spend. How many shirts can she buy? 3 shirts

10. A typical credit card has an area of 7.17 in^2. A billboard artist draws a scale drawing of the credit card using a scale factor of 50. What is the area of the drawing? *[Lesson 7-10]* 17,925 in^2

11. Social Science The population of Americans who speak a language other than English at home increased 6.5% from 1980 to 1990. If this population was 216 million in 1980, what was it in 1990? *[Lesson 8-7]* About 230 million

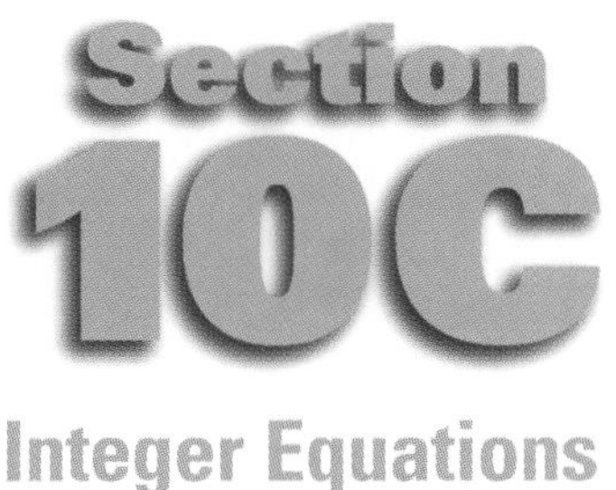

Integer Equations

LESSON PLANNING GUIDE

Student Edition / Ancillaries

LESSON		MATERIALS	VOCABULARY	DAILY	OTHER
	Section 10 Opener				
10-9	**Integer Addition and Subtraction Equations**	algebra tiles		10-9	Teaching Tool Trans. 12, 13 Lesson Enhancement Transparencies 48, 49 Technology Master
10-10	**Integer Multiplication and Division Equations**	algebra tiles		10-10	Teaching Tool Trans. 12, 13 Lesson Enhancement Trans. 50 Technology Master 50
10-11	**Solving Two-Step Equations**	algebra tiles		10-11	Teaching Tool Trans. 12, 13 Technology Master 51 Ch. 10 Project Master
10-12	**Problem Solving with Integer Equations**	graph paper		10-12	Teaching Tool Trans. 7 *WW Math*–Middle School
	Connect				Interdisc. Team Teaching 10C
	Review				Practice 10C; Quiz 10C; *TestWorks*
	Extend Key Ideas				
	Chapter 10 Summary and Review				
	Chapter 10 Assessment				Ch. 10 Tests Forms A–F; *TestWorks*; Ch. 10 Letter Home
	Cumulative Review Chapters 1–10				Cumulative Review Ch. 1–10

SKILLS TRACE

LESSON	SKILL	FIRST INTRODUCED GR. 5	GR. 6	GR. 7	DEVELOP	PRACTICE/ APPLY	REVIEW
10-9	**Solving addition and subtraction equations (integers).**		✘		pp. 524–526	pp. 527–528	pp. 544, 547, 609
10-10	**Solving multiplication and division equations (integers).**		✘		pp. 529–531	pp. 532–533	pp. 544, 547, 614
10-11	**Solving two-step equations (integers).**			✘ p. 534	pp. 534–536	pp. 537–538	pp. 544, 547, 604
10-12	**Solving real-world problems (integers).**		✘		pp. 539–540	pp. 541–542	pp. 544, 547

CONNECTED MATHEMATICS

The unit *Accentuate the Negative (Integers)*, from the **Connected Mathematics** series, can be used with Section 10C.

INTERDISCIPLINARY TEAM TEACHING

Math and Science/Technology

(Worksheet pages 43–44: Teacher pages T43–T44)

In this lesson, students solve integer equations using weather data.

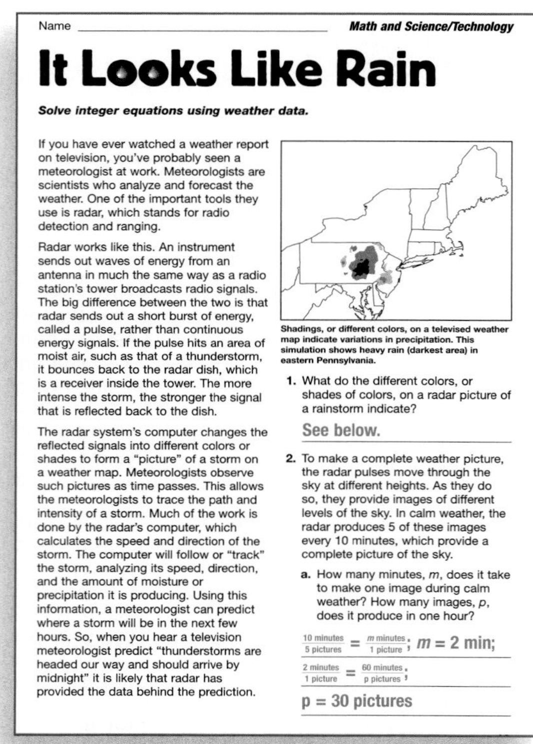

Name ______________________ *Math and Science/Technology*

It Looks Like Rain

Solve integer equations using weather data.

If you have ever watched a weather report on television, you've probably seen a meteorologist at work. Meteorologists are scientists who analyze and forecast the weather. One of the important tools they use is radar, which stands for radio detection and ranging.

Radar works like this. An instrument sends out waves of energy from an antenna in much the same way as a radio station's tower broadcasts radio signals. The big difference between the two is that radar sends out a short burst of energy, called a pulse, rather than continuous energy signals. If the pulse hits an area of moist air, such as that of a thunderstorm, it bounces back to the radar dish, which is a receiver inside the tower. The more intense the storm, the stronger the signal that is reflected back to the dish.

The radar system's computer changes the reflected signals into different colors or shades to form a "picture" of a storm on a weather map. Meteorologists observe such pictures as time passes. This allows the meteorologists to trace the path and intensity of a storm. Much of the work is done by the radar's computer, which calculates the speed and direction of the storm. The computer will follow or "track" the storm, analyzing its speed, direction, and the amount of moisture or precipitation it is producing. Using this information, a meteorologist can predict where a storm will be in the next few hours. So, when you hear a television meteorologist predict "thunderstorms are headed our way and should arrive by midnight" it is likely that radar has provided the data behind the prediction.

Shadings, or different colors, on a televised weather map indicate variations in precipitation. This simulation shows heavy rain (darkest area) in eastern Pennsylvania.

1. What do the different colors, or shades of colors, on a radar picture of a rainstorm indicate?

See below.

2. To make a complete weather picture, the radar pulses move through the sky at different heights. As they do so, they provide images of different levels of the sky. In calm weather, the radar produces 5 of these images every 10 minutes, which provide a complete picture of the sky.

a. How many minutes, *m*, does it take to make one image during calm weather? How many images, *p*, does it produce in one hour?

$\frac{10 \text{ minutes}}{5 \text{ pictures}} = \frac{m \text{ minutes}}{1 \text{ picture}}$; $m = 2$ min;

$\frac{2 \text{ minutes}}{1 \text{ picture}} = \frac{60 \text{ minutes}}{p \text{ pictures}}$;

$p = 30$ pictures

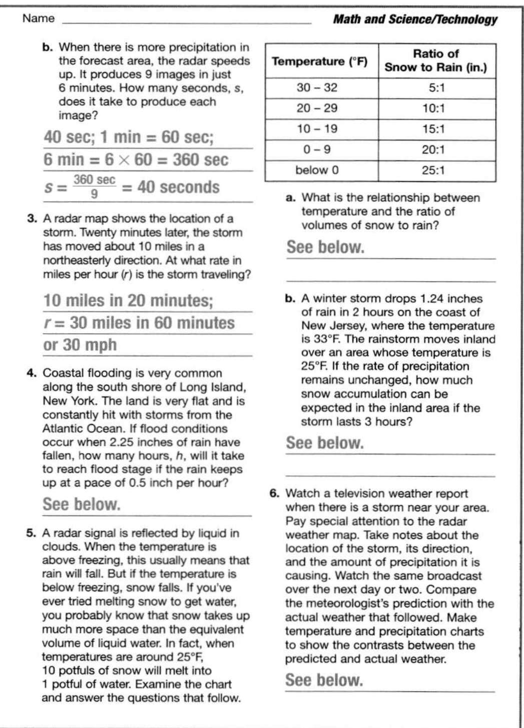

Name ______________________ *Math and Science/Technology*

b. When there is more precipitation in the forecast area, the radar speeds up. It produces 9 images in just 6 minutes. How many seconds, *s*, does it take to produce each image?

40 sec; 1 min = 60 sec;

6 min = $6 \times 60 = 360$ sec

$s = \frac{360 \text{ sec}}{9} = 40$ seconds

3. A radar map shows the location of a storm. Twenty minutes later, the storm has moved about 10 miles in a northeasterly direction. At what rate in miles per hour (*r*) is the storm traveling?

10 miles in 20 minutes;

$r = 30$ miles in 60 minutes

or 30 mph

4. Coastal flooding is very common along the south shore of Long Island, New York. The land is very flat and is constantly hit with storms from the Atlantic Ocean. If flood conditions occur when 2.25 inches of rain have fallen, how many hours, *h*, will it take to reach flood stage if the rain keeps up at a pace of 0.5 inch per hour?

See below.

5. A radar signal is reflected by liquid in clouds. When the temperature is above freezing, this usually means that rain will fall. But if the temperature is below freezing, snow falls. If you've ever tried melting snow to get water, you probably know that snow takes up much more space than the equivalent volume of liquid water. In fact, when temperatures are around 25°F, 10 potfuls of snow will melt into 1 potful of water. Examine the chart and answer the questions that follow.

Temperature (°F)	Ratio of Snow to Rain (in.)
30 – 32	5:1
20 – 29	10:1
10 – 19	15:1
0 – 9	20:1
below 0	25:1

a. What is the relationship between temperature and the ratio of volumes of snow to rain?

See below.

b. A winter storm drops 1.24 inches of rain in 2 hours on the coast of New Jersey, where the temperature is 33°F. The rainstorm moves inland over an area whose temperature is 25°F. If the rate of precipitation remains unchanged, how much snow accumulation can be expected in the inland area if the storm lasts 3 hours?

See below.

6. Watch a television weather report when there is a storm near your area. Pay special attention to the radar weather map. Take notes about the location of the storm, its direction, and the amount of precipitation it is causing. Watch the same broadcast over the next day or two. Compare the meteorologist's prediction with the actual weather that followed. Make temperature and precipitation charts to show the contrasts between the predicted and actual weather.

See below.

Answers

1. Different intensities of rainfall
4. $h = 2.25$ inches divided by rate of 0.5 inches per hour $= 4.5$ hours
5. a. The ratio increases with the decreasing temperature.

   b. The ratio increases with the decreasing temperature. 18.6 inches; .62 in./hr $\times$ 3 hrs = 1.86 in. of rain; ratio is 10:1; 10×1.86 in. = 18.6 in.
6. Students should show notes taken during the weather broadcast and use their charts to assess the accuracy of the weather forecast.

BIBLIOGRAPHY

FOR TEACHERS

Huxley, Anthony, ed. *Standard Encyclopedia of the World's Mountains.* New York, NY: Putnam, 1962.

O'Toole, Christopher, ed. *The Encyclopedia of Insects.* New York, NY: Facts on File, 1986.

Robinson, Andrew. *Earth Shock: Hurricanes, Volcanoes, Earthquakes, Tornadoes and Other Forces of Nature.* New York, NY: Thames and Hudson, 1993.

Ryden, Hope. *Wild Animals of Africa ABC.* New York, NY: Lodestar Books, 1989.

Thomas, Lowell. *Lowell Thomas' Book of High Mountains.* New York, NY: J. Messner, 1964.

FOR STUDENTS

Bungum, Jane E. *Money and Financial Institutions.* Minneapolis, MN: Lerner Publications, 1991.

Hare, Tony. *The Greenhouse Effect.* New York, NY: Gloucester Press, 1990.

SECTION **10C**

Integer Equations

▶ Science Link ▶ Geography Link ▶ www.mathsurf.com/7/ch10/weather

Weathering the Storm

On September 11, 1995, tropical storm Luis hit Newfoundland, Canada. Its strong winds and torrential rains washed out roads and flooded low-lying areas. The storm caused millions of dollars in damage and claimed one life. A fearsome storm, right? Yes, but …

This was only the last fizzling gasp of what was once Hurricane Luis. *As it smashed through the Caribbean, packing winds whose gusts reached 170 mi/hr, Hurricane Luis caused billions of dollars worth of damage. It destroyed hotels and hospitals on Antigua, and ripped the roofs off three-quarters of the homes in the island nation of St. Kitts-Nevis.*

Obviously, warning people about the approach of a storm such as Hurricane Luis can save thousands of lives. Meteorologists use physics, mathematics, and data from satellites to develop weather forecasts. Equations such as the ones you're about to investigate play an important role in predicting our wild, wild weather.

1 **Name some weather conditions that have affected your state in the past year.**

2 **Make a list of some information that you think is involved in predicting the weather.**

3 **Name some examples of mathematics used in weather reports.**

523

Where are we now?

In Section 10B, students learned to solve equations using graphs and tables.

They learned how to

- use tables to solve equations.
- use graphs to solve equations.
- graph inequalities on a number line.
- write inequalities represented on a graph.

Where are we going?

In Section 10C, students will

- solve addition and subtraction equations involving positive and negative integers.
- solve multiplication and division equations involving positive and negative integers.
- solve two-step equations involving integers.
- solve real-world problems by using integer equations.

Theme: Weather

World Wide Web

If your class has access to the World Wide Web, you might want to use the information found at the Web site address given. The interdisciplinary links relate to topics discussed in this section.

About the Page

This page introduces the theme of the section, weather, and discusses the tools meteorologists use to predict the weather.

Ask …

- Have you ever experienced a bad storm? Tell about your experience.
- What are some of the hazardous weather conditions faced by your community?

Extensions

The following activities do not require access to the World Wide Web.

Science
Have students report on the kind of weather information given in their local newspapers.

Geography
Have students research a violent storm that has been in the news. Have them use a map to show the areas affected by the storm.

Answers for Questions

1. Possible answers: Drought, hurricane, flood, blizzard, storm.
2. Previous weather patterns; satellite images.
3. Amount of rain; probabilities used in forecasting.

Connect

On page 543, students write and solve equations about Hurricane Luis.

10-9 Lesson Organizer

Objective

- Solve addition and subtraction equations involving positive and negative integers.

Materials

- Explore: Algebra tiles

NCTM Standards

- 1–4, 7, 9

Review

Simplify each expression.

1. $-4 - 5$ -9
2. $8 - (-5)$ 13
3. $-4 - (-5)$ 1
4. $6 - 9$ -3

Available on Daily Transparency 10-9

1 Introduce

Explore

You may want to use Lesson Enhancement Transparency 48 with **Explore**.

The Point

Students write addition and subtraction equations modeled by algebra tiles and solve the equations.

Ongoing Assessment

Point out to students that they can add either positive or negative tiles to each side, but they must add the same number to each side.

For Groups That Finish Early

Explain what you did to solve each equation in Step 1. (a) Add 3 negative tiles to each side, (b) add 3 positive tiles to each side, (c) add 3 negative tiles to each side.

Answers for Explore

1. a. $x + 3 = 5$; $x = 2$

   b. $x - 3 = 7$; $x = 10$

   c. $-3 = x + 3$; $x = -6$

2. Answers may vary.

10-9 Integer Addition and Subtraction Equations

You'll Learn ...

- to solve addition and subtraction equations involving positive and negative integers

... How It's Used

Addition and subtraction equations are important when you're keeping track of the balance in a bank account.

▶ **Lesson Link** You've solved equations using graphs and tables. Now you'll use algebra to solve equations involving addition and subtraction of integers. ◀

Explore Modeling Integer Equations

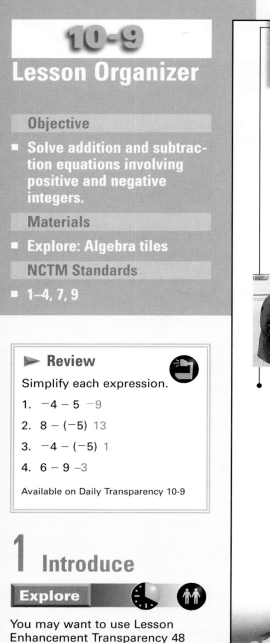

Tiling the Day Away

Materials: Algebra tiles

You must follow these rules when using algebra tiles to solve equations:

Zero Pairs: x, $-x$; -1, 1

- Whatever you do to one side of the equation, you must do to the other.
- Any zero pairs on one side of the equation can be removed.
- The equation is solved when a positive x-tile is alone on one side.

1. Write the equation modeled by each equation box. Then use algebra tiles and the rules to solve each equation. State your final equation for each problem, and give the solution.

a. 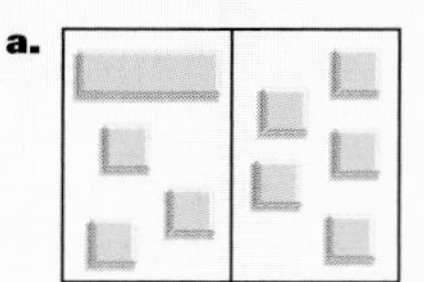

b. 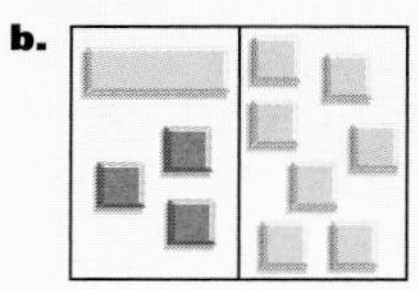

c. 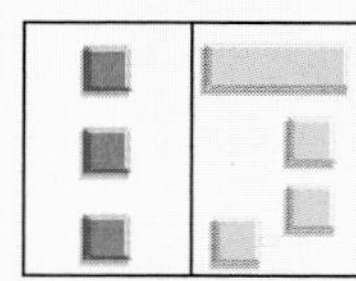

2. Make up and solve an equation that involves x and integers.

Learn Integer Addition and Subtraction Equations

When you solve an equation, it helps to think of a balanced scale.

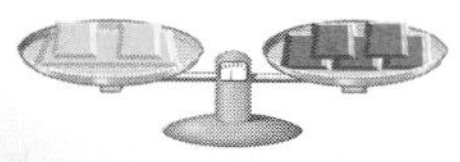

To preserve the balance, you must do the same thing to each side of the equation.

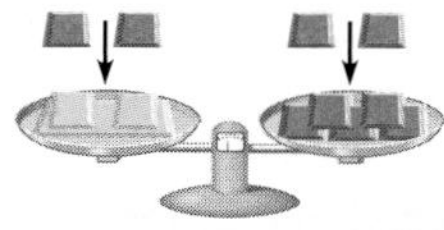

MEETING INDIVIDUAL NEEDS

Resources

- 10-9 Practice
- 10-9 Reteaching
- 10-9 Problem Solving
- 10-9 Enrichment
- 10-9 Daily Transparency
  - Problem of the Day
  - Review
  - Quick Quiz
- Teaching Tool Transparencies 12, 13
- Lesson Enhancement Transparencies 48, 49
- Technology Master 49

Learning Modalities

Verbal Have students write a set of guidelines that would help someone use algebra tiles in solving equations.

Kinesthetic Have students work with a balance scale to show how you must add or subtract the same amount to both sides in order for the scale to remain balanced. Have them discuss how this is related to equation solving.

Social Some students will have trouble using algebra tiles. Allow students to work together so that students can help each other.

English Language Development

Some students may have difficulty distinguishing between the two uses of a minus sign. When referring to a negative integer, have students use the word "negative" rather than "minus." For example, -8 would be "negative 8" rather than "minus 8." On the other hand, $10 - 8$ would be read as "10 minus 8."

Examples

1 Solve: $x + (-3) = -5$

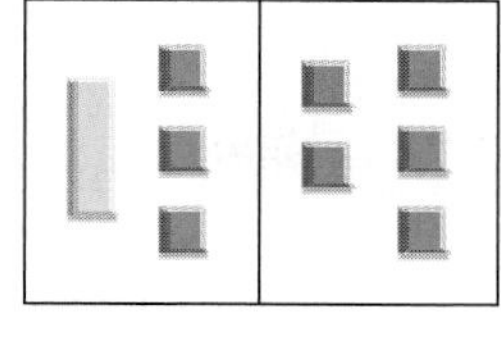

The algebra tiles illustrate the steps. Each side of the equation box represents a side of the equation.

$x + (-3) = -5$

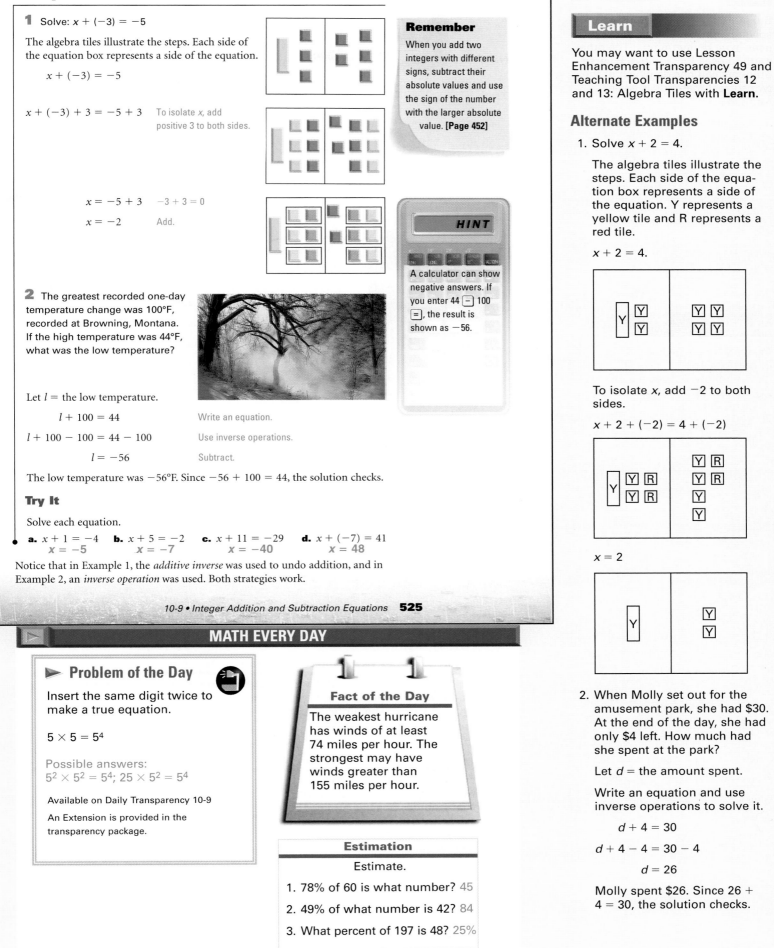

$x + (-3) + 3 = -5 + 3$ — To isolate x, add positive 3 to both sides.

$x = -5 + 3$ — $-3 + 3 = 0$

$x = -2$ — Add.

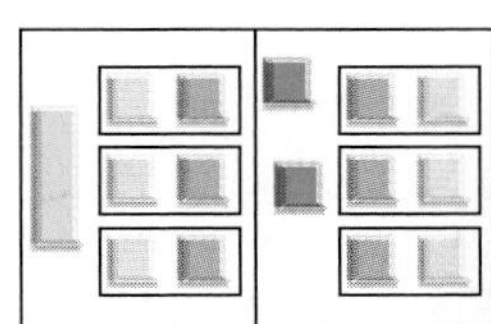

Remember

When you add two integers with different signs, subtract their absolute values and use the sign of the number with the larger absolute value. [Page 452]

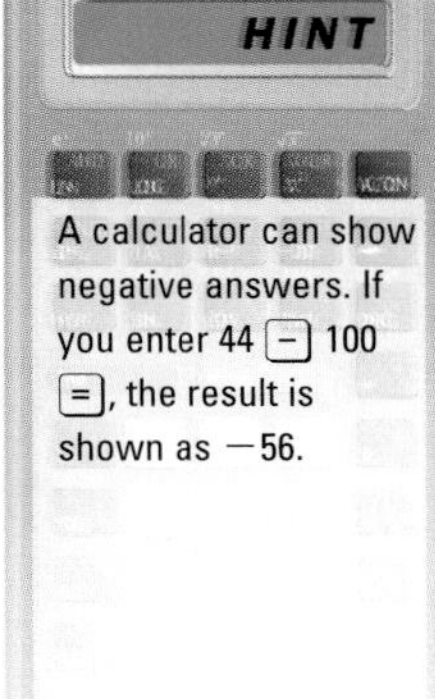

A calculator can show negative answers. If you enter 44 [−] 100 [=], the result is shown as −56.

2 The greatest recorded one-day temperature change was 100°F, recorded at Browning, Montana. If the high temperature was 44°F, what was the low temperature?

Let l = the low temperature.

$l + 100 = 44$ — Write an equation.

$l + 100 - 100 = 44 - 100$ — Use inverse operations.

$l = -56$ — Subtract.

The low temperature was −56°F. Since $-56 + 100 = 44$, the solution checks.

Try It

Solve each equation.

a. $x + 1 = -4$ $x = -5$ **b.** $x + 5 = -2$ $x = -7$ **c.** $x + 11 = -29$ $x = -40$ **d.** $x + (-7) = 41$ $x = 48$

Notice that in Example 1, the *additive inverse* was used to undo addition, and in Example 2, an *inverse operation* was used. Both strategies work.

2 Teach

Learn

You may want to use Lesson Enhancement Transparency 49 and Teaching Tool Transparencies 12 and 13: Algebra Tiles with **Learn.**

Alternate Examples

1. Solve $x + 2 = 4$.

   The algebra tiles illustrate the steps. Each side of the equation box represents a side of the equation. Y represents a yellow tile and R represents a red tile.

   $x + 2 = 4.$

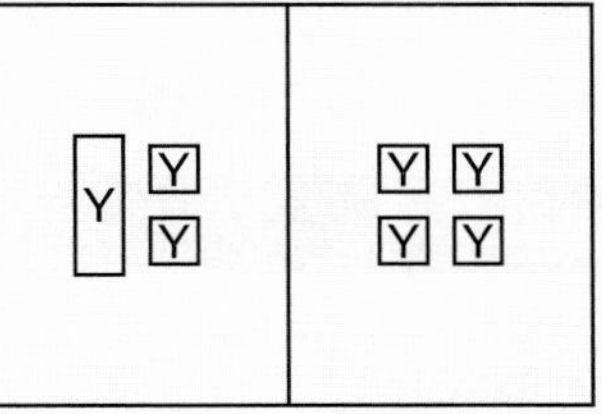

   To isolate x, add -2 to both sides.

   $x + 2 + (-2) = 4 + (-2)$

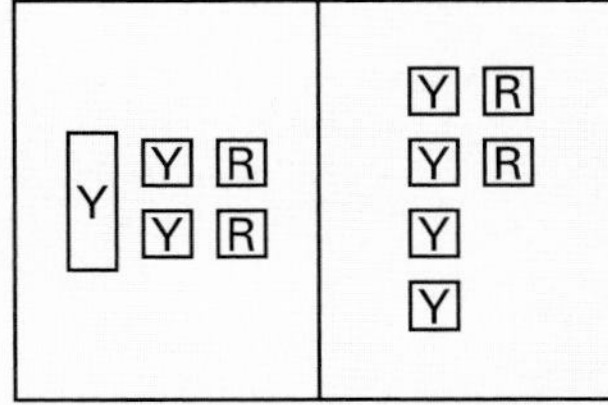

   $x = 2$

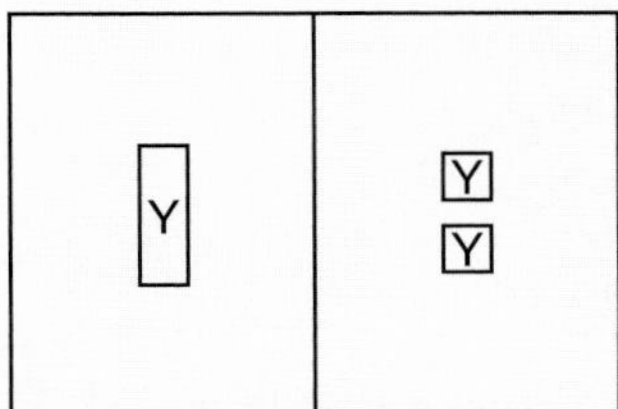

2. When Molly set out for the amusement park, she had $30. At the end of the day, she had only $4 left. How much had she spent at the park?

   Let d = the amount spent.

   Write an equation and use inverse operations to solve it.

   $d + 4 = 30$

   $d + 4 - 4 = 30 - 4$

   $d = 26$

   Molly spent $26. Since $26 + 4 = 30$, the solution checks.

MATH EVERY DAY

Problem of the Day

Insert the same digit twice to make a true equation.

$5 \times 5 = 5^4$

Possible answers: $5^2 \times 5^2 = 5^4$; $25 \times 5^2 = 5^4$

Available on Daily Transparency 10-9

An Extension is provided in the transparency package.

Fact of the Day

The weakest hurricane has winds of at least 74 miles per hour. The strongest may have winds greater than 155 miles per hour.

Estimation

Estimate.

1. 78% of 60 is what number? 45
2. 49% of what number is 42? 84
3. What percent of 197 is 48? 25%

Students see two methods of solving a problem. One method uses inverse operations. The other method uses the additive inverse. Students can decide which of the two correct methods is easier for them.

Answers for What Do You Think?

1. Subtracting a number from both sides of an equation is the same thing as adding that number's opposite to both sides.
2. $-7 - 15$ is the same as $-7 + (-15)$, which is -22.

3 Practice and Assess

Check

Answers for Check Your Understanding

1. A variable is on one side of the equals sign and a constant is on the other.
2. No; Adding -7 is the same as subtracting 7.

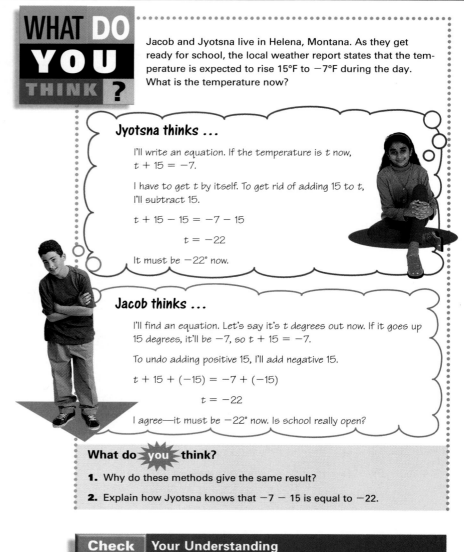

Jacob and Jyotsna live in Helena, Montana. As they get ready for school, the local weather report states that the temperature is expected to rise 15°F to −7°F during the day. What is the temperature now?

Jyotsna thinks ...

I'll write an equation. If the temperature is t now, $t + 15 = -7$.

I have to get t by itself. To get rid of adding 15 to t, I'll subtract 15.

$$t + 15 - 15 = -7 - 15$$

$$t = -22$$

It must be −22° now.

Jacob thinks ...

I'll find an equation. Let's say it's t degrees out now. If it goes up 15 degrees, it'll be −7, so $t + 15 = -7$.

To undo adding positive 15, I'll add negative 15.

$$t + 15 + (-15) = -7 + (-15)$$

$$t = -22$$

I agree—it must be −22° now. Is school really open?

What do you think?

1. Why do these methods give the same result?
2. Explain how Jyotsna knows that $-7 - 15$ is equal to -22.

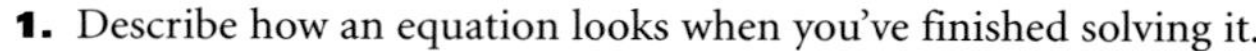

Check Your Understanding

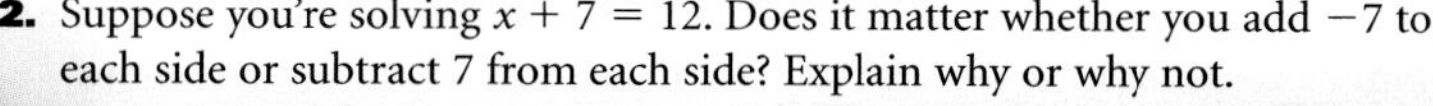

1. Describe how an equation looks when you've finished solving it.
2. Suppose you're solving $x + 7 = 12$. Does it matter whether you add -7 to each side or subtract 7 from each side? Explain why or why not.

MEETING MIDDLE SCHOOL CLASSROOM NEEDS

Tips from Middle School Teachers

Students need to be reminded that every subtraction of integers can be rewritten as an addition. For example, $8 - (-2)$ can be written as $8 + 2$ and $3 - 5$ can be written as $3 + (-5)$. Therefore, an equation such as $x - 6 = 10$ could be written as $x + (-6) = 10$.

Team Teaching

Work with a geography teacher to show how an almanac can be used to find a variety of information that involves positive and negative integers, for example, temperatures and elevations. Use this information to create problems that can be solved by using equations.

Industry Connection

The Dow Jones Industrial Average is the most widely cited indicator of how the stock market is doing. It consists of 30 stocks that are considered representative of all industrial stocks. The stocks are selected by the editors of the *Wall Street Journal*.

10-9 Exercises and Applications

Practice and Apply

1. **Getting Started** Follow the steps to solve $x + (-2) = (-11)$.
   a. To isolate x, you need to undo the addition of -2. To do this, add (positive) 2 to both sides of the equation.
   b. The left side of the equation simplifies to x. Use your rules for integer addition to simplify the right side of the equation.
   c. Check your answer by substituting it into the original equation.

Write the equation represented by each equation box. Then solve the equation.

2. 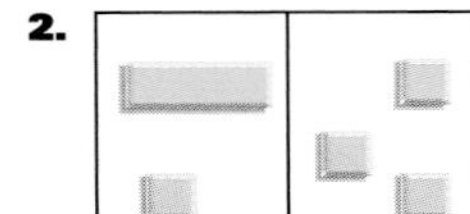
$x + 1 = 3$; $x = 2$

3. 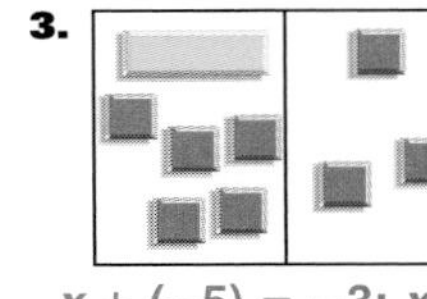
$x + (-5) = -3$; $x = 2$

4. 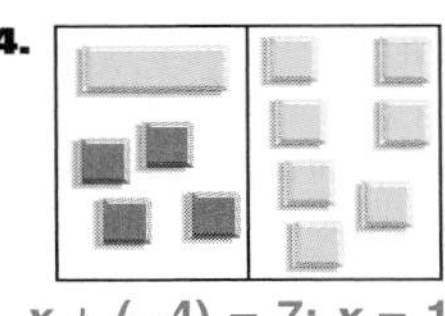
$x + (-4) = 7$; $x = 11$

For each equation, tell whether the number in bold is a solution.

5. $m - (-4) = -5$; **−1** No
6. $x + 18 = 3$; **−15** Yes
7. $24 + b = -2$; **26** No
8. $c + (-4) = -1$; **−5** No

Solve each equation. Check your solutions.

9. $x + 2 = -3$ $x = -5$
10. $m + 1 = -9$ $m = -10$
11. $z - 7 = -8$ $z = -1$
12. $x + (-7) = -8$ $x = -1$
13. $-10 + k = 17$ $k = 27$
14. $p - 45 = -32$ $p = 13$
15. $x - (-33) = 28$ $x = -5$
16. $(-4) + x = -19$ $x = -15$
17. $22 + x = 11$ $x = -11$
18. $n + 111 = 95$ $n = -16$
19. $x - (-59) = -1$ $x = -60$
20. $b + (-61) = -85$ $b = -24$

21. **Science** The fastest recorded temperature rise was 49° in 2 minutes, in Spearfish, South Dakota. If the temperature after the rise was 45°F, what was the temperature before the rise? −4°F

22. **Social Studies** The amount of profit a business (or a government) makes is equal to its income minus its expenses. As an equation: $P = I - E$. In 1994, the United States government had a deficit of about 203 billion dollars. (This means the same thing as a profit of −203 billion dollars.) If the government's expenses were about 1461 billion dollars that year, what was its income? $1258 billion

PRACTICE 10-9

10-9 Exercises and Applications

Assignment Guide

- **Basic** 1–16, 21, 23, 24, 26, 28–33
- **Average** 1–8, 11–18, 21–26, 28–33
- **Enriched** 2–8, 13–20, 22–28, 30–33

Exercise Notes

Exercises 2–4

Extension Have students show each step in solving each equation with words, with a picture, and with an equation that describes what the two sides of the box look like.

Exercises 11, 14, 15, and 19

Error Prevention Some students may confuse operations on both sides of an equation. They may solve equations such as $z - 7 = -8$ by finding $-8 - 7$. Ask them what number they should add to both sides of the equation to isolate the variable.

Exercise Answers

1. a. $x + (-2) + 2 = (-11) + 2$
   b. $x = -9$
   c. $-9 + (-2) = -11$; $-11 = -11$

PRACTICE

Name ____________

Practice 10-9

Integer Addition and Subtraction Equations

Write the equation represented by each equation box. Then solve the equation. The lighter tiles represent positive integers.

1. $x + (-3) = 2$ $x =$ 5
2. $x + 7 = 3$ $x =$ −4
3. $x + (-4) = -5$ $x =$ −1

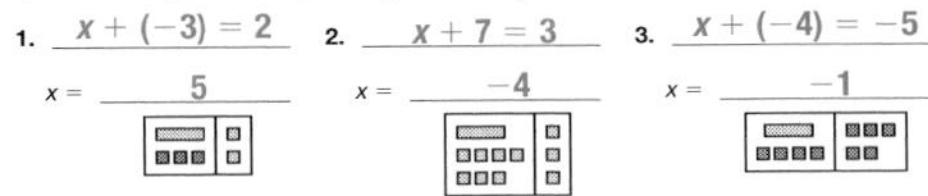

For each equation, tell whether the number in bold is a solution.

4. $x - 4 = 0$; **6** No
5. $h + (-3) = -13$; **16** No
6. $b - 1 = -4$; **−3** Yes
7. $m + (-6) = 8$; **2** No
8. $d - 7 = 6$; **13** Yes
9. $p + (-8) = -35$; **43** No

Solve each equation. Check your solutions.

10. $a - (-4) = -2$ $a =$ −6
11. $q + 2 = -47$ $q =$ −49
12. $s - (-5) = -7$ $s =$ −12
13. $t + 6 = 3$ $t =$ −3
14. $k + 8 = 2$ $k =$ −6
15. $f - (-7) = -24$ $f =$ −31
16. $c + (-2) = 51$ $c =$ 53
17. $y - 9 = 4$ $y =$ 13
18. $j + 15 = -9$ $j =$ −24
19. $u + (-21) = 18$ $u =$ 39
20. $g - 5 = 3$ $g =$ 8
21. $x - 31 = 74$ $x =$ 105
22. $w + (-45) = 11$ $w =$ 56
23. $r - 60 = -38$ $r =$ 22
24. $n + 3 = 26$ $n =$ 23
25. $z - (-72) = 62$ $z =$ −10

26. Yesterday's high temperature was 24°F. This was 33° higher than last night's low temperature. What was last night's low temperature? −9°F

27. The U.S. Postal Service handled 35.8 million pieces of library rate mail in 1994. This is 2.9 million pieces fewer than in 1993. How many library rate packages were mailed in 1993? 38.7 million

RETEACHING

Name ____________

Alternative Lesson 10-9

Integer Addition and Subtraction Equations

To solve an equation, you need to decide what was done to the variable. Then use *inverse operations* to undo it.

Example

Solve $x + 3 = -7$.

Step 1: Isolate x. Since 3 was added to x, you can undo the addition by subtracting 3. Think: $x + 3 - 3$ is the same as x.

Step 2: Since the amounts on each side of the equation are equal, you must perform the same operation on each side. $x + 3 - \mathbf{3} = -7 - \mathbf{3}$

Step 3: Simplify both sides of the equation. $x = -10$

So, the solution is $x = -10$.

Try It Solve $x - 5 = -1$.

a. Isolate x. What will you undo? Add 5 to undo subtraction of 5.

b. Solve the equation.

$x - 5 = -1$
$x - 5 + \underline{5} = -1 + \underline{5}$
$x = \underline{4}$

Solve each equation.

c. $x + 4 = 9$
$x + 4 - \underline{4} = 9 - \underline{4}$
$x = \underline{5}$

d. $x - 2 = 3$
$x - 2 + \underline{2} = 3 + \underline{2}$
$x = \underline{5}$

e. $x + 3 = 12$
$x + 3 - \underline{3} = 12 - \underline{3}$
$x = \underline{9}$

f. $x - 3 = 14$
$x - 3 + \underline{3} = 14 + \underline{3}$
$x = \underline{17}$

g. $x - 2 = 5$ $x = \underline{7}$

h. $x + 5 = 12$ $x = \underline{7}$

i. $x + 200 = 550$ $x = \underline{350}$

Reteaching

Activity

Materials: Cups, 2-color counters

- To solve $x + 2 = -6$, place a cup and 2 yellow counters on one side of your desk and 6 red counters on the other side.
- Put counters into the cup so that the value on both sides is the same. How many counters did you put into the cup? 8 What color are they? Red What is the value of x? $x = -8$
- Use the same method to solve other addition or subtraction equations involving integers.

Exercise Notes

Exercise 23

Problem-Solving Tip Some students may solve problems like this one by adding 948 and 73; ask them if there is another equation they could write for this problem.

Exercise Answers

25. Possible answer: After she paid him 5 cents, Christa still owed Danilo 55 cents. How much did she originally owe? $x = -60$

27. a. The variable has a negative sign.

    b. $x = 59$; Solve for $-x$ and take the opposite of that number.

28. 6, 12, 24; Possible answers: $\frac{2}{3} = \frac{4}{6}, \frac{2}{3} = \frac{8}{12}, \frac{8}{12} = \frac{16}{24}, \frac{2}{3} = \frac{16}{24}$.

29. 15, 20, 35; Possible answers: $\frac{1}{5} = \frac{3}{15}, \frac{3}{15} = \frac{4}{20}, \frac{4}{20} = \frac{7}{35}, \frac{3}{15} = \frac{7}{35}$.

30. $\frac{11}{24} = \frac{x}{100}$; $x = 45.8$

31. $\frac{1}{5} = \frac{12}{x}$; $x = 60$

32. $\frac{9}{10} = \frac{n}{1210}$; $n = 1089$

33. $\frac{1}{1000} = \frac{57}{m}$; $m = 57{,}000$

Alternate Assessment

Interview Have students use algebra tiles to solve an equation. The interview may be videotaped or audiotaped; in either case, students will need to explain each step of the solution aloud.

Quick Quiz

Solve each equation.

1. $x - 5 = -2$ $x = 3$
2. $x - (-3) = 2$ $x = -1$
3. $x + 4 = -9$ $x = -13$

Available on Daily Transparency 10-9

PROBLEM SOLVING 10-9

23. Science Atmospheric pressure is sometimes measured in *millibars.* Low pressure is associated with severe weather. The pressure at the center of Hurricane Luis dropped 73 millibars in ten days, to a low of 948 millibars. What was the original pressure? 1021 millibars

24. Test Prep At sunset on the moon, the temperature is about 58°F. After night falls, the temperature can drop to −261°F. Which equation could be used to find the difference between the two temperatures? C

Ⓐ $D = 261 - 58$ Ⓑ $D = 58 - 261$

Ⓒ $D = 58 - (-261)$ Ⓓ $D = -261 + 58$

Problem Solving and Reasoning

25. Communicate Write a problem that could be modeled by the equation $x + 5 = -55$. Then give the solution to your problem.

26. Choose a Strategy GPS The Dow Jones Industrial Average measures the prices of important stocks on the New York Stock Exchange. Suppose the Dow Jones average ends the week at 5602.10. The average lost 8.70 points on Monday, gained 37.70 on Tuesday, lost 11.25 on Wednesday, gained 24.90 on Thursday, and gained 27.15 on Friday. What was the Dow Jones average at the start of the week? 5532.30

Problem Solving STRATEGIES

- Look for a Pattern
- Make an Organized List
- Make a Table
- Guess and Check
- Work Backward
- Use Logical Reasoning
- Draw a Diagram
- Solve a Simpler Problem

27. Critical Thinking Suppose you're given the equation $-x + 27 = -32$.

a. What is the difference between this equation and other addition and subtraction equations you've solved?

b. Solve this equation. Explain how you found the solution.

Mixed Review

Complete each table to create equal ratios. Then write four proportions involving ratios in the table. *[Lesson 6-5]*

28.

2	4	8	16
3			

29.

1	3	4	7
5			

Write a proportion and solve each problem. If necessary, round answers to the nearest tenth. *[Lesson 8-6]*

30. What percent of 24 is 11?

31. 20% of what number is 12?

32. 90% of 1210 is what number?

33. 0.1% of what number is 57?

PROBLEM SOLVING

Name ____________

Guided Problem Solving 10-9

GPS PROBLEM 26, STUDENT PAGE 528

The Dow Jones Industrial Average measures the prices of important stocks on the New York Stock Exchange. Suppose the Dow Jones average ends the week at 5602.10. The average lost 8.70 points on Monday, gained 37.70 on Tuesday, lost 11.25 on Wednesday, gained 24.90 on Thursday, and gained 27.15 on Friday. What was the Dow Jones average at the start of the week?

— Understand —

1. Where was the Dow Jones average at the end of the week? 5602.10
2. How many changes were made during the week? 5 changes.
3. What are you asked to find? The Dow Jones average at the start of the week.

— Plan —

4. Which of the changes could be considered positive? Negative? Positive; 37.70, 24.90, 27.15; Negative: 8.70, 11.25
5. Let x represent the Dow Jones average at the start of the week. Write an equation to show the change from the start of the week to the end of the week. $x - 8.70 + 37.70 - 11.25 + 24.90 + 27.15 = 5602.10$

— Solve —

6. Solve the equation you wrote in Item 5. What was the Dow Jones average at the start of the week? 5532.30

— Look Back —

7. What other strategy could you use to find the answer? Possible answer: Work Backward

SOLVE ANOTHER PROBLEM

Suppose Jerome has an average of 87.2 in math. On the previous three tests, his average had gained 2.1 points, lost 3.4 points, and gained 1.5 points. What was his average before the last three tests? 87

ENRICHMENT

Name ____________

Extend Your Thinking 10-9

Visual Thinking

Which of these figures do you think will have the greatest area? The greatest perimeter? The least area? The least perimeter? Record your estimates inside each figure. Estimates will vary.

1.

2.

3.

4.

5.

Measure each figure to the nearest centimeter and complete the table.

Figure	Length (cm)	Width (cm)	Area	Perimeter
1	8 cm	3 cm	24 cm^2	22 cm
2	7 cm	3 cm	21 cm^2	20 cm
3	12 cm	2 cm	24 cm^2	28 cm
4	5 cm	5 cm	25 cm^2	20 cm
5	6 cm	4 cm	24 cm^2	20 cm

Which figure has the

6. greatest area? Figure 4
7. greatest perimeter? Figure 3
8. least area? Figure 2
9. least perimeter? Figures 2, 4, 5

Integer Multiplication and Division Equations

10-10

▶ Lesson Link You've solved equations that involve adding and subtracting integers. Now you'll solve equations with multiplication and division of integers. ◀

You'll Learn ...

- to solve multiplication and division equations involving positive and negative integers

... How It's Used

Submarine crews can solve an equation involving their ascent rate to determine when they will reach the surface.

Explore — Modeling Multiplication Equations

Divide and Conquer!

Materials: Algebra tiles

1. A set of equations is modeled by algebra tiles. Write the equation for each equation box.

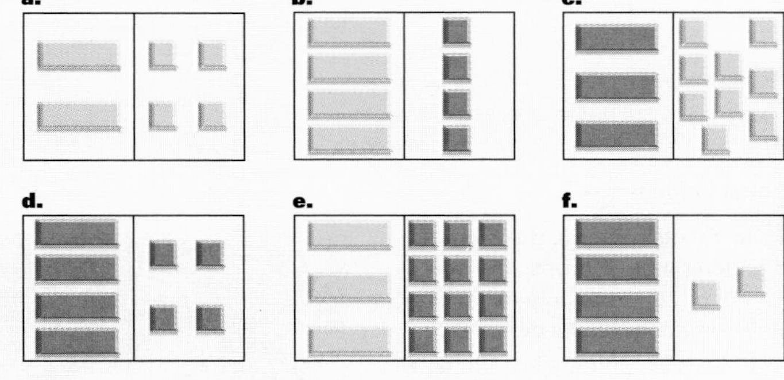

2. Use the tiles to solve each equation. Check your solutions.
3. Explain how you solved these equations. Tell why the method you used does not break any of the rules for solving equations.

Learn — Integer Multiplication and Division Equations

You've seen that multiplication and division are inverse operations. You can use this fact to solve multiplication and division equations with negative numbers.

When you solve these equations, you'll need to remember the rules for multiplication and division of signed numbers.

When two numbers have the same sign, their product or quotient is positive; when the numbers have different signs, their product or quotient is negative.

MEETING INDIVIDUAL NEEDS

Resources

- 10-10 Practice
- 10-10 Reteaching
- 10-10 Problem Solving
- 10-10 Enrichment
- 10-10 Daily Transparency
  - Problem of the Day
  - Review
  - Quick Quiz
- Teaching Tool Transparencies 12, 13
- Lesson Enhancement Transparency 50
- Technology Master 50

Learning Modalities

Kinesthetic Have students use algebra tiles to model the equations in Exercises 1 and 5.

Visual Have students make a poster with the procedures for solving addition and subtraction equations, as well as multiplication and division equations.

Challenge

Have students use real data to make up other problems similar to Example 2 on page 530. Point out that almanacs contain much weather information about various cities around the world.

10-10 Lesson Organizer

Objective

- Solve multiplication and division equations involving positive and negative integers.

Materials

- Explore: Algebra tiles

NCTM Standards

- 1–4, 9, 12

Review

Find each product or quotient.

1. $-20(-30)$ 600
2. $8(-40)$ -320
3. $\frac{-80}{40}$ -2
4. $\frac{-300}{-50}$ 6

Available on Daily Transparency 10-10

1 Introduce

Explore

You may want to use Lesson Enhancement Transparency 50 with **Explore**.

The Point

Students use algebra tiles to model equations involving multiplication and division and then solve the equations.

Ongoing Assessment

Some students may have difficulty with Step 1f since the solution is a fraction.

Answers for Explore

1. a. $2x = 4$ b. $4x = -4$ c. $-3x = 9$ d. $-4x = -4$ e. $3x = -12$ f. $-4x = 2$
2. a. $x = 2$ b. $x = -1$ c. $x = -3$ d. $x = 1$ e. $x = -4$ f. $x = -\frac{1}{2}$
3. Divide the number that is alone on one side by the number in front of the variable; Whatever is done to one side of the equation is done to the other.

2 Teach

Learn

You may want to use Teaching Tool Transparencies 12 and 13: Algebra Tiles with **Learn.**

Alternate Examples

1. Solve $4x = -12$.

   The algebra tiles illustrate the steps. Each side of the equation box represents a side of the equation.

   $4x = -12$

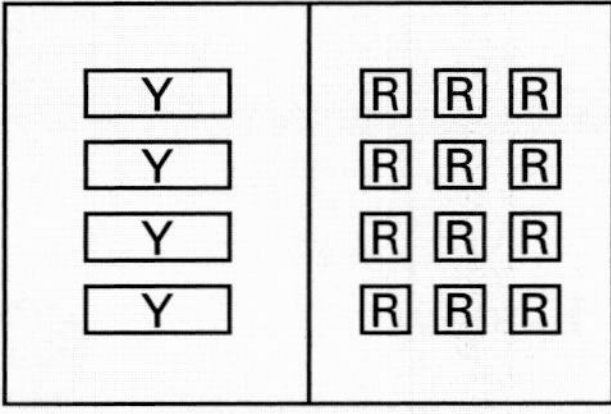

   To undo multiplying by 4, divide by 4.

   $\frac{4x}{4} = \frac{-12}{4}$

Y	R R R
Y	R R R
Y	R R R
Y	R R R

   The quotient of a negative and a positive number is negative.

Y	R R R

   $x = -3$

2. Suppose that the average high temperature drops 10°F each month from July to January. How long does it take before the average high temperature changes by −40°F?

   Define a variable and write an equation for the problem. Let m = the number of months. Use inverse operations to solve.

   $-10m = -40$

   $\frac{-10m}{-10} = \frac{-40}{-10}$

   $m = \frac{-40}{-10}$

   $= 4$ Divide.

   The quotient of two negative numbers is positive.

   The average high temperature changes by −40°F in 4 months.

Algebra tiles can be used to show why the steps for solving a multiplication equation work. Notice how division is shown in the equation boxes.

Examples

1 Solve: $3x = -9$

The algebra tiles illustrate the steps. Each side of the equation box represents a side of the equation.

$3x = -9$

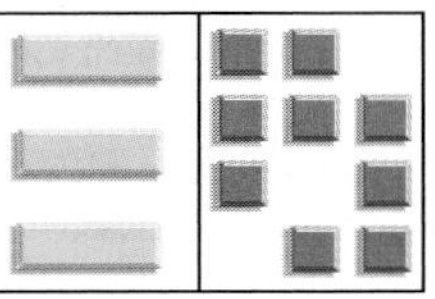

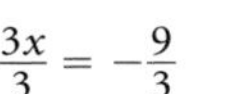

$\frac{3x}{3} = -\frac{9}{3}$ To undo multiplying by 3, divide by 3.

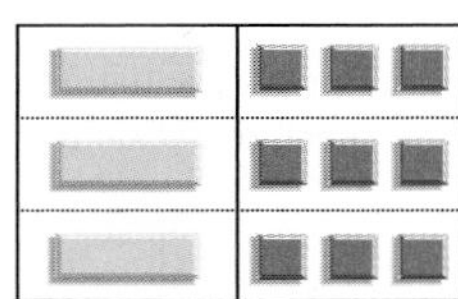

$x = -3$ Divide. The quotient of a negative and a positive number is negative.

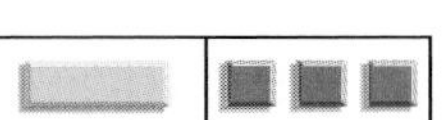

The solution is $x = -3$.

DID YOU KNOW?

In January, the average *high* temperature in Yakutsk is −46°F!

2 In Yakutsk, Russia, the average high temperature drops 20°F per month (−20°) from July to January. How long does it take before the average high temperature changes (drops) by −90°F?

Let m = the number of months. Define a variable.

$-20m = -90$ Write an equation for the problem.

$\frac{-20m}{-20} = \frac{-90}{-20}$ Use inverse operations.

$m = \frac{-90}{-20} = \frac{9}{2} = 4\frac{1}{2}$ Divide. The quotient of two negative numbers is positive.

The average high temperature changes by −90°F in $4\frac{1}{2}$ months.

Try It

Solve each equation.

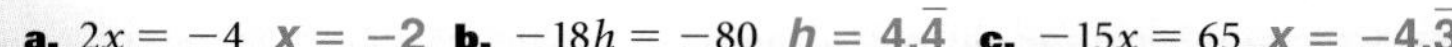

a. $2x = -4$ $x = -2$ **b.** $-18h = -80$ $h = 4.\overline{4}$ **c.** $-15x = 65$ $x = -4.\overline{3}$

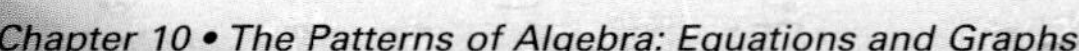

MATH EVERY DAY

Problem of the Day

Melissa had $250 in her savings account. On January 1, she put some money into her account. Each month she doubled the amount that she had put in her account the previous month. Excluding interest earned, her savings account balance on June 2 was $691. How much did she deposit on June 1? $224

Available on Daily Transparency 10-10

An Extension is provided in the transparency package.

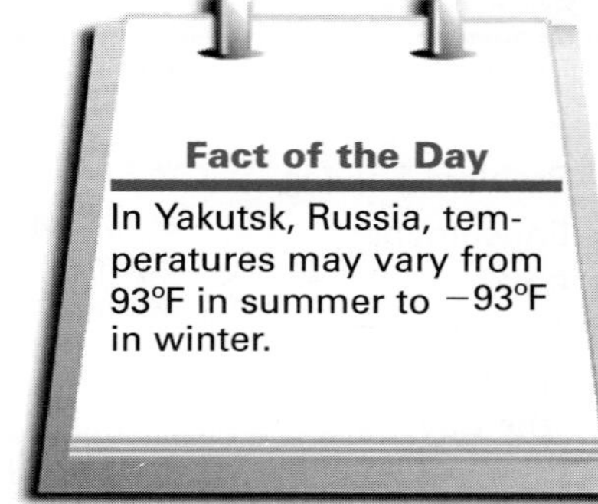

Fact of the Day

In Yakutsk, Russia, temperatures may vary from 93°F in summer to −93°F in winter.

Mental Math

Do these mentally.

1. $3\frac{1}{2} + 5\frac{1}{2} - 4\frac{1}{2}$ $4\frac{1}{2}$
2. $(3\frac{1}{2} + 5\frac{1}{2}) \div 2$ $4\frac{1}{2}$
3. $4 \bullet 5\frac{1}{2}$ 22
4. $5 \div \frac{1}{2}$ 10

It's difficult to model division equations with algebra tiles. However, these equations can be solved by using inverse operations.

Examples

3 Solve: $\frac{x}{-10} = 20$

$\frac{x}{-10}(-10) = 20(-10)$ Use inverse operations.

$x = -200$ Multiply.

The solution is $x = -200$. To check, substitute into the original equation.

$\frac{-200}{-10} = 20$

$20 = 20$ ✓

4 In a flood in Kansas City, Missouri, and Kansas City, Kansas, the Kansas River rose an average of 6 inches per hour for 40 hours, when it spilled over a restraining wall and flooded the cities. How much did the waters rise over this time?

Let r = the rise in the waters. Define a variable.

$\frac{r}{40} = 6$ Write an equation for the problem.

$\frac{r}{40} \cdot 40 = 6 \cdot 40$ Use inverse operations.

$r = 240$ Multiply.

The flood waters rose 240 inches, or 20 feet.

History Link

The Salton Sea in California did not exist until 1905, when the Colorado River flooded a human-made canal. The water rushed into a salt flat known as the Salton Sink, creating a huge inland lake.

Try It

Solve each equation.

a. $\frac{y}{5} = -30$ $y = -150$ **b.** $\frac{w}{-6} = -220$ $w = 1320$ **c.** $\frac{m}{-2} = -224$ $m = 448$

Check Your Understanding

1. Explain how you could use algebra tiles to solve $-3x = 6$.

2. Can you tell the sign of the answer to a multiplication equation before you solve it? If so, explain how. If not, explain why not.

Alternate Examples

3. Solve $\frac{x}{3} = -5$.

Use inverse operations.

$\frac{x}{3}(3) = -5(3)$

$x = -15$ Multiply.

The solution is $x = -15$. To check, substitute into the original equation.

$-\frac{15}{3} = -5$

$-5 = -5$ √

4. A submarine descends 10 feet each minute. It goes down for 24 minutes. How far below the surface is it?

Let f = the number of feet above or below the surface. Write an equation for the problem. Then use inverse operations.

$\frac{f}{-10} = 24$

$\frac{f}{-10}(-10) = 24(-10)$

$f = -240$

The submarine is 240 feet below the surface.

3 Practice and Assess

Check

Answers for Check Your Understanding

1. Use 3 red strips on the left and 6 yellow squares on the right. Make 3 equal groups on both sides. Each group on the left has one red strip and each group on the right has 2 yellow squares, showing $-x = 2$, or "the opposite of x equals 2." From this, we know that $x = -2$.
2. Yes; If both the number in front of the variable and the number on the opposite side of the equation have the same sign, the answer will be positive; if they have different signs, the answer will be negative.

MEETING MIDDLE SCHOOL CLASSROOM NEEDS

Tips from Middle School Teachers

My students seem to be much more comfortable multiplying than dividing. It seems as if they set up just about every problem by multiplying. I used to worry that this would not give them enough experience with division situations, but I realized that they can always use multiplication instead of division. Now I make sure that students have experiences with solving division equations, but I don't worry about whether they used division in setting up the equations.

Cooperative Learning

As a follow-up to the **Explore** activity, have each student write about how their group solved two of the equations illustrated. This follow-up allows you to assess the students individually and helps to establish accountability for participation in group activities.

Geography Connection

Yakutsk, Russia, is located in the region called Siberia. This region has long, cold winters and short, hot summers. A layer of permanently frozen ground called permafrost covers most of eastern Siberia.

Assignment Guide

- **Basic** 1–16, 22–26, 28–33
- **Average** 1–8, 11–18, 21–26, 28–33
- **Enriched** 2–8, 13–33

Exercise Notes

Exercise 15

Error Prevention Some students may solve an equation such as this one by dividing -12 by -3 instead of multiplying. Remind them to use the inverse operation and to check their solution by substituting it into the equation.

Exercise 21

Problem-Solving Tip Some students may write the equation $r = 6748 \div 13{,}486$ to solve this problem. They could also write $13{,}486r = 6743$.

Exercise Answers

1. a. $\frac{-3x}{-3} = \frac{-15}{-3}$
   b. $x = 5$
   c. $-3(5) = -15, -15 = -15$

Reteaching

Activity

Materials: Almanac

- Work with a partner. Each of you pick a city and then use the almanac to find the average high temperatures in that city for the months of July and January.
- Determine the average drop or rise per month. Write a problem similar to Example 2 on page 530 and then exchange problems and solve them.

10-10 Exercises and Applications

PRACTICE 10-10

Practice and Apply

1. **Getting Started** Follow the steps to solve $-3x = -15$.

a. To isolate x, you need to undo multiplication by -3. To do this, divide both sides of the equation by -3.

b. The left side of the equation simplifies to x. Use your rules for integer division to simplify the right side of the equation.

c. Check your answer by substituting it into the original equation.

Write the equation represented by each equation box. Then solve the equation.

2. 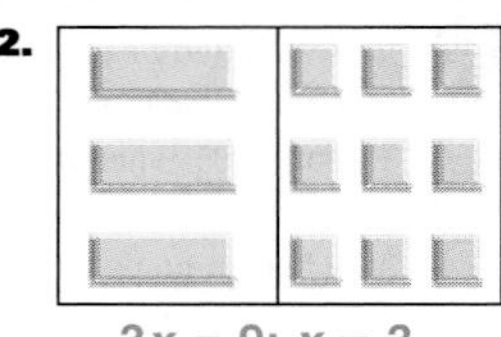
$3x = 9$; $x = 3$

3. 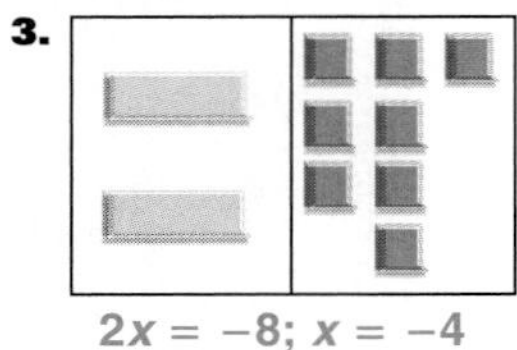
$2x = -8$; $x = -4$

4. 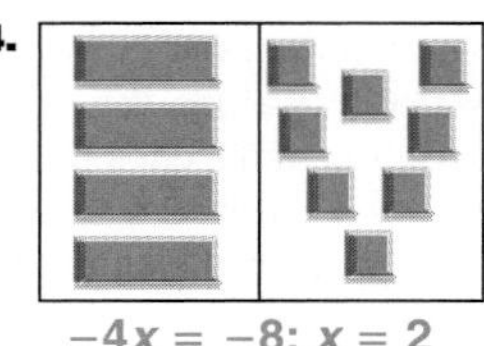
$-4x = -8$; $x = 2$

For each equation, tell whether the number in bold is a solution.

5. $-4p = -20$; $\mathbf{-5}$ No **6.** $\frac{x}{4} = -16$; $\mathbf{-4}$ No **7.** $8t = -168$; $\mathbf{-21}$ Yes **8.** $\frac{v}{-2} = 12$; $\mathbf{-24}$ Yes

Solve each equation. Check your solutions.

9. $3m = 99$ $m = 33$ **10.** $11g = -44$ $g = -4$ **11.** $-8z = -80$ $z = 10$ **12.** $84 = -2s$ $s = -42$

13. $\frac{c}{4} = -16$ $c = -64$ **14.** $\frac{g}{7} = -11$ $g = -77$ **15.** $\frac{d}{-3} = -12$ $d = 36$ **16.** $\frac{f}{-8} = -22$ $f = 176$

17. $-1x = 19$ $x = -19$ **18.** $\frac{n}{-25} = -101$ $n = 2525$ **19.** $-5.2x = -18.2$ $x = 3.5$ **20.** $\frac{y}{-107} = 0$ $y = 0$

21. **Science** The wettest inhabited place in the world is Buenaventura, Colombia. Its average annual rainfall is 6,743 mm—over 22 ft of rain! Buenaventura's rainfall is 13,486 times as great as the rainfall of the driest inhabited place, Aswan, Egypt. What is the annual rainfall in Aswan? 0.5 mm

Aswan, Egypt

PRACTICE

Name ______________________

Practice 10-10

Integer Multiplication and Division Equations

Write the equation represented by each equation box. Then solve the equation. The lighter tiles represent positive integers.

1. $-2x = 8$ $x =$ -4 2. $-4x = -12$ $x =$ 3 3. $3x = -6$ $x =$ -2

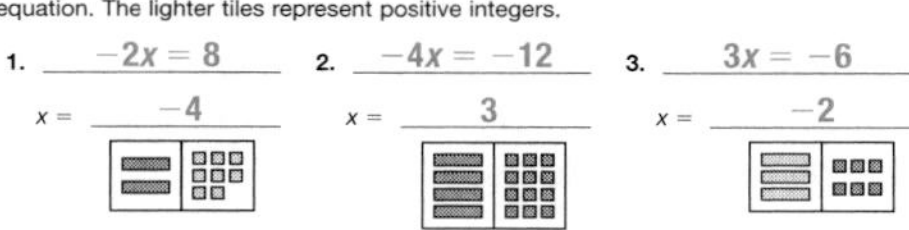

For each equation, tell whether the number in bold is a solution.

4. $\frac{x}{7} = 15$; **105** Yes 5. $3x = 21$; **63** No 6. $\frac{t}{-2} = 8$; **−4** No
7. $-5z = -34$; **7** No 8. $\frac{m}{4} = -9$; **−36** Yes 9. $-6t = -24$; **4** Yes

Solve each equation. Check your solutions.

10. $7n = 77$ $n =$ 11 11. $\frac{r}{-5} = 12$ $r =$ −60 12. $-2b = 34$ $b =$ −17 13. $\frac{g}{3} = 8$ $g =$ 24
14. $-8d = -64$ $d =$ 8 15. $-5k = 0$ $k =$ 0 16. $\frac{x}{10} = -6$ $x =$ −60 17. $\frac{u}{-8} = 15$ $u =$ −120
18. $-4a = 40$ $a =$ −10 19. $\frac{h}{-64} = 1$ $h =$ −64 20. $-7c = -56$ $c =$ 8 21. $\frac{f}{2} = -16$ $f =$ −32
22. $\frac{p}{-11} = -88$ $p =$ 968 23. $6t = -42$ $t =$ −7 24. $-12z = -96$ $z =$ 8 25. $\frac{y}{-18} = 3$ $y =$ −54

26. **Computer** Jerry recently bought a new modem for his computer. Yesterday, his new modem took 7 minutes to download a file. This is $\frac{1}{12}$ of the time it would have taken using his old modem. How long would it take to download the file using the old modem? 84 min

27. **Geography** In 1994, the population of Argentina was about 34,000,000 people This was about 170 times as great as the population of Belize. What was the population of Belize? About 200,000

RETEACHING

Name ______________________

Alternative Lesson 10-10

Integer Multiplication and Division Equations

To solve an equation, you need to decide what was done to the variable. Then use inverse operations to undo it.

Example

Solve $-2x = 14$.

Step 1: Isolate x. Since x is multiplied by -2, you can undo the multiplication by dividing by -2. Think: $\frac{-2x}{-2}$ is the same as x.

Step 2: Since the amounts on each side of an equation are equal, you must perform the same operation on each side. $\frac{-2x}{-2} = \frac{14}{-2}$

Step 3: Simplify both sides of the equation. $x = -7$

So, the solution is -7.

Try It Solve $\frac{x}{3} = 8$.

a. Isolate x. What will you undo? Multiply by 3 to undo division by 3.

b. Solve the equation.

$\frac{x}{3} = 8$
$\frac{x}{3} \cdot$ 3 $= 8 \cdot$ 3
$x =$ 24

Solve each equation.

c. $-4x = 28$
$-4x \div$ −4 $= 28 \div$ −4
$x =$ −7

d. $6x = 18$
$6x \div$ 6 $= 18 \div$ 6
$x =$ 3

e. $\frac{x}{5} = -7$
$\frac{x}{5} \cdot$ 5 $= -7 \cdot$ 5
$x =$ −35

f. $\frac{x}{-3} = -9$
$\frac{x}{-3} \cdot$ −3 $= -9 \cdot$ −3
$x =$ 27

22. Geometry If the area of a parallelogram is 42 cm^2 and its length is 14 cm, what is its width? Explain how you solved this problem.

23. Operation Sense Write two different division equations that have a solution of -4.

24. **Test Prep** Yakutat, Alaska, has an average annual rainfall of about 135 inches. This is about 5 times the annual rainfall of Minneapolis, Minnesota. Which equation can be used to find the approximate annual rainfall for Minneapolis? D

Ⓐ $r = 135 \cdot 5$ Ⓑ $r = 135 + 5$ Ⓒ $r = 135 - 5$ Ⓓ $r = \frac{135}{5}$

25. Consumer Using a sunscreen can help prevent skin cancer. A sunscreen with an SPF of 15 means you can stay in the sun 15 times as long without burning as you could with no sunscreen. Jules tends to burn after 30 minutes in the sun. If he is buying sunscreen for a 12-hour hike in a sunny canyon, what is the smallest SPF number he should look for? 24

Problem Solving TIP

Draw a picture to help you write an algebraic equation.

PROBLEM SOLVING 10-10

Problem Solving and Reasoning

26. Communicate Write a problem that could be modeled by the equation $-5x = -100$. Then give the solution to your problem.

27. Journal Although it's difficult to use algebra tiles to model a division equation, it's not impossible! Explain a way that you could use algebra tiles to solve a division equation. Then show how your method works by sketching the solution to a division equation.

28. Critical Thinking GPS Suppose the average low temperature for a 4-day period in Chicago, Illinois, is $-8°F$. After the next day, the 5-day average is $-9°F$. What was the low temperature for the fifth day? Explain your reasoning.

Mixed Review

29. George earned \$12.00 for working 2 hours and \$35.00 for working 5 hours. Are the rates proportional? *[Lesson 6-6]* No

Find the new amount after each increase or decrease. If necessary, round answers to the nearest tenth. *[Lesson 8-7]*

30. \$80 is increased by 55% \$124

31. 1580 is decreased by 90% 158

32. 22.7 is increased by 120% 49.9

33. \$108 is decreased by 34% \$71.30

Exercise Notes

Exercise 25

Problem-Solving Tip Some students may solve this problem by thinking that 12 hours is 24 times as long as one half-hour, without using any variables. Encourage them to also look for a way to use a variable in the problem.

Exercise Answers

22. 3 cm; $42 = 14x$; Solve for x.

23. Possible answers: $\frac{12}{m} = -3$ and $\frac{n}{-2} = 2$.

26. Possible answer: Jennifer descended 100 feet at a rate of 5 feet per minute. How many minutes did this descent take her? 20 minutes

27. Answers may vary. Possible answer: Let the variable tiles represent a fraction rather than one whole.

28. $-13°F$; The sum of the temperatures for the first four days was $-32°F$; therefore, set up and solve the equation $\frac{-32 + n}{5} = -12$.

Alternate Assessment

You may want to use the *Interactive CD-ROM Journal* with this assessment.

Journal Have students explain how solving addition/subtraction equations is like solving multiplication/division equations and how it is different.

PROBLEM SOLVING

Name ____________________

Guided Problem Solving 10-10

GPS PROBLEM 28, STUDENT PAGE 533

Suppose the average low temperature for a 4-day period in Chicago, Illinois, is -8°F. After the next day, the 5-day average is -9°F. What was the low temperature for the fifth day? Explain your reasoning.

— Understand —

1. How do you find the average of several temperatures? Add them; divide sum by the number of temperatures.

2. If the average is -8°F, could some of the temperatures be

a. above -8°F? Yes b. below -8°F? Yes

— Plan —

3. If the average for a 4-day period is -8°F, what is the sum of the temperatures for a 4-day period? Explain. -32°F, because $-32 \div 4 = -8$.

4. If the average for a 5-day period is -9°F, what is the sum of the temperatures for the 5-day period? Explain. -45°F, because $-45 \div 5 = -9$.

5. What is the change in temperature between the 4-day period and the 5-day period? 13° change.

— Solve —

6. What is the low temperature for the fifth day? -13°F

— Look Back —

7. How can you check to see if your answer is reasonable? Possible answer: Add your answer and the 4-day total, then divide by 5 to make sure the average is -9°F.

SOLVE ANOTHER PROBLEM

After 3 days, the average low temperature was -5°C. After the next day, the 4-day average was -9°C. What was the low temperature for the fourth day? -21°F

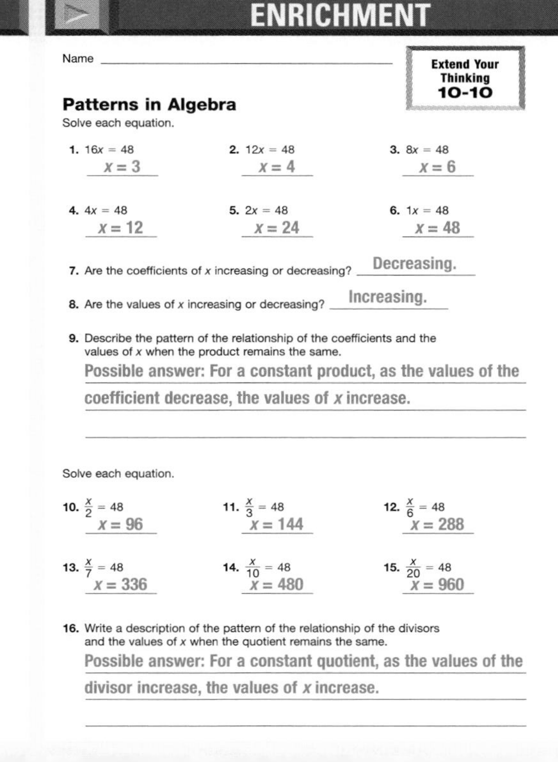

ENRICHMENT

Name ____________________

Extend Your Thinking 10-10

Patterns in Algebra

Solve each equation.

1. $16x = 48$ $x = 3$
2. $12x = 48$ $x = 4$
3. $8x = 48$ $x = 6$
4. $4x = 48$ $x = 12$
5. $2x = 48$ $x = 24$
6. $1x = 48$ $x = 48$

7. Are the coefficients of x increasing or decreasing? Decreasing.

8. Are the values of x increasing or decreasing? Increasing.

9. Describe the pattern of the relationship of the coefficients and the values of x when the product remains the same. Possible answer: For a constant product, as the values of the coefficient decrease, the values of x increase.

Solve each equation.

10. $\frac{x}{2} = 48$ $x = 96$
11. $\frac{x}{3} = 48$ $x = 144$
12. $\frac{x}{6} = 48$ $x = 288$
13. $\frac{x}{7} = 48$ $x = 336$
14. $\frac{x}{10} = 48$ $x = 480$
15. $\frac{x}{20} = 48$ $x = 960$

16. Write a description of the pattern of the relationship of the divisors and the values of x when the quotient remains the same. Possible answer: For a constant quotient, as the values of the divisor increase, the values of x increase.

Quick Quiz

Solve each equation.

1. $-6x = 36$ $x = -6$
2. $\frac{y}{5} = -15$ $y = -75$
3. $-28 = -7s$ $s = 4$
4. $-6 = \frac{n}{-2}$ $n = 12$

Available on Daily Transparency 10-10

10-11 Lesson Organizer

Objective

- Solve two-step equations involving positive and negative integers.

Materials

- Algebra tiles

NCTM Standards

- 1–4, 7, 9, 12

Review

Solve each equation.

1. $x + (-5) = -22$ $x = -17$
2. $x - (-8) = 14$ $x = 6$
3. $4x = -100$ $x = -25$
4. $-6x = -96$ $x = 16$

Available on Daily Transparency 10-11

1 Introduce

Explore

You may want to use Teaching Tool Transparencies 12 and 13: Algebra Tiles with **Explore.**

The Point
Students use algebra tiles to solve a two-step equation and then try to find a second way to solve the equation.

Ongoing Assessment
Some students may be able to solve the equation in one way but unable to come up with a second way. Suggest that they try to make three equal groups on the left by adding something to both sides.

Answers for Explore

1. See page C5.
2. $x = 2$
3. Addition of -2; To undo expressions, reverse the order of operations.
4. Possible solution: Add -1 to both sides, divide both sides by 3, and solve the resulting equation ($x - 1 = 1$).

10-11 Solving Two-Step Equations

You'll Learn ...

- to solve two-step equations involving positive and negative integers

... How It's Used

Two-step equations can help you analyze memberships or subscriptions that have a small initial payment plus a monthly fee.

▶ Lesson Link You've solved integer equations involving just one step. Now you'll solve two-step equations. ◀

Explore Modeling Two-Step Equations

Doing the Two-Step

Materials: Algebra tiles

1. Model the equation $3x + (-2) = 4$ with algebra tiles.
2. Use the rules for solving equations to solve this equation. Record each step and check your answer when you finish.
3. In solving this equation, which did you undo first, the addition of -2 to x or the multiplication of x by 3? Why did you choose to undo this operation first?
4. Try to use the tiles to solve the equation in Step 1 in a different way. If you are able to solve the equation another way, explain how you did it. If you can't solve the equation, explain why not.

Learn Solving Two-Step Equations

You may recall the idea of an inverse operation machine. This machine always gives back the same number that goes in. Notice that it undoes operations in the *opposite* of their original order.

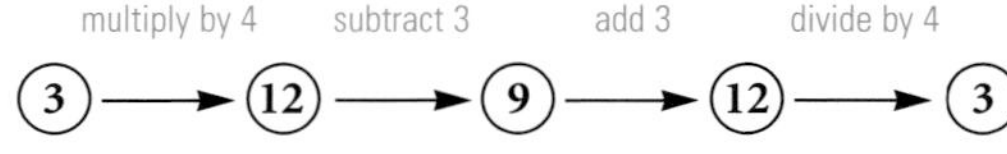

You can use this idea to help you solve two-step equations. Because you *do* addition and subtraction last in the order of operations, you need to *undo* them first when solving equations.

MEETING INDIVIDUAL NEEDS

Resources

- 10-11 Practice
- 10-11 Reteaching
- 10-11 Problem Solving
- 10-11 Enrichment
- 10-11 Daily Transparency
  - Problem of the Day
  - Review
  - Quick Quiz
- Teaching Tool Transparencies 12, 13
- Technology Master 51
- Chapter 10 Project Master

Learning Modalities

Visual Ask students to develop a visual display to help them in solving equations. Their display might include order of operations and a reminder to reverse the order of operations when solving equations.

Social Ask students who need an extra challenge to explain to the class how to do problems like Exercise 26. Encourage them to use additional examples, models, and/or overhead transparencies to create an interesting presentation.

English Language Development

Have students make flashcards with the names of the four operations and the words sum, difference, product, and quotient and another set with the symbols +, −, •, and ÷. Then have students match cards that are related.

Examples

1 Solve: $3 + 2x = -5$

$3 + 2x = -5$

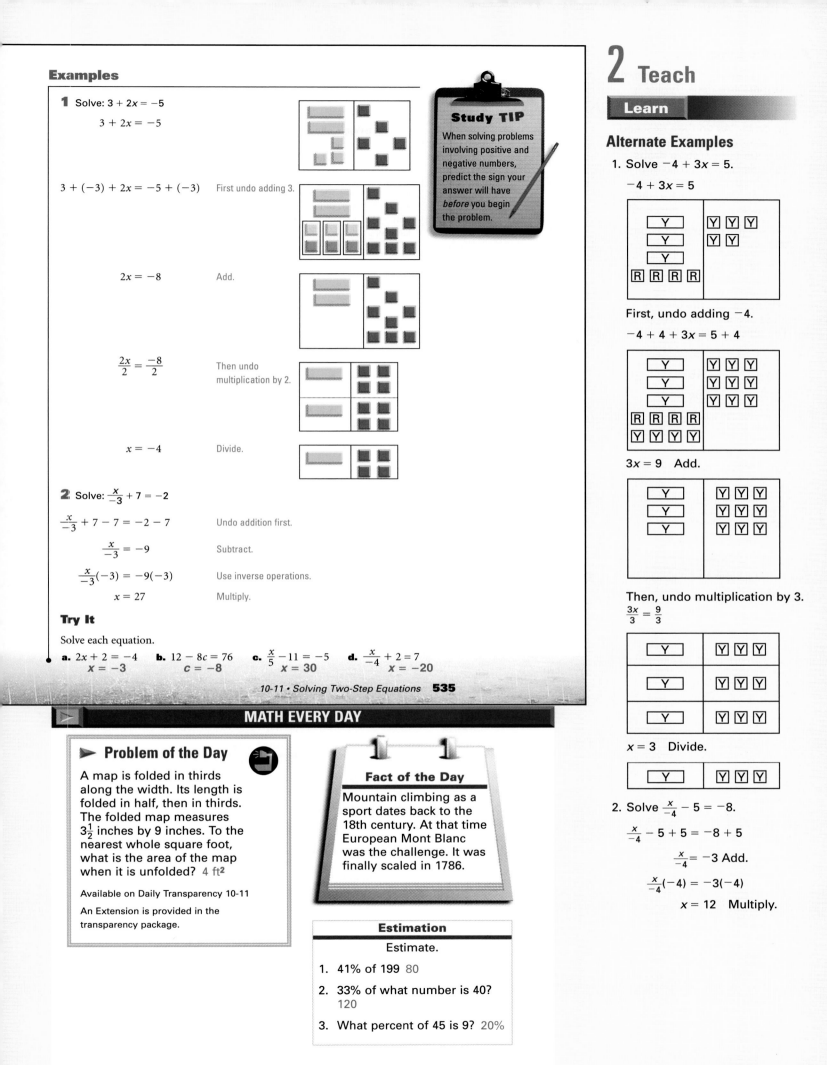

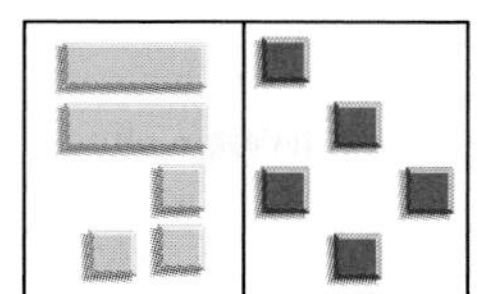

$3 + (-3) + 2x = -5 + (-3)$ First undo adding 3.

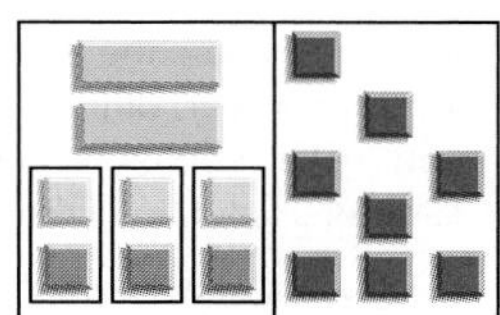

$2x = -8$ Add.

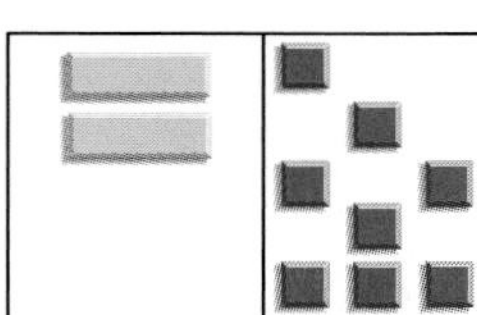

$\frac{2x}{2} = \frac{-8}{2}$ Then undo multiplication by 2.

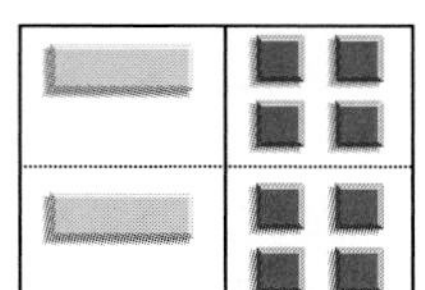

$x = -4$ Divide.

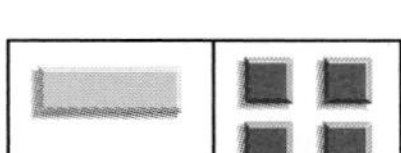

Study TIP

When solving problems involving positive and negative numbers, predict the sign your answer will have *before* you begin the problem.

2 Solve: $\frac{x}{-3} + 7 = -2$

$\frac{x}{-3} + 7 - 7 = -2 - 7$ Undo addition first.

$\frac{x}{-3} = -9$ Subtract.

$\frac{x}{-3}(-3) = -9(-3)$ Use inverse operations.

$x = 27$ Multiply.

Try It

Solve each equation.

a. $2x + 2 = -4$ $x = -3$ **b.** $12 - 8c = 76$ $c = -8$ **c.** $\frac{x}{5} - 11 = -5$ $x = 30$ **d.** $\frac{x}{-4} + 2 = 7$ $x = -20$

2 Teach

Learn

Alternate Examples

1. Solve $-4 + 3x = 5$.

$-4 + 3x = 5$

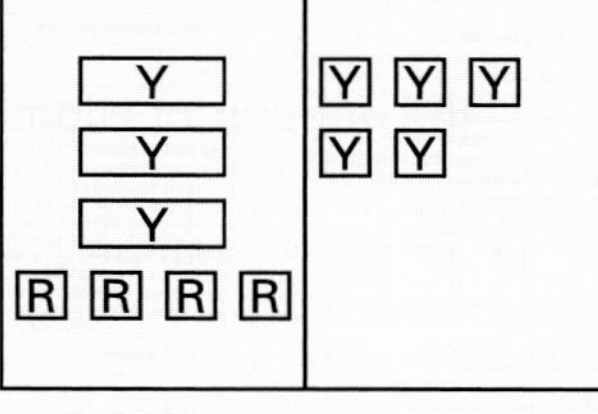

First, undo adding -4.

$-4 + 4 + 3x = 5 + 4$

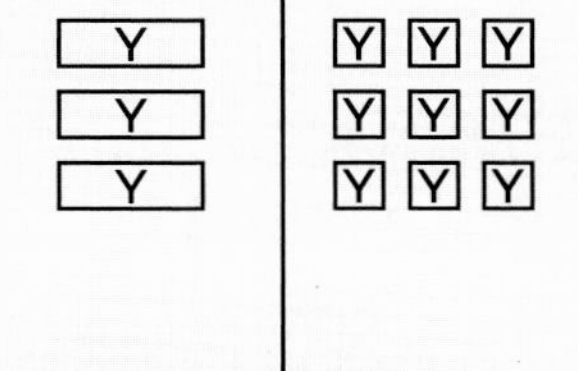

$3x = 9$ Add.

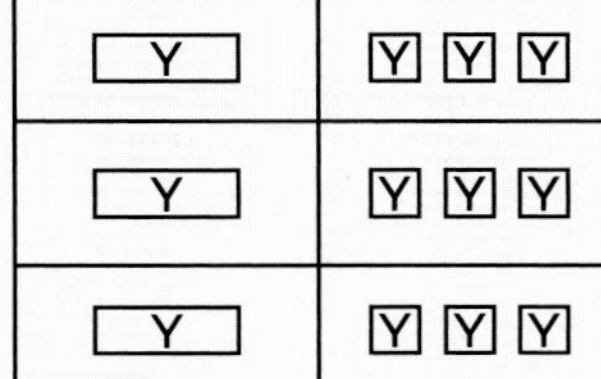

Then, undo multiplication by 3.

$\frac{3x}{3} = \frac{9}{3}$

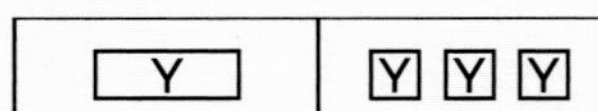

$x = 3$ Divide.

2. Solve $\frac{x}{-4} - 5 = -8$.

$\frac{x}{-4} - 5 + 5 = -8 + 5$

$\frac{x}{-4} = -3$ Add.

$\frac{x}{-4}(-4) = -3(-4)$

$x = 12$ Multiply.

MATH EVERY DAY

Problem of the Day

A map is folded in thirds along the width. Its length is folded in half, then in thirds. The folded map measures $3\frac{1}{2}$ inches by 9 inches. To the nearest whole square foot, what is the area of the map when it is unfolded? 4 ft^2

Available on Daily Transparency 10-11

An Extension is provided in the transparency package.

Fact of the Day

Mountain climbing as a sport dates back to the 18th century. At that time European Mont Blanc was the challenge. It was finally scaled in 1786.

Estimation

Estimate.

1. 41% of 199 80
2. 33% of what number is 40? 120
3. What percent of 45 is 9? 20%

Alternate Examples

3. As you go down in altitude, the temperature rises. Typically, there is an increase of about 6.5°C for every kilometer you go down. As you are descending a mountain on a particular day, the temperature drops 15°C. However, due to your altitude decline, you feel a drop of only 2°. How many kilometers did you descend?

   Let k = the number of kilometers you descended.

   The temperature change due to altitude is $6.5k$, since it gets warmer as you descend. Adding this to the drop of 15° gives the drop you feel of 2°. The equation is:

$$6.5k + (-15) = -2$$
$$6.5k + (-15) + 15 = -2 + 15$$
$$6.5k = 13$$
$$\frac{6.5k}{6.5} = \frac{13}{6.5}$$
$$k = 2$$

   You descended 2 kilometers.

3 Practice and Assess

Check

Possible Answers

1. To undo expressions, you must reverse the order of operations.
2. Yes; In a two-step equation, first undo the addition or subtraction, then undo the multiplication or division.

Some real-world situations can be modeled by two-step equations.

Example 3

As you go up in altitude, the temperature decreases. Typically, there is a decrease of about 6.5°C for every kilometer you go up.

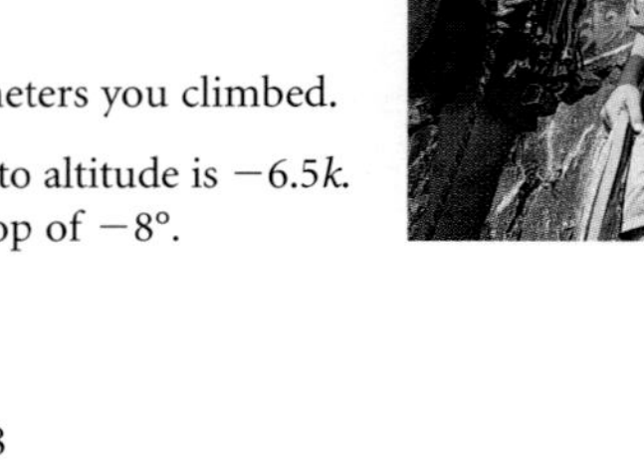

Suppose you begin a mountain climbing trip. During the day, the temperature increases 18°C. However, due to your altitude gain, you feel a drop of about 8°C. How many kilometers did you climb?

Let k = the number of kilometers you climbed.

The temperature change due to altitude is $-6.5k$. Adding this to 18° gives a drop of $-8°$. The equation is:

$$-6.5k + 18 = -8$$
$$-6.5k + 18 - 18 = -8 - 18$$
$$-6.5k = -26$$
$$\frac{-6.5k}{-6.5} = \frac{-26}{-6.5}$$
$$k = 4$$

You climbed 4 kilometers.

► Science Link

As elevation increases, climate changes dramatically. Above a particular altitude, the atmosphere cannot hold enough water vapor for trees to survive. This transition point is called the *tree line.*

Try It

a. In Example 3, suppose you feel an *increase* of 5°C instead of a decrease of 8°C. How many kilometers did you climb? 2 km

b. In Example 3, suppose you feel a decrease of 14.5°C. How many kilometers did you climb? 5 km

Check Your Understanding

1. When you solve a two-step equation, why do you undo addition or subtraction before you undo multiplication or division?

2. Suppose you're given a two-step equation to solve. Can you tell what you'll need to do to solve it just by looking at the equation? If so, explain how you can tell. If not, explain why it's not possible to tell.

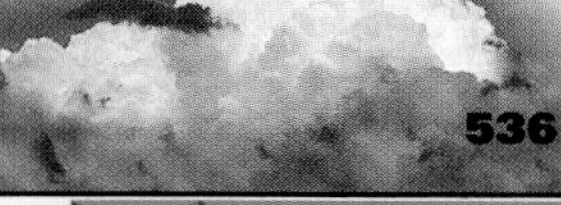

MEETING MIDDLE SCHOOL CLASSROOM NEEDS

Tips from Middle School Teachers

My students like to play "Find the Hidden Number." I use an overhead projector, but before turning it on I write an expression such as 4 • 5−6 = 14 and cover a number such as 5 with a penny. Then I turn on the overhead and ask the students to figure out what number is hidden.

Team Teaching

Work with a social studies teacher to discuss why the Gettysburg Address is considered one of the most famous speeches in history.

Geography Connection

The island of Réunion is in the Indian Ocean about 400 miles east of Madagascar. It is an overseas department of France.

10-11 Exercises and Applications

Practice and Apply

1. **Getting Started** Follow the steps to solve $-4x - 2 = -14$.
   a. First undo subtracting 2 by adding 2 to both sides of the equation.
   b. The left side of the equation simplifies to $-4x$. Use your rules for integer addition to simplify the right side of the equation.
   c. To isolate x, you need to undo multiplication by -4. To do this, divide both sides of the equation by -4.
   d. The left side of the equation simplifies to x. Use your rules for integer division to simplify the right side of the equation.
   e. Check your answer by substituting it into the original equation.

Write the equation represented by each equation box. Then solve the equation.

2. 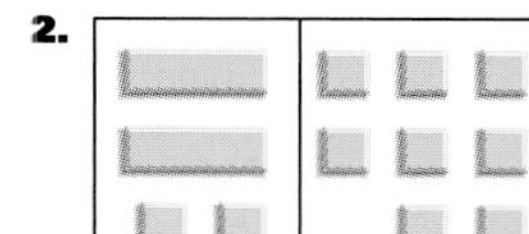
$2x + 2 = 8;\ x = 3$

3. 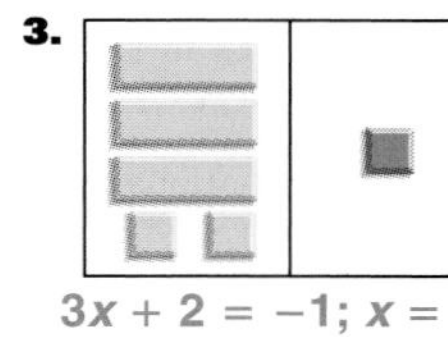
$3x + 2 = -1;\ x = -1$

4. 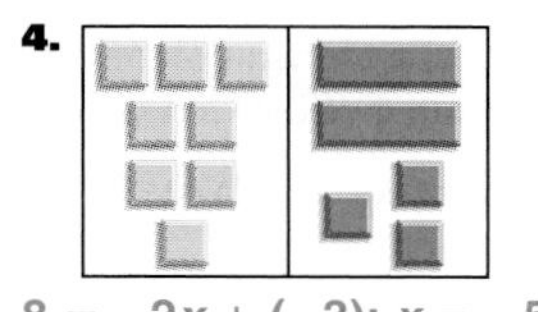
$8 = -2x + (-3);\ x = -5\frac{1}{2}$

For each equation, tell whether the number in bold is a solution.

5. $4 = 2x + 10;\ \mathbf{-3}$ Yes **6.** $\frac{m}{3} + 3 = 3;\ \mathbf{2}$ No **7.** $2j + (-5) = -3;\ \mathbf{-4}$ No **8.** $\frac{y}{-2} + 4 = -8;\ \mathbf{6}$ No

Solve each equation. Check your solutions.

9. $2x - 1 = 1$ $x = 1$ **10.** $2m + 3 = -5$ $m = -4$ **11.** $\frac{t}{6} - 1 = -7$ $t = -36$ **12.** $3 = 5w + (-2)$ $w = 1$

13. $8 = -5g - 7$ $g = -3$ **14.** $96 = \frac{v}{-2} + 90$ $v = -12$ **15.** $5n + 100 = 60$ $n = -8$ **16.** $2e + 6 = 6$ $e = 0$

17. $\frac{x}{-4} - (-8) = -12$ $x = 80$ **18.** $2k - 11 = -22$ $k = -5.5$ **19.** $\frac{f}{7} + 52 = -108$ $f = -1120$ **20.** $6p + 27 = -3$ $p = -5$

21. Science The greatest one-day rainfall ever recorded was 72 inches (six *feet!*) on January 7–8, 1966, on the island of Réunion. This is 14 inches less than twice the greatest recorded one-day rainfall in United States history. Find the greatest one-day United States rainfall.
43 inches

PRACTICE 10-11

10-11 Exercises and Applications

Assignment Guide

- Basic
  1–16, 22–24, 27–33
- Average
  2–8, 11–18, 21–25, 27–33
- Enriched
  2–8, 13–23, 24–33

Exercise Notes

Exercises 9–20

Extension Have students share as many different ways as they can find to solve each equation.

Exercise 21

Error Prevention Encourage students to read this problem very carefully; they may have difficulty figuring out whether to add 14 to the rainfall on Réunion or in the U.S.

Exercise Answers

1. a. $-4x - 2 + 2 = -14 + 2$
   b. -12
   c. $\frac{-4x}{-4} = \frac{-12}{-4}$
   d. $x = 3$
   e. $-4(3) - 2 = -14,\ -12 - 2 = -14,\ -14 = -14$

PRACTICE

Name ______________________

Practice 10-11

Solving Two-Step Equations

Write the equation represented by each equation box. Then solve the equation.

1. $-2x + 3 = -5$ $x = 4$ 2. $10 = 4x + (-2)$ $x = 3$ 3. $3x + 4 = -2$ $x = -2$

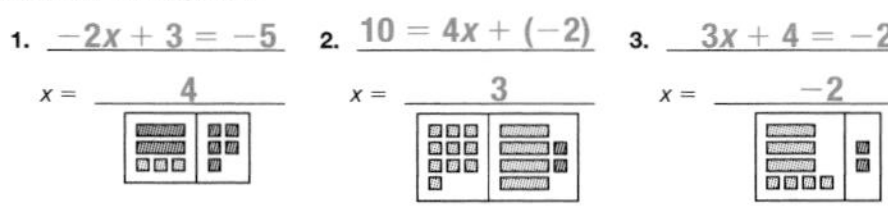

For each equation, tell whether the number in bold is a solution.

4. $\frac{p}{7} = -14;\ \mathbf{-98}$ Yes 5. $-2x + 3 = 5;\ \mathbf{2}$ No 6. $\frac{a}{-8} - 5 = -3;\ \mathbf{-16}$ Yes
7. $\frac{u}{-5} + 7 = 12;\ \mathbf{30}$ No 8. $4x + (-3) = 9;\ \mathbf{3}$ Yes 9. $\frac{q}{3} + (-4) = 11;\ \mathbf{-15}$ No

Solve each equation. Check your solutions.

10. $3b + (-7) = -25$ $b = -6$ 11. $\frac{n}{-4} + (-3) = 8$ $n = -44$ 12. $16 = 4h - 12$ $h = 7$ 13. $\frac{x}{6} - (-10) = 3$ $x = -42$
14. $8w - 17 = -89$ $w = -9$ 15. $\frac{c}{7} - 12 = -4$ $c = 56$ 16. $\frac{p}{-5} + 12 = 20$ $p = -40$ 17. $5j + (-16) = -76$ $j = -12$
18. $\frac{k}{-3} + (-8) = -8$ $k = 0$ 19. $-11z + 42 = 86$ $z = -4$ 20. $15 = \frac{d}{2} - (-12)$ $d = 6$ 21. $13r - (-12) = 103$ $r = 7$
22. $\frac{g}{12} + (-8) = -5$ $g = 36$ 23. $24 = \frac{m}{-5} + 17$ $m = -35$ 24. $42 = 7t - 42$ $t = 12$ 25. $-18y + 14 = -166$ $y = 10$

26. The area of a trapezoid is 32 cm^2. Its height is 8 cm and one base has length 3 cm. Write and solve an equation to find the length of the other base.
Possible answer: $\frac{1}{2} \cdot 8(3 + x) = 32$; 5 cm

27. **Science** Gorillas and chimpanzees can learn sign language to communicate with humans. By 1982, a gorilla named Koko had learned 700 words. This is 50 fewer than 5 times as many words as a chimp named Washoe knew a decade earlier. How many words did Washoe know? 150 words

RETEACHING

Name ______________________

Alternative Lesson 10-11

Solving Two-Step Equations

In some equations, more than one operation is used. To undo the operations, you reverse the original order of operations.

Example

Solve $3x - 1 = -7$.

In the equation, x was first multiplied by 3 and then 1 was subtracted. To undo the operations, you would work backward by first adding 1 and then dividing by 3.

$3x - 1 = -7$

Step 1: *Add 1* to each side. $3x - 1 + \mathbf{1} = -7 + \mathbf{1}$

Step 2: *Divide by 3* on each side. $\frac{3x}{\mathbf{3}} = \frac{-6}{3}$

So, the solution is –2. $x = -2$

Try It Solve $\frac{x}{-3} + 5 = 9$.

a. What will you undo first to isolate x? Subtract 5 to undo add 5.
b. What will you undo second? Multiply by –3 to undo divide by –3.
c. Solve the equation.

$\frac{x}{-3} + 5 = 9$
$\frac{x}{-3} + 5 - \underline{5} = 9 - \underline{5}$
$\frac{x}{-3} = \underline{4}$
$\frac{x}{-3} \cdot \underline{-3} = 4 \cdot \underline{-3}$
$x = \underline{-12}$

Solve each equation.

d.
$2x + 1 = 13$
$2x + 1 - \underline{1} = 13 - \underline{1}$
$2x = \underline{12}$
$\frac{2x}{\boxed{2}} = \frac{12}{\boxed{2}}$
$x = \underline{6}$

e.
$\frac{x}{4} - 6 = 3$
$\frac{x}{4} - 6 + \underline{6} = 3 + \underline{6}$
$\frac{x}{4} = \underline{9}$
$\frac{x}{4} \cdot \underline{4} = 9 \cdot \underline{4}$
$x = \underline{36}$

Reteaching

Activity

Materials: Algebra tiles

Model each equation with algebra tiles. Then solve the equation.

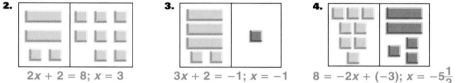

- $4x + 1 = 9$ $x = 2$
- $-2x - 3 = 5$ $x = -4$
- $-3x + 3 = 0$ $x = 1$
- $-4x - 5 = -1$ $x = -1$

Exercise Notes

■ Exercise 24

Extension Ask students to write an equation they could use to solve this problem.

■ Exercise 26

Error Prevention Remind students that dividing by a fraction is the same as multiplying by its reciprocal.

Project Progress

You may want to have students use Chapter 10 Project Master.

Exercise Answers

22. $2l + 12 = 32$; 10 m

24. a. 20; Set up and solve the equation $4x + 7 = 87$.

b. 1863

25. Possible answers: $3m + 11 = 2$ and $3 - 2n = 9$.

26. $x = -39$; Possible answer: Subtract 7 from both sides, then multiply both sides by $\frac{3}{2}$.

27. $0.\overline{2}$; Repeats.

28. $0.\overline{45}$ Repeats.

29. 0.875; Terminates.

30. $0.\overline{6}$; Repeats.

31. 0.4375; Terminates.

Alternate Assessment

Self Assessment Have students write a paragraph describing how to solve a two-step equation.

► Quick Quiz

Solve each equation.

1. $7x - 4 = -11$ $x = -1$
2. $-3x + 8 = -4$ $x = 4$
3. $\frac{x}{-2} + 3 = 6$ $x = -6$
4. $\frac{x}{5} - 11 = -9$ $x = 10$

Available on Daily Transparency 10-11

PROBLEM SOLVING 10-11

22. Geometry Write and solve an equation to find the length of this rectangle if its perimeter is 32 m.

6 m

l

23. **Test Prep** The snow depth at a ski resort is 64 in. now, and snow is falling at the rate of 2 in. per hour. Which equation could be used to find the number of hours it will take for the snow depth to reach 77 in.? A

Ⓐ $2h + 64 = 77$ Ⓑ $\frac{h}{2} + 64 = 77$

Ⓒ $2h - 64 = 77$ Ⓓ $\frac{h}{2} - 77 = 64$

Problem Solving and Reasoning

24. Critical Thinking Abraham Lincoln's famous speech, the Gettysburg Address, begins, "Four score and seven years ago." Lincoln was referring to the fact that the Declaration of Independence had been written 87 years earlier.

GPS

a. How many years are there in a score? Explain your answer.

b. If the Declaration of Independence was written in 1776, when did Lincoln give the Gettysburg Address?

25. Communicate Write two different two-step equations that each have a solution of -3.

26. Critical Thinking Solve the equation $\frac{2}{3}x + 7 = -19$. (Remember that your goal is to isolate x, and that you must do the same thing to both sides of the equation.) Explain how you were able to solve this equation.

Mixed Review

Convert to a decimal. Tell if the decimal terminates or repeats. *[Lesson 3-10]*

27. $\frac{2}{9}$ **28.** $\frac{5}{11}$ **29.** $\frac{7}{8}$ **30.** $\frac{26}{39}$ **31.** $\frac{7}{16}$

Corn is on sale at 5 ears for $1.25. Find each cost. *[Lesson 6-7]*

32. The cost of 1 ear of corn 25 cents **33.** The cost of 12 ears of corn $3.00

Project Progress

Choose a population figure that your town, city, or state seems to be moving toward. Then make a mathematical estimate of the year the population will reach that figure. You may choose to use graphs, tables, or equations to help make your estimate.

Problem Solving
Understand
Plan
Solve
Look Back

PROBLEM SOLVING

Name ______________ **Guided Problem Solving 10-11**

GPS **PROBLEM 24, STUDENT PAGE 538**

Abraham Lincoln's famous speech, the Gettysburg Address, begins, "Four score and seven years ago." Lincoln was referring to the fact that the Declaration of Independence had been written 87 years earlier.

a. How many years are there in a score? Explain your answer.

b. If the Declaration of Independence was written in 1776, when did Lincoln give the Gettysburg Address?

— Understand —

1. Underline the information you will need to answer Question a.
2. What does Question b ask you to find? In what year the Gettysburg Address was given.

— Plan —

3. Which equation shows the relationship between "four score and seven" and 87? Let s represent score. a

a. $4s + 7 = 87$ b. $4s = 87 + 7$ c. $4s - 7 = 87$

4. Which operation would you perform to find the year the Gettysburg Address is given? b

a. Subtract 87 from 1776. b. Add 87 to 1776.

— Solve —

5. To find how many years are in a score, solve the equation chosen in Item 3. Explain how you found your answer. $s = 20$ years; Subtract 7 from 87. Then divide by 4.

6. When did Lincoln give the Gettysburg Address? 1863

— Look Back —

7. How can you estimate to see if your answer to part b is reasonable? Possible answer: 1775 + 90 = 1865, 1865 is close to 1863.

SOLVE ANOTHER PROBLEM

Suppose "five glyphs and 3 years ago" means something happened 68 years ago. How long is a glyph? 13 years.

ENRICHMENT

Name ______________ **Extend Your Thinking 10-11**

Critical Thinking

Solve the equation $4x - 3 = 7$.

Jane solved the equation by reversing the normal order of operations.

$4x - 3 = 7$
$4x - 3 + 3 = 7 + 3$
$4x = 10$
$\frac{4x}{4} = \frac{10}{4}$
$x = \frac{10}{4} = \frac{5}{2} = 2\frac{1}{2}$

John solved the equation by first dividing all terms by 4, the coefficient of x.

$4x - 3 = 7$
$\frac{4x}{4} - \frac{3}{4} = \frac{7}{4}$
$x - \frac{3}{4} = \frac{7}{4}$
$x - \frac{3}{4} + \frac{3}{4} = \frac{7}{4} + \frac{3}{4}$
$x = \frac{10}{4} = \frac{5}{2} = 2\frac{1}{2}$

1. Did both students arrive at the same solution? Yes.

2. Compare the two approaches. Which one was easier? Explain. Possible answer: Jane's method, because she did not have to work with fractions.

Solve each of the following equations using both methods.

3. Jane's method $3x - 9 = 24$

$3x - 9 + 9 = 24 + 9$
$3x = 33$
$\frac{3x}{3} = \frac{33}{3}$
$x = 11$

John's method $3x - 9 = 24$

$\frac{3x}{3} - \frac{9}{3} = \frac{24}{3}$
$x - 3 = 8$
$x - 3 + 3 = 8 + 3$
$x = 11$

4. Jane's method $5x + 25 = 100$

$5x + 25 - 25 = 100 - 25$
$5x = 75$
$\frac{5x}{5} = \frac{75}{5}$
$x = 15$

John's method $5x + 25 = 100$

$\frac{5x}{5} + \frac{25}{5} = \frac{100}{5}$
$x + 5 = 20$
$x + 5 - 5 = 20 - 5$
$x = 15$

5. When does dividing first work best? Possible answer: When all coefficients and constant terms are divisible by the coefficient of x.

Problem Solving with Integer Equations

10-12

▶ Lesson Link You've solved equations with positive and negative numbers. Now you'll use those methods to solve real-world problems. ◀

You'll Learn ...

■ to solve real-world problems by using integer equations

... How It's Used

Movie producers need to solve equations involving integers to see whether or not a film will make a profit.

Explore Problem Solving with Integer Equations

Forecast: Flood!

Materials: Graph paper

Raging River is 8 ft deep at 9:00 A.M. Heavy rainfall is causing the river to rise.

1. The river will overflow its banks and flood the town if it reaches a depth of 32 ft. It is rising at a rate of 3 ft/hr. You need to know how long it will be until the river floods. Write an equation to model this problem.
2. Make a graph or a table to solve the equation you wrote in Step 1. At what time will the river flood? Check that your answer makes sense.
3. Write a short report explaining how you solved this problem.

Learn Problem Solving with Integer Equations

You can use your equation-solving abilities to answer real-world questions.

Example 1

After takeoff, a plane ascends at a rate of 750 feet per minute. How long will it take to reach a cruising altitude of 30,000 feet?

Let m = the number of minutes to reach cruising altitude.

$750m = 30{,}000$

$\frac{750m}{750} = \frac{30{,}000}{750}$

$m = 40$

The plane will take 40 minutes to reach an altitude of 30,000 feet.

MEETING INDIVIDUAL NEEDS

Resources

- 10-12 Practice
- 10-12 Reteaching
- 10-12 Problem Solving
- 10-12 Enrichment
- 10-12 Daily Transparency
  - Problem of the Day
  - Review
  - Quick Quiz
- Teaching Tool Transparency 7

Wide World of Mathematics Middle School: Student Engineers

Learning Modalities

Verbal Have students create a play or a story about problem situations that can be solved by algebra. If time permits, the students can present the play or read the story, stopping at appropriate points for the students in the class to find the answer to each problem posed.

Logical Have students compare the three methods of solving equations: using graphs, tables, or algebra. Students should apply all three methods to several problems and then decide which one they like best, under what circumstance, and why.

Inclusion

If there is a substantial range of abilities in the classroom, you may wish to have students in different groups do different word problems in this lesson. In such a case, it is important that the students not perceive that there are differences in the level of work expected of them.

10-12 Lesson Organizer

Objective

■ Solve real-world problems by using integer equations.

Materials

■ Explore: Graph paper

NCTM Standards

■ 1–4, 9

▶ Review

Simplify each expression.

1. $5(-3) + 2(-1)$ −17
2. $5 + 15 \div 5$ 8
3. $-6 - (7 - 4)$ −9

Available on Daily Transparency 10-12

1 Introduce

Explore

You may want to use Teaching Tool Transparency 7: $\frac{1}{4}$-Inch Graph Paper with **Explore.**

The Point

Students set up an equation to solve a real-world problem and use a table or a graph to help solve it. Then they write a report about what they did.

Ongoing Assessment

Check students' answers to Step 1 as they are working so they do not spend time working with an incorrect equation.

For Groups That Finish Early

If the river is rising at a rate of 4 ft/hr, how long will it take to overflow the banks? 6 hours

Answers for Explore

Possible Answers

1. $3r + 8 = 32$
2. At 5 P.M.; From 9 A.M. to 5 P.M. is an 8-hour time span. At a rate of 3 ft/hr, the river will rise 24 ft in 8 hr. It is already at 8 ft, and 24 + 8 = 32.
3. Answers may vary.

2 Teach

Learn

Alternate Examples

1. José earns \$55 a week as a cashier. How long will it take him to earn \$825?

   Let w = the number of weeks worked.

   $55w = 825$

   $\frac{55w}{55} = \frac{825}{55}$

   $w = 15$

   It will take 15 weeks for José to earn \$825.

2. Between 1890 and 1990, the population of Philadelphia increased by 538,613. If the 1990 population was 1,585,577, what was the 1890 population?

   Let p = the 1890 population.

   $p + 538{,}613 = 1{,}585{,}577$

   $p + 538{,}613 - 538{,}613 = 1{,}585{,}577 - 538{,}613$

   $p = 1{,}046{,}964$

   The 1890 population was 1,046,964.

3. Helga has saved \$450 for a trip. She needs \$40 each day she is away, and she wants to have \$90 left over for emergencies. How many days can Helga be away on her trip?

   Let d = the number of days Helga can be away.

   $450 - 40d = 90$

   $450 + (-40d) = 90$

   $450 - 450 + (-40d) = 90 - 450$

   $-40d = -360$

   $\frac{-40d}{-40} = \frac{-360}{-40}$

   $d = 9$

   Helga has enough money to be away for 9 days.

Problem Solving TIP

If you are having trouble solving an equation with large numbers, it may help to solve a similar equation with smaller numbers first. The method you use to solve the simpler equation may help you see how to solve the more difficult one.

Examples

2 Between 1990 and 1992, the population of St. Louis, Missouri, declined by 12,952 people. If the 1992 population was 383,733, what was the 1990 population?

Let p = the 1990 population.

$$p - 12{,}952 = 383{,}733$$

$$p - 12{,}952 + 12{,}952 = 383{,}733 + 12{,}952$$

$$p = 396{,}685$$

The 1990 population of St. Louis was 396,685.

3 In Bismarck, North Dakota, the average high temperature in July is about 28°C. Between July and January, the high temperature drops an average of 6°C each month. At this rate of decrease, how long will it be before the average high temperature is 4°C?

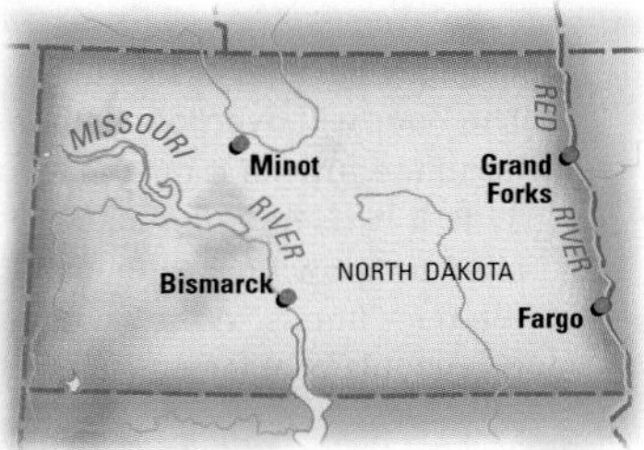

Let m = the number of months. The temperature change in m months is $-6m$.

The starting temperature is 28°C, so the temperature after m months is $28 + (-6m)$. We need to know when this number will equal 4°C.

$$28 + (-6m) = 4$$

$$28 - 28 + (-6m) = 4 - 28$$

$$-6m = -24$$

$$\frac{-6m}{-6} = \frac{-24}{-6}$$

$$m = 4$$

The temperature will equal 4°C in 4 months.

Try It

a. Between 1980 and 1990, the per capita income in the United States increased by \$9,202. If the 1990 per capita income was \$18,696, what was the per capita income in 1980? \$9,494

b. Luisa wants to buy a pair of basketball shoes that cost \$60. She earns about \$15 each week doing odd jobs. Before she can buy the shoes, she must pay her mother back \$15. How long will it take before Luisa can afford the shoes? 5 weeks

MATH EVERY DAY

Problem of the Day

Place 16 coins in a 4-by-4 arrangement. Then remove 6 coins so that an even number is left in each row and column.

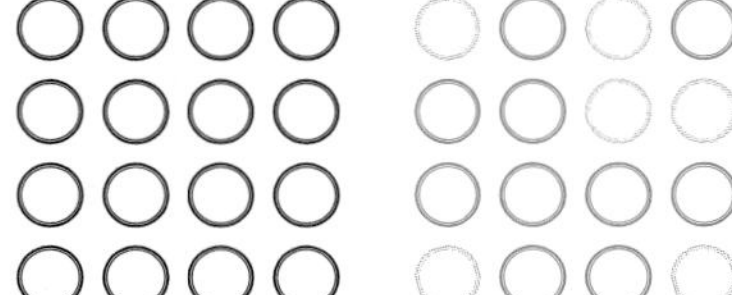

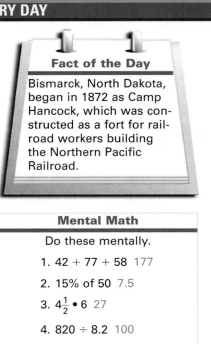

Available on Daily Transparency 10-12

An Extension is provided in the transparency package.

Fact of the Day

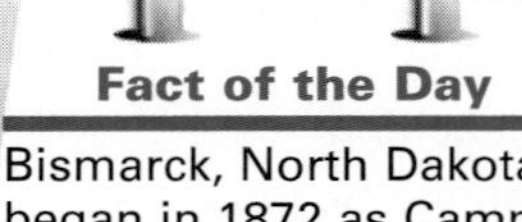

Bismarck, North Dakota, began in 1872 as Camp Hancock, which was constructed as a fort for railroad workers building the Northern Pacific Railroad.

Mental Math

Do these mentally.

1. $42 + 77 + 58$ 177
2. 15% of 50 7.5
3. $4\frac{1}{2} \cdot 6$ 27
4. $820 \div 8.2$ 100

Check Your Understanding

1. The equation in Example 2 could have been written with a negative integer instead of using subtraction. Write this form of the equation.
2. Suppose you solve a real-world problem and come up with a negative answer. Have you done something wrong? If not, in what kinds of problems might a negative answer make sense?

PRACTICE 10-12

10-12 Exercises and Applications

Practice and Apply

Getting Started **Write an equation for each statement. Do not solve the equation.**

1. The number of hours (h) increased by 2 equals 14. $h + 2 = 14$
2. The number of inches of snowfall (s) multiplied by 3 is 6. $3s = 6$
3. Twice the temperature (t) decreased by 7 equals -27. $2t - 7 = -27$
4. A number (x) divided by -5, then increased by 4, equals 100. $\frac{x}{-5} + 4 = 100$
5. **Problem Solving** Suppose that the temperature drops 17° to -12°F. What was the starting temperature? 5°F
6. **Industry** The formula $D = 2A + V$ is used by the Forest Department to describe the damage potential, D, that a forest fire can cause to an area. A represents the average age of the brush, and V is the *value class,* used to describe the worth of the resources and structures in the area. If the value class of an area is 5 and the damage potential is 25, what is the average age of the brush? 10

7. **Science** Bagdad, California, went over 2 years without measurable rainfall. This is $\frac{1}{7}$ the number of years that Arica, Chile, went without rain. How long did Arica go without rain? 14 years
8. **Science** The pressure at sea level is 1 *atmosphere.* Undersea divers must plan on 1 additional atmosphere of pressure for every 33 ft of depth. Pressure can be found using the formula $P = \frac{d}{33} + 1$, where P is the pressure in atmospheres and d is the depth in ft. Find the number of atmospheres experienced by:
   a. A diver at a depth of 33 ft. 2
   b. The record-holding bathyscaphe *Trieste* at a depth of 35,817 ft. $1086.\overline{36}$

10-12 Exercises and Applications

Assignment Guide

- **Basic** 1–10, 12–17, 20–34 evens
- **Average** 1–10, 14–19, 21–33 odds
- **Enriched** 1–11, 15–19, 21–33 odds

3 Practice and Assess

Check

Answers for Check Your Understanding

Possible Answers

1. $p + (-12{,}952) = 383{,}733$
2. No; Possible answers: Loss of yardage in football, descending a mountain, falling temperatures.

Exercise Notes

Exercises 1–4

Extension Have students solve each of the equations. Answers are $h = 12$, $s = 2$, $t = -10$, and $x = -480$.

PRACTICE

Name ______________________

Practice 10-12

Problem-Solving with Integer Equations

1. Suppose the temperature increases 8° to −7°F. What was the starting temperature? −15°F
2. **Science** A typical giant squid is about 240 in. long, which is 16 times the diameter of one of its eyes. What is the diameter of the eye? About 15 in.
3. **Consumer** James went to the store to return a defective $45 tape recorder for a refund. At the same time, he bought some batteries for $3 per package. If he received $33 of his refund, how many packages of batteries did he buy? 4 packages
4. The Rugyong Hotel in Pyongyang, North Korea, has 105 stories. This is 9 more than twice the number of stories of the Transamerica Pyramid in San Francisco, California. How many stories does the Transamerica Pyramid have? 48 stories
5. Rome, Italy, gets an average of 2 in. of rain in April. This is about $\frac{1}{4}$ the average April rainfall in Nairobi, Kenya. How much rain falls in Nairobi in April? About 8 in.
6. **Science** Neptune has 8 known moons. This is 2 more than $\frac{1}{3}$ of the number of known moons of Saturn. How many moons is Saturn known to have? 18 moons
7. **Science** Ohm's Law states that the electrical current, I, through a resistor is given by the formula $I = \frac{V}{R}$, where V is the voltage in volts and R is the resistance in ohms. If the current is 6 amperes and the resistance is 18 ohms, what is the voltage? 108 volts
8. During Super Bowl XX in 1986, the Chicago Bears scored 46 points against the New England Patriots. This was 24 less than 7 times the Patriots score. How many points did the Patriots score? 10 points
9. Fahrenheit and Celsius temperatures are related by the formula $F = \frac{9C}{5} + 32$. What is the Celsius temperature if
   a. the temperature is 77°F? 25°C
   b. the temperature is −22°F? −30°C

RETEACHING

Name ______________________

Alternative Lesson 10-12

Problem Solving with Integer Equations

You can use your equation-solving abilities to help you solve real-world problems.

Example

Cory wants to buy new track shoes that cost $75. So far, she has saved $25. She usually earns $10 each week cutting lawns. How many weeks will it take her to earn the rest of the money needed to buy the shoes?

You can often use these four steps to help you solve problems.

Step 1: Choose a variable to represent what you want to find. Let w = the number of weeks.

Step 2: Write an equation to show the information in the problem.

Cost of shoes = Money saved + Money earned

$75 = 25 + 10w$

Step 3: Solve your equation.

$$75 = 25 + 10w$$
$$75 - 25 = 25 - 25 + 10w$$
$$\frac{50}{10} = \frac{10w}{10}$$
$$5 = w$$

Step 4: Answer the question in the problem. It will take Cory 5 weeks to earn the money.

Try It

a. The area of Jared's computer room floor is 168 ft². The formula for area of a rectangle is $A = l \times w$. If the length of the room is 14 feet, what is the width? Let w = width.

Write an equation. Use the formula to help you. $168 = 14w$

Solve the equation. w = 12

Answer the question. The width is 12 feet.

b. A skirt costs $15 more than a blouse. The skirt costs $48. What is the price of the blouse? Write an equation. Then solve the problem.

$b + 15 = 48$; The price of the blouse is $33.

c. Mary ate one of the muffins she baked and had 12 left. How many muffins did Mary bake? Write an equation. Then solve the problem.

$m - 1 = 12$; Mary baked 13 muffins.

Reteaching

Activity

Materials: Algebra tiles

Make up a word problem to match each of the following equations and then solve the equation using algebra tiles.

1. $3x - 4 = 11$

   $x = 5$; Answers will vary.
2. $5x + 2 = -3$

   $x = -1$; Answers will vary.
3. $17 - 2x = 9$

   $x = 4$; Answers will vary.

Exercise Notes

■ Exercise 10

Extension Have students investigate current long-distance plans available locally and write formulas similar to the one given here. Students may also be interested in comparing the plans to find out which is most economical for whom.

Exercise Answers

11. a. In about 200 years.
    b. In about 600 years.
    c. In about 800 years.
    d. $0.0\overline{3}$° C per century; This is much lower than the current rate.

Alternate Assessment

Portfolio Have students include the report they prepare for **Explore** (or a similar problem) in their portfolios. If desired, students can prepare their reports individually after they have worked in pairs on solving the problem.

► Quick Quiz

Write an equation for each sentence and then solve the equation.

1. Ten times the number of dollars (d), increased by \$6, equals \$126.

   $10d + 6 = 126$; $d = 12$

2. The number of inches of rainfall (r) multiplied by 4 equals 28.

   $4r = 28$; $r = 7$

3. A number (y) divided by -3, then decreased by 2, equals -9.

   $\frac{y}{-3} - 2 = -9$; $y = 21$

Available on Daily Transparency 10-12

PROBLEM SOLVING 10-12

9. **Test Prep** Carole took a car trip through California. After leaving the lowest point in Death Valley, she gained 1597 meters in altitude to cross Towne Pass. If the elevation of Towne Pass is 1511 m, what is the elevation of the lowest point in Death Valley? **B**

Ⓐ −282 m Ⓑ −86 m Ⓒ 86 m Ⓓ 3108 m

Problem Solving and Reasoning

10. **Critical Thinking** Suppose it costs 25¢ for the first minute of a long distance phone call and 15¢ for each additional minute. The cost of a phone call can then be expressed by the formula $c = 0.25 + 0.15(m - 1)$, where c is the total cost in dollars and m is the number of minutes.

GPS

a. For \$1.75, how long can you talk? **11 min**

b. What is the cost of a call that lasts 1 hour 15 minutes? **\$11.35**

11. **Communicate** According to some scientists, the average temperature of the earth has increased about $\frac{1}{2}$°C over the last 100 years. This phenomenon is called *global warming.* If this trend continues, and the current average temperature is about 17°C, when will the earth's average temperature reach:

a. 18°C ? **b.** 20°C? **c.** 21°C?

d. In the last ice age, about 15,000 years ago, the average temperature was about 5°C less than it is today. Find the average rate of temperature increase over this 15,000-year period. How does it compare to the current rate of global warming?

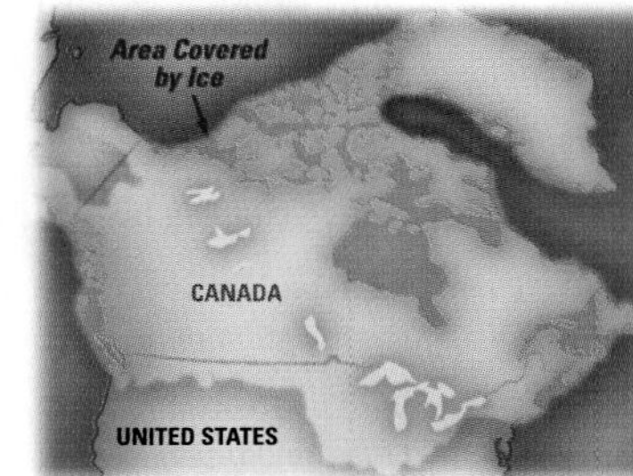

Mixed Review

Solve each proportion. *[Lesson 6-8]*

12. $\frac{x}{5} = \frac{4}{10}$ $x = 2$ **13.** $\frac{1}{6} = \frac{k}{18}$ $k = 3$ **14.** $\frac{5}{x} = \frac{25}{20}$ $x = 4$ **15.** $\frac{1}{10} = \frac{6}{x}$ $x = 60$

16. $\frac{8}{1} = \frac{t}{7}$ $t = 56$ **17.** $\frac{y}{9} = \frac{12}{27}$ $y = 4$ **18.** $\frac{4}{9} = \frac{6}{x}$ $x = 13.5$ **19.** $\frac{3}{2} = \frac{2}{x}$ $x = 1.\overline{3}$

Find each absolute value. *[Lesson 9-1]*

20. $|10|$ 10 **21.** $|-10|$ 10 **22.** $|-108|$ 108 **23.** $|0|$ 0 **24.** $|-4.6|$ 4.6

25. $|75|$ 75 **26.** $|8.14|$ 8.14 **27.** $|-32|$ 32 **28.** $|-3007|$ 3007 **29.** $|101|$ 101

30. $|5 + 9|$ 14 **31.** $|-5 + (-9)|$ 14 **32.** $|9 - 5|$ 4 **33.** $|-9 + 5|$ 4 **34.** $|-\pi|$ π

PROBLEM SOLVING

Name ______________________

Guided Problem Solving 10-12

GPS PROBLEM 10, STUDENT PAGE 542

Suppose it costs 25¢ for the first minute of a long distance phone call and 15¢ for each additional minute. The cost of a phone call can then be expressed by the formula $c = 0.25 + 0.15(m - 1)$, where c is the total cost in dollars and m is the number of minutes.

a. For \$1.75, how long can you talk?

b. What is the cost of a call that lasts 1 hour 15 minutes?

— Understand —

1. Underline the formula showing how to find the cost of a phone call.
2. What do c and m represent in the formula? c = cost in \$; m = minutes

— Plan —

3. You can substitute \$1.75 (from part a) for which variable in the formula? c
4. Write the formula, substituting 1.75 for the chosen variable. $1.75 = 0.25 + 0.15(m - 1)$
5. Look at part b. How many minutes are in 1 hour 15 minutes? 75 minutes.
6. Write the formula, substituting 75 for m. $c = 0.25 + 0.15(75 - 1)$

— Solve —

7. How long can you talk for \$1.75? Solve the formula in Item 4. 11 minutes.
8. What is the cost of a call that lasts 1 hour 15 minutes? Solve the formula in Item 6. \$11.35

— Look Back —

9. What other strategy might you use to help you solve this problem? Possible answer: Guess and Check; Make a Table

SOLVE ANOTHER PROBLEM

A car rental is \$25 for the day and 22¢ per mile.

a. For \$91, how many miles could you drive? 300 miles

b. What is the cost to rent the car for one day and drive 225 miles? \$74.50

ENRICHMENT

Name ______________________

Extend Your Thinking 10-12

Decision Making

You are in charge of redesigning the work stations in a 40-by-24 ft room. Each worker is to have at least 64 ft² and no more than 80 ft². The partitions used to separate work stations are 4 ft long and must be joined at the ends. Aisles must be at least 4 feet wide. All work stations must have direct access to an aisle.

Each square on the grid below represents a 4-ft-by-4-ft area, or 16 ft². On the left below is the current room arrangement for 10 workstations. Now you need to have 12 workstations. Draw your design on the grid at the right.

Possible answer:

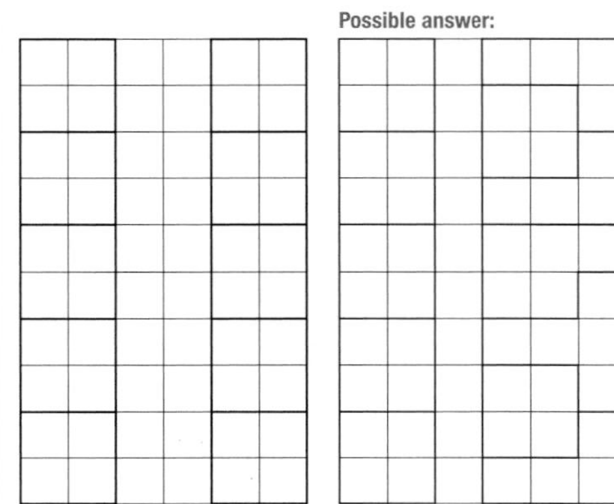

Current Arrangement
Number of work stations: 10

Your New Arrangement
Number of work stations: 12

Section 10C Connect

You've investigated many different ways to solve equations involving positive and negative integers. Now you'll apply your skills to solve some real-world problems about an important hurricane.

Weathering the Storm

Hurricane Luis was one of the most powerful storms of this century. It left a terrible path of destruction through the Caribbean Sea during August and September 1995.

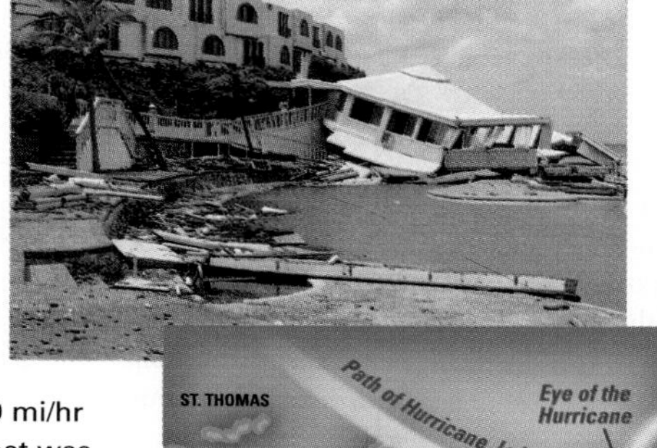

Write and solve an equation for each of the following questions. Explain how you solved each problem.

1. From August 30 to September 2, Luis's wind speeds increased by 100 mi/hr. If Luis's wind speed was 140 mi/hr on September 2, what was its wind speed on August 30?
2. On September 3, at 11:00 P.M., the *eye* (center) of Hurricane Luis was 355 miles east of the Leeward Islands. It was moving west at a speed of 14 mi/hr. If its path and speed did not change, when did Luis's center reach the Leeward Islands?
3. On September 6, Luis's wind speed was 130 mi/hr. During the next few days, this speed declined by about 8 mi/hr per day. By what day had Luis's sustained wind speed declined to 90 mi/hr?

10C Connect

Weathering the Storm

The Point

Hurricane Luis was discussed in *Weathering the Storm* on page 523. Now students use equations to solve problems about Hurricane Luis.

About the Page

- Suggest that students write the equation in words, then substitute numbers and variables, then solve the equation.
- Ask students what two things they need to determine to solve Question 2. Number of hours and time of day.

Ongoing Assessment

Check that students have written appropriate equations and solved each problem correctly.

Extension

Ask students to study the work of meteorologists in predicting hurricanes and alerting the public to prepare for these potentially destructive storms.

Answers for Connect

1. 40 mi/hr; Explanations may vary.
2. After 25.36 hours, at about 12:20 A.M. on Sept. 5; Explanations may vary.
3. After 5 days, by Sept. 11; Explanations may vary.

10C Review

Section 10C Review

REVIEW 10C

Write the equation represented by each equation box. Then solve the equation.

1. 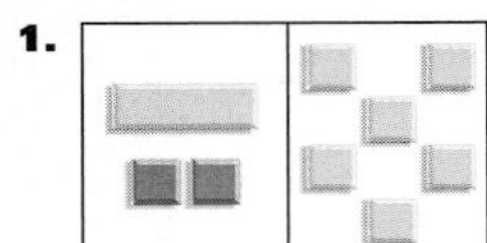

2. 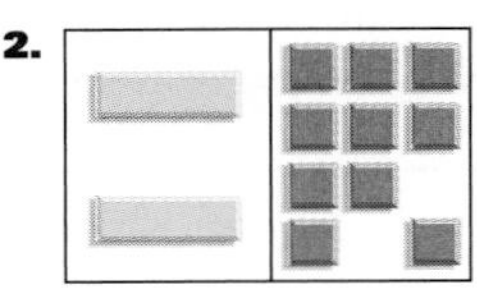

3. 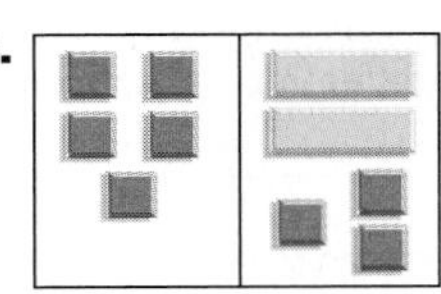

For each equation, tell whether the number in bold is a solution.

4. $x + (-7) = -22$; **−15** Yes

5. $\frac{g}{3} = -81$; **−27** No

6. $38 = -2p$; **−19** Yes

7. $-4g - 18 = (-22)$; **1** Yes

Solve each equation. Check your solutions.

8. $w + 70 = 65$ $w = -5$

9. $3p = -66$ $p = -22$

10. $s - 85 = 50$ $s = 135$

11. $\frac{x}{-6} = -30$ $x = 180$

12. $-19 = f + (-19)$ $f = 0$

13. $64 = \frac{d}{2}$ $d = 128$

14. $-2h + 6 = -24$ $h = 15$

15. $\frac{x}{-4} + 2 = 10$ $x = -32$

16. Science Since land heats up and cools down faster than water, areas far from oceans tend to have a wide temperature range. Verkhoyansk, Russia, has one of the widest temperature ranges in the world. According to the *Guinness Book of World Records,* the highest temperature there was 98°F. If this was 192° greater than the lowest recorded temperature, what was the lowest temperature? −94°F

Solve each equation using a table. Then solve it using a graph. *[Lesson 10-6]*

17. $4 = x - 1$ $x = 5$

18. $10 = x + 4$ $x = 6$

19. $2x = 8$ $x = 4$

20. $56 = 8x$ $x = 7$

Test Prep

When you're asked to identify an equation that describes a problem on a multiple choice test, use key words in the problem, like *times, less than,* or *added to,* to identify the operations that should be in the equation.

21. In the blizzard of 1888, Albany received about 48 inches of snow. This was 4 times the amount Boston received. Which equation would you use to find Boston's snowfall? D

Ⓐ $48 + 4 = s$ Ⓑ $48 - 4 = s$ Ⓒ $48 \cdot 4 = s$ Ⓓ $\frac{48}{4} = s$

Review Correlation

Item(s)	Lesson(s)
1, 4, 8, 10, 12	10-9
2, 5, 6, 9, 11, 13	10-10
3, 7, 14, 15	10-11
16, 21	10-12
17–20	10-6

Test Prep

Test-Taking Tip

Tell students to read each problem carefully for key words or phrases. Here, they should see the phrase "4 times the amount."

Answers for Review

1. $x - 2 = 6$; $x = 8$
2. $2y = -10$; $y = -5$
3. $-5 = 2w - 3$; $w = -1$

Resources

Practice Masters
Section 10C Review

Assessment Resources
Quiz 10C

TestWorks
Test and Practice Software

PRACTICE

Name ______________________

Practice

Section 10C Review

Write the equation represented by each equation box. Then solve the equation.

1. $-3x = 9$ $x =$ -3
2. $x + (-6) = 2$ $x =$ 8
3. $7 = 3x + 4$ $x =$ 1

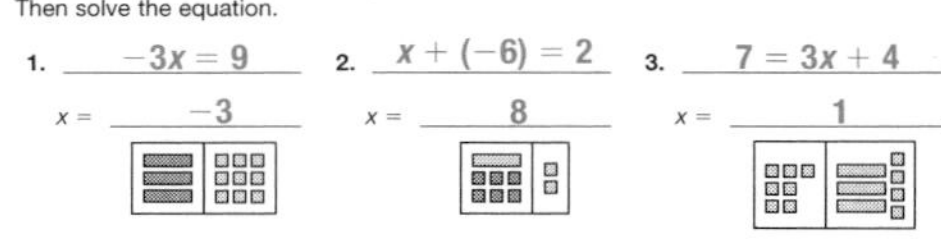

For each equation, tell whether the number in bold is a solution.

4. $k + (-16) = 4$; **20** Yes
5. $8z = -24$; **−3** Yes
6. $\frac{p}{-7} = 3$; **21** No
7. $\frac{w}{7} + (-4) = 10$; **2** No
8. $\frac{t}{5} - 12 = -2$; **50** Yes
9. $-4s + 16 = -12$; **7** Yes

Solve each equation. Check your solutions.

10. $b - 24 = -17$ $b =$ 7
11. $-7n = 49$ $n =$ -7
12. $\frac{h}{-3} + (-8) = -3$ $h =$ -15
13. $\frac{d}{5} = -8$ $d =$ -40
14. $8k + 4 = -20$ $k =$ -3
15. $c + 8 = -4$ $c =$ -12
16. $-6q = -78$ $q =$ 13
17. $\frac{s}{6} - 21 = -14$ $s =$ 42
18. $\frac{f}{-10} = 20$ $f =$ -200
19. $\frac{w}{7} = -17$ $w =$ -119
20. $y - (-12) = 43$ $y =$ 31
21. $4r + (-60) = -108$ $r =$ -12

22. A business lost $38,000 in 1996. This is the same as a profit of −$38,000, which is $85,000 less than the 1995 profit. What was the profit in 1995? $47,000

23. **Fine Arts** A mountain painting created by Kao K'o-kung in about 1300 is 32 in. wide and 48 in. tall. A reproduction of this painting in a book is 5 in. tall. How wide is the reproduction? *[Lesson 7-9]* $3\frac{1}{3}$ in.

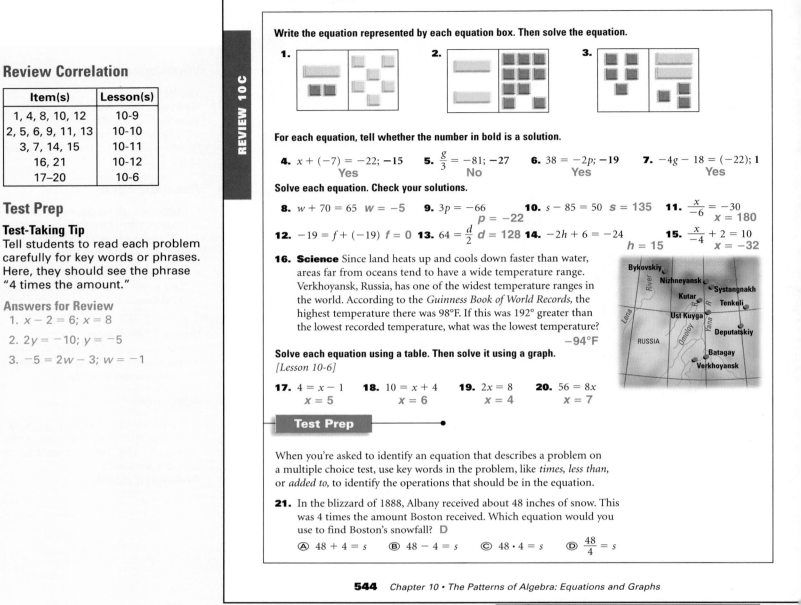

24. **Geography** Temperatures in Siberia average about −35°F during the coldest months of the year. Temperatures in the arctic region of North America are about 10° warmer than this. Find the North American temperature. *[Lesson 9-4]* About −25°F

Extend Key Ideas • Algebra

Quadratic and Absolute Value Graphs

Not all graphs of equations are straight lines.

The equation $y = x^2 - 5$ is *quadratic*. Quadratic equations have squared terms, such as the x^2 in this equation.

You can graph a quadratic equation by making a table of values. Here is a table for $y = x^2 - 5$.

x	−3	−2	−1	0	1	2	3
y	4	−1	−4	−5	−4	−1	4

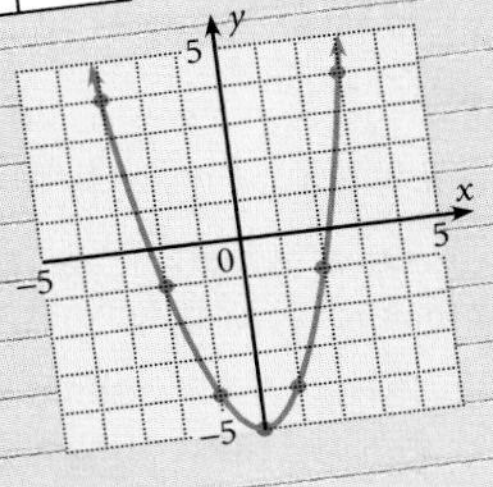

Plotting and connecting these points gives the graph of the quadratic equation. Notice that the equation is somewhat U-shaped. This shape is called a *parabola*.

You can also graph equations involving the absolute value of a variable.

To graph $y = |x| - 2$, begin by making a table of values.

x	−3	−2	−1	0	1	2	3
y	1	0	−1	−2	−1	0	1

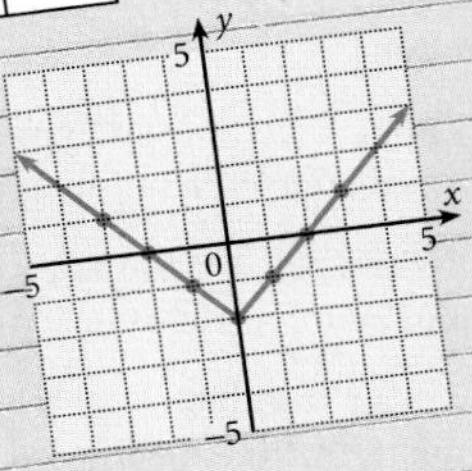

Then plot and connect the points.

Notice that the graph of this absolute value equation has a V shape. This is typical of the graphs of these equations. There is a V shape because the part of the equation inside the absolute value bars cannot be less than zero.

Try It

Graph each quadratic or absolute value equation on a coordinate plane.

1. $y = x^2$ **2.** $y = x^2 + 2$ **3.** $y = |x| - 5$ **4.** $y = |x - 5|$ **5.** $y = 5 - x^2$

545

Extend Key Ideas

Quadratic and Absolute Value Graphs

The Point

Students learn that the graph of a quadratic equation is a U-shaped parabola, and that the graph of an absolute value function is V-shaped.

About the Page

- Graphing utilities are useful for graphing both quadratic equations and absolute value equations. Almost all calculators have a key for squaring, usually x^2. Calculators do not have absolute value bars. Instead, there is either a key or a menu option for ABS, which is the absolute value function.
- It is important to graph enough points so that the shape of the graph is well defined.

Ask ...

- What might you conclude about the graph of $y = |x| - 2$ if only $x = -3, -2, -1$, and 0 were calculated? That the graph is a straight line.
- What point of either graph is the most important to know? The minimum (or maximum) point along the y-axis.

Extension

Have students draw the graphs of $y = 2|x|$ and $y = 2x^2$.

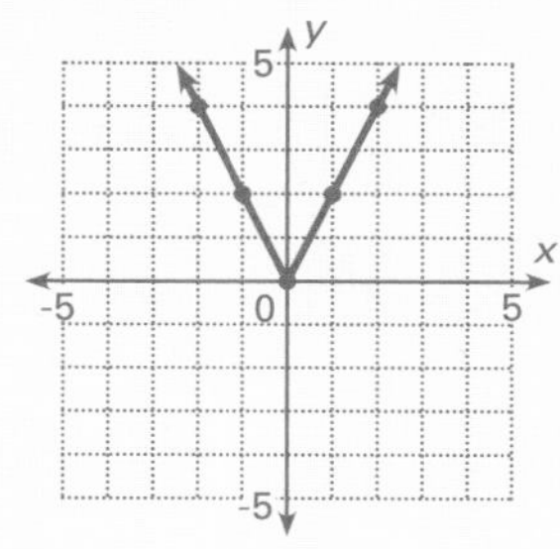

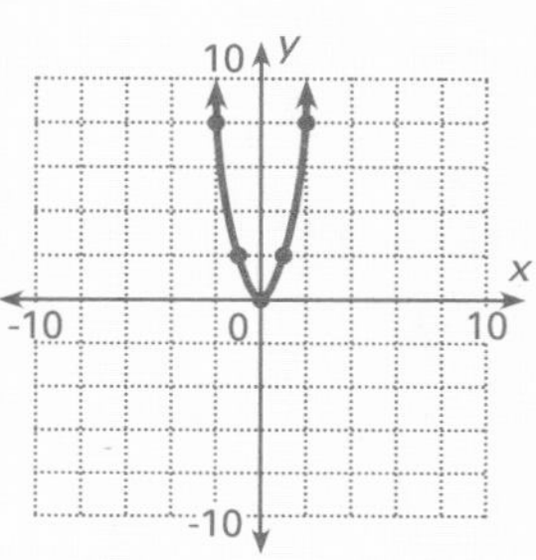

Answers for Try It

1.

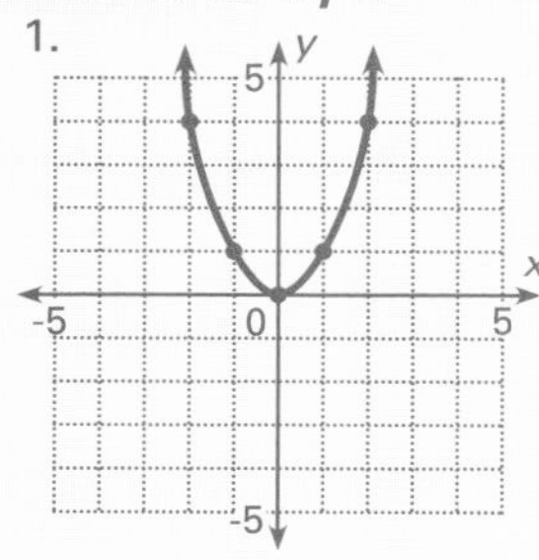

3.

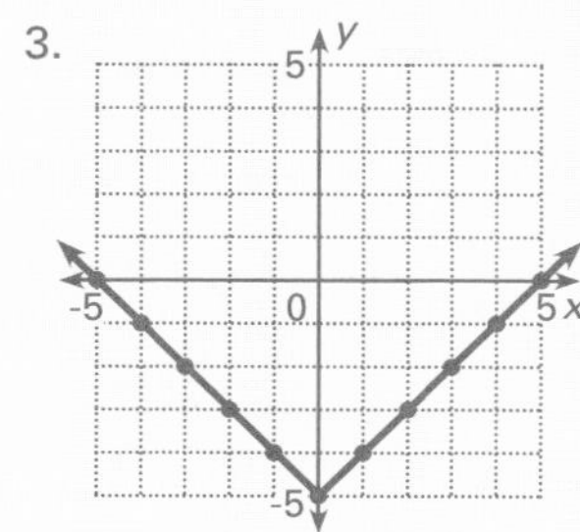

5.

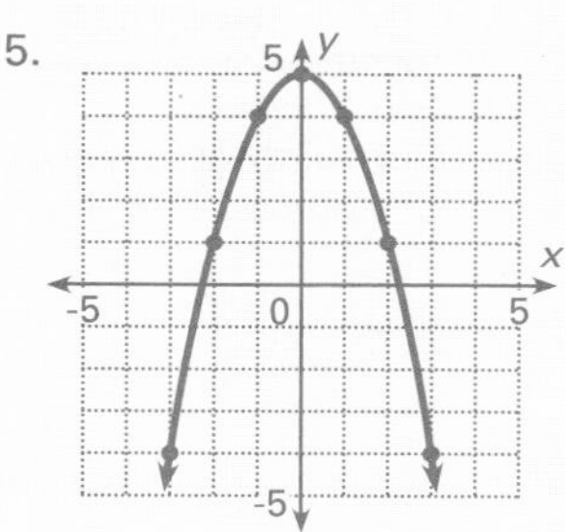

2.

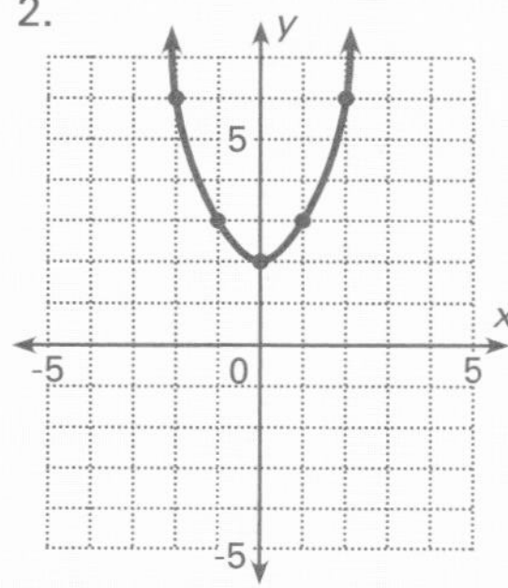

4.

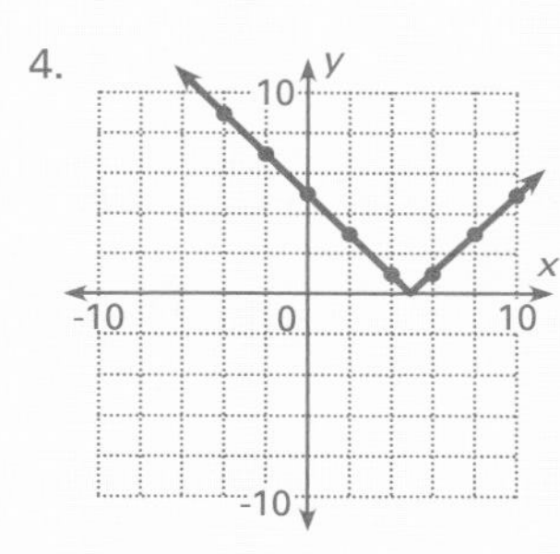

Chapter 10 Summary and Review

Review Correlation

Item(s)	Lesson(s)
1, 2	10-1
3, 4	10-3
5	10-2
6	10-4
7	10-5
8	10-6
9	10-7
10	10-8
11	10-11
12, 14	10-12
13, 17	10-10
15, 16	10-9

For additional review, see page 681.

Answers for Review

1. Possible answer: p = number of petals on a flower; 8–50 petals.
2. Possible answers: diameter, circumference, height.
3. Six is added to each previous term or $6n$; 600.
4.

x	1	2	3	4	5	6
y	7	9	11	13	15	17

5. Possible answer: Over a 3-month period a plant grew to 3 feet and then with lack of water over the next 3 months withered down to the ground.
6. $y = 4x$; 36
7. a.

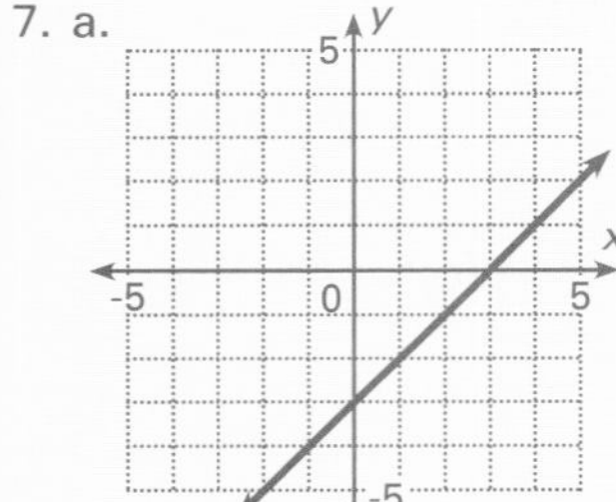

b.

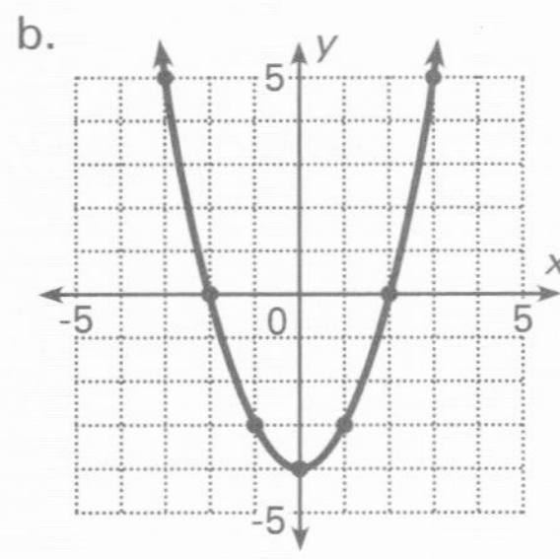

Chapter 10 Summary and Review

Graphic Organizer

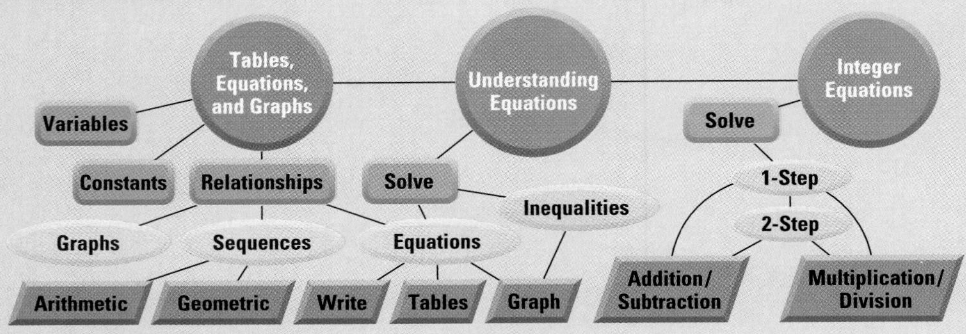

Section 10A Tables, Equations, and Graphs

Summary

- A quantity is a *variable* if its value may change and a **constant** otherwise.
- The direction of a graph (**increasing, decreasing,** or **constant**) can help show the relationship between the quantities on its axes.
- A **sequence** is a list of numbers, or **terms.** Sequences often follow a pattern that can be described using an expression.
- You can graph an equation by making a table of values, plotting the ordered pairs these values represent, and connecting the points.

Review

1. Define a variable and give a reasonable range of values for the number of petals on a flower.
2. Name a quantity that the volume of a cylinder might depend on.
3. Write a rule for the sequence 6, 12, 18, 24, …, and give the 100th term of the sequence.
4. Make a table of six pairs of values for the equation $y = 2x + 5$.
5. Tell a story that fits the graph.

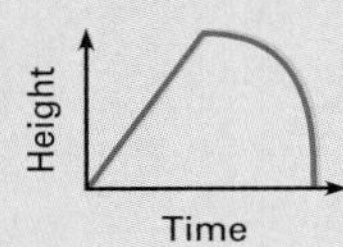

6. For the table below, write an equation to show the relationship between x and y. Use the equation to find y when $x = 9$.

x	1	2	3	4
y	4	8	12	16

7. Graph each equation on a coordinate plane.
   a. $y = x - 3$ **b.** $y = x^2 - 4$

Resources

Practice Masters
Cumulative Review Chapters 1–10

PRACTICE

Name ______

Practice

Cumulative Review Chapters 1–10

Solve each proportion. *[Lesson 6-8]*

1. $\frac{y}{16} = \frac{7}{8}$ y = 14
2. $\frac{8}{18} = \frac{20}{b}$ b = 45
3. $\frac{3}{m} = \frac{15}{20}$ m = 4
4. $\frac{25}{10} = \frac{j}{2}$ j = 5
5. $\frac{6}{2} = \frac{9}{p}$ p = 3
6. $\frac{8}{12} = \frac{r}{3}$ r = 2
7. $\frac{7}{a} = \frac{28}{36}$ a = 9
8. $\frac{n}{15} = \frac{30}{9}$ n = 50

A model of a building is 8 in. tall. Use each scale to find the height of the actual building. *[Lesson 7-2]*

9. Scale: 1 in. = 3 ft Actual height: 24 ft
10. Scale: 1 in. = 5 ft Actual height: 40 ft
11. Scale: 1 in. = $1\frac{1}{2}$ ft Actual height: 12 ft
12. Scale: 1 in. = $8\frac{1}{4}$ ft Actual height: 66 ft
13. Scale: 2 in. = 11 ft Actual height: 44 ft
14. Scale: 3 in. = 25 ft Actual height: $66\frac{2}{3}$ ft

Find each sum, difference, product, or quotient. *[Lessons 9-4 to 9-7]*

15. $3 + (-16)$ −13
16. $7 \cdot (-5)$ −35
17. $-64 \div 4$ −16
18. $-8 - (-12)$ 4
19. $-14 \div (-7)$ 2
20. $-9 + (-32)$ −41

Graph each equation on a coordinate plane. *[Lesson 10-5]*

21. $y = -x + 4$ 22. $y = 4x$ 23. $y = 2x - 3$

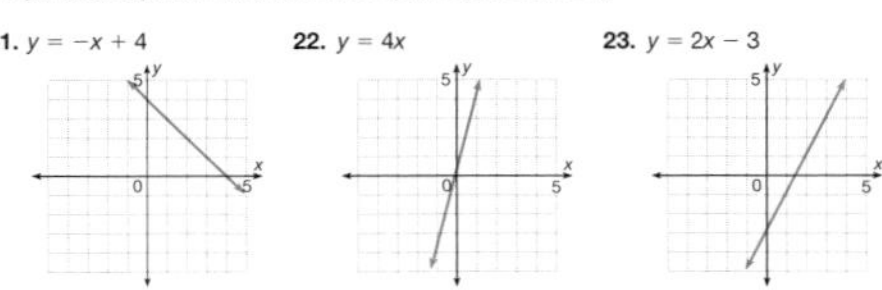

Solve each equation. Check your solutions. *[Lesson 10-12]*

24. $x + (-7) = 12$ x = 19
25. $-4p = 28$ p = −7
26. $\frac{t}{-5} + 8 = 13$ t = −25
27. $-6n + 3 = 45$ n = −7

Section 10B Understanding Equations

Summary

- You can use a table or a graph to solve an equation.
- An **inequality** uses an inequality sign to compare two expressions. The **solutions** of an inequality are the values of the variable that make the inequality true. They can be graphed on a number line.

Review

8. The table below was created from the equation $y = -2x + 3$. Use it to solve the following related equations.

a. $-3 = -2x + 3$ $x = 3$ **b.** $3 = -2x + 3$ $x = 0$

x	0	1	2	3	4
y	3	1	−1	−3	−5

9. Use a graph to solve $-7 = 3x + 5$. $x = -4$

10. Write and graph an inequality on a number line to show that the cost was less than $7.

Section 10C Integer Equations

Summary

- Solving equations with negative integers involves the same rules as solving equations with only positive integers. The goal is to isolate the variable, and whatever you do to one side of the equation, you must do to the other.
- You can use algebra tiles to model and solve equations. Solve the equation by getting a single *x*-tile on one side and unit tiles on the other.

Review

11. Solve the equation $-3s + 5 = 14$. Check your solution. -3

13. Solve each equation. Check your solutions.

a. $4x = -16$ $x = -4$ **b.** $\frac{t}{-2} = -10$ $t = 20$

15. Write the equation modeled in the equation box. Solve the equation. Sketch your steps.

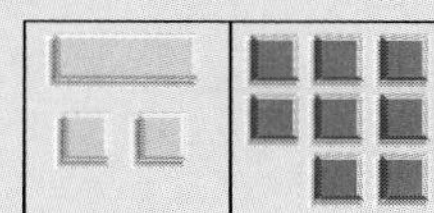

12. The length of a rectangle is 15 cm. If its perimeter is 36 cm, what is its width? 3 cm

14. Tapes are $9 each and there is a $5 shipping charge. Kadie paid $41 for some tapes. How many did she buy? 4 tapes

16. Solve each equation. Check your solutions.

a. $x + 3 = 7$ $x = 4$ **b.** $k + (-3) = -4$ $k = -1$

17. For each equation, tell whether the number in **bold** is a solution.

a. $-2x = 24$; $\mathbf{-12}$ Yes **b.** $\frac{g}{3} = -18$; $\mathbf{-6}$ No

Answers for Review

10. $y < 7$;

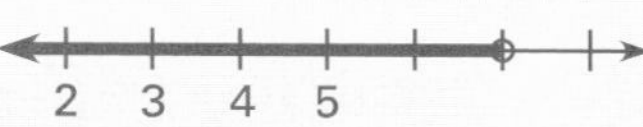

15. $x + 2 = -8$; $x = -10$

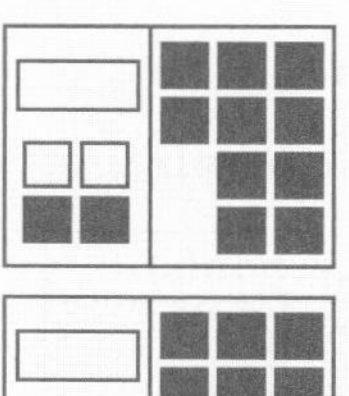

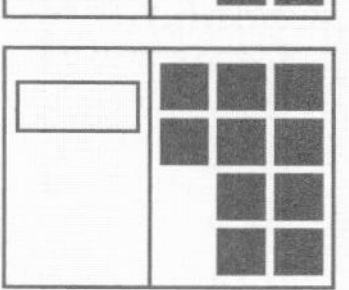

Chapter 10 Assessment

Assessment Correlation

Item(s)	Lesson(s)
1, 2	10-1
3	10-2
4, 5	10-3
6, 7	10-4
8	10-5
9	10-6
10, 11	10-8
12	10-9, 10-10, 10-11
13	10-12

Answers for Assessment

1. Constant
2. Possible answers: h = hours spent doing homework on a weeknight; 1 to 2.5 hr.
3. Possible answer:

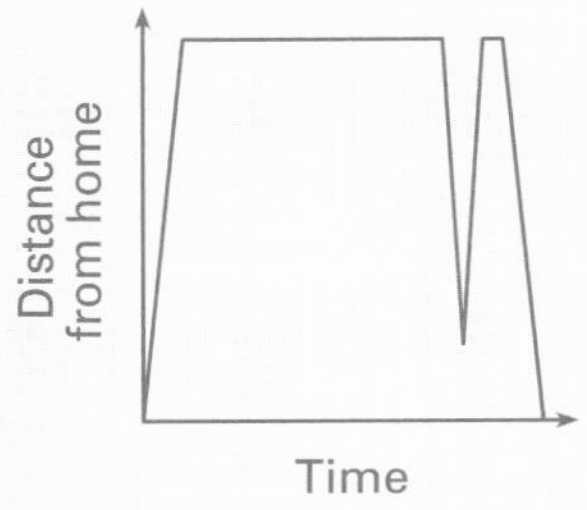

4. 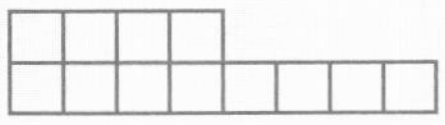

6. 18, 21; $v = 3u$
7. Possible table values for (x, y): $(1, -3)$, $(2, -1)$, $(3, 1)$, $(4, 3)$, $(5, 5)$, and $(6, 7)$
8. a.

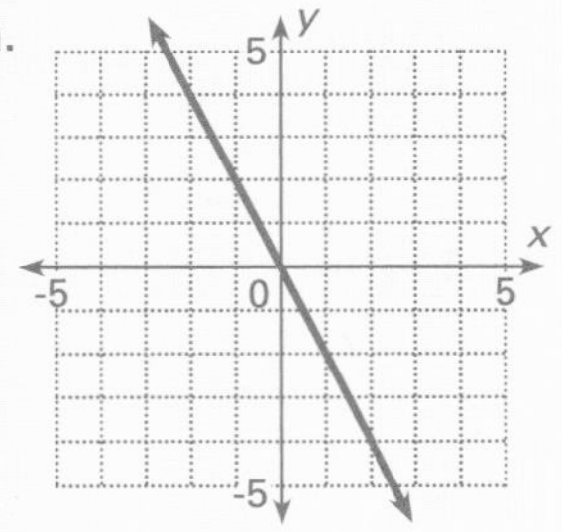

b.

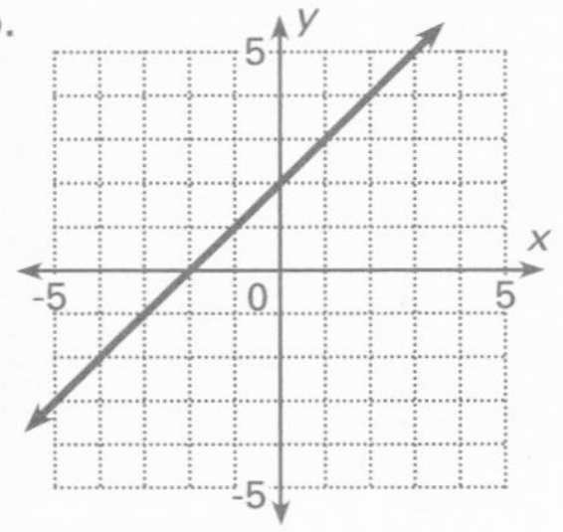

10.

Chapter 10 Assessment

1. Tell whether the number of ounces in 500 pounds is a variable or a constant.

2. Define a variable and give a reasonable range of values for the number of hours a student spends doing homework on a weeknight.

3. You ride your bicycle to school in the morning. After school, you ride most of the way home before remembering that you need your math book. You go back to get it, and then you ride home. Sketch a graph that shows the relationship between time and your distance from home.

4. Give the next picture in the pattern.

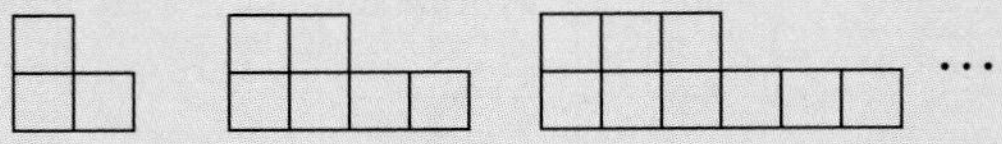

5. Write a rule for the sequence $-4, -3, -2, -1, \ldots$, and give the 100th term of the sequence. $n - 5$; 95

6. Complete the table and write an equation to show the relationship between the variables.

u	3	4	5	6	7
v	9	12	15		

7. Make a table of six pairs of values for the equation $y = 2x - 5$.

8. Graph each equation on a coordinate plane.

a. $y = -2x$ **b.** $y = x + 2$

9. The table at the right was created from the equation $u = 5t - 7$. Use it to solve the following related equations.

t	0	1	2	3	4
u	−7	−2	3	8	13

a. $13 = 5t - 7$ $t = 4$ **b.** $-2 = 5t - 7$ $t = 1$

10. Graph the inequality $x \geq -4$ on a number line.

11. Write an inequality for the graph. $x < -2$

12. Solve each equation. Check your solutions.

a. $z - 18 = -7$ $z = 11$ **b.** $\frac{w}{6} = -9$ $w = -54$ **c.** $-7t + 12 = 33$ $t = -3$

13. One winter day, the temperature rises 29° to reach a high of 12°F. What was the low temperature that day? −17°F

Performance Task Answers may vary.

Write a story describing your typical day at school. Choose a fixed location at school, such as your locker or your homeroom. Then sketch a graph that shows the relationship between time and your distance from your chosen location.

548 *Chapter 10 • The Patterns of Algebra: Equations and Graphs*

Performance Task Assessment

See Key on page 479.

Resources

Assessment Sourcebook
Chapter 10 Tests
- Forms A and B (free response)
- Form C (multiple choice)
- Form D (performance assessment)
- Form E (mixed response)
- Form F (cumulative chapter test)

TestWorks
Test and Practice Software

Home and Community Connections
Letter Home for Chapter 10 in English and Spanish

Suggested Scoring Rubric

4
- Gives accurate account of the school day and distances from a location.
- Graph is correctly labeled.
- Shows correct interpretation of relationship between time and distance.

3
- Gives reasonable account of most of the day and distances.
- Graph is labeled
- Shows satisfactory relationship between time and distance.

2
- Reasonable account of most of the day and distances are given.
- Graph is not labeled correctly.
- Has difficulty showing the relationship between time and distance.

1
- Account of day and distances lacks sufficient detail.
- Graph is not labeled correctly.
- Does not show the relationship.

Cumulative Review Chapters 1–10 — Test Prep

Multiple Choice

Choose the best answer.

1. For the data set below, which of the following is equal to 6.5? *[Lesson 1-4]* **A**

3, 7, 9, 9, 8, 5, 4, 6, 7, 7, 5, 8

Ⓐ Mean Ⓑ Median
Ⓒ Mode Ⓓ Mean and median

2. Evaluate: $8 \cdot 4 + 3 \cdot 5$ *[Lesson 2-2]* **A**

Ⓐ 47 Ⓑ 105 Ⓒ 152 Ⓓ 280

3. Round 6.938471 to the nearest thousandth. *[Lesson 3-2]* **B**

Ⓐ 6.94 Ⓑ 6.938
Ⓒ 6.9385 Ⓓ 6.939

4. Find the difference: $5\frac{5}{12} - 2\frac{11}{18}$ *[Lesson 4-3]* **B**

Ⓐ $2\frac{7}{18}$ Ⓑ $2\frac{29}{36}$ Ⓒ $3\frac{23}{36}$ Ⓓ $3\frac{29}{36}$

5. What is the sum of the angle measures in a hexagon? *[Lesson 5-4]* **C**

Ⓐ 360° Ⓑ 540° Ⓒ 720° Ⓓ 900°

6. Solve the proportion: $\frac{15}{z} = \frac{27}{99}$ *[Lesson 6-8]* **B**

Ⓐ $z = 45$ Ⓑ $z = 55$
Ⓒ $z = 66$ Ⓓ $z = 85$

7. Myra left home at 4:35 P.M. and rode her bike to the library at a rate of 12 mi/hr. If the library is 5 mi away from home, what time did she arrive? *[Lesson 7-3]* **C**

Ⓐ 4:40 Ⓑ 4:47 Ⓒ 5:00 Ⓓ 5:35

8. The value of Ron's coin collection has gone up 25% since last year. If it was worth $500 last year, how much is it worth now? *[Lesson 8-7]* **C**

Ⓐ $400 Ⓑ $525
Ⓒ $625 Ⓓ $12,500

9. Which quadrant contains (3, −2)? *[Lesson 9-3]* **D**

Ⓐ I Ⓑ II Ⓒ III Ⓓ IV

10. Fill in the blank: The sum of two positive numbers is ____ greater than the sum of a positive number and a negative number. *[Lesson 9-4]* **B**

Ⓐ Always Ⓑ Sometimes Ⓒ Never

11. Find the product: $-3 \cdot (-4)$ *[Lesson 9-6]* **D**

Ⓐ −12 Ⓑ −7 Ⓒ 7 Ⓓ 12

12. Where is the graph increasing? *[Lesson 10-2]* **A**

Ⓐ *P* to *Q*
Ⓑ *Q* to *R*
Ⓒ *R* to *S*
Ⓓ Nowhere

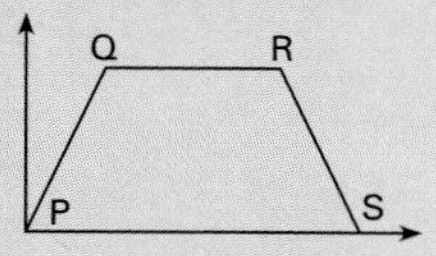

13. Which equation shows the relationship between the variables in the table shown below? *[Lesson 10-4]* **C**

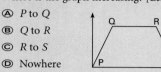

x	1	2	3	4
y	−6	−12	−18	−24

Ⓐ $y = 6x$ Ⓑ $y = x - 7$
Ⓒ $y = -6x$ Ⓓ $x = -6y$

14. Solve the equation: $k + (-18) = -11$ *[Lesson 10-9]* **C**

Ⓐ $k = -29$ Ⓑ $k = -7$
Ⓒ $k = 7$ Ⓓ $k = 29$

15. Solve the equation: $-3x = -27$ *[Lesson 10-10]* **C**

Ⓐ $x = -81$ Ⓑ $x = -9$
Ⓒ $x = 9$ Ⓓ $x = 81$

16. Solve the equation: $5x - 4 = 21$ *[Lesson 10-11]* **B**

Ⓐ $x = 4$ Ⓑ $x = 5$
Ⓒ $x = 6$ Ⓓ $x = 7$

Cumulative Review Test Prep

About Multiple-Choice Tests

The Cumulative Review found at the end of Chapters 2, 4, 6, 8, 10, and 12 can be used to prepare students for standardized tests.

Students sometimes do not perform as well on standardized tests as they do on other tests. There may be several reasons for this related to the format and content of the test.

- **Format**
Students may have limited experience with multiple-choice tests. For some questions, such tests are harder because having options may confuse the students.

- **Content**
A standardized test may cover a broader range of content than normally covered on a test, and the relative emphasis given to various strands may be different than given in class. Also, some questions may assess general aptitude or thinking skills and not include specific pieces of mathematical content.

It is important not to let the differences between standardized tests and other tests shake your students' confidence.

Chapter 11

▶ OVERVIEW

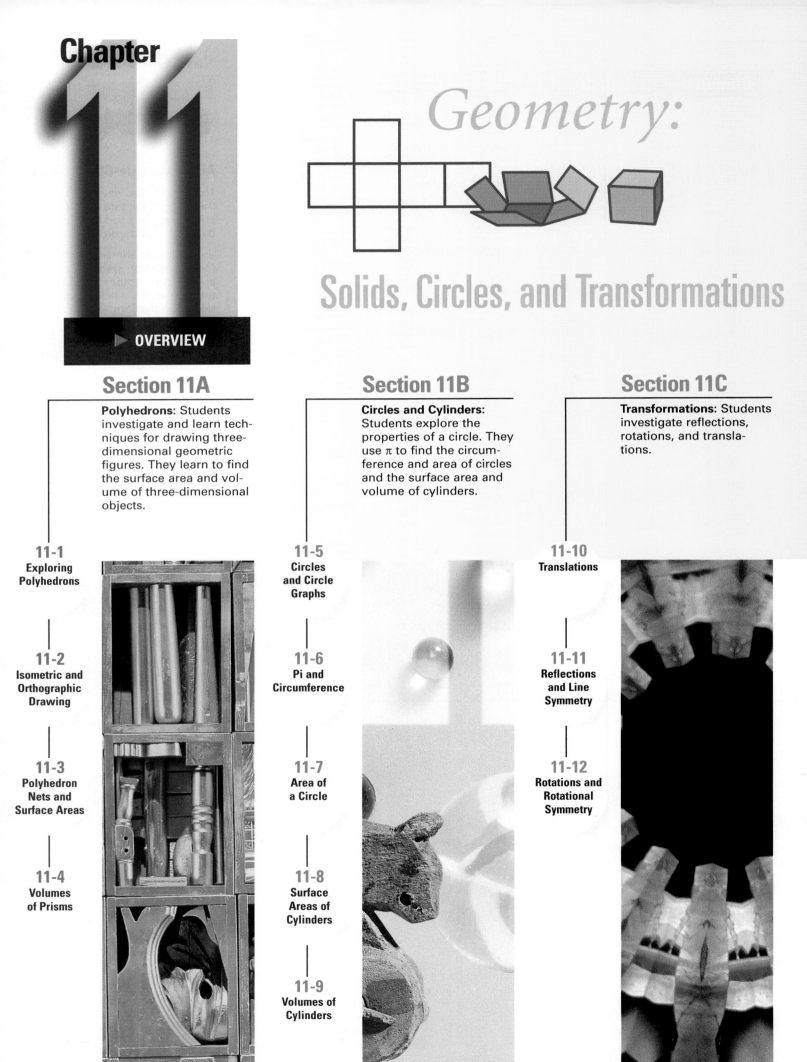

Geometry: Solids, Circles, and Transformations

Section 11A

Polyhedrons: Students investigate and learn techniques for drawing three-dimensional geometric figures. They learn to find the surface area and volume of three-dimensional objects.

11-1 Exploring Polyhedrons

11-2 Isometric and Orthographic Drawing

11-3 Polyhedron Nets and Surface Areas

11-4 Volumes of Prisms

Section 11B

Circles and Cylinders: Students explore the properties of a circle. They use π to find the circumference and area of circles and the surface area and volume of cylinders.

11-5 Circles and Circle Graphs

11-6 Pi and Circumference

11-7 Area of a Circle

11-8 Surface Areas of Cylinders

11-9 Volumes of Cylinders

Section 11C

Transformations: Students investigate reflections, rotations, and translations.

11-10 Translations

11-11 Reflections and Line Symmetry

11-12 Rotations and Rotational Symmetry

Meeting NCTM Standards

Curriculum Standards

STANDARD			pages
1	**Problem Solving**	Skills and Strategies	551, 552, 559, 570, *580*, 581, 584, 586, 591, 596, 609, 614
		Applications	556–557, 561–562, 565–566, 569–570, 571, 576–577, 580–581, 585–586, 590–591, 595–596, 597, 603–604, 608–609, 613–614, 615
		Exploration	554, 558, 563, 567, 574, 578, 583, 587, 592, 600, 605, 610
2	**Communication**	Oral	553, 560, 568, 573, 579, 584, 590, 599, 607
		Written	557, 562, *570*, 572, 581, 586, 596, 604, 614
		Cooperative Learning	*550, 558, 567, 578, 587, 592, 600, 605, 610*
3	**Reasoning**	Critical Thinking	557, 566, 570, 577, 581, 583, 586, 591, 596, 604, 609, 614
4	**Connections**	Mathematical	See Standards 5, 7, 9, 10, 12, 13 below.
		Interdisciplinary	Sports 576, 589; Social Studies 550, *576*, 586, 601, 614; Entertainment 550; Arts & Literature 550; Science 551, 555, 557, 576, 594, *599, 602*, 603, 608, 611, 614; Fine Arts *553*, 556, *560*, 569, 572, 613; History 560, 576, 581, 585, 591, 598; Consumer 565, 569; Literature 565, *607*; Geography 577, *585*, 604, 609; Language 579, 606, 616; Industry 573, 596
		Technology	552, 579, 582
		Cultural	*550–551, 594, 612*
5	**Number and Number Relationships**		576, 586, 591
7	**Computation and Estimation**		559, 566, 576, *579*, 586, 590, *593*, 595, *606*
8	**Patterns and Functions**		577, *591, 609*
9	**Algebra**		600–604, 609
10	**Statistics**		574–577, 598
12	**Geometry**		554–617
13	**Measurement**		563–572, 578–597

Italic type indicates Teacher Edition reference.

Teaching Standards

Focus on Mathematical Connections

A goal of teaching mathematics should be to expand each student's understanding of mathematical connections. Connections should occur frequently enough to convince students about

- the value of mathematics to society.
- its contributions to other disciplines.

Assessment Standards

Focus on Openness

Projects The Openness Standard urges teachers to share clear expectations of what skills students need to be able to perform and how they will show that ability. A chapter project provides an ongoing opportunity for the teacher to highlight the importance of each new skill and its possible application. Chapter 11 projects have students

- make 3-dimensional containers.
- use nets.
- draw symmetric figures.

TECHNOLOGY

For the Teacher

- **Resource Pro, a Teacher's Resource Planner CD-ROM**
Use the teacher planning CD-ROM to view resources available for Chapter 11. You can prepare custom lesson plans or use the default lesson plans provided.

- **World Wide Web**
Visit **www.kz.com** to view class summary reports, individual student reports, and more.

- **TestWorks**
TestWorks provides ready-made tests and can create custom tests and practice worksheets.

For the Parent

- **World Wide Web**
Parents can use the Web site at **www.kz.com.** to check on student progress or take a quick refresher course.

For the Student

- **Interactive CD-ROM**
Lessons 11-3 and 11-4 have an *Interactive CD-ROM Lesson*. The *Interactive CD-ROM Journal* and *Interactive CD-ROM Spreadsheet/Grapher Tool* are also used in Chapter 11.

- **Wide World of Mathematics**
Lesson 11-3 Geometry: Gateway Arch
Lesson 11-6 Geometry: Star Athlete
Lesson 11-7 Geometry: Warp Speed at the Arena
Lesson 11-9 Middle School: Chunnel
Lesson 11-10 Algebra: Living in 64 Squares
Lesson 11-11 Geometry: Miniature Golf

- **World Wide Web**
Use with Chapter and Section Openers; Students can go online to the Scott Foresman-Addison Wesley Web site at **www.mathsurf.com/7/ch11** to collect information about chapter themes. Students can also visit **www.kz.com** for tutorials and practice.

STANDARDIZED - TEST CORRELATION

SECTION 11A

LESSON	OBJECTIVE	ITBS Form M	CTBS 4th Ed.	CAT 5th Ed.	SAT 9th Ed.	MAT 7th Ed.	Your Form
11-1	• Name polyhedrons. • Sketch polyhedrons.	✘		✘	✘	✘	
11-2	• Match isometric and orthographic views. • Draw front, side, and top views of a solid. • Draw a figure in perspective from its front, top, and side views.						
11-3	• Find the surface area of a polyhedron.						
11-4	• Find the volume of a prism.				✘	✘	

SECTION 11B

LESSON	OBJECTIVE	ITBS Form M	CTBS 4th Ed.	CAT 5th Ed.	SAT 9th Ed.	MAT 7th Ed.	Your Form
11-5	• Make circle graphs.	✘	✘		✘		
11-6	• Know the meaning of π. • Find the circumference of a circle.		 ✘	✘ 	✘ ✘		
11-7	• Find the area of a circle.	✘	✘		✘		
11-8	• Find the surface area of a cylinder.						
11-9	• Find the volume of a cylinder.						

SECTION 11C

LESSON	OBJECTIVE	ITBS Form M	CTBS 4th Ed.	CAT 5th Ed.	SAT 9th Ed.	MAT 7th Ed.	Your Form
11-10	• Draw translations on a coordinate plane. • Reflect figures on a coordinate plane.				✘		
11-11	• Identify lines of symmetry. • Write rules for translations.		✘ ✘	✘ ✘	✘ ✘	✘ ✘	
11-12	• Identify figures with rotational symmetry. • Determine how far a figure has been rotated. • Rotate figures on a coordinate plane.				✘ ✘		

Key: ITBS - Iowa Test of Basic Skills; CTBS - Comprehensive Test of Basic Skills; CAT - California Achievement Test; SAT - Stanford Achievement Test; MAT - Metropolitan Achievement Test

ASSESSMENT PROGRAM

Traditional Assessment

QUICK QUIZZES	SECTION REVIEW	CHAPTER REVIEW	CHAPTER ASSESSMENT FREE RESPONSE	CHAPTER ASSESSMENT MULTIPLE CHOICE	CUMULATIVE REVIEW
TE: pp. 557, 562, 566, 570, 577, 581, 586, 591, 596, 604, 609, 614	SE: pp. 572, 598, 616 *Quiz 11A, 11B, 11C	SE: pp. 618–619	SE: p. 620 *Ch. 11 Tests Forms A, B, E	*Ch. 11 Tests Forms C, E	SE: p. 621 *Ch. 11 Test Form F

Alternate Assessment

INTERVIEW	JOURNAL	ONGOING	PERFORMANCE	PORTFOLIO	PROJECT	SELF
TE: p. 586	SE: pp. 557, 572, 577, 586, 609 TE: pp. 552, 562, 570, 591, 596	TE: pp. 558, 567, 574, 578, 583, 587, 592, 600, 605, 610	SE: pp. 620, 621 TE: p. 604 *Ch. 11 Tests Forms D, E	TE: pp. 557, 581	SE: pp. 570, 596, 614 TE: pp. 561, 566, 614	TE: pp. 577, 609

*Tests and quizzes are in *Assessment Sourcebook*. Test Form E is a mixed response test. Forms for Alternate Assessment are also available in *Assessment Sourcebook*.

TestWorks: Test and Practice Software

MIDDLE SCHOOL PACING CHART

REGULAR PACING

Day	5 classes per week
1	Chapter 11 Opener; Problem Solving Focus
2	Section **11A** Opener; Lesson **11-1**
3	Lesson **11-2**
4	Lesson **11-3**
5	Lesson **11-4**
6	**11A** Connect; **11A** Review
7	Section **11B** Opener; Lesson **11-5**
8	Lesson **11-6**; Technology
9	Lesson **11-7**
10	Lesson **11-8**
11	Lesson **11-9**
12	**11B** Connect; **11B** Review
13	Section **11C** Opener; Lesson **11-10**
14	Lesson **11-11**
15	Lesson **11-12**
16	**11C** Connect; **11C** Review; Extend Key Ideas
17	Chapter 11 Summary and Review
18	Chapter 11 Assessment; Cumulative Review, Chapter 1–11

BLOCK SCHEDULING OPTIONS

Block Scheduling for
Complete Course

Chapter 11 may be presented in

- eleven 90-minute blocks
- fourteen 75-minute blocks

Each block consists of a combination of

- Chapter and Section Openers
- Explores
- Lesson Development
- Problem Solving Focus
- Technology
- Extend Key Ideas
- Connect
- Review
- Assessment

For details, see *Block Scheduling Handbook*.

Block Scheduling for
Interdisciplinary Course

Each block integrates math with another subject area.

In Chapter 11, interdisciplinary topics include

- Geometric Sculpture
- Round Toys of the World
- Kaleidoscopes

Themes for Interdisciplinary Team Teaching 11A, 11B, and 11C are

- Polyhedra and Art
- Map Projections
- Eye and Mirror Images

For details, see *Block Scheduling Handbook*.

Block Scheduling for
Lab-Based Course

In each block, 30–40 minutes is devoted to lab activities including

- Explores in the Student Edition
- Connect pages in the Student Edition
- Technology options in the Student Edition
- Reteaching Activities in the Teacher Edition

For details, see *Block Scheduling Handbook*.

Block Scheduling for
Course with *Connected Mathematics*

In each block, investigations from **Connected Mathematics** replace or enhance the lessons in Chapter 11.

Connected Mathematics topics for Chapter 11 can be found in

- *Filling and Wrapping*
- *Stretching and Shrinking*

For details, see *Block Scheduling Handbook*.

INTERDISCIPLINARY BULLETIN BOARD

Set Up

Prepare a bulletin board showing how to make a tessellation. Give students several index cards to use in making their designs.

Procedure

- Have students make a tessellation by following the steps shown.
- After students have created their own tessellations, display their designs on the bulletin board.

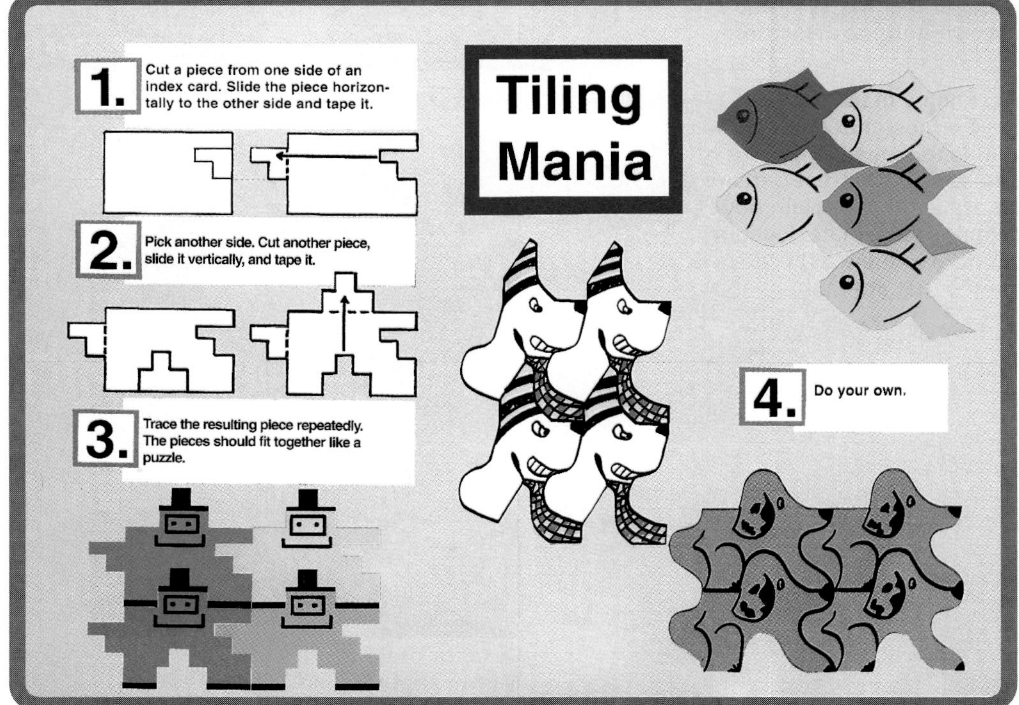

Chapter 11

The information on these pages shows how geometric ideas are applied in real-life situations.

World Wide Web

If your class has access to the World Wide Web, you might want to use the information found at the Web site addresses given.

Extensions

The following activities do not require access to the World Wide Web.

Social Studies
Have students find lines of longitude and latitude on a globe and then determine the latitude and longitude of your community.

Arts & Literature
Ask students to locate Granada, Spain, on a map and give its longitude and latitude. Then have students research the history of the Alhambra Palace and describe the mosaic patterns it contains.

Entertainment
Ask students to investigate different ways music is recorded. Ask what effect CD players have had on the recording industry.

Science
Suggest that students use mirrors to discover the line symmetry in objects around the classroom.

People of the World
Suggest that students work in groups to investigate types of homes built in different parts of the world. Have them explain how such things as climate, location, and culture influence the kinds of structures that are built.

11 Geometry: Solids, Circles, and

Social Studies Link
www.mathsurf.com/7/ch11/social

Arts & Literature Link
www.mathsurf.com/7/ch11/arts

Social Studies

Longitude and latitude lines are imaginary circles. The circles that make longitude lines are all the same size. The longest latitude line is the equator.

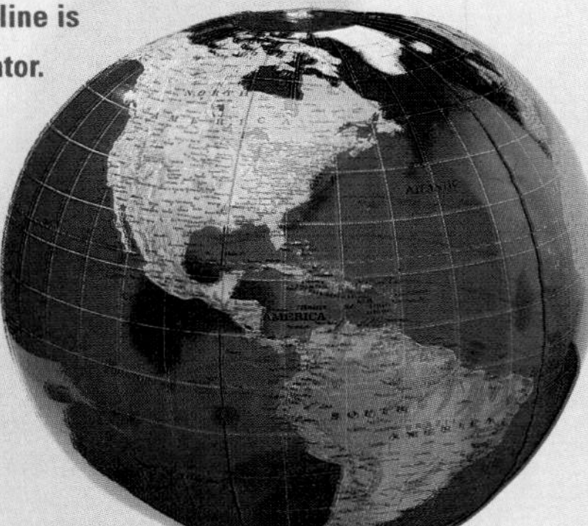

Arts & Literature

The Alhambra palace was built for the Islamic rulers of Granada, Spain. Tile patterns on the walls and floors of the Alhambra show reflections and rotations of geometric figures.

Entertainment

Old music boxes play music that is "recorded" on cylinders. Indentations or bumps in the cylinders represent notes.

TEACHER TALK

Meet James. E Hopkins

Director of Education
Muckleshoot Indian Tribe
Auburn, Washington

Within Native American cultures the circle is the center of most teachings concerning all living creatures. Most students are interested in the significance the circle plays in my culture. For example, I illustrate why we must know how to measure a circle in order to build a tipi or to find the area of the traditional dance arbor. Students find it interesting that a tipi is built with strips of canvas or animal hides in a half-circle and then wrapped into a cone; the radius becomes the measuring factor when determining the size of the tipi. The book, *The Indian Tipi, Its History, Construction, and Use,* by Reginald and Gladys Laubin, University of Oklahoma Press, 1957/1977, is an invaluable resource when teaching this material.

Transformations

Geography Link
www.mathsurf.com/7/ch11/people

Science

Most animals have right and left sides that are mirror images of each other.

People of the World

Many cultures build homes that do not have square corners. Mongolian nomads live in cylindrical tents called *yurts.*

KEY MATH IDEAS

A polyhedron is a three-dimensional figure whose surfaces, or faces, are polygons.

The surface area of a three-dimensional figure is the total area of all its faces. The volume of the figure is the amount of space it takes up.

A circle is a set of points that are at the same distance (the radius) from its center point. A circle's perimeter is called its circumference.

A cylinder has two circular bases. The formula for the area of a circle is important for finding the surface area and volume of a cylinder.

A figure has symmetry if a reflection or rotation of the figure is identical to the original. When you slide (translate), reflect, or rotate a geometric figure, you create a transformation.

CHAPTER PROJECT

Problem Solving
Understand
Plan
Solve
Look Back

In this project, you'll design and build a single-serving beverage container. Begin the project by thinking about the different shapes of the containers that juices and soft drinks are sold in.

551

Chapter Project

Students create two single-serving beverage containers, one shaped like a rectangular prism and the other shaped like a cylinder.

Materials
Art supplies

Resources
Chapter 11 Project Master

Introduce the Project

- Begin by talking about what kind of shapes would be appropriate for a beverage container. If possible, have some containers to display, such as milk cartons, juice bottles, and soft drink cans.
- Have students sketch how an appropriate container might look. Would it be tall and narrow, or short and wide?

Project Progress

Section A, page 570 Students design a prism-shaped container with a volume of 360 cm^3. They draw a net for the prism and give the dimensions.

Section B, page 596 Students design a cylindrical beverage container with a volume of 360 cm^3. They draw a net for the cylinder and give the dimensions.

Section C, page 614 Students decide which of the two containers they prefer, design a label for it, decorate the net, and make the container.

Community Project

A community project for Chapter 11 is available in *Home and Community Connections.*

Cooperative Learning

You may want to use Teaching Tool Transparency 1: Cooperative Learning Checklist with **Explore** and other group activities in this chapter.

PROJECT ASSESSMENT

You may choose to use this project as a performance assessment for the chapter.

Performance Assessment Key

Level 4 Full Accomplishment

Level 3 Substantial Accomplishment

Level 2 Partial Accomplishment

Level 1 Little Accomplishment

Suggested Scoring Rubric

Level	Criteria
4	• Both containers have appropriate dimensions and the given volume. • Nets are correctly drawn and container is neatly assembled.
3	• Both containers have given volume. • Nets are correctly drawn and container is assembled.
2	• An attempt is made to give dimensions for containers with given volume. • Drawing of nets and final assembly are attempted with only some success.
1	• Dimensions for only one container are given. • Drawing of net and final assembly are not acceptable.

Problem Solving Focus

Checking the Rules of the Problem

The Point
Students focus on checking to see if answers fit the various conditions given in the problem.

Resources
Teaching Tool Transparency 16: Problem-Solving Guidelines

 *Interactive CD-ROM Journal*

About the Page

Using the Problem-Solving Process
Once students have solved a problem, they should look back and determine if the solution is reasonable and fits all the conditions in the problem. Discuss these suggestions for looking back:

- Determine what the problem asked you to find.
- Decide if your solution answers the question in the problem.
- Check that each part of your answer fits all the given facts.

Ask ...
- What is one fact you would check in Problem 1? Is it enough to check only that fact? Explain. Possible answer: That the sum of the weights is correct; No, sum could be correct but individual weights could be wrong.
- In Problem 2, which animal has the longest life span, the elephant or the Komodo monitor? The elephant, because the monitor's life span is less than the giraffe's and the giraffe's is less than the elephant's.

Answers for Problems
1. Answer 2; Answer 1 doesn't have a total weight of 17,000 lb; In Answer 3 the rhinoceros doesn't weigh 100 lb more than the giraffe.
2. Answer 3; In Answer 1 the Komodo monitor's life span isn't $\frac{5}{7}$ of the giraffe's; Answer 2 doesn't have a total age of 175 years.

Journal

Have students choose one of the animals mentioned and write a short paragraph about it.

Problem Solving
Understand
Plan
Solve
Look Back

Checking the Rules of the Problem

After you solve a problem, look back to make sure your answer or answers satisfy the rules described in the problem.

Problem Solving Focus

Identify the correct answer. Tell which rule the other two answers didn't follow.

1. A wild animal park has an African elephant, a black rhinoceros, a giraffe, and a Komodo monitor. Their weights total 17,000 lb. The rhinoceros weighs 100 lb more than the giraffe. The giraffe weighs 15 times as much as the Komodo monitor. The monitor weighs 10,500 lb less than the elephant. How much does each weigh?

   Answer 1: Komodo monitor, 100 lb; giraffe, 1,500 lb; elephant, 10,600 lb; rhinoceros, 1,600 lb.

   Answer 2: Komodo monitor, 200 lb; giraffe, 3,000 lb; elephant, 10,700 lb; rhinoceros, 3,100 lb.

   Answer 3: Komodo monitor, 150 lb; giraffe, 2,250 lb; elephant, 10,650 lb; rhinoceros, 3,950 lb.

2. The Komodo monitor, giraffe, elephant, and rhinoceros can reach a total age of 175 years in captivity. The Komodo monitor's life span is $\frac{5}{7}$ of the giraffe's. The giraffe's life span is 50% of the elephant's. The rhino's life span is 10 years longer than the giraffe's. What is the life span of each animal?

   Answer 1: Komodo monitor, 45 years; giraffe, 30 years; elephant, 60 years; rhinoceros, 40 years.

   Answer 2: Komodo monitor, 35 years; giraffe, 49 years; elephant, 98 years; rhinoceros, 59 years.

   Answer 3: Komodo monitor, 25 years; giraffe, 35 years; elephant, 70 years; rhinoceros, 45 years.

552

Additional Problem

Australia uses more water per capita per day than any other country—476 gallons. Other countries use far less. During a particular year, Costa Rica's daily per capita use is $1\frac{1}{2}$ times Kenya's, which is one gallon per day less than India's. Iraq uses four times as much as Costa Rica, but together these four countries use only 77 gallons per day per capita. How much water per day per capita does each country use?

1. Rank the four countries—Costa Rica, Kenya, India, and Iraq—in order by water use. Iraq, Costa Rica, India, Kenya.
2. Identify the correct answer. Tell which rule the other answer did not follow.

   Answer 1: Iraq, 48, Costa Rica, 12, India, 9, Kenya, 8.

   Answer 2: Iraq, 3, Costa Rica, 12, India, 9, Kenya, 8.

   Answer 1 is correct; In Answer 2, Iraq's total is not four times Costa Rica's, so the total is not correct.

Section 11A

Polyhedrons

LESSON PLANNING GUIDE

Student Edition / Ancillaries

LESSON		MATERIALS	VOCABULARY	DAILY	OTHER
	Chapter 11 Opener				Ch. 11 Project Master Ch. 11 Community Project Teaching Tool Trans. 1
	Problem Solving Focus				Teaching Tool Trans. 16 *Interactive CD-ROM Journal*
	Section 11A Opener				
11-1	**Exploring Polyhedrons**		solid, face, polyhedron, edge, vertex, prism, base, pyramid	11-1	Lesson Enhancement Transparencies 51, 52
11-2	**Isometric and Orthographic Drawing**	centimeter cubes	isometric drawing, orthographic drawing	11-2	Teaching Tool Trans. 9 Lesson Enhancement Transparencies 53, 54 Technology Master 52
11-3	**Polyhedron Nets and Surface Areas**	graph paper, scissors, tape	surface area	11-3	Teaching Tool Transparency 7 Technology Master 53 *Interactive CD-ROM Lesson 11* WW Math–Geometry
11-4	**Volumes of Prisms**	centimeter cubes, centimeter graph paper, scissors, tape	volume, height	11-4	Teaching Tool Trans. 2, 3, 7 Technology Master 54 Ch. 11 Project Master *Interactive CD-ROM Lesson 11*
	Connect	construction paper, ruler, scissors, tape			Interdisc. Team Teaching 11A
	Review				Practice 11A; Quiz 11A; *TestWorks*

SKILLS TRACE

LESSON	SKILL	FIRST INTRODUCED GR. 5	GR. 6	GR. 7	DEVELOP	PRACTICE/ APPLY	REVIEW
11-1	**Naming and sketching polyhedrons.**		✘		pp. 554–555	pp. 556–557	pp. 572, 618, 630
11-2	**Matching and sketching different views.**			✘ p. 558	pp. 558–560	pp. 561–562	pp. 572, 618, 630
11-3	**Finding surface area of polyhedrons.**	✘			pp. 563–564	pp. 565–566	pp. 572, 618, 635
11-4	**Finding volumes of prisms.**	✘			pp. 567–568	pp. 569–570	pp. 572, 618, 635

CONNECTED MATHEMATICS

Investigations 1–3 in the unit *Filling and Wrapping (Three-Dimensional Measurement)*, from the **Connected Mathematics** series, can be used with Section 11A.

INTERDISCIPLINARY TEAM TEACHING

Math and Fine Arts

(Worksheet pages 45–46: Teacher pages T45–T46)

In this lesson, students use information about polyhedrons to evaluate art works.

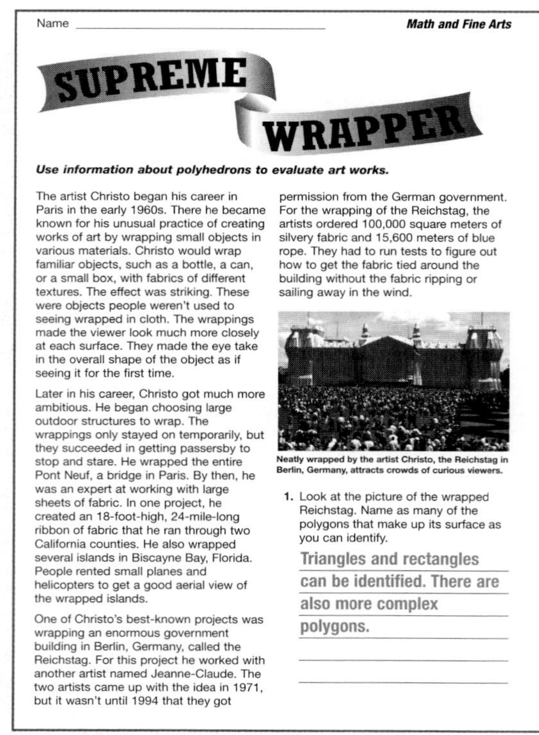

Name ______________________ *Math and Fine Arts*

SUPREME WRAPPER

Use information about polyhedrons to evaluate art works.

The artist Christo began his career in Paris in the early 1960s. There he became known for his unusual practice of creating works of art by wrapping small objects in various materials. Christo would wrap familiar objects, such as a bottle, a can, or a small box, with fabrics of different textures. The effect was striking. These were objects people weren't used to seeing wrapped in cloth. The wrappings made the viewer look much more closely at each surface. They made the eye take in the overall shape of the object as if seeing it for the first time.

Later in his career, Christo got much more ambitious. He began choosing large outdoor structures to wrap. The wrappings only stayed on temporarily, but they succeeded in getting passersby to stop and stare. He wrapped the entire Pont Neuf, a bridge in Paris. By then, he was an expert at working with large sheets of fabric. In one project, he created an 18-foot-high, 24-mile-long ribbon of fabric that he ran through two California counties. He also wrapped several islands in Biscayne Bay, Florida. People rented small planes and helicopters to get a good aerial view of the wrapped islands.

One of Christo's best-known projects was wrapping an enormous government building in Berlin, Germany, called the Reichstag. For this project he worked with another artist named Jeanne-Claude. The two artists came up with the idea in 1971, but it wasn't until 1994 that they got permission from the German government. For the wrapping of the Reichstag, the artists ordered 100,000 square meters of silvery fabric and 15,600 meters of blue rope. They had to run tests to figure out how to get the fabric tied around the building without the fabric ripping or sailing away in the wind.

Neatly wrapped by the artist Christo, the Reichstag in Berlin, Germany, attracts crowds of curious viewers.

1. Look at the picture of the wrapped Reichstag. Name as many of the polygons that make up its surface as you can identify.

   Triangles and rectangles can be identified. There are also more complex polygons.

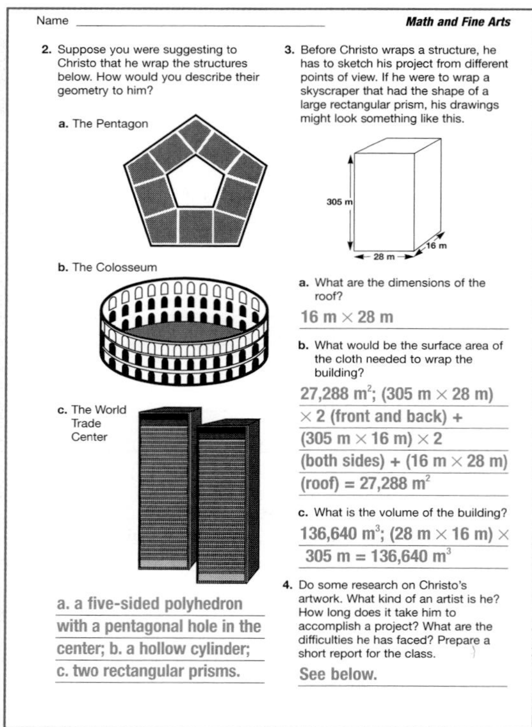

Name ______________________ *Math and Fine Arts*

2. Suppose you were suggesting to Christo that he wrap the structures below. How would you describe their geometry to him?

   a. The Pentagon

   b. The Colosseum

   c. The World Trade Center

   a. a five-sided polyhedron with a pentagonal hole in the center; b. a hollow cylinder; c. two rectangular prisms.

3. Before Christo wraps a structure, he has to sketch his project from different points of view. If he were to wrap a skyscraper that had the shape of a large rectangular prism, his drawings might look something like this.

   a. What are the dimensions of the roof?

   16 m × 28 m

   b. What would be the surface area of the cloth needed to wrap the building?

   27,288 m²; (305 m × 28 m) × 2 (front and back) + (305 m × 16 m) × 2 (both sides) + (16 m × 28 m) (roof) = 27,288 m²

   c. What is the volume of the building?

   136,640 m³; (28 m × 16 m) × 305 m = 136,640 m³

4. Do some research on Christo's artwork. What kind of an artist is he? How long does it take him to accomplish a project? What are the difficulties he has faced? Prepare a short report for the class.

   See below.

Answers

4. Students will find that Christo is considered to be a conceptual artist, one for whom an idea or concept is sometimes more important than the work itself or its visual qualities. He is also somewhat controversial. His large projects, which are temporary, are expensive and face the challenge of many engineering difficulties. The time required to complete a project varies from project to project.

BIBLIOGRAPHY

FOR TEACHERS

Cunningham, Scott. *Cunningham's Encyclopedia of Crystal, Gem and Metal Magic.* St. Paul, MN: Llewellyn Publications, 1988.

Irving, Washington. *The Alhambra, Palace of Mystery and Splendor.* New York, NY: Macmillan, 1953.

Spangler, David. *Math for Real Kids.* Glenview, IL: Good Year Books, 1997.

Tomecek, Steve. *Bouncing & Bending Light: Phantastic Physical Phenomena.* New York, NY: Scientific American Books for Young Readers, 1995.

FOR STUDENTS

Brown, Jeff. *Flat Stanley.* New York, NY: Harper & Row, 1964.

Stangl, Jean. *Crystals and Crystal Gardens You Can Grow.* New York, NY: F. Watts, 1990.

Symes, R. F. *Crystal & Gem.* New York, NY: Knopf, 1991.

Section 11A

SECTION 11A

Polyhedrons

▶ Fine Arts Link ▶ www.mathsurf.com/7/ch11/sculpture

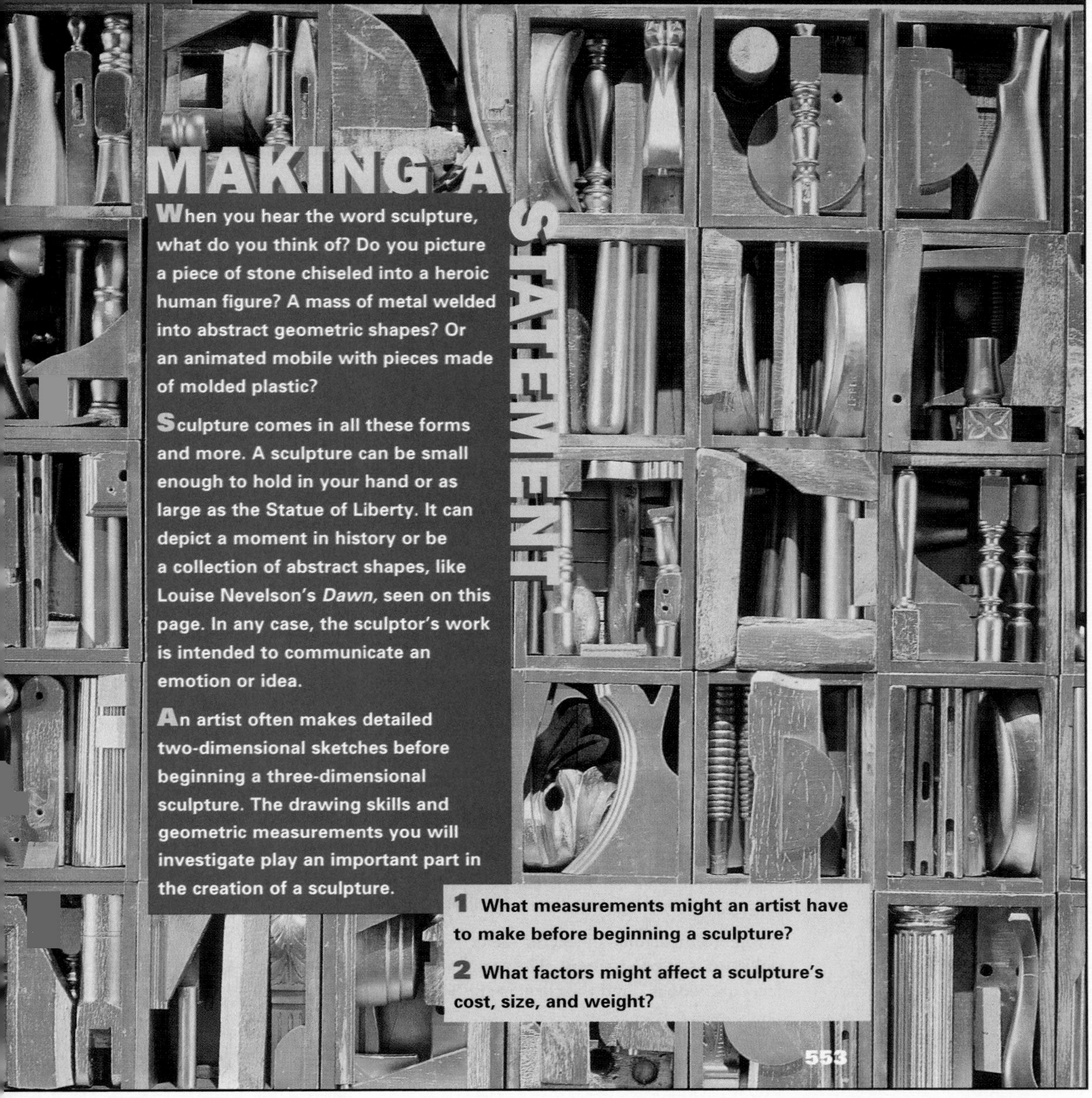

MAKING A STATEMENT

When you hear the word sculpture, what do you think of? Do you picture a piece of stone chiseled into a heroic human figure? A mass of metal welded into abstract geometric shapes? Or an animated mobile with pieces made of molded plastic?

Sculpture comes in all these forms and more. A sculpture can be small enough to hold in your hand or as large as the Statue of Liberty. It can depict a moment in history or be a collection of abstract shapes, like Louise Nevelson's *Dawn*, seen on this page. In any case, the sculptor's work is intended to communicate an emotion or idea.

An artist often makes detailed two-dimensional sketches before beginning a three-dimensional sculpture. The drawing skills and geometric measurements you will investigate play an important part in the creation of a sculpture.

1 What measurements might an artist have to make before beginning a sculpture?

2 What factors might affect a sculpture's cost, size, and weight?

553

Where are we now?

In Chapter 5, students explored lines, angles, and two-dimensional polygons.

They learned how to

- identify and name angles.
- identify parallel and perpendicular lines.
- find the areas and perimeters of rectangles.
- find the areas and perimeters of triangles.
- find the areas and perimeters of parallelograms and trapezoids.

Where are we going?

In Chapter 11, Section 11A, students will

- name and sketch polyhedrons.
- investigate techniques for drawing three-dimensional objects.
- find the surface area of a polyhedron.
- find the volume of a prism.

Theme: Geometric Sculpture

World Wide Web

If your class has access to the World Wide Web, you might want to use the information found at the Web site address given. The interdisciplinary link relates to topics discussed in this section.

About the Page

This page introduces the theme of the section, geometric sculpture, and discusses sculpture and the skills of the sculptor.

Ask ...

- What sculptures have you seen? Where? Describe what you saw.
- Have you ever seen a mobile? Where? Did you realize that it was a sculpture?
- Have you ever seen a sculpture that was made out of unusual materials?

Extension

The following activity does not require access to the World Wide Web.

Fine Arts

A hologram is a three-dimensional picture that is made on photographic film. It consists of a pattern of interference produced by a beam of radiation and light. A hologram is illuminated from behind for viewing. Have students research holograms and their uses. If possible, bring one to class to show to the students.

Answers for Questions

1. Possible answers: Size, proportion, balance.
2. Possible answers: What it's made of, where it's to go, who it's for.

Connect

On page 571, students design and make a piece of sculpture out of three-dimensional geometric shapes.

11-1 Lesson Organizer

Objectives

- Name polyhedrons.
- Sketch polyhedrons.

Vocabulary

- Solid, face, polyhedron, edge, vertex, prism, base, pyramid

NCTM Standards

- 1–4, 12, 13

Review

Answer the following questions.

1. When you look at an ordinary cardboard box, what is the greatest number of sides of the box you can see from any vantage point? 3
2. When you look at a cardboard box, is it possible you could see only one side? Explain. Yes, you might be looking directly at that side.

Available on Daily Transparency 11-1

Lesson Link

Have students discuss the types of polygons they have studied.

1 Introduce

Explore

You may wish to use Lesson Enhancement Transparency 51 with **Explore**.

The Point
Students explore different ways to classify three-dimensional figures. This helps them understand the similarities and differences among prisms, pyramids, cones, and cylinders.

For Groups That Finish Early
Which figures involve only polygons? A, D, E, F

11-1 Exploring Polyhedrons

You'll Learn ...

- to name polyhedrons
- to sketch polyhedrons

... How It's Used

Gemologists grind and polish irregularly shaped stones into polyhedrons.

Vocabulary

solid
face
polyhedron
edge
vertex
prism
base
pyramid

Lesson Link You've worked with two-dimensional polygons. Now you'll investigate three-dimensional geometric figures.

Explore Three-Dimensional Figures

A Touch of Classification

1. Several three-dimensional figures are shown. Decide on a way to sort these figures into at least three categories. Explain your classification system.

A. 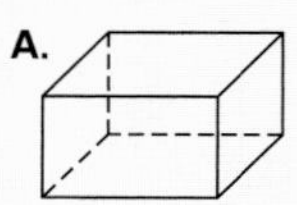
B. 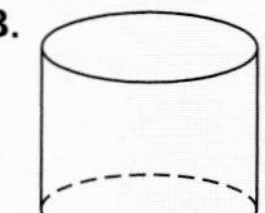
C. 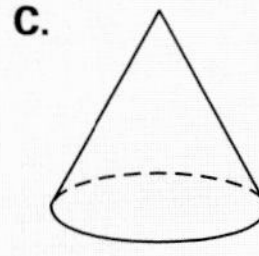
D. 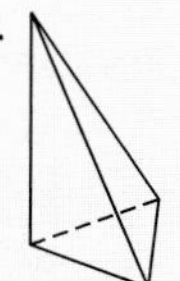
E. 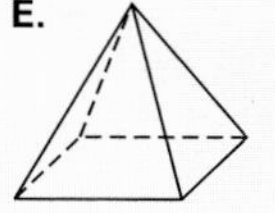
F. 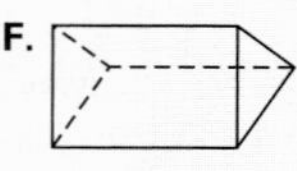
G. 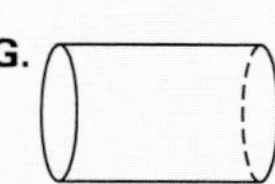
H. 

2. Find and explain two other ways to classify these figures.
3. Suppose you're describing one of these figures to an artist who is making a preliminary sketch for a sculpture. What are some characteristics you would include in your description?

Learn Exploring Polyhedrons

The geometric figures you've investigated so far are two-dimensional, since they are flat. However, anything that takes up space is a three-dimensional object.

A three-dimensional object, or **solid**, whose **faces** are polygons is a **polyhedron**. The segments joining the faces are **edges**, and the corners are **vertices**.

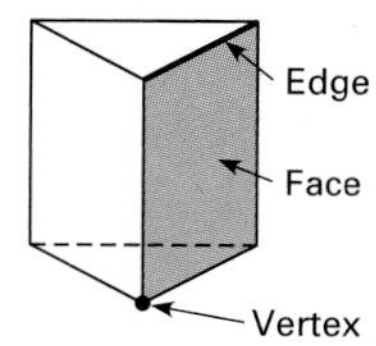

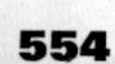

MEETING INDIVIDUAL NEEDS

Resources

- 11-1 Practice
- 11-1 Reteaching
- 11-1 Problem Solving
- 11-1 Enrichment
- 11-1 Daily Transparency
  - Problem of the Day
  - Review
  - Quick Quiz

Lesson Enhancement Transparencies 51, 52

Learning Modalities

Visual Have students find photos in newspapers or magazines that illustrate polyhedrons.

Kinesthetic Students can benefit from examining models of figures like those in **Explore.** If commercial models are not available, cereal boxes, coffee cans, ice cream cones, and other similar models can be just as useful.

Social Some students have more artistic talent than others. This lesson is a good place to allow these students to work with other students who have trouble drawing three-dimensional figures.

English Language Development

Use a cardboard box. Point to various parts of the box and have students identify each part as an edge, a face, or a vertex.

Have students work in groups to make charts of the vocabulary words for this lesson. Charts might include drawings and students' native language equivalents of the terms.

A **prism** is a polyhedron whose **bases** are congruent and parallel. A **pyramid** has a polygonal base but comes to a point.

The name of a prism or pyramid tells the shape of its base.

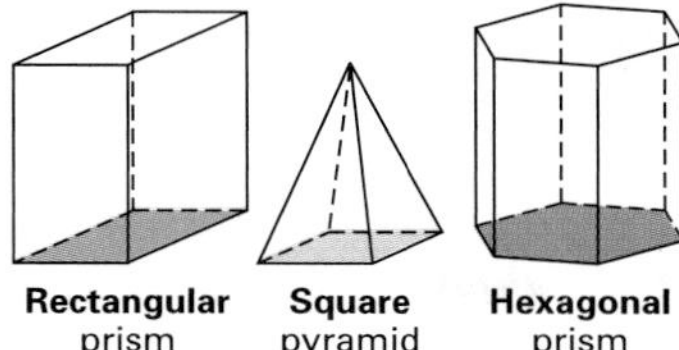

Rectangular prism **Square** pyramid **Hexagonal** prism

When you're drawing a three-dimensional figure, you can show depth by imagining that you're in front of and above the object. Show hidden edges as dashed lines.

> **Science Link**
>
> Many minerals form crystals that are prisms. Fluorite has cubic crystals. Quartz, staurolite, and vanadinite are sometimes found as hexagonal prisms.

Examples

1 Name the polyhedrons in the sculpture.

In the sculpture, you can see cubes and other rectangular prisms.

2 Sketch a right triangular prism.

Sketch one base.

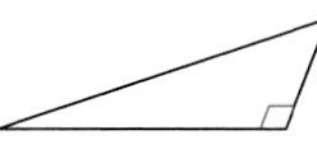

Draw an identical base below the first.

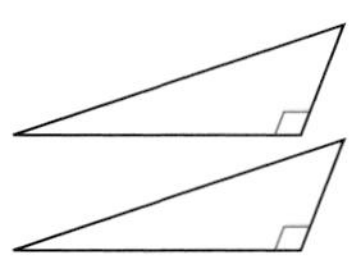

Add vertical lines joining the vertices of the bases. Make the hidden edge dashed.

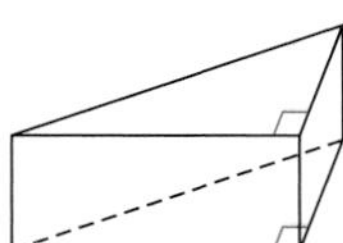

Try It

Name each polyhedron.

a.

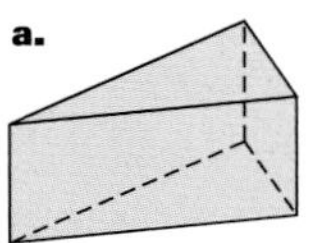

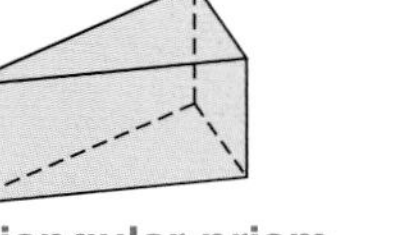

Triangular prism

b.

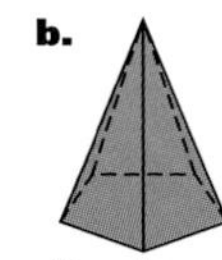

Pentagonal pyramid

c. Sketch a pentagonal prism. See students' drawings.

> **Remember**
>
> A polygon is named according to the number of sides it has. A *triangle* has three sides, a *quadrilateral* has four, a *pentagon* has five, and a *hexagon* has six. [Page 227]

Check Your Understanding

1. Is a cube a prism? Explain. What is another name for a cube?

2. Give real-world examples of at least three polyhedrons.

MATH EVERY DAY

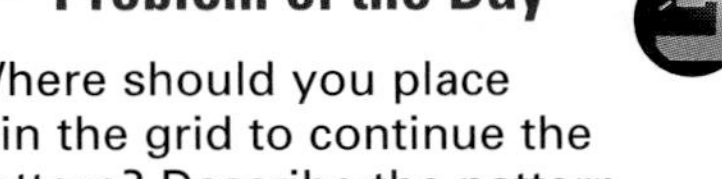

Problem of the Day

Where should you place 6 in the grid to continue the pattern? Describe the pattern.

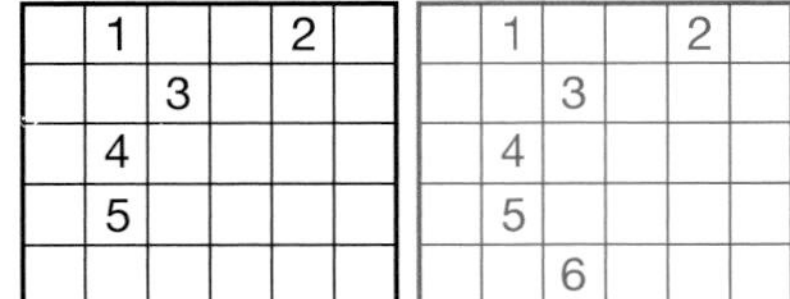

The number, *n*, reflects the number of empty squares directly before it, going from left to right and top to bottom.

Available on Daily Transparency 11-1

An Extension is provided in the transparency package.

Fact of the Day

In 1876 France presented the United States with a 151-ft sculpture entitled "Liberty Enlightening the World." Today the sculpture is known as the Statue of Liberty.

Mental Math

Do these mentally.

1. 8.89 × 10 88.9
2. 0.023 × 100 2.3
3. 0.14 × 1000 140
4. 18.9 × 10,000 189,000

Answers for Explore

1. Possible answers: A, F: mostly rectangular sides; B, C, G, H: mostly circular sides; D, E: mostly triangular sides
2. C, D, E, H: figures with one base; A, D, E, F: figures with no circles.
3. Number of vertices, number of straight edges, number of sides, shapes of sides.

2 Teach

Learn

You may wish to use Lesson Enhancement Transparency 52 with **Learn.**

Alternate Examples

1. Name the polyhedrons.

a.

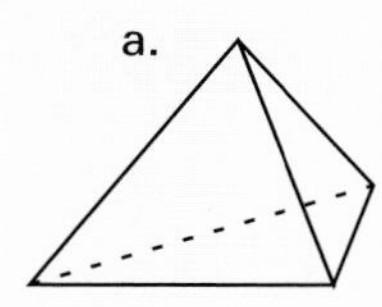

b.

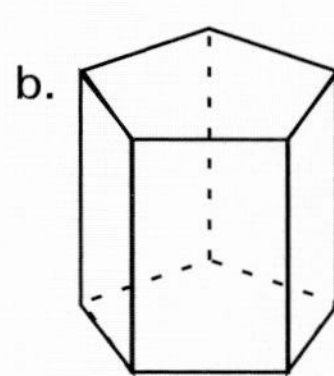

Figure *a* is a triangular pyramid.

Figure *b* is a pentagonal prism.

2. Sketch a hexagonal pyramid.

Sketch the base. Then pick a point above the base and connect each vertex of the base with that point. Make the hidden edges dashed.

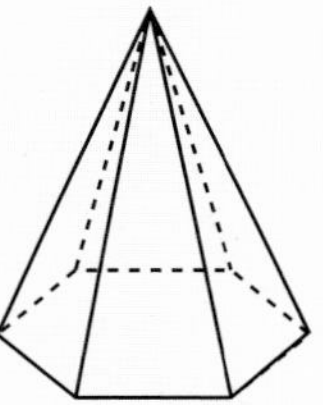

3 Practice and Assess

Check

Be sure students understand that all faces of a polyhedron are polygons.

Answers for Check Your Understanding

1. Yes; Its bases are congruent and parallel; Rectangular prism or square prism.
2. Possible answers: Most containers with lids, a flat-sided lunch box.

11-1 Exercises and Applications

Assignment Guide

- Basic
  1–9, 11, 13, 16, 18–25
- Average
  2–11, 13, 15–25
- Enriched
  5–25

Exercise Notes

Exercise 15

Extension Have students determine the names for the other two Platonic solids and briefly describe them. Dodecahedron, 12 pentagonal faces; icosahedron, 20 triangular faces

Exercise Answers

1. Possible answer:

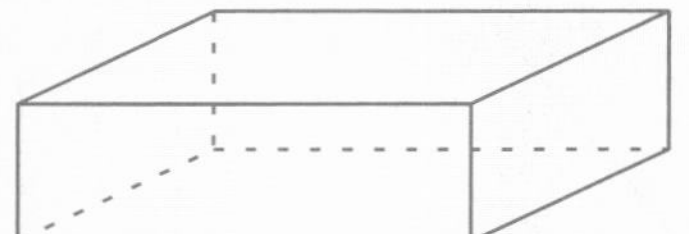

8. Possible answer:

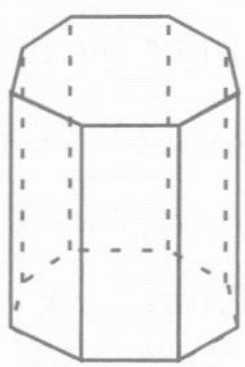

9. Possible answer:

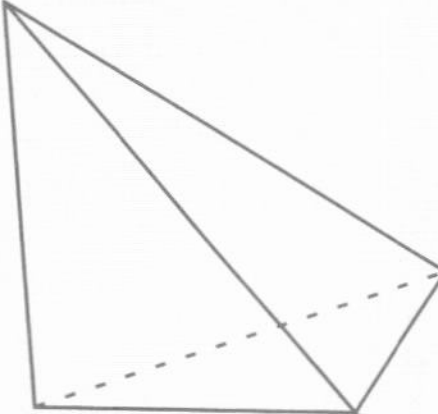

10. Possible answer:

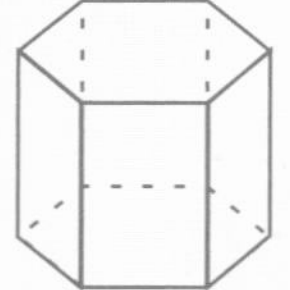

11. Square pyramid

12. Cube (square prism)

Reteaching

Activity

Materials: Cardboard box

Work with a partner. Use a cardboard box. Point out all the faces, edges, and vertices.

11-1 Exercises and Applications

Practice and Apply

1. **Getting Started** Follow these steps to sketch a rectangular prism.
   a. Draw a parallelogram to show one rectangular base in perspective.
   b. Draw a second parallelogram directly below the first.
   c. Add vertical lines joining the vertices of the bases.
   d. Decide which edges are hidden. Make these dashed lines.

Geometry Use the sketch of the prism to answer each question.

2. Name the polyhedron. Triangular prism
3. Name the polygons that are the faces of the prism. How many of each type of polygon are there? 2 triangles, 3 rectangles
4. How many edges, faces, and vertices does the polyhedron have? 9 edges, 5 faces, 6 vertices

Name each polyhedron.

5. 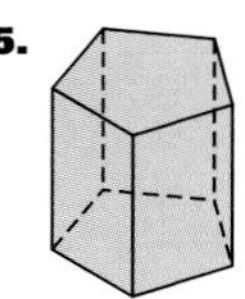 Pentagonal prism

6. 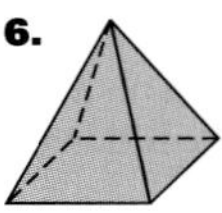 Square pyramid

7. 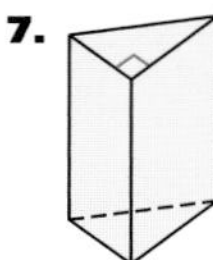 Right triangular prism

Sketch each polyhedron.

8. An octagonal prism
9. A triangular pyramid
10. A hexagonal prism

Fine Arts Name the polyhedrons in each sculpture.

11. 

12. 

13. **Test Prep** How many faces, edges, and vertices does a square pyramid have? C
    Ⓐ 4 faces, 8 edges, 6 vertices
    Ⓑ 4 faces, 6 edges, 4 vertices
    Ⓒ 5 faces, 8 edges, 5 vertices
    Ⓓ 5 faces, 9 edges, 6 vertices

PRACTICE

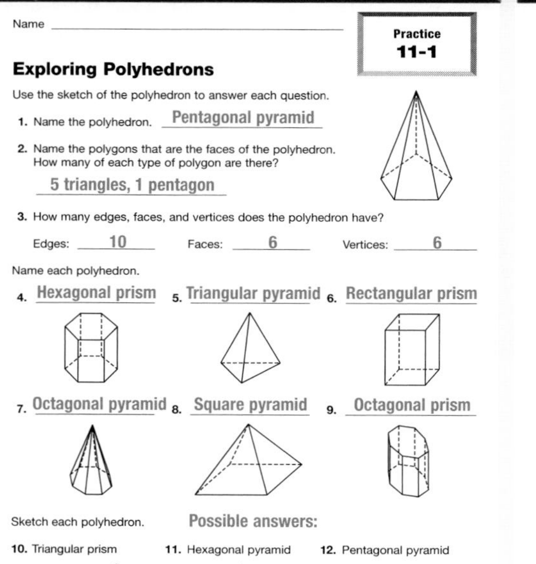

Name ______

Practice 11-1

Exploring Polyhedrons

Use the sketch of the polyhedron to answer each question.

1. Name the polyhedron. Pentagonal pyramid
2. Name the polygons that are the faces of the polyhedron. How many of each type of polygon are there? 5 triangles, 1 pentagon
3. How many edges, faces, and vertices does the polyhedron have?
   Edges: 10 Faces: 6 Vertices: 6

Name each polyhedron.

4. Hexagonal prism
5. Triangular pyramid
6. Rectangular prism
7. Octagonal pyramid
8. Square pyramid
9. Octagonal prism

Sketch each polyhedron. Possible answers:

10. Triangular prism
11. Hexagonal pyramid
12. Pentagonal pyramid

RETEACHING

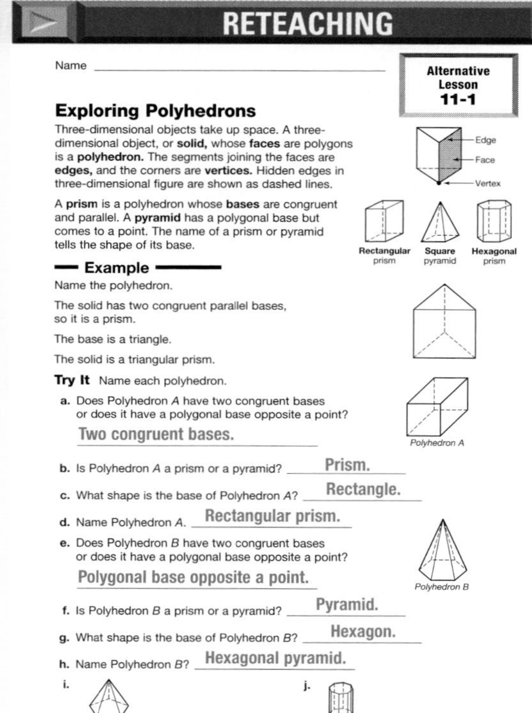

Name ______

Alternative Lesson 11-1

Exploring Polyhedrons

Three-dimensional objects take up space. A three-dimensional object, or **solid,** whose **faces** are polygons is a **polyhedron.** The segments joining the faces are **edges,** and the corners are **vertices.** Hidden edges in three-dimensional figure are shown as dashed lines.

A **prism** is a polyhedron whose **bases** are congruent and parallel. A **pyramid** has a polygonal base but comes to a point. The name of a prism or pyramid tells the shape of its base.

Example

Name the polyhedron.

The solid has two congruent parallel bases, so it is a prism.

The base is a triangle.

The solid is a triangular prism.

Try It Name each polyhedron.

a. Does Polyhedron *A* have two congruent bases or does it have a polygonal base opposite a point? Two congruent bases.
b. Is Polyhedron *A* a prism or a pyramid? Prism.
c. What shape is the base of Polyhedron *A*? Rectangle.
d. Name Polyhedron *A*. Rectangular prism.
e. Does Polyhedron *B* have two congruent bases or does it have a polygonal base opposite a point? Polygonal base opposite a point.
f. Is Polyhedron *B* a prism or a pyramid? Pyramid.
g. What shape is the base of Polyhedron *B*? Hexagon.
h. Name Polyhedron *B*? Hexagonal pyramid.

i. Pentagonal pyramid.
j. Octagonal prism.

14. Science Different minerals form differently shaped crystals. Name the shape of each mineral.

a. Halite (rock salt) Cube

b. Beryl Hexagonal prism

Problem Solving and Reasoning

15. Critical Thinking *Platonic solids,* named for the Greek philosopher Plato, are polyhedrons whose faces are all regular polygons. Three of the five Platonic solids are shown.

Tetrahedron

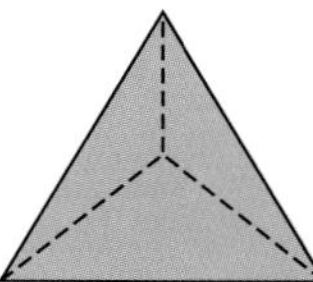

Hexahedron (cube)

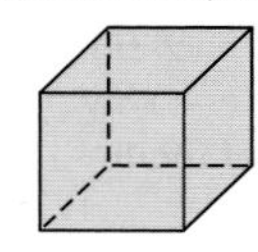

Octahedron

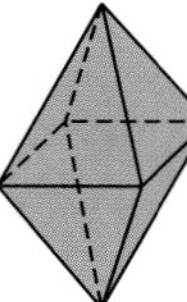

a. Find the number of faces, edges, and vertices in each Platonic solid.

b. There is an equation relating the number of faces, vertices, and edges of a polyhedron. Use your results from **a** to find the equation.

16. Journal In your own words, describe the similarities and differences between pyramids and prisms.

17. Critical Thinking The sculpture *Untitled,* by Donald Judd, is made up of ten identical rectangular prisms. What is the total number of faces, edges, and vertices for the prisms in this sculpture?

Mixed Review

Draw each pair of angles. *[Lesson 5-1]*

18. Two complementary angles, one with measure 45°

19. Two supplementary angles, one with measure 105°

20. Two complementary angles, one with measure 80°

Plot and label each point on the same coordinate plane. Name the quadrant or axis that contains each point. *[Lesson 9-3]*

21. $(-3, 4)$ II **22.** $(0, -2)$ *y*-axis **23.** $(-5, -3)$ III **24.** $(5, 0)$ *x*-axis **25.** $(6, 2)$ I

PROBLEM SOLVING 11-1

Exercise Answers

15. a. Tetrahedron: 4 faces, 6 edges, 4 vertices; Hexahedron: 6 faces, 12 edges, 8 vertices; Octahedron: 8 faces, 12 edges, 6 vertices.

b. Faces + Vertices − Number of edges = 2

16. Possible answers: Prisms and pyramids are polyhedrons; The faces of both are polygons; The bases of a prism are congruent and parallel; A pyramid has only one base.

17. 60 faces, 120 edges, 80 vertices

18.–20.

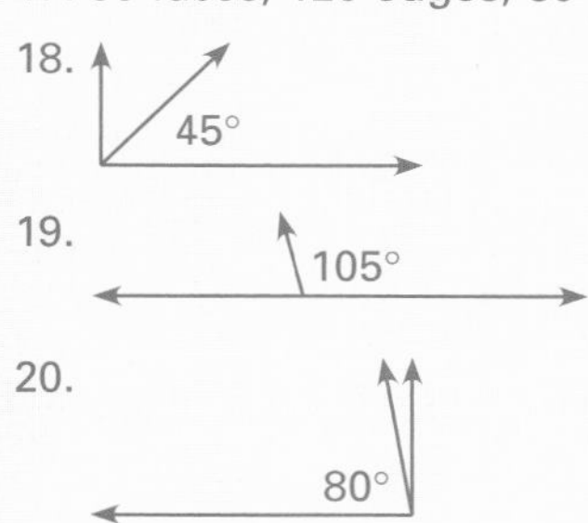

21–25.

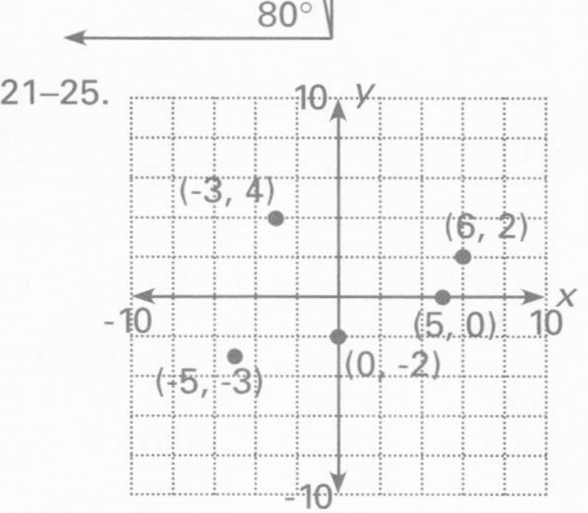

Alternate Assessment

Portfolio Have students choose and draw two polyhedrons that were discussed in this lesson.

Quick Quiz

Refer to the polyhedron.

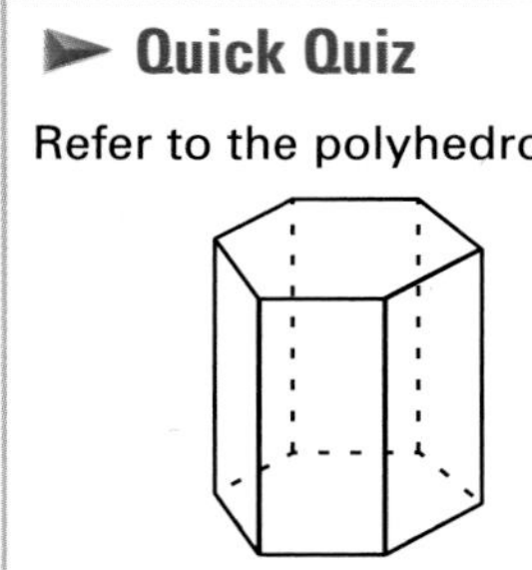

1. Name the polyhedron. hexagonal prism
2. Give the number of edges, faces, and vertices. 18, 8, 12

Available on Daily Transparency 11-1

PROBLEM SOLVING

Name ______

Guided Problem Solving 11-1

GPS PROBLEM 13, STUDENT PAGE 556

How many faces, edges, and vertices does a square pyramid have?

A. 4 faces, 8 edges, 6 vertices B. 4 faces, 6 edges, 4 vertices
C. 5 faces, 8 edges, 5 vertices D. 5 faces, 9 edges, 6 vertices

— Understand —

1. What figure is the base of a square pyramid? Possible answer: Items 3-6, and 9 Square.
2. Does a pyramid have two congruent parallel bases or one base opposite a point? One base opposite a point.

— Plan —

3. Draw a square pyramid. Label the vertices *A, B, C,* and so on.

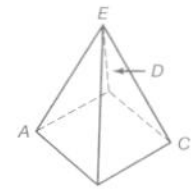

4. List the vertices. *A, B, C, D, E*
5. List the edges. *AB, AD, AE, BC, BE, CD, CE, DE*
6. List the faces. *ABCD, ADE, ABE, BCE, CDE*

— Solve —

7. Use your answers to Items 4–6 to tell how many of each there are in a square pyramid.

a. Vertices 5 vertices. b. Edges 8 edges. c. Faces 5 faces.

8. Which choice is the correct answer. C

— Look Back —

9. How did making an organized list help you know that you counted all the edges? Made sure all were counted, and none were counted more than one time.

SOLVE ANOTHER PROBLEM

How many faces, edges, and vertices does a hexagonal prism have? 8 faces, 18 edges, 12 vertices.

ENRICHMENT

Name ______

Extend Your Thinking 11-1

Decision Making

Your family has decided to buy a pet. The choices have been narrowed to a long-haired cat, a golden retriever (large dog) or a toy poodle (small dog). Since you will be the person who takes care of the pet, you can make the final decision about which type of animal to buy.

1. What basic care does a pet require each day? Possible answers: food, water, play, affection, walks for a dog.
2. What other things will you need to do for the pet? Possible answers: groom, vet visits, obedience class, clean litter box.
3. What factors would you need to consider before making your decision? Possible answers: time to care for animal, enjoyment animal will bring you, cost of care.
4. Which animal would you choose? Explain. Possible answers: cat; less time is needed for its care.

At a pet store, a small can of cat food costs 40¢ and a 5-pound bag of dry food costs \$6.40. The recommended feeding is 2 cans or $\frac{1}{2}$ cup of dry food for a 10-pound cat each day. A $\frac{1}{2}$ cup of food weighs about 1 oz.

A can of dog food costs 70¢ and a 20-pound bag of dry food costs \$16.00. The recommended feeding is 3 cans or $5\frac{1}{2}$ cups of dry food for a large dog each day. A small dog eats 1 can or $1\frac{1}{2}$ cups of dry food each day.

5. Complete the table to determine the cost of feeding each pet for one week.

	Only canned	Only dry	Combination $\frac{1}{2}$ canned-$\frac{1}{2}$ dry
Cat	\$5.60	\$0.56	\$3.08
Large dog	\$14.70	\$3.85	\$9.28
Small dog	\$4.90	\$1.05	\$2.98

6. Which diet would you feed your pet? Explain. Possible answer: Combination, it provides variety at reasonable cost.
7. Would this expense affect your decision about which pet to buy? Explain. Possible answer: No, family can afford food costs.

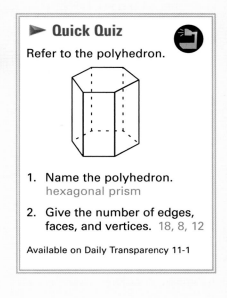

11-2 Lesson Organizer

Objectives

- Match isometric and orthographic views.
- Draw front, side, and top views of a solid.
- Draw a figure in perspective from its front, top, and side views.

Vocabulary

- Isometric drawing, orthographic drawing

Materials

- Explore: Centimeter cubes

NCTM Standards

- 1–2, 4, 12

Review

Think of looking at an ordinary cube. Then answer the following questions.

1. How many faces? 6
2. How many edges? 12
3. How many vertices? 8
4. What is the greatest number of faces you can see when you look at a cube? 3

Available on Daily Transparency 11-2

1 Introduce

Explore

You may wish to use Lesson Enhancement Transparency 53 with **Explore**.

The Point
To investigate the issues involved in drawing 3-dimensional figures, students construct models of buildings. Then they sketch views of the buildings.

Ongoing Assessment
Watch for students who do not realize that the views shown represent "head-on" views. If they view the cubes from an angle, the views will be different.

11-2 Isometric and Orthographic Drawing

You'll Learn ...

- to match isometric and orthographic views
- to draw front, side, and top views of a solid
- to draw a figure in perspective from its front, top, and side views

... How It's Used

Draftspeople make orthographic drawings to show exact specifications for a manufactured part.

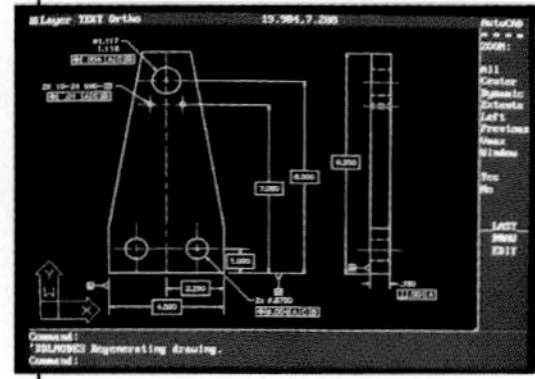

Vocabulary

isometric drawing

orthographic drawing

► Lesson Link You've named and sketched different polyhedrons. Now you'll investigate techniques for drawing any three-dimensional object. ◄

Explore Three-Dimensional Figures

What's Your View?

Materials: Centimeter cubes

You're the construction crew! Front, side, and top views of three simple buildings are shown.

1. Use cubes to construct each building. Is there more than one way to construct any or all of them?
2. Sketch the buildings you made in Step 1. Do your best to make your sketches look three-dimensional.
3. Design and build a cube building of your own. Draw front, side, and top views of your building.
4. When you're describing a building, what advantages and disadvantages do front, side, and top views have compared to drawings such as the one you made in Step 2?

A.

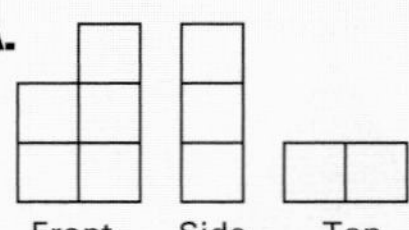

B.

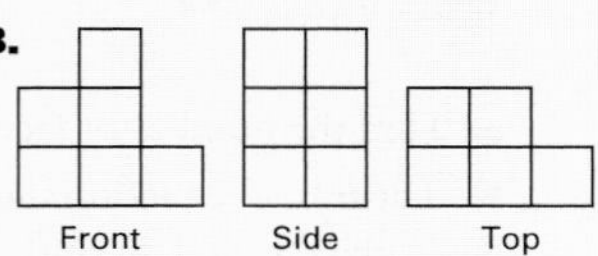

C.

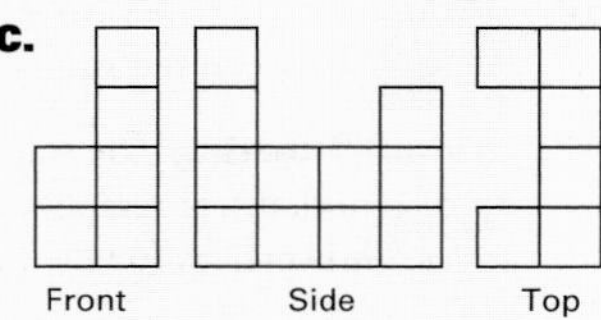

Learn Isometric and Orthographic Drawing

Artists of many cultures have tried to give the illusion of depth to their paintings. In Babylonian sculpture, the figures in front partially block our view of those in back. During the Renaissance, European artists developed a mathematical way to show perspective.

MEETING INDIVIDUAL NEEDS

Resources

- **11-2** Practice
- **11-2** Reteaching
- **11-2** Problem Solving
- **11-2** Enrichment
- **11-2** Daily Transparency
  - Problem of the Day
  - Review
  - Quick Quiz
- Teaching Tool Transparency 9
- Lesson Enhancement Transparencies 53, 54
- Technology Master 52

Learning Modalities

Visual Use photos of buildings from magazines and newspapers. Have students draw front, side, and top views.

Kinesthetic Give students as much practice as possible working with cubes and building models similar to those shown in the exercises.

Social Have students work together in constructing the models described in **Explore**.

English Language Development

Most students, even those for whom English is a native language, will find the words *orthographic* and *isometric* intimidating. Be sure to allow time for discussing these words and their pronunciations.

Pair English language learners with students who are more proficient in English.

Isometric drawing is one method used to give perspective to a drawing. Using isometric dot paper makes isometric drawing easier.

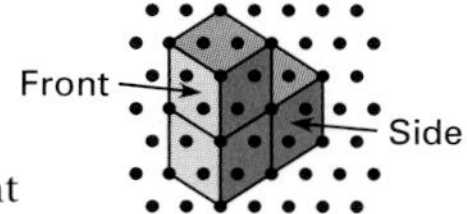

However, isometric drawing can distort angles. The right angles of the cube look like obtuse and acute angles.

Orthographic drawing shows angles and lengths accurately. In an orthographic view, you look directly at the object from front, side, and top views. More than one view is needed to describe the object completely.

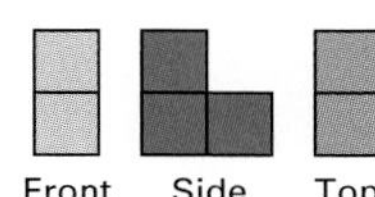

Example 1

Match each isometric drawing with a set of orthographic views.

1.

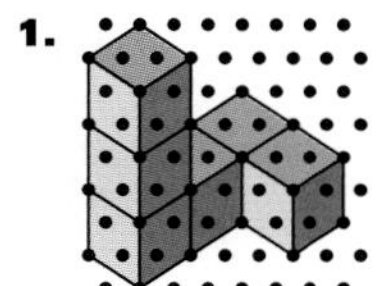

A.

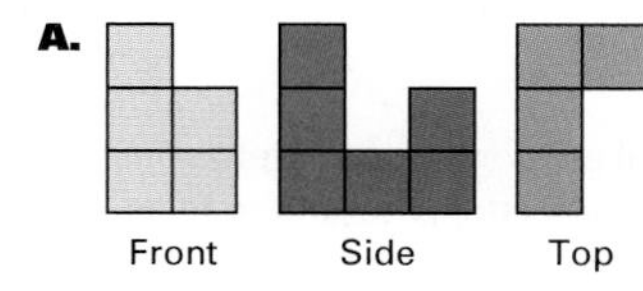

2.

B.

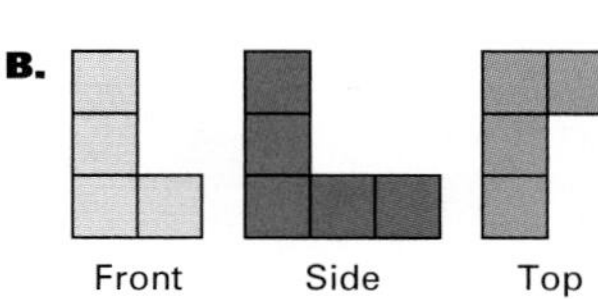

Use the heights of the stacks of cubes to help you match isometric and orthographic drawings.

Isometric drawing 2 has a stack of two cubes; drawing 1 does not. The front and side views of **A** show stacks of two cubes in the proper location to match drawing 2.

Drawing 1 matches with **B** and drawing 2 with **A**.

Try It

Match the isometric drawing with a set of orthographic views.

1. A

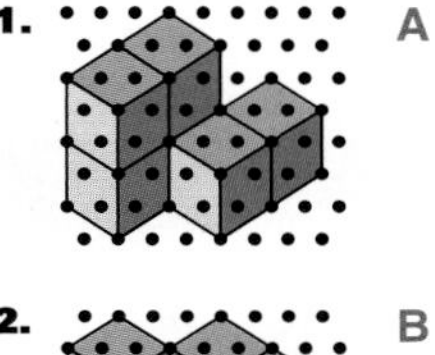

A.

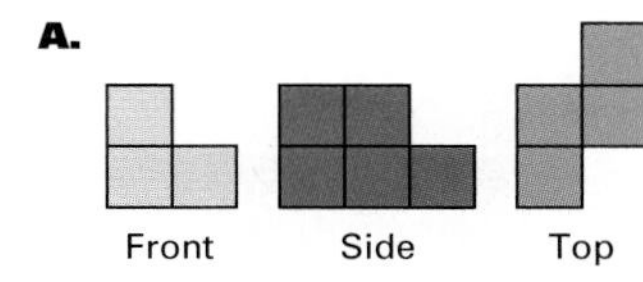

2. B

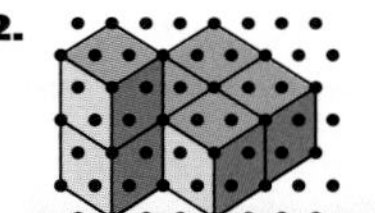

B.

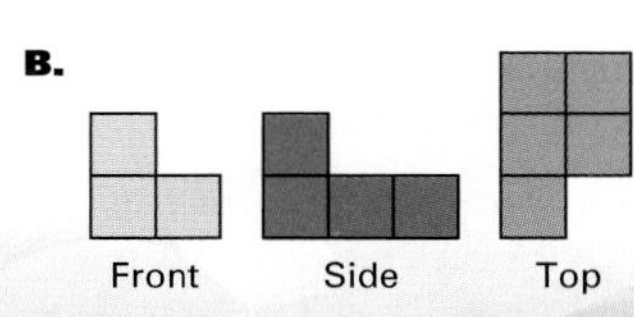

MATH EVERY DAY

► Problem of the Day

Milton had a penny, nickel, dime, and quarter in his pocket. When he bent over to pick up a dime that was on the floor, one coin fell out of his pocket and was lost. He put the dime he found in his pocket. What are the chances that he has more money in his pocket now than before he picked up the dime? 2 chances out of 4, or 1 chance out of 2 (If either the penny or nickel fell out, he has more money now. If the dime fell out he has the same amount. If the quarter fell out, he has less.)

Available on Daily Transparency 11-2

An Extension is provided in the transparency package.

Fact of the Day
Artists in Western civilizations developed different perspective techniques from those of non-Western cultures.

Estimation

Estimate.

1. 51 × 89 4500
2. 99 × 79 8000
3. 42 × 602 24,000
4. 789 × 910 720,000

Answers for Explore

1. B and C can be constructed in more than one way.
2. Possible answers

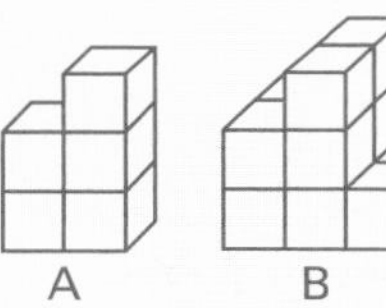

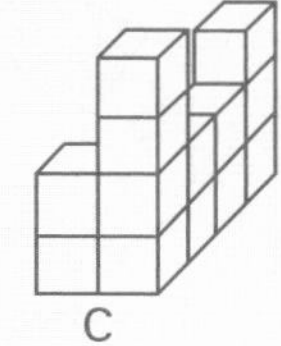

3. Answers may vary.
4. One view does not always show all the parts. Buildings like B or C could be built incorrectly since there is more than one way to construct them. However, front, top, and side views do not show perspective.

2 Teach

Learn

You may wish to use Lesson Enhancement Transparency 54 and Teaching Tool Transparency 9: Isometric Dot Paper with **Learn**.

Alternate Examples

1. Match each isometric drawing with a set of orthographic views.

1. 2.

A.

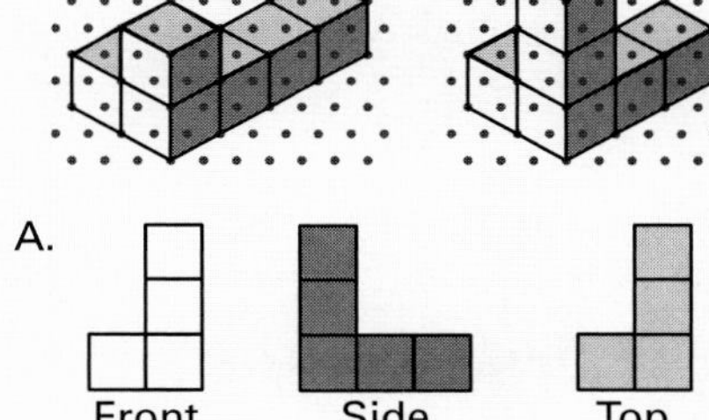

B.

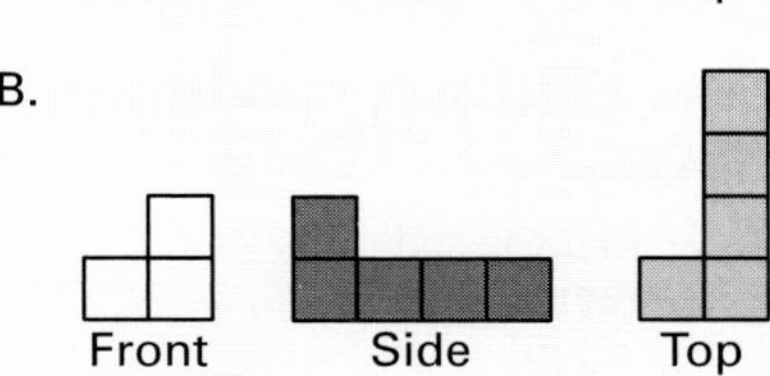

Isometric drawing **2** has a stack of three cubes, while **1** does not. The front and side views of A show stacks of cubes in the proper location to match drawing **2**.

Drawing 1 matches with B and drawing 2 with A.

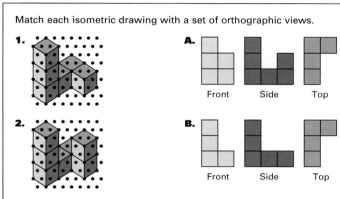

Alternate Examples

2. Sketch front, top, and side views of the object shown.

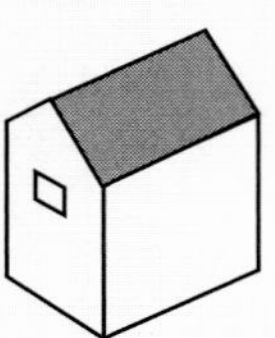

The three views are shown.

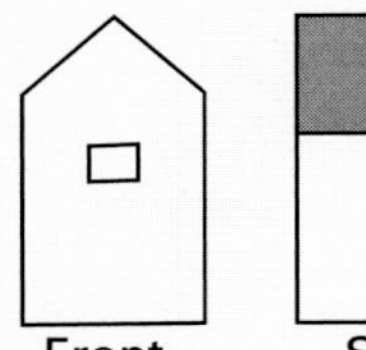

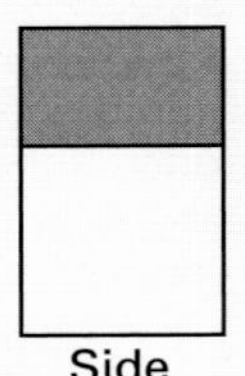

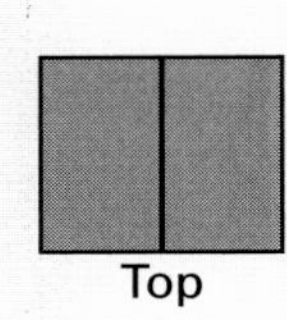

Front Side Top

3. Make a perspective sketch of the object shown.

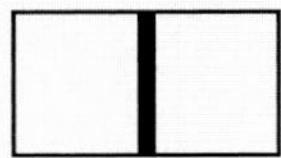

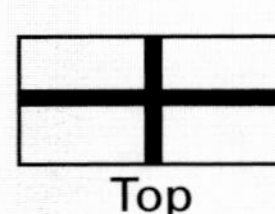

Front Side Top

The sketch is shown.

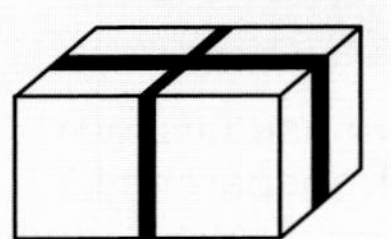

Answers for Try It

a.

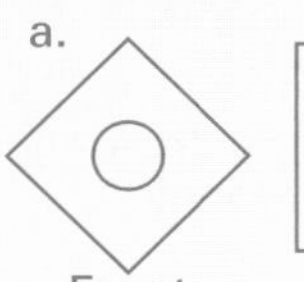

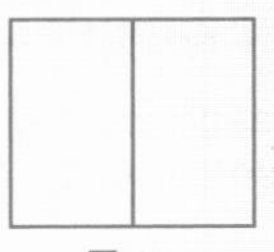

Front Top Side

b.

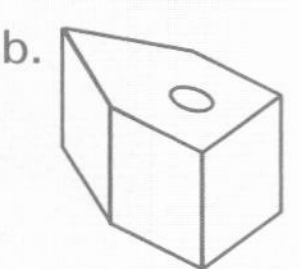

3 Practice and Assess

Check

Answers for Check Your Understanding

1. Possible answers: Orthographic views are more useful if you only want to see a particular view or you want to see the angles and lines as they actually appear. Isometric drawings are useful when you need to see how different views relate to each other and how the whole object looks.
2. Not always. Sometimes other cubes could be hidden behind the front view of a set of cubes.

Examples

2 Sketch front, top, and side views of the object shown.

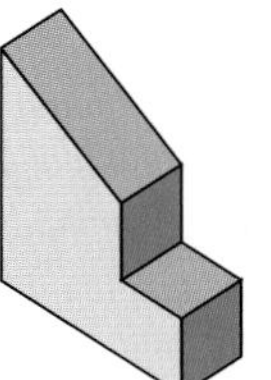

The three views are shown. Notice how the lines in the side and top views show changes in the object.

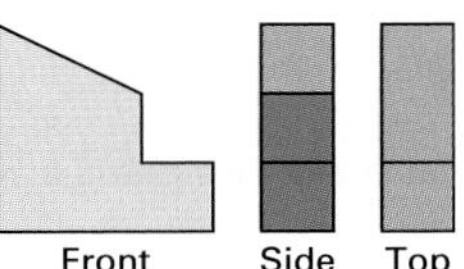

3 Make a perspective sketch of the metal plate. (The dotted lines represent the two holes.)

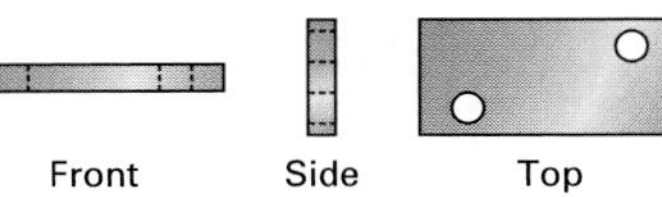

The sketch is shown.

Try It

a. The sculpture shown is in downtown New York City. Sketch front, top, and side views of the sculpture.

b. Make a perspective sketch of the object shown.

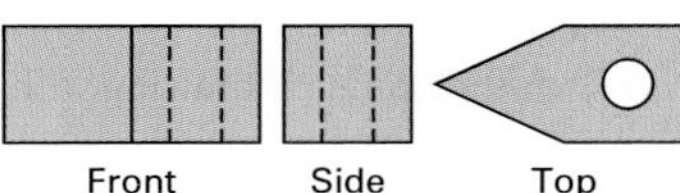

History Link

The Colossus of Rhodes was one of the seven ancient wonders of the world. The bronze statue of Apollo was 120 ft tall and stood atop a 25 ft tall marble base. About 220 B.C., just 60 years after its completion, the Colossus broke at the knees and fell during an earthquake. It was later sold as scrap metal.

Check Your Understanding

1. Name some situations where orthographic views would be more useful than an isometric drawing. When might the isometric drawing be more helpful?
2. If you were given the front view of a set of cubes, would you be able to sketch the back view? If so, explain how; if not, explain why not.

MEETING MIDDLE SCHOOL CLASSROOM NEEDS

Tips from Middle School Teachers

I like to have students use ordinary children's alphabet blocks to make models. Even though they invariably make jokes about playing with blocks, I feel this makes the topic less intimidating for those who find this lesson difficult.

Team Teaching

Work with an art teacher. Show pictures of modern sculptures that involve geometric designs.

Fine Arts Connection

Point out that many architects provide their clients with orthographic drawings called *elevations.* They are usually labeled north elevation, east elevation, south elevation, and west elevation. Each elevation shows what the building looks like when viewed from that direction.

11-2 Exercises and Applications

Practice and Apply

1. **Getting Started** Follow these steps to draw front, side, and top orthographic views of the cubes.

   a. Imagine yourself in front of the cubes. Decide how many stacks of cubes you would see. Then decide how many cubes you would see in each stack. Draw the front view.

   b. Imagine that you move to the side of the "building" to your right. Repeat **a** to draw the side view.

   c. Imagine yourself directly above the cubes. Repeat **a** to draw the top view.

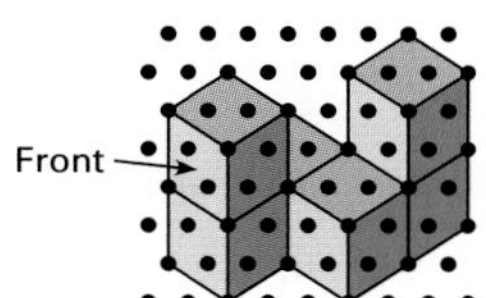

Find the number of cubes in each figure. Assume all cubes are visible.

2. 5 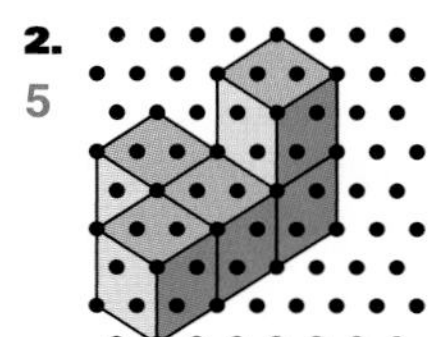

3. 7 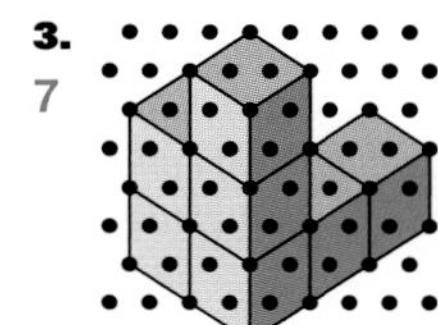

4. 8 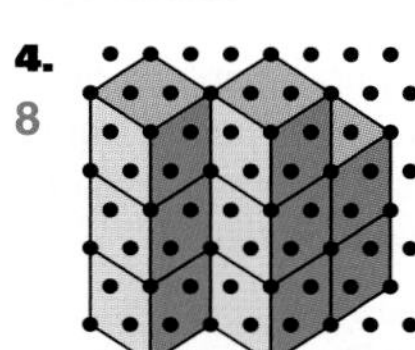

Match each isometric drawing with a set of orthographic views.

5. C 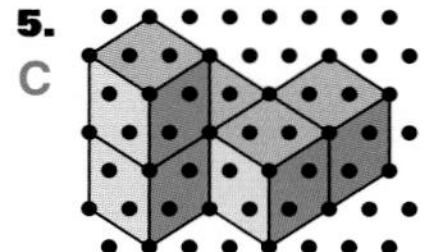

6. B 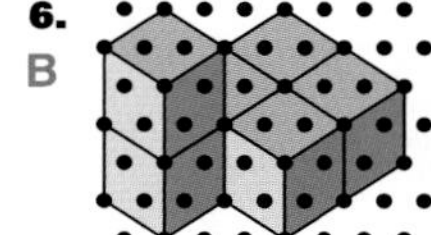

7. A 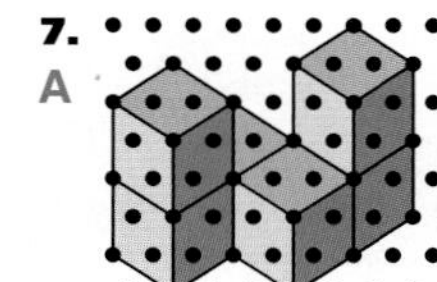

8. D 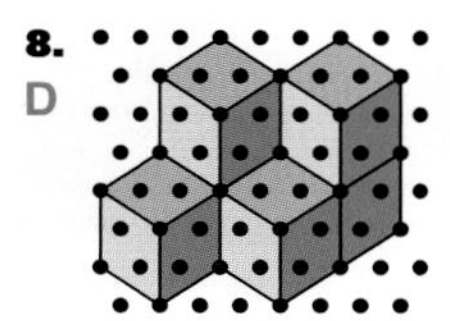

A. 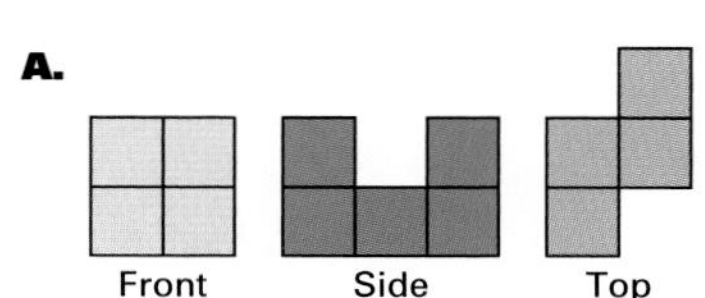 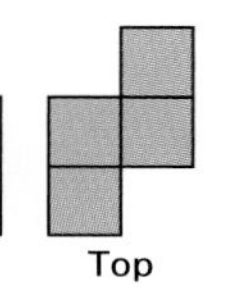

B. 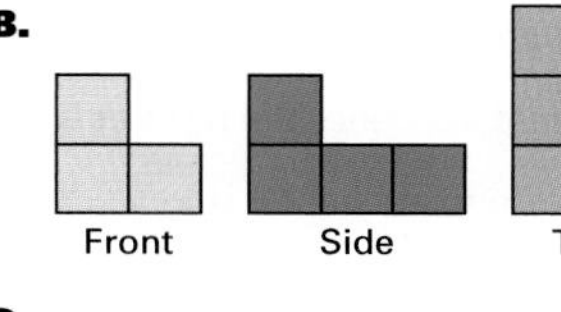 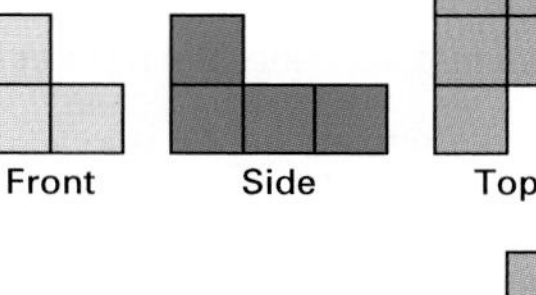

C. 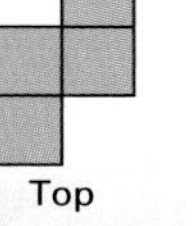

D. 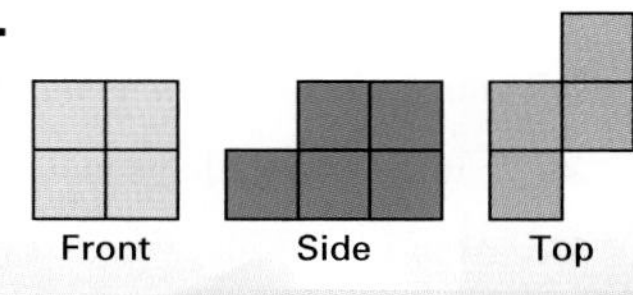

PRACTICE

Name ______________________

Practice 11-2

Isometric and Orthographic Drawing

Find the number of cubes in each figure. Assume all cubes are visible.

1. 8 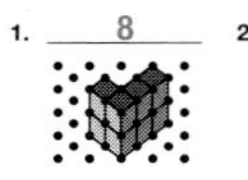
2. 7 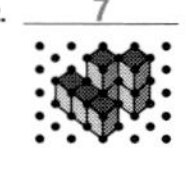
3. 6 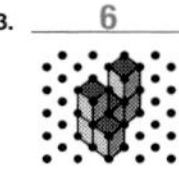
4. 7 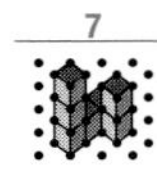

Match each isometric drawing with a set of orthographic views.

5. D 

A. 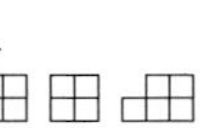

6. B 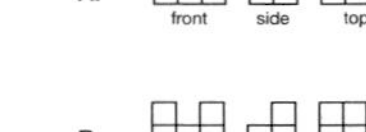

B. 

7. C 

C. 

8. A 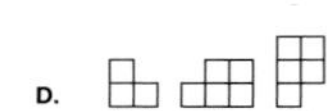

D. 

9. Sketch front, side, and top views of the object.

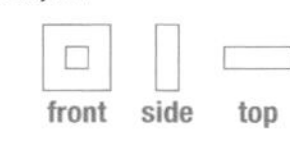

10. Make a perspective sketch of the object.

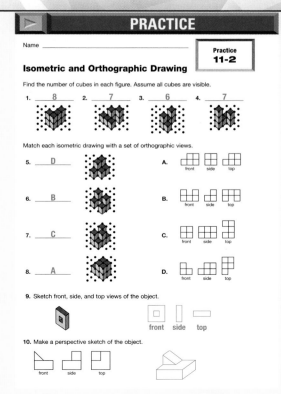

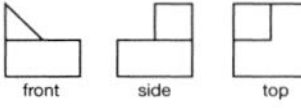

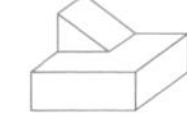

RETEACHING

Name ______________________

Alternative Lesson 11-2

Isometric and Orthographic Drawing

Isometric drawing is one method used to give perspective to a drawing. Using isometric dot paper makes isometric drawing easier. However, the angles may be distorted.

Orthographic drawing shows angles and lengths accurately. In an orthographic view, you look directly at the object from front, side, and top views.

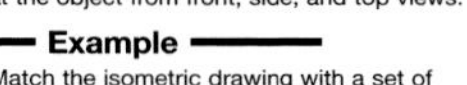

Example

Match the isometric drawing with a set of orthographic views.

Compare the heights of the stacks. The tallest stack in the isometric drawing is two cubes high, so the side and front orthographic views should also have stacks with two cubes.

Determine that the number of cubes and their position is correct in each view. There should be 4 cubes in the side and top views and 3 cubes in the front view. View *A* has the correct number and placement of cubes.

Set *A* matches the isometric drawing.

Try It Match each isometric drawing with a set of orthographic views.

a. How many cubes high is Drawing *A*? 2 cubes.

b. How many cubes would be viewed from the front of Drawing *A*? 3 cubes.

c. How many cubes would be viewed from the side of Drawing *A*? 3 cubes.

d. How many cubes would be viewed from the top of Drawing *A*? 3 cubes.

e. Which set of orthographic views correctly represents Drawing *A*? Set *E*.

f. How many cubes high is Drawing *B*? 3 cubes.

g. How many cubes would be viewed from the front of Drawing *B*? 4 cubes.

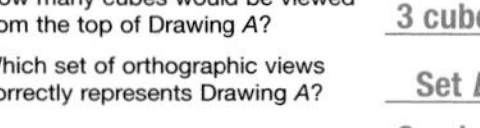

h. How many cubes would be viewed from the side of Drawing *B*? 4 cubes.

i. How many cubes would be viewed from the top of Drawing *B*? 3 cubes.

j. Which set of orthographic views correctly represents Drawing *B*? Set *C*.

11-2 Exercises and Applications

Assignment Guide

- **Basic** 1–10, 14, 16–22 evens
- **Average** 2–12, 14, 16–23
- **Enriched** 4–23

Exercise Notes

Exercises 2–4

Extension Have students draw the front, side, and top view for each figure.

Exercises 5–8

Error Prevention Some students will confuse "front" and "side" in the isometric drawings. You might give them a clue: front is to the left, side is to the right.

Exercise Answers

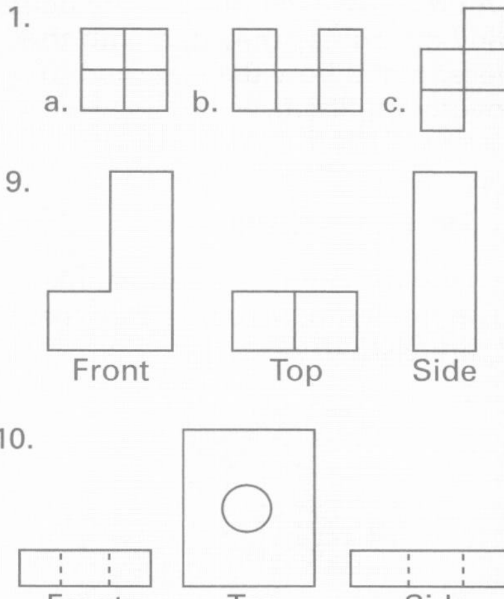

Reteaching

Activity

Materials: Centimeter cubes

Work with a partner. Make two models using cubes. The models should have these qualities.

- The front, side, and top orthographic views are the same.
- The number of cubes needed to make each model is different.

Possible Answer: A cube that is 2 × 2 × 2 and a figure that is almost the same except that 1 cube is missing from the back corner.

Exercise Answers

9–10. See page 561.

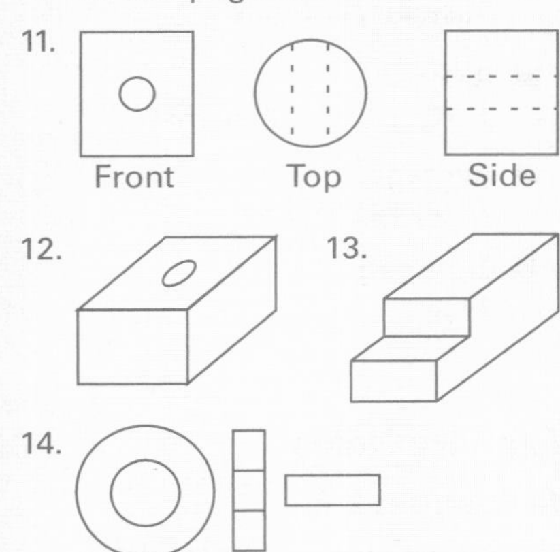

15. A perspective view would distort their shapes, so they would be more difficult to manufacture precisely.

Alternate Assessment

You may want to use the *Interactive CD-ROM Journal* with this assessment.

Journal Have students write about any difficulties they had with this lesson and how they learned to overcome them.

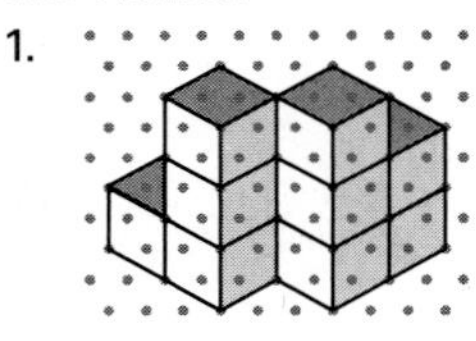

Quick Quiz

Find the number of cubes in the figure. Assume all cubes are visible.

1.

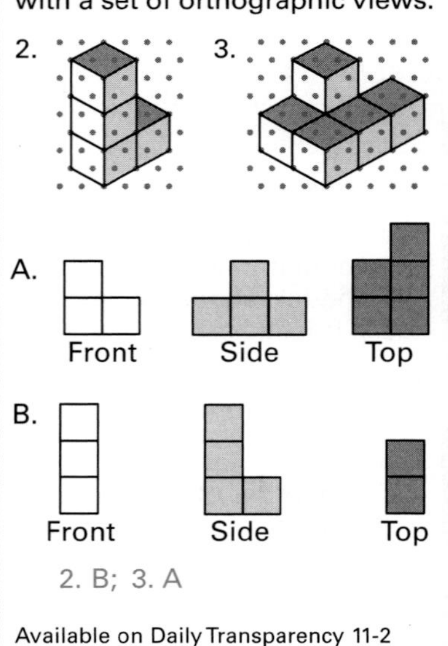

9 cubes

Match each isometric drawing with a set of orthographic views.

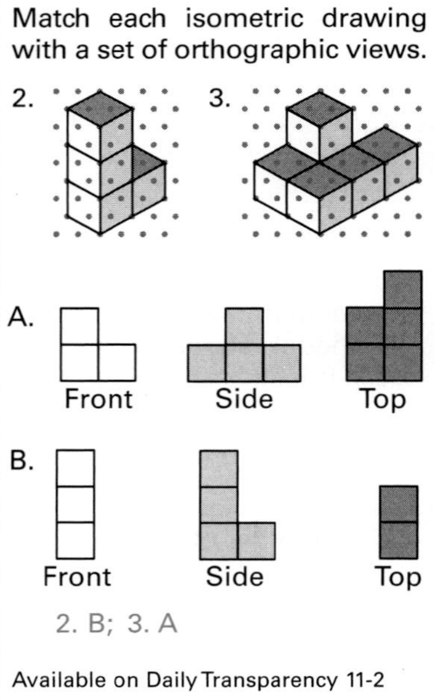

2. B; 3. A

Available on Daily Transparency 11-2

Sketch front, top, and side views of each object.

9. GPS

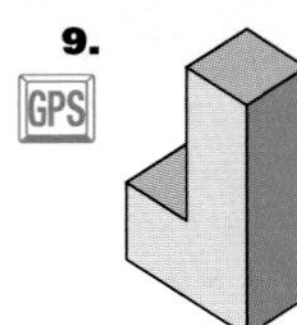

10.

11.

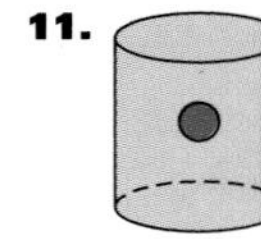

Make a perspective sketch of each object.

12.

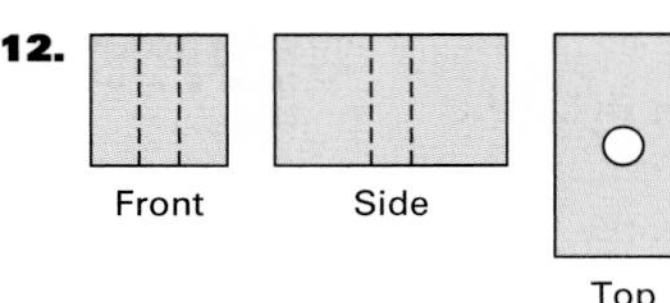

13.

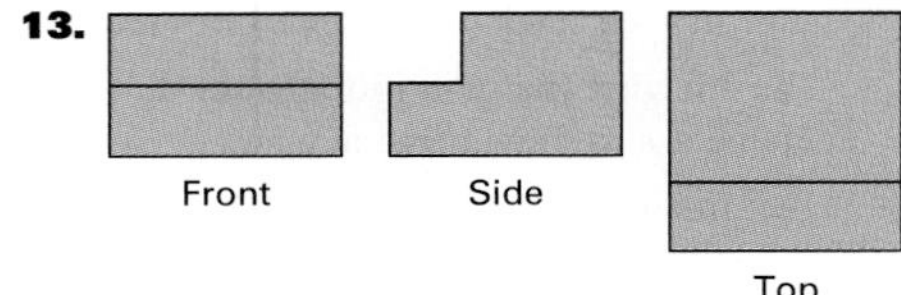

Problem Solving and Reasoning

14. **Communicate** The photograph of *Black Sun*, by Isamu Noguchi, is nearly a front view of the sculpture. Sketch what you think the top and side views look like.

15. **Communicate** Technical drawings of manufactured parts are orthographic drawings. Explain why orthographic drawings are used to picture these parts.

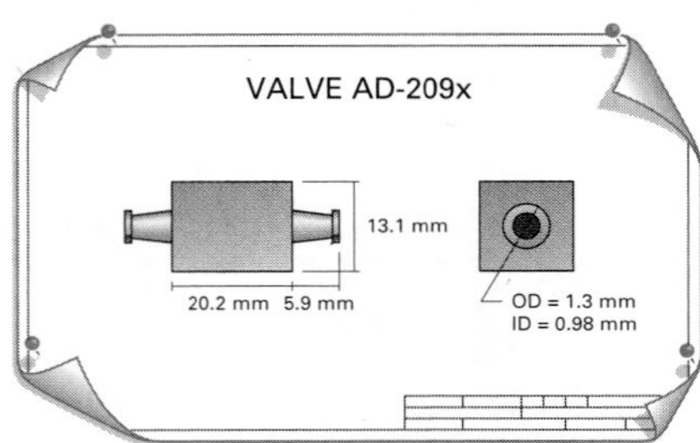

Mixed Review

Write the word that describes the lines or line segments. *[Lesson 5-2]*

16. A double yellow line on the street **Parallel**

17. The top and side edges of a door **Perpendicular**

18. The sideline and end line of a playing field **Perpendicular**

19. Joined edges of a floppy disk **Perpendicular**

Tell which quantities are variables and which are constants. *[Lesson 10-1]*

20. Number of students in a classroom **Variable**

21. Number of inches in a foot **Constant**

22. Amount of water you drink in a day **Variable**

23. Number of leaves on a tree **Variable**

PROBLEM SOLVING 11-2

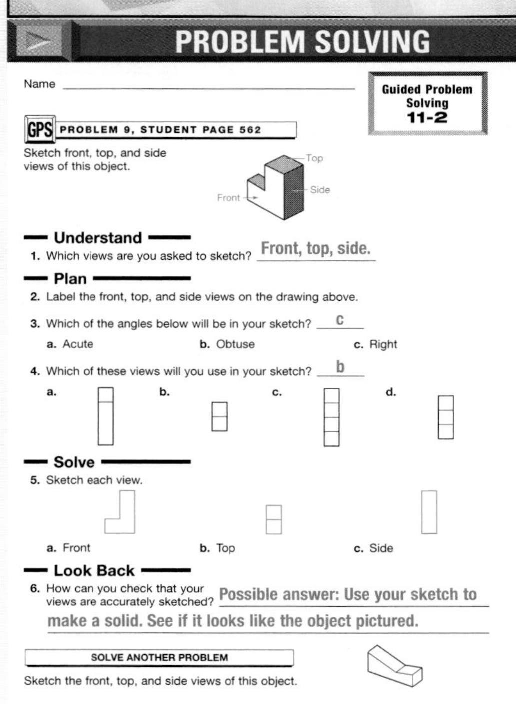

PROBLEM SOLVING

Name

Guided Problem Solving 11-2

GPS PROBLEM 9, STUDENT PAGE 562

Sketch front, top, and side views of this object.

Understand

1. Which views are you asked to sketch? Front, top, side.

Plan

2. Label the front, top, and side views on the drawing above.
3. Which of the angles below will be in your sketch? c
   a. Acute b. Obtuse c. Right
4. Which of these views will you use in your sketch? b

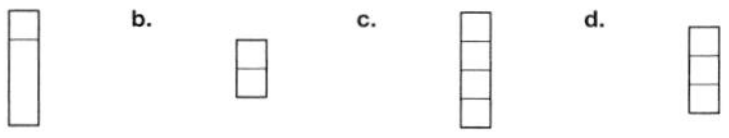

Solve

5. Sketch each view.
   a. Front b. Top c. Side

Look Back

6. How can you check that your views are accurately sketched? Possible answer: Use your sketch to make a solid. See if it looks like the object pictured.

SOLVE ANOTHER PROBLEM

Sketch the front, top, and side views of this object.

a. Front b. Top c. Side

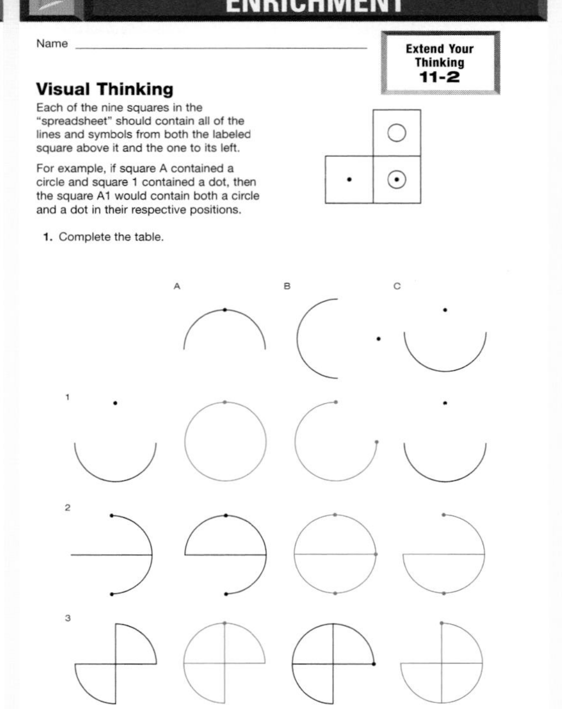

ENRICHMENT

Name

Extend Your Thinking 11-2

Visual Thinking

Each of the nine squares in the "spreadsheet" should contain all of the lines and symbols from both the labeled square above it and the one to its left.

For example, if square A contained a circle and square 1 contained a dot, then the square A1 would contain both a circle and a dot in their respective positions.

1. Complete the table.

Polyhedron Nets and Surface Areas

11-3

▶ Lesson Link You know how to calculate areas of two-dimensional figures. Now you'll apply those skills to find surface areas of three-dimensional figures. ◀

You'll Learn ...

■ to find the surface area of a polyhedron

... How It's Used

Parade volunteers must know the surface area of a float to decide how much decorative material they need.

Vocabulary

surface area

Explore Nets for Polyhedrons

Polyhedron Wrap

Materials: Graph paper, Scissors, Tape

A *net* is a two-dimensional pattern that folds up into a three-dimensional object.

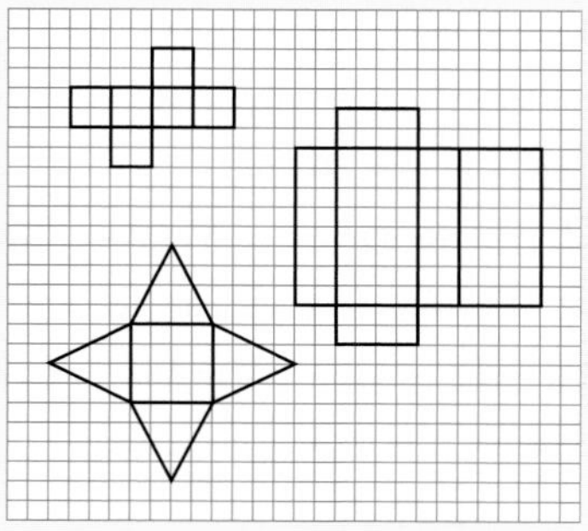

1. Copy each net onto graph paper. Cut out each net, then fold and tape the sides together to make a polyhedron.
2. Name the polyhedron for each net. Then give the name of each of its faces. How many of each type of face are there?
3. Can you look at a net and predict the polyhedron it will make? Explain.
4. Create your own net for a polyhedron. Test it to see if it works.

Learn Polyhedron Nets and Surface Areas

The **surface area** of a three-dimensional figure is the sum of the areas of its faces. The faces include the base(s) of the polyhedron.

The surface area of a gift box is equal to the area of the paper you'd need to wrap it, assuming no gaps or overlap.

By drawing a net for a polyhedron, you can see the shapes and dimensions of its faces. Then you can use area formulas to help you calculate surface areas.

MEETING INDIVIDUAL NEEDS

Resources

- 11-3 Practice
- 11-3 Reteaching
- 11-3 Problem Solving
- 11-3 Enrichment
- 11-3 Daily Transparency
  - Problem of the Day
  - Review
  - Quick Quiz
- Teaching Tool Transparency 7
- Technology Master 53

Interactive CD-ROM Lesson 11

Wide World of Mathematics Geometry: Gateway Arch

Learning Modalities

Verbal Show students an example of a polyhedron. Then have them write a step-by-step description of how they would find the surface area.

Kinesthetic Give students as much practice as possible in actually making nets and folding them to form polyhedrons.

Inclusion

Some students have trouble finding surface area by looking at diagrams. Show them three-dimensional models and point to one face at a time. Have them find the area of each face as you point to it.

Make sure students understand the difference between two- and three-dimensional models. Have students manipulate both. Add new vocabulary to reference book.

INTERACTIVE LESSON

11-3 Lesson Organizer

Objective

- Find the surface area of a polyhedron.

Vocabulary

- Surface area

Materials

- Explore: Graph paper, scissors, tape

NCTM Standards

- 1–4, 7, 12, 13

▶ Review

Find the area of each figure.

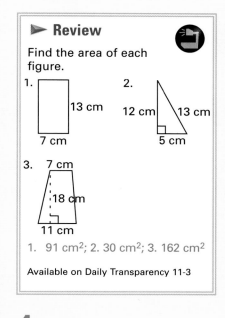

1. Rectangle: 13 cm, 7 cm
2. Right triangle: 12 cm, 13 cm, 5 cm
3. Trapezoid: 7 cm, 18 cm, 11 cm

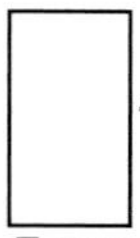

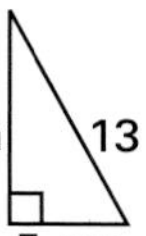

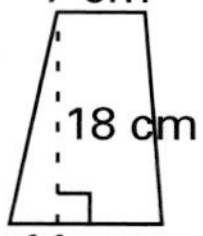

1. 91 cm²; 2. 30 cm²; 3. 162 cm²

Available on Daily Transparency 11-3

1 Introduce

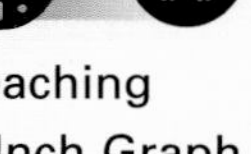

Explore

You may wish to use Teaching Tool Transparency 7: $\frac{1}{4}$-Inch Graph Paper with **Explore**.

The Point

Students discover the relationship between two-dimensional nets and three-dimensional polyhedrons.

Answers for Explore

2. Square prism or cube: 6 square faces; Rectangular prism: 6 rectangular faces; Square pyramid: 1 square face, 4 triangular faces.
3. Sometimes you can look at a net and visualize the polyhedron, but sometimes the figure is too complex to visualize.
4. Answers may vary.

2 Teach

Learn

Alternate Examples

1. Sketch a net for the polyhedron. Then find its surface area.

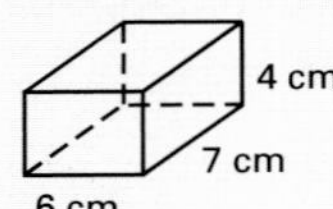

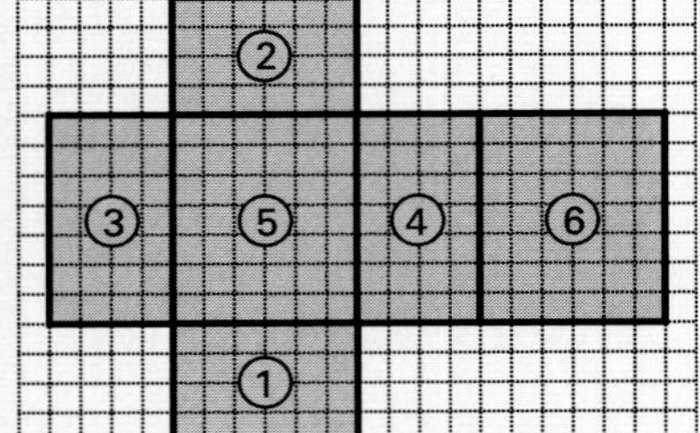

Faces 1 and 2: Area = 48 cm^2

Faces 3 and 4: Area = 56 cm^2

Faces 5 and 6: Area = 84 cm^2

Surface area = 48 cm^2 + 56 cm^2 + 84 cm^2 = 188 cm^2

2. Find the surface area of the prism.

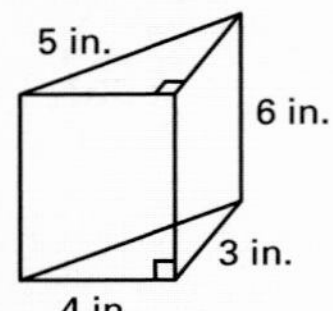

Rectangle area = 24 in^2

Rectangle area = 18 in^2

Rectangle area = 30 in^2

Two triangles, base 4 in. and height 3 in.: area = 12 in^2

Surface area = 24 in^2 + 18 in^2 + 30 in^2 + 12 in^2 = 84 in^2

Answers for Try It

a. 

Surface area: 112 ft^2

3 Practice and Assess

Check

Answers for Check Your Understanding

1. You can see the shapes and dimensions of the polyhedron's faces, and then use area formulas to calculate the area.
2. Surface area is the sum of the areas of a figure's faces. Since each area is in square units, so is surface area.

Study TIP

On the day of a test, take a few minutes to skim the material you studied the night before. A quick review can help refresh your memory.

Examples

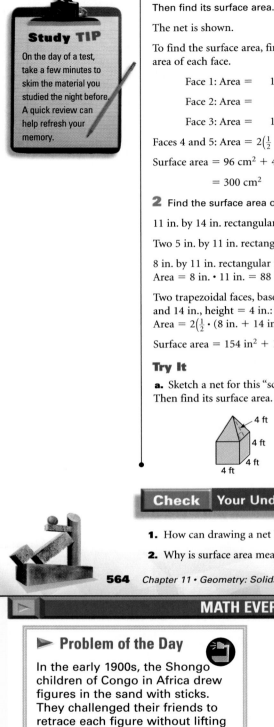

1 Sketch a net for the polyhedron. Then find its surface area.

The net is shown.

To find the surface area, first find the area of each face.

Face 1: Area = 12 cm • 8 cm = 96 cm^2

Face 2: Area = 5 cm • 8 cm = 40 cm^2

Face 3: Area = 13 cm • 8 cm = 104 cm^2

Faces 4 and 5: Area = $2(\frac{1}{2} \cdot 12 \text{ cm} \cdot 5 \text{ cm}) = 60 \text{ cm}^2$

Surface area = 96 cm^2 + 40 cm^2 + 104 cm^2 + 60 cm^2

= 300 cm^2

2 Find the surface area of the prism.

11 in. by 14 in. rectangular face: Area = 11 in. • 14 in. = 154 in^2

Two 5 in. by 11 in. rectangular faces: Area = 2(5 in. • 11 in.) = 110 in^2

8 in. by 11 in. rectangular face:
Area = 8 in. • 11 in. = 88 in^2

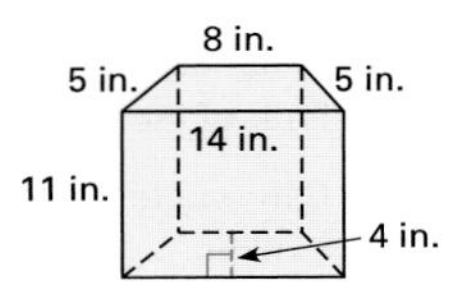

Two trapezoidal faces, bases 8 in. and 14 in., height = 4 in.:
Area = $2(\frac{1}{2} \cdot (8 \text{ in.} + 14 \text{ in.}) \cdot 4 \text{ in.}) = 88 \text{ in}^2$

Surface area = 154 in^2 + 110 in^2 + 88 in^2 + 88 in^2 = 440 in^2

Try It

a. Sketch a net for this "sculpture." Then find its surface area. 112 ft^2

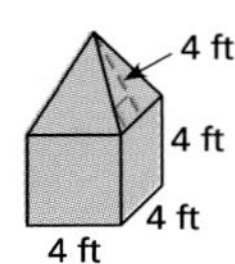

b. Find the surface area of the prism. 610 mm^2

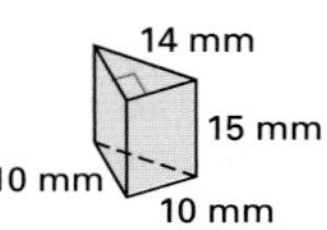

Check Your Understanding

1. How can drawing a net help you find the surface area of a polyhedron?
2. Why is surface area measured in square units?

MATH EVERY DAY

Problem of the Day

In the early 1900s, the Shongo children of Congo in Africa drew figures in the sand with sticks. They challenged their friends to retrace each figure without lifting the stick or retracing any line segment. To retrace the figure, where must you start?

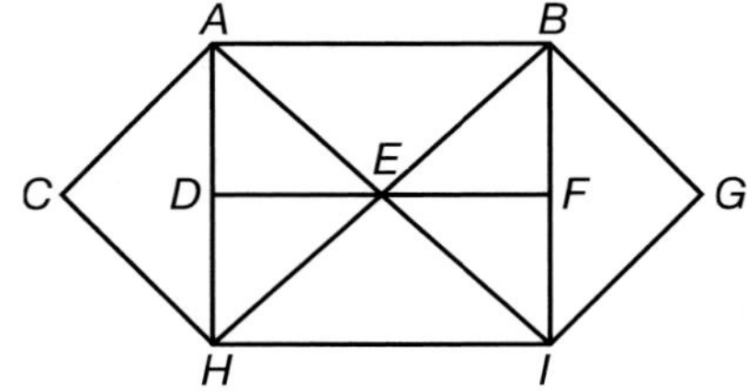

At *D* or *F*

Available on Daily Transparency 11-3

An Extension is provided in the transparency package.

Fact of the Day

Lake Superior, the largest freshwater lake in the world, has a surface area of 31,820 square miles and is 350 miles long.

Mental Math

Do these mentally.

1. 80 + 90 170
2. 170 + 30 200
3. 4000 + 8000 12,000
4. 100 + 90 + 7 197
5. 7000 + 600 + 40 + 8 7648

11-3 Exercises and Applications

Practice and Apply

1. **Getting Started** Follow the steps to find the surface area of the triangular prism.
   a. Find the area of the 10 by 4 rectangular face. 40 cm^2
   b. Find the area of the 10 by 13 rectangular face. 130 cm^2
   c. Find the area of the 10 by 15 rectangular face. 150 cm^2
   d. Find the total area of the two triangular bases. 48 cm^2
   e. Add the areas in **a–d** to find the surface area. 368 cm^2

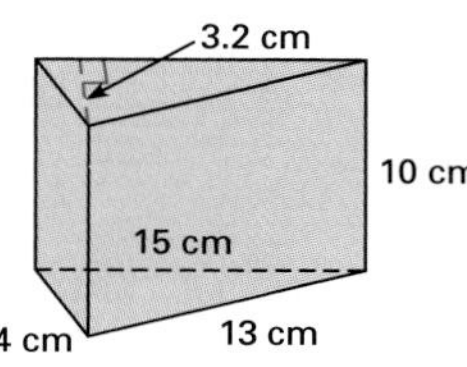

Sketch a net for each polyhedron.

2. 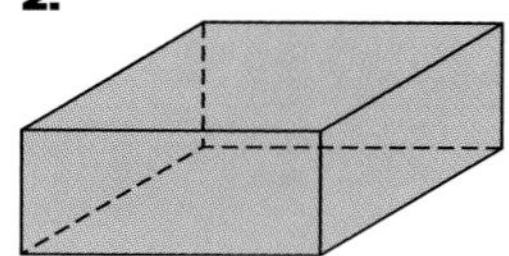

3. 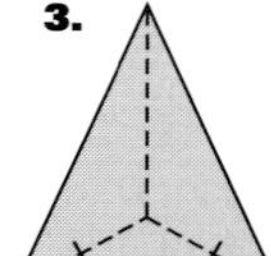

4. 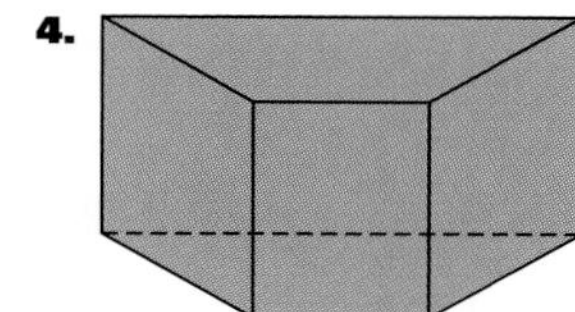

Sketch a net for each polyhedron, then find its surface area.

5. 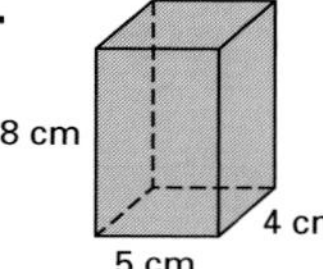

6. 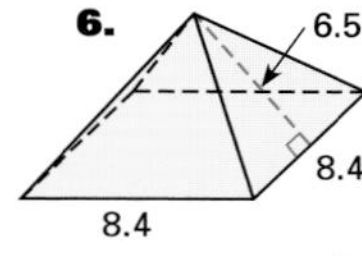

square pyramid

7. 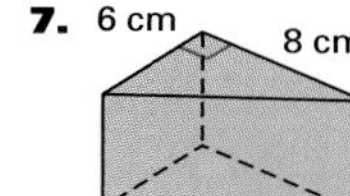

triangular prism

8. 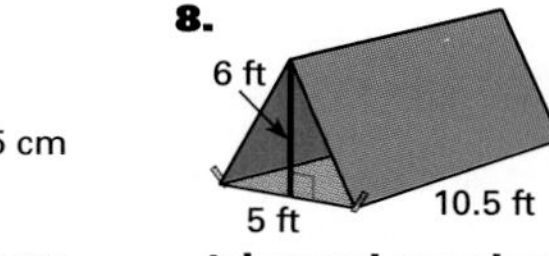

triangular prism

9. **Consumer** You need to paint the outside of the house shown. A gallon of paint covers between 300 and 400 square feet. How many gallons will you need to buy? (Ignore the areas of windows and doors, and do not paint the roof!) ≈ 7 gal

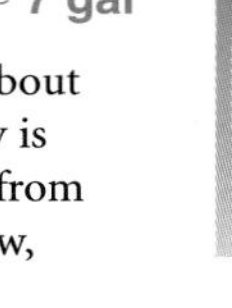

10. **Literature** In *Flat Stanley,* Stanley is, "four feet tall, about a foot wide, and half an inch thick." Assuming Stanley is a rectangular solid, what is his surface area? (Excerpt from *Flat Stanley* by Jeff Brown (New York: Harper and Row, 1964.) Copyright ©1964 by Jeff Brown.) 1212 in^2

11. **Test Prep** Which formula gives the surface area of a cube whose sides are s units long? C

Ⓐ s^2 Ⓑ $3s^2$ Ⓒ $6s^2$ Ⓓ s^3

PRACTICE 11-3

PRACTICE

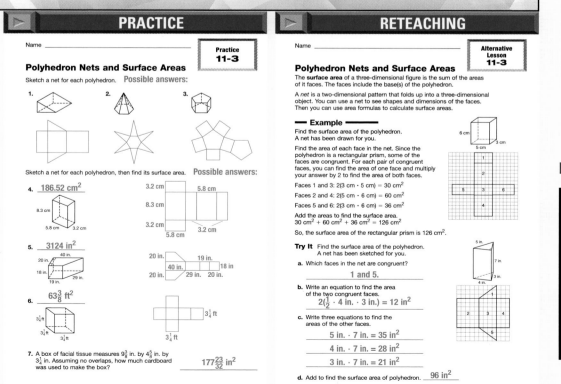

Name ______

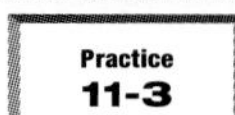

Polyhedron Nets and Surface Areas

Sketch a net for each polyhedron. Possible answers:

1. 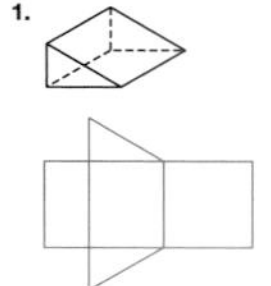

2. 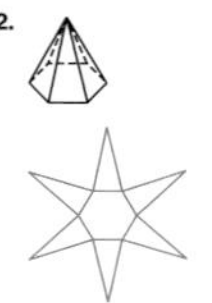

3. 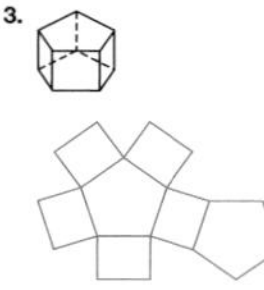

Sketch a net for each polyhedron, then find its surface area. Possible answers:

4. 186.52 cm^2

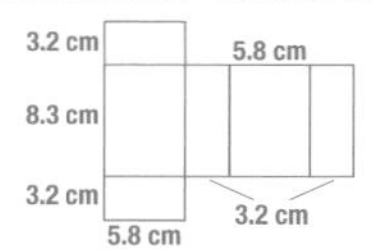

5. 3124 in^2

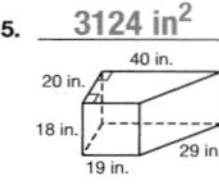

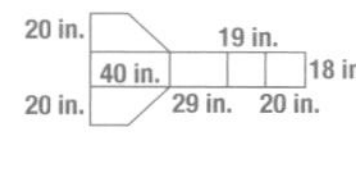

6. $63\frac{3}{8}\text{ ft}^2$

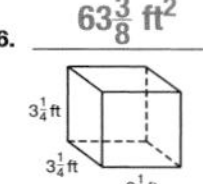

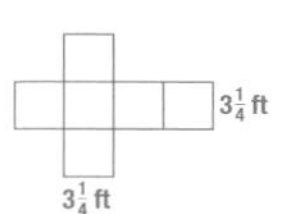

7. A box of facial tissue measures $9\frac{3}{8}$ in. by $4\frac{5}{8}$ in. by $3\frac{1}{4}$ in. Assuming no overlaps, how much cardboard was used to make the box? $177\frac{23}{32}\text{ in}^2$

RETEACHING

Name ______

Alternative Lesson 11-3

Polyhedron Nets and Surface Areas

The **surface area** of a three-dimensional figure is the sum of the areas of it faces. The faces include the base(s) of the polyhedron.

A *net* is a two-dimensional pattern that folds up into a three-dimensional object. You can use a net to see shapes and dimensions of the faces. Then you can use area formulas to calculate surface areas.

Example

Find the surface area of the polyhedron. A net has been drawn for you.

Find the area of each face in the net. Since the polyhedron is a rectangular prism, some of the faces are congruent. For each pair of congruent faces, you can find the area of one face and multiply your answer by 2 to find the area of both faces.

Faces 1 and 3: $2(3\text{ cm} \cdot 5\text{ cm}) = 30\text{ cm}^2$

Faces 2 and 4: $2(5\text{ cm} \cdot 6\text{ cm}) = 60\text{ cm}^2$

Faces 5 and 6: $2(3\text{ cm} \cdot 6\text{ cm}) = 36\text{ cm}^2$

Add the areas to find the surface area.
$30\text{ cm}^2 + 60\text{ cm}^2 + 36\text{ cm}^2 = 126\text{ cm}^2$

So, the surface area of the rectangular prism is 126 cm^2.

Try It Find the surface area of the polyhedron. A net has been sketched for you.

a. Which faces in the net are congruent? 1 and 5.

b. Write an equation to find the area of the two congruent faces. $2(\frac{1}{2} \cdot 4\text{ in.} \cdot 3\text{ in.}) = 12\text{ in}^2$

c. Write three equations to find the areas of the other faces.
$5\text{ in.} \cdot 7\text{ in.} = 35\text{ in}^2$
$4\text{ in.} \cdot 7\text{ in.} = 28\text{ in}^2$
$3\text{ in.} \cdot 7\text{ in.} = 21\text{ in}^2$

d. Add to find the surface area of polyhedron. 96 in^2

11-3 Exercises and Applications

Assignment Guide

- **Basic** 1–11 odds, 13–15, 17–22
- **Average** 2–8 evens, 9–15, 17–22
- **Enriched** 5–22

Exercise Notes

Exercises 5–8

Error Prevention If students have trouble determining the surface areas, have them label each edge on the net with the correct measurements.

Exercise Answers

2. 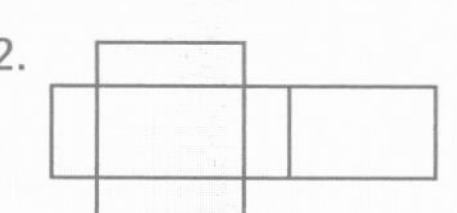

3. 

4. 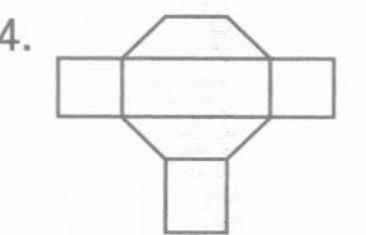

5. 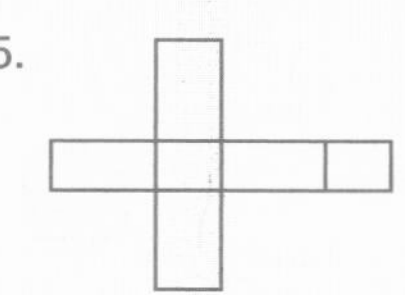

Surface area: 184 cm^2

6. 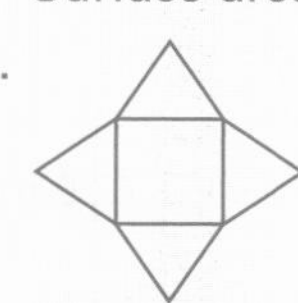

Surface area: 179.76 units^2

7–8. See page C6.

Reteaching

Activity

Materials: Cardboard box

Work with a partner. Bring a cardboard box to class.

- Measure the length, width, and height.
- Cut the box apart and lay it flat to illustrate its net. Then determine the surface area.

Exercise Answers

14. a. About 3528.4 in^2
    b. Possible answer:

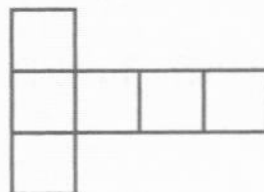

15. a. Yes; Remove any cube that is not a corner.
    b. No
    c. Yes; Remove any corner piece.
16. $2(hw) + 2(hl) + lw$; The formula finds the area of the two sides measuring h by w, the two sides measuring h by l, and the bottom measuring l by w.
17. Quadrilateral, parallelogram, rectangle, rhombus, square.
18. Right, scalene triangle.
19. Obtuse, scalene triangle.
20. Amount of gas.
21. Length of base or height.
22. Total number of test points.

Alternate Assessment

Project Have students take home an example of a net that can be folded to form a polyhedron. Then have them work with a family member to discover at least one example of a polyhedron and find the surface area.

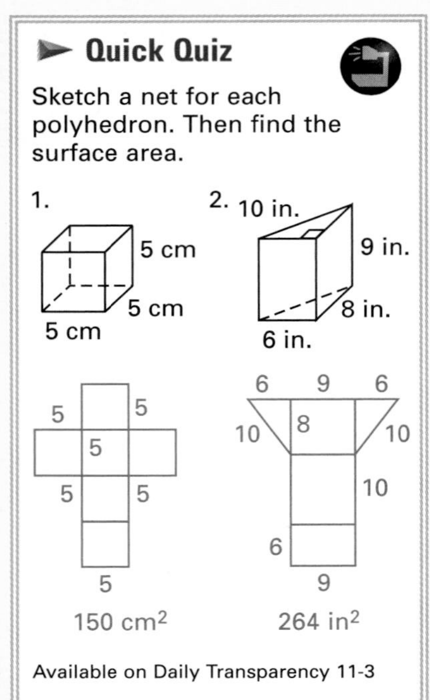

Quick Quiz

Sketch a net for each polyhedron. Then find the surface area.

150 cm^2

264 in^2

Available on Daily Transparency 11-3

PROBLEM SOLVING 11-3

12. Estimation Estimate the surface area of the polyhedron. **94 m^2**

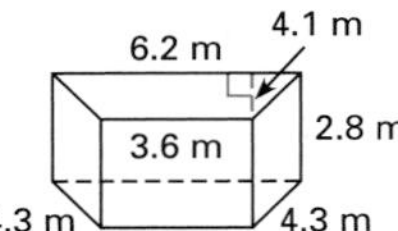

13. Identify the nets that can be folded into a cube. **a and c**

a.

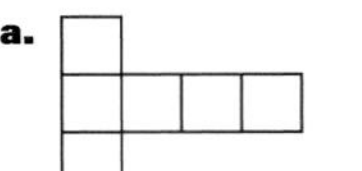

b.

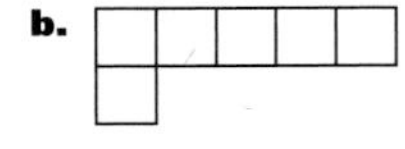

c.

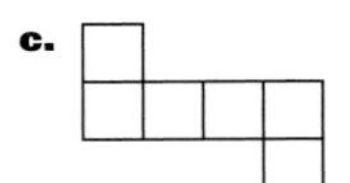

d.

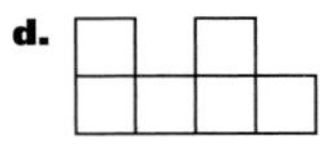

14. Fine Arts Artist Larry Bell created this cube-shaped sculpture entitled *Memories of Mike*. Each side of the cube is $24\frac{1}{4}$ inches long.

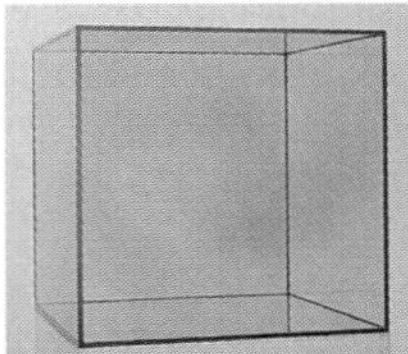

a. What is the surface area of the sculpture?

b. Draw a net of this sculpture. Label the measure of each side.

Problem Solving and Reasoning

15. Critical Thinking A large cube is made of small cubes as shown. Can you remove one cube from the figure and

a. Increase its surface area? If so, how?

b. Decrease its surface area? If so, how?

c. Keep its surface area the same? If so, how?

16. Communicate Find a formula for the surface area of the outside of an *open* box whose length is l, width is w, and height is h. Explain why your formula works.

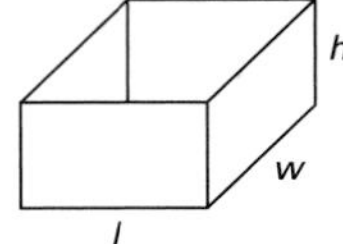

Mixed Review

Classify each polygon in as many ways as you can. *[Lesson 5-3]*

17.

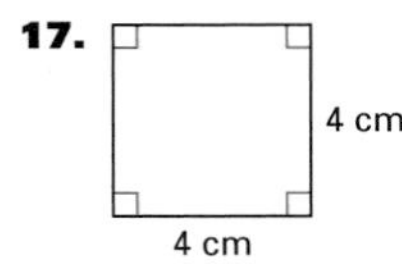

18.

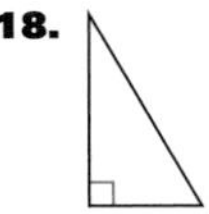

19.

Name a quantity each value might depend on. *[Lesson 10-2]* **Answers may vary.**

20. Distance traveled in a car **21.** Area of a triangle **22.** Your grade in a class

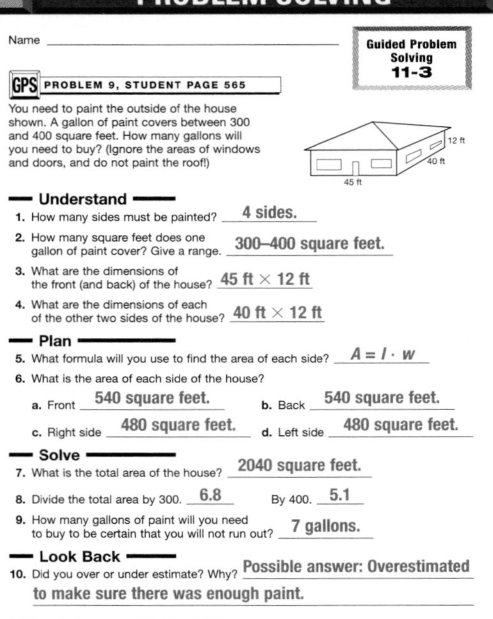

PROBLEM SOLVING

Name ____________

Guided Problem Solving 11-3

GPS PROBLEM 9, STUDENT PAGE 565

You need to paint the outside of the house shown. A gallon of paint covers between 300 and 400 square feet. How many gallons will you need to buy? (Ignore the areas of windows and doors, and do not paint the roof!)

Understand

1. How many sides must be painted? **4 sides.**
2. How many square feet does one gallon of paint cover? Give a range. **300–400 square feet.**
3. What are the dimensions of the front (and back) of the house? **45 ft × 12 ft**
4. What are the dimensions of each of the other two sides of the house? **40 ft × 12 ft**

Plan

5. What formula will you use to find the area of each side? $A = l \cdot w$
6. What is the area of each side of the house?
   a. Front **540 square feet.** b. Back **540 square feet.**
   c. Right side **480 square feet.** d. Left side **480 square feet.**

Solve

7. What is the total area of the house? **2040 square feet.**
8. Divide the total area by 300. **6.8** By 400. **5.1**
9. How many gallons of paint will you need to buy to be certain that you will not run out? **7 gallons.**

Look Back

10. Did you over or under estimate? Why? **Possible answer: Overestimated to make sure there was enough paint.**

SOLVE ANOTHER PROBLEM

A gallery is 30 feet long and 24 feet wide. The walls are 10 feet high. Assume that a gallon of paint will cover 300 to 400 square feet. How many gallons of paint will you need to buy to be sure you have enough to paint all four walls of the gallery? **4 gallons.**

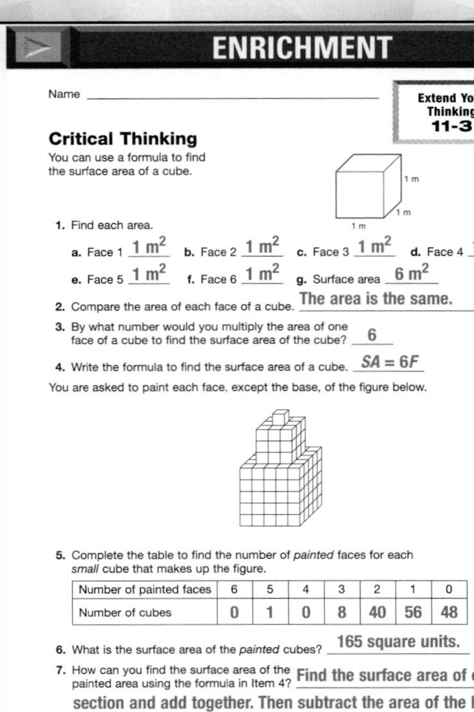

ENRICHMENT

Name ____________

Extend Your Thinking 11-3

Critical Thinking

You can use a formula to find the surface area of a cube.

1. Find each area.
   a. Face 1 **1 m^2** b. Face 2 **1 m^2** c. Face 3 **1 m^2** d. Face 4 **1 m^2**
   e. Face 5 **1 m^2** f. Face 6 **1 m^2** g. Surface area **6 m^2**
2. Compare the area of each face of a cube. **The area is the same.**
3. By what number would you multiply the area of one face of a cube to find the surface area of the cube? **6**
4. Write the formula to find the surface area of a cube. $SA = 6F$

You are asked to paint each face, except the base, of the figure below.

5. Complete the table to find the number of *painted* faces for each *small* cube that makes up the figure.

Number of painted faces	6	5	4	3	2	1	0
Number of cubes	0	1	0	8	40	56	48

6. What is the surface area of the *painted* cubes? **165 square units.**
7. How can you find the surface area of the painted area using the formula in Item 4? **Find the surface area of each section and add together. Then subtract the area of the base of the bottom sections and 2 times the areas of the bases of the middle and top sections.**

Volumes of Prisms

11-4

▶ Lesson Link You know how to find the surface area of a prism. Now you'll investigate another measure of a prism's size—its volume. ◀

You'll Learn ...

■ to find the volume of a prism

... How It's Used

Packaging designers calculate volumes as they decide the best ways to create packages that are both efficient and attractive.

Vocabulary

volume

height

Explore — Filling Rectangular Solids

Box 'Em Up!

Materials: Centimeter cubes, Centimeter graph paper, Scissors, Tape

You can make a box out of graph paper by cutting a square out of each corner, then folding up the sides. What's the *largest* box you can make?

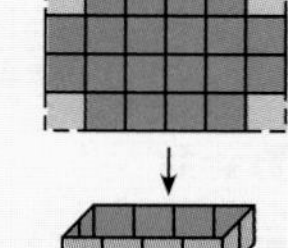

1. Cut a 16 cm by 12 cm rectangle from your graph paper. Cut a 1 cm square out of each corner, then fold and tape the sides to make a box.
2. How many centimeter cubes does your box hold? Record the dimensions of the box and the number of cubes it can hold.
3. Now make a box by cutting 2 by 2 squares out of a 16 by 12 rectangle. Find out how many cubes it holds. Repeat, cutting out larger and larger squares, until you find the box that holds the most cubes.
4. What are the dimensions of the box that holds the most cubes? How many cubes does it hold? Why are you sure this is the largest box?

Learn — Volumes of Prisms

The **volume** of a three-dimensional object is the amount of space it takes up. Volume describes the number of cubes an object can hold, so it is measured in cubic units.

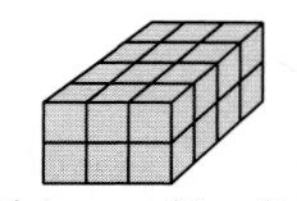

Volume = 24 units^3

A prism has two identical bases. The distance between the bases is the **height**, h, of the prism. Thinking of the prism as a stack of bases h units tall leads to a formula for the volume of a prism.

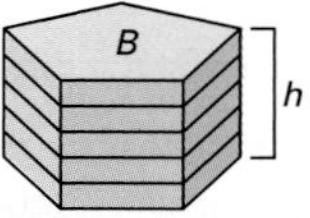

MEETING INDIVIDUAL NEEDS

Resources

- 11-4 Practice
- 11-4 Reteaching
- 11-4 Problem Solving
- 11-4 Enrichment
- 11-4 Daily Transparency
  - Problem of the Day
  - Review
  - Quick Quiz
- Teaching Tool Transparencies 2, 3
- Technology Master 54
- Chapter 11 Project Master

Interactive CD-ROM Lesson 11

Learning Modalities

Verbal Show students an example of a polyhedron. Then have them write a step-by-step description of how they would find the volume.

Kinesthetic Give students several different boxes and have them use cubes to discover the volume.

Challenge

Have students discuss the following problem: One student found the surface area of a prism to be 216 cm^2. For the same prism, another student found the volume to be 216 cm^3. Is that possible? Explain. Yes, a cube with each edge 6 cm in length would have a surface area of 216 cm^2 and a volume of 216 cm^3.

INTERACTIVE LESSON

11-4 Lesson Organizer

Objective

- Find the volume of a prism.

Vocabulary

- Volume, height

Materials

- Explore: Centimeter cubes, centimeter graph paper, scissors, tape

NCTM Standards

- 1–5, 12, 13

▶ Review

Find each product.

1. 24 • 10 • 5 1200
2. $\frac{1}{2}$ • 10 • 12 60
3. 2.4 • 6 • 4 57.6
4. $\frac{1}{2}$ •12 • (9 + 11) 120

Available on Daily Transparency 11-4

1 Introduce

Explore

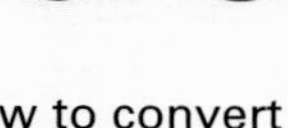

The Point

Students discover how to convert a sheet of paper into a box with the greatest volume.

Ongoing Assessment

Be sure students understand that they use a 16 cm by 12 cm rectangle in each case.

For Groups That Finish Early

Can two different boxes with different dimensions hold the same number of cubes? Explain. Yes. For example, a 4 by 2 by 1 box and a 2 by 2 by 2 box would both hold 8 cubes.

Answers for Explore on next page.

Follow Up
Have students discuss how their results would compare if they used inch graph paper and inch cubes instead of centimeter graph paper and centimeter cubes. The number of cubes to fill the boxes would be the same, but the overall sizes of the boxes would be larger.

Answers for Explore

2. 140; The box is 1 cm high, 14 cm long, 10 cm wide.
3. 192; The box is 2 cm high, 12 cm long, 8 cm wide.
4. 2 cm high by 12 cm long by 8 cm wide; 192; Make all combinations and see that this is the largest.

2 Teach

Learn

Alternate Examples

1. Find the volume of the right triangular prism.

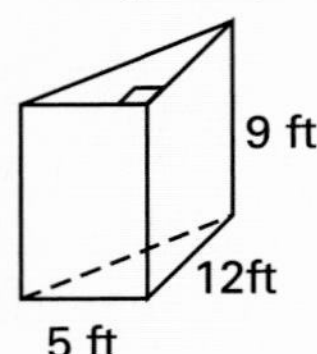

$B = \frac{1}{2} \cdot 12 \cdot 5 = 30 \text{ ft}^2$

$h = 9$ ft

$V = Bh$
$= 30 \text{ ft}^2 \cdot 9 \text{ ft}$
$= 270 \text{ ft}^3$

2. Find the volume of the flower pot where $B = 80 \text{ cm}^2$ and $h = 40$ cm.

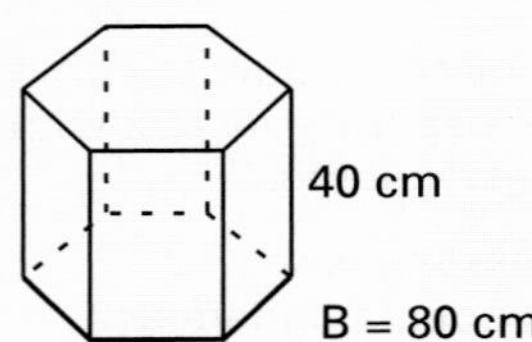

$V = Bh = 80 \text{ cm} \cdot 40 \text{ cm} = 3200 \text{ cm}^3$

3. Find the volume of a rectangular prism whose height is 12 mm, length is 8 mm, and width is 9 mm.

Use $V = lwh$ for a rectangular prism.

$V = 12 \text{ mm} \cdot 8 \text{ mm} \cdot 9 \text{ mm}$
$= 864 \text{ mm}^3$

VOLUME OF A PRISM
The volume of a prism whose base area is B and height is h is given by $V = Bh$.

Examples

1 Find the volume of the right triangular prism.

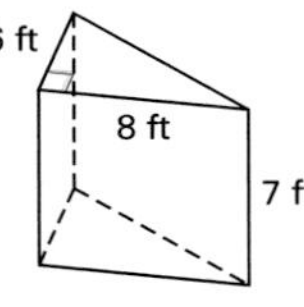

The volume is equal to the base area times the height.

$B = \frac{1}{2} \cdot 8 \cdot 6 = 24 \text{ ft}^2$ $\qquad h = 7$ ft

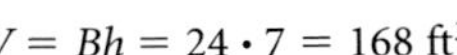

$V = Bh = 24 \cdot 7 = 168 \text{ ft}^3$

2 A prism has a base area of 32 cm² and a height of 7 cm. Find its volume.

$V = Bh = 32 \cdot 7 = 224 \text{ cm}^3$

The prism has a volume of 224 cm³.

Test Prep
Remember to include units in your answers to surface area and volume problems. Surface area is measured in square units, and volume is measured in cubic units.

Try It

a. At Devil's Postpile National Monument, basalt, a volcanic rock, forms hexagonal columns. If one column has a base area of 2 ft² and a height of 24 ft, what is the volume of the column? 48 ft³

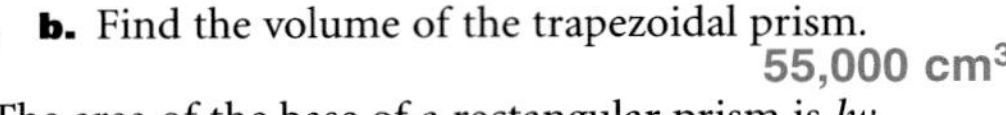

b. Find the volume of the trapezoidal prism. 55,000 cm³

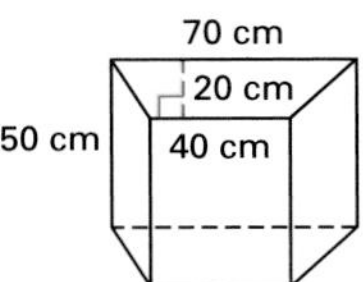

The area of the base of a rectangular prism is lw, so the formula for the volume of a rectangular prism is $V = lwh$.

Example 3

Find the volume of a rectangular prism whose height is 4 mm, length is 10 mm, and width is 8 mm.

Use $V = lwh$ for a rectangular prism.

$V = 10 \cdot 8 \cdot 4 = 320 \text{ mm}^3$

Check Your Understanding

1. Describe the difference between surface area and volume.
2. If you measure the volume of a prism in cubic centimeters, do you get a greater volume than if you measure the volume in cubic inches? Explain.

MATH EVERY DAY

Problem of the Day

On a 33-question test, three points are deducted for each wrong answer and eight points are added for each correct answer. You answer all the questions and get a score of 0. How many questions did you get correct? 9 correct ($3x = 8y$; $x + y = 33$; $x = 24$, $y = 9$)

Available on Daily Transparency 11-4

An Extension is provided in the transparency package.

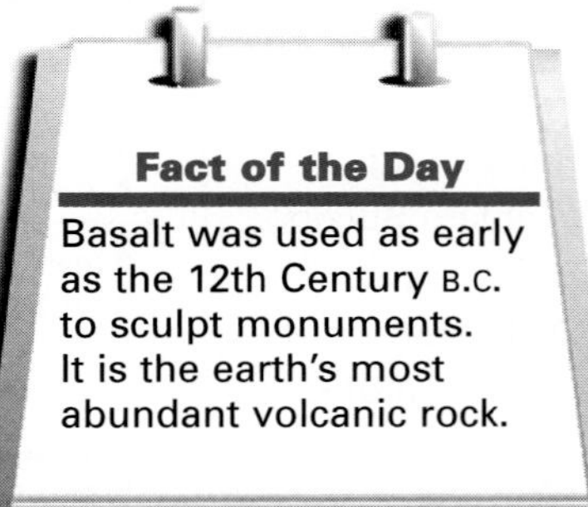

Fact of the Day
Basalt was used as early as the 12th Century B.C. to sculpt monuments. It is the earth's most abundant volcanic rock.

Estimation

Estimate.

1. $\frac{1}{2}$ of 989 500
2. $\frac{1}{3}$ of 489 160
3. $\frac{1}{4}$ of 805 200
4. $\frac{3}{4}$ of 390 300

11-4 Exercises and Applications

Practice and Apply

1. **Getting Started** Follow these steps to find the volume of the prism.

   a. Find the area of the base. Since the base of this prism is a triangle, use the formula for the area of a triangle. 24 cm^2

   b. Multiply the base area by the height. $24 \cdot 9 = 216$

   c. Write your answer. Be sure to use cubic units. 216 cm^3

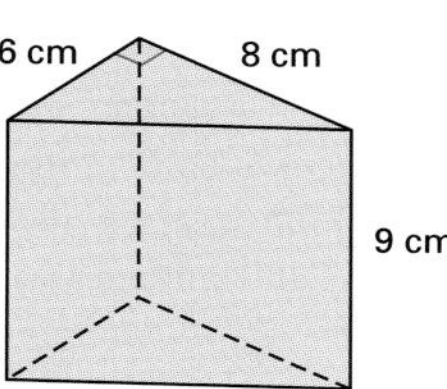

Find the volume of each prism.

2. 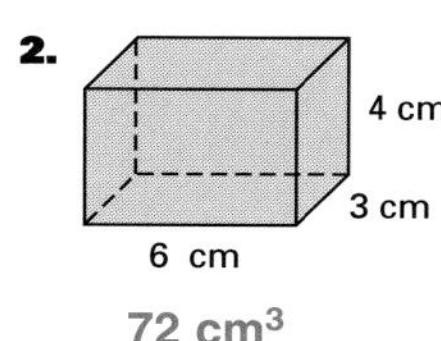

72 cm^3

3. 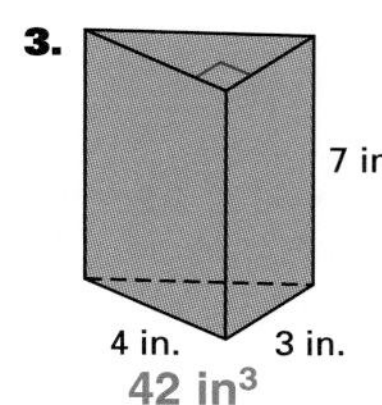

42 in^3

4. 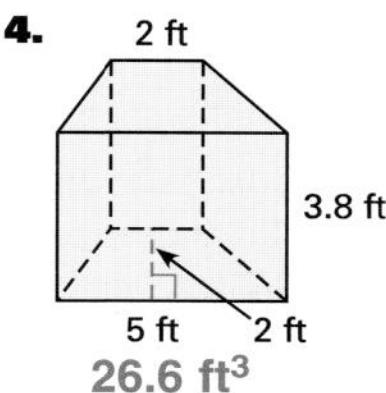

26.6 ft^3

5. 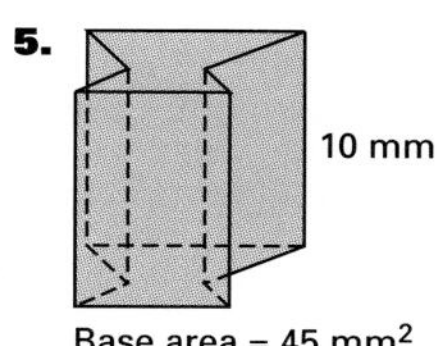

450 mm^3

6. **Fine Arts** The sculpture *Untitled*, by Donald Judd, is made up of ten rectangular prisms. The length of each prism is 40 in., the width is 31 in., and the height is 9 in. What is the volume of one of these prisms? $11{,}160 \text{ in}^3$

7. Sarah's family is thinking of installing a swimming pool in their backyard, and they want to know how much it will increase their water use. The pool would be a rectangular prism with dimensions 10 m by 8 m by 2 m. What is the maximum volume of water it could hold? 160 m^3

8. **Consumer** The two boxes of sugar are the same price. Which one is the better buy? Explain your answer.

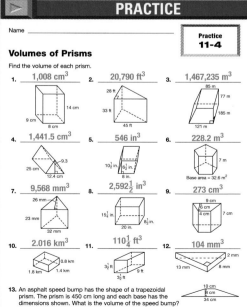

GPS

A. 

B. 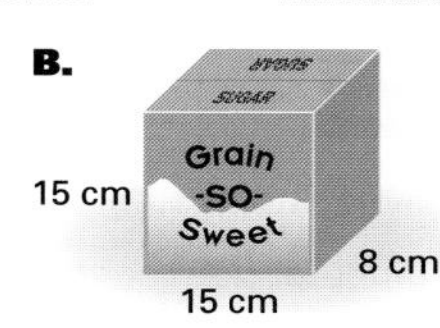

PRACTICE

Name ______________________

Practice 11-4

Volumes of Prisms

Find the volume of each prism.

1. $1{,}008 \text{ cm}^3$ 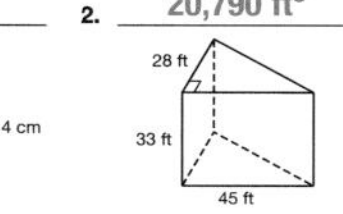
2. $20{,}790 \text{ ft}^3$ 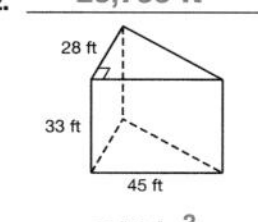
3. $1{,}467{,}235 \text{ m}^3$ 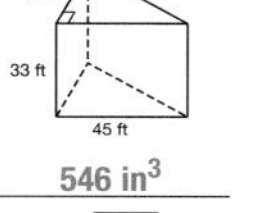
4. $1{,}441.5 \text{ cm}^3$ 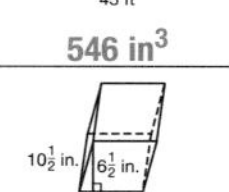
5. 546 in^3 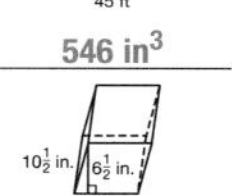
6. 228.2 m^3 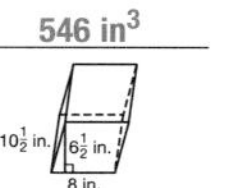
7. $9{,}568 \text{ mm}^3$ 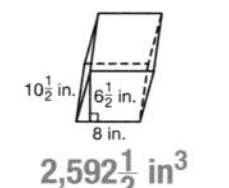
8. $2{,}592\frac{1}{2} \text{ in}^3$ 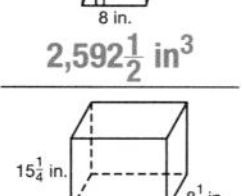
9. 273 cm^3 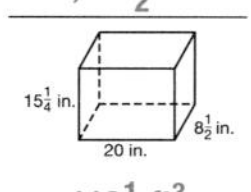
10. 2.016 km^3 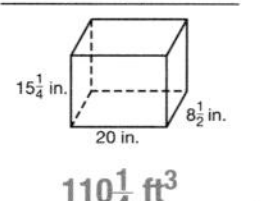
11. $110\frac{1}{4} \text{ ft}^3$ 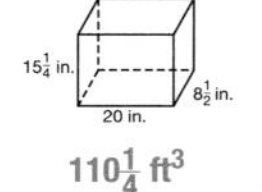
12. 104 mm^3 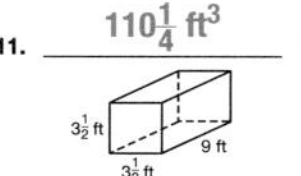

13. An asphalt speed bump has the shape of a trapezoidal prism. The prism is 450 cm long and each base has the dimensions shown. What is the volume of the speed bump?

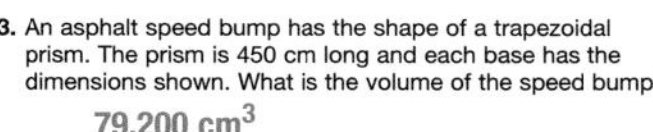

$79{,}200 \text{ cm}^3$

14. The tunnel on Yerba Buena Island near San Francisco, California, is about 78 ft wide, 56 ft tall, and 540 ft long. Estimate the amount of air in the tunnel by assuming that the tunnel has the shape of a rectangular prism.

About $2{,}400{,}000 \text{ ft}^3$

RETEACHING

Name ______________________

Alternative Lesson 11-4

Volumes of Prisms

The **volume** of a three-dimensional object is the amount of space it takes up. Volume describes the number of cubes an object can hold, so it is measured in cubic units.

A prism has two identical bases. The distance between the bases is the **height**, *h*, of the prism. Think of the prism as a stack of bases *h* units tall.

The formula to find the volume of a prism whose base area is *B* and height is *h* is given by $V = Bh$.

Example

Find the volume of the rectangular prism.

The volume is equal to the base area times the height.

Find the area of the base: $8 \times 3 = 24 \text{ in}^2$

Multiply the area of the base by the height, 5 in.

$24 \cdot 5 = 120 \text{ in}^3$

So, the volume of the rectangular prism is 120 in^3.

Try It Find the volume of each prism.

a. What shape is the base in Prism *A*? Triangle.

b. Write an equation to find the area of the base of Prism *A*. $(\frac{1}{2} \cdot 2 \cdot 3) = 3 \text{ cm}^2$

c. What is the height of Prism *A*? 5 cm

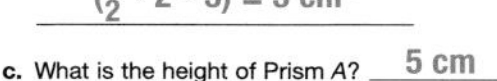

d. Multiply to find the volume. 15 cm^3

e. What shape is the base in Prism *B*? Square.

f. Write an equation to find the area of the base of Prism *B*. $4 \cdot 4 = 16 \text{ m}^2$

g. What is the height of Prism *B*? 6 m

h. Multiply to find the volume. 96 m^3

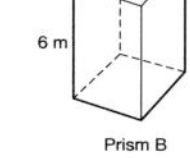

Prism B

11-4 Exercises and Applications

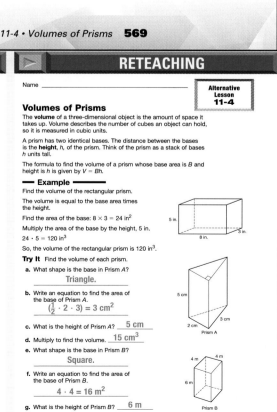

Assignment Guide

- **Basic** 1–6, 8–9, 11, 13–19 odds
- **Average** 2–9, 11, 12–18 evens
- **Enriched** 3–12, 13–19 odds

3 Practice and Assess

Check

Answers for Check Your Understanding

1. Surface area is the sum of the areas of the figure's faces; It is measured in units squared. Volume is the amount of space a figure takes up; It is measured in units cubed.
2. The volume is the same, but the number of cubic centimeters would be greater than the number of cubic inches.

Exercise Notes

Exercise 4

Error Prevention Some students may treat the figure as if it is a rectangular prism and give 38 ft^3 as the answer. Remind them that the base is a trapezoid.

Exercise Answers

8. B; B holds 1800 cm^3 and A holds only 1200 cm^3.

Reteaching

Activity

Materials: Cardboard boxes

Work in small groups. Bring several cardboard boxes to class. Play the following game.

- Each person first secretly estimates the volume of the box and writes the estimate on a slip of paper.
- The group then works together to measure the length, width, and height and find the actual volume.
- The person whose estimate is nearest the actual volume is the winner for that round Use a different box for each round.

PRACTICE 11-4

Exercise Notes

■ Exercise 9

Test Prep If students selected D, they multiplied 2280 by 152. In order to solve 2280 = 152h, they need to divide 2280 by 152.

■ Exercise 12

Problem-Solving Tip You may want to use Teaching Tool Transparencies 2 and 3: Guided Problem Solving, pages 1–2.

Exercise Answers

10. c. The volume doesn't change. The surface area becomes 28 cm^3.

11. The volume of the prism would be 3 times the volume of the pyramid.

12. a. The volume is 8 times as great.

b. The volume is 27 times as great.

c. The volume is 64 times as great.

d. The volume is $\frac{1}{8}$ the original.

e. The volume differs by the cube of the amount changed.

Project Progress

You may want to have students use Chapter 11 Project Master.

Alternate Assessment

You may want to use the *Interactive CD-ROM Journal* with this assessment.

Journal Have students write a paragraph comparing and contrasting the process of finding the volume of a prism with that of finding the surface area.

Quick Quiz

Find the volume of each prism.

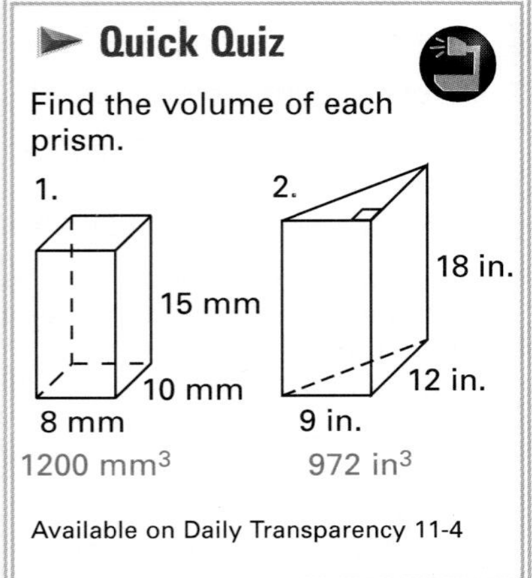

1200 mm^3 972 in^3

Available on Daily Transparency 11-4

PROBLEM SOLVING 11-4

9. **Test Prep** An artist uses 2280 cm^3 of modeling clay to make a prism. If the area of the prism's base is 152 cm^2, what is its height? **A**

Ⓐ 15 cm Ⓑ 25 cm Ⓒ 2128 cm Ⓓ 346,560 cm

10. Assume that the edges of the cubes in the figures are 1 cm long. All cubes are visible.

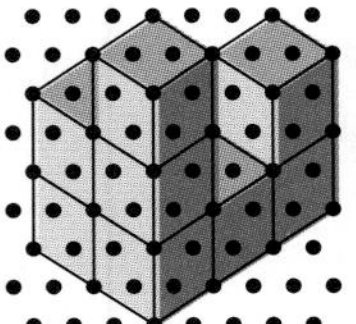

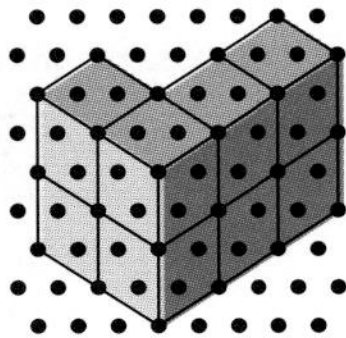

a. What is the volume of the first figure? **8 cm^3**

b. What is its surface area? **32 cm^2**

c. Suppose the top cube in the stack of three is moved to "fill in" the stack of one as shown. How do the volume and surface area change?

Problem Solving and Reasoning

11. Critical Thinking The volume of a pyramid is given by the formula $V = \frac{1}{3}Bh$. Suppose you had a rectangular pyramid with the same base and height measurements as a rectangular prism. How would their volumes compare?

12. Choose a Strategy Suppose each dimension (length, width, and height) of a rectangular solid is changed as described. How does the volume of the box change? Try several examples for each change.

a. Each dimension is doubled. **b.** Each dimension is tripled.

c. Each dimension is quadrupled. **d.** Each dimension is halved.

e. Describe any pattern you see in your results.

Problem Solving STRATEGIES
- Look for a Pattern
- Make an Organized List
- Make a Table
- Guess and Check
- Work Backward
- Use Logical Reasoning
- Draw a Diagram
- Solve a Simpler Problem

Mixed Review

Find the sums of the measures of the angles of each polygon. *[Lesson 5-4]*

13. 12-sided polygon **1800°** **14.** 14-sided polygon **2160°** **15.** 17-sided polygon **2700°**

Give the next term in each sequence. Write a rule for each. *[Lesson 10-3]*

16. 5, 9, 13, 17, **21** — **4n + 1**

17. 3, 3, 3, 3, **3** — **Always 3**

18. −4, −2, 0, 2, **4** — **2n − 6**

19. $\frac{1}{6}, \frac{1}{8}, \frac{1}{10}, \frac{1}{12}$, $\frac{1}{14}$ — $\frac{1}{2n+4}$

Project Progress

Design a beverage container in the shape of a prism. The container must have a volume of 360 cm^3. Sketch a net for your container and show its dimensions on the net.

Problem Solving: Understand, Plan, Solve, Look Back

PROBLEM SOLVING

Name ______ **Guided Problem Solving 11-4**

GPS PROBLEM 8, STUDENT PAGE 569

The two boxes of sugar are the same price. Which one is the better buy? Explain your answer.

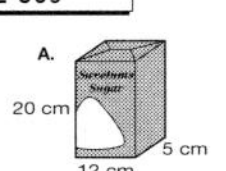

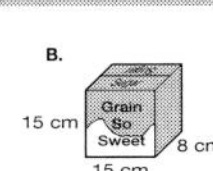

Understand

1. Assume that the size of the box relates to the amount it holds. How will you find the amount each box holds? **Find the volume.**
2. What shape are the boxes? **Rectangular prisms.**
3. What are the dimensions in cm of each box?
   a. Sweetums Sugar **20 × 12 × 5** b. Grain So Sweet **15 × 15 × 8**

Plan

4. What formula will you use to find the volume of each box? **$V = B \cdot h$**
5. What is the area of the base of each package?
   a. Sweetums Sugar **60 cm^2** b. Grain So Sweet **120 cm^2**

Solve

6. What is the volume of the package of each product?
   a. Sweetums Sugar? **1200 cm^3** b. Grain So Sweet? **1800 cm^3**
7. Which is the better buy? Explain. **Possible answer: Grain So Sweet because the package has a greater volume.**

Look Back

8. Does the sugar necessarily fill the volume of the package? What else might you consider in your decision? **Possible answer: No, Weight of the sugar.**

SOLVE ANOTHER PROBLEM

Two white porcelain boxes are the same price. Box *A* has a 3 cm by 2 cm rectangular base and a height of 4 cm. Box *B* has a 3 cm by 4 cm rectangular base and a height of 3 cm. Which is the better buy? **Box *B*.**

ENRICHMENT

Name ______ **Extend Your Thinking 11-4**

Critical Thinking

Find the volume and surface area for each rectangular prism.

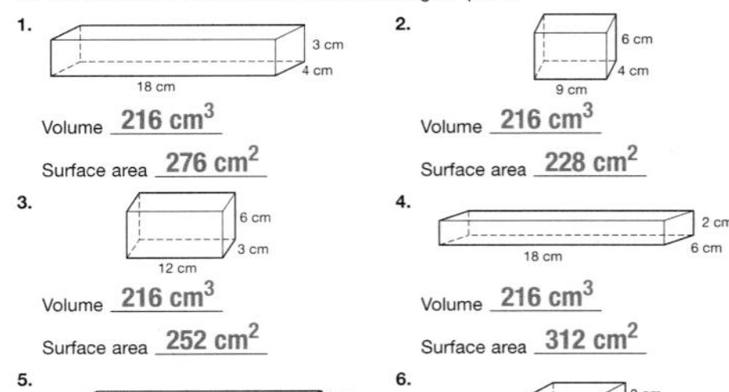

1. Volume **216 cm^3** Surface area **276 cm^2**
2. Volume **216 cm^3** Surface area **228 cm^2**
3. Volume **216 cm^3** Surface area **252 cm^2**
4. Volume **216 cm^3** Surface area **312 cm^2**
5. 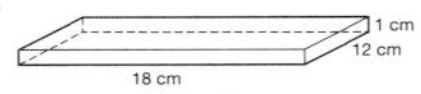 Volume **216 cm^3** Surface area **492 cm^2**
6. 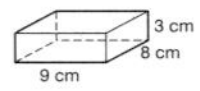 Volume **216 cm^3** Surface area **246 cm^2**
7. 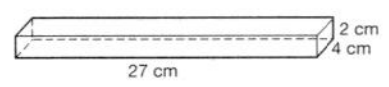 (27 cm, 2 cm, 4 cm) Volume **216 cm^3** Surface area **340 cm^2**
8. 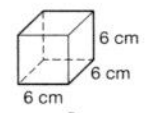 (6 cm, 6 cm, 6 cm) Volume **216 cm^3** Surface area **216 cm^2**
9. Which figure has the smallest surface area? **The cube.**
10. Describe the relationship between volume and surface area. How does this compare with the relationship between the perimeters of rectangles with the same area? **Given rectangular prisms with equal volume, the cube has the smallest surface area. In rectangles with the same area, the square has the smallest perimeter.**

You've explored ways to sketch polyhedrons, and you've calculated their surface areas and volumes. Now you'll use all these skills to design and analyze a sculpture of your own.

Making a Statement

Materials: Construction paper, Ruler, Scissors, Tape

Many artists and sculptors use geometric figures in their art. Now you'll make a piece of geometric sculpture that uses polyhedrons.

1. Decide how you want your sculpture to look. (Include at least one prism in the design.) Sketch a three-dimensional picture of your sculpture. Then sketch front, side, and top views.

2. Use construction paper, scissors, and tape to construct your sculpture.

3. *Gold leaf* is solid gold that has been rolled into a thin sheet. It costs about 11¢ per square inch. How much would it cost to cover your sculpture with gold leaf?

4. An overseas museum wants to display your sculpture! The sculpture must be packed for shipping in a crate that is a rectangular prism. Find the dimensions and volume of a crate large enough to hold your sculpture. Explain how you found your answers.

Making a Statement

The Point

Geometric sculpture was discussed in *Making a Statement* on page 553. Now students will make their own geometric sculptures.

Materials

Construction paper, ruler, scissors, tape

About the Page

- Review the techniques for drawing three-dimensional objects.
- If students have difficulty visualizing their sculpture, suggest that they stack some blocks and other geometric shapes and try to sketch what they see. If these materials are not available, students could try sketching a stack of boxes or books.
- Ask students what information they will need before they can determine the cost of covering their sculpture with gold leaf. The surface area of the shapes.
- Discuss with students how they might determine the size of the shipping crate they will need for their sculpture.

Ongoing Assessment

Check that students have sketched and constructed a reasonable sculpture.

Extension

Assume that you could also make your sculpture out of a thin colored plastic material that costs $12.50 per square foot. Would it cost more to make it out of plastic than to cover it with gold leaf? What is the difference in cost per square foot? No; $15.84 per sq ft for gold leaf, $12.50 for plastic; $3.34 more per sq ft to cover in gold leaf.

Answers for Connect

Answers may vary.

11A Review

Review Correlation

Item(s)	Lesson(s)
1–7	11-1
8	11-3
9–11	11-3, 11-4
12	11-2
13	11-3, 11-4
14	11-4

Test Prep

Test-Taking Tip

Tell students that when the possible answers given for a multiple-choice test are not close together, it might make sense to estimate the answer.

Answers for Review

1. True
2. False; A prism has two bases. A pyramid has only one base.
3. True
4. False; No polygon faces.
5. 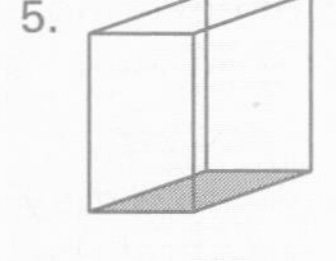
6. 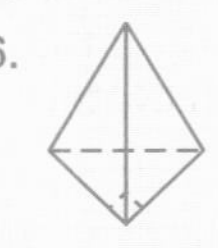
7. 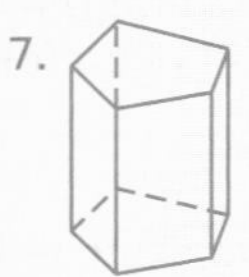
8. 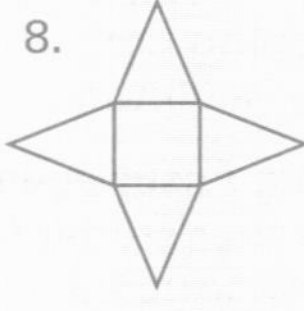

   340 cm^2
9. SA: 30 cm^2; Volume: 7 cm^3.
10. SA = 2720 in^2 (without top); V = $12,800\text{ in}^3$
11. SA: 339.042 in^2; Volume: 678.368 in^3.
12. Accept any sketches that show the overall shape accurately. Possible sketches:

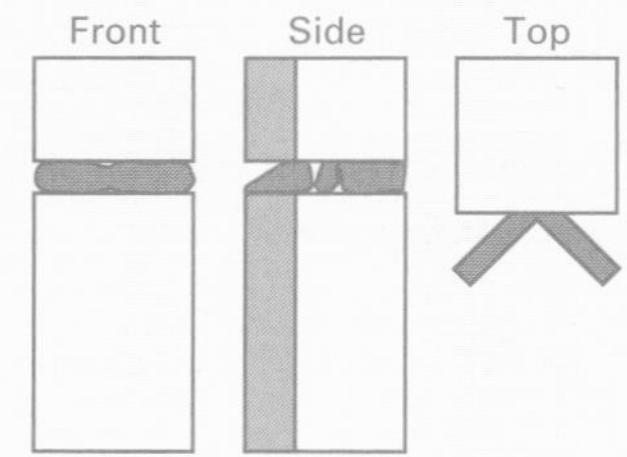

13. Both; Possible answers: To paint the doghouse, you need to know its surface area. You need to think about the volume to see if the dog will be able to fit inside.
14. C

Section 11A Review

REVIEW 11-A

Tell whether each statement is true or false. If it is false, explain why.

1. A cube is a rectangular prism.

2. Some pyramids are prisms.

3. A square pyramid has five vertices.

4. A cylinder is a polyhedron.

Sketch each polyhedron.

5. A rectangular prism

6. A right triangular pyramid

7. A pentagonal prism

8. Sketch a net for the square pyramid at right. Then find its surface area.

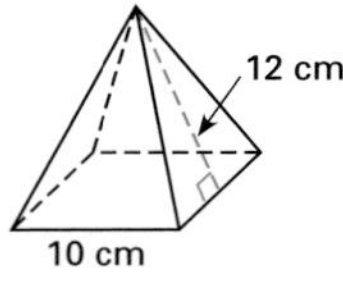

Find the surface area and volume of each figure.

9. 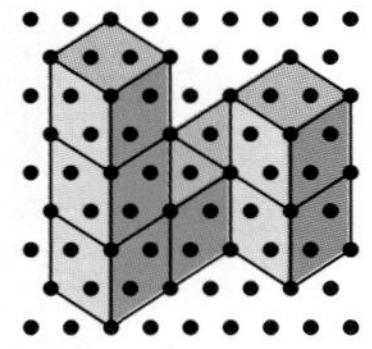

Each edge is 1 cm long.

10. 

11. 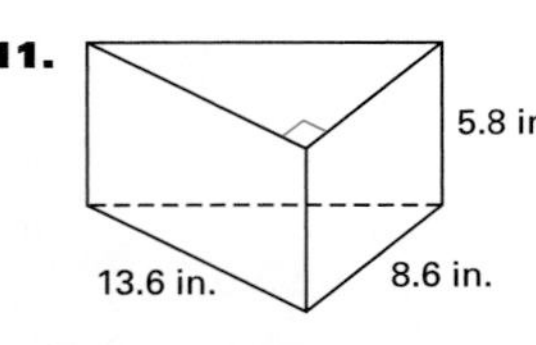

triangular prism

12. Fine Arts This sculpture, by Hubert Dalwood, is made of aluminum, wood, and gilt. Sketch front, top, and side views of the sculpture.

13.  Journal Suppose you wanted to build a doghouse for your dog Melvin. When planning the doghouse, would you need to think about its surface area, its volume, or both? Explain your answer.

Test Prep

When asked to find a volume on a multiple choice test, you may be able to use mental math to eliminate some of the answer choices.

14. Find the volume of the rectangular prism.

Ⓐ 10.5 in^3 Ⓑ 842 in^3 Ⓒ $1,050\text{ in}^3$ Ⓓ $13,500\text{ in}^3$

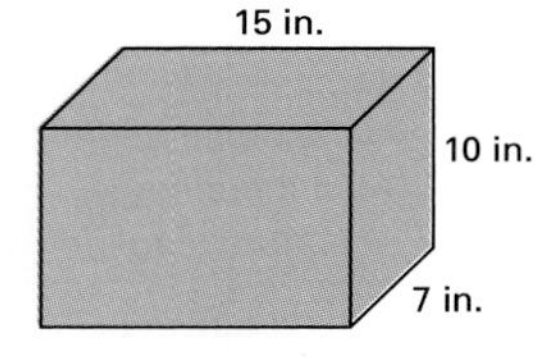

Resources

Practice Masters
Section 11A Review

Assessment Sourcebook
Quiz 11A

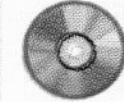
TestWorks
Test and Practice Software

PRACTICE

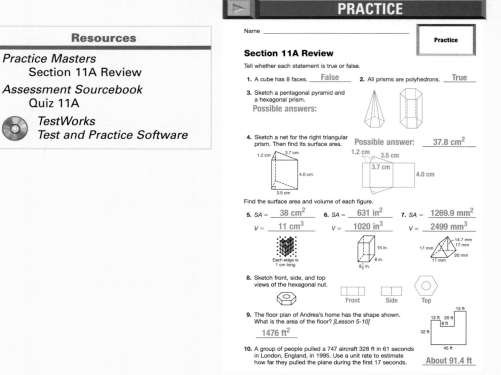

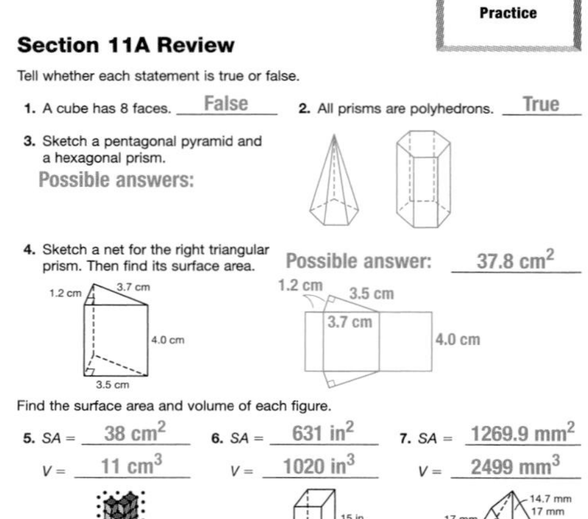

Name ______________________ Practice

Section 11A Review

Tell whether each statement is true or false.

1. A cube has 8 faces. False
2. All prisms are polyhedrons. True
3. Sketch a pentagonal pyramid and a hexagonal prism. Possible answers:
4. Sketch a net for the right triangular prism. Then find its surface area. Possible answer: 37.8 cm^2

1.2 cm 3.7 cm 4.0 cm 3.5 cm

Find the surface area and volume of each figure.

5. SA = 38 cm^2 V = 11 cm^3 (Each edge is 1 cm long)
6. SA = 631 in^2 V = 1020 in^3 (15 in., 8 in., $8\frac{1}{2}$ in.)
7. SA = 1269.9 mm^2 V = 2499 mm^3 (14.7 mm, 17 mm, 17 mm, 20 mm, 17 mm)
8. Sketch front, side, and top views of the hexagonal nut. Front Side Top
9. The floor plan of Andrea's home has the shape shown. What is the area of the floor? *[Lesson 5-10]* 1476 ft^2

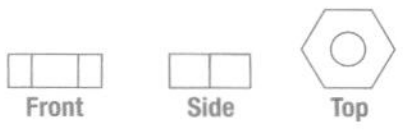

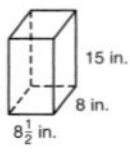

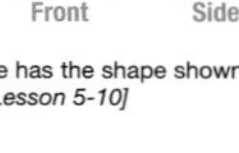

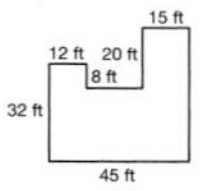

10. A group of people pulled a 747 aircraft 328 ft in 61 seconds in London, England, in 1995. Use a unit rate to estimate how far they pulled the plane during the first 17 seconds. About 91.4 ft

Section 11B

Circles and Cylinders

LESSON PLANNING GUIDE

Student Edition / **Ancillaries**

LESSON	MATERIALS	VOCABULARY	DAILY	OTHER
Section 11B Opener				
11-5 Circles and Circle Graphs	compass, protractor, colored pencils	circle, center, sector, central angle	11-5	Teaching Tool Trans. 15 Lesson Enhancement Trans. 55
11-6 Pi and Circumference	spreadsheet software, tape measure, round objects	diameter, radius, circumference, π (pi)	11-6	Teaching Tool Trans. 2, 3 Technology Master 55 *Interactive CD-ROM Spreadsheet/Grapher Tool* *WW Math*–Geometry
Technology	Dynamic geometry software			*CD-ROM Geometry Tool* *WW Math*–Geometry
11-7 Area of a Circle	graph paper, compass, spreadsheet software		11-7	Teaching Tool Trans. 7 Lesson Enhancement Trans. 56 Technology Master 56 WW Math–Geometry
11-8 Surface Area of Cylinders	conical/cylindrical objects, scissors, tape, graph paper	cylinder, cone, sphere		Teaching Tool Trans. 7 Lesson Enhancement Trans. 57 Technology Master 56 *WW Math*–Geometry
11-9 Volumes of Cylinders	centimeter cubes, ruler, cylindrical jar, glass, or mug			Technology Master 58 Ch. 11 Project Master *WW Math*–Middle School
Connect				Lesson Enhancement Trans. 58 Interdisc. Team Teaching 11B
Review				Practice 11B; Quiz 11B; *TestWorks*

SKILLS TRACE

LESSON	SKILL	FIRST INTRODUCED GR. 5	GR. 6	GR. 7	DEVELOP	PRACTICE/ APPLY	REVIEW
11-5	**Making circle graphs.**			✘ p. 574	pp. 574–575	pp. 576–577	pp. 598, 619, 640
11-6	**Finding circumferences of circles.**	✘			pp. 578–579	pp. 580–581	pp. 598, 619, 640
11-7	**Finding areas of circles.**		✘		pp. 583–584	pp. 585–586	pp. 598, 619, 648
11-8	**Finding surface areas of cylinders.**		✘		pp. 587–589	pp. 590–591	pp. 598, 619, 648
11-9	**Finding volumes of cylinders.**			✘ p. 595	pp. 592–594	pp. 595–596	pp. 598, 619, 653

CONNECTED MATHEMATICS

Investigations 1–3 in the unit *Filling and Wrapping (Three-Dimensional Measurement)*, from the **Connected Mathematics** series, can be used with Section 11B.

INTERDISCIPLINARY TEAM TEACHING

Math and Social Studies

(Worksheet pages 47–48: Teacher pages T47–T48)

In this lesson, students use information about circles and cylinders to investigate map projections.

Name ________________ *Math and Social Studies*

When the Earth Is Flat

Use information about circles and cylinders to investigate map projections.

For centuries mapmakers have struggled with the problem of portraying a round Earth on a flat page. Three basic needs have to be taken into account when drawing a map of the Earth. First, information about land masses, bodies of water, distances, and locations should be easy to interpret. Second, the scale of the map has to be accurate so that the size of different features is proportional to those on Earth. And third, the shapes of bodies of land and water should be drawn as accurately as possible.

Mapmakers use colors, symbols, and shading to communicate information on a map. They also place a grid pattern over the map to represent the lines of longitude, which run north and south, and latitude, which run east and west.

1. a. Which line of latitude shown has the largest circumference?
   the equator or 0 degrees
   b. Which line of latitude shown has the smallest circumference?
   90 degrees

2. The lines of longitude all pass through the poles. How do their lengths compare?
   They're all the same length.

3. The greatest problem in portraying a round Earth on a flat map is that either the proportion between the different features or the shapes of land and water masses may be distorted. Many maps look like the one below, which is called a *cylindrical projection*.

A cylindrical projection is like an unrolled cylinder. The cylinder would fit around the globe. The middle of the cylinder would touch the globe at the equator. Near the middle of the cylinder, the shapes are very accurate, but they get more distorted toward the top and bottom.

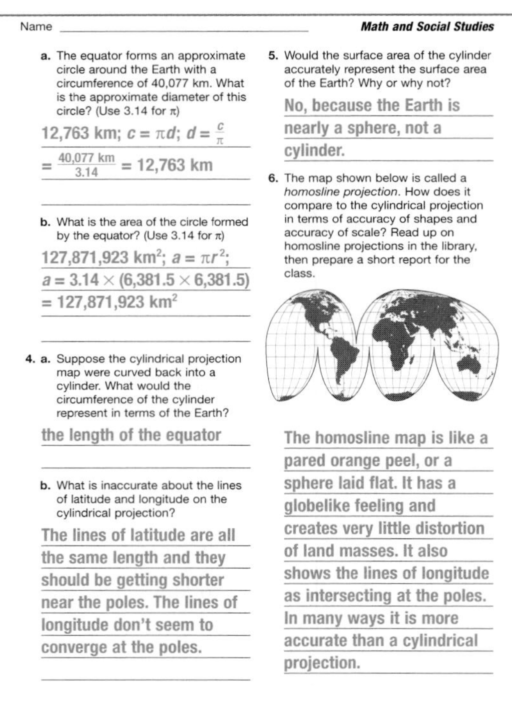

Name ________________ *Math and Social Studies*

a. The equator forms an approximate circle around the Earth with a circumference of 40,077 km. What is the approximate diameter of this circle? (Use 3.14 for π)
12,763 km; $c = \pi d$; $d = \frac{c}{\pi}$
$= \frac{40{,}077 \text{ km}}{3.14} = 12{,}763$ km

b. What is the area of the circle formed by the equator? (Use 3.14 for π)
127,871,923 km^2; $a = \pi r^2$;
$a = 3.14 \times (6{,}381.5 \times 6{,}381.5)$
$= 127{,}871{,}923$ km^2

4. a. Suppose the cylindrical projection map were curved back into a cylinder. What would the circumference of the cylinder represent in terms of the Earth?
   the length of the equator
   b. What is inaccurate about the lines of latitude and longitude on the cylindrical projection?
   The lines of latitude are all the same length and they should be getting shorter near the poles. The lines of longitude don't seem to converge at the poles.

5. Would the surface area of the cylinder accurately represent the surface area of the Earth? Why or why not?
   No, because the Earth is nearly a sphere, not a cylinder.

6. The map shown below is called a *homosline projection*. How does it compare to the cylindrical projection in terms of accuracy of shapes and accuracy of scale? Read up on homosline projections in the library, then prepare a short report for the class.
   The homosline map is like a pared orange peel, or a sphere laid flat. It has a globelike feeling and creates very little distortion of land masses. It also shows the lines of longitude as intersecting at the poles. In many ways it is more accurate than a cylindrical projection.

BIBLIOGRAPHY

FOR TEACHERS

Cunningham, Scott. *Cunningham's Encyclopedia of Crystal, Gem and Metal Magic.* St. Paul, MN: Llewellyn Publications, 1988.

Irving, Washington. *The Alhambra, Palace of Mystery and Splendor.* New York, NY: Macmillan, 1953.

Spangler, David. *Math for Real Kids.* Glenview, IL: Good Year Books, 1997.

Tomecek, Steve. *Bouncing & Bending Light: Phantastic Physical Phenomena.* New York, NY: Scientific American Books for Young Readers, 1995.

FOR STUDENTS

Greising, Cynthia Hedges. *Toys Everywhere.* Chicago, IL: Childrens Press, 1995.

Jensen, Vicki. *Carving a Totem Pole.* New York, NY: H. Holt, 1996.

Townsend, Richard. *The Aztecs.* New York, NY: Thames and Hudson, 1992.

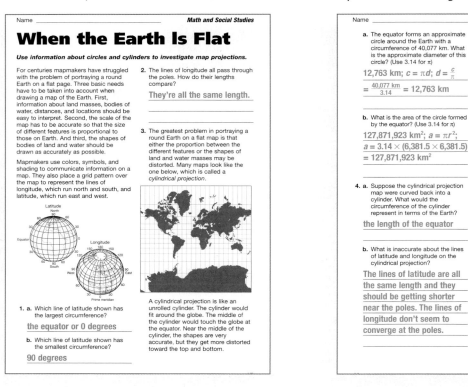

Section 11B

SECTION **11B**

Circles and Cylinders

▶ Industry Link ▶ www.mathsurf.com/7/ch11/round_toys

What do a Frisbee®, a marble, a soccer ball, a Hula Hoop®, and a yo-yo have in common? They're all fun to play with, of course. But they wouldn't be nearly as much fun (and some would be downright dangerous!) if it weren't for their other common trait. All of these toys are *round* in some way.

People have been making toys with circular shapes almost since they discovered that round things roll. A 3800-year-old toy cart was found at Mohenjo Daro, in what is now Pakistan. The wooden horse on wheels shown at lower left was made by Egyptians about A.D. 200. All around the world, people have fun rolling hoops, bouncing balls, and spinning disks.

As you explore the mathematics of circles and circular objects, you'll learn more about the measurements that describe round toys.

1 Which of the toys listed in the first paragraph would be impossible to play with if they were square instead of round? Explain your answer.

2 Although a marble, a Hula Hoop, and a yo-yo are all "round," they have different shapes. Describe the differences in the shapes of these toys.

573

Where are we now?

In Section 11A, students explored three-dimensional figures.

They learned how to

- name and sketch polyhedrons.
- investigate techniques for drawing three-dimensional objects.
- find the surface area of a polyhedron.
- find the volume of a prism.

Where are we going?

In Section 11B, students will

- make circle graphs.
- understand and use π.
- find the circumference of a circle.
- find the area of a circle.
- find the surface area of a cylinder.
- find the volume of a cylinder.

Theme: Round Toys

World Wide Web

If your class has access to the World Wide Web, you might want to use the information found at the Web site address given. The interdisciplinary link relates to topics discussed in this section.

About the Page

This page introduces the theme of the section, round toys, and discusses features of toys that are made in circular shapes.

Ask ...

- Why do you think we like to play with toys that have circular shapes?
- What are some games, other than those played with round balls, that are played with circular objects? Possible answers: Ring toss, marbles, checkers, darts (dart board), discus, and hockey.

Extension

The following activity does not require access to the World Wide Web.

Industry

Have interested students research one of the toys mentioned on this page. Tell them to find out such things as who invented the toy, what company first produced it, how many have been sold, and so on. Suggest that they report their findings to the class.

Answers for Questions

1. Marbles and soccer balls wouldn't roll and hula hoops wouldn't spin.
2. A marble is like a ball. A hula hoop is a disc, with no middle. A yo-yo can be round like a marble, but usually it has flat sides.

Connect

On page 597, students use their knowledge of circles to analyze a Slinky® toy.

11-5 Lesson Organizer

Objective

- Make circle graphs.

Vocabulary

- Circle, center, central angle

Materials

- Explore: Compass, colored pencils or markers

NCTM Standards

- 1–4, 7, 10, 12, 13

Review

Change each fraction to a decimal and a percent. Round decimals to the nearest hundredth.

1. $\frac{3}{5}$ 0.6, 60%
2. $\frac{1}{6}$ 0.17, 17%
3. $\frac{27}{35}$ 0.77, 77%
4. $\frac{73}{92}$ 0.79, 79%

Available on Daily Transparency 11-5

1 Introduce

Explore

You may want to use Teaching Tool Transparency 15: Protractors with this lesson.

The Point
Students take a survey and make a frequency table. Then they use their knowledge of percents to make a circle graph showing the results.

Ongoing Assessment
Some students may need help in determining numbers in the percent column.

For Groups That Finish Early
Suppose there had been more toys to pick from. How would that affect the sizes of the slices? Each slice would be smaller or the same size as it is now.

Answers for Explore
Answers should consist of a table with percents and a circle graph.

11-5 Circles and Circle Graphs

You'll Learn ...

- to make circle graphs

... How It's Used

Newspaper editors use circle graphs to show the data in a news story.

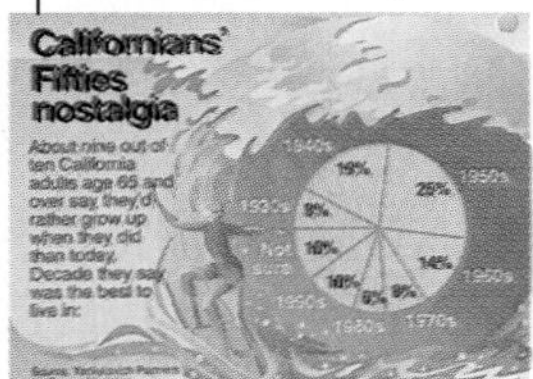

Vocabulary

circle
center
central angle

► Lesson Link You've interpreted data shown on circle graphs. Now you'll explore properties of a circle and draw your own circle graphs. ◄

Explore: Making Circle Graphs

Materials: Compass, Colored pencils or markers

Circular Reasoning

Which of these toys would you have liked best when you were younger?

1. Survey the class to find the number of students who prefer each toy.
2. Copy the frequency table. Enter the number of votes for each toy. Then find the percent of the class that voted for each toy.
3. Draw a circle and mark its center. Using your knowledge of percents, make a circle graph showing the results from Step 2.
4. Explain how you made your circle graph.

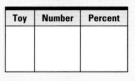

Toy	Number	Percent

Learn: Circles and Circle Graphs

The circle graph shows where the world's computers were in 1993. It also shows important parts of a circle.

All of the points on a **circle** are the same distance from its **center**.

Each "slice" of the circle graph is a *sector* of the circle. The **central angle** that determines the size of the sector has its vertex at the center of the circle.

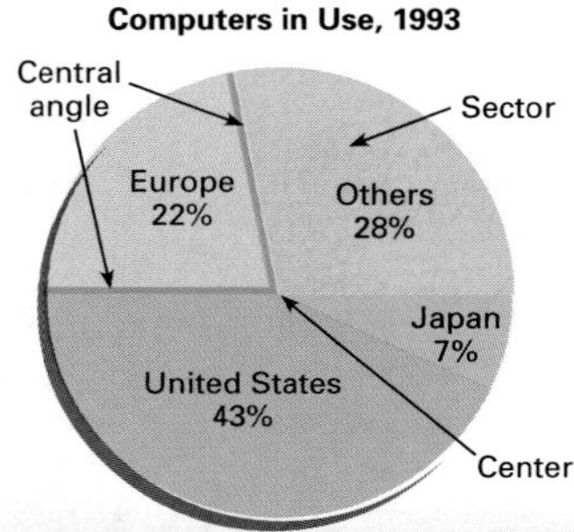

MEETING INDIVIDUAL NEEDS

Resources

- 11-5 Practice
- 11-5 Reteaching
- 11-5 Problem Solving
- 11-5 Enrichment
- 11-5 Daily Transparency
  - Problem of the Day
  - Review
  - Quick Quiz
- Teaching Tool Transparency 15
- Lesson Enhancement Transparency 55

Learning Modalities

Visual Have students find examples of circle graphs in newspapers or magazines.

Kinesthetic Give students a large circular piece of cardboard or paper that has been divided into sectors of various sizes. Have them measure the central angle for each sector and label it in degrees.

English Language Development

Show students a diagram of a circle graph. As you pronounce *circle, center,* and *central* angle, have them point to appropriate portions of the diagram to show that they understand the meanings of the terms.

Invite students who are learning English to research information about their native countries (for example, population makeup, products, exports, and so on), and make circle graphs to present the information to the class.

To make a circle graph, you must find out how large the central angle of each sector should be. You can use the fact that there are 360° in a circle to find the central angles.

Example 1

In 1996, the Pittsburgh Penguins played 82 regular-season hockey matches. They won 49 matches, lost 29, and tied 4. Draw a circle graph to display this data.

Find the percent of wins, losses, and ties.

Wins $= \frac{49}{82} \approx 0.60 = 60\%$ Losses $= \frac{29}{82} \approx 0.35 = 35\%$

Ties $= \frac{4}{82} \approx 0.05 = 5\%$

To find each central angle, multiply the percent (in decimal form) by 360°.

Wins: $0.60 \cdot 360° = 216°$ Losses: $0.35 \cdot 360° = 126°$ Ties: $0.05 \cdot 360° = 18°$

Draw a circle. Use a protractor to draw each central angle that measures less than 180°. Label each sector of the circle graph, and give the graph a title.

Notice that since the Penguins won more than 50% of their games, the central angle of the "Wins" sector measures *more* than 180°. The angle is *past* a straight line.

1996 Pittsburgh Penguins Record

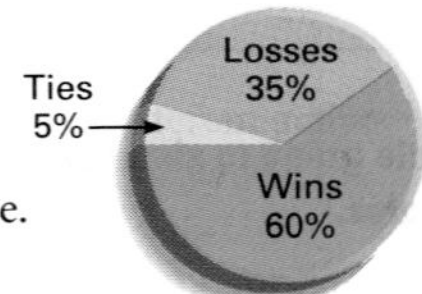

Remember

To draw an angle with a protractor, place the protractor along a side of the angle and mark your paper at the desired angle measure. Draw the second side of the angle through the mark. **[Page 213]**

Try It

Draw a circle graph to show each data set.

a. A recent survey showed that 89% of the people in the United States had heard of a Slinky®. (*Hint:* What percent had *not* heard of a Slinky?)

b. In the 1992 presidential election, about 44 million people voted for Bill Clinton, 39 million for George Bush, and 20 million for Ross Perot.

DID YOU KNOW?

The Slinky® was invented when Richard Jones, who was trying to make a spring for use in navigational instruments, knocked a spring off a shelf. Instead of falling, the spring "walked" to the floor.

Check Your Understanding

1. Suppose 25% of the people in a survey name pizza as their favorite food. How large would the central angle in the "pizza" sector be in a circle graph? How do you know?
2. Can a circle graph have two central angles that measure more than 180°? Explain.

MATH EVERY DAY

Problem of the Day

Write down your age. Add 7. Multiply that sum by 50. Add the number formed by the last two digits of the year in which you were born. Multiply the sum by 2. Subtract 700. Subtract the number formed by the last two digits of the year in which you were born. How is your answer related to your age and birth year? The first two digits of the answer show the age, and the last two digits show the last two digits of the birth year.

Available on Daily Transparency 11-5

An Extension is provided in the transparency package.

Fact of the Day

The speed of a hockey puck shot across the ice has been known to exceed 100 miles per hour.

Mental Math

Do these mentally.

1. $\frac{800}{40}$ 20
2. $\frac{15,000}{300}$ 50
3. $\frac{7200}{9}$ 800
4. $\frac{63,000}{7000}$ 9

2 Teach

Learn

You may wish to use Lesson Enhancement Transparency 55 with **Learn**.

Alternate Example

In one season, a football team won 10 games, lost 6 games, and tied 2 games. Draw a circle graph to show this data.

Wins $= \frac{10}{18} \approx 0.56 = 56\%$

Losses $= \frac{6}{18} \approx 0.33 = 33\%$

Ties $\frac{2}{18} \approx 0.11 = 11\%$.

Find each central angle:

Wins: $0.56 \cdot 360° = 202°$

Losses: $0.33 \cdot 360° = 119°$

Ties: $0.11 \cdot 360° = 40°$

Draw a circle. Label each sector and give the graph a title.

Win–Loss Record

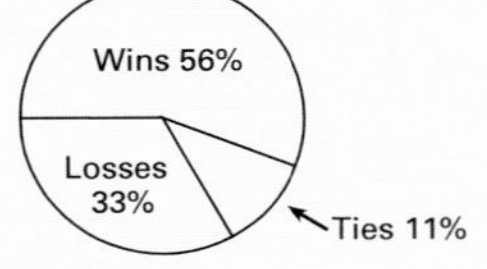

Answers for Try It

a. People Who've Heard of Slinky

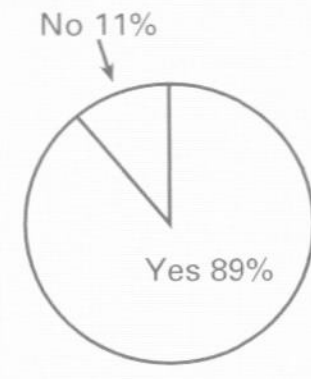

b. 1992 Presidential Votes (millions)

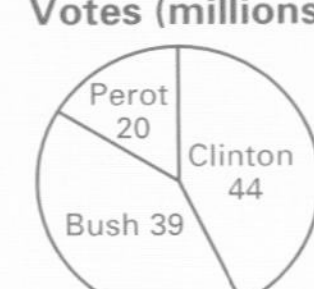

3 Practice and Assess

Check

Answers for Check Your Understanding

1. 90°; 25% of 360° is 90°.
2. No; The sum of central angles of a circle is exactly 360°.

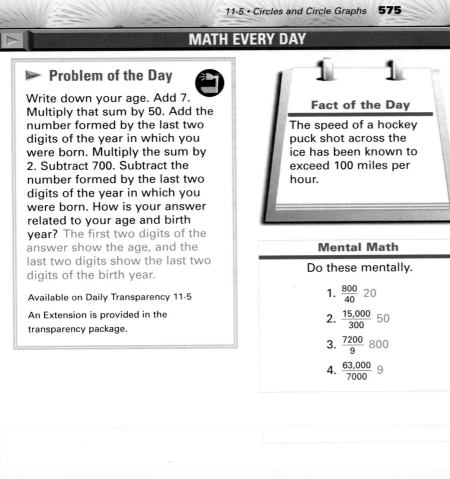

10. $r = 18\frac{1}{4}$ in. $A \approx$ 1045.8 in²
11. $d = 27$ cm $A \approx$ 572.3 cm²
12. $r = 38$ mi $A \approx$ 4534.2 mi²
13. $d = 5$ ft $A \approx$ 19.6 ft²
14. $r = 9.1$ cm $A \approx$ 260.0 cm²
15. $d = \frac{5}{8}$ in. $A \approx$ 0.3 in²
16. Find the area of a pizza if the diameter is 15 in. About 176.6 in²
17. The radius of a U.S. quarter is about 12 mm. Find the area of a quarter. About 452.2 mm²

d. What is the radius of Circle *B*? 10 cm

e. Substitute for the radius and π in the formula $A = \pi r^2$. $A \approx 3.14 \cdot 10^2$

f. What is the area? ≈ 314 cm²

g. 16 m — 200.96 m²

h. 100 yd — 7850 yd²

i. 12 mm — 113.04 mm²

- Measure the base and height of the resulting figure and estimate the area.

Follow Up
Have students discuss how they arrived at their estimated areas in **Explore**.

Answers for Explore
1–2. Answers may vary.

AREA OF A CIRCLE
The area of a circle whose radius is r is given by $A = \pi r^2$.

11B Review

Review Correlation

Item(s)	Lesson(s)
1	11-5
2–4	11-6, 11-7
5	11-6
6, 7	11-8, 11-9
8	11-3, 11-4
9	11-6

Test Prep

Test-Taking Tip
Tell students they can work backwards on some problems. Here, they can use each answer in the formula for circumference and see which answer comes closest to the given circumference.

Answers for Review

1. Expenses for Average Two-Income Family in 1994

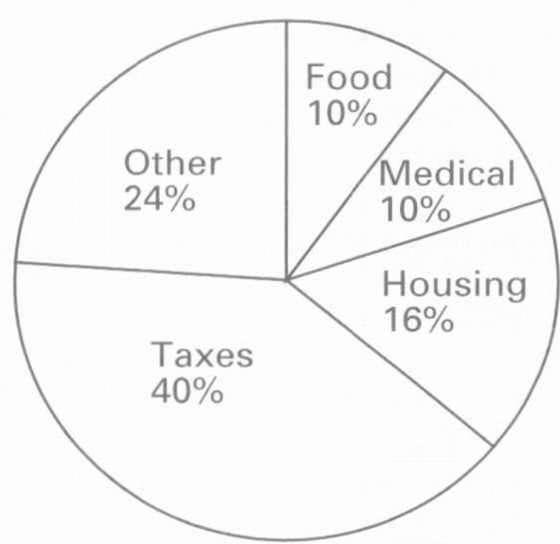

Section 11B Review

REVIEW 11B

1. **Data** In 1994, an average two-income family in the United States spent its money as shown in the table. Draw a circle graph to show this data.

Category	Taxes	Housing and Household	Medical Care	Food	Other
Percent	40%	16%	10%	10%	24%

Find the circumference and area of each circle given its diameter or radius. Use $\pi \approx 3.14$, and round answers to the nearest tenth.

2. 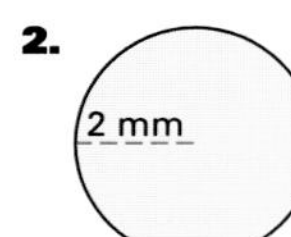

3. 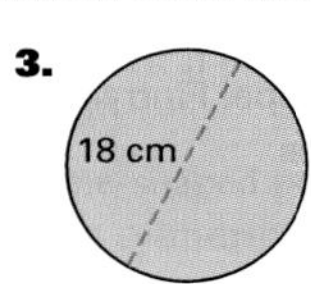

4. 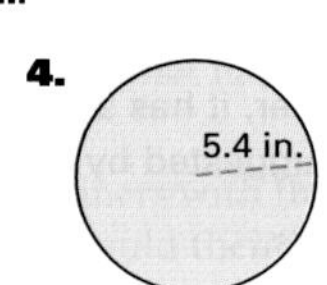

2. $C = 12.6$ mm; $A = 12.6$ mm^2
3. $C = 56.5$ cm; $A = 254.3$ cm^2
4. $C = 33.9$ in.; $A = 91.6$ in.^{2}

5. **History** In the 1800s, children sometimes used steel wheel rims as hoop toys. If the circumference of a wagon wheel was 10 ft, find the radius of the hoop. About 1.6 ft

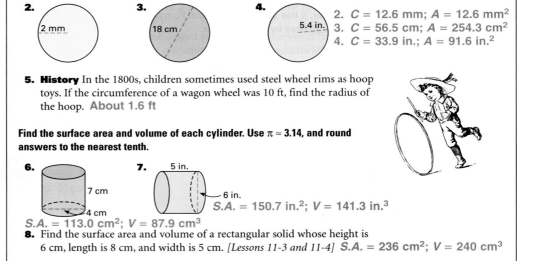

Find the surface area and volume of each cylinder. Use $\pi \approx 3.14$, and round answers to the nearest tenth.

6. 7 cm, 4 cm
$S.A. = 113.0$ cm^2; $V = 87.9$ cm^3

7. 5 in., 6 in.
$S.A. = 150.7$ in.^{2}; $V = 141.3$ in.^{3}

8. Find the surface area and volume of a rectangular solid whose height is 6 cm, length is 8 cm, and width is 5 cm. *[Lessons 11-3 and 11-4]* $S.A. = 236$ cm^2; $V = 240$ cm^3

Test Prep

When you're given the circumference of a circle and are asked to find its radius on a multiple choice test, it may be faster to check which one of the answers works instead of solving the equation for the radius.

9. The circumference of a circle is 18.8 cm. Find its radius to the nearest cm. A
Ⓐ 3 cm Ⓑ 4 cm Ⓒ 5 cm Ⓓ 6 cm

Resources

Practice Masters
Section 11B Review

Assessment Sourcebook
Quiz 11B

TestWorks
Test and Practice Software

Name ____________________

Practice

Section 11B Review

1. The table gives data about 1993 retail car sales in the U.S. Draw a circle graph to show the data.

Category	Small	Midsize	Large	Luxury
Percent of Sales	33%	43%	11%	13%

U.S. Car Sales, 1993: Luxury 13%, Large 11%, Small 33%, Midsize 43%

Find the circumference and area of each circle given its diameter or radius. Use $\pi \approx 3.14$, and round answers to the nearest tenth.

2. $C \approx$ 87.9 cm, $A \approx$ 615.4 cm^2 (14 cm)
3. $C \approx$ 47.1 in., $A \approx$ 176.6 in^2 ($7\frac{1}{2}$ in.)
4. $C \approx$ 25.7 m, $A \approx$ 52.8 m^2 (8.2 m)

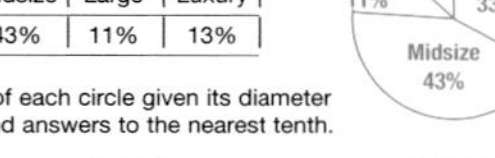

5. **Science** The length of Mercury's equator is about 9522 mi. Find the diameter of Mercury. About 3032 mi

Find the surface area and volume of each cylinder. Use $\pi \approx 3.14$, and round answers to the nearest tenth.

6. $SA \approx$ 3,504.2 in^2, $V \approx$ 13,225.7 in^3 (18 in., 13 in.)
7. $SA \approx$ 229.6 ft^2, $V \approx$ 265.3 ft^3 ($6\frac{1}{2}$ ft, 8 ft)
8. $SA \approx$ 1,011.1 m^2, $V \approx$ 2,461.8 m^3 (7 m, 16 m)

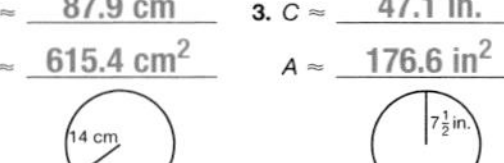

9. A skydiver jumps out of an airplane flying at an elevation of 940 ft above sea level. She lands in Death Valley, California, (elevation −282 ft). How far did she fall? *[Lesson 9-5]* 1222 ft

10. **Science** The saltopus was a small dinosaur that lived in Scotland and weighed 2 lb. An equation to represent the weight of several of these creatures is $w = 2s$, where w represents the weight in pounds and s represents the number of saltopuses. Graph this equation on a coordinate plane. *[Lesson 10-5]*

Weight (lb); Number of saltopuses

Transformations

LESSON PLANNING GUIDE

Student Edition / Ancillaries*

LESSON	MATERIALS	VOCABULARY	DAILY	OTHER
Section 11C Opener				
11-10 Translations	graph paper, scissors	transformation, translation	11-10	Teaching Tool Trans. 7 Lesson Enhancement Trans. 59 Technology Master 59 *WW Math*–Algebra
11-11 Reflections and Line Symmetry	graph paper, markers	symmetry, line symmetry, line of symmetry, reflection	11-11	Teaching Tool Trans. 7 Technology Master 60 WW Math–Geometry
11-12 Rotations and Rotational Symmetry	graph paper, push pin, ruler, scissors, cardboard	rotation, rotational symmetry, point symmetry	11-12	Lesson Enhancement Trans. 60 Technology Master 61 Ch. 11 Project Master
Connect				Interdisc. Team Teaching 11C
Review		scatter plot, trend		Practice 11C; Quiz 11C; *TestWorks*
Extend Key Ideas				
Chapter 11 Summary and Review				
Chapter 11 Assessment				Ch. 11 Tests Forms A–F *TestWorks*; Ch. 11 Letter Home
Cumulative Review Chapters 1–11	compass, rectangular mirrors, coin, protractor			Cumulative Review Ch. 1–11

* Daily Ancillaries include Practice, Reteaching, Problem Solving, Enrichment, and Daily Transparency. Teaching Tool Transparencies are in *Teacher's Toolkits*. Lesson Enhancement Transparencies are in *Overhead Transparency Package*.

SKILLS TRACE

LESSON	SKILL	FIRST INTRODUCED GR. 5	GR. 6	GR. 7	DEVELOP	PRACTICE/ APPLY	REVIEW
11-10	**Drawing and describing translations.**	✘			pp. 600–602	pp. 603–604	pp. 616, 619, 653
11-11	**Reflecting figures on a coordinate plane.**		✘		pp. 605–607	pp. 608–609	pp. 616, 619, 658
11-12	**Rotating figures on a coordinate plane.**		✘		pp. 610–612	pp. 613–614	pp. 616, 619

CONNECTED MATHEMATICS

Investigations 1–3 in the unit *Stretching and Shrinking (Similarity)*, from the **Connected Mathematics** series, can be used with Section 11C.

INTERDISCIPLINARY TEAM TEACHING

Math and Science/Technology

(Worksheet pages 49–50: Teacher pages T49–T50)

In this lesson, students use transformations to understand how the eye produces images.

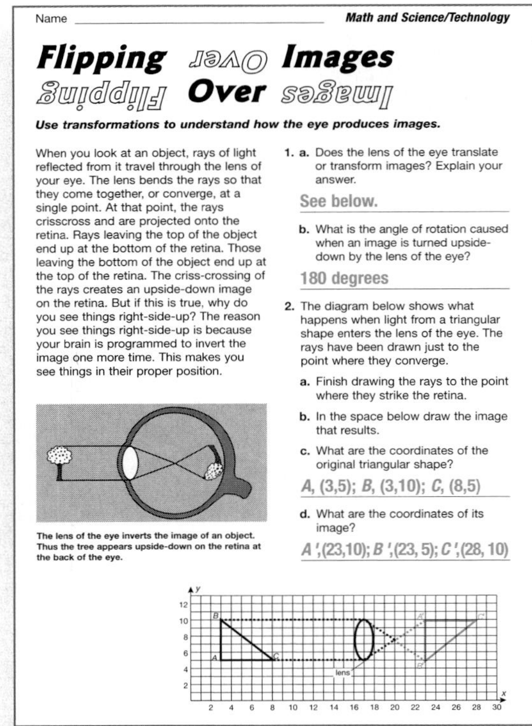

Name ______________________ *Math and Science/Technology*

Flipping Over Images

Use transformations to understand how the eye produces images.

When you look at an object, rays of light reflected from it travel through the lens of your eye. The lens bends the rays so that they come together, or converge, at a single point. At that point, the rays crisscross and are projected onto the retina. Rays leaving the top of the object end up at the bottom of the retina. Those leaving the bottom of the object end up at the top of the retina. The criss-crossing of the rays creates an upside-down image on the retina. But if this is true, why do you see things right-side-up? The reason you see things right-side-up is because your brain is programmed to invert the image one more time. This makes you see things in their proper position.

The lens of the eye inverts the image of an object. Thus the tree appears upside-down on the retina at the back of the eye.

1. a. Does the lens of the eye translate or transform images? Explain your answer.

See below.

b. What is the angle of rotation caused when an image is turned upside-down by the lens of the eye?

180 degrees

2. The diagram below shows what happens when light from a triangular shape enters the lens of the eye. The rays have been drawn just to the point where they converge.

a. Finish drawing the rays to the point where they strike the retina.

b. In the space below draw the image that results.

c. What are the coordinates of the original triangular shape?

A, (3,5); B, (3,10); C, (8,5)

d. What are the coordinates of its image?

A′,(23,10); B′,(23, 5); C′,(28, 10)

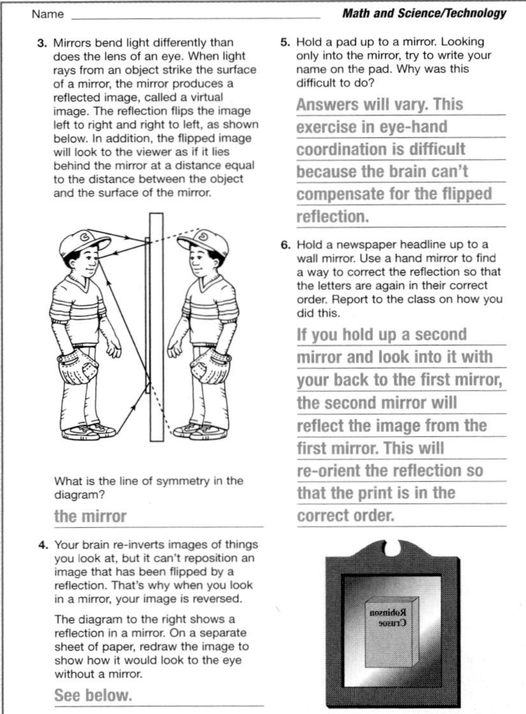

Name ______________________ *Math and Science/Technology*

3. Mirrors bend light differently than does the lens of an eye. When light rays from an object strike the surface of a mirror, the mirror produces a reflected image, called a virtual image. The reflection flips the image left to right and right to left, as shown below. In addition, the flipped image will look to the viewer as if it lies behind the mirror at a distance equal to the distance between the object and the surface of the mirror.

What is the line of symmetry in the diagram?

the mirror

4. Your brain re-inverts images of things you look at, but it can't reposition an image that has been flipped by a reflection. That's why when you look in a mirror, your image is reversed.

The diagram to the right shows a reflection in a mirror. On a separate sheet of paper, redraw the image to show how it would look to the eye without a mirror.

See below.

5. Hold a pad up to a mirror. Looking only into the mirror, try to write your name on the pad. Why was this difficult to do?

Answers will vary. This exercise in eye-hand coordination is difficult because the brain can't compensate for the flipped reflection.

6. Hold a newspaper headline up to a wall mirror. Use a hand mirror to find a way to correct the reflection so that the letters are again in their correct order. Report to the class on how you did this.

If you hold up a second mirror and look into it with your back to the first mirror, the second mirror will reflect the image from the first mirror. This will re-orient the reflection so that the print is in the correct order.

Answers

1. a. The lens transforms images, because it changes their orientation from right-side-up to upside-down. A translation, on the other hand, is the sliding of a figure without changing its orientation.

4. The spine of the book would be on the left and the letters would read:

ROBINSON

CRUSOE

BIBLIOGRAPHY

FOR TEACHERS

Cunningham, Scott. *Cunningham's Encyclopedia of Crystal, Gem and Metal Magic.* St. Paul, MN: Llewellyn Publications, 1988.

Irving, Washington. *The Alhambra, Palace of Mystery and Splendor.* New York, NY: Macmillan, 1953.

Spangler, David. *Math for Real Kids.* Glenview, IL: Good Year Books, 1997.

Tomecek, Steve. *Bouncing & Bending Light: Phantastic Physical Phenomena.* New York, NY: Scientific American Books for Young Readers, 1995.

FOR STUDENTS

Boswell, Thomas, ed. *The Kaleidoscope Book: A Spectrum of Spectacular Scopes to Make.* New York, NY: Sterling Pub. Co. 1992.

Hargittai, Istvan. *Symmetry: A Unifying Concept.* Bolinas, CA: Shelter Publications, 1994.

Mayers, Florence Cassen. *A Russian ABC.* New York, NY: Harry N. Abrams, Inc. Publishers, 1992.

Voss, Gisela. *Museum Shapes.* Boston, MA: Museum of Fine Arts, 1993.

Section 11C

SECTION 11C

Transformations

▶ Science Link ▶ www.mathsurf.com/7/ch11/kaleidoscope

When Worlds Kaleide

Question: What's less than a foot long and filled with millions of intricate works of art? *Hint:* If you don't like the art, you can change it with a twist of your wrist.

Answer: A kaleidoscope!

In 1816, a Scottish scientist, Sir David Brewster, discovered that if he placed a chamber full of colored glass objects at the end of a cylinder with mirrors inside it, the reflections created beautiful geometric patterns. The kaleidoscope was born!

Over the years, kaleidoscopes have been made with different mirror arrangements that create a wide variety of pattern types. The objects used to make those patterns include seashells, stones, beads, fake pearls floating in oil, and the world itself.

When you look through a kaleidoscope, the sections of the pattern you see are copies of each other in different positions. Now you'll begin to investigate the slides, flips, and twists that describe these patterns.

1 Look at the circled kaleidoscope pattern. Describe two ways you could fold this pattern so the two halves are mirror images of each other.

2 Look at the top half and bottom half of the circled kaleidoscope image. What do you notice? What about the left side and right side?

3 Describe any slides, flips, or twists you see in the circled kaleidoscope pattern.

599

Theme: Kaleidoscopes

World Wide Web

If your class has access to the World Wide Web, you might want to use the information found at the Web site address given. The interdisciplinary link relates to topics discussed in this section.

About the Page

This page introduces the theme of the section, kaleidoscopes, and discusses the patterns you see when you look through one.

Ask ...

- What happens when you turn a kaleidoscope?
- What do the patterns look like inside a kaleidoscope?
- How many times do you think the patterns in a kaleidoscope are repeated? If you have a kaleidoscope, have students try to count the number of repeats.

Extension

Science

Sir David Brewster was very interested in the effect of light. Besides the kaleidoscope, he invented many optical devices. Have interested students investigate David Brewster's inventions.

Answers for Questions

1. Answers may vary. Folds can be made either through the black lines that separate the blue "feathers" or through the red "spikes."
2. Possible answer: They could be mirror images of each other.
3. No slides. You can flip this image over any of several lines and get the same image. Any twist of $\frac{1}{14}$, $\frac{2}{14}$, $\frac{3}{14}$, etc., of a turn gives you the same image.

Connect

On page 615, students use transformations to create a kaleidoscopic tessellation.

Where are we now?

In Section 11B, students made circle graphs and explored the properties of circles.

They learned how to

- make circle graphs.
- understand and use π.
- find the circumference of a circle.
- find the area of a circle.
- find the surface area of a cylinder.
- find the volume of a cylinder.

Where are we going?

In Section 11C, students will

- draw translations on a coordinate plane.
- identify lines of symmetry.
- reflect figures on a coordinate plane.
- identify figures with rotational symmetry.
- determine how far a figure has been rotated.
- rotate figures on a coordinate plane.

11-10 Lesson Organizer

Objectives

- Draw translations on a coordinate plane.
- Write rules for translations.

Vocabulary

- Transformation, translation

Materials

- Explore: Graph paper, scissors

NCTM Standards

- 1–4, 9, 12

Review

Give the final location if you start with a point located at (2, 3) and then move as directed.

1. right 5, up 2 (7, 5)
2. right 4, down 5 (6, −2)
3. left 5, up 2 (−3, 5)
4. left 10, down 10 (−8, −7)

Available on Daily Transparency 11-10

1 Introduce

Explore

You may wish to use Lesson Enhancement Transparency 59 and Teaching Tool Transparency 7: $\frac{1}{4}$-Inch Graph Paper with **Explore**.

The Point
Students explore translations by sliding triangles to other locations on a grid. They then give verbal descriptions of the slides.

Ongoing Assessment
Watch for students who slide the triangle so that the top vertex is moved to a vertex other than the top vertex.

11-10 Translations

You'll Learn ...

- to draw translations on a coordinate plane
- to write rules for translations

... How It's Used

Computer animators use translations to move figures across a scene.

Vocabulary

transformation

translation

► Lesson Link You've plotted points in all four quadrants of a coordinate plane. Now you'll use those skills to investigate slides of geometric figures. ◄

Explore Slides on a Coordinate Plane

Which Way Did He Go?

Materials: Graph paper, Scissors

1. On graph paper, trace and cut out a copy of one of the right triangles shown on the coordinate plane. Then copy the axes and triangles onto another sheet of graph paper.

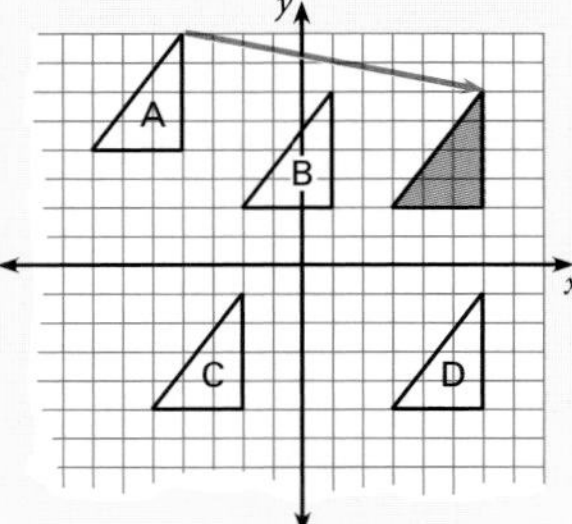

2. Draw an arrow to show the path of a slide from the top vertex of triangle *A* to the top vertex of the shaded triangle. Then draw arrows for triangles B, C, and D.
3. Position the cutout triangle on top of triangle A. Slide it along the arrow until it exactly matches the shaded triangle. Think of a way to describe this slide to someone whose graph paper does not show the shaded triangle.
4. Repeat Step 3 to describe slides from triangles B, C, and D to the shaded triangle.
5. Have a classmate test your directions from Steps 3 and 4.

Learn Translations

When you change the position or size of a figure, you have performed a **transformation**. A **translation** is a transformation that slides a figure without changing its size or orientation.

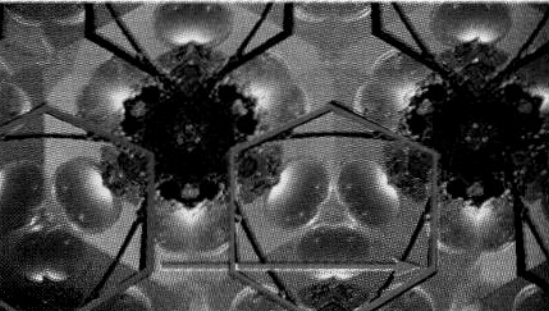

MEETING INDIVIDUAL NEEDS

Resources

11-10 Practice
11-10 Reteaching
11-10 Problem Solving
11-10 Enrichment
11-10 Daily Transparency
- Problem of the Day
- Review
- Quick Quiz

Teaching Tool Transparency 7

Lesson Enhancement Transparency 59

Technology Master 59

Wide World of Mathematics
Algebra: Living in 64 Squares

Learning Modalities

Visual Have students look in magazines or newspapers for photos that illustrate translations.

Kinesthetic Have students use objects such as buttons or coins and lay these objects on a grid. Then have them translate the objects according to various rules.

English Language Development

Students probably will be familiar with the word *translation* with regard to languages. Point out that the word *translation* has a different meaning when used in mathematics.

Example 1

Which lettered figure is a translation of the shaded figure?

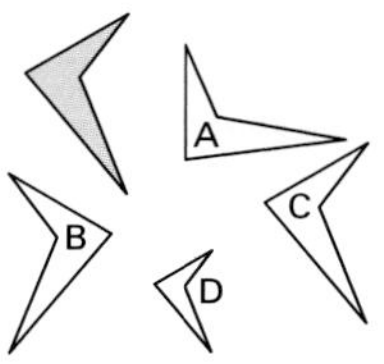

Although all the figures are moved to new positions, A has also been twisted, B has been flipped, and D has been reduced.

C is a translation of the shaded figure.

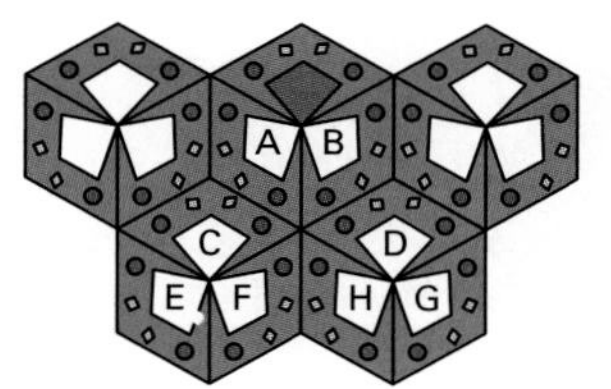

Try It

Identify the lettered figures in the kaleidoscope pattern that are translations of the shaded quadrilateral. C and D

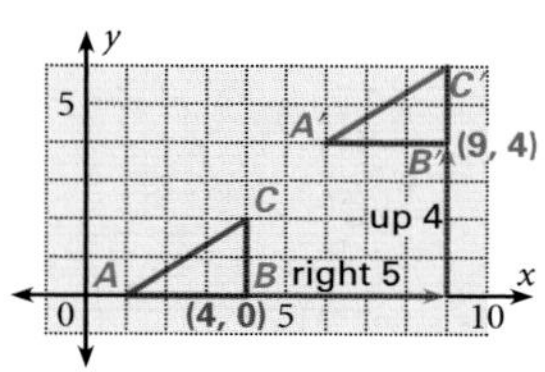

When a figure is translated on a coordinate plane, you can use coordinates to describe the translation.

In the translation shown, every point is moved right 5 units and up 4 units. For instance, (4, 0) slides to (9, 4). The translation of point A is labeled A' ("A prime").

Since every point moves 5 units to the right, every x-coordinate increases by 5. Since every point moves 4 units up, every y-coordinate increases by 4.

To describe the translation "right 5, up 4," we can write the rule $(x, y) \rightarrow (x + 5, y + 4)$.

> **Social Studies Link**
>
> Clothing designs in many cultures show repeating patterns that involve translations. African, Greek, and Native American embroidery often use translation-based designs.

> **Remember**
>
> The ***x*-coordinate** of a point tells how far to the left or right of the origin the point is along the x-axis. The ***y*-coordinate** tells how far up or down the point is along the y-axis. **[Page 443]**

Examples

2 Write a rule for the translation "left 6, down 3."

Left and down are negative directions. *Subtract* from both coordinates.

The rule is $(x, y) \rightarrow (x - 6, y - 3)$.

3 A line segment has endpoints at (0, 0) and (−3, −2). Give the endpoints of its translated segment using the rule $(x, y) \rightarrow (x + 1, y - 3)$.

$(0, 0) \rightarrow (0 + 1, 0 - 3) = (1, -3)$
$(-3, -2) \rightarrow (-3 + 1, -2 - 3) = (-2, -5)$

Try It

A triangle has vertices at (0, 0), (0, 4), and (2, 3). Give the vertices of its translation using the rule $(x, y) \rightarrow (x - 5, y + 1)$. (−5, 1), (−5, 5), (−3, 4)

MATH EVERY DAY

Problem of the Day

On July 26, 1969, Sharon Sites Adams, a California homemaker, sailed her 31-ft ketch into San Diego harbor. She became the first woman ever to sail alone across the Pacific Ocean. She left Yokohama, Japan and sailed 5618 miles at an average speed of 3.133 mi/hr. How many days did her journey last? Round to the nearest tenth. 74.7 days

Available on Daily Transparency 11-10

An Extension is provided in the transparency package.

Fact of the Day

A kaleidoscope created with two mirrors will present a circular design. One with three mirrors will present an endless field of patterns.

Mental Math

Do these mentally.

1. $\frac{1}{4}$ of 12 3
2. $\frac{1}{10}$ of 100 10
3. $\frac{1}{5}$ of 200 40
4. $\frac{1}{8}$ of 160 20

Answers for Explore

2.

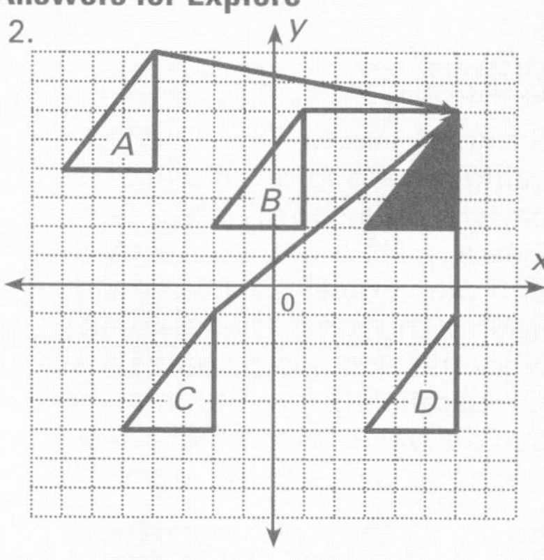

3. Slide the triangle 10 units right and 2 units down.
4. B: Slide the triangle 5 units right; C: Slide the triangle 8 units right and 7 units up. D: Slide the triangle 7 units up.

2 Teach

Learn

Alternate Examples

1. Which lettered figure is a translation of the shaded figure?

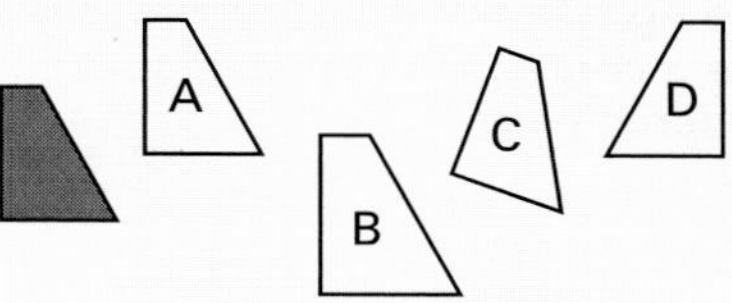

Figure B has been enlarged, C has been twisted, and D has been flipped.

Figure A is a translation of the shaded figure.

2. Write a rule for the translation, "right 5, down 3."

Right is a positive direction and down is a negative direction. Add 5 to the x-coordinate and subtract 3 from the y-coordinate.

The rule is $(x, y) \rightarrow (x + 5, y - 3)$.

3. A line segment has endpoints at (0, 0) and (−6, 4). Give the endpoints of its translated segment using the rule

$(x, y) \rightarrow (x - 2, y + 4)$

$(0, 0) \rightarrow (0 - 2, 0 + 4) = (-2, 4)$

$(-6, 4) \rightarrow (-6 - 2, 4 + 4) = (-8, 8)$

Students see two methods of using a translation to create a pattern on a coordinate plane. One applies the rule directly to find the vertices of the translated figure. The other thinks about what the rule means and slides the parallelogram. Students can decide which of the two correct methods is easier for them.

Answers for What Do You Think?

1. They use the same rule.
2. Shawon; Lorena has to use a coordinate grid and that would be hard with large numbers.

3 Practice and Assess

Check

Point out that translations could be described by first giving the up or down direction and then the right or left direction. But the conventional method is to give the right or left direction first since the x-coordinate comes first in an ordered pair.

Answers for Check Your Understanding

1. Answers may vary.
2. Possible answers: Draw the figures; See if you can find a rule.

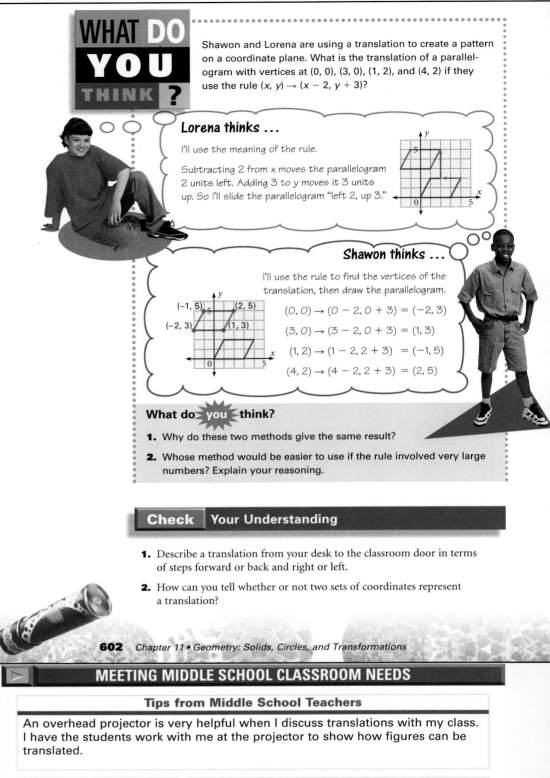

Shawon and Lorena are using a translation to create a pattern on a coordinate plane. What is the translation of a parallelogram with vertices at (0, 0), (3, 0), (1, 2), and (4, 2) if they use the rule $(x, y) \rightarrow (x - 2, y + 3)$?

Lorena thinks ...

I'll use the meaning of the rule.

Subtracting 2 from x moves the parallelogram 2 units left. Adding 3 to y moves it 3 units up. So I'll slide the parallelogram "left 2, up 3."

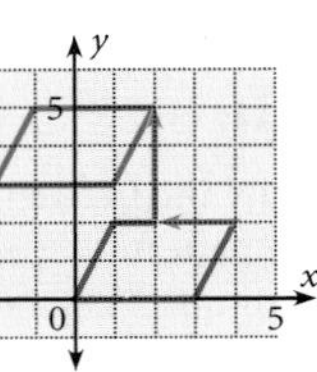

Shawon thinks ...

I'll use the rule to find the vertices of the translation, then draw the parallelogram.

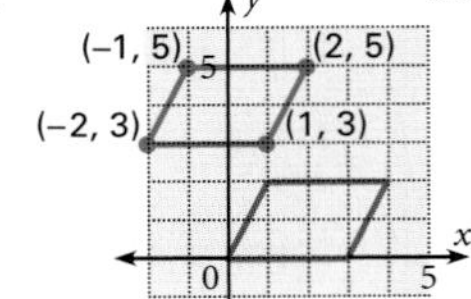

$(0, 0) \rightarrow (0 - 2, 0 + 3) = (-2, 3)$

$(3, 0) \rightarrow (3 - 2, 0 + 3) = (1, 3)$

$(1, 2) \rightarrow (1 - 2, 2 + 3) = (-1, 5)$

$(4, 2) \rightarrow (4 - 2, 2 + 3) = (2, 5)$

What do you think?

1. Why do these two methods give the same result?
2. Whose method would be easier to use if the rule involved very large numbers? Explain your reasoning.

Check Your Understanding

1. Describe a translation from your desk to the classroom door in terms of steps forward or back and right or left.
2. How can you tell whether or not two sets of coordinates represent a translation?

602 *Chapter 11 • Geometry: Solids, Circles, and Transformations*

MEETING MIDDLE SCHOOL CLASSROOM NEEDS

Tips from Middle School Teachers

An overhead projector is very helpful when I discuss translations with my class. I have the students work with me at the projector to show how figures can be translated.

Team Teaching

Work with an art teacher to show wallpaper designs that illustrate translations.

Science Connection

The earliest mirrors were made of polished pieces of metal which dulled easily. The process of chemically depositing silver on glass to prevent dullness was developed in 1835 by German chemist Justus von Liebig. This method is still applied today for commonly used mirrors.

11-10 Exercises and Applications

Practice and Apply

1. **Getting Started** Sketch the translation of $\triangle MNP$ using the rule $(x, y) \rightarrow (x + 2, y - 1)$.
   a. Find the coordinates of point M' by adding 2 to M's x-coordinate and subtracting 1 from its y-coordinate. Plot M'.
   b. Repeat **a** to plot points N' and P'.
   c. Draw the translated triangle $\triangle M'N'P'$ by connecting its vertices.

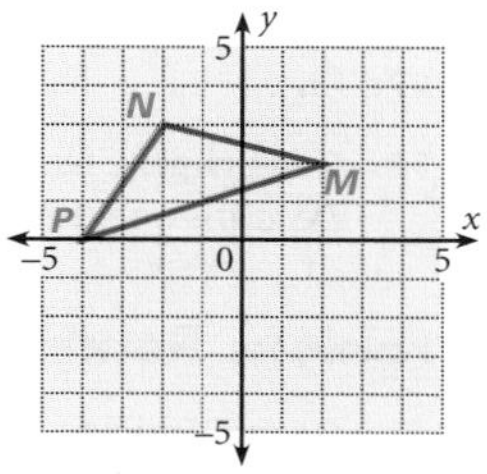

For each group of figures, identify all lettered polygons that are translations of the shaded polygon.

2. D
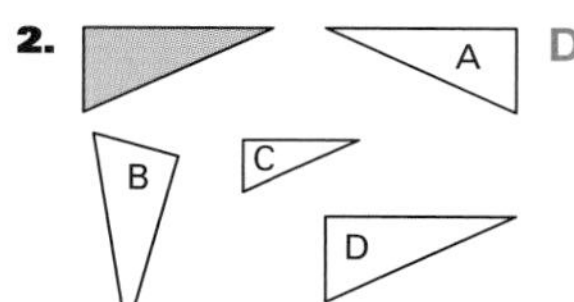

3. C
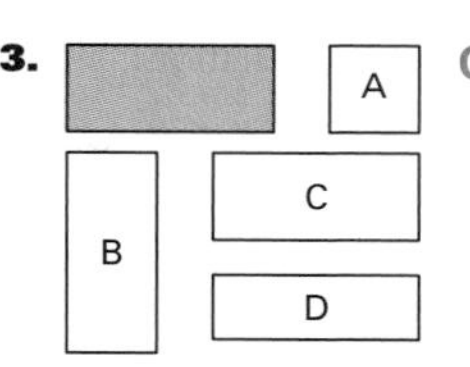

4. C and D
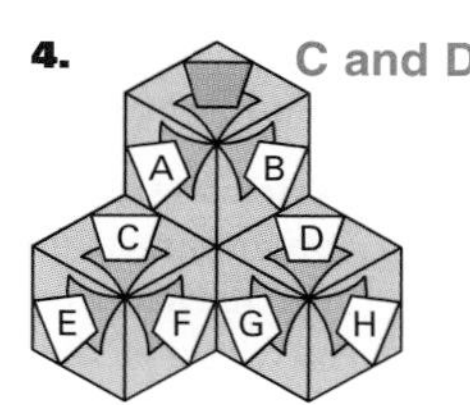

5. **Science** Some kaleidoscopes use four perpendicular mirrors. These kaleidoscopes produce images like the one shown. Use transformations to describe this image.

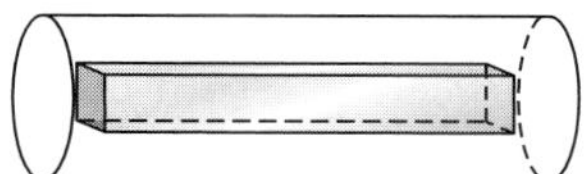
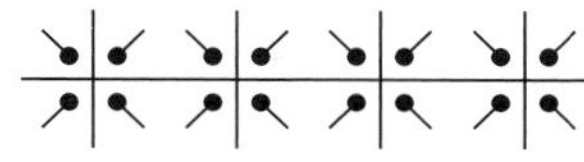

Write a rule for each translation.

6. Right 1, up 2 $(x, y) \rightarrow (x + 1, y + 2)$
7. Left 5, up 7 $(x, y) \rightarrow (x - 5, y + 7)$
8. Left 6, down 5 $(x, y) \rightarrow (x - 6, y - 5)$
9. Down 3 $(x, y) \rightarrow (x, y - 3)$

Point A is at $(2, -3)$. Use each rule to find the coordinates of A'.

10. $(x, y) \rightarrow (x + 3, y - 1)$ $(5, -4)$
11. $(x, y) \rightarrow (x - 2, y + 3)$ $(0, 0)$
12. $(x, y) \rightarrow (x, y - 4)$ $(2, -7)$
13. $(x, y) \rightarrow (x - 5, y + 7)$ $(-3, 4)$
14. **Test Prep** If you translate $(4, -2)$ three units to the right and five units down, what are the coordinates of the translated point? A

   Ⓐ $(7, -7)$ Ⓑ $(1, -7)$ Ⓒ $(7, 3)$ Ⓓ $(1, 3)$

PRACTICE 11-10

PRACTICE

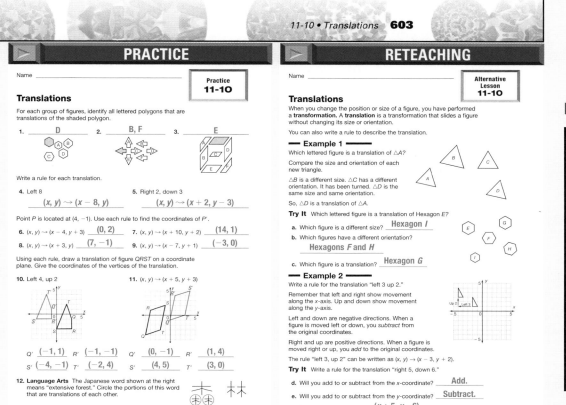

Name ______________________

Practice 11-10

Translations

For each group of figures, identify all lettered polygons that are translations of the shaded polygon.

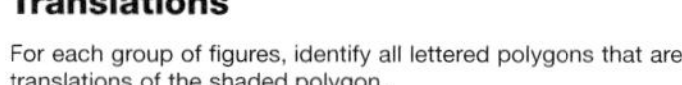

1. D
2. B, F
3. E

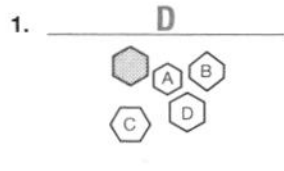

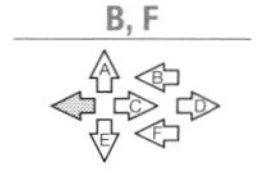

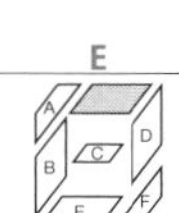

Write a rule for each translation.

4. Left 8 $(x, y) \rightsquigarrow (x - 8, y)$
5. Right 2, down 3 $(x, y) \rightsquigarrow (x + 2, y - 3)$

Point P is located at $(4, -1)$. Use each rule to find the coordinates of P'.

6. $(x, y) \rightsquigarrow (x - 4, y + 3)$ $(0, 2)$
7. $(x, y) \rightsquigarrow (x + 10, y + 2)$ $(14, 1)$
8. $(x, y) \rightsquigarrow (x + 3, y)$ $(7, -1)$
9. $(x, y) \rightsquigarrow (x - 7, y + 1)$ $(-3, 0)$

Using each rule, draw a translation of figure $QRST$ on a coordinate plane. Give the coordinates of the vertices of the translation.

10. Left 4, up 2 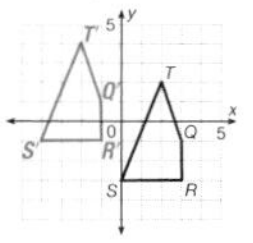
11. $(x, y) \rightsquigarrow (x + 5, y + 3)$

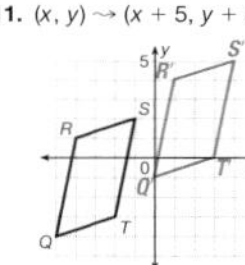

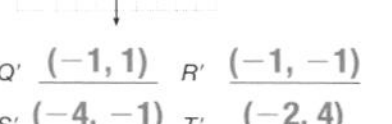
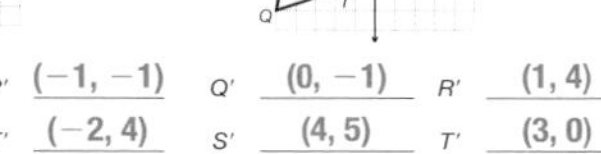

10. Q' $(-1, 1)$ R' $(-1, -1)$ S' $(-4, -1)$ T' $(-2, 4)$

11. Q' $(0, -1)$ R' $(1, 4)$ S' $(4, 5)$ T' $(3, 0)$

12. **Language Arts** The Japanese word shown at the right means "extensive forest." Circle the portions of this word that are translations of each other.

RETEACHING

Name ______________________

Alternative Lesson 11-10

Translations

When you change the position or size of a figure, you have performed a **transformation.** A **translation** is a transformation that slides a figure without changing its size or orientation.

You can also write a rule to describe the translation.

Example 1

Which lettered figure is a translation of $\triangle A$?

Compare the size and orientation of each new triangle.

$\triangle B$ is a different size. $\triangle C$ has a different orientation. It has been turned. $\triangle D$ is the same size and same orientation.

So, $\triangle D$ is a translation of $\triangle A$.

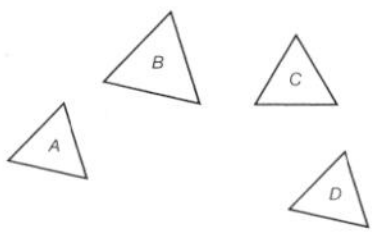

Try It Which lettered figure is a translation of Hexagon E?

a. Which figure is a different size? Hexagon I

b. Which figures have a different orientation? Hexagons F and H

c. Which figure is a translation? Hexagon G

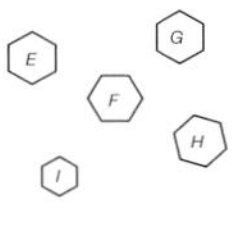

Example 2

Write a rule for the translation "left 3 up 2."

Remember that left and right show movement along the x-axis. Up and down show movement along the y-axis.

Left and down are negative directions. When a figure is moved left or down, you *subtract* from the original coordinates.

Right and up are positive directions. When a figure is moved right or up, you *add* to the original coordinates.

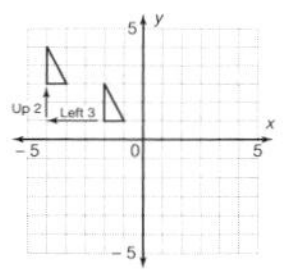

The rule "left 3, up 2" can be written as $(x, y) \rightarrow (x - 3, y + 2)$.

Try It Write a rule for the translation "right 5, down 6."

d. Will you add to or subtract from the x-coordinate? Add.

e. Will you add to or subtract from the y-coordinate? Subtract.

f. Complete the rule. $(x, y) \rightarrow$ $(x + 5, y - 6)$

11-10 Exercises and Applications

Assignment Guide

- **Basic** 1–13 odds, 14–16, 19, 21–27 odds
- **Average** 2–12 evens, 14–16, 19–20, 22–34 evens
- **Enriched** 5–13 odds, 14–20, 21–33 odds

Exercise Notes

Exercises 14

Test Prep If students give an answer other than A, they are moving left instead of right and/or down instead of up to find the translated point.

Exercise Answers

1. a–c.

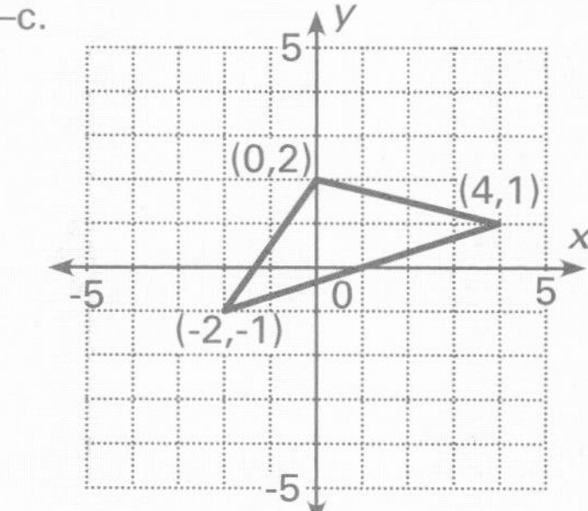

5. Possible answer: The image is a series of translations of a basic figure.

Reteaching

Activity

Materials: Graph paper

Work with a partner. Follow these steps.

- One person should draw a set of axes and then draw a triangle on the grid.
- The second person names a rule for translating the triangle.
- The first person then draws the translated triangle.
- Switch roles and have the other person draw the triangles.

Exercise Answers

15.

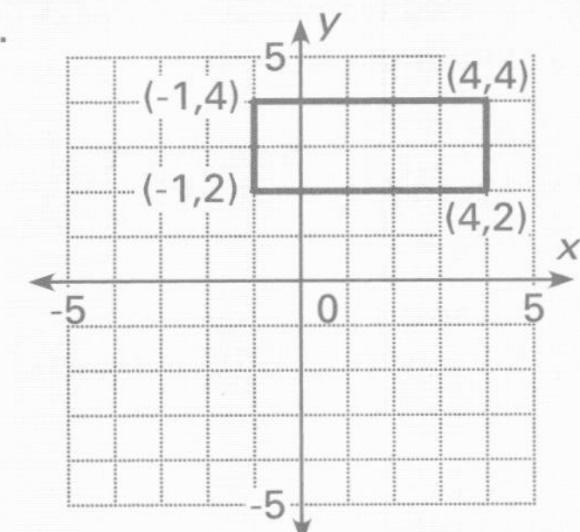

16.

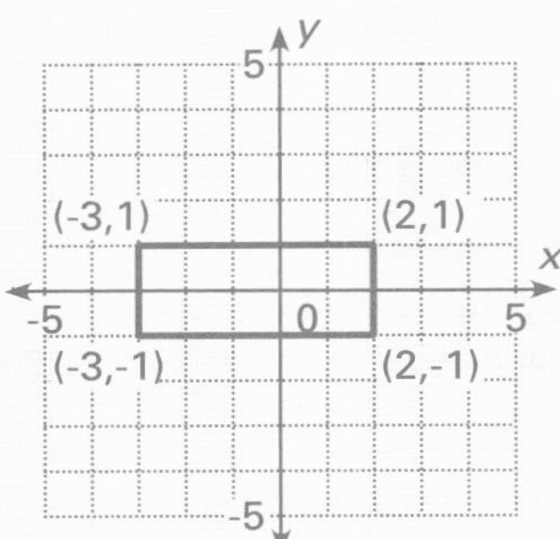

17.

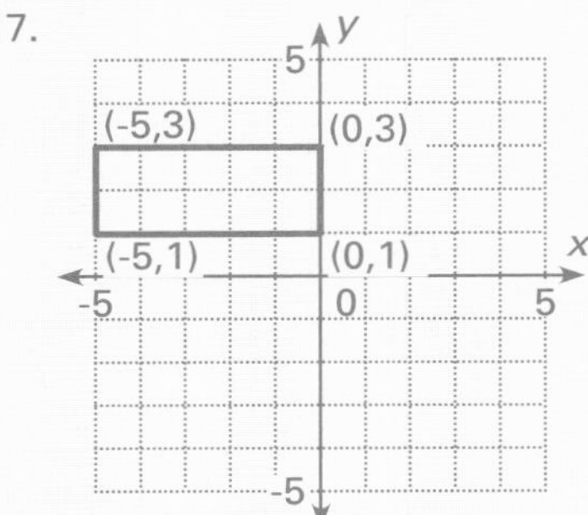

18. Possible answer: Montgomery County can be seen as a leftward translation of Adams County or Union County.

19. Yes; $(x, y) \rightarrow (x - 2, y + 1)$

Alternate Assessment

Performance Have students draw a picture of a rectangle on a grid, name a rule for translating the rectangle, and then show the translated rectangle on the same grid.

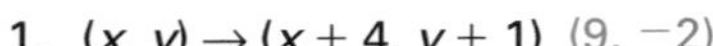

Quick Quiz

Point X is at $(5, -3)$. Use each rule to find the coordinates of X.

1. $(x, y) \rightarrow (x + 4, y + 1)$ (9, −2)
2. $(x, y) \rightarrow (x - 2, y + 3)$ (3, 0)
3. $(x, y) \rightarrow (x + 1, y - 5)$ (6, −8)
4. $(x, y) \rightarrow (x - 3, y - 6)$ (2, −9)

Available on Daily Transparency 11-10

Using each rule, draw a translation of figure *ABCD* on a coordinate plane. Give the coordinates of the vertices of the translation.

15. Right 3 units

16. $(x, y) \rightarrow (x + 1, y - 3)$

17. $(x, y) \rightarrow (x - 1, y - 1)$

18. Geography The map shows counties in southern Iowa. Describe any translations that you see.

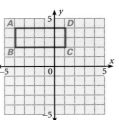

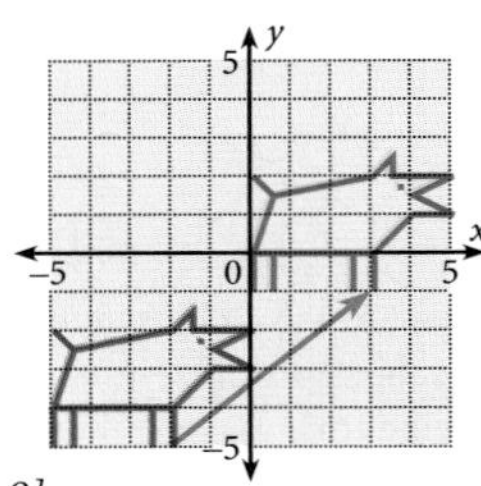

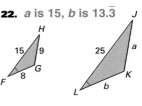

Problem Solving and Reasoning

19. Communicate A transformation of $\triangle ABC$ moves $A(2, -3)$ to $D(0, -2)$, $B(1, 4)$ to $E(-1, 5)$, and $C(-2, 1)$ to $F(-4, 2)$. Is $\triangle DEF$ a translation of $\triangle ABC$? If so, what is the rule for the translation? If not, why not?

20. Critical Thinking When creating animations, computer programmers use translations to describe the ways images will move across a screen. Suppose that the figure moves as shown by the arrow. Write a rule for the translation of this figure. $(x, y) \rightarrow (x + 5, y + 4)$

PROBLEM SOLVING 11-10

Mixed Review

Find the missing side lengths in each pair of similar figures. *[Lesson 7-9]*

21.

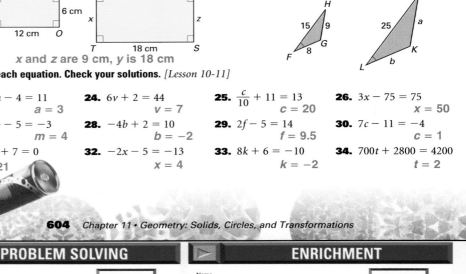

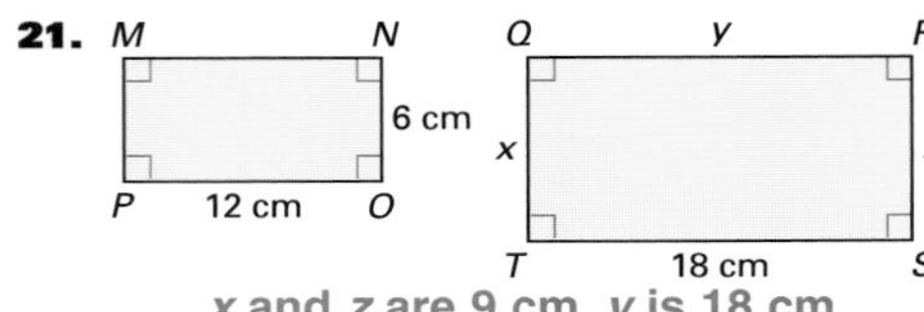

x and z are 9 cm, y is 18 cm

22. a is 15, b is 13.$\overline{3}$

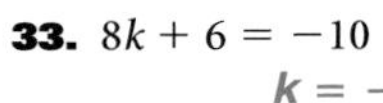

Solve each equation. Check your solutions. *[Lesson 10-11]*

23. $5a - 4 = 11$ $a = 3$

24. $6v + 2 = 44$ $v = 7$

25. $\frac{c}{10} + 11 = 13$ $c = 20$

26. $3x - 75 = 75$ $x = 50$

27. $\frac{m}{2} - 5 = -3$ $m = 4$

28. $-4b + 2 = 10$ $b = -2$

29. $2f - 5 = 14$ $f = 9.5$

30. $7c - 11 = -4$ $c = 1$

31. $\frac{c}{3} + 7 = 0$ $c = -21$

32. $-2x - 5 = -13$ $x = 4$

33. $8k + 6 = -10$ $k = -2$

34. $700t + 2800 = 4200$ $t = 2$

604 Chapter 11 • Geometry: Solids, Circles, and Transformations

PROBLEM SOLVING

Name ______ Guided Problem Solving 11-10

GPS PROBLEM 19, STUDENT PAGE 604

A transformation of $\triangle ABC$ moves $A(2, -3)$ to $D(0, -2)$, $B(1, 4)$ to $E(-1, 5)$, and $C(-2, 1)$ to $F(-4, 2)$. Is $\triangle DEF$ a translation of $\triangle ABC$? If so, what is the rule for the translation? If not, why not?

Understand

1. Does each point in a translation move in the same or in a different direction? Same direction.
2. Does each point in a translation move the same or a different number of units in each direction? Same number.
3. Write the coordinates for each point.
   a. Point A (2, −3) b. Point B (1, 4) c. Point C (−2, 1)
   d. Point D (0, −2) e. Point E (−1, 5) f. Point F (−4, 2)

Plan

4. Use the words left or right and up or down to describe the movement between each point.
   a. Point A to Point D Left 2, Up 1 b. Point B to Point E Left 2, Up 1
   c. Point C to Point F Left 2, Up 1
5. Which movements are written as addition when you write a rule? Right, up.

Solve

6. If the movement is a translation, write the rule using (x, y) notation. If it is not a translation, explain. $(x, y) \rightarrow (x - 2, y + 1)$

Look Back

7. What other strategy could you use to find the answer? Possible answer: Draw a Diagram (Graph)

SOLVE ANOTHER PROBLEM

A transformation of $\triangle GHI$ moves $G(-2, -1)$ to $J(0, 4)$, $H(5, -1)$ to $K(0, -2)$, and $I(2, 3)$ to $L(7, -2)$. Is $\triangle JKL$ a translation of $\triangle GHI$? If so, what is the rule for the translation? If not, why not? No, each point moves different number of units in different directions.

ENRICHMENT

Name ______ Extend Your Thinking 11-10

Visual Thinking

In each row, the net on the left shows a pattern that can be folded to make one of the cubes on the right. Circle the letter of cube that can be made with the net.

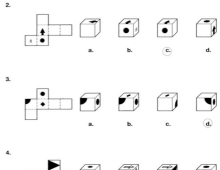

1.

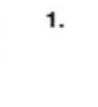
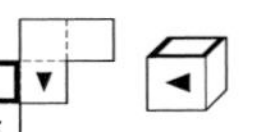

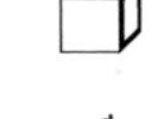

(a.) b. c. d.

2.

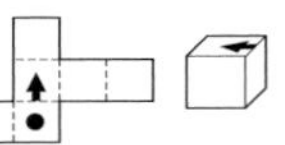
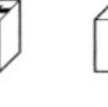

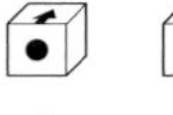

a. b. (c.) d.

3.

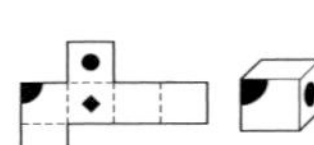

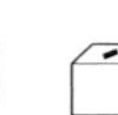
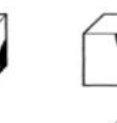
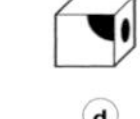

a. b. c. (d.)

4.

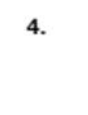
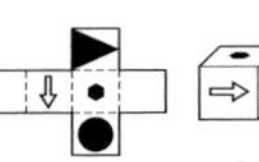

(a.) b. c. d.

Reflections and Line Symmetry

11-11

▶ Lesson Link You've transformed figures by sliding them. Now you'll investigate transformations made by flipping figures. ◀

Explore Reflections

Mirror, Mirror, on the Graph

Materials: Graph paper, Markers

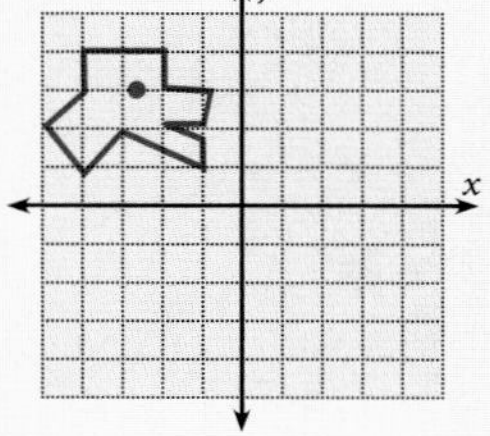

1. Set up *x*- and *y*-axes on your graph paper. Use a marking pen to sketch a simple cartoon character or irregular design in the second quadrant of your coordinate system.
2. Fold your paper along the *y*-axis so the original figure is on the outside. Turn your paper over and trace your figure onto the other half of the paper.
3. Unfold your paper. Compare your original figure to the tracing. Are the figures identical? If not, what differences do you see?
4. Choose a point on your original figure. How far is the point from the *y*-axis? How far is the matching point on your tracing from the *y*-axis?

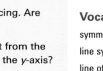

You'll Learn ...

- to identify lines of symmetry
- to reflect figures on a coordinate plane

... How It's Used

Judges at dog shows look for symmetry when choosing champion dogs.

Vocabulary

symmetry

line symmetry

line of symmetry

reflection

Learn Reflections and Line Symmetry

A balance, or **symmetry**, is often found in nature and in art.

When one half of an object is a mirror image of the other, the object has **line symmetry**, and the imaginary "mirror" is the **line of symmetry**.

Since kaleidoscopes use several mirrors, the patterns they produce have many lines of symmetry.

MEETING INDIVIDUAL NEEDS

Resources

- **11-11** Practice
- **11-11** Reteaching
- **11-11** Problem Solving
- **11-11** Enrichment
- **11-11** Daily Transparency
  - Problem of the Day
  - Review
  - Quick Quiz
- Teaching Tool Transparency 7
- Technology Master 60

Wide World of Mathematics Geometry: Miniature Golf

Learning Modalities

Visual Have students look for objects in the classroom that illustrate line symmetry.

Verbal Have students write a series of steps they would follow for reflecting a polygon across the *x*-axis and then across the *y*-axis.

Challenge

Have students find a word (in block letters) that looks the same when reflected across the *y*-axis and another word that looks the same when reflected across the *x*-axis. Possible answers: For *y*-axis, MOM, TOOT. For *x*-axis, OX, HOOK

11-11 Lesson Organizer

Objectives

- Identify lines of symmetry.
- Reflect figures on a coordinate plane.

Vocabulary

- Symmetry, line symmetry, line of symmetry, reflection

Materials

- Explore: Graph paper, marking pens

NCTM Standards

- 1–4, 7, 12

▶ Review

Answer the following questions.

1. What point is directly across the *y*-axis from $(-5, 3)$ and the same distance from the *y*-axis? $(5, 3)$
2. What point is directly across the *x*-axis from $(-5, 3)$ and the same distance from the *x*-axis? $(-5, -3)$

Available on Daily Transparency 11-11

1 Introduce

Explore

You may want to use Teaching Tool Transparency 7: $\frac{1}{4}$-Inch Graph Paper with **Explore.**

The Point

Students reflect a figure across the *y*-axis by folding and tracing.

Ongoing Assessment

Check that students fold the paper so that the figure is on the outside.

Answers for Explore

1–2. Answers may vary.

3. No; The figures are mirror images of each other.
4. The distances are the same.

2 Teach

Learn

Alternate Examples

Decide whether each figure has line symmetry. If it does, copy the figure and draw and number the lines of symmetry.

1. non-regular hexagon

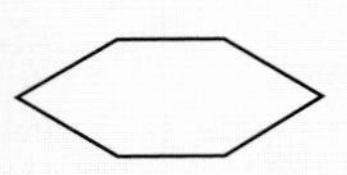

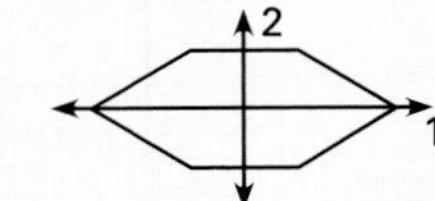

The non-regular hexagon has 2 lines of symmetry.

2. parallelogram

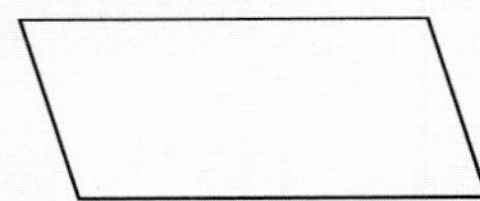

The parallelogram has no lines of symmetry.

3. trapezoid

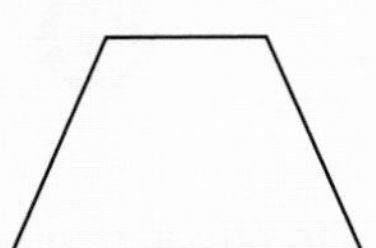

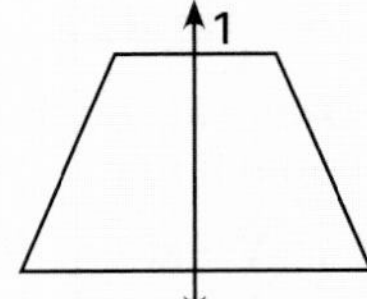

The trapezoid has 1 line of symmetry.

Answers for Try It

a.

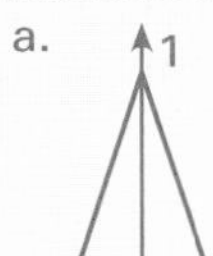

b.

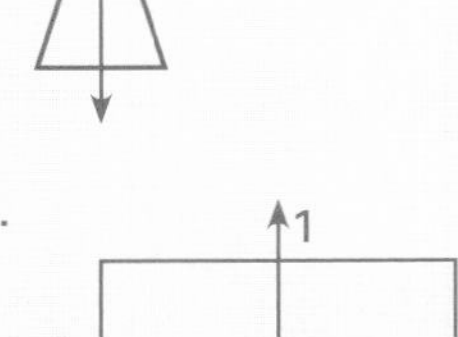

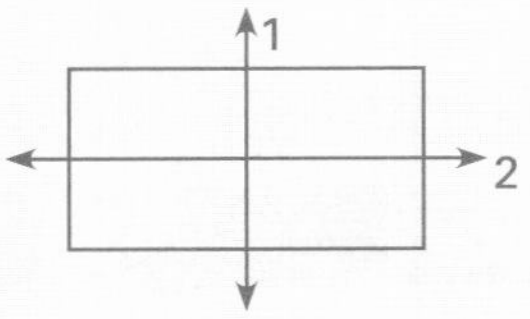

c.

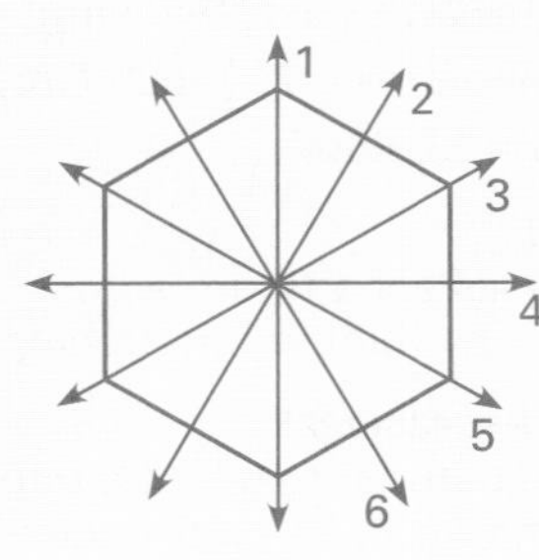

Examples

Decide whether each figure has line symmetry. If it does, copy the figure, then draw and number the lines of symmetry.

1 Regular pentagon

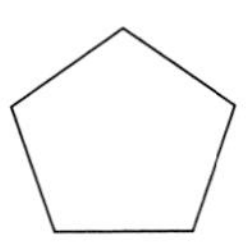

A regular pentagon has 5 lines of symmetry.

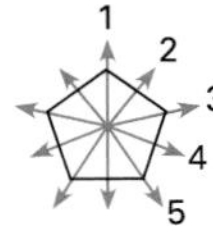

2 Square

A square has 4 lines of symmetry.

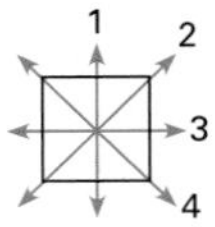

3 Scalene triangle

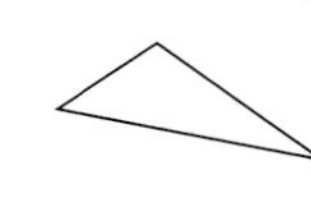

A scalene triangle has no lines of symmetry.

Try It

Decide whether each figure has line symmetry. If it does, copy the figure, then draw and number the lines of symmetry.

a. Isosceles triangle

b. Rectangle

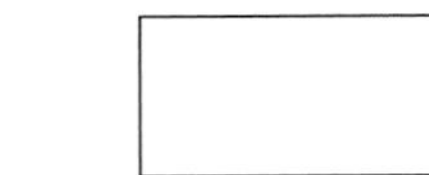

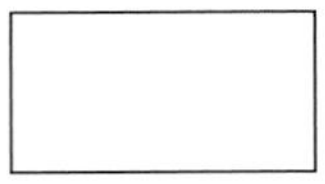

c. Regular hexagon

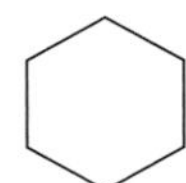

Language Link

The word *kaleidoscope* comes from the Greek *kalos* (beautiful) + *eidos* (form) + *scopos* (to look at).

Whether it has line symmetry or not, any figure can be reflected in a mirror. The reflections in kaleidoscope images can be produced by irregular objects.

The transformation created by flipping a figure is a **reflection**.

When you reflect a figure across a line, every point on the original figure is the same distance from the line as the matching point on its reflection.

You can use this idea to help you draw reflections on a coordinate plane.

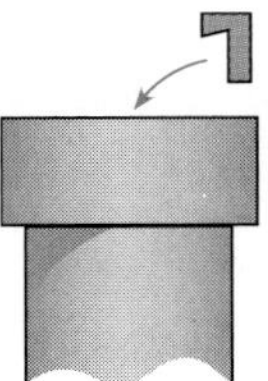

MATH EVERY DAY

Problem of the Day

A group of math students were working together and noticed that each name could be written using reflections. Name the members of the group.

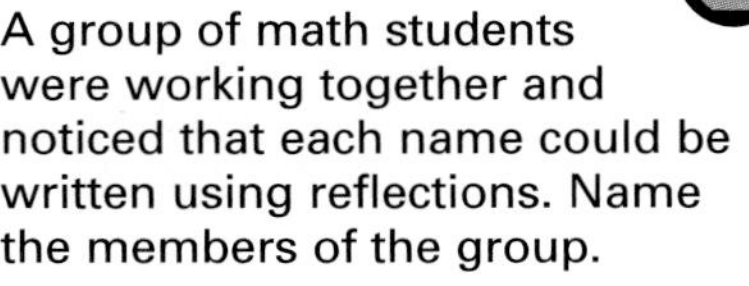

Tammy, Dixie, Dick, Cho, Otto

Available on Daily Transparency 11-11

An Extension is provided in the transparency package.

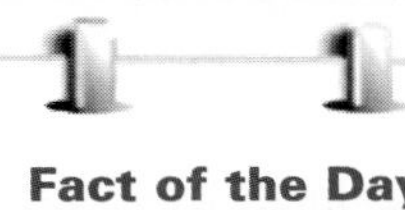

Fact of the Day

The most common diamond crystal is an octahedron seen as two symmetrical four-sided pyramids positioned base to base.

Estimation

Estimate.

1. 50% of $49.95 $25
2. 25% of $23.50 $6
3. 20% of $9.69 $2
4. 75% of $101.59 $75
5. 40% of $59 $24

Example 4

The vertices of $\triangle FGH$ are $F(-4, 1)$, $G(-2, 5)$, and $H(4, 3)$. Draw the reflection of $\triangle FGH$ across the x-axis. Give the coordinates of the reflection's vertices.

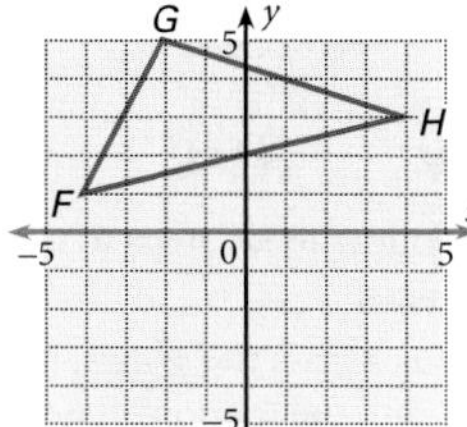

Draw the reflection by reflecting the vertices, then connecting the points.

To reflect a point, find the distance to the line of reflection. Go the same distance on the other side of the line and mark the reflection point.

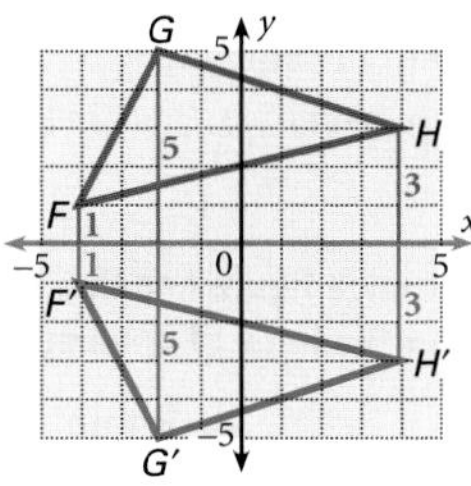

For instance, since point F is one unit *above* the x-axis, its reflection F' is one unit *below* the axis.

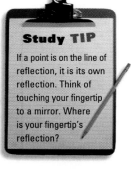

The coordinates of the vertices of the reflection are $F'(-4, -1)$, $G'(-2, -5)$, and $H'(4, -3)$.

Try It

The vertices of $\triangle ABC$ are $A(3, 2)$, $B(-3, 4)$, and $C(0, 5)$. Draw a reflection of $\triangle ABC$ across the x-axis, and give the coordinates of its vertices.

The coordinates of points in Example 4 demonstrate an important pattern. When a point is reflected across the x-axis:

- its x-coordinate stays the same
- its y-coordinate is multiplied by -1

There is a similar rule for reflections across the y-axis. When a point is reflected across the y-axis:

- its x-coordinate is multiplied by -1
- its y-coordinate stays the same

Study TIP

If a point is on the line of reflection, it is its own reflection. Think of touching your fingertip to a mirror. Where is your fingertip's reflection?

Check Your Understanding

1. How are the ideas of line symmetry and reflection related? What are some differences between them?
2. Explain how to sketch the reflection of a polygon across a line.
3. If a figure is reflected across a line, does the reflection have line symmetry? Explain your answer.

MEETING MIDDLE SCHOOL CLASSROOM NEEDS

Tips from Middle School Teachers

I have students write their initials in block letters on a sheet of grid paper. Then I have them reflect the letters across the y-axis. They are fascinated that some letters look the same even after they are reflected, while others are reversed.

Team Teaching

Work with a science teacher to show students a kaleidoscope and then explain how mirrors and reflections are used to create the patterns.

Literature Connection

A mirror and its reflected images are often important to the plot in fantasy literature. *Alice in Wonderland, Through the Looking Glass,* and *Snow White* are three such stories in which a mirror plays a significant part.

Alternate Example

4. The vertices of $\triangle ABC$ are $A(-6, 2)$, $B(-6, 5)$, and $C(-2, 4)$. Draw the reflection of $\triangle ABC$ across the y-axis. Give the coordinates of the reflection's vertices.

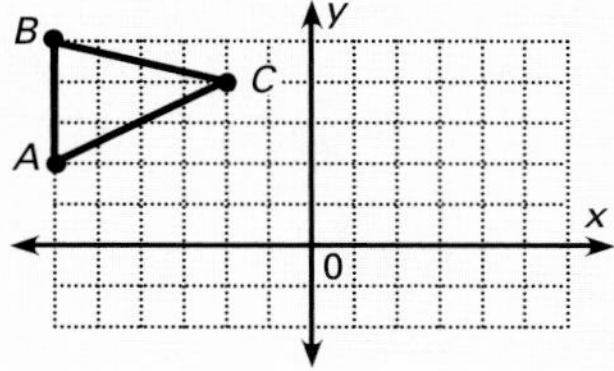

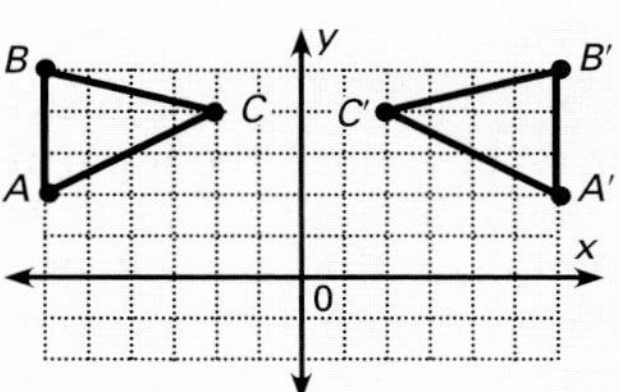

Reflection coordinates are $A'(6, 2)$, $B'(6, 5)$, and $C'(2, 4)$.

Answer for Try It

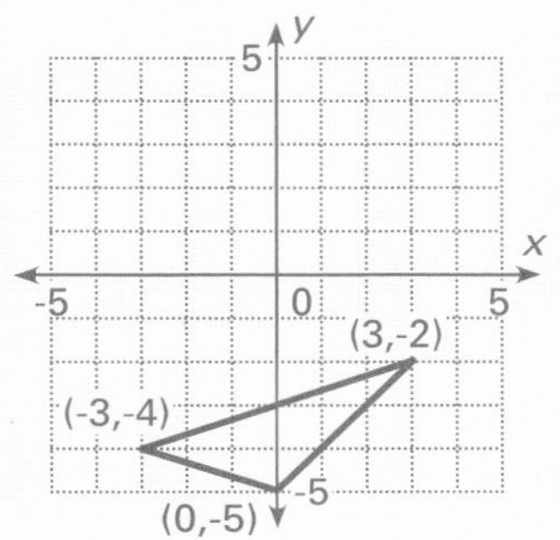

3 Practice and Assess

Check

Answers for Check Your Understanding

1. Possible answer: A figure with line symmetry has a line of symmetry that splits it into two parts, each a mirror image of the other. A reflection is a mirror image. A figure lacking line symmetry can have a reflection.
2. For every point on the polygon, draw a point on the other side of the line that is the same distance from the line as the matching point on the polygon. The reflection of the polygon will have the same shape.
3. If the original figure has line symmetry, the reflection will too. If the original figure does not, the reflection won't either.

11-11 Exercises and Applications

Assignment Guide

- Basic
  1–8, 10, 14, 15–23 odds
- Average
  2–10, 14, 16–24 evens
- Enriched
  4–15, 17–25 odds

Exercise Notes

Exercise 4

Error Prevention Some students will overlook the lines of symmetry through the vertices. Remind them that some lines of symmetry are neither horizontal or vertical.

Exercise Answers

Answers for Exercises 1–5 on page C6.

6. Answers should show two lines of symmetry, one vertical and one horizontal.

11-11 Exercises and Applications

PRACTICE 11-11

Practice and Apply

1. **Getting Started** Follow these steps to draw the reflection of $\triangle DEF$ across the *y*-axis.

a. Since the reflection is across the *y*-axis, find the coordinates of point D' by multiplying the *x*-coordinate of D by -1 and keeping the *y*-coordinate the same. Plot point D'.

b. Repeat **a** to plot points E' and F'.

c. Draw the reflected triangle $\triangle D'E'F'$ by connecting its vertices.

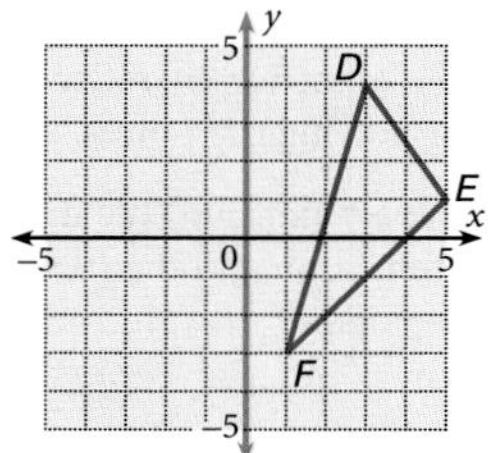

Geometry Decide whether each figure has line symmetry. If it does, copy the figure, then draw and number the lines of symmetry.

2. Equilateral triangle

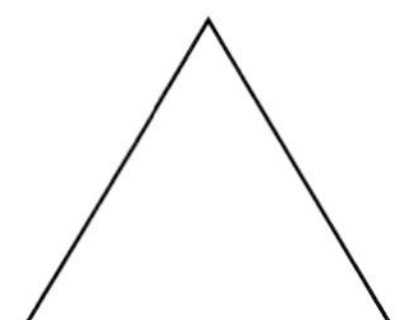

3. Rhombus

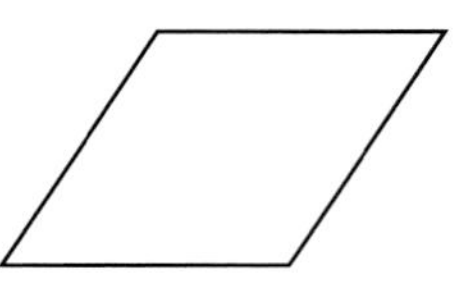

4. Regular octagon

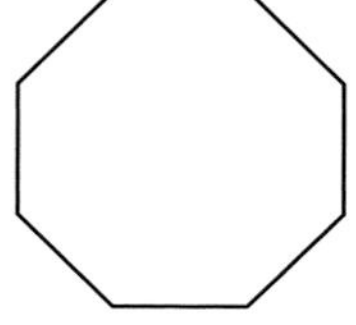

Decide whether each pattern or object has line symmetry. If it does, make a simplified copy of the figure, then draw and number the lines of symmetry.

5. Kaleidoscope pattern

6. **Science** Diatom (microscopic plant)

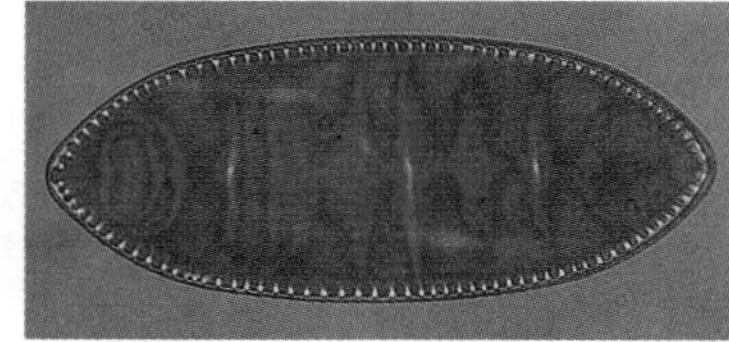

7. **Test Prep** If you reflect the point $(3, -5)$ over the *y*-axis, what are the coordinates of the reflection? B

Ⓐ $(3, 5)$ Ⓑ $(-3, -5)$ Ⓒ $(3, -5)$ Ⓓ $(-3, 5)$

PRACTICE

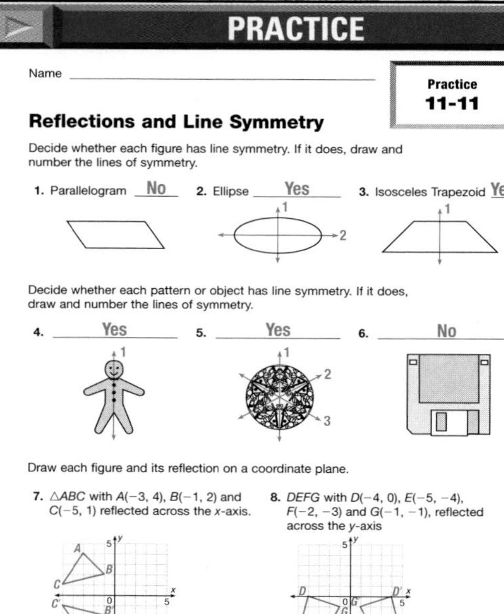

Name ______________________

Practice 11-11

Reflections and Line Symmetry

Decide whether each figure has line symmetry. If it does, draw and number the lines of symmetry.

1. Parallelogram No 2. Ellipse Yes 3. Isosceles Trapezoid Yes

Decide whether each pattern or object has line symmetry. If it does, draw and number the lines of symmetry.

4. Yes 5. Yes 6. No

Draw each figure and its reflection on a coordinate plane.

7. $\triangle ABC$ with $A(-3, 4)$, $B(-1, 2)$ and $C(-5, 1)$ reflected across the *x*-axis.

8. $DEFG$ with $D(-4, 0)$, $E(-5, -4)$, $F(-2, -3)$ and $G(-1, -1)$, reflected across the *y*-axis

Geography Tell how many lines of symmetry are in each flag.

9. Sweden 1 10. Japan 2 11. Trinidad and Tobago 0

RETEACHING

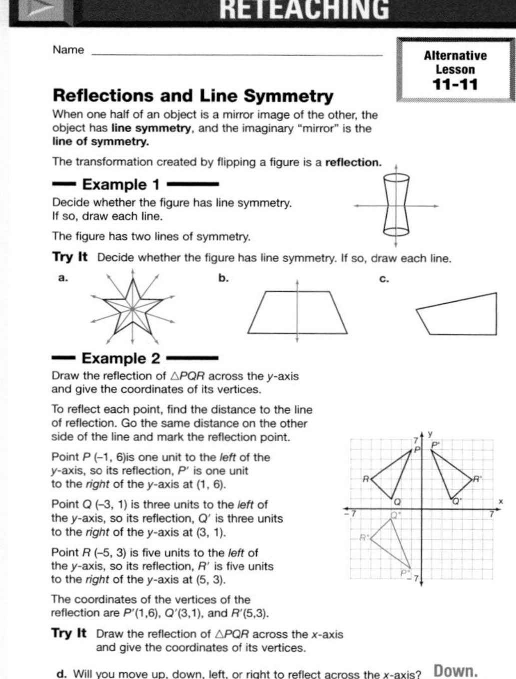

Name ______________________

Alternative Lesson 11-11

Reflections and Line Symmetry

When one half of an object is a mirror image of the other, the object has **line symmetry**, and the imaginary "mirror" is the **line of symmetry.**

The transformation created by flipping a figure is a **reflection.**

Example 1

Decide whether the figure has line symmetry. If so, draw each line.

The figure has two lines of symmetry.

Try It Decide whether the figure has line symmetry. If so, draw each line.

a. b. c.

Example 2

Draw the reflection of $\triangle PQR$ across the *y*-axis and give the coordinates of its vertices.

To reflect each point, find the distance to the line of reflection. Go the same distance on the other side of the line and mark the reflection point.

Point P (–1, 6)is one unit to the *left* of the *y*-axis, so its reflection, P' is one unit to the *right* of the *y*-axis at (1, 6).

Point Q (–3, 1) is three units to the *left* of the *y*-axis, so its reflection, Q' is three units to the *right* of the *y*-axis at (3, 1).

Point R (–5, 3) is five units to the *left* of the *y*-axis, so its reflection, R' is five units to the *right* of the *y*-axis at (5, 3).

The coordinates of the vertices of the reflection are $P'(1,6)$, $Q'(3,1)$, and $R'(5,3)$.

Try It Draw the reflection of $\triangle PQR$ across the *x*-axis and give the coordinates of its vertices.

d. Will you move up, down, left, or right to reflect across the *x*-axis? Down.

e. What are the coordinates of each point?

Point P'' (–1, –6) Point Q'' (–3, –1) Point R'' (–5, –3)

Reteaching

Activity

Materials: Graph paper

Work in groups of three. Use graph paper and follow these steps.

- One person first draws a triangle on the grid. The second person reflects the triangle across the *y*-axis.
- The third person uses the triangle from the preceding step and reflects it across the *x*-axis.
- Repeat the preceding steps but start with a different person in the group.

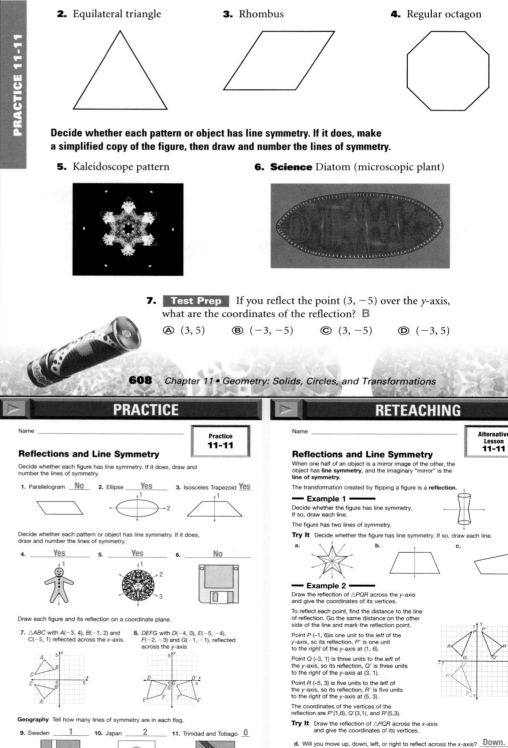

8. Draw the reflection of $\triangle JKL$ across the x-axis. Give the coordinates of the reflection's vertices.

9. Draw the reflection of $\triangle JKL$ across the y-axis. Give the coordinates of the reflection's vertices.

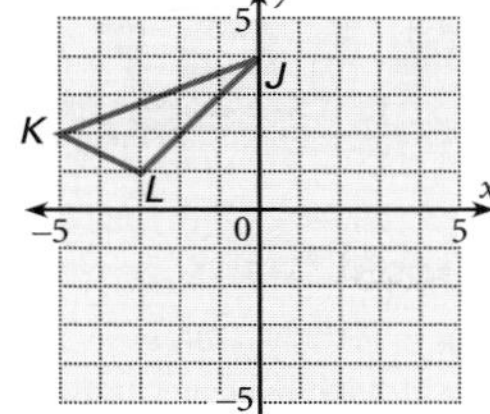

Draw each figure and its reflection on a coordinate plane.

10. $\triangle RST$ with $R(1, 3)$, $S(5, 4)$, and $T(4, 1)$, reflected across the y-axis.

11. $VWXY$ with $V(1, 2)$, $W(2, 4)$, $X(5, 5)$, and $Y(6, 1)$, reflected across the x-axis.

12. Geography Tell how many lines of symmetry there are in each state flag.

a. 
Arizona 1

b. 
Colorado 1

c. 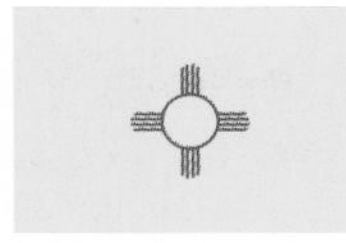
New Mexico 2

d. 
Texas 0

Problem Solving and Reasoning

13. Communicate Sketch regular polygons with different numbers of sides, and see how many lines of symmetry each has. What do you notice? Explain the pattern you see.

Look for a pattern.

14. Critical Thinking Draw a quadrilateral with exactly two lines of symmetry. What type did you draw? Are other types possible? Explain.

15. Journal Explain why reflecting a point across the x-axis multiplies its y-coordinate by -1 but does not change its x-coordinate.

PROBLEM SOLVING 11-11

Mixed Review

Suppose two figures are similar. For each scale factor of the smaller to the larger, find the unknown perimeter and area. *[Lesson 7-10]*

16. Scale factor $= \frac{1}{4}$, perimeter of smaller $= 15$ cm, area of smaller $= 9$ cm^2. Find the perimeter and area of the larger figure. perimeter = 60 cm; area = 144 cm^2

17. Scale factor $= \frac{1}{3}$, perimeter of larger $= 90$ in., area of larger $= 450$ in^2. Find the perimeter and area of the smaller figure. perimeter = 30 in.; area = 50 in.^{2}

Solve each equation. Check your solutions. *[Lesson 10-9]*

18. $-6 + x = 26$ $x = 32$

19. $m + 42 = -3$ $m = -45$

20. $t - 12 = 144$ $t = 156$

21. $y + 100 = 100$ $y = 0$

22. $-72 + a = 100$ $a = 172$

23. $d + (-4) = 38$ $d = 42$

24. $22 - r = 38$ $r = -16$

25. $17 - z = -35$ $z = 52$

PROBLEM SOLVING

Name ______

Guided Problem Solving 11-11

GPS PROBLEM 8, STUDENT PAGE 609

Draw the reflection of $\triangle JKL$ across the x-axis. Give the coordinates of the reflection's vertices.

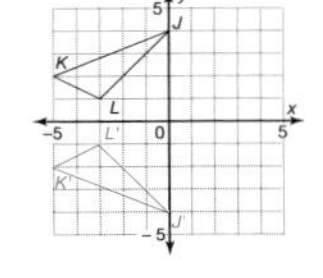

Understand

1. Which axis will you draw the reflection across? x-axis.
2. Will the x-coordinate or the y-coordinate change? y-coordinate.
3. Write the coordinates for each point.
   a. Point J (0, 4) b. Point K (–5, 2) c. Point L (–3, 1)

Plan

4. How many units above the x-axis is each point?
   a. Point J 4 units. b. Point K 2 units. c. Point L 1 unit.
5. How many units left of the y-axis is each point?
   a. Point J 0 units. b. Point K 5 units. c. Point L 3 units.

Solve

6. Draw the reflection of $\triangle JKL$ on the coordinate plane at the top of the page. Label the points J', K', and L'.
7. Write each coordinate.
   a. Point J' (0, –4) b. Point K' (–5, –2) c. Point L' (–3, 1)

Look Back

8. What is the line of symmetry in your reflection? x-axis.

SOLVE ANOTHER PROBLEM

Draw the reflection of $\triangle STU$ across the y-axis. Give the coordinates of the reflection's vertices.

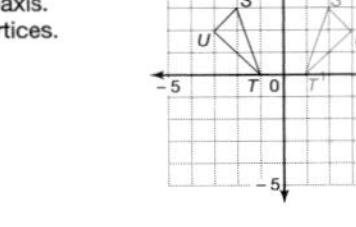

a. Point S' (2, 3)
b. Point T' (1, 0)
c. Point U' (3, 2)

ENRICHMENT

Name ______

Extend Your Thinking 11-11

Patterns in Geometry

Draw lines of symmetry for each regular polygon.

1. Lines of symmetry: 3 lines. 2. Lines of symmetry: 4 lines.

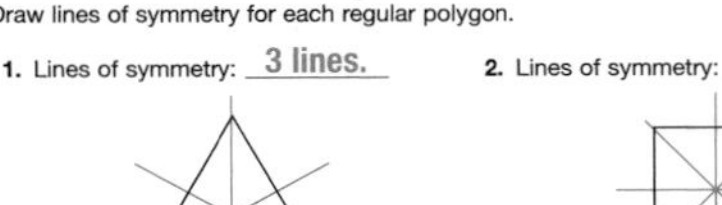

3. Lines of symmetry: 5 lines. 4. Lines of symmetry: 6 lines.

5. Lines of symmetry: 7 lines. 6. Lines of symmetry: 8 lines.

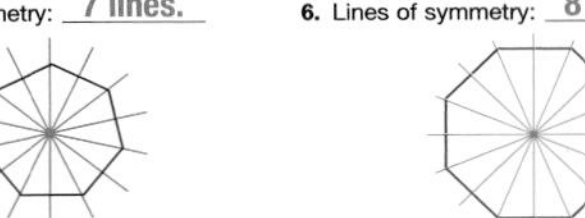

7. What pattern do you see in the lines of symmetry of the regular polygons? The number of lines of symmetry equals the number of sides.

8. Predict how many lines of symmetry you would find in a polygon with 12 sides. With 20 sides. With 100 sides. 12 lines of symmetry; 20 lines of symmetry; 100 lines of symmetry.

9. Do you think this pattern will be true for irregular polygons? On another sheet of paper, sketch some irregular figures to support your answer. Write *Yes* or *No* below each drawing. No. Check student's drawings.

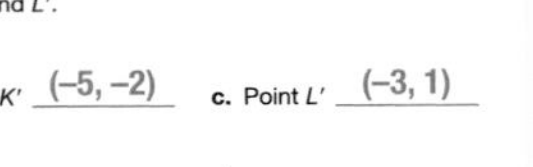

Exercise Answers

8–9. See page C6

10. 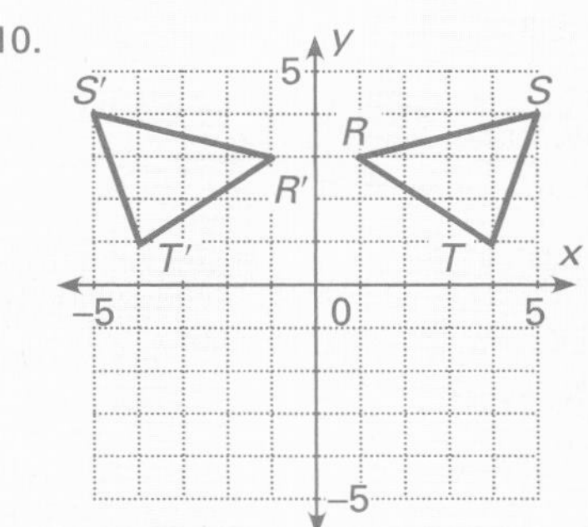

11. 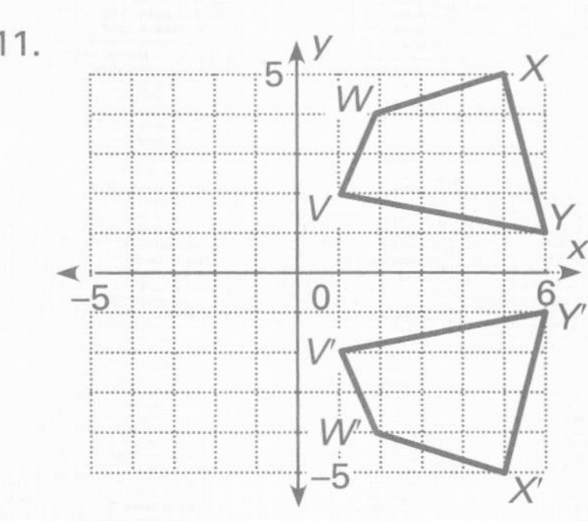

13. Regular polygons have the same number of lines of symmetry as they have sides.

14. Only a rectangle or a rhombus has exactly two lines of symmetry.

15. When you reflect a point across the x-axis, it does not move right or left, so its x-coordinate doesn't change. Its y-coordinate has the opposite sign since it is reflected from the positive to the negative or from the negative to the positive side of the y-axis.

Alternate Assessment

Self Assessment Have students write a paragraph explaining how reflecting a point across the x-axis is different from reflecting a point across the y-axis.

Quick Quiz

Draw $\triangle HJK$ with $H(-4, 0)$, $J(-6, 3)$, and $K(-2, 3)$. Then reflect it across the y-axis.

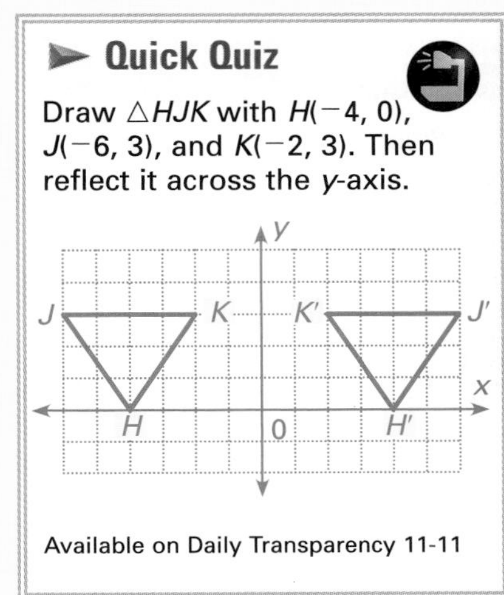

Available on Daily Transparency 11-11

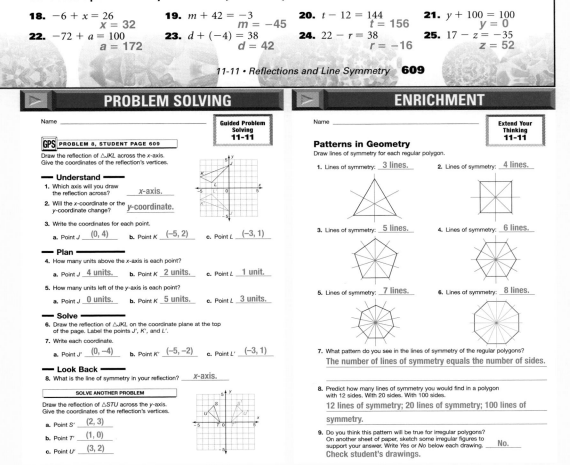

11-12 Lesson Organizer

Objectives

- Identify figures with rotational symmetry.
- Determine how far a figure has been rotated.
- Rotate figures on a coordinate plane.

Vocabulary

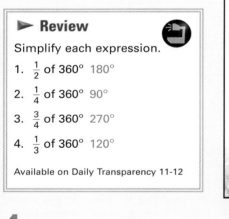

- Rotation, rotational symmetry, point symmetry

Materials

- Explore: Graph paper, push pin, ruler, scissors, cardboard

NCTM Standards

- 1–4, 12

Review

Simplify each expression.

1. $\frac{1}{2}$ of 360° 180°
2. $\frac{1}{4}$ of 360° 90°
3. $\frac{3}{4}$ of 360° 270°
4. $\frac{1}{3}$ of 360° 120°

Available on Daily Transparency 11-12

1 Introduce

Explore

The Point

Students explore rotations of polygons. They determine how many times rotated figures overlap themselves before returning to their starting positions.

Ongoing Assessment

Point out that overlap refers to the *shape* of the entire figure, not specific points on the figure. Specific points will not overlap until the figures rotate through 360°.

Answers for Explore

3. 3
4. 1 overlap
5. 5 overlaps

11-12 Rotations and Rotational Symmetry

You'll Learn ...

- to identify figures with rotational symmetry
- to determine how far a figure has been rotated
- to rotate figures on a coordinate plane

... How It's Used

Woodworkers use rotating lathes to create symmetric designs.

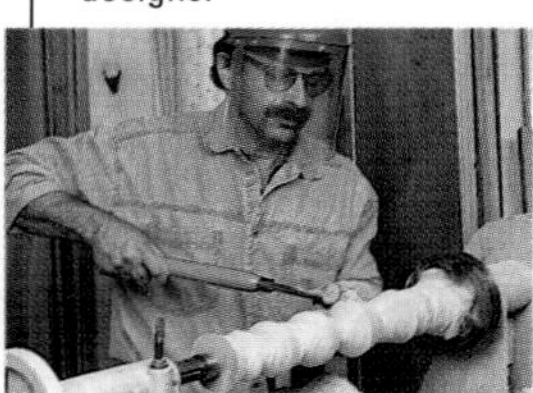

Vocabulary

rotation

rotational symmetry

point symmetry

Lesson Link You've explored translations and reflections. Now you'll see a transformation that turns a figure.

Explore The Symmetry of Turns

A Big Turnaround

Materials: Graph paper, Push pin, Ruler, Scissors, Cardboard

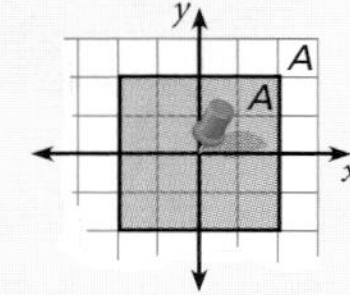

1. Set up *x*- and *y*-axes on a sheet of graph paper. Then cut a 4 by 4 square and a 2 by 4 rectangle out of another sheet.
2. Place the cardboard behind your coordinate plane. Use the push pin to attach the center of your square to the origin of the graph. Label the upper right vertex *A* on the graph paper *and* on the square. Trace around the square.
3. Turn the square clockwise until it matches its starting position. Notice where *A* is. Continue turning the square. How many perfect overlaps are there before the square returns to its starting position?
4. Repeat Steps 2 and 3 for the rectangle.
5. Trace and cut out the regular hexagon shown, then repeat Steps 2 and 3 for this figure.

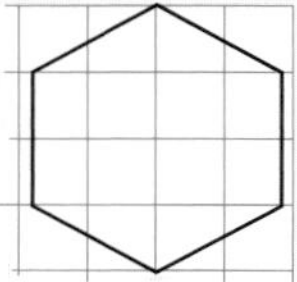

Learn Rotations and Rotational Symmetry

A **rotation** is a transformation that pivots a figure around a point. A full turn is a 360° rotation. So a $\frac{1}{4}$ turn is a 90° rotation, a $\frac{1}{2}$ turn is a 180° rotation, and a $\frac{3}{4}$ turn is a 270° rotation.

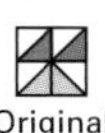
Original position

90° clockwise rotation

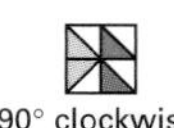
180° clockwise rotation

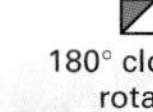
270° clockwise rotation

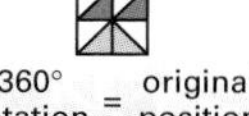
360° rotation = original position

MEETING INDIVIDUAL NEEDS

Resources

- 11-12 Practice
- 11-12 Reteaching
- 11-12 Problem Solving
- 11-12 Enrichment
- 11-12 Daily Transparency
  - Problem of the Day
  - Review
  - Quick Quiz
- Lesson Enhancement Transparency 60
- Chapter 11 Project Master
- Technology Master 61

Learning Modalities

Visual Have students make a bulletin board display of photos or drawings that illustrate rotational symmetry.

Kinesthetic Have students cut out cardboard figures of various shapes and rotate them through different fractional turns to determine if any have rotational symmetry.

English Language Development

Have students discuss various objects that rotate or turn around a fixed point. Then have them discuss how this is related to rotational symmetry. Have students write and illustrate their explanations.

A figure has **rotational symmetry** if a rotation of less than 360° rotates the figure onto itself. If a figure has 180° (half-turn) rotational symmetry, it has **point symmetry**.

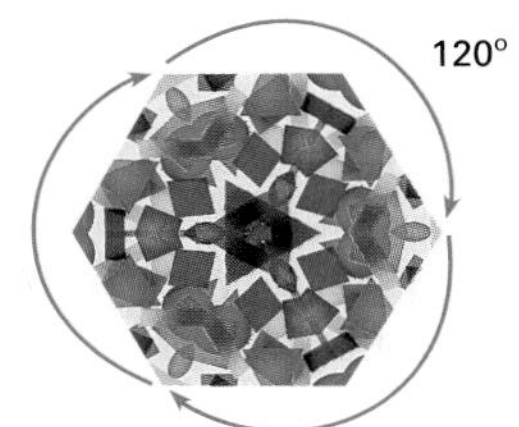

Examples

1 Decide whether this parallelogram has rotational symmetry. If it does, name all clockwise fractional turns that rotate the figure onto itself.

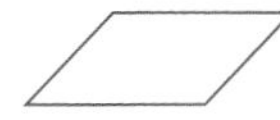

Imagine the figure rotating around its center. The original figure is shown in blue.

$\frac{1}{4}$ turn — $\frac{1}{2}$ turn **overlaps** — $\frac{3}{4}$ turn

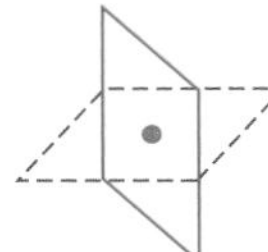
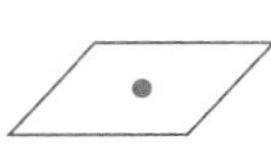
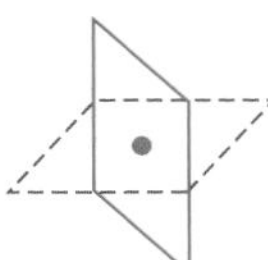

The parallelogram has half-turn rotational symmetry (point symmetry).

2 Give the smallest fractional turn that this figure has been rotated clockwise. Then express your answer in degrees.

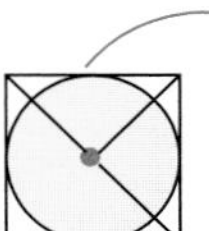
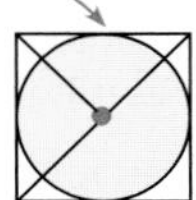

Imagine the figure rotating around its center.

$\frac{1}{4}$ turn — $\frac{1}{2}$ turn — $\frac{3}{4}$ turn

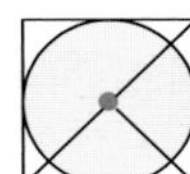
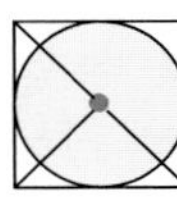
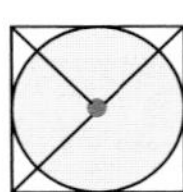

The figure has been rotated $\frac{3}{4}$ of a turn, or 270°.

Try It

Decide whether this trapezoid has rotational symmetry. If it does, name all clockwise fractional turns that rotate the figure onto itself. No

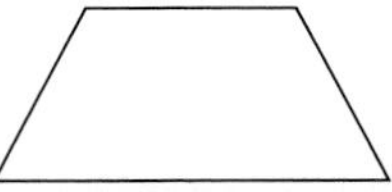

Science Link

Different arrangements of mirrors in a kaleidoscope produce different types of images. Three-mirror kaleidoscopes produce patterns with 120° and 240° rotational symmetry.

DID YOU KNOW?

When someone says an object has "symmetry," they usually mean it has *line* symmetry.

2 Teach

Learn

You may wish to use Lesson Enhancement Transparency 60 with **Learn**.

Alternate Examples

1. Decide whether this figure has rotational symmetry. If it does, name the clockwise fractional turn(s) that rotate the figure onto itself.

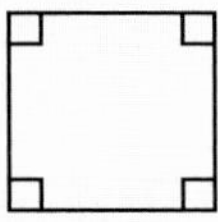

Imagine the figure rotating about its center.

$\frac{1}{4}$ turn — $\frac{1}{2}$ turn — $\frac{3}{4}$ turn

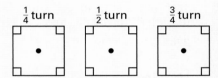

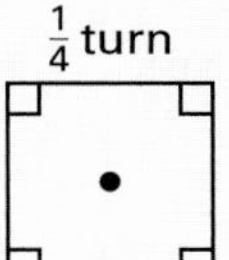
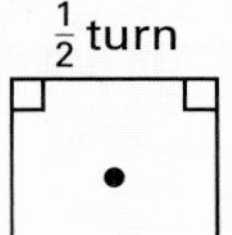
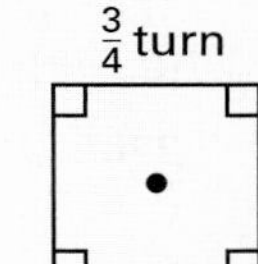

The figure rotates onto itself after $\frac{1}{4}$ turn, $\frac{1}{2}$ turn, and $\frac{3}{4}$ turn. It has rotational symmetry.

2. Give the smallest fractional turn that this figure has been rotated clockwise. Then express your answer in degrees.

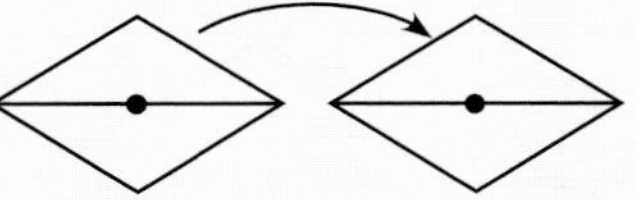

Imagine the figure rotating around its center.

$\frac{1}{4}$ turn — $\frac{1}{2}$ turn — $\frac{3}{4}$ turn

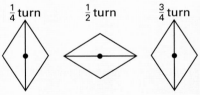

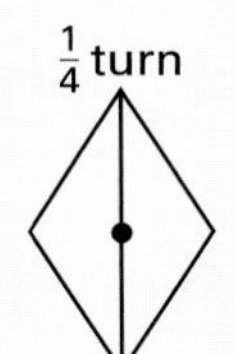
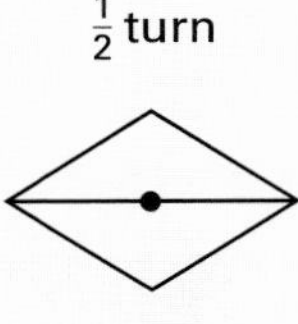
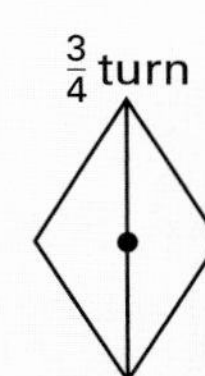

The figure has been rotated $\frac{1}{2}$ turn or 180°.

MATH EVERY DAY

Problem of the Day

Insert the numbers from 1 to 16 to make a magic square. What is the sum of each row, column and diagonal? Some numbers have been given to help you get started.

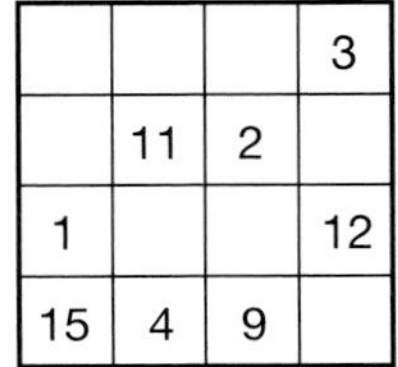

			3
	11	2	
1			12
15	4	9	

10	5	16	3
8	11	2	13
1	14	7	12
15	4	9	6

Magic sum = 34

Available on Daily Transparency 11-12

An Extension is provided in the transparency package.

Fact of the Day

Mathematician and graphic artist M.C. Escher was known for creating designs using rotations and tessellations.

Mental Math

Do these mentally.

1. 540 ÷ 60 9
2. 6300 ÷ 70 90
3. 72,000 ÷ 8 9000
4. 140,000 ÷ 20 7000
5. 210,000 ÷ 3000 70

Alternate Example

3. Give the coordinates of rotations of $\triangle DEF$ after clockwise rotations of 90° ($\frac{1}{4}$ turn), 180° ($\frac{1}{2}$ turn), and 270° ($\frac{3}{4}$ turn) around the origin.

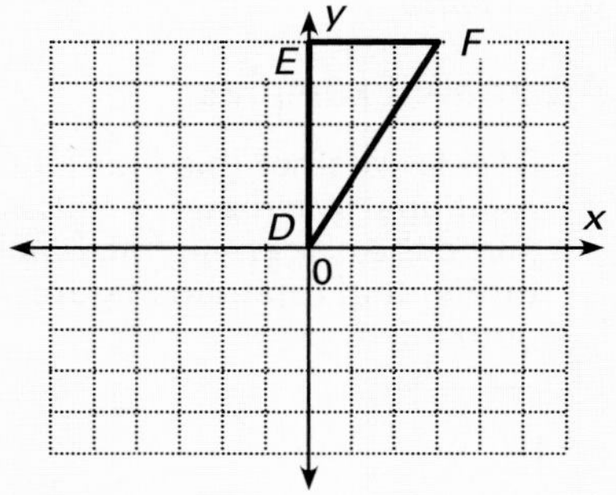

90°: D' is at (0, 0). E' is on the x-axis. E' is at (5, 0). F' is at (5, −3).

180°: D'' is at (0, 0). E'' is at (0, −5). F'' is at (−3, −5).

270°: D''' is at (0, 0). E''' is at (−5, 0). F''' is at (−5, 3).

360°: The triangle is back in its original position, with vertex coordinates (0, 0), (0, 5), and (3, 5).

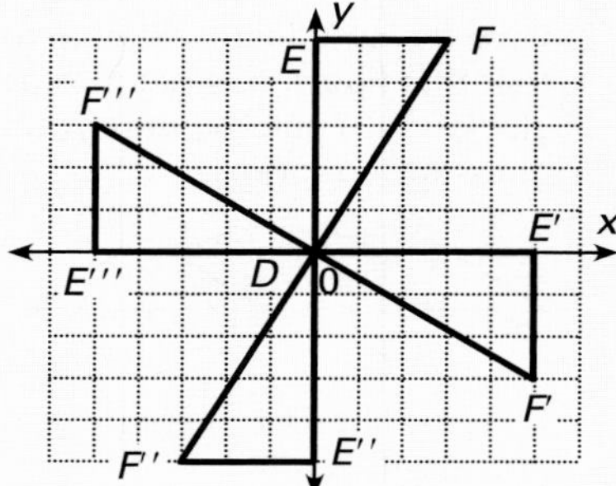

You can use coordinates to help describe rotations.

Study TIP

It is helpful to remember that a 90° rotation of a point on the x-axis falls on the y-axis, and vice versa.

Example 3

Give the coordinates of rotations of $\triangle RST$ after clockwise rotations of 90° ($\frac{1}{4}$ turn), 180° ($\frac{1}{2}$ turn), 270° ($\frac{3}{4}$ turn), and 360° (full turn) around the origin.

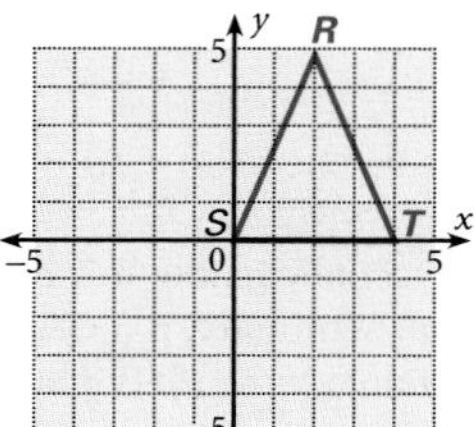

90°: Since S is the center of the rotation, its "rotations" do not move. So S' is at (0, 0). T' is on the y-axis. It is still 4 units from the origin, so T' is at (0, −4). R' is at (5, −2).

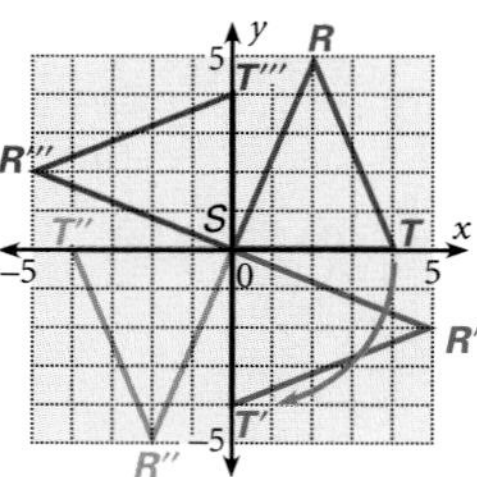

180°: S'' is at (0, 0). T'' is on the negative side of the x-axis, 4 units from S, at (−4, 0). R'' is at (−2, −5).

270°: S''' is at (0, 0). T''' is on the positive side of the y-axis, so its coordinates are (0, 4). R''' is at (−5, 2).

360°: The triangle is back in its original position, with vertex coordinates (0, 0), (4, 0), and (2, 5).

DID YOU KNOW?

Some kaleidoscopes do not contain beads, but reflect images from the outside world. They are called *teleidoscopes.* The image on page 615 comes from a teleidoscope.

Notice that the *shape* of a figure does not change as it is rotated.

When you rotate an object, the only point that does not move is the center of the rotation. You can use this fact to identify the center of a rotation.

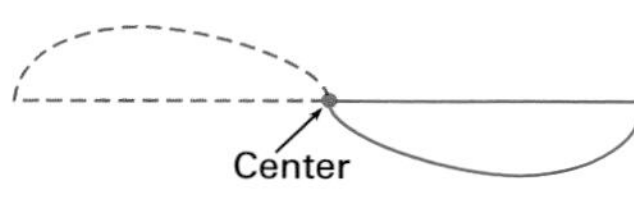

Check Your Understanding

1. What happens when you rotate a figure 360°?
2. Identify some objects in your classroom that have rotational symmetry.
3. If a figure has point symmetry, does it have rotational symmetry? If it has rotational symmetry, does it have point symmetry? Explain your answer.
4. Is it possible for a figure to have line symmetry but not rotational symmetry? If it is, sketch such a figure; if not, explain why it is not possible.

3 Practice and Assess

Check

Answers for Check Your Understanding

1. It returns to its original position.
2. Possible answers: Clocks, desks, floor tiles, posters.
3. A figure with point symmetry has rotational symmetry. A figure with rotational symmetry does not have to have point symmetry.
4. Yes;

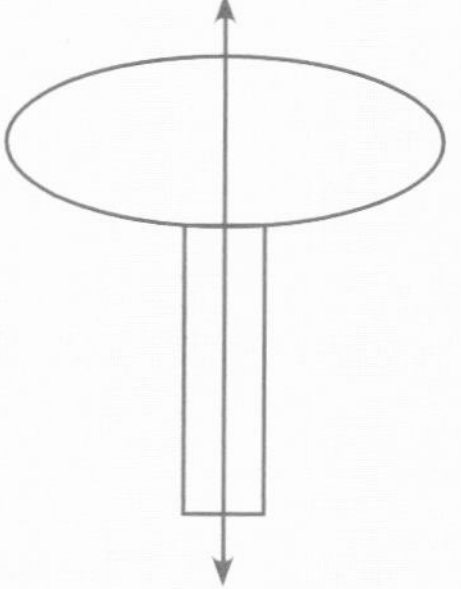

MEETING MIDDLE SCHOOL CLASSROOM NEEDS

Tips from Middle School Teachers

I find that paper plates make a great tool for helping students understand rotational symmetry. The plates can be marked in various ways with ink markers to illustrate figures with different types of rotational symmetry.

Team Teaching

Work with an art teacher to show various designs illustrating rotational symmetry.

Cultural Connection

Have students from various cultures bring examples of crafts or artwork that illustrate rotational symmetry.

11-12 Exercises and Applications

Practice and Apply

1. **Getting Started** Follow the steps to decide whether the figure has rotational symmetry.

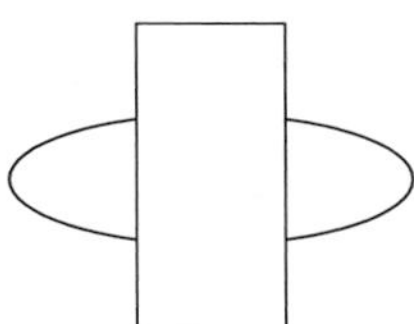

a. Copy the original figure.

b. Slowly rotate your copy. As you turn the figure, check to see whether it matches the original. Be especially sure to check after each $\frac{1}{4}$ turn.

c. If the copy matches the original at any time before you have made a full turn, it has rotational symmetry.

Decide whether each figure has rotational symmetry. If it does, name all clockwise fractional turns that rotate the figure onto itself.

2. Square $\frac{1}{4}, \frac{1}{2}, \frac{3}{4}$

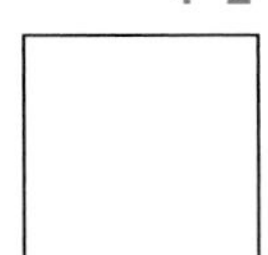

3. Parallelogram $\frac{1}{2}$

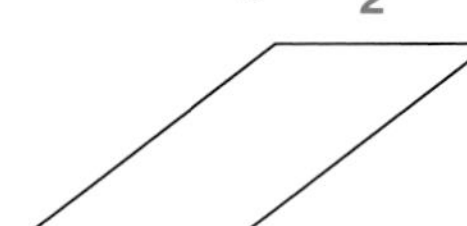

4. Isosceles triangle None

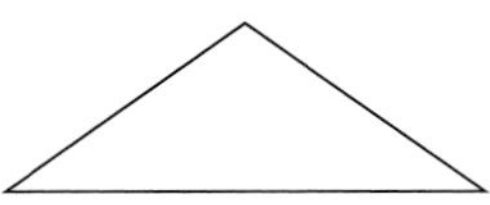

5. Computer-generated kaleidoscope pattern

$\frac{1}{4}, \frac{1}{2}, \frac{3}{4}$

6. **Fine Arts** Ellsworth Kelly's *Blue, Green, Yellow, Orange, Red* None

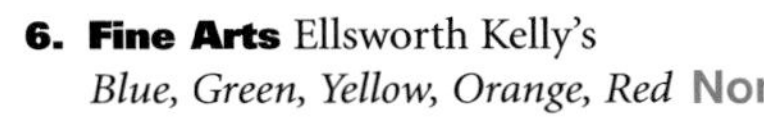

7. List all the images in Exercises 2–6 that have point symmetry. 2, 3, 5

8. On a coordinate plane, draw rectangle $WXYZ$ with $W(0, 0)$, $X(2, 0)$, $Y(2, 3)$, and $Z(0, 3)$. Give the coordinates of rotations of $WXYZ$ after clockwise rotations around the origin of:

a. 90° $\left(\frac{1}{4}\text{ turn}\right)$ **b.** 180° $\left(\frac{1}{2}\text{ turn}\right)$ **c.** 270° $\left(\frac{3}{4}\text{ turn}\right)$ **d.** 360° (full turn)

9. **Test Prep** How many degrees does $\frac{3}{4}$ of a rotation represent? C

Ⓐ 90° Ⓑ 180° Ⓒ 270° Ⓓ 360°

PRACTICE 11-12

11-12 Exercises and Applications

Assignment Guide

- **Basic**
  1–12, 13–15, 16–26 evens
- **Average**
  2–11, 13–15, 17–25 odds
- **Enriched**
  3–15, 17–26

Exercise Notes

Exercises 7

Error Prevention Some students may think that for a figure to have point symmetry, it must have only 180° rotational symmetry. Point out that it might also have other rotational symmetries.

Exercise Answers

1. Yes, it has 180° rotational symmetry.

8.

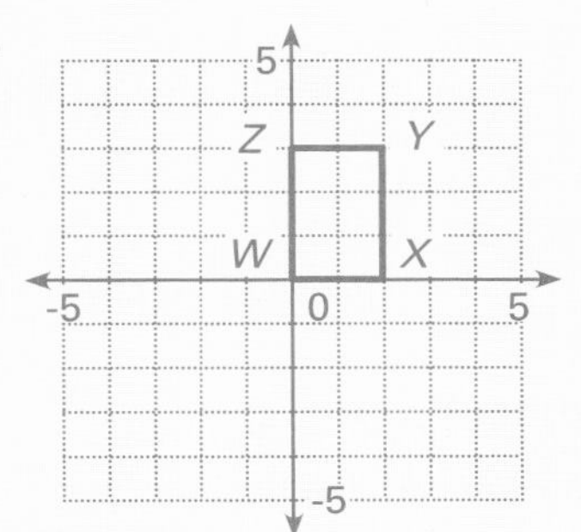

a. $W'(0, 0)$, $X'(0, -2)$, $Y'(3, -2)$, $Z'(3, 0)$

b. $W''(0, 0)$, $X''(-2, 0)$, $Y''(-2, -3)$, $Z''(0, -3)$

c. $W'''(0, 0)$, $X'''(0, 2)$, $Y'''(-3, 2)$, $Z'''(-3, 0)$

d. $W(0, 0)$, $X(2, 0)$, $Y(2, 3)$, $Z(0, 3)$

PRACTICE

Name ______________________

Practice 11-12

Rotations and Rotational Symmetry

Decide whether each figure has rotational symmetry. If it does, name the fractional turns that rotate the figure onto itself.

1. Rhombus Yes; $\frac{1}{2}$ turn 2. Rectangle Yes; $\frac{1}{2}$ turn 3. Scalene triangle No

4. List all of the images in Exercises **1–3** that have point symmetry. 1, 2

Give the smallest fractional turn that each figure has been rotated clockwise. Express your answer in degrees.

5. Clock face 90° 6. Dumb bell 180° 7. Puerto Rican flag 360°

8. Give the coordinates of $\triangle PQR$ after clockwise rotations around the origin of:

a. 90° $\left(\frac{1}{4}\text{ turn}\right)$ P' (4, −2) Q' (5, −4) R' (1, −4)

b. 180° $\left(\frac{1}{2}\text{ turn}\right)$ P'' (−2, −4) Q'' (−4, −5) R'' (−4, −1)

c. 270° $\left(\frac{3}{4}\text{ turn}\right)$ P''' (−4, 2) Q''' (−5, 4) R''' (−1, 4)

d. 360° (full turn) P'''' (2, 4) Q'''' (4, 5) R'''' (4, 1)

9. Draw rectangle $STUV$ with $S(0, 3)$, $T(1, 4)$, $U(3, 2)$ and $V(2, 1)$. Give the coordinates of rotations of $STUV$ after clockwise rotations of:

a. 90° $\left(\frac{1}{4}\text{ turn}\right)$ S' (3, 0) T' (4, −1) U' (2, −3) V' (1, −2)

b. 180° $\left(\frac{1}{2}\text{ turn}\right)$ S'' (0, −3) T'' (−1, −4) U'' (−3, −2) V'' (−2, −1)

c. 270° $\left(\frac{3}{4}\text{ turn}\right)$ S''' (−3, 0) T''' (−4, 1) U''' (−2, 3) V''' (−1, 2)

d. 360° (full turn) S'''' (0, 3) T'''' (1, 4) U'''' (3, 2) V'''' (2, 1)

RETEACHING

Name ______________________

Alternative Lesson 11-12

Rotations and Rotational Symmetry

A **rotation** is a transformation that pivots a figure around a point. A full turn is a 360° rotation.

Original position | $\frac{1}{4}$ clockwise turn 90° clockwise rotation | $\frac{1}{2}$ clockwise turn 180° clockwise rotation | $\frac{3}{4}$ clockwise turn 270° clockwise rotation | Full turn 360° rotation

A figure has **rotational symmetry** if a rotation of less than 360° rotates the figure onto itself.

Example 1

Decide whether the figure has rotational symmetry. If it does, name all clockwise fractional turns that rotate the figure onto itself.

Imagine the figure rotating around its center. Turn the figure until it rotates onto itself.

$\frac{1}{4}$ turn $\frac{1}{2}$ turn $\frac{3}{4}$ turn

The figure has rotational symmetry. It overlaps at $\frac{1}{4}$ turn, $\frac{1}{2}$ turn, and $\frac{3}{4}$ turn.

Try It Decide whether each figure has rotational symmetry. If it does, name all clockwise fractional turns that rotate the figure onto itself. If you need help, cut out the figure and turn it to see the overlaps.

a. Yes, $\frac{1}{2}$ turn. b. No. c. Yes, $\frac{1}{4}, \frac{1}{2}, \frac{3}{4}$ turns.

Example 2

Give the smallest fractional turn that each figure has been rotated clockwise. Then express your answer in degrees.

Imagine the figure rotating around its center.

The figure has been rotated $\frac{1}{2}$ turn, which is a 180° rotation.

Try It Give the smallest fractional turn that each figure has been rotated clockwise. Then express your answer in degrees. If you need help, cut out the figure and turn it to see the overlaps.

d. $\frac{1}{4}$ turn, 90° e. Full turn, 360° f. $\frac{1}{2}$ turn, 180°

Reteaching

Activity

Work in groups of four. Use graph paper and follow these steps.

- One person first draws a triangle on the grid.
- The second person rotates the triangle 90° clockwise.
- The third person takes the triangle and rotates it another 90° clockwise.
- The fourth person takes the triangle and rotates it another 90° clockwise.
- Repeat the preceding steps but start with a different person in the group.

Exercise Answers

13. a. $D'(0, 0)$, $E'(4, -1)$, $F'(0, -3)$
    b. $D''(0, 0)$, $E''(-1, -4)$, $F''(-3, 0)$
    c. $D'''(0, 0)$, $E'''(-4, 1)$, $F'''(0, 3)$
14. Possible answer: A reflection reverses the orientation of a figure; a rotation preserves its orientation. For example, if the vertices of $\triangle ABC$ read A,B,C in a clockwise direction, the vertices of $\triangle A'B'C'$ read A',C',B' for a reflection, but still read A',B',C' for a rotation.
15. a. $\frac{1}{3}, \frac{2}{3}$
    b. $\frac{1}{4}, \frac{1}{2}, \frac{3}{4}$
    c. $\frac{1}{5}, \frac{2}{5}, \frac{3}{5}, \frac{4}{5}$
    d. $\frac{1}{6}, \frac{1}{3}, \frac{1}{2}, \frac{2}{3}, \frac{5}{6}$
    e. A regular polygon with n sides has rotational symmetry for every multiple of the quotient of $\frac{360°}{n}$.
16. $\frac{30}{100} = \frac{x}{220}$; $x = 66$
17. $\frac{x}{100} = \frac{25}{125}$; $x = 20$
18. $\frac{5}{100} = \frac{12}{x}$; $x = 240$

Project Progress

You may want to have students use Chapter 11 Project Master.

Alternate Assessment

Project Have students draw diagrams to illustrate one figure with 90° rotational symmetry, another figure with 180° rotational symmetry, and one with no rotational symmetry.

Quick Quiz

Decide whether each figure has rotational symmetry. If it does, name the clockwise fractional turns that rotate the figure onto itself.

1. 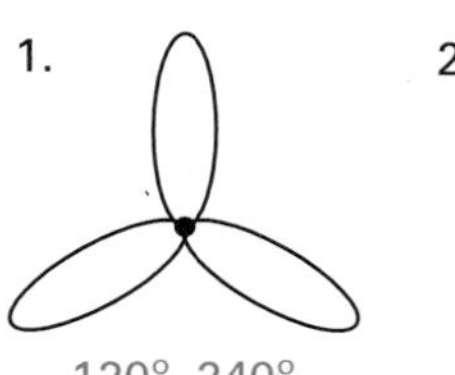
   120°, 240°
2. 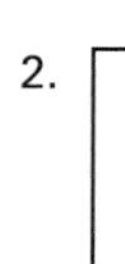
   No

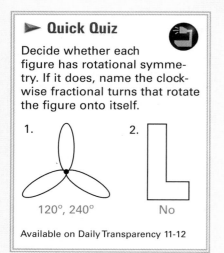

Available on Daily Transparency 11-12

Give the smallest fractional turn that each figure has been rotated clockwise. Then express your answer in degrees.

10. Social Studies Swiss flag 90°

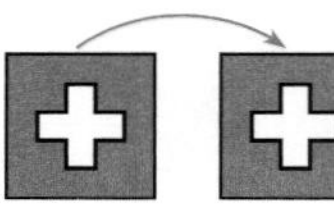

11. 180°

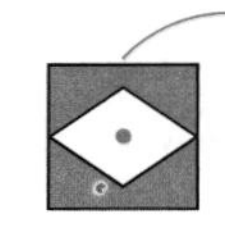
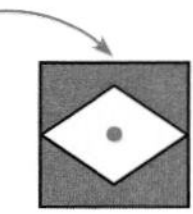

12. Science Water (H_2O) molecule None

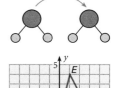

13. Give the coordinates of rotations of $\triangle DEF$ after clockwise rotations around the origin of:

a. 90° $\left(\frac{1}{4}\text{ turn}\right)$ **b.** 180° $\left(\frac{1}{2}\text{ turn}\right)$ **c.** 270° $\left(\frac{3}{4}\text{ turn}\right)$

Problem Solving and Reasoning

14. Critical Thinking How can you tell if a figure has been rotated 180° or reflected over a line?

15. Communicate Decide whether each of these regular polygons has rotational symmetry. If it does, name all clockwise fractional turns that rotate the figure onto itself.

a. Equilateral triangle **b.** Square **c.** Regular pentagon **d.** Regular hexagon

e. What pattern of rotational symmetry is there for regular polygons?

Mixed Review

Write a proportion and solve each problem. If necessary, round answers to the nearest tenth. *[Lesson 8-6]*

16. What is 30% of 220? **17.** 25 is what percent of 125? **18.** 12 is 5% of what number?

Solve each equation. Check your solutions. *[Lesson 10-10]*

19. $5x = 105$ $x = 21$
20. $\frac{y}{12} = 3$ $y = 36$
21. $4m = 52$ $m = 13$
22. $\frac{g}{-3} = 5$ $g = -15$
23. $7v = 56$ $v = 8$
24. $\frac{h}{11} = 11$ $h = 121$
25. $-12x = 12$ $x = -1$
26. $15n = 30$ $n = 2$

Project Progress

Decide which of your containers you prefer. Then design a label for your container, using transformations and symmetry. Finally, copy the net for the container you chose, decorate it with the label design, and make the container.

Problem Solving: Understand, Plan, Solve, Look Back

PROBLEM SOLVING

Name ____________

Guided Problem Solving 11-12

GPS PROBLEM 15, STUDENT PAGE 614

Decide whether each of these regular polygons has rotational symmetry. If it does, name all clockwise fractional turns that rotate the figure onto itself.

a. Equilateral triangle b. Square
c. Regular pentagon d. Regular hexagon
e. What pattern of rotational symmetry is there for regular polygons?

— Understand — Possible answers: Items 4 and 5

1. What do equilateral triangles, squares, and other regular polygons have in common? Sides and angles within each figure have the same measure.

— Plan —

2. Sketch each regular polygon.

Equilateral triangle Square Pentagon Hexagon

— Solve —

3. Imagine each polygon rotating around its center. Then complete the table. Write *yes* or *no* to describe the rotational symmetry.

	Triangle	Square	Pentagon	Hexagon
Rotational symmetry	Yes.	Yes.	Yes.	Yes.
Fractional turns	$\frac{1}{3}, \frac{2}{3}$	$\frac{1}{4}, \frac{1}{2}, \frac{3}{4}$	$\frac{1}{5}, \frac{2}{5}, \frac{3}{5}, \frac{4}{5}$	$\frac{1}{6}, \frac{1}{3}, \frac{1}{2}, \frac{2}{3}, \frac{5}{6}$

4. What pattern of rotational symmetry is there for regular polygons? Each turn is $\frac{1}{\text{number of sides}}$.

— Look Back —

5. How could you prove your answer to someone who doesn't understand rotational symmetry? Model with cut-outs.

SOLVE ANOTHER PROBLEM

Possible answer:

What clockwise fractional turns would rotate a regular octagon onto itself? Explain.

$\frac{1}{8}, \frac{1}{4}, \frac{3}{8}, \frac{1}{2}, \frac{5}{8}, \frac{3}{4}, \frac{7}{8}$; Number of rotations to return to original position is 8, each turn is $\frac{1}{8}$.

ENRICHMENT

Name ____________

Extend Your Thinking 11-12

Decision Making

For their community service project, a group of ten students are going to paint a mural.

Three businesses have agreed to let the students paint a mural on one of their walls. The students can paint part of a wood fence around the library, the front wall of a parking garage, or a wall at the animal shelter that faces a popular bus route.

Possible answers: Items 1-5

1. Which location do you think is the best place to paint the mural? Explain your reasoning.
   Animal shelter because it is visible to more people.
2. Your group will have two four-hour time periods and five cans of paint to complete the mural. Each can will cover 200 square feet. What size do you think the mural should be? Why?
   a. Give the dimensions of the largest size mural you can make. Explain.
   10 ft by 100 ft, since 5 cans cover 1000 sq ft.
   b. What size section will each student paint if each paints a same-size section?
   Each student paints a 10-ft by 10-ft section.
3. Why might you want to paint a smaller mural?
   Section may be easier to draw and paint in allotted time; you can give greater attention to detail; you can use more coats of paint if necessary.
4. The border of the mural will be drawn using a transformation. Show the border you would use. Identify each transformation.
   Check students' answers.

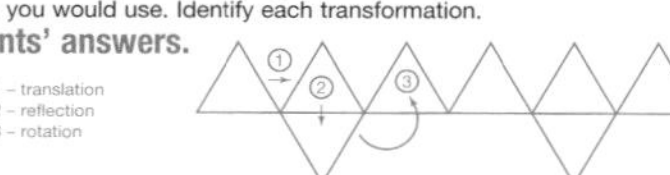

5. What do you need to plan before you get to the location? Why is it important to plan each of these things? What the mural will look like, who will perform each activity, the time needed to clean up, transportation; Important, so that the mural can be completed in the time frame.

Section 11C Connect

You've used reflections, rotations, and translations to transform objects. Now you'll use transformations to create a kaleidoscopic tessellation.

When Worlds Kaleide

A *tessellation* is a pattern of congruent shapes that covers a flat surface without gaps or overlaps.

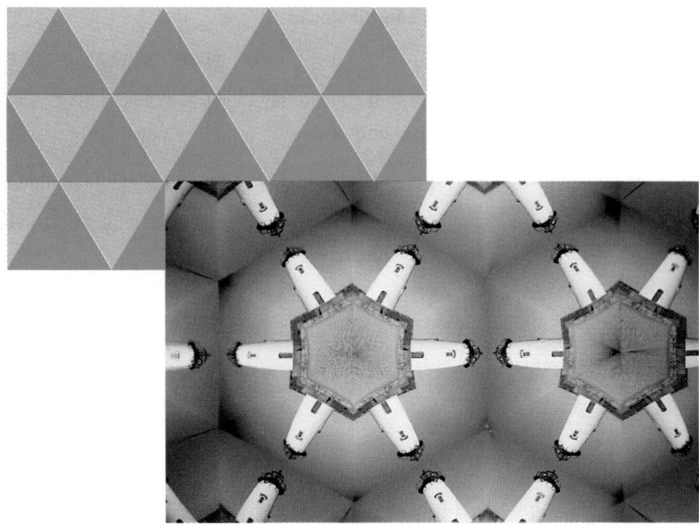

1. Look at the kaleidoscope pattern that tessellates. Identify the basic (largest) geometric figure in the kaleidoscope tessellation.
2. Examine the pattern within one of the basic figures (*cells*) you identified in Step 1. Describe some of the symmetries—line or rotational—you see.
3. Design one cell of a simple kaleidoscope pattern that uses at least one transformation. Then repeat the pattern to make a tessellation.

When Worlds Kaleide

The Point

In *When Worlds Kaleide* on page 599 students discussed kaleidoscopes. Now they use transformations to design a kaleidoscope tessellation.

About the Page

- Discuss rotational symmetry and how it is used in a kaleidoscope.
- Ask students the shape of the pattern they will use in their tessellation. Ask them if a square, rectangle, or pentagon could be the pattern shape for their kaleidoscope tessellation.
- Remind students that some kaleidoscopes use mirrors to create the different images seen in a kaleidoscope.
- Have students use a mirror to reflect their pattern and design and to see the mirror image created.

Ongoing Assessment

Check that students have drawn a reasonable tessellation for a kaleidoscope.

Extension

After students have designed their tessellations, have them use markers or colored pencils to enhance the beauty of their designs. Display the designs in the classroom.

Answers for Connect

1. Hexagon
2. Clockwise rotational symmetry of 60°, 120°, 180°, 240°, and 300°. 6 lines of symmetry: 3 through pairs of opposite vertices of the hexagon, 3 through centers of lighthouses.
3. Answers may vary.

11C Review

Review Correlation

Item(s)	Lesson(s)
1	11-11
2	11-12
3, 4	11-10
5, 6	11-11, 11-12
7	11-12

Test Prep

Test-Taking Tip

Tell students that they can act out some problems. Here, students could trace each shape on a piece of scratch paper and test each by turning it about a pencil point.

Answers for Review

1. 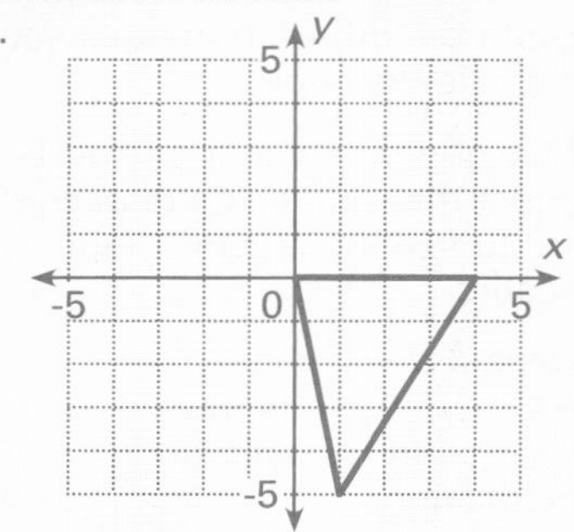

Coordinates of vertices: (0, 0), (1, −5), (4, 0)

2. a. (0, 0), (5, −1), (0, −4)
   b. (0, 0), (−1, −5), (−4, 0)
   c. (0, 0), (−5, 1), (0, 4)
   d. (0, 0), (1, 5), (4, 0)

5. Students may identify many different translations, rotations, and reflections. Each part of the image has a corresponding translation about 1 in. to its right. Several lines of reflection can be identified (at angles of 0°, 60°, and 120° to the vertical). The hexagonal cells of the image have rotational symmetries of 120° and 240°.

Section 11C Review

REVIEW 11C

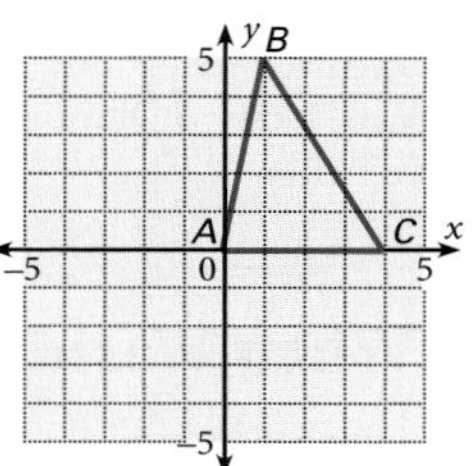

1. Copy the coordinate plane and draw the reflection of $\triangle ABC$ across the x-axis. Give the coordinates of the reflection's vertices.
2. Give the coordinates of rotations of $\triangle ABC$ after clockwise rotations around the origin of:
   a. $90° \left(\frac{1}{4} \text{ turn}\right)$
   b. $180° \left(\frac{1}{2} \text{ turn}\right)$
   c. $270° \left(\frac{3}{4} \text{ turn}\right)$
   d. $360°$ (full turn)

Point D is at (−4, −1). Use each translation rule to find the coordinates of D'.

3. $(x, y) \rightarrow (x + 5, y + 3)$ (1, 2)
4. $(x, y) \rightarrow (x - 3, y - 4)$ (−7, −5)

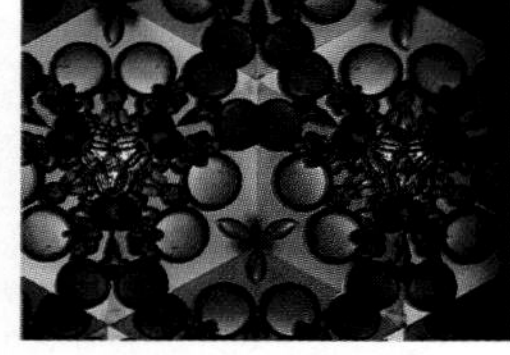

5. Explain how the kaleidoscope image shows reflections and rotations.
6. **Language Arts** The Cyrillic alphabet is used in Russia and other Eastern European countries. Ten of its thirty-two letters are shown.

Б Д Е Ж И К П Ф т Щ

   a. Which letters have a horizontal line of symmetry? 3rd, 4th, 8th
   b. Which letters have a vertical line of symmetry? 4th, 7th, 8th, 9th
   c. Which letters have rotational symmetry? 4th, 5th, 8th

Test Prep

When you are asked to identify a figure with point symmetry on a multiple choice test, remember that point symmetry means half-turn rotational symmetry.

7. Which of these figures has point symmetry? D

Ⓐ 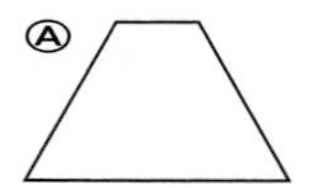
Ⓑ 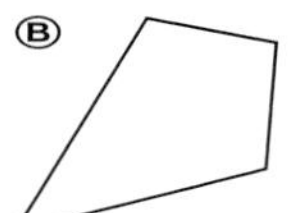
Ⓒ 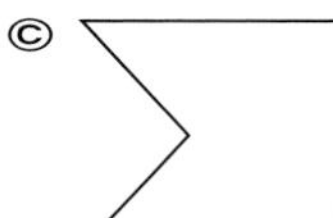
Ⓓ 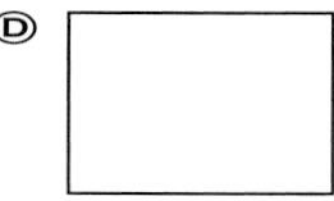

Resources

Practice Masters
Section 11C Review

Assessment Sourcebook
Quiz 11C

TestWorks
Test and Practice Software

PRACTICE

Name ______________________

Practice

Section 11C Review

Point K is at (5, −3). Use each translation rule to find the coordinates of K'.

1. $(x, y) \rightarrow (x, y - 7)$ (5, −10)
2. $(x, y) \rightarrow (x + 3, y + 3)$ (8, 0)
3. $(x, y) \rightarrow (x - 5, y + 6)$ (0, 3)
4. $(x, y) \rightarrow (x - 12, y)$ (−7, −3)

5. Draw the reflection of $\triangle LMN$ across the y-axis. Give the coordinates of the vertices of the reflection.

L' (−1, 5) M' (−5, 4) N' (−3, 1)

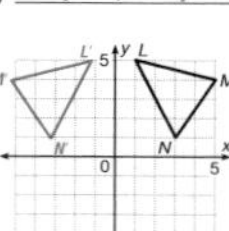

6. Give the coordinates of the vertices of rotations of $\triangle LMN$ after clockwise rotations around the origin of:

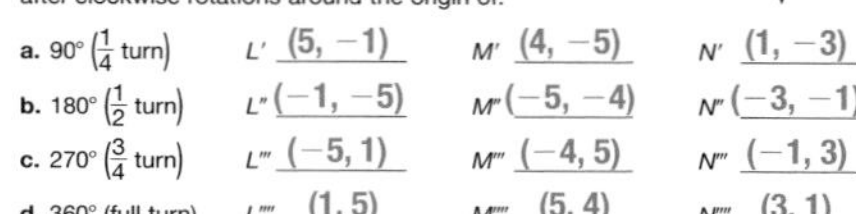

a. $90° \left(\frac{1}{4} \text{ turn}\right)$	L' (5, −1)	M' (4, −5)	N' (1, −3)
b. $180° \left(\frac{1}{2} \text{ turn}\right)$	L'' (−1, −5)	M'' (−5, −4)	N'' (−3, −1)
c. $270° \left(\frac{3}{4} \text{ turn}\right)$	L''' (−5, 1)	M''' (−4, 5)	N''' (−1, 3)
d. 360° (full turn)	L'''' (1, 5)	M'''' (5, 4)	N'''' (3, 1)

7. **Language Arts** Blind people can read using the Braille alphabet of raised dot patterns. Eleven of these patterns are shown below.

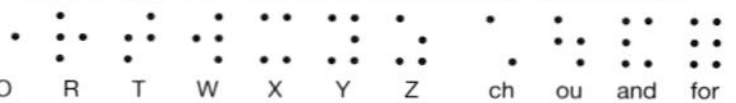

   a. Which patterns have a horizontal line of symmetry? O, R, W, X, Y, and, for
   b. Which patterns have a vertical line of symmetry? X, for
   c. Which patterns have rotational symmetry? T, X, ch, ou, for

8. The number of motorcycles in the U.S. decreased from 5,444,400 in 1985 to 4,259,500 in 1990. Find the percent decrease. *[Lesson 8-7]* About 21.8%

9. The Fujiyama roller coaster in Japan is designed to travel at speeds up to 118.8 feet per second. Convert this speed to miles per hour *[Lesson 7-7]* 81 mi/hr

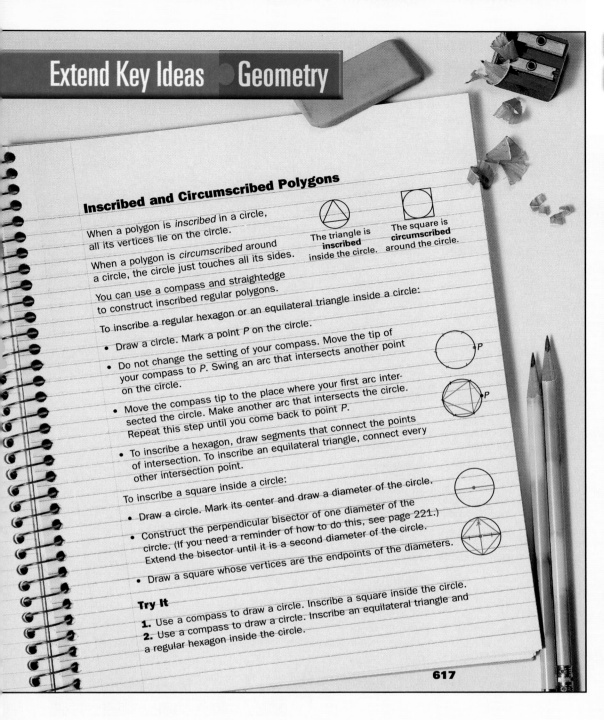

Extend Key Ideas Geometry

Inscribed and Circumscribed Polygons

When a polygon is *inscribed* in a circle, all its vertices lie on the circle.

When a polygon is *circumscribed* around a circle, the circle just touches all its sides.

The triangle is **inscribed** inside the circle.

The square is **circumscribed** around the circle.

You can use a compass and straightedge to construct inscribed regular polygons.

To inscribe a regular hexagon or an equilateral triangle inside a circle:

- Draw a circle. Mark a point *P* on the circle.
- Do not change the setting of your compass. Move the tip of your compass to *P*. Swing an arc that intersects another point on the circle.
- Move the compass tip to the place where your first arc intersected the circle. Make another arc that intersects the circle. Repeat this step until you come back to point *P*.
- To inscribe a hexagon, draw segments that connect the points of intersection. To inscribe an equilateral triangle, connect every other intersection point.

To inscribe a square inside a circle:

- Draw a circle. Mark its center and draw a diameter of the circle.
- Construct the perpendicular bisector of one diameter of the circle. (If you need a reminder of how to do this, see page 221.) Extend the bisector until it is a second diameter of the circle.
- Draw a square whose vertices are the endpoints of the diameters.

Try It

1. Use a compass to draw a circle. Inscribe a square inside the circle.
2. Use a compass to draw a circle. Inscribe an equilateral triangle and a regular hexagon inside the circle.

617

Extend Key Ideas

Inscribed and Circumscribed Polygons

The Point
Students learn to construct inscribed and circumscribed polygons.

About the Page

- Instructions for inscribing three figures are given. You might demonstrate any or all of these, then have students do them in the **Try It** section.
- The size of the circle does not matter. Have students choose a length for the compass that is easy to manipulate.

Ask ...

- What does it mean for a figure to be inscribed in a circle? Its vertices lie on the circle and the figure is inside the circle.
- What does it mean for a figure to be circumscribed around a circle? The figure lies outside the circle and its sides are tangent to the circle.

Extension
How could you construct a square so that it circumscribes the circle with the inscribed square? Construct tangent lines at each point where the inscribed square touches the circle. Pairs of tangent lines intersect at the vertices of the circumscribed square.

Answers for Try It

1.
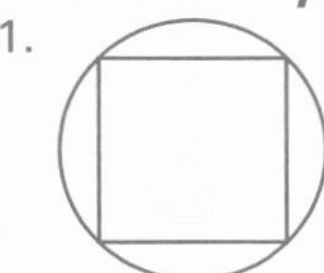

2.
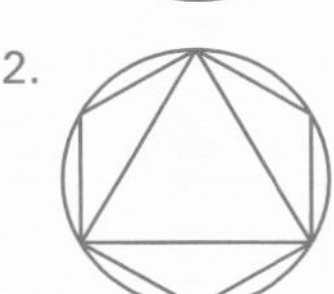

Chapter 11 Summary and Review

Review Correlation

Item(s)	Lesson(s)
1	11-2
2	11-1
3	11-3, 11-4
4	11-5
5	11-6, 11-7
6	11-8, 11-9
7	11-11, 11-12
8	11-10
9	11-11, 11-12

For additional review, see page 682.

Answers for Review

2.

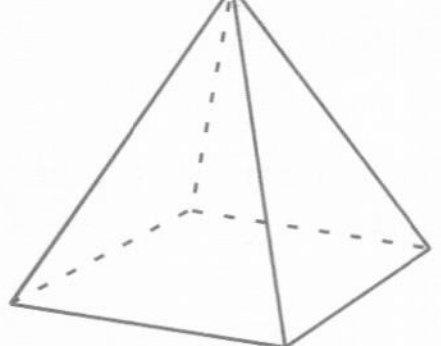

8 edges; 5 faces; 5 vertices

Chapter 11 Summary and Review

Graphic Organizer

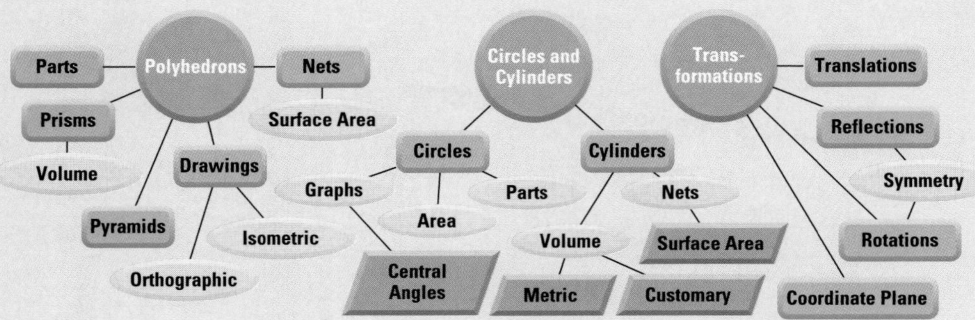

Section 11A Polyhedrons

Summary

- A **polyhedron** is a 3-dimensional object, or **solid,** whose **faces** are polygons. A **prism** is a polyhedron whose **bases** are congruent and parallel. A **pyramid** has a polygonal base and one more vertex above or below the base.
- **Isometric drawing** shows perspective. **Orthographic drawing** shows angles and lengths accurately in front, top, and side views.
- The **surface area** of a polyhedron is the sum of the areas of its faces. You can use a net to help calculate surface area.
- The **volume** of a 3-dimensional object is the amount of space it takes up. Prism volumes are given by the formulas $V = Bh$ and $V = lwh$.

Review

1. Find the number of cubes in the figure at the right. Assume all cubes are visible. 6

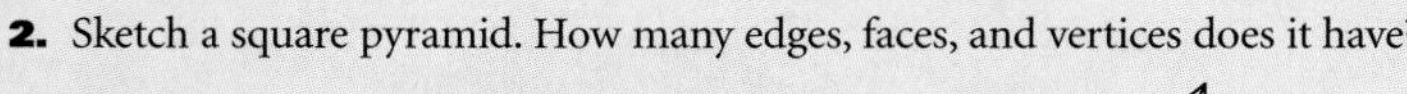

2. Sketch a square pyramid. How many edges, faces, and vertices does it have?
3. The bases of the prism are right triangles.
   a. Sketch a net for this prism. Answers will vary
   b. Find its surface area and volume.
   S.A. = 540 in^2; *V* = 600 in^3

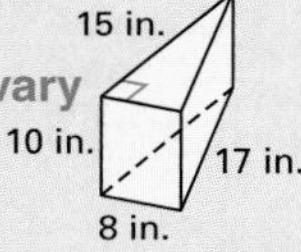

Resources

Practice Masters
Cumulative Review Chapters 1–11

PRACTICE

Name ____________

Practice

Cumulative Review Chapters 1–11

Find the area of each figure. *[Lesson 5-10]*

1. 805 ft^2 (19 ft, 22 ft, 31 ft, 24 ft)
2. 14.8 cm^2 (1.6 cm, 1.4 cm, 2.9 cm, 3.8 cm)
3. $10\frac{7}{16}$ in^2 ($1\frac{3}{4}$ in., 2 in., $2\frac{1}{4}$ in., $2\frac{3}{4}$ in., $5\frac{1}{2}$ in.)

Find the missing side lengths in each pair of similar figures. *[Lesson 7-9]*

4. t = 72 u = 75 (50, 14, 48, u, 21, t)
5. v = 30 cm w = 40 cm (45 cm, w, v, 18 cm, 27 cm, 24 cm)
6. x = 52 y = 36 z = 48 (63, 84, 91, 28, 16, x, z, y)

Write each fraction or decimal as a percent. Where necessary, use a repeating decimal to help express your percent. *[Lesson 8-2]*

7. 0.67 67%
8. 0.045 4.5%
9. $\frac{3}{20}$ 15%
10. $\frac{17}{25}$ 68%
11. $\frac{5}{6}$ $83.\overline{3}\%$
12. $\frac{3}{50}$ 6%
13. $\frac{5}{8}$ 62.5%
14. $\frac{2}{5}$ 40%

Find the area of the circle, given its diameter or radius. Use $\pi \approx 3.14$, and round answers to the nearest tenth. *[Lesson 11-7]*

15. 113.0 ft^2
16. 298.5 in^2
17. 961.6 m^2

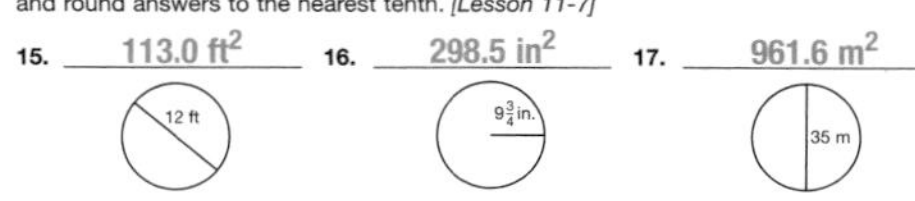

For each group of figures, identify all lettered polygons that are translations of the shaded polygon. *[Lesson 11-10]*

18. B, D
19. D
20. C

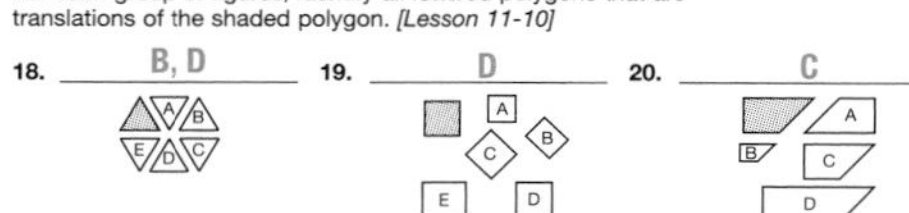

Section 11B Circles and Cylinders

Summary

- A **circle** is the set of all points in a plane that are the same distance (the **radius**) from the center. The **diameter** is twice the radius.
- The **circumference** is the distance around a circle: $C = \pi d$ or $C = 2\pi r$. The area of a circle is given by $A = \pi r^2$. **Pi** (π) is the ratio of the circumference of a circle to its diameter.
- A **cylinder** has two circular bases and a **cone** has one circular base.

Review

4. The data shows Hal's time at work. Make a circle graph. Label each sector.

Typing	Filing	Telephone	Meetings
35%	25%	30%	10%

5. Find the circumference and area of a circle whose radius is 21.98 m. Use 3.14 for π. Round to the nearest tenth.
$C = 138.0$ m, $A = 1517.0$ m^2

6. Find the surface area and the volume of the cylinder. Use 3.14 for π.
S.A. ≈ 533.8 cm^2; $V \approx 942$ cm^3

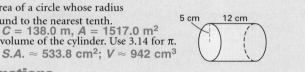

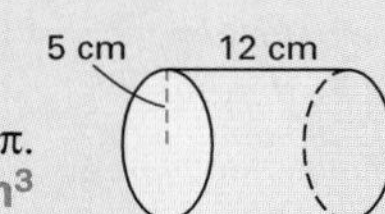

Section 11C Transformations

Summary

- A **translation** slides every point on a figure.
- A **line of symmetry** divides a figure into two mirror-image halves. The **reflection** of a figure is its mirror image across a line.
- A **rotation** turns a figure. A figure has **rotational symmetry** if you can rotate it a fraction of 360° and it matches the original figure exactly.

Review

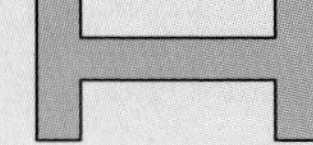

7. Copy the figure. Draw all lines of symmetry. Then tell whether or not it has rotational symmetry.

8. Point A is at $(-4, -1)$. Use the translation rule $(x, y) \rightarrow (x - 3, y + 2)$ to find the coordinates of A'. $(-7, 1)$

9. $ABCD$ has coordinates $A(0, 0)$, $B(4, 0)$, $C(6, 3)$, and $D(2, 5)$.

a. Draw the figure on a coordinate plane.

b. Draw the reflection of $ABCD$ across the x-axis. Give the coordinates of the reflection's vertices.

c. Give the coordinates of a rotation of $ABCD$ for a 90° clockwise rotation around the origin.

Answers for Review

4.

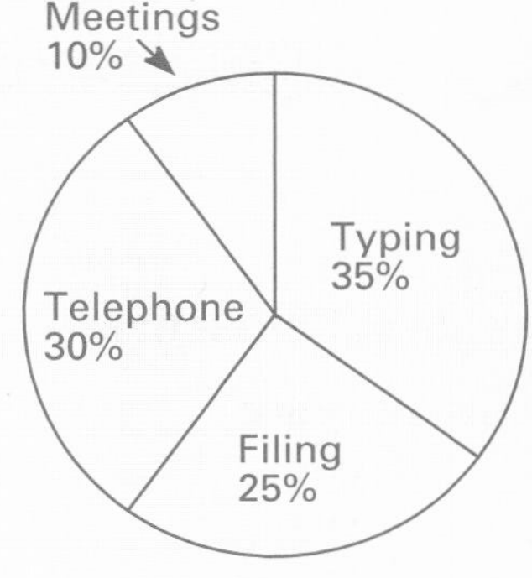

7.

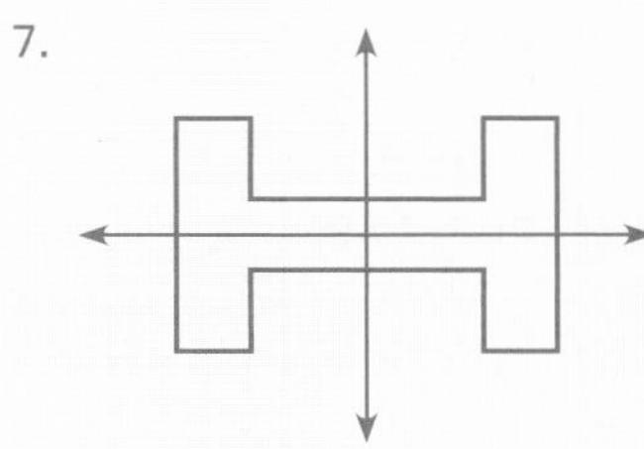

Yes, the figure has rotational symmetry.

9. a.

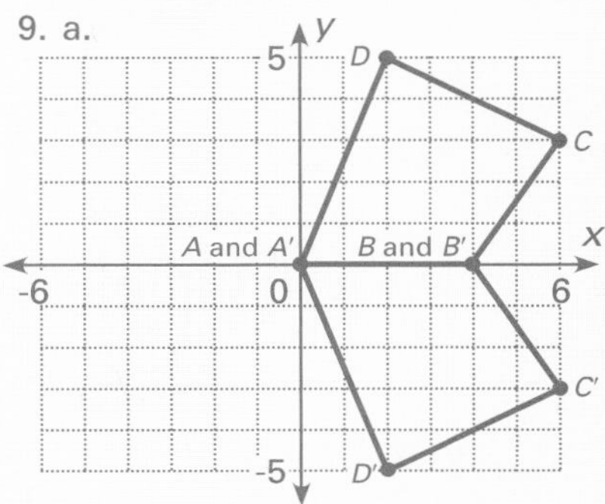

b. Coordinates of reflection's vertices: $A'(0, 0)$, $B'(4, 0)$, $C'(6, -3)$, and $D'(2, -5)$

c. Coordinates of rotated figure: $A''(0, 0)$, $B''(0, -4)$, $C''(3, -6)$, and $D''(5, -2)$

Chapter 11 Assessment

Assessment Correlation

Item(s)	Lesson(s)
1	11-1
2	11-2
3	11-5
4	11-3, 11-4
5	11-6, 11-7
6	11-7
7	11-8, 11-9
8	11-11
9	11-12
10	11-10
11	11-11, 11-12

Answers for Assessment

1.

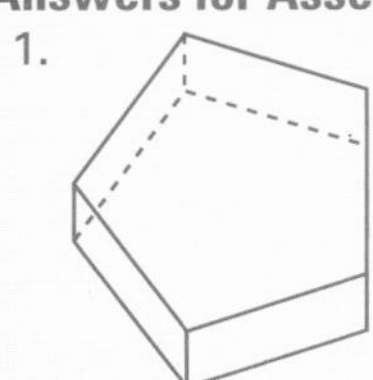

15 edges; 7 faces; 10 vertices

2.

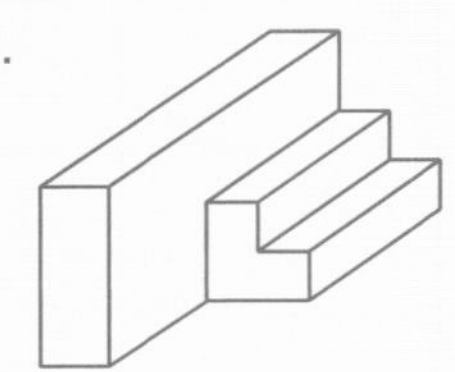

3.

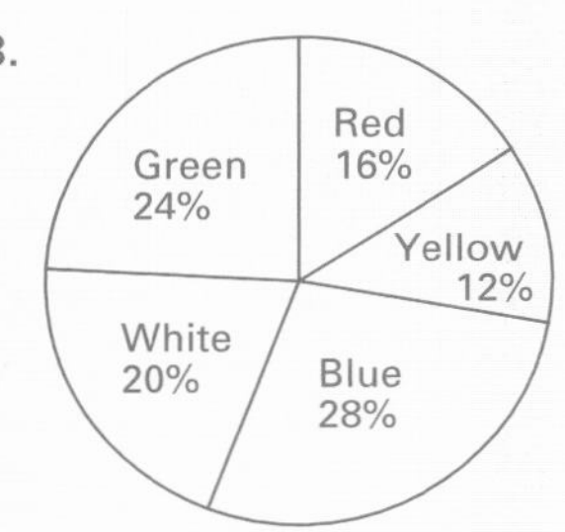

4. a. Possible answer:

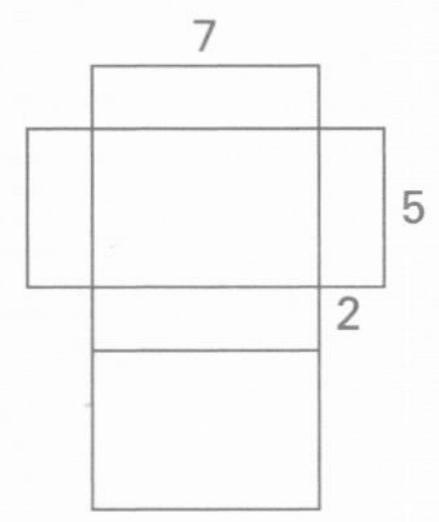

b. Surface area, 118 ft^2; Volume, 70 ft^3

5. Radius, 4 cm; Circumference, 25.1 cm; Area, 50.2 cm^2

8–10. See page C6.

Chapter 11 Assessment

1. Sketch a pentagonal prism. How many edges, faces, and vertices does it have?

2. Make a perspective sketch of the object shown at the right.

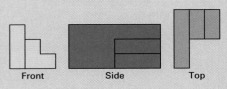

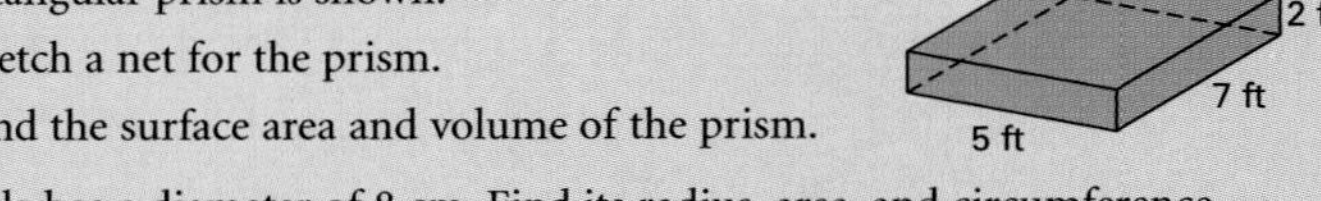

3. Last week, Auto Imports sold 3 yellow cars, 7 blue cars, 5 white cars, 4 red cars, and 6 green cars. Make a circle graph to show this data.

4. A rectangular prism is shown.

a. Sketch a net for the prism.

b. Find the surface area and volume of the prism.

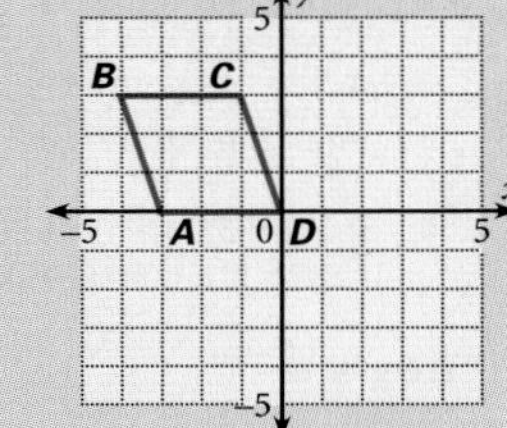

5. A circle has a diameter of 8 cm. Find its radius, area, and circumference. Use 3.14 for π. Round to the nearest tenth.

6. Marc jogged one circuit around a large circular lawn with area 15,000 m^2. How far did Marc jog? About 434 m

7. A child's cylindrical block is 4 in. long and has a diameter of 2 in. Find its surface area and volume. Use 3.14 for π. Round to the nearest tenth. *S.A.* = 31.4 in^2; *V* = 12.6 in^3

Use the figure at the right for Exercises 8–10.

8. Draw the reflection of *ABCD* across the *x*-axis. Give the coordinates of the reflection's vertices.

9. Give the coordinates of a rotation of *ABCD* for a 180° clockwise rotation around the origin.

10. Sketch the image formed by translating *ABCD* using the translation rule $(x, y) \rightarrow (x + 4, y - 5)$.

11. For the digits **1, 2, 3, 6,** and **8:**

a. Which have no lines of symmetry? 1, 2, 6

b. Which have just one line of symmetry? 3

c. Which have two lines of symmetry? 8

d. Which have rotational symmetry? 8

Performance Task

Wheelchair ramps are often triangular prisms. Design a wheelchair ramp with a horizontal length of 40 ft. The angle between the ground and the ramp must measure 4°. Use a net to make a scale model of your ramp, and calculate its surface area and volume.

Performance Assessment Key

See key on page 551.

Resources

Assessment Sourcebook

Chapter 11 Tests
- Forms A and B (free response)
- Form C (multiple choice)
- Form D (performance assessment)
- Form E (mixed response)
- Form F (cumulative chapter test)

TestWorks
Tests and Practice Software

Home and Community Connections
Letter Home for Chapter 11 in English and Spanish

Suggested Scoring Rubric

Score	Criteria
4	•Ramp has given shape and reasonable dimensions based on given angle and scale of the length. •Net is accurately drawn and labeled. •Surface area and volume are correct.
3	•Ramp has given shape and acceptable dimensions based on given angle and scale of length. •Net is drawn and labeled. •Surface area and volume are correct.
2	•Ramp has given shape but dimensions chosen are not reasonable. •Net is attempted but not accurate. •Shows some understanding of surface area and volume.
1	•Ramp design is not acceptable. •Net is not accurate. •Shows little understanding of surface area and volume.

Cumulative Review Test Prep

Cumulative Review Chapters 1–11 — Test Prep

Performance Assessment

Choose one problem.

BLOCK SCHEDULE

Design a set of four building blocks using the shapes you have learned about in this chapter. Draw top, front, and side views of each block. Make a net for each one, then build your set of blocks. Calculate or estimate the volume and surface area of each of your blocks.

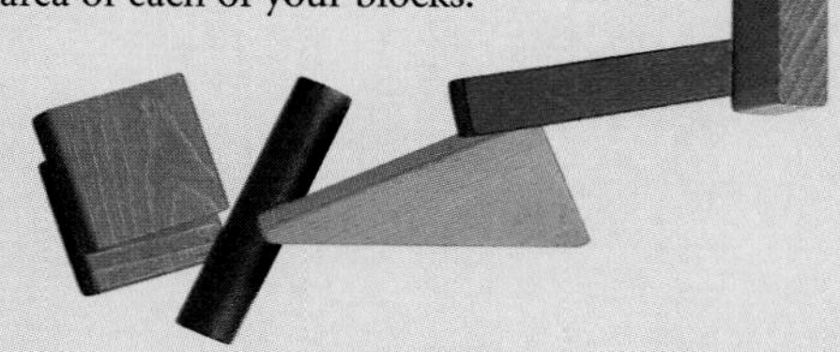

Rolling Along

Each number on a number cube has a $\frac{1}{6}$ probability of coming up on any roll. Sometimes game designers want to use a solid where all of the probabilities are *not* $\frac{1}{6}$.

Five special polyhedrons are called *Platonic solids.* All of the faces of these polyhedrons are regular polygons. Research the names and shapes of the five Platonic solids. Build a model of each one and number its faces. Which solid would you roll if you wanted each number to come up $\frac{1}{4}$ of the time? $\frac{1}{6}$? $\frac{1}{8}$? $\frac{1}{12}$? $\frac{1}{20}$?

Circles, Circles, Circles

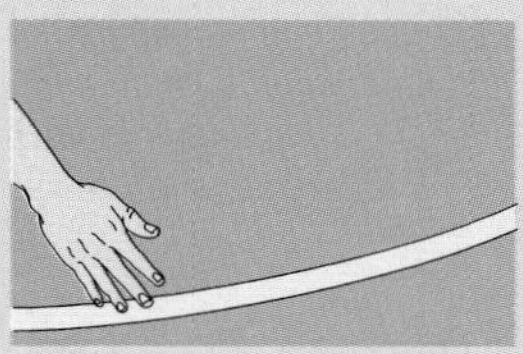

Use a compass to draw circles that have the same center and the following radii: $\frac{1}{2}$ in., 1 in., $1\frac{1}{2}$ in., 2 in., $2\frac{1}{2}$ in., 3 in., $3\frac{1}{2}$ in., and 4 in. How does the circumference of each circle compare to that of the one inside it? Now imagine that $\frac{1}{2}$ in. masking tape is used to make a circle with a radius of 1 mile. There are really *two* circles, one corresponding to the inside border of the tape and one corresponding to the outside border of the tape. How do the circumferences of these two circles compare?

Making Money

For this experiment, you will need two small rectangular mirrors, a coin, and a protractor.

Place the coin on a tabletop. Set the two mirrors together so that you can see the coin's reflection. How many coins do you see?

Experiment with the angle between the mirrors. Use a protractor to measure the angles that give different numbers of reflections. Make a table that shows the relationship between the angle and the number of coins you see.

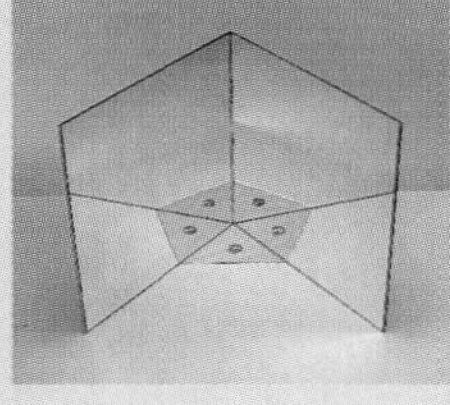

Is there a way to "make" an infinite amount of money with your mirrors? If so, explain how.

About Performance Assessment

The Performance Assessment options ...

- provide an alternate means of assessing students.
- address different learning modalities.
- allow students to choose one problem.

Teachers may encourage students to choose the most challenging problem.

Learning Modalities
Block Schedule **Visual** Students use models to find surface area and volume.
Rolling Along **Individual** Students research Platonic solids and probability.
Circles, Circles, Circles **Logical** Students solve a circumference problem.
Making Money **Verbal** Students describe ways to use mirrors to make money.

Suggested Scoring Rubric

See key on page 551.

Block Schedule

4
- Gives reasonable dimensions and scale for each block.
- Views and nets are accurate.
- Finds correct volumes and surface areas.

3
- Uses reasonable dimensions and scale.
- Makes accurate views and nets of at least three blocks.
- Finds volumes and surface areas.

2
- Shows some understanding of scale in choosing dimensions.
- Makes fairly accurate views of at least two blocks.
- Has difficulty calculating volumes and/or surface areas.

1
- Shows little understanding of scale or dimensions, and has difficulty drawing views.
- Does not make nets or find volumes and surface areas.

Answers for Assessment

• Rolling Along

The names of the five Platonic solids are given below, along with the number of faces and the shape of each face.

Cube (6 faces; squares)

Octahedron, (8 faces; triangles)

Tetrahedron (4 faces, triangles)

Icosahedron (20 faces, triangles)

Dodecahedron (12 faces; pentagons)

• Circles, Circles, Circles

Possible answer: Each circle is 3.14 in. more in circumference than the circle inside it. The circumference of the circle on the outside edge of the tape is 3.14 in. more in circumference than the circle on the inside edge.

Suggested Scoring Rubrics for *Rolling Along* and *Making Money* on page C7.

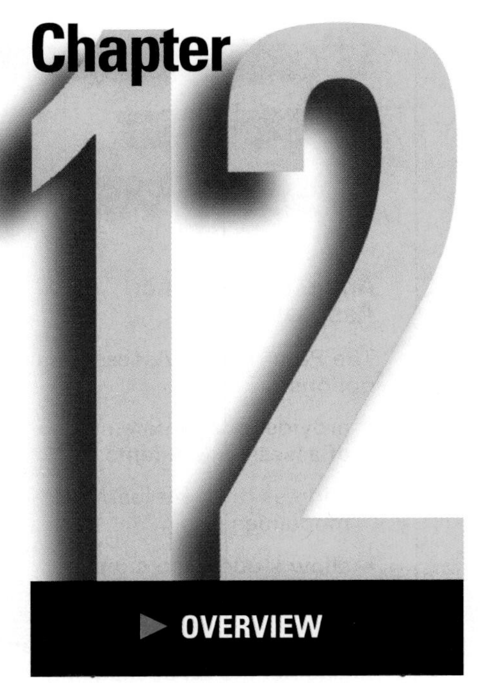

▶ OVERVIEW

Counting and Probability

Section 12A

Counting: Students explore ways to determine the number of outcomes for a series of events. They learn to count the number of ways to choose things when the order matters, and when the order does not matter.

12-1 Counting Methods

12-2 Arrangements

12-3 Choosing a Group

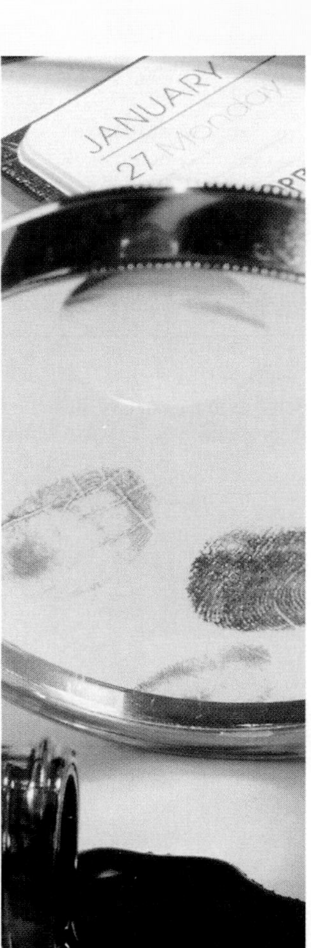

Section 12B

Chance and Probability: Students find the odds of an event occurring. They explore the relationship between odds and probability.

12-4 Odds and Fairness

12-5 Probability

12-6 Experimental Probability

12-7 Independent and Dependent Events

Meeting NCTM Standards

Curriculum Standards

STANDARD			pages
1	**Problem Solving**	Skills and Strategies	623, 624, 634, 635, 639, 640, 642, 650, 658, 663
		Applications	629–630, 634–635, 639–640, 641, 647–648, 652–653, 657–658, 662–663, 665
		Exploration	626, 631, 636, 644, 649, 654, 659
2	**Communication**	Oral	625, 628, 633, 638, 643, 646, 648, 651, *653*, 656, 661
		Written	624, 630, 635, 640, 642, 648, 653, 658, 663, 666
		Cooperative Learning	622, *626*, *631*, *636*, *638*, *644*, *648*, *653*, *654*, *656*, *658*, *659*
3	**Reasoning**	Critical Thinking	630, 640, 648, 653, 663
4	**Connections**	Mathematical	See Standards 5, 7, 8, 10, 11 below.
		Interdisciplinary	History 645, 657; Social Studies 622, *625*, *628*, 629, 647, *647*, 661, 662, 666; Science 622, *625*, *633*, 634, 642, 656, 662; Arts & Literature 622; Entertainment *622*, 623; Language 632; Consumer 634; Literature 637, 638; Geography *640*; Language Arts *647*; Industry *643*; Recreation 652; Sports *633*, 634, *651*
		Technology	624, 630, 633, 664
		Cultural	*623*, *633*, 634, *646*, *651*, *656*, *661*, *662*
5	**Number and Number Relationships**		629, 634, 642
7	**Computation and Estimation**		624, *637*
8	**Patterns and Functions**		648, 658, 667
10	**Statistics**		646, 652
11	**Probability**		625–667
12	**Geometry**		635, 653, 656–658

Italic type indicates Teacher Edition reference.

Teaching Standards

Focus on Major Shifts

Throughout the NCTM Professional Standards for Teaching Mathematics are woven several major shifts. These include a shift

- toward logic and mathematical evidence as verification—away from the teacher as the sole authority for right answers.
- toward conjecturing, inventing, and problem solving—away from an emphasis on mechanistic answer-finding.

Assessment Standards

Focus on Coherence

Journals Matching assessment activities to the goals of the curriculum is the focus of the Coherence Standard. If one goal is for students to be able to use and make connections between different methods of solving the same problem, journal prompts can encourage them to verbalize those connections. Students' journal entries in Chapter 12 include

- finding all the outcomes for a set of choices.
- explaining the results of a probability experiment.

TECHNOLOGY

For the Teacher

- **Resource Pro, a Teacher's Resource Planner CD-ROM**
  Use the teacher planning CD-ROM to view resources available for Chapter 12. You can prepare custom lesson plans or use the default lesson plans provided.

- **World Wide Web**
  Visit **www.kz.com** to view class summary reports, individual student reports, and more.

- **Test Works**
  TestWorks provides ready-made tests and can create custom tests and practice worksheets.

For the Parent

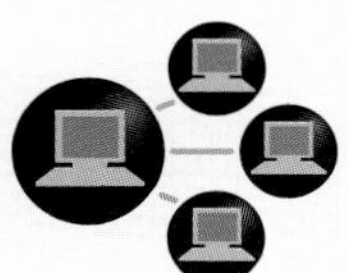

- **World Wide Web**
  Parents can use the web site at **www.kz.com** to check on student progress or take a quick refresher course.

For the Student

- **Interactive CD-ROM**
  Lesson 12-6 has an *Interactive CD-ROM Lesson*. The *Interactive CD-ROM Journal* and *Interactive CD-ROM Probability Tool* are also used in Chapter 12.

- **Wide World of Mathematics**
  Lesson 12-5 *Middle School*: Hurricane Prediction
  Lesson 12-7 *Middle School*: Two-Sport Athlete

- **World Wide Web**
  Use with Chapter and Section Openers; Students can go online to the Scott Foresman-Addison Wesley Web site at **www.mathsurf.com/7/ch12** to collect information about chapter themes. Students can also visit **www.kz.com** for tutorials and practice.

STANDARDIZED - TEST CORRELATION

SECTION 12A	LESSON	OBJECTIVE	ITBS FORM M	CTBS FORM A	CAT FORM A	SAT FORM S	MAT FORM S	YOUR FORM
	12-1	• Use tree diagrams and the Counting Principle to find all of the outcomes for a set of choices.	✘	✘		✘		
	12-2	• Count the number of ways items can be arranged. • Use factorial products to count arrangements.				✘		
	12-3	• Calculate the number of ways to choose some items out of a larger group when the order is unimportant.						

SECTION 12B	LESSON	OBJECTIVE	ITBS FORM M	CTBS FORM A	CAT FORM A	SAT FORM S	MAT FORM S	YOUR FORM
	12-4	• Find the odds that an event happens.						
	12-5	• Find the probability of an event.	✘	✘	✘	✘	✘	
	12-6	• Use experimental probability to estimate probabilities. • Find probabilities involving geometric figures.	✘	✘	✘	✘	✘	
	12-7	• Decide whether two events are dependent or independent. • Find probabilities of dependent and independent events.						

Key: ITBS - Iowa Test of Basic Skills; CTBS - Comprehensive Test of Basic Skills; CAT - California Achievement Test; SAT - Stanford Achievement Test; MAT - Metropolitan Achievement Test

ASSESSMENT PROGRAM

Traditional Assessment	QUICK QUIZZES	SECTION REVIEW	CHAPTER REVIEW	CHAPTER ASSESSMENT FREE RESPONSE	CHAPTER ASSESSMENT MULTIPLE CHOICE	CUMULATIVE REVIEW
	TE: pp. 630, 635, 640, 648, 653, 658, 663	SE: pp. 642, 666 *Quiz 12A, 12B	SE: pp. 668–669	SE: p. 670 *Ch. 12 Tests Forms A, B, E	*Ch. 12 Tests Forms C, E	SE: p. 671 *Ch. 12 Test Form F; Quarterly Test Ch. 1–12

Alternate Assessment	INTERVIEW	JOURNAL	ONGOING	PERFORMANCE	PORTFOLIO	PROJECT	SELF
	TE: pp. 648, 653	SE: pp. 630, 642, 648, 658, 663, 666 TE: pp. 624, 630, 658	TE: pp. 626, 631, 636, 644, 649, 654, 659	SE: p. 670 *Ch. 12 Tests Forms D, E	TE: pp. 635, 663	SE: pp. 640, 663 TE: p. 623	TE: p. 640

*Tests and quizzes are in *Assessment Sourcebook*. Test Form E is a mixed response test. Forms for Alternate Assessment are also available in *Assessment Sourcebook*.

TestWorks: Test and Practice Software

MIDDLE SCHOOL PACING CHART

REGULAR PACING

Day	5 classes per week
1	Chapter 12 Opener; Problem Solving Focus
2	Section **12A** Opener; Lesson **12-1**
3	Lesson **12-2**
4	Lesson **12-3**
5	**12A** Connect; **12A** Review
6	Section **12B** Opener; Lesson **12-4**
7	Lesson **12-5**
8	Lesson **12-6**
9	Lesson **12-7**; Technology
10	**12B** Connect; **12B** Review; Extend Key Ideas
11	Chapter 12 Summary and Review
12	Chapter 12 Assessment; Cumulative Review, Chapters 1–12

BLOCK SCHEDULING OPTIONS

Block Scheduling for
Complete Course

Chapter 12 may be presented in

- seven 90-minute blocks
- ten 75-minute blocks

Each block consists of a combination of

- Chapter and Section Openers
- Explores
- Lesson Development
- Problem Solving Focus
- Technology
- Extend Key Ideas
- Connect
- Review
- Assessment

For details, see *Block Scheduling Handbook*.

Block Scheduling for
Interdisciplinary Course

Each block integrates math with another subject area.

In Chapter 12, interdisciplinary topics include

- Detective Work
- Games

Themes for Interdisciplinary Team Teaching 12A and12B are

- Probability of Flooding
- Fairness of Games

For details, see *Block Scheduling Handbook*.

Block Scheduling for
Lab-Based Course

In each block, 30–40 minutes is devoted to lab activities including

- Explores in the Student Edition
- Connect pages in the Student Edition
- Technology options in the Student Edition
- Reteaching Activities in the Teacher Edition

For details, see *Block Scheduling Handbook*.

Block Scheduling for
Course with *Connected Mathematics*

In each block, investigations from **Connected Mathematics** replace or enhance the lessons in Chapter 12.

Connected Mathematics topics for Chapter 12 can be found in

- *What Do You Expect?*

For details, see *Block Scheduling Handbook*.

INTERDISCIPLINARY BULLETIN BOARD

Set Up

Draw an oval-shaped outline of a human head on a bulletin board. You might attach a large manila envelope for storing attachments to the figure.

Procedure

- Small groups of students should draw different kinds of hats, hairdos, eyes, noses, mouths, ears, collars, or ties that could be attached to the head.
- Students should cut out their drawings. They might store the cut-outs in the envelope near the bulletin board.
- Students can choose features to attach each day. Items can be interchanged daily to vary the appearance of the head until all possible combinations have been used.

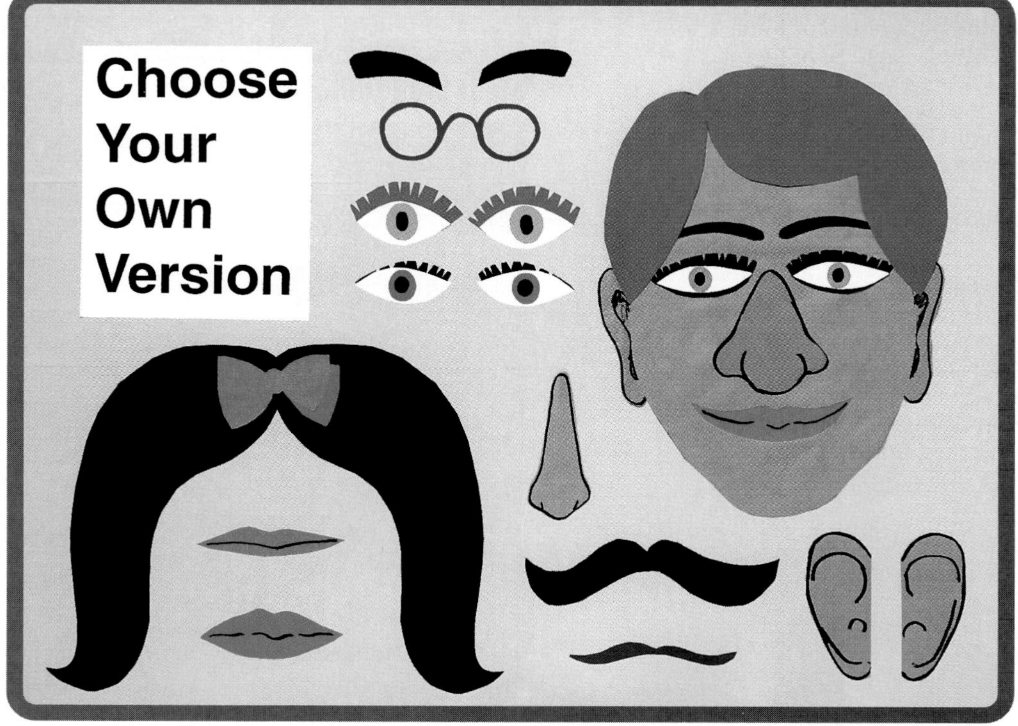

Chapter 12

The information on these pages shows how probability and counting are applied to real-life situations.

World Wide Web

If your class has access to the World Wide Web, you might want to use the information found at the Web site addresses given.

Extensions

The following activities do not require access to the World Wide Web.

Social Studies
Suggest that students research the Underground Railroad. Have them draw a map showing the various routes and final destinations that made up this railroad system.

Science
Ask students to look in newspapers, magazines, or books for other statements about odds in science, and compare them with the one given here.

Arts & Literature
Have students select two favorite books and describe why they feel the books were selected for publication.

People of the World
Ask students to write a sentence about the population of India based on the statement given here. Possible answer: About 1 in every 6 people live in India. You also might have students compare the current population of India with the current population of the United States.

Entertainment
Have students work in groups and investigate probabilities in other games, such as getting a hole in one in golf, picking a certain letter in Scrabble®, winning a sweepstakes, and so on.

12 Counting and Probability

Science Link
www.mathsurf.com/7/ch12/science

Social Studies

Before the Civil War, the Underground Railroad helped thousands of slaves reach free states and Canada. Harriet Tubman was the most famous "conductor" on the Railroad. For each of the 300 or more people she guided, the probability of reaching freedom was 100%.

Science

According to NASA, the odds of the earth colliding with an asteroid or comet over 1 km in diameter in the next century is less than 1 out of 1000.

Arts & Literature

According to *What the Odds Are*, by Les Krantz, once you submit a book to a publisher, the odds of having it published are between 1:50 and 1:100.

A Tail Of Two Cities

by Chuck Dickens

REJECT

Chapter 1

It was the best of times, it was pretty lame, it was the age of wisdom, it was the age of really dumb stuff,

622

TEACHER TALK

Meet Vera Holliday

Westlane Middle School
Indianapolis, Indiana

Two weeks prior to beginning the unit on probability, I introduce the following activity.

I prepare a bag of 85 white and 15 red marbles. Each day of the first week, as students enter the classroom, they take a marble from the bag. We tally the results, noting which students drew a red marble, and return the marbles to the bag. The next week the process is altered so that the marbles are not returned to the bag. When we study probability, we use our activity to discuss under which of the two conditions it was easier to pick a red marble—when the marbles were replaced or when they were not replaced.

Cultural Link
www.mathsurf.com/7/ch12/people

People of the World

The probability that a randomly chosen person lives in India is about 16%.

Entertainment

According to *Numbers,* by Andrea Sutcliffe, the odds that you will go to jail during a game of Monopoly® are 1 to 1.74.

KEY MATH IDEAS

You can find the number of different **outcomes** for a series of events by using a **tree diagram,** or by multiplying the number of possibilities for each item.

A **permutation** is a possible way to put a set of items in order. A **combination** is an arrangement of items where the order does not matter.

The **odds** of an **event** are the ratio of the number of ways it could happen to the number of ways it could not happen. The **(theoretical) probability** of an event is the ratio of the number of ways it could happen to the total number of possible outcomes.

Two events are **independent** if the outcome of one does not change the probabilities of the outcome for the second; otherwise, the events are **dependent**.

CHAPTER PROJECT

Problem Solving
Understand
Plan
Solve
Look Back

In this project, you'll design an experiment to simulate the typical performance of a favorite player, such as the free-throw percentage of a basketball player or the batting average of a baseball or softball player. Begin the project by choosing a sports star whose skills you'll simulate.

623

Chapter Project

Students design an experiment to simulate the performance of a favorite sports star.

Materials

Chapter 12 Project Master

Introduce the Project

- Discuss the kinds of activities that can be simulated, such as free-throw percentage or batting average. Have students describe sports statistics with which they are familiar.
- Describe what is meant by a simulation.
- Talk about where students can find information about sports stars, such as in almanacs, in newspapers, and on the Internet.

Project Progress

Section A, page 640 Students think about what could happen when a person performs the skill they selected. They list all the possible outcomes of performing the skill twice.

Section B, page 663 Students give outcomes and probabilities of performing their chosen skill once. Then they choose one outcome and find the probability of this outcome happening twice in a row.

Community Project

A community project for Chapter 12 is available in *Home and Community Connections.*

Cooperative Learning

You may want to use Teaching Tool Transparency 1: Cooperative Learning Checklist with **Explore** and other group activities in this chapter.

PROJECT ASSESSMENT

You may choose to use this project as a performance assessment for the chapter.

Performance Assessment Key

Level 4 Full Accomplishment

Level 3 Substantial Accomplishment

Level 2 Partial Accomplishment

Level 1 Little Accomplishment

Suggested Scoring Rubric

Level	Criteria
4	•Skill selected is appropriate and list of possible outcomes is complete. •Outcomes and probabilities of performing the skill once are correct. •Probability of one outcome happening twice in a row is correct.
3	•List of possible outcomes is complete. •Outcomes and probabilities of performing the skill once are acceptable. •Probability of one outcome happening twice in a row is acceptable.
2	•Some possible outcomes are listed. •Attempts to give outcomes and probabilities of performing the skill once. •Probability of one outcome happening twice in a row is incorrect.
1	•List of possible outcomes is not complete. •Outcomes and probabilities are not given.

Problem Solving Focus

Checking for a Reasonable Answer

The Point
Students focus on determining if an answer is reasonable, especially if they have used a calculator.

Resources
Teaching Tool Transparency 16: Problem-Solving Guidelines

 *Interactive CD-ROM Journal*

About the Page

Using the Problem-Solving Process
It is very important that students check the reasonableness of their answers using estimation and common sense. Discuss these suggestions:

- Does your solution answer the question?
- Use estimation. Is the result of your computation reasonable?
- Think about the problem. Is your answer sensible?

Ask ...

- Should your answers in Problems 1 and 2 be greater or less than the number of viewers? Explain. Less; The percent of viewers is less than 100%.
- In Problem 3, describe a sensible answer. Possible answer: 129% is about 100% + 25%; $160 + \frac{1}{4}(160) = 160 + 40 = 200$.
- In Problem 4, how can you estimate 199%? Multiply by 2.

Journal

Ask students to write a paragraph describing how they determine a reasonable answer to a problem.

Answers for Problems

1. Too high; The number of teens is greater than the total number of viewers.
2. Close enough; There are about 18,000,000 situation comedy viewers, 30% of 18,000,000 is 5,400,000.
3. Too high; 320 minutes is 200% of 160, and actual viewing time is 129% of 160.
4. Close enough; 199% is close to 200%; and 2 • 160 = 320 minutes.

Problem Solving
Understand
Plan
Solve
Look Back

Checking for a Reasonable Answer

Even if you use a calculator to help you solve a problem, you should look back to check whether your answer is reasonable. You can use estimation and common sense to help you.

Problem Solving Focus

Each of the problems below has an answer, but the answer is not exactly right. Tell if each answer is "close enough," "too low," or "too high," and explain why.

1. A 1996 television viewing survey showed that 15,440,000 viewers watched suspense and mystery programming. Approximately 4% of this audience was made up of teens between the ages of 12 and 17. About how many teens watched suspense and mystery programming?
Answer: 61,760,000

2. The survey found that 2,720,000 more viewers watched situation comedies than suspense and mystery programs. About 30% of situation comedy viewers were men aged 18 or older. About how many men 18 or older watched situation comedies?
Answer: 5,400,000

3. A 1995 survey found that female teenagers spent less time watching television than any other age group, averaging 160 minutes per day. Male teens' viewing time was about 129% of that amount. About how many minutes per day did male teens watch television?
Answer: 320 minutes

4. Women aged 55 or older spent the most time watching television. Their average daily viewing time was 199% of the viewing time of female teenagers. About how many minutes per day did women 55 or older watch television?
Answer: 320 minutes

624

Additional Problem

The population of Oregon in 2010 is predicted to be 2,922,000. Of these people, 68.5% are predicted to live in metropolitan areas. How many people will live outside metropolitan areas?

1. Janeen predicted that 3,000,000 people will live outside metropolitan areas. Do you agree with her estimate? No, the actual number will be less than the total number of people living in Oregon.
2. Kenji predicted that 2,000,000 people will live outside metropolitan areas. Do you think his answer is too low, too high, or close enough? Explain. Too high; Kenji probably used the percent in metropolitan areas in his estimate instead of the percent outside metropolitan areas.
3. Give an estimate that you think is close enough. Possible answer: $\frac{1}{3}$ of 3,000,000, or about 1,000,000 people.

Counting

LESSON PLANNING GUIDE

Student Edition / Ancillaries*

LESSON		MATERIALS	VOCABULARY	DAILY	OTHER
	Chapter 12 Opener				Ch. 12 Project Master Ch. 12 Community Project Teaching Tool Trans. 1
	Problem Solving Focus				Teaching Tool Trans. 16 *Interactive CD-ROM Journal*
	Section 12A Opener				
12-1	**Counting Methods**		tree diagram, outcome, Counting Principle	12-1	Lesson Enhancement Trans. 61
12-2	**Arrangements**	index cards or slips of paper	permutation	12-2	Teaching Tool Trans. 2, 3, 22 Technology Master 62
12-3	**Choosing a Group**	index cards or slips of paper	combination	12-3	Ch. 12 Project Master Technology Master 63
	Connect	tape, index cards, magnifying glass-es, calculators			Lesson Enhancement Trans. 62 Interdisc. Team Teaching 12A
	Review				Practice 12A; Quiz 12A; *TestWorks*

* Daily Ancillaries include Practice, Reteaching, Problem Solving, Enrichment, and Daily Transparency. Teaching Tool Transparencies are in *Teacher's Toolkits*. Lesson Enhancement Transparencies are in *Overhead Transparency Package*.

SKILLS TRACE

LESSON	SKILL	FIRST INTRODUCED GR. 5	GR. 6	GR. 7	DEVELOP	PRACTICE/ APPLY	REVIEW
12-1	**Using tree diagrams and the Counting Principle.**		✘		pp. 626–628	pp. 629–630	pp. 642, 658, 666, 668
12-2	**Counting arrangements/using factorials.**			✘ p. 631	pp. 631–633	pp. 634–635	pp. 642, 663, 668
12-3	**Calculating choices (order not important).**			✘ p. 636	pp. 636–638	pp. 639–640	pp. 642, 663, 668

CONNECTED MATHEMATICS

Investigation 4 in the unit *What Do You Expect?*, from the **Connected Mathematics** series, can be used with Section 12A.

INTERDISCIPLINARY TEAM TEACHING

Math and Science/Technology

(Worksheet pages 51–52: Teacher pages T51–T52)

In this lesson, students use probability to answer questions about rainfall and its effect on flooding.

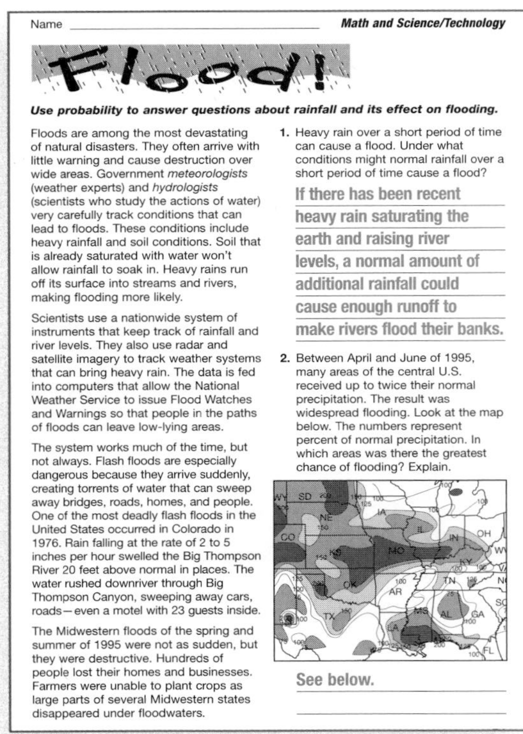

Name ______________________ *Math and Science/Technology*

Flood!

Use probability to answer questions about rainfall and its effect on flooding.

Floods are among the most devastating of natural disasters. They often arrive with little warning and cause destruction over wide areas. Government *meteorologists* (weather experts) and *hydrologists* (scientists who study the actions of water) very carefully track conditions that can lead to floods. These conditions include heavy rainfall and soil conditions. Soil that is already saturated with water won't allow rainfall to soak in. Heavy rains run off its surface into streams and rivers, making flooding more likely.

Scientists use a nationwide system of instruments that keep track of rainfall and river levels. They also use radar and satellite imagery to track weather systems that can bring heavy rain. The data is fed into computers that allow the National Weather Service to issue Flood Watches and Warnings so that people in the paths of floods can leave low-lying areas.

The system works much of the time, but not always. Flash floods are especially dangerous because they arrive suddenly, creating torrents of water that can sweep away bridges, roads, homes, and people. One of the most deadly flash floods in the United States occurred in Colorado in 1976. Rain falling at the rate of 2 to 5 inches per hour swelled the Big Thompson River 20 feet above normal in places. The water rushed downriver through Big Thompson Canyon, sweeping away cars, roads—even a motel with 23 guests inside.

The Midwestern floods of the spring and summer of 1995 were not as sudden, but they were destructive. Hundreds of people lost their homes and businesses. Farmers were unable to plant crops as large parts of several Midwestern states disappeared under floodwaters.

1. Heavy rain over a short period of time can cause a flood. Under what conditions might normal rainfall over a short period of time cause a flood?
   If there has been recent heavy rain saturating the earth and raising river levels, a normal amount of additional rainfall could cause enough runoff to make rivers flood their banks.
2. Between April and June of 1995, many areas of the central U.S. received up to twice their normal precipitation. The result was widespread flooding. Look at the map below. The numbers represent percent of normal precipitation. In which areas was there the greatest chance of flooding? Explain.
   See below.

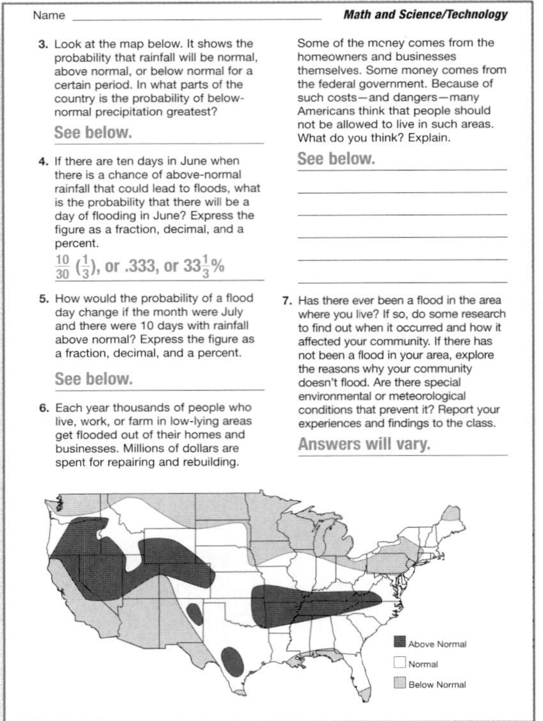

Name ______________________ *Math and Science/Technology*

3. Look at the map below. It shows the probability that rainfall will be normal, above normal, or below normal for a certain period. In what parts of the country is the probability of below-normal precipitation greatest?
   See below.
4. If there are ten days in June when there is a chance of above-normal rainfall that could lead to floods, what is the probability that there will be a day of flooding in June? Express the figure as a fraction, decimal, and a percent.
   $\frac{10}{30}$ ($\frac{1}{3}$), or .333, or $33\frac{1}{3}$%
5. How would the probability of a flood day change if the month were July and there were 10 days with rainfall above normal? Express the figure as a fraction, decimal, and a percent.
   See below.
6. Each year thousands of people who live, work, or farm in low-lying areas get flooded out of their homes and businesses. Millions of dollars are spent for repairing and rebuilding. Some of the money comes from the homeowners and businesses themselves. Some money comes from the federal government. Because of such costs—and dangers—many Americans think that people should not be allowed to live in such areas. What do you think? Explain.
   See below.
7. Has there ever been a flood in the area where you live? If so, do some research to find out when it occurred and how it affected your community. If there has not been a flood in your area, explore the reasons why your community doesn't flood. Are there special environmental or meteorological conditions that prevent it? Report your experiences and findings to the class.
   Answers will vary.

Answers

2. The areas that received 200 percent of normal precipitation (darkest areas on the map), because they received the most rainfall. These include large parts of Kansas, Missouri, Oklahoma, Illinois, Indiana, Wyoming, Colorado, South Dakota, Nebraska, Mississippi, and Louisiana.
3. The Pacific Northwest and across the northern tier of states to Pennsylvania and New York; most of California and the Southwest; the southern tip of Texas; the Gulf coast of Louisiana, Mississippi, and Alabama; the Florida panhandle, and southern tip of Florida.
5. The probability would decrease slightly to 10/31, or .3225, or 32.3%
6. Opinions will vary. Accept any reasonable answer. Students who think that people should not be allowed to live where flooding is very likely might state that it is too dangerous or that it isn't fair to use government money (taxpayers' money) to help people rebuild homes and businesses in places that are likely to flood. Students who think that people should be allowed to live in such areas might state that people have the right to live where they please, that most places are prone to some type of natural disaster, or that people should be allowed to live in flood plains if they pay for rebuilding themselves.

BIBLIOGRAPHY

FOR TEACHERS

Adler, Henry L. *Introduction to Probability & Statistics.* San Francisco, CA: W. H. Freeman, 1972.

Johnson, Christine V. *Investigating Apples: Real-World Mathematics Through Science.* Menlo Park, CA: Innovative Learning Publications; Addison-Wesley Publications, 1995.

Krantz, Les. *The Best and Worst of Everything.* New York, NY: Prentice Hall General Reference, 1991.

Nichols, Judith E. *By the Numbers: Using Demographics and Psychographics. . . .* Chicago, IL: Bonus Books, 1990.

Spangler, David. *Math for Real Kids.* Glenview, IL: Good Year Books, 1997.

FOR STUDENTS

Bode, Janet. *New Kids in Town: Oral Histories of Immigrant Teens.* New York, NY: Scholastic, Inc. 1991.

Froman, Robert. *Venn Diagrams.* New York, NY: Crowell, 1972.

Krantz, Les. *What the Odds Are.* New York, NY: HarperPerennial, 1992.

Riedel, Manfred G. *Winning with Numbers: A Kid's Guide to Statistics.* Englewood Cliffs, NJ: Prentice-Hall, 1978.

Ungar, Sanford J. *Fresh Blood: The New American Immigrants.* New York, NY: Simon & Schuster, 1995.

Section 12A

SECTION 12A

Counting

▶ Science Link ▶ Social Studies Link ▶ www.mathsurf.com/7/ch12/detective

Someday My Prints Will Come

"It is a capital mistake to theorize before you have all the evidence [said Sherlock Holmes]. It biases the judgment."

—Arthur Conan Doyle
A Study in Scarlet

Ever since Arthur Conan Doyle introduced the world to Sherlock Holmes, people have enjoyed reading detective stories. It's fun to try to solve the mystery along with (or faster than!) a super-sleuth like Agatha Christie's Miss Marple.

In real life, a fingerprint is one of a detective's most important clues. Every person has unique fingerprints, so a match between a suspect and a fingerprint at a crime scene is powerful evidence.

Fingerprint experts use a classification system based on 3 basic patterns. Along with the computerized Automated Fingerprint Identification System, this classification system helps compare a fingerprint to the millions on file. The mathematics of arranging and counting you are about to investigate is an important part of this system.

1 Look at one of your fingertips closely. Describe any patterns you see in your fingerprint.

2 Compare the fingerprints on your two little fingers. What do you notice?

3 Why do you think fingerprint experts needed to devise a system for classifying fingerprints?

625

Where are we now?

In Grade 6, students explored the ways events can happen.

They learned how to

- find the probability of an event from sample data.
- find the probability of an event from geometric models.
- make tree diagrams.

Where are we going?

In Section 12A, students will

- use tree diagrams and the Counting Principle to find all of the outcomes for a set of choices.
- count the number of ways items can be arranged.
- use factorial products to count arrangements.
- calculate the number of ways to choose some item out of a larger group when order is important.

Theme: Detective Work

World Wide Web

If your class has access to the World Wide Web, you might want to use the information found at the Web site address given. The interdisciplinary links relate to the topics discussed in this section.

About the Page

This page introduces the theme of the section, detective work, and discusses how forensic scientists use fingerprints to solve crimes.

Ask …

- How do you think computers have helped to organize the fingerprint identification system?
- What other kinds of physical evidence do forensic scientists study to identify criminals? Possible answers: Blood, physical and facial features.

Extension

The following activities do not require access to the World Wide Web.

Science

In the late 19th century, Sir Francis Galton showed that a person's fingerprints were unique. Have students research the history of fingerprinting.

Social Studies

Forensic scientists are frequently called upon to help in criminal investigations. Ask students to investigate how these people help local law enforcement officials.

Answers for Questions

1. Possible answers: Students may describe arcs and loops.
2. They are nearly perfect reflections of one another.
3. Without a system, they would need to compare a fingerprint from a crime scene to fingerprints on file one at a time. Since there are millions on file, this would not be possible.

Connect

On page 641, students will analyze their own fingerprints.

12-1 Lesson Organizer

Objective

- Use tree diagrams and the Counting Principle to find all the outcomes for a set of choices.

Vocabulary

- Tree diagram, outcome, Counting Principle

NCTM Standards

- 1–4, 11

► Review

Find each product.

1. 5 × 6 × 2 60
2. 2 × 4 × 5 × 2 80
3. 3 × 5 × 4 60
4. 3 × 3 × 4 × 2 72

Available on Daily Transparency 12-1

1 Introduce

Explore

The Point
Students investigate ways to organize information by listing possible characteristics that could be used to describe a burglary suspect, and discuss how a witness might use these characteristics to describe a burglar.

Ongoing Assessment
Have groups share their lists to be sure that they understand the assignment.

For Groups That Finish Early
Discuss which characteristics you think would be most helpful and which would be least helpful in describing a burglar. Answers will vary.

12-1 Counting Methods

You'll Learn ...

- to use tree diagrams and the Counting Principle to find all the outcomes for a set of choices

... How It's Used

Biologists use tree diagrams to analyze what might happen in different generations of animals.

Vocabulary

tree diagram
outcome
Counting Principle

► Lesson Link You've had experience making organized lists. Now you'll see how organized lists can help you count efficiently. ◄

Explore Classifying Characteristics

I Spy a Crook

You are a detective interviewing witnesses at a burglary scene. Your goal is to get an accurate description of the suspect.

1. Make a list of all the characteristics you can think of that you will ask the witnesses about.
2. For each characteristic, what are the possible responses? (For instance, possible responses for observed hair color might include blonde, brown, red, and black.)
3. How many of your characteristics would you expect a witness to be able to remember? Explain your answer.
4. Give some different possibilities for the description of your suspect.

Learn Counting Methods

Suppose a witness sees a burglar running from a robbery and can describe the color and length of the suspect's hair. You can make an organized list to count the number of possible descriptions.

Hair Color	Hair Length	Hair Color	Hair Length
Black	Short	Brown	Short
Black	Medium	Brown	Medium
Black	Long	Brown	Long
Blonde	Short	Red	Short
Blonde	Medium	Red	Medium
Blonde	Long	Red	Long

MEETING INDIVIDUAL NEEDS

Resources

12-1 Practice
12-1 Reteaching
12-1 Enrichment
12-1 Problem Solving
12-1 Daily Transparency
- Problem of the Day
- Review
- Quick Quiz

Lesson Enhancement Transparency 61

Wide World of Mathematics Geometry: One Long Detour

Learning Modalities

Visual Encourage students to draw tree diagrams to display the number of outcomes for selecting several items. Have them label each column with the appropriate description.

Social Have students work in groups of 3 or 4 to complete the **Explore** exercises.

Inclusion

For students who are having difficulty in drawing tree diagrams, it is sometimes helpful to give them partially completed diagrams and then have them complete the diagrams.

You can see that, if there are 4 hair colors and 3 lengths, there are 12 different combinations of hair length and color.

There are other organized ways to count the information shown in this table. One is to use a **tree diagram**. The structure of the tree shows all the possibilities, or **outcomes**, in a given situation.

Example 1

Use a tree diagram to show all of the different outcomes for 4 hair colors (black, blonde, brown, and red) and 3 hair lengths (short, medium, and long).

From the starting point, draw a "branch" for each of the 4 hair colors.

For each color, draw 3 "twigs," one for each possible length.

Counting the twigs shows that there are 12 different outcomes for hair length and color.

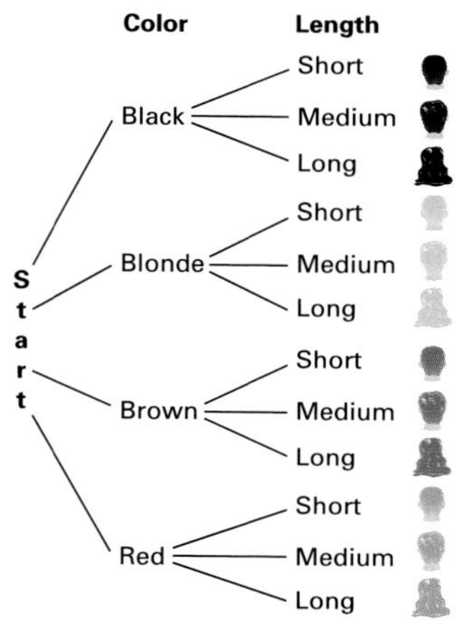

Only about 8% of the people in the United States have red hair.

Try It

Hector's Juice-O-Rama sells 2 types of juice, orange and apple. You can order a small, medium, or large glass of either type. Use a tree diagram to show how many different juice orders are possible.

In Example 1, the tree diagram had 4 branches and each branch had 3 twigs. Notice that the number of possible combinations, 12, is equal to 4 • 3.

4 branches times 3 twigs equals 12 combinations.

$4 \times 3 = 12$

This idea is summarized in the **Counting Principle**.

COUNTING PRINCIPLE

To find the number of different outcomes for making choices in a sequence, multiply together the number of possibilities for each item.

Answers for Explore

1. Height, weight, hair color, age, sex, race, eye color, etc.
2. Height and weight: ranges, 4–7 ft, 70–350 lb; hair color: red, blonde, black, brown, etc.
3. Responses should indicate that not every witness will remember every characteristic.
4. Possible description: White female, 20–25 years old, medium height, brown hair.

2 Teach

Learn

You may wish to use Lesson Enhancement Transparency 61 with Example 1.

Alternate Examples

1. Use a tree diagram to show all of the outcomes for 4 hair colors (black, blonde, brown, and red) and 4 eye colors (brown, blue, green, and hazel).

   From the starting point, draw a "branch" for each hair color. Then for each color, draw four "twigs," one for each eye color.

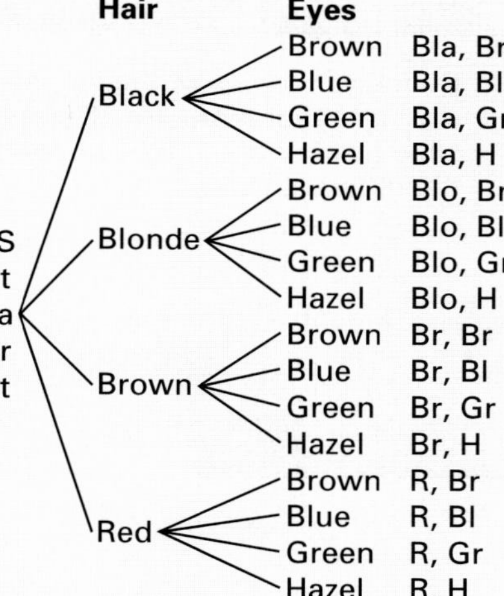

There are 16 different outcomes for hair color and eye color.

Answers for Try It

There are 6 possible outcomes for juice orders.

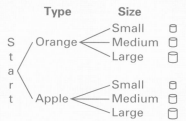

Type / Size

Start
- Orange: Small, Medium, Large
- Apple: Small, Medium, Large

MATH EVERY DAY

Problem of the Day

Draw the figure that continues the pattern.

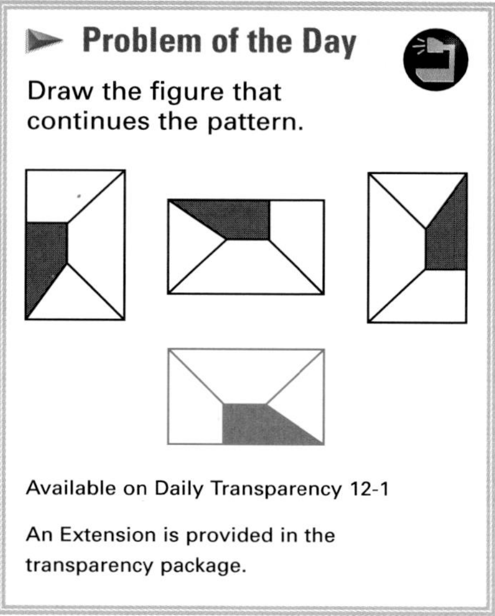

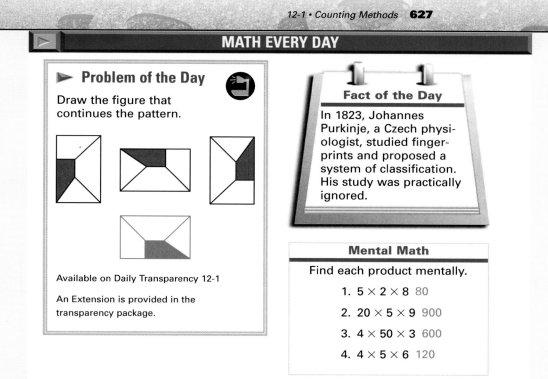

Available on Daily Transparency 12-1

An Extension is provided in the transparency package.

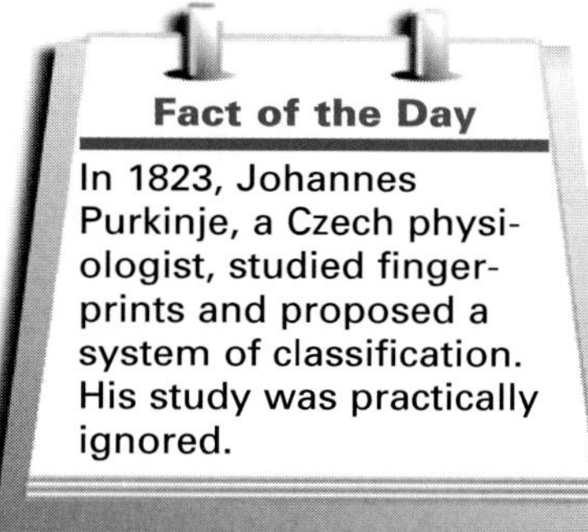

Fact of the Day
In 1823, Johannes Purkinje, a Czech physiologist, studied fingerprints and proposed a system of classification. His study was practically ignored.

Mental Math

Find each product mentally.

1. $5 \times 2 \times 8$ 80
2. $20 \times 5 \times 9$ 900
3. $4 \times 50 \times 3$ 600
4. $4 \times 5 \times 6$ 120

Alternate Examples

2. A school has 5 math teachers, 2 music teachers, and 5 history teachers. Use the Counting Principle to find how many different sets of teachers a student could have for these three subjects.

   $5 \times 2 \times 5 = 50$

   There are 50 possible sets of teachers.

3. Sandy makes trays. She uses 2 shapes (square or circular), 2 colors (white or gray), and 3 designs (plain, striped, or plaid). How many different types of trays does she make, and what are they?

   You can use the Counting Principle to find the number of groupings: $2 \times 2 \times 3 = 12$. But we need to make an organized list, such as a tree diagram, to describe the trays.

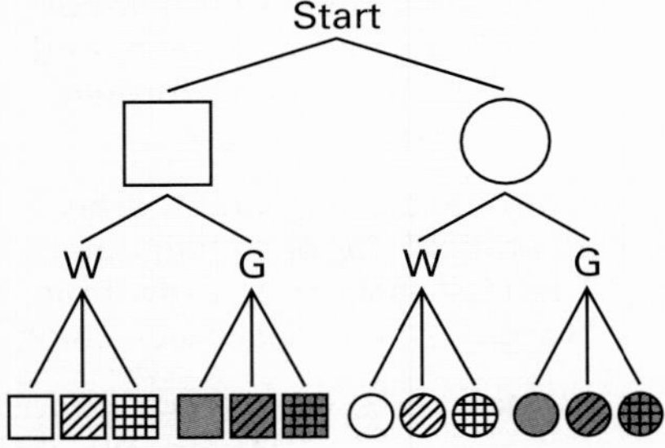

   Counting the tips of the twigs confirms that there are 12 possible trays, while the tips show the different trays.

Examples

2 A school has 3 mathematics teachers, 4 English teachers, and 2 Spanish teachers. Using the Counting Principle, find how many different sets of teachers a student could have for these 3 subjects.

Multiply the number of choices for each type of teacher.

$3 \cdot 4 \cdot 2 = 24$

There are 24 possible sets of teachers.

3 A detective is planning a disguise. He can choose from 2 wigs (red or blonde), 2 fake noses (bulbous or pointy), and 2 pairs of glasses (green or mirrored). How many different disguises can he create, and what are they?

Using the Counting Principle, there are $2 \cdot 2 \cdot 2 = 8$ disguises. However, we need to make an organized list, such as a tree diagram, to describe the disguises.

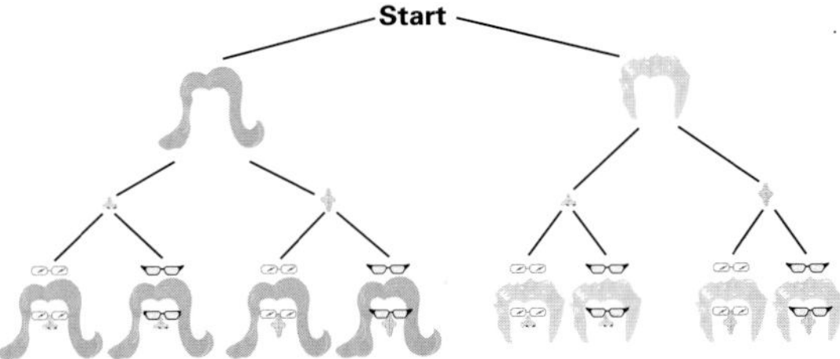

Counting the tips of the twigs confirms that there are 8 possible disguises. The tips of the twigs show the different disguises.

Try It

A softball coach has 5 pitchers, 2 catchers, and 2 shortstops on her team. Using the Counting Principle, find out how many different sets of players she can use for these positions. 20

Check Your Understanding

1. In the tree diagram in Example 1, would you get a different number of outcomes if the branches were hair lengths and the twigs were colors? Explain.
2. Describe a situation where the Counting Principle is more useful than a tree diagram. Describe a situation where a tree diagram is more useful.

3 Practice and Assess

Check

Answers for Check Your Understanding

1. No; there would be three branches, each with four twigs, giving 12 outcomes.
2. Possible answer: The Counting Principle is more useful when you need to know only the number of possibilities; The tree diagram is more useful when you need to know what those possibilities are.

MEETING MIDDLE SCHOOL CLASSROOM NEEDS

Tips from Middle School Teachers

I have students work in small groups to determine how many outcomes are possible in situations where several choices are given. For example,

Kinds of chicken: regular or crispy? plain or spicy? white meat, dark meat, or wings? 12

Sizes of jeans: Possible waists are 26″, 28″, 30″, 32″, 34″, 36″, 38″ and possible lengths are 28″, 30″, 32″, 34″, 36″. 35

Team Teaching

Have the curriculum director supply a list of classes available for different periods of the school day. Then have students determine how many different ways they could arrange a schedule including all the courses they wish to take.

Social Studies Connection

In 1924, The United States established the Identification Division of the Federal Bureau of Investigation. This division helped law enforcement agencies by having all the fingerprint records in one place rather than having separate records throughout the country. The FBI has fingerprint records for over 170 million people.

12-1 Exercises and Applications

Practice and Apply

1. **Getting Started** Follow the steps to find out how many different sundaes you can make choosing one flavor of ice cream, one sauce, and one topping from the list.

Ice Cream Flavors	Sauce Flavors	Toppings
Vanilla	Chocolate	Nuts
Chocolate	Caramel	Whipped Cream
Strawberry	Butterscotch	Sprinkles
Peach		

a. Multiply the number of ice cream flavors by the number of sauce flavors. 12

b. Multiply your answer to **a** by the number of toppings. The product is the number of different sundaes you can make. 36

c. What is the name of the principle you used to solve this problem? Counting Principle

Operation Sense Use the Counting Principle to find the number of outcomes in each situation.

2. Parakeets: 2 types, 5 colors. How many choices? 10

3. Clothing: 3 shirts, 4 pairs of pants, 2 pairs of shoes. How many outfits? 24

4. Bicycles: 5 colors, 3 sizes, 3 styles. How many choices? 45

5. Lunch: 2 drinks, 4 different sandwiches, 3 kinds of fruit. How many choices? 24

6. **Logic** You are taking a true-false test. The test has 3 questions, and there are 2 choices (T and F) for each.

a. Make a tree diagram to show the possible outcomes for answers for this test. How many outcomes are there? What are the outcomes?

b. Suppose the correct answers are FFT. How many of the outcomes in **a** give all 3 right answers? 2 right answers? 1 right answer?

7. **Social Studies** On a 1996 ballot in San Jose, California, there were 8 candidates for President, 5 for U.S. Representative, and 3 for State Senator. How many different ways could a voter select one candidate for each office? 120

8. GPS The Out To Lunch restaurant chain offers customers their choice of one kind of soup and one sandwich. On Monday, the soups are chicken noodle and tomato, and the sandwiches are roast beef, turkey, and veggie. How many different lunches can be selected, and what are they?

PRACTICE 12-1

12-1 Exercises and Applications

Assignment Guide

- Basic
  1–7 odds, 8–11, 13–17 odds
- Average
  2–12 evens, 13, 16, 18
- Enriched
  2–12 evens, 13, 14–18 evens

Exercise Notes

Exercises 2–5

Extension Have students make tree diagrams to verify their numerical answers and then identify the possible choices.

Exercise Answers

6. a.

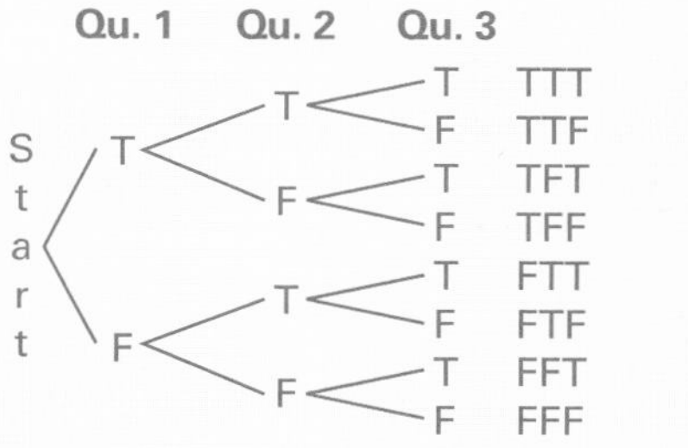

There are 8 outcomes; TTT, TTF, TFT, TFF, FTT, FTF, FFT, FFF

b. 1 way; 3 ways; 3 ways

8. 6 lunches; Chicken noodle and roast beef, chicken noodle and turkey, chicken noodle and veggie, tomato and roast beef, tomato and turkey, tomato and veggie.

PRACTICE

Name ______________________

Practice 12-1

Counting Methods

Use the Counting Principle to find the number of outcomes in each situation.

1. Magazine subscriptions: 4 magazines, 3 subscription lengths. How many choices? 12
2. Jeans: 3 colors, 6 waist sizes, 10 lengths. How many choices? 180
3. Computers: 3 motherboards, 3 hard drives, 4 monitors. How many choices? 36
4. Stereos: 5 receivers, 3 CD players, 4 types of speakers. How many systems? 60
5. Dinner: 4 main courses, 3 side dishes, salad with one of 6 dressings. How many choices? 72
6. You are taking a multiple-choice test. Each of the 2 questions has 4 choices (A, B, C, and D).

Possible answer:

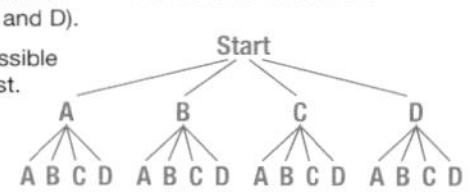

a. Make a tree diagram to show the possible outcomes for the answers for this test. How many outcomes are there? 16

What are the outcomes?

AA, AB, AC, AD, BA, BB, BC, BD, CA, CB, CC, CD, DA, DB, DC, DD

b. Suppose the correct answers are CB. How many of the outcomes in **a** provide a correct response for both questions? 1

For only one question? 6 For neither question? 9

7. Lloyd is trying to guess a 3-digit number. He knows that the hundreds digit is 4 or 7, the tens digit is 3, 6, or 9, and the units digit is 0 or 5.

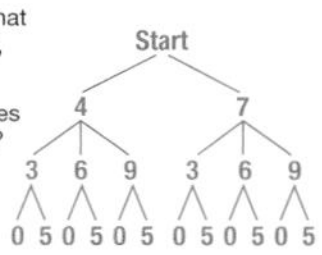

a. Make a tree diagram to show the possible outcomes for the number. How many outcomes are possible? 12

List the outcomes.

430, 435, 460, 465, 490, 495, 730, 735, 760, 765, 790, 795

b. Lloyd finds out that the units digit is 5. Now how many outcomes are possible? 6

RETEACHING

Name ______________________

Alternative Lesson 12-1

Counting Methods

When there are several ways that choices can be made, you need an organized way to count them.

A **tree diagram** is one way to show all possibilities, or **outcomes**, in a given situation. Another way to find the number of possible outcomes is to use the **counting principle**.

Counting Principle
To find the number of different outcomes for making choices in a sequence, multiply together the number of possibilities for each item.

Example

Find the number of possible outcomes if you toss two coins. What are they? You can use the Counting Principle to find the number of possible outcomes.

Outcomes for 1st coin		Outcomes for 2nd coin		Total number of outcomes
2	×	2	=	4

There are 4 possible outcomes.

To find what each outcome may be, you can make a tree diagram.

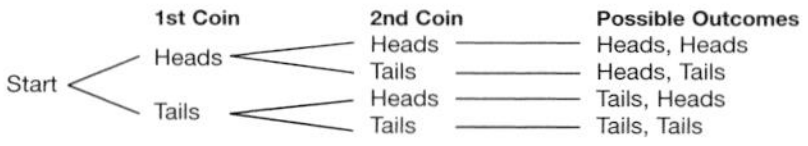

The four possible outcomes are: 2 heads, 2 tails, 1 tail and 1 head, and 1 head and 1 tail.

Try It

a. Use the Counting Principle to find the number of possible outcomes if you toss three coins. 8 possible outcomes

b. Complete the tree diagram to show what each outcome might be.

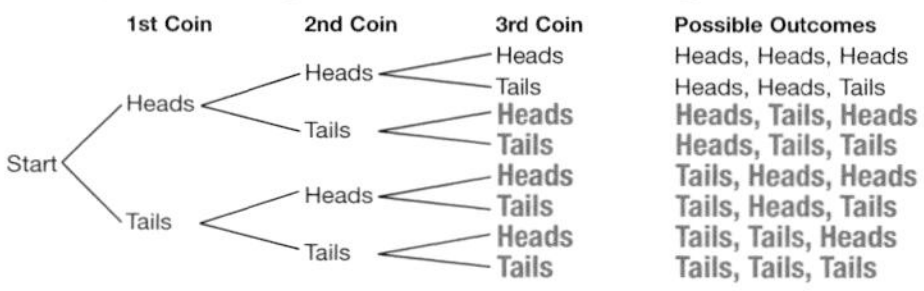

Find the number of possible outcomes if you toss

c. four coins. 16 outcomes. d. five coins. 32 outcomes.

Reteaching

Activity

Materials: Number cube, index cards

Work with a partner. Each person should write his or her name on an index card. Then complete the following steps:

- Put the cards in a stack and shuffle them. Pick a card from the stack and then toss the number cube. Record the results as follows: NAME, NUMBER.
- Make a list and count all possible results for the preceding step. 12
- Keep repeating the first step above until all possible results have been obtained. Discuss why this might require more steps than appear in the tree diagram.

Exercise Notes

■ Exercise 10

Test Prep If students selected A, they added the outcomes instead of applying the Counting Principle.

Exercise Answers

12. a. *xyz*

b. Any three numbers whose product is 42 are correct; possible answers: 3, 2, 7 and 1, 14, 3

13. Answers may vary.

14.

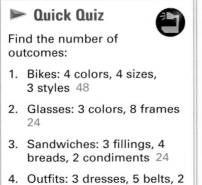

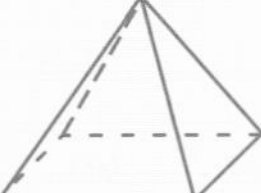

15.

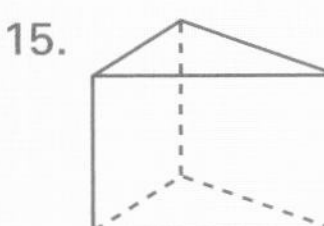

16.

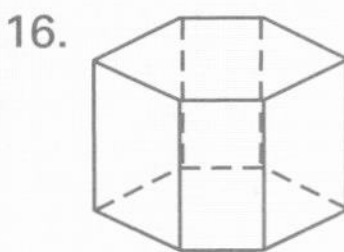

17.

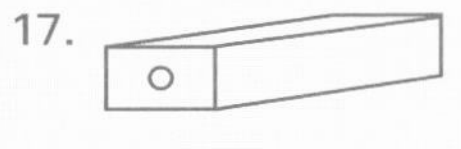

18.

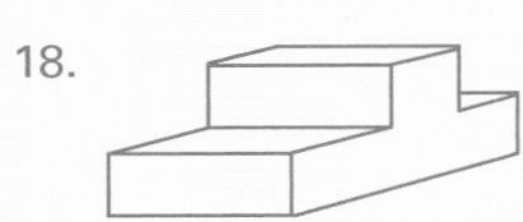

Alternate Assessment

You may want to use the *Interactive CD-ROM Journal* with this assessment.

Journal Have students write if they would use an organized list, tree diagram, or the Counting Principle to solve this problem: Jon has 3 shirts (red, green, and blue), 3 slacks (blue, khaki, and gray), and 2 pairs of shoes (black and white). How many different outfits can he wear?

► Quick Quiz

Find the number of outcomes:

1. Bikes: 4 colors, 4 sizes, 3 styles 48
2. Glasses: 3 colors, 8 frames 24
3. Sandwiches: 3 fillings, 4 breads, 2 condiments 24
4. Outfits: 3 dresses, 5 belts, 2 scarves 30

Available on Daily Transparency 12-1

9. Police artists draw *composite sketches* of suspects. The FaceKit imaging system allows detectives to create composite sketches on a computer. Among other features, FaceKit has 96 different head shapes, 248 noses, 176 mouths, and 224 chins. How many combinations of these features can FaceKit make? 938,606,592

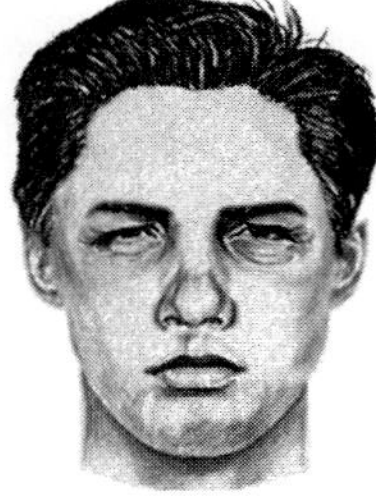

Image created by FaceKit Pacer Infotec, Inc.

10. **Test Prep** There are 4 roads from City A to City B, 2 from B to C, and only 1 highway from C to D. How many different routes are there from A to B to C to D? B

Ⓐ 7 Ⓑ 8 Ⓒ 9 Ⓓ 10

Problem Solving and Reasoning

11. **Critical Thinking** Ms. Potatohead® comes with: a straw hat, a yellow visor, a red baseball cap, a flowered bonnet; eyes with glasses, eyes without glasses; open lips with teeth, closed lips, open lips with tongue sticking out; green, purple, and pink shoes; and two different noses. How many different versions of Ms. Potatohead could you create if you use one choice for each feature? 144

12. **Critical Thinking** Suppose you have x choices for your first period class, y choices for your second period class, and z choices for your third period class.

a. How many possible ways are there to select these classes?

b. Give possible values of x, y, and z if there are 42 ways to select the classes.

13. Journal Write an interactive story where the reader is allowed to make 2 decisions. (For instance, at one point you could ask, "Should Ana go into the dragon's cave? If you answer yes, go on to the next paragraph. If no, go to paragraph 5.") There should be at least 6 possible versions of the story.

Mixed Review

Sketch each polyhedron. *[Lesson 11-1]*

14. Square pyramid **15.** Triangular prism **16.** Hexagonal prism

Make a perspective sketch of each object. *[Lesson 11-2]*

17.

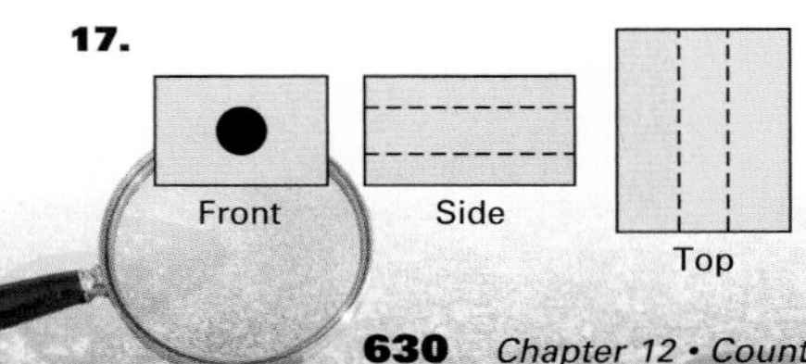

18.

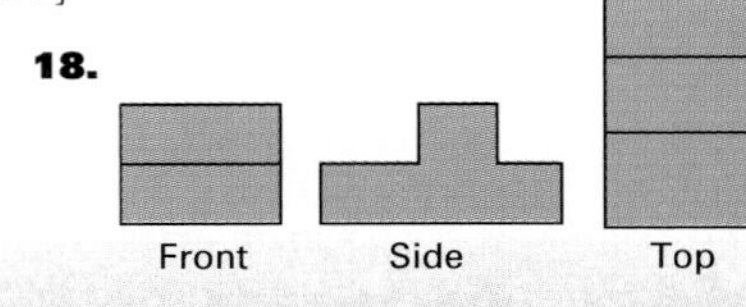

PROBLEM SOLVING 12-1

PROBLEM SOLVING

Name ______________ **Guided Problem Solving 12-1**

GPS PROBLEM 8, STUDENT PAGE 629

The Out To Lunch restaurant chain offers customers their choice of one kind of soup and one sandwich. On Monday, the soups are chicken noodle and tomato, and the sandwiches are roast beef, turkey, and veggie. How many different lunches can be selected, and what are they?

— Understand —

1. Underline what you are asked to find.

— Plan —

2. Which method can you use to find the number of possible outcomes? d

a. Organized list b. Tree diagram c. Counting Principle d. Any of them

— Solve —

3. Use one of the counting methods to show each possible outcome.

Start
- Chicken Noodle
  - Roast Beef — Chicken noodle, roast beef
  - Turkey — Chicken noodle, turkey
  - Veggie — Chicken noodle, veggie
- Tomato
  - Roast Beef — Tomato, roast beef
  - Turkey — Tomato, turkey
  - Veggie — Tomato, veggie

4. How many different lunches can be selected? 6 different lunches.

— Look Back —

5. How can you use the Counting Principle to make sure you have listed all the possible outcomes?

Possible answer: Multiply to find possible outcomes; then check to see that your list has the same number.

SOLVE ANOTHER PROBLEM

On Tuesday, the restaurant offers these choices. Soups are barley, corn chowder, and potato. Sandwiches are ham, veggie, salami, and turkey. How many different lunches can be selected and what are they?

12: BH, BV, BS, BT, CH, CV, CS, CT, PH, PV, PS, PT

ENRICHMENT

Name ______________ **Extend Your Thinking 12-1**

Visual Thinking

Find the way through the maze.

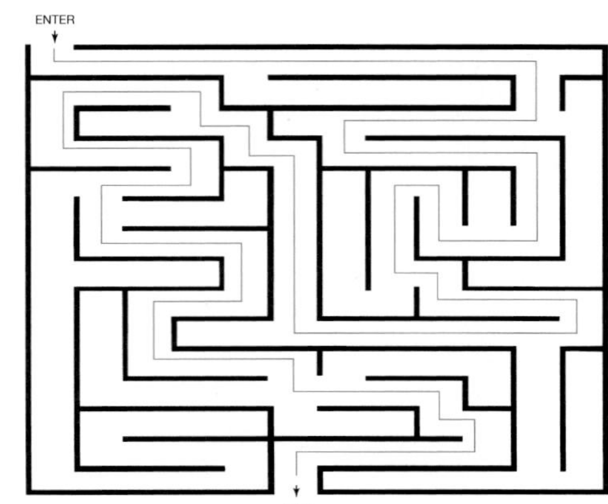

Arrangements

12-2

▶ Lesson Link You've found the number of outcomes for a series of events. Now you will investigate situations where the *order* of the events is important. ◀

Explore Arrangements

This Isn't a Chorus Line!

Materials: Index cards or slips of paper

Police Chief Iva Gottam is planning a police *lineup,* where witnesses to a crime try to pick the criminal out of a group of people. How many different ways can she line up 3 people from left to right?

1. Write the names of the 3 people in the lineup on cards and arrange them in all the possible orders. (You'll need several cards for each person.) Record your results and count the arrangements.
2. Take the cards and arrange them in a tree diagram to show all the possibilities. Again, record your results and count the arrangements.
3. After you placed the first person in a lineup, how many choices did you have for the second? After the first two were placed, how many choices did you have for the third?
4. How is this situation different from the combinations you've investigated so far?

Learn Arrangements

When you arrange a set of books on a shelf, each one you place leaves one less possibility for the next. When the order of the items in an arrangement is important, each possible ordering is called a **permutation**.

The fact that you have one less choice at each stage of the decision is very important when finding the number of permutations.

You'll Learn ...

- to count the number of ways items can be arranged
- to use factorial products to count arrangements

... How It's Used

You use permutations when arranging a selection of photographs in a frame.

Vocabulary

permutation

MEETING INDIVIDUAL NEEDS

Resources

12-2 Practice
12-2 Reteaching
12-2 Enrichment
12-2 Problem Solving
12-2 Daily Transparency
Problem of the Day
Review
Quick Quiz
Teaching Tool Transparencies 2, 3, 22
Technology Master 62

Learning Modalities

Logical Have students list some situations in daily life where the order of items in a group is important.

Visual As in Lesson 12-1, tree diagrams are again a valuable visual aid for students in picturing permutations.

English Language Development

Be sure that students do not confuse the meaning of the factorial sign (!) with an exclamation point. Relate the term *factorial* to the term *factor*. The number with the factorial symbol tells how many factors are to be multiplied and is the greatest of the factors. Each succeeding factor is 1 less than the one before it.

12-2 Lesson Organizer

Objectives

- Count the number of ways items can be arranged.
- Use factorial products to count arrangements.

Vocabulary

- Permutation

Materials

- Explore: Index cards or slips of paper

NCTM Standards

- 1–2, 4, 11

▶ Review

Find each product.

1. 6 • 5 • 4 120
2. 5 • 4 • 3 60
3. 7 • 6 • 5 210
4. 6 • 5 • 4 • 3 360
5. 5 • 4 • 3 • 2 120

Available on Daily Transparency 12-2

1 Introduce

Explore

The Point
Students use cards containing three names to model all the possible order arrangements.

Ongoing Assessment
Be sure students understand that once a suspect has been placed in the lineup, he or she cannot appear in another position.

Answers for Explore on next page.

For Groups That Finish Early

Tell how many different ways the four letters A, E, L, and P can be ordered. 24 List the arrangements and tell if any words are formed. LEAP, PALE, PEAL, PLEA

Answers for Explore

1. 6 arrangements.
2. 6 arrangements.
3. 2 choices for the second; 1 choice for the third.
4. Previous decisions eliminate possibilities for the next choice.

2 Teach

Learn

You may wish to use Teaching Tool Transparency 22: Scientific Calculator with **Try It**.

Use six different books to physically demonstrate the concept of permutation developed in **Learn**. Discuss the number of ways the books can be arranged in order.

Alternate Examples

1. In how many different orders can you arrange a math book, a science book, and a history book on your bookshelf?

   There are 3 possibilities for the first place. Once the first book has been placed, there are 2 books possible for the second place. Finally, there is only 1 book left for the third place. There are 6 possible orders.

	Book 1	Book 2	Book 3	Orders
Start	M	S	H	MSH
		H	S	MHS
	S	M	H	SMH
		H	M	SHM
	H	M	S	HMS
		S	M	HSM

2. How many different orders are possible for the numbers 5, 6, 7, and 8?

   There are 4 possibilities for the first position, 3 possibilities for the second position, 2 possibilities for the third position, and 1 possibility for the last position.

   By the Counting Principle there are $4 \cdot 3 \cdot 2 \cdot 1 = 24$ ways to arrange the numbers 5, 6, 7, and 8.

Example 1

Language Link

The word *permutation* comes from the Latin *permutare,* "to change thoroughly."

Today, Azucena, Bert, and Chao-Yee are going to give their reports in math class. In how many orders can these students give their reports?

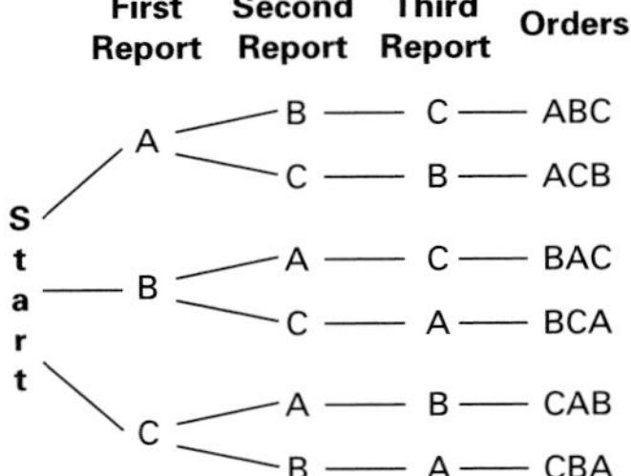

There are 3 possibilities for the first report.

Once the first student gives his or her report, there are 2 choices (shown by the branches) for the second.

Finally, there is only 1 person left for the third report, as shown by having 1 twig for each branch.

There are 6 possible orders for the student reports.

Notice that there are 3 "trunks," each trunk has 2 "branches," and each branch has 1 "twig," resulting in the $3 \cdot 2 \cdot 1 = 6$ permutations.

The Counting Principle can help determine the number of possible permutations in a given situation.

Example 2

There are 4 people in Darryl's family. In how many different ways can they line up for a family portrait?

There are 4 possible choices for the person on the left. There are 3 choices for the second spot, 2 for the third, and the remaining person must stand on the right.

By the Counting Principle, there are $4 \cdot 3 \cdot 2 \cdot 1 = 24$ ways Darryl's family can line up for the portrait.

Try It

The Fotomatic Camera Store, Gemie's Jewelry, Handy Hardware, Igloo Yogurt, and Joe's Junque Shoppe were burglarized in Napoleonville last night. In how many different orders could the burglaries have taken place? 120

Did you notice a pattern in the multiplications in Examples 1 and 2? The factors decreased by 1 each time, since every step reduced the number of choices by 1.

MATH EVERY DAY

Problem of the Day

The Egyptians used a rope with 12 evenly spaced knots to make triangles when building geometric structures. What kinds of triangles and angles can they make using such a rope? Possible answer: The rope was used to create right angles by making a 3-4-5 right triangle. It can be used to create 60° angles by making an equilateral triangle.

Available on Daily Transparency 12-2

An Extension is provided in the transparency package.

Fact of the Day

Fingerprints were first used to identify criminals in the 1890s by Sir Edward Richard Henry, the British police offical in Bengal, India.

Mental Math

Find each product mentally.

1. $5 \times 4 \times 3 \times 2$ 120
2. $4 \times 3 \times 2 \times 1$ 24
3. $10 \times 9 \times 8$ 720
4. $6 \times 5 \times 4$ 120

Another way to write 4 • 3 • 2 • 1 is 4!. This is read "four factorial" (not "four!!"). The exclamation point is the sign for factorial.

Factorial products, and portions of factorial products, are important in calculating numbers of permutations.

Study TIP

To remember what factorial means, use the dot in "!" to remind you to multiply, and the line to remind you that the last number to multiply is 1.

Examples

Give each factorial product.

3 5!

5! = 5 • 4 • 3 • 2 • 1 = 120

4 8!

8! = 8 • 7 • 6 • 5 • 4 • 3 • 2 • 1 = 40,320

5 Cycleville uses a 3-digit number for each of its bicycle license plates. Zeros are not used, and no digit appears more than once in a license. Chief Pedals wants to know how many different licenses he can issue.

There are 9 possibilities (1–9) for the first digit. Suppose you choose a 7 for the first digit.

Then there are only 8 possibilities left for the second: 1, 2, 3, 4, 5, 6, 8, and 9.

If you choose a 4 for the second digit, there are 7 possibilities left for the third: 1, 2, 3, 5, 6, 8, and 9.

Once you choose the third digit, the license is finished.

There are 9 • 8 • 7 = 504 different license numbers.

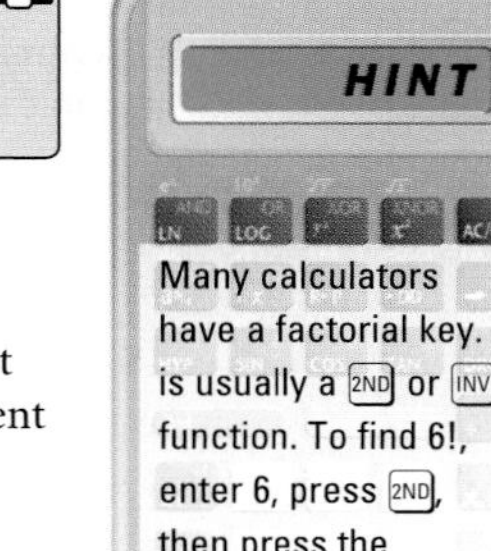

HINT

Many calculators have a factorial key. It is usually a 2ND or INV function. To find 6!, enter 6, press 2ND, then press the factorial key.

Try It

Give each factorial product.

a. 4! 24

b. 10! 3,628,800

c. Chief Pedals (from Example 5) decides that 504 license numbers are not enough for Cycleville. If he uses 4-digit numbers instead, how many different license plate numbers will there be? 3024

Check Your Understanding

1. Write the values of 2! through 6! and see how quickly the size of a factorial product grows. Why do you think these products grow so quickly?

2. Explain why, when you order a set of items, the number of possibilities decreases by 1 at each step in the ordering process.

Alternate Examples

Give each factorial product.

3. 6!

 6! = 6 • 5 • 4 • 3 • 2 • 1 = 720

4. 9!

 9! = 9 • 8 • 7 • 6 • 5 • 4 • 3 • 2 • 1 = 362,880

5. Gary wants to use only even numbers with no repetitions for a 3-digit code for his combination lock. How many different codes can he have?

 There are 5 possibilities (0, 2, 4, 6, and 8) for the first number in the code. Suppose Gary chooses 4 as the first number. Then there are 4 possibilities (0, 2, 6, and 8) for the second number. If he chooses 0 for the second number, there are 3 possibilities (2, 6, and 8) left for the last number.

 Gary can have 5 • 4 • 3 = 60 different codes.

3 Practice and Assess

Check

Answers for Check Your Understanding

1. 2! = 2, 3! = 6, 4! = 24, 5! = 120, 6! = 720; As the number in the factorial increases, you multiply by greater and greater numbers.
2. Once an item is placed, you cannot choose it for the next position in the arrangement. So, every time you place an item, the number of items left to choose from decreases by 1.

MEETING MIDDLE SCHOOL CLASSROOM NEEDS

Tips from Middle-School Teachers

I like to have students physically act out various ways 4 students can be elected class president, vice-president, secretary, and treasurer to reinforce the concept of permutations.

Sports Connection

The marathon is a long-distance race, covering 26 miles, 385 yards (42.2 kilometers). The race commemorates the run in 490 B.C. by the Greek soldier Pheidippides, who ran 22.5 miles from the battle of Marathon to Athens to announce the Greek victory over the Persians. The first modern Olympic marathon in 1896 was won by a Greek. The women's marathon did not become an Olympic event until 1984.

Team Teaching

A Physical Education teacher might have students find the number of possible batting orders for a 9-player softball team. Then, discuss why a coach does not have to consider all the possibilites because only a few players are suited for particular places in the lineup.

12-2 Exercises and Applications

Assignment Guide

- **Basic**
  1–3, 6–13, 15, 18
- **Average**
  4–5, 7–11, 13 –14, 16, 19
- **Enriched**
  4–5, 7–11, 13 –14, 17, 20

Exercise Notes

Exercises 1–5

Extension Have students use their calculators to check the factorials. They can either multiply or use a factorial key.

Exercise 10

Consumer Ask students what the letters ATM represent. Automated Teller Machine Ask how an ATM operates.

Exercise 11

Test Prep If students chose D, they found the value of 9!

Exercise 14

Problem-Solving Tip You may want to use Teaching Tool Transparencies 2 and 3: Guided Problem Solving, pages 1–2.

Exercise Answers

7. ARY, AYR, RAY, RYA, YAR, YRA (A = Arimori, R = Roba, Y = Yegorova)

9. ABCD, ABDC, ACBD, ACDB, ADBC, ADCB, BACD, BADC, BCAD, BCDA, BDAC, BDCA, CABD, CADB, CBAD, CBDA, CDAB, CDBA, DABC, DACB, DBAC, DBCA, DCAB, DCBA; None of the orderings form words.

Reteaching

Activity

Materials: Four sets of number cards, each set labeled 1–9

Use the number cards to make all possible arrangements for each exercise. Do not repeat any numbers. Then tell how many arrangements are possible.

1. Two-digit numbers using 1–5. 20
2. Three-digit numbers using 6–9. 24
3. Four-digit numbers using 2, 4, 6, and 8. 24
4. Two-digit numbers using 1–6. 30

12-2 Exercises and Applications

Practice and Apply

1. **Getting Started** On a Saturday, you plan to go shopping, eat lunch, call a friend, and see a movie. Follow the steps to determine how many different orders there are for these activities.
   a. Decide how many choices there are for the first activity. 4
   b. After you do the first activity, how many choices do you have for the second? 3
   c. How many choices are left for the third activity? 2
   d. How many choices are left for the fourth? 1
   e. Multiply your answers to **a, b, c,** and **d** to find the number of different orders for these activities. 24

Operation Sense Give each factorial product.

2. 3! 6 **3.** 7! 5040 **4.** 11! 39,916,800 **5.** 9! 362,880

6. Problem Solving A detective plans to dust a crime scene for fingerprints, make casts of footprints, collect hair samples, and collect fiber samples. In how many different orders can he do these tasks? 24

7. Sports In the 1996 Olympics, the gold, silver, and bronze medalists in the women's marathon were Yuko Arimori, Japan; Fatuma Roba, Ethiopia; and Valentina Yegorova, Russia — but not in that order. List all of the possible orders of finish for these athletes.

8. Science Many animal groups have *pecking orders.* An animal dominates those below it in the pecking order. Use factorial notation to give the number of possible pecking orders for:

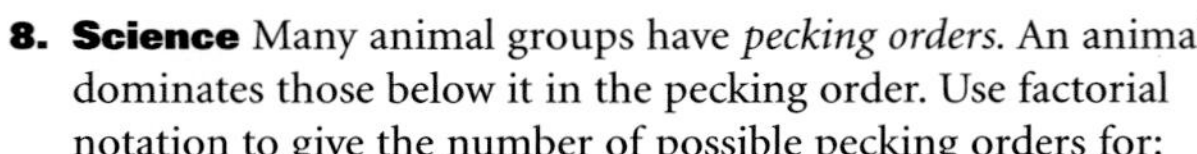

a. A flock of 15 chickens 15! **b.** A pack of 22 wolves 22!

9. List all possible orderings of the letters A, B, C, and D (without repeating letters). Do any of these orderings form words?

10. Consumer Polly must make up a 4-digit secret code for her ATM card. If she can choose any of the digits 1–6, but is not allowed to repeat digits, how many possibilities are there for her code? 360

11. Test Prep How many different 4-digit license plates can be made from the digits 0–9 if no digits are repeated? C

Ⓐ 10 Ⓑ 3,024 Ⓒ 5,040 Ⓓ 362,880

PRACTICE 12-2

PRACTICE

Name ____________

Practice 12-2

Arrangements

Give each factorial product.

1. 6! 720 2. 2! 2 3. 4! 24 4. 5! 120
5. 1! 1 6. 9! 362,880 7. 8! 40,320 8. 12! 479,001,600

9. Every morning Harold feeds his dog, takes a shower, eats breakfast, and reads the newspaper. In how many different orders can he do these tasks? 24

10. Matt, Nat, and Pat are having a swimming race. List all the possible orders in which they can finish the race.
Matt, Nat, Pat; Matt, Pat, Nat; Nat, Matt, Pat; Nat, Pat, Matt; Pat, Nat, Matt; Pat, Matt, Nat

11. Sandra displays her collection of compact discs on a shelf. Use factorial notation to give the number of ways she can arrange her discs if she has:
a. 5 discs 5! **b.** 15 discs 15! **c.** 34 discs 34! **d.** 182 discs 182!

12. List all of the possible ways to order the letters in the word MATH (without repeating letters).
AHMT, AHTM, AMHT, AMTH, ATHM, ATMH, HAMT, HATM, HMAT, HMTA, HTAM, HTMA, MAHT, MATH, MHAT, MHTA, MTAH, MTHA, TAHM, TAMH, THAM, THMA, TMAH, TMHA

13. Keith must choose a 3-letter password for a computer account. He can use any of the 26 upper-case letters of the alphabet, but he cannot repeat letters. How many passwords are possible? 15,600

14. Jarita is making a simple jigsaw puzzle for her very young cousin. She plans to arrange the shapes shown in a row. How many ways can she arrange the shapes? (The shapes are not to be rotated.) 720
⬡△□○⇧☆

15. The president, vice president, secretary, and treasurer of a school club are lining up for a photograph. In how many different orders can they line up? 24

RETEACHING

Name ____________

Alternative Lesson 12-2

Arrangements

When the order of items in an arrangement is important, each possible ordering is called a **permutation.** Each time you choose an item in a permutation, you have one less choice for the next item.

Example 1

Jared and Leroy want to play miniature golf, shoot some basketball goals, and watch a movie. In how many different ways (orders) can they do these activities?

A tree diagram shows all their options.

	First	Second	Third	Orders
Start	Golf	Basketball	Movie	Golf, Basketball, Movie
		Movie	Basketball	Golf, Movie, Basketball
	Basketball	Golf	Movie	Basketball, Golf, Movie
		Movie	Golf	Basketball, Movie, Golf
	Movie	Golf	Basketball	Movie, Golf, Basketball
		Basketball	Golf	Movie, Basketball, Golf

Use the Counting Principle to find the number of ways to order the activities.

First choice		Second choice		Third choice		Number of ways
3 ways	×	2 ways	×	1 way	=	6 ways

Both methods show that there are 6 ways in which the boys can choose to do these activities.

Try It

a. Janelle plans to shop, eat lunch, go to a movie, and visit the library. How many choices are there for each activity?
1st activity 4 2nd activity 3 3rd activity 2 4th activity 1

b. Use the Counting Principle to find the different ways Janelle can choose to do these activities. $4 \times 3 \times 2 \times 1 = 24$

c. In how many ways (orders) can Cora read a mystery book, a science fiction book, and a historical novel? 6 ways.

Example 2

Give the factorial product of 7!

7! is a short way to write $7 \times 6 \times 5 \times 4 \times 3 \times 2 \times 1$.

The product of 7! is 5040.

Try It

Give each factorial product.

d. 3! 6 e. 4! 24 f. 5! 120 g. 6! 720

12. Kadim and Mary have been asked to design a school flag. They have decided to make a flag with three horizontal stripes, similar to the flag of Sierra Leone at right. They can choose from green, white, red, and yellow stripes. How many different possibilities are there for the design if the three stripes must have different colors? (Assume a green-white-red flag is different from a red-white-green flag.) 24

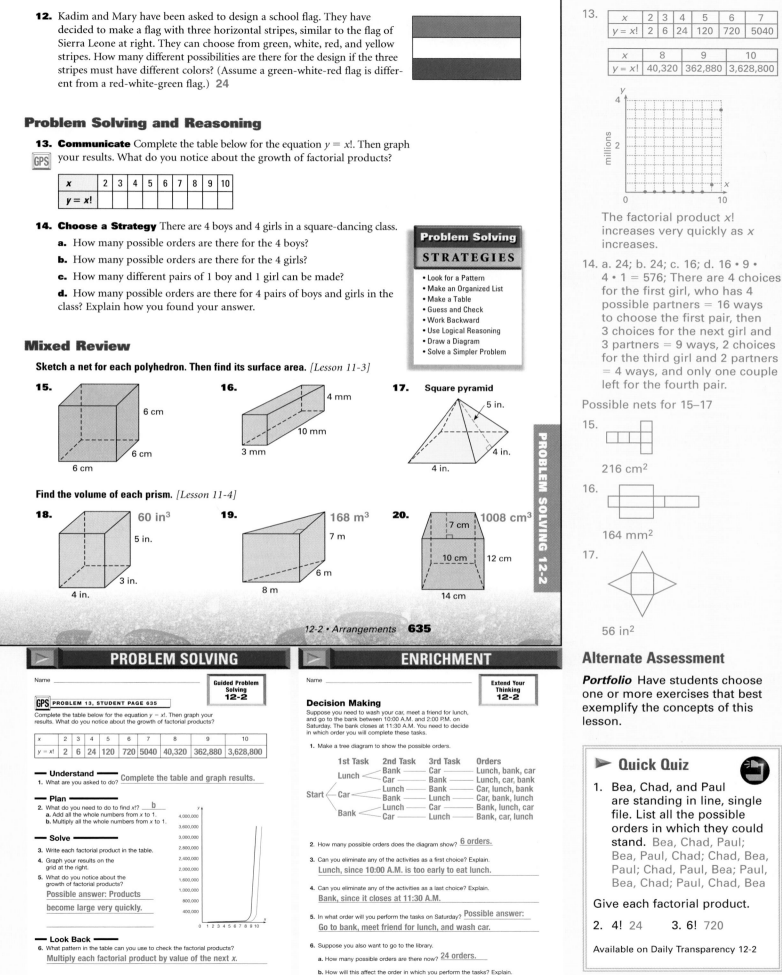

Problem Solving and Reasoning

13. Communicate Complete the table below for the equation $y = x!$. Then graph your results. What do you notice about the growth of factorial products?

GPS

x	2	3	4	5	6	7	8	9	10
$y = x!$									

14. Choose a Strategy There are 4 boys and 4 girls in a square-dancing class.

a. How many possible orders are there for the 4 boys?

b. How many possible orders are there for the 4 girls?

c. How many different pairs of 1 boy and 1 girl can be made?

d. How many possible orders are there for 4 pairs of boys and girls in the class? Explain how you found your answer.

Problem Solving STRATEGIES

- Look for a Pattern
- Make an Organized List
- Make a Table
- Guess and Check
- Work Backward
- Use Logical Reasoning
- Draw a Diagram
- Solve a Simpler Problem

Mixed Review

Sketch a net for each polyhedron. Then find its surface area. *[Lesson 11-3]*

15.

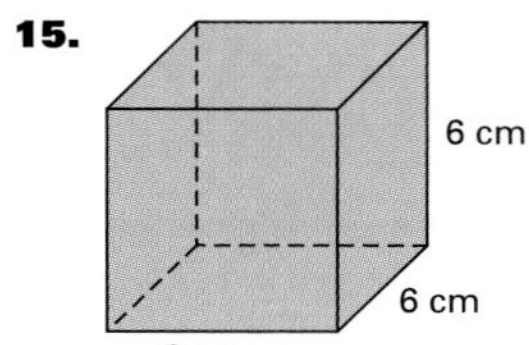

16.

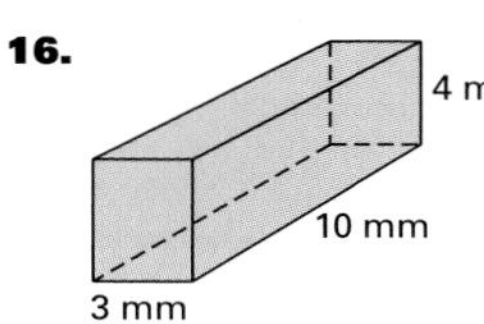

17. Square pyramid

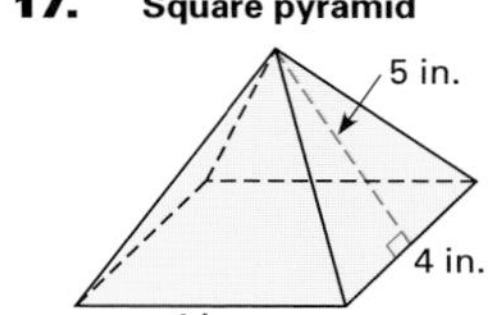

Find the volume of each prism. *[Lesson 11-4]*

18. 60 in³

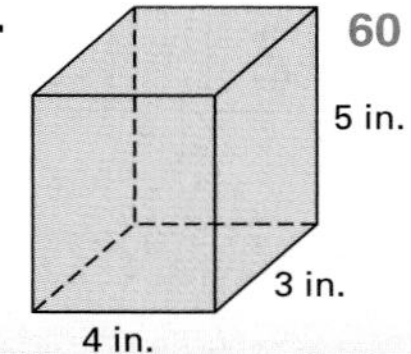

19. 168 m³

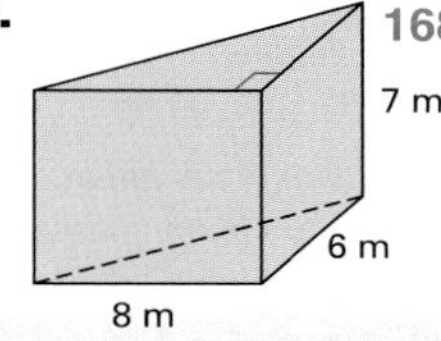

20. 1008 cm³

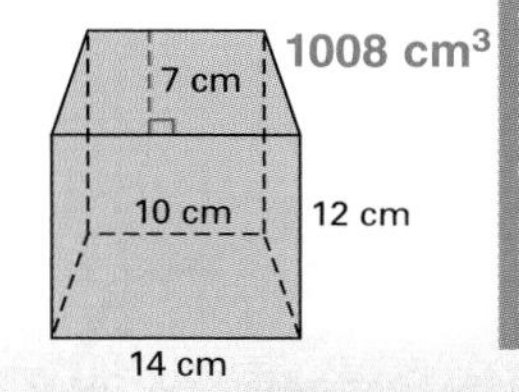

PROBLEM SOLVING 12-2

PROBLEM SOLVING

Name ______________________

Guided Problem Solving 12-2

GPS **PROBLEM 13, STUDENT PAGE 635**

Complete the table below for the equation $y = x!$. Then graph your results. What do you notice about the growth of factorial products?

x	2	3	4	5	6	7	8	9	10
$y = x!$	2	6	24	120	720	5040	40,320	362,880	3,628,800

Understand

1. What are you asked to do? Complete the table and graph results.

Plan

2. What do you need to do to find $x!$? b
   a. Add all the whole numbers from x to 1.
   b. Multiply all the whole numbers from x to 1.

Solve

3. Write each factorial product in the table.
4. Graph your results on the grid at the right.
5. What do you notice about the growth of factorial products? Possible answer: Products become large very quickly.

y; 4,000,000; 3,600,000; 3,000,000; 2,800,000; 2,400,000; 2,000,000; 1,600,000; 1,000,000; 800,000; 400,000; x; 0 1 2 3 4 5 6 7 8 9 10

Look Back

6. What pattern in the table can you use to check the factorial products? Multiply each factorial product by value of the next x.

SOLVE ANOTHER PROBLEM

On the grid above, graph $y = (x - 1)!$. Use x values 2 through 11. How does your graph compare to the one in the problem above?
The new graph is moved 1 unit to the right of the old graph.

ENRICHMENT

Name ______________________

Extend Your Thinking 12-2

Decision Making

Suppose you need to wash your car, meet a friend for lunch, and go to the bank between 10:00 A.M. and 2:00 P.M. on Saturday. The bank closes at 11:30 A.M. You need to decide in which order you will complete these tasks.

1. Make a tree diagram to show the possible orders.

	1st Task	2nd Task	3rd Task	Orders
Start	Lunch	Bank	Car	Lunch, bank, car
		Car	Bank	Lunch, car, bank
	Car	Lunch	Bank	Car, lunch, bank
		Bank	Lunch	Car, bank, lunch
	Bank	Lunch	Car	Bank, lunch, car
		Car	Lunch	Bank, car, lunch

2. How many possible orders does the diagram show? 6 orders.
3. Can you eliminate any of the activities as a first choice? Explain. Lunch, since 10:00 A.M. is too early to eat lunch.
4. Can you eliminate any of the activities as a last choice? Explain. Bank, since it closes at 11:30 A.M.
5. In what order will you perform the tasks on Saturday? Possible answer: Go to bank, meet friend for lunch, and wash car.
6. Suppose you also want to go to the library.
   a. How many possible orders are there now? 24 orders.
   b. How will this affect the order in which you perform the tasks? Explain. Possible answers: Go to bank first, then to the library either before or after lunch to get the run-around tasks done before doing the messy task of washing the car.

Exercise Answers

13.

x	2	3	4	5	6	7
$y = x!$	2	6	24	120	720	5040

x	8	9	10
$y = x!$	40,320	362,880	3,628,800

y; 4; 2; millions; x; 0; 10

The factorial product $x!$ increases very quickly as x increases.

14. a. 24; b. 24; c. 16; d. 16 • 9 • 4 • 1 = 576; There are 4 choices for the first girl, who has 4 possible partners = 16 ways to choose the first pair, then 3 choices for the next girl and 3 partners = 9 ways, 2 choices for the third girl and 2 partners = 4 ways, and only one couple left for the fourth pair.

Possible nets for 15–17

15. 216 cm²

16. 164 mm²

17.

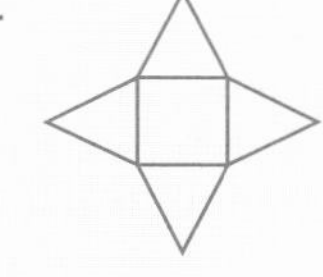

56 in²

Alternate Assessment

Portfolio Have students choose one or more exercises that best exemplify the concepts of this lesson.

Quick Quiz

1. Bea, Chad, and Paul are standing in line, single file. List all the possible orders in which they could stand. Bea, Chad, Paul; Bea, Paul, Chad; Chad, Bea, Paul; Chad, Paul, Bea; Paul, Bea, Chad; Paul, Chad, Bea

Give each factorial product.

2. 4! 24
3. 6! 720

Available on Daily Transparency 12-2

Lesson Organizer

Objective

- Calculate the number of ways to choose some items out of a larger group when the order is unimportant.

Vocabulary

- Combination

Materials

- Explore: Index cards or slips of paper

NCTM Standards

- 1–4, 7, 11

Review 

Suppose you have 4 flowers–a rose, a daisy, a mum, and a carnation.

1. List all the ways you could use 3 of the flowers to make a bouquet. Rose, daisy, mum; Rose, mum, carnation; Rose, daisy, carnation; Daisy, mum, carnation
2. Does the order in which you put the flowers in the vase make any difference in the resulting bouquet? No

Available on Daily Transparency 12-3

1 Introduce

Explore  

The Point
Students use index cards to model all the possible combinations of four names.

Ongoing Assessment
Be sure students have no duplicate pairs in their lists of suspects.

For Groups That Finish Early
Tell how many different ways the four suspects could be grouped in threes and then list the groups.
4; ARL, ARK, ALK, RLK

12-3 Choosing a Group

You'll Learn ...

- how to calculate the number of ways to choose some items out of a larger group when the order is unimportant

... How It's Used

Coaches use combinations when they're selecting a starting lineup.

Vocabulary

combination

► Lesson Link You've found the number of permutations, where the order of a set of items is important. Now you'll explore methods to count the number of ways to choose things where the order does not matter. ◄

Explore Choosing a Group

Pick a Pair of Perpetrators

Materials: Index cards or slips of paper

Eyewitnesses say that 2 burglars stole the Secret Sauce recipe at the Burger Bungalow. The detectives have narrowed down the list of suspects to Ally Eagle, Ray Kinn, Lars Sonny, and Kat Berglar. Help the detectives discover how many possible pairs of these suspects there are.

1. Write the names or initials of the suspects on index cards.
2. Find all the possible pairs that can be made with these suspects.
3. When you think you've found all the possible pairs, check your answer by making a list or drawing a picture.
4. How many pairs of burglars can you make from the list of 4 suspects? Explain how you know that you've found all the possibilities.

Ally Eagle

Ray Kinn

Lars Sonny

Kat Berglar

Learn Choosing a Group

When you solved problems involving permutations, you were concerned with the order the items were in.

≠

Now you will count the number of ways a few items can be selected from a larger group. In these problems, the order does *not* matter.

 = 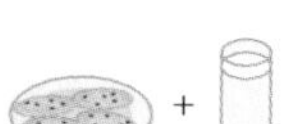

A selection of items where the order does not matter is a **combination**.

MEETING INDIVIDUAL NEEDS

Resources

- 12-3 Practice
- 12-3 Reteaching
- 12-3 Enrichment
- 12-3 Problem Solving
- 12-3 Daily Transparency
  - Problem of the Day
  - Review
  - Quick Quiz
- Chapter 12 Project Master
- Technology Master 63

Learning Modalities

Verbal Have students make a list of people in their class and then choose from the list to show all possible committees of 2 people, 3 people, and so on.

Visual Have students draw a tree diagram on the board showing all the permutations of 3 letters that can be made from A, B, C, and D. Circle the grouping ABC. Then have a volunteer cross out any groupings that contain A, B, and C. Follow the same procedure for ABD, ACD, and so on. Tell students that the groupings ABE, ABD, ACD, and so on, are combinations of 4 things taken 3 at a time, and that the order of the letters does not matter.

English Language Development

You can help students distinguish between permutations and combinations by relating the word *permutation* to the root *mutate*, or change. We change the positions of the items in different permutations. Thus, there are generally more permutations than combinations for a given set of items.

Examples

1 At a crime scene, a detective collected 3 clothing fiber samples labeled A, B, and C. The crime lab has time to analyze 2 samples before the case goes to trial. How many different pairs of the samples could be analyzed? What are the pairs?

You can use a tree diagram to answer this question.

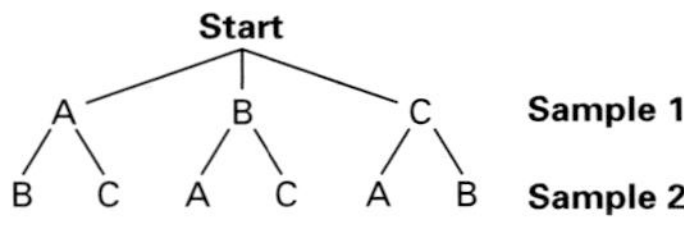

AB AC ~~BA~~ BC ~~CA~~ ~~CB~~ **Outcomes**

There are 6 pairs listed at the bottom of the tree diagram. However, the pairs in red are duplicates of those in black.

There are 3 different pairs of samples that could be analyzed. They are AB, AC, and BC.

2 There are 4 candidates, Winnie, Xavier, Yolanda, and Zeke, running for 3 positions on the student council. How many different ways are there to choose 3 of the 4?

You can make an organized list of the possibilities to answer this question.

First find all the choices that include Winnie. Be sure to list all the possibilities for the other 2 candidates.

WXY WXZ WYZ

Then find all the choices that don't include Winnie. Since there are only 3 other candidates, there's only 1 possibility.

XYZ

There are 4 different ways to choose 3 candidates.

Try It

a. Suppose you can choose 2 out of these 3 electives: Drawing, Metal Shop, or Journalism. How many different options do you have? 3

b. In Example 2, suppose there is a fifth candidate to choose from, Victor. How many different combinations are there for 3 of the 5 candidates? 10

Literature Link

Sherlock Holmes, the famous detective created by Arthur Conan Doyle, popularized the science of criminology.

Test Prep

When you check your answer to a combination problem, make sure you've eliminated all the possibilities that are duplicates of each other.

MATH EVERY DAY

Problem of the Day

Alyssia baled hay last month. She used half of what was baled to feed her dairy cattle. She sold half of the bales she had left. Then she donated 42 bales to a local animal shelter and still had 120 bales left. How many bales of hay did she bale last month? 648 bales [Work backwards. 120 + 42 = 162; So she sold 162 of 324. Her dairy cattle were fed 324 of 648 bales.]

Available on Daily Transparency 12-3

An Extension is provided in the transparency package.

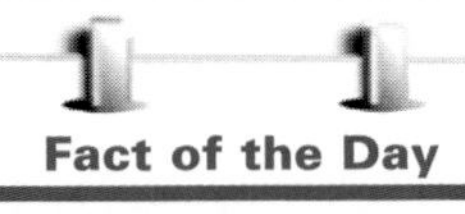

Fact of the Day

After Allan Pinkerton captured a gang of counterfeiters in Chicago, he was elected sheriff of Cook County. In 1850, he became Chicago's first city detective.

Estimation

Estimate each product.

1. 52 × 5 250
2. 431 × 4 1600
3. 187 × 9 1800
4. 62 × 59 3600
5. 73 × 490 35,000

Answers for Explore

1–3. Ally and Rae, Ally and Lars, Ally and Kat, Rae and Lars, Rae and Kat, Lars and Kat

4. 6 pairs; Explanations should tell why the list or picture must include all possibilities.

2 Teach

Learn

Alternate Examples

1. There are 5 suspects for a robbery committed by 2 people. How many different pairs are possible? List the pairs. Use A, B, C, D, and E to represent the subjects.

   Use a tree diagram. There are 20 pairs listed. Cross out the duplicate pairs.

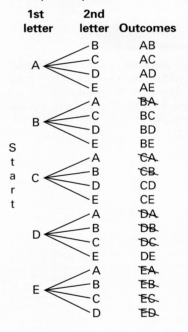

	1st letter	2nd letter	Outcomes
Start	A	B	AB
		C	AC
		D	AD
		E	AE
	B	A	~~BA~~
		C	BC
		D	BD
		E	BE
	C	A	~~CA~~
		B	~~CB~~
		D	CD
		E	CE
	D	A	~~DA~~
		B	~~DB~~
		C	~~DC~~
		E	DE
	E	A	~~EA~~
		B	~~EB~~
		C	~~EC~~
		D	~~ED~~

   There are 10 different pairs of suspects: AB, AC, AD, AE, BC, BD, BE, CD, CE, and DE.

2. Five candidates, Joe, Kay, Lee, May, and Nan, are running for 4 positions on the school newspaper. How many different ways are there to choose 4 of the 5 students?

   You can make an organized list of the possibilities. First, find the choices that include Joe.

   JKLM JKLN JLMN JKMN

   Then find the choices that include Kay but not Joe.

   KLMN

   Use the same idea to finish your list. There are no other possibilities. There are 5 different ways to choose 4 students.

Students see two methods for finding the number of combinations of 4 things taken 2 at a time. One method utilizes an organized list and the other employs a tree diagram. Students can decide which of the two correct methods is easier for them.

Answers for What Do You Think?

1. To make the tree diagram, Lorena had to choose one item "first" and another "second," so it showed all possible orders of the combinations.
2. He listed all possible combinations with green peppers in the first row.

3 Practice and Assess

Check

Have students make a tree diagram to confirm the number of different combinations in Example 2. Have a volunteer draw the diagram on the chalkboard.

Answers for Check Your Understanding

1. In a combination of items, the order does not matter; AB is the same as BA. In permutations, the order of the items makes a difference.
2. By making an organized list, you can make sure that you have accounted for all possibilities. Start by listing all possibilities that include one of the items. Then list all the remaining possibilities for each of the other items. In each case, you must remember to *not* include the items you've already listed completely.

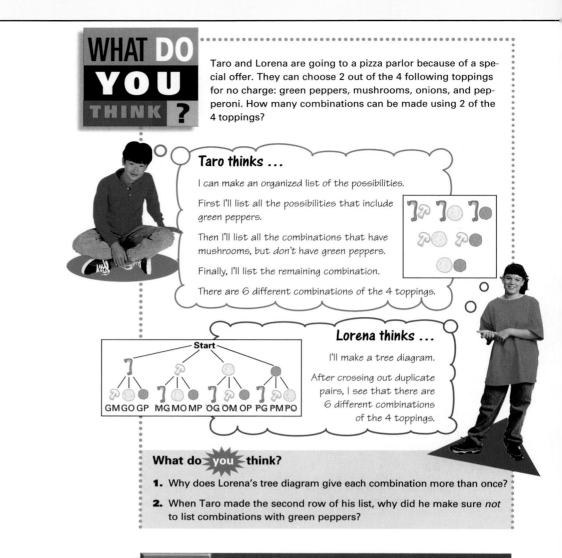

Taro and Lorena are going to a pizza parlor because of a special offer. They can choose 2 out of the 4 following toppings for no charge: green peppers, mushrooms, onions, and pepperoni. How many combinations can be made using 2 of the 4 toppings?

Taro thinks ...

I can make an organized list of the possibilities.

First I'll list all the possibilities that include green peppers.

Then I'll list all the combinations that have mushrooms, but *don't* have green peppers.

Finally, I'll list the remaining combination.

There are 6 different combinations of the 4 toppings.

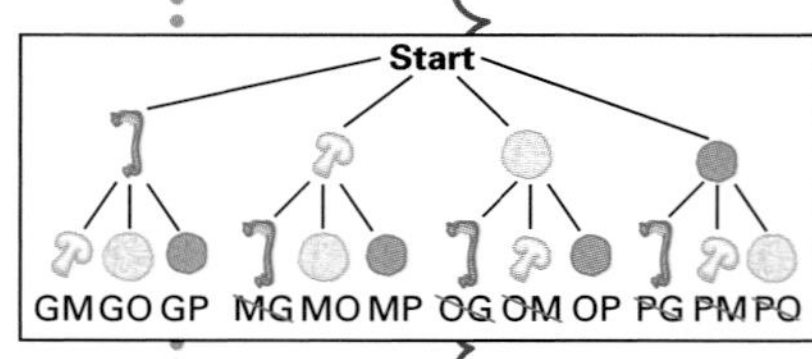

Lorena thinks ...

I'll make a tree diagram.

After crossing out duplicate pairs, I see that there are 6 different combinations of the 4 toppings.

What do you think?

1. Why does Lorena's tree diagram give each combination more than once?
2. When Taro made the second row of his list, why did he make sure *not* to list combinations with green peppers?

Check Your Understanding

1. How are combinations different from permutations?
2. How can writing an organized list help you find all of the possible combinations for a given situation? What do you need to remember to do?

MEETING MIDDLE SCHOOL CLASSROOM NEEDS

Tips from Middle-School Teachers

I like to use names of my own students when I discuss examples of combinations. Students always enjoy seeing their own names included in examples.

Literature Connection

After Conan Doyle's Sherlock Holmes became popular, many writers sought to follow his lead. One such writer was G. K. Chesterton, who created the character of Father Brown, a priest-detective. In 1920, another English writer, Agatha Christie, created crime-solver Hercule Poirot, a Belgian detective. At about the same time in the United States, the Ellery Queen series was begun.

Cooperative Learning

Have students work together to develop a list of several items that could be used to make a tossed salad. Then have them develop various lists showing combinations of two items, three items, and so on.

12-3 Exercises and Applications

Practice and Apply

1. **Getting Started** Alex, Bess, and Chandra are running for two seats on the student council. Follow the steps to find all possible combinations of two of these candidates.

   a. List all pairs of candidates that include Alex. Remember that the order does not matter. Alex and Bess, Alex and Chandra

   b. List all pairs of candidates that *do not* include Alex. Again, remember that the order does not matter. Bess and Chandra

   c. The results of **a** and **b** give a complete list of the possible combinations. How many combinations are there? 3

Decide whether or not order matters in each situation. Write *Yes* or *No*.

2. Choosing 4 CDs out of a list of 100 in a record club offer No
3. Choosing digits for an alarm code Yes
4. Seating students in a classroom Yes

You are at a pizza parlor that offers four toppings: anchovies, olives, pineapple, and sausage. How many different combinations of these items can you make if you choose:

5. Two toppings? 6
6. Three toppings? 4
7. Four toppings? 1

8. Secret agents 001, 002, 003, 004, and 005 are available to be sent on a case. Their boss, Agent 000, decides to send only two of them. How many different pairs of these agents are there? 10

9. **Problem Solving** A florist uses 6 different types of flowers to make bouquets: asters, begonias, carnations, daisies, roses, and zinnias. In how many different ways can he select 3 of these types of flowers? 20

10. Five stores in town were recently burglarized: Alice's Aquariums, Boris's Bagels, Carlos's Candy, Dorinda's Dolls, and Ellis's Electronics. Detective Wilson knows the same person committed 3 of the crimes. How many different combinations of 3 of these stores are there? 10

11. **Test Prep** How many different ways can a student choose 2 books from a reading list of 5 books? B

    Ⓐ 5 Ⓑ 10 Ⓒ 20 Ⓓ 50

Problem Solving TIP

Use a letter to represent each store. Then make an organized list of the possibilities, starting with all of the possibilities that include A (Alice's Aquariums).

PRACTICE 12-3

12-3 Exercises and Applications

Assignment Guide

- Basic
  1–5, 9–11, 12– 18 evens
- Average
  2–4, 6, 9, 11–17
- Enriched
  2–4, 7–9, 11–17, 19

Exercise Notes

Exercises 5–11

Error Prevention If students are having difficulty, encourage them to make lists or tree diagrams to picture each situation.

Project Progress

You may want to have students use Chapter 12 Project Master.

Exercise Answers

10. ABC, ABD, ABE, ACD, ACE, ADE, BCD, BCE, BDE, CDE (A = Alice's, B = Boris's, C = Carlos's, D = Dorinda's, E = Ellis's)

PRACTICE

Name ______________________

Practice 12-3

Choosing a Group

Decide whether or not order matters in each situation. Write *Yes* or *No*.

1. Choosing the digits in a lock combination Yes
2. Choosing 5 books to check out from the library No
3. Electing the president, vice president, and secretary of a club Yes
4. Choosing 5 club members to serve on a committee No

You plan to paint a clay pot. The hobby store offers appropriate paints in 6 colors. How many different ways can you choose the colors for your design if you plan to use:

5. Two colors? 15 6. Three colors? 20 7. Five colors? 6

8. At the video store, you've selected 4 videos you want to watch, but you only have time to watch 2 of them. How many ways can you select 2 of the 4 videos? 6

9. Abe, Bo, Cal, Duc, and Eve are student council members. Two of them need to meet with the school principal today.

   a. How many different ways are there to choose two of these students? 10

   b. List the possibilities.

   Abe and Bo, Abe and Cal, Abe and Duc, Abe and Eve, Bo and Cal, Bo and Duc, Bo and Eve, Cal and Duc, Cal and Eve, Duc and Eve

10. A bakery makes 3 kinds of bread: white, whole what, and nine-grain. You want to buy 2 different loaves. How many ways can you make your selection? 3

11. You have 3 extra tickets for a concert. How many ways can you choose 3 of your 5 best friends to go with you? 10

12. **History** In 1849, President Zachary Taylor chose 7 men as cabinet members. How many ways could Taylor choose 2 cabinet members with whom to consult about a particular issue? 21

RETEACHING

Name ______________________

Alternative Lesson 12-3

Choosing a Group

Sometimes the order in which items are chosen is not important. A selection of items where order does not matter is a **combination.**

— Example —

At summer camp, Conchita and Rosa can choose two daily activities from this selection: crafts, swimming, and archery. The order in which they choose the activities is not important.

Conchita made a tree diagram and crossed out the duplicates.

	First	Second	Outcomes
Start	Crafts	Swimming	Crafts, Swimming
		Archery	Crafts, Archery
	Swimming	Crafts	~~Swimming, Crafts~~
		Archery	Swimming, Archery
	Archery	Crafts	~~Archery, Crafts~~
		Swimming	~~Archery, Swimming~~

Rosa made an organized list.

First, she listed all the choices that include crafts.

Crafts and swimming
Crafts and archery

Then she listed all the choices that don't include crafts.

Swimming and archery

Both girls found 3 different ways to choose 2 activities.

— Try It —

You are at an ice cream store that offers five flavors: vanilla (V), chocolate (C), strawberry (S), butter pecan (B), and mint chocolate (M). List all the different combinations of these flavors you can make and tell how many combinations there are in all for each number of scoops.

a. Four scoops of ice cream
List all the choices that include vanilla. VCSB, VSBM, VSMC, VCBM

List all the choices that do not include vanilla. CSBM

How many different combinations can you make? 5 combinations

b. Three scoops of ice cream 10 combinations: VCS, VSB, VCB, VBM, VSM, VMC, CSB, CSM, CBM, SBM

c. Two scoops of ice cream 10 combinations: VC, VS, VB, VM, CS, CB, CM, SB, SM, BM

Reteaching

Activity

Materials: Ten number cards labeled 0–9

Use the number cards to help you answer the questions. You may want to list the groupings. Order does not matter.

From the cards 0–4, how many ways can you choose

1. 5 cards? 1
2. 4 cards? 5
3. 3 cards? 10
4. 2 cards? 10

Exercise Notes

■ Exercise 13

Geography Display a globe or a world map and have students find the South American countries named.

■ Exercise 15

Problem-Solving Tip Remind students that there are 360° in a circle.

Exercise Answers

12.

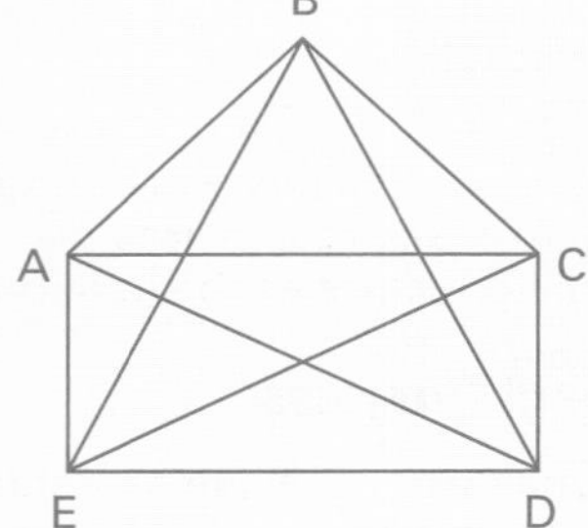

The ten possibilities are shown by the 5 sides of the pentagon and the 5 diagonals.

13. a. 20

b. 120

c. The number in b is greater; For any set of 3 countries, there are several orders in which you can visit them.

15.

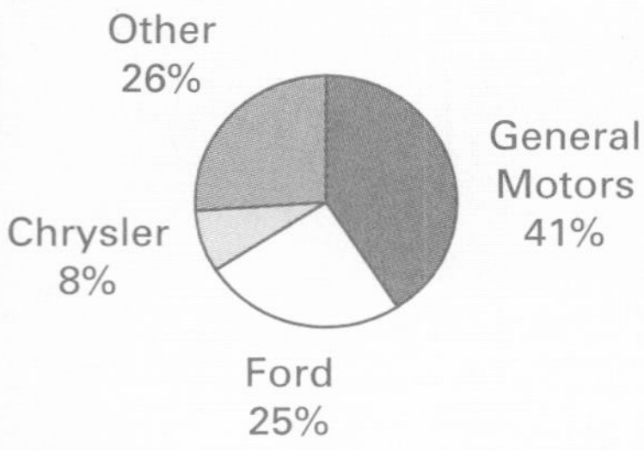

Alternate Assessment

Self Assessment Have students describe the differences between permutations and combinations, giving examples of each.

▶ Quick Quiz

Suzy's Diner offers omelets with the following items added: Swiss cheese, bacon, tomatoes, onions, and green peppers. How many different omelets can you have if you have a choice of:

1. 4 items? 5
2. 3 items? 10
3. 2 items? 10
4. 1 item? 5

Available on Daily Transparency 12-3

Problem Solving and Reasoning

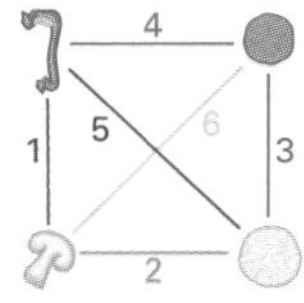

12. Critical Thinking There is another way to answer the question in the What Do You Think scenario on page 638. You can find all of the ways to choose 2 out of 4 toppings by drawing all of the segments that can connect them. Using this method, show how you can use a pentagon to solve Exercise 11.

13. Communicate Mr. Marble won an all expenses paid trip for being Outstanding Detective of the Year. He can choose to visit any 3 of the following countries: Argentina, Brazil, Chile, Ecuador, Peru, and Uruguay.

a. How many different trips can Mr. Marble take if the order of the countries is not considered?

b. How many different trips can he take if the order is considered?

c. Which number is greater, the one you found in **a** or the one you found in **b**? Explain why this makes sense.

14. Critical Thinking Suppose you can choose 1, 2, 3, *or* 4 of the following fruits for a fruit shake: banana, blueberry, pineapple, and strawberry. How many different shakes are possible? 15

GPS

Mixed Review

15. In 1994, about 41% of the cars made in the United States were made by General Motors, 25% by Ford, 8% by Chrysler, and 26% by other companies. Draw a circle graph to show this data. *[Lesson 11-5]*

Find the circumference of each circle given its radius or diameter. Use $\pi \approx 3.14$, and round answers to the nearest tenth. *[Lesson 11-6]*

16.

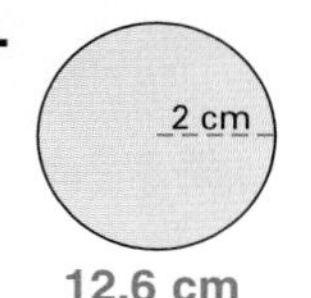

12.6 cm

17.

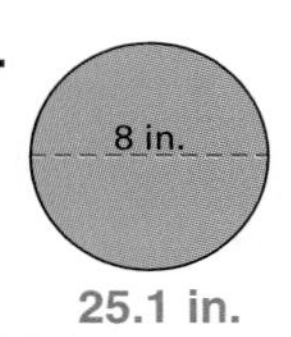

25.1 in.

18.

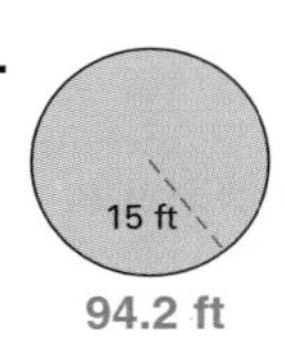

94.2 ft

19.

34.5 mm

Project Progress

Think about all of the things that could possibly happen when your sports star performs the skill you are interested in, like shooting a free throw or going to bat. Then list all of the possible outcomes of performing this skill twice.

Problem Solving
Understand
Plan
Solve
Look Back

PROBLEM SOLVING 12-3

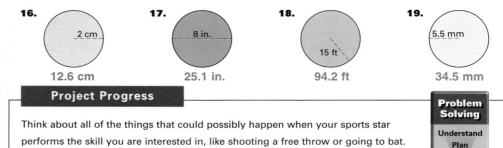

PROBLEM SOLVING

Name ______________________

Guided Problem Solving 12-3

GPS **PROBLEM 14, STUDENT PAGE 640**

Suppose you can choose 1, 2, 3, *or* 4 of the following fruits for a fruit shake: Banana, blueberry, pineapple, and strawberry. How many different shakes are possible?

— Understand —

1. How many fruits can you use in your choice of shake? 1, 2, 3, *or* 4.
2. Name the fruits from which you can choose. Banana, blueberry, pineapple, strawberry.

— Plan —

3. List all the possible choices if you choose only 1 fruit. Let Ba represent banana, Bl represent blueberry, P represent pineapple, and S represent strawberry in your lists. Ba, Bl, P, and S.
4. List all the possible choices if you choose 2 fruits. Ba-Bl, Ba-P, Ba-S, Bl-P, Bl-S, P-S.
5. List all the possible choices if you choose 3 fruits. Ba-Bl-P, Ba-Bl-S, Ba-P-S, Bl-P-S.
6. List all the possible choices if you choose 4 fruits. Ba-Bl-P-S.

— Solve —

7. How many different shakes are possible? 15 different shakes.

— Look Back —

8. How can you use a tree diagram to check your answer? Find all possible outcomes and cross out duplicates.

SOLVE ANOTHER PROBLEM

Suppose you can choose 1, 2, or 3 toppings for your pizza: extra cheese, sausage, or pepperoni. How many different pizzas are possible?
7 different pizzas: C, S, P, C-S, C-P, S-P, C-S-P.

ENRICHMENT

Name ______________________

Extend Your Thinking 12-3

Critical Thinking

An arrangement of items in a particular order is called a **permutation.** You can use this formula to find the number of permutations of *n* different items, taken *r* items at a time with no repetitions, when only part of a set is used:

$$_nP_r = \frac{n!}{(n-r)!}$$

For example: How many permutations are there if 5 students are to be selected 3 at a time? To find the number of permutations of 5 students, substitute 5 for *n* and 3 for *r*.

$$_5P_3 = \frac{5!}{(5-3)!} = \frac{5!}{2!} = \frac{5 \cdot 4 \cdot 3 \cdot 2 \cdot 1}{2 \cdot 1} = 5 \cdot 4 \cdot 3 = 60$$

There are 60 different ways students can be selected 3 at a time.

A set of items in which order is not important is called a **combination.** You can use this formula to find the number of combinations of n different items, taken r items at a time:

$$_nC_r = \frac{n!}{(n-r)!r!}$$

For example: How many combinations are there if 5 letters are chosen 3 at a time? To find the number of combinations of 5 letters, substitute 5 for *n* and 3 for *r*.

$$_5C_3 = \frac{5!}{(5-3)!3!} = \frac{5!}{2!3!} = \frac{5 \cdot 4 \cdot 3 \cdot 2 \cdot 1}{2 \cdot 1 \cdot 3 \cdot 2 \cdot 1} = \frac{5 \cdot 4}{2} = \frac{20}{2} = 10$$

There are 10 different combinations of 5 letters chosen 3 at a time.

Tell which formula you will use to solve each problem. Then find the answer.

1. A random drawing is held to select 2 out of 5 students to be sent to a sporting event. How many different pairs of students can be selected?
$_nC_r = \frac{n!}{(n-r)!r!} = \frac{5!}{(5-2)!2!} = 10$; 10 pairs.
2. How many permutations are there if you have 7 books and need to put four of them on display?
$_nP_r = \frac{n!}{(n-r)!} = \frac{7!}{(7-4)!} = 840$; 840 permutations.
3. How many 3-letter "words," real or imaginary, can you make from these letters: T H A N K S? A letter cannot be used twice.
$_nP_r = \frac{n!}{(n-r)!} = \frac{6!}{(6-3)!} = 120$; 120 "words"

Section 12A Connect

You've seen how you can use tree diagrams, organized lists, and the Counting Principle to help count the possibilities in different situations. Now you'll use some of those skills to analyze your own fingerprints.

Someday My Prints Will Come

Materials: Tape, Index cards, Magnifying glasses, Calculators

There are 3 basic types of fingerprint patterns: *whorls, loops,* and *arches.*

Whorl

1. You may have a different fingerprint pattern (whorl, loop, or arch) on each finger. How many different combinations of these patterns can occur on your right hand? (*Hint:* Does the order make a difference?)

2. Suppose you have a different fingerprint pattern on the ring and pinky fingers of your left hand. How many possible pairs of patterns are there for those two fingers?
3. Take a #2 pencil and rub it so that you cover about 1 square inch of paper with the graphite. Rub the index finger of your nonwriting hand over the graphite. Then take a piece of tape and wrap it around your fingertip. Remove the tape carefully and place it on a card.

Loop

4. Compare your fingerprint to the patterns. How would you characterize your fingerprint?

Arch

641

Someday My Prints Will Come

The Point

Students discussed fingerprinting in *Someday My Prints Will Come* on page 625. Now they will analyze their own fingerprints.

Materials

Tape, index cards, magnifying glasses, calculators

Resources

Lesson Enhancement Transparency 62

About the Page

- Have students make a tree diagram showing all of the possible combinations of fingerprint patterns and characteristics.
- Tell students to use the side of the pencil point when rubbing it against the paper. They need only smudge their index finger with the black graphite for it to show up clearly on the transparent tape.
- Have students compare their fingerprints with the fingerprints of other students to see the unique and varying characteristics of fingerprints.

Ongoing Assessment

Check that students' fingerprints show clear patterns.

Extension

Many hospitals make a footprint of newborn infants for identification purposes. Have students ask at home if there is a record of their birth footprint. Ask those students who have these records to share them with the class.

Answers for Connect

1. 243
2. 6

3–4. Answers may vary.

12A Review

Review Correlation

Item(s)	Lesson(s)
1–3	12-1
4–7	12-2
8	12-3
9, 10	12-2
11	12-3

Test Prep

Test-Taking Tip

Tell students to review key concepts shortly before taking a test. Here, students should review "order" versus "belong" concepts in counting problems.

Answers for Review

3.

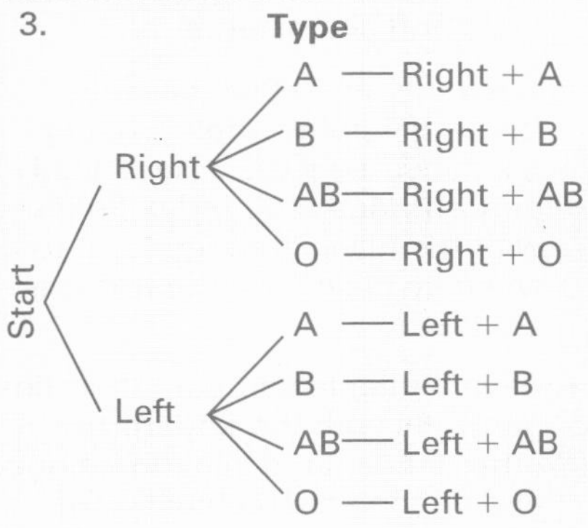

There are 8 possibilities.

10. Possible answer: In a permutation, each time you place an item in the ordering, there is one less choice for the next position. So the number you multiply by goes down by 1 each time, which is a factorial pattern.

Section 12A Review

Operation Sense Use the Counting Principle to find the number of outcomes in each situation.

1. Drinks: 3 flavors, 4 sizes. How many choices? 12
2. Entertainment: 6 movies, 2 ways to get there, 12 rows. How many choices? 144
3. **Problem Solving** A burglar cut his hand during a car break-in, and tests will reveal whether the blood he left behind is type A, B, AB, or O. Also, by analyzing scratches from the break-in, detectives will be able to tell whether he is right- or left-handed. Make a tree diagram to show all the possibilities for blood type and handedness. How many possibilities are there?

Distribution of Blood Types

Type O 44%
Type AB 5%
Type A 41%
Type B 10%

Operation Sense Give each factorial product.

4. 4! 24
5. 8! 40,320
6. 10! 3,628,800
7. 6! 720
8. **Science** The genetic coding in our bodies is called DNA. The "rungs" in the spiral ladder of a strand of DNA are made of 2 out of 4 *bases:* adenine, cytosine, guanine, and thymine.
   a. How many ways can you select 2 out of these 4 bases? 6
   b. Adenine and thymine are always paired. How many pairs of bases are actually possible, and what are they? 2; adenine - thymine and cytosine - guanine

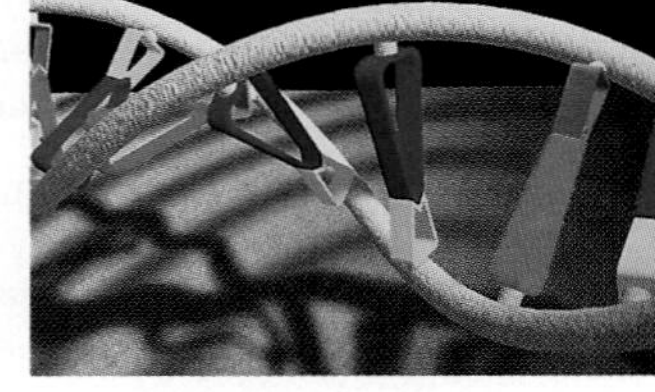

Computer model of DNA strand

9. How many different three-number license plates can be made from the digits 0–9 if:
   a. Digits can be repeated? 1000
   b. Digits can't be repeated? 720
10. Journal Explain why factorial products and partial factorial products are important for calculating numbers of permutations.

REVIEW 12A

Test Prep

When you're solving a counting problem on a multiple choice test, be sure to think about whether or not the order makes a difference.

11. How many different combinations of 3 letters can be made from the letters A, B, C, and D? A

Ⓐ 4 Ⓑ 12 Ⓒ 16 Ⓓ 24

Resources

Practice Masters
Section 12A Review

Assessment Sourcebook
Quiz 12A

TestWorks
Test and Practice Software

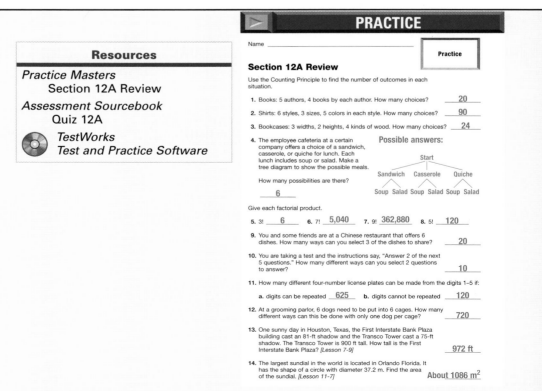

PRACTICE

Name ______________________ Practice

Section 12A Review

Use the Counting Principle to find the number of outcomes in each situation.

1. Books: 5 authors, 4 books by each author. How many choices? 20
2. Shirts: 6 styles, 3 sizes, 5 colors in each style. How many choices? 90
3. Bookcases: 3 widths, 2 heights, 4 kinds of wood. How many choices? 24
4. The employee cafeteria at a certain company offers a choice of a sandwich, casserole, or quiche for lunch. Each lunch includes soup or salad. Make a tree diagram to show the possible meals.
   How many possibilities are there? 6

Possible answers:
Start
Sandwich Casserole Quiche
Soup Salad Soup Salad Soup Salad

Give each factorial product.

5. 3! 6
6. 7! 5,040
7. 9! 362,880
8. 5! 120
9. You and some friends are at a Chinese restaurant that offers 6 dishes. How many ways can you select 3 of the dishes to share? 20
10. You are taking a test and the instructions say, "Answer 2 of the next 5 questions." How many different ways can you select 2 questions to answer? 10
11. How many different four-number license plates can be made from the digits 1–5 if:
    a. digits can be repeated 625
    b. digits cannot be repeated 120
12. At a grooming parlor, 6 dogs need to be put into 6 cages. How many different ways can this be done with only one dog per cage? 720
13. One sunny day in Houston, Texas, the First Interstate Bank Plaza building cast an 81-ft shadow and the Transco Tower cast a 75-ft shadow. The Transco Tower is 900 ft tall. How tall is the First Interstate Bank Plaza? *[Lesson 7-9]* 972 ft
14. The largest sundial in the world is located in Orlando Florida. It has the shape of a circle with diameter 37.2 m. Find the area of the sundial. *[Lesson 11-7]* About 1086 m^2

Chance and Probability

LESSON PLANNING GUIDE

Student Edition | **Ancillaries**

LESSON		MATERIALS	VOCABULARY	DAILY	OTHER
	Section 12B Opener				
12-4	**Odds and Fairness**	number cubes	experiment, event, odds, fair games	12-4	
12-5	**Probability**		probability	12-5	*WW Math*–Middle School
12-6	**Experimental Probability**	number cubes	theoretical probability, experimental probability, geometric probability	12-6	Lesson Enhancement Trans. 63 Teaching Tool Trans. 2, 3 Technology Master 64 *Interactive CD-ROM Lesson 12*
12-7	**Independent and Dependent Events**	number cubes	independent events, dependent events, compound event, sample space	12-7	Ch. 12 Project Master *WW Math*–Middle School
	Technology	graphing calculator			Teaching Tool Trans. 23
	Connect	compass, protractor, cardboard, pushpin, paper clip, number cubes			Interdisc. Team Teaching 12B Teaching Tool Trans. 15
	Review				Practice/Quiz 12B; *TestWorks*
	Extend Key Ideas				
	Chapter 12 Summary/Review				
	Chapter 12 Assessment				Ch. 12 Tests Forms A–F; *TestWorks*; Ch. 12 Letter Home
	Cumulative Review Chapters 1–12				Cumulative Review Ch. 1–12 Quarterly Test Ch. 1–12

SKILLS TRACE

LESSON	SKILL	FIRST INTRODUCED GR. 5	GR. 6	GR. 7	DEVELOP	PRACTICE/ APPLY	REVIEW
12-4	**Finding odds.**			✘ p. 644	pp. 644–646	pp. 647–648	pp. 666, 669
12-5	**Finding probabilities.**		✘	✘ p. 649	pp. 649–651	pp. 652–653	pp. 666, 669
12-6	**Finding experimental probabilities.**		✘	✘ p. 654	pp. 654–656	pp. 657–658	
12-7	**Finding probabilities for dependent/ independent events.**			✘ p. 659	pp. 659–661	p. 662	p. 666

CONNECTED MATHEMATICS

Investigation 4 in the unit *What Do You Expect?*, from the **Connected Mathematics** series, can be used with Section 12B.

10 POINT BONUS

INTERDISCIPLINARY TEAM TEACHING

Math and Social Studies

(Worksheet pages 53–54: Teacher pages T53–T54)

In this lesson, students use knowledge of probability and mathematical fairness to answer questions about playing card games.

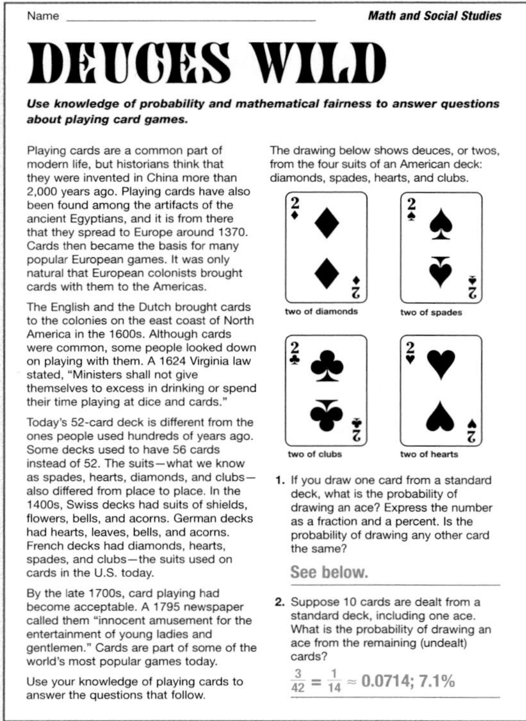

Name ______________________ *Math and Social Studies*

DEUCES WILD

Use knowledge of probability and mathematical fairness to answer questions about playing card games.

Playing cards are a common part of modern life, but historians think that they were invented in China more than 2,000 years ago. Playing cards have also been found among the artifacts of the ancient Egyptians, and it is from there that they spread to Europe around 1370. Cards then became the basis for many popular European games. It was only natural that European colonists brought cards with them to the Americas.

The English and the Dutch brought cards to the colonies on the east coast of North America in the 1600s. Although cards were common, some people looked down on playing with them. A 1624 Virginia law stated, "Ministers shall not give themselves to excess in drinking or spend their time playing at dice and cards."

Today's 52-card deck is different from the ones people used hundreds of years ago. Some decks used to have 56 cards instead of 52. The suits—what we know as spades, hearts, diamonds, and clubs—also differed from place to place. In the 1400s, Swiss decks had suits of shields, flowers, bells, and acorns. German decks had hearts, leaves, bells, and acorns. French decks had diamonds, hearts, spades, and clubs—the suits used on cards in the U.S. today.

By the late 1700s, card playing had become acceptable. A 1795 newspaper called them "innocent amusement for the entertainment of young ladies and gentlemen." Cards are part of some of the world's most popular games today.

Use your knowledge of playing cards to answer the questions that follow.

The drawing below shows deuces, or twos, from the four suits of an American deck: diamonds, spades, hearts, and clubs.

two of diamonds — two of spades — two of clubs — two of hearts

1. If you draw one card from a standard deck, what is the probability of drawing an ace? Express the number as a fraction and a percent. Is the probability of drawing any other card the same?
   See below.
2. Suppose 10 cards are dealt from a standard deck, including one ace. What is the probability of drawing an ace from the remaining (undealt) cards?
   $\frac{3}{42} = \frac{1}{14} \approx 0.0714$; 7.1%

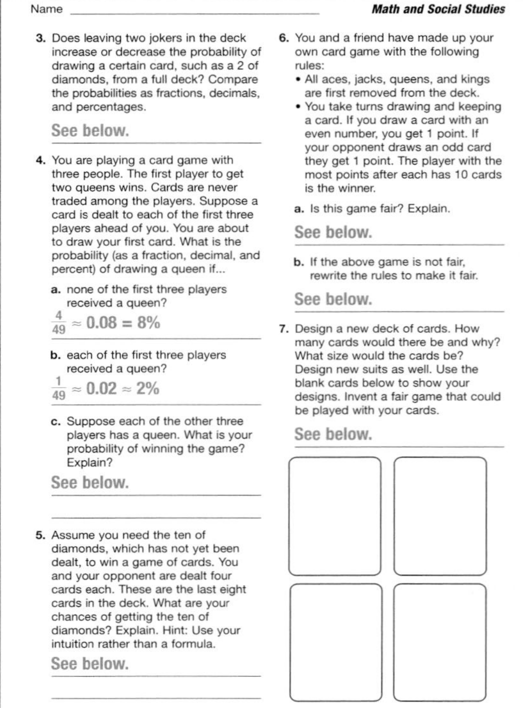

Name ______________________ *Math and Social Studies*

3. Does leaving two jokers in the deck increase or decrease the probability of drawing a certain card, such as a 2 of diamonds, from a full deck? Compare the probabilities as fractions, decimals, and percentages.
   See below.
4. You are playing a card game with three people. The first player to get two queens wins. Cards are never traded among the players. Suppose a card is dealt to each of the first three players ahead of you. You are about to draw your first card. What is the probability (as a fraction, decimal, and percent) of drawing a queen if...
   a. none of the first three players received a queen?
      $\frac{4}{49} \approx 0.08 = 8\%$
   b. each of the first three players received a queen?
      $\frac{1}{49} \approx 0.02 \approx 2\%$
   c. Suppose each of the other three players has a queen. What is your probability of winning the game? Explain?
      See below.
5. Assume you need the ten of diamonds, which has not yet been dealt, to win a game of cards. You and your opponent are dealt four cards each. These are the last eight cards in the deck. What are your chances of getting the ten of diamonds? Explain. Hint: Use your intuition rather than a formula.
   See below.
6. You and a friend have made up your own card game with the following rules:
   - All aces, jacks, queens, and kings are first removed from the deck.
   - You take turns drawing and keeping a card. If you draw a card with an even number, you get 1 point. If your opponent draws an odd card they get 1 point. The player with the most points after each has 10 cards is the winner.

   a. Is this game fair? Explain.
      See below.
   b. If the above game is not fair, rewrite the rules to make it fair.
      See below.
7. Design a new deck of cards. How many cards would there be and why? What size would the cards be? Design new suits as well. Use the blank cards below to show your designs. Invent a fair game that could be played with your cards.
   See below.

Answers

1. Your chances of drawing an ace are $\frac{4}{52}$ or 7.7%.

   You have the same chance of drawing any other card at the beginning of the game. (See page T53.)

3. Leaving the jokers in decreases your chances of getting the 2 of diamonds, but only slightly. Your chance without the jokers is $\frac{1}{52}$ or .019 or about 1.9%. Your chance with the jokers is $\frac{1}{54}$ or .0185 or about 1.85%.
4. c. 0: There is only one queen remaining in the deck, so there is no chance for being dealt 2 queens.
5. $\frac{1}{2}$, .50, or 50%; since both you and your opponent are getting the same number of cards, you each have the same probability of getting the ten of diamonds, that is, one chance in two.
6. a. No. There are 20 cards with even numbers, but only 16 cards with odd numbers.

   b. Possible answer: Keep the aces in the deck and give them the value of the number 1.
7. Answers will vary widely depending on students' senses of design and humor. Accept any new card deck designs, but have students share their drawings and explanations with the rest of the class.

BIBLIOGRAPHY

FOR TEACHERS

Adler, Henry L. *Introduction to Probability & Statistics.* San Francisco, CA: W. H. Freeman, 1972.

Johnson, Christine V. *Investigating Apples: Real-World Mathematics Through Science.* Menlo Park, CA: Innovative Learning Publications; Addison-Wesley Publications, 1995.

Krantz, Les. *The Best and Worst of Everything.* New York, NY: Prentice Hall General Reference, 1991.

Nichols, Judith E. *By the Numbers: Using Demographics and Psychographics. . . .* Chicago, IL: Bonus Books, 1990.

Spangler, David. *Math for Real Kids.* Glenview, IL: Good Year Books, 1997.

FOR STUDENTS

Bulloch, Ivan. *Games.* New York, NY: Thompson Learning, 1994.

Kalman, Bobbie and Schimpky, David. *Games from Long Ago.* New York, NY: Crabtree, 1995.

Smithsonian Institution. *Games, Puzzles and Toys: Step-by-Step Science Activity Projects. . . .* Milwaukee, WI: Gareth Stevens, 1993.

Stienecker, David. *Numbers.* New York, NY: Benchmark Books, 1996.

Straffin, Phillip D. *Game Theory and Strategy.* New York, NY: The Mathematical Association of America.

SECTION **12B**

Chance and Probability

▶ Industry Link ▶ www.mathsurf.com/7/ch12/games

Do NOT Pass Go!

What's your favorite board game? Do you prefer a game of pure skill, like chess or Go? Or would you rather play a game like Monopoly®, where all of your skill and cunning can be destroyed by an unlucky roll of the dice?

People have played games where luck is involved for hundreds of years. Cubes with dots have been found in Egyptian tombs, and 2500-year-old dice have been unearthed in Chinese excavations. In ancient India, instead of rolling a cube when playing a game, people tossed six cowrie shells.

Whether you play Chutes and Ladders®, Scrabble®, or a modern version of an ancient game like Pachisi (from India) or Hyena Chase (from North Africa), winning or losing depends, at least in part, on chance. As you investigate chance and probability, you'll get a better understanding of the mathematics of games.

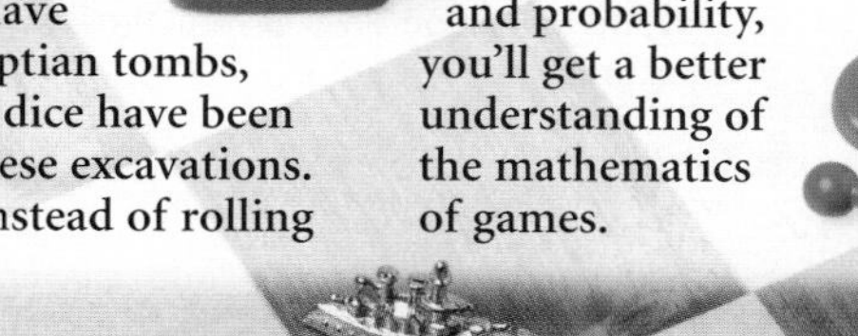

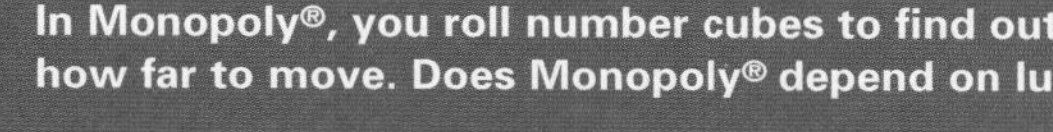

1. In Monopoly®, you roll number cubes to find out how far to move. Does Monopoly® depend on luck?
2. What number or numbers would you use to describe the chance that a tossed coin lands heads? How did you decide on the number(s)?
3. A cowrie shell has a flat side and a rounded side. How do you think six cowrie shells might have been used when playing a game?

643

Where are we now?

In Section 12A, students found ways to count all of the ways something can happen.

They learned how to

- use tree diagrams and the Counting Principle to find all of the outcomes for a set of choices.
- count the number of ways items can be arranged.
- use factorial products to count arrangements.
- calculate the number of ways to choose some item out of a larger group when order is important.

Where are we going?

In Section 12B, students will

- find the odds that an event can happen.
- find the probability of an event.
- use experimental probability to estimate probabilities.
- decide whether two events are dependent or independent.
- find probabilities of dependent and independent events.

Section 12B

Theme: Games

World Wide Web

If your class has access to the World Wide Web, you might want to use the information found at the Web site address given. The interdisciplinary link relates to the topics discussed in this section.

About the Page

This page introduces the theme of the section, games, and discusses the history of games of chance and some games we play today.

Ask ...

- What games of chance do you play? Do you win or lose most of the time?
- Do you think skill or luck is involved in spinning a spinner, tossing number cubes, or tossing a coin?

Extension

The following activity does not require access to the World Wide Web.

Industry

Some games of chance, such as lotteries and sweepstakes, are "big business," with very high odds, as well as very high profits for the promoters. Usually, the odds of winning are printed on the ticket or sweepstakes entry form. Have students examine a sweepstakes entry form or lottery ticket. Discuss the odds shown and the chances of winning the prizes. Also discuss what the game's promoters expect to gain.

Answers for Questions

1. Yes.
2. Possible answer: $\frac{1}{2}$ or one out of two; numbers chosen because one of the two sides of a coin is a head.
3. Possible answer: The "roll" might have been the number of shells that landed flat side up (or down).

Connect

On page 665, students design a game of chance.

Lesson Organizer

Objective

- Find the odds that an event happens.

Vocabulary

- Experiment, event, odds, fair games

Materials

- Explore: Number cubes

NCTM Standards

- 1–4, 11

Review 

Suppose you have ten number cards labeled 1–10.

1. How many ways can you choose an even number? 5
2. How many ways can you choose a number that is not even? 5
3. How many ways can you choose a prime number? 4
4. How many ways can you choose a number that is not prime? 6

Available on Daily Tranparency 12-4

1 Introduce

Explore  

The Point
Students play a game with number cubes and decide whether or not the game is fair.

Ongoing Assessment
Check that students are playing the game correctly and that they are switching roles.

For Groups That Finish Early
Use the rules of Multiplication Toss to play a game finding even and odd sums instead of products. Answers may vary.

12-4 Odds and Fairness

You'll Learn ...

■ to find the odds that an event happens

... How It's Used

Bird breeders need to know the odds of certain traits appearing in their chicks.

Vocabulary

experiment
event
odds
fair games

▶ Lesson Link In the last section, you found methods of counting all the ways that something can happen. Now you'll see how knowing all the possible outcomes can help you find the odds of an event. ◀

Explore Fairness

Materials: Number cubes

Multiplication Toss

You and a partner are about to play a game of chance called Multiplication Toss. Here are the rules of the game.

- Decide which player will be "even" and which will be "odd."
- Take turns rolling the cubes. For each roll, find the product of the numbers rolled. If the product is odd, the odd player gets a point; if it's even, the even player gets a point.
- Repeat until each player has rolled 10 times. The player with the most points wins.

1. Play Multiplication Toss several times. Switch from "even" to "odd" each time.
2. If you could choose to be the "even" player or the "odd" player, which would you prefer? Why?
3. Would you ever expect the "odd" player to win this game? Explain.
4. Is Multiplication Toss a fair game? Explain why or why not.

Learn Odds and Fairness

When you hear the word *experiment,* you probably think of a science lab. In probability, an **experiment** can be anything that involves chance—like the toss of a coin or the roll of a number cube.

The result of an experiment is an *outcome.* For a coin toss, the possible outcomes are heads and tails.

MEETING INDIVIDUAL NEEDS

Resources

- 12-4 Practice
- 12-4 Reteaching
- 12-4 Enrichment
- 12-4 Problem Solving
- 12-4 Daily Transparency
  - Problem of the Day
  - Review
  - Quick Quiz

Learning Modalities

Verbal Discuss the various meanings of the words *odd* and *odds. Odd* meaning strange or unusual, of course, has no mathematical connotation. However, *odd* used with numbers and *odds* used with probability have very specific meanings.

Logical Ask students what the odds are of rolling a 7 or a 0 on a number cube. 0:6 Then ask what the odds are of rolling a 1, 2, 3, 4, 5, or 6. 6:0 Be sure they see that a number in an odds ratio can be zero.

Social Have students work in pairs to play Multiplication Toss.

Challenge

Have groups of 3 or 4 students work together to make up their own games using cards, spinners, number cubes, or coins to share with the class. Have them be prepared to explain mathematically why their games are fair or unfair.

Examples

Name the possible outcomes of each experiment.

1 Rolling a number cube.

The possible outcomes are the numbers 1, 2, 3, 4, 5, and 6.

2 Drawing one marble from a bag with red, white, and blue marbles.

The possible outcomes are drawing a red marble, drawing a white marble, and drawing a blue marble.

An **event** is any outcome (or set of outcomes) we're interested in. We can use **odds** to describe the chance that an event will happen.

ODDS OF AN EVENT

The odds of an event are:
number of ways the event can happen : number of ways it cannot happen

Examples

Give the odds of each event.

3 Rolling a 2 on a number cube.

There is only one way for the event to happen—you roll a 2. The other five rolls (1, 3, 4, 5, and 6) are ways it does *not* happen.

The odds of rolling a 2 on a roll of a number cube are 1:5.

4 Drawing a blue marble from a bag with 2 blue, 5 red, and 4 white marbles.

There are two ways for the event to happen—the 2 blue marbles. The other 9 marbles are ways it does not happen.

The odds of drawing a blue marble are 2:9.

Try It

Give the odds of each event.

a. Getting heads on the toss of a coin. 1:1

b. Getting a 2 or a 5 on a roll of a number cube. 2:4

History Link

There have been 44 vice presidents of the United States before Al Gore. So far, the odds that a vice president will eventually become president are 14:30.

In some games, both players start with equal forces. In others, like the South Asian game of Cows and Leopards, one player starts at a disadvantage.

A game where all players have the same odds of winning is a **fair game**.

Answers for Explore

1–2. It is better to be the "even" player because more products are even than odd.

3. It is possible for the "odd" player to win, but unlikely. (Theoretically, the "odd" player will win a 10-point game about 2% of the time and tie about 6% of the time.)

4. It is not a fair game, because the "even" player is more likely to win.

2 Teach

Learn

You might discuss the fact that odds can be rewritten the same way that fractions are. So, odds of 5:10 can be given as 1:2.

Alternate Examples

Name the possible outcomes for each experiment.

1. Spinning the spinner below.

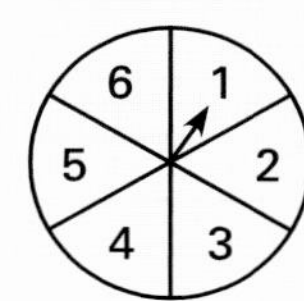

The possible outcomes are 1, 2, 3, 4, 5, and 6.

2. Choosing a nut from a bag of mixed nuts containing cashews, almonds, pecans, walnuts, and peanuts.

The possible outcomes are drawing a cashew, an almond, a pecan, a walnut, and a peanut.

Give the odds for each event.

3. Rolling a prime number on a number cube.

There are **3** ways for the event to happen–rolling a 2, a 3, or a 5. The other **3** rolls (1, 4, 6) are ways the event does *not* happen.

The odds of rolling a prime number on a number cube are 3:3.

4. Drawing a red marble from a bag containing 3 blue, 4 red, and 5 white marbles.

There are 4 ways for the event to happen, the 4 red marbles. The other 8 marbles are ways the event does not happen.

The odds of drawing a red marble are 4:8.

MATH EVERY DAY

Problem of the Day

You are given six coins. One of the coins is counterfeit and weighs slightly more than the real coins. You are given a balance scale. How many weighings will you need to find the counterfeit coin? 2 weighings; Put three coins on each side of the scale. One of the three coins on the heavier side is counterfeit. Put two of these three on the scale. If they balance, the coin not on the balance is counterfeit. If they do not balance, the heavier coin is counterfeit.

Available on Daily Transparency 12-4

An Extension is provided in the transparency package.

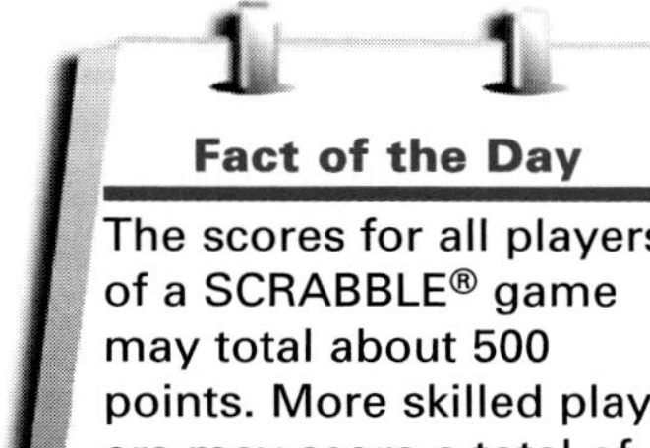

Fact of the Day

The scores for all players of a SCRABBLE® game may total about 500 points. More skilled players may score a total of 700 points or more.

Mental Math

Give each fraction in lowest terms.

1. $\frac{5}{20}$ $\frac{1}{4}$
2. $\frac{4}{12}$ $\frac{1}{3}$
3. $\frac{50}{100}$ $\frac{1}{2}$
4. $\frac{6}{8}$ $\frac{3}{4}$
5. $\frac{3}{15}$ $\frac{1}{5}$
6. $\frac{9}{72}$ $\frac{1}{8}$

Tad's odds: 3 : 2 Jill's odds: 2 : 3 Fair? No

10. Roll a number cube. Ed gets a point for a 1 or 2. Fred gets a point for a 3 or 6. Gwen gets a point for a 4 or 5.
Ed's odds: 1 : 2 Fred's odds: 1 : 2 Gwen's odds: 1 : 2 Fair? Yes

f. Give the odds by writing the ratio of the number in **d** to the number in **e.** 2:3

Suppose you choose a card at random from eleven cards that can spell out the word **P R O B A B I L I T Y**. You hope to choose a B.

g. In how many ways can the event you are looking for happen? 2

h. In how many ways can the event not happen? 9

i. Give the odds by writing the ratio of the number in **g** to the number in **h.** 2:9

found? 10

Alternate Examples

For each game described, give

Examples

Exercise Notes

■ Exercises 22–26

You may need to review with students the formulas for area of a circle and surface area of a cylinder.

Exercise Answers

17. Odds for A = 1:5; odds for B = 4:2; odds for C = 1:5; Unfair

19. Possible answer: No, because the lambs outnumber the tigers.

20. a. Answers may vary.
    b. Answers may vary, but the sum of the numbers in each ratio should be 50.
    c. Possible answer: No; different languages use different mixes of sounds.

21. Yes; although the yellow team wins $\frac{1}{3}$ as often, each win is worth 3 times a green win.

Alternate Assessment

Interview Show students a bag containing a mixture of colored marbles. First have them examine the contents of the bag. Then have them give the odds of drawing any one color of marble from the bag.

► Quick Quiz

Find the odds for each event.

1. Drawing a vowel from the first ten letters of the alphabet 3:7
2. Rolling a 1 or a 2 on a number cube 2:4
3. Choosing a multiple of 10 from the numbers 1–100 10:90

Available on Daily Transparency 12-4

Logic For each game described, give each player's odds of winning. Then tell whether the game is fair.

16. Toss a coin. Player A gets a point for heads; player B, for tails. 1:1 odds for both; Fair

17. Roll a number cube. Player A gets a point for a 1, player B gets a point for 2, 3, 4, or 5, and player C gets a point for 6.

18. **Test Prep** What are the odds of rolling a 3 or a 4 on a number cube? B

Ⓐ 1:3 Ⓑ 2:4 Ⓒ 3:4 Ⓓ 4:2

Problem Solving and Reasoning

19. Journal Lambs and Tigers is a game played in India. One player has 3 pieces called tigers, and the other has 15 lambs. Tigers remove lambs by jumping them, and lambs remove tigers by trapping them. Is this likely to be a fair game? Why or why not?

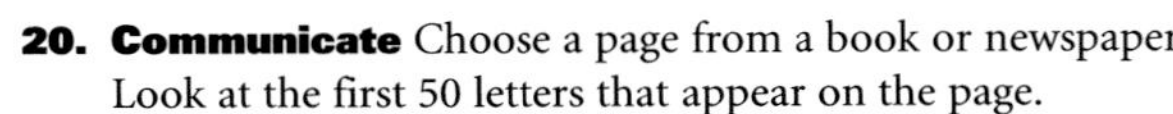

20. Communicate Choose a page from a book or newspaper. Look at the first 50 letters that appear on the page.

a. How many of the letters are vowels? How many are consonants?

b. Based on your results, what are the odds that a letter chosen at random is a vowel? A consonant?

c. Do you think your results would be similar for any language? Explain.

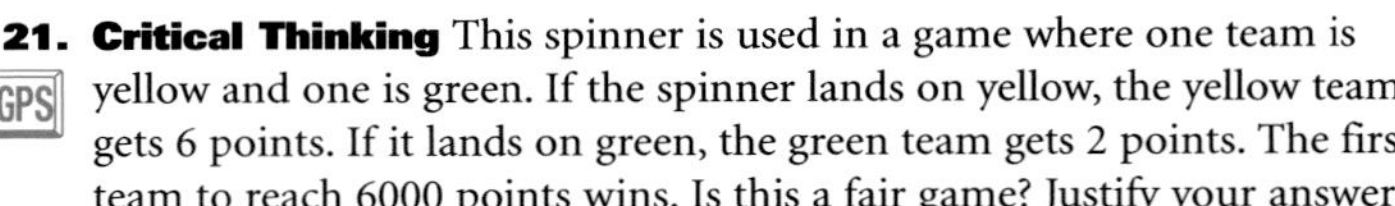

21. Critical Thinking GPS This spinner is used in a game where one team is yellow and one is green. If the spinner lands on yellow, the yellow team gets 6 points. If it lands on green, the green team gets 2 points. The first team to reach 6000 points wins. Is this a fair game? Justify your answer.

Mixed Review

Find the area of each circle given its radius or diameter. Use $\pi \approx 3.14$, and round answers to the nearest tenth. *[Lesson 11-7]*

22.
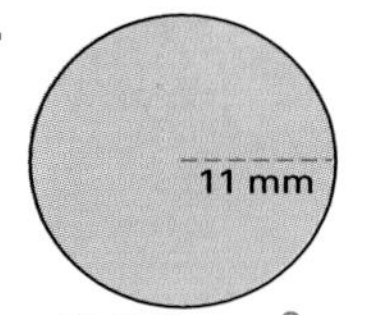

379.9 mm²

23.
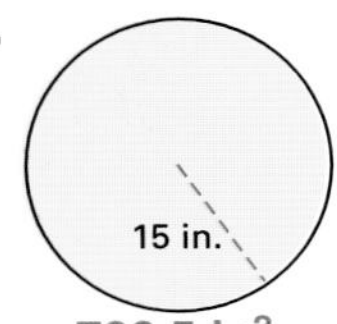

706.5 in²

24.
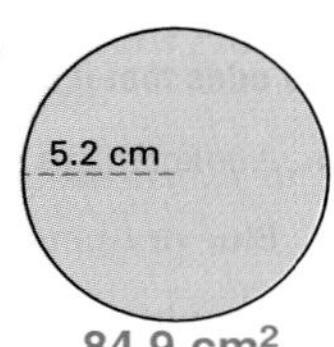

84.9 cm²

25.
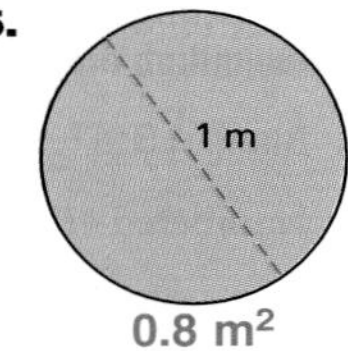

0.8 m²

26. Find the surface area of a cylinder whose height is 12 cm and radius is 8 cm. Use $\pi \approx 3.14$, and round your answer to the nearest tenth. *[Lesson 11-8]* 1004.8 cm²

PROBLEM SOLVING 12-4

PROBLEM SOLVING

Name ______

Guided Problem Solving 12-4

GPS PROBLEM 21, STUDENT PAGE 648

This spinner is used in a game where one team is yellow and one is green. If the spinner lands on yellow, the yellow team gets 6 points. If it lands on green, the green team gets 2 points. The first team to reach 6000 points wins. Is this a fair game? Justify your answer.

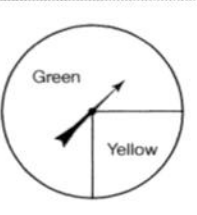
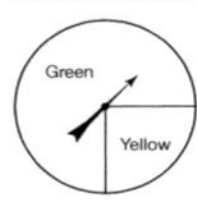

— Understand —

1. Which color is the spinner more likely to land on? Explain. Green, because the section is larger.

— Plan —

2. Suppose the circle were divided into fourths. How many fourths would be
   a. green? 3 fourths b. yellow? 1 fourth
3. How many times larger than the yellow section is the green section? 3 times
4. How should the number of points for spinning yellow compare to the number of points for spinning green? The points for yellow should be 3 times the points for green.

— Solve —

5. If the spinner lands on yellow, the yellow team scores 6 points. If it lands on green, the green team scores 2 points. Is this a fair game? Justify your answer. Yes, because the likelihood of spinning green is 3 times that of spinning yellow, and 3 × 2 = 6.

— Look Back —

6. Write the odds of winning and the number of points as two ratios. Do they form a proportion? $\frac{3}{1} \stackrel{?}{=} \frac{6}{2}$; Yes.

SOLVE ANOTHER PROBLEM

If the spinner lands on red, the red team scores 8 points. If it lands on blue, the blue team scores 2 points. Is this a fair game? Justify your answer.

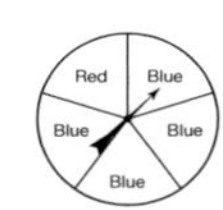

Yes, because the likelihood of spinning blue is 4 times that of spinning red, and 4 × 2 = 8.

ENRICHMENT

Name ______

Extend Your Thinking 12-4

Patterns in Numbers

As you know, a set of items in which order is not important is called a combination. You can use this formula to find the number of combinations of n different items, taken r items at a time:

$${}_nC_r = \frac{n!}{(n-r)!r!}.$$

1. Find the number that goes in each square. Some are already completed for you.

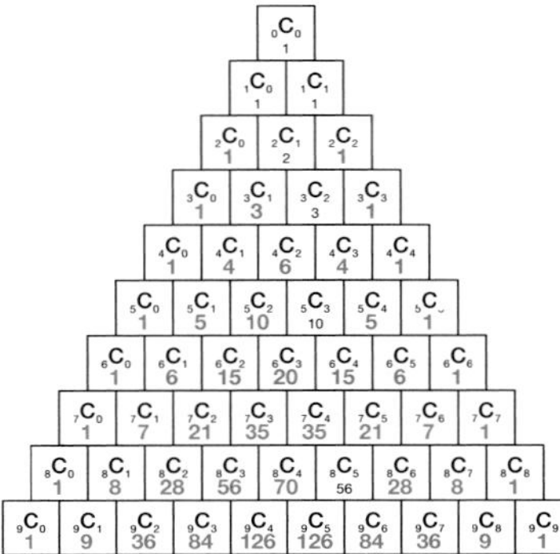

${}_0C_0$: 1
${}_1C_0$: 1, ${}_1C_1$: 1
${}_2C_0$: 1, ${}_2C_1$: 2, ${}_2C_2$: 1
${}_3C_0$: 1, ${}_3C_1$: 3, ${}_3C_2$: 3, ${}_3C_3$: 1
${}_4C_0$: 1, ${}_4C_1$: 4, ${}_4C_2$: 6, ${}_4C_3$: 4, ${}_4C_4$: 1
${}_5C_0$: 1, ${}_5C_1$: 5, ${}_5C_2$: 10, ${}_5C_3$: 10, ${}_5C_4$: 5, ${}_5C_5$: 1
${}_6C_0$: 1, ${}_6C_1$: 6, ${}_6C_2$: 15, ${}_6C_3$: 20, ${}_6C_4$: 15, ${}_6C_5$: 6, ${}_6C_6$: 1
${}_7C_0$: 1, ${}_7C_1$: 7, ${}_7C_2$: 21, ${}_7C_3$: 35, ${}_7C_4$: 35, ${}_7C_5$: 21, ${}_7C_6$: 7, ${}_7C_7$: 1
${}_8C_0$: 1, ${}_8C_1$: 8, ${}_8C_2$: 28, ${}_8C_3$: 56, ${}_8C_4$: 70, ${}_8C_5$: 56, ${}_8C_6$: 28, ${}_8C_7$: 8, ${}_8C_8$: 1
${}_9C_0$: 1, ${}_9C_1$: 9, ${}_9C_2$: 36, ${}_9C_3$: 84, ${}_9C_4$: 126, ${}_9C_5$: 126, ${}_9C_6$: 84, ${}_9C_7$: 36, ${}_9C_8$: 9, ${}_9C_9$: 1

2. Describe any patterns you see. Possible answers: A number in any square is the sum of the two numbers directly above it. All numbers in the left and right squares on the drawing are 1s. The answers form a pattern known as Pascal's triangle.

Probability

12-5

▶ Lesson Link You've used odds to describe the likelihood of an event. Now you'll use *probability* to describe how likely an event is to happen. ◀

You'll Learn ...

■ to find the probability of an event

... How It's Used

Geologists use probabilities to describe the likelihood that an earthquake will occur on a fault within a certain number of years.

Vocabulary

probability

Explore Measuring Likelihood

A Likely Story?

1. Sketch a "likelihood line" like the one shown.

Impossible ———————|——————— Certain

2. Use your intuition to estimate the likelihood of each event below. Place each event on the likelihood line.
   a. Getting a head on a coin toss
   b. Getting a 3 on a roll of a number cube
   c. Getting either a head or a tail on a coin toss
   d. Drawing a red marble out of a bag full of green and white marbles
   e. That tomorrow will be a sunny day
   f. Getting an odd number on a roll of a number cube
   g. That you will see a train this week
   h. That you will travel to the moon during your lifetime
3. Explain how you placed these events on the line. Did you place any of the events at the halfway point? If so, which one(s), and why?

Learn Probability

When you play a game that involves chance, you think about how likely different events are. Should you risk rolling the dice once more if a total of 12 will put you in jail? What's the chance that the spinner will land on "Lose a Turn"?

You can use probability to assign numbers to these chances.

12-5 Lesson Organizer

Objective

- Find the probability of an event.

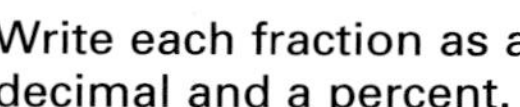

Vocabulary

- Probability

NCTM Standards

- 1–4, 10

➤ Review

Write each fraction as a decimal and a percent.

1. $\frac{3}{4}$ 0.75, 75%
2. $\frac{42}{100}$ 0.42, 42%
3. $\frac{3}{10}$ 0.3, 30%
4. $\frac{5}{8}$ 0.625, 62.5%
5. $\frac{2}{3}$ $0.\overline{6}$, $66\frac{2}{3}$%

Available on Daily Transparency 12-5

1 Introduce

Explore

You may want to use the *Interactive CD-ROM Probability Tool* with this lesson.

The Point

Students rate the likelihood of events, from impossible to certain, by placing the events on a "likelihood line."

Ongoing Assessment

Some students may be bothered that some answers are hard to estimate. Stress that answers are estimates and may vary from student to student.

For Groups That Finish Early

Think of other events that are impossible and certain, and events that you would place somewhere between the two endpoints of a likelihood line.
Answers may vary.

Answers for Explore on next page.

MEETING INDIVIDUAL NEEDS

Resources

- **12-5** Practice
- **12-5** Reteaching
- **12-5** Enrichment
- **12-5** Problem Solving
- **12-5** Daily Transparency
  - Problem of the Day
  - Review
  - Quick Quiz

Wide World of Mathematics Middle School: Hurricane Prediction

Learning Modalities

Kinesthetic Using a variety of games is generally helpful in reinforcing basic ideas of probability.

Social Have students discuss various games they have played that involve dice, spinners, and so on. Ask if they think the games are constructed to be fair or unfair, and why.

English Language Development

Draw a likelihood line, including a halfway mark, on the chalkboard. Then describe a variety of certain and impossible events. Have students tell in which category each event falls, and point to the appropriate word. Then describe some events which are neither certain nor impossible and have students suggest where on the line these events would fall.

12–5 Exercises and Applications

Assignment Guide

- **Basic**
  1, 3, 4–20 evens, 21, 24–30 evens
- **Average**
  2, 4, 5–19 odds, 20–22, 23–29 odds
- **Enriched**
  2, 4, 5–19 odds, 20–22, 23–29

Exercise Notes

Exercise 2

Error Prevention Be sure that students realize that rolling a 1, 3, 4, *or* 5 constitutes 4 ways for the event to happen.

Exercise Answers

4. a. $\frac{4}{7} \approx 0.571 = 57.1\%$

b. $\frac{1}{1} = 1 = 100\%$

c. $\frac{0}{1} = 0 = 0\%$

Reteaching

Activity

Materials: Ten number cards labeled 0–9

Use the number cards to answer these questions. You might display the cards and model each situation. Give probability answers as fractions.

1. What is the total number of cards, or outcomes? 10
2. How many cards have a 4? What is the probability of drawing a 4? 1; $\frac{1}{10}$
3. How many cards do *not* have a 4? What is the probability of *not* drawing a 4? 9; $\frac{9}{10}$
4. What is the sum of the probabilities in Exercises 2 and 3? 1
5. What is the probability of drawing a 10? 0
6. What is the probability of drawing a 0–9? 1
7. What is the sum of the probabilities in Exercises 5 and 6? 1

12-5 Exercises and Applications

Practice and Apply

1. **Getting Started** Follow the steps to find the probability of drawing a red marble out of a bag containing 3 red, 5 blue, and 4 yellow marbles.
   a. Find the total number of marbles. 12
   b. Write a fraction with the number of red marbles in the numerator and the total number of marbles in the denominator. $\frac{3}{12}$
   c. Rewrite the fraction in lowest terms. $\frac{1}{4}$

Give the probability of each event as a fraction, a percent, and a decimal.

2. Rolling a 1, 3, 4, or 5 on a number cube
3. Spinning "Spin Again" on the spinner at right
4. Drawing a purple marble from a bag containing:
   a. 2 yellow, 4 purple, and 1 red marble
   b. 5 purple marbles
   c. 2 pink marbles

Move Ahead 1
Move Ahead 2
Spin Again
Lose a Turn

2. $\frac{2}{3} \approx 66.7\% = 0.667$

3. $\frac{1}{6} \approx 16.7\% = 0.167$

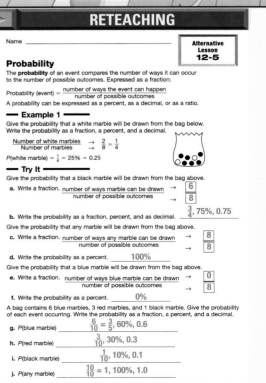

5. **Data** The circle graph shows commuting habits of 26- to 44-year-olds. What is the probability that a randomly selected person in this age group:
   a. Drives alone to work 75.1%
   b. Does *not* drive alone 24.9%
   c. Uses either public transit or carpools 18.4%

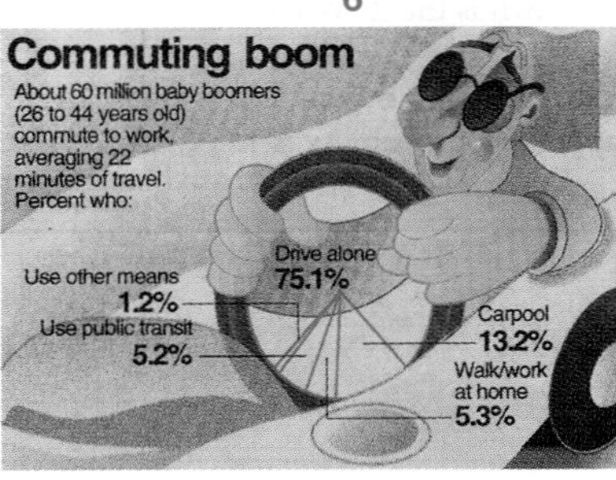

Copy and complete the table.

	Probability of Event	Probability That Event Does Not Happen	Odds of Event
6.	$\frac{1}{4}$	$\frac{3}{4}$	1:3
7.	$\frac{1}{8}$	$\frac{7}{8}$	1:7
8.	$\frac{4}{10}$	$\frac{6}{10}$	4:6
9.	$\frac{1}{2}$	$\frac{1}{2}$	1:1

PRACTICE 12-5

PRACTICE

Name ______________________

Practice 12-5

Probability

Give the probability of each event as a fraction, a percent, and a decimal.

1. Spinning "Draw a Card" on the spinner shown $\frac{1}{4} = 25\% = 0.25$
2. Spinning "Get 100 Points" on the spinner shown $\frac{1}{8} = 12.5\% = 0.125$

Draw a Card
Lose a Turn
Get 100 Points
Move Ahead 5
Move Ahead 2

3. Drawing a green marble from a bag containing the following marbles:
   a. 21 green $1 = 100\% = 1.0$
   b. 5 black and 7 white $0 = 0\% = 0.0$
   c. 3 green, 7 yellow $\frac{3}{10} = 30\% = 0.3$
4. **Social Studies** The circle graph shows the percent of the population of Arizona that lived in its five largest cities in 1990. What is the probability that a randomly selected resident:
   a. Lives in Phoenix? $\frac{27}{100} = 27\% = 0.27$
   b. Does *not* live in Phoenix? $\frac{73}{100} = 73\% = 0.73$
   c. Lives in Tempe, Mesa, or Glendale? $\frac{4}{25} = 16\% = 0.16$

Phoenix, 27%
Other, 46%
Tucson, 11%
Mesa, 8%
Tempe, 4%
Glendale, 4%

5. Complete the table.

Probability of event	$\frac{1}{3}$	$\frac{4}{5}$	$\frac{1}{6}$	$\frac{3}{8}$	$\frac{7}{10}$	$\frac{3}{4}$
Probability that event does not happen	$\frac{2}{3}$	$\frac{1}{5}$	$\frac{5}{6}$	$\frac{5}{8}$	$\frac{3}{10}$	$\frac{1}{4}$
Odds of event	1 : 2	4 : 1	2 : 10	3 : 5	7 : 3	12 : 4

Give the probability that corresponds to each of the odds. Express each answer as a fraction in lowest terms.

6. 5 : 7 $\frac{5}{12}$
7. 8 : 2 $\frac{4}{5}$
8. 21 : 21 $\frac{1}{2}$
9. 16 : 20 $\frac{4}{9}$
10. 24 : 1 $\frac{24}{25}$
11. 44 : 56 $\frac{11}{25}$
12. 35 : 15 $\frac{7}{10}$
13. 27 : 81 $\frac{1}{4}$

Assume you are drawing the first tile in a Scrabble® game. Use the table on page 653 of your textbook to find each probability. Express each as a percent.

14. *P*(W) 2%
15. *P*(Not an A) 91%
16. *P*(E, F, or G) 17%

RETEACHING

Name ______________________

Alternative Lesson 12-5

Probability

The **probability** of an event compares the number of ways it can occur to the number of possible outcomes. Expressed as a fraction:

$$\text{Probability (event)} = \frac{\text{number of ways the event can happen}}{\text{number of possible outcomes}}$$

A probability can be expressed as a percent, as a decimal, or as a ratio.

Example 1

Give the probability that a white marble will be drawn from the bag below. Write the probability as a fraction, a percent, and a decimal.

$$\frac{\text{Number of white marbles}}{\text{Number of marbles}} \rightarrow \frac{2}{8} = \frac{1}{4}$$

$P(\text{white marble}) = \frac{1}{4} = 25\% = 0.25$

Try It

Give the probability that a black marble will be drawn from the bag above.

a. Write a fraction. $\frac{\text{number of ways marble can be drawn}}{\text{number of possible outcomes}} \rightarrow \frac{6}{8}$

b. Write the probability as a fraction, percent, and as decimal. $\frac{3}{4}$, 75%, 0.75

Give the probability that any marble will be drawn from the bag above.

c. Write a fraction. $\frac{\text{number of ways any marble can be drawn}}{\text{number of possible outcomes}} \rightarrow \frac{8}{8}$

d. Write the probability as a percent. 100%

Give the probability that a blue marble will be drawn from the bag above.

e. Write a fraction. $\frac{\text{number of ways blue marble can be drawn}}{\text{number of possible outcomes}} \rightarrow \frac{0}{8}$

f. Write the probability as a percent. 0%

A bag contains 6 blue marbles, 3 red marbles, and 1 black marble. Give the probability of each event occurring. Write the probability as a fraction, a percent, and a decimal.

g. *P*(blue marble) $\frac{6}{10} = \frac{3}{5}$, 60%, 0.6

h. *P*(red marble) $\frac{3}{10}$, 30%, 0.3

i. *P*(black marble) $\frac{1}{10}$, 10%, 0.1

j. *P*(any marble) $\frac{10}{10} = 1$, 100%, 1.0

10. In Yahtzee®, players have 3 turns to roll any or all of 5 number cubes. The highest-scoring result is a Yahtzee, where all 5 dice have the same number. Suppose 4 of the cubes show a 4, and you roll the fifth cube again. What is the probability that you get a Yahtzee on this roll? $\frac{1}{6}$

Give the probability that corresponds to each of the odds.

11. 1:1 $\frac{1}{2}$ **12.** 3:2 $\frac{3}{5}$ **13.** 1:7 $\frac{1}{8}$ **14.** 11:9 $\frac{11}{20}$ **15.** 55:44 $\frac{55}{99} = \frac{5}{9}$

Assume you are drawing the first tile in a Scrabble® game. Use the table to find each probability. Express each as a percent.

Tile	Number	Tile	Number	Tile	Number
A	9	J	1	S	4
B	2	K	1	T	6
C	2	L	4	U	4
D	4	M	2	V	2
E	12	N	6	W	2
F	2	O	8	X	1
G	3	P	2	Y	2
H	2	Q	1	Z	1
I	9	R	6	Blank	2

16. $P(E)$ 12% **17.** $P(Q)$ 1%

18. P(blank) 2% **19.** P(consonant) 56%

20. Test Prep Which of these odds means the same thing as a probability of 25%? C

GPS

Ⓐ 1:5 Ⓑ 1:4 Ⓒ 1:3 Ⓓ 1:2

Problem Solving and Reasoning

21. Critical Thinking Name an event that has a probability of 1 and another that has a probability of 0.

22. Communicate Tell whether you would express each probability as a fraction, a decimal, or a percent. Explain each answer.

a. The probability that you will catch the flu this winter

b. The probability that you will roll a 1 or a 3 on a number cube

c. The probability that it will rain tomorrow

Mixed Review

Find the volume of each cylinder. Use $\pi \approx 3.14$ and round answers to the nearest tenth. *[Lesson 11-9]*

23.

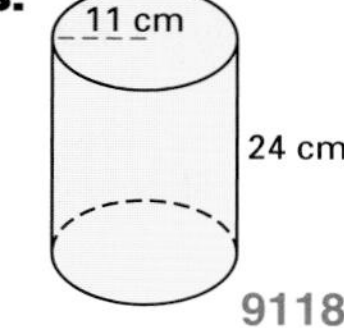

9118.6 cm³

24.

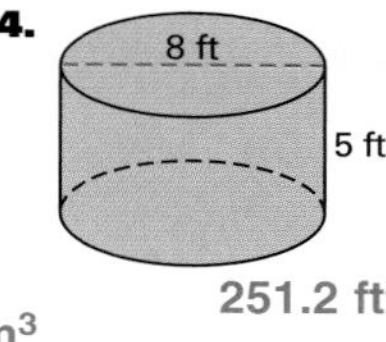

251.2 ft³

25.

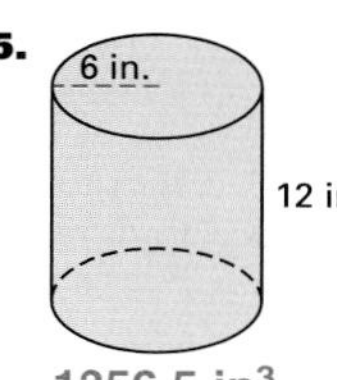

1356.5 in³

26.

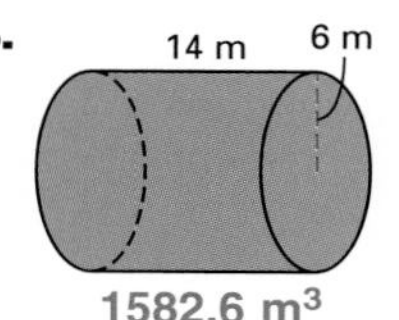

1582.6 m³

Write a rule for each translation. *[Lesson 11-10]*

27. Right 4, down 6 $(x + 4, y - 6)$ **28.** Right 2, up 7 $(x + 2, y + 7)$ **29.** Left 0.2, up 7 $(x - 0.2, y + 7)$ **30.** Up 6 $(x, y + 6)$

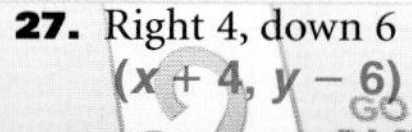

PROBLEM SOLVING 12-5

PROBLEM SOLVING

Name ________ **Guided Problem Solving 12-5**

GPS PROBLEM 20, STUDENT PAGE 653

Which of these odds means the same thing as a probability of 25%?

(A) 1:5 (B) 1:4 (C) 1:3 (D) 1:2

— Understand —

1. What fraction means the same as 25%? $\frac{1}{4}$
2. What does a probability of 25% mean? There is 1 desired event out of 4 possible outcomes.
3. Which describes how to find the probability of an event? B
   a. number of ways the event can happen:number of ways it cannot happen
   b. number of ways the event can happen:number of possible outcomes

— Plan —

4. What does the first number mean when given odds of an event? Tells how many ways event can happen.
5. What does the second number mean when given odds of an event? Tells how many ways event cannot happen.
6. When given the odds of an event, how can you find the number of possible outcomes? A
   a. Add both numbers. b. Multiply both numbers.
7. Write each odds as a probability the event will happen.
   a. 1:5 $\frac{1}{6}$ b. 1:4 $\frac{1}{5}$ c. 1:3 $\frac{1}{4}$ d. 1:2 $\frac{1}{3}$

— Solve —

8. Which is the correct choice? C

— Look Back —

9. How can you determine probability when given the odds? Write first number in odds over sum of both numbers.

SOLVE ANOTHER PROBLEM

Which of these odds means the same thing as a probability of 10%? D

(A) 1:5 (B) 1:11 (C) 1:10 (D) 1:9

ENRICHMENT

Name ________ **Extend Your Thinking 12-5**

Critical Thinking

Suppose a bag contains ten slips with classroom enrichment tasks you can do for extra credit. The tasks include problems related to probability, geometry, and algebra. The number of tasks related to probability is twice the number of tasks related to algebra. There is at least one task devoted to each type of problem.

1. If the odds of choosing an algebra task are 1:9, how many slips for each task will there be? 2 probability tasks, 1 algebra task, 7 geometry tasks.
2. If the odds of choosing an algebra task are 1:4, how many slips for each task will there be? 4 probability tasks, 2 algebra tasks, 4 geometry tasks.
3. If the odds of choosing a probability task are 3:2, how many slips for each task will there be? 6 probability tasks, 3 algebra tasks, 1 geometry task.
4. Suppose a bag contains 15 slips, each listing one of these sports: basketball, baseball, football, volleyball. There are three times as many slips for basketball as baseball and twice as many slips for football as for volleyball. There is at least one slip for each sport.
   a. What are the odds for drawing a slip that shows each of the following sports?
   basketball 9:6 or 3:2 baseball 3:12 or 1:4
   football 2:13 volleyball 1:14
   b. Which sport is more likely to be picked in a random drawing? Explain. Basketball, since 9 chances out of 15 is more likely to happen than 3 out of 15, 2 out of 15, or 1 out of 15.
5. Record several school subjects on the chalkboard. Have each person in the room write his or her favorite subject on a slip of paper and put the slips in a bag. What are the odds of drawing a slip at random that shows your favorite subject? That shows each of the other subjects? Check students' answers.

Exercise Notes

■ Exercise 20

Test Prep If students selected B, they confused odds with probability.

■ Exercises 23–26

Error Prevention Some students may confuse the diameter of a circle with the radius. Point out that the formula for volume of a cylinder involves the radius.

Exercise Answers

21. Possible answers: A dropped ball will fall down (probability 1); A person will jump to the moon tomorrow (probability 0).
22. Possible answers:
    a. A percent; Most people can get a sense of the size of a percent more easily than the size of a fraction.
    b. A fraction; $\frac{1}{3}$ is a familiar fraction, and the decimal and percent forms involve repeating digits.
    c. A percent; People are used to hearing percents given with weather forecasts.

Alternate Assessment

Interview Show students a bag containing a mixture of colored marbles. First have them examine the contents. Then have them give the probability of drawing any one color of marble from the bag.

Quick Quiz

Find the probability for each event. Give a fraction, a decimal, and a percent.

1. Drawing a consonant from the first ten letters of the alphabet $\frac{7}{10}$, 0.7, 70%
2. Rolling an 8 on a number cube $\frac{0}{1}$, 0, 0%
3. Rolling a 4, a 5, or a 6 on a number cube $\frac{3}{6} = \frac{1}{2}$, 0.5, 50%
4. Choosing a multiple of 20 from the numbers 1–100 $\frac{5}{100} = \frac{1}{20}$, 0.05, 5%

Available on Daily Transparency 12-5

INTERACTIVE LESSON

12-6 Lesson Organizer

Objectives

- Use experimental probability to estimate probabilities.
- Find probabilities involving geometric figures.

Vocabulary

- Theoretical probability, experimental probability, geometric probability

Materials

- Explore: Number cubes

NCTM Standards

- 1–2, 4, 11

Review

Find the area of each figure.

1. Square with side length 8 cm 64 cm²
2. Right triangle with legs measuring 4 in. and 8 in. 16 in²
3. Rectangle with sides 7 m and 9 m long 63 m²
4. Trapezoid with height 6 ft and bases 13 ft and 9 ft 66 ft²

Available on Daily Transparency 12-6

1 Introduce

Explore

You may want to use the *Interactive CD-ROM Probability Tool* with this lesson.

The Point
Students conduct a number-cube experiment and compare the probabilities with expected probabilities.

Ongoing Assessment
Be sure that students realize that for **Explore** Step 3 they need to calculate the probability for all 24 rolls of the number cube.

12-6 Experimental Probability

You'll Learn ...

- to use experimental probability to estimate probabilities
- to find probabilities involving geometric figures

... How It's Used

A batting average is the experimental probability that the batter will get a hit.

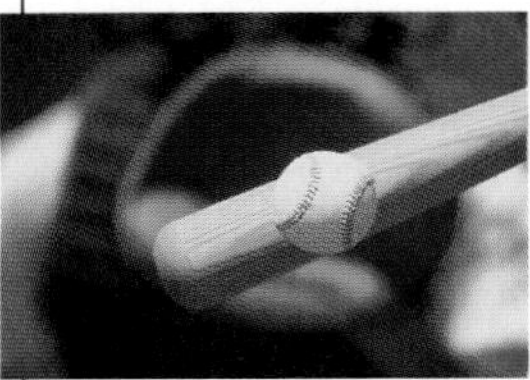

Vocabulary

theoretical probability
experimental probability
geometric probability

▶ Lesson Link You've computed the probabilities of many different events. Now you'll use probability experiments to estimate the probability of an event. ◀

Explore Experimental Probability

Rolling Right Along

Materials: Number cubes

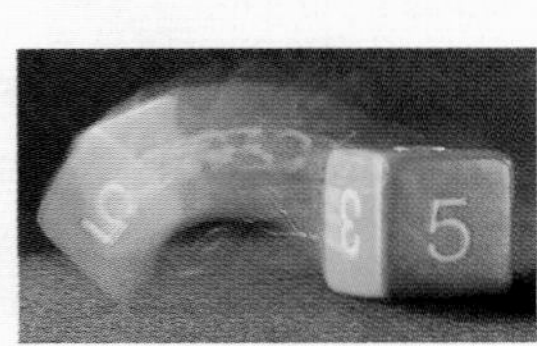

1. Write down the possible outcomes for a roll of a number cube. What is the probability of rolling a 6? Of rolling any even number? Express your probabilities as percents.
2. Roll a number cube 12 times. Record your results. What percent of the rolls came up 6? What percent came up even? Are these percents equal to the probabilities you found in Step 1?
3. Roll the number cube 12 more times. Compute the percent of sixes and of even rolls for all 24 rolls. Compare these percents to the probabilities of a 6 and of an even number. What do you notice? What changes do you see from your Step 2 results?
4. Combine the results for your 24 rolls with those of another student. How do the combined results compare to the probabilities?
5. What do you think would give percents closer to the true probabilities, rolling a number cube 6 times or rolling a number cube 600 times? Explain.

Learn Experimental Probability

To calculate the probability that a tossed coin lands heads, you don't need to toss a coin. Since heads represents one out of the two sides, the **theoretical probability** of heads is $\frac{1}{2} = 50\%$.

However, while mathematician John Kerrich was a prisoner of war during World War II, he tossed a coin 10,000 times and got 5,067 heads. His **experimental probability** of heads was $\frac{\text{number of heads}}{\text{number of tosses}} = \frac{5,067}{10,000} = 50.67\%$.

MEETING INDIVIDUAL NEEDS

Resources

- **12-6** Practice
- **12-6** Reteaching
- **12-6** Enrichment
- **12-6** Problem Solving
- **12-6** Daily Transparency
  - Problem of the Day
  - Review
  - Quick Quiz
- Lesson Enhancement Transparency 63
- Teaching Tool Transparencies 2, 3
- Technology Master 64

Interactive CD-ROM Lesson 12

Learning Modalities

Kinesthetic It is important to have students understand the difference between theoretical and experimental probabilities. Give them many experiences with conducting their own experiments with number cubes,coins, and so on, and have them figure both the theoretical and experimental probabilities for various events.

Logical For **Explore** Step 3, collect the data for the entire class and have students compute the experimental probabilities.

Challenge

Have groups of students determine the geometric probability for each section of a standard dart board. Then have them evaluate whether the point values in the sections make the board fair or unfair for random tosses of a dart.

It's easy to find the probability of tossing heads or tails. But other theoretical probabilities are difficult—or even impossible—to calculate. In these cases, we may be able to estimate the probability by doing an experiment.

Example 1

Of Kerrich's first 10 coin tosses, 6 were tails. What is the experimental probability of tails for these tosses? Express the answer as a decimal.

The experimental probability is $\frac{\text{number of tails}}{\text{total number of tosses}} = \frac{6}{10} = 0.6$.

Since there are 6 numbers on a number cube, the Counting Principle tells us that there are $6 \cdot 6 = 36$ possible outcomes for a roll of two cubes, as shown.

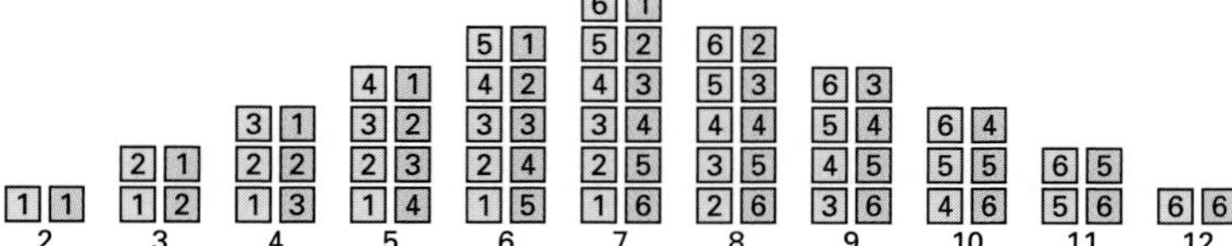

Example 2

In Monopoly®, one way to get out of jail is to roll a "double" with two number cubes. Suppose you roll a pair of number cubes 24 times and get doubles 6 times. What is the experimental probability of getting doubles? Compare this to the theoretical probability of getting doubles.

Experimental probability $= \frac{\text{number of doubles}}{\text{number of rolls}} = \frac{6}{24} = \frac{1}{4}$

From the chart: Theoretical probability $= \frac{\text{ways a double can happen}}{\text{number of outcomes}} = \frac{6}{36} = \frac{1}{6}$

The experimental probability of $\frac{1}{4}$ is larger than the theoretical probability of $\frac{1}{6}$.

The idea for Monopoly® was first developed by Lizzie Magie in 1904, but it was rejected by toy companies. During the Great Depression, the idea for the game was modified and sold to Parker Brothers.

Try It

a. If you drop a piece of bread with jelly on one side 100 times, and it lands "jelly side down" 58 times, what is the experimental probability of "jelly side down"? Express your answer as a decimal. 0.58

b. Suppose you roll a pair of number cubes 72 times and get a sum of 7 eight of those times. What is the experimental probability of a sum of 7? Use the figure above to compare this to the theoretical probability of this sum.
Experimental $\frac{1}{9}$; Theoretical $\frac{1}{6}$

MATH EVERY DAY

Problem of the Day

Each of the 40 students wrote his or her choice for group leader on a sheet of paper. Six girls chose James. The rest of the girls chose Andrea. Five of the boys chose Andrea. The rest of the boys chose James. If one sheet of paper was to be drawn at random, the probability was 3 out of 8 that Andrea's name would be drawn. How many girls and how many boys are there? 16 girls, 24 boys

Available on Daily Transparency 12-6

An Extension is provided in the transparency package.

Fact of the Day

The first World Champion chess player was Wilhelm Steinitz of Austria. He defeated Adolph Anderssen in 1866 and held the title until 1894.

Mental Math

Give the theoretical probability of each event as a fraction.

1. Tossing heads with a coin $\frac{1}{2}$
2. Rolling a 1, a 2, or a 3 with a number cube $\frac{1}{2}$
3. Rolling a 9 with a number cube 0

For Groups That Finish Early

Repeat the **Explore** activity until you have a total of 100 rolls. Then compare your probabilities for 100 rolls with the probabilities in Step 1.
Answers may vary.

Answers for Explore

1. 1, 2, 3, 4, 5, 6; 16.7%; 50%

2–4. Answers will vary. As the number of rolls increases, the percents are likely to get closer to the probabilities in Step 1.

5. Rolling a cube 600 times; Any "unusual" results for a few rolls are likely to smooth out over many rolls.

2 Teach

Learn

You may wish to use Lesson Enhancement Transparency 63 with **Learn.**

Alternate Examples

1. Of Barb's 20 rolls of a number cube, 4 were 2s. What is the experimental probability of a 2 for these rolls? Express the answer as a decimal.

   Experimental probability = $\frac{\text{number of 2s}}{\text{total number of rolls}} = \frac{4}{20} = 0.2$.

2. Suppose you roll a pair of number cubes 30 times and get a pair of 6s two times. What is your experimental probability of getting a pair of 6s? Compare this to the theoretical probability of getting a pair of 6s.

   Experimental probability = $\frac{\text{number of pairs of 6s}}{\text{number of rolls}} = \frac{2}{30} = \frac{1}{15}$.

   Refer to the diagram on this page.

   Theoretical probability = $\frac{\text{number of ways a pair of 6s can happen}}{\text{number of possible outcomes}}$ $= \frac{1}{36}$.

   The experimental probability of $\frac{1}{15}$ is greater than the theoretical probability of $\frac{1}{36}$.

Alternate Examples

3. What is the theoretical probability that a coin tossed randomly onto this game board will land on a shaded square?

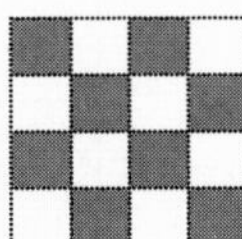

P (shaded) = $\frac{\text{number of shaded squares}}{\text{total number of squares}} = \frac{8}{16} = \frac{1}{2}$

4. In the game shown below, you win a prize if you toss a marker onto the shaded square of the square table. While Tony watched, 8 out of 50 tosses won a prize.

   a. If the markers land randomly on the table, what is the theoretical probability of winning a prize?

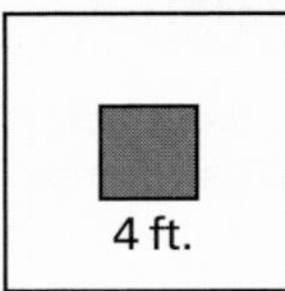

   The area of the shaded region is $4^2 = 16$ ft^2, and the area of the table is $12^2 = 144$ ft^2. The theoretical probability of winning is $\frac{\text{area of winning region}}{\text{total area}} = \frac{16}{144} = \frac{1}{9} \approx 11\%$.

   b. What was the experimental probability of winning? The experimental probability of winning was $\frac{\text{games won}}{\text{total games}} = \frac{8}{50} = 16\%$.

   Is the theoretical probability of an event always the same? Yes, but experimental probability will vary.

▶ Science Link

According to some geologists, there is a 50% probability of a strong earthquake (Richter scale magnitude of 6 or more) on the New Madrid fault in Missouri before the year 2000.

When a probability involves a geometric figure, you can find the theoretical probability by comparing areas, perimeters, or other measurements. A probability calculated in this way is called a **geometric probability**.

Examples

3 What is the geometric probability that a coin tossed randomly onto this "chessboard" lands mostly on a red square?

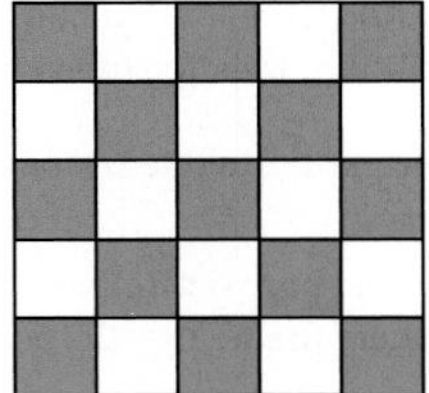

$$P(\text{red}) = \frac{\text{number of red squares}}{\text{total number of squares}} = \frac{13}{25}$$

4 In the carnival game shown, you win a prize if you toss a marker onto the shaded area of the square table. While Saskia watches, 15 out of 80 tosses win a prize.

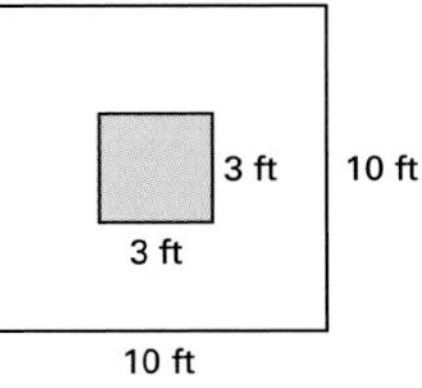

a. If the markers land randomly on the table, what is the theoretical probability of winning a prize? Express your answer as a percent.

The area of the shaded region is $3^2 = 9$ ft^2, and the area of the table is $10^2 = 100$ ft^2.

The theoretical probability of winning is $\frac{\text{area of winning region}}{\text{total area}} = \frac{9}{100} = 9\%$.

b. What is the experimental probability of winning a prize?

The experimental probability of winning is $\frac{\text{games won}}{\text{total games}} = \frac{15}{80} = 18.75\%$.

Try It

If a dart lands randomly on this "dart board," what is the theoretical probability that it lands in the triangular region? $\frac{6}{128} \approx 4.7\%$

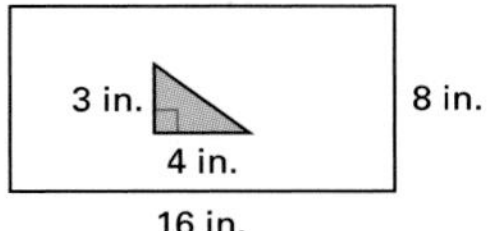

Check Your Understanding

1. Is the experimental probability of an event always the same? Explain.
2. What would you think if the experimental probability for a coin toss turned out to be very different from its theoretical probability?
3. In Example 4, why do you think the experimental probability of winning the game might have been higher than the theoretical probability?

3 Practice and Assess

Check

Answers for Check Your Understanding

1. No; Experimental probability depends on results of a series of trials which may be different for different experiments.
2. The coin was not "fair," or the experiment had too few trials.
3. The markers did not actually land randomly because people were aiming at the target.

MEETING MIDDLE SCHOOL CLASSROOM NEEDS

Tips from Middle-School Teachers

I give small groups of students a choice of number cubes, coins, spinners, or boards with which to conduct a probability experiment. They make up their own procedures, but I insist that they record outcomes and find both the theoretical and experimental probabilities involved. Groups then share with each other the comparisons of the two probabilities for their experiment.

Cultural Connection

Cowrie shells are the shells of small sea snails. Oval-shaped, they can be from $\frac{1}{2}$"–6" long and are usually very colorful and beautifully patterned. There are more than 150 kinds of cowries, some of which are so rare that collectors will pay hundreds of dollars for them. They were once used as money in China, India, and Africa; and at one time they were a badge of office for Fiji Island chieftains.

Cooperative Learning

Have students conduct experiments to see how close their experimental results are to the experimental results and the theoretical results for Exercises 2–13.

12-6 Exercises and Applications

Practice and Apply

1. **Getting Started** A dart lands randomly on the dart board shown. Follow the steps to find the geometric probability that the dart lands in the shaded area.

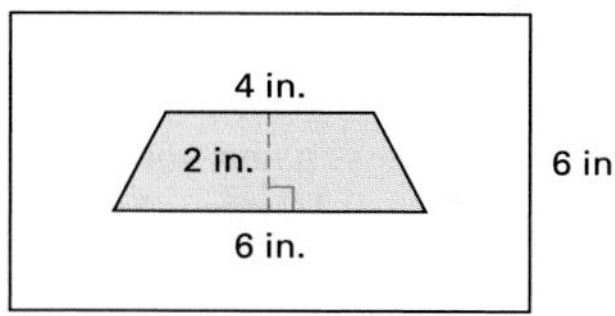

   a. Find the area of the shaded region. Use the area formula for a trapezoid. 10 in^2

   b. Find the area of the dart board. Use the area formula for a rectangle. 60 in^2

   c. Write a fraction with the area of the shaded region in the numerator and the area of the entire dart board in the denominator. Rewrite the fraction in lowest terms. $\frac{10}{60} = \frac{1}{6}$

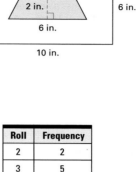

The tally sheet shows the results for several rolls of two number cubes. Use the sheet to find the experimental probability of each event.

Roll	Frequency
2	2
3	5
4	9
5	8
6	10
7	15
8	7
9	8
10	5
11	2
12	1

2. Rolling a 3 $\frac{5}{72}$
3. Rolling a 4 $\frac{9}{72} = \frac{1}{8}$
4. Rolling a 6 $\frac{10}{72} = \frac{5}{36}$
5. Rolling a 7 $\frac{15}{72} = \frac{5}{24}$
6. Rolling an 8 $\frac{7}{72}$
7. Rolling a 12 $\frac{1}{72}$

8–13. Use the figure on page 655 to find the *theoretical* probability of each event in Exercises 2–7. Compare the probabilities.

14. **Test Prep** You roll a pair of number cubes 36 times and roll a sum of 8 five times. How does the experimental probability of rolling a sum of 8 compare to the theoretical probability? B

   Ⓐ Less than Ⓑ Equal to

   Ⓒ Greater than Ⓓ Not enough information

15. **History** Over the years, many cultures have used cowrie shells as a kind of dice. African cultures have used them in games of chance, and they were the dice in early versions of the Indian game of Pachisi. If a cowrie shell lands "mouth up" in 48 of 80 tosses, what is the experimental probability of "mouth up" for a cowrie shell? Express your answer as a percent. 60%

PRACTICE 12-6

12–6 Exercises and Applications

Assignment Guide

- **Basic** 1–13 odds, 14, 15, 17, 20, 21, 23–26
- **Average** 2–22 evens, 23–26
- **Enriched** 2–14 evens, 16, 19, 20, 22–26

Exercise Notes

Exercises 2–7

Review the term *frequency*.

Exercises 8–13

Error Prevention Be sure students know how to interpret the diagram on page 655. Suggest that they express the fractions with denominators of 72 so that the probabilities are more easily compared.

Exercise Answers

8. $\frac{2}{36} = \frac{1}{18}$; Less than experimental
9. $\frac{3}{36} = \frac{1}{12}$; Less than experimental
10. $\frac{5}{36}$; Equal to experimental
11. $\frac{6}{36} = \frac{1}{6}$; Less than experimental
12. $\frac{5}{36}$; Greater than experimental
13. $\frac{1}{36}$; Greater than experimental

Reteaching

Activity

Materials: Bag with 5 red chips, 3 white chips, 2 blue chips

- Use a table like the one below. Draw a chip from the bag and tally the result in the appropriate row. Replace the chip in the bag and draw again. Tally this result. Draw 20 chips in all.
- Fill in the remaining columns of the table. Remember, if you drew a red chip 13 times, the experimental probability would be $\frac{13}{20}$.

Color	Red	White	Blue
Tally			
Number			
Exper. Probabil.			
Theoret. Probabil.	$\frac{1}{2}$	$\frac{3}{10}$	$\frac{1}{5}$

PRACTICE

Name ______________________

Practice 12-6

Experimental Probability

The tally shows the results for several rolls of two number cubes.
a. Use the sheet to find the experimental probability of each event.
b. Use the figure on page 655 of your textbook to find the theoretical probability of each event. Give your answers as fractions in lowest terms.

Roll	Frequency
2	1
3	3
4	4
5	6
6	8
7	7
8	9
9	5
10	3
11	2
12	2

1. Rolling a 2 **a.** $\frac{1}{50}$ **b.** $\frac{1}{36}$
2. Rolling a 3 **a.** $\frac{3}{50}$ **b.** $\frac{1}{18}$
3. Rolling a 5 **a.** $\frac{3}{25}$ **b.** $\frac{1}{9}$
4. Rolling a 7 **a.** $\frac{7}{50}$ **b.** $\frac{1}{6}$
5. Rolling an 8 **a.** $\frac{9}{50}$ **b.** $\frac{5}{36}$
6. Rolling a 10 **a.** $\frac{3}{50}$ **b.** $\frac{1}{12}$
7. Rolling an 11 **a.** $\frac{1}{25}$ **b.** $\frac{1}{18}$

A speck of dust lands on the grid shown. What is the probability that it:

8. Lands on the dark shaded area? $\frac{12}{25} = 48\% = 0.48$
9. Lands on the light shaded area? $\frac{8}{25} = 32\% = 0.32$
10. Lands on the unshaded area? $\frac{1}{5} = 20\% = 0.2$

In a coin toss game, you earn points for landing on the shaded figures. Assume coins land randomly in the large square. What is the probability that a coin:

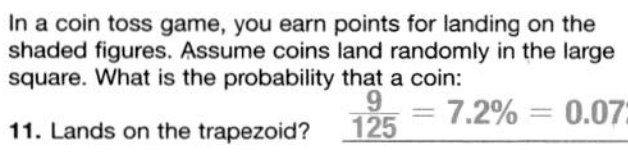

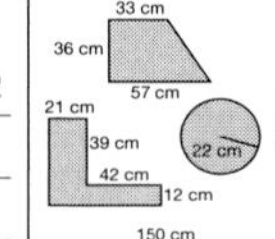

11. Lands on the trapezoid? $\frac{9}{125} = 7.2\% = 0.072$
12. Lands on the circle? $\approx 6.75\% = 0.0675$
13. Lands on the "L" shape? $\frac{7}{100} = 7\% = 0.07$
14. During the 1994–1995 basketball season, the Charlotte Hornets won 50 out of 82 games. Based on these results, what is the experimental probability that the Hornets will win a game? Express your answer as a percent. About 61.0%

RETEACHING

Name ______________________

Alternative Lesson 12-6

Experimental Probability

You have calculated the **theoretical probability** of an event occurring by using the ratio:

$$\text{Probability (event)} = \frac{\text{number of ways the event can happen}}{\text{number of possible outcomes}}$$

This probability is theoretical because it is based on what should occur.

Suppose you perform an experiment and record your results. You can then use the data to find the **experimental probability** of an event occurring by using this ratio.

$$\text{Probability (event)} = \frac{\text{number of ways the event happened}}{\text{number of possible outcomes}}$$

The probability is experimental because it is based on what actually occurs.

Example

A tile is drawn out of a bag containing 4 tiles imprinted with Ds, 3 with As, 2 with Bs, and 1 with a C. It is replaced and another tile is drawn. The results of ten draws are shown in the table.

Draw	1	2	3	4	5	6	7	8	9	10
Letter	B	C	A	A	D	D	B	A	A	D

Give the experimental probability of drawing D generated by the data. Then compare it to the theoretical probability.

Experimental probability The letter D was drawn 3 times. → 3; There are 10 possible outcomes. → 10: $\frac{3}{10}$

Theoretical probability There are 4 Ds in the bag → 4; There are 10 possible outcomes. → 10: $\frac{4}{10}$

The experimental probability of drawing D is $\frac{3}{10}$. The theoretical probability is $\frac{4}{10}$. It is larger than the experimental probability.

Try It

Suppose you tossed a number cube 8 times and recorded your results. The recorded data shows you tossed 2 fives.

a. What is the experimental probability of tossing a 5? $\frac{2}{8} = \frac{1}{4}$

b. What is the theoretical probability of tossing a 5? $\frac{1}{6}$

c. Compare the probabilities. The experimental probability is greater than the theoretical probability: $\frac{1}{4} > \frac{1}{6}$.

Exercise Notes

Exercise 21

Problem-Solving Tip You may want to use Teaching Tool Transparencies 2 and 3: Guided Problem Solving, pages 1–2.

Exercises 23–25

Error Prevention You may need to review the notion of line symmetry.

Exercise Answers

17. Answers may vary. An estimate from 1000 trials would give you more confidence; 10 trials might contain some unusual results that would even out over a long series of trials.
21. a. Experimental
    b. Possible answer: 10 injured firefighters, 36 uninjured; I found two whole numbers whose ratio is 1:3.6.
22. Answers will vary.

23–25. See page C7.

Alternate Assessment

You may want to use the *Interactive CD-ROM Journal* with this assessment.

Journal Give each group of 3 students a bag containing a mixture of colored marbles. Have them conduct an experiment by drawing and replacing a marble at least 40 times. Then in their journal have them make a table showing the colors, the number of times each color was chosen, the experimental probability for each color, and the theoretical probability for each color.

Quick Quiz

Find the experimental and theoretical probabilities for each event. Give fraction answers. Tell which probability is greater.

1. Kiyoko rolled a 6 four times in 20 rolls of a number cube.
   $\frac{4}{20} = \frac{1}{5}, \frac{1}{6}$; experimental
2. Maria rolled an odd number twelve times in 30 rolls of a number cube.
   $\frac{12}{30} = \frac{2}{5}, \frac{1}{2}$; theoretical
3. Guy tossed heads ten times in 24 tosses of a coin.
   $\frac{10}{24} = \frac{5}{12}, \frac{1}{2}$; theoretical

Available on Daily Transparency 12-6

---

16. A fly lands on the checkered picnic blanket shown. What is the theoretical probability that it lands on a green square? $\frac{25}{49}$

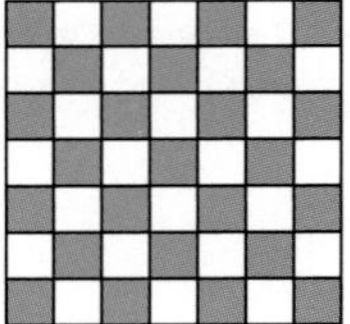

17. An experimental probability is an estimate of the true probability of an event. Would you be more confident of an experimental probability that came from 10 trials or 1000 trials? Explain.

In a coin toss game, you earn points for landing on the shaded figures. Assume coins land randomly in the large square. What is the probability that a coin:

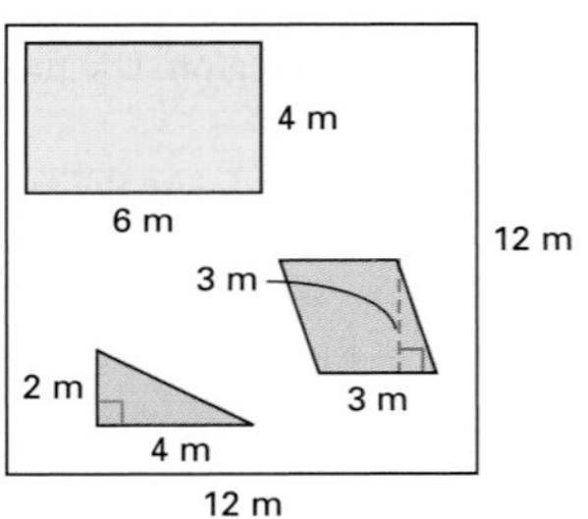

18. Lands on the shaded rectangle? $\frac{24}{144} = \frac{1}{6}$
19. Lands on the non-rectangular parallelogram? $\frac{9}{144} = \frac{1}{16}$
20. GPS Lands on the right triangle? $\frac{4}{144} = \frac{1}{36}$

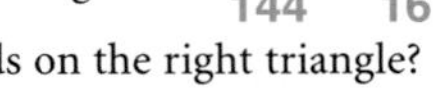

Problem Solving and Reasoning

21. **Choose a Strategy** Fire fighting is an occupation with a high probability of injury. For every fire fighter who is injured, 3.6 are not.
    a. Do these numbers represent an experimental or a theoretical probability?
    b. Create a data set that would give this probability of injury. Explain how you created the data set.

Problem Solving STRATEGIES
- Look for a Pattern
- Make an Organized List
- Make a Table
- Guess and Check
- Work Backward
- Use Logical Reasoning
- Draw a Diagram
- Solve a Simpler Problem

22. Journal Find the theoretical probability of an event. Then design an experiment, and calculate an experimental probability for the event. Compare your findings.

PROBLEM SOLVING 12-6

Mixed Review

Decide whether each figure has line symmetry. If it does, copy the figure and draw and number the lines of symmetry. *[Lesson 11-11]*

23. Isosceles right triangle
24. Regular pentagon

25. Isosceles trapezoid

26. Suppose a jacket comes in 3 colors, 2 styles, and 5 sizes. Use the Counting Principle to find the number of different jackets. *[Lesson 12-1]* 30

PROBLEM SOLVING

Name ________

Guided Problem Solving 12-6

GPS **PROBLEM 20, STUDENT PAGE 658**

In a coin toss game you earn points for landing on the shaded figures. Assume coins land randomly in the large square. What is the probability that a coin lands on the right triangle?

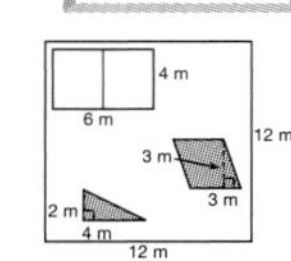

Understand

1. Underline what you are asked to find.
2. Which ratio will you use to find the probability? a
   a. Area of right triangle : area of square
   b. Area of right triangle : perimeter of square

Plan

3. Which formula will you use to find the area of the large square? b
   a. $A = \frac{1}{2}bh$ b. $A = l \times w$ c. $A = \pi r^2$
4. Which formula will you use to find the area of the right triangle? a
   a. $A = \frac{1}{2}bh$ b. $A = l \times w$ c. $A = \pi r^2$

Solve

5. Find the area of the large square. $144\ m^2$
6. Find the area of the right triangle. $4\ m^2$
7. Find the probability that a coin lands on the right triangle. $\frac{4}{144} = \frac{1}{36}$

Look Back

8. What strategy could help you decide if your answer is reasonable?
   Divide diagram into 100 squares. Count squares inside triangle; total is about 3 squares, which is close to $\frac{1}{36}$.

SOLVE ANOTHER PROBLEM

Coins are randomly tossed on the rectangle at the right. Find the probability that a coin lands on the shaded parallelogram. Assume coins land randomly in the large square.

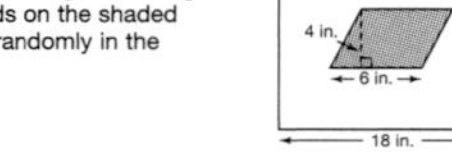

$\frac{24}{216} = \frac{1}{9}$

ENRICHMENT

Name ________

Extend Your Thinking 12-6

Patterns in Geometry

1. The radius of the center circle in the dart game is 1 inch. Each larger circle has a radius that is 1 inch greater than the next smallest circle. Complete the table by finding the area of each ring in the target. Then find the geometric probability of hitting each ring expressed as a percent.

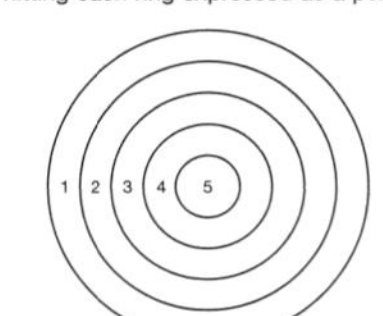

Ring	Area	Probability
1	$28.26\ in^2$	36%
2	$21.98\ in^2$	28%
3	$15.7\ in^2$	20%
4	$9.42\ in^2$	12%
5	$3.14\ in^2$	4%

2. What pattern do you see in the table?
   The probability decreases by 8% for each ring as you move from the outer ring to the middle circle.
3. The length of the side of the smallest square in the target below is 1 cm. Each larger square has a side length that is twice the size of the next smallest square. Complete the table by finding the area of each figure in the target. Then find the geometric probability of hitting each figure expressed as a percent.

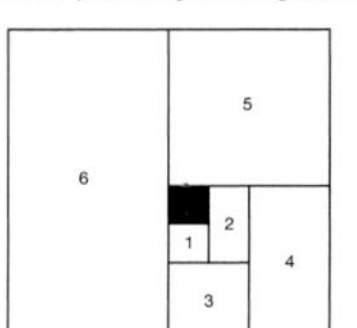

Figure	Area	Probability
1	$1\ cm^2$	1.5625%
2	$2\ cm^2$	3.125%
3	$4\ cm^2$	6.25%
4	$8\ cm^2$	12.5%
5	$16\ cm^2$	25%
6	$32\ cm^2$	50%

4. What pattern do you see in the table?
   The probability doubles as you move from a smaller figure to the next larger one.

Independent and Dependent Events

12-7

▶ **Lesson Link** You've found probabilities for many different types of events. Now you'll use these skills to help you find the probability that *two* particular things will happen. ◀

You'll Learn ...

- to decide whether two events are dependent or independent
- to find probabilities of dependent and independent events

... How It's Used

Genetic researchers use dependent probabilities when they identify genes causing diseases such as cystic fibrosis.

Vocabulary

independent events

dependent events

compound event

sample space

Explore Independent and Dependent Events

Eight Is for Elephant

Materials: Number cubes

An ancient African dice game matches numbers with animals. Suppose that a sum of 8 on a roll of two cubes stands for "elephant."

Use experimental probability to investigate each question. Roll the number cube 20 times for each experiment.

1. What is the probability that you roll "elephant" on a roll of the cubes?
2. Suppose you roll the cubes one at a time. If you roll a 1 on the first cube, what is the probability of "elephant"? Explain how you know.
3. If you roll a 4 on the first cube, what is the probability of "elephant"? Explain.
4. If your answers for Steps 1–3 were the same, explain why this makes sense. If not, explain why you think the probabilities are different.

Learn Independent and Dependent Events

Now, how did I land the last time?

If a coin lands heads several times in a row, many people think that the probability of heads on the next toss will be less than 50%. But even though it has a head, a coin doesn't have a memory! The probability of the next toss landing heads is still $\frac{1}{2}$.

When the outcome of one event does not change the probability of another, the events are **independent**. Two coin tosses are independent, since the result of the first toss doesn't affect the second.

MEETING INDIVIDUAL NEEDS

Resources

12-7 Practice
12-7 Reteaching
12-7 Enrichment
12-7 Problem Solving
12-7 Daily Transparency
- Problem of the Day
- Review
- Quick Quiz

Chapter 12 Project Master

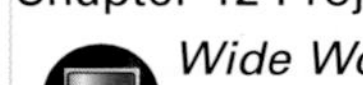
Wide World of Mathematics
Middle School: Two-Sport Athlete

Learning Modalities

Verbal Have students verbalize the meanings of dependent and independent events and give examples of both. This will help them clarify the distinction between the two. Seventh graders should have a fairly good idea of the general meanings of these terms.

Social Have students work in pairs on **Explore**. Encourage them to actually roll the number cubes to investigate the probabilities involved.

English Language Development

Distinguishing between independent and dependent events is sometimes difficult for students with limited English proficiency. Give examples from their daily experience such as whether catching the flu and owning a goldfish are independent or dependent. Independent Then ask whether catching the flu and staying home from school the next day are independent or dependent. Dependent

12-7 Lesson Organizer

Objectives

- Decide whether two events are dependent or independent.
- Find probabilities of dependent and independent events.

Vocabulary

- Independent events, dependent events, compound event, sample space

Materials

- Explore: Number cubes

NCTM Standards

- 1–4, 11

▶ Review

Find each product. Give each answer in lowest terms.

1. $\frac{1}{3} \times \frac{1}{4}$ $\frac{1}{12}$
2. $\frac{2}{3} \times \frac{3}{4}$ $\frac{1}{2}$
3. $\frac{9}{10} \times \frac{8}{9}$ $\frac{4}{5}$
4. $\frac{5}{6} \times \frac{4}{5}$ $\frac{2}{3}$
5. $\frac{11}{12} \times \frac{10}{11}$ $\frac{5}{6}$

Available on Daily Transparency 12-7

1 Introduce

Explore

The Point

Students explore an African dice game involving the roll of two dice. This introduces them to independent and dependent events.

Ongoing Assessment

Student pairs may actually roll number cubes or refer to the diagram on page 655 for the theoretical probability.

Answers for Explore on next page.

For Groups That Finish Early
Repeat **Explore** Step 3, assuming a 2 on the first cube. Students should conclude that the probability is still $\frac{1}{6}$.

Answers for Explore

1. Answers may vary.
2. Probability = 0; If you roll a 1 on the first cube, you can't roll a large enough number on the second to add up to 8.
3. Answers may vary.
4. The probabilities are different; The number you get on the first roll affects the likelihood that the sum of the rolls will be 8.

2 Teach

Learn

Alternate Examples

Tell whether the events are *dependent* or *independent*.

1. Rolling a 5 on the first roll of a number cube and then rolling another 5 on the second.

   The first roll does not affect the second, so the events are independent.

2. Choosing a red jellybean from a bag containing a mixture of colors and eating it before choosing another jellybean.

   Because you did not replace the jellybean, there are fewer jellybeans for your second choice. So your first choice affects the second, and the events are dependent.

3. Give the sample space for 2 tosses of a coin. There are four possible outcomes: (heads, heads), (heads, tails), (tails, heads), and (tails, tails).

Suppose there are 11 jellybeans in a bag, and 2 are purple. If you take a jellybean out of the bag and don't put it back, you change the probability of getting a purple jellybean on the next draw.

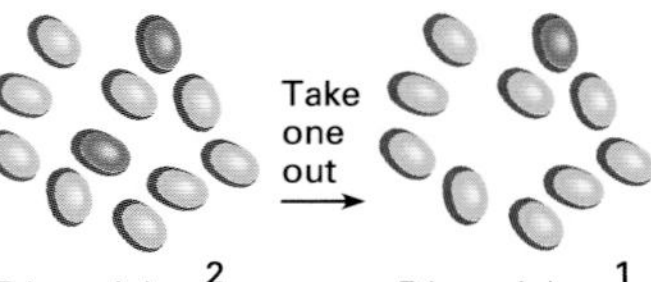

$P(\text{purple}) = \frac{2}{11}$ $P(\text{purple}) = \frac{1}{10}$

The two draws of a jellybean are **dependent events** —the probability of the second depends on the results of the first.

Study TIP
When deciding whether two events are dependent, decide whether knowing the results of the first would help predict the results of the second.

Examples

Tell whether the events are dependent or independent.

1 Rolling an even number on the first roll of a number cube, then rolling an odd number on the second.

The first roll does not affect the second. The events are independent.

2 Being sick on Monday, then being sick on Tuesday.

If you are sick one day, you are more likely than usual to be sick the next. The events are dependent.

A **compound event** is made up of two or more individual events. To find the **sample space**, or set of all possible outcomes, for a compound event, make an organized list of all the possibilities for each event.

Examples

3 A marble bag holds 1 red marble and 3 green marbles. Give the sample space for drawing two marbles if you replace the first.

The possibilities for the first draw are red and green. The possibilities for the second are also red and green.

The sample space is (red, red), (red, green), (green, red), and (green, green).

4 To win a game, you must roll a 5 on a number cube, then spin "Return to Base" on the spinner. Use the Counting Principle to determine the probability you will win the game.

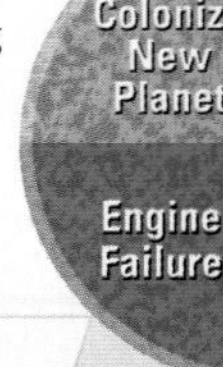

There are 6 possible rolls of the cube, and 4 equal sectors on the spinner. According to the Counting Principle, there are $6 \cdot 4 = 24$ possible outcomes. Only 1 of those 24 is the winning combination.

The probability that you will win is $\frac{1}{24}$.

MATH EVERY DAY

Problem of the Day

How many isosceles triangles can you find in the figure below?

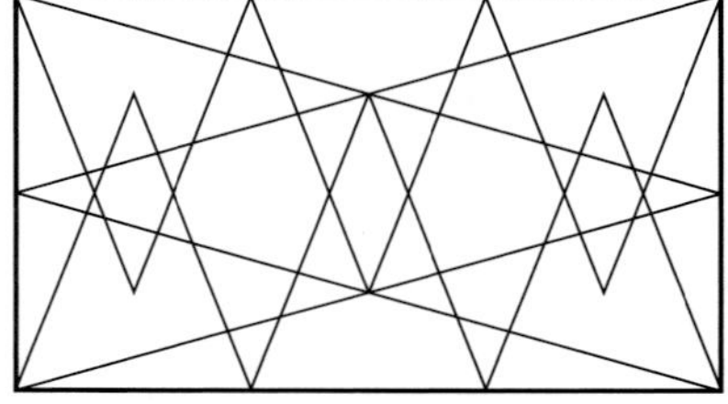

16 isosceles triangles

Available on Daily Transparency 12-7

An Extension is provided in the transparency package.

Fact of the Day

Indian elephants were used as work animals possibly as early as 2000 B.C. Hannibal, a North African ruler, used elephants with his army around 218 B.C.

Mental Math

Give each product in lowest terms.

1. $\frac{1}{6} \times \frac{1}{5}$ $\frac{1}{30}$
2. $\frac{1}{5} \times \frac{1}{4}$ $\frac{1}{20}$
3. $\frac{7}{8} \times \frac{6}{7}$ $\frac{3}{4}$
4. $\frac{2}{3} \times \frac{1}{2}$ $\frac{1}{3}$
5. $\frac{3}{4} \times \frac{2}{3}$ $\frac{1}{2}$

In Example 4, notice that $P(5) = \frac{1}{6}$ and $P(\text{Return to Base}) = \frac{1}{4}$. The product $\frac{1}{6} \times \frac{1}{4}$ equals $\frac{1}{24}$, which is the probability that these independent events *both* happen.

PROBABILITY OF TWO INDEPENDENT EVENTS

The probability that two independent events A and B both happen is given by: $P(A, B) = P(A) \times P(B)$.

Examples

5 For a coin toss and a roll of a number cube, find *P*(heads, 4).

The events are independent. $P(\text{heads}) = \frac{1}{2}$, and $P(4) = \frac{1}{6}$.

Therefore, $P(\text{heads}, 4) = \frac{1}{2} \times \frac{1}{6} = \frac{1}{12}$.

6 Cheryl is drawing the first 2 tiles in a Scrabble® game. What is the probability that both are A's? (Note: 9 of the 100 tiles are A's.)

The first draw changes the number of tiles left, and may change the number of A's, so the events are dependent.

The probability of an A on the first draw is $\frac{9}{100}$. The probability of getting an A on the second draw *after* getting an A on the first is $\frac{8}{99}$, since there are 8 A's and 99 tiles left after the first A is drawn.

$P(\text{A, then A}) = \frac{9}{100} \times \frac{8}{99} = \frac{72}{9900} = \frac{2}{275}$.

Social Studies Link

Once a person in the United States has been in prison, the probability that he or she will return to jail at some time is greater than 60%.

Try It a. (red, green), (green, red), (green, green)

a. Find the sample space for the marble bag in Example 3 if you do *not* replace the first marble.

b. For a coin toss and a spin of the spinner, find *P*(tails, red). $\frac{1}{10}$

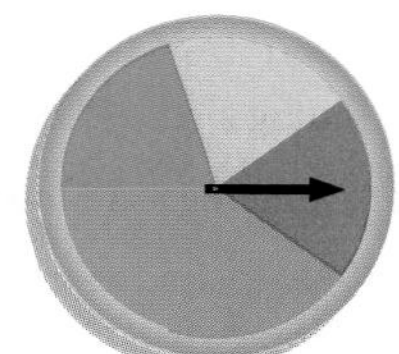

c. A drawer contains 8 black socks and 8 blue socks. If you draw 2 socks out of the drawer in the dark, what is the probability that both are blue? $\frac{7}{30}$

Check Your Understanding

1. Explain the difference between dependent and independent events.
2. Give two ways to find the probability of two independent events.

MEETING MIDDLE SCHOOL CLASSROOM NEEDS

Tips from Middle-School Teachers

To help students distinguish between independent and dependent events, I have them work with groups of playing cards, for instance, using all the face cards or all cards of one suit. I have them model the probabilities of drawing certain cards with and without replacement. I stress that *with* replacement gives independent events and *without* replacement gives dependent events.

Cultural Connection

Hanukkah, also spelled *Chanukah*, is a Jewish festival celebrated in December to commemorate the reconsecration of the Temple of Jerusalem after the temple was taken back from the Syrian Greeks around 165 B.C.

Hanukkah is also known as the *Festival of Lights* because candles are lit every day for 8 festival days. Two candles are lit on the first day, and one additional candle is lit each succeeding day. Ask students to calculate how many candles are lit for a total of 8 days. 44

Team Teaching

Ask the science teachers to discuss with students how probability is involved in weather forecasting.

Alternate Examples

4. To win a game, you must roll a 6 on a number cube and spin an 8 on the spinner shown below. What is the probability that you will win?

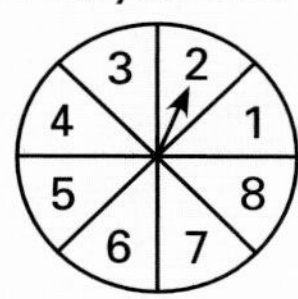

There are 6 possible rolls of the cube and 8 congruent sectors on the spinner. By the Counting Principle, there are $6 \cdot 8 = 48$ possible outcomes. Only one of those 48 is the winning combination. The probability that you will win $= \frac{1}{48}$.

5. For a coin toss and a roll of a number cube, find *P* (tails, 2).

   The events are *independent*. $P(\text{tails}) = \frac{1}{2}$, and $P(2) = \frac{1}{6}$. So, $P(\text{tails}, 2) = \frac{1}{2} \times \frac{1}{6} = \frac{1}{12}$.

6. Mike is drawing the first two tiles in a Scrabble® game. What is the probability that both will be Es? (Remember, 12 of the 100 tiles are Es.)

   The first draw changes the number of tiles left and may change the number of Es, so the events are *dependent*.

   The probability of E on the first draw is $\frac{12}{100}$. The probability of E on the second draw *after* getting E on the first is $\frac{11}{99}$, since there are 11 Es and 99 tiles left after the first draw. So, $P(E, E) = \frac{12}{100} \times \frac{11}{99} = \frac{132}{9900} = \frac{1}{75}$.

3 Practice and Assess

Check

Answers for Check Your Understanding

1. Two events are dependent if the outcome of one affects the probability of the other. They are independent otherwise.
2. Multiply the probabilities of the individual events, or find all of the possible outcomes for *both* and count the number of ways the two events you are looking for can happen.

Assignment Guide

- **Basic**
  1–8, 11–15 odds
- **Average**
  2–12, 14
- **Enriched**
  4–16

Exercise Notes

Exercise 8

Cultural The Hebrew letters on the driedel are called *nun, gimmel, hay,* and *shin.*

Exercise Answers

9. a. $\frac{1}{16}$ = 6.25%; b. No; The probability that it will rain tomorrow increases if a weather pattern has made rain more likely today.

Reteaching

Activity

Materials: Red and blue chips

Suppose you have a bag containing 1 blue and 2 red chips. Use the chips to model all the possibilities of drawing 2 red chips if you draw a chip, replace it, and draw again.

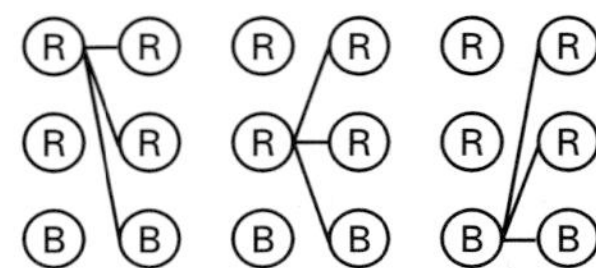

How many outcomes show 2 red chips? 4 How many outcomes are there in all? 9 What is the probability of drawing 2 red chips? $\frac{4}{9}$

Repeat the activity above, except do not replace the chip. The possibilities are:

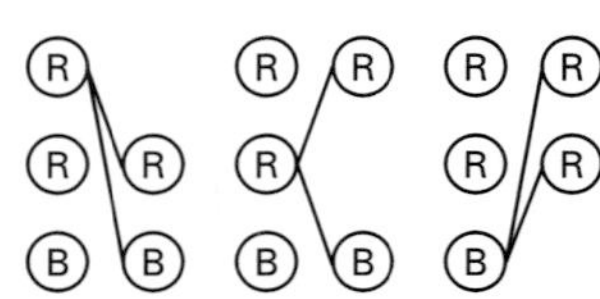

How many outcomes show 2 red chips? 2 How many outcomes are there in all? 6 What is the probability of drawing 2 red chips? $\frac{2}{6} = \frac{1}{3}$

Tell whether each experiment is dependent or independent. The first is independent; the second is dependent.

12-7 Exercises and Applications

Practice and Apply

1. **Getting Started** Five red cubes and five green cubes are in a bag. Follow the steps to find *P*(green, green)—the probability that you pull two green cubes out of the bag in a row.

   a. What is the probability that the first cube taken from the bag is green? $\frac{5}{10}$
   b. After a green cube is taken out of the bag, how many green cubes are left? How many cubes are left all together? 4 green cubes; 9 cubes
   c. What is the probability that the second cube taken from the bag is green? $\frac{4}{9}$
   d. Find the product of your answers from **a** and **c.** Write your answer in lowest terms. $\frac{2}{9}$

Tell whether the events are dependent or independent.

2. One tossed coin landing heads and the next landing tails Independent
3. Rolling two sixes in a row on a number cube Independent
4. Being the tallest person in your class one year, then being the tallest again the next year Dependent

Exercises 5–7 refer to rolling a number cube, then spinning the spinner shown. Find each probability.

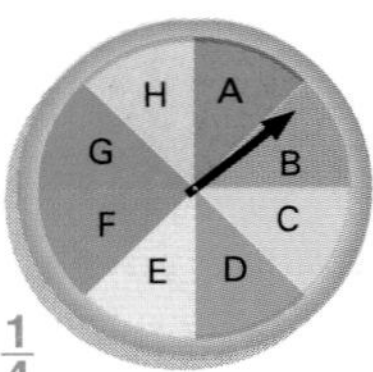

5. *P*(rolling a 2, spinning an A) $\frac{1}{48}$
6. *P*(rolling an even number, spinning a vowel) $\frac{1}{8}$
7. *P*(rolling a number less than 3, spinning a consonant) $\frac{1}{4}$
8. **Social Studies** During Hanukkah, children play with a *dreidel.* The dreidel has four sides, with the Hebrew letters that correspond to the letters N, G, S, and H. The children spin the dreidel like a top, and the letter that comes up determines the result for each turn. GPS
   a. Are the spins of a dreidel dependent or independent events? Independent
   b. What is the probability of spinning 2 Hs in a row? $\frac{1}{16}$
9. **Science** Suppose the weather report says there is a 25% chance of rain for the next two days.
   a. If the events are independent, what is the probability that it rains *both* days?
   b. Do you think these events are actually independent? Explain why or why not.

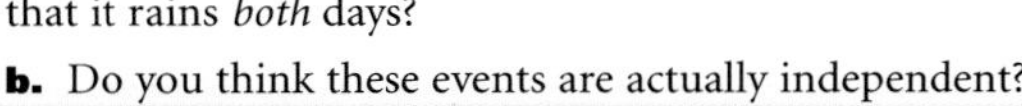

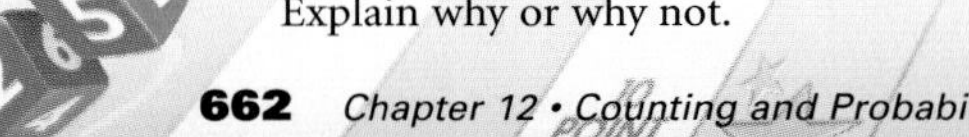

PRACTICE 12-7

PRACTICE

Name ____________

Practice 12-7

Independent and Dependent Events

Tell whether the events are dependent or independent.

1. A coin toss landing tails and a number cube coming up 5 Independent
2. Sunshine in Boston, Massachusetts, and sunshine in Hartford, Connecticut Dependent
3. Drawing a blue Rummikub® tile, then drawing a red tile (after replacing the first tile) Independent

Exercises 4–6 refer to tossing a coin, then spinning the spinner shown. Find each probability.

4. *P*(coin landing heads and spinning a 5) $\frac{1}{14}$
5. *P*(coin landing heads and spinning a prime number) $\frac{2}{7}$
6. *P*(coin landing tails and spinning a 3, 4, 5, 6, or 7) $\frac{5}{14}$

Exercises 7–9 refer to rolling a green number cube, then rolling a red number cube. Find each probability.

7. *P*(rolling a green 3 and a red 2) $\frac{1}{36}$
8. *P*(rolling a green 4 and a red prime number) $\frac{1}{12}$
9. *P*(rolling a green number less than 6 and a red number greater than 3) $\frac{5}{12}$
10. A set of Scrabble® tiles includes 12 E's and 9 I's out of 100 tiles. Suppose you draw a tile, and then draw another tile without replacing the first.
    a. Are the two tile draws dependent or independent events? Dependent
    b. What is the probability that the first tile is an E and the second tile is an I? $\frac{3}{275} = 1.0\overline{9}\% = 0.01\overline{09}$
11. Some role-playing games use dice with different numbers of sides. You roll a four-sided die (numbered 1 to 4) and then a ten-sided die (numbered 1 to 10). What is the probability that the first number is greater than 1 and the second number is less than 7 ? $\frac{9}{20} = 45\% = 0.45$

RETEACHING

Name ____________

Alternative Lesson 12-7

Independent and Dependent Events

When the outcome of one event does not change the probability of another, the events are **independent.** If the probability of the second outcome depends on the results of the first, then the events are **dependent** events.

Example 1

A bag contains 1 red marble, 1 blue marble, and 1 black marble. The faces of a number cube show the numbers 1 through 6. Find the probability of drawing a red marble and tossing a 3.

The events are independent. Find the probability of each event and multiply.

***P*(red marble)**		***P*(tossing a 3)**		
$\frac{1}{3}$	×	$\frac{1}{6}$	=	$\frac{1}{18}$

The probability of drawing a red marble and tossing a 3 is $\frac{1}{18}$.

Example 2

Give the probability of drawing 1, then 6, from cards showing **1 2 3 4 5 6.** The first card drawn is not replaced before drawing the other card.

The events are dependent. Find the probability of each event and multiply.

***P*(1)**		***P*(6)**		
$\frac{1}{6}$	×	$\frac{1}{5}$	=	$\frac{1}{30}$

The probability of drawing 1, then 6, is $\frac{1}{30}$.

Try It

Find the probability of spinning A on the first spinner and B on the second spinner.

a. Are the events dependent or independent? Independent.
b. What is the probability of spinning A? $\frac{1}{3}$ Of spinning B? $\frac{2}{4} = \frac{1}{2}$
c. What is the probability of spinning A, then B? $\frac{1}{6}$

Find the probability of drawing A, then B from six cards that can spell out the word **B A N A N A.** The first card is not replaced.

d. Are the events dependent or independent? Dependent.
e. What is the probability of drawing A? $\frac{1}{2}$ Of drawing B? $\frac{1}{5}$
f. What is the probability of drawing A, then B? $\frac{1}{10}$

Give the sample space for each compound event.

10. A toss of a coin and a roll of a number cube.

11. Two draws of a marble from a bag with 3 red marbles, 2 blue marbles, and 1 yellow marble. The first marble is not replaced before the second draw.

12. Problem Solving A teacher has students change desks every month. To do this, he has students draw desk numbers from a hat. You and your best friend draw the first two numbers. If there are 20 desks, what is the probability that you will choose desk 1 and she will choose desk 2? $\frac{1}{380}$

Problem Solving TIP
Cutting out slips of paper and acting out the draws may help you understand the problem better.

13. **Test Prep** A spinner is divided into five equal sections, numbered 1 through 5. What is the probability of spinning two 5s in a row? D

Ⓐ $\frac{1}{5}$ Ⓑ $\frac{1}{10}$ Ⓒ $\frac{1}{15}$ Ⓓ $\frac{1}{25}$

Problem Solving and Reasoning

14. Journal Suppose you toss a coin several times.

a. What is the theoretical probability that the first two tosses land heads? Toss coins to find an experimental probability for this event. Conduct at least 20 experiments. How do your experimental results compare to the theoretical probability?

b. What is the theoretical probability that the first three tosses land heads? The first four?

c. What is the theoretical probability of n heads in a row? Explain your thinking.

15. Critical Thinking The circle graphs show results of a survey by the American Games Association. If the preferences for game type and group size are independent, what is the probability that a person prefers solitaire card games? 5% Large group word games? 14%

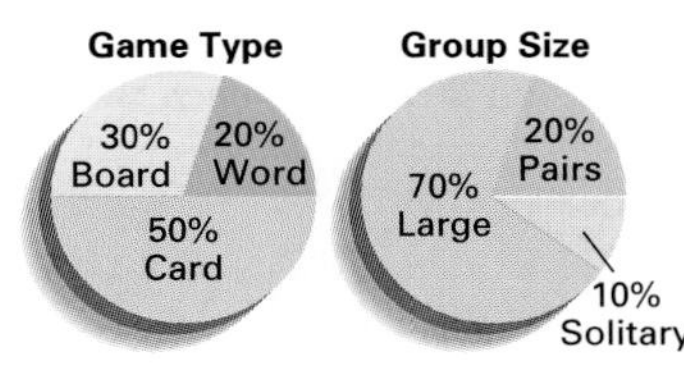

Mixed Review

16. This summer, you plan to visit Austin, Houston, and San Antonio, Texas. In how many different orders can you visit those cities? *[Lesson 12-2]* 6

You are joining a book club. You get free books for joining the club. How many choices do you have in each situation? *[Lesson 12-3]*

17. If you can choose 2 out of 4 books 6

18. If you can choose 3 out of 4 books 4

PROBLEM SOLVING 12-7

Exercise Notes

Exercise 12

Extension Have students find the probability described using the number of desks in your classroom.

Exercise 14

Extension Use the answers to **a** and **b** to help students see that $(\frac{1}{2})^n = \frac{1}{2^n}$.

Exercise Answers

10. (H, 1), (H, 2), (H, 3), (H, 4), (H, 5), (H, 6), (T, 1), (T, 2), (T, 3), (T, 4), (T, 5), (T, 6)

11. (R, R), (B, B), (R, B), (R, Y), (B, Y), (B, R), (Y, R), (Y, B)

14. a. $\frac{1}{4}$; The experimental probabilities will vary, but are likely to be close to $\frac{1}{4}$.

b. $\frac{1}{8}$; $\frac{1}{16}$

c. $(\frac{1}{2})^n = \frac{1}{2^n}$; The probability is $\frac{1}{2}$ multiplied together n times.

Alternate Assessment

Portfolio Have students pick an exercise that best exemplifies the concepts of this lesson.

Quick Quiz

A bag contains 3 blue chips, 2 red chips, and 1 white chip. Give each probability.

1. Drawing 2 red chips in a row if you
   a. replace the first chip drawn. $\frac{4}{36} = \frac{1}{9}$
   b. do not replace the first chip drawn. $\frac{2}{30} = \frac{1}{15}$
2. Drawing 2 blue chips in a row if you
   a. replace the first chip drawn. $\frac{9}{36} = \frac{1}{4}$
   b. do not replace the first chip drawn. $\frac{6}{30} = \frac{1}{5}$

Available on Daily Transparency 12-7

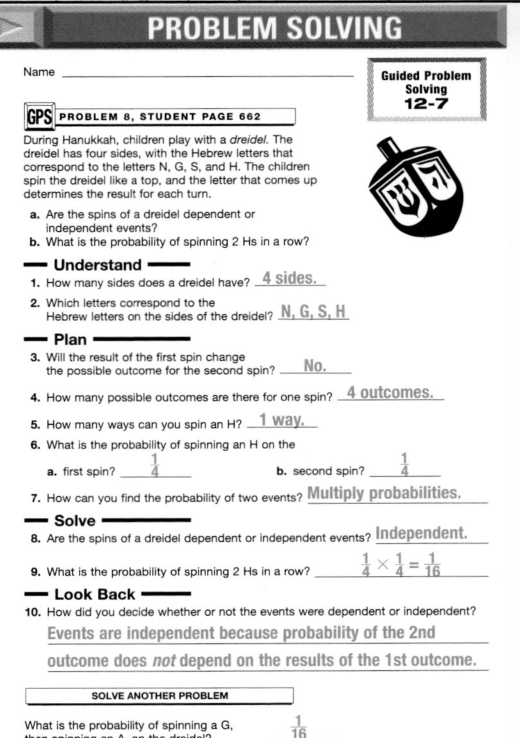

PROBLEM SOLVING

Name ______

Guided Problem Solving 12-7

GPS PROBLEM 8, STUDENT PAGE 662

During Hanukkah, children play with a *dreidel*. The dreidel has four sides, with the Hebrew letters that correspond to the letters N, G, S, and H. The children spin the dreidel like a top, and the letter that comes up determines the result for each turn.

a. Are the spins of a dreidel dependent or independent events?
b. What is the probability of spinning 2 Hs in a row?

Understand

1. How many sides does a dreidel have? 4 sides.
2. Which letters correspond to the Hebrew letters on the sides of the dreidel? N, G, S, H

Plan

3. Will the result of the first spin change the possible outcome for the second spin? No.
4. How many possible outcomes are there for one spin? 4 outcomes.
5. How many ways can you spin an H? 1 way.
6. What is the probability of spinning an H on the
   a. first spin? $\frac{1}{4}$ b. second spin? $\frac{1}{4}$
7. How can you find the probability of two events? Multiply probabilities.

Solve

8. Are the spins of a dreidel dependent or independent events? Independent.
9. What is the probability of spinning 2 Hs in a row? $\frac{1}{4} \times \frac{1}{4} = \frac{1}{16}$

Look Back

10. How did you decide whether or not the events were dependent or independent? Events are independent because probability of the 2nd outcome does *not* depend on the results of the 1st outcome.

SOLVE ANOTHER PROBLEM

What is the probability of spinning a G, then spinning an A, on the dreidel? $\frac{1}{16}$

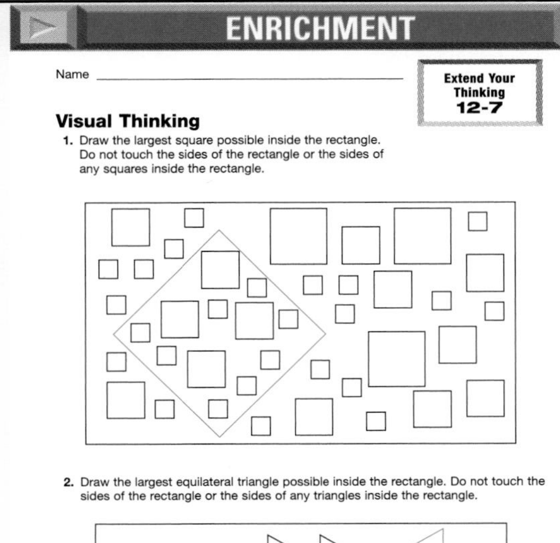

ENRICHMENT

Name ______

Extend Your Thinking 12-7

Visual Thinking

1. Draw the largest square possible inside the rectangle. Do not touch the sides of the rectangle or the sides of any squares inside the rectangle.

2. Draw the largest equilateral triangle possible inside the rectangle. Do not touch the sides of the rectangle or the sides of any triangles inside the rectangle.

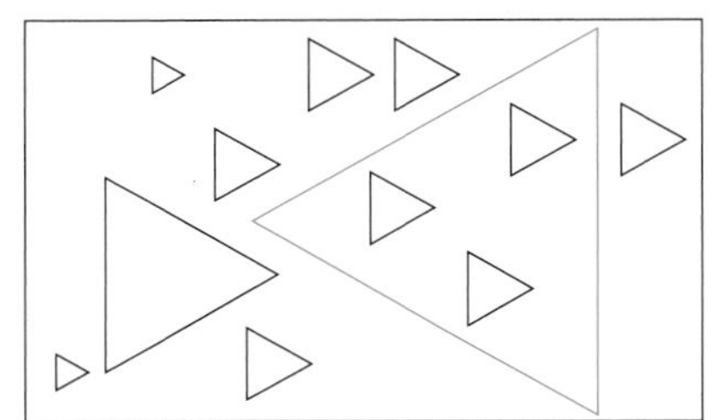

Technology

Using a Graphing Calculator • Simulations with Random Numbers

The Point
Students use the random number feature of the graphing calculator to simulate data for probability.

Materials
Graphing calculator

Resources
Teaching Tool Transparency 23: Graphing Calculator

About the Page
- The random number feature does not generate integers, but numbers between 0 and 1.
- In order to get some sense of realistic results, many trial weeks must be generated. As with any empirical probability, the more data gathered, the more credible are the results.

Ask ...
- In Part b of **Try It,** suppose the first two random numbers generated are both less than 0.310. Is it safe to conclude that the probability that the player gets two hits in a row is 1? No. More trials need to be conducted.
- What is the theoretical probability that the player gets two hits in a row? $0.310^2 \approx 0.096$

Answers for Try It
a. Probability is very small (theoretical probability ≈ 0.03%).
b. Theoretical probability is about 9.6%; Student answers will vary but should be within 10% of this.

On Your Own
Another method might be to enter this formula: INT(11*Rand). INT is the greatest integer function, and truncates any decimal part of a number. It may be found by pressing MATH and NUM.

Answers for On Your Own
Possible answer: Use the first digit of the random number as the number of the spin.

TECHNOLOGY

Using a Graphing Calculator • Simulations with Random Numbers

Problem: Washington, DC, has about 124 days with precipitation each year. How can you estimate the probability that there will be precipitation in a given week?

You can use a graphing or scientific calculator to answer this question.

1. **Find the probability of precipitation on a particular day and express the answer as a decimal. The probability is $\frac{124}{365} \approx 0.34$.**
2. **Press the** MATH **button on your graphing calculator, then choose** PRB **and** Rand.
3. **When you press** ENTER **twice, you get a random number between 0 and 1. If this number is less than 0.34, it represents a day with precipitation. (The number on the screen does not, since it is greater than 0.34.)**
4. **Pressing** ENTER **six more times gives you a whole "week." Determine whether there was precipitation during the week, and record this result. (In the week modeled here there was precipitation on days 4 and 6.)**
5. **Generate several more weeks. Record whether or not it rained in each one.**

Solution: To estimate the probability of precipitation in a given week, divide the number of weeks with rain in your simulation by the total number of weeks.

TRY IT

a. Belem, Brazil, has about 251 days of rain each year. Use random numbers to estimate the probability that it doesn't rain for 3 consecutive days in Belem.

b. Suppose the probability that a baseball player gets a hit is 0.310. Use random numbers to estimate the probability that he gets two hits in a row.

ON YOUR OWN

▶ Suppose you wanted to use random numbers to simulate spins of a spinner with numbers from 0 to 9. How could you do this?

Section 12B Connect

You've investigated odds, fair games, and several ways to find probabilities. Now you'll combine those skills to design a game of your own.

Do NOT Pass Go!

Materials: Compass, Protractor, Cardboard, Pushpin, Paper clip, Number cubes

In this investigation, you'll make a game of your own. If you choose to use a spinner in your game, here's how you can make one.

- Use a compass to draw a circle.
- Decide how many sectors you want your spinner to have. Use your protractor to measure the central angles, then draw the sectors.
- Put the paper with your circle on top of the cardboard, and place the paper clip over the center of the circle. Then push the pushpin into the center of the circle so the clip can be used as a spinner.

1. Use what you've learned about probability to design a game of chance. Your game must use at least two different ways to generate outcomes (for instance, a coin and a number cube). Once you've come up with a game you like, play a few rounds to see if any changes are needed.

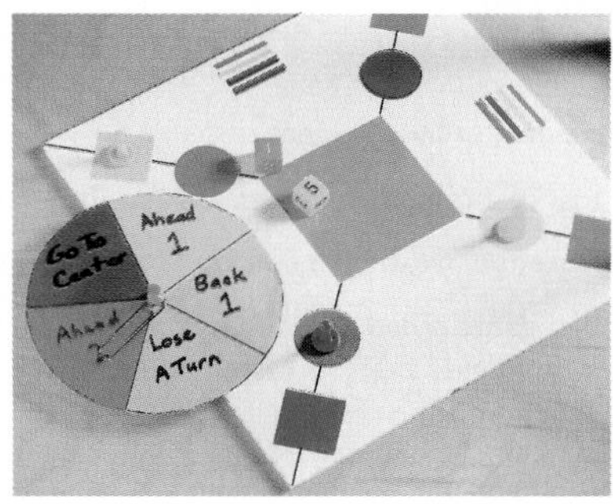

2. Is your game a fair game? Explain why or why not.
3. Does your game involve dependent events? If it does, tell what they are.
4. Identify at least two events that could happen in your game. Find the probability of each of these events. Explain how you found each probability.

Do NOT Pass Go!

The Point

Students discussed games of chance in *Do NOT Pass Go!* on page 643. Now they will design their own game of chance.

Materials

Compass, protractor, cardboard, pushpin, paper clip, number cubes

Resources

Teaching Tool Transparency 15: Protractor

About the Page

- Discuss with students some of the board games they have played. Ask students the possible ways that outcomes are generated. Possible answers: Tossing number cubes, spinning a spinner, drawing a card or number, tossing a coin.
- Discuss some events that happen in games.
- Suggest that students choose the two different ways their game will generate outcomes before designing the game.
- Students could work in small groups to design their games.

Ongoing Assessment

Check that students have designed a reasonable game that generates outcomes in two ways.

Extension

Give students the opportunity to play some of the games they have designed. As they play, ask students to determine if the game is a fair game and if the game involves dependent events.

Answers for Connect

1–4. Answers may vary.

Section 12B Review

Review Correlation

Item(s)	Lesson(s)
1–5	12-4
6–9	12-5
10	12-5, 12-6
11, 12	12-7
13	12-6
14	12-4, 12-7

Test Prep

Test-Taking Tip

Tell students to rephrase formulas in different ways to help them remember the formula. Here, students might think of odds as "number of wins to number of losses."

Answers for Review

5. The game is fair; P(heads, even) = P(tails, odd) = $\frac{1}{4}$.

Name the possible outcomes for each experiment.

1. Spinning a spinner whose sectors are numbered 1 through 10. 1, 2, 3, 4, 5, 6, 7, 8, 9, 10

2. Rolling two number cubes and finding the sum of the two numbers. 2, 3, 4, 5, 6, 7, 8, 9, 10, 11, 12

Give the odds of each event.

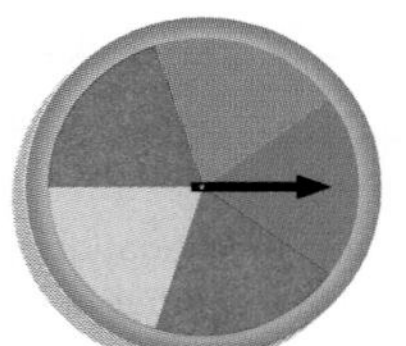

3. Rolling a number less than or equal to 4 on a number cube. 4:2

4. Spinning red on the spinner at the right. 2:3

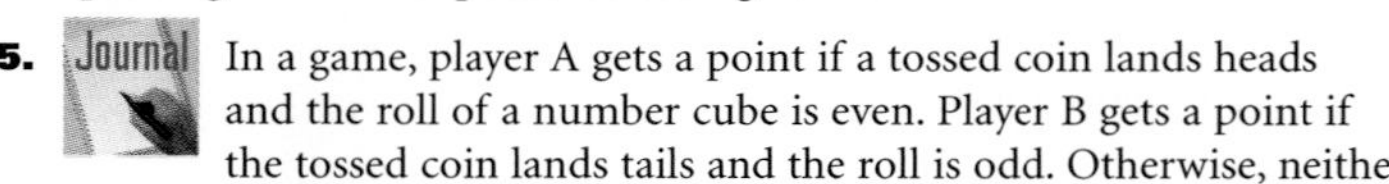

5. Journal In a game, player A gets a point if a tossed coin lands heads and the roll of a number cube is even. Player B gets a point if the tossed coin lands tails and the roll is odd. Otherwise, neither player gets a point. Is this game fair? Explain why or why not.

A bag contains 5 red, 3 blue, and 2 yellow marbles. Give the probability of each event as a fraction, a percent, and a decimal. (Round answers if necessary.)

6. P(red) **7.** P(blue) **8.** P(orange) **9.** P(*not* yellow)

6. $\frac{1}{2}$ = 50% = 0.5
7. $\frac{3}{10}$ = 30% = 0.3
8. $\frac{0}{1}$ = 0% = 0
9. $\frac{4}{5}$ = 80% = 0.8

10. If you draw two marbles out of the bag, what is P(blue, blue)? Assume you don't put the first marble back. $\frac{1}{15} \approx 6.7\% = 0.067$

Tell whether the events are dependent or independent.

11. Getting heads on the first toss of a coin, then getting tails on the second. Independent

12. Sunny weather one day, then rainy weather the next. Dependent

13. **Social Studies** A Hawaiian game called Lu-Lu uses disks of volcanic stone that are marked on one side. If a disk is tossed twice, what is the probability that both tosses land on the marked side? $\frac{1}{4}$

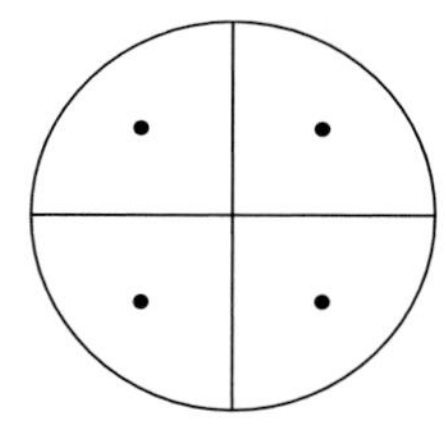

Lu-Lu disk

Test Prep

When you're asked to find the odds of an event on a multiple choice test, remember that the second number in the ratio represents the number of ways it can *not* happen, not the total number of possible outcomes.

14. What are the odds of rolling a sum of 12 on two number cubes? B

Ⓐ 1:36 Ⓑ 1:35 Ⓒ 2:12 Ⓓ 12:2

Resources

Practice Masters
Section 12B Review

Assessment Sourcebook
Quiz 12B

TestWorks
Test and Practice Software

PRACTICE

Name ______________ Practice

Section 12B Review

Name the possible outcomes for each experiment.

1. Spinning a spinner whose 7 sectors are labeled with the days of the week Sun., Mon., Tues., Wed., Thu., Fri., Sat.
2. Tossing a coin twice Heads-heads, heads-tails, tails-heads, tails-tails

Give the odds of each event.

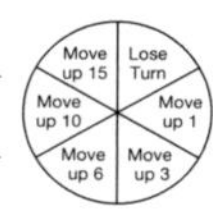

3. Spinning "Move Up 3" on the spinner at the right 1 : 5
4. Drawing an A, B, or C from a set of Scrabble® tiles (There are 9 A's, 2 B's, and 2 C's out of 100 tiles.) 13 : 87

A box contains 7 yellow, 3 green, and 4 blue pencils. Give the probability of each event as a fraction, a percent, and a decimal. (Round percent and decimal answers to two digits if necessary.)

5. P(blue) $\frac{2}{7} \approx 29\% = 0.29$
6. P(yellow) $\frac{1}{2} = 50\% = 0.5$
7. P(not blue) $\frac{5}{7} \approx 71\% = 0.71$
8. P(not yellow) $\frac{1}{2} = 50\% = 0.5$
9. If you select two pencils from the box, what is P(green, then yellow)? Assume you do not put the first pencil back. $\frac{3}{26} \approx 12\% = 0.12$

Tell whether the events are dependent or independent.

10. Getting an even number on the first roll of a number cube, then getting an even number on the second roll Independent
11. Getting a face card on the first draw from a deck of playing cards, then getting a face card on the second draw (The first card is not replaced. A deck of 52 cards has 12 face cards.) Dependent
12. Refer to the spinner in Exercise **3.** If you spin the spinner twice, what is the probability that you move up 6 or more on the first spin, and then lose a turn? $\frac{1}{12} = 8.\bar{3}\% = 0.08\bar{3}$
13. **Geography** Bulgaria has 220 miles of coastline. This is 200 miles less than three times Romania's coastline. How much coastline does Romania have? *[Lesson 10-11]* 140 mi
14. A shelf is $\frac{1}{2}$ in. thick, 10 in. wide, and 48 in. long. Find the volume of the shelf. *[Lesson 11-4]* 240 in^3

Extend Key Ideas • Logic

Venn Diagrams and If-Then Statements

A Venn diagram shows relationships between sets of items, or *elements*.

If regions in a Venn diagram do not overlap, they have no common elements.

Mammals | Reptiles

Overlapping regions contain elements that are in both sets. The overlapping region in this Venn diagram contains bats, since bats are mammals that fly.

Mammals | Flying Animals

If one region contains another, all elements in the smaller region also belong in the larger. The diagram shows that *if* a figure is a triangle, *then* it is also a polygon.

Polygons | Triangles

If-then statements like the one above are an important part of the language of logic. The "if" part of an if-then statement is its *hypothesis*, and the "then" part is its *conclusion*. For the statement to be true, the conclusion must be true whenever the hypothesis is true.

True or false? If a figure is a square, then it is a rectangle.

The statement is true. Suppose a figure is a square. The conclusion *must* be true, since all squares have four sides and four right angles. In the Venn diagram, the oval that shows the hypothesis "fits" the conclusion.

Rectangles | Squares

True or false? If an animal is a bird, then it can fly.

This statement is false. Some types of birds cannot fly. In the Venn diagram, the oval representing the hypothesis goes outside the oval that shows the conclusion.

Birds | Flying Animals

Try It

Draw a Venn diagram to show the relationships between:

1. Triangles and squares **2.** Lions, bears, and animals

Explain whether each if-then statement is true or false. Draw a Venn diagram.

3. If an angle measures 30°, then it is acute.

4. If a vehicle has four wheels, then it is a car.

667

Extend Key Ideas

Venn Diagrams and If-Then Statements

The Point

Students learn to interpret Venn diagrams as they relate to if-then statements.

About the Page

- Venn diagrams provide a way for students to understand relationships visually.
- Have students discuss if-then statements and when they have heard them used.

Ask ...

- In an if-then statement, what is the "if" part called? the "then" part? Hypothesis; conclusion
- In order for an if-then statement to be true, what must be the relationship of the ovals in the Venn Diagram? The "if" part oval must be entirely contained within the "then" part oval.

Answers for Try It

1.

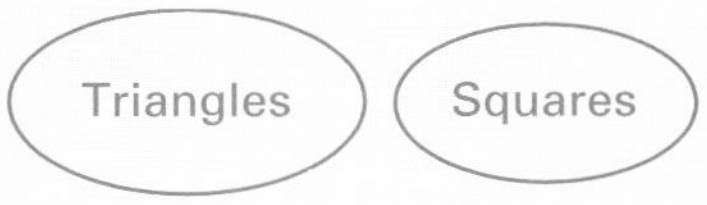

Triangles | Squares

2.

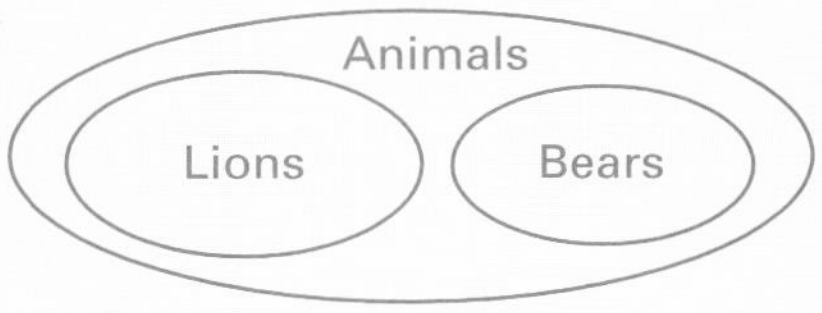

Animals | Lions | Bears

3. True

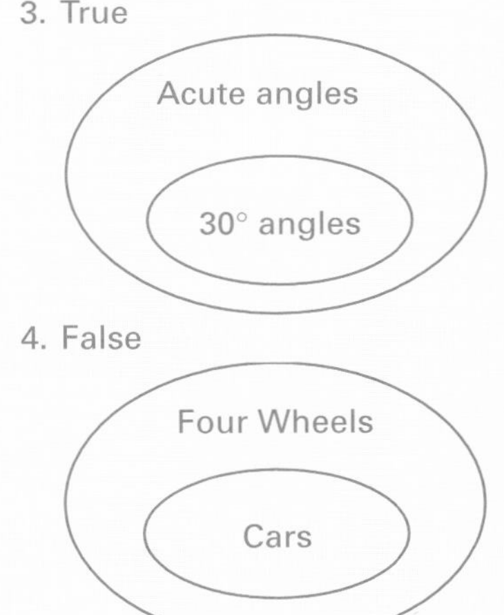

Extension

Have students create their own if-then statements and accompanying Venn diagrams, stating whether each is true or false.

Chapter 12 Summary and Review

Review Correlation

Item(s)	Lesson(s)
1–3	12-1
4, 5	12-2
6	12-3
7, 8	12-4
9, 10	12-5
11	12-6
12	12-5
13, 14	12-7

For additional review, see page 683.

Answers for Review

2.

The store needs 8 bins.

5. TUV, TVU, UVT, UTV, VTU, VUT.

Chapter 12 Summary and Review

Graphic Organizer

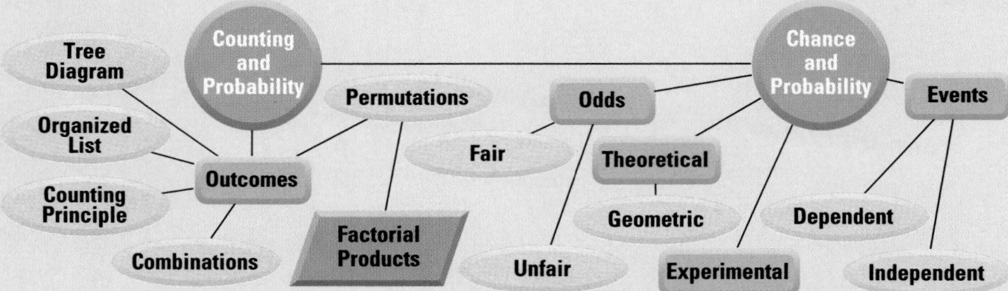

Section 12A Counting

Summary

- You can count the possible **outcomes** for a series of choices by making an organized list, making a **tree diagram,** or using the **Counting Principle.**
- A **permutation** is the number of possible arrangements of a collection of items. You can use the Counting Principle or **factorials** to count permutations.
- A **combination** is a selection of items where the order does not matter.

Review

1. For lunch, Jo's Restaurant offers 3 soups, 4 main courses, and 5 desserts. Use the Counting Principle to find the number of different lunches consisting of soup, main course, and dessert. 60

2. A used-music store has separate bins for CDs and cassettes in each category: jazz, popular, classical, and other. Make a tree diagram to show how many bins the store needs.

3. Fifth State Bank offers 3 different checking accounts and 5 different savings accounts. How many ways are there to open both a checking account and a savings account? 15

4. A club is electing a president, vice president, secretary, and treasurer. Only Jed, Karl, Lori, and Marti are eligible to hold office. In how many ways can the officers be chosen? 24

5. List all the possible orderings of the letters T, U, and V, without repeating letters.

6. Reggie has 7 books he intends to read. How many different ways can he choose 2 of the books to take on a vacation? 21

Resources

Practice Masters
Cumulative Review Chapters 1–12

Assessment Sourcebook
Quarterly Test Chapters 1–12

PRACTICE

Name ______________________

Practice

Cumulative Review Chapters 1–12

Find the area of each figure. *[Lessons 5-8, 5-9]*

1. $336\ m^2$ (16 m, 21 m)
2. $16\frac{7}{8}\ in^2$ ($2\frac{1}{4}$ in., $7\frac{1}{2}$ in.)
3. $13.92\ cm^2$ (3.2 cm, 8.7 cm)
4. $57\ ft^2$ (8 ft, 6 ft, 11 ft)

Solve each problem. If necessary, round answers to the nearest tenth. *[Lessons 8-5, 8-6]*

5. 84% of 365 is what number? 306.6
6. 23% of what number is 17? 73.9
7. 65 is what percent of 127? 51.2%
8. 863 is 128% of what number? 674.2

Solve each equation. Check your solution. *[Lesson 10-11]*

9. $\frac{m}{16} + (-5) = 4$ $m =$ 144
10. $6g - 43 = 35$ $g =$ 13
11. $\frac{t}{-4} + 31 = -8$ $t =$ 156
12. $5y + 123 = 68$ $y =$ −11

Find the surface area and volume of each polyhedron or cylinder. Where necessary, use $\pi \approx 3.14$ and round answers to the nearest tenth. *[Lessons 11-3, 11-4, 11-8, and 11-9]*

13. $SA =$ $79.2\ m^2$ $V =$ $45.5\ m^3$ (2.6 m, 3.5 m, 5.0 m)
14. $SA \approx$ $2{,}725.5\ ft^2$ $V \approx$ $10{,}462.5\ ft^3$ (14 ft, 17 ft)
15. $SA \approx$ $471\ in^2$ $V \approx$ $696.0\ in^3$ (3 in., 3 in., 3 in., 3 in., 3 in., 3 in., 16 in.; Base area ≈ 43.5 in^2)

Give the probability of each event as a fraction, a percent, and a decimal. *[Lesson 12-5]*

16. Spinning "Dog" on the spinner shown $\frac{1}{5}$, 20%, 0.2

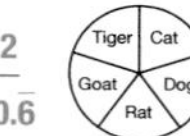

17. Rolling a number less than 5 on a number cube $\frac{2}{3}$, $66.\overline{6}\%$, $0.\overline{6}$

18. Drawing a yellow marble from a bag containing the following marbles:

a. 9 red $0 = 0\% = 0.0$

b. 6 red and 4 yellow $\frac{2}{5} = 40\% = 0.4$

c. 12 yellow $1 = 100\% = 1.0$

Chapter 12 Summary and Review

Section 12B Chance and Probability

Summary

- In probability, an **experiment** is anything that involves chance. The possible results of an experiment are outcomes. An **event** is any outcome (or set of outcomes) we are interested in.
- The **odds** of an event are the ratio of the number of ways the event can happen to the number of ways it can fail to happen.
- In a **fair** game, all players have the same odds of winning.
- The **probability,** or **theoretical probability,** of an event is given by Probability(event) $= \frac{\text{number of ways the event can happen}}{\text{number of possible outcomes}}$. An impossible event has probability 0. An event that is certain to happen has probability 1.
- The **experimental probability** of an event is the number of times the event occurred divided by the number of times the experiment was carried out.
- When the occurrence of one event does not change the probability of another, the events are **independent**. Otherwise, they are **dependent**.

Review

7. A bag contains 5 red marbles and 3 blue marbles. A marble is chosen at random. Find the odds that the marble is red. 5:3

8. A spinner has 7 equal sections, numbered 1 to 7. Melanie wins if an odd number is spun, and Nathan wins if an even number is spun. Give each player's odds of winning. Then determine whether the game is fair. Melanie 4:3; Nathan 3:4; No

9. A number cube is rolled. Find the probability of rolling a number:

a. Less than 5 $\frac{4}{6} = \frac{2}{3}$ **b.** *Not* less than 5 $\frac{2}{6} = \frac{1}{3}$

10. Use the table on page 653 to find the probability of choosing a U, V, or W when drawing the first tile in a Scrabble® game. Express your answer as a percent. 8%

11. Paula flipped a coin 25 times and got heads 14 times. Find the experimental probability of tails. $\frac{11}{25}$

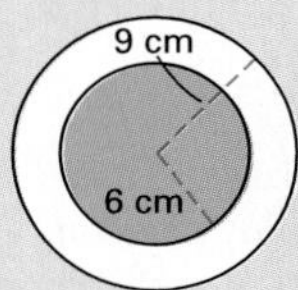

12. A fly lands on the dart board. What is the probability that it lands in the shaded region? $\frac{4}{9}$

13. A number cube is rolled twice. What is the probability of getting a 5 on the first roll, then an even number on the second? $\frac{1}{12}$

14. Sandy draws 2 marbles from a bag with 5 green and 6 black marbles. What is the probability that both are green? $\frac{2}{11}$

Chapter 12 Assessment

Assessment Correlation

Item(s)	Lesson(s)
1, 2	12-1
3, 4	12-2
5	12-3
6, 7	12-4
8	12-6
9	12-5
10, 11	12-7

Answers for Assessment

2.

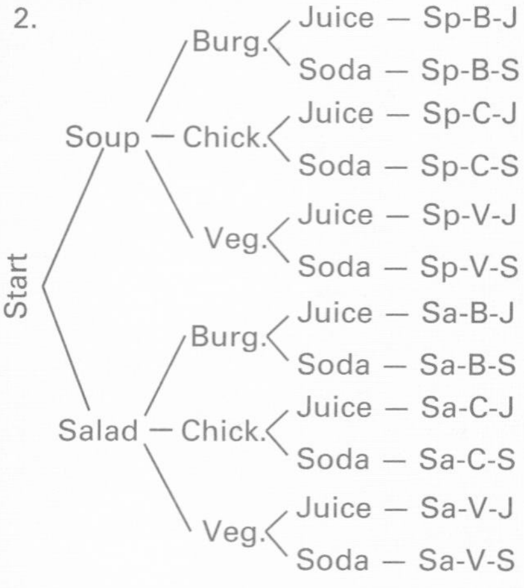

There are 12 outcomes.

6. Yellow marble, purple marble, clear marble.

7. All have odds of 2:4; Fair.

Chapter 12 Assessment

1. Crafty Computer Company offers a choice of 4 processors, 3 hard drives, and 3 installed software packages. Use the Counting Principle to find the number of different computers. 36

2. A cafeteria's lunch special includes a choice of soup or salad; hamburger, chicken, or vegetable casserole; and fruit juice or soda. Make a tree diagram to show the number of ways to order a lunch special. How many outcomes are there?

3. Calculate 6!. 720

4. Pearl, Quan, Raul, Sally, and Tim need to line up in single file to buy movie tickets. In how many different orders can they line up? 120

5. Vanilla Heaven offers only one flavor of ice cream, but customers can choose any 3 of 4 available toppings. How many different combinations of 3 toppings are there? 4

6. A bag contains 3 yellow marbles, 4 purple marbles, and 7 clear marbles. Give the possible outcomes for drawing 1 marble.

7. In a game, a number cube is rolled. Xien wins if a 1 or a 3 is rolled; Yoshi wins if a 2 or a 6 is rolled; and Zelda wins if a 4 or a 5 is rolled. Give each player's odds of winning. Then tell if the game is fair.

8. Sam drew a Scrabble® tile from a bag 100 times, replacing his selection each time. If his draws included 10 A's, 3 B's, and 2 C's, what was the experimental probability of drawing an A, B, or C? $\frac{15}{100} = \frac{3}{20} = 15\%$

9. A coin lands randomly on the board shown. Find the probability that it lands in the shaded region. $\frac{48}{128} = \frac{3}{8}$

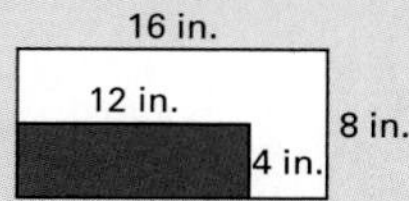

10. Hans drew a marble from the bag described in Exercise 6. He then drew another one without replacing the first. Are his results for the two draws *independent* or *dependent* events? Dependent

11. Art tossed a coin and a number cube at the same time. Find $P(\text{heads}, 6)$. $\frac{1}{12}$

Performance Task

Roll a pair of number cubes 36 times and record the sums. Find the experimental probability of rolling a 2, of rolling a 3, and so on. Compare your results to the theoretical probabilities. Then roll the cubes another 36 times and combine your results for all 72 rolls. Which results are closer to the theoretical probabilities, those for 36 rolls or those for 72 rolls?

Performance Assessment Key

See key on page 623.

Resources

Assessment Sourcebook

Chapter 12 Tests
- Forms A and B (free response)
- Form C (multiple choice)
- Form D (performance assessment)
- Form E (mixed response)
- Form F (cumulative chapter test)

TestWorks
Test and Practice Software

Home and Community Connections
- Letter Home for Chapter 12 in English and Spanish

Suggested Scoring Rubric for Performance Task

4
- All probabilities are calculated correctly.
- Comparison is clear, and shows understanding that more trials should give experimental probabilities closer to theoretical values.

3
- Almost all probabilities are calculated correctly.
- Comparison is clear, but does not show understanding that more trials should give experimental probabilities closer to theoretical values.

2
- Most probabilities are calculated correctly.
- Comparison is vague or inaccurate.

1
- Few probabilities are calculated correctly.
- Comparison is poorly done or missing.

Cumulative Review Chapters 1–12

Test Prep

Multiple Choice

Choose the best answer.

1. Which number is divisible by 2, 3, and 5? *[Lesson 3-6]* A

Ⓐ 270 Ⓑ 276 Ⓒ 280 Ⓓ 285

2. Find the product: $3\frac{3}{8} \cdot 2\frac{2}{3}$ *[Lesson 4-5]* D

Ⓐ $1\frac{17}{64}$ Ⓑ $6\frac{1}{4}$ Ⓒ $8\frac{17}{24}$ Ⓓ 9

3. The hypotenuse of a right triangle is 12 ft long and one leg is 7 ft long. Which of the following is the approximate length of the other leg? *[Lesson 5-7]* C

Ⓐ 5.0 ft Ⓑ 8.3 ft Ⓒ 9.7 ft Ⓓ 13.9 ft

4. Use unit rates to determine which is the best buy for avocados. *[Lesson 6-2]* C

Ⓐ \$3.45 for 3 Ⓑ \$3.60 for 4
Ⓒ \$4.30 for 5 Ⓓ \$6.00 for 6

5. 32 is 8% of which number? *[Lesson 8-5]* D

Ⓐ 2.56 Ⓑ 4 Ⓒ 256 Ⓓ 400

6. Which point is in quadrant II? *[Lesson 9-3]* A

Ⓐ $(-3, 4)$ Ⓑ $(-5, -7)$
Ⓒ $(2, 2)$ Ⓓ $(4, -1)$

7. The graph of which equation does *not* include the origin? *[Lesson 10-5]* C

Ⓐ $y = -x$ Ⓑ $y = 2x$
Ⓒ $y = 3x - 3$ Ⓓ $y = x^2$

8. How many faces does a rectangular pyramid have? *[Lesson 11-1]* B

Ⓐ 4 Ⓑ 5 Ⓒ 6 Ⓓ 8

9. A building is a rectangular prism whose base measures 65 ft by 80 ft. Its volume is 624,000 ft^3. How tall is it? *[Lesson 11-4]* B

Ⓐ 96 ft Ⓑ 120 ft Ⓒ 520 ft Ⓓ 7800 ft

10. Which net *cannot* be folded into a cube? *[Lesson 11-3]* C

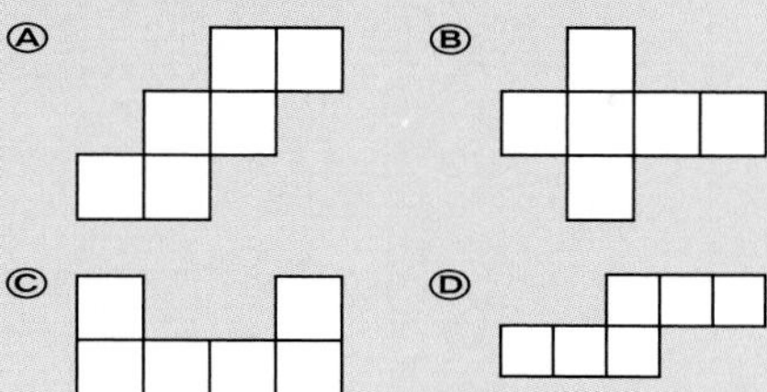

11. Find the surface area of a cylinder with radius 8 m and height 5 m. Use 3.14 for π. *[Lesson 11-8]* D

Ⓐ 251.2 m^2 Ⓑ 408.2 m^2
Ⓒ 452.16 m^2 Ⓓ 653.12 m^2

12. Soap is available in 3 scents. Each is available in 4 sizes. How many different choices are there? *[Lesson 12-1]* D

Ⓐ 3 Ⓑ 4 Ⓒ 7 Ⓓ 12

13. Stella is joining a music club. If the available selections include 5 albums she wants, how many ways can she choose 3 selections? *[Lesson 12-3]* B

Ⓐ 6 Ⓑ 10 Ⓒ 60 Ⓓ 120

14. A bag contains 8 blue marbles and 5 black ones. Find the probability of drawing a black marble. *[Lesson 12-5]* C

Ⓐ $\frac{8}{5}$ Ⓑ $\frac{5}{8}$ Ⓒ $\frac{5}{13}$ Ⓓ $\frac{8}{13}$

15. Which of the following describes the results of 2 consecutive rolls of a number cube? *[Lesson 12-7]* A

Ⓐ Independent events Ⓑ Unfair game
Ⓒ Dependent events Ⓓ Fair game

Cumulative Review Test Prep

About Multiple-Choice Tests

The Cumulative Review found at the end of Chapters 2, 4, 6, 8, 10, and 12 can be used to prepare students for standardized tests.

Students sometimes do not perform as well on standardized tests as they do on other tests. There may be several reasons for this related to the format and content of the test.

- **Format**
  Students may have limited experience with multiple-choice tests. For some questions, such tests are harder because having options may confuse the student.
- **Content**
  A standardized test may cover a broader range of content than normally covered on a test, and the relative emphasis given to various strands may be different than given in class. Also, some questions may assess general aptitude or thinking skills and not include specific pieces of mathematical content.

It is important not to let the differences between standardized tests and other tests shake your students' confidence.

STUDENT RESOURCES

CONTENTS

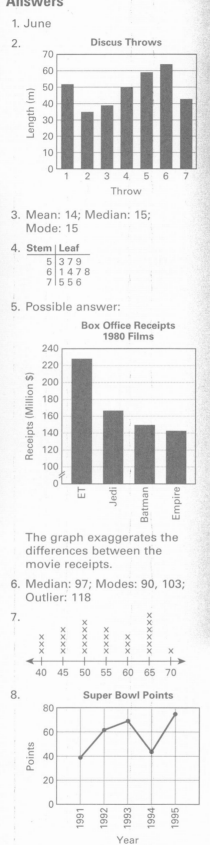

Answers

1. June

2.

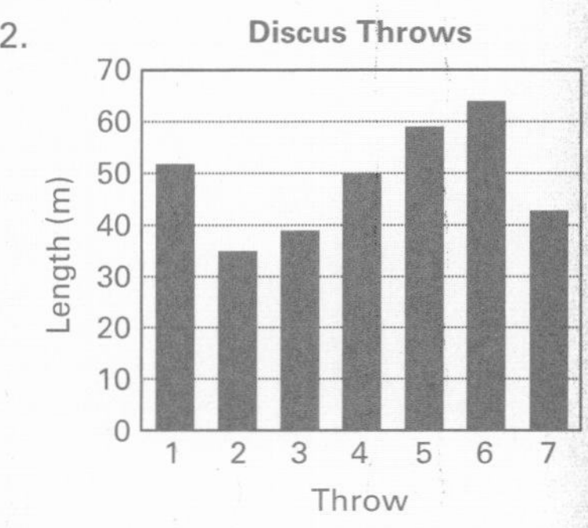

3. Mean: 14; Median: 15; Mode: 15

4.

Stem	Leaf
5	3 7 9
6	1 4 7 8
7	5 5 6

5. Possible answer:

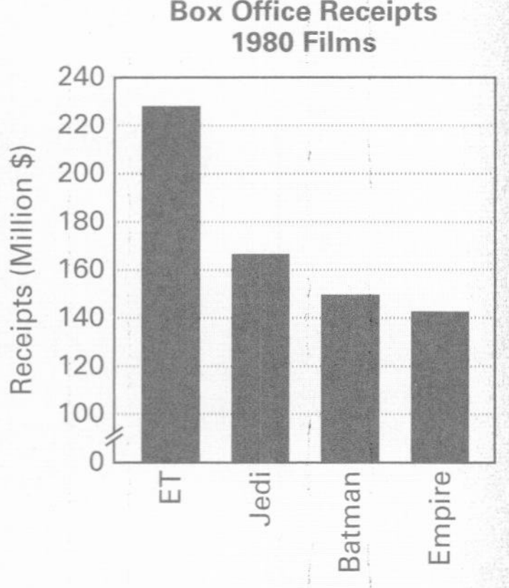

The graph exaggerates the differences between the movie receipts.

6. Median: 97; Modes: 90, 103; Outlier: 118

7.

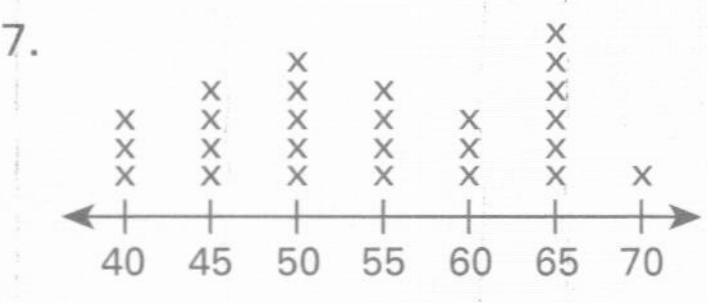

8.

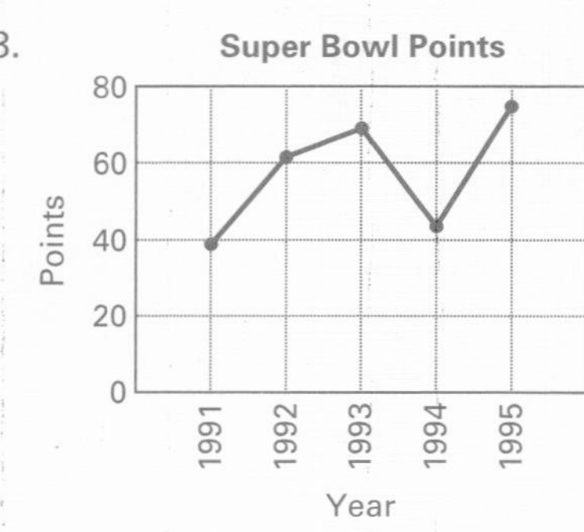

Chapter Review

Chapter 1 Review

1. Use estimation to identify the month with the largest difference between cost and revenue.

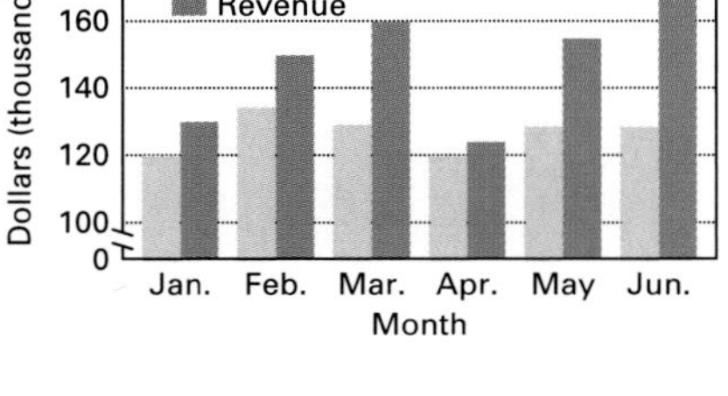

2. The lengths of seven discus throws, in meters, were 52, 34, 39, 50, 59, 64, 43. Make a bar graph of the data.

3. Find the mean, median, and mode(s) of the data values: 9, 19, 15, 4, 23, 14, 20, 15, 7

4. Make a stem-and-leaf diagram of the data: 57, 76, 75, 61, 53, 68, 75, 59, 64, 67

5. Make a bar graph with a broken vertical axis to display this data for the four most popular films of the 1980s. Explain why your graph could be misleading.

Box Office Receipts—1980s Films

Movie	Receipts ($ million)
E.T.—The Extra-Terrestrial	228
Return of the Jedi	168
Batman	151
The Empire Strikes Back	142

6. Find the median and mode(s) of the data values displayed in the stem-and-leaf diagram. Are there any outliers?

Stem	Leaf
8	4 5 5 6 9 9
9	0 0 0 1 4 5 7 7 9 9
10	1 1 2 3 3 3 5 6
11	8

7. Make a line plot to show the finishing times of swimmers in a race.

Seconds	40	45	50	55	60	65	70
Finishers	3	4	5	4	3	6	1

8. The table gives the total number of points scored in the Super Bowl for each year. Make a line graph to display the data.

Total Points Scored in Super Bowl

Year	1991	1992	1993	1994	1995
Points	39	61	69	43	75

9. Make a scatterplot of the data for the players on a tennis team. Draw a trend line and use it to predict the expected number of winners for a player with 15 unforced errors.

Winners	24	12	17	20	10
Unforced Errors	19	8	14	14	5

9.

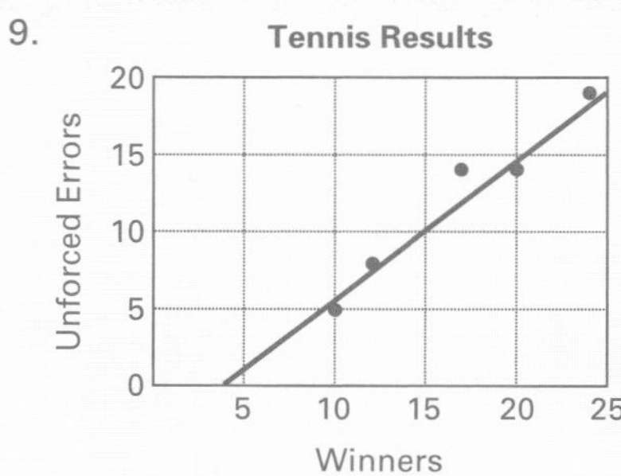

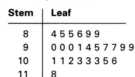

About 20 winners

Chapter 2 Review

1. A long distance call costs $1.50 plus $0.80 for each minute. Let $C = 0.8m + 1.5$, where C is the cost and m is the number of minutes. How much would a 12-minute call cost?

Evaluate each expression.

2. $7 + 3 \times 5$
3. $48 - 36 \div (11 - 2)$
4. Tell which operation you would do first to evaluate $\frac{3 \times (9 - 5)}{6}$.
5. Find a formula relating the variables.

x	1	2	3	4	5	6	7
y	5	6	7	8	9	10	11

6. Which property is suggested by the formulas $A = lw$ and $A = wl$?
7. Use the formula $r = \frac{d}{t}$ to make a table of values showing the speed (r) needed to travel a distance (d) of 120 miles in 2, 3, 4, 5, and 6 hours (t).
8. Name the inverse action of walking 3 miles west.

Tell if the number in bold is a solution to the equation.

9. $x - 24 = 9$; **15**
10. $j \cdot 14 = 56$; **4**

Solve each equation. Check your answer.

11. $a - 31 = 47$
12. $53 = c + 17$
13. $18m = 396$
14. $\frac{n}{7} = 6$
15. $15k + 32 = 77$
16. $7 = \frac{n}{3} - 5$
17. A number is multiplied by 2, then 13 is added to the result. What operations are needed to return the original number?
18. Write an equation for this statement: The number of students decreased by 4 is 31.
19. Write an algebraic expression for the product of 8 and a number (n).
20. Lauren bought 6 chewing bones for each of her dogs. She bought 24 bones all together. Write and solve an equation to find the number of dogs (d) she has.

Write a phrase for each algebraic expression.

21. $a + 4$
22. $8n - 1$
23. $\frac{h}{3} - 2$
24. $\frac{5}{x + 9}$

CHAPTER 2 REVIEW

Chapter 2 Review

Answers

1. $11.10
2. 22
3. 44
4. $9 - 5$
5. $y = x + 4$
6. The Commutative Property of Multiplication
7.

Time (hr)	2	3	4	5	6
Speed (mi/hr)	60	40	30	24	20

8. Walking 3 miles east
9. No
10. Yes
11. $a = 78$
12. $c = 36$
13. $m = 22$
14. $n = 42$
15. $k = 3$
16. $n = 36$
17. Subtract 13, then divide by 2
18. $s - 4 = 31$
19. $8n$
20. $6d = 24$; $d = 4$
21. Four more than a number a
22. One less than 8 times a number n
23. Two less than a number h divided by 3
24. Five divided by the sum of a number x and 9

CHAPTER REVIEW

Chapter 3 Review

Answers

1. The first 6 represents 60; The second represents $\frac{6}{10000}$.
2. $2.89 > 2.091$
3. 4.928
4. 1800
5. 450
6. 220
7. 25
8. $x = 266.99$
9. $y = 13.4$
10. $n = 47.32$
11. $x = 33.4$
12. $x = 101$
13. $w = 480.703$
14. 4,597,000
15. 3.85×10^5
16. $2^2 \cdot 3 \cdot 5^2$
17. 24
18. 80
19. Possible answer: $\frac{8}{13}, \frac{16}{26}$
20. $\frac{8}{11}$
21. $\frac{5}{8}$
22. $\frac{1}{3}$
23. $\frac{2}{11}$
24. $\frac{1}{4}$
25. $\frac{9}{20}$
26. $\frac{8}{11} < \frac{16}{21}$
27. $\frac{15}{24} = \frac{35}{56}$
28. $\frac{18}{45} = \frac{24}{60}$
29. $\frac{31}{250}$
30. $\frac{17}{20}$
31. $\frac{1}{4}$
32. $\frac{5}{8}$
33. $\frac{8}{25}$
34. $\frac{1}{20}$
35. 0.777...; Repeats

CHAPTER REVIEW

Chapter 3 Review

CHAPTER 3 REVIEW

1. Give the value of each 6 in 4168.9206.

2. Use <, >, or = to compare: 2.89 ☐ 2.091

3. Round 4.9275 to the nearest thousandth.

Estimate.

4. $294.91 \cdot 5.81$

5. $141.83 + 308.11$

6. Find the sum: $129.56 + 85.403$

7. Find the quotient: $\frac{766.38}{31.8}$

Solve each equation.

8. $x + 64.1 = 331.09$

9. $129.98 = 9.7y$

10. $\frac{n}{5.2} = 9.1$

11. $x - 10.5 = 22.9$

12. $1.01x = 102.01$

13. $\frac{w}{35.74} = 13.45$

14. Write 4.597×10^6 in standard form.

15. Write 385,000 in scientific notation.

16. Use a factor tree to find the prime factorization of 300.

17. Find the GCF of 120 and 144.

18. Find the LCM of 16 and 20.

19. Give two fractions that are equivalent to $\frac{24}{39}$.

Rewrite each fraction in lowest terms.

20. $\frac{56}{77}$ **21.** $\frac{40}{64}$ **22.** $\frac{75}{225}$ **23.** $\frac{18}{99}$ **24.** $\frac{13}{52}$ **25.** $\frac{72}{160}$

Compare using <, >, or =.

26. $\frac{8}{11}$ ☐ $\frac{16}{21}$ **27.** $\frac{15}{24}$ ☐ $\frac{35}{56}$ **28.** $\frac{18}{45}$ ☐ $\frac{24}{60}$

Convert each decimal to a fraction in lowest terms.

29. 0.124 **30.** 0.85 **31.** 0.25 **32.** 0.625 **33.** 0.32 **34.** 0.05

35. Convert $\frac{14}{18}$ to a decimal. Tell if the decimal terminates or repeats.

Chapter 4 Review

Estimate each sum or difference.

1. $\frac{4}{5} + \frac{1}{10}$ **2.** $\frac{7}{15} - \frac{1}{4}$

3. Use compatible numbers to estimate the quotient $48\frac{1}{3} \div 5\frac{5}{8}$.

4. About how many $4\frac{3}{4}$-inch pieces can be cut from a string measuring $32\frac{7}{8}$ inches? Estimate to find your answer.

Find each sum or difference. Write answers in lowest terms.

5. $\frac{4}{15} + \frac{8}{15}$ **6.** $\frac{7}{8} - \frac{2}{3}$ **7.** $\frac{2}{5} + \frac{1}{4}$

8. $\frac{5}{6} - \frac{1}{3}$ **9.** $\frac{7}{18} + \frac{11}{24}$ **10.** $\frac{10}{50} - \frac{1}{10}$

11. Solve the equation: $x - \frac{1}{4} = \frac{2}{5}$

12. Write $4\frac{5}{6}$ as an improper fraction.

Find each sum or difference.

13. $6\frac{7}{9} - 4\frac{8}{9}$ **14.** $14\frac{3}{5} + 9\frac{2}{3}$ **15.** $9\frac{1}{6} - 8\frac{1}{3}$

16. $22\frac{3}{7} + 19\frac{8}{21}$ **17.** $9\frac{9}{99} - 8\frac{8}{88}$ **18.** $1\frac{17}{18} + 3\frac{2}{3}$

19. Find the area of a picture frame with dimensions $\frac{11}{12}$ ft by $\frac{3}{4}$ ft.

20. One package is $2\frac{1}{3}$ times as heavy as another. If the lighter package weighs 9 lb, how much does the heavier package weigh?

Find each product or quotient. Write answers in lowest terms.

21. $\frac{4}{5} \cdot \frac{7}{12}$ **22.** $6\frac{2}{5} \cdot 4\frac{7}{8}$ **23.** $\frac{5}{7} \div \frac{25}{4}$

24. $4\frac{5}{8} \div 1\frac{7}{12}$ **25.** $1\frac{2}{5} \cdot 3\frac{3}{4}$ **26.** $\frac{1}{4} \div \frac{16}{64}$

27. The area of one plot of land is $1\frac{1}{4}$ acres. How many plots with this area are contained in 20 acres of land?

28. A jar holds $\frac{7}{8}$ of a gallon. How many jars of this size are needed to hold 28 gallons?

CHAPTER 4 REVIEW

Chapter 4 Review

Answers

1. ≈ 1
2. $\approx \frac{1}{4}$
3. About 8
4. About 6
5. $\frac{4}{5}$
6. $\frac{5}{24}$
7. $\frac{13}{20}$
8. $\frac{1}{2}$
9. $\frac{61}{72}$
10. $\frac{1}{10}$
11. $x = \frac{13}{20}$
12. $\frac{29}{6}$
13. $1\frac{8}{9}$
14. $24\frac{4}{15}$
15. $\frac{5}{6}$
16. $41\frac{17}{21}$
17. 1
18. $5\frac{11}{18}$
19. $\frac{11}{16}$ ft^2
20. 21 lb
21. $\frac{7}{15}$
22. $31\frac{1}{5}$
23. $\frac{4}{35}$
24. $2\frac{35}{38}$
25. $5\frac{1}{4}$
26. 1
27. 16 plots
28. 32 jars

CHAPTER REVIEW

Answers

1. Possible answer:

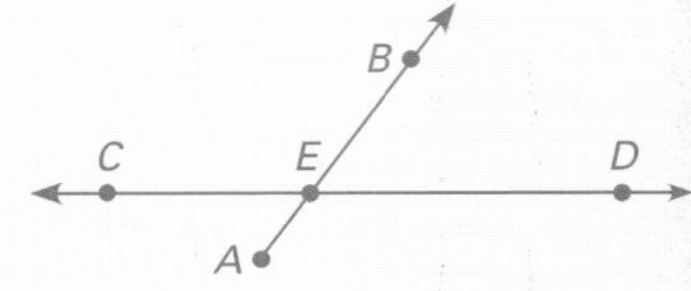

2. 1080°
3. a. 27°
   b. 117°
4. $\angle CFE \cong \angle BEF$ because they are alternate interior angles, $\angle CFE \cong \angle AGE$ because they are corresponding angles, $\angle CFE \cong \angle DFH$ because they are vertical angles.
5. Area: 1872 ft^2; Perimeter: 176 ft
6. Congruent; Congruent; Congruent
7. 64
8. 6.481
9. 5 m
10. 16 in^2
11. 115 cm^2
12. 1068 ft^2

CHAPTER REVIEW

Chapter 5 Review

CHAPTER 5 REVIEW

1. Draw a ray $\overrightarrow{AB}$ and a line $\overleftrightarrow{CD}$ intersecting to form $\angle BEC$.

2. What is the sum of the measures of the angles of an octagon?

3. If $\angle ABC$ measures 63°:

a. What is the measure of an angle complementary to $\angle ABC$?

b. What is the measure of an angle supplementary to $\angle ABC$?

4. Lines $\overleftrightarrow{AB}$ and $\overleftrightarrow{CD}$ are parallel. List the angles congruent to $\angle CFE$, and explain why they are congruent.

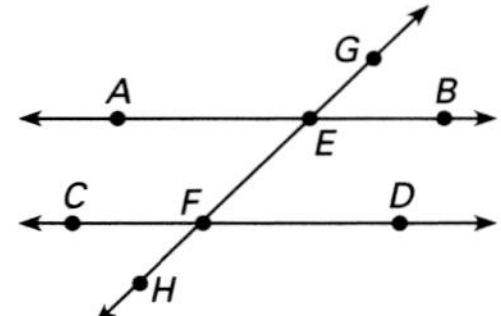

5. Find the area and perimeter of the base of a rectangular building 36 ft wide and 52 ft long.

6. Fill in the blanks: All sides of a square are _____. All sides of an equilateral triangle are _____. The sides of any other regular polygon are _____.

7. Find a perfect square between 60 and 70.

8. Find $\sqrt{42}$ to three decimal places.

9. Find the length of the shorter leg of a right triangle whose hypotenuse is 13 m long and whose longer leg is 12 m long.

10. Find the area of a triangle whose height is 6.4 in. and whose base is 5 in.

11. Find the area of the trapezoid.

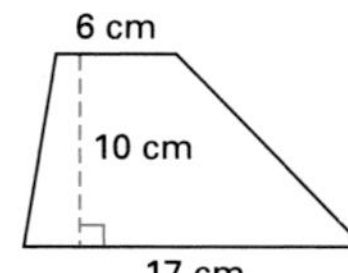

12. Find the area of the stage.

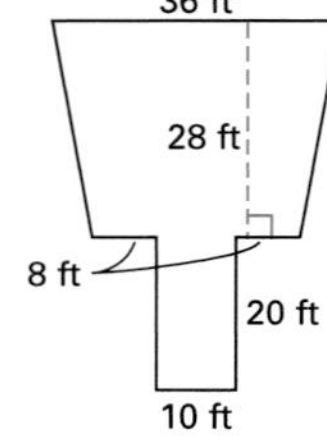

Chapter 6 Review

1. Estimate the ratio of the width to the length of the rectangle shown.

2. Find the rate: 144 feet in 6 seconds. Remember to include units in your rate.
3. Express the rate as a unit rate: $46.00 for 8 hours of work
4. Use unit rates to find the better gas mileage: 162 miles on 6 gallons of gas or 203 miles on 7 gallons
5. Corner Market sells 3 pounds of apples for $6.45. At this rate, how much will 5 pounds of apples cost?
6. Multiply and divide to find two ratios equivalent to $\frac{14}{24}$.
7. Use a table to find two rates equivalent to 45 jumping jacks in 2 minutes.
8. Using multiplication, complete the table to find five ratios equivalent to $\frac{2}{5}$.

2	4	6	8	10	12
5					

9. Using division, complete the table to find five ratios equivalent to $\frac{288}{216}$.

288	144	48	16	8	4
216					

10. Complete the ratio table. Then write four proportions involving the ratios.

5	10	15	20
6			

11. Sam baked one apple pie using 4 apples and 3 tablespoons of sugar, and a larger pie using 6 apples and 5 tablespoons of sugar. Are these ratios proportional?
12. Decide whether these ratios form a proportion: $\frac{84}{124} \stackrel{?}{=} \frac{42}{60}$
13. Decide if these ratios are proportional and give a reason: $\frac{5}{8} \stackrel{?}{=} \frac{17}{24}$
14. Find the unit rate: 54 pages in 9 minutes
15. Kamilah's mother drove 138 miles on 6 gallons of gas. Find the gas mileage for her car.
16. Solve the proportion: $\frac{16}{20} = \frac{n}{35}$

CHAPTER 6 REVIEW

Chapter 6 Review

Answers

1. 1:2
2. $\frac{24 \text{ ft}}{1 \text{ sec}}$
3. $\frac{\$5.75}{1 \text{ hr}}$
4. 203 miles on 7 gallons
5. $10.75
6. Possible answer: $\frac{28}{48}, \frac{7}{12}$
7. Possible answer:

min	2	4	6
jumps	45	90	135

8.

2	4	6	8	10	12
5	10	15	20	25	30

$\frac{4}{10}, \frac{6}{15}, \frac{8}{20}, \frac{10}{25}, \frac{12}{30}$

9.

288	144	48	16	8	4
216	108	36	12	6	3

$\frac{144}{108}, \frac{48}{36}, \frac{16}{12}, \frac{8}{6}, \frac{4}{3}$

10.

5	10	15	20
6	12	18	24

Possible answer: $\frac{5}{6} = \frac{10}{12}, \frac{10}{12} = \frac{15}{18}, \frac{10}{12} = \frac{20}{24}, \frac{20}{24} = \frac{5}{6}$

11. No
12. No
13. No. Possible reason: because $\frac{5}{8} = \frac{15}{24}$
14. 6 pages per minute
15. 23 miles per gallon
16. $n = 28$

CHAPTER REVIEW

Answers

1. Possible answer: 1 cm:4 m; 15 cm:60 m
2. 3 cm:14 km
3. 21 ft
4. $x = 21$ mi
5. At or before 8:18 A.M.
6. 5:00 P.M.
7. Possible answer: 1 in.:1 ft
8. 1:14
9. Possible answer: Centimeters per month
10. $0.25 per 1 gal
11. 7 ft per sec
12. $29\frac{1}{3}$ ft per sec
13. No; $\frac{10}{6} = \frac{20}{12} \neq \frac{26}{12}$
14. Perimeter: 45 cm; Area: 180 cm^2
15. Perimeter ratio: 6:1; Scale factor: 6
16. 15 cm

Chapter 7 Review

1. Write 5 cm:20 m in two other ways.

2. Find the scale of a map if a 42 km wide lake is 9 cm wide on the map.

3. A scale model of a truck is 3.5 in. long. Find the length of the actual truck if the scale is 1 in.:6 ft.

4. Solve the proportion: $\frac{8 \text{ in.}}{6 \text{ mi}} = \frac{28 \text{ in.}}{x}$

5. Paul needs to be at school at 8:30 A.M. If the school is 6 miles away from his home and the bus travels at 30 mi/hr, when does the bus need to leave his home?

6. Anne begins running at 4:15 P.M. and runs at a rate of 8 km/hr. If she runs 6 km, what time does she finish?

7. A model of an 82 ft long train has to fit in a display case that is 10 in. long. Suggest an appropriate scale for the model.

8. A photograph is 4 in. by 6 in. What is the largest scale that can be used to make an enlargement to fit in a 60 in. by 85 in. frame?

9. Suggest appropriate units for the rate at which your hair grows.

10. Give a reciprocal unit rate that has the same meaning as 4 gal for $1.

11. Convert 84 inches per second to feet per second.

12. Ting bicycles at a speed of 20 miles per hour. Convert this rate to feet per second.

13. Tell whether the triangles at right are similar. If they are, write a similarity statement using ~ and give the scale factor. If they are not, explain why not.

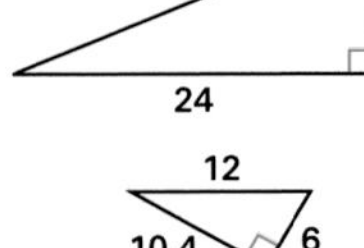

14. Two trapezoids are similar, with scale factor 3:1. The smaller trapezoid has perimeter 15 cm and area 20 cm^2. Find the perimeter and area of the larger trapezoid.

15. Two similar pentagons have an area ratio of 36:1. Find the ratio of their perimeters and the scale factor.

16. Rectangle *ABCD* has an area of 44 cm^2 and a perimeter of 30 cm. Rectangle *EFGH* is similar to *ABCD*. If the area of *EFGH* is 11 cm^2, what is its perimeter?

Chapter 8 Review

1. Rewrite $\frac{19}{25}$ as a percent. **2.** Rewrite 56% as a fraction. **3.** Rewrite 31% as a decimal.

Rewrite each decimal as a fraction and a percent.

4. 0.24 **5.** 1.5 **6.** 0.002 **7.** 0.75

Rewrite each percent as a fraction and a decimal.

8. 0.2% **9.** 96% **10.** 120% **11.** 36%

Find each of the following mentally.

12. 10% of 340 **13.** 50% of 410 **14.** 1% of $50

15. 80% of 35 is what number? **16.** What percent of 72 is 40?

17. 12% of what number is 60? **18.** 220% of 145 is what number?

19. A compact disc player is on sale for $119. This is 85% of the regular price. Find the regular price.

20. In one town, 20% of the 165 restaurants sell pizza. How many restaurants sell pizza?

21. Of the 700 students at Central School, 112 went on a field trip. What percent of the students went on the field trip?

22. A $15 book is on sale at a 30% discount. What is the sale price of the book?

23. Nate bought a $42 sweater on sale for $36.96. What percent is this of the regular price? What percent discount did he get?

24. Over a holiday weekend, the number of cats at a kennel increased from 35 to 48. What was the percent increase?

25. After Janine received a salary increase of 6%, her salary was $44,520. What was her salary before the raise?

26. Maria was given 120 raffle tickets to sell. She sold 29 of them in one week. What percent decrease in the tickets was this?

27. The number of birds on a nature reserve increased from 2980 to 3610. What was the percent increase?

28. There were 650 students at an all-day concert. By the time the last band played, 480 students were left. Find the percent decrease in the number of students.

CHAPTER 8 REVIEW

Chapter 8 Review

Answers

1. 76%
2. $\frac{14}{25}$
3. 0.31
4. $\frac{6}{25}$, 24%
5. $\frac{3}{2}$, 150%
6. $\frac{1}{500}$, 0.2%
7. $\frac{3}{4}$, 75%
8. $\frac{1}{500}$, 0.002
9. $\frac{24}{25}$, 0.96
10. $\frac{6}{5}$, 1.2
11. $\frac{9}{25}$, 0.36
12. 34
13. 205
14. $0.50
15. 28
16. About 55.6%
17. 500
18. 319
19. $140
20. 33 restaurants
21. 16%
22. $10.50
23. 88%; 12%
24. About 37.1%
25. $42,000
26. About 24.2%
27. About 21.1%
28. About 26.2%

CHAPTER REVIEW

Answers

1. No
2. −2000 ft
3. 19
4. 53
5. −47 < −35
6. −13, −6, −2, 7, 24
7. Sometimes
8. 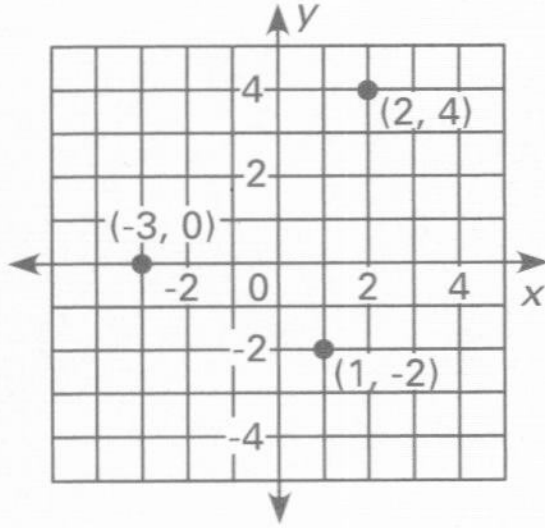

9. Quadrant III
10. Possible answer:
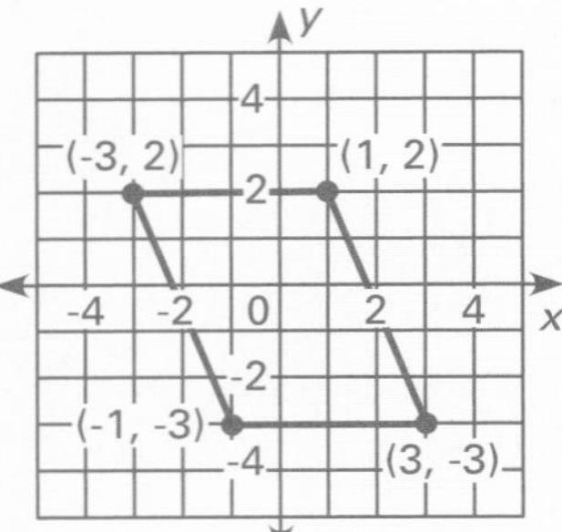

11. 4+ −7 = −3
12. 13
13. 13
14. −16
15. 28
16. −1
17. −7
18. 3
19. −74
20. 0
21. 167°F
22. 40
23. −36
24. −180
25. −504
26. −7
27. 9
28. 6
29. −13
30. −$500

Chapter 9 Review

1. Tell whether −4.5 is an integer.
2. Use a sign to write this number: 2000 feet below sea level
3. Write the opposite of −19.
4. Find the absolute value: $|-53|$
5. Use >, <, or = to compare: −47 ☐ −35
6. Order this set of numbers from least to greatest: 24, −6, 7, −13, −2
7. Fill in the blank with *sometimes, always,* or *never:* An integer is ____ equal to its absolute value.
8. Plot each point on the same coordinate plane.
   a. (2, 4) **b.** (1, −2) **c.** (−3, 0)
9. Name the quadrant or axis that contains the point (−4, −7).
10. Draw a parallelogram so that each of its vertices is in a different quadrant. Label the coordinates of each point.
11. Write the addition problem and the sum modeled in the picture.

12. Write the next integer in the pattern: −14, −5, 4, ____.

Find each sum or difference.

13. 24 + (−11)	**14.** −9 + (−7)	**15.** −63 + 91	**16.** 37 + (−38)
17. 8 − 15	**18.** −4 − (−7)	**19.** −29 − 45	**20.** −18 − (−57) − 39

21. The highest average temperature in the world is 95°F, in Dalol Danakil Depression, Ethiopia. The lowest average temperature is −72°F, in Plateau Station, Antarctica. Subtract to find the range of average temperatures.

Find each product or quotient.

22. −8 • (−5)	**23.** −12 • 3	**24.** 15 • (−4) • 3	**25.** −7 • (−9) • (−8)
26. 84 ÷ (−12)	**27.** −54 ÷ (−6)	**28.** −90 ÷ 3 ÷ (−5)	**29.** −39 ÷ 3

30. The profits from Rocia's business for the first five months of 1996 were $3500, −$2200, −$2900, $800, and −$1700. What was the average monthly profit?

Chapter 10 Review

1. Tell a story that fits the graph at right. 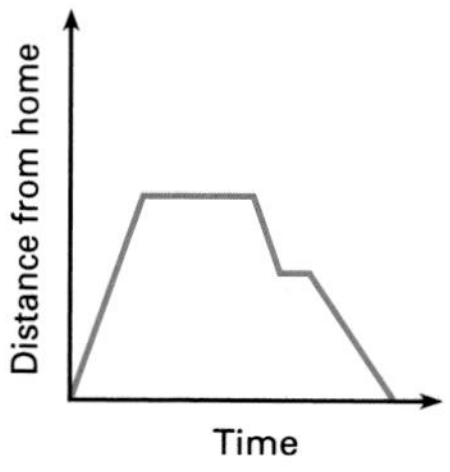
2. Define a variable and give a reasonable range of values for the height of a car.
3. Name a quantity that the volume of a cone might depend on.
4. Write a rule for the sequence 5, 10, 15, 20, …, and give the 100th term of the sequence.
5. For the table below, write an equation to show the relationship between x and y. Use the equation to find y when $x = 7$.

Distance from home

Time

x	1	2	3	4
y	3	4	5	6

6. Make a table of six pairs of values for the equation $y = 3x - 7$.

Graph each equation on a coordinate plane.

7. $y = x + 2$
8. $y = x^2 + 1$
9. The table below was created from the equation $y = -4x + 2$. Use it to solve each related equation.

x	0	1	2	3	4
y	2	−2	−6	−10	−14

a. $-2 = -4x + 2$
b. $-14 = -4x + 2$

10. Use a graph to solve $-11 = 2x - 5$.
11. Write the equation modeled in the equation box. Solve the equation. Sketch your steps.

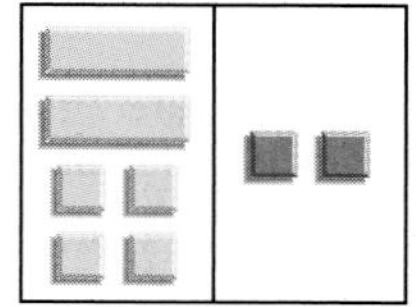

12. Write and graph an inequality to show that at least 150 students attended a play.

Solve each equation. Check your solution.

13. $p - 14 = -6$
14. $a + 11 = 36$
15. $\frac{d}{-6} = -72$
16. $-9r = 63$
17. $3x + 4 = 1$
18. $\frac{c}{3} - 2 = 5$
19. A cab ride costs \$3 plus \$2 per mile. Alonzo paid \$17 for a cab ride. How many miles did he travel?

CHAPTER 10 REVIEW

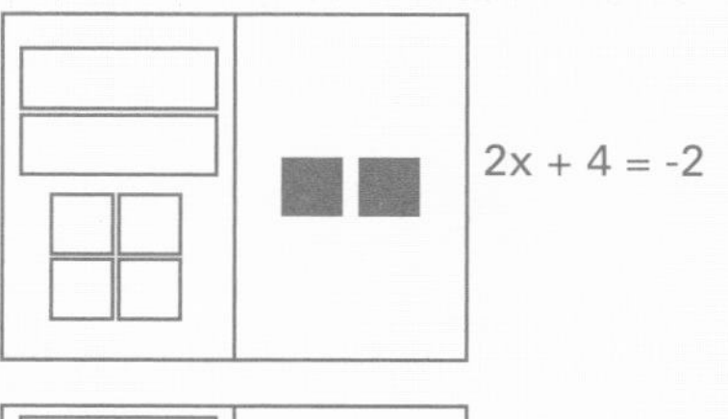

$2x + 4 = -2$

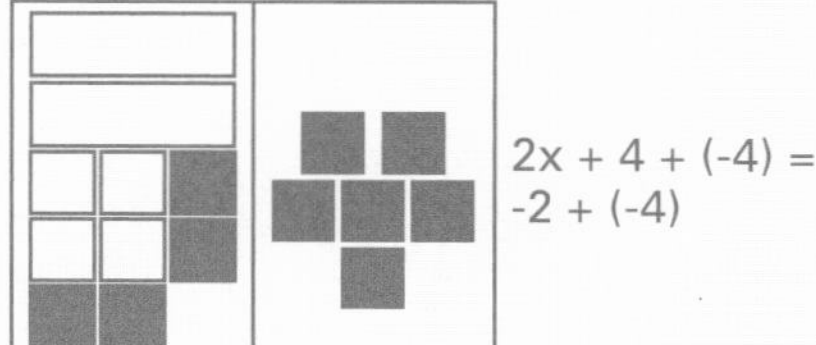

$2x + 4 + (-4) = -2 + (-4)$

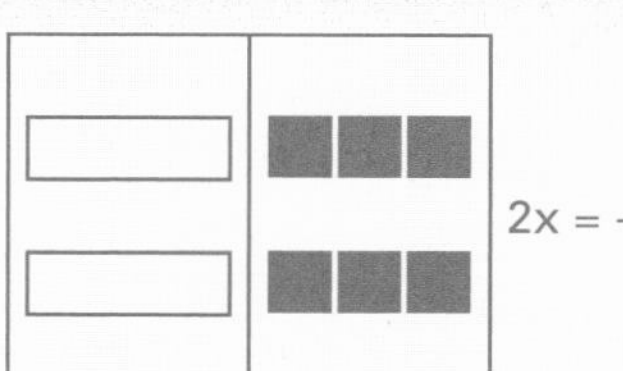

$2x = -6$

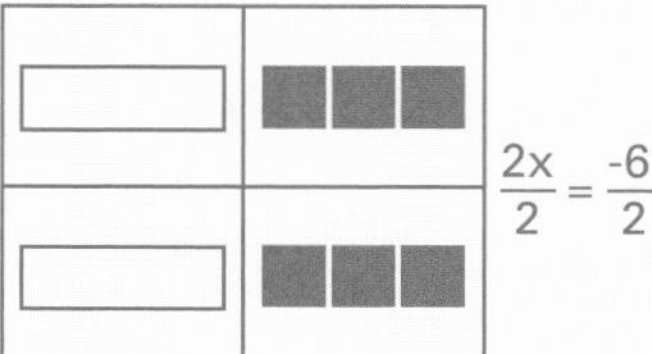

$\frac{2x}{2} = \frac{-6}{2}$

$x = -3$

Chapter 10 Review

Answers

1. Possible answer: A boy walked to a friend's house, stayed there a while, then went home, stopping to get a drink of water at a park.
2. Possible answer: h = height; Range = 4 to 6 ft
3. Possible answers: Height, area of base, radius of base
4. $5n$; 500
5. $y = x + 2$; 9
6. Possible answer:

x	0	1	2	3	4	5
y	-7	-4	-1	2	5	8

7.

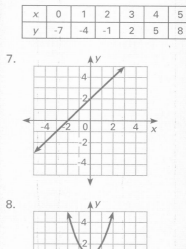

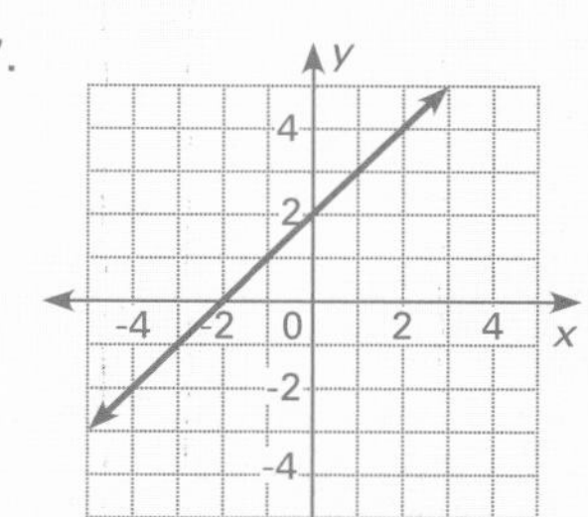

8.

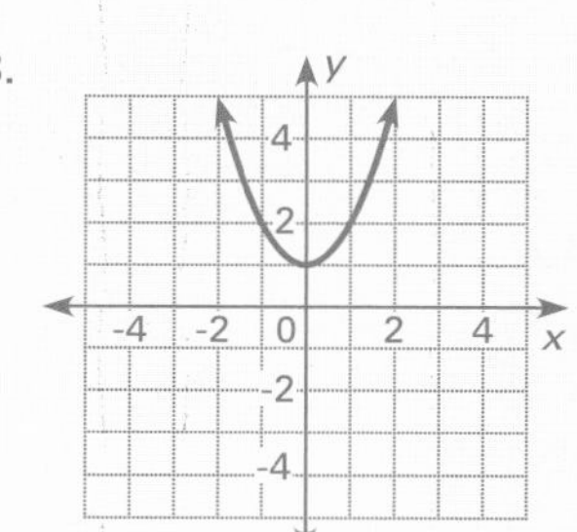

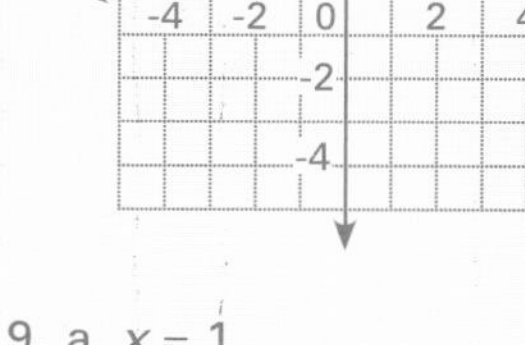

9. a. $x = 1$

b. $x = 4$

10.

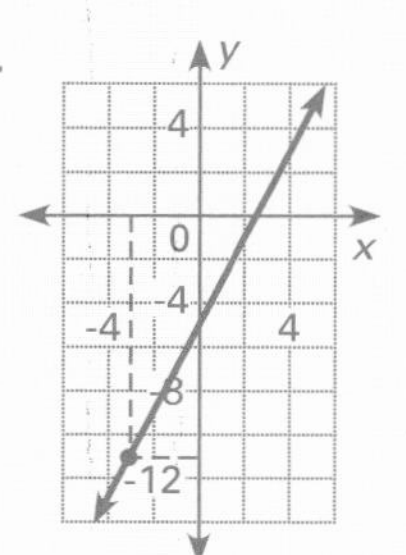

When $y = -11$, $x = -3$

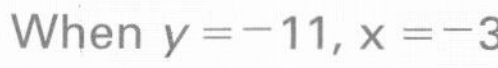

11. $2x + 4 = -2$
Steps shown at the left.

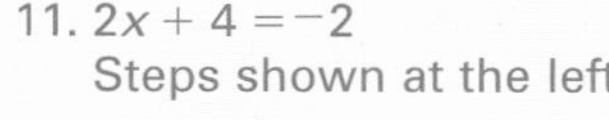

12. $s \geq 150$

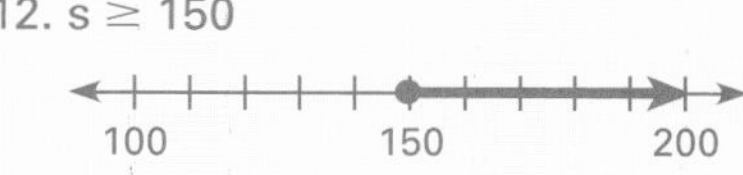

13. $p = 8$
14. $a = 25$
15. $d = 432$
16. $r = -7$
17. $x = -1$
18. $c = 21$
19. 7 mi

CHAPTER REVIEW

Answers

1.

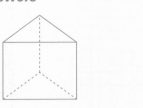

9 edges, 5 faces, 6 vertices

2. 7

3. a. Possible answer:

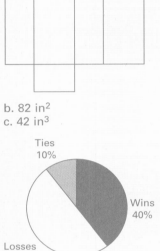

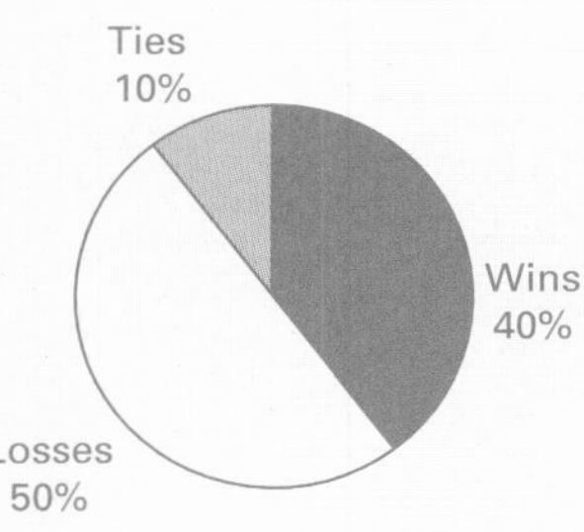

b. 82 in^2
c. 42 in^3

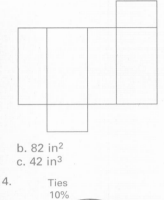

4.

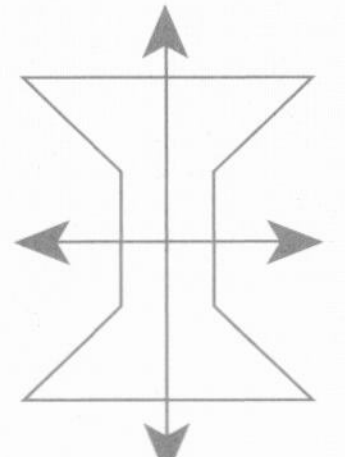

5. Circumference: 39.38 cm; Area: 123.44 cm^2

6. Surface area: 6041.4 ft^2; Volume: $23{,}349.0 \text{ ft}^3$

7.

Yes, it has rotational symmetry.

8. $A'(-1, -2)$

9. a–b.

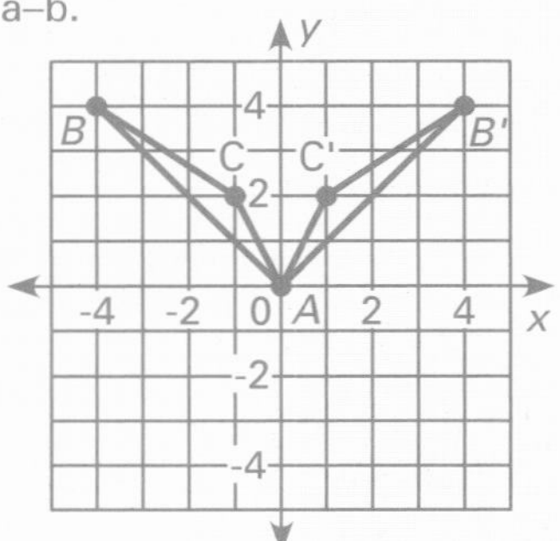

Reflection vertices: $A'(0, 0)$, $B'(4, 4)$, $C'(1, 2)$

c. Rotation vertices: $A'(0, 0)$, $B'(4, 4)$, $C'(2, 1)$.

Chapter 11 Review

1. Sketch a triangular prism. How many edges, faces, and vertices does it have?

2. Find the number of cubes in the figure at right. Assume all cubes are visible.

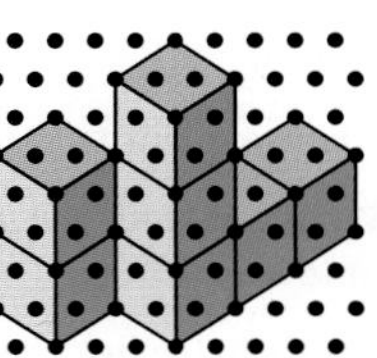

3. A rectangular prism is shown below.

a. Sketch a net for this prism.

b. Find its surface area.

c. Find its volume.

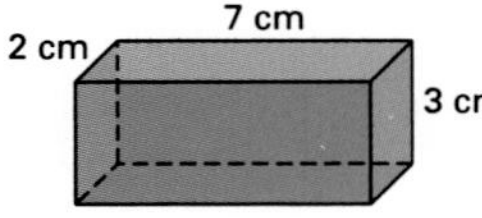

4. The data shows the season summary for Phil's baseball team. Make a circle graph. Label each sector.

Wins	Losses	Ties
40%	50%	10%

5. Find the circumference and area of a circle whose diameter is 12.54 cm. Use 3.14 for π. Round to the nearest hundredth.

6. Find the surface area and the volume of the cylinder shown. Use 3.14 for π. Round to the nearest tenth.

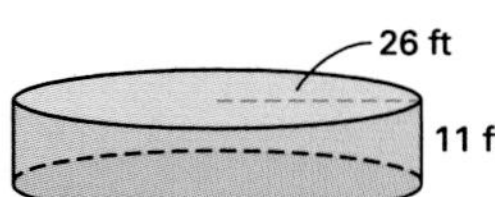

7. Copy the figure. Draw all lines of symmetry. Then tell whether or not it has rotational symmetry.

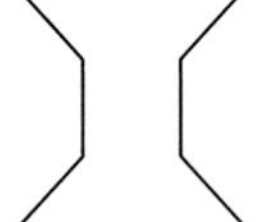

8. Point A is at $(3, -1)$. Use the translation rule $(x, y) \rightarrow (x - 4, y - 1)$ to find the coordinates of A'.

9. The coordinates of a triangle are $A(0, 0)$, $B(-4, 4)$, and $C(-1, 2)$.

a. Draw the figure on the coordinate plane.

b. Draw the reflection of ABC across the y-axis. Give the coordinates of the reflection's vertices.

c. Give the coordinates of a rotation of ABC for a 90° clockwise rotation around the origin.

Chapter 12 Review

1. Mama's Pizza Parlor offers 3 types of crust, 2 choices of cheese, and 6 choices of toppings. Use the Counting Principle to find the number of different pizzas consisting of one type of crust, cheese, and topping.

2. A bookstore has separate sections for hardcover and paperback books in each of these categories: fiction, mystery, nonfiction, science fiction, and poetry. Make a tree diagram to show the possible outcomes. How many sections does the bookstore need?

3. A contest awards four prizes. Sandra, Miguel, Tasha, and Jimmy are the four finalists. In how many ways can first, second, third, and fourth place be assigned?

4. List all of the possible orderings of the numbers 1, 2, and 3, without repeating digits.

5. Elena has 10 CDs she wants to take on a trip, but she can't fit all of them into her luggage. How many different ways can she choose 4 of the CDs to take?

6. A bag contains 4 red, 6 blue, and 3 yellow marbles. A marble is chosen at random. Find the odds that the marble is:

   a. Blue
   b. Yellow

7. A spinner has 6 equal sections, labeled A, B, C, D, E, and F. Pramit wins if a vowel is spun and Molly wins if a consonant is spun. Give each player's odds of winning. Then determine whether the game is fair.

8. A number cube is rolled. Find the probability of each event.

   a. Rolling a number greater than 4
   b. Rolling a number that is *not* greater than 4

9. Find the probability of rolling a sum of 9 when rolling two number cubes. Express your answer as a percent.

10. Mike flipped a coin 20 times and got heads 7 times. Find each of the following:

    a. Theoretical probability of getting heads
    b. Experimental probability of getting heads

11. A dart hits the dart board shown. What is the probability that it lands in the shaded region?

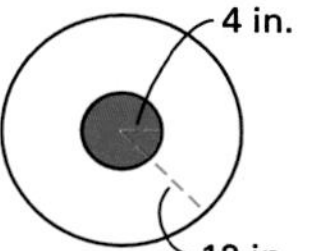

12. A number cube is rolled twice. What is the probability of getting a number less than 3 on the first roll, then a 6 on the second?

13. Roberto draws two coins from his pocket, which contains 4 quarters and 5 nickels. What is the probability that both coins are quarters?

Chapter 12 Review

Answers

1. 36 different pizzas
2. 10 sections
3. 24 ways
4. 1, 2, 3; 1, 3, 2; 2, 3, 1; 2, 1, 3; 3, 1, 2; 3, 2, 1
5. 5040 ways
6. a. 6:7
   b. 3:10
7. Pramit: 1:3; Molly: 2:3; Not fair
8. a. $\frac{1}{3}$
   b. $\frac{2}{3}$
9. About 11.1%
10. a. 50%
    b. 35%
11. $\frac{1}{9}$
12. $\frac{1}{18}$
13. $\frac{1}{6}$

Geometric Formulas

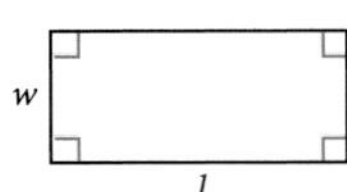 **Rectangle** Area: $A = lw$ Perimeter: $p = 2l + 2w$	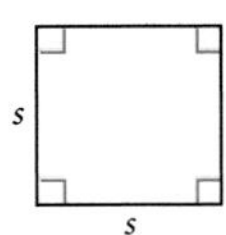 **Square** Area: $A = s^2$ Perimeter: $p = 4s$	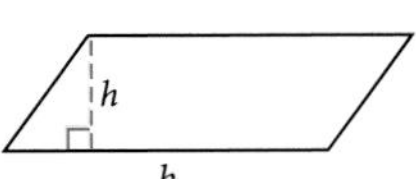 **Parallelogram** Area: $A = bh$
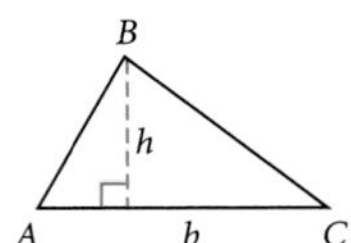 **Triangle** Area: $A = \frac{1}{2}bh$ $m\angle A + m\angle B + m\angle C = 180°$	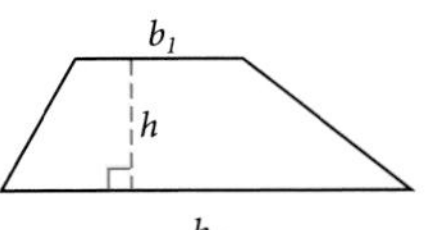 **Trapezoid** Area: $A = \frac{1}{2}h(b_1 + b_2)$	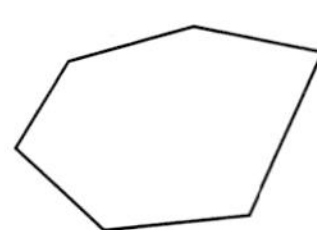 **Polygon** Sum of angle measures for n-sided polygon: $S = (n - 2)180°$ Perimeter: sum of measures of all sides
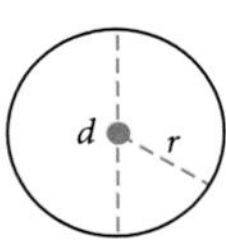 **Circle** Area: $A = \pi r^2$ Circumference: $C = \pi d = 2\pi r$	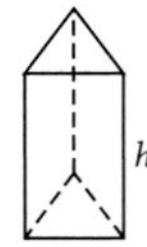 **Prism** Volume: $V = Bh$ Surface Area: $SA = ph + 2B$	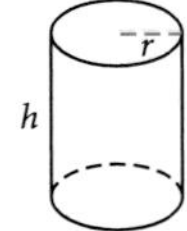 **Cylinder** Volume: $V = \pi r^2 h$ Surface Area: $SA = 2\pi rh + 2\pi r^2$

Measurement Conversion Factors

Metric Measures of Length
1000 meters (m) = 1 kilometer (km)
100 centimeters (cm) = 1 m
10 decimeters (dm) = 1 m
1000 millimeters (mm) = 1 m
10 cm = 1 decimeter (dm)
10 mm = 1 cm

Customary Measures of Length
12 inches (in.) = 1 foot (ft)
3 ft = 1 yard (yd)
36 in. = 1 yd
5280 ft = 1 mile (mi)
1760 yd = 1 mi
6076 ft = 1 nautical mile

Area
100 square millimeters (mm^2) = 1 square centimeter (cm^2)
10,000 cm^2 = 1 square meter (m^2)
10,000 m^2 = 1 hectare (ha)

Area
144 square inches (in^2) = 1 square foot (ft^2)
9 ft^2 = 1 square yard (yd^2)
43,560 sq ft^2 = 1 acre (A)

Volume
1000 cubic millimeters (mm^3) = 1 cubic centimeter (cm^3)
1000 cm^3 = 1 cubic decimeter (dm^3)
1,000,000 cm^3 = 1 cubic meter (m^3)

Volume
1728 cubic inches (cu in.) = 1 cubic foot (cu ft)
27 cu ft = 1 cubic yard (cu yard)

Capacity
1000 milliliters (mL) = 1 liter (L)
1000 L = 1 kiloliter (kL)

Capacity
8 fluid ounces (fl oz) = 1 cup (c)
2 c = 1 pint (pt)
2 pt = 1 quart (qt)
4 qt = 1 gallon (gal)

Mass
1000 kilograms (kg) = 1 metric ton (t)
1000 grams (g) = 1 kg
1000 milligrams (mg) = 1 g

Weight
16 ounces (oz) = 1 pound (lb)
2000 lb = 1 ton (T)

Temperatures in Degrees Celsius (°C)
0°C = freezing point of water
37°C = normal body temperature
100°C = boiling point of water

Temperatures in Degrees Fahrenheit (°F)
32°F = freezing point of water
98.6°F = normal body temperature
212°F = boiling point of water

Time
60 seconds (sec) = 1 minute (min)
60 min = 1 hour (hr)
24 hr = 1 day

TABLES

685

Symbols

$+$	plus or positive
$-$	minus or negative
$\cdot$	times
$\times$	times
$\div$	divided by
$\pm$	positive or negative
$=$	is equal to
$\neq$	is not equal to
$<$	is less than
$>$	is greater than
$\leq$	is less than or equal to
$\geq$	is greater than or equal to
$\approx$	is approximately equal to
%	percent
$a:b$	the ratio of a to b, or $\frac{a}{b}$
$\cong$	is congruent to
$\sim$	is similar to
$^\circ$	degree(s)
$\overleftrightarrow{AB}$	line containing points A and B
$\overline{AB}$	line segment with endpoints A and B
$\overrightarrow{AB}$	ray with endpoint A and containing B
⊾	right angle
$\perp$	is perpendicular to
$\parallel$	is parallel to
AB	length of $\overline{AB}$; distance between A and B
$\triangle ABC$	triangle with vertices A, B, and C
$\angle ABC$	angle with sides $\overrightarrow{BA}$ and $\overrightarrow{BC}$
$\angle B$	angle with vertex B
$m\angle ABC$	measure of angle ABC
$'$	prime
a^n	the nth power of a
$\lvert x \rvert$	absolute value of x
$\sqrt{x}$	principal square root of x
π	pi (approximately 3.1416)
(a, b)	ordered pair with x-coordinate a and y-coordinate b
$P(\text{A})$	the probability of event A
$n!$	n factorial

TABLES

TABLES

Squares and Square Roots

N	N^2	$\sqrt{N}$
1	1	1
2	4	1.414
3	9	1.732
4	16	2
5	25	2.236
6	36	2.449
7	49	2.646
8	64	2.828
9	81	3
10	100	3.162
11	121	3.317
12	144	3.464
13	169	3.606
14	196	3.742
15	225	3.873
16	256	4
17	289	4.123
18	324	4.243
19	361	4.359
20	400	4.472
21	441	4.583
22	484	4.690
23	529	4.796
24	576	4.899
25	625	5
26	676	5.099
27	729	5.196
28	784	5.292
29	841	5.385
30	900	5.477
31	961	5.568
32	1,024	5.657
33	1,089	5.745
34	1,156	5.831
35	1,225	5.916
36	1,296	6
37	1,369	6.083
38	1,444	6.164
39	1,521	6.245
40	1,600	6.325
41	1,681	6.403
42	1,764	6.481
43	1,849	6.557
44	1,936	6.633
45	2,025	6.708
46	2,116	6.782
47	2,209	6.856
48	2,304	6.928
49	2,401	7
50	2,500	7.071
51	2,601	7.141
52	2,704	7.211
53	2,809	7.280
54	2,916	7.348
55	3,025	7.416
56	3,136	7.483
57	3,249	7.550
58	3,364	7.616
59	3,481	7.681
60	3,600	7.746
61	3,721	7.810
62	3,844	7.874
63	3,969	7.937
64	4,096	8
65	4,225	8.062
66	4,356	8.124
67	4,489	8.185
68	4,624	8.246
69	4,761	8.307
70	4,900	8.367
71	5,041	8.426
72	5,184	8.485
73	5,329	8.544
74	5,476	8.602
75	5,625	8.660
76	5,776	8.718
77	5,929	8.775
78	6,084	8.832
79	6,241	8.888
80	6,400	8.944
81	6,561	9
82	6,724	9.055
83	6,889	9.110
84	7,056	9.165
85	7,225	9.220
86	7,396	9.274
87	7,569	9.327
88	7,744	9.381
89	7,921	9.434
90	8,100	9.487
91	8,281	9.539
92	8,464	9.592
93	8,649	9.644
94	8,836	9.695
95	9,025	9.747
96	9,216	9.798
97	9,409	9.849
98	9,604	9.899
99	9,801	9.950
100	10,000	10

Glossary

absolute value A number's distance from zero, shown by | |. Example: |−7| = 7 [p. 434]

acute angle An angle that measures less than 90°. [p. 213]

acute triangle A triangle with three acute angles. [p. 223]

addend A number added to one or more others.

additive inverse A number's opposite. Example: The additive inverse of 2 is −2. [p. 451]

algebraic expression An expression containing a variable. Example: $2(x - 9)$ [p. 78]

alternate interior angles A pair of angles formed by two lines and a transversal. In the figure below, ∠1 and ∠3 are a pair of alternate interior angles, and ∠2 and ∠4 are a pair of alternate interior angles. [p. 218]

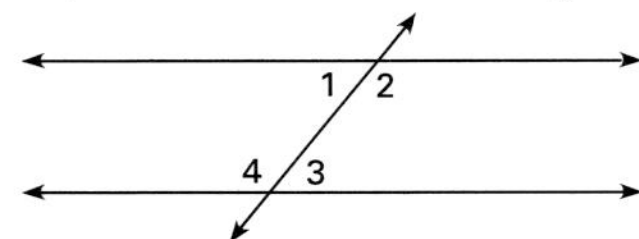

angle Two rays with a common endpoint. [p. 213]

angle bisector A ray bisecting an angle. [p. 214]

area The number of square units needed to cover a figure. [p. 233]

arithmetic sequence A sequence where the difference between consecutive terms is always the same. Example: 3, 6, 9, ... [p. 492]

Associative Property of Addition The fact that grouping does not affect the sum of three or more numbers. $a + (b + c) = (a + b) + c$ [p. 62]

Associative Property of Multiplication The fact that grouping does not affect the product of three or more numbers. $a(bc) = (ab)c$ [p. 62]

average See *mean.*

axes See *x-axis* and *y-axis.*

bar graph A graph that uses bars to display data. [p. 7]

base (in numeration) A number multiplied by itself the number of times shown by an exponent. Example: $5^2 = 5 \cdot 5$, where 5 is the base and 2 is the exponent. [p. 125]

base (of a polygon) Any side of the polygon, or the length of that side. [pp. 233, 249]

base (of a solid) See examples below. [pp. 555, 587]

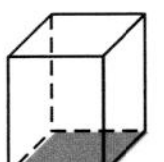

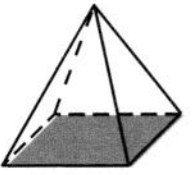

binary number system A base-two place value system. [p. 159]

bisect To divide an angle or segment into two congruent angles or segments. [pp. 214, 218]

box-and-whisker plot A graph showing how a collection of data is distributed. [p. 26]

capacity The volume of a figure, given in terms of liquid measure. [p. 594]

center The point at the exact middle of a circle or sphere. [pp. 574, 587]

central angle An angle whose vertex is at the center of a circle. [p. 574]

circle A plane figure whose points are all the same distance from its center. [p. 574]

circle graph A circular graph that uses wedges to represent portions of the data set. [p. 7]

circumference The perimeter of a circle. [p. 578]

circumscribed figure A figure containing another. A polygon is circumscribed around a circle if the circle touches each of its sides. [p. 617]

combination A selection of items where the order does not matter. [p. 636]

common denominator A denominator that is the same in two or more fractions. [p. 150]

common factor If a number is a factor of two or more numbers, it is a common factor of that set of numbers. [p. 139]

common multiple A number that is a multiple of each of two given numbers. Example: 24 is a common multiple of 4 and 3. [p. 141]

Commutative Property of Addition The fact that ordering does not affect the sum of two or more numbers. $a + b = b + a$ [p. 62]

Commutative Property of Multiplication The fact that ordering does not affect the product of two or more numbers. $ab = ba$ [p. 62]

complementary angles Two angles whose measures add up to 90°. [p. 214]

composite number A whole number greater than 1 that has more than two factors. [p. 136]

GLOSSARY

688

cone A solid with one circular base. [p. 587]

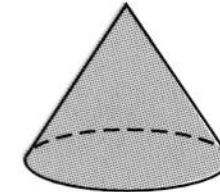

congruent angles Two angles that have equal measures. [p. 214]

congruent segments Two segments that have equal lengths. [p. 218]

constant A quantity whose value cannot change. [p. 482]

constant graph A graph in which the height of the line does not change. [p. 486]

conversion factor A fraction, equal to 1, whose numerator and denominator represent the same quantity but use different units. [p. 349]

coordinates A pair of numbers used to locate a point on a coordinate plane. [p. 443]

coordinate system (coordinate plane) A system of intersecting horizontal and vertical number lines, used to locate points. [p. 443]

corresponding angles Angles formed by two lines and a transversal. $\angle 1$ and $\angle 5$, $\angle 2$ and $\angle 6$, $\angle 4$ and $\angle 8$, and $\angle 3$ and $\angle 7$ are corresponding angles. [p. 218]

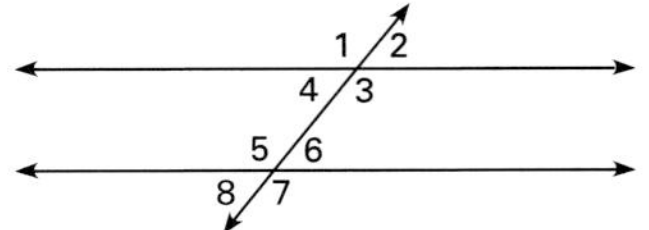

corresponding angles (in similar figures) Matching angles on similar figures. [p. 361]

corresponding sides Matching sides on similar figures. [p. 361]

counterexample An example that shows a statement is false. [p. 265]

Counting Principle To find the number of outcomes for selecting several items, multiply the number of possibilities for each item. [p. 627]

cross product In a proportion, the product of a numerator on one side with the denominator on the other. [p. 308]

cube (geometric figure) A 6-sided prism whose faces are congruent squares.

cube (in numeration) A number raised to the third power.

customary system of measurement The measurement system often used in the United States: inches, feet, miles, ounces, pounds, tons, cups, quarts, gallons, etc.

cylinder A solid with two parallel circular bases with the same radius. [p. 587]

decagon A polygon with 10 sides.

decimal system A base-10 place value system.

decreasing graph A graph in which the height of the line decreases from left to right. [p. 486]

deductive reasoning Using logic to show that a statement is true. [p. 265]

degree (°) A unit of measure for angles. [p. 213]

denominator The bottom number in a fraction. [p. 144]

dependent events Events for which the outcome of one affects the probability of the other. [p. 660]

diameter The distance across a circle through its center. [p. 578]

difference The answer to a subtraction problem.

Distributive Property The fact that $a(b + c) = ab + ac$. [p. 62]

dividend The number to be divided in a division problem. In $8 \div 4 = 2$, 8 is the dividend, 4 is the *divisor,* and 2 is the *quotient.*

divisible A number is divisible by a second number if it can be divided by that number with no remainder. [p. 134]

divisor See *dividend.*

double-bar graph A single graph comparing bar graphs for two related data sets. [p. 12]

double-line graph A single graph comparing line graphs for two related data sets. [p. 32]

edge A segment joining two faces of a polyhedron. [p. 554]

equally-likely outcomes Outcomes that have the same probability.

equation A mathematical statement that two expressions are equal. Example: $x - 10 = 6$ [p. 82]

equilateral triangle A triangle whose sides are all the same length. [p. 222]

equivalent fractions Two fractions representing the same number, such as $\frac{1}{2}$ and $\frac{8}{16}$. [p. 144]

equivalent rates Rates corresponding to equivalent fractions. [p. 282]

equivalent ratios Ratios corresponding to equivalent fractions. [p. 282]

estimate An approximation for the result of a calculation.

event An outcome or set of outcomes of an experiment or situation. Example: Rolling a 3 or higher is one possible event produced by a dice roll. [p. 645]

GLOSSARY

GLOSSARY

689

experiment In probability, any activity involving chance (such as a dice roll). [p. 644]

experimental probability A probability based on the statistical results of an experiment. [p. 654]

exponent A number telling how many times the base is being used as a factor. Example: $8^3 = 8 \cdot 8 \cdot 8$, where 3 is the exponent and 8 is the base. [p. 125]

expression A mathematical phrase made up of variables and/or numbers and operations. Example: $3x - 11$ [p. 60]

face A flat surface on a solid. [p. 554]

factor A whole number that divides another whole number evenly. Example: 8 is a factor of 48. [p. 134]

factorial The factorial of a number is the product of all whole numbers from 1 to that number. The symbol for factorial is an "!" [p. 633]

factor tree A diagram showing how a whole number breaks down into its prime factors. [p. 136]

fair games Games where all players have the same odds of winning. [p. 645]

formula A rule showing relationships among quantities. Example: $A = bh$ [p. 56]

fractal A pattern with self-similarity. If you zoom in on a small part of a fractal, the enlarged region looks similar to the original figure. [p. 377]

fraction A number in the form $\frac{a}{b}$. [p. 144]

function A rule that matches two sets of numbers. [p. 97]

geometric probability A probability based on comparing measurements of geometric figures. [p. 656]

geometric sequence A sequence where the ratio between consecutive terms is always the same. Example: 3, 6, 12, ... [p. 492]

greatest common factor (GCF) The largest factor two numbers have in common. Example: 6 is the GCF of 24 and 18. [p. 139]

height On a triangle or quadrilateral, the distance from the base to the opposite vertex or side. On a prism or cylinder, the distance between the bases. [pp. 233, 249, 567, 587]

heptagon A seven-sided polygon.

hexadecimal number system A base-16 place value system. [p. 159]

hexagon A six-sided polygon. [p. 227]

histogram A type of bar graph where the categories are equal ranges of numbers. [p. 47]

hypotenuse The side opposite the right angle in a right triangle. [p. 244]

if-then statement A logical statement that uses *if* and *then* to show a relationship between two conditions. Example: *If* a triangle is scalene, *then* none of its sides are congruent. [p. 667]

improper fraction A fraction greater than 1. [p. 178]

increasing graph A graph in which the height of the line increases from left to right. [p. 486]

independent events Events for which the outcome of one does not affect the probability of the other. [p. 660]

inductive reasoning Using a pattern to draw a conclusion. [p. 265]

inequality A statement that two expressions are not equal. Examples: $3x < 11$, $x + 2 \leq 6$ [p. 517]

inscribed figure A figure that just fits inside another. A polygon is inscribed in a circle if all of its vertices lie on the circle. [p. 617]

integer A whole number, its opposite, or zero. The integers are the numbers ... –3, –2, –1, 0, 1, 2, 3, ... [p. 433]

interval The space between marked values on a bar graph's scale. [p. 11]

inverse operations Operations that "undo" each other, such as addition and subtraction. [p. 75]

isometric drawing A perspective drawing. [p. 559]

isosceles triangle A triangle with at least two congruent sides. [p. 222]

least common denominator (LCD) The least common multiple (LCM) of two or more denominators. [p. 174]

least common multiple (LCM) The smallest common multiple of two numbers. Example: 56 is the LCM of 8 and 14. [p. 141]

leg A side of a right triangle other than the hypotenuse. [p. 244]

line A straight set of points that extends without end in both directions. [p. 212]

line graph A graph that uses a line to show how data changes over time. [p. 30]

line of symmetry The imaginary "mirror" in line symmetry. [p. 605]

line plot A plot, using stacked x's, showing the distribution of values in a data set. [p. 17]

line segment Two points, called the *endpoints* of the segment, and all points between them. [p. 218]

line symmetry A figure has line symmetry if one half is the mirror image of the other half. [p. 605]

lowest terms A fraction with a numerator and denominator whose only common factor is 1. [p. 145]

mean The sum of the values in a data set divided by the number of values. Also known as the *average.* [p. 22]

measurement error The uncertainty in a measurement. The greatest possible error in a measurement is half the smallest unit used. [p. 203]

median The middle value in a data set when the values are arranged in order. [p. 22]

metric system of measurement The most commonly used measurement system throughout the world: centimeters, meters, kilometers, grams, kilograms, milliliters, liters, etc.

midpoint The point that divides a segment into two congruent smaller segments. [p. 218]

mixed number A number made up of a nonzero whole number and a fraction. [p. 169]

mode The value(s) that occur most often in a data set. [p. 22]

multiple The product of a given number and another whole number. Example: Since $3 \cdot 7 = 21$, 21 is a multiple of both 3 and 7. [p. 141]

negative numbers Numbers that are less than zero. [p. 433]

negative relationship Two data sets have a negative relationship when the data values in one set increase as the values in the other decrease. [p. 37]

no relationship Two data sets have no relationship when there is no positive or negative relationship. [p. 37]

numerator The top number in a fraction. [p. 144]

obtuse angle An angle that measures more than 90° and less than 180°. [p. 213]

obtuse triangle A triangle with one obtuse angle. [p. 223]

octagon An eight-sided polygon. [p. 227]

odds The ratio of the number of ways an event can happen to the number of ways it cannot. [p. 645]

opposite numbers Numbers that are the same distance from zero but on opposite sides, such as 5 and –5. [p. 433]

ordered pair A pair of numbers, such as (12, –8), used to locate points on a coordinate plane. [p. 443]

order of operations A rule telling in what order a series of operations should be done. The order of operations is (1) compute within grouping symbols; (2) compute powers; (3) multiply and divide from left to right; (4) add and subtract from left to right. [p. 61]

origin The zero point on a number line, or the point (0, 0) where the axes of a coordinate system intersect. [pp. 433, 443]

orthographic drawing A drawing of an object using front, side, and top views. [p. 559]

outcome (in probability) One way an experiment or situation could turn out. [p. 627]

outlier A value widely separated from the others in a data set. [p. 17]

parallel lines Lines in a plane that never meet. [p. 217]

parallelogram A quadrilateral with parallel and congruent opposite sides. [p. 223]

pentagon A five-sided polygon. [p. 227]

percent A ratio comparing a number to 100. Example: $29\% = \frac{29}{100}$ [p. 386]

percent change The amount of a change, divided by the original amount, times 100. [p. 415]

percent decrease A percent change describing a decrease in a quantity. [p. 415]

percent increase A percent change describing an increase in a quantity. [p. 415]

perfect square The square of a whole number. [p. 240]

perimeter The distance around the outside of a figure. [p. 233]

permutation One of the ways to order a set of items. [p. 631]

perpendicular Lines, rays, or line segments that intersect at right angles. [p. 219]

perpendicular bisector A line, ray, or segment that intersects a segment at its midpoint and is perpendicular to it. [p. 219]

pi (π) The ratio of a circle's circumference to its diameter: $\pi \approx 3.14159265....$ [p. 579]

place value The value given to the place a digit occupies.

plane A flat surface that extends forever. [p. 217]

point symmetry A figure has point symmetry if it looks unchanged after a 180° rotation. [p. 611]

polygon A geometric figure with at least three sides. [p. 227]

polyhedron A solid whose faces are polygons. [p. 554]

positive numbers Numbers greater than zero. [p. 433]

positive relationship Two data sets have a positive relationship when their data values increase or decrease together. [p. 37]

GLOSSARY

691

power A number produced by raising a base to an exponent. Example: $16 = 2^4$, so 16 is the 4th power of 2. [p. 125]

prime factorization Writing a number as a product of prime numbers. Example: $60 = 2^2 \cdot 3 \cdot 5$ [p. 136]

prime number A whole number greater than 1 whose only factors are 1 and itself. The primes start with 2, 3, 5, 7, 11, ... [p. 136]

prism A polyhedron whose bases are congruent and parallel. [p. 555]

probability The number of ways an event can occur divided by the total number of possible outcomes. [p. 650]

product The answer to a multiplication problem.

proportion A statement showing two ratios are equal. [p. 294]

protractor A tool for measuring angles. [p. 213]

pyramid A polyhedron with one polygonal base. [p. 555]

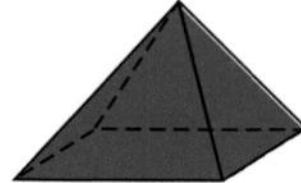

Pythagorean Theorem In a right triangle where c is the length of the hypotenuse and a and b are the lengths of the legs, $a^2 + b^2 = c^2$. [p. 245]

quadrants The four regions determined by the axes of a coordinate plane. [p. 443]

quadratic equation An equation with squared terms. Example: $x^2 + 3 = 12$ [p. 545]

quadrilateral A four-sided polygon. [p. 223]

quotient See *dividend.*

radical sign $\sqrt{\ }$, used to represent a square root. [p. 241]

radius The distance from the center of a circle to a point on the circle. [p. 578]

range (in statistics) The difference between the least and greatest numbers in a data set. [p. 22]

rate A ratio showing how quantities with different units are related. Example: $\frac{72 \text{ dollars}}{8 \text{ hours}}$ [p. 278]

ratio A comparison of two quantities, often written as a fraction. [p. 274]

ray Part of a line that has one endpoint and extends forever. [p. 212]

reciprocals Two numbers whose product is 1. Example: $\frac{5}{7}$ and $\frac{7}{5}$ are reciprocals. [p. 198]

rectangle A quadrilateral with four right angles. [p. 223]

reflection A transformation that flips a figure over a line. [p. 606]

regular polygon A polygon with all sides and angles congruent. [p. 228]

repeating decimal A decimal number that repeats a pattern of digits. Example: $2.313131... = 2.\overline{31}$ [p. 154]

rhombus A parallelogram with all sides congruent. [p. 223]

right angle An angle that measures 90°. [p. 213]

right triangle A triangle with one right angle. [p. 223]

rotation A transformation that turns a figure around a point. [p. 610]

rotational symmetry A figure has rotational symmetry if it looks unchanged after a rotation of less than 360°. [p. 611]

rounding Estimating a number to a given place value. Example: 2153 rounded to the nearest hundred is 2200. [p. 110]

scale (graphical) The evenly spaced marks on a bar graph's vertical axis, used to measure the heights of the bars. [p. 11]

scale (in scale drawings and maps) The ratio of the distance between two points on the map or drawing to the actual distance. [p. 324]

scale drawing A drawing that uses a scale to make an enlarged or reduced picture of an object. [p. 328]

scale factor The ratio used to enlarge or reduce similar figures. [p. 361]

scalene triangle A triangle whose sides have different lengths. [p. 222]

scatterplot A graph showing paired data values as points. [p. 35]

scientific notation A number written as a decimal greater than or equal to 1 and less than 10, times a power of 10. Example: $937 = 9.37 \times 10^2$ [p. 126]

sector A wedge-shaped part of a circle. [p. 7]

segment See *line segment.*

segment bisector A line, ray, or segment through the midpoint of a segment. [p. 218]

sequence A list of numbers, such as –1, 4, 9, 14, ... [p. 490]

similar figures Figures with the same shape but not necessarily the same size. [p. 360]

simulation (in probability) A model of a probability experiment. [p. 664]

solid A three-dimensional object. [p. 554]

solutions of an equation or inequality Values of a variable that make an equation or inequality true. [pp. 82, 517]

GLOSSARY

GLOSSARY

692

solve To find the solutions of an equation or inequality. [p. 82]

sphere A solid whose points are all the same distance from the center. [p. 587]

square (geometric figure) A quadrilateral with four congruent sides and four right angles. [p. 223]

square (in numeration) A number raised to the second power. [p. 240]

square root The length of the side of a square with an area equal to a given number. [p. 240]

standard form The usual way of writing numbers (in contrast to scientific notation). [p. 126]

stem-and-leaf diagram A table showing the distribution of values in a data set by splitting each value into a stem and a leaf. [p. 17]

straight angle An angle that measures 180°. [p. 213]

substitute To replace a variable with a known value. [p. 57]

sum The answer to an addition problem.

supplementary angles Two angles whose measures add up to 180°. [p. 214]

surface area For a solid, the sum of the areas of its surfaces. [p. 563]

symmetry See *line symmetry, point symmetry,* and *rotational symmetry.*

tangent line A line that touches a circle at only one point. [p. 582]

tangent ratio In a right triangle, the tangent of an angle is the ratio of the length of the side opposite the angle to the length of the side adjacent to it. [p. 315]

term One number in a sequence. [p. 490]

terminating decimal A decimal number that ends. Example: 2.31 [p. 154]

tessellation A set of repeating figures that fills a flat surface with no gaps or overlaps. [p. 615]

theoretical probability The ratio of the number of ways an event can happen to the total number of possible outcomes. [p. 654]

transformation A change in the size or position of a figure. [p. 600]

translation A transformation that slides a figure. [p. 600]

transversal A line intersecting two or more lines. [p. 217]

trapezoid A quadrilateral with exactly two parallel sides. [p. 223]

tree diagram A branching diagram showing all possible outcomes for a given situation. [p. 627]

trend A clear direction in a line graph suggesting how the data will behave in the future. [p. 31]

trend line A line drawn through a set of data points to show a trend in the data values. [p. 41]

triangle A three-sided polygon.

unit price A unit rate giving the cost of one item. [p. 279]

unit rate A rate in which the second quantity is one unit. Example: $\frac{55 \text{ miles}}{1 \text{ hour}}$ [p. 278]

variable A quantity whose values may vary. [p. 56]

Venn diagram A diagram that uses regions to show relationships. [p. 667]

vertex On an angle, the endpoint of the rays forming the angle. On a polygon, a corner where two sides meet. On a polyhedron, a corner where edges meet. [pp. 213, 227, 554]

vertical angles Angles on opposite sides of the intersection of two lines. ∠1 and ∠2 are a pair of vertical angles. [p. 218]

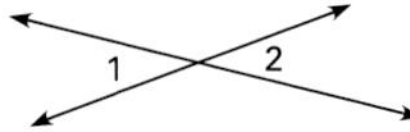

volume The amount of space taken up by a solid. [p. 567]

whole number A number in the set {0, 1, 2, 3, ...}.

***x*-axis** The horizontal line in an *x-y* coordinate system. [p. 443]

***x*-coordinate** The first number in an ordered pair. [p. 443]

***x-y* coordinate plane** A coordinate system for locating points based on two number lines, the *x*- and *y*-axes. [p. 443]

***y*-axis** The vertical line in an *x-y* coordinate system. [p. 443]

***y*-coordinate** The second number in an ordered pair. [p. 443]

zero pair A number and its opposite. Example: 23 and (–23) [p. 451]

GLOSSARY

693

Chapter 1

1-1 Try It (Examples 1–2)

Public service and trade

Try It (Examples 3–4)

A bar graph

1-1 Exercises & Applications

1. a. Ruiz; Hekla **b.** Colima and Etna **c.** Height in feet **3. a.** Bar graph **b.** Circle graph **c.** Circle graph **5.** C **7.** Gardening **13.** 16,002 **15.** 133 **17.** 938 **19.** 108

1-2 Try It

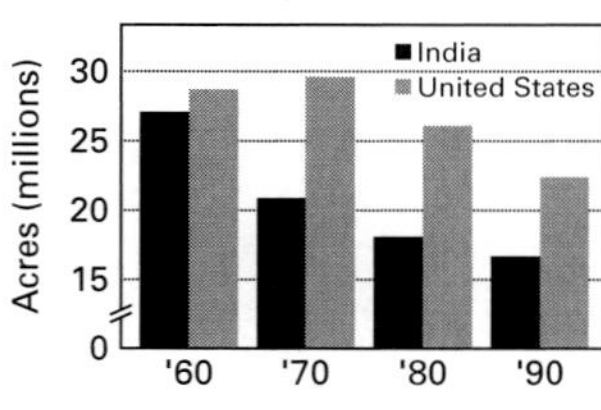

1-2 Exercises & Applications

1. a. 250,000,000 **b.** 50,000,000 **3.** B **5.** Possible answer: Scale 1000–5000, Interval 1000. **7.** Possible answer: Scale 120–360, Interval 40. **13.** four hundred twenty-eight **15.** forty-three thousand one hundred eighty-five **17.** three million seven hundred thirty-four thousand seven hundred ninety **19.** 16 **21.** 186

1-3 Try It

a.

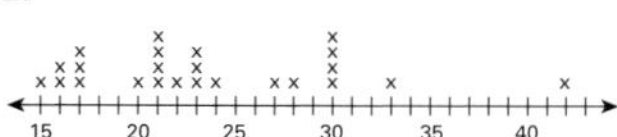

b.

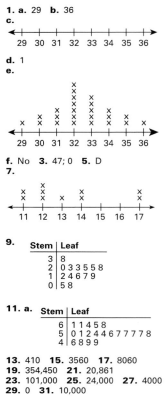

Stem	Leaf
4	2
3	0, 0, 0, 0, 3
2	0, 1, 1, 1, 1, 2, 3, 3, 3, 4, 7, 8
1	5, 6, 6, 7, 7, 7

1-3 Exercises & Applications

1. a. 29 **b.** 36

c.

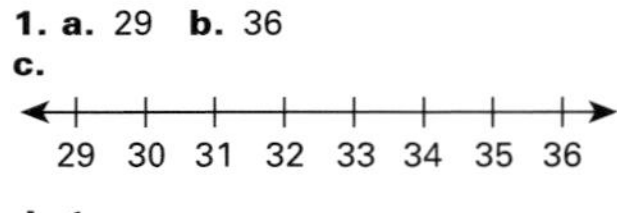

d. 1

e.

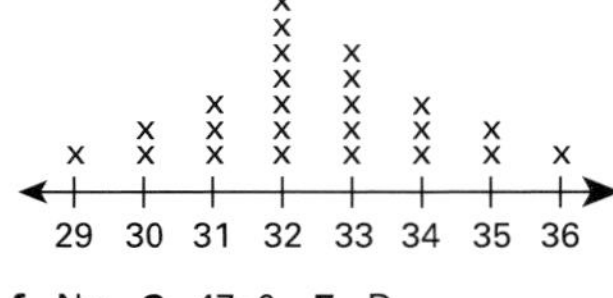

f. No **3.** 47; 0 **5.** D

7.

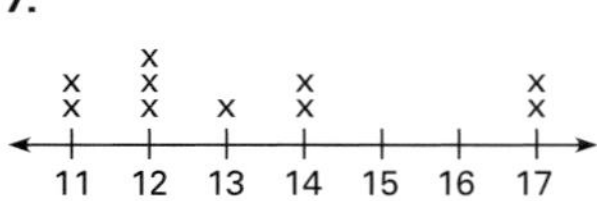

9.

Stem	Leaf
3	8
2	0 3 3 5 5 8
1	2 4 6 7 9
0	5 8

11. a.

Stem	Leaf
6	1 1 4 5 8
5	0 1 2 4 4 6 7 7 7 7 8
4	6 8 9 9

13. 410 **15.** 3560 **17.** 8060 **19.** 354,450 **21.** 20,861 **23.** 101,000 **25.** 24,000 **27.** 4000 **29.** 0 **31.** 10,000

1-4 Try It

a. Mean 38.4, median 41, range 45.
b. Mean 46, median 40.5, range 67.

1-4 Exercises & Applications

1. a. 5, 6, 17, 19, 23, 26, 34; Median is 19. **b.** 27, 38, 39, 45, 47, 48, 49, 52; Median is 46. **3. a.** Mean ≈ 59.7 in., median 59.5 in., range 7 in., mode 59 in. **5.** Mean ≈ 320.1; Median 321.5; Modes 320 and 327; Range 202. **7. a.** ≈ 6,000,000 people **9.** Mean 11.87, median 10, mode 6. **11.** C **17.** 9 R2 **19.** 97 R3 **21.** 6999; 7286; 8003 **23.** 28; 82; 288; 2228; 8282; 8822; 8882

Section 1A Review

1. 25% **3.** Yes

5.

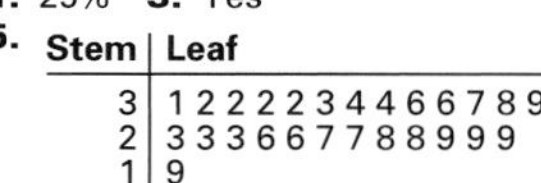

Stem	Leaf
3	1 2 2 2 2 3 4 4 6 6 7 8 9
2	3 3 3 6 6 7 7 8 8 9 9 9
1	9

7. China

1-5 Try It

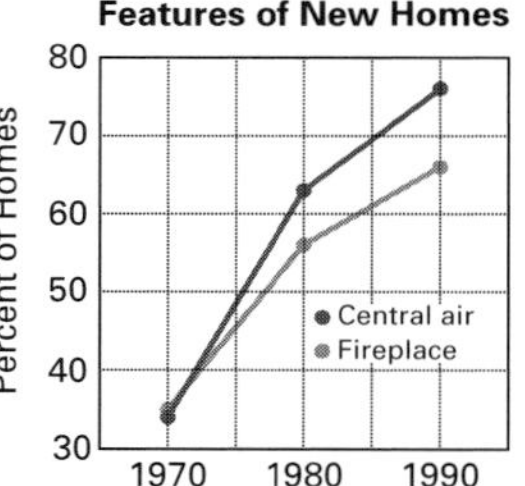

1-5 Exercises & Applications

1. An increasing trend—more nations compete each time.

3.

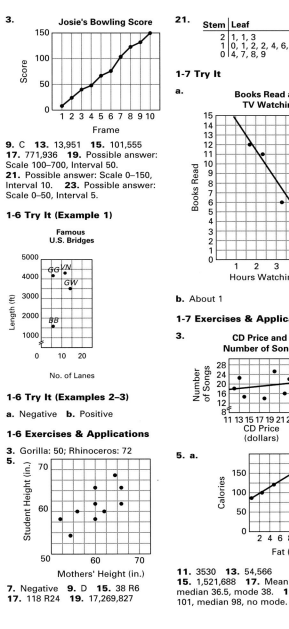

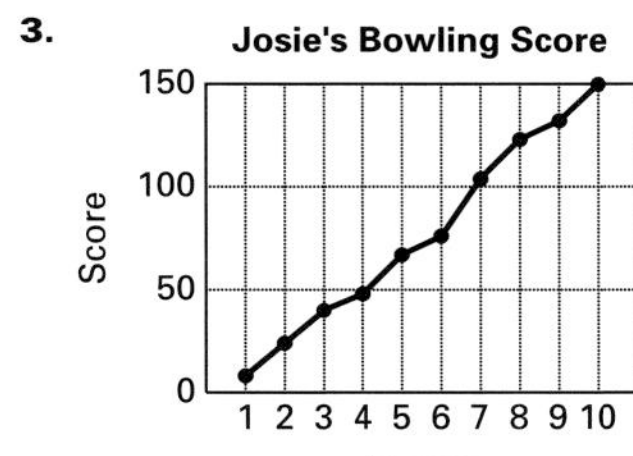

9. C **13.** 13,951 **15.** 101,555 **17.** 771,936 **19.** Possible answer: Scale 100–700, Interval 50. **21.** Possible answer: Scale 0–150, Interval 10. **23.** Possible answer: Scale 0–50, Interval 5.

1-6 Try It (Example 1)

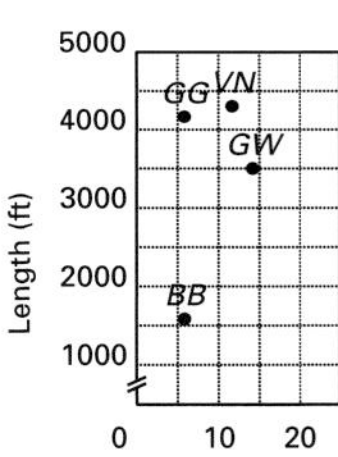

1-6 Try It (Examples 2–3)

a. Negative **b.** Positive

1-6 Exercises & Applications

3. Gorilla: 50; Rhinoceros: 72

5.

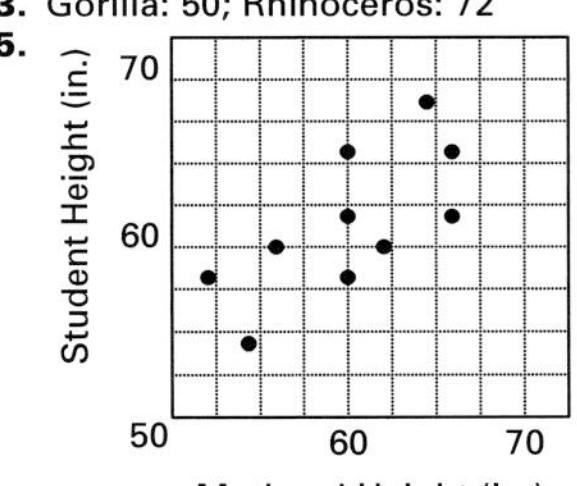

7. Negative **9.** D **15.** 38 R6 **17.** 118 R24 **19.** 17,269,827

21.

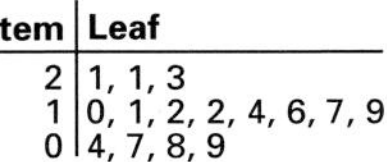

Stem	Leaf
2	1, 1, 3
1	0, 1, 2, 2, 4, 6, 7, 9
0	4, 7, 8, 9

1-7 Try It

a.

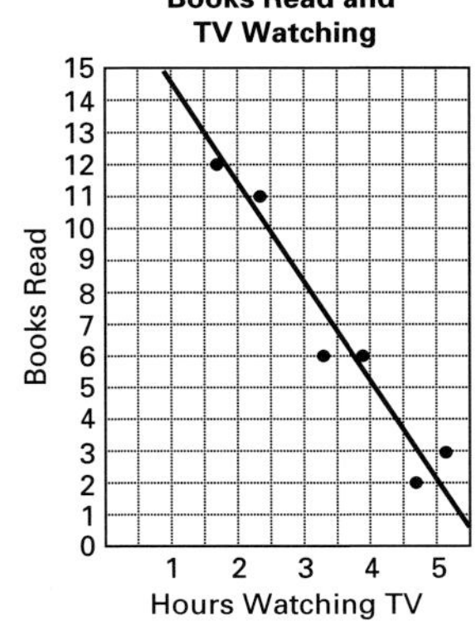

b. About 1

1-7 Exercises & Applications

3.

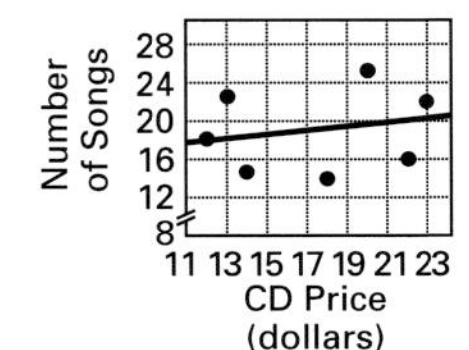

5. a.

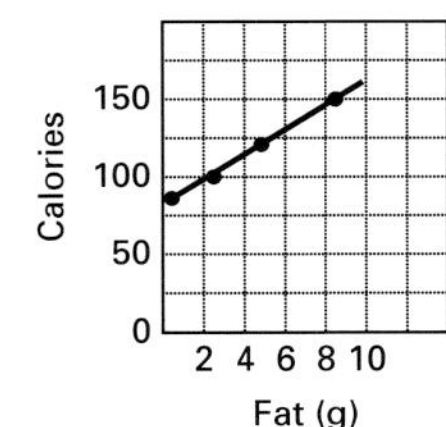

11. 3530 **13.** 54,566 **15.** 1,521,688 **17.** Mean 34.67, median 36.5, mode 38. **19.** Mean 101, median 98, no mode.

Section 1B Review

1. a.

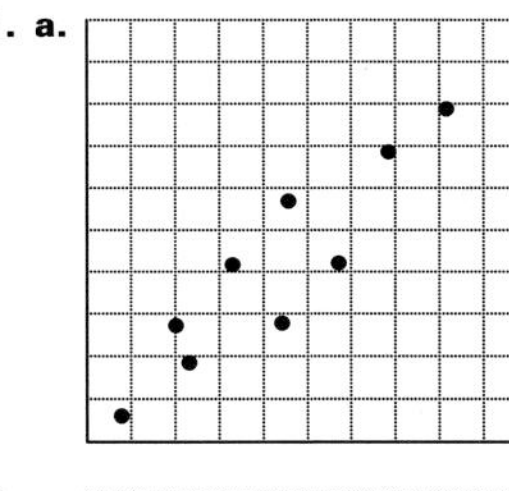

b.

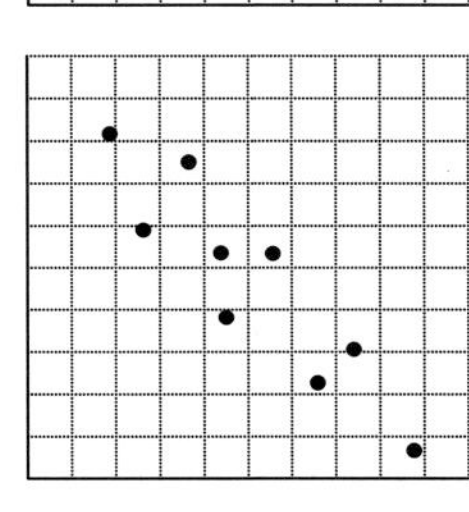

c.

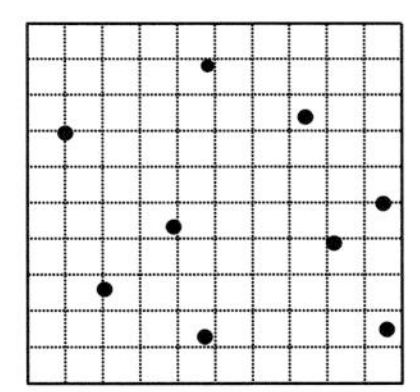

5.

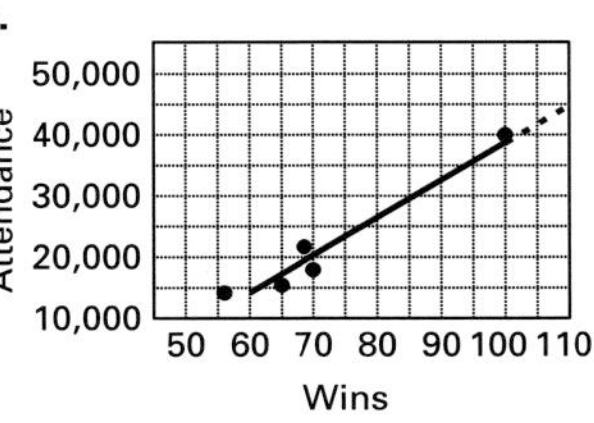

Chapter 1 Summary & Review

1.

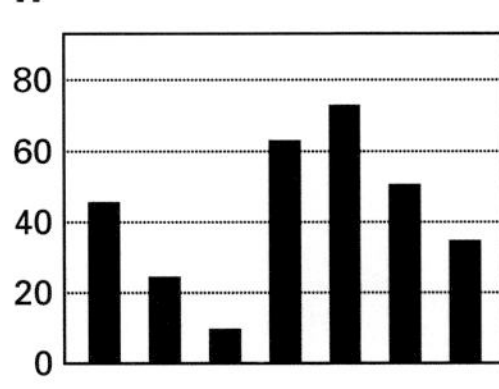

SELECTED ANSWERS

SELECTED ANSWERS

695

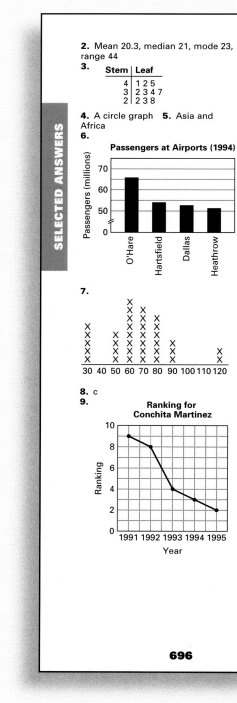

2. Mean 20.3, median 21, mode 23, range 44

3.

Stem	Leaf
4	1 2 5
3	2 3 4 7
2	2 3 8

4. A circle graph **5.** Asia and Africa

6.

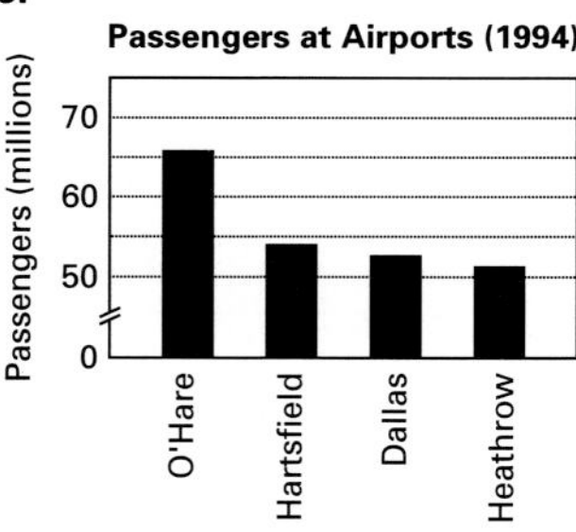

7.

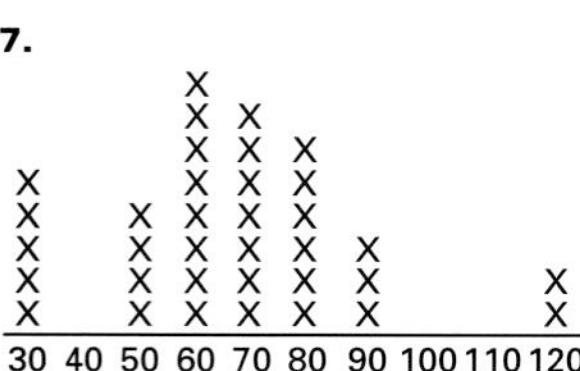

8. c

9.

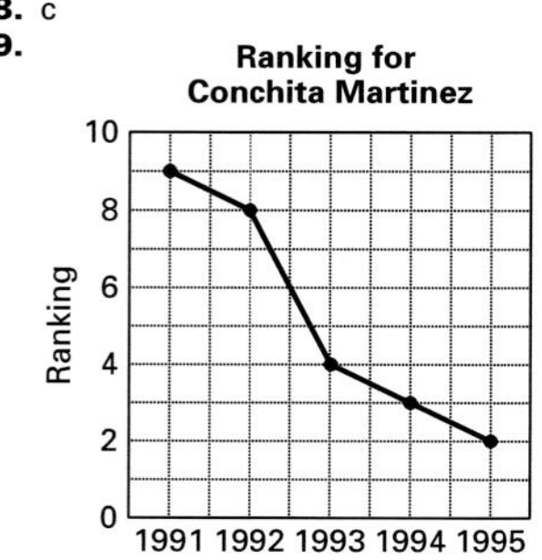

10.

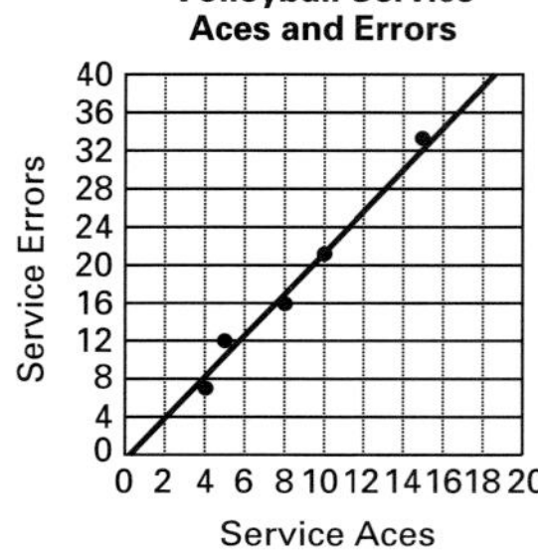

Chapter 2

2-1 Try It

a. 14 **b.** $160

2-1 Exercises & Applications

1. a. *p*, *l* and *w* **b.** 20 cm **3.** 230 m^2 **5.** 240 ft^2 **7.** ≈ 0.435 km/hr **9.** 0.6 km/hr **11.** 9 miles **13.** B **17.** 24,000 **19.** 7,500 **21.** 296,000 **23.** 74,600 **25.** 146,000 **27.** 3,820,000

2-2 Try It (Examples 1–2)

a. 7 **b.** 2 **c.** 14 **d.** 26

2-2 Try It (Example 3)

a. 2430 **b.** 2456 **c.** 2460

2-2 Exercises & Applications

1. Multiplication **3.** Division **5.** Yes; Parentheses **7.** Yes; Division bar **9.** 13 **11.** 89 **13.** 66 **15.** B **17.** $18 + 12 \div (3 + 1) = 21$ **19.** $7 \times (2 + 3 \times 6) = 140$ **21.** Associative Property of Multiplication **23.** Commutative Property of Multiplication **25.** Commutative Property of Multiplication **27. a.** $65.10 **b.** $65.10 **31.** 80 **33.** 190 **35.** 170 **37.** 220

2-3 Try It (Example 1)

s (in.)	2	3	5	8	10	12
A (in^2)	4	9	25	64	100	144

2-3 Try It (Example 2)

a. $y = 8x$ **b.** $n = m - 4$

2-3 Exercises & Applications

1. a. 72 **b.** 96

c.

Days	3	4	5	6	7	8
Hours	72	96	120	144	168	192

3.

C	0°	20°	40°	60°	80°	100°
K	273°	293°	313°	333°	353°	373°

5. $y = 5x$ **7.** $n = 6m$ **9.** $v = 0.1w$

11.

A	4	8	12	16
C	1	2	3	4

15. 50 **17.** 170 **19.** 270 **21.** 4600

Section 2A Review

1. 10 **3.** 7 **5.** 16 **7.** $9 \times (9 - 9) \div 9 = 0$ **9.** $(9 \times 9) - (9 \div 9) = 80$ **11.** 120 **13.** $y = 3x$ **16.** B

2-4 Try It

a. 12 **b.** Subtract 3, then multiply by 2

2-4 Exercises & Applications

1. Drive 5 mi west **3.** Run down 3 flights of stairs **5.** Subtract $4.50 **7.** 25, 30, 240, 30, 25 **9.** 44, 49, 392, 49, 44 **11.** Multiply by 4, subtract 7 **13.** Set his watch ahead 3 hours **15.** 2 **19.** 240 **21.** 1500 **23.** 52,000 **25.** 3,000,000 **27.** 1000 **29.** 125 **31.** 10,000 **33.** 100,000 **35.** 32,768

2-5 Try It (Examples 1–2)

a. $h \div 2$ **b.** $25 + *d* **c.** $d(v - 5)$

2-5 Try It (Examples 3–4)

a. Twelve decreased by a number (*g*) **b.** The sum of the products of 3 and a number (*a*) and 4 and a number (*b*) **c.** The product of 11 and the difference between 5 and a number (*r*).

SELECTED ANSWERS

2-5 Exercises & Applications

1. Subtraction **3.** Addition **5.** $2k$ **7.** $u - 4$ **9.** $2c + 8$ **11.** $4(n - 6)$ **13.** $3(x + 15)$ **15.** 6 decreased by a number (x) **17.** The sum of twice a number (r) and 3 **19.** Half a number (f) **21.** The product of 3 and the sum of a number (d) and 3 **23.** 4 more than the quotient of 3 and the sum of a number (c) and 2 **25. a.** $267n$ **b.** $267n - 25$ **27.** $5 + 2y$ **29. a.** $2x + 6$ **b.** $2(x + 3)$ **33.** 16 **35.** 4 **37.** 20 **39.** 40 **41.** $P = 102$ ft; $A = 620$ ft^2 **43.** $P = 204$ m; $A = 2480$ m^2

2-6 Try It

a. $x = 181$ **b.** $b + 67 = 122$; $b = 55$; $55

2-6 Exercises & Applications

1. Add 80 to both sides: $d - 80 + 80 = 70 + 80$ **3.** Subtract 16 from both sides: $f + 16 - 16 = 32 - 16$ **5.** Yes **7.** No **9.** $d = 9$ **11.** $f = 9$ **13.** $x = 88$ **15.** $p = 0$ **17.** $h = 68$ **19.** $f = 1000$ **21.** $g = 12$ **23.** $c = 149$ **25.** D **27.** $p - 25 = 180$ **29.** $n = 59 - 17$; $n = 42$ **31.** $n + 127 = 250$; $n = 123$ **33.** $t \approx 1400$ **35.** $s \approx 6000$ **37.** 13 was added to both sides. **39.** $h = 1300 - 115$, $h = 1185$ **41.** Add 17 **43.** Divide by 20 **45.** 7 **47.** 3 **49.** 16 **51.** 18

2-7 Try It

a. $x = 245$ **b.** $s = 222$ **c.** 120 kilowatts

2-7 Exercises & Applications

1. Divide both sides by 15: $15d \div 15 = 1200 \div 15$ **3.** Multiply both sides by 16: $\frac{f}{16} \times 16 = 32 \times 16$ **5.** No **7.** No **9.** $m = 2$ **11.** $p = 1$ **13.** $d = 15$ **15.** $y = 1$ **17.** $r = 21$ **19.** $h = 3484$ **21.** A **23.** Rectangle with 4 cm base has a height of 3 cm and rectangle with 6 cm base has a height of 2 cm. **25.** About 3,775,000 mi^2 **27.** $k \approx 30$ **29.** $t \approx 20{,}000$ **31.** C **35.** $n = 1235 \div 36$; $n \approx 34.31$; Hua must buy 35 rolls of film. **37.** About $\frac{1}{4}$ mi **41.** $2c - 3$ **43.** $r - 10$

2-8 Try It

a. $x = 51$ **b.** $5t + 48 = 73$. He worked 5 hours.

2-8 Exercises & Applications

1. Addition **3.** Subtraction **5.** $n = 1$ **7.** $u = 1$ **9.** $m = 7.5$ **11.** $s = 1$ **13.** $u = 4$ **15.** $s = 5$ **17.** $x = 7$ **19.** $s = 16$ **21.** $8 = 4 + 2x$; 2 oz **23. a.** 176 chirps per minute **b.** 16 chirps per minute **25.** No **27.** 4 days **29.** First 6 was subtracted from both sides, then both sides were multiplied by 4. **31.** $x = 26$ **33.** $x = 76$ **35.** $x = 63$ **37.** $x = 857$ **39.** $e = d + 4$ **41.** $y = 9x$

Section 2B Review

1. She unfastens her seatbelt, opens the door, stands up, gets out of the car, closes the door. **3.** $32 + y$ **5.** 28 decreased by a number (f) **7.** The product of 6 and the difference of g and 8 **9.** 1 **11.** 21 **15.** $k = 8$ **17.** $z = 38$ **19.** $x = 2$ **21.** $k = 49$ **23.** $m = 4$

Chapter 2 Summary & Review

1. 20 ft^2 **2.** It will cost $20 to travel 6 miles. **3.** 23 **4.** 10 **5.** Addition **6.** The distributive property **7.** $y = 4x$ **8.**

Time (t) in hr	0	1	2	3	4	5
Distance (d) in mi	0	40	80	120	160	200

9. Flying 260 miles south. **10.** Yes, $35 \div 5 = 7$ **11.** $d + 7 = 23$; $d = 16$ **12.** Multiplication by 11 **13.** No, $18 + 6 \neq 26$. **14.** $x = 13$ **15.** $a = 17$ **16.** $n = 96$ **17.** $x = 135$ **18.** $x = 120$ **19.** Division by 3, and subtraction of 18. **20. a.** $k + 21$ **b.** $10u$ **21.** $x = 7$ **22. a.** The product of 5 and a number (z). **b.** The product of 12 and 4 less than a number (j). **c.** The quotient of 5 more than a number (d) and 14.

Cumulative Review Chapters 1–2

1. B **2.** B **3.** C **4.** A **5.** B **6.** D **7.** C **8.** A **9.** C **10.** A

Chapter 3

3-1 Try It

a. $>$ **b.** $=$

3-1 Exercises & Applications

1. Thirty-six and five-tenths **3.** Four thousand, seven hundred ninety-two and six hundred thirty-nine thousandths **5.** $\frac{6}{100}$ **7.** $\frac{6}{10}$ **9.** 6 thousands, 6 hundreds, $\frac{6}{10}$, $\frac{6}{100}$ **11.** $<$ **13.** $<$ **15.** $<$ **17.** Greatest: 1993; Least: 1991 **19. a.** Country Yogurt **25.** 23, 29, 34, 43, 45, 46, 65, 78, 89; Median is 45 **27.** 2, 3, 3, 3, 4, 5, 5, 6, 6, 6, 7, 8, 8, 9; Median is 5.5 **29.** 7 less than a number (x) **31.** The product of 8 and 4 less than a number (n) **33.** The quotient of 3 more than a number (d) and 4 **35.** 5 reduced by a number (n)

3-2 Try It (Example 1)

7.9; 7.87; 7.865

3-2 Try It (Examples 2–4)

a. $\approx 68 - 32 = 36$ **b.** $\approx 10 \times 60 = 600$ **c.** $\approx 450 \div 90 \approx 5$

3-2 Exercises & Applications

1. 3.1 **3.** 17.5 **5.** 15 **7.** 10 **9.** 15, 1; 15 **11.** 2, 9; 18 **13.** ≈ 800 **15.** ≈ 9 **17.** ≈ 290 **19.** ≈ 240 **21.** ≈ 9600 **23.** ≈ 7 **25.** ≈ 2.5 **27.** ≈ 550 **29. a.** 23.38 **b.** 23.4 **c.** 23.383 **31. a.** 19.01 **b.** 19.0 **c.** 19.010 **33. a.** 0.05 **b.** 0.0 **c.** 0.046 **35. a.** 43.43 **b.** 43.4 **c.** 43.434 **37.** $\approx$ $240 **39.** B **41.** Mars: 0.2 years; Jupiter: 1.3 years; Saturn: 2.7 years; Neptune: 9.3 years **47.** $x = 22$ **49.** $m = 197$ **51.** $y = 3$ **53.** $n = 55$

3-3 Try It

a. $x = 13.1$ **b.** $x = 21.35$

SELECTED ANSWERS

697

3-3 Exercises & Applications

1. a. $42.4 > 42.268$ **d.** 0.132 **3.** ≈ 170 **5.** ≈ 0.4 **7.** ≈ 0.6 **9.** ≈ 0.01 **11.** ≈ 0.04 **13.** ≈ 0.26 **15.** $x = 84.304$ **17.** $x = 16.395$ **19.** $x = 0.015667$ **21.** A **23.** 2.3125 points **25.** Fuel used = 33.39 kg; Fuel remaining = 22.31 kg **31.** $v = 12$ **33.** $c = 140$ **35.** $w = 60$ **37.** $d = 72$

3-4 Try It (Example 1)

a. $x = 1.6173$ **b.** $x = 152.165$

3-4 Try It (Examples 2–3)

a. 34.5 **b.** 0.66

3-4 Try It (Example 4)

a. $x \approx 9.47$ **b.** $n \approx 197.95$

3-4 Exercises & Applications

1. a. $\frac{x}{9} \approx 4$; $x \approx 36$ **b.** 38.22 **c.** 38.22 and 36 are close, so the answer is reasonable. **3.** ≈ 36 **5.** ≈ 12.5 **7.** 2 **9.** 20 **11.** 0.5 **13.** ≈ 0.4 **15.** ≈ 0.004 **17.** ≈ 20 **19.** ≈ 24 **21.** ≈ 0.05 **23.** $u = 0.46552$ **25.** $x \approx 2.8147$ **27.** $a = 0.9968$ **29.** $k = 0.5068$ **31.** B **33.** $10.68 **35.** $w \approx 3.0698$ **37.** 364 **39.** 1 **41.** $g = 7$ **43.** $x = 14$ **45.** $w = 826$ **47.** $c = 306$

3-5 Try It

a. 3.17×10^{10} **b.** 9.6005×10^3 **c.** 410,000 **d.** 2,894,000,000,000

3-5 Exercises & Applications

1. a. 1.6120000 **b.** 7 **c.** 1.612×10^7 **3.** 9 **5.** 10,000 **7.** 9.37×10^9 **9.** 1.75×10^2 **11.** 1.01×10^9 **13.** 3.654×10^7 **15.** 9.9×10^{17} **17.** 2.43×10^8 **19.** C **21.** 600,000,000 **23.** 1,200,000,000,000 **25.** 498,000 **27.** 5,690,000 **29.** $18,157.69 **31.** 2.2744×10^9 **33.** $5,446 **37.** Subtract 5 **39.** Sit down **41.** 12.0 **43.** 6.5 **45.** 109 **47.** 88

Section 3A Review

1. a. $>$ **b.** $<$ **c.** $=$ **3.** ≈ 69 **5.** ≈ 82 **7.** 2 **9.** 0.2 **11.** $x \approx 9$; $x = 8.96$ **13.** $x \approx 5.3$; $x \approx 4.90$ **15. a.** 1.21×10^4 **b.** 5.206×10^6 **c.** 4.86×10^9 **19.** About $6 **21.** C

3-6 Try It (Example 2)

a. 2, 3, 4, and 6 **b.** 5 **c.** 2, 4, and 8 **d.** 2, 3, 6, and 9

3-6 Try It (Example 3)

a. $2^2 \times 31$ **b.** $3^2 \times 7$ **c.** $2^2 \times 7 \times 11$ **d.** $2 \times 3 \times 17$

3-6 Exercises & Applications

1. No **3.** Yes **5.** Yes **7.** Yes **9.** 3 **11.** 3, 5, and 9 **13.** 2, 4, 5, 8, and 10 **15.** 2, 3, 6, and 9 **17.** Composite **19.** Composite **21.** Composite **23.** Composite **25.** 2×3^2 **27.** 5×37 **29.** $2^3 \times 3^2 \times 5$ **31.** $3^2 \times 5^3$ **33.** C **35.** 1, 2, 3, 6, 7, 9, 14, 18, 21, 27, 42, 54, 63, 126, and 189 seconds **43.** 1,758,289,144

45.

Stem	Leaf
4	13
3	18
2	369
1	57

47.

Stem	Leaf
11	7
10	35
9	459
8	67

49. $>$ **51.** $<$ **53.** $>$ **55.** $>$

3-7 Try It (Example 2)

a. 18 **b.** 24 **c.** 13 **d.** 2

3-7 Try It (Examples 3–4)

a. 15 **b.** 48 **c.** 60 **d.** 63

3-7 Exercises & Applications

1. a. 1, 2, 3, 6, 7, 14, 21, 42 **b.** 1, 3, 7, 9, 21, 63 **c.** 1, 3, 7, 21 **d.** 21 **3.** 12 **5.** 17 **7.** 54 **9.** 81 **11.** 45 **13.** 60 **15.** 56 **17.** 120 **19.** The 300th customer **21.** 85 bars **31.** ≈ 160 **33.** ≈ 0.28 **35.** ≈ 4 **37.** ≈ 100

3-8 Try It (Example 1)

Possible answers: **a.** $\frac{2}{3}, \frac{12}{18}$ **b.** $\frac{5}{6}, \frac{50}{60}$ **c.** $\frac{5}{6}, \frac{30}{36}$ **d.** $\frac{5}{7}, \frac{30}{42}$

3-8 Try It (Example 2)

a. No **b.** No **c.** Yes **d.** Yes

3-8 Exercises & Applications

1. a. 1, 2, 4, 8, 16 **b.** 1, 2, 3, 4, 6, 8, 12, 24 **c.** GCF = 8 **d.** $\frac{2}{3}$ **3.** $\frac{5}{9}, \frac{30}{54}$ **5.** $\frac{8}{11}, \frac{32}{44}$ **7.** $\frac{2}{3}$ **9.** $\frac{7}{9}$ **11.** $\frac{4}{5}$ **13.** $\frac{2}{3}$ **15.** $\frac{3}{4}$ **17.** $\frac{3}{4}$ **19.** $\frac{2}{3}$ **21.** $\frac{1}{7}$ **23.** $\frac{13}{27}$ **25.** $\frac{18}{25}$ **27.** $\frac{5}{22}$ **29.** $\frac{24}{53}$ **31.** C **33.** About $\frac{11}{20}$ **35.** $x = 21$ **37.** $x = 75$ **41.** $t = 9$ **43.** $x = 2$ **45.** $n = 204$ **47.** $y = 408$ **49.** 31 **51.** 470 **53.** 87 **55.** 56

3-9 Try It

a. $>$ **b.** $>$ **c.** $<$

3-9 Exercises & Applications

1. a. $\frac{48}{56}$ **b.** $\frac{49}{56}$ **c.** $\frac{7}{8} > \frac{6}{7}$ **3.** $=$ **5.** $<$ **7.** $>$ **9.** $>$ **11.** $=$ **13.** $=$ **15.** $=$ **17.** $=$ **27.** 4.756×10^5 **29.** 9.3×10^7 **31.** 8.3×10^2 **33.** 5.0×10 **35.** 46,000 **37.** 620,000,000 **39.** 347,000 **41.** 749,000,000,000,000 **43.** $\frac{25}{51}$

3-10 Try It (Example 1)

a. $\frac{3}{10}$ **b.** $\frac{3}{4}$ **c.** $\frac{46}{125}$

3-10 Try It (Examples 2–3)

a. 0.85; terminating **b.** $0.\overline{6}$; repeating **c.** 0.28125; terminating

3-10 Exercises & Applications

1. a. $\frac{25}{1000}$ **b.** $\frac{1}{40}$ **3.** $\frac{3}{25}$ **5.** $\frac{1}{25}$ **7.** $\frac{27}{250}$ **9.** $\frac{203}{250}$ **11.** $0.\overline{571428}$, repeating **13.** $0.\overline{6}$, repeating **15.** 0.8, terminating **17.** 0.52, terminating

SELECTED ANSWERS

698

19. C **21.** $\frac{5}{6}$ **23.** $\frac{2}{11}$ **27.** 63.25
29. 56.625
31.

Gallons	1	2	3	4	5
Miles	36	72	108	144	180

Section 3B Review

1. $<$ **3.** $>$ **5.** $>$ **7.** $>$ **9.** $w = 8.5$ **11.** $c = 26.72$ **13.** 2×3^3 **15.** $5^2 \times 7$ **17.** $2^4 \times 3^2$ **19.** GCF: 9; LCM: 810 **21.** GCF: 27; LCM: 810

23. $\frac{1}{32}$; one thirty-second

25. $0.\overline{428571}$ **27.** $0.\overline{6}$

Chapter 3 Summary & Review

1. 400, $\frac{4}{1000}$ **2.** $8.041 > 8.04$
3. 18.64 **4.** ≈ 840 **5.** ≈ 6
6. 343.615 **7.** $y = 43.783$
8. 29.555 **9.** $e = 58.824$ **10.** $p = 45.3$ **11.** 723,400 **12.** 1.739×10^6
13. 2, 3, 5, 6, and 10 **14.** $2^2 \times 3 \times 23$ **15.** 5 **16.** 60 **17.** Possible answer: $\frac{5}{6}, \frac{30}{36}$ **18.** $\frac{1}{4}$ **19.** $\frac{5}{11}$
20. $\frac{24}{31} > \frac{23}{31}$ **21.** $\frac{9}{16} > \frac{5}{9}$ **22.** $\frac{6}{25}$
23. $\frac{66}{125}$ **24.** $0.\overline{81}$; the decimal repeats

Chapter 4

4-1 Try It (Example 1)

a. $\approx \frac{1}{2}$ **b.** ≈ 1 **c.** ≈ 2

4-1 Try It (Example 2)

a. ≈ 9 **b.** ≈ 4 **c.** ≈ 21

4-1 Try It (Examples 3–4)

a. ≈ 5 **b.** ≈ 5 **c.** ≈ 176

4-1 Exercises & Applications

1. $\frac{1}{2}$ **3.** 0 **5.** 0 **7.** $\approx \frac{1}{2}$ **9.** ≈ 0
11. ≈ 1 **13.** $\approx \frac{1}{2}$ **15.** ≈ 1
17. ≈ 12 **19.** ≈ 1 **21.** ≈ 14
23. ≈ 4 **25.** ≈ 4 **27.** ≈ 8
29. ≈ 7 **31.** ≈ 9 **33.** 30–35 times
35. ≈ 5 pieces **39.** South; Mountain **41.** $>$ **43.** $>$ **45.** $<$

4-2 Try It

a. $d = \frac{7}{12}$ **b.** $w = \frac{14}{15}$ **c.** $h = \frac{1}{3}$

4-2 Exercises & Applications

1. As written **3.** Rewritten **5.** As written **7.** 12 **9.** 24 **11.** 20
13. $\frac{4}{5}$ **15.** $\frac{7}{8}$ **17.** $\frac{5}{12}$ **19.** $\frac{13}{18}$ **21.** $\frac{1}{2}$
23. $y = \frac{2}{9}$ **25.** $n = \frac{9}{28}$ **27.** $\frac{7}{8}$
29. A **31.** Stock A **33.** $p = 7$
35. $u \approx 7.\overline{09}$ **37.** $a = 996$ **39.** $x = 2976$ **41.** ≈ 49 **43.** ≈ 1260
45. ≈ 111 **47.** ≈ 1500 **49.** ≈ 55
51. ≈ 470 **53.** ≈ 130 **55.** ≈ 5000

4-3 Try It

a. $8\frac{1}{8}$ **b.** $1\frac{2}{3}$ **c.** $3\frac{9}{10}$

4-3 Exercises & Applications

1. $3\frac{3}{7}$ **3.** $3\frac{7}{9}$ **5.** $4\frac{7}{8}$ **7.** $\frac{25}{8}$ **9.** $\frac{31}{4}$
11. $\frac{55}{8}$ **13.** $4\frac{1}{4}$ **15.** $2\frac{2}{7}$ **17.** $6\frac{4}{5}$
19. $2\frac{7}{8}$ **21.** $n = 3\frac{5}{21}$ **23.** $y = 6\frac{13}{20}$
25. **a.** $1\frac{4}{5}$ in. **b.** $1\frac{3}{4}$ in. **27.** $5\frac{1}{5}$ AU
29. **a.** $\frac{1}{8}$ **b.** $\frac{1}{16}$ **33.** $d = 50$ mi

35. $d = 375$ km **37.** $d = 220$ mi

39. $x = 68.86$ **41.** $x = 45.56$

43. $p = 0.049$

Section 4A Review

1. ≈ 1 **3.** $\approx 1\frac{1}{2}$ **5.** ≈ 0 **7.** ≈ 8
9. ≈ 21 **11.** $\frac{19}{24}$ **13.** $\frac{43}{45}$ **15.** $8\frac{1}{5}$
17. $4\frac{4}{5}$ **19.** $6\frac{5}{8}$ **21.** $z = 3\frac{7}{20}$
23. $x = 9\frac{7}{8}$ **25.** 2 ft $5\frac{1}{4}$ in. **27.** D

4-4 Try It (Examples 1–2)

a. $\frac{15}{56}$ **b.** $\frac{2}{3}$ **c.** $\frac{1}{4}$ **d.** $\frac{1}{6}$ **e.** $\frac{1}{10}$

4-4 Try It (Examples 3–4)

a. $\frac{8}{9}$ **b.** $\frac{1}{3}$ **c.** $\frac{27}{125}$ **d.** $\frac{1}{2}$ **e.** $\frac{1}{4}$

4-4 Exercises & Applications

1. $\frac{1}{3}$ **3.** $\frac{8}{45}$ **5.** $\frac{3}{20}$ **7.** $\frac{2}{5}$ **9.** $\frac{1}{3}$
11. $\frac{3}{10}$ **13.** $\frac{1}{7}$ **15.** $\frac{1}{6}$ **17.** $\frac{1}{4}$ **19.** $\frac{5}{14}$
21. $\frac{4}{25}$ **23.** $\frac{3}{14}$ **25.** $\frac{1}{5}$ **27.** B
29. $\approx 13{,}000$ **31.** $1\frac{1}{3}$ **37.** $p = 1.15$
39. $u = 3.8$ **41.** $x = 2.65$
43. $y = 9.26$

4-5 Try It

a. 18 **b.** 6 **c.** $4\frac{1}{2}$ **d.** $16\frac{1}{2}$ **e.** $17\frac{1}{3}$

4-5 Exercises & Applications

1. $\frac{27}{8}$ **3.** $\frac{71}{8}$ **5.** $\frac{13}{6}$ **7.** 14
9. 16 **11.** 16 **13.** 56 **15.** 9
17. $6\frac{2}{3}$ **19.** $73\frac{1}{8}$ **21.** $3\frac{23}{27}$ **23.** $43\frac{1}{2}$
25. $9\frac{2}{7}$ **29.** 26 **31.** $6\frac{3}{8}$ grams
39. 1.8×10^1 **41.** 4.21×10^7
43. 1.27×10^8 **45.** 1.933×10^4
47. 2.7×10^2 **49.** 9.3×10^7

4-6 Try It

a. 35 **b.** $\frac{3}{4}$ **c.** $1\frac{1}{3}$

4-6 Exercises & Applications

1. 2 **3.** $\frac{10}{3}$ **5.** 4 **7.** $\frac{7}{2}; \frac{2}{7}$ **9.** $\frac{19}{4}; \frac{4}{19}$
11. $\frac{3}{8} \times 4 = 1\frac{1}{2}$ **13.** $\frac{3}{5} \times 3 = 1\frac{4}{5}$
15. $\frac{5}{8} \times \frac{2}{7} = \frac{5}{28}$ **17.** $\frac{12}{5} \times \frac{6}{5} = 2\frac{22}{25}$
19. $\frac{5}{7}$ **21.** $2\frac{1}{2}$ **23.** $1\frac{25}{44}$ **25.** $4\frac{13}{20}$
27. C **29.** $13\frac{1}{3}$ or 14 hats

31. Possible answer: A whole number is the sum of that many ones. A proper fraction is less than one, so there must be more of them contained in the whole number.

33. **a.** $x = 1\frac{5}{9}$ **b.** $x = 8\frac{8}{25}$ **37.** 2, 3, 6 **39.** 2, 5, 10

Section 4B Review

1. $\frac{5}{21}$ **3.** $3\frac{7}{8}$ **5.** $\frac{1}{8}$ **7.** $1\frac{7}{10}$ **9.** $\frac{7}{12}$
11. $1\frac{2}{25}$ **13.** $5\frac{4}{9}$ **15.** 2 **17.** $\frac{1}{8}$
19. $\frac{8}{25}$ **21.** $\frac{203}{325}$ **23.** $\frac{65}{96}$ **25.** ≈ 42 ft
27. A

Chapter 4 Summary & Review

1. $\approx 1\frac{1}{2}$ **2.** ≈ 0 **3.** ≈ 5
4. ≈ 29 **5.** $1\frac{17}{30}$ **6.** $\frac{13}{18}$ **7.** $\frac{19}{60}$
8. $\frac{31}{8}$ **9.** $9\frac{3}{8}$ **10.** $5\frac{13}{15}$ **11.** $\frac{6}{11}$
12. $1\frac{3}{7}$ **13.** $\frac{5}{16}$ ft^2 **14.** 36 yr
15. 18 **16.** $61\frac{39}{40}$ **17.** $\frac{9}{16}$
18. $1\frac{13}{55}$ **19.** $41\frac{2}{3}$ or 42 disks
20. 8

SELECTED ANSWERS

699

SELECTED ANSWERS

Cumulative Review Chapters 1–4

1. C **2.** C **3.** B **4.** C **5.** B **6.** C **7.** B **8.** C **9.** C **10.** B **11.** A **12.** D **13.** C **14.** C

Chapter 5

5-1 Try It

Complement: 47°; Supplement: 137°

5-1 Exercises & Applications

3. $\angle XYZ$; 140° **5.** $\angle LMN$; 100° **7.** None; 45° **9.** 56°; 146° **11.** 145° **13.** 13° **15.** Obtuse **17.** Acute **19.** A **23.** $<$ **25.** $>$ **27.** $>$ **29.** $>$ **31.** GCF = 5; LCM = 2805 **33.** GCF = 12; LCM = 672 **35.** GCF = 33; LCM = 2178 **37.** GCF = 4; LCM = 504

5-2 Try It (Example 1)

a. Corresponding **b.** Vertical **c.** Alternate Interior **d.** 59° **e.** 121° **f.** 121° **g.** 59°

5-2 Try It (Example 2)

a. The midpoint of the shorter "stick" is at the point where it is intersected by the longer one.
b. The longer stick is the perpendicular bisector of the shorter; The longer stick intersects the shorter at its midpoint and forms a right angle.

5-2 Exercises & Applications

1. Parallel **3.** Perpendicular **5.** Parallel **7.** Perpendicular **9.** Perpendicular **11.** $\overleftrightarrow{EF}$ and $\overleftrightarrow{GH}$ **13.** Possible answer: $\angle 1$ and $\angle 2$ **19.** A **25.** ≈ 85 **27.** ≈ 15 **29.** ≈ 35 **31.** ≈ 1000 **33.** $\frac{1}{3}$ **35.** $\frac{6}{13}$ **37.** $\frac{24}{35}$ **39.** $\frac{9}{16}$

5-3 Try It

a. 90°

5-3 Exercises & Applications

1. a. Known: 87°, 76°, 98°; Unknown: m **b.** $87 + 76 + 98 + m = 360$ **c.** $261 - 261 + m = 360 - 261$ **d.** 99 **3.** Right scalene **5.** Right isosceles **7.** Quadrilateral, parallelogram **9.** Quadrilateral, rectangle, parallelogram **11.** Quadrilateral, rhombus, parallelogram **13.** $t =$ 38° **15.** $x =$ 177° **21.** $y = 31.95$ **23.** $x = 12.78$ **25.** $k = 106.575$ **27.** $>$ **29.** $<$ **31.** $<$ **33.** $<$

5-4 Try It

a. 1080° **b.** 1800°

5-4 Exercises & Applications

1. Regular hexagon **3.** Nonregular quadrilateral **5.** Sides are not congruent. **7.** Sides and angles not congruent. **11.** 900° **13.** 3240° **17.** C **19.** 13 **21.** 108° **23.** 135° **27.** $m = 3.6$ **29.** $y = 1.46$ **31.** $x = 9.84$ **33.** $b = 12.8$ **35.** $0.\overline{4375}$; Terminates **37.** $0.\overline{428571}$; Repeats **39.** 0.13125; Terminates **41.** 0.875; Terminates

5-5 Try It

a. 268 ft **b.** 4200 ft^2

5-5 Exercises & Applications

1. a. 48 ft **b.** $A = 14$ ft × 10 ft **c.** 140 ft^2 **3.** P: 80 m; A: 364 m^2 **5.** P: 346 yd; A: 6360 yd^2 **7.** P: 9,232 ft; A: 5,270,220 ft^2 **9.** P: 42 ft; A: 108 ft^2 **11.** 2760 m^2 **17.** 10% **19.** ≈ 12 **21.** ≈ 16 **23.** ≈ 12 **25.** ≈ 34 **27.** ≈ 35

Section 5A Review

1. 143° **3.** 13° **5.** Nonregular hexagon **7.** 1260° **9.** 2520° **11.** P: 800 ft; A: 33,600 ft^2

5-6 Try It (Example 1)

a. 9 **b.** 11 **c.** 15 **d.** 100 **e.** 8

5-6 Try It (Examples 2–3)

a. 9.22 **b.** 6.40 **c.** 8.54 **d.** 9.49 **e.** 17.32

5-6 Exercises & Applications

1. 16 **3.** 625 **5.** 81 **7.** 0.0121 **9.** $\frac{9}{64}$ **11.** Yes **13.** Yes **15.** No **17.** 10 **19.** 9 **21.** 15 **23.** 100 **25.** 25 **27.** 23.32 **29.** 27.04 **31.** 9.90 **33.** 7.55 **35.** 3.46 **37.** 1 **39.** ≈ 115 ft **41.** B **43.** 36 and 64 **47.** $\frac{1}{6}$ **49.** $\frac{43}{75}$ **51.** $1\frac{1}{80}$ **53.** $\frac{87}{91}$ **55.** $\frac{11}{60}$ **57.** $\frac{189}{1100}$

5-7 Try It

a. $c = 25$ ft **b.** $b \approx 10.39$ ft

5-7 Exercises & Applications

1. Hypotenuse r; legs p and q **3.** Hypotenuse s; legs t and u **5.** $j^2 + h^2 = k^2$ **7.** $w^2 + v^2 = u^2$ **9.** Yes **11.** No **13.** $a = 9$ in. **15.** $y = 35$ cm **17.** ≈ 127.3 ft **19.** C **25.** $20\frac{7}{48}$ **27.** $22\frac{18}{35}$ **29.** $3\frac{51}{70}$ **31.** $36\frac{1}{21}$

5-8 Try It

a. 42 in^2 **b.** 152 in^2 **c.** 60 ft^2

5-8 Exercises & Applications

1. a. 9 **b.** 4 **c.** 36 **d.** 18 sq. units **3.** $62\frac{1}{2}$ ft^2 **5.** $6\frac{2}{3}$ in^2 **7.** 22 ft^2 **9.** 810 m^2 **11.** 18 ft **13.** 90 in. **15.** 18 yd **17.** 26 in. **19.** 7 in^2 **25.** 3 **27.** 5 **29.** 2, 4 **31.** None **33.** $\frac{7}{12}$ **35.** $\frac{7}{15}$ **37.** $\frac{2}{9}$ **39.** $\frac{56}{225}$ **41.** $\frac{55}{96}$ **43.** 1

5-9 Try It (Example 1)

a. $\frac{15}{4}$ in^2 **b.** 253 m^2 **c.** 2.88 km^2

5-9 Try It (Example 3)

a. 19.5 in^2 **b.** 13.25 cm^2 **c.** 8.4375 in^2

5-9 Exercises & Applications

1. Height n; base m **3.** Height x; base y **5.** $A = \frac{1}{2}h(b_1 + b_2)$ **7.** $A = bh$ **9.** 175.2 cm^2 **11.** $\frac{2}{9}$ in^2 **13.** 96 cm^2 **15.** $\frac{9}{16}$ in^2 **17.** 64 cm^2 **19.** A **25.** GCF = 2; LCM = 2376 **27.** GCF = 42; LCM = 840 **29.** GCF = 30; LCM = 13,260 **31.** GCF = 30; LCM = 3780

700

33. $18\frac{6}{7}$ **35.** $55\frac{1}{4}$ **37.** $16\frac{11}{18}$
39. $14\frac{7}{12}$

5-10 Try It

700 ft^2

5-10 Exercises & Applications

1. c. Area = 39 m^2 **3.** 328 ft^2 **5.** 615 in^2 **7.** 690 yd^2 **9.** 191.5 in^2 **11.** 6144 m^2 **13.** 864 in^2 **15.** $\frac{5}{7}$ **17.** $\frac{2}{9}$ **19.** $\frac{21}{32}$ **21.** $\frac{13}{25}$ **23.** $\frac{27}{56}$ **25.** 4 **27.** $\frac{55}{108}$ **29.** $\frac{5}{12}$

Section 5B Review

1. Perimeter = 74 m; Area = 300 m^2 **3.** Perimeter = $15\frac{1}{4}$ in.; Area = $14\frac{7}{32}$ in^2 **5.** 11 **7.** $\frac{81}{100}$ **9.** 30 in. **11.** 2 yd **13.** 17.1 cm^2 **15.** 0.9 mi^2 **19.** A

Chapter 5 Summary & Review

1.

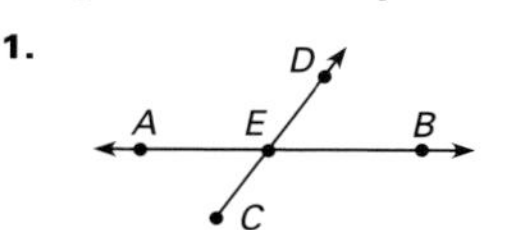

2. 1440° **3. a.** 132° **b.** 42° **4.** $\angle EFD$, an alternate interior angle **5.** Area: 24 ft^2; Perimeter: 20 ft **6.** Right; acute; obtuse **7.** 49 **8.** 4.123 **9.** 10 ft **10.** 28 cm^2 **11.** 5.425 cm^2 **12.** 260 ft^2

Chapter 6

6-1 Try It

1:2

6-1 Exercises & Applications

1. a. 12 **b.** 36 **c.** $\frac{12}{36}$; $\frac{1}{3}$ **3.** $\frac{7}{8}$; 7:8; 7 to 8 **5.** $\frac{4}{3}$; 4:3; 4 to 3 **7.** 44; 44:1; 44 to 1 **9.** $\frac{37}{1}$ **11.** $\frac{22}{70}$ **13.** $\frac{29}{99}$ **15.** 1:7 **17.** B **21.** 40 sec **23.** Obtuse; 133°

6-2 Try It

a. $\frac{1}{4}$ inch per hour **b.** $8.42 for 5 videotapes

6-2 Exercises & Applications

1. a. $\frac{480}{8}$ **b.** $\frac{60}{1}$ **c.** 60 miles per hour **3.** $\frac{65 \text{ miles}}{2 \text{ gallons}} = \frac{32.5 \text{ miles}}{1 \text{ gallon}}$ **5.** $4.00 per notebook **7.** 3 cookies per student **9.** $5.50 per hour of work **11.** $2.07 for 3 baskets **13.** $3.36 for 24 slices **15.** No **17.** Yes **19.** No **21.** $\frac{12}{1000} = \frac{3}{250}$ **23.** 108,000 mi/hr **25.** A **29.** 144 **31.** 13 **33.** 9 **35.** 8 **37.** $\overleftrightarrow{AD}$ and $\overleftrightarrow{AC}$

6-3 Try It

a. Possible answer: $\frac{3}{7}$ and $\frac{12}{28}$
b. 2 cups

6-3 Exercises & Applications

1–11. Possible answers given.
1. a. 2 **b.** $\frac{16}{40}$ **c.** 4 **d.** $\frac{4}{10}$ **3.** $\frac{20}{28}$; $\frac{5}{7}$ **5.** $\frac{44}{48}$; $\frac{11}{12}$ **7.** $\frac{54}{90}$; $\frac{3}{5}$ **9.** $\frac{80}{150}$; $\frac{8}{15}$ **11.** $\frac{200}{350}$; $\frac{4}{7}$ **13.** 1000 pesetas **15.** 60 sec **17.** 720; $\frac{720 \text{ frames}}{30 \text{ seconds}}$ **21.** $<$ **23.** $<$ **25.** $>$ **27.** $<$ **29.** Right isosceles

6-4 Try It

$\frac{4}{10}$; $\frac{6}{15}$; $\frac{8}{20}$; $\frac{10}{25}$; $\frac{12}{30}$

6-4 Exercises & Applications

1. a–d.

4	8	12	16	20	24
7	14	21	28	35	42

3. $\frac{24}{36}$; $\frac{16}{24}$; $\frac{12}{18}$; $\frac{8}{12}$; $\frac{6}{9}$ **5.** $\frac{16}{32}$; $\frac{4}{8}$; $\frac{1}{2}$; $\frac{64}{128}$ **7.** 11 video games **15.** B **19.** $\frac{1}{4}$ **21.** $\frac{671}{1000}$ **23.** $\frac{19}{50}$ **25.** $\frac{617}{5000}$ **27.** 540°

Section 6A Review

1. 1:5 **3.** $\frac{1}{7}$ **5.** $\frac{5}{6}$ **7.** 21 push-ups per minute **9.** $2.22 for 2 baskets

6-5 Try It

a. Missing table entries are 10, 15, 20; $\frac{2}{5} = \frac{4}{10}$; $\frac{2}{5} = \frac{6}{15}$; $\frac{2}{5} = \frac{8}{20}$
b. $\frac{3 \text{ gray whales}}{8 \text{ killer whales}} = \frac{6 \text{ gray whales}}{16 \text{ killer whales}}$, $\frac{3 \text{ gray whales}}{8 \text{ killer whales}} = \frac{9 \text{ gray whales}}{24 \text{ killer whales}}$

6-5 Exercises & Applications

1. a–b.

2	4	6	8
7	14	21	28

c. $\frac{2}{7} = \frac{4}{14}$; $\frac{2}{7} = \frac{6}{21}$; $\frac{2}{7} = \frac{8}{28}$

3.

5	10	20	50
9	18	36	90

$\frac{5}{9} = \frac{10}{18}$; $\frac{5}{9} = \frac{20}{36}$; $\frac{5}{9} = \frac{50}{90}$; $\frac{10}{18} = \frac{20}{36}$

5.

7	14	21	28
8	16	24	32

$\frac{7}{8} = \frac{14}{16}$; $\frac{7}{8} = \frac{21}{24}$; $\frac{7}{8} = \frac{28}{32}$

7.

13	26	39	52
15	30	45	60

$\frac{13}{15} = \frac{26}{30}$; $\frac{13}{15} = \frac{39}{45}$; $\frac{13}{15} = \frac{52}{60}$

9.

10	20	30	40
14	28	42	56

$\frac{10}{14} = \frac{20}{28}$; $\frac{10}{14} = \frac{30}{42}$; $\frac{10}{14} = \frac{40}{56}$

11.

2	4	6	8
100	200	300	400

$\frac{2}{100} = \frac{4}{200}$; $\frac{2}{100} = \frac{6}{300}$; $\frac{2}{100} = \frac{8}{400}$

13.

17	34	51	68
19	38	57	76

$\frac{17}{19} = \frac{34}{38}$; $\frac{17}{19} = \frac{51}{57}$; $\frac{17}{19} = \frac{68}{76}$ **19.** C **23.** $x = 10$; $y = 63$ **25.** $g = 100$; $h = 144$ **37.** P = 68 ft; A = 280 ft^2 **39.** P = 34 m; A = 72 m^2

6-6 Try It (Example 3)

a. Yes, both are equal to $\frac{1}{5}$. **b.** No **c.** Yes: 7 • 3 = 21 and 10 • 3 = 30

SELECTED ANSWERS

701

6-6 Try It (Example 4)

a. Proportional

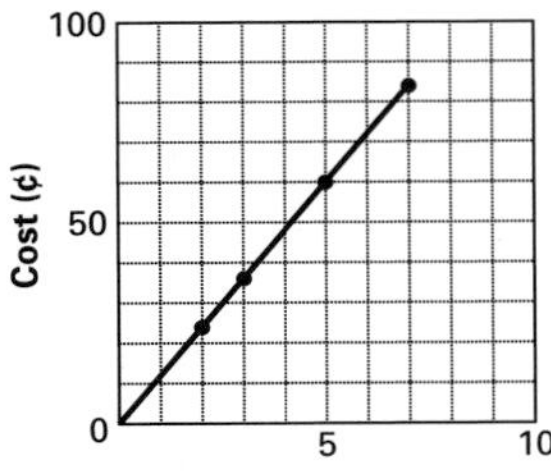

b. Not proportional

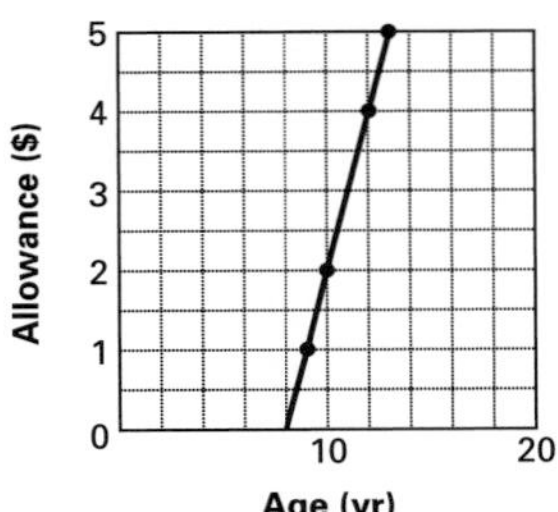

6-6 Exercises & Applications

1. a. $\frac{3}{4}$ **b.** $\frac{3}{4}$ **c.** They are equal and proportional. **3.** Yes **5.** Yes **7.** Yes **9.** Yes **11.** No **13.** No **15.** Yes **19.** Yes **21.** D **23.** No **27.** Subtract 45 **29.** Multiply by 10 **31.** Multiply by 7, then subtract 24 **33.** 9 **35.** 60 **37.** 10 **39.** 17

6-7 Try It

$58.80

6-7 Exercises & Applications

1. 4 pages per minute **3.** $0.12 for one **5. a.** $0.33 **b.** $0.66 **7. a.** 74.6 miles per hour **b.** 149.2 miles **c.** 0.0134 hours per mile **d.** 5.36 hours **9. a.** 12.8 days **b.** 2187.5 miles **11.** 17 **15.** $u - 5$ **17.** $g + 12$ **19.** 10 **21.** 26 ft

6-8 Try It

a. No **b.** Yes **c.** $x = 48$ **d.** $k = 72$ **e.** $n = 5.8\overline{3}$

6-8 Exercises & Applications

1. a. 3 **b.** 15 **d.** $x = 3.75$ **3.** 18 **5.** 320 **7.** No **9.** Yes **11.** No **13.** Yes **15.** $x = 2$ **17.** $x = 5.\overline{45}$ **19.** $t = 36$ **21.** $x = 22.5$ **23.** C **25.** No **27.** 2394 g **31.** $x = 33$ **33.** $y = 52$ **35.** 24 units^2

Section 6B Review

7. No **9.** Yes **11.** Yes **13.** 12.5 **15.** 20 **17.** $0.65; 120

Chapter 6 Summary & Review

1. 4 to 3; 4:3; $\frac{4}{3}$ **2.** $\frac{3}{5}$ **3.** 65 miles per hour **4.** 17 houses per mile **5.** $3.20 for 2 loaves **6.** 189 miles **7.** Possible answer: $\frac{32}{40}, \frac{8}{10}$ **8.** Possible answer: $\frac{30 \text{ points}}{8 \text{ games}}, \frac{45 \text{ points}}{12 \text{ games}}$ **9.** $\frac{6}{8}, \frac{9}{12}, \frac{12}{16}, \frac{15}{20}, \frac{18}{24}$ **10.** $\frac{60}{40}, \frac{30}{20}, \frac{24}{16}, \frac{12}{8}, \frac{6}{4}$ **11.** No

12.

4	8	12	16
7	14	21	28

$\frac{4}{7} = \frac{8}{14}; \frac{4}{7} = \frac{12}{21}; \frac{4}{7} = \frac{16}{28}; \frac{8}{14} = \frac{12}{21}$

13.

5	10	15	20
13	26	39	52

$\frac{5}{13} = \frac{10}{26}; \frac{5}{13} = \frac{15}{39}; \frac{5}{13} = \frac{20}{52}$ **14.** No; Their cross products are not equal. **15.** $0.85 per muffin **16.** $n = 30$ **17.** Yes **18.** $8.25 per hour

Cumulative Review Chapters 1–6

1. B **2.** C **3.** B **4.** D **5.** B **6.** A **7.** B **8.** D **9.** C **10.** A **11.** A **12.** B **13.** B

Chapter 7

7-1 Try It (Examples 1–2)

A little less than 2 inches: ≈ 1.9 inches

7-1 Try It (Example 3)

≈ 150 km

7-1 Exercises & Applications

1. a. 75 miles **b.** ≈ 1.9 miles **c.** ≈ 76.9 miles **3.** 1 in.:225 mi, $\frac{1 \text{ in.}}{225 \text{ mi}}$ **5.** 6 cm = 100 km, $\frac{6 \text{ cm}}{100 \text{ km}}$ **7.** 1 in.:10–12 mi **9.** 1 in.:7–8 mi **11.** ≈ 2 cm **13.** ≈ 9000 km **15.** ≈ 100 mi **17.** 25 ft:3000 mi ≈ 1 ft:100 mi **19.** ≈ 7 in. long, ≈ 5 in. wide **21.** 1 in.:100 ft **23.** $\approx \frac{1}{2}$ **25.** ≈ 1 **27.** ≈ 0 **29.** $\approx \frac{1}{2}$ **31.** ≈ 1 **33.** 36 sq. units

7-2 Try It

5 feet

7-2 Exercises & Applications

1. a. 3 cm **b.** $\frac{3 \text{ cm}}{x \text{ m}} = \frac{1 \text{ cm}}{3 \text{ m}}$ **c.** 9 m **3.** 12.75 ft **5.** 18.375 ft **7.** 20 m **9.** 250 mi **11.** $x = 20$ ft **13.** $x =$ 125 mi **15.** 2860 km **17.** 160 ft × 255 ft **21.** $\frac{1}{30}$ **23.** $\frac{59}{60}$ **25.** 82.5 sq. units **27.** 71 sq. units

7-3 Try It

About 5:35 P.M.

7-3 Exercises & Applications

1. a. 6 km **b.** $1\frac{1}{2}$ hours **c.** 5:00 P.M. **3.** 8:00 P.M. **5.** ≈ 5:45 P.M. **7. a.** ≈ 30 mi **b.** ≈ 45 min **c.** ≈ 7:15 P.M. **9. a.** 12:30 P.M. **b.** 7:50 P.M. **11. a.** 1,375 mi **b.** 125 gallons **c.** $162.50 **15.** $2\frac{4}{5}$ **17.** $1\frac{11}{56}$ **19.** $16\frac{19}{63}$ **21.** $18\frac{2}{21}$ **23.** 3 pounds:1 dollar; $\frac{3 \text{ pounds}}{1 \text{ dollar}}$; 3 pounds = 1 dollar

7-4 Try It

1:11

7-4 Exercises & Applications

1. a. 2.5 in. **b.** 14.4:1 **c.** 2 in.; 10.5:1 **d.** Scale is 10.5:1 **3.** 1 ft:3 ft **5.** 1 in.:3.6 ft **7.** ≈ 4.25:1 **9.** 1 in.:200 mi **11.** 27 ft:5 in. = 1 ft:$0.\overline{185}$ in. **13. a.** ≈ 1:7,326,300,000 **b.** ≈ 20.4 m **c.** ≈ 812.1 m **d.** ≈ 0.06 m = 6 cm **15.** $q = 60$ **17.** $n = 5$ **19.** $t = 21$ **21.** $r = 2$ **23.** $w = 40$ **25.** 3 sections per day

SELECTED ANSWERS

702

27. 33.4 miles per gallon **29.** 24 cans per case

Section 7A Review

1. $\frac{4 \text{ in.}}{200 \text{ mi}}$, 4 in. = 200 mi **3.** 10 cm:4 km, 10 cm = 4 km **5.** 2 cm:400 km **7.** 60 in.

7-5 Try It (Example 1)

a. Miles per hour **b.** Problems per hour

7-5 Try It (Example 2)

Yes

7-5 Try It (Example 3)

$\frac{1 \text{ wk}}{25 \text{ lbs}}$; $\frac{0.04 \text{ wk}}{1 \text{ lb}}$

7-5 Exercises & Applications

1. a. $\frac{20 \text{ miles}}{1 \text{ gallon}}$ **b.** $\frac{1 \text{ gallon}}{20 \text{ miles}}$ **c.** $\frac{0.05 \text{ gallons}}{\text{mile}}$ **3–5.** Possible answers given: **3.** Gallons per mile **5.** Dollars per hour **7.** $\frac{1}{2}$ quart of soup per student **9.** 10 meters per second **11.** Yes **13.** Yes **15.** $\frac{\$0.20}{1 \text{ lb}}$ **17.** $\frac{0.5 \text{ ton}}{\text{week}}$ **19.** No **23.** Yes **25.** $q = 75$ **27.** $n = 3$ **29.** 3 mm per second **31.** 33 desks per classroom **33.** 1000 mL per L

7-6 Try It

a. 3 hrs **b.** 30 yds

7-6 Exercises & Applications

1. a. $\frac{1000 \text{ m}}{1 \text{ km}}$ and $\frac{1 \text{ km}}{1000 \text{ m}}$ **b.** $\frac{1 \text{ km}}{1000 \text{ m}}$ **c.** 3 km **3.** $\frac{365 \text{ days}}{1 \text{ year}}$, $\frac{1 \text{ year}}{365 \text{ days}}$ **5.** $\frac{1 \text{ pound}}{16 \text{ ounces}}$, $\frac{16 \text{ ounces}}{1 \text{ pound}}$ **7.** $\frac{1000 \text{ grams}}{1 \text{ kilogram}}$, $\frac{1 \text{ kilogram}}{1000 \text{ grams}}$ **9.** 240 inches **11.** 42 pounds **13.** 2 gallons **15.** 12.5 feet **17.** 40 quarts **21.** C **25.** 4.00452×10^4 **27.** 4.3567×10^1 **29.** 5.77×10^2 **31.** 4.03770×10^2

7-7 Try It (Example 1)

a. ≈ 29,762 trees per hour
b. 12,000 millimeters per second
c. 720,000 millimeters per minute

7-7 Try It (Example 2)

a. ≈ 1083.3 meters per minute
b. 15 cents per ounce

7-7 Exercises & Applications

1. a. $\frac{1 \text{ gal}}{4 \text{ qt}}$; $\frac{4 \text{ qt}}{1 \text{ gal}}$ **b.** $\frac{4 \text{ qt}}{1 \text{ gal}}$ **c.** $\frac{64 \text{ qt}}{1 \text{ day}}$ **3.** $10\frac{2}{3}$ feet per second **5.** $4\frac{1}{2}$ cups per day **7.** ≈ 137,000 flea collars per day **9.** ≈ 46,000 ounces per hour **11.** A **13.** ≈ 216.8 miles per hour **17.** $\frac{13}{52} < \frac{5}{16}$ **19.** $\frac{23}{92} = \frac{1}{4}$ **21.** $\frac{5}{3} = \frac{10}{6}$; $\frac{10}{6} = \frac{15}{9}$; $\frac{15}{9} = \frac{20}{12}$ **23.** $\frac{11}{44} = \frac{22}{88}$; $\frac{22}{88} = \frac{33}{132}$; $\frac{33}{132} = \frac{44}{176}$ **25.** $\frac{27}{36} = \frac{9}{12}$; $\frac{9}{12} = \frac{3}{4}$; $\frac{3}{4} = \frac{54}{72}$

Section 7B Review

1. Possible answer: Pages per hour **3.** $\frac{2.5 \text{ pizzas}}{1 \text{ student}}$; $\frac{0.4 \text{ pizza}}{1 \text{ student}}$ **5.** No **7.** Yes **9.** 3.5 days **11.** 600 miles per day **13.** 2880 gallons per day **15.** 208 ounces per year **17.** B

7-8 Try It

Yes; Scale factor is $\frac{4}{3}$; $\triangle UVW \sim \triangle XZY$

7-8 Exercises & Applications

1. a. $\angle E, \angle D, \angle F$ **b.** Corresponding angles are congruent. **c.** $\overline{ED}, \frac{1}{3}$; $\overline{DF}, \frac{1}{3}$; $\overline{EF}, \frac{1}{3}$ **d.** The ratios are equal; scale factor is $\frac{1}{3}$. **3.** Not similar **7.** $m\angle U = 38°$; $m\angle V = 46°$; $m\angle W = 96°$ **9.** $\frac{1}{960}$ **11.** B **13.**

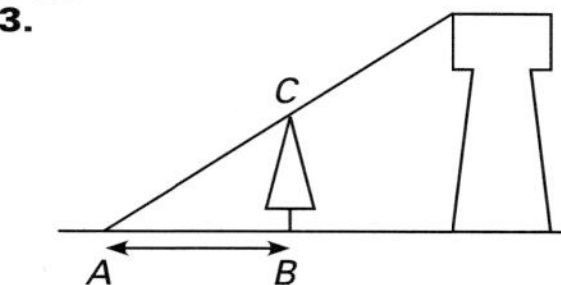

Anywhere on line segment $\overline{AB}$.

15. $\frac{2}{15}$ **17.** 1 **19.** 1 **21.** Yes **23.** Yes

7-9 Try It

$a = 9$, $b = 18$, $c = 21$

7-9 Exercises & Applications

1. a. $\overline{AB}$ **b.** $\frac{x}{18}$ **c.** $\overline{HE}$ **d.** $\overline{DA}$; $\frac{1}{3}$ **e.** $\frac{x}{18} = \frac{1}{3}$; $x = 6$ **3.** $x = 45$ **5.** 50 m **7.** $t = 3$, $s = 5$, $u = 3$ **9.** A **13.** Yes **15.** $25\frac{11}{24}$ **17.** $24\frac{7}{10}$ **19.** 40 words per minute **21.** \$1.699 per gallon

7-10 Try It

Perimeter = 96 units; Area = 99 square units

7-10 Exercises & Applications

1. a. 42 **b.** 9 **c.** 252 sq. units **3.** 16 **5.** Perimeter = 30 cm; Area = 54 cm^2 **7.** Perimeter = 21 ft; Area = 58.5 ft^2 **9.** 5 **11.** 0.62 **13.** B **15.** 1875 m^2 **17.** $\frac{9}{20}$ **19.** $3\frac{1}{3}$ **21.** 64 **23.** $p = 9$ **25.** $n = 10$

Section 7C Review

1. Yes; $\triangle XYZ \sim \triangle RQP$; 2 **3.** No **5.** Perimeter = 40 ft; Area = 96 ft^2 **7.** $12\frac{1}{3}$ miles per minute

Chapter 7 Summary & Review

1. 1 in.:25 mi; 1 in. = 25 mi **2.** x = 8 yd **3.** 450 ft **4.** 14 cm = 63 km or 1 cm = 4.5 km **5.** 4:27 p.m. **6.** About 1:3 **7.** Answers may vary. **8.** $\frac{0.2 \text{ sec}}{\text{foot}}$ **9.** 6 miles per minute **10.** ≈ 1.5 cents per second **11.** Similar **12.** Perimeter = 28 in.; Area = 80 in^2 **13.** Perimeter ratio = 9; Scale factor = 9

Chapter 8

8-1 Try It

a. $\frac{1}{2} = 50\%$; $\frac{3}{5} = 60\%$; $\frac{1}{2} < \frac{3}{5}$ **b.** $\frac{7}{10} = 70\%$; $\frac{3}{4} = 75\%$; $\frac{7}{10} < \frac{3}{4}$ **c.** $\frac{13}{20} = 65\%$; $\frac{16}{25} = 64\%$; $\frac{13}{20} > \frac{16}{25}$

SELECTED ANSWERS

703

SELECTED ANSWERS

8-1 Exercises & Applications

1. a. 4 **b.** $\frac{28}{100}$ **c.** 28% **3.** 75% **5.** 48.3% **7.** 75% **9.** 13.5% **11.** 80% **13.** $\frac{11}{25} = 44\%, \frac{1}{2} = 50\%; \frac{11}{25} < \frac{1}{2}$ **15.** $\frac{3}{4} = 75\%, \frac{4}{5} = 80\%; \frac{3}{4} < \frac{4}{5}$ **17.** $9\% < 15\%$ **19.** $16\% < 28\%$ **21.** 1% **23.** 63% **25.** 100% **27.** 1% of a dollar **29.** 100% of a dollar **31.** D **35.** $\frac{44}{125}$ **37.** $\frac{1101}{2000}$ **39.** $\frac{49}{80}$ **41.** 0.375 **43.** 0.46 **45.** $0.\overline{3}$ **47.** 1 cm:20 m **49.** 1 in.:20 ft

8-2 Try It

a. $\frac{27}{50}$ **b.** 91% **c.** 60% **d.** 13.5%

8-2 Exercises & Applications

1. a. 0.1875 **b.** 18.75% **3.** 0.75 **5.** 0.05 **7.** 1.0 **9.** 0.143 **11.** 0.475 **13.** $\frac{1}{5}$ **15.** $\frac{17}{20}$ **17.** $\frac{11}{20}$ **19.** $\frac{7}{25}$ **21.** $\frac{3}{8}$ **23.** 8% **25.** 87.5% **27.** 50% **29.** $44.\overline{4}\%$ **31.** 80% **33.** 45% **35.** 15.5% **37.** ≈ 3% **39.** C **41.** No; 54 of the 130 calories ≈ 41.5%. **43.** ≈ 1 **45.** ≈ 1 **47.** $\approx \frac{1}{2}$ **49.** $\approx \frac{1}{2}$ **51.** $\approx \frac{1}{2}$ **53.** $x = 25$ in. **55.** $x = 0.8$ in. **57.** $x = 250$ m **59.** $x = 52.5$ mm **61.** $x = 110$ km

8-3 Try It

a. $\frac{1}{250}$, 0.004 **b.** $1\frac{1}{4}$, 1.25

8-3 Exercises & Applications

1. a. $\frac{0.8}{100}$ **b.** $\frac{8}{1000}$ **c.** $\frac{1}{125}$ **3.** A **5.** B **7.** C **9.** A **11.** B **13.** $>$ **15.** $<$ **17.** 0.03% **19.** 350% **21.** 130% **23.** 280% **25.** 0.8% **27.** 0.7% **29.** 0.125% **31.** 6.04% **33.** 1.25 **35.** 0.002 **37.** 0.065 **39.** 0.00375 **41.** 0.000067 **43.** ≈ 0.27% **45.** B **49.** $\frac{11}{12}$ **51.** $\frac{25}{36}$ **53.** $\frac{19}{21}$ **55.** $\frac{5}{39}$ **57.** $\frac{11}{30}$ **59.** 3:20 P.M. **61.** 2:45 P.M.

8-4 Try It

a. 3 **b.** 16 **c.** 15 **d.** 450

8-4 Exercises & Applications

1. a. 3,400 **b.** 1,700 **c.** 5,100 **3.** 2,900; 580; 58 **5.** 122; 24.4; 2.44 **7.** 1,230 **9.** 5,740 **11.** 3,280 **13.** 125 **15.** $56 **17.** 105 **19.** 240 **21.** 35 **23.** ≈ 4 **25.** ≈ 12 **27.** ≈ 2000 **29.** C **31. a.** 2,000,000 died; 2,000,000 survived **b.** 500,000 died; 1,500,000 returned to Texas. **c.** 37.5 **33.** 256 **35.** 529 **37.** 1 **39.** 22 **41.** 19 **43.** 14 in.:100 mi ≈ 1 in.:7.1 mi

Section 8A Review

1. 17% **3.** 30% **5.** 71.6% **7.** 60% **9.** 45.6% **11.** 89% **13.** 49.8% **15.** 307% **17.** 0.3 **19.** 4.23 **21.** 0.001 **23.** $\frac{7}{10}$ **25.** $3\frac{3}{50}$ **27.** 85 **29.** $5.40 **31.** 305

8-5 Try It

a. 30% **b.** 75

8-5 Exercises & Applications

1. a. Let regular price be *r*. **b.** $25.20 is 60% of the regular price. **c.** $25.20 = 0.6 \cdot r$ **d.** $\frac{25.20}{0.6} = \frac{0.6}{0.6} \cdot r$ **e.** $r = 42$. The regular price is $42.00. **3.** 31.4% **5.** 54 **7.** 327.3 **9.** 38 **11.** 200 **13.** 12,000 **15. a.** 75% **b.** $5.25 **17.** It is not possible to tell. **21.** Greater than 45; Less than 45 **23.** Yes Possible answers for Exercises 25 and 27: **25.** Breaths per minute **27.** Cubic centimeters per minute

8-6 Try It (Examples 1–2)

a. 172.38 **b.** $53.\overline{3}\%$

8-6 Try It (Example 3)

a. 164 **b.** 1,312,500 African elephants

8-6 Exercises & Applications

1. a. x **b.** $\frac{38}{100} = \frac{52}{x}$ **c.** $38x = 5200$ **d.** $\frac{38x}{38} = \frac{5200}{38}$ **e.** 136.8 **3.** 17.3 **5.** 9.1% **7.** 238.9 **9.** 240% **11.** 3.3% **13.** 2.5 **15.** 7,500,000% **17.** Possible answer: $\frac{4}{12}, \frac{8}{24}, \frac{16}{48}$ **19. a.** 6.25 grams **b.** 2.5 grams **23.** $b = 10$ cm **25.** $h = 12$ m **27.** 120 feet per minute **29.** 30.48 centimeters per foot

8-7 Try It

a. 60% **b.** 29¢

8-7 Exercises & Applications

1. a. 119 **b.** $\frac{c}{100} = \frac{119}{140}$ **c.** $140c = 11{,}900$ **d.** 85% **3.** 25% **5.** 98.4% **7.** 66.7% **9.** 30 **11.** 42 **13.** 9.4 **15.** 40.1 **17.** ≈ 23.1% **19.** Tax: $4.41; Price: $57.90 **21.** Tax: $5.20; Price: $85.18 **23.** 56.25% **25.** 224% **27.** C **29.** 7,499,900% **31.** 48 yd^2 **33.** 21 in^2 **35.** $28.\overline{63}$ miles per hour

Section 8B Review

1. 22.2% **3.** 105.4 **5.** 125% **7.** 67.2 **9.** $23.76 **11.** $83\frac{1}{9}\%$ **13.** $5 **15.** $4.80

Chapter 8 Summary & Review

1. 27% **2.** $\frac{1}{4} = 25\%; \frac{1}{5} = 20\%; \frac{1}{4} > \frac{1}{5}$ **3.** $\frac{11}{50}$ **4.** 0.86 **5.** 73%, $\frac{73}{100}$ **6.** $\frac{9}{20}$, 0.45 **7.** $\frac{1}{125}$, 0.008 **8.** $\frac{5}{4}$, 1.25 **9.** 240, 24 **10.** 276 **11.** 14 **12.** $6.60 **13.** 20 **14.** ≈ 46.2% **15.** $66\frac{2}{3}$ **16.** 184 **17.** $212.50 **18.** $15.00 **19.** 99 **20.** ≈ 21.5% **21.** 84%; 16% **22.** ≈ 23.1% **23.** $31\frac{1}{9}\%$ **24.** ≈ 74.2%

Cumulative Review Chapters 1–8

1. C **2.** B **3.** C **4.** D **5.** A **6.** B **7.** B **8.** C **9.** C **10.** B **11.** C **12.** B **13.** C

704

Chapter 9

9-1 Try It (Examples 1–2)

3, 4, 5; −1, −3, −5; −3 and 3, −5 and 5

9-1 Try It (Example 3)

a. 17 **b.** 5.25 **c.** 3298 **d.** 0

9-1 Exercises & Applications

1. a.

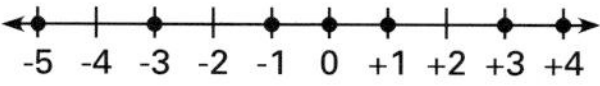

b. 1, 3, 4 **c.** −1, −3, −5 **d.** −1 and 1, −3 and 3 **3.** No **5.** Yes **7.** −31,441 **9.** −6 **11.** −2 **13.** −3 **15.** 222 **17.** −5640 **19.** 23 **21.** 66 **23.** 4771 **25.** 2435 **27.** 90,121 **29.** 136°; 129°; −129° **31.** 13,796; −19,680 **35.** $\frac{2}{1}$, 2:1, 2 to 1 **37.** $\frac{12}{10}$, 12:10, 12 to 10 **39.** $x = 15$

9-2 Try It

a. 45°F **b.** −1 > −22 **c.** −313, −262, −252, −245

9-2 Exercises & Applications

1. a.

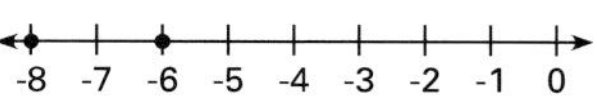

b. −6 **3.** −5 > −7 **5.** 5 > −8 **7.** −7 > −9 **9.** −2 > −3 **11.** 3 > −4 **13.** < **15.** > **17.** = **19.** > **21.** $12, $11, $8, $0, −$2, −$5, −$7 **23.** −3151, −3155, −3515, −3551, −3555 **25. a.** Always **b.** Sometimes **c.** Never **d.** Always **27.** B **29. a.** Lost $2.75 **b.** Lost $3.25 **c.** Gained $1.25 **d.** Lost $4.00 **31.** A half a page per minute **33.** 2 hours per day **35.** Perimeter of first: 24; Area of first: 36; Perimeter of second: 72; Area of second: 324

9-3 Try It (Examples 1–2)

a–d.

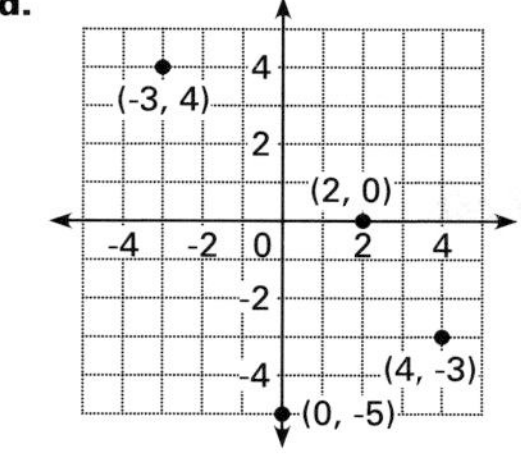

e. II **f.** IV **g.** x-axis **h.** y-axis

9-3 Try It (Example 3)

$B(-4, 1)$, $C(1, 3)$, $D(0, -3)$, $E(2, -2)$

9-3 Try It (Example 4)

They are negative.

9-3 Exercises & Applications

1. a–d.

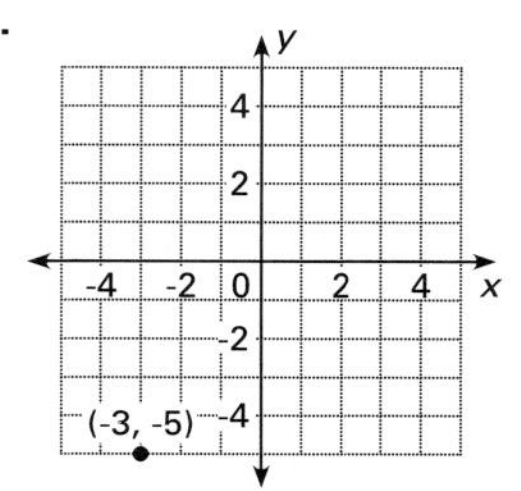

3. (0, 0) **5.** (−2, 0) **7.** (3, −1) **19. a.** (200, −100); (500, −200) **b.**

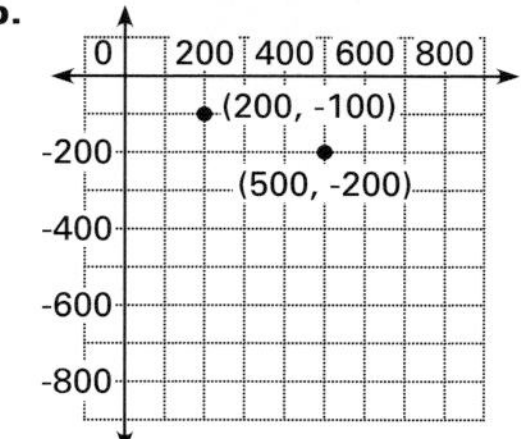

21. IV **23.** I **25.** III **27.** IV **29.** I **31.** C **33.** Cairo: 30° north, 31° east; Zanzibar: 6° south, 39° east Possible answers for 35–39: **35.** $\frac{4}{11}$, $\frac{16}{44}$ **37.** $\frac{10}{21}$, $\frac{40}{84}$ **39.** $\frac{21}{50}$, $\frac{84}{200}$ **41.** 67% **43.** 34%

Section 9A Review

1. 4 **3.** 0 **5.** −201 **7.** 6 **9.** 613 **11.** > **13.** > **15.** −5, −25 **23.** C

9-4 Try It (Example 1)

a. −3 **b.** 5 **c.** −8 **d.** 6

9-4 Try It (Examples 2–3)

a. 3 **b.** −1 **c.** −1 **d.** 0

9-4 Exercises & Applications

1. a–b. □□ ■■■■■

c.

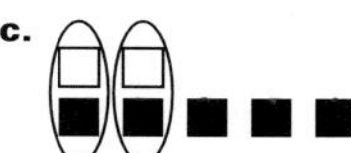

d. −3 **3.** 4 + (−6) = −2 **5.** 6 **7.** 15 **9.** 0 **11.** −10 **13.** 5 **15.** 4 **17.** −10 **19.** 0 **21.** 11 **23.** −46 **25.** 22 **27.** −110 **29.** 4 tokens **31.** −10 **33.** B **35. a.** 264 + (−127) **b.** 137 ft **37.** $\frac{6}{14}$, $\frac{9}{21}$, $\frac{12}{28}$, $\frac{15}{35}$, $\frac{18}{42}$ **39.** $\frac{1}{2}$ **41.** $\frac{1}{20}$ **43.** $\frac{9}{20}$ **45.** $\frac{14}{125}$ **47.** $\frac{13}{25}$

9-5 Try It (Example 1)

a. 1 **b.** −3 **c.** −6 **d.** 4

9-5 Try It (Example 2)

a. 2 **b.** −5 **c.** 3 **d.** 2

9-5 Try It (Example 3)

69 feet

9-5 Exercises & Applications

1. a–b. □□□□□ ■■■■

c. □□□□□

d. 5 **3.** −9 **5.** 10 **7.** 12 **9.** 56 **11.** 60 **13.** −21 **15.** −30 **17.** −91 **19.** 583 **21.** 130 **23.** −14 **25.** 12 **27.** −7 **29.** Alaska: 180; California: 179; Hawaii: 86; North Dakota: 181; West Virginia: 149; Widest: North Dakota; Narrowest: Hawaii **31. a.** −10 − 20 = −30

SELECTED ANSWERS

705

b. 20 − (−10) = 30 **c.** −10 − (−10) = 0 **d.** 20 − 20 = 0 **33.** 2^{10}
35. $2 \times 3 \times 11$ **37.** $2^4 \times 3^2$
39. $2 \times 3 \times 5 \times 7 \times 13$ **41.** $2^5 \times 3$
43. 52% **45.** 90% **47.** 243%
49. 987.654% **51.** 1020%

9-6 Try It (Examples 1–3)

a. −16 **b.** 20 **c.** −54 **d.** −33
e. −140 **f.** 0

9-6 Try It (Examples 4–6)

a. 64 **b.** −30 **c.** 24

9-6 Exercises & Applications

1. 8, 4, −4, −8 **3.** −27, 0, 9, 18
5. − **7.** + **9.** 72 **11.** −72
13. 45 **15.** −100 **17.** −135
19. 125 **21.** −112 **23.** −8
25. −84 **27.** −512 **29.** −136
31. C **33.** You can multiply integers as you would whole numbers, but you have to look at the signs to figure out what sign the product is.
35. 15 **37.** 17 **39.** 21 **41.** 3
43. 60 **45.** 90 **47.** 1.5 **49.** $5.40

9-7 Try It (Examples 1–4)

a. 4 **b.** 5 **c.** −2 **d.** −3

9-7 Try It (Example 5)

−4

9-7 Exercises & Applications

1. a. −724 **b.** −181 **c.** −181
d. a drop **3.** − **5.** + **7.** −3 **9.** 8
11. −2 **13.** −8 **15.** 81 **17.** −16
19. 15 **21.** −8 **23.** 4 **25.** −1
27. 0 **29.** $\frac{11}{25}$ **31.** $\frac{1}{5}$ **33.** $\frac{4}{5}$ **35.** $\frac{1}{5}$
37. 50% **39.** 22 **41.** 25%

Section 9B Review

1. 0 **3.** −50 **5.** 9 **7.** 150
9. −240 **11.** 382 **13.** −16
15. −170,017 **17.** −160 **19.** 0
27. 265°F; 147°C

Chapter 9 Summary & Review

1. No **2.** −$25 **3.** −42 **4.** 87
5. > **6.** −8, −4, 0, 10, 18

7. Possible answer:

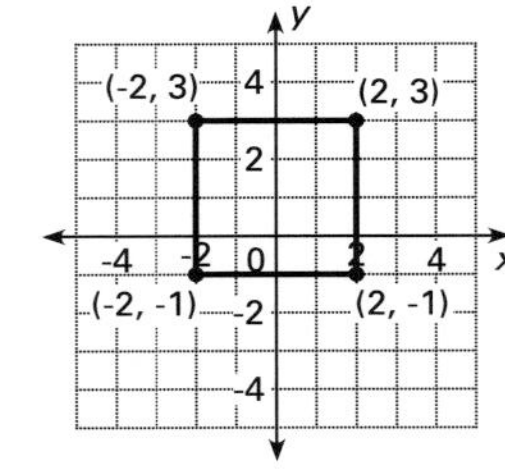

8.

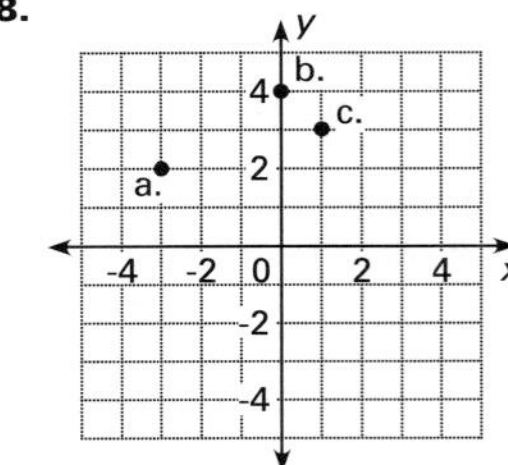

9. 5 + (−9) = −4
10. Possible answer:

□□□
■■■■■■■

Sum is −4.
11. 2 **12. a.** 6 **b.** −11 **c.** −65
d. −62 **13. a.** −3 **b.** 4 **c.** −101
d. 0 **14. a.** −84 **b.** 40 **c.** −252
d. 480 **15. a.** −22 **b.** 4 **c.** −6
d. 21 **16.** −$5250 **17.** 20,602 ft

Chapter 10

10-1 Try It (Examples 1–2)

a. Variable **b.** Constant
c. Variable **d.** Constant

10-1 Try It (Examples 3–4)

Possible answers: **a.** Let T = the time it takes to get to school; Between 5 and 60 minutes **b.** Let W = wingspan of a butterfly; Between 1 cm and 10 cm

10-1 Exercises & Applications

1. a. Variables **b.** Constants
3. Variable **5.** Variable

7. Variable Possible answers for Exercises 9–17: **9.** Let W = weight of newborn; Between 5 and 12 lb
11. Let T = time it takes to eat lunch; Between 5 and 45 min
13. Let H = height of desk; Between 2 and 4 ft **15.** Feet or meters
17. Minutes or hours **19.** The measurements of the area, the base, and the height can change; The $\frac{1}{2}$ is constant. **21.** D **23.** The length is constant. **25.** About 12 in.
27. 41°, 32°, 3°, −3°, −15°, −42°
29. −4111, −4122, −4212, −4221, −4222

10-2 Try It (Example 1)

b

10-2 Try It (Example 2)

There were no students at the start of the day, a few students arrived and stayed for the first class, more students came and stayed for a second class, some students left before a third class, then everyone left the room.

10-2 Exercises & Applications

1. a. Decreases **b.** Decreases
c. Stays constant **d.** Increases
Possible answers for Exercises 3 and 5: **3.** The length of a side **5.** The age of the teenager **7.** a
9. Possible answer: You start with a full tank. You stop driving for a while, then drive for a bit longer. Then you fill the tank. **13.** b
15. 8 m **17.** 14 m

10-3 Try It (Examples 1–3)

$3n$

10-3 Try It (Example 4)

x	1	2	3	4	5	6
10x	10	20	30	40	50	60

10-3 Exercises & Applications

1.

Term #	1	2	3	4	5	n
# in Seq.	7	14	21	28	35	$7n$

SELECTED ANSWERS

706

3. 0 **5.** 5 **7.** 16 **11.** $n + 10$; 110 **13.** $\frac{n}{2}$; 50 **15.** $\frac{n}{10}$; 10 **17.** n^2; 10,000 **19. a.** 8000n **b.** 2,920,000 **25. b.** 3n **c.** 300 **27.** Arithmetic; 9, 11 **29.** Arithmetic; 55, 66 **31.** Geometric; 100,000; 1,000,000 **33.** Neither; $\frac{5}{6}$, $\frac{6}{7}$ **35.** 625,000,000 **37.** 9:00 P.M. **39.** 5:24 P.M. **41.** 8 **43.** −27 **45.** −48 **47.** −179 **49.** −468

10-4 Try It (Examples 1–2)

$y = \frac{x}{4}$; $y = 4.25$

10-4 Try It (Example 3)

Possible answers:

y	1	2	3	4	5	6
p	20 kg	40 kg	60 kg	80 kg	100 kg	120 kg

10-4 Exercises & Applications

1. Possible answer:

x	1	2	3	4	5
y	-1	2	5	8	11

3. $y = -5x$; $y = -35$ **5.** $C = 21.00$, $C = 28.00$; $C = 3.5n$ **7.** $d = 105$, $d = 140$, $d = 175$; $d = 35t$ **19.** C **23.** 1 in.:4 ft **25.** 1 in.:2.4 ft **27.** 5 **29.** 102 **31.** 789

10-5 Try It (Example 1)

a.

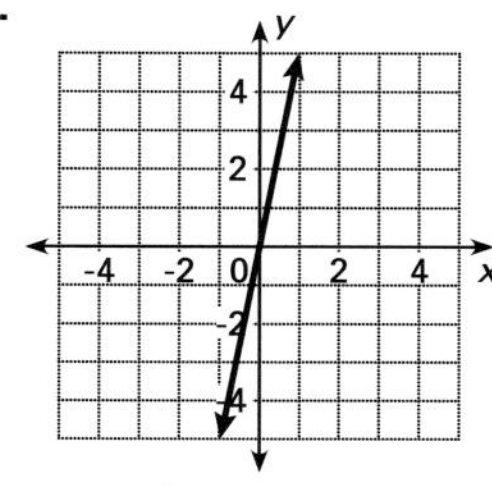

b.

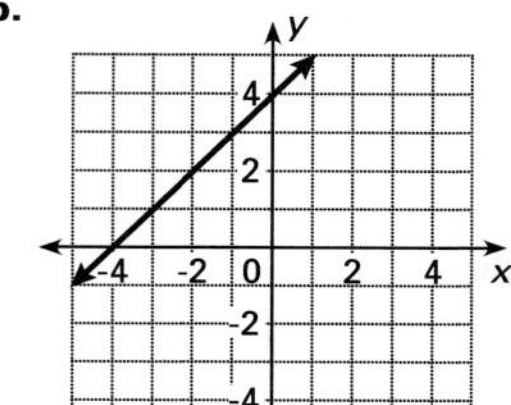

c.

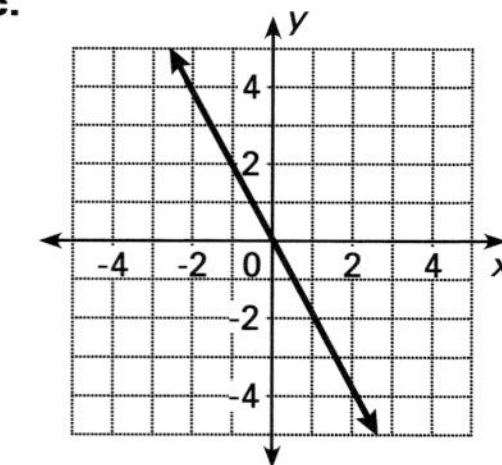

10-5 Try It (Example 2)

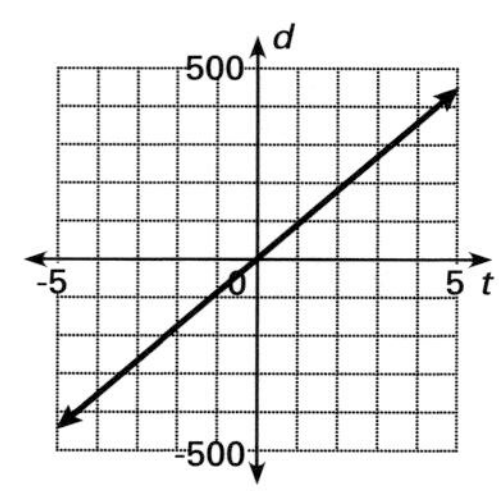

10-5 Exercises & Applications

1.

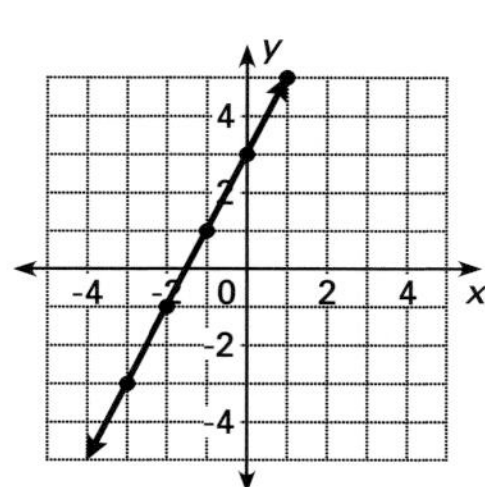

3.

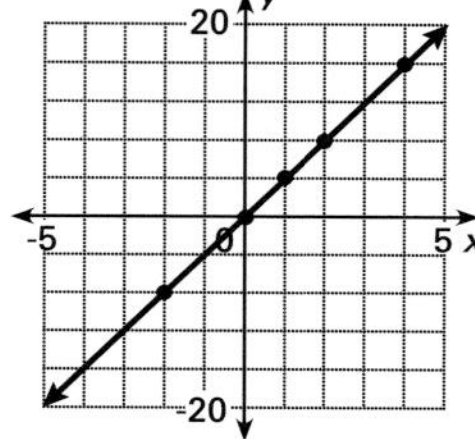

11. The graphs that go through the origin don't have a number subtracted or added at the end of the equation.
13, 15.

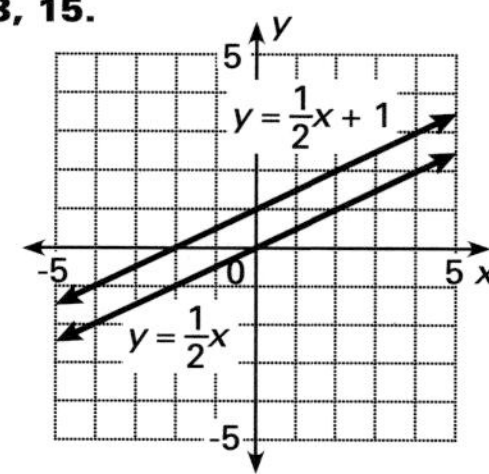

17. They are parallel lines. **19. a.** Let r = rate and m = minutes; r = 140m and $r = \frac{m}{60}$. **b.** The line with the steeper slope represents the greater rate. **21. d.** The lines are images of each other reflected over the y-axis. **23.** $\frac{9}{20} = 45\%$; $\frac{1}{2} = 50\%$; $\frac{9}{20} < \frac{1}{2}$ **25.** $\frac{1}{4} = 25\%$; $\frac{1}{5} = 20\%$; $\frac{1}{4} > \frac{1}{5}$ **27.** 63 **29.** −44 **31.** 0 **33.** 108 **35.** −270

Section 10A Review

1. b **3.** 2n; 200 **5.** −5n; −500 **7.** $y = x - 6$; 3
9.

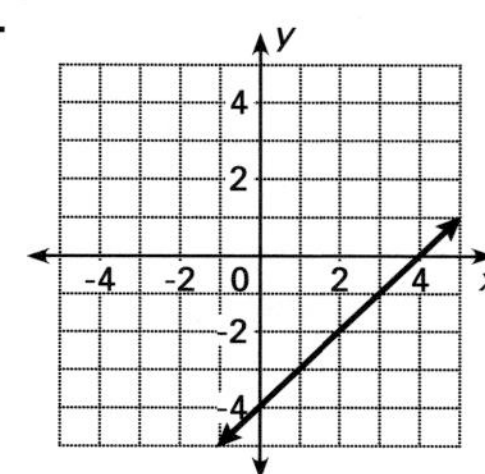

SELECTED ANSWERS

707

11.

10-6 Try It

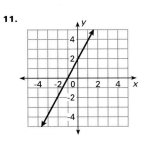

a. $x = 10$ **b.** $x = -6$ **c.** $k = 4\frac{1}{3}$ **d.** $x = -7$

10-6 Exercises & Applications

1. a. $y = x + 3$ **c.** $x = 5$ **3.** $x = -2$ **5.** $x = 4$ **7.** $x = 6$ **9.** $r = -4$ **11.** $x = 3\frac{1}{2}$ **13.** $z = -5$ **15. b.** $d \approx 3\frac{1}{2}$cm **17.** 200 times **19.** Possible answer: About 63.4% **21.** 0.5 **23.** 0.9 **25.** 0.07 **27.** 0.056 **29.** 0.8462 **31.** 3 **33.** 0 **35.** 7 **37.** −4 **39.** −34

10-7 Try It

a. $x = 6$ **b.** $x = -4$ **c.** $x = -3$

10-7 Exercises & Applications

1. $x = -1$ **3.** $x = 1$ **5.** $x = -2\frac{1}{2}$ **7.** $x = 2$ **9.** $p = -1$ **11.** $x = 4\frac{1}{2}$ **13.** $t \approx -15\frac{1}{3}$ **15.** 10 months **17. a.** $2n$ **b.** $1200 **c.** $y = 2n - 1200$ **d.** 2100 items **19. a.** $A = 5 + 0.25c$ **b.** $7.50 **c.** 15 checks **21.** 135% **23.** 0.5% **25.** −7 **27.** 417 **29.** 114 **31.** 22,714 **33.** -4×10^4

10-8 Try It (Examples 1–2)

a.

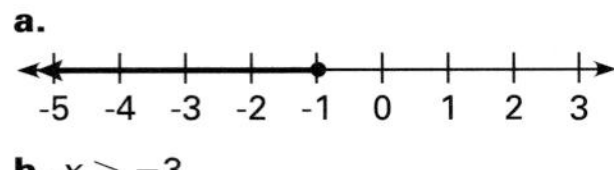

b. $x > -3$

10-8 Try It (Examples 3–4)

$A < 450$

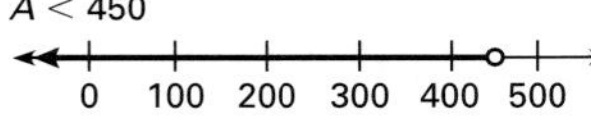

10-8 Exercises & Applications

1. a–c.

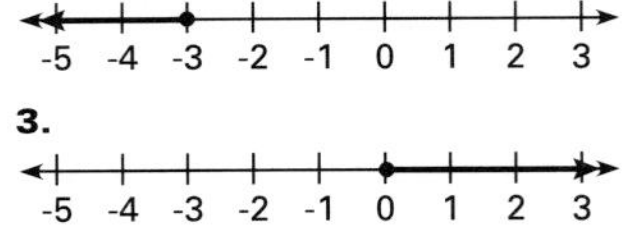

3.

5.

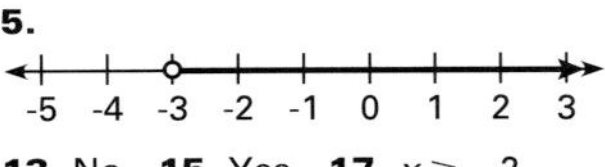

13. No **15.** Yes **17.** $x \geq -2$ **19.** $x > 40$ **21.** The number of tickets sold was greater than 150. **23.** The plane needed at least 90 gallons of fuel. **25.** There were no more than 65 sofas in the shipment. **27.** $C \leq 1$ **29.** No **31.** A **33.** Tables may vary; Any values of x greater than 4 solve the inequality. **35.** ≈ 4 **37.** ≈ $2.10 **39.** < **41.** < **43.** > **45.** >

Section 10B Review

1. $x = 0$ **3.** $x = -2$ **5.** $x = 0$ **7.** $x = -4$ **11. a.** $m = 72p$ **b.** Need to sell about 55 pillows to make $4000. **13.** $6n$; 600 **15.** n^3; 1,000,000

10-9 Try It

a. $x = -5$ **b.** $x = -7$ **c.** $x = -40$ **d.** $x = 48$

10-9 Exercises & Applications

1. a. $x + (-2) + 2 = (-11) + 2$ **b.** $x = -9$ **c.** $(-9) + (-2) = (-11)$; $-11 = -11$ **3.** $x + (-5) = -3$; $x = 2$ **5.** No **7.** No **9.** $x = -5$ **11.** $z = -1$ **13.** $k = 27$ **15.** $x = -5$ **17.** $x = -11$ **19.** $x = -60$ **21.** −4°F **23.** 1021 millibars **25.** $x = -60$ **27. a.** The variable is preceded by a minus sign. **b.** $x = 59$ **29.** 15, 20, 35; Possible answers: $\frac{1}{5} = \frac{3}{15}$, $\frac{3}{15} = \frac{4}{20}$, $\frac{4}{20} = \frac{7}{35}$, $\frac{3}{15} = \frac{7}{35}$ **31.** $\frac{1}{5} = \frac{12}{x}$; $x = 60$ **33.** $\frac{1}{1000} = \frac{57}{m}$; $m = 57{,}000$

10-10 Try It (Examples 1–2)

a. $x = -2$ **b.** $h = 4.\overline{4}$ **c.** $x = -4.\overline{3}$

10-10 Try It (Examples 3–4)

a. $y = -150$ **b.** $w = 1320$ **c.** $m = 448$

10-10 Exercises & Applications

1. a. $\frac{-3x}{-3} = \frac{-15}{-3}$ **b.** $x = 5$ **c.** $-3(5) = -15$, $-15 = -15$ **3.** $2x = -8$; $x = -4$ **5.** No **7.** Yes **9.** $m = 33$ **11.** $z = 10$ **13.** $c = -64$ **15.** $d = 36$ **17.** $x = -19$ **19.** $x = 3.5$ **21.** 0.5 mm **23.** Possible answers: $\frac{12}{m} = -3$ and $\frac{n}{-2} = 2$ **25.** 24 **29.** No **31.** 158 **33.** $71.30

10-11 Try It (Examples 1–2)

a. $x = -3$ **b.** $c = -8$ **c.** $x = 30$ **d.** $x = -20$

10-11 Try It (Example 3)

a. 2 km **b.** 5 km

10-11 Exercises & Applications

1. a. $-4x - 2 + 2 = -14 + 2$ **b.** −12 **c.** $\frac{-4x}{-4} = \frac{-12}{-4}$ **d.** $x = 3$ **e.** $-4(3) - 2 = -14$, $-12 - 2 = -14$, $-14 = -14$ **3.** $3x + 2 = -1$; $x = -1$ **5.** Yes **7.** No **9.** $x = 1$ **11.** $t = -36$ **13.** $g = -3$ **15.** $n = -8$ **17.** $x = 80$ **19.** $f = -1120$ **21.** 43 inches **23.** A **25.** Possible answers: $3m + 11 = 2$ and $3 - 2n = 9$ **27.** $0.\overline{2}$; Repeats **29.** 0.875; Terminates **31.** 0.4375; Terminates **33.** $3.00

10-12 Try It

a. $9494 **b.** 5 weeks

10-12 Exercises & Applications

1. $h + 2 = 14$ **3.** $2t - 7 = -27$ **5.** 5°F **7.** 14 years **9.** B **11. a.** In 200 years **b.** In 600 years **c.** In 800 years **d.** $0.000\overline{3}$°C per year; This is $\frac{1}{15}$ of the current rate. **13.** $k = 3$ **15.** $x = 60$ **17.** $y = 4$ **19.** $x = 1.\overline{3}$ **21.** 10 **23.** 0 **25.** 75 **27.** 32 **29.** 101 **31.** 14 **33.** 4

SELECTED ANSWERS

708

Section 10C Review

1. $x - 2 = 6$; $x = 8$ **3.** $-5 = 2x - 3$; $x = -1$ **5.** No **7.** Yes **9.** $p = -22$ **11.** $x = 180$ **13.** $d = 128$ **15.** $x = -32$ **17.** $x = 5$ **19.** $x = 4$ **21.** D

Chapter 10 Summary & Review

1. Possible answer: p = number of petals on a flower; 5–50 petals **2.** Possible answers: diameter, circumference, height **3.** $6n$; 600 **4.** Possible table values for (x, y): (1, 7), (2, 9), (3, 11), (4, 13), (5, 15), (6, 17) **5.** Possible answer: Over a 3-month period a plant grew to 3 feet and then with lack of water over the next 3 months withered down to the ground. **6.** $y = 4x$; 36
7. a.

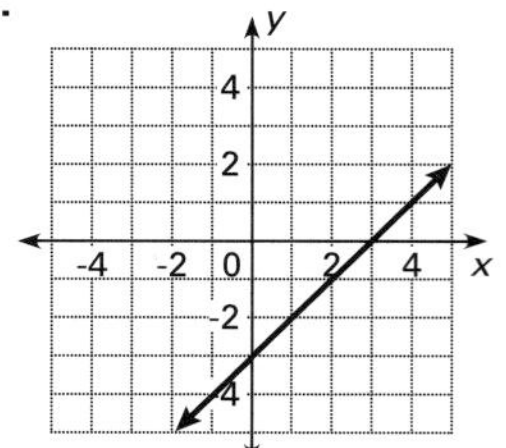

b.

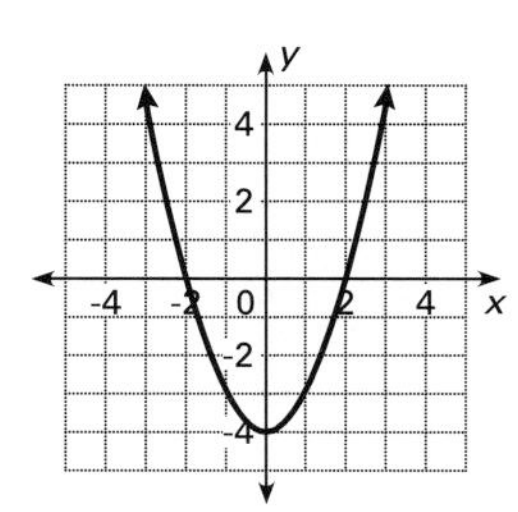

8. a. $x = 3$ **b.** $x = 0$ **9.** $x = -4$
10. $y < 7$

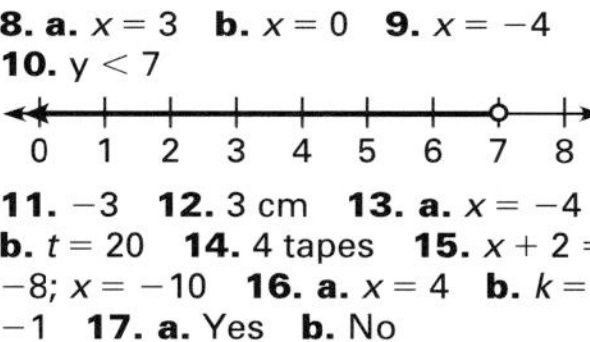

11. -3 **12.** 3 cm **13. a.** $x = -4$ **b.** $t = 20$ **14.** 4 tapes **15.** $x + 2 = -8$; $x = -10$ **16. a.** $x = 4$ **b.** $k = -1$ **17. a.** Yes **b.** No

Cumulative Review Chapters 1–10

1. A **2.** A **3.** B **4.** B **5.** C **6.** B **7.** C **8.** C **9.** D **10.** B **11.** D **12.** A **13.** C **14.** C **15.** C **16.** B

Chapter 11

11-1 Try It

a. Triangular prism **b.** Pentagonal pyramid
c.

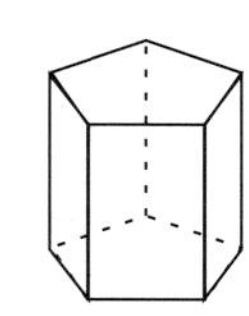

11-1 Exercises & Applications

1. Possible answer:

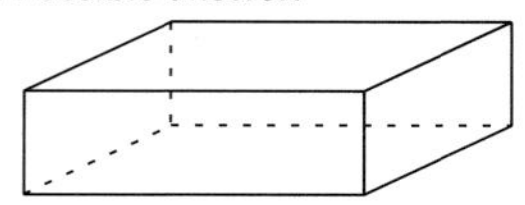

3. 2 triangles, 3 rectangles **5.** Pentagonal prism **7.** Right triangular prism **11.** Rectangular pyramid **13.** C **15. a.** Tetrahedron: 4 faces, 6 edges, 4 vertices; Hexahedron: 6 faces, 12 edges, 8 vertices; Octahedron: 8 faces, 12 edges, 6 vertices **b.** Number of faces + Number of vertices − Number of edges = 2 **17.** 60 faces, 120 edges, 80 vertices
19.

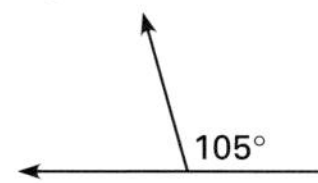

21. II **23.** III **25.** I

11-2 Try It (Example 1)

1. A **2.** B

11-2 Try It (Examples 2–3)

a.

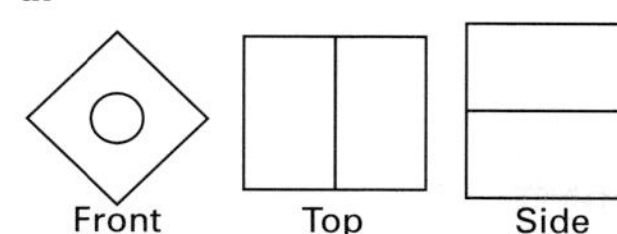

b.

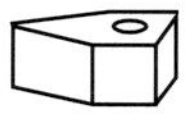

11-2 Exercises & Applications

1. a–c. Front Side Top

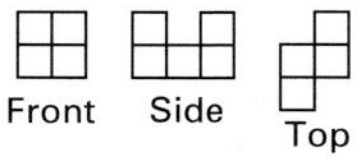

3. 7 **5.** C **7.** A **17.** Perpendicular **19.** Perpendicular **21.** Constant **23.** Variable

11-3 Try It

a.

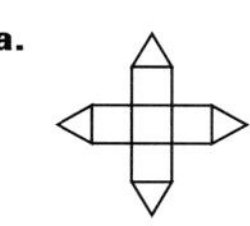

112 ft^2 **b.** 610 mm^2

11-3 Exercises & Applications

1. a. 40 cm^2 **b.** 130 cm^2 **c.** 150 cm^2 **d.** 48 cm^2 **e.** 368 cm^2 **5.** 184 cm^2 **7.** 168 cm^2 **9.** 7 gal **11.** C **13.** a and c **15. a.** Yes; Any piece other than a corner **b.** No **c.** Yes; Any corner piece **17.** Quadrilateral, parallelogram, rectangle, rhombus, square **19.** Obtuse, scalene triangle **21.** Measure of base or height

11-4 Try It

a. 48 ft^3 **b.** 55,000 cm^3

11-4 Exercises & Applications

1. a. 24 cm^2 **b.** $24 \cdot 9 = 216$ **c.** 216 cm^3 **3.** 42 in^3 **5.** 450 mm^3 **7.** 160 m^3 **9.** A **11.** The volume of the prism would be 3 times the volume of the pyramid. **13.** 1800° **15.** 2700° **17.** 3; Always 3 **19.** $\frac{1}{14}$; $\frac{1}{2n+4}$

SELECTED ANSWERS

SELECTED ANSWERS

709

Section 11A Review

1. True **3.** True **9.** Area: 30 cm^2; Volume: 7 cm^3 **11.** Area: ≈ 339 in^2; Volume: 339.184 in^3

11-5 Try It

a.

No 11%

Yes 89%

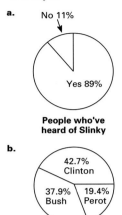

People who've heard of Slinky

b.

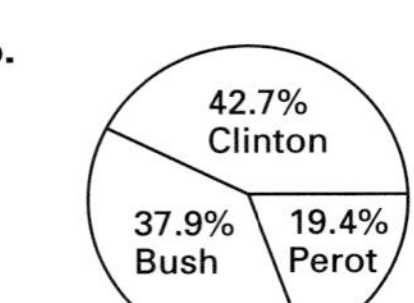

11-5 Exercises & Applications

1. a. 104.4° **b.** 40% is 144°; 31% is 111.6°

c–e.

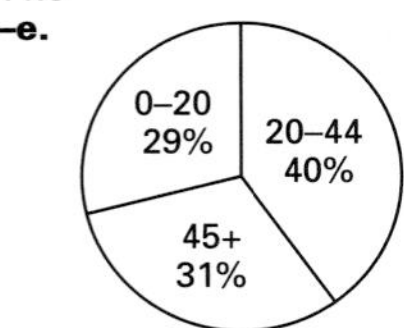

Ages of People in the US, 1990

3. Republican; The sector is greater than 50% of the circle. **7.** 864 **15.** A = 68 in^2; P = 42 in. **17.** A = 7.2 cm^2; P = 36.8 cm **19.** A = 10,875 mi^2; P = 440 mi **21.** y = −8, −9, −10, −11, −12, −13

11-6 Try It

d = 64 in.; C ≈ 201 in.

11-6 Exercises & Applications

1. a. 10 cm **b.** 31.4 cm **3.** d = 8 cm; C = 25.1 cm **5.** d = 16.4 m; C = 51.5 m **7.** ≈ $23\frac{4}{7}$ ft **9.** d = 16 cm; C ≈ 50.2 cm **11.** d ≈ 1.9 mm; r ≈ 1.0 mm **13.** r = 25.5 ft; C ≈ 160.1 ft **15.** d = 200 in.; C ≈ 628.0 in. **17.** d ≈ 28.0 ft; r ≈ 14.0 ft **19.** D **21.** 157 in. **23.** The $\frac{\text{circumference}}{\text{diameter}}$ ratio for all circles is π. It doesn't matter how big or small the circle is. **25.** 51 mi/hr **27.** 17 students for 1 teacher

11-7 Try It

a. 1256 in^2 **b.** 122.7 cm^2

11-7 Exercises & Applications

1. a. 8 in. **b.** A ≈ 200.96 in^2 **3.** 28.3 cm^2 **5.** 1589.6 ft^2 **7.** $38\frac{1}{2}$ ft^2 **9.** 12.6 cm^2 **11.** 73,504.3 ft^2 **13.** 78.5 cm^2 **15.** 60.8 m^2 **17.** ≈ 113.04 ft^2 **19.** $\frac{22}{7}$ = 3.1428571... is closer. **23.** ≈ 286 in^2 **25.** 48 hr **27.** 5 lb **29.** 42 gallons **31.** x = 5 **33.** x = −25

11-8 Try It

a. 81.6 in^2 **b.** 366.2 in^2

11-8 Exercises & Applications

1. a. ≈ 78.5 cm^2 **b.** 157 cm^2 **c.** 31.4 cm **d.** 628 cm^2 **e.** 785 cm^2 **5.** D **7.** 113.0 cm^2 **9.** 117.8 m^2 **11.** ≈ 25.1 in^2 **13.** ≈ 125.6 in^2 **17.** 184,800 ft/hr **19.** x = 3 **21.** x = 2

11-9 Try It (Examples 1–2)

a. ≈ 1152 cm^3 **b.** 1384.7 in^3

11-9 Try It (Example 3)

577 mL

11-9 Exercises & Applications

1. a. ≈ 28.26 in^2 **b.** 113.04 in^3 **c.** 113.0 in^3 **3.** 300 cm^3 **5.** 8164 mm^3 **7.** 1256 in^3 **9.** 52.2 cm^3 **11.** About 15.3 in^3 **13.** 1130.4 mL **15.** 879.6 mL **17.** Liquid foods, or foods packed in liquid, tend to come in cans; dry foods tend to come in boxes. Liquids need to be packed in metal (or plastic), not cardboard, and metal boxes are difficult to make (and dangerous to have on tall shelves). **19.** No **21.** Yes

Section 11B Review

3. C = 56.5 cm; A = 254.3 cm^2 **5.** About 1.6 ft **7.** V = 141.3 in^3; SA = 150.7 in^2 **9.** A

11-10 Try It (Example 1)

C and D

11-10 Try It (Examples 2–3)

(−5, 1), (−5, 5), (−3, 4)

11-10 Exercises & Applications

1. a-c.

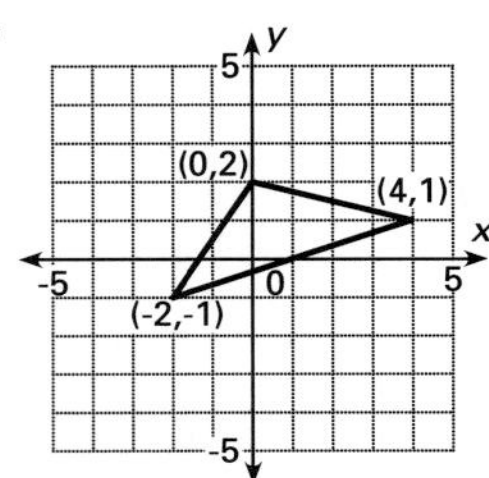

3. C **5.** The image shows horizontal translations of a basic pattern. **7.** $(x, y) \rightarrow (x - 5, y + 7)$ **9.** $(x, y) \rightarrow (x, y - 3)$ **11.** (0, 0) **13.** (−3, 4) **15.** (−1, 4), (4, 4), (−1, 2), and (4, 2) **17.** (−5, 3), (0, 3), (−5, 1), and (0, 1) **19.** Yes; $(x, y) \rightarrow (x - 2, y + 1)$ **21.** x and z are 9 cm, y is 18 cm **23.** a = 3 **25.** c = 20 **27.** m = 4 **29.** f = 9.5 **31.** c = −21 **33.** k = −2

11-11 Try It (Examples 1–3)

a.

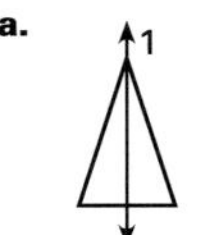

b.

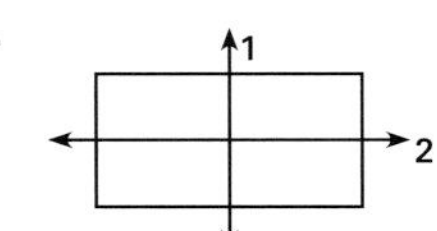

SELECTED ANSWERS

710

c.

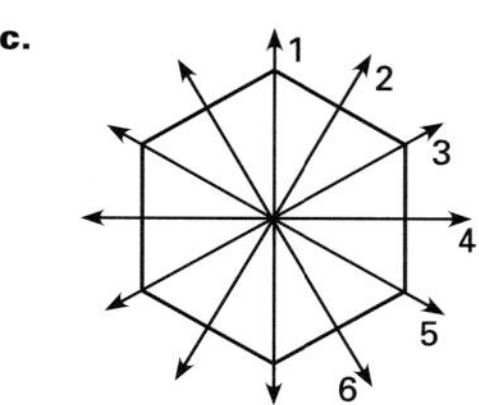

11-11 Try It (Example 4)

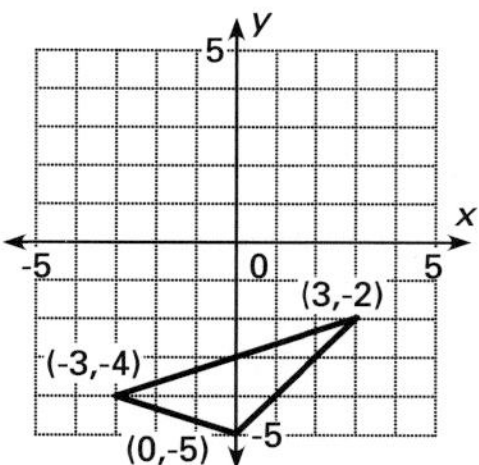

$A'(3, -2)$, $B'(-3, -4)$, $C'(0, -5)$

11-11 Exercises & Applications

1. a–c.

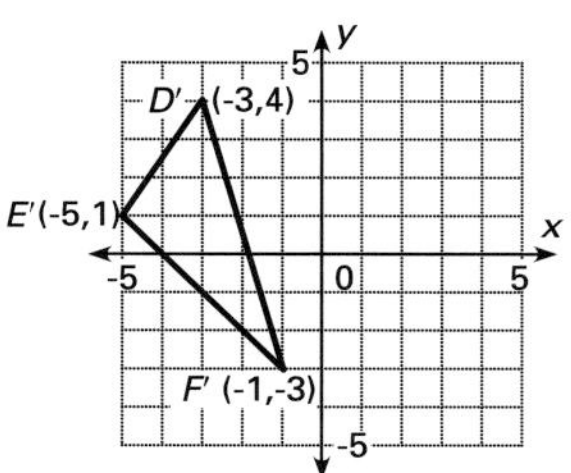

3. Yes **5.** Yes **7.** B **9.** (0, 4), (3, 1), and (5, 2) **13.** Regular polygons have the same number of lines of symmetry as they have sides. **17.** Perimeter: 30 in.; Area: 50 in^2 **19.** $m = -45$ **21.** $y = 0$ **23.** $d = 42$ **25.** $z = 52$

11-12 Try It

No

11-12 Exercises & Applications

1. Yes, it has 180° rotational symmetry. **3.** $\frac{1}{2}$ **5.** $\frac{1}{4}, \frac{1}{2}, \frac{3}{4}$ **7.** 2, 3, 5 **9.** C **11.** 180° **13. a.** $D'(0, 0)$, $E'(4, -1)$, $F'(0, -3)$ **b.** $D'(0, 0)$, $E'(-1, -4)$, $F'(-3, 0)$ **c.** $D'(0, 0)$, $E'(-4, 1)$, $F'(0, 3)$ **15. a.** $\frac{1}{3}, \frac{2}{3}$ **b.** $\frac{1}{4}, \frac{1}{2}, \frac{3}{4}$ **c.** $\frac{1}{5}, \frac{2}{5}, \frac{3}{5}, \frac{4}{5}$ **d.** $\frac{1}{6}, \frac{1}{3}, \frac{1}{2}, \frac{2}{3}, \frac{5}{6}$ **e.** A regular polygon with n sides has rotational symmetry for every multiple of the quotient of $\frac{360°}{n}$. **17.** $\frac{x}{100} = \frac{25}{125}$; $x = 20$ **19.** $x = 21$ **21.** $m = 13$ **23.** $v = 8$ **25.** $x = -1$

Section 11C Review

1. (0, 0), (4, 0), and (1, −5) **3.** (1, 2) **7.** D

Chapter 11 Summary & Review

1. 6
2.

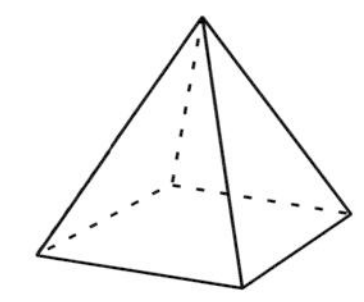

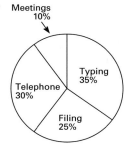

8 edges, 5 faces, 5 vertices
3. a. Answers will vary. **b.** SA = 520 in^2, V = 600 in^3
4.

Meetings 10%
Typing 35%
Telephone 30%
Filing 25%

5. Circumference, 138.0 m; Area, 1517.0 m^2 **6.** Surface area, 533.8 cm^2; Volume, 942 cm^3

7.

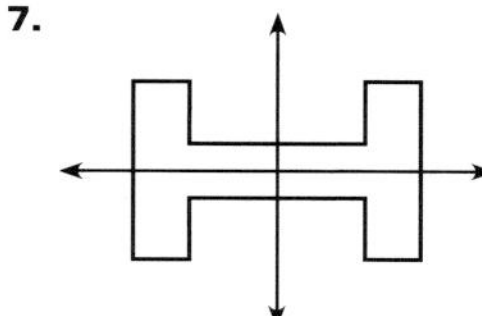

Yes **8.** $A'(-7, 1)$ **9. b.** $A'(0, 0)$, $B'(4, 0)$, $C'(6, -3)$, and $D'(2, -5)$ **c.** $A'(0, 0)$, $B'(0, -4)$, $C'(3, -6)$, and $D'(5, -2)$

Chapter 12

12-1 Try It (Example 1)

There are 6 different outcomes for juice orders.

12-1 Try It (Examples 2–3)

20

12-1 Exercises & Applications

1. a. 12 **b.** 36 **c.** Counting Principle **3.** 24 **5.** 24 **7.** 120 **9.** 144 **11.** 144

12-2 Try It (Examples 1–2)

120

12-2 Try It (Examples 3–5)

a. 24 **b.** 3,628,800 **c.** 3024

12-2 Exercises & Applications

1. a. 4 **b.** 3 **c.** 2 **d.** 1 **e.** 24 **3.** 5040 **5.** 362,880 **7.** ARY, AYR, RAY, RYA, YAR, YRA (A = Arimora, R = Roba, Y = Yegorova) **9.** ABCD, ABDC, ACBD, ACDB, ADBC, ADCB, BACD, BADC, BCAD, BCDA, BDAC, BDCA, CABD, CADB, CBAD, CBDA, CDAB, CDBA, DABC, DACB, DBAC, DBCA, DCAB, DCBA; None of the orderings form words. **11.** C **13.** The factorial product $x!$ increases very quickly as x increases. **15.** Surface area = 216 cm^2 **17.** Surface area = 56 in^2 **19.** 168 m^3

12-3 Try It

a. 3 **b.** 10

SELECTED ANSWERS

711

SELECTED ANSWERS

12-3 Exercises & Applications

1. a. Alex and Bess, Alex and Chandra **b.** Bess and Chandra **c.** 3 **3.** Yes **5.** 6 **7.** 1 **9.** 20 **11.** B **13. a.** 20 **b.** 120 **c.** The number in b is greater **17.** 25.1 in. **19.** 34.5 mm

Section 12A Review

1. 12 **3.** There are 8 possibilities. **5.** 40,320 **7.** 720 **9. a.** 1000 **b.** 720 **11.** A

12-4 Try It (Examples 3–4)

a. 1:1 **b.** 2:4

12-4 Try It (Examples 5–6)

a. 1:1 odds for both; Fair **b.** Odds for A = 2:1, odds for B = 1:2; Unfair **c.** Odds for Evan = 3:3, odds for Primo = 3:3, odds for Trace = 2:4; Unfair

12-4 Exercises & Applications

1. a. 2 **b.** 4 **c.** 2:4 **3.** 1, 2, 3, 4, 5, 6, 7, or 8 **5.** 1:1 **7.** 2:3 **9.** 104:66 **11.** 2:52 **13.** 26:28 **15.** 16:38 **17.** Odds for A = 1:5, odds for B = 4:2, odds for C = 1:5; Unfair **21.** Yes **23.** 706.5 in^2 **25.** 0.8 m^2

12-5 Try It (Examples 1–3)

a. $\frac{1}{3} \approx 33.3\% = 0.333$ **b.** $\frac{1}{2} = 50\% = 0.5$ **c.** $\frac{3}{10} = 30\% = 0.3$

12-5 Try It (Examples 4–5)

a. $\frac{7}{8}$ **b.** $\frac{1}{100}$; 1:99

12-5 Exercises & Applications

1. a. 12 **b.** $\frac{3}{12}$ **c.** $\frac{1}{4}$ **3.** $\frac{1}{6} \approx 16.7\% = 0.167$ **5. a.** 75.1% **b.** 24.9% **c.** 18.4% **7.** Probability does not = $\frac{7}{8}$; Odds = 1:7 **9.** Probability = $\frac{1}{2}$; Odds = 1:1 **11.** $\frac{1}{2}$ **13.** $\frac{1}{8}$ **15.** $\frac{55}{99} = \frac{5}{9}$ **17.** 1% **19.** 56%

21. Possible answers: A dropped ball will fall down (probability 1); A person will jump to the moon tomorrow (probability 0). **23.** 9118.6 cm^3 **25.** 1356.5 in^3 **27.** $(x + 4, y - 6)$ **29.** $(x - 0.2, y + 7)$

12-6 Try It (Examples 1–2)

a. 0.58 **b.** $\frac{8}{72} = \frac{1}{9}$; Less than the theoretical probability of $\frac{6}{36} = \frac{1}{6}$

12-6 Try It (Examples 3–4)

$\frac{6}{128} = \frac{3}{64}$

12-6 Exercises & Applications

1. a. 10 in^2 **b.** 60 in^2 **c.** $\frac{10}{60} = \frac{1}{6}$ **3.** $\frac{9}{72} = \frac{1}{8}$ **5.** $\frac{15}{72} = \frac{5}{24}$ **7.** $\frac{1}{72}$ **9.** $\frac{3}{36} = \frac{1}{12}$; Less than experimental **11.** $\frac{6}{36} = \frac{1}{6}$; Less than experimental **13.** $\frac{1}{36}$; Greater than experimental **15.** $\frac{48}{80} = 60\%$ **17.** An estimate from 1000 trials would give more confidence. **19.** $\frac{9}{144} = \frac{1}{16}$ **21. a.** Experimental **b.** Possible data set: 10 injured fire fighters, 36 uninjured **23.** Figure has one line of symmetry. **25.** Figure has one line of symmetry.

12-7 Try It (Examples 1–2)

a. Dependent **b.** Independent

12-7 Try It (Examples 4–5)

a. $\frac{1}{10}$ **b.** $\frac{7}{30}$

12-7 Exercises & Applications

1. a. $\frac{5}{10}$ **b.** 4 green cubes; 9 cubes **c.** $\frac{4}{9}$ **d.** $\frac{2}{9}$ **3.** Independent **5.** $\frac{1}{48}$ **7.** $\frac{1}{4}$ **9. a.** $\frac{1}{16} = 6.25\%$ **b.** No **13.** D **15.** 5%, 14% **17.** 6

Section 12B Review

1. 1, 2, 3, 4, 5, 6, 7, 8, 9, 10 **3.** 4:2 **7.** $\frac{3}{10} = 30\% = 0.3$ **9.** $\frac{4}{5} = 80\% = 0.8$ **11.** Independent **13.** $\frac{1}{4}$

Chapter 12 Summary & Review

1. 60 **2.** The store needs 8 bins. **3.** 15 **4.** 24 **5.** TUV, TVU, UVT, UTV, VTU, VUT **6.** 21 **7.** 5:3 **8.** Melanie's odds = 4:3, Nathan's odds = 3:4; Unfair **9. a.** $\frac{4}{6} = \frac{2}{3}$ **b.** $\frac{2}{6} = \frac{1}{3}$ **10.** 8% **11.** $\frac{11}{25}$ **12.** $\frac{4}{9}$ **13.** $\frac{1}{12}$ **14.** $\frac{5}{11} \cdot \frac{4}{10} = \frac{2}{11}$

Cumulative Review Chapters 1–12

1. A **2.** D **3.** C **4.** C **5.** D **6.** A **7.** C **8.** B **9.** B **10.** C **11.** D **12.** D **13.** B **14.** C **15.** A

SELECTED ANSWERS

712

Photographs

Cover/Spine Dugald Bremner/Tony Stone Images

Front Matter **iii** GHP Studio* **iii (background)** John Banagan/The Image Bank **v–xvi T (border)** GHP Studio* **xviii BC** GHP Studio* **xviii TC** Thomas Johnson/Earthviews **xviii BL** David Madison **xviii BR** Adam Peiperl/The Stock Market **xix T** Parker/Boon Productions and Dorey Sparre Photography* **xix B** Dennis Geaney,* Ken Karp* and Parker/Boon Productions and Dorey Sparre Photography* **xxi** Anne Dowie* **xxii** Anne Dowie* **xxiii** Anne Dowie* **xxiv** Roz Chast © 1995 from The New Yorker Magazine, Inc. **xxv** Richard Steinheimer **xxvi** Ken Karp* **xxviii** Ken Karp* **xxix** William R. Sallaz/Duomo

Chapter 1 **2–3 (background)** Allen Lee Page/The Stock Market **2 TL** Giraudon/Art Resource, NY **2 BL** SEF/Art Resource, NY **2 R** Reed Saxon/AP Photo **2 TR** Cheryl Fenton* **3** Ken Karp* **4** Cheryl Fenton* **5 L** Don Mason/The Stock Market **5 R** Geoffrey Nilsen Photography* **6** Lawrence Migdale/Tony Stone Images **8** Shaw McCutcheon/Bruce Coleman Inc. **10** Nathan T. Wright/Bruce Coleman Inc. **11 L** J. Messerschmidt/ Bruce Coleman Inc. **11 R** ©1996, USA TODAY. Reprinted with permission. Photo by Cheryl Fenton* **12** UPI/Corbis-Bettmann **13 T** Cameramann/The Image Works **13 B** Rich Iwasaki/Tony Stone Images **15** Library of Congress **16** Tim Davis* **18** Chad Ehlers/ Tony Stone Images **19** GHP Studio* **20** Stanley King Collection **21 R** Dan Dancer/Herd/Sipa Press **21 L** Ken Karp* **24** Robie Price* **27 T** Don Mason/The Stock Market **27 R** Geoffrey Nilsen Photography* **28** Will & Deni McIntyre/Photo Researchers **29 TL** David Madison **29 TR** David Madison/Bruce Coleman Inc. **29 B** Jim Cummins/FPG International **30** Court Mast/FPG International **31** Culver Pictures **32** Cheryl Fenton* **33** Andrea Sperling/FPG International **34** Otto Greule/Allsport **35** Geoffrey Nilsen Photography* **36** Bill Losh/FPG International **38** Andy Lyons/Allsport **40 R** David Madison **40 L** Clive Mason/Allsport **41** The Image Bank **42 R** Parker/Boon Productions and Dorey Sparre Photography* **42 L** Dennis Geaney* **43 T** David Madison **43 B** Cheryl Fenton* **44 T** Stephen Dunn/Allsport **45** Jim Cummins/FPG International **46** Stephen Dunn/Allsport **47** Geoffrey Nilsen Photography* **51 TL** David Madison **51 BL (capitol)** Richard Pasley/Stock, Boston **51 BL (tiles)** Cheryl Fenton* **51 TR** Cheryl Fenton* **51 BR** George B. Fry III*

Chapter 2 **52–53 (background)** GHP Studio* **52 B** Photo © Michael Holford/Collection British Museum **52 TL** David Madison **52 TR** Jenny Thomas* **53 B** Cheryl Fenton* **53 T** Joe McDonald/Animals, Animals **54 T** E. R. Degginger/Animals, Animals **54 B** Johnny Johnson/DRK Photo **55** Cindy Lewis **56** Will & Deni McIntyre/Tony Stone Images **58** Renee Lynn/Davis-Lynn Images **59** Ford Motor Company **60 L** Phil Degginger/Bruce Coleman Inc. **60 R** Cheryl Fenton* **61** GHP Studio* **62** Cindy Lewis **63** Tim Davis/Davis-Lynn Images **66** Anne Dowie* **68** Ken Karp* **69** Archive Photos **70** Maxell Corporation of America **71** Cindy Lewis **72** Tony Arruza/The Image Works **73 (inset)** The Bancroft Library, University of California **73 (background)** Steve Solum/Bruce Coleman Inc. **74 L** Mindscape, Inc. **74 R** Jenny Thomas* **77** Art Wolfe/Tony Stone Images **78** Cheryl Fenton.* Drawing from the collection of Jeff Kelly **80** Detroit Industry, North Wall (detail of fresco), 1932–1933 by Diego Rivera. Accession no. 33.10N (detail). Photograph © 1996 The Detroit Institute of Arts, Gift of Edsel B. Ford. **81** Long Term Parking, sculpture by Arman. Photo by Gianfranco Gorgoni/Sygma **82** Rene Sheret/Tony Stone Images **83** Photo © Michael Holford/Collection British Museum **84 L** Charles D. Winters/ Photo Researchers **84 R** Eric Gravé/ Photo Researchers **85** Culver Pictures **86** Dr. Jeremy Burgess/SPL/Photo Researchers **87** NMAI/Smithsonian Institution **88** Ken Karp* **89** David J. Sams/Stock, Boston **90** Cheryl Fenton* **91** Jose L. Pelaez/The Stock Market **92** Corbis-Bettmann **93** GHP Studio* **94** David Madison **95** Steve Solum/Bruce Coleman Inc. **97** Geoffrey Nilsen Photography*

Chapter 3 **102–103 (background)** M. L. Sinibaldi/The Stock Market **102 TL** Cheryl Fenton* **102 TC** Ulrike Welsch **102 TR** Ulrike Welsch **102 BL** Alfred Pasieka/G&J Images/The Image Bank **103 T** Cheryl Fenton* **103 B** Naomi Duquid/Asia Access **104 T** Cheryl Fenton* **104 B** Aneal F. Vohra/Unicorn Stock Photos **105** World Perspectives/Tony Stone Images **106** Topham/The Image Works **110 L** Richard Hutchings/Photo Researchers **110 R** USGS/NASA **111** Finley Holiday Films **113** Ken Karp* **114** Julian Baum/SPL/Photo Researchers **115 L** NASA/JPL Special Services **115 R** Cheryl Fenton* **116** James Balog/Tony Stone Images **117 T** Ken Karp* **117 B** Parker/Boon Productions and Dorey Sparre Photography* **118** fotos international/Archive Photos **119** Finley Holiday Film **120** John Lei* **121** NASA **123** Francois Gohier/Photo Researchers **124** Finley Holiday Film **125** John Lei* **127** Yerkes Observatory Photograph **129** Biophoto Associates/Photo Researchers **130** Cheryl Fenton* **131** World Perspectives/Tony Stone Images **132** NASA/Dan McCoy/The Stock Market **133** Ken Karp* **134 L** Peter Beck/The Stock Market **134 R** G. Holz/ The Image Works **137** Jane Lidz **139 L** GHP Studio* **139 R** Mike Greenlar/The Image Works **140** Ken Karp* **141** Ken Karp **143** Cheryl Fenton* **144 L** Mark Loader/Uniphoto Picture Agency **144 R** Cheryl Fenton* **146** Ken Karp* **147** Courtesy of The Selmer Company **148** Wolfgang Kaehler **149** Anne Dowie* **150** Cheryl Fenton* **151** G. C. Kelley/Photo Researchers **152** Bob Daemmrich/Stock, Boston **153 L** Cheryl Fenton* **153 R** Anne Dowie* **154** Richard Pasley/Liaison International **155 T** JPL/NASA **155 B** GHP Studio* **156** Cheryl Fenton* **157 L** GHP Studio* **157 R** Ken Karp* **158** Cheryl Fenton* **159** Geoffrey Nilsen Photography* **163 TL** Ken Karp* **163 TR** Cheryl Fenton* **163 BL** Renee Lynn/Davis-Lynn Images **163 BR** GHP Studio*

Chapter 4 **164–165 (background)** Cheryl Fenton* **164 TL** Cheryl Fenton* **164 TR** GHP Studio* **164 B** Photo © Michael Holford/Collection British Museum **165 T** Anne Dowie* **165 B T.** A. Wiewandt/DRK Photo **166 T** GHP Studio* **166 B** John Margolies/Esto **167 T** Jonathan Kirn/Liaison International **167 C** Jon Riley/Tony Stone Images **167 B** Tim Flach/Tony Stone Images **168** Ed Bock/The Stock Market **169** Ken Karp* **170** Bryan F. Peterson/The Stock Market **171 L** Joe McDonald/Animals, Animals **171 C** Stephen Green-Armytage/The Stock Market **171 R** Roy Morsch/The Stock Market **172** Roger Tully/Tony Stone Images **173** Pierre Boulat/Cosmos/Woodfin Camp & Associates **175** Laima Druskis/Photo Researchers **176** Adam Lubroth/Liaison International **178** Joe Quever* **179** Ed Lallo/Liaison International **180 L** Dennis Geaney* **180 R** Ken Karp* **181** UPI/Corbis-Bettmann **183 L** Ken Karp* **183 TR** Jonathan Kirn/Liaison International **183 CR** Jon Riley/Tony Stone Images **183 BR** Tim Flach/Tony Stone Images **184** Tim Davis/Photo Researchers **185** Ken Karp* **186** Crandall/The Image Works **187** Union Pacific Railroad **189** Ken Karp* **190** Tim Fitzharris/Masterfile **191** Joe Quever* **193 L** Ken Karp* **193 R** Dennis Geaney* **194** Porter Gifford/Liaison International **195** Cheryl Fenton* **197** Cheryl Fenton* **200** Bob Daemmrich/Stock, Boston **201** Ken Karp* **202 L** Zefa Germany/The Stock Market **202 R** Tim Davis/Tony Stone Images **203** Geoffrey Nilsen Photography*

Chapter 5 **208–209 (background)** Rafael Macía/Photo Researchers **208 TR** GHP Studio* **208 L** ©1997 photo by Kunio Hirano/ORION PRESS, Tokyo **209 T** Roberto de Gugliemo/SPL/Photo Researchers **209 B** Bob Burch/Bruce Coleman Inc. **210 T** Cheryl Fenton* **210 B** Parker/Boon Productions and Dorey Sparre Photography* **211** Jon Simon/Liaison International **212 L** Marty Katz/Woodfin Camp & Associates **212 R** David Barnes/Tony Stone Images **213** Cheryl Fenton* **214** Ron Sanford/Tony Stone Images **216** Ken Kay/Fundamental Photographs **217 TL** Ken Karp* **217 TR** Greg Stott/Masterfile **217 B** Robert Fried/Stock, Boston **219** GHP Studio* **220** 1994 by Rand McNally R.L. 94-S-140 **221 L** Bob Krist/The Stock Market **221 R** P. Hammerschmidt/Okapia/Photo Researchers **222 L** Lisl Dennis/The Image Bank **223** Cheryl Fenton* **224** Harvey Lloyd/The Stock Market **226 L** Rafael Macia/Photo Researchers **226 C** Catherine Karnow/Woodfin Camp & Associates **226 R** M. Granitsas/The Image Works **227 T** Michal Heron/The Stock Market **227 TL** Cheryl Fenton* **227 B** Tony Craddock/SPL/Photo Researchers **228** J. C. Carton/Bruce Coleman Inc. **229 L** Ken Karp* **229 R** Parker/Boon Productions and Dorey Sparre Photography* **230 L** Wendell Metzen/Bruce Coleman Inc. **230 R** Springer/Liaison International **230 B** GHP Studio* **233** Charles Gupton/Stock, Boston **234** Kevin R. Morris/Tony Stone Images **235** Kay Chernush **236** Peter Mauss/Esto **237 L** Kevin Schafer/Tony Stone Images **237 R** Jon Simon/Liaison International **239** Cheryl Fenton* **240 L** M. Douglas/The Image Works **240 R** GHP Studio* **241** Cheryl Fenton* **242 L** Ken Karp* **242 R** Miles Ertman/Masterfile **244** Renee Lynn* **247** David Madison **248** Lee Foster/Bruce Coleman Inc. **250** Cheryl Fenton* **251** Schiller/The Image Works **252** Cheryl Fenton* **253** GHP Studio* **254** Lionello Fabbri/Photo Researchers **258 L** Baron Wolman **258 R** John Margolies/ESTO **260** Parker/Boon Productions and Dorey Sparre Photography* **261** Kal Muller/Woodfin Camp & Associates **262** Craig Wells/Liaison International **263** Cheryl Fenton* **264** Claus Andersen/Masterfile **265** Geoffrey Nilsen Photography* **269 L** John Elk/Stock, Boston **269 TR** GHP Studio* **269 B** David Rosenberg/Tony Stone Images

Chapter 6 **270–271 (background)** Cheryl Fenton* **270 L** Cheryl Fenton* **270 TR** Jack Vartoogian **270 BR** The Oakland Museum of California **271 T** Peter Menzel/Stock, Boston **271 B** Nancy Fix/Stock, Boston **272 B** NASA **272 T** Warren Faidley/Weatherstock **273** Will & Deni McIntyre/Photo Researchers **274** David Sailors/The Stock Market **275 T** Scala/Art Resource, NY **275 B** Jeff Hunter/The Image Bank **276** Ned Gillette/The Stock Market **277** Dale O'Dell/The Stock Market **278** David Pollack/The Stock Market **279** Jim Pickerell/The Image Works **280** M. Siluk/The Image Works **281** William Johnson/Stock, Boston **282** Ken Karp*

283 Howard Sochurek/Woodfin Camp & Associates **284** Donald Dietz/Stock, Boston **285** © Aardman Animations/Wallace and Gromit Ltd. 1995 **286 L** Brownie Harris/The Stock Market **286 R** Erwin and Peggy Bauer/Bruce Coleman Inc. **287** Ken Karp* **288 L** Ken Karp* **288 R** Dennis Geaney* **289** David Madison **290** Art Wolfe/Tony Stone Images **291 TL** Ken Karp* **291 BL** Scala/Art Resource, NY **291 R** Will & Deni McIntyre/Photo Researchers **292** David Madison **293** Art Wolfe/Tony Stone Images **294 L** Cheryl Fenton* **294 R** Pieter Arend Folkens **297** Richard Ellis/Photo Researchers **298 L** Alvis Upitis/The Image Bank **298 R** Thomas Johnson/Earthviews **299** Francois Gohier/Photo Researchers **301** Stuart Westmorland/Tony Stone Images **302** Joseph Van/The Image Bank **304 L** Anne Dowie* **304 BR** Tim Davis* **305** Stephen Frink/The Stock Market **306** Culver Pictures **307** Cheryl Fenton* **308 L** Ken Karp* **308 R** Paul Souders/Tony Stone Images **309** Steinhart Aquarium, photo by Tom McHugh/Photo Researchers **310** Ken Karp* **311** Nicholas Conte/Bruce Coleman Inc. **313** Art Wolfe/Tony Stone Images **314** Joe Cavaretta/Wide World Photos **315** Geoffrey Nilsen Photography*

Chapter 7 **320–321 (background)** GHP Studio* **320 TL** Katrine Naleid* **320 TR** Judith Canty/Stock, Boston **320 B** Corbis-Bettmann **321 T** European Space Agency/SPL/Photo Researchers **321 C** GHP Studio* **321 B** New York Public Library, courtesy of Map Division, Astor, Lenox & Tilden Foundations **322 T** Ken Karp* **322 B** George B. Fry III* **323** Smithsonian Institution, photo #83.3049 **324 L** © AAA, reproduced by permission. Photo by Cheryl Fenton* **324 TR** Quattrocchi Architects **324 B** Minnesota State Map ©Rand McNally 352-2-9611. Photo by Ken Karp* **325** Ken Karp* **326** RAGA/The Stock Market **327 T** Brent Jones **327 B** Illustration from THE HOBBIT. Copyright © 1966 by J.R.R. Tolkien. Reprinted by permission of Houghton Mifflin Company. All rights reserved. **328** Bob Daemmrich/Stock, Boston **330 L** Ken Karp* **330 R** Parker/Boon Productions and Dorey Sparre Photography* **331** GHP Studio* **332 L** Blumb/Liaison International **332 R** GHP Studio* **333** Ken Karp* **335** Corbis-Bettmann **336** Courtesy Northampton East High School, Conway, North Carolina **337** Bill Gallery/Stock, Boston **339** William R. Sallaz/Duomo **340** Oscar Mayer, the Oscar Mayer Rhomboid, and the Oscar Mayer Wienermobile are registered trademarks of Kraft Foods, Inc., Madison, Wisconsin and are used with permission. **341** Smithsonian Institution, photo #83.3049 **342** Giraudon/Art Resource, NY **343** Ken Karp* **344 L** John Lei* **344 R** Katrine Naleid* **346** Liza Loeffler* **348** Cheryl Fenton* **349 L** John Lei* **349 R** Eric Carle/Stock, Boston **350 T** Hans Reinhard/Bruce Coleman Inc. **350 B** Vanessa Vick/Photo Researchers **351** Michael Holford **352** William Strode/Woodfin Camp & Associates **353** Nancy Pierce/Photo Researchers **354** Tim Bieber Inc./The Image Bank **355** Gary Holscher/Tony Stone Images **356 T** Laguna Photo/Liaison International **356 B** Katrine Naleid* **357** Ken Karp* **358** Bob Daemmrich/Stock, Boston **359** Cheryl Fenton* **360 L** John Lei* **360 R** Alan Schein/The Stock Market **360 BR** Ken Karp* **364** Cheryl Fenton* **366** Robb Kendrick/Aurora **368 L** Parker/Boon Productions and Dorey Sparre Photography* **368 R** Ken Karp* **371 L** Steve Starr/Stock, Boston **371 R** Cheryl Fenton* **373** Archive Photos **374 T** John Elk III/Stock, Boston **374 B** Everett Collection **375** Cheryl Fenton* **376 T** Tim Davis/Tony Stone Images **376 B** Everett Collection **377** Geoffrey Nilsen Photography* **381 TL** Photofest **381 TR** California State Railroad Museum **381 BL** GHP Studio*

Chapter 8 **382–383 (background)** Tom Bean/DRK Photo **382 TL** Cheryl Fenton* **382 TR** Alan Schein/The Stock Market **382 B** Cheryl Fenton* **383 T** David Madison/Duomo **383 B** Jon Feingersh/The Stock Market **384 T** GHP Studio* **384 B** Ken Karp* **385** Jane Burton/Bruce Coleman Inc. **386 L** Joe Quever* **386 R** Merlin D. Tuttle **387** John Elk/Stock, Boston **388** ©1996 Cordon Art, Baarn, Holland **389** Merlin D. Tuttle/Bat Conservation International, Inc. **390** Cheryl Fenton* **391** J. McDonald/Bruce Coleman Inc. **393** Michael Fogden/DRK Photo **394** Mark Burnett/Stock, Boston **395** Merlin D. Tuttle **396** Ken Karp* **397** Michael Fogden/DRK Photo **398** Merlin D. Tuttle **399** Jenny Thomas* **400** Wayne Lankinen/DRK Photo **401** Mark Tomalty/Masterfile **402** Michael Fogden/DRK Photo **403 L** Stephen J. Krasemann/DRK Photo **403 R** Jane Burton/Bruce Coleman Inc. **404** Merlin D. Tuttle **405 (background)** Kevin R. Morris/Tony Stone Images **405 (insets)** Cheryl Fenton* **406** Anne Dowie* **407** GHP Studio* **408** Anne Dowie* **409** Cheryl Fenton* **410** Cheryl Fenton* **411** Cheryl Fenton* **412** Brian Stablyk/Tony Stone Images **414** Robert A. Tyrell **414** Will & Deni McIntyre/Tony Stone Images **415** Joe Quever* **416** Marc Biggins/Liaison International **417** Parker/Boon Productions and Dorey Sparre Photography* **421 (background)** Kevin R. Morris/Tony Stone Images **421 (inset)** Cheryl Fenton* **422** Corbis-Bettmann **423** Geoffrey Nilsen Photography*

Chapter 9 **428–429 (background)** Cheryl Fenton* **428 TL** Robert Fried/Stock, Boston **428 TR** NASA **428 B** Cheryl Fenton* **429 T** Dr. Peter W. Sloss/NOAA/NGDC **429 B** Cheryl Fenton* **430** Cheryl Fenton* **432** Tom Bean/DRK Photo **433** Barbara Gerlach/DRK Photo **434 L** Peter Essick/Aurora **434 R** Tom McHugh/Cal. Acad. of Sciences/Photo Researchers **435** NASA, Goddard Institute for Space Studies/SPL/Photo Researchers **436** Guido Cozzi/Bruce Coleman Inc. **437 L** Sally Beyer/Tony Stone Images **437 R** Ted Horowitz/The Stock Market **439 L** Parker/Boon Productions and Dorey Sparre Photography* **439 R** Ken Karp* **442 T** Roger Richards/Liaison International **442 B** Map Art Corporation **447 L** Leo Touchet/Woodfin Camp & Associates **449** Susan Van Etten/Stock, Boston **450** © 1996, USA TODAY. Reprinted with permission. Photo by Cheryl Fenton* **451** Liza Loeffler* **452** Liza Loeffler* **453** Liza Loeffler* **454** UPI/Corbis-Bettmann **455** Cheryl Fenton* **457** Dan Feicht/ Cedar Point **458** David M. Schleser/Photo Researchers **461** Jeff Hunter/The Image Bank **464** Dallas & John Heaton/Stock, Boston **465 T** Rocky Widner **465 B** Jeff Greenberg/MRp/Photo Researchers **466 L** Cheryl Fenton* **466 R** Paramount's Great America **467** Liza Loeffler* **468 L** Parker/Boon Productions and Dorey Sparre Photography* **468 R** Ken Karp* **469** J. L. Bulcao/Liaison International **470** Michele Burgess/The Stock Market **471 L** C. Bruce Forster/Tony Stone Images **471 R** Susan Van Etten/Stock, Boston **472** Underwood Photo Archives, SF **473** Geoffrey Nilsen Photography* **477 TL** Cheryl Fenton* **477 BL** Stacy Pick/Stock, Boston **477 BR** Cheryl Fenton*

Chapter 10 **478–479 (background)** Gregory Sams/SPL/Photo Researchers **478 TL** Scala/Art Resource, NY **478 TR** GHP Studio* **478 B** Cheryl Fenton* **479** Lifesmith Classic Fractals **480 T** John Elk III **480 B** Rich Buzzelli/Tom Stack & Associates **481** (ants) Runk-Schoenberger/Grant Heilman Photography **481** (bees) Charles Krebs/Tony Stone Images **481** Katrine Naleid* **482 L** Bryan Peterson/The Stock Market **482 R** Dr. Jeremy Burgess/SPL/Photo Researchers **483** Michael Lustbader/Photo Researchers **484** David Overcash/Bruce Coleman Inc. **485** Richard R. Hansen/Photo Researchers **486** Donald C. Johnson/The Stock Market **487** Aaron Strong/Liaison International **488** Wolfgang Kaehler/Liaison International **490** Phil Degginger/Bruce Coleman Inc. **491 L** ©1997 photo by Noriyuki Yoshida/ORION PRESS, Tokyo **491 R** Kim Taylor/Bruce Coleman Inc. **493** Kjell B. Sandved/Photo Researchers **494** J. M. Burnley/Bruce Coleman Inc. **495** Ken Karp* **498 T** Michael Lustbader/Photo Researchers **498 B** Daniel J. Cox/Liaison International **500** Mark Burnett/Stock, Boston **502 L** Kim Taylor/Bruce Coleman Inc. **502 R** Jeff Lepore/Photo Researchers **503** E. R. Degginger/Bruce Coleman Inc. **504** Scott Camazine/Photo Researchers **505 L** G & J Images/The Image Bank **505 R** Katrine Naleid* **505 R(inset)** Charles Krebs/Tony Stone Images **506** Richard Hurley/Courtesy of the John Carter Brown Library at Brown University **507** Cheryl Fenton* **508 L** GHP Studio* **508 R** David Katzenstein **509** David Katzenstein **510** Paul F. Gero/KDI-Champ Cookies **511** Cheryl Fenton* **512 L** Ted Horowitz/The Stock Market **512 R** David Katzenstein **514 L** Parker/Boon Productions and Dorey Sparre Photography* **514 R** Ken Karp* **516** John Zich **517 L** Rex Rystedt Photography **517 R** Ken Karp* **519** Katherine Lambert **520** Charles D. Winters/Photo Researchers **521 L** Jim McHugh **521 R** Cheryl Fenton* **523** NASA Space Photo/The Image Bank **524** Ken Karp* **525** Gary Withey/Bruce Coleman Inc. **526 L** Ken Karp* **526 R** Parker/Boon Productions and Dorey Sparre Photography* **527** Cheryl Fenton* **528** NASA/Liaison International **529** Mark M. Lawrence/Stock Market **530** TASS/Sovfoto/Eastfoto **531** Mike Maple/Woodfin Camp & Associates **532** Robert Caputo/Stock, Boston **533** Coco McCoy/Rainbow **534 L** Spencer Grant/Stock, Boston **534 R** Ken Karp* **536** B. Seitz/Photo Researchers **537** Dagmar Fabricius/Stock, Boston **538** Inga Spence/Tom Stack & Associates **539 L** Keith Gunnar/Bruce Coleman Inc. **539 R** Archive Photos **541** Erwin & Peggy Bauer/Bruce Coleman Inc. **543 L** Christopher Pfau/Wide World Photos **543 R** NASA Space Photo/The Image Bank **545** Geoffrey Nilsen Photography*

Chapter 11 **550–551 (background)** Ken Lax* **550 TL** GHP Studio* **550 TR** Adam Woolfitt/Woodfin Camp & Associates **550 B** GHP Studio* **551 T** Mark Newman/Photo Researchers **551 B** Keren Su/Stock, Boston **552 T** Tim Davis/Photo Researchers **552 B** Jim Tuten/Animals, Animals **553** Dawn (1962), by Louise Nevelson. Gold painted wood, 94-1/2 × 75-1/2 × 7-3/4." Photograph courtesy PaceWildenstein, New York **554** Antonio Ribeiro/Liaison International **555** Cubi XIX (1964), by David Smith. © Copyright VAGA, NY. Tate Gallery, London/Art Resource, NY **556 L** John Elk III/Stock, Boston **556 R** Peter Menzel/Stock, Boston **557 TL** Breck P. Kent/Earth Scenes **557 TR** Geoffrey Nilsen* **557 B** Untitled (1975), by Donald Judd. Galvanized iron in ten units, 31" × 9" × 40" each. Donald Judd Estate/VAGA. Photo by Flavin Judd **558 T** Illustration by Amanda Smith, photo by Joe Quever* **558 B** Relief from Sennacherib's Palace at Nineveh. Photo © Michael Holford/Collection British Museum **560** Coco McCoy/Rainbow

562 Black Sun (1969), by Isamu Noguchi. Courtesy of the Seattle City Light 1% for Art Collection **563** Joe Sohm/The Stock Market **566** Memories of Mike (1966), by Larry Bell. Vacuum-plated glass with metal binding. 24" × 24" × 24". Photograph courtesy PaceWildenstein, New York. Photo by Boesch **567** Cheryl Fenton* **568** Brenda Tharp/ Photo Researchers **569** Untitled (1975), by Donald Judd. Galvanized iron in ten units, 31" × 9" × 40" each. Donald Judd Estate/VAGA. Photo by Flavin Judd **571 L** Two Open Modular Cubes/Half-Off (1972) by Sol LeWitt. Tate Gallery, London/Art Resource, NY **571 R** Dawn (1962), by Louise Nevelson. Gold painted wood, 94-1/2 × 75-1/2 × 7-3/4." Photograph courtesy PaceWildenstein, New York **572 T** Kathleen Culbert-Aguilar* **572 B** Una Grande Liberta (1963), by Hubert Dalwood. Aluminum, gilt and wood. 60 × 30 × 10 3/4 (153 × 77 × 27). Collection and photo: Gimpel Fils, London **573 (background)** GHP Studio* **573 (inset)** Wooden horse on wheels from Akhmun, 200 A.D. Photo © Michael Holford/Collection British Museum **574 L** ©1996, USA TODAY. Reprinted with permission. Photo by GHP Studio* **574 R** Cheryl Fenton* **575** Cheryl Fenton* **577** Scott Halleran/Allsport **578** Joe Quever* **579** GHP Studio* **581 L** George Holton/Photo Researchers **581 R** Dr. Tom Kuhn **583** Robert Rathe/Stock, Boston **584 T** Cheryl Fenton* **584 B** GHP Studio* **585** Wolfgang Kaehler **586 T** Cheryl Fenton* **586 B** GHP Studio* **587 L** Ken Karp* **587 R** Kaz Mori/The Image Bank **588** Cheryl Fenton* **589 T** Ken Karp* **589 B** Dennis Geaney* **591 T** GHP Studio* **591 B** Rachel Canto/Rainbow **592 L** Jim Corwin/Tony Stone Images **592 R** GHP Studio* **593 T** GHP Studio* **593 C** Cheryl Fenton* **593 B** Cheryl Fenton* **594** GHP Studio* **595** GHP Studio* **596** Ken Lax* **597** GHP Studio* **598** Corbis-Bettmann **599 (background)** Adam Peiperl/The Stock Market **599 (inset)** Adam Peiperl/The Stock Market **600 T** The Kobal Collection/Touchstone Pictures **600 B** C. Bennett through Scopelens **602** Ken Karp* **605 T** John Eastcott-Yva Momatiuk/Photo Researchers **605 B** Adam Peiperl/The Stock Market **608 L** Adam Peiperl/The Stock Market **608 R** Eric Grave/Photo Researchers **610** Joe Quever* **611** Alfred Pasieka-Science Photo Library/Photo Researchers **613 L** Adam Peiperl/The Stock Market **613 R** Blue, Green, Yellow, Orange, Red (1966), by Ellsworth Kelly. Guggenheim Museum, New York. Photograph by David Heald. © The Solomon R. Guggenheim Foundation, New York. (FN 67.1833) **615 L** Viviane Moos **615 R** Adam Peiperl/The Stock Market **616** C. Bennett through Scopelens **617** Geoffrey Nilsen Photography* **621 TL** Ken Lax* **621 TR** Joe Quever* **621 B** Ken Karp*

Chapter 12 **622–623 (background)** Joe Quever* **622 TL** Jacob Lawrence: Harriet Tubman Series No. 16. Casein tempera on gessoed hardboard, 12 × 17-7/8". Hampton University Museum, Hampton, Virginia **622 TR** Lowell Observatory/NOAO **622 B** Cheryl Fenton* **623 T** Jonathan T. Wright/Bruce Coleman Inc. **623 B** Cheryl Fenton* **624 T** Cheryl Fenton* **624 B** Weinberg-Clark/The Image Bank **625** Cheryl Fenton* **626 L** Stephen J. Krasemann/DRK Photo **626 R** Jenny Thomas* **629** Elliott Smith* **630 T** Pacer Infotec Inc. **630 B** Cheryl Fenton* **631** Cheryl Fenton* **632** Jenny Thomas* **634 T** Richard Pasley/Stock, Boston **634 B** Jeff Lepore/ Photo Researchers **636** Michael Topolovac/David Madison **637** Bruce Iverson **638 L** Parker/Boon Productions and Dorey Sparre Photography* **638 R** Ken Karp* **639** Cheryl Fenton* **641** Cheryl Fenton* **642** Bert Blokhuis/Tony Stone Images **643** Joe Quever* **644 L** J. M. Labat/ Jacana/Photo Researchers **644 R** Cheryl Fenton* **647** Cesar Rubio* **649** Hires Chip/Liaison International **651** GHP Studio* **652** ©1996, USA TODAY. Reprinted with permission. Photo by GHP Studio* **653** Cheryl Fenton* **654 L** David Madison/Bruce Coleman Inc. **654 R** Cheryl Fenton* **657** Cheryl Fenton* **659** Geoff Tomkinson/SPL/Photo Researchers **662** GHP Studio* **665 L** Cheryl Fenton* **665 R** Joe Quever* **667** Geoffrey Nilsen Photography*

*Photographs provided expressly for Addison Wesley Longman, Inc.

Illustrations

Brian Evans: **93b** Terry Guyer: **3d, 9a, 9b, 10b, 12b, 33c, 35a, 36c, 38a, 39f, 43a, 44b, 108a, 109a, 115a, 128a, 138a, 163e, 218b, 219b, 249e, 341a, 347b, 361b, 370b, 381c, 431b, 432a, 432d, 448a, 477a, 479a, 486a, 500a, 500b** Gary Hallgren: **96a** Joe Heiner Studio: All icons and borders. Paul Koziarz: **106a, 173a, 178a, 233a, 248a, 248b, 248c, 248d, 248e, 253a, 253b, 360a, 372a, 375a, 375b, 430a, 430b, 430c, 430d, 563a, 563b, 583a, 583b, 583c, 600a, 610a, 610b, 610c, 659a** Maryland Cartographics: **337a** Marlene May-Howerton: **309b** Patrick Merewether: **631a, 636a, 659b** Precision Graphics: All illustrative technical artwork throughout; all generated electronically. Laurie O'Keefe: **274b, 282b** William Pasini: **7c, 14b, 16b, 24b, 25b, 76a, 172b, 187a, 187b, 192a, 198a, 235a, 257a, 312a, 325a, 326b, 330a, 332a, 336b, 339b, 342b, 392a, 398a, 402b, 403b, 434a, 440c, 442a, 446a, 446b, 540a, 542a, 543b, 544d** QYA Design: **49d, 286b, 300b, 317b, 318b, C3c, C3e, C3f, C6b** Doug Roy: **95a** Rob Schuster: **56a, 64a, 67a, 82a, 86a, 91a, 168a, 177b, 182a, 203a, 263a, 269d, 278a, 284b, 284c, 329a, 329b, 334a, 363e, 367b, 369e, 380c, 410a, 426a, 445b, 459a, 461a, 461b, 469a, 477b, 484b, 489d, 495a, 502b, 629b, 645a, 648a, 660b**

Chapter 7

Page 361

7-8 Answers for Explore

3.

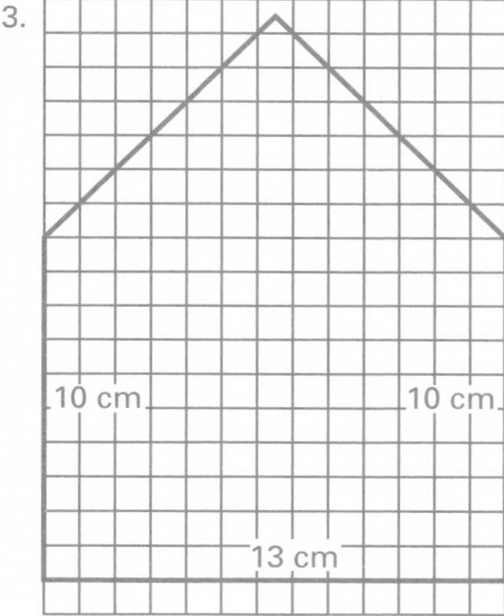

No, houses are not the same shape.

4. The right angles are unchanged. The other angles vary.

5.

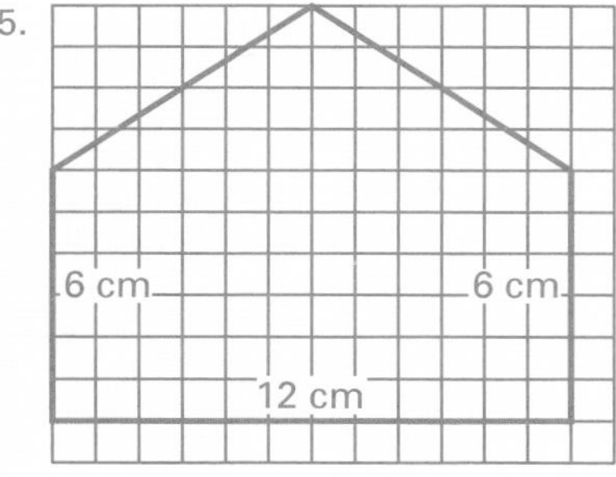

Yes, houses are the same shape.

6. The angles are the same as in the original drawing.

Page 371

7-10 Answers for Explore

1.

Lot space costs $1,000,000. Fence costs $6,000.

Total cost = $1,006,000.

2.

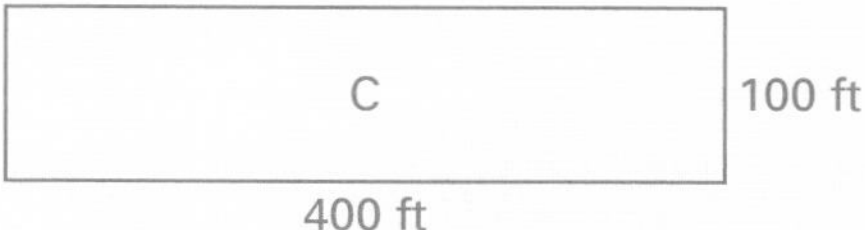

Lot space costs $2,000,000. Fence costs $7,200.
Total cost = $2,007,200.

Lot space costs $4,000,000. Fence costs $12,000.
Total cost = $4,012,000.

3.

Lot	A	B	C
Space	$1,000,000	$2,000,000	$4,000,000
Fencing	$6,000	$7,200	$12,000
Total	$1,006,000	$2,007,200	$4,012,000

The space cost of B is twice the space cost for A, but the perimeter cost for C is twice the fence cost for A; Answers may vary.

4. Fencing: perimeter; Size: area.

Page 381

Suggested Scoring Rubric

You Be The Guide!

4
- Tour is well-planned in terms of time available and use of maps.
- Travel times correlate with distance.
- Letter clearly outlines the plan.

3
- A good attempt at planning a tour is made.
- Travel times are fairly reasonable and correlate reasonably with distance.
- Plans are outlined in the letter.

2
- Plans too many or too few activities.
- Either misjudges travel times or distances.
- Letter does not clearly state plan.

1
- Little attempt made to plan or use maps.
- Does not make allowance for travel time.
- Letter poorly written or nonexistent.

Chapter 8

Page 387

8-1 Answers for Explore

1.

2.

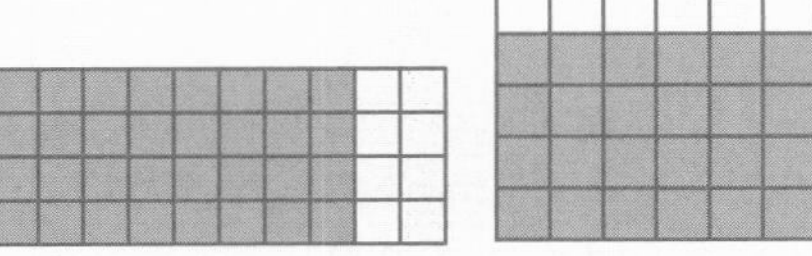

The 10-by-10 grid was easiest; 8 columns of 10 easily show 0.8.

Page 391

8-2 Answers for Explore

1.

Fraction	$\frac{91}{100}$	$\frac{23}{100}$	$\frac{67}{100}$	$\frac{39}{100}$	$\frac{87}{100}$	$\frac{11}{50}$	$\frac{3}{25}$	$\frac{4}{5}$
Decimal	0.91	0.23	0.67	0.39	0.87	0.22	0.12	0.8
Percent	91%	23%	67%	39%	87%	22%	12%	80%

Page 416

8-7 Answers for Explore

1–2.

Old Price	New Price	Price Change
20¢	25¢	+5¢
20¢	15¢	-5¢

$\frac{\text{New Price}}{\text{Old Price}}$	$\frac{\text{Price Change}}{\text{Old Price}}$	$\frac{\text{Price Change}}{\text{New Price}}$
125%	25%	20%
75%	25%	$33\frac{1}{3}$%

3.

Old Price	New Price	Price Change
20¢	30¢	+10¢
20¢	10¢	-10¢

$\frac{\text{New Price}}{\text{Old Price}}$	$\frac{\text{Price Change}}{\text{Old Price}}$	$\frac{\text{Price Change}}{\text{New Price}}$
150%	50%	$33\frac{1}{3}$%
50%	50%	100%

Chapter 9

Page 437

9-2 Answers for Explore

2.

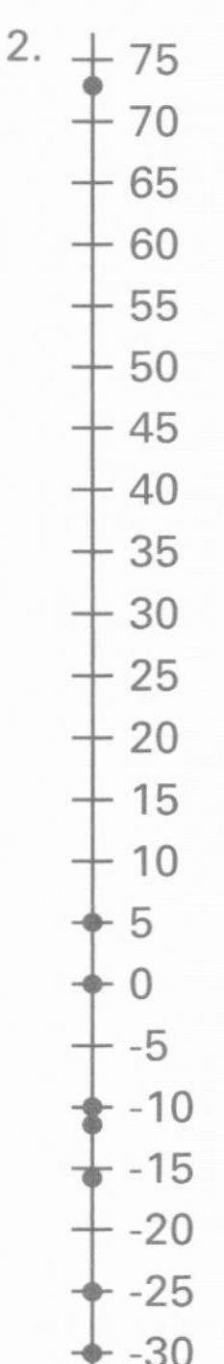

Page 445

9-3 Exercise Answers

1.

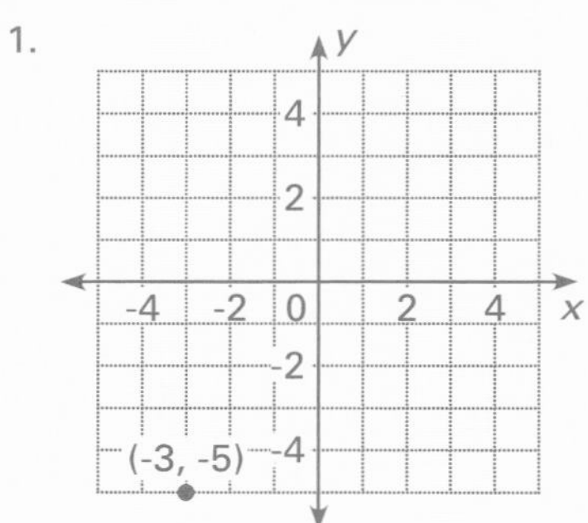

9–13.

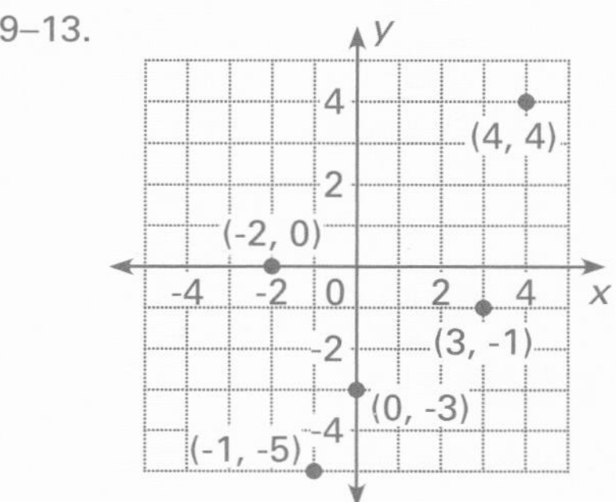

Answers continue on next page.

14–18.

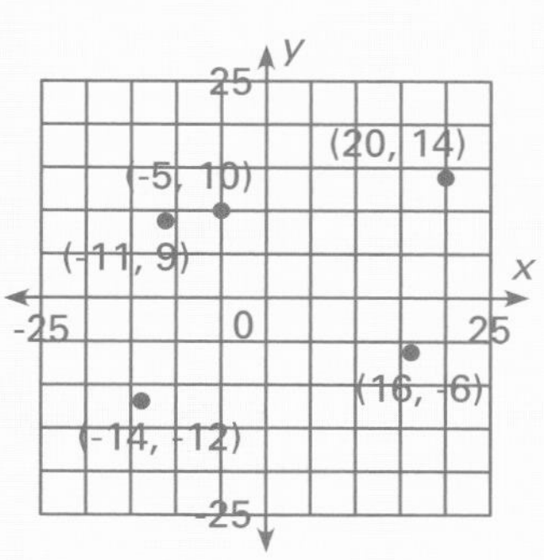

19. b.

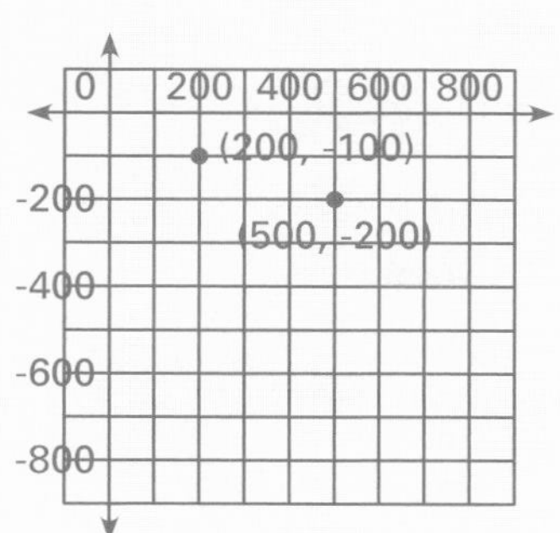

20. Possible Answer

Chapter 10

Page 493

10-3 Exercise Answers

19. a. $8000n$

 b. If there are 365 days in the year, she can lay 8000 • 365 or 2,920,000.

20.

Term Number, n	1	2	3	4
Number in Sequence, $6n$	6	12	18	24

21.

Term Number, n	1	2	3	4
Number in Sequence, $n + 8$	9	10	11	12

22.

Term Number, x	1	2	3	4
Number in Sequence, $-7x$	−7	−14	−21	−28

23.

Term Number, c	1	2	3	4
Number in Sequence, $2c + 5$	7	9	11	13

24.

Term Number, n	1	2	3	4
Number in Sequence, 3^n	3	9	27	81

Page 497

10-4 Exercise Answers

1. Possible answer:

x	1	2	3	4	5
y	−1	2	5	8	11

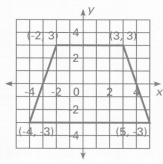

4. $D = 120$, $D = 130$; $D = 2r$
5. $C = 21.00$, $C = 28.00$; $C = 3.5n$
6. $A = 16$, $A = 36$; $A = s^2$
7. $d = 105$, $d = 140$, $d = 175$; $d = 35t$

Possible answers for Exercises 8–17:

8.

x	1	2	3	4	5	6
y	2	4	6	8	10	12

9.

x	1	2	3	4	5	6
y	9	10	11	12	13	14

10.

b	1	2	3	4	5	6
c	−7	−14	−21	−28	−35	−42

11.

g	1	2	3	4	5	6
k	−2	−1	0	1	2	3

12.

x	3	6	9	12	15	18
y	1	2	3	4	5	6

13.

x	1	2	3	4	5	6
y	4	7	10	13	16	19

14.

t	1	2	3	4	5	6
d	−36	−50	−64	−78	−92	−106

15.

x	1	2	3	4	5	6
y	0.22	0.44	0.66	0.88	1.1	1.32

16.

x	1	2	3	4	5	6
y	−1	−2	−3	−4	−5	−6

17.

k	4	8	12	16	20	24
h	2	3	4	5	6	7

Page 501

10-5 Answers for Try It

a.

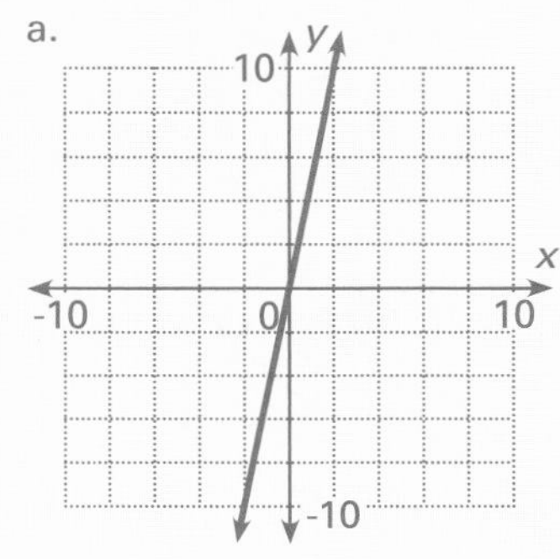

b.

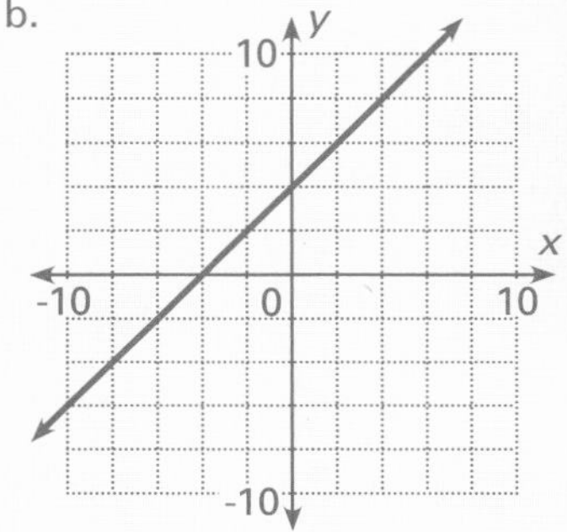

c.

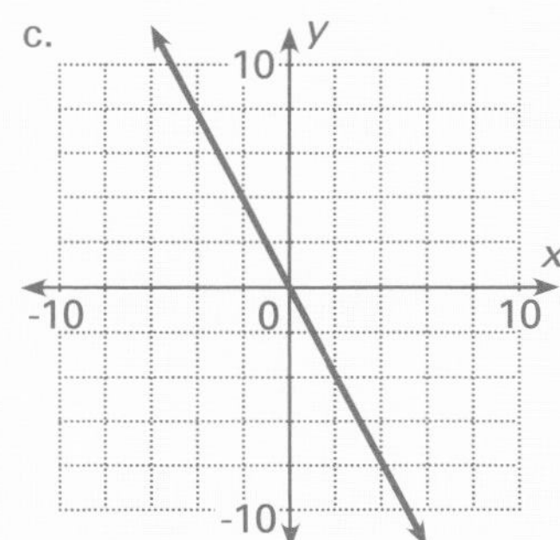

Page 503

10-5 Exercise Answers

1.

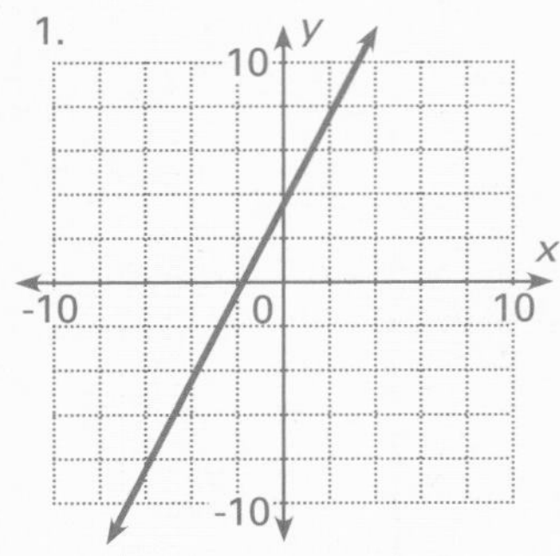

2.

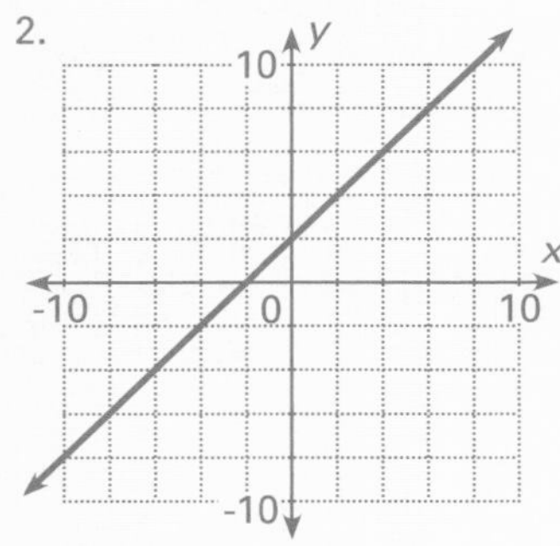

3.

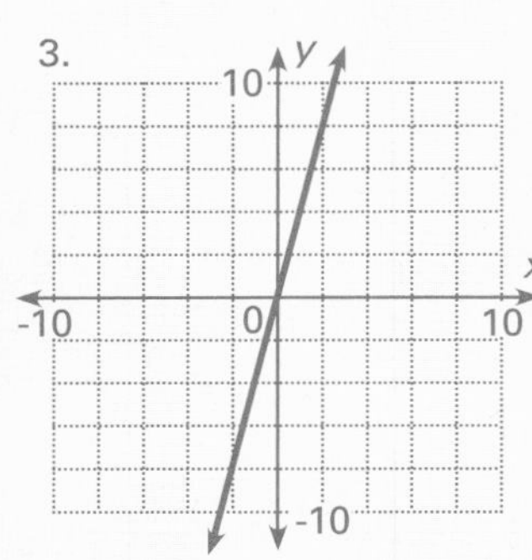

4.

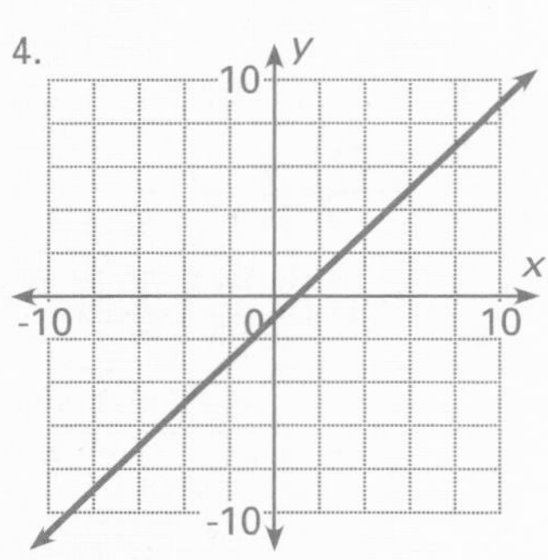

5.

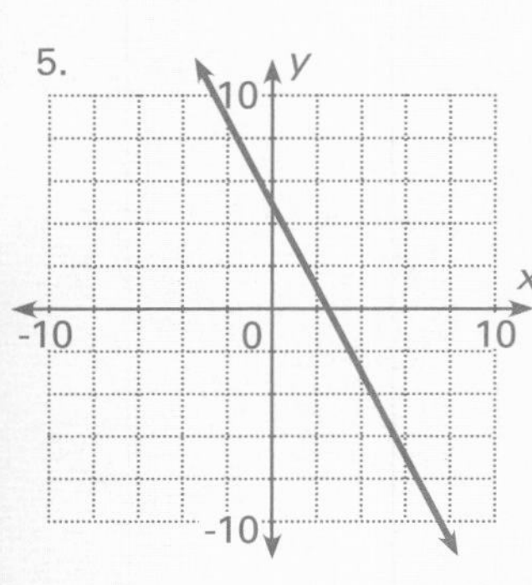

6.

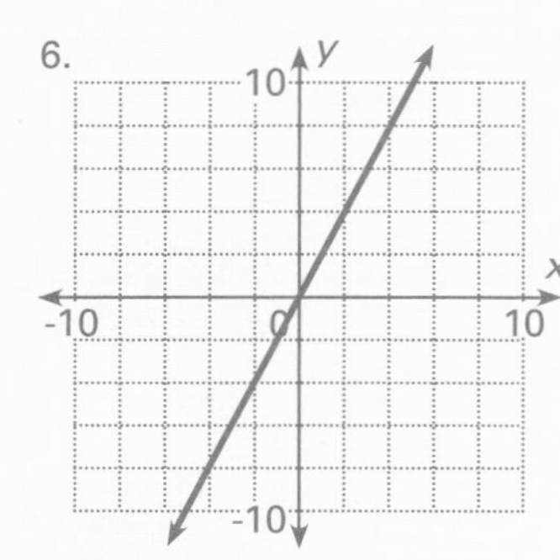

7.

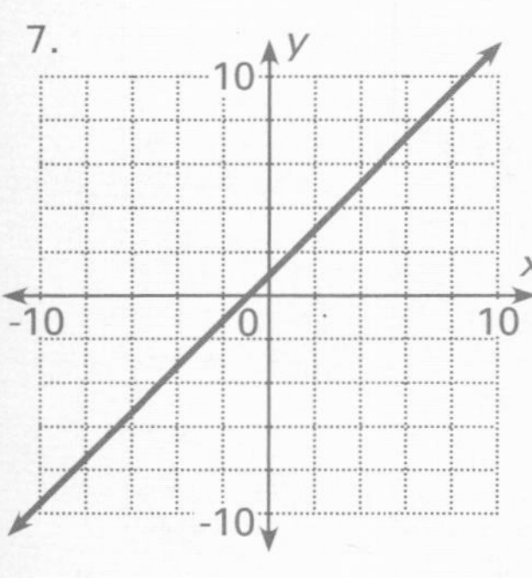

8.

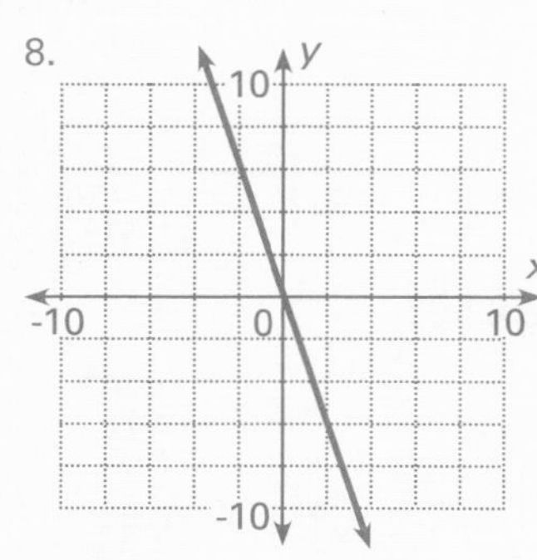

9.

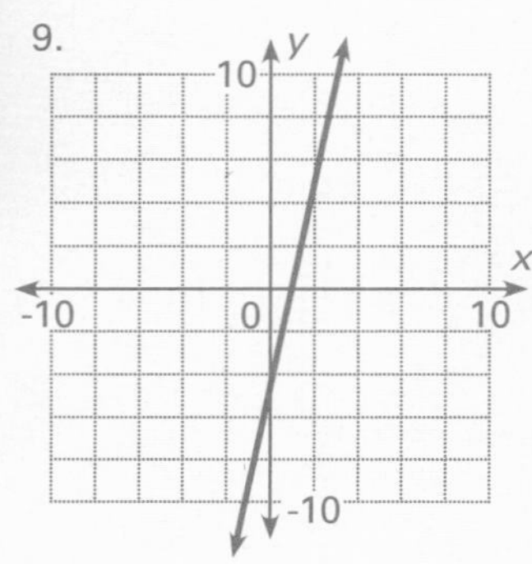

10.

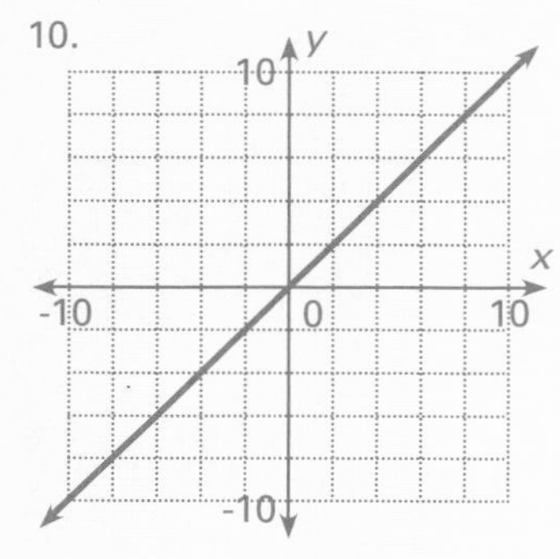

11. The graphs that go through the origin don't have a number subtracted or added at the end of the equation.

12.

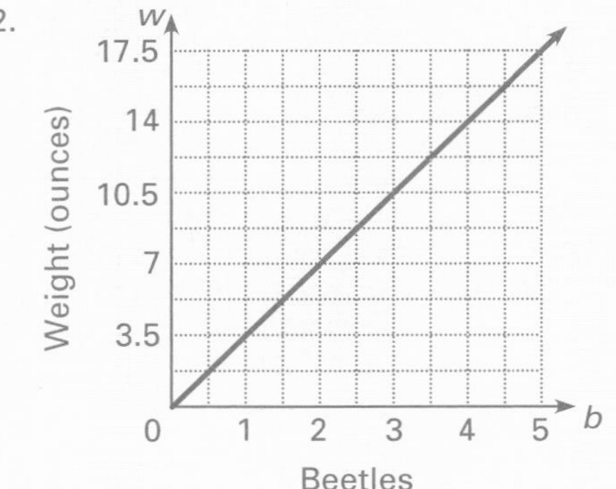

Page 504

10-5 Exercise Answers

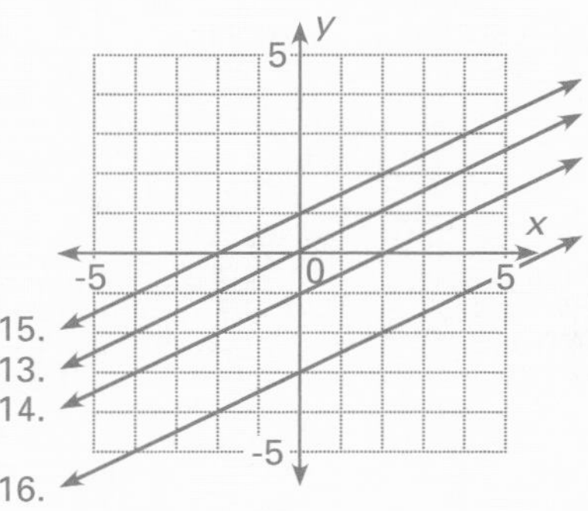

17. They are parallel lines.

19. a. Let b = beats and m = minutes; $b = 140m$ and $b = \frac{m}{60}$.

b. The line with the steeper slope represents the greater rate.

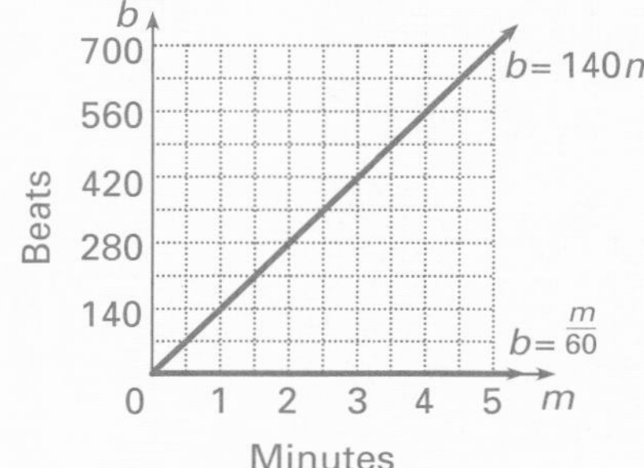

20. Use the equation and $x = 2$ to find the corresponding y value. The only y value is 5, so only the point (2, 5) is on the graph.

21. a.

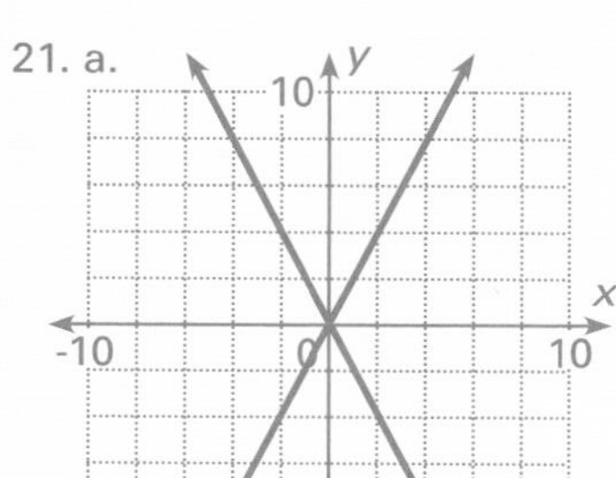

b.

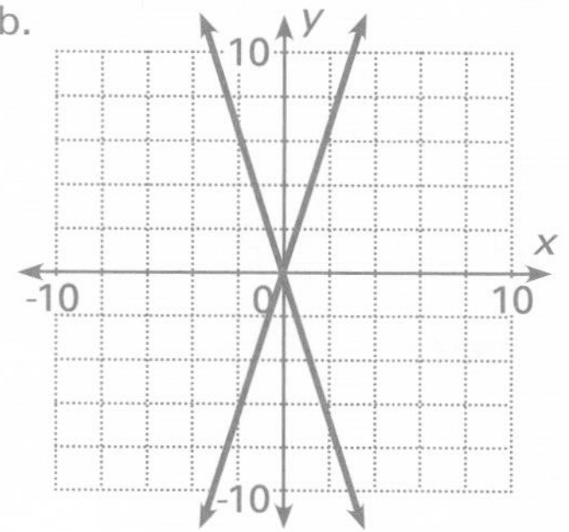

c.

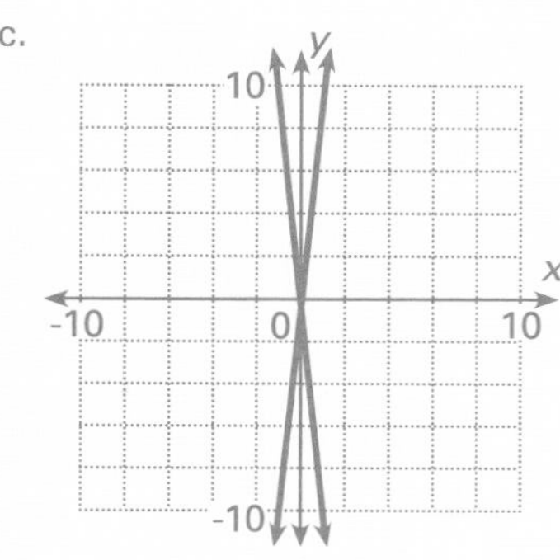

d. The lines are images of each other reflected over the *y*-axis.

Page 506

Answers for 10A Review

11.

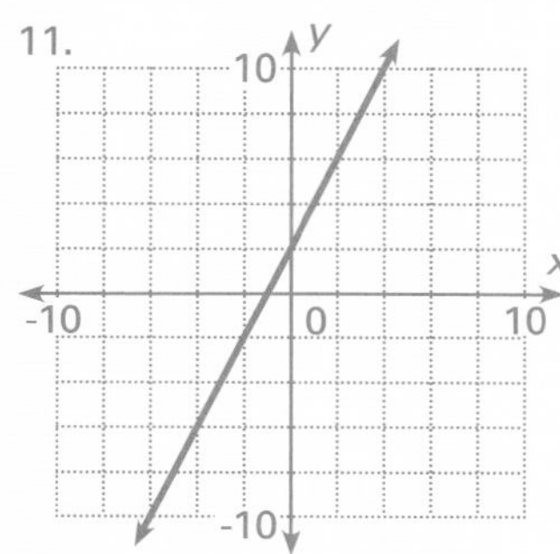

12.

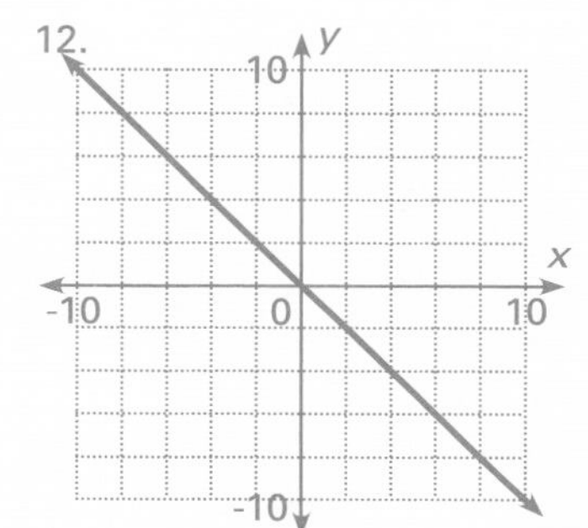

13. Possible answer: An equation uses variables and constants to show that two quantities are equal to each other. A table of values shows specific values of the variables that make the equation true. A graph is a visual representation of the equation.

Page 508

10-6 Answers for Explore

2.

n	1	2	3	4	5	6	7	8	9	10	11	12
c	$5	$10	$15	$20	$25	$30	$35	$40	$45	$50	$55	$60

Page 517

10-8 Answers for Explore

1.

Players	1	2	3	4	5	6	7	8	9	10
Income	$22	$44	$66	$88	$110	$132	$154	$176	$198	$220

Page 519

10-8 Exercise Answers

1.a–c.

2.

3. -5 -4 -3 -2 -1 0 1 2 3 4 5

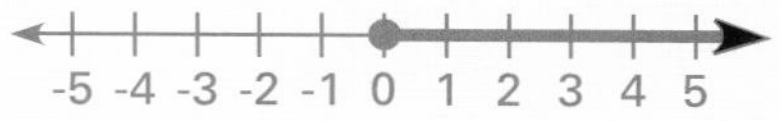

4. -5 -4 -3 -2 -1 0 1 2 3 4 5

5. -5 -4 -3 -2 -1 0 1 2 3 4 5

6. 0 1 2 3 4 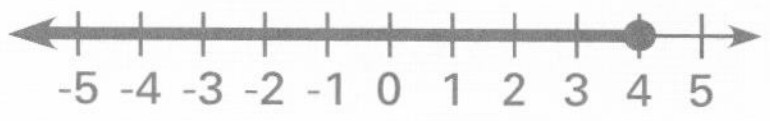 5  6  7 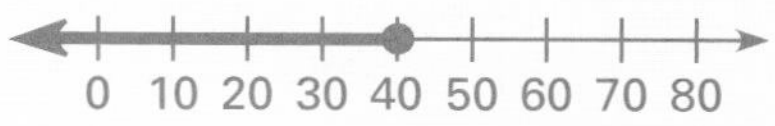 8 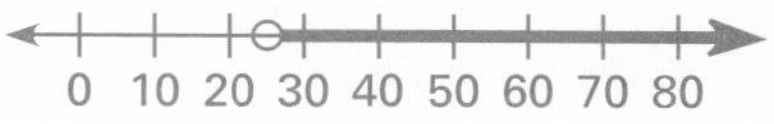 9  10

7. 0 10 20 30 40 50 60 70 80

8. 0 10 20 30 40 50 60 70 80

9. 0 100 200 300 400 500

10. -100 -80 -60 -40 -20 0

11. 0 1000 2000 3000 4000 5000

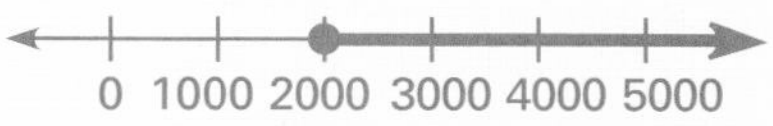

21. The number of tickets sold was greater than 150.

22. The amount of time was less than or equal to 12 seconds.

23. The plane needed at least 90 gallons of fuel.

24. The sales tax was less than or equal to 6%.

25. There were no more than 65 sofas in the shipment.

26. a. $c \leq 80$

b. 0 10 20 30 40 50 60 70 80

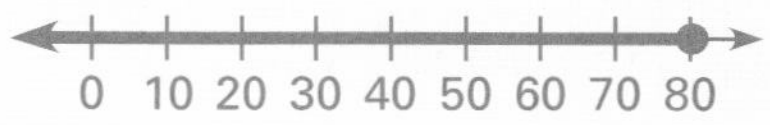

27. $c \leq 1$

0.50 0.75 1.00 1.25

28. $p \geq 1{,}000{,}000{,}000$

Page 534

10-11 Answers for Explore

1.

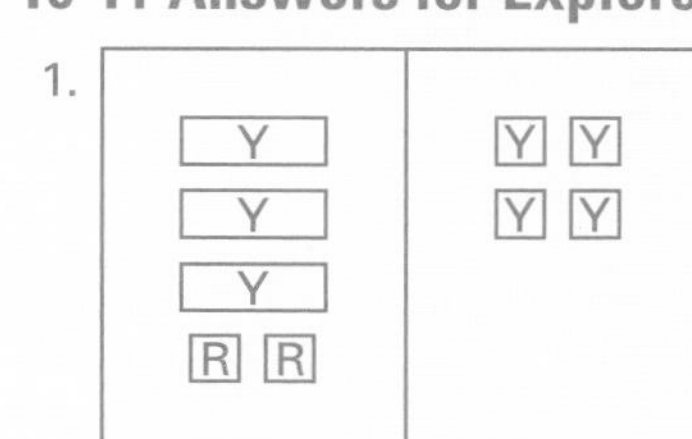

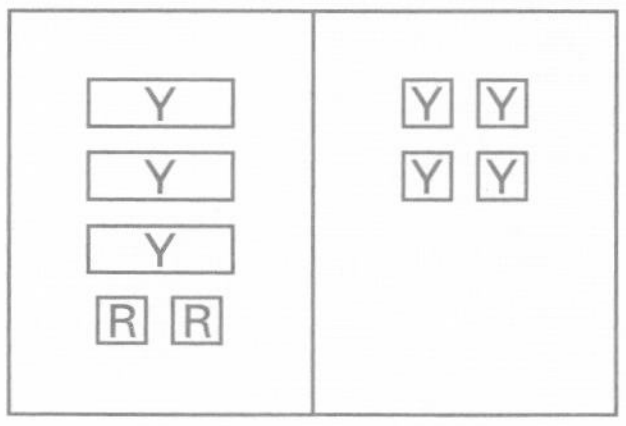

Chapter 11

Page 565

11-3 Exercise Answers

7. 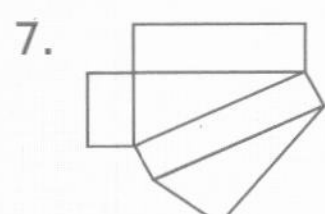

Surface Area: 168 cm^2

8. 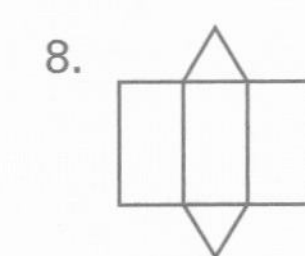

Surface Area: 219 ft^2

Page 576

11-5 Exercise Answers

4. 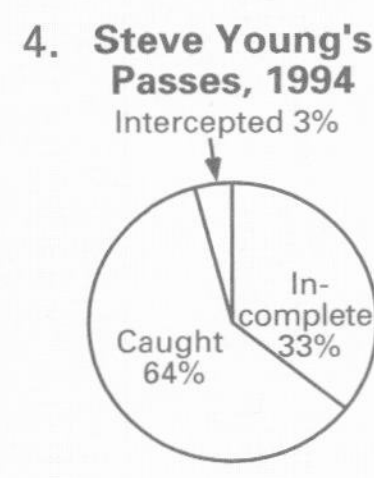

5. 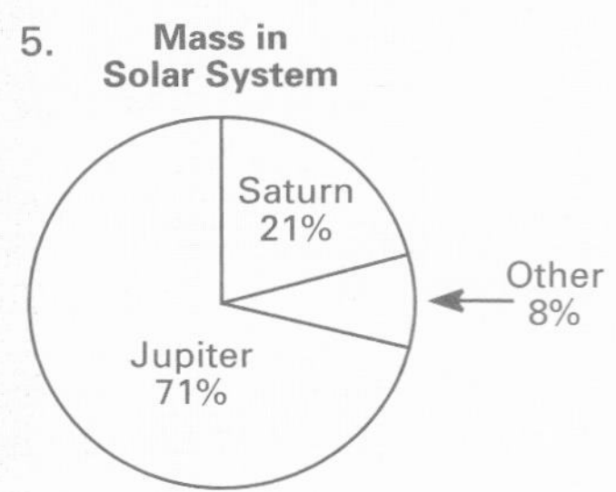

Page 577

11-5 Exercise Answers

8. 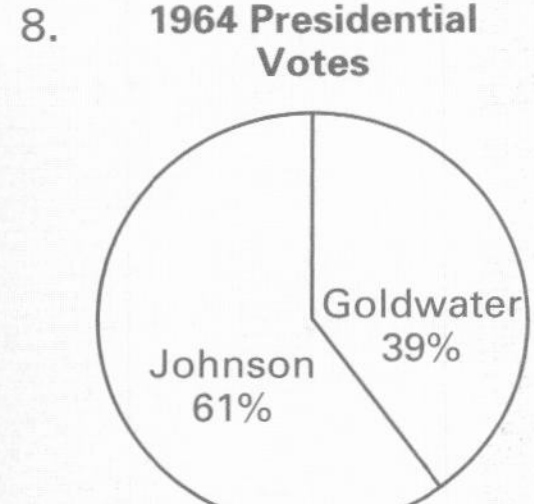

9. 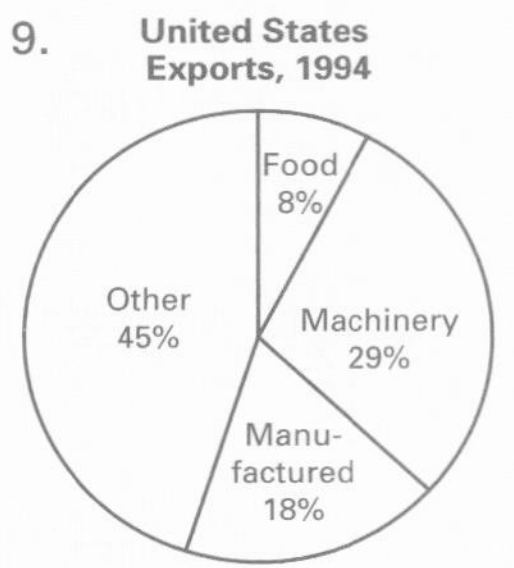

Page 608

11-11 Exercise Answers

1. a–c.

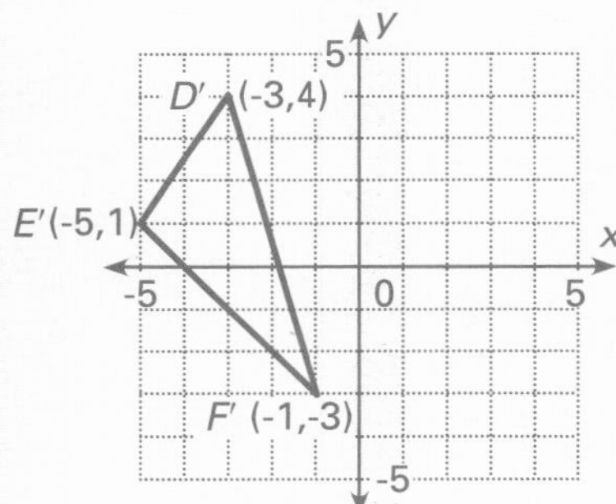

2. 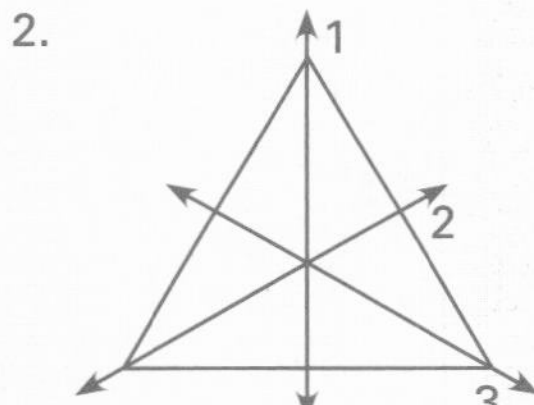

3. 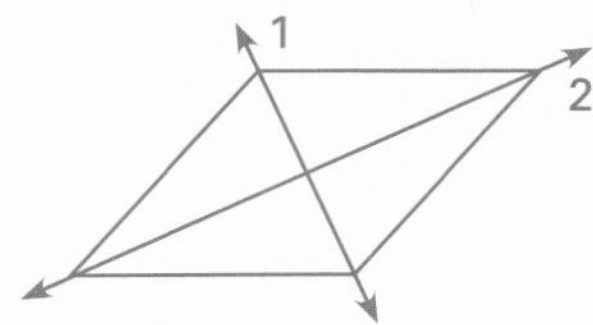

4. 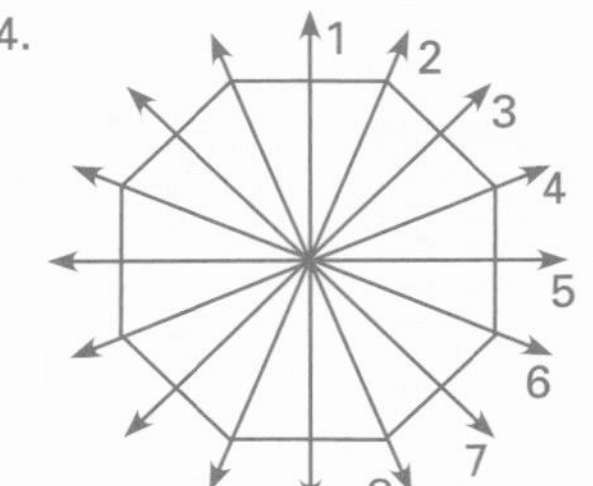

5. Possible figure: A regular hexagon with lines of symmetry numbered 1–6. See solution manual.

Page 609

11-11 Exercise Answers

8. 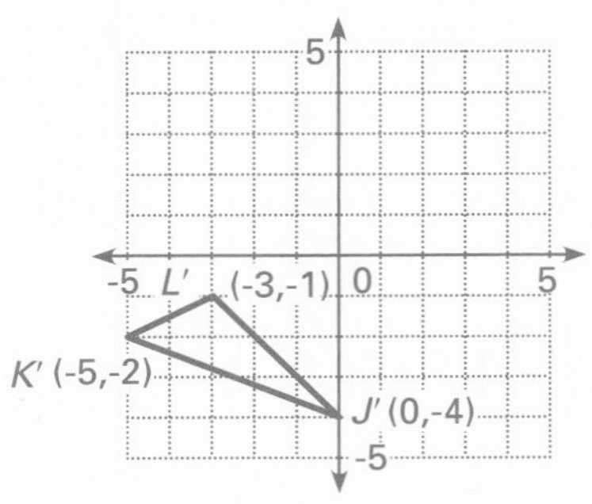

9. 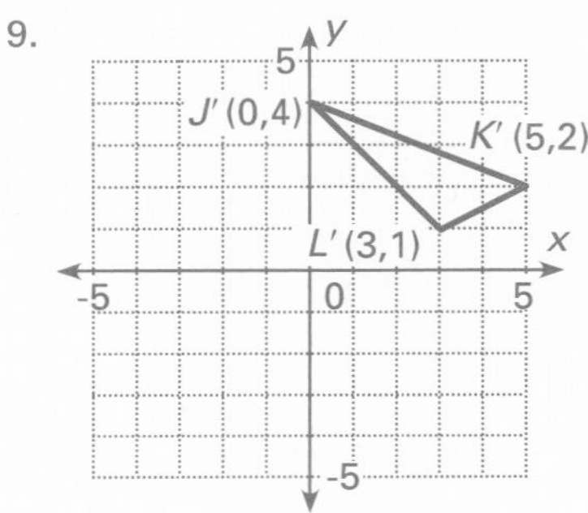

Page 620

Answers for Assessment

8. 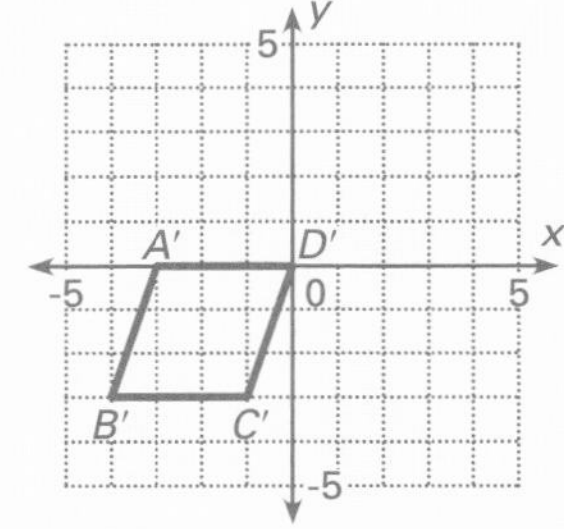

$A'(-3, 0)$, $B'(-4, -3)$, $C'(-1, -3)$, $D'(0, 0)$

9. $A'(3, 0)$, $B'(4, -3)$, $C'(1, -3)$, $D'(0, 0)$

10. 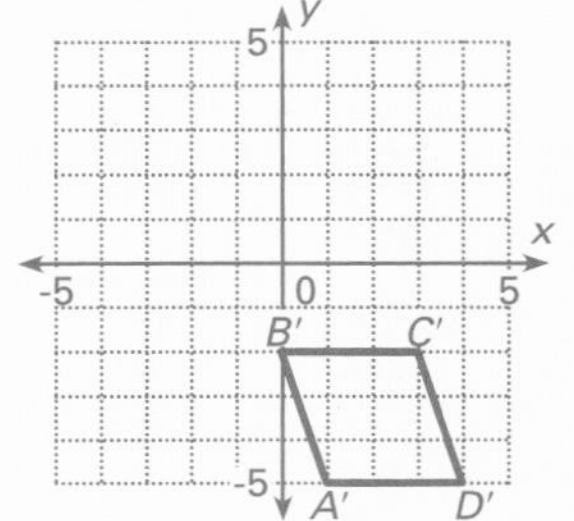

Page 621

Suggested Scoring Rubrics

Rolling Along

4
- Identifies the 5 Platonic solids.
- Builds models of at least three solids and numbers the faces.
- Correctly matches each solid with a given probability.

3
- Identifies the 5 Platonic solids.
- Builds model of at least two solids and numbers the faces.
- Correctly matches each of two solids with given probabilities.

2
- Identifies the 5 Platonic solids.
- Builds model of one solid and numbers the faces.
- Matches at least one of solids with given probabilities.

1
- Fails to identify the solids.
- Has difficulty building models.
- Cannot relate the number of faces to given probabilities.

Making Money

4
- Sets up the experiment and measures the angles.
- Table shows a relationship between the angle and the number of coins seen.
- Explains how to see an infinite amount of money.

3
- Sets up the experiment and measures the angles.
- Table shows a relationship between the angle and the coins seen.
- Attempts to explain how to see an infinite amount of money.

2
- Sets up the experiment but has difficulty measuring.
- Fails to show a relationship between angle and coins.
- Cannot explain how to see an infinite amount of money.

1
- Attempts to set up experiment.
- Table is not appropriate.
- Does not explain how to see an infinite amount of money.

Page 658

12-6 Exercise Answers

23. Figure has one line of symmetry.

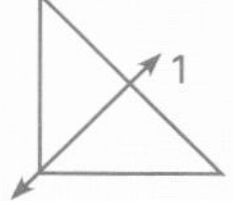

24. Figure has five lines of symmetry.

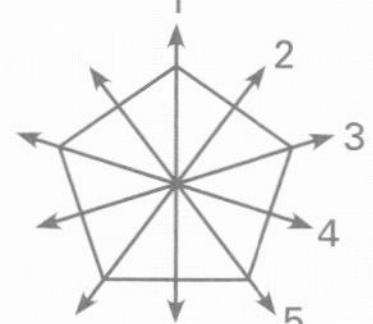

25. Figure has one line of symmetry.

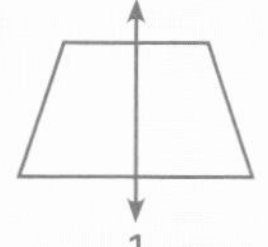

INDEX

INDEX